The Frederick Douglass Collection
By
Frederick Douglass

RECONSTRUCTION

THE assembling of the Second Session of the Thirty-ninth Congress may very properly be made the occasion of a few earnest words on the already much-worn topic of reconstruction.

Seldom has any legislative body been the subject of a solicitude more intense, or of aspirations more sincere and ardent. There are the best of reasons for this profound interest. Questions of vast moment, left undecided by the last session of Congress, must be manfully grappled with by this. No political skirmishing will avail. The occasion demands statesmanship.

Whether the tremendous war so heroically fought and so victoriously ended shall pass into history a miserable failure, barren of permanent results, -- a scandalous and shocking waste of blood and treasure, -- a strife for empire, as Earl Russell characterized it, of no value to liberty or civilization, -- an attempt to re-establish a Union by force, which must be the merest mockery of a Union, -- an effort to bring under Federal authority States into which no loyal man from the North may safely enter, and to bring men into the national councils who deliberate with daggers and vote with revolvers, and who do not even conceal their deadly hate of the country that conquered them; or whether, on the other hand, we shall, as the rightful reward of victory over treason, have a solid nation, entirely delivered from all contradictions and social antagonisms, based upon loyalty, liberty, and equality, must be determined one way or the other by the present session of Congress. The last session really did nothing which can be considered final as to these questions. The Civil Rights Bill and the Freedmen's Bureau Bill and the proposed constitutional amendments, with the amendment already adopted and recognized as the law of the land, do not reach the difficulty, and cannot, unless the whole structure of the government is changed from a government by States to something like a despotic central government, with power to control even the municipal regulations of States, and to make them conform to its own despotic will. While there remains such an idea as the right of each State to control its own local affairs, -- an idea, by the way, more deeply rooted in the minds of men of all sections of the country than perhaps any one other political idea, -- no general assertion of human rights can be of any practical value. To change the character of the government at this point is neither possible nor desirable. All that is necessary to be done is to make the government consistent with itself, and render the rights of the States compatible with the sacred rights of human nature.

The arm of the Federal government is long, but it is far too short to protect the rights of individuals in the interior of distant States. They must have the power to protect themselves, or they will go unprotected, spite of all the laws the Federal government can put upon the national statute-book.

Slavery, like all other great systems of wrong, founded in the depths of human selfishness, and existing for ages, has not neglected its own conservation. It has steadily exerted an influence upon all around it favorable to its own continuance. And to-day it is so strong that it could exist, not only without law, but even against law. Custom, manners, morals, religion, are all on its side everywhere in the South; and when you add the ignorance and servility of the ex-slave to the intelligence and accustomed authority of the master, you have the conditions, not out of which slavery will again grow, but under which it is impossible for the Federal government to wholly destroy it, unless the Federal government be armed with despotic power, to blot out State authority, and to station a Federal officer at every cross-road. This, of course, cannot be done, and ought not even if it could. The true way and the easiest way is to make our government entirely consistent with itself, and give to every loyal citizen the elective franchise, -- a right and power which will be ever present, and will form a wall of fire for his protection.

One of the invaluable compensations of the late Rebellion is the highly instructive disclosure it made of the true source of danger to republican government. Whatever may be tolerated in monarchical and despotic governments, no republic is safe that tolerates a privileged class, or denies to any of its citizens equal rights and equal means to maintain them. What was theory before the war has been made fact by the war.

There is cause to be thankful even for rebellion. It is an impressive teacher, though a stern and terrible one. In both characters it has come to us, and it was perhaps needed in both. It is an instructor never a day before its time, for it comes only when all other means of progress and enlightenment have failed. Whether the oppressed and despairing bondman, no longer able to repress his deep yearnings for manhood, or the tyrant, in his pride and impatience, takes the initiative, and strikes the blow for a firmer hold and a longer lease of oppression, the result is the same, -- society is instructed, or may be.

Such are the limitations of the common mind, and so thoroughly engrossing are the cares of common life, that only the few among men can discern through the glitter and dazzle of present prosperity the dark outlines of approaching disasters, even though they may have come up to our very gates, and are already within striking distance. The yawning seam and corroded bolt conceal their defects from the mariner until the storm calls all hands to the pumps. Prophets, indeed, were abundant before the war; but who cares for prophets while their predictions remain unfulfilled, and the calamities of which they tell are masked behind a blinding blaze of national prosperity?

It is asked, said Henry Clay, on a memorable occasion, Will slavery never come to an end? That question, said he, was asked fifty years ago, and it has been answered by fifty years of unprecedented prosperity. Spite of the eloquence of the earnest Abolitionists, -- poured out against slavery during thirty years, -- even they must confess, that, in all the probabilities of the case, that system of barbarism would have continued its horrors far beyond the limits of the nineteenth century but for the Rebellion, and perhaps only have disappeared at last in a fiery conflict, even more fierce and bloody than that which has now been suppressed.

It is no disparagement to truth, that it can only prevail where reason prevails. War begins where reason ends. The thing worse than rebellion is the thing that causes rebellion. What that thing is, we have been taught to our cost. It remains now to be seen whether we have the needed courage to have that cause entirely removed from the Republic. At any rate, to this grand work of national regeneration and entire purification Congress must now address Itself, with full purpose that the work shall this time be thoroughly done. The deadly upas, root and branch, leaf and fibre, body and sap, must be utterly destroyed. The country is evidently not in a condition to listen patiently to pleas for postponement, however plausible, nor will it permit the responsibility to be shifted to other shoulders. Authority and power are here commensurate with the duty imposed. There are no cloud-flung shadows to obscure the way. Truth shines with brighter light and intenser heat at every moment, and a country torn and rent and bleeding implores relief from its distress and agony.

If time was at first needed, Congress has now had time. All the requisite materials from which to form an intelligent judgment are now before it. Whether its members look at the origin, the progress, the termination of the war, or at the mockery of a peace now existing, they will find only one unbroken chain of argument in favor of a radical policy of reconstruction. For the omissions of the last session, some excuses may be allowed. A treacherous President stood in the way; and it can be easily seen how reluctant good men might be to admit an apostasy which involved so much of baseness and ingratitude. It was natural that they should seek to save him by bending to him even when he leaned to the side of error. But all is changed now. Congress knows now that it must go on without his aid, and even against his machinations. The advantage of the present session over the last is immense. Where that investigated, this has the facts. Where that walked by faith, this may walk by sight. Where that halted, this must go forward, and where that failed, this must succeed, giving the country whole measures where that gave us half-measures, merely as a means of saving the elections in a few doubtful districts. That Congress saw what was right, but distrusted the enlightenment of the loyal masses; but what was forborne in distrust of the people must now be done with a full knowledge that the people expect and require it. The members go to Washington fresh from the inspiring presence of the people. In every considerable public meeting, and in almost every conceivable way, whether at court-house, school-house, or cross-roads, in doors and out, the subject has been discussed, and the people have emphatically pronounced in favor of a radical policy. Listening to the doctrines of expediency and compromise with pity, impatience, and disgust, they have everywhere broken into demonstrations of the wildest enthusiasm when a brave word has been spoken in favor of equal rights and impartial suffrage. Radicalism, so far from being odious, is not the popular passport to power. The men most bitterly charged with it go to Congress with the largest majorities, while the timid and doubtful are sent by lean majorities, or else left at home. The strange controversy between the President and the Congress, at one time so threatening, is disposed of by the people. The high reconstructive powers which he so confidently, ostentatiously, and haughtily claimed, have been disallowed, denounced, and utterly repudiated; while those claimed by Congress have been confirmed.

Of the spirit and magnitude of the canvass nothing need be said. The appeal was to the people, and the verdict was worthy of the tribunal. Upon an occasion of his own selection, with the advice and approval of his astute Secretary, soon after the members of the Congress had returned to their constituents, the President quitted the executive mansion, sandwiched himself between two recognized heroes, -- men whom the whole country delighted to honor, -- and, with all the advantage which such company could give him, stumped the country from the Atlantic to the Mississippi, advocating everywhere his policy as against that of Congress. It was a strange sight, and perhaps the most disgraceful exhibition ever made by any President; but, as no evil is entirely unmixed, good has come of this, as from many others. Ambitious, unscrupulous, energetic, indefatigable, voluble, and plausible, -- a political gladiator, ready for a "set-to" in any crowd, -- he is beaten in his own chosen field, and stands to-day before the country as a convicted usurper, a political criminal, guilty of a bold and persistent attempt to possess himself of the legislative powers solemnly secured to Congress by the Constitution. No vindication could be more complete, no condemnation could be more absolute and humiliating. Unless reopened by the sword, as recklessly threatened in some circles, this question is now closed for all time.

Without attempting to settle here the metaphysical and somewhat theological question (about which so much has already been said and written), whether once in the Union means always in the Union, -- agreeably to the formula, Once in grace always in grace, -- it is obvious to common sense that the rebellious States stand to-day, in point of law, precisely where they stood when, exhausted, beaten, conquered, they fell powerless at the feet of Federal authority. Their State governments were overthrown, and the lives and property of the leaders of the Rebellion were forfeited. In reconstructing the institutions of these shattered and overthrown States, Congress should begin with a clean slate, and make clean work of it. Let there be no hesitation. It would be a cowardly deference to a defeated and treacherous President, if any account were made of the illegitimate, one-sided, sham governments hurried into existence for a malign purpose in the absence of Congress. These pretended governments, which were never submitted to the people, and from participation in which four millions of the loyal people were excluded by Presidential order, should now be treated according to their true character, as shams and impositions, and supplanted by true and legitimate governments, in the formation of which loyal men, black and white, shall participate.

It is not, however, within the scope of this paper to point out the precise steps to be taken, and the means to be employed. The people are less concerned about these than the grand end to be attained. They demand such a reconstruction as shall put an end to the present anarchical state of things in the late rebellious States, -- where frightful murders and wholesale massacres are perpetrated in the very presence of Federal soldiers. This horrible business they require shall cease. They want a reconstruction such as will protect loyal men, black and white, in their persons and property; such a one as will cause Northern industry, Northern capital, and Northern civilization to flow into the South, and make a man from New England as much at home in Carolina as elsewhere in the Republic. No Chinese wall can now be tolerated. The South must be opened to the light of law and liberty, and this session of Congress is relied upon to accomplish this important work.

The plain, common-sense way of doing this work, as intimated at the beginning, is simply to establish in the South one law, one government, one administration of justice, one condition to the exercise of the elective franchise, for men of all races and colors alike. This great measure is sought as earnestly by loyal white men as by loyal blacks, and is needed alike by both. Let sound political prescience but take the place of an unreasoning prejudice, and this will be done.

Men denounce the negro for his prominence in this discussion; but it is no fault of his that in peace as in war, that in conquering Rebel armies as in reconstructing the rebellious States, the right of the negro is the true solution of our national troubles. The stern logic of events, which goes directly to the point, disdaining all concern for the color or features of men, has determined the interests of the country as identical with and inseparable from those of the negro.

The policy that emancipated and armed the negro -- now seen to have been wise and proper by the dullest -- was not certainly more sternly demanded than is now the policy of enfranchisement. If with the negro was success in war, and without him failure, so in peace it will be found that the nation must fall or flourish with the negro.

Fortunately, the Constitution of the United States knows no distinction between citizens on account of color. Neither does it know any difference between a citizen of a State and a citizen of the United States. Citizenship evidently includes all the rights of citizens, whether State or national. If the Constitution knows none, it is clearly no part of the duty of a Republican Congress now to institute one. The mistake of the last session was the attempt to do this very thing, by a renunciation of its power to secure political rights to any class of citizens, with the obvious purpose to allow the rebellious States to disfranchise, if they should see fit, their colored citizens. This unfortunate blunder must now be retrieved, and the emasculated citizenship given to the negro supplanted by that contemplated in the Constitution of the United States, which declares that the citizens of each State shall enjoy all the rights and immunities of citizens of the several States, -- so that a legal voter in any State shall be a legal voter in all the States.

By a principle essential to Christianity, a PERSON is eternally differenced from a THING; so that the idea of a HUMAN BEING, necessarily excludes the idea of PROPERTY IN THAT BEING. —COLERIDGE

Entered according to Act of Congress in 1855 by Frederick Douglass in the Clerk's Office of the District Court of the Northern District of New York

TO

HONORABLE GERRIT SMITH,
AS A SLIGHT TOKEN OF
ESTEEM FOR HIS CHARACTER,
ADMIRATION FOR HIS GENIUS AND BENEVOLENCE,
AFFECTION FOR HIS PERSON, AND
GRATITUDE FOR HIS FRIENDSHIP,
AND AS
A Small but most Sincere Acknowledgement of
HIS PRE-EMINENT SERVICES IN BEHALF OF THE RIGHTS AND LIBERTIES
OF AN
AFFLICTED, DESPISED AND DEEPLY OUTRAGED PEOPLE,
BY RANKING SLAVERY WITH PIRACY AND MURDER,
AND BY
DENYING IT EITHER A LEGAL OR CONSTITUTIONAL EXISTENCE,
This Volume is Respectfully Dedicated,
BY HIS FAITHFUL AND FIRMLY ATTACHED FRIEND,

FREDERICK DOUGLAS.
ROCHESTER, N.Y.

MY BONDAGE and MY FREEDOM

EDITOR'S PREFACE

If the volume now presented to the public were a mere work of ART, the history of its misfortune might be written in two very simple words—TOO LATE. The nature and character of slavery have been subjects of an almost endless variety of artistic representation; and after the brilliant achievements in that field, and while those achievements are yet fresh in the memory of the million, he who would add another to the legion, must possess the charm of transcendent excellence, or apologize for something worse than rashness. The reader is, therefore, assured, with all due promptitude, that his attention is not invited to a work of ART, but to a work of FACTS—Facts, terrible and almost incredible, it may be yet FACTS, nevertheless.

I am authorized to say that there is not a fictitious name nor place in the whole volume; but that names and places are literally given, and that every transaction therein described actually transpired.

Perhaps the best Preface to this volume is furnished in the following letter of Mr. Douglass, written in answer to my urgent solicitation for such a work:

ROCHESTER, N. Y. July 2, 1855.

DEAR FRIEND: I have long entertained, as you very well know, a somewhat positive repugnance to writing or speaking anything for the public, which could, with any degree of plausibilty, make me liable to the imputation of seeking personal notoriety, for its own sake. Entertaining that feeling very sincerely, and permitting its control, perhaps, quite unreasonably, I have often refused to narrate my personal experience in public anti-slavery meetings, and in sympathizing circles, when urged to do so by friends, with whose views and wishes, ordinarily, it were a pleasure to comply. In my letters and speeches, I have generally aimed to discuss the question of Slavery in the light of fundamental principles, and upon facts, notorious and open to all; making, I trust, no more of the fact of my own former enslavement, than circumstances seemed absolutely to require. I have never placed my opposition to slavery on a basis so narrow as my own enslavement, but rather upon the indestructible and unchangeable laws of human nature, every one of which is perpetually and flagrantly violated by the slave system. I have also felt that it was best for those having histories worth the writing—or supposed to be so—to commit such work to hands other than their own. To write of one's self, in such a manner as not to incur the imputation of weakness, vanity, and egotism, is a work within the ability of but few; and I have little reason to believe that I belong to that fortunate few.

These considerations caused me to hesitate, when first you kindly urged me to prepare for publication a full account of my life as a slave, and my life as a freeman.

Nevertheless, I see, with you, many reasons for regarding my autobiography as exceptional in its character, and as being, in some sense, naturally beyond the reach of those reproaches which honorable and sensitive minds dislike to incur. It is not to illustrate any heroic achievements of a man, but to vindicate a just and beneficent principle, in its application to the whole human family, by letting in the light of truth upon a system, esteemed by some as a blessing, and by others as a curse and a crime. I agree with you, that this system is now at the bar of public opinion—not only of this country, but of the whole civilized world—for judgment. Its friends have made for it the usual plea—"not guilty;" the case must, therefore, proceed. Any facts, either from slaves, slaveholders, or by-standers, calculated to enlighten the public mind, by revealing the true nature, character, and tendency of the slave system, are in order, and can scarcely be innocently withheld.

I see, too, that there are special reasons why I should write my own biography, in preference to employing another to do it. Not only is slavery on trial, but unfortunately, the enslaved people are also on trial. It is alleged, that they are, naturally, inferior; that they are so low in the scale of humanity, and so utterly stupid, that they are unconscious of their wrongs, and do not apprehend their rights. Looking, then, at your request, from this stand-point, and wishing everything of which you think me capable to go to the benefit of my afflicted people, I part with my doubts and hesitation, and proceed to furnish you the desired manuscript; hoping that you may be able to make such arrangements for its publication as shall be best adapted to accomplish that good which you so enthusiastically anticipate.

FREDERICK DOUGLASS

There was little necessity for doubt and hesitation on the part of Mr. Douglass, as to the propriety of his giving to the world a full account of himself. A man who was born and brought up in slavery, a living witness of its horrors; who often himself experienced its cruelties; and who, despite the depressing influences surrounding his birth, youth and manhood, has risen, from a dark and almost absolute obscurity, to the distinguished position which he now occupies, might very well assume the existence of a commendable curiosity, on the part of the public, to know the facts of his remarkable history.

EDITOR

INTRODUCTION

When a man raises himself from the lowest condition in society to the highest, mankind pay him the tribute of their admiration; when he accomplishes this elevation by native energy, guided by prudence and wisdom, their admiration is increased; but when his course, onward and upward, excellent in itself, furthermore proves a possible, what had hitherto been regarded as an impossible, reform, then he becomes a burning and a shining light, on which the aged may look with gladness, the young with hope, and the down-trodden, as a representative of what they may themselves become. To such a man, dear reader, it is my privilege to introduce you.

The life of Frederick Douglass, recorded in the pages which follow, is not merely an example of self-elevation under the most adverse circumstances; it is, moreover, a noble vindication of the highest aims of the American anti-slavery movement. The real object of that movement is not only to disenthrall, it is, also, to bestow upon the Negro the exercise of all those rights, from the possession of which he has been so long debarred.

But this full recognition of the colored man to the right, and the entire admission of the same to the full privileges, political, religious and social, of manhood, requires powerful effort on the part of the enthralled, as well as on the part of those who would disenthrall them. The people at large must feel the conviction, as well as admit the abstract logic, of human equality; the Negro, for the first time in the world's history, brought in full contact with high civilization, must prove his title first to all that is demanded for him; in the teeth of unequal chances, he must prove himself equal to the mass of those who oppress him—therefore, absolutely superior to his apparent fate, and to their relative ability. And it is most cheering to the friends of freedom, today, that evidence of this equality is rapidly accumulating, not from the ranks of the half-freed colored people of the free states, but from the very depths of slavery itself; the indestructible equality of man to man is demonstrated by the ease with which black men, scarce one remove from barbarism—if slavery can be honored with such a distinction—vault into the high places of the most advanced and painfully acquired civilization. Ward and Garnett, Wells Brown and Pennington, Loguen and Douglass, are banners on the outer wall, under which abolition is fighting its most successful battles, because they are living exemplars of the practicability of the most radical abolitionism; for, they were all of them born to the doom of slavery, some of them remained slaves until adult age, yet they all have not only won equality to their white fellow citizens, in civil, religious, political and social rank, but they have also illustrated and adorned our common country by their genius, learning and eloquence. The characteristics whereby Mr. Douglass has won first rank among these remarkable men, and is still rising toward highest rank among living Americans, are abundantly laid bare in the book before us. Like the autobiography of Hugh Miller, it carries us so far back into early childhood, as to throw light upon the question, "when positive and persistent memory begins in the human being." And, like Hugh Miller, he must have been a shy old-fashioned child, occasionally oppressed by what he could not well account for, peering and poking about among the layers of right and wrong, of tyrant and thrall, and the wonderfulness of that hopeless tide of things which brought power to one race, and unrequited toil to another, until, finally, he stumbled upon his "first-found Ammonite," hidden away down in the depths of his own nature, and which revealed to him the fact that liberty and right, for all men, were anterior to slavery and wrong. When his knowledge of the world was bounded by the visible horizon on Col. Lloyd's plantation, and while every thing around him bore a fixed, iron stamp, as if it had always been so, this was, for one so young, a notable discovery.

To his uncommon memory, then, we must add a keen and accurate insight into men and things; an original breadth of common sense which enabled him to see, and weigh, and compare whatever passed before him, and which kindled a desire to search out and define their relations to other things not so patent, but which never succumbed to the marvelous nor the supernatural; a sacred thirst for liberty and for learning, first as a means of attaining liberty, then as an end in itself most desirable; a will; an unfaltering energy and determination to obtain what his soul pronounced desirable; a majestic self-hood; determined courage; a deep and agonizing sympathy with his embruted, crushed and bleeding fellow slaves, and an extraordinary depth of passion, together with that rare alliance between passion and intellect, which enables the former, when deeply roused, to excite, develop and sustain the latter.

With these original gifts in view, let us look at his schooling; the fearful discipline through which it pleased God to prepare him for the high calling on which he has since entered—the advocacy of emancipation by the people who are not slaves. And for this special mission, his plantation education was better than any he could have acquired in any lettered school. What he needed, was facts and experiences, welded to acutely wrought up sympathies, and these he could not elsewhere have obtained, in a manner so peculiarly adapted to his nature. His physical being was well trained, also, running wild until advanced into boyhood; hard work and light diet, thereafter, and a skill in handicraft in youth.

For his special mission, then, this was, considered in connection with his natural gifts, a good schooling; and, for his special mission, he doubtless "left school" just at the proper moment. Had he remained longer in slavery—had he fretted under bonds until the ripening of manhood and its passions, until the drear agony of slave-wife and slave-children had been piled upon his already bitter experiences—then, not only would his own history have had another termination, but the drama of American slavery would have been essentially varied; for I cannot resist the belief, that the boy who learned to read and write as he did, who taught his fellow slaves these precious acquirements as he did, who plotted for their mutual escape as he did, would, when a man at bay, strike a blow which would make slavery reel and stagger. Furthermore, blows and insults he bore, at the moment, without resentment; deep but suppressed emotion rendered him insensible to their sting; but it was afterward, when the memory of them went seething through his brain, breeding a fiery indignation at his injured self-hood, that the resolve came to resist, and the time fixed when to resist, and the plot laid, how to resist; and he always kept his self-pledged word. In what he undertook, in this line, he looked fate in the face, and had a cool, keen look at the relation of means to ends. Henry Bibb, to avoid chastisement, strewed his master's bed with charmed leaves and was whipped. Frederick Douglass quietly pocketed a like fetiche, compared his muscles with those of Covey—and whipped him.

In the history of his life in bondage, we find, well developed, that inherent and continuous energy of character which will ever render him distinguished. What his hand found to do, he did with his might; even while conscious that he was wronged out of his daily earnings, he worked, and worked hard. At his daily labor he went with a will; with keen, well set eye, brawny chest, lithe figure, and fair sweep of arm, he would have been king among calkers, had that been his mission.

It must not be overlooked, in this glance at his education, that Mr. Douglass lacked one aid to which so many men of mark have been deeply indebted—he had neither a mother's care, nor a mother's culture, save that which slavery grudgingly meted out to him. Bitter nurse! may not even her features relax with human feeling, when she gazes at such offspring! How susceptible he was to the kindly influences of mother-culture, may be gathered from his own words, on page 57: "It has been a life-long standing grief to me, that I know so little of my mother, and that I was so early separated from her. The counsels of her love must have been beneficial to me. The side view of her face is imaged on my memory, and I take few steps in life, without feeling her presence; but the image is mute, and I have no striking words of hers treasured up."

From the depths of chattel slavery in Maryland, our author escaped into the caste-slavery of the north, in New Bedford, Massachusetts. Here he found oppression assuming another, and hardly less bitter, form; of that very handicraft which the greed of slavery had taught him, his half-freedom denied him the exercise for an honest living; he found himself one of a class—free colored men—whose position he has described in the following words:

"Aliens are we in our native land. The fundamental principles of the republic, to which the humblest white man, whether born here or elsewhere, may appeal with confidence, in the hope of awakening a favorable response, are held to be inapplicable to us. The glorious doctrines of your revolutionary fathers, and the more glorious teachings of the Son of God, are construed and applied against us. We are literally scourged beyond the beneficent range of both authorities, human and divine. * * * * American humanity hates us, scorns us, disowns and denies, in a thousand ways, our very personality. The outspread wing of American christianity, apparently broad enough to give shelter to a perishing world, refuses to cover us. To us, its bones are brass, and its features iron. In running thither for shelter and succor, we have only fled from the hungry blood-hound to the devouring wolf—from a corrupt and selfish world, to a hollow and hypocritical church."—Speech before American and Foreign Anti-Slavery Society, May, 1854.

Four years or more, from 1837 to 1841, he struggled on, in New Bedford, sawing wood, rolling casks, or doing what labor he might, to support himself and young family; four years he brooded over the scars which slavery and semi-slavery had inflicted upon his body and soul; and then, with his wounds yet unhealed, he fell among the Garrisonians—a glorious waif to those most ardent reformers. It happened one day, at Nantucket, that he, diffidently and reluctantly, was led to address an anti-slavery meeting. He was about the age when the younger Pitt entered the House of Commons; like Pitt, too, he stood up a born orator.

William Lloyd Garrison, who was happily present, writes thus of Mr. Douglass' maiden effort; "I shall never forget his first speech at the convention—the extraordinary emotion it excited in my own mind—the powerful impression it created upon a crowded auditory, completely taken by surprise. * * * I think I never hated slavery so intensely as at that moment; certainly, my perception of the enormous outrage which is inflicted by it on the godlike nature of its victims, was rendered far more clear than ever. There stood one in physical proportions and stature commanding and exact—in intellect richly endowed—in natural eloquence a prodigy." 1

It is of interest to compare Mr. Douglass's account of this meeting with Mr. Garrison's. Of the two, I think the latter the most correct. It must have been a grand burst of eloquence! The pent up agony, indignation and pathos of an abused and harrowed boyhood and youth, bursting out in all their freshness and overwhelming earnestness!

This unique introduction to its great leader, led immediately to the employment of Mr. Douglass as an agent by the American Anti-Slavery Society. So far as his self-relying and independent character would permit, he became, after the strictest sect, a Garrisonian. It is not too much to say, that he formed a complement which they needed, and they were a complement equally necessary to his "make-up." With his deep and keen sensitiveness to wrong, and his wonderful memory, he came from the land of bondage full of its woes and its evils, and painting them in characters of living light; and, on his part, he found, told out in sound Saxon phrase, all those principles of justice and right and liberty, which had dimly brooded over the dreams of his youth, seeking definite forms and verbal expression. It must have been an electric flashing of thought, and a knitting of soul, granted to but few in this life, and will be a life-long memory to those who participated in it. In the society, moreover, of Wendell Phillips, Edmund Quincy, William Lloyd Garrison, and other men of earnest faith and refined culture, Mr. Douglass enjoyed the high advantage of their assistance and counsel in the labor of self-culture, to which he now addressed himself with wonted energy. Yet, these gentlemen, although proud of Frederick Douglass, failed to fathom, and bring out to the light of day, the highest qualities of his mind; the force of their own education stood in their own way: they did not delve into the mind of a colored man for capacities which the pride of race led them to believe to be restricted to their own Saxon blood. Bitter and vindictive sarcasm, irresistible mimicry, and a pathetic narrative of his own experiences of slavery, were the intellectual manifestations which they encouraged him to exhibit on the platform or in the lecture desk.

A visit to England, in 1845, threw Mr. Douglass among men and women of earnest souls and high culture, and who, moreover, had never drank of the bitter waters of American caste. For the first time in his life, he breathed an atmosphere congenial to the longings of his spirit, and felt his manhood free and unrestricted. The cordial and manly greetings of the British and Irish audiences in public, and the refinement and elegance of the social circles in which he mingled, not only as an equal, but as a recognized man of genius, were, doubtless, genial and pleasant resting places in his hitherto thorny and troubled journey through life. There are joys on the earth, and, to the wayfaring fugitive from American slavery or American caste, this is one of them.

But his sojourn in England was more than a joy to Mr. Douglass. Like the platform at Nantucket, it awakened him to the consciousness of new powers that lay in him. From the pupilage of Garrisonism he rose to the dignity of a teacher and a thinker; his opinions on the broader aspects of the great American question were earnestly and incessantly sought, from various points of view, and he must, perforce, bestir himself to give suitable answer. With that prompt and truthful perception which has led their sisters in all ages of the world to gather at the feet and support the hands of reformers, the gentlewomen of England 2 were foremost to encourage and strengthen him to carve out for himself a path fitted to his powers and energies, in the life-battle against slavery and caste to which he was pledged. And one stirring thought, inseparable from the British idea of the evangel of freedom, must have smote his ear from every side—

Hereditary bondmen! know ye not
Who would be free, themselves mast strike the blow?

The result of this visit was, that on his return to the United States, he established a newspaper. This proceeding was sorely against the wishes and the advice of the leaders of the American Anti-Slavery Society, but our author had fully grown up to the conviction of a truth which they had once promulged, but now forgotten, to wit: that in their own elevation—self-elevation— colored men have a blow to strike "on their own hook," against slavery and caste. Differing from his Boston friends in this matter, diffident in his own abilities, reluctant at their dissuadings, how beautiful is the loyalty with which he still clung to their principles in all things else, and even in this.

Now came the trial hour. Without cordial support from any large body of men or party on this side the Atlantic, and too far distant in space and immediate interest to expect much more, after the much already done, on the other side, he stood up, almost alone, to the arduous labor and heavy expenditure of editor and lecturer. The Garrison party, to which he still adhered, did not want a colored newspaper—there was an odor of caste about it; the Liberty party could hardly be expected to give warm support to a man who smote their principles as with a hammer; and the wide gulf which separated the free colored people from the Garrisonians, also separated them from their brother, Frederick Douglass.

The arduous nature of his labors, from the date of the establishment of his paper, may be estimated by the fact, that anti-slavery papers in the United States, even while organs of, and when supported by, anti-slavery parties, have, with a single exception, failed to pay expenses. Mr. Douglass has maintained, and does maintain, his paper without the support of any party, and even in the teeth of the opposition of those from whom he had reason to expect counsel and encouragement. He has been compelled, at one and the same time, and almost constantly, during the past seven years, to contribute matter to its columns as editor, and to raise funds for its support as lecturer. It is within bounds to say, that he has expended twelve thousand dollars of his own hard earned money, in publishing this paper, a larger sum than has been contributed by any one individual for the general advancement of the colored people. There had been many other papers published and edited by colored men, beginning as far back as 1827, when the Rev. Samuel E. Cornish and John B. Russworm (a graduate of Bowdoin college, and afterward Governor of Cape Palmas) published the Freedom's Journal, in New York City; probably not less than one hundred newspaper enterprises have been started in the United States, by free colored men, born free, and some of them of liberal education and fair talents for this work; but, one after another, they have fallen through, although, in several instances, anti-slavery friends contributed to their support. 3 It had almost been given up, as an impracticable thing, to maintain a colored newspaper, when Mr. Douglass, with fewest early advantages of all his competitors, essayed, and has proved the thing perfectly practicable, and, moreover, of great public benefit. This paper, in addition to its power in holding up the hands of those to whom it is especially devoted, also affords irrefutable evidence of the justice, safety and practicability of Immediate Emancipation; it further proves the immense loss which slavery inflicts on the land while it dooms such energies as his to the hereditary degradation of slavery.

It has been said in this Introduction, that Mr. Douglass had raised himself by his own efforts to the highest position in society. As a successful editor, in our land, he occupies this position. Our editors rule the land, and he is one of them. As an orator and thinker, his position is equally high, in the opinion of his countrymen. If a stranger in the United States would seek its most distinguished men—the movers of public opinion—he will find their names mentioned, and their movements chronicled, under the head of "BY MAGNETIC TELEGRAPH," in the daily papers. The keen caterers for the public attention, set down, in this column, such men only as have won high mark in the public esteem. During the past winter—1854-5—very frequent mention of Frederick Douglass was made under this head in the daily papers; his name glided as often—this week from Chicago, next week from Boston—over the lightning wires, as the name of any other man, of whatever note. To no man did the people more widely nor more earnestly say, "Tell me thy thought!" And, somehow or other, revolution seemed to follow in his wake. His were not the mere words of eloquence which Kossuth speaks of, that delight the ear and then pass away. No! They were work-able, do-able words, that brought forth fruits in the revolution in Illinois, and in the passage of the franchise resolutions by the Assembly of New York.

And the secret of his power, what is it? He is a Representative American man—a type of his countrymen. Naturalists tell us that a full grown man is a resultant or representative of all animated nature on this globe; beginning with the early embryo state, then representing the lowest forms of organic life, 4 and passing through every subordinate grade or type, until he reaches the last and highest—manhood. In like manner, and to the fullest extent, has Frederick Douglass passed through every gradation of rank comprised in our national make-up, and bears upon his person and upon his soul every thing that is American. And he has not only full sympathy with every thing American; his proclivity or bent, to active toil and visible progress, are in the strictly national direction, delighting to outstrip "all creation."

Nor have the natural gifts, already named as his, lost anything by his severe training. When unexcited, his mental processes are probably slow, but singularly clear in perception, and wide in vision, the unfailing memory bringing up all the facts in their every aspect; incongruities he lays hold of incontinently, and holds up on the edge of his keen and telling wit. But this wit never descends to frivolity; it is rigidly in the keeping of his truthful common sense, and always used in illustration or proof of some point which could not so readily be reached any other way. "Beware of a Yankee when he is feeding," is a shaft that strikes home in a matter never so laid bare by satire before. "The Garrisonian views of disunion, if carried to a successful issue, would only place the people of the north in the same relation to American slavery which they now bear to the slavery of Cuba or the Brazils," is a statement, in a few words, which contains the result and the evidence of an argument which might cover pages, but could not carry stronger conviction, nor be stated in less pregnable form. In proof of this, I may say, that having been submitted to the attention of the Garrisonians in print, in March, it was repeated before them at their business meeting in May—the platform, par excellence, on which they invite free fight, a l'outrance, to all comers. It was given out in the clear, ringing tones, wherewith the hall of shields was wont to resound of old, yet neither Garrison, nor Phillips, nor May, nor Remond, nor Foster, nor Burleigh, with his subtle steel of "the ice brook's temper," ventured to break a lance upon it! The doctrine of the dissolution of the Union, as a means for the abolition of American slavery, was silenced upon the lips that gave it birth, and in the presence of an array of defenders who compose the keenest intellects in the land.

"The man who is right is a majority" is an aphorism struck out by Mr. Douglass in that great gathering of the friends of freedom, at Pittsburgh, in 1852, where he towered among the highest, because, with abilities inferior to none, and moved more deeply than any, there was neither policy nor party to trammel the outpourings of his soul. Thus we find, opposed to all disadvantages which a black man in the United States labors and struggles under, is this one vantage ground—when the chance comes, and the audience where he may have a say, he stands forth the freest, most deeply moved and most earnest of all men.

It has been said of Mr. Douglass, that his descriptive and declamatory powers, admitted to be of the very highest order, take precedence of his logical force. Whilst the schools might have trained him to the exhibition of the formulas of deductive logic, nature and circumstances forced him into the exercise of the higher faculties required by induction. The first ninety pages of this "Life in Bondage," afford specimens of observing, comparing, and careful classifying, of such superior character, that it is difficult to believe them the results of a child's thinking; he questions the earth, and the children and the slaves around him again and again, and finally looks to "God in the sky" for the why and the wherefore of the unnatural thing, slavery. "Yes, if indeed thou art, wherefore dost thou suffer us to be slain?" is the only prayer and worship of the God-forsaken Dodos in the heart of Africa. Almost the same was his prayer. One of his earliest observations was that white children should know their ages, while the colored children were ignorant of theirs; and the songs of the slaves grated on his inmost soul, because a something told him that harmony in sound, and music of the spirit, could not consociate with miserable degradation.

To such a mind, the ordinary processes of logical deduction are like proving that two and two make four. Mastering the intermediate steps by an intuitive glance, or recurring to them as

Ferguson resorted to geometry, it goes down to the deeper relation of things, and brings out what may seem, to some, mere statements, but which are new and brilliant generalizations, each resting on a broad and stable basis. Thus, Chief Justice Marshall gave his decisions, and then told Brother Story to look up the authorities—and they never differed from him. Thus, also, in his "Lecture on the Anti-Slavery Movement," delivered before the Rochester Ladies' Anti-Slavery Society, Mr. Douglass presents a mass of thought, which, without any showy display of logic on his part, requires an exercise of the reasoning faculties of the reader to keep pace with him. And his "Claims of the Negro Ethnologically Considered," is full of new and fresh thoughts on the dawning science of race-history.

If, as has been stated, his intellection is slow, when unexcited, it is most prompt and rapid when he is thoroughly aroused. Memory, logic, wit, sarcasm, invective pathos and bold imagery of rare structural beauty, well up as from a copious fountain, yet each in its proper place, and contributing to form a whole, grand in itself, yet complete in the minutest proportions. It is most difficult to hedge him in a corner, for his positions are taken so deliberately, that it is rare to find a point in them undefended aforethought. Professor Reason tells me the following: "On a recent visit of a public nature, to Philadelphia, and in a meeting composed mostly of his colored brethren, Mr. Douglass proposed a comparison of views in the matters of the relations and duties of 'our people;' he holding that prejudice was the result of condition, and could be conquered by the efforts of the degraded themselves. A gentleman present, distinguished for logical acumen and subtlety, and who had devoted no small portion of the last twenty-five years to the study and elucidation of this very question, held the opposite view, that prejudice is innate and unconquerable. He terminated a series of well dove-tailed, Socratic questions to Mr. Douglass, with the following: 'If the legislature at Harrisburgh should awaken, to-morrow morning, and find each man's skin turned black and his hair woolly, what could they do to remove prejudice?' 'Immediately pass laws entitling black men to all civil, political and social privileges,' was the instant reply—and the questioning ceased."

The most remarkable mental phenomenon in Mr. Douglass, is his style in writing and speaking. In March, 1855, he delivered an address in the assembly chamber before the members of the legislature of the state of New York. An eye witness 5 describes the crowded and most intelligent audience, and their rapt attention to the speaker, as the grandest scene he ever witnessed in the capitol. Among those whose eyes were riveted on the speaker full two hours and a half, were Thurlow Weed and Lieutenant Governor Raymond; the latter, at the conclusion of the address, exclaimed to a friend, "I would give twenty thousand dollars, if I could deliver that address in that manner." Mr. Raymond is a first class graduate of Dartmouth, a rising politician, ranking foremost in the legislature; of course, his ideal of oratory must be of the most polished and finished description.

The style of Mr. Douglass in writing, is to me an intellectual puzzle. The strength, affluence and terseness may easily be accounted for, because the style of a man is the man; but how are we to account for that rare polish in his style of writing, which, most critically examined, seems the result of careful early culture among the best classics of our language; it equals if it does not surpass the style of Hugh Miller, which was the wonder of the British literary public, until he unraveled the mystery in the most interesting of autobiographies. But Frederick Douglass was still calking the seams of Baltimore clippers, and had only written a "pass," at the age when Miller's style was already formed.

I asked William Whipper, of Pennsylvania, the gentleman alluded to above, whether he thought Mr. Douglass's power inherited from the Negroid, or from what is called the Caucasian side of his make up? After some reflection, he frankly answered, "I must admit, although sorry to do so, that the Caucasian predominates." At that time, I almost agreed with him; but, facts narrated in the first part of this work, throw a different light on this interesting question.

We are left in the dark as to who was the paternal ancestor of our author; a fact which generally holds good of the Romuluses and Remuses who are to inaugurate the new birth of our republic. In the absence of testimony from the Caucasian side, we must see what evidence is given on the other side of the house.

"My grandmother, though advanced in years, * * * was yet a woman of power and spirit. She was marvelously straight in figure, elastic and muscular." (p. 46.)

After describing her skill in constructing nets, her perseverance in using them, and her widespread fame in the agricultural way he adds, "It happened to her—as it will happen to any careful and thrifty person residing in an ignorant and improvident neighborhood—to enjoy the reputation of being born to good luck." And his grandmother was a black woman.

"My mother was tall, and finely proportioned; of deep black, glossy complexion; had regular features; and among other slaves was remarkably sedate in her manners." "Being a field hand, she was obliged to walk twelve miles and return, between nightfall and daybreak, to see her children" (p. 54.) "I shall never forget the indescribable expression of her countenance when I told her that I had had no food since morning. * * * There was pity in her glance at me, and a fiery indignation at Aunt Katy at the same time; * * * * she read Aunt Katy a lecture which she never forgot." (p. 56.) "I learned after my mother's death, that she could read, and that she was the only one of all the slaves and colored people in Tuckahoe who enjoyed that advantage. How she acquired this knowledge, I know not, for Tuckahoe is the last place in the world where she would be apt to find facilities for learning." (p. 57.) "There is, in Prichard's Natural History of Man, the head of a figure—on page 157—the features of which so resemble those of my mother, that I often recur to it with something of the feeling which I suppose others experience when looking upon the pictures of dear departed ones." (p. 52.)

The head alluded to is copied from the statue of Ramses the Great, an Egyptian king of the nineteenth dynasty. The authors of the Types of Mankind give a side view of the same on page 148, remarking that the profile, "like Napoleon's, is superbly European!" The nearness of its resemblance to Mr. Douglass' mother rests upon the evidence of his memory, and judging from his almost marvelous feats of recollection of forms and outlines recorded in this book, this testimony may be admitted.

These facts show that for his energy, perseverance, eloquence, invective, sagacity, and wide sympathy, he is indebted to his Negro blood. The very marvel of his style would seem to be a development of that other marvel—how his mother learned to read. The versatility of talent which he wields, in common with Dumas, Ira Aldridge, and Miss Greenfield, would seem to be the result of the grafting of the Anglo-Saxon on good, original, Negro stock. If the friends of "Caucasus" choose to claim, for that region, what remains after this analysis—to wit: combination—they are welcome to it. They will forgive me for reminding them that the term "Caucasian" is dropped by recent writers on Ethnology; for the people about Mount Caucasus, are, and have ever been, Mongols. The great "white race" now seek paternity, according to Dr. Pickering, in Arabia—"Arida Nutrix" of the best breed of horses &c. Keep on, gentlemen; you will find yourselves in Africa, by-and-by. The Egyptians, like the Americans, were a mixed race, with some Negro blood circling around the throne, as well as in the mud hovels.

This is the proper place to remark of our author, that the same strong self-hood, which led him to measure strength with Mr. Covey, and to wrench himself from the embrace of the Garrisonians, and which has borne him through many resistances to the personal indignities offered him as a colored man, sometimes becomes a hyper-sensitiveness to such assaults as men of his mark will meet with, on paper. Keen and unscrupulous opponents have sought, and not unsuccessfully, to pierce him in this direction; for well they know, that if assailed, he will smite back.

It is not without a feeling of pride, dear reader, that I present you with this book. The son of a self-emancipated bond-woman, I feel joy in introducing to you my brother, who has rent his own bonds, and who, in his every relation—as a public man, as a husband and as a father—is such as does honor to the land which gave him birth. I shall place this book in the hands of the only child spared me, bidding him to strive and emulate its noble example. You may do likewise. It is an American book, for Americans, in the fullest sense of the idea. It shows that

the worst of our institutions, in its worst aspect, cannot keep down energy, truthfulness, and earnest struggle for the right. It proves the justice and practicability of Immediate Emancipation. It shows that any man in our land, "no matter in what battle his liberty may have been cloven down, * * * * no matter what complexion an Indian or an African sun may have burned upon him," not only may "stand forth redeemed and disenthralled," but may also stand up a candidate for the highest suffrage of a great people—the tribute of their honest, hearty admiration. Reader, Vale! New York
JAMES M'CUNE SMITH

CHAPTER I. Childhood

PLACE OF BIRTH—CHARACTER OF THE DISTRICT—TUCKAHOE—ORIGIN OF THE
NAME—CHOPTANK RIVER—TIME OF BIRTH—GENEALOGICAL TREES—MODE OF
COUNTING TIME—NAMES OF GRANDPARENTS—THEIR POSITION—GRANDMOTHER
ESPECIALLY ESTEEMED—"BORN TO GOOD LUCK"—SWEET
POTATOES—SUPERSTITION—THE LOG CABIN—ITS CHARMS—SEPARATING
CHILDREN—MY AUNTS—THEIR NAMES—FIRST KNOWLEDGE OF BEING A SLAVE—OLD
MASTER—GRIEFS AND JOYS OF CHILDHOOD—COMPARATIVE HAPPINESS OF THE
SLAVE-BOY AND THE SON OF A SLAVEHOLDER.

In Talbot county, Eastern Shore, Maryland, near Easton, the county town of that county, there is a small district of country, thinly populated, and remarkable for nothing that I know of more than for the worn-out, sandy, desert-like appearance of its soil, the general dilapidation of its farms and fences, the indigent and spiritless character of its inhabitants, and the prevalence of ague and fever.

The name of this singularly unpromising and truly famine stricken district is Tuckahoe, a name well known to all Marylanders, black and white. It was given to this section of country probably, at the first, merely in derision; or it may possibly have been applied to it, as I have heard, because some one of its earlier inhabitants had been guilty of the petty meanness of stealing a hoe—or taking a hoe that did not belong to him. Eastern Shore men usually pronounce the word took, as tuck; Took-a-hoe, therefore, is, in Maryland parlance, Tuckahoe. But, whatever may have been its origin—and about this I will not be positive—that name has stuck to the district in question; and it is seldom mentioned but with contempt and derision, on account of the barrenness of its soil, and the ignorance, indolence, and poverty of its people. Decay and ruin are everywhere visible, and the thin population of the place would have quitted it long ago, but for the Choptank river, which runs through it, from which they take abundance of shad and herring, and plenty of ague and fever.

It was in this dull, flat, and unthrifty district, or neighborhood, surrounded by a white population of the lowest order, indolent and drunken to a proverb, and among slaves, who seemed to ask, "Oh! what's the use?" every time they lifted a hoe, that I—without any fault of mine was born, and spent the first years of my childhood.

The reader will pardon so much about the place of my birth, on the score that it is always a fact of some importance to know where a man is born, if, indeed, it be important to know anything about him. In regard to the time of my birth, I cannot be as definite as I have been respecting the place. Nor, indeed, can I impart much knowledge concerning my parents. Genealogical trees do not flourish among slaves. A person of some consequence here in the north, sometimes designated father, is literally abolished in slave law and slave practice. It is only once in a while that an exception is found to this statement. I never met with a slave who could tell me how old he was. Few slave-mothers know anything of the months of the year, nor of the days of the month. They keep no family records, with marriages, births, and deaths. They measure the ages of their children by spring time, winter time, harvest time, planting time, and the like; but these soon become undistinguishable and forgotten. Like other slaves, I cannot tell how old I am. This destitution was among my earliest troubles. I learned when I grew up, that my master—and this is the case with masters generally—allowed no questions to be put to him, by which a slave might learn his age. Such questions deemed evidence of impatience, and even of impudent curiosity. From certain events, however, the dates of which I have since learned, I suppose myself to have been born about the year 1817.

The first experience of life with me that I now remember—and I remember it but hazily—began in the family of my grandmother and grandfather. Betsey and Isaac Baily. They were quite advanced in life, and had long lived on the spot where they then resided. They were considered old settlers in the neighborhood, and, from certain circumstances, I infer that my grandmother, especially, was held in high esteem, far higher than is the lot of most colored persons in the slave states. She was a good nurse, and a capital hand at making nets for catching shad and herring; and these nets were in great demand, not only in Tuckahoe, but at Denton and Hillsboro, neighboring villages. She was not only good at making the nets, but was also somewhat famous for her good fortune in taking the fishes referred to. I have known her to be in the water half the day. Grandmother was likewise more provident than most of her neighbors in the preservation of seedling sweet potatoes, and it happened to her—as it will happen to any careful and thrifty person residing in an ignorant and improvident community—to enjoy the reputation of having been born to "good luck." Her "good luck" was owing to the exceeding care which she took in preventing the succulent root from getting bruised in the digging, and in placing it beyond the reach of frost, by actually burying it under the hearth of her cabin during the winter months. In the time of planting sweet potatoes, "Grandmother Betty," as she was familiarly called, was sent for in all directions, simply to place the seedling potatoes in the hills; for superstition had it, that if "Grandmamma Betty but touches them at planting, they will be sure to grow and flourish." This high reputation was full of advantage to her, and to the children around her. Though Tuckahoe had but few of the good things of life, yet of such as it did possess grandmother got a full share, in the way of presents. If good potato crops came after her planting, she was not forgotten by those for whom she planted; and as she was remembered by others, so she remembered the hungry little ones around her.

The dwelling of my grandmother and grandfather had few pretensions. It was a log hut, or cabin, built of clay, wood, and straw. At a distance it resembled—though it was smaller, less commodious and less substantial—the cabins erected in the western states by the first settlers. To my child's eye, however, it was a noble structure, admirably adapted to promote the comforts and conveniences of its inmates. A few rough, Virginia fence-rails, flung loosely over the rafters above, answered the triple purpose of floors, ceilings, and bedsteads. To be sure, this upper apartment was reached only by a ladder—but what in the world for climbing could be better than a ladder? To me, this ladder was really a high invention, and possessed a sort of charm as I played with delight upon the rounds of it. In this little hut there was a large family of children: I dare not say how many. My grandmother—whether because too old for field service, or because she had so faithfully discharged the duties of her station in early life, I know not—enjoyed the high privilege of living in a cabin, separate from the quarter, with no other burden than her own support, and the necessary care of the little children, imposed. She evidently esteemed it a great fortune to live so. The children were not her own, but her grandchildren—the children of her daughters. She took delight in having them around her, and in attending to their few wants. The practice of separating children from their mother, and hiring the latter out at distances too great to admit of their meeting, except at long intervals, is a marked feature of the cruelty and barbarity of the slave system. But it is in harmony with the grand aim of slavery, which, always and everywhere, is to reduce man to a level with the brute. It is a successful method of obliterating from the mind and heart of the slave, all just ideas of the sacredness of the family, as an institution.

Most of the children, however, in this instance, being the children of my grandmother's daughters, the notions of family, and the reciprocal duties and benefits of the relation, had a better chance of being understood than where children are placed—as they often are in the hands of strangers, who have no care for them, apart from the wishes of their masters. The daughters of my grandmother were five in number. Their names were JENNY, ESTHER, MILLY, PRISCILLA, and HARRIET. The daughter last named was my mother, of whom the reader shall learn more by-and-by.

Living here, with my dear old grandmother and grandfather, it was a long time before I knew myself to be a slave. I knew many other things before I knew that. Grandmother and grandfather were the greatest people in the world to me; and being with them so snugly in their own little cabin—I supposed it be their own—knowing no higher authority over me or the other children than the authority of grandmamma, for a time there was nothing to disturb me; but, as I grew larger and older, I learned by degrees the sad fact, that the "little hut," and the lot on which it stood, belonged not to my dear old grandparents, but to some person who lived a great distance off, and who was called, by grandmother, "OLD MASTER." I further learned the sadder fact, that not only the house and lot, but that grandmother herself, (grandfather was free,) and all the little children around her, belonged to this mysterious personage, called by grandmother, with every mark of reverence, "Old Master." Thus early did clouds and shadows begin to fall upon my path. Once on the track—troubles never come singly—I was not long in finding out another fact, still more grievous to my childish heart. I was told that this "old master," whose name seemed ever to be mentioned with fear and shuddering, only allowed the children to live with grandmother for a limited time, and that in fact as soon as they were big enough, they were promptly taken away, to live with the said "old master." These were distressing revelations indeed; and though I was quite too young to comprehend the full import of the intelligence, and mostly spent my childhood days in gleesome sports with the other children, a shade of disquiet rested upon me.

The absolute power of this distant "old master" had touched my young spirit with but the point of its cold, cruel iron, and left me something to brood over after the play and in moments of repose. Grandmammy was, indeed, at that time, all the world to me; and the thought of being separated from her, in any considerable time, was more than an unwelcome intruder. It was intolerable.

Children have their sorrows as well as men and women; and it would be well to remember this in our dealings with them. SLAVE-children are children, and prove no exceptions to the general rule. The liability to be separated from my grandmother, seldom or never to see her again, haunted me. I dreaded the thought of going to live with that mysterious "old master," whose name I never heard mentioned with affection, but always with fear. I look back to this as among the heaviest of my childhood's sorrows. My grandmother! my grandmother! and the little hut, and the joyous circle under her care, but especially she, who made us sorry when she left us but for an hour, and glad on her return,—how could I leave her and the good old home? But the sorrows of childhood, like the pleasures of after life, are transient. It is not even within the power of slavery to write indelible sorrow, at a single dash, over the heart of a child.

> The tear down childhood's cheek that flows,
> Is like the dew-drop on the rose—
> When next the summer breeze comes by,
> And waves the bush—the flower is dry.

There is, after all, but little difference in the measure of contentment felt by the slave-child neglected and the slaveholder's child cared for and petted. The spirit of the All Just mercifully holds the balance for the young.

The slaveholder, having nothing to fear from impotent childhood, easily affords to refrain from cruel inflictions; and if cold and hunger do not pierce the tender frame, the first seven or eight years of the slave-boy's life are about as full of sweet content as those of the most favored and petted white children of the slaveholder. The slave-boy escapes many troubles which befall and vex his white brother. He seldom has to listen to lectures on propriety of behavior, or on anything else. He is never chided for handling his little knife and fork improperly or awkwardly, for he uses none. He is never reprimanded for soiling the table-cloth, for he takes his meals on the clay floor. He never has the misfortune, in his games or sports, of soiling or tearing his clothes, for he has almost none to soil or tear. He is never expected to act like a nice little gentleman, for he is only a rude little slave. Thus, freed from all restraint, the slave-boy can be, in his life and conduct, a genuine boy, doing whatever his boyish nature suggests; enacting, by turns, all the strange antics and freaks of horses, dogs, pigs, and barn-door fowls, without in any manner compromising his dignity, or incurring reproach of any sort. He literally runs wild; has no pretty little verses to learn in the nursery; no nice little speeches to make for aunts, uncles, or cousins, to show how smart he is; and, if he can only manage to keep out of the way of the heavy feet and fists of the older slave boys, he may trot on, in his joyous and roguish tricks, as happy as any little heathen under the palm trees of Africa. To be sure, he is occasionally reminded, when he stumbles in the path of his master—and this he early learns to avoid—that he is eating his "white bread," and that he will be made to "see sights" by-and-by. The threat is soon forgotten; the shadow soon passes, and our sable boy continues to roll in the dust, or play in the mud, as bests suits him, and in the veriest freedom. If he feels uncomfortable, from mud or from dust, the coast is clear; he can plunge into the river or the pond, without the ceremony of undressing, or the fear of wetting his clothes; his little tow-linen shirt—for that is all he has on—is easily dried; and it needed ablution as much as did his skin. His food is of the coarsest kind, consisting for the most part of cornmeal mush, which often finds it way from the wooden tray to his mouth in an oyster shell. His days, when the weather is warm, are spent in the pure, open air, and in the bright sunshine. He always sleeps in airy apartments; he seldom has to take powders, or to be paid to swallow pretty little sugar-coated pills, to cleanse his blood, or to quicken his appetite. He eats no candies; gets no lumps of loaf sugar; always relishes his food; cries but little, for nobody cares for his crying; learns to esteem his bruises but slight, because others so esteem them. In a word, he is, for the most part of the first eight years of his life, a spirited, joyous, uproarious, and happy boy, upon whom troubles fall only like water on a duck's back. And such a boy, so far as I can now remember, was the boy whose life in slavery I am now narrating.

CHAPTER II. Removed from My First Home

THE NAME "OLD MASTER" A TERROR—COLONEL LLOYD'S PLANTATION—WYE RIVER—WHENCE ITS NAME—POSITION OF THE LLOYDS—HOME ATTRACTION—MEET
OFFERING—JOURNEY FROM TUCKAHOE TO WYE RIVER—SCENE ON REACHING OLD
MASTER'S—DEPARTURE OF GRANDMOTHER—STRANGE MEETING OF SISTERS AND
BROTHERS—REFUSAL TO BE COMFORTED—SWEET SLEEP.

That mysterious individual referred to in the first chapter as an object of terror among the inhabitants of our little cabin, under the ominous title of "old master," was really a man of some consequence. He owned several farms in Tuckahoe; was the chief clerk and butler on the home plantation of Col. Edward Lloyd; had overseers on his own farms; and gave directions to overseers on the farms belonging to Col. Lloyd. This plantation is situated on Wye river—the river receiving its name, doubtless, from Wales, where the Lloyds originated. They (the Lloyds) are an old and honored family in Maryland, exceedingly wealthy. The home plantation, where they have resided, perhaps for a century or more, is one of the largest, most fertile, and best appointed, in the state.

About this plantation, and about that queer old master—who must be something more than a man, and something worse than an angel—the reader will easily imagine that I was not only curious, but eager, to know all that could be known. Unhappily for me, however, all the information I could get concerning him increased my great dread of being carried thither—of being separated from and deprived of the protection of my grandmother and grandfather. It was, evidently, a great thing to go to Col. Lloyd's; and I was not without a little curiosity to see the place; but no amount of coaxing could induce in me the wish to remain there. The fact is, such was my dread of leaving the little cabin, that I wished to remain little forever, for I knew the taller I grew the shorter my stay. The old cabin, with its rail floor and rail bedsteads upstairs, and its clay floor downstairs, and its dirt chimney, and windowless sides, and that most curious piece of workmanship dug in front of the fireplace, beneath which grandmammy placed the sweet potatoes to keep them from the frost, was MY HOME—the only home I ever had; and I loved it, and all connected with it. The old fences around it, and the stumps in the edge of the woods near it, and the squirrels that ran, skipped, and played upon them, were objects of interest and affection. There, too, right at the side of the hut, stood the old well, with its stately and skyward-pointing beam, so aptly placed between the limbs of what had once been a tree, and so nicely balanced that I could move it up and down with only one hand, and could get a drink myself without calling for help. Where else in the world could such a well be found, and where could such another home be met with? Nor were these all the attractions of the place. Down in a little valley, not far from grandmammy's cabin, stood Mr. Lee's mill, where the people came often in large numbers to get their corn ground. It was a watermill; and I never shall be able to tell the many things thought and felt, while I sat on the bank and watched that mill, and the turning of that ponderous wheel. The mill-pond, too, had its charms; and with my pinhook, and thread line, I could get nibbles, if I could catch no fish. But, in all my sports and plays, and in spite of them, there would, occasionally, come the painful foreboding that I was not long to remain there, and that I must soon be called away to the home of old master.

I was A SLAVE—born a slave and though the fact was in comprehensible to me, it conveyed to my mind a sense of my entire dependence on the will of somebody I had never seen; and, from some cause or other, I had been made to fear this somebody above all else on earth. Born for another's benefit, as the firstling of the cabin flock I was soon to be selected as a meet offering to the fearful and inexorable demigod, whose huge image on so many occasions haunted my childhood's imagination. When the time of my departure was decided upon, my grandmother, knowing my fears, and in pity for them, kindly kept me ignorant of the dreaded event about to transpire. Up to the morning (a beautiful summer morning) when we were to start, and, indeed, during the whole journey—a journey which, child as I was, I remember as well as if it were yesterday—she kept the sad fact hidden from me. This reserve was necessary; for, could I have known all, I should have given grandmother some trouble in getting me started. As it was, I was helpless, and she—dear woman!—led me along by the hand, resisting, with the reserve and solemnity of a priestess, all my inquiring looks to the last. The distance from Tuckahoe to Wye river—where my old master lived—was full twelve miles, and the walk was quite a severe test of the endurance of my young legs. The journey would have proved too severe for me, but that my dear old grandmother—blessings on her memory!—afforded occasional relief by "toting" me (as Marylanders have it) on her shoulder. My grandmother, though advanced in years—as was evident from more than one gray hair, which peeped from between the ample and graceful folds of her newly-ironed bandana turban—was yet a woman of power and spirit. She was marvelously straight in figure, elastic, and muscular. I seemed hardly to be a burden to her. She would have "toted" me farther, but that I felt myself too much of a man to allow it, and insisted on walking. Releasing dear grandmamma from carrying me, did not make me altogether independent of her, when we happened to pass through portions of the somber woods which lay between Tuckahoe and Wye river. She often found me increasing the energy of my grip, and holding her clothing, lest something should come out of the woods and eat me up. Several old logs and stumps imposed upon me, and got themselves taken for wild beasts. I could see their legs, eyes, and ears, or I could see something like eyes, legs, and ears, till I got close enough to them to see that the eyes were knots, washed white with rain, and the legs were broken limbs, and the ears, only ears owing to the point from which they were seen. Thus early I learned that the point from which a thing is viewed is of some importance.

As the day advanced the heat increased; and it was not until the afternoon that we reached the much dreaded end of the journey. I found myself in the midst of a group of children of many colors; black, brown, copper colored, and nearly white. I had not seen so many children before. Great houses loomed up in different directions, and a great many men and women were at work in the fields. All this hurry, noise, and singing was very different from the stillness of Tuckahoe. As a new comer, I was an object of special interest; and, after laughing and yelling around me, and playing all sorts of wild tricks, they (the children) asked me to go out and play with them. This I refused to do, preferring to stay with grandmamma. I could not help feeling that our being there boded no good to me. Grandmamma looked sad. She was soon to lose another object of affection, as she had lost many before. I knew she was unhappy, and the shadow fell from her brow on me, though I knew not the cause.

All suspense, however, must have an end; and the end of mine, in this instance, was at hand. Affectionately patting me on the head, and exhorting me to be a good boy, grandmamma told me to go and play with the little children. "They are kin to you," said she; "go and play with them." Among a number of cousins were Phil, Tom, Steve, and Jerry, Nance and Betty. Grandmother pointed out my brother PERRY, my sister SARAH, and my sister ELIZA, who stood in the group. I had never seen my brother nor my sisters before; and, though I had sometimes heard of them, and felt a curious interest in them, I really did not understand what they were to me, or I to them. We were brothers and sisters, but what of that? Why should they be attached to me, or I to them? Brothers and sisters we were by blood; but slavery had made us strangers. I heard the words brother and sisters, and knew they must mean something; but slavery had robbed these terms of their true meaning. The experience through which I was passing, they had passed through before. They had already been initiated into the mysteries of old master's domicile, and they seemed to look upon me with a certain degree of compassion; but my heart clave to my grandmother. Think it not strange, dear reader, that so little sympathy of feeling existed between us. The conditions of brotherly and sisterly feeling were wanting— we had never nestled and played together. My poor mother, like many other slave-women, had many children, but NO FAMILY! The domestic hearth, with its holy lessons and precious endearments, is abolished in the case of a slave-mother and her children. "Little children, love one another," are words seldom heard in a slave cabin.

I really wanted to play with my brother and sisters, but they were strangers to me, and I was full of fear that grandmother might leave without taking me with her. Entreated to do so, however, and that, too, by my dear grandmother, I went to the back part of the house, to play with them and the other children. Play, however, I did not, but stood with my back against the wall, witnessing the playing of the others. At last, while standing there, one of the children, who had been in the kitchen, ran up to me, in a sort of roguish glee, exclaiming, "Fed, Fed! grandmammy gone! grandmammy gone!" I could not believe it; yet, fearing the worst, I ran into the kitchen, to see for myself, and found it even so. Grandmammy had indeed gone, and was now far away, "clean" out of sight. I need not tell all that happened now. Almost heart-broken at the discovery, I fell upon the ground, and wept a boy's bitter tears, refusing to be comforted. My brother and sisters came around me, and said, "Don't cry," and gave me peaches and pears, but I flung them away, and refused all their kindly advances. I had never been deceived before; and I felt not only grieved at parting—as I supposed forever—with my grandmother, but indignant that a trick had been played upon me in a matter so serious. It was now late in the afternoon. The day had been an exciting and wearisome one, and I knew not how or where, but I suppose I sobbed myself to sleep. There is a healing in the angel wing of sleep, even for the slave-boy; and its balm was never more welcome to any wounded soul than it was to mine, the first night I spent at the domicile of old master. The reader may be surprised that I narrate so minutely an incident apparently so trivial, and which must have occurred when I was not more than seven years old; but as I wish to give a faithful history of my experience in slavery, I cannot withhold a circumstance which, at the time, affected me so deeply. Besides, this was, in fact, my first introduction to the realities of slavery.

CHAPTER III. Parentage

MY FATHER SHROUDED IN MYSTERY—MY MOTHER—HER PERSONAL APPEARANCE—INTERFERENCE OF SLAVERY WITH THE NATURAL AFFECTIONS OF
MOTHER AND CHILDREN—SITUATION OF MY MOTHER—HER NIGHTLY VISITS TO HER
BOY—STRIKING INCIDENT—HER DEATH—HER PLACE OF BURIAL.
If the reader will now be kind enough to allow me time to grow bigger, and afford me an opportunity for my experience to become greater, I will tell him something, by-and-by, of slave life, as I saw, felt, and heard it, on Col. Edward Lloyd's plantation, and at the house of old master, where I had now, despite of myself, most suddenly, but not unexpectedly, been dropped. Meanwhile, I will redeem my promise to say something more of my dear mother.
I say nothing of father, for he is shrouded in a mystery I have never been able to penetrate. Slavery does away with fathers, as it does away with families. Slavery has no use for either fathers or families, and its laws do not recognize their existence in the social arrangements of the plantation. When they do exist, they are not the outgrowths of slavery, but are antagonistic to that system. The order of civilization is reversed here. The name of the child is not expected to be that of its father, and his condition does not necessarily affect that of the child. He may be the slave of Mr. Tilgman; and his child, when born, may be the slave of Mr. Gross. He may be a freeman; and yet his child may be a chattel. He may be white, glorying in the purity of his Anglo-Saxon blood; and his child may be ranked with the blackest slaves. Indeed, he may be, and often is, master and father to the same child. He can be father without being a husband, and may sell his child without incurring reproach, if the child be by a woman in whose veins courses one thirty-second part of African blood. My father was a white man, or nearly white. It was sometimes whispered that my master was my father.
But to return, or rather, to begin. My knowledge of my mother is very scanty, but very distinct. Her personal appearance and bearing are ineffaceably stamped upon my memory. She was tall, and finely proportioned; of deep black, glossy complexion; had regular features, and, among the other slaves, was remarkably sedate in her manners. There is in Prichard's Natural History of Man, the head of a figure—on page 157—the features of which so resemble those of my mother, that I often recur to it with something of the feeling which I suppose others experience when looking upon the pictures of dear departed ones.
Yet I cannot say that I was very deeply attached to my mother; certainly not so deeply as I

should have been had our relations in childhood been different. We were separated, according to the common custom, when I was but an infant, and, of course, before I knew my mother from any one else.

The germs of affection with which the Almighty, in his wisdom and mercy, arms the hopeless infant against the ills and vicissitudes of his lot, had been directed in their growth toward that loving old grandmother, whose gentle hand and kind deportment it was in the first effort of my infantile understanding to comprehend and appreciate. Accordingly, the tenderest affection which a beneficent Father allows, as a partial compensation to the mother for the pains and lacerations of her heart, incident to the maternal relation, was, in my case, diverted from its true and natural object, by the envious, greedy, and treacherous hand of slavery. The slave-mother can be spared long enough from the field to endure all the bitterness of a mother's anguish, when it adds another name to a master's ledger, but not long enough to receive the joyous reward afforded by the intelligent smiles of her child. I never think of this terrible interference of slavery with my infantile affections, and its diverting them from their natural course, without feelings to which I can give no adequate expression.

I do not remember to have seen my mother at my grandmother's at any time. I remember her only in her visits to me at Col. Lloyd's plantation, and in the kitchen of my old master. Her visits to me there were few in number, brief in duration, and mostly made in the night. The pains she took, and the toil she endured, to see me, tells me that a true mother's heart was hers, and that slavery had difficulty in paralyzing it with unmotherly indifference.

My mother was hired out to a Mr. Stewart, who lived about twelve miles from old master's, and, being a field hand, she seldom had leisure, by day, for the performance of the journey. The nights and the distance were both obstacles to her visits. She was obliged to walk, unless chance flung into her way an opportunity to ride; and the latter was sometimes her good luck. But she always had to walk one way or the other. It was a greater luxury than slavery could afford, to allow a black slave-mother a horse or a mule, upon which to travel twenty-four miles, when she could walk the distance. Besides, it is deemed a foolish whim for a slave-mother to manifest concern to see her children, and, in one point of view, the case is made out—she can do nothing for them. She has no control over them; the master is even more than the mother, in all matters touching the fate of her child. Why, then, should she give herself any concern? She has no responsibility. Such is the reasoning, and such the practice. The iron rule of the plantation, always passionately and violently enforced in that neighborhood, makes flogging the penalty of failing to be in the field before sunrise in the morning, unless special permission be given to the absenting slave. "I went to see my child," is no excuse to the ear or heart of the overseer.

One of the visits of my mother to me, while at Col. Lloyd's, I remember very vividly, as affording a bright gleam of a mother's love, and the earnestness of a mother's care.

"I had on that day offended "Aunt Katy," (called "Aunt" by way of respect,) the cook of old master's establishment. I do not now remember the nature of my offense in this instance, for my offenses were numerous in that quarter, greatly depending, however, upon the mood of Aunt Katy, as to their heinousness; but she had adopted, that day, her favorite mode of punishing me, namely, making me go without food all day—that is, from after breakfast. The first hour or two after dinner, I succeeded pretty well in keeping up my spirits; but though I made an excellent stand against the foe, and fought bravely during the afternoon, I knew I must be conquered at last, unless I got the accustomed reenforcement of a slice of corn bread, at sundown. Sundown came, but no bread, and, in its stead, their came the threat, with a scowl well suited to its terrible import, that she "meant to starve the life out of me!" Brandishing her knife, she chopped off the heavy slices for the other children, and put the loaf away, muttering, all the while, her savage designs upon myself. Against this disappointment, for I was expecting that her heart would relent at last, I made an extra effort to maintain my dignity; but when I saw all the other children around me with merry and satisfied faces, I could stand it no longer. I went out behind the house, and cried like a fine fellow! When tired of this, I returned to the kitchen, sat by the fire, and brooded over my hard lot. I was too hungry to sleep. While I sat in the corner, I caught sight of an ear of Indian corn on an upper shelf of the kitchen. I watched my chance, and got it, and, shelling off a few grains, I put it back again. The grains in my hand, I quickly put in some ashes, and covered them with embers, to roast them. All this I did at the risk of getting a brutal thumping, for Aunt Katy could beat, as well as starve me. My corn was not long in roasting, and, with my keen appetite, it did not matter even if the grains were not exactly done. I eagerly pulled them out, and placed them on my stool, in a clever little pile. Just as I began to help myself to my very dry meal, in came my dear mother. And now, dear reader, a scene occurred which was altogether worth beholding, and to me it was instructive as well as interesting. The friendless and hungry boy, in his extremest need— and when he did not dare to look for succor—found himself in the strong, protecting arms of a mother; a mother who was, at the moment (being endowed with high powers of manner as well as matter) more than a match for all his enemies. I shall never forget the indescribable expression of her countenance, when I told her that I had had no food since morning; and that Aunt Katy said she "meant to starve the life out of me." There was pity in her glance at me, and a fiery indignation at Aunt Katy at the same time; and, while she took the corn from me, and gave me a large ginger cake, in its stead, she read Aunt Katy a lecture which she never forgot. My mother threatened her with complaining to old master in my behalf; for the latter, though harsh and cruel himself, at times, did not sanction the meanness, injustice, partiality and oppressions enacted by Aunt Katy in the kitchen. That night I learned the fact, that I was, not only a child, but somebody's child. The "sweet cake" my mother gave me was in the shape of a heart, with a rich, dark ring glazed upon the edge of it. I was victorious, and well off for the moment; prouder, on my mother's knee, than a king upon his throne. But my triumph was short. I dropped off to sleep, and waked in the morning only to find my mother gone, and myself left at the mercy of the sable virago, dominant in my old master's kitchen, whose fiery wrath was my constant dread.

I do not remember to have seen my mother after this occurrence. Death soon ended the little communication that had existed between us; and with it, I believe, a life judging from her weary, sad, down-cast countenance and mute demeanor—full of heartfelt sorrow. I was not allowed to visit her during any part of her long illness; nor did I see her for a long time before she was taken ill and died. The heartless and ghastly form of slavery rises between mother and child, even at the bed of death. The mother, at the verge of the grave, may not gather her children, to impart to them her holy admonitions, and invoke for them her dying benediction. The bond-woman lives as a slave, and is left to die as a beast; often with fewer attentions than are paid to a favorite horse. Scenes of sacred tenderness, around the death-bed, never forgotten, and which often arrest the vicious and confirm the virtuous during life, must be looked for among the free, though they sometimes occur among the slaves. It has been a life-long, standing grief to me, that I knew so little of my mother; and that I was so early separated from her. The counsels of her love must have been beneficial to me. The side view of her face is imaged on my memory, and I take few steps in life, without feeling her presence; but the image is mute, and I have no striking words of her's treasured up.

I learned, after my mother's death, that she could read, and that she was the only one of all the slaves and colored people in Tuckahoe who enjoyed that advantage. How she acquired this knowledge, I know not, for Tuckahoe is the last place in the world where she would be apt to find facilities for learning. I can, therefore, fondly and proudly ascribe to her an earnest love of knowledge. That a "field hand" should learn to read, in any slave state, is remarkable; but the achievement of my mother, considering the place, was very extraordinary; and, in view of that fact, I am quite willing, and even happy, to attribute any love of letters I possess, and for which I have got—despite of prejudices only too much credit, not to my admitted Anglo-Saxon paternity, but to the native genius of my sable, unprotected, and uncultivated mother—a woman, who belonged to a race whose mental endowments it is, at present, fashionable to hold in disparagement and contempt.

Summoned away to her account, with the impassable gulf of slavery between us during her entire illness, my mother died without leaving me a single intimation of who my father was. There was a whisper, that my master was my father; yet it was only a whisper, and I cannot say that I ever gave it credence. Indeed, I now have reason to think he was not; nevertheless, the fact remains, in all its glaring odiousness, that, by the laws of slavery, children, in all cases, are reduced to the condition of their mothers. This arrangement admits of the greatest license to brutal slaveholders, and their profligate sons, brothers, relations and friends, and gives to the pleasure of sin, the additional attraction of profit. A whole volume might be written on this single feature of slavery, as I have observed it.

One might imagine, that the children of such connections, would fare better, in the hands of their masters, than other slaves. The rule is quite the other way; and a very little reflection will satisfy the reader that such is the case. A man who will enslave his own blood, may not be safely relied on for magnanimity. Men do not love those who remind them of their sins unless they have a mind to repent—and the mulatto child's face is a standing accusation against him who is master and father to the child. What is still worse, perhaps, such a child is a constant offense to the wife. She hates its very presence, and when a slaveholding woman hates, she wants not means to give that hate telling effect. Women—white women, I mean—are IDOLS at the south, not WIVES, for the slave women are preferred in many instances; and if these idols but nod, or lift a finger, woe to the poor victim: kicks, cuffs and stripes are sure to follow. Masters are frequently compelled to sell this class of their slaves, out of deference to the feelings of their white wives; and shocking and scandalous as it may seem for a man to sell his own blood to the traffickers in human flesh, it is often an act of humanity toward the slave-child to be thus removed from his merciless tormentors.

It is not within the scope of the design of my simple story, to comment upon every phase of slavery not within my experience as a slave.

But, I may remark, that, if the lineal descendants of Ham are only to be enslaved, according to the scriptures, slavery in this country will soon become an unscriptural institution; for thousands are ushered into the world, annually, who—like myself—owe their existence to white fathers, and, most frequently, to their masters, and master's sons. The slave-woman is at the mercy of the fathers, sons or brothers of her master. The thoughtful know the rest.

After what I have now said of the circumstances of my mother, and my relations to her, the reader will not be surprised, nor be disposed to censure me, when I tell but the simple truth, viz: that I received the tidings of her death with no strong emotions of sorrow for her, and with very little regret for myself on account of her loss. I had to learn the value of my mother long after her death, and by witnessing the devotion of other mothers to their children.

There is not, beneath the sky, an enemy to filial affection so destructive as slavery. It had made my brothers and sisters strangers to me; it converted the mother that bore me, into a myth; it shrouded my father in mystery, and left me without an intelligible beginning in the world.

My mother died when I could not have been more than eight or nine years old, on one of old master's farms in Tuckahoe, in the neighborhood of Hillsborough. Her grave is, as the grave of the dead at sea, unmarked, and without stone or stake.

CHAPTER IV. A General Survey of the Slave Plantation

ISOLATION OF LLOYD S PLANTATION—PUBLIC OPINION THERE NO PROTECTION TO
THE SLAVE—ABSOLUTE POWER OF THE OVERSEER—NATURAL AND

ARTIFICIAL CHARMS

OF THE PLACE—ITS BUSINESS-LIKE APPEARANCE—SUPERSTITION ABOUT THE BURIAL GROUND—GREAT IDEAS OF COL. LLOYD—ETIQUETTE AMONG SLAVES—THE
COMIC SLAVE DOCTOR—PRAYING AND FLOGGING—OLD MASTER LOSING ITS TERRORS—HIS BUSINESS—CHARACTER OF AUNT KATY—SUFFERINGS FROM HUNGER—OLD MASTER'S HOME—JARGON OF THE PLANTATION—GUINEA SLAVES—MASTER DANIEL—FAMILY OF COL. LLOYD—FAMILY OF CAPT. ANTHONY—HIS SOCIAL POSITION—NOTIONS OF RANK AND STATION.

It is generally supposed that slavery, in the state of Maryland, exists in its mildest form, and that it is totally divested of those harsh and terrible peculiarities, which mark and characterize the slave system, in the southern and south-western states of the American union. The argument in favor of this opinion, is the contiguity of the free states, and the exposed condition of slavery in Maryland to the moral, religious and humane sentiment of the free states.

I am not about to refute this argument, so far as it relates to slavery in that state, generally; on the contrary, I am willing to admit that, to this general point, the arguments is well grounded. Public opinion is, indeed, an unfailing restraint upon the cruelty and barbarity of masters, overseers, and slave-drivers, whenever and wherever it can reach them; but there are certain secluded and out-of-the-way places, even in the state of Maryland, seldom visited by a single ray of healthy public sentiment—where slavery, wrapt in its own congenial, midnight darkness, can, and does, develop all its malign and shocking characteristics; where it can be indecent without shame, cruel without shuddering, and murderous without apprehension or fear of exposure.

Just such a secluded, dark, and out-of-the-way place, is the "home plantation" of Col. Edward Lloyd, on the Eastern Shore, Maryland. It is far away from all the great thoroughfares, and is proximate to no town or village. There is neither school-house, nor town-house in its neighborhood. The school-house is unnecessary, for there are no children to go to school. The children and grand-children of Col. Lloyd were taught in the house, by a private tutor—a Mr. Page a tall, gaunt sapling of a man, who did not speak a dozen words to a slave in a whole year. The overseers' children go off somewhere to school; and they, therefore, bring no foreign or dangerous influence from abroad, to embarrass the natural operation of the slave system of the place. Not even the mechanics—through whom there is an occasional out-burst of honest and telling indignation, at cruelty and wrong on other plantations—are white men, on this plantation. Its whole public is made up of, and divided into, three classes—SLAVEHOLDERS, SLAVES and OVERSEERS. Its blacksmiths, wheelwrights, shoemakers, weavers, and coopers, are slaves. Not even commerce, selfish and iron-hearted at it is, and ready, as it ever is, to side with the strong against the weak—the rich against the poor—is trusted or permitted within its secluded precincts. Whether with a view of guarding against the escape of its secrets, I know not, but it is a fact, the every leaf and grain of the produce of this plantation, and those of the neighboring farms belonging to Col. Lloyd, are transported to Baltimore in Col. Lloyd's own vessels; every man and boy on board of which—except the captain—are owned by him. In return, everything brought to the plantation, comes through the same channel. Thus, even the glimmering and unsteady light of trade, which sometimes exerts a civilizing influence, is excluded from this "tabooed" spot.

Nearly all the plantations or farms in the vicinity of the "home plantation" of Col. Lloyd, belong to him; and those which do not, are owned by personal friends of his, as deeply interested in maintaining the slave system, in all its rigor, as Col. Lloyd himself. Some of his neighbors are said to be even more stringent than he. The Skinners, the Peakers, the Tilgmans, the Lockermans, and the Gipsons, are in the same boat; being slaveholding neighbors, they may have strengthened each other in their iron rule. They are on intimate terms, and their interests and tastes are identical.

Public opinion in such a quarter, the reader will see, is not likely to very efficient in protecting the slave from cruelty. On the contrary, it must increase and intensify his wrongs. Public opinion seldom differs very widely from public practice. To be a restraint upon cruelty and vice, public opinion must emanate from a humane and virtuous community. To no such humane and virtuous community, is Col. Lloyd's plantation exposed. That plantation is a little nation of its own, having its own language, its own rules, regulations and customs. The laws and institutions of the state, apparently touch it nowhere. The troubles arising here, are not settled by the civil power of the state. The overseer is generally accuser, judge, jury, advocate and executioner. The criminal is always dumb. The overseer attends to all sides of a case. There are no conflicting rights of property, for all the people are owned by one man; and they can themselves own no property. Religion and politics are alike excluded. One class of the population is too high to be reached by the preacher; and the other class is too low to be cared for by the preacher. The poor have the gospel preached to them, in this neighborhood, only when they are able to pay for it. The slaves, having no money, get no gospel. The politician keeps away, because the people have no votes, and the preacher keeps away, because the people have no money. The rich planter can afford to learn politics in the parlor, and to dispense with religion altogether.

In its isolation, seclusion, and self-reliant independence, Col. Lloyd's plantation resembles what the baronial domains were during the middle ages in Europe. Grim, cold, and unapproachable by all genial influences from communities without, there it stands; full three hundred years behind the age, in all that relates to humanity and morals.

This, however, is not the only view that the place presents. Civilization is shut out, but nature cannot be. Though separated from the rest of the world; though public opinion, as I have said, seldom gets a chance to penetrate its dark domain; though the whole place is stamped with its own peculiar, ironlike individuality; and though crimes, high-handed and atrocious, may there be committed, with almost as much impunity as upon the deck of a pirate ship—it is, nevertheless, altogether, to outward seeming, a most strikingly interesting place, full of life, activity, and spirit; and presents a very favorable contrast to the indolent monotony and languor of Tuckahoe. Keen as was my regret and great as was my sorrow at leaving the latter, I was not long in adapting myself to this, my new home. A man's troubles are always half disposed of, when he finds endurance his only remedy. I found myself here; there was no getting away; and what remained for me, but to make the best of it? Here were plenty of children to play with, and plenty of places of pleasant resort for boys of my age, and boys older. The little tendrils of affection, so rudely and treacherously broken from around the darling objects of my grandmother's hut, gradually began to extend, and to entwine about the new objects by which I now found myself surrounded.

There was a windmill (always a commanding object to a child's eye) on Long Point—a tract of land dividing Miles river from the Wye a mile or more from my old master's house. There was a creek to swim in, at the bottom of an open flat space, of twenty acres or more, called "the Long Green"—a very beautiful play-ground for the children.

In the river, a short distance from the shore, lying quietly at anchor, with her small boat dancing at her stern, was a large sloop—the Sally Lloyd; called by that name in honor of a favorite daughter of the colonel. The sloop and the mill were wondrous things, full of thoughts and ideas. A child cannot well look at such objects without thinking.

Then here were a great many houses; human habitations, full of the mysteries of life at every stage of it. There was the little red house, up the road, occupied by Mr. Sevier, the overseer. A little nearer to my old master's, stood a very long, rough, low building, literally alive with slaves, of all ages, conditions and sizes. This was called "the Longe Quarter." Perched upon a hill, across the Long Green, was a very tall, dilapidated, old brick building—the architectural dimensions of which proclaimed its erection for a different purpose—now occupied by slaves, in a similar manner to the Long Quarter. Besides these, there were numerous other slave houses and huts, scattered around in the neighborhood, every nook and corner of which was completely occupied. Old master's house, a long, brick building, plain, but substantial, stood in the center of the plantation life, and constituted one independent establishment on the premises of Col. Lloyd.

Besides these dwellings, there were barns, stables, store-houses, and tobacco-houses; blacksmiths' shops, wheelwrights' shops, coopers' shops—all objects of interest; but, above all, there stood the grandest building my eyes had then ever beheld, called, by every one on the plantation, the "Great House." This was occupied by Col. Lloyd and his family. They occupied it; I enjoyed it. The great house was surrounded by numerous and variously shaped out-buildings. There were kitchens, wash-houses, dairies, summer-house, green-houses, hen-houses, turkey-houses, pigeon-houses, and arbors, of many sizes and devices, all neatly painted, and altogether interspersed with grand old trees, ornamental and primitive, which afforded delightful shade in summer, and imparted to the scene a high degree of stately beauty. The great house itself was a large, white, wooden building, with wings on three sides of it. In front, a large portico, extending the entire length of the building, and supported by a long range of columns, gave to the whole establishment an air of solemn grandeur. It was a treat to my young and gradually opening mind, to behold this elaborate exhibition of wealth, power, and vanity. The carriage entrance to the house was a large gate, more than a quarter of a mile distant from it; the intermediate space was a beautiful lawn, very neatly trimmed, and watched with the greatest care. It was dotted thickly over with delightful trees, shrubbery, and flowers. The road, or lane, from the gate to the great house, was richly paved with white pebbles from the beach, and, in its course, formed a complete circle around the beautiful lawn. Carriages going in and retiring from the great house, made the circuit of the lawn, and their passengers were permitted to behold a scene of almost Eden-like beauty. Outside this select inclosure, were parks, where as about the residences of the English nobility—rabbits, deer, and other wild game, might be seen, peering and playing about, with none to molest them or make them afraid. The tops of the stately poplars were often covered with the red-winged black-birds, making all nature vocal with the joyous life and beauty of their wild, warbling notes. These all belonged to me, as well as to Col. Edward Lloyd, and for a time I greatly enjoyed them.

A short distance from the great house, were the stately mansions of the dead, a place of somber aspect. Vast tombs, embowered beneath the weeping willow and the fir tree, told of the antiquities of the Lloyd family, as well as of their wealth. Superstition was rife among the slaves about this family burying ground. Strange sights had been seen there by some of the older slaves. Shrouded ghosts, riding on great black horses, had been seen to enter; balls of fire had been seen to fly there at midnight, and horrid sounds had been repeatedly heard. Slaves know enough of the rudiments of theology to believe that those go to hell who die slaveholders; and they often fancy such persons wishing themselves back again, to wield the lash. Tales of sights and sounds, strange and terrible, connected with the huge black tombs, were a very great security to the grounds about them, for few of the slaves felt like approaching them even in the day time. It was a dark, gloomy and forbidding place, and it was difficult to feel that the spirits of the sleeping dust there deposited, reigned with the blest in the realms of eternal peace.

The business of twenty or thirty farms was transacted at this, called, by way of eminence, "great house farm." These farms all belonged to Col. Lloyd, as did, also, the slaves upon them. Each farm was under the management of an overseer. As I have said of the overseer of the home plantation, so I may say of the overseers on the smaller ones; they stand between the slave and all civil constitutions—their word is law, and is implicitly obeyed.

The colonel, at this time, was reputed to be, and he apparently was, very rich. His slaves, alone, were an immense fortune. These, small and great, could not have been fewer than one thousand in number, and though scarcely a month passed without the sale of one or more lots to the Georgia traders, there was no apparent diminution in the number of his human stock: the home plantation merely groaned at a removal of the young increase, or human crop, then proceeded as lively as ever. Horse-shoeing, cart-mending, plow-repairing, coopering, grinding, and weaving, for all the neighboring farms, were performed here, and slaves were employed in all these branches. "Uncle Tony" was the blacksmith; "Uncle Harry" was the cartwright; "Uncle Abel" was the shoemaker; and all these had hands to assist them in their several departments.

These mechanics were called "uncles" by all the younger slaves, not because they really sustained that relationship to any, but according to plantation etiquette, as a mark of respect, due from the younger to the older slaves. Strange, and even ridiculous as it may seem, among a people so uncultivated, and with so many stern trials to look in the face, there is not to be found, among any people, a more rigid enforcement of the law of respect to elders, than they maintain. I set this down as partly constitutional with my race, and partly conventional. There is no better material in the world for making a gentleman, than is furnished in the African. He shows to others, and exacts for himself, all the tokens of respect which he is compelled to manifest toward his master. A young slave must approach the company of the older with hat in hand, and woe betide him, if he fails to acknowledge a favor, of any sort, with the accustomed "tank'ee," &c. So uniformly are good manners enforced among slaves, I can easily detect a "bogus" fugitive by his manners.

Among other slave notabilities of the plantation, was one called by everybody Uncle Isaac Copper. It is seldom that a slave gets a surname from anybody in Maryland; and so completely has the south shaped the manners of the north, in this respect, that even abolitionists make very little of the surname of a Negro. The only improvement on the "Bills," "Jacks," "Jims," and "Neds" of the south, observable here is, that "William," "John," "James," "Edward," are substituted. It goes against the grain to treat and address a Negro precisely as they would treat and address a white man. But, once in a while, in slavery as in the free states, by some extraordinary circumstance, the Negro has a surname fastened to him, and holds it against all conventionalities. This was the case with Uncle Isaac Copper. When the "uncle" was dropped, he generally had the prefix "doctor," in its stead. He was our doctor of medicine, and doctor of divinity as well. Where he took his degree I am unable to say, for he was not very communicative to inferiors, and I was emphatically such, being but a boy seven or eight years old. He was too well established in his profession to permit questions as to his native skill, or his attainments. One qualification he undoubtedly had—he was a confirmed cripple; and he could neither work, nor would he bring anything if offered for sale in the market. The old man, though lame, was no sluggard. He was a man that made his crutches do him good service. He was always on the alert, looking up the sick, and all such as were supposed to need his counsel. His remedial prescriptions embraced four articles. For diseases of the body, Epsom salts and castor oil; for those of the soul, the Lord's Prayer, and hickory switches!

I was not long at Col. Lloyd's before I was placed under the care of Doctor Issac Copper. I was sent to him with twenty or thirty other children, to learn the "Lord's Prayer." I found the old gentleman seated on a huge three-legged oaken stool, armed with several large hickory switches; and, from his position, he could reach—lame as he was—any boy in the room. After standing awhile to learn what was expected of us, the old gentleman, in any other than a devotional tone, commanded us to kneel down. This done, he commenced telling us to say everything he said. "Our Father"—this was repeated after him with promptness and uniformity; "Who art in heaven"—was less promptly and uniformly repeated; and the old gentleman paused in the prayer, to give us a short lecture upon the consequences of inattention, both immediate and future, and especially those more immediate. About these he was absolutely certain, for he held in his right hand the means of bringing all his predictions and warnings to pass. On he proceeded with the prayer; and we with our thick tongues and unskilled ears, followed him to the best of our ability. This, however, was not sufficient to please the old gentleman. Everybody, in the south, wants the privilege of whipping somebody else. Uncle Isaac shared the common passion of his country, and, therefore, seldom found any means of keeping his disciples in order short of flogging. "Say everything I say;" and bang would come the switch on some poor boy's undevotional head. "What you looking at there"— "Stop that pushing"—and down again would come the lash.

The whip is all in all. It is supposed to secure obedience to the slaveholder, and is held as a sovereign remedy among the slaves themselves, for every form of disobedience, temporal or spiritual. Slaves, as well as slaveholders, use it with an unsparing hand. Our devotions at Uncle Isaac's combined too much of the tragic and comic, to make them very salutary in a spiritual point of view; and it is due to truth to say, I was often a truant when the time for attending the praying and flogging of Doctor Isaac Copper came on.

The windmill under the care of Mr. Kinney, a kind hearted old Englishman, was to me a source of infinite interest and pleasure. The old man always seemed pleased when he saw a troop of darkey little urchins, with their tow-linen shirts fluttering in the breeze, approaching to view and admire the whirling wings of his wondrous machine. From the mill we could see other objects of deep interest. These were, the vessels from St. Michael's, on their way to Baltimore. It was a source of much amusement to view the flowing sails and complicated rigging, as the little crafts dashed by, and to speculate upon Baltimore, as to the kind and quality of the place. With so many sources of interest around me, the reader may be prepared to learn that I began to think very highly of Col. L.'s plantation. It was just a place to my boyish taste. There were fish to be caught in the creek, if one only had a hook and line; and crabs, clams and oysters were to be caught by wading, digging and raking for them. Here was a field for industry and enterprise, strongly inviting; and the reader may be assured that I entered upon it with spirit.

Even the much dreaded old master, whose merciless fiat had brought me from Tuckahoe, gradually, to my mind, parted with his terrors. Strange enough, his reverence seemed to take no particular notice of me, nor of my coming. Instead of leaping out and devouring me, he scarcely seemed conscious of my presence. The fact is, he was occupied with matters more weighty and important than either looking after or vexing me. He probably thought as little of my advent, as he would have thought of the addition of a single pig to his stock!

As the chief butler on Col. Lloyd's plantation, his duties were numerous and perplexing. In almost all important matters he answered in Col. Lloyd's stead. The overseers of all the farms were in some sort under him, and received the law from his mouth. The colonel himself seldom addressed an overseer, or allowed an overseer to address him. Old master carried the keys of all store houses; measured out the allowance for each slave at the end of every month; superintended the storing of all goods brought to the plantation; dealt out the raw material to all the handicraftsmen; shipped the grain, tobacco, and all saleable produce of the plantation to market, and had the general oversight of the coopers' shop, wheelwrights' shop, blacksmiths' shop, and shoemakers' shop. Besides the care of these, he often had business for the plantation which required him to be absent two and three days.

Thus largely employed, he had little time, and perhaps as little disposition, to interfere with the children individually. What he was to Col. Lloyd, he made Aunt Katy to him. When he had anything to say or do about us, it was said or done in a wholesale manner; disposing of us in classes or sizes, leaving all minor details to Aunt Katy, a person of whom the reader has already received no very favorable impression. Aunt Katy was a woman who never allowed herself to act greatly within the margin of power granted to her, no matter how broad that authority might be. Ambitious, ill-tempered and cruel, she found in her present position an ample field for the exercise of her ill-omened qualities. She had a strong hold on old master she was considered a first rate cook, and she really was very industrious. She was, therefore, greatly favored by old master, and as one mark of his favor, she was the only mother who was permitted to retain her children around her. Even to these children she was often fiendish in her brutality. She pursued her son Phil, one day, in my presence, with a huge butcher knife, and dealt a blow with its edge which left a shocking gash on his arm, near the wrist. For this, old master did sharply rebuke her, and threatened that if she ever should do the like again, he would take the skin off her back. Cruel, however, as Aunt Katy was to her own children, at times she was not destitute of maternal feeling, as I often had occasion to know, in the bitter pinches of hunger I had to endure. Differing from the practice of Col. Lloyd, old master, instead of allowing so much for each slave, committed the allowance for all to the care of Aunt Katy, to be divided after cooking it, amongst us. The allowance, consisting of coarse corn-meal, was not very abundant—indeed, it was very slender; and in passing through Aunt Katy's hands, it was made more slender still, for some of us. William, Phil and Jerry were her children, and it is not to accuse her too severely, to allege that she was often guilty of starving myself and the other children, while she was literally cramming her own. Want of food was my chief trouble the first summer at my old master's. Oysters and clams would do very well, with an occasional supply of bread, but they soon failed in the absence of bread. I speak but the simple truth, when I say, I have often been so pinched with hunger, that I have fought with the dog—"Old Nep"—for the smallest crumbs that fell from the kitchen table, and have been glad when I won a single crumb in the combat. Many times have I followed, with eager step, the waiting-girl when she went out to shake the table cloth, to get the crumbs and small bones flung out for the cats. The water, in which meat had been boiled, was as eagerly sought for by me. It was a great thing to get the privilege of dipping a piece of bread in such water; and the skin taken from rusty bacon, was a positive luxury. Nevertheless, I sometimes got full meals and kind words from sympathizing old slaves, who knew my sufferings, and received the comforting assurance that I should be a man some day. "Never mind, honey—better day comin'," was even then a solace, a cheering consolation to me in my troubles. Nor were all the kind words I received from slaves. I had a friend in the parlor, as well, and one to whom I shall be glad to do justice, before I have finished this part of my story.

I was not long at old master's, before I learned that his surname was Anthony, and that he was generally called "Captain Anthony"—a title which he probably acquired by sailing a craft in the Chesapeake Bay. Col. Lloyd's slaves never called Capt. Anthony "old master," but always Capt. Anthony; and me they called "Captain Anthony Fred." There is not, probably, in the whole south, a plantation where the English language is more imperfectly spoken than on Col. Lloyd's. It is a mixture of Guinea and everything else you please. At the time of which I am now writing, there were slaves there who had been brought from the coast of Africa. They never used the "s" in indication of the possessive case. "Cap'n Ant'ney Tom," "Lloyd Bill," "Aunt Rose Harry," means "Captain Anthony's Tom," "Lloyd's Bill," &c. "Oo you dem long to?" means, "Whom do you belong to?" "Oo dem got any peachy?" means, "Have you got any peaches?" I could scarcely understand them when I first went among them, so broken was their speech; and I am persuaded that I could not have been dropped anywhere on the globe, where I could reap less, in the way of knowledge, from my immediate associates, than on this plantation. Even "MAS' DANIEL," by his association with his father's slaves, had measurably adopted their dialect and their ideas, so far as they had ideas to be adopted. The equality of nature is strongly asserted in childhood, and childhood requires children for associates. Color makes no difference with a child. Are you a child with wants, tastes and pursuits common to children, not put on, but natural? then, were you black as ebony you would be welcome to the child of alabaster whiteness. The law of compensation holds here, as well as elsewhere. Mas' Daniel could not associate with ignorance without sharing its shade; and he could not give his black playmates his company, without giving them his intelligence, as well. Without knowing this, or caring about it, at the time, I, for some cause or other, spent much of my time with Mas' Daniel, in preference to spending it with most of the other boys.

Mas' Daniel was the youngest son of Col. Lloyd; his older brothers were Edward and Murray—both grown up, and fine looking men. Edward was especially esteemed by the children, and by me among the rest; not that he ever said anything to us or for us, which could be called especially kind; it was enough for us, that he never looked nor acted scornfully toward us. There were also three sisters, all married; one to Edward Winder; a second to Edward Nicholson; a third to Mr. Lownes.

The family of old master consisted of two sons, Andrew and Richard; his daughter, Lucretia, and her newly married husband, Capt. Auld. This was the house family. The kitchen family consisted of Aunt Katy, Aunt Esther, and ten or a dozen children, most of them older than myself. Capt. Anthony was not considered a rich slaveholder, but was pretty well off in the world. He owned about thirty "head" of slaves, and three farms in Tuckahoe. The most valuable part of his property was his slaves, of whom he could afford to sell one every year. This crop, therefore, brought him seven or eight hundred dollars a year, besides his yearly salary, and other revenue from his farms.

The idea of rank and station was rigidly maintained on Col. Lloyd's plantation. Our family never visited the great house, and the Lloyds never came to our home. Equal non-intercourse was observed between Capt. Anthony's family and that of Mr. Sevier, the overseer.

Such, kind reader, was the community, and such the place, in which my earliest and most lasting impressions of slavery, and of slave-life, were received; of which impressions you will learn more in the coming chapters of this book.

CHAPTER V. Gradual Initiation to the Mysteries of Slavery

GROWING ACQUAINTANCE WITH OLD MASTER—HIS CHARACTER—EVILS OF UNRESTRAINED PASSION—APPARENT TENDERNESS—OLD MASTER A MAN OF TROUBLE—CUSTOM OF MUTTERING TO HIMSELF—NECESSITY OF BEING AWARE OF
HIS WORDS—THE SUPPOSED OBTUSENESS OF SLAVE-CHILDREN—BRUTAL OUTRAGE—DRUNKEN OVERSEER—SLAVEHOLDER'S IMPATIENCE—WISDOM OF APPEALING
TO SUPERIORS—THE SLAVEHOLDER S WRATH BAD AS THAT OF THE OVERSEER—A
BASE AND SELFISH ATTEMPT TO BREAK UP A COURTSHIP—A HARROWING SCENE.

Although my old master—Capt. Anthony—gave me at first, (as the reader will have already seen) very little attention, and although that little was of a remarkably mild and gentle description, a few months only were sufficient to convince me that mildness and gentleness were not the prevailing or governing traits of his character. These excellent qualities were displayed only occasionally. He could, when it suited him, appear to be literally insensible to the claims of humanity, when appealed to by the helpless against an aggressor, and he could himself commit outrages, deep, dark and nameless. Yet he was not by nature worse than other men. Had he been brought up in a free state, surrounded by the just restraints of free society—restraints which are necessary to the freedom of all its members, alike and equally—Capt. Anthony might have been as humane a man, and every way as respectable, as many who now oppose the slave system; certainly as humane and respectable as are members of society generally. The slaveholder, as well as the slave, is the victim of the slave system. A man's character greatly takes its hue and shape from the form and color of things about him. Under the whole heavens there is no relation more unfavorable to the development of honorable character, than that sustained by the slaveholder to the slave. Reason is imprisoned here, and passions run wild. Like the fires of the prairie, once lighted, they are at the mercy of every wind, and must burn, till they have consumed all that is combustible within their remorseless grasp. Capt. Anthony could be kind, and, at times, he even showed an affectionate disposition. Could the reader have seen him gently leading me by the hand—as he sometimes did—patting me on the head, speaking to me in soft, caressing tones and calling me his "little Indian boy," he would have deemed him a kind old man, and really, almost fatherly. But the pleasant moods of a slaveholder are remarkably brittle; they are easily snapped; they neither come often, nor remain long. His temper is subjected to perpetual trials; but, since these trials are never borne patiently, they add nothing to his natural stock of patience.

Old master very early impressed me with the idea that he was an unhappy man. Even to my child's eye, he wore a troubled, and at times, a haggard aspect. His strange movements excited my curiosity, and awakened my compassion. He seldom walked alone without muttering to himself; and he occasionally stormed about, as if defying an army of invisible foes. "He would do this, that, and the other; he'd be d—d if he did not,"—was the usual form of his threats. Most of his leisure was spent in walking, cursing and gesticulating, like one possessed by a demon. Most evidently, he was a wretched man, at war with his own soul, and with all the world around him. To be overheard by the children, disturbed him very little. He made no more of our presence, than of that of the ducks and geese which he met on the green. He little thought that the little black urchins around him, could see, through those vocal crevices, the very secrets of his heart. Slaveholders ever underrate the intelligence with which they have to grapple. I really understood the old man's mutterings, attitudes and gestures, about as well as he did himself. But slaveholders never encourage that kind of communication, with the slaves, by which they might learn to measure the depths of his knowledge. Ignorance is a high virtue in a human chattel; and as the master studies to keep the slave ignorant, the slave is cunning enough to make the master think he succeeds. The slave fully appreciates the saying, "where ignorance is bliss, 'tis folly to be wise." When old master's gestures were violent, ending with a threatening shake of the head, and a sharp snap of his middle finger and thumb, I deemed it wise to keep at a respectable distance from him; for, at such times, trifling faults stood, in his eyes, as momentous offenses; and, having both the power and the disposition, the victim had only to be near him to catch the punishment, deserved or undeserved.

One of the first circumstances that opened my eyes to the cruelty and wickedness of slavery, and the heartlessness of my old master, was the refusal of the latter to interpose his authority, to protect and shield a young woman, who had been most cruelly abused and beaten by his overseer in Tuckahoe. This overseer—a Mr. Plummer—was a man like most of his class, little better than a human brute; and, in addition to his general profligacy and repulsive coarseness, the creature was a miserable drunkard. He was, probably, employed by my old master, less on account of the excellence of his services, than for the cheap rate at which they could be obtained. He was not fit to have the management of a drove of mules. In a fit of drunken madness, he committed the outrage which brought the young woman in question down to my old master's for protection. This young woman was the daughter of Milly, an own aunt of mine. The poor girl, on arriving at our house, presented a pitiable appearance. She had left in haste, and without preparation; and, probably, without the knowledge of Mr. Plummer. She had traveled twelve miles, bare-footed, bare-necked and bare-headed. Her neck and shoulders were covered with scars, newly made; and not content with marring her neck and shoulders, with the cowhide, the cowardly brute had dealt her a blow on the head with a hickory club, which cut a horrible gash, and left her face literally covered with blood. In this condition, the poor young woman came down, to implore protection at the hands of my old master. I expected to see him boil over with rage at the revolting deed, and to hear him fill the air with curses upon the brutal Plummer; but I was disappointed. He sternly told her, in an angry tone, he "believed she deserved every bit of it," and, if she did not go home instantly, he would himself take the remaining skin from her neck and back. Thus was the poor girl compelled to return, without redress, and perhaps to receive an additional flogging for daring to appeal to old master against the overseer.

Old master seemed furious at the thought of being troubled by such complaints. I did not, at that time, understand the philosophy of his treatment of my cousin. It was stern, unnatural, violent. Had the man no bowels of compassion? Was he dead to all sense of humanity? No. I think I now understand it. This treatment is a part of the system, rather than a part of the man. Were slaveholders to listen to complaints of this sort against the overseers, the luxury of owning large numbers of slaves, would be impossible. It would do away with the office of overseer, entirely; or, in other words, it would convert the master himself into an overseer. It would occasion great loss of time and labor, leaving the overseer in fetters, and without the necessary power to secure obedience to his orders. A privilege so dangerous as that of appeal, is, therefore, strictly prohibited; and any one exercising it, runs a fearful hazard. Nevertheless, when a slave has nerve enough to exercise it, and boldly approaches his master, with a well-founded complaint against an overseer, though he may be repulsed, and may even have that of which he complains repeated at the time, and, though he may be beaten by his master, as well as by the overseer, for his temerity, in the end the policy of complaining is, generally, vindicated by the relaxed rigor of the overseer's treatment. The latter becomes more careful, and less disposed to use the lash upon such slaves thereafter. It is with this final result in view, rather than with any expectation of immediate good, that the outraged slave is induced to meet his master with a complaint. The overseer very naturally dislikes to have the ear of the master disturbed by complaints; and, either upon this consideration, or upon advice and warning privately given him by his employers, he generally modifies the rigor of his rule, after an outbreak of the kind to which I have been referring.

Howsoever the slaveholder may allow himself to act toward his slave, and, whatever cruelty he may deem it wise, for example's sake, or for the gratification of his humor, to inflict, he cannot, in the absence of all provocation, look with pleasure upon the bleeding wounds of a defenseless slave-woman. When he drives her from his presence without redress, or the hope of redress, he acts, generally, from motives of policy, rather than from a hardened nature, or from innate brutality. Yet, let but his own temper be stirred, his own passions get loose, and the slave-owner will go far beyond the overseer in cruelty. He will convince the slave that his wrath is far more terrible and boundless, and vastly more to be dreaded, than that of the underling overseer. What may have been mechanically and heartlessly done by the overseer, is now done with a will. The man who now wields the lash is irresponsible. He may, if he pleases, cripple or kill, without fear of consequences; except in so far as it may concern profit or loss. To a man of violent temper—as my old master was—this was but a very slender and inefficient restraint. I have seen him in a tempest of passion, such as I have just described—a passion into which entered all the bitter ingredients of pride, hatred, envy, jealousy, and the thrist(sic) for revenge.

The circumstances which I am about to narrate, and which gave rise to this fearful tempest of passion, are not singular nor isolated in slave life, but are common in every slaveholding community in which I have lived. They are incidental to the relation of master and slave, and exist in all sections of slave-holding countries.

The reader will have noticed that, in enumerating the names of the slaves who lived with my old master, Esther is mentioned. This was a young woman who possessed that which is ever a curse to the slave-girl; namely—personal beauty. She was tall, well formed, and made a fine appearance. The daughters of Col. Lloyd could scarcely surpass her in personal charms. Esther was courted by Ned Roberts, and he was as fine looking a young man, as she was a woman. He was the son of a favorite slave of Col. Lloyd. Some slaveholders would have been glad to promote the marriage of two such persons; but, for some reason or other, my old master took it upon him to break up the growing intimacy between Esther and Edward. He strictly ordered her to quit the company of said Roberts, telling her that he would punish her severely if he ever found her again in Edward's company. This unnatural and heartless order was, of course, broken. A woman's love is not to be annihilated by the peremptory command of any one, whose breath is in his nostrils. It was impossible to keep Edward and Esther apart. Meet they would, and meet they did. Had old master been a man of honor and purity, his motives, in this matter, might have been viewed more favorably. As it was, his motives were as abhorrent, as his methods were foolish and contemptible. It was too evident that he was not concerned for the girl's welfare. It is one of the damning characteristics of the slave system, that it robs its victims of every earthly incentive to a holy life. The fear of God, and the hope of heaven, are found sufficient to sustain many slave-women, amidst the snares and dangers of their strange lot; but, this side of God and heaven, a slave-woman is at the mercy of the power, caprice and passion of her owner. Slavery provides no means for the honorable continuance of the race. Marriage as imposing obligations on the parties to it—has no existence here, except in such hearts as are purer and higher than the standard morality around them. It is one of the consolations of my life, that I know of many honorable instances of persons who maintained their honor, where all around was corrupt.

Esther was evidently much attached to Edward, and abhorred—as she had reason to do—the tyrannical and base behavior of old master. Edward was young, and fine looking, and he loved and courted her. He might have been her husband, in the high sense just alluded to; but WHO and what was this old master? His attentions were plainly brutal and selfish, and it was as natural that Esther should loathe him, as that she should love Edward. Abhorred and circumvented as he was, old master, having the power, very easily took revenge. I happened to see this exhibition of his rage and cruelty toward Esther. The time selected was singular. It was early in the morning, when all besides was still, and before any of the family, in the house or kitchen, had left their beds. I saw but few of the shocking preliminaries, for the cruel work had begun before I awoke. I was probably awakened by the shrieks and piteous cries of poor Esther. My sleeping place was on the floor of a little, rough closet, which opened into the kitchen; and through the cracks of its unplaned boards, I could distinctly see and hear what was going on, without being seen by old master. Esther's wrists were firmly tied, and the twisted rope was fastened to a strong staple in a heavy wooden joist above, near the fireplace. Here she stood, on a bench, her arms tightly drawn over her breast. Her back and shoulders were bare to the waist. Behind her stood old master, with cowskin in hand, preparing his barbarous work with all manner of harsh, coarse, and tantalizing epithets. The screams of his victim were most piercing. He was cruelly deliberate, and protracted the torture, as one who was delighted with the scene. Again and again he drew the hateful whip through his hand, adjusting it with a view of dealing the most pain-giving blow. Poor Esther had never yet been severely whipped, and her shoulders were plump and tender. Each blow, vigorously laid on, brought screams as well as blood. "Have mercy; Oh! have mercy" she cried; "I won't do so no more;" but her piercing cries seemed only to increase his fury. His answers to them are too coarse and blasphemous to be produced here. The whole scene, with all its attendants, was revolting and shocking, to the last degree; and when the motives of this brutal castigation are considered,—language has no power to convey a just sense of its awful criminality. After laying on some thirty or forty stripes, old master untied his suffering victim, and let her get down. She could scarcely stand, when untied. From my heart I pitied her, and—child though I was—the outrage kindled in me a feeling far from peaceful; but I was hushed, terrified, stunned, and could do nothing, and the fate of Esther might be mine next. The scene here described was often repeated in the case of poor Esther, and her life, as I knew it, was one of wretchedness.

CHAPTER VI. Treatment of Slaves on Lloyd's Plantation

EARLY REFLECTIONS ON SLAVERY—PRESENTIMENT OF ONE DAY BEING A FREEMAN—COMBAT BETWEEN AN OVERSEER AND A SLAVEWOMAN—THE ADVANTAGES
OF RESISTANCE—ALLOWANCE DAY ON THE HOME PLANTATION—THE SINGING
OF SLAVES—AN EXPLANATION—THE SLAVES FOOD AND CLOTHING—NAKED CHILDREN—LIFE IN THE QUARTER—DEPRIVATION OF SLEEP—NURSING CHILDREN

CARRIED TO THE FIELD—DESCRIPTION OF THE COWSKIN—THE ASH-CAKE—MANNER
OF MAKING IT—THE DINNER HOUR—THE CONTRAST.

The heart-rending incidents, related in the foregoing chapter, led me, thus early, to inquire into the nature and history of slavery. Why am I a slave? Why are some people slaves, and others masters? Was there ever a time this was not so? How did the relation commence? These were the perplexing questions which began now to claim my thoughts, and to exercise the weak powers of my mind, for I was still but a child, and knew less than children of the same age in the free states. As my questions concerning these things were only put to children a little older, and little better informed than myself, I was not rapid in reaching a solid footing. By some means I learned from these inquiries that "God, up in the sky," made every body; and that he made white people to be masters and mistresses, and black people to be slaves. This did not satisfy me, nor lessen my interest in the subject. I was told, too, that God was good, and that He knew what was best for me, and best for everybody. This was less satisfactory than the first statement; because it came, point blank, against all my notions of goodness. It was not good to let old master cut the flesh off Esther, and make her cry so. Besides, how did people know that God made black people to be slaves? Did they go up in the sky and learn it? or, did He come down and tell them so? All was dark here. It was some relief to my hard notions of the goodness of God, that, although he made white men to be slaveholders, he did not make them to be bad slaveholders, and that, in due time, he would punish the bad slaveholders; that he would, when they died, send them to the bad place, where they would be "burnt up." Nevertheless, I could not reconcile the relation of slavery with my crude notions of goodness. Then, too, I found that there were puzzling exceptions to this theory of slavery on both sides, and in the middle. I knew of blacks who were not slaves; I knew of whites who were not slaveholders; and I knew of persons who were nearly white, who were slaves. Color, therefore, was a very unsatisfactory basis for slavery.

Once, however, engaged in the inquiry, I was not very long in finding out the true solution of the matter. It was not color, but crime, not God, but man, that afforded the true explanation of the existence of slavery; nor was I long in finding out another important truth, viz: what man can make, man can unmake. The appalling darkness faded away, and I was master of the subject. There were slaves here, direct from Guinea; and there were many who could say that their fathers and mothers were stolen from Africa—forced from their homes, and compelled to serve as slaves. This, to me, was knowledge; but it was a kind of knowledge which filled me with a burning hatred of slavery, increased my suffering, and left me without the means of breaking away from my bondage. Yet it was knowledge quite worth possessing. I could not have been more than seven or eight years old, when I began to make this subject my study. It was with me in the woods and fields; along the shore of the river, and wherever my boyish wanderings led me; and though I was, at that time, quite ignorant of the existence of the free states, I distinctly remember being, even then, most strongly impressed with the idea of being a freeman some day. This cheering assurance was an inborn dream of my human nature a constant menace to slavery—and one which all the powers of slavery were unable to silence or extinguish.

Up to the time of the brutal flogging of my Aunt Esther—for she was my own aunt—and the horrid plight in which I had seen my cousin from Tuckahoe, who had been so badly beaten by the cruel Mr. Plummer, my attention had not been called, especially, to the gross features of slavery. I had, of course, heard of whippings and of savage rencontres between overseers and slaves, but I had always been out of the way at the times and places of their occurrence. My plays and sports, most of the time, took me from the corn and tobacco fields, where the great body of the hands were at work, and where scenes of cruelty were enacted and witnessed. But, after the whipping of Aunt Esther, I saw many cases of the same shocking nature, not only in my master's house, but on Col. Lloyd's plantation. One of the first which I saw, and which greatly agitated me, was the whipping of a woman belonging to Col. Lloyd, named Nelly. The offense alleged against Nelly, was one of the commonest and most indefinite in the whole catalogue of offenses usually laid to the charge of slaves, viz: "impudence." This may mean almost anything, or nothing at all, just according to the caprice of the master or overseer, at the moment. But, whatever it is, or is not, if it gets the name of "impudence," the party charged with it is sure of a flogging. This offense may be committed in various ways; in the tone of an answer; in answering at all; in not answering; in the expression of countenance; in the motion of the head; in the gait, manner and bearing of the slave. In the case under consideration, I can easily believe that, according to all slaveholding standards, here was a genuine instance of impudence. In Nelly there were all the necessary conditions for committing the offense. She was a bright mulatto, the recognized wife of a favorite "hand" on board Col. Lloyd's sloop, and the mother of five sprightly children. She was a vigorous and spirited woman, and one of the most likely, on the plantation, to be guilty of impudence. My attention was called to the scene, by the noise, curses and screams that proceeded from it; and, on going a little in that direction, I came upon the parties engaged in the skirmish. Mr. Siever, the overseer, had hold of Nelly, when I caught sight of them; he was endeavoring to drag her toward a tree, which endeavor Nelly was sternly resisting; but to no purpose, except to retard the progress of the overseer's plans. Nelly—as I have said—was the mother of five children; three of them were present, and though quite small (from seven to ten years old, I should think) they gallantly came to their mother's defense, and gave the overseer an excellent pelting with stones. One of the little fellows ran up, seized the overseer by the leg and bit him; but the monster was too busily engaged with Nelly, to pay any attention to the assaults of the children. There were numerous bloody marks on Mr. Sevier's face, when I first saw him, and they increased as the struggle went on. The imprints of Nelly's fingers were visible, and I was glad to see them. Amidst the wild screams of the children—"Let my mammy go"—"let my mammy go"—there escaped, from between the teeth of the bullet-headed overseer, a few bitter curses, mingled with threats, that "he would teach the d—d b—h how to give a white man impudence." There is no doubt that Nelly felt herself superior, in some respects, to the slaves around her. She was a wife and a mother; her husband was a valued and favorite slave. Besides, he was one of the first hands on board of the sloop, and the sloop hands—since they had to represent the plantation abroad—were generally treated tenderly. The overseer never was allowed to whip Harry; why then should he be allowed to whip Harry's wife? Thoughts of this kind, no doubt, influenced her; but, for whatever reason, she nobly resisted, and, unlike most of the slaves, seemed determined to make her whipping cost Mr. Sevier as much as possible. The blood on his (and her) face, attested her skill, as well as her courage and dexterity in using her nails. Maddened by her resistance, I expected to see Mr. Sevier level her to the ground by a stunning blow; but no; like a savage bull-dog—which he resembled both in temper and appearance—he maintained his grip, and steadily dragged his victim toward the tree, disregarding alike her blows, and the cries of the children for their mother's release. He would, doubtless, have knocked her down with his hickory stick, but that such act might have cost him his place. It is often deemed advisable to knock a man slave down, in order to tie him, but it is considered cowardly and inexcusable, in an overseer, thus to deal with a woman. He is expected to tie her up, and to give her what is called, in southern parlance, a "genteel flogging," without any very great outlay of strength or skill. I watched, with palpitating interest, the course of the preliminary struggle, and was saddened by every new advantage gained over her by the ruffian. There were times when she seemed likely to get the better of the brute, but he finally overpowered her, and succeeded in getting his rope around her arms, and in firmly tying her to the tree, at which he had been aiming. This done, and Nelly was at the mercy of his merciless lash; and now, what followed, I have no heart to describe. The cowardly creature made good his every threat; and wielded the lash with all the hot zest of furious revenge. The cries of the woman, while undergoing the terrible infliction, were mingled with those of the children, sounds which I hope the reader may never be called upon to hear. When Nelly was untied, her back was covered with blood. The red stripes were all over her shoulders. She was whipped—

severely whipped; but she was not subdued, for she continued to denounce the overseer, and to call him every vile name. He had bruised her flesh, but had left her invincible spirit undaunted. Such floggings are seldom repeated by the same overseer. They prefer to whip those who are most easily whipped. The old doctrine that submission is the very best cure for outrage and wrong, does not hold good on the slave plantation. He is whipped oftenest, who is whipped easiest; and that slave who has the courage to stand up for himself against the overseer, although he may have many hard stripes at the first, becomes, in the end, a freeman, even though he sustain the formal relation of a slave. "You can shoot me but you can't whip me," said a slave to Rigby Hopkins; and the result was that he was neither whipped nor shot. If the latter had been his fate, it would have been less deplorable than the living and lingering death to which cowardly and slavish souls are subjected. I do not know that Mr. Sevier ever undertook to whip Nelly again. He probably never did, for it was not long after his attempt to subdue her, that he was taken sick, and died. The wretched man died as he had lived, unrepentant; and it was said—with how much truth I know not—that in the very last hours of his life, his ruling passion showed itself, and that when wrestling with death, he was uttering horrid oaths, and flourishing the cowskin, as though he was tearing the flesh off some helpless slave. One thing is certain, that when he was in health, it was enough to chill the blood, and to stiffen the hair of an ordinary man, to hear Mr. Sevier talk. Nature, or his cruel habits, had given to his face an expression of unusual savageness, even for a slave-driver. Tobacco and rage had worn his teeth short, and nearly every sentence that escaped their compressed grating, was commenced or concluded with some outburst of profanity. His presence made the field alike the field of blood, and of blasphemy. Hated for his cruelty, despised for his cowardice, his death was deplored by no one outside his own house—if indeed it was deplored there; it was regarded by the slaves as a merciful interposition of Providence. Never went there a man to the grave loaded with heavier curses. Mr. Sevier's place was promptly taken by a Mr. Hopkins, and the change was quite a relief, he being a very different man. He was, in all respects, a better man than his predecessor; as good as any man can be, and yet be an overseer. His course was characterized by no extraordinary cruelty; and when he whipped a slave, as he sometimes did, he seemed to take no especial pleasure in it, but, on the contrary, acted as though he felt it to be a mean business. Mr. Hopkins stayed but a short time; his place much to the regret of the slaves generally—was taken by a Mr. Gore, of whom more will be said hereafter. It is enough, for the present, to say, that he was no improvement on Mr. Sevier, except that he was less noisy and less profane.

I have already referred to the business-like aspect of Col. Lloyd's plantation. This business-like appearance was much increased on the two days at the end of each month, when the slaves from the different farms came to get their monthly allowance of meal and meat. These were gala days for the slaves, and there was much rivalry among them as to who should be elected to go up to the great house farm for the allowance, and, indeed, to attend to any business at this (for them) the capital. The beauty and grandeur of the place, its numerous slave population, and the fact that Harry, Peter and Jake the sailors of the sloop—almost always kept, privately, little trinkets which they bought at Baltimore, to sell, made it a privilege to come to the great house farm. Being selected, too, for this office, was deemed a high honor. It was taken as a proof of confidence and favor; but, probably, the chief motive of the competitors for the place, was, a desire to break the dull monotony of the field, and to get beyond the overseer's eye and lash. Once on the road with an ox team, and seated on the tongue of his cart, with no overseer to look after him, the slave was comparatively free; and, if thoughtful, he had time to think. Slaves are generally expected to sing as well as to work. A silent slave is not liked by masters or overseers. "Make a noise," "make a noise," and "bear a hand," are the words usually addressed to the slaves when there is silence amongst them. This may account for the almost constant singing heard in the southern states. There was, generally, more or less singing among the teamsters, as it was one means of letting the overseer know where they were, and that they were moving on with the work. But, on allowance day, those who visited the great house farm were peculiarly excited and noisy. While on their way, they would make the dense old woods, for miles around, reverberate with their wild notes. These were not always merry because they were wild. On the contrary, they were mostly of a plaintive cast, and told a tale of grief and sorrow. In the most boisterous outbursts of rapturous sentiment, there was ever a tinge of deep melancholy. I have never heard any songs like those anywhere since I left slavery, except when in Ireland. There I heard the same wailing notes, and was much affected by them. It was during the famine of 1845-6. In all the songs of the slaves, there was ever some expression in praise of the great house farm; something which would flatter the pride of the owner, and, possibly, draw a favorable glance from him.

I am going away to the great house farm,
O yea! O yea! O yea!
My old master is a good old master,
O yea! O yea! O yea!

This they would sing, with other words of their own improvising—jargon to others, but full of meaning to themselves. I have sometimes thought, that the mere hearing of those songs would do more to impress truly spiritual-minded men and women with the soul-crushing and death-dealing character of slavery, than the reading of whole volumes of its mere physical cruelties. They speak to the heart and to the soul of the thoughtful. I cannot better express my sense of them now, than ten years ago, when, in sketching my life, I thus spoke of this feature of my plantation experience:

I did not, when a slave, understand the deep meanings of those rude, and apparently incoherent songs. I was myself within the circle, so that I neither saw or heard as those without might see and hear. They told a tale which was then altogether beyond my feeble comprehension; they were tones, loud, long and deep, breathing the prayer and complaint of souls boiling over with the bitterest anguish. Every tone was a testimony against slavery, and a prayer to God for deliverance from chains. The hearing of those wild notes always depressed my spirits, and filled my heart with ineffable sadness. The mere recurrence, even now, afflicts my spirit, and while I am writing these lines, my tears are falling. To those songs I trace my first glimmering conceptions of the dehumanizing character of slavery. I can never get rid of that conception. Those songs still follow me, to deepen my hatred of slavery, and quicken my sympathies for my brethren in bonds. If any one wishes to be impressed with a sense of the soul-killing power of slavery, let him go to Col. Lloyd's plantation, and, on allowance day, place himself in the deep, pine woods, and there let him, in silence, thoughtfully analyze the sounds that shall pass through the chambers of his soul, and if he is not thus impressed, it will only be because "there is no flesh in his obdurate heart."

The remark is not unfrequently made, that slaves are the most contended and happy laborers in the world. They dance and sing, and make all manner of joyful noises—so they do; but it is a great mistake to suppose them happy because they sing. The songs of the slave represent the sorrows, rather than the joys, of his heart; and he is relieved by them, only as an aching heart is relieved by its tears. Such is the constitution of the human mind, that, when pressed to extremes, it often avails itself of the most opposite methods. Extremes meet in mind as in matter. When the slaves on board of the "Pearl" were overtaken, arrested, and carried to prison—their hopes for freedom blasted—as they marched in chains they sang, and found (as Emily Edmunson tells us) a melancholy relief in singing. The singing of a man cast away on a desolate island, might be as appropriately considered an evidence of his contentment and happiness, as the singing of a slave. Sorrow and desolation have their songs, as well as joy and peace. Slaves sing more to make themselves happy, than to express their happiness.

It is the boast of slaveholders, that their slaves enjoy more of the physical comforts of life than the peasantry of any country in the world. My experience contradicts this. The men and the women slaves on Col. Lloyd's farm, received, as their monthly allowance of food, eight pounds of pickled pork, or their equivalent in fish. The pork was often tainted, and the fish was of the poorest quality—herrings, which would bring very little if offered for sale in any northern market. With their pork or fish, they had one bushel of Indian meal—unbolted—of which quite fifteen per cent was fit only to feed pigs. With this, one pint of salt was given; and this was the entire monthly allowance of a full grown slave, working constantly in the open field, from morning until night, every day in the month except Sunday, and living on a fraction more than a quarter of a pound of meat per day, and less than a peck of corn-meal per week. There is no kind of work that a man can do which requires a better supply of food to prevent physical exhaustion, than the field-work of a slave. So much for the slave's allowance of food; now for his raiment. The yearly allowance of clothing for the slaves on this plantation, consisted of two tow-linen shirts—such linen as the coarsest crash towels are made of; one pair of trowsers of the same material, for summer, and a pair of trowsers and a jacket of woolen, most slazily put together, for winter; one pair of yarn stockings, and one pair of shoes of the coarsest description. The slave's entire apparel could not have cost more than eight dollars per year. The allowance of food and clothing for the little children, was committed to their mothers, or to the older slavewomen having the care of them. Children who were unable to work in the field, had neither shoes, stockings, jackets nor trowsers given them. Their clothing consisted of two coarse tow-linen shirts—already described—per year; and when these failed them, as they often did, they went naked until the next allowance day. Flocks of little children from five to ten years old, might be seen on Col. Lloyd's plantation, as destitute of clothing as any little heathen on the west coast of Africa; and this, not merely during the summer months, but during the frosty weather of March. The little girls were no better off than the boys; all were nearly in a state of nudity.

As to beds to sleep on, they were known to none of the field hands; nothing but a coarse blanket—not so good as those used in the north to cover horses—was given them, and this only to the men and women. The children stuck themselves in holes and corners, about the quarters; often in the corner of the huge chimneys, with their feet in the ashes to keep them warm. The want of beds, however, was not considered a very great privation. Time to sleep was of far greater importance, for, when the day's work is done, most of the slaves have their washing, mending and cooking to do; and, having few or none of the ordinary facilities for doing such things, very many of their sleeping hours are consumed in necessary preparations for the duties of the coming day.

The sleeping apartments—if they may be called such—have little regard to comfort or decency. Old and young, male and female, married and single, drop down upon the common clay floor, each covering up with his or her blanket,—the only protection they have from cold or exposure. The night, however, is shortened at both ends. The slaves work often as long as they can see, and are late in cooking and mending for the coming day; and, at the first gray streak of morning, they are summoned to the field by the driver's horn.

More slaves are whipped for oversleeping than for any other fault. Neither age nor sex finds any favor. The overseer stands at the quarter door, armed with stick and cowskin, ready to whip any who may be a few minutes behind time. When the horn is blown, there is a rush for the door, and the hindermost one is sure to get a blow from the overseer. Young mothers who worked in the field, were allowed an hour, about ten o'clock in the morning, to go home to nurse their children. Sometimes they were compelled to take their children with them, and to leave them in the corner of the fences, to prevent loss of time in nursing them. The overseer generally rides about the field on horseback. A cowskin and a hickory stick are his constant companions. The cowskin is a kind of whip seldom seen in the northern states. It is made entirely of untanned, but dried, ox hide, and is about as hard as a piece of well-seasoned live oak. It is made of various sizes, but the usual length is about three feet. The part held in the hand is nearly an inch in thickness; and, from the extreme end of the butt or handle, the cowskin tapers its whole length to a point. This makes it quite elastic and springy. A blow with it, on the hardest back, will gash the flesh, and make the blood start. Cowskins are painted red, blue and green, and are the favorite slave whip. I think this whip worse than the "cat-o'nine-tails." It condenses the whole strength of the arm to a single point, and comes with a spring that makes the air whistle. It is a terrible instrument, and is so handy, that the overseer can always have it on his person, and ready for use. The temptation to use it is ever strong; and an overseer can, if disposed, always have cause for using it. With him, it is literally a word and a blow, and, in most cases, the blow comes first.

As a general rule, slaves do not come to the quarters for either breakfast or dinner, but take their "ash cake" with them, and eat it in the field. This was so on the home plantation; probably, because the distance from the quarter to the field, was sometimes two, and even three miles.

The dinner of the slaves consisted of a huge piece of ash cake, and a small piece of pork, or two salt herrings. Not having ovens, nor any suitable cooking utensils, the slaves mixed their meal with a little water, to such thickness that a spoon would stand erect in it; and, after the wood had burned away to coals and ashes, they would place the dough between oak leaves and lay it carefully in the ashes, completely covering it; hence, the bread is called ash cake. The surface of this peculiar bread is covered with ashes, to the depth of a sixteenth part of an inch, and the ashes, certainly, do not make it very grateful to the teeth, nor render it very palatable. The bran, or coarse part of the meal, is baked with the fine, and bright scales run through the bread. This bread, with its ashes and bran, would disgust and choke a northern man, but it is quite liked by the slaves. They eat it with avidity, and are more concerned about the quantity than about the quality. They are far too scantily provided for, and are worked too steadily, to be much concerned for the quality of their food. The few minutes allowed them at dinner time, after partaking of their coarse repast, are variously spent. Some lie down on the "turning row," and go to sleep; others draw together, and talk; and others are at work with needle and thread, mending their tattered garments. Sometimes you may hear a wild, hoarse laugh arise from a circle, and often a song. Soon, however, the overseer comes dashing through the field. "Tumble up! Tumble up, and to work, work," is the cry; and, now, from twelve o'clock (mid-day) till dark, the human cattle are in motion, wielding their clumsy hoes; hurried on by no hope of reward, no sense of gratitude, no love of children, no prospect of bettering their condition; nothing, save the dread and terror of the slave-driver's lash. So goes one day, and so comes and goes another.

But, let us now leave the rough usage of the field, where vulgar coarseness and brutal cruelty spread themselves and flourish, rank as weeds in the tropics; where a vile wretch, in the shape of a man, rides, walks, or struts about, dealing blows, and leaving gashes on broken-spirited men and helpless women, for thirty dollars per month—a business so horrible, hardening and disgraceful, that, rather, than engage in it, a decent man would blow his own brains out—and let the reader view with me the equally wicked, but less repulsive aspects of slave life; where pride and pomp roll luxuriously at ease; where the toil of a thousand men supports a single family in easy idleness and sin. This is the great house; it is the home of the LLOYDS! Some idea of its splendor has already been given—and, it is here that we shall find that height of luxury which is the opposite of that depth of poverty and physical wretchedness that we have just now been contemplating. But, there is this difference in the two extremes; viz: that in the case of the slave, the miseries and hardships of his lot are imposed by others, and, in the master's case, they are imposed by himself. The slave is a subject, subjected by others; the slaveholder is a subject, but he is the author of his own subjection. There is more truth in the saying, that slavery is a greater evil to the master than to the slave, than many, who utter it, suppose. The self-executing laws of eternal justice follow close on the heels of the evil-doer here, as well as elsewhere; making escape from all its penalties impossible. But, let others philosophize; it is my province here to relate and describe; only allowing myself a word or two, occasionally, to assist the reader in the proper understanding of the facts narrated.

CHAPTER VII. Life in the Great House

COMFORTS AND LUXURIES—ELABORATE EXPENDITURE—HOUSE SERVANTS—MEN
SERVANTS AND MAID SERVANTS—APPEARANCES—SLAVE ARISTOCRACY—STABLE AND
CARRIAGE HOUSE—BOUNDLESS HOSPITALITY—FRAGRANCE OF RICH DISHES—THE
DECEPTIVE CHARACTER OF SLAVERY—SLAVES SEEM HAPPY—SLAVES
AND SLAVEHOLDERS ALIKE WRETCHED—FRETFUL DISCONTENT
OF SLAVEHOLDERS—FAULT-FINDING—OLD BARNEY—HIS
PROFESSION—WHIPPING—HUMILIATING SPECTACLE—CASE EXCEPTIONAL—WILLIAM
WILKS—SUPPOSED SON OF COL. LLOYD—CURIOUS INCIDENT—SLAVES PREFER RICH
MASTERS TO POOR ONES.

The close-fisted stinginess that fed the poor slave on coarse corn-meal and tainted meat; that clothed him in crashy tow-linen, and hurried him to toil through the field, in all weathers, with wind and rain beating through his tattered garments; that scarcely gave even the young slave-mother time to nurse her hungry infant in the fence corner; wholly vanishes on approaching the sacred precincts of the great house, the home of the Lloyds. There the scriptural phrase finds an exact illustration; the highly favored inmates of this mansion are literally arrayed "in purple and fine linen," and fare sumptuously every day! The table groans under the heavy and blood-bought luxuries gathered with painstaking care, at home and abroad. Fields, forests, rivers and seas, are made tributary here. Immense wealth, and its lavish expenditure, fill the great house with all that can please the eye, or tempt the taste. Here, appetite, not food, is the great desideratum. Fish, flesh and fowl, are here in profusion. Chickens, of all breeds; ducks, of all kinds, wild and tame, the common, and the huge Muscovite; Guinea fowls, turkeys, geese, and pea fowls, are in their several pens, fat and fatting for the destined vortex. The graceful swan, the mongrels, the black-necked wild goose; partridges, quails, pheasants and pigeons; choice water fowl, with all their strange varieties, are caught in this huge family net. Beef, veal, mutton and venison, of the most select kinds and quality, roll bounteously to this grand consumer. The teeming riches of the Chesapeake bay, its rock, perch, drums, crocus, trout, oysters, crabs, and terrapin, are drawn hither to adorn the glittering table of the great house. The dairy, too, probably the finest on the Eastern Shore of Maryland—supplied by cattle of the best English stock, imported for the purpose, pours its rich donations of fragant cheese, golden butter, and delicious cream, to heighten the attraction of the gorgeous, unending round of feasting. Nor are the fruits of the earth forgotten or neglected. The fertile garden, many acres in size, constituting a separate establishment, distinct from the common farm—with its scientific gardener, imported from Scotland (a Mr. McDermott) with four men under his direction, was not behind, either in the abundance or in the delicacy of its contributions to the same full board. The tender asparagus, the succulent celery, and the delicate cauliflower; egg plants, beets, lettuce, parsnips, peas, and French beans, early and late; radishes, cantelopes, melons of all kinds; the fruits and flowers of all climes and of all descriptions, from the hardy apple of the north, to the lemon and orange of the south, culminated at this point. Baltimore gathered figs, raisins, almonds and juicy grapes from Spain. Wines and brandies from France; teas of various flavor, from China; and rich, aromatic coffee from Java, all conspired to swell the tide of high life, where pride and indolence rolled and lounged in magnificence and satiety.

Behind the tall-backed and elaborately wrought chairs, stand the servants, men and maidens—fifteen in number—discriminately selected, not only with a view to their industry and faithfulness, but with special regard to their personal appearance, their graceful agility and captivating address. Some of these are armed with fans, and are fanning reviving breezes toward the over-heated brows of the alabaster ladies; others watch with eager eye, and with fawn-like step anticipate and supply wants before they are sufficiently formed to be announced by word or sign.

These servants constituted a sort of black aristocracy on Col. Lloyd's plantation. They resembled the field hands in nothing, except in color, and in this they held the advantage of a velvet-like glossiness, rich and beautiful. The hair, too, showed the same advantage. The delicate colored maid rustled in the scarcely worn silk of her young mistress, while the servant men were equally well attired from the over-flowing wardrobe of their young masters; so that, in dress, as well as in form and feature, in manner and speech, in tastes and habits, the distance between these favored few, and the sorrow and hunger-smitten multitudes of the quarter and the field, was immense; and this is seldom passed over.

Let us now glance at the stables and the carriage house, and we shall find the same evidences of pride and luxurious extravagance. Here are three splendid coaches, soft within and lustrous without. Here, too, are gigs, phaetons, barouches, sulkeys and sleighs. Here are saddles and harnesses—beautifully wrought and silver mounted—kept with every care. In the stable you will find, kept only for pleasure, full thirty-five horses, of the most approved blood for speed and beauty. There are two men here constantly employed in taking care of these horses. One of these men must be always in the stable, to answer every call from the great house. Over the way from the stable, is a house built expressly for the hounds—a pack of twenty-five or thirty—whose fare would have made glad the heart of a dozen slaves. Horses and hounds are not the only consumers of the slave's toil. There was practiced, at the Lloyd's, a hospitality which would have astonished and charmed any health-seeking northern divine or merchant, who might have chanced to share it. Viewed from his own table, and not from the field, the colonel was a model of generous hospitality. His house was, literally, a hotel, for weeks during the summer months. At these times, especially, the air was freighted with the rich fumes of baking, boiling, roasting and broiling. The odors I shared with the winds; but the meats were under a more stringent monopoly except that, occasionally, I got a cake from Mas' Daniel. In Mas' Daniel I had a friend at court, from whom I learned many things which my eager curiosity was excited to know. I always knew when company was expected, and who they were, although I was an outsider, being the property, not of Col. Lloyd, but of a servant of the wealthy colonel. On these occasions, all that pride, taste and money could do, to dazzle and charm, was done.

Who could say that the servants of Col. Lloyd were not well clad and cared for, after witnessing one of his magnificent entertainments? Who could say that they did not seem to glory in being the slaves of such a master? Who, but a fanatic, could get up any sympathy for persons whose every movement was agile, easy and graceful, and who evinced a consciousness of high superiority? And who would ever venture to suspect that Col. Lloyd was subject to the troubles of ordinary mortals? Master and slave seem alike in their glory here? Can it all be seeming? Alas! it may only be a sham at last! This immense wealth; this gilded splendor; this profusion of luxury; this exemption from toil; this life of ease; this sea of plenty; aye, what of it all? Are the pearly gates of happiness and sweet content flung open to such suitors? far from it! The poor slave, on his hard, pine plank, but scantily covered with his thin blanket, sleeps more soundly than the feverish voluptuary who reclines upon his feather bed and downy pillow. Food, to the indolent lounger, is poison, not sustenance. Lurking beneath all their dishes, are invisible spirits of evil, ready to feed the self-deluded gormandizers which aches, pains, fierce temper, uncontrolled passions, dyspepsia, rheumatism, lumbago and gout; and of these the Lloyds got their full share. To the pampered love of ease, there is no resting place. What is pleasant today, is repulsive tomorrow; what is soft now, is hard at another time; what is sweet in the morning, is bitter in the evening. Neither to the wicked, nor to the idler, is there any solid peace: "Troubled, like the restless sea."

I had excellent opportunities of witnessing the restless discontent and the capricious irritation of the Lloyds. My fondness for horses—not peculiar to me more than to other boys attracted me, much of the time, to the stables. This establishment was especially under the care of "old" and "young" Barney—father and son. Old Barney was a fine looking old man, of a brownish complexion, who was quite portly, and wore a dignified aspect for a slave. He was, evidently, much devoted to his profession, and held his office an honorable one. He was a farrier as well as an ostler; he could bleed, remove lampers from the mouths of the horses, and was well instructed in horse medicines. No one on the farm knew, so well as Old Barney, what to do with a sick horse. But his gifts and acquirements were of little advantage to him. His office was by no means an enviable one. He often got presents, but he got stripes as well; for in nothing was Col. Lloyd more unreasonable and exacting, than in respect to the management of his pleasure horses. Any supposed inattention to these animals were sure to be visited with degrading punishment. His horses and dogs fared better than his men. Their beds must be softer and cleaner than those of his human cattle. No excuse could shield Old Barney, if the colonel only suspected something wrong about his horses; and, consequently, he was often punished when faultless. It was absolutely painful to listen to the many unreasonable and fretful scoldings, poured out at the stable, by Col. Lloyd, his sons and sons-in-law. Of the latter, he had three—Messrs. Nicholson, Winder and Lownes. These all lived at the great house a portion of the year, and enjoyed the luxury of whipping the servants when they pleased, which was by no means unfrequently. A horse was seldom brought out of the stable to which no objection could be raised. "There was dust in his hair;" "there was a twist in his reins;" "his mane did not lie straight;" "he had not been properly grained;" "his head did not look well;" "his fore-top was not combed out;" "his fetlocks had not been properly trimmed;" something was always wrong. Listening to complaints, however groundless, Barney must stand, hat in hand, lips sealed, never answering a word. He must make no reply, no explanation; the judgment of the master must be deemed infallible, for his power is absolute and irresponsible. In a free state, a master, thus complaining without cause, of his ostler, might be told—"Sir, I am sorry I cannot please you, but, since I have done the best I can, your remedy is to dismiss me." Here, however, the ostler must stand, listen and tremble. One of the most heart-saddening and humiliating scenes I ever witnessed, was the whipping of Old Barney, by Col. Lloyd himself. Here were two men, both advanced in years; there were the silvery locks of Col. L., and there was the bald and toil-worn brow of Old Barney; master and slave; superior and inferior here, but equals at the bar of God; and, in the common course of events, they must both soon meet in another world, in a world where all distinctions, except those based on obedience and disobedience, are blotted out forever. "Uncover your head!" said the imperious master; he was obeyed. "Take off your jacket, you old rascal!" and off came Barney's jacket. "Down on your knees!" down knelt the old man, his shoulders bare, his bald head glistening in the sun, and his aged knees on the cold, damp ground. In his humble and debasing attitude, the master—that master to whom he had given the best years and the best strength of his life—came forward, and laid on thirty lashes, with his horse whip. The old man bore it patiently, to the last, answering each blow with a slight shrug of the shoulders, and a groan. I cannot think that Col. Lloyd succeeded in marring the flesh of Old Barney very seriously, for the whip was a light, riding whip; but the spectacle of an aged man—a husband and a father—humbly kneeling before a worm of the dust, surprised and shocked me at the time; and since I have grown old enough to think on the wickedness of slavery, few facts have been of more value to me than this, to which I was a witness. It reveals slavery in its true color, and in its maturity of repulsive hatefulness. I owe it to truth, however, to say, that this was the first and the last time I ever saw Old Barney, or any other slave, compelled to kneel to receive a whipping.

I saw, at the stable, another incident, which I will relate, as it is illustrative of a phase of slavery to which I have already referred in another connection. Besides two other coachmen, Col. Lloyd owned one named William, who, strangely enough, was often called by his surname, Wilks, by white and colored people on the home plantation. Wilks was a very fine looking man. He was about as white as anybody on the plantation; and in manliness of form, and comeliness of features, he bore a very striking resemblance to Mr. Murray Lloyd. It was whispered, and pretty generally admitted as a fact, that William Wilks was a son of Col. Lloyd, by a highly favored slave-woman, who was still on the plantation. There were many reasons for believing this whisper, not only in William's appearance, but in the undeniable freedom which he enjoyed over all others, and his apparent consciousness of being something more than a slave to his master. It was notorious, too, that William had a deadly enemy in Murray Lloyd, whom he so much resembled, and that the latter greatly worried his father with importunities to sell William. Indeed, he gave his father no rest until he did sell him, to Austin Woldfolk, the great slave-trader at that time. Before selling him, however, Mr. L. tried what giving William a whipping would do, toward making things smooth; but this was a failure. It was a compromise, and defeated itself; for, immediately after the infliction, the heart-sickened colonel atoned to William for the abuse, by giving him a gold watch and chain. Another fact, somewhat curious, is, that though sold to the remorseless Woldfolk, taken in irons to Baltimore and cast into prison, with a view to being driven to the south, William, by some means—always a mystery to me—outbid all his purchasers, paid for himself, and now resides in Baltimore, a FREEMAN. Is there not room to suspect, that, as the gold watch was presented to atone for the whipping, a purse of gold was given him by the same hand, with which to effect his purchase, as an atonement for the indignity involved in selling his own flesh and blood. All the circumstances of William, on the great house farm, show him to have occupied a different position from the other slaves, and, certainly, there is nothing in the supposed hostility of slaveholders to amalgamation, to forbid the supposition that William Wilks was the son of Edward Lloyd. Practical amalgamation is common in every neighborhood where I have been in slavery.

Col. Lloyd was not in the way of knowing much of the real opinions and feelings of his slaves respecting him. The distance between him and them was far too great to admit of such knowledge. His slaves were so numerous, that he did not know them when he saw them. Nor, indeed, did all his slaves know him. In this respect, he was inconveniently rich. It is reported of him, that, while riding along the road one day, he met a colored man, and addressed him in the usual way of speaking to colored people on the public highways of the south: "Well, boy, who do you belong to?" "To Col. Lloyd," replied the slave. "Well, does the colonel treat you well?" "No, sir," was the ready reply. "What? does he work you too hard?" "Yes, sir." "Well, don't he give enough to eat?" "Yes, sir, he gives me enough, such as it is." The colonel, after ascertaining where the slave belonged, rode on; the slave also went on about his business, not dreaming that he had been conversing with his master. He thought, said and heard nothing more of the matter, until two or three weeks afterwards. The poor man was then informed by his overseer, that, for having found fault with his master, he was now to be sold to a Georgia trader. He was immediately chained and handcuffed; and thus, without a moment's warning he was snatched away, and forever sundered from his family and friends, by a hand more unrelenting than that of death. This is the penalty of telling the simple truth, in answer to a series of plain questions. It is partly in consequence of such facts, that slaves, when inquired of as to their condition and the character of their masters, almost invariably say they are contented, and that their masters are kind. Slaveholders have been known to send spies among their slaves, to ascertain, if possible, their views and feelings in regard to their condition. The frequency of this had the effect to establish among the slaves the maxim, that a still tongue makes a wise head. They suppress the truth rather than take the consequence of telling it, and, in so doing, they prove themselves a part of the human family. If they have anything to say of their master, it is, generally, something in his favor, especially when speaking to strangers. I was frequently asked, while a slave, if I had a kind master, and I do not remember ever to have given a negative reply. Nor did I, when pursuing this course, consider myself as uttering what was utterly false; for I always measured the kindness of my master by the standard of kindness set up by slaveholders around us. However, slaves are like other people, and imbibe similar prejudices. They are apt to think their condition better than that of others. Many, under the influence of this prejudice, think their own masters are better than the masters of other slaves; and this, too, in some cases, when the very reverse is true. Indeed, it is not uncommon for slaves even to fall out and quarrel among themselves about the relative kindness of their masters, contending for the superior goodness of his own over that of others. At the very same time, they mutually execrate their masters, when viewed separately. It was so on our plantation. When Col. Lloyd's slaves met those of Jacob Jepson, they seldom parted without a quarrel about their masters; Col. Lloyd's slaves contending that he was the richest, and Mr. Jepson's slaves that he was the smartest, man of the two. Col. Lloyd's slaves would boost his ability to buy and sell Jacob Jepson; Mr. Jepson's slaves would boast his ability to whip Col. Lloyd. These quarrels would almost always end in a fight between the parties; those that beat were supposed to have gained the point at issue. They seemed to think that the greatness of their masters was transferable to themselves. To be a SLAVE, was thought to be bad enough; but to be a poor man's slave, was deemed a disgrace, indeed.

CHAPTER VIII. A Chapter of Horrors

AUSTIN GORE—A SKETCH OF HIS CHARACTER—OVERSEERS AS A CLASS—THEIR
PECULIAR CHARACTERISTICS—THE MARKED INDIVIDUALITY OF AUSTIN
GORE—HIS SENSE OF DUTY—HOW HE WHIPPED—MURDER OF POOR DENBY—HOW IT
OCCURRED—SENSATION—HOW GORE MADE PEACE WITH COL. LLOYD—THE
MURDER
UNPUNISHED—ANOTHER DREADFUL MURDER NARRATED—NO LAWS FOR THE
PROTECTION
OF SLAVES CAN BE ENFORCED IN THE SOUTHERN STATES.
As I have already intimated elsewhere, the slaves on Col. Lloyd's plantation, whose hard lot, under Mr. Sevier, the reader has already noticed and deplored, were not permitted to enjoy the comparatively moderate rule of Mr. Hopkins. The latter was succeeded by a very different man. The name of the new overseer was Austin Gore. Upon this individual I would fix particular attention; for under his rule there was more suffering from violence and bloodshed than had—according to the older slaves ever been experienced before on this plantation. I confess, I hardly know how to bring this man fitly before the reader. He was, it is true, an overseer, and possessed, to a large extent, the peculiar characteristics of his class; yet, to call him merely an overseer, would not give the reader a fair notion of the man. I speak of overseers as a class. They are such. They are as distinct from the slaveholding gentry of the south, as are the fishwomen of Paris, and the coal-heavers of London, distinct from other members of society. They constitute a separate fraternity at the south, not less marked than is the fraternity of Park Lane bullies in New York. They have been arranged and classified by that great law of attraction, which determines the spheres and affinities of men; which ordains, that men, whose malign and brutal propensities predominate over their moral and intellectual endowments, shall, naturally, fall into those employments which promise the largest gratification to those predominating instincts or propensities. The office of overseer takes this raw material of vulgarity and brutality, and stamps it as a distinct class of southern society. But, in this class, as in all other classes, there are characters of marked individuality, even while they bear a general resemblance to the mass. Mr. Gore was one of those, to whom a general characterization would do no manner of justice. He was an overseer; but he was

something more. With the malign and tyrannical qualities of an overseer, he combined something of the lawful master. He had the artfulness and the mean ambition of his class; but he was wholly free from the disgusting swagger and noisy bravado of his fraternity. There was an easy air of independence about him; a calm self-possession, and a sternness of glance, which might well daunt hearts less timid than those of poor slaves, accustomed from childhood and through life to cower before a driver's lash. The home plantation of Col. Lloyd afforded an ample field for the exercise of the qualifications for overseership, which he possessed in such an eminent degree.

Mr. Gore was one of those overseers, who could torture the slightest word or look into impudence; he had the nerve, not only to resent, but to punish, promptly and severely. He never allowed himself to be answered back, by a slave. In this, he was as lordly and as imperious as Col. Edward Lloyd, himself; acting always up to the maxim, practically maintained by slaveholders, that it is better that a dozen slaves suffer under the lash, without fault, than that the master or the overseer should seem to have been wrong in the presence of the slave. Everything must be absolute here. Guilty or not guilty, it is enough to be accused, to be sure of a flogging. The very presence of this man Gore was painful, and I shunned him as I would have shunned a rattlesnake. His piercing, black eyes, and sharp, shrill voice, ever awakened sensations of terror among the slaves. For so young a man (I describe him as he was, twenty-five or thirty years ago) Mr. Gore was singularly reserved and grave in the presence of slaves. He indulged in no jokes, said no funny things, and kept his own counsels. Other overseers, how brutal soever they might be, were, at times, inclined to gain favor with the slaves, by indulging a little pleasantry; but Gore was never known to be guilty of any such weakness. He was always the cold, distant, unapproachable overseer of Col. Edward Lloyd's plantation, and needed no higher pleasure than was involved in a faithful discharge of the duties of his office. When he whipped, he seemed to do so from a sense of duty, and feared no consequences. What Hopkins did reluctantly, Gore did with alacrity. There was a stern will, an iron-like reality, about this Gore, which would have easily made him the chief of a band of pirates, had his environments been favorable to such a course of life. All the coolness, savage barbarity and freedom from moral restraint, which are necessary in the character of a pirate-chief, centered, I think, in this man Gore. Among many other deeds of shocking cruelty which he perpetrated, while I was at Mr. Lloyd's, was the murder of a young colored man, named Denby. He was sometimes called Bill Denby, or Demby; (I write from sound, and the sounds on Lloyd's plantation are not very certain.) I knew him well. He was a powerful young man, full of animal spirits, and, so far as I know, he was among the most valuable of Col. Lloyd's slaves. In something—I know not what—he offended this Mr. Austin Gore, and, in accordance with the custom of the latter, he under took to flog him. He gave Denby but few stripes; the latter broke away from him and plunged into the creek, and, standing there to the depth of his neck in water, he refused to come out at the order of the overseer; whereupon, for this refusal, Gore shot him dead! It is said that Gore gave Denby three calls, telling him that if he did not obey the last call, he would shoot him. When the third call was given, Denby stood his ground firmly; and this raised the question, in the minds of the by-standing slaves—"Will he dare to shoot?" Mr. Gore, without further parley, and without making any further effort to induce Denby to come out of the water, raised his gun deliberately to his face, took deadly aim at his standing victim, and, in an instant, poor Denby was numbered with the dead. His mangled body sank out of sight, and only his warm, red blood marked the place where he had stood. This devilish outrage, this fiendish murder, produced, as it was well calculated to do, a tremendous sensation. A thrill of horror flashed through every soul on the plantation, if I may except the guilty wretch who had committed the hell-black deed. While the slaves generally were panic-struck, and howling with alarm, the murderer himself was calm and collected, and appeared as though nothing unusual had happened. The atrocity roused my old master, and he spoke out, in reprobation of it; but the whole thing proved to be less than a nine days' wonder. Both Col. Lloyd and my old master arraigned Gore for his cruelty in the matter, but this amounted to nothing. His reply, or explanation—as I remember to have heard it at the time was, that the extraordinary expedient was demanded by necessity; that Denby had become unmanageable; that he had set a dangerous example to the other slaves; and that, without some such prompt measure as that to which he had resorted, were adopted, there would be an end to all rule and order on the plantation. That very convenient covert for all manner of cruelty and outrage that cowardly alarm-cry, that the slaves would "take the place," was pleaded, in extenuation of this revolting crime, just as it had been cited in defense of a thousand similar ones. He argued, that if one slave refused to be corrected, and was allowed to escape with his life, when he had been told that he should lose it if he persisted in his course, the other slaves would soon copy his example; the result of which would be, the freedom of the slaves, and the enslavement of the whites. I have every reason to believe that Mr. Gore's defense, or explanation, was deemed satisfactory—at least to Col. Lloyd. He was continued in his office on the plantation. His fame as an overseer went abroad, and his horrid crime was not even submitted to judicial investigation. The murder was committed in the presence of slaves, and they, of course, could neither institute a suit, nor testify against the murderer. His bare word would go further in a court of law, than the united testimony of ten thousand black witnesses. All that Mr. Gore had to do, was to make his peace with Col. Lloyd. This done, and the guilty perpetrator of one of the most foul murders goes unwhipped of justice, and uncensured by the community in which he lives. Mr. Gore lived in St. Michael's, Talbot county, when I left Maryland; if he is still alive he probably yet resides there; and I have no reason to doubt that he is now as highly esteemed, and as greatly respected, as though his guilty soul had never been stained with innocent blood. I am well aware that what I have now written will by some be branded as false and malicious. It will be denied, not only that such a thing ever did transpire, as I have now narrated, but that such a thing could happen in Maryland. I can only say—believe it or not—that I have said nothing but the literal truth, gainsay it who may.

I speak advisedly when I say this,—that killing a slave, or any colored person, in Talbot county, Maryland, is not treated as a crime, either by the courts or the community. Mr. Thomas Lanman, ship carpenter, of St. Michael's, killed two slaves, one of whom he butchered with a hatchet, by knocking his brains out. He used to boast of the commission of the awful and bloody deed. I have heard him do so, laughingly, saying, among other things, that he was the only benefactor of his country in the company, and that when "others would do as much as he had done, we should be relieved of the d—d niggers."

As an evidence of the reckless disregard of human life where the life is that of a slave I may state the notorious fact, that the wife of Mr. Giles Hicks, who lived but a short distance from Col. Lloyd's, with her own hands murdered my wife's cousin, a young girl between fifteen and sixteen years of age—mutilating her person in a most shocking manner. The atrocious woman, in the paroxysm of her wrath, not content with murdering her victim, literally mangled her face, and broke her breast bone. Wild, however, and infuriated as she was, she took the precaution to cause the slave-girl to be buried; but the facts of the case coming abroad, very speedily led to the disinterment of the remains of the murdered slave-girl. A coroner's jury was assembled, who decided that the girl had come to her death by severe beating. It was ascertained that the offense for which this girl was thus hurried out of the world, was this: she had been set that night, and several preceding nights, to mind Mrs. Hicks's baby, and having fallen into a sound sleep, the baby cried, waking Mrs. Hicks, but not the slave-girl. Mrs. Hicks, becoming infuriated at the girl's tardiness, after calling several times, jumped from her bed and seized a piece of fire-wood from the fireplace; and then, as she lay fast asleep, she deliberately pounded in her skull and breast-bone, and thus ended her life. I will not say that this most horrid murder produced no sensation in the community. It did produce a sensation; but, incredible to tell, the moral sense of the community was blunted too entirely by the ordinary nature of slavery horrors, to bring the murderess to punishment. A warrant was issued for her arrest, but, for some reason or other, that warrant was never served. Thus did Mrs. Hicks not only escape condign punishment, but even the pain and mortification of being arraigned before a court of justice.

Whilst I am detailing the bloody deeds that took place during my stay on Col. Lloyd's plantation, I will briefly narrate another dark transaction, which occurred about the same time as the murder of Denby by Mr. Gore.

On the side of the river Wye, opposite from Col. Lloyd's, there lived a Mr. Beal Bondley, a wealthy slaveholder. In the direction of his land, and near the shore, there was an excellent oyster fishing ground, and to this, some of the slaves of Col. Lloyd occasionally resorted in their little canoes, at night, with a view to make up the deficiency of their scanty allowance of food, by the oysters that they could easily get there. This, Mr. Bondley took it into his head to regard as a trespass, and while an old man belonging to Col. Lloyd was engaged in catching a few of the many millions of oysters that lined the bottom of that creek, to satisfy his hunger, the villainous Mr. Bondley, lying in ambush, without the slightest ceremony, discharged the contents of his musket into the back and shoulders of the poor old man. As good fortune would have it, the shot did not prove mortal, and Mr. Bondley came over, the next day, to see Col. Lloyd—whether to pay him for his property, or to justify himself for what he had done, I know not; but this I can say, the cruel and dastardly transaction was speedily hushed up; there was very little said about it at all, and nothing was publicly done which looked like the application of the principle of justice to the man whom chance, only, saved from being an actual murderer. One of the commonest sayings to which my ears early became accustomed, on Col. Lloyd's plantation and elsewhere in Maryland, was, that it was "worth but half a cent to kill a nigger, and a half a cent to bury him;" and the facts of my experience go far to justify the practical truth of this strange proverb. Laws for the protection of the lives of the slaves, are, as they must needs be, utterly incapable of being enforced, where the very parties who are nominally protected, are not permitted to give evidence, in courts of law, against the only class of persons from whom abuse, outrage and murder might be reasonably apprehended. While I heard of numerous murders committed by slaveholders on the Eastern Shores of Maryland, I never knew a solitary instance in which a slaveholder was either hung or imprisoned for having murdered a slave. The usual pretext for killing a slave is, that the slave has offered resistance. Should a slave, when assaulted, but raise his hand in self defense, the white assaulting party is fully justified by southern, or Maryland, public opinion, in shooting the slave down. Sometimes this is done, simply because it is alleged that the slave has been saucy. But here I leave this phase of the society of my early childhood, and will relieve the kind reader of these heart-sickening details.

CHAPTER IX. Personal Treatment

MISS LUCRETIA—HER KINDNESS—HOW IT WAS MANIFESTED—"IKE"—A BATTLE
WITH HIM—THE CONSEQUENCES THEREOF—MISS LUCRETIA'S BALSAM—BREAD—HOW
I OBTAINED IT—BEAMS OF SUNLIGHT AMIDST THE GENERAL DARKNESS—SUFFERING
FROM COLD—HOW WE TOOK OUR MEALS—ORDERS TO PREPARE
FOR BALTIMORE—OVERJOYED AT THE THOUGHT OF QUITTING THE
PLANTATION—EXTRAORDINARY CLEANSING—COUSIN TOM'S VERSION OF
BALTIMORE—ARRIVAL THERE—KIND RECEPTION GIVEN ME BY MRS. SOPHIA
AULD—LITTLE TOMMY—MY NEW POSITION—MY NEW DUTIES—A TURNING
POINT IN

MY HISTORY.

I have nothing cruel or shocking to relate of my own personal experience, while I remained on Col. Lloyd's plantation, at the home of my old master. An occasional cuff from Aunt Katy, and a regular whipping from old master, such as any heedless and mischievous boy might get from his father, is all that I can mention of this sort. I was not old enough to work in the field, and, there being little else than field work to perform, I had much leisure. The most I had to do, was, to drive up the cows in the evening, to keep the front yard clean, and to perform small errands for my young mistress, Lucretia Auld. I have reasons for thinking this lady was very kindly disposed toward me, and, although I was not often the object of her attention, I constantly regarded her as my friend, and was always glad when it was my privilege to do her a service. In a family where there was so much that was harsh, cold and indifferent, the slightest word or look of kindness passed, with me, for its full value. Miss Lucretia—as we all continued to call her long after her marriage—had bestowed upon me such words and looks as taught me that she pitied me, if she did not love me. In addition to words and looks, she sometimes gave me a piece of bread and butter; a thing not set down in the bill of fare, and which must have been an extra ration, planned aside from either Aunt Katy or old master, solely out of the tender regard and friendship she had for me. Then, too, I one day got into the wars with Uncle Able's son, "Ike," and had got sadly worsted; in fact, the little rascal had struck me directly in the forehead with a sharp piece of cinder, fused with iron, from the old blacksmith's forge, which made a cross in my forehead very plainly to be seen now. The gash bled very freely, and I roared very loudly and betook myself home. The coldhearted Aunt Katy paid no attention either to my wound or my roaring, except to tell me it served me right; I had no business with Ike; it was good for me; I would now keep away "from dem Lloyd niggers." Miss Lucretia, in this state of the case, came forward; and, in quite a different spirit from that manifested by Aunt Katy, she called me into the parlor (an extra privilege of itself) and, without using toward me any of the hard-hearted and reproachful epithets of my kitchen tormentor, she quietly acted the good Samaritan. With her own soft hand she washed the blood from my head and face, fetched her own balsam bottle, and with the balsam wetted a nice piece of white linen, and bound up my head. The balsam was not more healing to the wound in my head, than her kindness was healing to the wounds in my spirit, made by the unfeeling words of Aunt Katy. After this, Miss Lucretia was my friend. I felt her to be such; and I have no doubt that the simple act of binding up my head, did much to awaken in her mind an interest in my welfare. It is quite true, that this interest was never very marked, and it seldom showed itself in anything more than in giving me a piece of bread when I was hungry; but this was a great favor on a slave plantation, and I was the only one of the children to whom such attention was paid. When very hungry, I would go into the back yard and play under Miss Lucretia's window. When pretty severely pinched by hunger, I had a habit of singing, which the good lady very soon came to understand as a petition for a piece of bread. When I sung under Miss Lucretia's window, I was very apt to get well paid for my music. The reader will see that I now had two friends, both at important points—Mas' Daniel at the great house, and Miss Lucretia at home. From Mas' Daniel I got protection from the bigger boys; and from Miss Lucretia I got bread, by singing when I was hungry, and sympathy when I was abused by that termagant, who had the reins of government in the kitchen. For such friendship I felt deeply grateful, and bitter as are my recollections of slavery, I love to recall any instances of kindness, any sunbeams of humane treatment, which found way to my soul through the iron grating of my house of bondage. Such beams seem all the brighter from the general darkness into which they penetrate, and the impression they make is vividly distinct and beautiful.

As I have before intimated, I was seldom whipped—and never severely—by my old master. I suffered little from the treatment I received, except from hunger and cold. These were my two great physical troubles. I could neither get a sufficiency of food nor of clothing; but I suffered less from hunger than from cold. In hottest summer and coldest winter, I was kept almost in a state of nudity; no shoes, no stockings, no jacket, no trowsers; nothing but coarse sackcloth or tow-linen, made into a sort of shirt, reaching down to my knees. This I wore night and day, changing it once a week. In the day time I could protect myself pretty well, by keeping on the sunny side of the house; and in bad weather, in the corner of the kitchen chimney. The great difficulty was, to keep warm during the night. I had no bed. The pigs in the pen had leaves, and the horses in the stable had straw, but the children had no beds. They lodged anywhere in the ample kitchen. I slept, generally, in a little closet, without even a blanket to cover me. In very cold weather. I sometimes got down the bag in which corn meal was usually carried to the mill, and crawled into that. Sleeping there, with my head in and feet out, I was partly protected, though not comfortable. My feet have been so cracked with the frost, that the pen with which I am writing might be laid in the gashes. The manner of taking our meals at old master's, indicated but little refinement. Our corn-meal mush, when sufficiently cooled, was placed in a large wooden tray, or trough, like those used in making maple sugar here in the north. This tray was set down, either on the floor of the kitchen, or out of doors on the ground; and the children were called, like so many pigs; and like so many pigs they would come, and literally devour the mush—some with oyster shells, some with pieces of shingles, and none with spoons. He that eat fastest got most, and he that was strongest got the best place; and few left the trough really satisfied. I was the most unlucky of any, for Aunt Katy had no good feeling for me; and if I pushed any of the other children, or if they told her anything unfavorable of me, she always believed the worst, and was sure to whip me.

As I grew older and more thoughtful, I was more and more filled with a sense of my wretchedness. The cruelty of Aunt Katy, the hunger and cold I suffered, and the terrible reports of wrong and outrage which came to my ear, together with what I almost daily witnessed, led me, when yet but eight or nine years old, to wish I had never been born. I used to contrast my condition with the black-birds, in whose wild and sweet songs I fancied them so happy! Their apparent joy only deepened the shades of my sorrow. There are thoughtful days in the lives of children—at least there were in mine when they grapple with all the great, primary subjects of knowledge, and reach, in a moment, conclusions which no subsequent experience can shake. I was just as well aware of the unjust, unnatural and murderous character of slavery, when nine years old, as I am now. Without any appeal to books, to laws, or to authorities of any kind, it was enough to accept God as a father, to regard slavery as a crime.

I was not ten years old when I left Col. Lloyd's plantation for Balitmore(sic). I left that plantation with inexpressible joy. I never shall forget the ecstacy with which I received the intelligence from my friend, Miss Lucretia, that my old master had determined to let me go to Baltimore to live with Mr. Hugh Auld, a brother to Mr. Thomas Auld, my old master's son-in-law. I received this information about three days before my departure. They were three of the happiest days of my childhood. I spent the largest part of these three days in the creek, washing off the plantation scurf, and preparing for my new home. Mrs. Lucretia took a lively interest in getting me ready. She told me I must get all the dead skin off my feet and knees, before I could go to Baltimore, for the people there were very cleanly, and would laugh at me if I looked dirty; and, besides, she was intending to give me a pair of trowsers, which I should not put on unless I got all the dirt off. This was a warning to which I was bound to take heed; for the thought of owning a pair of trowsers, was great, indeed. It was almost a sufficient motive, not only to induce me to scrub off the mange (as pig drovers would call it) but the skin as well. So I went at it in good earnest, working for the first time in the hope of reward. I was greatly excited, and could hardly consent to sleep, lest I should be left. The ties that, ordinarily, bind children to their homes, were all severed, or they never had any existence in my case, at least so far as the home plantation of Col. L. was concerned. I therefore found no severe trail at the moment of my departure, such as I had experienced when separated from my home in Tuckahoe. My home at my old master's was charmless to me; it was not home, but a prison to me; on parting from it, I could not feel that I was leaving anything which I could have enjoyed by staying. My mother was now long dead; my grandmother was far away, so that I seldom saw her; Aunt Katy was my unrelenting tormentor; and my two sisters and brothers, owing to our early separation in life, and the family-destroying power of slavery, were, comparatively, strangers to me. The fact of our relationship was almost blotted out. I looked for home elsewhere, and was confident of finding none which I should relish less than the one I was leaving. If, however, I found in my new home to which I was going with such blissful anticipations—hardship, whipping and nakedness, I had the questionable consolation that I should not have escaped any one of these evils by remaining under the management of Aunt Katy. Then, too, I thought, since I had endured much in this line on Lloyd's plantation, I could endure as much elsewhere, and especially at Baltimore; for I had something of the feeling about that city which is expressed in the saying, that being "hanged in England, is better than dying a natural death in Ireland." I had the strongest desire to see Baltimore. My cousin Tom—a boy two or three years older than I—had been there, and though not fluent (he stuttered immoderately) in speech, he had inspired me with that desire, by his eloquent description of the place. Tom was, sometimes, Capt. Auld's cabin boy; and when he came from Baltimore, he was always a sort of hero amongst us, at least till his Baltimore trip was forgotten. I could never tell him of anything, or point out anything that struck me as beautiful or powerful, but that he had seen something in Baltimore far surpassing it. Even the great house itself, with all its pictures within, and pillars without, he had the hardihood to say "was nothing to Baltimore." He bought a trumpet (worth six pence) and brought it home; told what he had seen in the windows of stores; that he had heard shooting crackers, and seen soldiers; that he had seen a steamboat; that there were ships in Baltimore that could carry four such sloops as the "Sally Lloyd." He said a great deal about the market-house; he spoke of the bells ringing; and of many other things which roused my curiosity very much; and, indeed, which heightened my hopes of happiness in my new home.

We sailed out of Miles river for Baltimore early on a Saturday morning. I remember only the day of the week; for, at that time, I had no knowledge of the days of the month, nor, indeed, of the months of the year. On setting sail, I walked aft, and gave to Col. Lloyd's plantation what I hoped would be the last look I should ever give to it, or to any place like it. My strong aversion to the great farm, was not owing to my own personal suffering, but the daily suffering of others, and to the certainty that I must, sooner or later, be placed under the barbarous rule of an overseer, such as the accomplished Gore, or the brutal and drunken Plummer. After taking this last view, I quitted the quarter deck, made my way to the bow of the sloop, and spent the remainder of the day in looking ahead; interesting myself in what was in the distance, rather than what was near by or behind. The vessels, sweeping along the bay, were very interesting objects. The broad bay opened like a shoreless ocean on my boyish vision, filling me with wonder and admiration.

Late in the afternoon, we reached Annapolis, the capital of the state, stopping there not long enough to admit of my going ashore. It was the first large town I had ever seen; and though it was inferior to many a factory village in New England, my feelings, on seeing it, were excited to a pitch very little below that reached by travelers at the first view of Rome. The dome of the state house was especially imposing, and surpassed in grandeur the appearance of the great house. The great world was opening upon me very rapidly, and I was eagerly acquainting myself with its multifarious lessons.

We arrived in Baltimore on Sunday morning, and landed at Smith's wharf, not far from Bowly's wharf. We had on board the sloop a large flock of sheep, for the Baltimore market; and, after assisting in driving them to the slaughter house of Mr. Curtis, on Loudon Slater's Hill, I was speedily conducted by Rich—one of the hands belonging to the sloop—to my new home in Alliciana street, near Gardiner's ship-yard, on Fell's Point. Mr. and Mrs. Hugh Auld, my new mistress and master, were both at home, and met me at the door with their rosy cheeked little son, Thomas, to take care of whom was to constitute my future occupation. In fact, it was to "little Tommy," rather than to his parents, that old master made a present of me; and though there was no legal form or arrangement entered into, I have no doubt that Mr. and

Mrs. Auld felt that, in due time, I should be the legal property of their bright-eyed and beloved boy, Tommy. I was struck with the appearance, especially, of my new mistress. Her face was lighted with the kindliest emotions; and the reflex influence of her countenance, as well as the tenderness with which she seemed to regard me, while asking me sundry little questions, greatly delighted me, and lit up, to my fancy, the pathway of my future. Miss Lucretia was kind; but my new mistress, "Miss Sophy," surpassed her in kindness of manner. Little Thomas was affectionately told by his mother, that "there was his Freddy," and that "Freddy would take care of him;" and I was told to "be kind to little Tommy"—an injunction I scarcely needed, for I had already fallen in love with the dear boy; and with these little ceremonies I was initiated into my new home, and entered upon my peculiar duties, with not a cloud above the horizon.

I may say here, that I regard my removal from Col. Lloyd's plantation as one of the most interesting and fortunate events of my life. Viewing it in the light of human likelihoods, it is quite probable that, but for the mere circumstance of being thus removed before the rigors of slavery had fastened upon me; before my young spirit had been crushed under the iron control of the slave-driver, instead of being, today, a FREEMAN, I might have been wearing the galling chains of slavery. I have sometimes felt, however, that there was something more intelligent than chance, and something more certain than luck, to be seen in the circumstance. If I have made any progress in knowledge; if I have cherished any honorable aspirations, or have, in any manner, worthily discharged the duties of a member of an oppressed people; this little circumstance must be allowed its due weight in giving my life that direction. I have ever regarded it as the first plain manifestation of that

Divinity that shapes our ends,
Rough hew them as we will.

I was not the only boy on the plantation that might have been sent to live in Baltimore. There was a wide margin from which to select. There were boys younger, boys older, and boys of the same age, belonging to my old master some at his own house, and some at his farm—but the high privilege fell to my lot.

I may be deemed superstitious and egotistical, in regarding this event as a special interposition of Divine Providence in my favor; but the thought is a part of my history, and I should be false to the earliest and most cherished sentiments of my soul, if I suppressed, or hesitated to avow that opinion, although it may be characterized as irrational by the wise, and ridiculous by the scoffer. From my earliest recollections of serious matters, I date the entertainment of something like an ineffaceable conviction, that slavery would not always be able to hold me within its foul embrace; and this conviction, like a word of living faith, strengthened me through the darkest trials of my lot. This good spirit was from God; and to him I offer thanksgiving and praise.

CHAPTER X. Life in Baltimore

CITY ANNOYANCES—PLANTATION REGRETS—MY MISTRESS, MISS SOPHA—HER
HISTORY—HER KINDNESS TO ME—MY MASTER, HUGH AULD—HIS SOURNESS—MY
INCREASED SENSITIVENESS—MY COMFORTS—MY OCCUPATION—THE BANEFUL EFFECTS
OF SLAVEHOLDING ON MY DEAR AND GOOD MISTRESS—HOW SHE COMMENCED TEACHING

ME TO READ—WHY SHE CEASED TEACHING ME—CLOUDS GATHERING OVER MY
BRIGHT PROSPECTS—MASTER AULD'S EXPOSITION OF THE TRUE PHILOSOPHY OF
SLAVERY—CITY SLAVES—PLANTATION SLAVES—THE CONTRAST—EXCEPTIONS—MR.
HAMILTON'S TWO SLAVES, HENRIETTA AND MARY—MRS. HAMILTON'S CRUEL
TREATMENT OF THEM—THE PITEOUS ASPECT THEY PRESENTED—NO POWER MUST COME
BETWEEN THE SLAVE AND THE SLAVEHOLDER.

Once in Baltimore, with hard brick pavements under my feet, which almost raised blisters, by their very heat, for it was in the height of summer; walled in on all sides by towering brick buildings; with troops of hostile boys ready to pounce upon me at every street corner; with new and strange objects glaring upon me at every step, and with startling sounds reaching my ears from all directions, I for a time thought that, after all, the home plantation was a more desirable place of residence than my home on Alliciana street, in Baltimore. My country eyes and ears were confused and bewildered here; but the boys were my chief trouble. They chased me, and called me "Eastern Shore man," till really I almost wished myself back on the Eastern Shore. I had to undergo a sort of moral acclimation, and when that was over, I did much better. My new mistress happily proved to be all she seemed to be, when, with her husband, she met me at the door, with a most beaming, benignant countenance. She was, naturally, of an excellent disposition, kind, gentle and cheerful. The supercilious contempt for the rights and feelings of the slave, and the petulance and bad humor which generally characterize slaveholding ladies, were all quite absent from kind "Miss" Sophia's manner and bearing toward me. She had, in truth, never been a slaveholder, but had—a thing quite unusual in the south—depended almost entirely upon her own industry for a living. To this fact the dear lady, no doubt, owed the excellent preservation of her natural goodness of heart, for slavery can change a saint into a sinner, and an angel into a demon. I hardly knew how to behave toward "Miss Sopha," as I used to call Mrs. Hugh Auld. I had been treated as a pig on the plantation; I was treated as a child now. I could not even approach her as I had formerly approached Mrs. Thomas Auld. How could I hang down my head, and speak with bated breath, when there was no pride to scorn me, no coldness to repel me, and no hatred to inspire me with fear? I therefore soon learned to regard her as something more akin to a mother, than a slaveholding mistress. The crouching servility of a slave, usually so acceptable a quality to the haughty slaveholder, was not understood nor desired by this gentle woman. So far from deeming it impudent in a slave to look her straight in the face, as some slaveholding ladies do, she seemed ever to say, "look up, child; don't be afraid; see, I am full of kindness and good will toward you." The hands belonging to Col. Lloyd's sloop, esteemed it a great privilege to be the bearers of parcels or messages to my new mistress; for whenever they came, they were sure of a most kind and pleasant reception. If little Thomas was her son, and her most dearly beloved child, she, for a time, at least, made me something like his half-brother in her affections. If dear Tommy was exalted to a place on his mother's knee, "Feddy" was honored by a place at his mother's side. Nor did he lack the caressing strokes of her gentle hand, to convince him that, though motherless, he was not friendless. Mrs. Auld was not only a kind-hearted woman, but she was remarkably pious; frequent in her attendance of public worship, much given to reading the bible, and to chanting hymns of praise, when alone. Mr. Hugh Auld was altogether a different character. He cared very little about religion, knew more of the world, and was more of the world, than his wife. He set out, doubtless to be—as the world goes—a respectable man, and to get on by becoming a successful ship builder, in that city of ship building. This was his ambition, and it fully occupied him. I was, of course, of very little consequence to him, compared with what I was to good Mrs. Auld; and, when he smiled upon me, as he sometimes did, the smile was borrowed from his lovely wife, and, like all borrowed light, was transient, and vanished with the source whence it was derived. While I must characterize Master Hugh as being a very sour man, and of forbidding appearance, it is due to him to acknowledge, that he was never very cruel to me, according to the notion of cruelty in Maryland. The first year or two which I spent in his house, he left me almost exclusively to the management of his wife. She was my law-giver. In hands so tender as hers, and in the absence of the cruelties of the plantation, I became, both physically and mentally, much more sensitive to good and ill treatment; and, perhaps, suffered more from a frown from my mistress, than I formerly did from a cuff at the hands of Aunt Katy. Instead of the cold, damp floor of my old master's kitchen, I found myself on carpets; for the corn bag in winter, I now had a good straw bed, well furnished with covers; for the coarse corn-meal in the morning, I now had good bread, and mush occasionally; for my poor tow-lien shirt, reaching to my knees, I had good, clean clothes. I was really well off. My employment was to run errands, and to take care of Tommy; to prevent his getting in the way of carriages, and to keep him out of harm's way generally. Tommy, and I, and his mother, got on swimmingly together, for a time. I say for a time, because the fatal poison of irresponsible power, and the natural influence of slavery customs, were not long in making a suitable impression on the gentle and loving disposition of my excellent mistress. At first, Mrs. Auld evidently regarded me simply as a child, like any other child; she had not come to regard me as property. This latter thought was a thing of conventional growth. The first was natural and spontaneous. A noble nature, like hers, could not, instantly, be wholly perverted; and it took several years to change the natural sweetness of her temper into fretful bitterness. In her worst estate, however, there were, during the first seven years I lived with her, occasional returns of her former kindly disposition.

The frequent hearing of my mistress reading the bible for she often read aloud when her husband was absent soon awakened my curiosity in respect to this mystery of reading, and roused in me the desire to learn. Having no fear of my kind mistress before my eyes, (she had then given me no reason to fear,) I frankly asked her to teach me to read; and, without hesitation, the dear woman began the task, and very soon, by her assistance, I was master of the alphabet, and could spell words of three or four letters. My mistress seemed almost as proud of my progress, as if I had been her own child; and, supposing that her husband would be as well pleased, she made no secret of what she was doing for me. Indeed, she exultingly told him of the aptness of her pupil, of her intention to persevere in teaching me, and of the duty which she felt it to teach me, at least to read the bible. Here arose the first cloud over my Baltimore prospects, the precursor of drenching rains and chilling blasts.

Master Hugh was amazed at the simplicity of his spouse, and, probably for the first time, he unfolded to her the true philosophy of slavery, and the peculiar rules necessary to be observed by masters and mistresses, in the management of their human chattels. Mr. Auld promptly forbade continuance of her instruction; telling her, in the first place, that the thing itself was unlawful; that it was also unsafe, and could only lead to mischief. To use his own words, further, he said, "if you give a nigger an inch, he will take an ell;" "he should know nothing but the will of his master, and learn to obey it." "if you teach that nigger—speaking of myself—how to read the bible, there will be no keeping him;" "it would forever unfit him for the duties of a slave;" and "as to himself, learning would do him no good, but probably, a great deal of harm—making him disconsolate and unhappy." "If you learn him now to read, he'll want to know how to write; and, this accomplished, he'll be running away with himself." Such was the tenor of Master Hugh's oracular exposition of the true philosophy of training a human chattel; and it must be confessed that he very clearly comprehended the nature and the requirements of the relation of master and slave. His discourse was the first decidedly anti-slavery lecture to which it had been my lot to listen. Mrs. Auld evidently felt the force of his remarks; and, like an obedient wife, began to shape her course in the direction indicated by her husband. The effect of his words, on me, was neither slight nor transitory. His iron sentences—cold and harsh—sunk deep into my heart, and stirred up not only my feelings into a sort of rebellion, but awakened within me a slumbering train of vital thought. It was a new and special revelation, dispelling a painful mystery, against which my youthful understanding had struggled, and struggled in vain, to wit: the white man's power to perpetuate the enslavement of the black man. "Very well," thought I; "knowledge unfits a child to be a slave." I instinctively assented to the proposition; and from that moment I understood the direct pathway from slavery to freedom. This was just what I needed; and I got it at a time, and from a source, whence I least expected it. I was saddened at the thought of losing the assistance of my kind mistress; but the information, so instantly derived, to some extent compensated me for the loss I had sustained in this direction. Wise as Mr. Auld was, he evidently underrated my comprehension, and had little idea of the use to which I was capable of putting the impressive lesson he was giving to his wife. He wanted me to be a slave; I had already voted against that on the home plantation of Col. Lloyd. That which he most loved I most hated; and the very determination which he expressed to keep me in ignorance, only rendered me the more resolute in seeking intelligence. In learning to read, therefore, I am not sure that I do not owe quite as much to the opposition of my master, as to the kindly assistance of my amiable mistress. I acknowledge the benefit rendered me by the one, and by the other; believing, that but for my mistress, I might have grown up in ignorance.

I had resided but a short time in Baltimore, before I observed a marked difference in the manner of treating slaves, generally, from which I had witnessed in that isolated and out-of-the-way part of the country where I began life. A city slave is almost a free citizen, in Baltimore, compared with a slave on Col. Lloyd's plantation. He is much better fed and clothed, is less dejected in his appearance, and enjoys privileges altogether unknown to the whip-driven slave on the plantation. Slavery dislikes a dense population, in which there is a majority of non-slaveholders. The general sense of decency that must pervade such a population, does much to check and prevent those outbreaks of atrocious cruelty, and those dark crimes without a name, almost openly perpetrated on the plantation. He is a desperate slaveholder who will shock the humanity of his non-slaveholding neighbors, by the cries of the lacerated slaves; and very few in the city are willing to incur the odium of being cruel masters. I found, in Baltimore, that no man was more odious to the white, as well as to the colored people, than he, who had the reputation of starving his slaves. Work them, flog them, if need be, but don't starve them. These are, however, some painful exceptions to this rule. While it is quite true that most of the slaveholders in Baltimore feed and clothe their slaves well, there are others who keep up their country cruelties in the city.

An instance of this sort is furnished in the case of a family who lived directly opposite to our house, and were named Hamilton. Mrs. Hamilton owned two slaves. Their names were Henrietta and Mary. They had always been house slaves. One was aged about twenty-two, and the other about fourteen. They were a fragile couple by nature, and the treatment they received was enough to break down the constitution of a horse. Of all the dejected, emaciated, mangled and excoriated creatures I ever saw, those two girls—in the refined, church going and Christian city of Baltimore were the most deplorable. Of stone must that heart be made, that could look upon Henrietta and Mary, without being sickened to the core with sadness. Especially was Mary a heart-sickening object. Her head, neck and shoulders, were literally cut to pieces. I have frequently felt her head, and found it nearly covered over with festering sores, caused by the lash of her cruel mistress. I do not know that her master ever whipped her, but I have often been an eye witness of the revolting and brutal inflictions by Mrs. Hamilton; and what lends a deeper shade to this woman's conduct, is the fact, that, almost in the very moments of her shocking outrages of humanity and decency, she would charm you by the sweetness of her voice and her seeming piety. She used to sit in a large rocking chair, near the middle of the room, with a heavy cowskin, such as I have elsewhere described; and I speak within the truth when I say, that these girls seldom passed that chair, during the day, without a blow from that cowskin, either upon their bare arms, or upon their shoulders. As they passed her, she would draw her cowskin and give them a blow, saying, "move faster, you black jip!" and, again, "take that, you black jip!" continuing, "if you don't move faster, I will give you more." Then the lady would go on, singing her sweet hymns, as though her righteous soul were sighing for the holy realms of paradise.

Added to the cruel lashings to which these poor slave-girls were subjected—enough in themselves to crush the spirit of men—they were, really, kept nearly half starved; they seldom knew what it was to eat a full meal, except when they got it in the kitchens of neighbors, less mean and stingy than the psalm-singing Mrs. Hamilton. I have seen poor Mary contending for the offal, with the pigs in the street. So much was the poor girl pinched, kicked, cut and pecked to pieces, that the boys in the street knew her only by the name of "pecked," a name derived from the scars and blotches on her neck, head and shoulders.

It is some relief to this picture of slavery in Baltimore, to say—what is but the simple truth— that Mrs. Hamilton's treatment of her slaves was generally condemned, as disgraceful and shocking; but while I say this, it must also be remembered, that the very parties who censured the cruelty of Mrs. Hamilton, would have condemned and promptly punished any attempt to interfere with Mrs. Hamilton's right to cut and slash her slaves to pieces. There must be no force between the slave and the slaveholder, to restrain the power of the one, and protect the weakness of the other; and the cruelty of Mrs. Hamilton is as justly chargeable to the upholders of the slave system, as drunkenness is chargeable on those who, by precept and example, or by indifference, uphold the drinking system.

CHAPTER XI. "A Change Came O'er the Spirit of My Dream"

HOW I LEARNED TO READ—MY MISTRESS—HER SLAVEHOLDING DUTIES— THEIR
DEPLORABLE EFFECTS UPON HER ORIGINALLY NOBLE NATURE—THE CONFLICT IN HER
MIND—HER FINAL OPPOSITION TO MY LEARNING TO READ—TOO LATE—SHE HAD
GIVEN ME THE INCH, I WAS RESOLVED TO TAKE THE ELL—HOW I PURSUED MY EDUCATION—MY TUTORS—HOW I COMPENSATED THEM—WHAT PROGRESS I
MADE—SLAVERY—WHAT I HEARD SAID ABOUT IT—THIRTEEN YEARS OLD— THE
Columbian Orator—A RICH SCENE—A DIALOGUE—SPEECHES OF CHATHAM, SHERIDAN, PITT AND FOX—KNOWLEDGE EVER INCREASING—MY EYES OPENED—LIBERTY—HOW I PINED FOR IT—MY SADNESS—THE DISSATISFACTION OF
MY POOR MISTRESS—MY HATRED OF SLAVERY—ONE UPAS TREE OVERSHADOWED US
BOTH.

I lived in the family of Master Hugh, at Baltimore, seven years, during which time—as the almanac makers say of the weather—my condition was variable. The most interesting feature of my history here, was my learning to read and write, under somewhat marked disadvantages. In attaining this knowledge, I was compelled to resort to indirections by no means congenial to my nature, and which were really humiliating to me. My mistress—who, as the reader has already seen, had begun to teach me was suddenly checked in her benevolent design, by the strong advice of her husband. In faithful compliance with this advice, the good lady had not only ceased to instruct me, herself, but had set her face as a flint against my learning to read by any means. It is due, however, to my mistress to say, that she did not adopt this course in all its stringency at the first. She either thought it unnecessary, or she lacked the depravity indispensable to shutting me up in mental darkness. It was, at least, necessary for her to have some training, and some hardening, in the exercise of the slaveholder's prerogative, to make her equal to forgetting my human nature and character, and to treating me as a thing destitute of a moral or an intellectual nature. Mrs. Auld—my mistress—was, as I have said, a most kind and tender-hearted woman; and, in the humanity of her heart, and the simplicity of her mind, she set out, when I first went to live with her, to treat me as she supposed one human being ought to treat another.

It is easy to see, that, in entering upon the duties of a slaveholder, some little experience is needed. Nature has done almost nothing to prepare men and women to be either slaves or slaveholders. Nothing but rigid training, long persisted in, can perfect the character of the one or the other. One cannot easily forget to love freedom; and it is as hard to cease to respect that natural love in our fellow creatures. On entering upon the career of a slaveholding mistress, Mrs. Auld was singularly deficient; nature, which fits nobody for such an office, had done less for her than any lady I had known. It was no easy matter to induce her to think and to feel that the curly-headed boy, who stood by her side, and even leaned on her lap; who was loved by little Tommy, and who loved little Tommy in turn; sustained to her only the relation of a chattel. I was more than that, and she felt me to be more than that. I could talk and sing; I could laugh and weep; I could reason and remember; I could love and hate. I was human, and she, dear lady, knew and felt me to be so. How could she, then, treat me as a brute, without a mighty struggle with all the noble powers of her own soul. That struggle came, and the will and power of the husband was victorious. Her noble soul was overthrown; but, he that overthrew it did not, himself, escape the consequences. He, not less than the other parties, was injured in his domestic peace by the fall.

When I went into their family, it was the abode of happiness and contentment. The mistress of the house was a model of affection and tenderness. Her fervent piety and watchful uprightness made it impossible to see her without thinking and feeling—"that woman is a Christian." There was no sorrow nor suffering for which she had not a tear, and there was no innocent joy for which she did not a smile. She had bread for the hungry, clothes for the naked, and comfort for every mourner that came within her reach. Slavery soon proved its ability to divest her of these excellent qualities, and her home of its early happiness. Conscience cannot stand much violence. Once thoroughly broken down, who is he that can repair the damage? It may be broken toward the slave, on Sunday, and toward the master on Monday. It cannot endure such shocks. It must stand entire, or it does not stand at all. If my condition waxed bad, that of the family waxed not better. The first step, in the wrong direction, was the violence done to nature and to conscience, in arresting the benevolence that would have enlightened my young mind. In ceasing to instruct me, she must begin to justify herself to herself; and, once consenting to take sides in such a debate, she was riveted to her position. One needs very little knowledge of moral philosophy, to see where my mistress now landed. She finally became even more violent in her opposition to my learning to read, than was her husband himself. She was not satisfied with simply doing as well as her husband had commanded her, but seemed resolved to better his instruction. Nothing appeared to make my poor mistress—after her turning toward the downward path—more angry, than seeing me, seated in some nook or corner, quietly reading a book or a newspaper. I have had her rush at me, with the utmost fury, and snatch from my hand such newspaper or book, with something of the wrath and consternation which a traitor might be supposed to feel on being discovered in a plot by some dangerous spy. Mrs. Auld was an apt woman, and the advice of her husband, and her own experience, soon demonstrated, to her entire satisfaction, that education and slavery are incompatible with each other. When this conviction was thoroughly established, I was most narrowly watched in all my movements. If I remained in a separate room from the family for any considerable length of time, I was sure to be suspected of having a book, and was at once called upon to give an account of myself. All this, however, was entirely too late. The first, and never to be retraced, step had been taken. In teaching me the alphabet, in the days of her simplicity and kindness, my mistress had given me the "inch," and now, no ordinary precaution could prevent me from taking the "ell."

Seized with a determination to learn to read, at any cost, I hit upon many expedients to accomplish the desired end. The plea which I mainly adopted, and the one by which I was most successful, was that of using my young white playmates, with whom I met in the streets as teachers. I used to carry, almost constantly, a copy of Webster's spelling book in my pocket; and, when sent of errands, or when play time was allowed me, I would step, with my young friends, aside, and take a lesson in spelling. I generally paid my tuition fee to the boys, with bread, which I also carried in my pocket. For a single biscuit, any of my hungry little comrades would give me a lesson more valuable to me than bread. Not every one, however, demanded this consideration, for there were those who took pleasure in teaching me, whenever I had a chance to be taught by them. I am strongly tempted to give the names of two or three of those little boys, as a slight testimonial of the gratitude and affection I bear them, but prudence forbids; not that it would injure me, but it might, possibly, embarrass them; for it is almost an unpardonable offense to do any thing, directly or indirectly, to promote a slave's freedom, in a slave state. It is enough to say, of my warm-hearted little play fellows, that they lived on Philpot street, very near Durgin & Bailey's shipyard.

Although slavery was a delicate subject, and very cautiously talked about among grown up people in Maryland, I frequently talked about it—and that very freely—with the white boys. I would, sometimes, say to them, while seated on a curb stone or a cellar door, "I wish I could be free, as you will be when you get to be men." "You will be free, you know, as soon as you are twenty-one, and can go where you like, but I am a slave for life. Have I not as good a right to be free as you have?" Words like these, I observed, always troubled them; and I had no small satisfaction in wringing from the boys, occasionally, that fresh and bitter condemnation of slavery, that springs from nature, unseared and unperverted. Of all consciences let me have those to deal with which have not been bewildered by the cares of life. I do not remember ever to have met with a boy, while I was in slavery, who defended the slave system; but I have often had boys to console me, with the hope that something would yet occur, by which I might be made free. Over and over again, they have told me, that "they believed I had as good a right to be free as they had;" and that "they did not believe God ever made any one to be a slave." The reader will easily see, that such little conversations with my play fellows, had no tendency to weaken my love of liberty, nor to render me contented with my condition as a slave.

When I was about thirteen years old, and had succeeded in learning to read, every increase of knowledge, especially respecting the FREE STATES, added something to the almost intolerable burden of the thought—I AM A SLAVE FOR LIFE. To my bondage I saw no end. It was a terrible reality, and I shall never be able to tell how sadly that thought chafed my young spirit. Fortunately, or unfortunately, about this time in my life, I had made enough money to buy what was then a very popular school book, viz: the Columbian Orator. I bought this addition to my library, of Mr. Knight, on Thames street, Fell's Point, Baltimore, and paid him fifty cents for it. I was first led to buy this book, by hearing some little boys say they were going to learn some little pieces out of it for the Exhibition. This volume was, indeed, a rich treasure, and every opportunity afforded me, for a time, was spent in diligently perusing it. Among much other interesting matter, that which I had perused and reperused with unflagging satisfaction, was a short dialogue between a master and his slave. The slave is represented as having been recaptured, in a second attempt to run away; and the master opens the dialogue with an upbraiding speech, charging the slave with ingratitude, and demanding to know what he has to say in his own defense. Thus upbraided, and thus called upon to reply, the slave rejoins, that he knows how little anything that he can say will avail, seeing that he is completely in the hands of his owner; and with noble resolution, calmly says, "I submit to my fate." Touched by the slave's answer, the master insists upon his further speaking, and recapitulates the many acts of kindness which he has performed toward the slave, and tells him he is permitted to speak for himself. Thus invited to the debate, the quondam slave made a spirited defense of himself, and thereafter the whole argument, for and against slavery, was brought out. The master was vanquished at every turn in the argument; and seeing himself to be thus vanquished, he generously and meekly emancipates the slave, with his best wishes for his prosperity. It is scarcely neccessary(sic) to say, that a dialogue, with such an origin, and such an ending—read when the fact of my being a slave was a constant burden of grief—powerfully affected me; and I could not help feeling that the day might come, when the well-directed answers made by the slave to the master, in this instance, would find their counterpart in myself.

This, however, was not all the fanaticism which I found in this Columbian Orator. I met there one of Sheridan's mighty speeches, on the subject of Catholic Emancipation, Lord Chatham's speech on the American war, and speeches by the great William Pitt and by Fox. These were all choice documents to me, and I read them, over and over again, with an interest that was ever increasing, because it was ever gaining in intelligence; for the more I read them, the better I understood them. The reading of these speeches added much to my limited stock of language, and enabled me to give tongue to many interesting thoughts, which had frequently flashed through my soul, and died away for want of utterance. The mighty power and heart-searching directness of truth, penetrating even the heart of a slaveholder, compelling him to yield up his earthly interests to the claims of eternal justice, were finely illustrated in the dialogue, just referred to; and from the speeches of Sheridan, I got a bold and powerful denunciation of oppression, and a most brilliant vindication of the rights of man. Here was, indeed, a noble acquisition. If I ever wavered under the consideration, that the Almighty, in some way, ordained slavery, and willed my enslavement for his own glory, I wavered no longer. I had now penetrated the secret of all slavery and oppression, and had ascertained their true foundation to be in the pride, the power and the avarice of man. The dialogue and the speeches were all redolent of the principles of liberty, and poured floods of light on the nature and character of slavery. With a book of this kind in my hand, my own human nature, and the facts of my experience, to help me, I was equal to a contest with the religious advocates of slavery, whether among the whites or among the colored people, for blindness, in this matter, is not confined to the former. I have met many religious colored people, at the south, who are under the delusion that God requires them to submit to slavery, and to wear their chains with meekness and humility. I could entertain no such nonsense as this; and I almost lost my patience when I found any colored man weak enough to believe such stuff. Nevertheless, the increase of knowledge was attended with bitter, as well as sweet results. The more I read, the more I was led to abhor and detest slavery, and my enslavers. "Slaveholders," thought I, "are only a band of successful robbers, who left their homes and went into Africa for the purpose of stealing and reducing my people to slavery." I loathed them as the meanest and the most wicked of men. As I read, behold! the very discontent so graphically pre dicted by Master Hugh, had already come upon me. I was no longer the light-hearted, gleesome boy, full of mirth and play, as when I landed first at Baltimore. Knowledge had come; light had penetrated the moral dungeon where I dwelt; and, behold! there lay the bloody whip, for my back, and here was the iron chain; and my good, kind master, he was the author of my situation. The revelation haunted me, stung me, and made me gloomy and miserable. As I writhed under the sting and torment of this knowledge, I almost envied my fellow slaves their stupid contentment. This knowledge opened my eyes to the horrible pit, and revealed the teeth of the frightful dragon that was ready to pounce upon me, but it opened no way for my escape. I have often wished myself a beast, or a bird—anything, rather than a slave. I was wretched and gloomy, beyond my ability to describe. I was too thoughtful to be happy. It was this everlasting thinking which distressed and tormented me; and yet there was no getting rid of the subject of my thoughts. All nature was redolent of it. Once awakened by the silver trump of knowledge, my spirit was roused to eternal wakefulness. Liberty! the inestimable birthright of every man, had, for me, converted every object into an asserter of this great right. It was heard in every sound, and beheld in every object. It was ever present, to torment me with a sense of my wretched condition. The more beautiful and charming were the smiles of nature, the more horrible and desolate was my condition. I saw nothing without seeing it, and I heard nothing without hearing it. I do not exaggerate, when I say, that it looked from every star, smiled in every calm, breathed in every wind, and moved in every storm.

I have no doubt that my state of mind had something to do with the change in the treatment adopted, by my once kind mistress toward me. I can easily believe, that my leaden, downcast, and discontented look, was very offensive to her. Poor lady! She did not know my trouble, and I dared not tell her. Could I have freely made her acquainted with the real state of my mind, and given her the reasons therefor, it might have been well for both of us. Her abuse of me fell upon me like the blows of the false prophet upon his ass; she did not know that an angel stood in the way; and—such is the relation of master and slave I could not tell her. Nature had made us friends; slavery made us enemies. My interests were in a direction opposite to hers, and we both had our private thoughts and plans. She aimed to keep me ignorant; and I resolved to know, although knowledge only increased my discontent. My feelings were not the result of any marked cruelty in the treatment I received; they sprung from the consideration of my being a slave at all. It was slavery—not its mere incidents—that I hated. I had been cheated. I saw through the attempt to keep me in ignorance; I saw that slaveholders would have gladly made me believe that they were merely acting under the authority of God, in making a slave of me, and in making slaves of others; and I treated them as robbers and deceivers. The feeding and clothing me well, could not atone for taking my liberty from me. The smiles of my mistress could not remove the deep sorrow that dwelt in my young bosom. Indeed, these, in time, came only to deepen my sorrow. She had changed; and the reader will see that I had changed, too. We were both victims to the same overshadowing evil—she, as mistress, I, as slave. I will not censure her harshly; she cannot censure me, for she knows I speak but the truth, and have acted in my opposition to slavery, just as she herself would have acted, in a reverse of circumstances.

CHAPTER XII. Religious Nature Awakened

ABOLITIONISTS SPOKEN OF—MY EAGERNESS TO KNOW WHAT THIS WORD MEANT—MY
CONSULTATION OF THE DICTIONARY—INCENDIARY INFORMATION—HOW AND WHERE
DERIVED—THE ENIGMA SOLVED—NATHANIEL TURNER'S INSURRECTION—THE
CHOLERA—RELIGION—FIRST AWAKENED BY A METHODIST MINISTER NAMED HANSON—MY DEAR AND GOOD OLD COLORED FRIEND, LAWSON—HIS CHARACTER AND
OCCUPATION—HIS INFLUENCE OVER ME—OUR MUTUAL ATTACHMENT—THE COMFORT
I DERIVED FROM HIS TEACHING—NEW HOPES AND ASPIRATIONS—HEAVENLY LIGHT AMIDST EARTHLY DARKNESS—THE TWO IRISHMEN ON THE WHARF—THEIR
CONVERSATION—HOW I LEARNED TO WRITE—WHAT WERE MY AIMS.

Whilst in the painful state of mind described in the foregoing chapter, almost regretting my very existence, because doomed to a life of bondage, so goaded and so wretched, at times, that I was even tempted to destroy my own life, I was keenly sensitive and eager to know any, and every thing that transpired, having any relation to the subject of slavery. I was all ears, all eyes, whenever the words slave, slavery, dropped from the lips of any white person, and the occasions were not unfrequent when these words became leading ones, in high, social debate, at our house. Every little while, I could hear Master Hugh, or some of his company, speaking with much warmth and excitement about "abolitionists." Of who or what these were, I was totally ignorant. I found, however, that whatever they might be, they were most cordially hated and soundly abused by slaveholders, of every grade. I very soon discovered, too, that slavery was, in some sort, under consideration, whenever the abolitionists were alluded to. This made the term a very interesting one to me. If a slave, for instance, had made good his escape from slavery, it was generally alleged, that he had been persuaded and assisted by the abolitionists. If, also, a slave killed his master—as was sometimes the case—or struck down his overseer, or set fire to his master's dwelling, or committed any violence or crime, out of the common way, it was certain to be said, that such a crime was the legitimate fruits of the abolition movement. Hearing such charges often repeated, I, naturally enough, received the impression that abolition—whatever else it might be—could not be unfriendly to the slave, nor very friendly to the slaveholder. I therefore set about finding out, if possible, who and what the abolitionists were, and why they were so obnoxious to the slaveholders. The dictionary afforded me very little help. It taught me that abolition was the "act of abolishing;" but it left me in ignorance at the very point where I most wanted information—and that was, as to the thing to be abolished. A city newspaper, the Baltimore American, gave me the incendiary information denied me by the dictionary. In its columns I found, that, on a certain day, a vast number of petitions and memorials had been presented to congress, praying for the abolition of slavery in the District of Columbia, and for the abolition of the slave trade between the states of the Union. This was enough. The vindictive bitterness, the marked caution, the studied reverse, and the cumbrous ambiguity, practiced by our white folks, when alluding to this subject, was now fully explained. Ever, after that, when I heard the words "abolition," or "abolition movement," mentioned, I felt the matter one of a personal concern; and I drew near to listen, when I could do so, without seeming too solicitous and prying. There was HOPE in those words. Ever and anon, too, I could see some terrible denunciation of slavery, in our papers—copied from abolition papers at the north—and the injustice of such denunciation commented on. These I read with avidity. I had a deep satisfaction in the thought, that the rascality of slaveholders was not concealed from the eyes of the world, and that I was not alone in abhorring the cruelty and brutality of slavery. A still deeper train of thought was stirred. I saw that there was fear, as well as rage, in the manner of speaking of the abolitionists. The latter, therefore, I was compelled to regard as having some power in the country; and I felt that they might, possibly, succeed in their designs. When I met with a slave to whom I deemed it safe to talk on the subject, I would impart to him so much of the mystery as I had been able to penetrate. Thus, the light of this grand movement broke in upon my mind, by degrees; and I must say, that, ignorant as I then was of the philosophy of that movement, I believe in it from the first—and I believed in it, partly, because I saw that it alarmed the consciences of slaveholders. The insurrection of Nathaniel Turner had been quelled, but the alarm and terror had not subsided. The cholera was on its way, and the thought was present, that God was angry with the white people because of their slaveholding wickedness, and, therefore, his judgments were abroad in the land. It was impossible for me not to hope much from the abolition movement, when I saw it supported by the Almighty, and armed with DEATH!

Previous to my contemplation of the anti-slavery movement, and its probable results, my mind had been seriously awakened to the subject of religion. I was not more than thirteen years old, when I felt the need of God, as a father and protector. My religious nature was awakened by the preaching of a white Methodist minister, named Hanson. He thought that all men, great and small, bond and free, were sinners in the sight of God; that they were, by nature, rebels against His government; and that they must repent of their sins, and be reconciled to God, through Christ. I cannot say that I had a very distinct notion of what was required of me; but one thing I knew very well—I was wretched, and had no means of making myself otherwise. Moreover, I knew that I could pray for light. I consulted a good colored man, named Charles Johnson; and, in tones of holy affection, he told me to pray, and what to pray for. I was, for weeks, a poor, brokenhearted mourner, traveling through the darkness and misery of doubts and fears. I finally found that change of heart which comes by "casting all one's care" upon God, and by having faith in Jesus Christ, as the Redeemer, Friend, and Savior of those who diligently seek Him.

After this, I saw the world in a new light. I seemed to live in a new world, surrounded by new objects, and to be animated by new hopes and desires. I loved all mankind—slaveholders not excepted; though I abhorred slavery more than ever. My great concern was, now, to have the world converted. The desire for knowledge increased, and especially did I want a thorough acquaintance with the contents of the bible. I have gathered scattered pages from this holy book, from the filthy street gutters of Baltimore, and washed and dried them, that in the moments of my leisure, I might get a word or two of wisdom from them. While thus religiously seeking knowledge, I became acquainted with a good old colored man, named Lawson. A more devout man than he, I never saw. He drove a dray for Mr. James Ramsey, the owner of a rope-walk on Fell's Point, Baltimore. This man not only prayed three time a day, but he prayed as he walked through the streets, at his work—on his dray everywhere. His life was a life of prayer, and his words (when he spoke to his friends,) were about a better world. Uncle Lawson lived near Master Hugh's house; and, becoming deeply attached to the old man, I went often with him to prayer-meeting, and spent much of my leisure time with him on Sunday. The old man could read a little, and I was a great help to him, in making out the hard words, for I was a better reader than he. I could teach him "the letter," but he could teach me "the spirit;" and high, refreshing times we had together, in singing, praying and glorifying God. These meetings with Uncle Lawson went on for a long time, without the knowledge of Master Hugh or my mistress. Both knew, how ever, that I had become religious, and they seemed to respect my conscientious piety. My mistress was still a professor of religion, and belonged to class. Her leader was no less a person than the Rev. Beverly Waugh, the presiding elder, and now one of the bishops of the Methodist Episcopal church. Mr. Waugh was then stationed over Wilk street church. I am careful to state these facts, that the reader may be able to form an idea of the precise influences which had to do with shaping and directing my mind. In view of the cares and anxieties incident to the life she was then leading, and, especially, in view of the separation from religious associations to which she was subjected, my mistress had, as I have before stated, become lukewarm, and needed to be looked up by her leader. This brought Mr. Waugh to our house, and gave me an opportunity to hear him exhort and pray. But my chief instructor, in matters of religion, was Uncle Lawson. He was my spiritual father; and I loved him intensely, and was at his house every chance I got.

This pleasure was not long allowed me. Master Hugh became averse to my going to Father Lawson's, and threatened to whip me if I ever went there again. I now felt myself persecuted by a wicked man; and I would go to Father Lawson's, notwithstanding the threat. The good old man had told me, that the "Lord had a great work for me to do;" and I must prepare to do it; and that he had been shown that I must preach the gospel. His words made a deep impression on my mind, and I verily felt that some such work was before me, though I could not see how I should ever engage in its performance. "The good Lord," he said, "would bring it to pass in his own good time," and that I must go on reading and studying the scriptures. The advice and the suggestions of Uncle Lawson, were not without their influence upon my character and destiny. He threw my thoughts into a channel from which they have never entirely diverged. He fanned my already intense love of knowledge into a flame, by assuring me that I was to be a useful man in the world. When I would say to him, "How can these things be and what can I do?" his simple reply was, "Trust in the Lord." When I told him that "I was a slave, and a slave FOR LIFE," he said, "the Lord can make you free, my dear. All things are possible with him, only have faith in God." "Ask, and it shall be given." "If you want liberty," said the good old man, "ask the Lord for it, in faith, AND HE WILL GIVE IT TO YOU."

Thus assured, and cheered on, under the inspiration of hope, I worked and prayed with a light heart, believing that my life was under the guidance of a wisdom higher than my own. With all other blessings sought at the mercy seat, I always prayed that God would, of His great mercy, and in His own good time, deliver me from my bondage.

I went, one day, on the wharf of Mr. Waters; and seeing two Irishmen unloading a large scow of stone, or ballast I went on board, unasked, and helped them. When we had finished the work, one of the men came to me, aside, and asked me a number of questions, and among them, if I were a slave. I told him "I was a slave, and a slave for life." The good Irishman gave his shoulders a shrug, and seemed deeply affected by the statement. He said, "it was a pity so fine a little fellow as myself should be a slave for life." They both had much to say about the matter, and expressed the deepest sympathy with me, and the most decided hatred of slavery. They went so far as to tell me that I ought to run away, and go to the north; that I should find friends there, and that I would be as free as anybody. I, however, pretended not to be interested in what they said, for I feared they might be treacherous. White men have been known to encourage slaves to escape, and then—to get the reward—they have kidnapped them, and returned them to their masters. And while I mainly inclined to the notion that these men were honest and meant me no ill, I feared it might be otherwise. I nevertheless remembered their words and their advice, and looked forward to an escape to the north, as a possible means of gaining the liberty for which my heart panted. It was not my enslavement, at the then present time, that most affected me; the being a slave for life, was the saddest thought. I was too young to think of running away immediately; besides, I wished to learn how to write, before going, as I might have occasion to write my own pass. I now not only had the hope of freedom, but a foreshadowing of the means by which I might, some day, gain that inestimable boon. Meanwhile, I resolved to add to my educational attainments the art of writing.

After this manner I began to learn to write: I was much in the ship yard—Master Hugh's, and that of Durgan & Bailey—and I observed that the carpenters, after hewing and getting a piece of timber ready for use, wrote on it the initials of the name of that part of the ship for which it was intended. When, for instance, a piece of timber was ready for the starboard side, it was marked with a capital "S." A piece for the larboard side was marked "L;" larboard forward, "L. F.;" larboard aft, was marked "L. A.;" starboard aft, "S. A.;" and starboard forward "S. F." I soon learned these letters, and for what they were placed on the timbers.

My work was now, to keep fire under the steam box, and to watch the ship yard while the carpenters had gone to dinner. This interval gave me a fine opportunity for copying the letters named. I soon astonished myself with the ease with which I made the letters; and the thought was soon present, "if I can make four, I can make more." But having made these easily, when I met boys about Bethel church, or any of our play-grounds, I entered the lists with them in the art of writing, and would make the letters which I had been so fortunate as to learn, and ask them to "beat that if they could." With playmates for my teachers, fences and pavements for my copy books, and chalk for my pen and ink, I learned the art of writing. I, however, afterward adopted various methods of improving my hand. The most successful, was copying the italics in Webster's spelling book, until I could make them all without looking on the book. By this time, my little "Master Tommy" had grown to be a big boy, and had written over a number of copy books, and brought them home. They had been shown to the neighbors, had elicited due praise, and were now laid carefully away. Spending my time between the ship yard and house, I was as often the lone keeper of the latter as of the former. When my mistress left me in charge of the house, I had a grand time; I got Master Tommy's copy books and a pen and ink, and, in the ample spaces between the lines, I wrote other lines, as nearly like his as possible. The process was a tedious one, and I ran the risk of getting a flogging for marring the highly prized copy books of the oldest son. In addition to those opportunities, sleeping, as I did, in the kitchen loft—a room seldom visited by any of the family—I got a flour barrel up there, and a chair; and upon the head of that barrel I have written (or endeavored to write) copying from the bible and the Methodist hymn book, and other books which had accumulated on my hands, till late at night, and when all the family were in bed and asleep. I was supported in my endeavors by renewed advice, and by holy promises from the good Father Lawson, with whom I continued to meet, and pray, and read the scriptures. Although Master Hugh was aware of my going there, I must say, for his credit, that he never executed his threat to whip me, for having thus, innocently, employed-my leisure time.

CHAPTER XIII. The Vicissitudes of Slave Life

DEATH OF OLD MASTER'S SON RICHARD, SPEEDILY FOLLOWED BY THAT OF OLD
MASTER—VALUATION AND DIVISION OF ALL THE PROPERTY, INCLUDING THE SLAVES—MY PRESENCE REQUIRED AT HILLSBOROUGH TO BE APPRAISED AND ALLOTTED TO A NEW OWNER—MY SAD PROSPECTS AND GRIEF—PARTING—THE UTTER
POWERLESSNESS OF THE SLAVES TO DECIDE THEIR OWN DESTINY—A GENERAL
DREAD OF MASTER ANDREW—HIS WICKEDNESS AND CRUELTY—MISS LUCRETIA MY NEW
OWNER—MY RETURN TO BALTIMORE—JOY UNDER THE ROOF OF MASTER HUGH—DEATH
OF MRS. LUCRETIA—MY POOR OLD GRANDMOTHER—HER SAD FATE—THE LONE COT
IN THE WOODS—MASTER THOMAS AULD'S SECOND MARRIAGE—AGAIN REMOVED FROM
MASTER HUGH'S—REASONS FOR REGRETTING THE CHANGE—A PLAN OF ESCAPE
ENTERTAINED.

I must now ask the reader to go with me a little back in point of time, in my humble story, and to notice another circumstance that entered into my slavery experience, and which, doubtless, has had a share in deepening my horror of slavery, and increasing my hostility toward those men and measures that practically uphold the slave system.

It has already been observed, that though I was, after my removal from Col. Lloyd's plantation, in form the slave of Master Hugh, I was, in fact, and in law, the slave of my old master, Capt. Anthony. Very well.

In a very short time after I went to Baltimore, my old master's youngest son, Richard, died; and, in three years and six months after his death, my old master himself died, leaving only his son, Andrew, and his daughter, Lucretia, to share his estate. The old man died while on a visit to his daughter, in Hillsborough, where Capt. Auld and Mrs. Lucretia now lived. The former, having given up the command of Col. Lloyd's sloop, was now keeping a store in that town. Cut off, thus unexpectedly, Capt. Anthony died intestate; and his property must now be equally divided between his two children, Andrew and Lucretia.

The valuation and the division of slaves, among contending heirs, is an important incident in slave life. The character and tendencies of the heirs, are generally well understood among the slaves who are to be divided, and all have their aversions and preferences. But, neither their aversions nor their preferences avail them anything.

On the death of old master, I was immediately sent for, to be valued and divided with the other property. Personally, my concern was, mainly, about my possible removal from the home of

Master Hugh, which, after that of my grandmother, was the most endeared to me. But, the whole thing, as a feature of slavery, shocked me. It furnished me anew insight into the unnatural power to which I was subjected. My detestation of slavery, already great, rose with this new conception of its enormity.

That was a sad day for me, a sad day for little Tommy, and a sad day for my dear Baltimore mistress and teacher, when I left for the Eastern Shore, to be valued and divided. We, all three, wept bitterly that day; for we might be parting, and we feared we were parting, forever. No one could tell among which pile of chattels I should be flung. Thus early, I got a foretaste of that painful uncertainty which slavery brings to the ordinary lot of mortals. Sickness, adversity and death may interfere with the plans and purposes of all; but the slave has the added danger of changing homes, changing hands, and of having separations unknown to other men. Then, too, there was the intensified degradation of the spectacle. What an assemblage! Men and women, young and old, married and single; moral and intellectual beings, in open contempt of their humanity, level at a blow with horses, sheep, horned cattle and swine! Horses and men—cattle and women—pigs and children—all holding the same rank in the scale of social existence; and all subjected to the same narrow inspection, to ascertain their value in gold and silver—the only standard of worth applied by slaveholders to slaves! How vividly, at that moment, did the brutalizing power of slavery flash before me! Personality swallowed up in the sordid idea of property! Manhood lost in chattelhood!

After the valuation, then came the division. This was an hour of high excitement and distressing anxiety. Our destiny was now to be fixed for life, and we had no more voice in the decision of the question, than the oxen and cows that stood chewing at the haymow. One word from the appraisers, against all preferences or prayers, was enough to sunder all the ties of friendship and affection, and even to separate husbands and wives, parents and children. We were all appalled before that power, which, to human seeming, could bless or blast us in a moment. Added to the dread of separation, most painful to the majority of the slaves, we all had a decided horror of the thought of falling into the hands of Master Andrew. He was distinguished for cruelty and intemperance.

Slaves generally dread to fall into the hands of drunken owners. Master Andrew was almost a confirmed sot, and had already, by his reckless mismanagement and profligate dissipation, wasted a large portion of old master's property. To fall into his hands, was, therefore, considered merely as the first step toward being sold away to the far south. He would spend his fortune in a few years, and his farms and slaves would be sold, we thought, at public outcry; and we should be hurried away to the cotton fields, and rice swamps, of the sunny south. This was the cause of deep consternation.

The people of the north, and free people generally, I think, have less attachment to the places where they are born and brought up, than have the slaves. Their freedom to go and come, to be here and there, as they list, prevents any extravagant attachment to any one particular place, in their case. On the other hand, the slave is a fixture; he has no choice, no goal, no destination; but is pegged down to a single spot, and must take root here, or nowhere. The idea of removal elsewhere, comes, generally, in the shape of a threat, and in punishment of crime. It is, therefore, attended with fear and dread. A slave seldom thinks of bettering his condition by being sold, and hence he looks upon separation from his native place, with none of the enthusiasm which animates the bosoms of young freemen, when they contemplate a life in the far west, or in some distant country where they intend to rise to wealth and distinction. Nor can those from whom they separate, give them up with that cheerfulness with which friends and relations yield each other up, when they feel that it is for the good of the departing one that he is removed from his native place. Then, too, there is correspondence, and there is, at least, the hope of reunion, because reunion is possible. But, with the slave, all these mitigating circumstances are wanting. There is no improvement in his condition probable,—no correspondence possible,—no reunion attainable. His going out into the world, is like a living man going into the tomb, who, with open eyes, sees himself buried out of sight and hearing of wife, children and friends of kindred tie.

In contemplating the likelihoods and possibilities of our circumstances, I probably suffered more than most of my fellow servants. I had known what it was to experience kind, and even tender treatment; they had known nothing of the sort. Life, to them, had been rough and thorny, as well as dark. They had—most of them—lived on my old master's farm in Tuckahoe, and had felt the reign of Mr. Plummer's rule. The overseer had written his character on the living parchment of most of their backs, and left them callous; my back (thanks to my early removal from the plantation to Baltimore) was yet tender. I had left a kind mistress at Baltimore, who was almost a mother to me. She was in tears when we parted, and the probabilities of ever seeing her again, trembling in the balance as they did, could not be viewed without alarm and agony. The thought of leaving that kind mistress forever, and, worse still, of being the slave of Andrew Anthony—a man who, but a few days before the division of the property, had, in my presence, seized my brother Perry by the throat, dashed him on the ground, and with the heel of his boot stamped him on the head, until the blood gushed from his nose and ears—was terrible! This fiendish proceeding had no better apology than the fact, that Perry had gone to play, when Master Andrew wanted him for some trifling service. This cruelty, too, was of a piece with his general character. After inflicting his heavy blows on my brother, on observing me looking at him with intense astonishment, he said, "That is the way I will serve you, one of these days;" meaning, no doubt, when I should come into his possession. This threat, the reader may well suppose, was not very tranquilizing to my feelings. I could see that he really thirsted to get hold of me. But I was there only for a few days. I had not received any orders, and had violated none, and there was, therefore, no excuse for flogging me.

At last, the anxiety and suspense were ended; and they ended, thanks to a kind Providence, in accordance with my wishes. I fell to the portion of Mrs. Lucretia—the dear lady who bound up my head, when the savage Aunt Katy was adding to my sufferings her bitterest maledictions. Capt. Thomas Auld and Mrs. Lucretia at once decided on my return to Baltimore. They knew how sincerely and warmly Mrs. Hugh Auld was attached to me, and how delighted Mr. Hugh's son would be to have me back; and, withal, having no immediate use for one so young, they willingly let me off to Baltimore.

I need not stop here to narrate my joy on returning to Baltimore, nor that of little Tommy; nor the tearful joy of his mother; nor the evident saticfaction(sic) of Master Hugh. I was just one month absent from Baltimore, before the matter was decided; and the time really seemed full six months.

One trouble over, and on comes another. The slave's life is full of uncertainty. I had returned to Baltimore but a short time, when the tidings reached me, that my friend, Mrs. Lucretia, who was only second in my regard to Mrs. Hugh Auld, was dead, leaving her husband and only one child—a daughter, named Amanda.

Shortly after the death of Mrs. Lucretia, strange to say, Master Andrew died, leaving his wife and one child. Thus, the whole family of Anthonys was swept away; only two children remained. All this happened within five years of my leaving Col. Lloyd's.

No alteration took place in the condition of the slaves, in consequence of these deaths, yet I could not help feeling less secure, after the death of my friend, Mrs. Lucretia, than I had done during her life. While she lived, I felt that I had a strong friend to plead for me in any emergency. Ten years ago, while speaking of the state of things in our family, after the events just named, I used this language:

Now all the property of my old master, slaves included, was in the hands of strangers—strangers who had nothing to do in accumulating it. Not a slave was left free. All remained slaves, from youngest to oldest. If any one thing in my experience, more than another, served to deepen my conviction of the infernal character of slavery, and to fill me with unutterable loathing of slaveholders, it was their base ingratitude to my poor old grandmother. She had served my old master faithfully from youth to old age. She had been the source of all his wealth; she had peopled his plantation with slaves; she had become a great-grandmother in his service. She had rocked him in infancy, attended him in childhood, served him through life, and at his death wiped from his icy brow the cold death-sweat, and closed his eyes forever. She was nevertheless left a slave—a slave for life—a slave in the hands of strangers; and in their hands she saw her children, her grandchildren, and her great-grandchildren, divided, like so many sheep, without being gratified with the small privilege of a single word, as to their or her own destiny. And, to cap the climax of their base ingratitude and fiendish barbarity, my grandmother, who was now very old, having outlived my old master and all his children, having seen the beginning and end of all of them, and her present owners finding she was of but little value, her frame already racked with the pains of old age, and complete helplessness fast stealing over her once active limbs, they took her to the woods, built her a little hut, put up a little mud-chimney, and then made her welcome to the privilege of supporting herself there in perfect loneliness; thus virtually turning her out to die! If my poor old grandmother now lives, she lives to suffer in utter loneliness; she lives to remember and mourn over the loss of children, the loss of grandchildren, and the loss of great-grandchildren. They are, in the language of the slave's poet, Whittier—

> Gone, gone, sold and gone,
> To the rice swamp dank and lone,
> Where the slave-whip ceaseless swings,
> Where the noisome insect stings,
> Where the fever-demon strews
> Poison with the falling dews,
> Where the sickly sunbeams glare
> Through the hot and misty air:—
> > Gone, gone, sold and gone
> > To the rice swamp dank and lone,
> > From Virginia hills and waters—
> > Woe is me, my stolen daughters!

The hearth is desolate. The children, the unconscious children, who once sang and danced in her presence, are gone. She gropes her way, in the darkness of age, for a drink of water. Instead of the voices of her children, she hears by day the moans of the dove, and by night the screams of the hideous owl. All is gloom. The grave is at the door. And now, when weighed down by the pains and aches of old age, when the head inclines to the feet, when the beginning and ending of human existence meet, and helpless infancy and painful old age combine together—at this time, this most needful time, the time for the exercise of that tenderness and affection which children only can exercise toward a declining parent—my poor old grandmother, the devoted mother of twelve children, is left all alone, in yonder little hut, before a few dim embers.

Two years after the death of Mrs. Lucretia, Master Thomas married his second wife. Her name was Rowena Hamilton, the eldest daughter of Mr. William Hamilton, a rich slaveholder on the Eastern Shore of Maryland, who lived about five miles from St. Michael's, the then place of my master's residence.

Not long after his marriage, Master Thomas had a misunderstanding with Master Hugh, and, as a means of punishing his brother, he ordered him to send me home.

As the ground of misunderstanding will serve to illustrate the character of southern chivalry, and humanity, I will relate it.

Among the children of my Aunt Milly, was a daughter, named Henny. When quite a child, Henny had fallen into the fire, and burnt her hands so bad that they were of very little use to her. Her fingers were drawn almost into the palms of her hands. She could make out to do something, but she was considered hardly worth the having—of little more value than a horse with a broken leg. This unprofitable piece of human property, ill shapen, and disfigured, Capt. Auld sent off to Baltimore, making his brother Hugh welcome to her services.

After giving poor Henny a fair trial, Master Hugh and his wife came to the conclusion, that they had no use for the crippled servant, and they sent her back to Master Thomas. Thus, the latter took as an act of ingratitude, on the part of his brother; and, as a mark of his displeasure, he required him to send me immediately to St. Michael's, saying, if he cannot keep "Hen," he shall not have "Fred."

Here was another shock to my nerves, another breaking up of my plans, and another severance of my religious and social alliances. I was now a big boy. I had become quite useful to several young colored men, who had made me their teacher. I had taught some of them to read, and was accustomed to spend many of my leisure hours with them. Our attachment was strong, and I greatly dreaded the separation. But regrets, especially in a slave, are unavailing. I was only a slave; my wishes were nothing, and my happiness was the sport of my masters.

My regrets at now leaving Baltimore, were not for the same reasons as when I before left that city, to be valued and handed over to my proper owner. My home was not now the pleasant place it had formerly been. A change had taken place, both in Master Hugh, and in his once pious and affectionate wife. The influence of brandy and bad company on him, and the influence of slavery and social isolation upon her, had wrought disastrously upon the characters of both. Thomas was no longer "little Tommy," but was a big boy, and had learned to assume the airs of his class toward me. My condition, therefore, in the house of Master Hugh, was not, by any means, so comfortable as in former years. My attachments were now outside of our family. They were felt to those to whom I imparted instruction, and to those little white boys from whom I received instruction. There, too, was my dear old father, the pious Lawson, who was, in christian graces, the very counterpart of "Uncle" Tom. The resemblance is so perfect, that he might have been the original of Mrs. Stowe's christian hero. The thought of leaving these dear friends, greatly troubled me, for I was going without the hope of ever returning to Baltimore again; the feud between Master Hugh and his brother being bitter and irreconcilable, or, at least, supposed to be so.

In addition to thoughts of friends from whom I was parting, as I supposed, forever, I had the grief of neglected chances of escape to brood over. I had put off running away, until now I was to be placed where the opportunities for escaping were much fewer than in a large city like Baltimore.

On my way from Baltimore to St. Michael's, down the Chesapeake bay, our sloop—the "Amanda"—was passed by the steamers plying between that city and Philadelphia, and I watched the course of those steamers, and, while going to St. Michael's, I formed a plan to escape from slavery; of which plan, and matters connected therewith the kind reader shall learn more hereafter.

CHAPTER XIV. Experience in St. Michael's

THE VILLAGE—ITS INHABITANTS—THEIR OCCUPATION AND LOW PROPENSITIES
CAPTAN(sic) THOMAS AULD—HIS CHARACTER—HIS SECOND WIFE, ROWENA—WELL
MATCHED—SUFFERINGS FROM HUNGER—OBLIGED TO TAKE FOOD—MODE OF ARGUMENT
IN VINDICATION THEREOF—NO MORAL CODE OF FREE SOCIETY CAN APPLY TO SLAVE SOCIETY—SOUTHERN CAMP MEETING—WHAT MASTER THOMAS DID THERE—HOPES—SUSPICIONS ABOUT HIS CONVERSION—THE RESULT—FAITH AND

WORKS ENTIRELY AT VARIANCE—HIS RISE AND PROGRESS IN THE CHURCH—POOR
COUSIN "HENNY"—HIS TREATMENT OF HER—THE METHODIST PREACHERS—THEIR
UTTER DISREGARD OF US—ONE EXCELLENT EXCEPTION—REV. GEORGE
COOKMAN—SABBATH SCHOOL—HOW BROKEN UP AND BY WHOM—A FUNERAL PALL CAST
OVER ALL MY PROSPECTS—COVEY THE NEGRO-BREAKER.

St. Michael's, the village in which was now my new home, compared favorably with villages in slave states, generally. There were a few comfortable dwellings in it, but the place, as a whole, wore a dull, slovenly, enterprise-forsaken aspect. The mass of the buildings were wood; they had never enjoyed the artificial adornment of paint, and time and storms had worn off the bright color of the wood, leaving them almost as black as buildings charred by a conflagration.

St. Michael's had, in former years, (previous to 1833, for that was the year I went to reside there,) enjoyed some reputation as a ship building community, but that business had almost entirely given place to oyster fishing, for the Baltimore and Philadelphia markets—a course of life highly unfavorable to morals, industry, and manners. Miles river was broad, and its oyster fishing grounds were extensive; and the fishermen were out, often, all day, and a part of the night, during autumn, winter and spring. This exposure was an excuse for carrying with them, in considerable quanties(sic), spirituous liquors, the then supposed best antidote for cold. Each canoe was supplied with its jug of rum; and tippling, among this class of the citizens of St. Michael's, became general. This drinking habit, in an ignorant population, fostered coarseness, vulgarity and an indolent disregard for the social improvement of the place, so that it was admitted, by the few sober, thinking people who remained there, that St. Michael's had become a very unsaintly, as well as unsightly place, before I went there to reside.

I left Baltimore for St. Michael's in the month of March, 1833. I know the year, because it was the one succeeding the first cholera in Baltimore, and was the year, also, of that strange phenomenon, when the heavens seemed about to part with its starry train. I witnessed this gorgeous spectacle, and was awe-struck. The air seemed filled with bright, descending messengers from the sky. It was about daybreak when I saw this sublime scene. I was not without the suggestion, at the moment, that it might be the harbinger of the coming of the Son of Man; and, in my then state of mind, I was prepared to hail Him as my friend and deliverer. I had read, that the "stars shall fall from heaven"; and they were now falling. I was suffering much in my mind. It did seem that every time the young tendrils of my affection became attached, they were rudely broken by some unnatural outside power; and I was beginning to look away to heaven for the rest denied me on earth.

But, to my story. It was now more than seven years since I had lived with Master Thomas Auld, in the family of my old master, on Col. Lloyd's plantation. We were almost entire strangers to each other; for, when I knew him at the house of my old master, it was not as a master, but simply as "Captain Auld," who had married old master's daughter. All my lessons concerning his temper and disposition, and the best methods of pleasing him, were yet to be learnt. Slaveholders, however, are not very ceremonious in approaching a slave; and my ignorance of the new material in shape of a master was but transient. Nor was my mistress long in making known her animus. She was not a "Miss Lucretia," traces of whom I yet remembered, and the more especially, as I saw them shining in the face of little Amanda, her daughter, now living under a step-mother's government. I had not forgotten the soft hand, guided by a tender heart, that bound up with healing balsam the gash made in my head by Ike, the son of Abel. Thomas and Rowena, I found to be a well-matched pair. He was stingy, and she was cruel; and—what was quite natural in such cases—she possessed the ability to make him as cruel as herself, while she could easily descend to the level of his meanness. In the house of Master Thomas, I was made—for the first time in seven years to feel the pinchings of hunger, and this was not very easy to bear.

For, in all the changes of Master Hugh's family, there was no change in the bountifulness with which they supplied me with food. Not to give a slave enough to eat, is meanness intensified, and it is so recognized among slaveholders generally, in Maryland. The rule is, no matter how coarse the food, only let there be enough of it. This is the theory, and—in the part of Maryland I came from—the general practice accords with this theory. Lloyd's plantation was an exception, as was, also, the house of Master Thomas Auld.

All know the lightness of Indian corn-meal, as an article of food, and can easily judge from the following facts whether the statements I have made of the stinginess of Master Thomas, are borne out. There were four slaves of us in the kitchen, and four whites in the great house Thomas Auld, Mrs. Auld, Hadaway Auld (brother of Thomas Auld) and little Amanda. The names of the slaves in the kitchen, were Eliza, my sister; Priscilla, my aunt; Henny, my cousin; and myself. There were eight persons in the family. There was, each week, one half bushel of corn-meal brought from the mill; and in the kitchen, corn-meal was almost our exclusive food, for very little else was allowed us. Out of this bushel of corn-meal, the family in the great house had a small loaf every morning; thus leaving us, in the kitchen, with not quite a half a peck per week, apiece. This allowance was less than half the allowance of food on Lloyd's plantation. It was not enough to subsist upon; and we were, therefore, reduced to the wretched necessity of living at the expense of our neighbors. We were compelled either to beg, or to steal, and we did both. I frankly confess, that while I hated everything like stealing, as such, I nevertheless did not hesitate to take food, when I was hungry, wherever I could find it. Nor was this practice the mere result of an unreasoning instinct; it was, in my case, the result of a clear apprehension of the claims of morality. I weighed and considered the matter closely, before I ventured to satisfy my hunger by such means. Considering that my labor and person were the property of Master Thomas, and that I was by him deprived of the necessaries of life necessaries obtained by my own labor—it was easy to deduce the right to supply myself with what was my own. It was simply appropriating what was my own to the use of my master, since the health and strength derived from such food were exerted in his service. To be sure, this was stealing, according to the law and gospel I heard from St. Michael's pulpit; but I had already begun to attach less importance to what dropped from that quarter, on that point, while, as yet, I retained my reverence for religion. It was not always convenient to steal from master, and the same reason why I might, innocently, steal from him, did not seem to justify me in stealing from others. In the case of my master, it was only a question of removal—the taking his meat out of one tub, and putting it into another; the ownership of the meat was not affected by the transaction. At first, he owned it in the tub, and last, he owned it in me. His meat house was not always open. There was a strict watch kept on that point, and the key was on a large bunch in Rowena's pocket. A great many times have we, poor creatures, been severely pinched with hunger, when meat and bread have been moulding under the lock, while the key was in the pocket of our mistress. This had been so when she knew we were nearly half starved; and yet, that mistress, with saintly air, would kneel with her husband, and pray each morning that a merciful God would bless them in basket and in store, and save them, at last, in his kingdom. But I proceed with the argument.

It was necessary that right to steal from others should be established; and this could only rest upon a wider range of generalization than that which supposed the right to steal from my master.

It was sometime before I arrived at this clear right. The reader will get some idea of my train of reasoning, by a brief statement of the case. "I am," thought I, "not only the slave of Thomas, but I am the slave of society at large. Society at large has bound itself, in form and in fact, to assist Master Thomas in robbing me of my rightful liberty, and of the just reward of my labor; therefore, whatever rights I have against Master Thomas, I have, equally, against those confederated with him in robbing me of liberty. As society has marked me out as privileged plunder, on the principle of self-preservation I am justified in plundering in turn. Since each slave belongs to all; all must, therefore, belong to each."

I shall here make a profession of faith which may shock some, offend others, and be dissented from by all. It is this: Within the bounds of his just earnings, I hold that the slave is fully justified in helping himself to the gold and silver, and the best apparel of his master, or that of any other slaveholder; and that such taking is not stealing in any just sense of that word. The morality of free society can have no application to slave society. Slaveholders have made it almost impossible for the slave to commit any crime, known either to the laws of God or to the laws of man. If he steals, he takes his own; if he kills his master, he imitates only the heroes of the revolution. Slaveholders I hold to be individually and collectively responsible for all the evils which grow out of the horrid relation, and I believe they will be so held at the judgment, in the sight of a just God. Make a man a slave, and you rob him of moral responsibility. Freedom of choice is the essence of all accountability. But my kind readers are, probably, less concerned about my opinions, than about that which more nearly touches my personal experience; albeit, my opinions have, in some sort, been formed by that experience. Bad as slaveholders are, I have seldom met with one so entirely destitute of every element of character capable of inspiring respect, as was my present master, Capt. Thomas Auld.

When I lived with him, I thought him incapable of a noble action. The leading trait in his character was intense selfishness. I think he was fully aware of this fact himself, and often tried to conceal it. Capt. Auld was not a born slaveholder—not a birthright member of the slaveholding oligarchy. He was only a slaveholder by marriage-right; and, of all slaveholders, these latter are, by far, the most exacting. There was in him all the love of domination, the pride of mastery, and the swagger of authority, but his rule lacked the vital element of consistency. He could be cruel; but his methods of showing it were cowardly, and evinced his meanness rather than his spirit. His commands were strong, his enforcement weak.

Slaves are not insensible to the whole-souled characteristics of a generous, dashing slaveholder, who is fearless of consequences; and they prefer a master of this bold and daring kind—even with the risk of being shot down for impudence to the fretful, little soul, who never uses the lash but at the suggestion of a love of gain.

Slaves, too, readily distinguish between the birthright bearing of the original slaveholder and the assumed attitudes of the accidental slaveholder; and while they cannot respect either, they certainly despise the latter more than the former.

The luxury of having slaves wait upon him was something new to Master Thomas; and for it he was wholly unprepared. He was a slaveholder, without the ability to hold or manage his slaves. We seldom called him "master," but generally addressed him by his "bay craft" title— "Capt. Auld." It is easy to see that such conduct might do much to make him appear awkward, and, consequently, fretful. His wife was especially solicitous to have us call her husband "master." Is your master at the store?"—"Where is your master?"—"Go and tell your master"—"I will make your master acquainted with your conduct"—she would say; but we were inapt scholars. Especially were I and my sister Eliza inapt in this particular. Aunt Priscilla was less stubborn and defiant in her spirit than Eliza and myself; and, I think, her road was less rough than ours.

In the month of August, 1833, when I had almost become desperate under the treatment of Master Thomas, and when I entertained more strongly than ever the oft-repeated determination to run away, a circumstance occurred which seemed to promise brighter and better days for us all. At a Methodist camp-meeting, held in the Bay Side (a famous place for campmeetings) about eight miles from St. Michael's, Master Thomas came out with a profession of religion. He had long been an object of interest to the church, and to the ministers, as I had seen by the repeated visits and lengthy exhortations of the latter. He was a fish quite worth catching, for he had money and standing. In the community of St. Michael's he was equal to the best citizen. He was strictly temperate; perhaps, from principle, but most likely, from interest. There was very little to do for him, to give him the appearance of piety, and to make him a pillar in the church. Well, the camp-meeting continued a week; people gathered from all parts of the county, and two steamboat loads came from Baltimore. The ground was happily chosen; seats were arranged; a stand erected; a rude altar fenced in, fronting the preachers' stand, with straw in it for the accommodation of mourners. This latter would hold at least one hundred persons. In front, and on the sides of the preachers' stand, and outside the long rows of seats, rose the first class of stately tents, each vieing with the other in strength, neatness, and capacity for accommodating its inmates. Behind this first circle of tents was another, less imposing, which reached round the camp-ground to the speakers' stand. Outside this second class of tents were covered wagons, ox carts, and vehicles of every shape and size. These served as tents to their owners. Outside of these, huge fires were burning, in all directions, where roasting, and boiling, and frying, were going on, for the benefit of those who were attending to their own spiritual welfare within the circle. Behind the preachers' stand, a narrow space was marked out for the use of the colored people. There were no seats provided for this class of persons; the preachers addressed them, "over the left," if they addressed them at all. After the preaching was over, at every service, an invitation was given to mourners to come into the pen; and, in some cases, ministers went out to persuade men and women to come in. By one of these ministers, Master Thomas Auld was persuaded to go inside the pen. I was deeply interested in that matter, and followed; and, though colored people were not allowed either in the pen or in front of the preachers' stand, I ventured to take my stand at a sort of half-way place between the blacks and whites, where I could distinctly see the movements of mourners, and especially the progress of Master Thomas.

"If he has got religion," thought I, "he will emancipate his slaves; and if he should not do so much as this, he will, at any rate, behave toward us more kindly, and feed us more generously than he has heretofore done." Appealing to my own religious experience, and judging my master by what was true in my own case, I could not regard him as soundly converted, unless some such good results followed his profession of religion.

But in my expectations I was doubly disappointed; Master Thomas was Master Thomas still. The fruits of his righteousness were to show themselves in no such way as I had anticipated. His conversion was not to change his relation toward men—at any rate not toward BLACK men—but toward God. My faith, I confess, was not great. There was something in his appearance that, in my mind, cast a doubt over his conversion. Standing where I did, I could see his every movement. I watched narrowly while he remained in the little pen; and although I saw that his face was extremely red, and his hair disheveled, and though I heard him groan, and saw a stray tear halting on his cheek, as if inquiring "which way shall I go?"—I could not wholly confide in the genuineness of his conversion. The hesitating behavior of that tear-drop and its loneliness, distressed me, and cast a doubt upon the whole transaction, of which it was a part. But people said, "Capt. Auld had come through," and it was for me to hope for the best. I was bound to do this, in charity, for I, too, was religious, and had been in the church full three years, although now I was not more than sixteen years old. Slaveholders may, sometimes, have confidence in the piety of some of their slaves; but the slaves seldom have confidence in the piety of their masters. "He cant go to heaven with our blood in his skirts," is a settled point in the creed of every slave; rising superior to all teaching to the contrary, and standing forever as a fixed fact. The highest evidence the slaveholder can give the slave of his acceptance with God, is the emancipation of his slaves. This is proof that he is willing to give up all to God, and for the sake of God. Not to do this, was, in my estimation, and in the opinion of all the slaves, an evidence of half-heartedness, and wholly inconsistent with the idea of genuine conversion. I had read, also, somewhere in the Methodist Discipline, the following question and answer:

"Question. What shall be done for the extirpation of slavery?

"Answer. We declare that we are much as ever convinced of the great evil of slavery; therefore, no slaveholder shall be eligible to any official station in our church."

These words sounded in my ears for a long time, and encouraged me to hope. But, as I have before said, I was doomed to disappointment. Master Thomas seemed to be aware of my hopes and expectations concerning him. I have thought, before now, that he looked at me in answer to my glances, as much as to say, "I will teach you, young man, that, though I have parted with my sins, I have not parted with my sense. I shall hold my slaves, and go to heaven too." Possibly, to convince us that we must not presume too much upon his recent conversion, he became rather more rigid and stringent in his exactions. There always was a scarcity of good nature about the man; but now his whole countenance was soured over with the seemings of piety. His religion, therefore, neither made him emancipate his slaves, nor caused him to treat them with greater humanity. If religion had any effect on his character at all, it made him more cruel and hateful in all his ways. The natural wickedness of his heart had not been removed, but only reinforced, by the profession of religion. Do I judge him harshly? God forbid. Facts are facts. Capt. Auld made the greatest profession of piety. His house was, literally, a house of prayer. In the morning, and in the evening, loud prayers and hymns were heard there, in which both himself and his wife joined; yet, no more meal was brought from the mill, no more attention was paid to the moral welfare of the kitchen; and nothing was done to make us feel that the heart of Master Thomas was one whit better than it was before he went into the little pen, opposite to the preachers' stand, on the camp ground.

Our hopes (founded on the discipline) soon vanished; for the authorities let him into the church at once, and before he was out of his term of probation, I heard of his leading class! He distinguished himself greatly among the brethren, and was soon an exhorter. His progress was almost as rapid as the growth of the fabled vine of Jack's bean. No man was more active than he, in revivals. He would go many miles to assist in carrying them on, and in getting outsiders interested in religion. His house being one of the holiest, if not the happiest in St. Michael's, became the "preachers' home." These preachers evidently liked to share Master Thomas's hospitality; for while he starved us, he stuffed them. Three or four of these ambassadors of the gospel—according to slavery—have been there at a time; all living on the fat of the land, while we, in the kitchen, were nearly starving. Not often did we get a smile of recognition from these holy men. They seemed almost as unconcerned about our getting to heaven, as they were about our getting out of slavery. To this general charge there was one exception—the Rev. GEORGE COOKMAN. Unlike Rev. Messrs. Storks, Ewry, Hickey, Humphrey and Cooper (all whom were on the St. Michael's circuit) he kindly took an interest in our temporal and spiritual welfare. Our souls and our bodies were all alike sacred in his sight; and he really had a good deal of genuine anti-slavery feeling mingled with his colonization ideas. There was not a slave in our neighborhood that did not love, and almost venerate, Mr. Cookman. It was pretty generally believed that he had been chiefly instrumental in bringing one of the largest slaveholders—Mr. Samuel Harrison—in that neighborhood, to emancipate all his slaves, and, indeed, the general impression was, that Mr. Cookman had labored faithfully with slaveholders, whenever he met them, to induce them to emancipate their bondmen, and that he did this as a religious duty. When this good man was at our house, we were all sure to be called in to prayers in the morning; and he was not slow in making inquiries as to the state of our minds, nor in giving us a word of exhortation and of encouragement. Great was the sorrow of all the slaves, when this faithful preacher of the gospel was removed from the Talbot county circuit. He was an eloquent preacher, and possessed what few ministers, south of Mason Dixon's line, possess, or dare to show, viz: a warm and philanthropic heart. The Mr. Cookman, of whom I speak, was an Englishman by birth, and perished while on his way to England, on board the ill-fated "President". Could the thousands of slaves in Maryland know the fate of the good man, to whose words of comfort they were so largely indebted, they would thank me for dropping a tear on this page, in memory of their favorite preacher, friend and benefactor.

But, let me return to Master Thomas, and to my experience, after his conversion. In Baltimore, I could, occasionally, get into a Sabbath school, among the free children, and receive lessons, with the rest; but, having already learned both to read and to write, I was more of a teacher than a pupil, even there. When, however, I went back to the Eastern Shore, and was at the house of Master Thomas, I was neither allowed to teach, nor to be taught. The whole community—with but a single exception, among the whites—frowned upon everything like imparting instruction either to slaves or to free colored persons. That single exception, a pious young man, named Wilson, asked me, one day, if I would like to assist him in teaching a little Sabbath school, at the house of a free colored man in St. Michael's, named James Mitchell. The idea was to me a delightful one, and I told him I would gladly devote as much of my Sabbath as I could command, to that most laudable work. Mr. Wilson soon mustered up a dozen old spelling books, and a few testaments; and we commenced operations, with some twenty scholars, in our Sunday school. Here, thought I, is something worth living for; here is an excellent chance for usefulness; and I shall soon have a company of young friends, lovers of knowledge, like some of my Baltimore friends, from whom I now felt parted forever. Our first Sabbath passed delightfully, and I spent the week after very joyously. I could not go to Baltimore, but I could make a little Baltimore here. At our second meeting, I learned that there was some objection to the existence of the Sabbath school; and, sure enough, we had scarcely got at work—good work, simply teaching a few colored children how to read the gospel of the Son of God—when in rushed a mob, headed by Mr. Wright Fairbanks and Mr. Garrison West—two class-leaders —and Master Thomas; who, armed with sticks and other missiles, drove us off, and commanded us never to meet for such a purpose again. One of this pious crew told me, that as for my part, I wanted to be another Nat Turner; and if I did not look out, I should get as many balls into me, as Nat did into him. Thus ended the infant Sabbath school, in the town of St. Michael's. The reader will not be surprised when I say, that the breaking up of my Sabbath school, by these class-leaders, and professedly holy men, did not serve to strengthen my religious convictions. The cloud over my St. Michael's home grew heavier and blacker than ever.

It was not merely the agency of Master Thomas, in breaking up and destroying my Sabbath school, that shook my confidence in the power of southern religion to make men wiser or better; but I saw in him all the cruelty and meanness, after his conversion, which he had exhibited before he made a profession of religion. His cruelty and meanness were especially displayed in his treatment of my unfortunate cousin, Henny, whose lameness made her a burden to him. I have no extraordinary personal hard usage toward myself to complain of, against him, but I have seen him tie up the lame and maimed woman, and whip her in a manner most brutal, and shocking; and then, with blood-chilling blasphemy, he would quote the passage of scripture, "That servant which knew his lord's will, and prepared not himself, neither did according to his will, shall be beaten with many stripes." Master would keep this lacerated woman tied up by her wrists, to a bolt in the joist, three, four and five hours at a time. He would tie her up early in the morning, whip her with a cowskin before breakfast; leave her tied up; go to his store, and, returning to his dinner, repeat the castigation; laying on the rugged lash, on flesh already made raw by repeated blows. He seemed desirous to get the poor girl out of existence, or, at any rate, off his hands. In proof of this, he afterwards gave her away to his sister Sarah (Mrs. Cline) but, as in the case of Master Hugh, Henny was soon returned on his hands. Finally, upon a pretense that he could do nothing with her (I use his own words) he "set her adrift, to take care of herself." Here was a recently converted man, holding, with tight grasp, the well-framed, and able bodied slaves left him by old master—the persons, who, in freedom, could have taken care of themselves; yet, turning loose the only cripple among them, virtually to starve and die.

No doubt, had Master Thomas been asked, by some pious northern brother, why he continued to sustain the relation of a slaveholder, to those whom he retained, his answer would have been precisely the same as many other religious slaveholders have returned to that inquiry, viz: "I hold my slaves for their own good."

Bad as my condition was when I lived with Master Thomas, I was soon to experience a life far more goading and bitter. The many differences springing up between myself and Master Thomas, owing to the clear perception I had of his character, and the boldness with which I defended myself against his capricious complaints, led him to declare that I was unsuited to his wants; that my city life had affected me perniciously; that, in fact, it had almost ruined me for every good purpose, and had fitted me for everything that was bad. One of my greatest faults, or offenses, was that of letting his horse get away, and go down to the farm belonging to his father-in-law. The animal had a liking for that farm, with which I fully sympathized. Whenever I let it out, it would go dashing down the road to Mr. Hamilton's, as if going on a grand frolic. My horse gone, of course I must go after it. The explanation of our mutual attachment to the place is the same; the horse found there good pasturage, and I found there plenty of bread. Mr. Hamilton had his faults, but starving his slaves was not among them. He gave food, in abundance, and that, too, of an excellent quality. In Mr. Hamilton's cook—Aunt Mary—I found a most generous and considerate friend. She never allowed me to go there without giving me bread enough to make good the deficiencies of a day or two. Master Thomas at last resolved to endure my behavior no longer; he could neither keep me, nor his horse, we liked so well to be at his father-in-law's farm. I had now lived with him nearly nine months, and he had given me a number of severe whippings, without any visible improvement in my character, or my conduct; and now he was resolved to put me out—as he said—"to be broken."

There was, in the Bay Side, very near the camp ground, where my master got his religious impressions, a man named Edward Covey, who enjoyed the execrated reputation, of being a first rate hand at breaking young Negroes. This Covey was a poor man, a farm renter; and this reputation (hateful as it was to the slaves and to all good men) was, at the same time, of immense advantage to him. It enabled him to get his farm tilled with very little expense, compared with what it would have cost him without this most extraordinary reputation. Some slaveholders thought it an advantage to let Mr. Covey have the government of their slaves a year or two, almost free of charge, for the sake of the excellent training such slaves got under his happy management! Like some horse breakers, noted for their skill, who ride the best horses in the country without expense, Mr. Covey could have under him, the most fiery bloods of the neighborhood, for the simple reward of returning them to their owners, well broken. Added to the natural fitness of Mr. Covey for the duties of his profession, he was said to "enjoy religion," and was as strict in the cultivation of piety, as he was in the cultivation of his farm. I was made aware of his character by some who had been under his hand; and while I could not look forward to going to him with any pleasure, I was glad to get away from St. Michael's. I was sure of getting enough to eat at Covey's, even if I suffered in other respects. This, to a hungry man, is not a prospect to be regarded with indifference.

CHAPTER XV. Covey, the Negro Breaker

JOURNEY TO MY NEW MASTER'S—MEDITATIONS BY THE WAY—VIEW OF COVEY'S
RESIDENCE—THE FAMILY—MY AWKWARDNESS AS A FIELD HAND—A CRUEL BEATING—WHY IT WAS GIVEN—DESCRIPTION OF COVEY—FIRST ADVENTURE AT OX
DRIVING—HAIR BREADTH ESCAPES—OX AND MAN ALIKE PROPERTY—COVEY'S MANNER
OF PROCEEDING TO WHIP—HARD LABOR BETTER THAN THE WHIP FOR BREAKING
DOWN THE SPIRIT—CUNNING AND TRICKERY OF COVEY—FAMILY WORSHIP—SHOCKING
CONTEMPT FOR CHASTITY—I AM BROKEN DOWN—GREAT MENTAL

AGITATION IN
CONTRASTING THE FREEDOM OF THE SHIPS WITH HIS OWN SLAVERY—
ANGUISH
BEYOND DESCRIPTION.

The morning of the first of January, 1834, with its chilling wind and pinching frost, quite in harmony with the winter in my own mind, found me, with my little bundle of clothing on the end of a stick, swung across my shoulder, on the main road, bending my way toward Covey's, whither I had been imperiously ordered by Master Thomas. The latter had been as good as his word, and had committed me, without reserve, to the mastery of Mr. Edward Covey. Eight or ten years had now passed since I had been taken from my grandmother's cabin, in Tuckahoe; and these years, for the most part, I had spent in Baltimore, where—as the reader has already seen—I was treated with comparative tenderness. I was now about to sound profounder depths in slave life. The rigors of a field, less tolerable than the field of battle, awaited me. My new master was notorious for his fierce and savage disposition, and my only consolation in going to live with him was, the certainty of finding him precisely as represented by common fame. There was neither joy in my heart, nor elasticity in my step, as I started in search of the tyrant's home. Starvation made me glad to leave Thomas Auld's, and the cruel lash made me dread to go to Covey's. Escape was impossible; so, heavy and sad, I paced the seven miles, which separated Covey's house from St. Michael's—thinking much by the solitary way—averse to my condition; but thinking was all I could do. Like a fish in a net, allowed to play for a time, I was now drawn rapidly to the shore, secured at all points. "I am," thought I, "but the sport of a power which makes no account, either of my welfare or of my happiness. By a law which I can clearly comprehend, but cannot evade nor resist, I am ruthlessly snatched from the hearth of a fond grandmother, and hurried away to the home of a mysterious 'old master;' again I am removed from there, to a master in Baltimore; thence am I snatched away to the Eastern Shore, to be valued with the beasts of the field, and, with them, divided and set apart for a possessor; then I am sent back to Baltimore; and by the time I have formed new attachments, and have begun to hope that no more rude shocks shall touch me, a difference arises between brothers, and I am again broken up, and sent to St. Michael's; and now, from the latter place, I am footing my way to the home of a new master, where, I am given to understand, that, like a wild young working animal, I am to be broken to the yoke of a bitter and life-long bondage."

With thoughts and reflections like these, I came in sight of a small wood-colored building, about a mile from the main road, which, from the description I had received, at starting, I easily recognized as my new home. The Chesapeake bay—upon the jutting banks of which the little wood-colored house was standing—white with foam, raised by the heavy north-west wind; Poplar Island, covered with a thick, black pine forest, standing out amid this half ocean; and Kent Point, stretching its sandy, desert-like shores out into the foam-cested bay—were all in sight, and deepened the wild and desolate aspect of my new home.

The good clothes I had brought with me from Baltimore were now worn thin, and had not been replaced; for Master Thomas was as little careful to provide us against cold, as against hunger. Met here by a north wind, sweeping through an open space of forty miles, I was glad to make any port; and, therefore, I speedily pressed on to the little wood-colored house. The family consisted of Mr. and Mrs. Covey; Miss Kemp (a broken-backed woman) a sister of Mrs. Covey; William Hughes, cousin to Edward Covey; Caroline, the cook; Bill Smith, a hired man; and myself. Bill Smith, Bill Hughes, and myself, were the working force of the farm, which consisted of three or four hundred acres. I was now, for the first time in my life, to be a field hand; and in my new employment I found myself even more awkward than a green country boy may be supposed to be, upon his first entrance into the bewildering scenes of city life; and my awkwardness gave me much trouble. Strange and unnatural as it may seem, I had been at my new home but three days, before Mr. Covey (my brother in the Methodist church) gave me a bitter foretaste of what was in reserve for me. I presume he thought, that since he had but a single year in which to complete his work, the sooner he began, the better. Perhaps he thought that by coming to blows at once, we should mutually better understand our relations. But to whatever motive, direct or indirect, the cause may be referred, I had not been in his possession three whole days, before he subjected me to a most brutal chastisement. Under his heavy blows, blood flowed freely, and wales were left on my back as large as my little finger. The sores on my back, from this flogging, continued for weeks, for they were kept open by the rough and coarse cloth which I wore for shirting. The occasion and details of this first chapter of my experience as a field hand, must be told, that the reader may see how unreasonable, as well as how cruel, my new master, Covey, was. The whole thing I found to be characteristic of the man; and I was probably treated no worse by him than scores of lads who had previously been committed to him, for reasons similar to those which induced my master to place me with him. But, here are the facts connected with the affair, precisely as they occurred.

On one of the coldest days of the whole month of January, 1834, I was ordered, at day break, to get a load of wood, from a forest about two miles from the house. In order to perform this work, Mr. Covey gave me a pair of unbroken oxen, for, it seems, his breaking abilities had not been turned in this direction; and I may remark, in passing, that working animals in the south, are seldom so well trained as in the north. In due form, and with all proper ceremony, I was introduced to this huge yoke of unbroken oxen, and was carefully told which was "Buck," and which was "Darby"—which was the "in hand," and which was the "off hand" ox. The master of this important ceremony was no less a person than Mr. Covey, himself; and the introduction was the first of the kind I had ever had. My life, hitherto, had led me away from horned cattle, and I had no knowledge of the art of managing them. What was meant by the "in ox," as against the "off ox," when both were equally fastened to one cart, and under one yoke, I could not very easily divine; and the difference, implied by the names, and the peculiar duties of each, were alike Greek to me. Why was not the "off ox" called the "in ox?" Where and what is the reason for this distinction in names, when there is none in the things themselves? After initiating me into the "woa," "back" "gee," "hither"—the entire spoken language between oxen and driver—Mr. Covey took a rope, about ten feet long and one inch thick, and placed one end of it around the horns of the "in hand ox," and gave the other end to me, telling me that if the oxen started to run away, as the scamp knew they would, I must hold on to the rope and stop them. I need not tell any one who is acquainted with either the strength of the disposition of an untamed ox, that this order was about as unreasonable as a command to shoulder a mad bull! I had never driven oxen before, and I was as awkward, as a driver, as it is possible to conceive. It did not answer for me to plead ignorance, to Mr. Covey; there was something in his manner that quite forbade that. He was a man to whom a slave seldom felt any disposition to speak. Cold, distant, morose, with a face wearing all the marks of captious pride and malicious sternness, he repelled all advances. Covey was not a large man; he was only about five feet ten inches in height, I should think; short necked, round shoulders; of quick and wiry motion, of thin and wolfish visage; with a pair of small, greenish-gray eyes, set well back under a forehead without dignity, and constantly in motion, and floating his passions, rather than his thoughts, in sight, but denying them utterance in words. The creature presented an appearance altogether ferocious and sinister, disagreeable and forbidding, in the extreme. When he spoke, it was from the corner of his mouth, and in a sort of light growl, like a dog, when an attempt is made to take a bone from him. The fellow had already made me believe him even worse than he had been presented. With his directions, and without stopping to question, I started for the woods, quite anxious to perform my first exploit in driving, in a creditable manner. The distance from the house to the woods gate a full mile, I should think—was passed over with very little difficulty; for although the animals ran, I was fleet enough, in the open field, to keep pace with them; especially as they pulled me along at the end of the rope; but, on reaching the woods, I was speedily thrown into a distressing plight. The animals took fright, and started off ferociously into the woods, carrying the cart, full tilt, against trees, over stumps, and dashing from side to side, in a manner altogether frightful. As I held the rope, I expected every moment to be crushed between the cart and the huge trees, among which they were so furiously dashing. After running thus for several minutes, my oxen were, finally, brought to a stand, by a tree, against which they dashed themselves with great violence, upsetting the cart, and entangling themselves among sundry young saplings. By the shock, the body of the cart was flung in one direction, and the wheels and tongue in another, and all in the greatest confusion. There I was, all alone, in a thick wood, to which I was a stranger; my cart upset and shattered; my oxen entangled, wild, and enraged; and I, poor soul! but a green hand, to set all this disorder right. I knew no more of oxen than the ox driver is supposed to know of wisdom. After standing a few moments surveying the damage and disorder, and not without a presentiment that this trouble would draw after it others, even more distressing, I took one end of the cart body, and, by an extra outlay of strength, I lifted it toward the axle-tree, from which it had been violently flung; and after much pulling and straining, I succeeded in getting the body of the cart in its place. This was an important step out of the difficulty, and its performance increased my courage for the work which remained to be done. The cart was provided with an ax, a tool with which I had become pretty well acquainted in the ship yard at Baltimore. With this, I cut down the saplings by which my oxen were entangled, and again pursued my journey, with my heart in my mouth, lest the oxen should again take it into their senseless heads to cut up a caper. My fears were groundless. Their spree was over for the present, and the rascals now moved off as soberly as though their behavior had been natural and exemplary. On reaching the part of the forest where I had been, the day before, chopping wood, I filled the cart with a heavy load, as a security against another running away. But, the neck of an ox is equal in strength to iron. It defies all ordinary burdens, when excited. Tame and docile to a proverb, when well trained, the ox is the most sullen and intractable of animals when but half broken to the yoke.

I now saw, in my situation, several points of similarity with that of the oxen. They were property, so was I; they were to be broken, so was I. Covey was to break me, I was to break them; break and be broken—such is life.

Half the day already gone, and my face not yet homeward! It required only two day's experience and observation to teach me, that such apparent waste of time would not be lightly overlooked by Covey. I therefore hurried toward home; but, on reaching the lane gate, I met with the crowning disaster for the day. This gate was a fair specimen of southern handicraft. There were two huge posts, eighteen inches in diameter, rough hewed and square, and the heavy gate was so hung on one of these, that it opened only about half the proper distance. On arriving here, it was necessary for me to let go the end of the rope on the horns of the "in hand ox;" and now as soon as the gate was open, and I let go of it to get the rope, again, off went my oxen—making nothing of their load—full tilt; and in doing so they caught the huge gate between the wheel and the cart body, literally crushing it to splinters, and coming only within a few inches of subjecting me to a similar crushing, for I was just in advance of the wheel when it struck the left gate post. With these two hair-breadth escape, I thought I could sucessfully(sic) explain to Mr. Covey the delay, and avert apprehended punishment. I was not without a faint hope of being commended for the stern resolution which I had displayed in accomplishing the difficult task—a task which, I afterwards learned, even Covey himself would not have undertaken, without first driving the oxen for some time in the open field, preparatory to their going into the woods. But, in this I was disappointed. On coming to him, his countenance assumed an aspect of rigid displeasure, and, as I gave him a history of the casualties of my trip, his wolfish face, with his greenish eyes, became intensely ferocious. "Go back to the woods again," he said, muttering something else about wasting time. I hastily obeyed; but I had not gone far on my way, when I saw him coming after me. My oxen now behaved themselves with singular propriety, opposing their present conduct to my representation of their former antics. I almost wished, now that Covey was coming, they would do something in keeping with the character I had given them; but no, they had already had their spree, and they could afford now to be extra good, readily obeying my orders, and seeming to understand them quite as well as I did myself. On reaching the woods, my tormentor—who seemed all the way to be remarking upon the good behavior of his oxen—came up to me, and ordered me to stop the cart, accompanying the same with the threat that he would now teach me how to break gates, and idle away my time, when he sent me to the woods. Suiting the action to the word, Covey paced off, in his own wiry fashion, to a large, black gum tree, the young shoots of which are generally used for ox goads, they being exceedingly tough. Three of these goads, from four to six feet long, he cut off, and trimmed up, with his large jack-knife. This done, he ordered me to take off my clothes. To this unreasonable order I made no reply, but sternly refused to take off my clothing. "If you will beat me," thought I, "you shall do so over my clothes." After many threats, which made no impression on me, he rushed at me with something of the savage fierceness of a wolf, tore off the few and thinly worn clothes I had on, and proceeded to wear out, on my back, the heavy goads which he had cut from the gum tree. This flogging was the first of a series of floggings; and though very severe, it was less so than many which came after it, and these, for offenses far lighter than the gate breaking.

I remained with Mr. Covey one year (I cannot say I lived with him) and during the first six months that I was there, I was whipped, either with sticks or cowskins, every week. Aching bones and a sore back were my constant companions. Frequent as the lash was used, Mr. Covey thought less of it, as a means of breaking down my spirit, than that of hard and long continued labor. He worked me steadily, up to the point of my powers of endurance. From the dawn of day in the morning, till the darkness was complete in the evening, I was kept at hard work, in the field or the woods. At certain seasons of the year, we were all kept in the field till eleven and twelve o'clock at night. At these times, Covey would attend us in the field, and urge us on with words or blows, as it seemed best to him. He had, in his life, been an overseer, and he well understood the business of slave driving. There was no deceiving him. He knew just what a man or boy could do, and he held both to strict account. When he pleased, he would work himself, like a very Turk, making everything fly before him. It was, however, scarcely necessary for Mr. Covey to be really present in the field, to have his work go on industriously. He had the faculty of making us feel that he was always present. By a series of adroitly managed surprises, which he practiced, I was prepared to expect him at any moment. His plan was, never to approach the spot where his hands were at work, in an open, manly and direct manner. No thief was ever more artful in his devices than this man Covey. He would creep and crawl, in ditches and gullies; hide behind stumps and bushes, and practice so much of the cunning of the serpent, that Bill Smith and I—between ourselves—never called him by any other name than "the snake." We fancied that in his eyes and his gait we could see a snakish resemblance. One half of his proficiency in the art of Negro breaking, consisted, I should think, in this species of cunning. We were never secure. He could see or hear us nearly all the time. He was, to us, behind every stump, tree, bush and fence on the plantation. He carried this kind of trickery so far, that he would sometimes mount his horse, and make believe he was going to St. Michael's; and, in thirty minutes afterward, you might find his horse tied in the woods, and the snake-like Covey lying flat in the ditch, with his head lifted above its edge, or in a fence corner, watching every movement of the slaves! I have known him walk up to us and give us special orders, as to our work, in advance, as if he were leaving home with a view to being absent several days; and before he got half way to the house, he would avail himself of our inattention to his movements, to turn short on his heels, conceal himself behind a fence corner or a tree, and watch us until the going down of the sun. Mean and contemptible as is all this, it is in keeping with the character which the life of a slaveholder is calculated to produce. There is no earthly inducement, in the slave's condition, to incite him to labor faithfully. The fear of punishment is the sole motive for any sort of industry, with him. Knowing this fact, as the slaveholder does, and judging the slave by himself, he naturally concludes the slave will be idle whenever the cause for this fear is absent. Hence, all sorts of petty deceptions are practiced, to inspire this fear.

But, with Mr. Covey, trickery was natural. Everything in the shape of learning or religion, which he possessed, was made to conform to this semi-lying propensity. He did not seem conscious that the practice had anything unmanly, base or contemptible about it. It was a part of an important system, with him, essential to the relation of master and slave. I thought I saw, in his very religious devotions, this controlling element of his character. A long prayer at night made up for the short prayer in the morning; and few men could seem more devotional than he, when he had nothing else to do.

Mr. Covey was not content with the cold style of family worship, adopted in these cold latitudes, which begin and end with a simple prayer. No! the voice of praise, as well as of prayer, must be heard in his house, night and morning. At first, I was called upon to bear some part in these exercises; but the repeated flogging given me by Covey, turned the whole thing into mockery. He was a poor singer, and mainly relied on me for raising the hymn for the family, and when I failed to do so, he was thrown into much confusion. I do not think that he ever abused me on account of these vexations. His religion was a thing altogether apart from his worldly concerns. He knew nothing of it as a holy principle, directing and controlling his daily life, making the latter conform to the requirements of the gospel. One or two facts will illustrate his character better than a volume of generalties(sic).

I have already said, or implied, that Mr. Edward Covey was a poor man. He was, in fact, just commencing to lay the foundation of his fortune, as fortune is regarded in a slave state. The first condition of wealth and respectability there, being the ownership of human property, every nerve is strained, by the poor man, to obtain it, and very little regard is had to the manner of obtaining it. In pursuit of this object, pious as Mr. Covey was, he proved himself to be as unscrupulous and base as the worst of his neighbors. In the beginning, he was only able—as he said—"to buy one slave;" and, scandalous and shocking as is the fact, he boasted that he bought her simply "as a breeder." But the worst is not told in this naked statement. This young woman (Caroline was her name) was virtually compelled by Mr. Covey to abandon herself to the object for which he had purchased her; and the result was, the birth of twins at the end of the year. At this addition to his human stock, both Edward Covey and his wife, Susan, were ecstatic with joy. No one dreamed of reproaching the woman, or of finding fault with the hired man—Bill Smith—the father of the children, for Mr. Covey himself had locked the two up together every night, thus inviting the result.

But I will pursue this revolting subject no further. No better illustration of the unchaste and demoralizing character of slavery can be found, than is furnished in the fact that this professedly Christian slaveholder, amidst all his prayers and hymns, was shamelessly and boastfully encouraging, and actually compelling, in his own house, undisguised and unmitigated fornication, as a means of increasing his human stock. I may remark here, that, while this fact will be read with disgust and shame at the north, it will be laughed at, as smart and praiseworthy in Mr. Covey, at the south; for a man is no more condemned there for buying a woman and devoting her to this life of dishonor, than for buying a cow, and raising stock from her. The same rules are observed, with a view to increasing the number and quality of the former, as of the latter.

I will here reproduce what I said of my own experience in this wretched place, more than ten years ago:

If at any one time of my life, more than another, I was made to drink the bitterest dregs of slavery, that time was during the first six months of my stay with Mr. Covey. We were worked all weathers. It was never too hot or too cold; it could never rain, blow, snow, or hail too hard for us to work in the field. Work, work, work, was scarcely more the order of the day than the night. The longest days were too short for him, and the shortest nights were too long for him. I was somewhat unmanageable when I first went there; but a few months of his discipline tamed me. Mr. Covey succeeded in breaking me. I was broken in body, soul and spirit. My natural elasticity was crushed; my intellect languished; the disposition to read departed; the cheerful spark that lingered about my eye died; the dark night of slavery closed in upon me; and behold a man transformed into a brute!

Sunday was my only leisure time. I spent this in a sort of beast-like stupor, between sleep and wake, under some large tree. At times, I would rise up, a flash of energetic freedom would dart through my soul, accompanied with a faint beam of hope, flickered for a moment, and then vanished. I sank down again, mourning over my wretched condition. I was sometimes prompted to take my life, and that of Covey, but was prevented by a combination of hope and fear. My sufferings on this plantation seem now like a dream rather than a stern reality.

Our house stood within a few rods of the Chesapeake bay, whose broad bosom was ever white with sails from every quarter of the habitable globe. Those beautiful vessels, robed in purest white, so delightful to the eye of freemen, were to me so many shrouded ghosts, to terrify and torment me with thoughts of my wretched condition. I have often, in the deep stillness of a summer's Sabbath, stood all alone upon the banks of that noble bay, and traced, with saddened heart and tearful eye, the countless number of sails moving off to the mighty ocean. The sight of these always affected me powerfully. My thoughts would compel utterance; and there, with no audience but the Almighty, I would pour out my soul's complaint in my rude way, with an apostrophe to the moving multitude of ships:

"You are loosed from your moorings, and free; I am fast in my chains, and am a slave! You move merrily before the gentle gale, and I sadly before the bloody whip! You are freedom's swift-winged angels, that fly around the world; I am confined in bands of iron! O, that I were free! O, that I were on one of your gallant decks, and under your protecting wing! Alas! betwixt me and you the turbid waters roll. Go on, go on. O that I could also go! Could I but swim! If I could fly! O, why was I born a man, of whom to make a brute! The glad ship is gone; she hides in the dim distance. I am left in the hottest hell of unending slavery. O God, save me! God, deliver me! Let me be free! Is there any God? Why am I a slave? I will run away. I will not stand it. Get caught, or get clear, I'll try it. I had as well die with ague as with fever. I have only one life to lose. I had as well be killed running as die standing. Only think of it; one hundred miles straight north, and I am free! Try it? Yes! God helping me, I will. It cannot be that I shall live and die a slave. I will take to the water. This very bay shall yet bear me into freedom. The steamboats steered in a north-east coast from North Point. I will do the same; and when I get to the head of the bay, I will turn my canoe adrift, and walk straight through Delaware into Pennsylvania. When I get there, I shall not be required to have a pass; I will travel without being disturbed. Let but the first opportunity offer, and come what will, I am off. Meanwhile, I will try to bear up under the yoke. I am not the only slave in the world. Why should I fret? I can bear as much as any of them. Besides, I am but a boy, and all boys are bound to some one. It may be that my misery in slavery will only increase my happiness when I get free. There is a better day coming."

I shall never be able to narrate the mental experience through which it was my lot to pass during my stay at Covey's. I was completely wrecked, changed and bewildered; goaded almost to madness at one time, and at another reconciling myself to my wretched condition.

Everything in the way of kindness, which I had experienced at Baltimore; all my former hopes and aspirations for usefulness in the world, and the happy moments spent in the exercises of religion, contrasted with my then present lot, but increased my anguish.

I suffered bodily as well as mentally. I had neither sufficient time in which to eat or to sleep, except on Sundays. The overwork, and the brutal chastisements of which I was the victim, combined with that ever-gnawing and soul-devouring thought—"I am a slave—a slave for life—a slave with no rational ground to hope for freedom"—rendered me a living embodiment of mental and physical wretchedness.

CHAPTER XVI. Another Pressure of the Tyrant's Vice

EXPERIENCE AT COVEY'S SUMMED UP—FIRST SIX MONTHS SEVERER THAN THE SECOND—PRELIMINARIES TO THE CHANCE—REASONS FOR NARRATING THE CIRCUMSTANCES—SCENE IN TREADING YARD—TAKEN ILL—UNUSUAL BRUTALITY OF COVEY—ESCAPE TO ST. MICHAEL'S—THE PURSUIT—SUFFERING IN THE WOODS—DRIVEN BACK AGAIN TO COVEY'S—BEARING OF MASTER THOMAS—THE SLAVE IS NEVER SICK—NATURAL TO EXPECT SLAVES TO FEIGN SICKNESS—LAZINESS OF SLAVEHOLDERS.

The foregoing chapter, with all its horrid incidents and shocking features, may be taken as a fair representation of the first six months of my life at Covey's. The reader has but to repeat, in his own mind, once a week, the scene in the woods, where Covey subjected me to his merciless lash, to have a true idea of my bitter experience there, during the first period of the breaking process through which Mr. Covey carried me. I have no heart to repeat each separate transaction, in which I was victim of his violence and brutality. Such a narration would fill a volume much larger than the present one. I aim only to give the reader a truthful impression of my slave life, without unnecessarily affecting him with harrowing details.

As I have elsewhere intimated that my hardships were much greater during the first six months of my stay at Covey's, than during the remainder of the year, and as the change in my condition was owing to causes which may help the reader to a better understanding of human nature, when subjected to the terrible extremities of slavery, I will narrate the circumstances of this change, although I may seem thereby to applaud my own courage. You have, dear reader, seen me humbled, degraded, broken down, enslaved, and brutalized, and you understand how it was done; now let us see the converse of all this, and how it was brought about; and this will take us through the year 1834.

On one of the hottest days of the month of August, of the year just mentioned, had the reader been passing through Covey's farm, he might have seen me at work, in what is there called the "treading yard"—a yard upon which wheat is trodden out from the straw, by the horses' feet. I was there, at work, feeding the "fan," or rather bringing wheat to the fan, while Bill Smith was feeding. Our force consisted of Bill Hughes, Bill Smith, and a slave by the name of Eli; the latter having been hired for this occasion. The work was simple, and required strength and activity, rather than any skill or intelligence, and yet, to one entirely unused to such work, it came very hard. The heat was intense and overpowering, and there was much hurry to get the wheat, trodden out that day, through the fan; since, if that work was done an hour before sundown, the hands would have, according to a promise of Covey, that hour added to their night's rest. I was not behind any of them in the wish to complete the day's work before sundown, and, hence, I struggled with all my might to get the work forward. The promise of one hour's repose on a week day, was sufficient to quicken my pace, and to spur me on to extra endeavor. Besides, we had all planned to go fishing, and I certainly wished to have a hand in that. But I was disappointed, and the day turned out to be one of the bitterest I ever experienced. About three o'clock, while the sun was pouring down his burning rays, and not a breeze was stirring, I broke down; my strength failed me; I was seized with a violent aching of the head, attended with extreme dizziness, and trembling in every limb. Finding what was coming, and feeling it would never do to stop work, I nerved myself up, and staggered on until I fell by the side of the wheat fan, feeling that the earth had fallen upon me. This brought the entire work to a dead stand. There was work for four; each one had his part to perform, and each part depended on the other, so that when one stopped, all were compelled to stop. Covey, who had now become my dread, as well as my tormentor, was at the house, about a hundred yards from where I was fanning, and instantly, upon hearing the fan stop, he came down to the treading yard, to inquire into the cause of our stopping. Bill Smith told him I was sick, and that I was unable longer to bring wheat to the fan.

I had, by this time, crawled away, under the side of a post-and-rail fence, in the shade, and was exceeding ill. The intense heat of the sun, the heavy dust rising from the fan, the stooping, to take up the wheat from the yard, together with the hurrying, to get through, had caused a rush of blood to my head. In this condition, Covey finding out where I was, came to me; and, after standing over me a while, he asked me what the matter was. I told him as well as I could, for it was with difficulty that I could speak. He then gave me a savage kick in the side, which jarred my whole frame, and commanded me to get up. The man had obtained complete control over me; and if he had commanded me to do any possible thing, I should, in my then state of mind, have endeavored to comply. I made an effort to rise, but fell back in the attempt, before gaining my feet. The brute now gave me another heavy kick, and again told me to rise. I again tried to rise, and succeeded in gaining my feet; but upon stooping to get the tub with which I was feeding the fan, I again staggered and fell to the ground; and I must have so fallen, had I been sure that a hundred bullets would have pierced me, as the consequence. While down, in this sad condition, and perfectly helpless, the merciless Negro breaker took up the hickory slab, with which Hughes had been striking off the wheat to a level with the sides of the half bushel measure (a very hard weapon) and with the sharp edge of it, he dealt me a heavy blow on my head which made a large gash, and caused the blood to run freely, saying, at the same time, "If you have got the headache, I'll cure you." This done, he ordered me again to rise, but I made no effort to do so; for I had made up my mind that it was useless, and that the heartless monster might now do his worst; he could but kill me, and that might put me out of my misery. Finding me unable to rise, or rather despairing of my doing so, Covey left me, with a view to getting on with the work without me. I was bleeding very freely, and my face was soon covered with my warm blood. Cruel and merciless as was the motive that dealt that blow, dear reader, the wound was fortunate for me. Bleeding was never more efficacious. The pain in my head speedily abated, and I was soon able to rise. Covey had, as I have said, now left me to my fate; and the question was, shall I return to my work, or shall I find my way to St. Michael's, and make Capt. Auld acquainted with the atrocious cruelty of his brother Covey, and beseech him to get me another master? Remembering the object he had in view, in placing me under the management of Covey, and further, his cruel treatment of my poor crippled cousin, Henny, and his meanness in the matter of feeding and clothing his slaves, there was little ground to hope for a favorable reception at the hands of Capt. Thomas Auld. Nevertheless, I resolved to go straight to Capt. Auld, thinking that, if not animated by motives of humanity, he might be induced to interfere on my behalf from selfish considerations. "He cannot," thought I, "allow his property to be thus bruised and battered, marred and defaced; and I will go to him, and tell him the simple truth about the matter." In order to get to St. Michael's, by the most favorable and direct road, I must walk seven miles; and this, in my sad condition, was no easy performance. I had already lost much blood; I was exhausted by over exertion; my sides were sore from the heavy blows planted there by the stout boots of Mr. Covey; and I was, in every way, in an unfavorable plight for the journey. I however watched my chance, while the cruel and cunning Covey was looking in an opposite direction, and started off, across the field, for St. Michael's. This was a daring step; if it failed, it would only exasperate Covey, and increase the rigors of my bondage, during the remainder of my term of service under him; but the step was taken, and I must go forward. I succeeded in getting nearly half way across the broad field, toward the woods, before Mr. Covey observed me. I was still bleeding, and the exertion of running had started the blood afresh. "Come back! Come back!" vociferated Covey, with threats of what he would do if I did not return instantly. But, disregarding his calls and his threats, I pressed on toward the woods as fast as my feeble state would allow. Seeing no signs of my stopping, Covey caused his horse to be brought out and saddled, as if he intended to pursue me. The race was now to be an unequal one; and, thinking

I might be overhauled by him, if I kept the main road, I walked nearly the whole distance in the woods, keeping far enough from the road to avoid detection and pursuit. But, I had not gone far, before my little strength again failed me, and I laid down. The blood was still oozing from the wound in my head; and, for a time, I suffered more than I can describe. There I was, in the deep woods, sick and emaciated, pursued by a wretch whose character for revolting cruelty beggars all opprobrious speech—bleeding, and almost bloodless. I was not without the fear of bleeding to death. The thought of dying in the woods, all alone, and of being torn to pieces by the buzzards, had not yet been rendered tolerable by my many troubles and hardships, and I was glad when the shade of the trees, and the cool evening breeze, combined with my matted hair to stop the flow of blood. After lying there about three quarters of an hour, brooding over the singular and mournful lot to which I was doomed, my mind passing over the whole scale or circle of belief and unbelief, from faith in the overruling providence of God, to the blackest atheism, I again took up my journey toward St. Michael's, more weary and sad than in the morning when I left Thomas Auld's for the home of Mr. Covey. I was bare-footed and bare-headed, and in my shirt sleeves. The way was through bogs and briers, and I tore my feet often during the journey. I was full five hours in going the seven or eight miles; partly, because of the difficulties of the way, and partly, because of the feebleness induced by my illness, bruises and loss of blood. On gaining my master's store, I presented an appearance of wretchedness and woe, fitted to move any but a heart of stone. From the crown of my head to the sole of my feet, there were marks of blood. My hair was all clotted with dust and blood, and the back of my shirt was literally stiff with the same. Briers and thorns had scarred and torn my feet and legs, leaving blood marks there. Had I escaped from a den of tigers, I could not have looked worse than I did on reaching St. Michael's. In this unhappy plight, I appeared before my professedly Christian master, humbly to invoke the interposition of his power and authority, to protect me from further abuse and violence. I had begun to hope, during the latter part of my tedious journey toward St. Michael's, that Capt. Auld would now show himself in a nobler light than I had ever before seen him. I was disappointed. I had jumped from a sinking ship into the sea; I had fled from the tiger to something worse. I told him all the circumstances, as well as I could; how I was endeavoring to please Covey; how hard I was at work in the present instance; how unwilling I sunk down under the heat, toil and pain; the brutal manner in which Covey had kicked me in the side; the gash cut in my head; my hesitation about troubling him (Capt. Auld) with complaints; but, that now I felt it would not be best longer to conceal from him the outrages committed on me from time to time by Covey. At first, master Thomas seemed somewhat affected by the story of my wrongs, but he soon repressed his feelings and became cold as iron. It was impossible—as I stood before him at the first—for him to seem indifferent. I distinctly saw his human nature asserting its conviction against the slave system, which made cases like mine possible; but, as I have said, humanity fell before the systematic tyranny of slavery. He first walked the floor, apparently much agitated by my story, and the sad spectacle I presented; but, presently, it was his turn to talk. He began moderately, by finding excuses for Covey, and ending with a full justification of him, and a passionate condemnation of me. "He had no doubt I deserved the flogging. He did not believe I was sick; I was only endeavoring to get rid of work. My dizziness was laziness, and Covey did right to flog me, as he had done." After thus fairly annihilating me, and rousing himself by his own eloquence, he fiercely demanded what I wished him to do in the case!

With such a complete knock-down to all my hopes, as he had given me, and feeling, as I did, my entire subjection to his power, I had very little heart to reply. I must not affirm my innocence of the allegations which he had piled up against me; for that would be impudence, and would probably call down fresh violence as well as wrath upon me. The guilt of a slave is always, and everywhere, presumed; and the innocence of the slaveholder or the slave employer, is always asserted. The word of the slave, against this presumption, is generally treated as impudence, worthy of punishment. "Do you contradict me, you rascal?" is a final silencer of counter statements from the lips of a slave.

Calming down a little in view of my silence and hesitation, and, perhaps, from a rapid glance at the picture of misery I presented, he inquired again, "what I would have him do?" Thus invited a second time, I told Master Thomas I wished him to allow me to get a new home and to find a new master; that, as sure as I went back to live with Mr. Covey again, I should be killed by him; that he would never forgive my coming to him (Capt. Auld) with a complaint against him (Covey); that, since I had lived with him, he almost crushed my spirit, and I believed that he would ruin me for future service; that my life was not safe in his hands. This, Master Thomas (my brother in the church) regarded as "nonsence(sic)." "There was no danger of Mr. Covey's killing me; he was a good man, industrious and religious, and he would not think of removing me from that home; besides," said he and this I found was the most distressing thought of all to him—"if you should leave Covey now, that your year has but half expired, I should lose your wages for the entire year. You belong to Mr. Covey for one year, and you must go back to him, come what will. You must not trouble me with any more stories about Mr. Covey; and if you do not go immediately home, I will get hold of you myself." This was just what I expected, when I found he had prejudged the case against me. "But, Sir," I said, "I am sick and tired, and I cannot get home to-night." At this, he again relented, and finally he allowed me to remain all night at St. Michael's; but said I must be off early in the morning, and concluded his directions by making me swallow a huge dose of epsom salts—about the only medicine ever administered to slaves.

It was quite natural for Master Thomas to presume I was feigning sickness to escape work, for he probably thought that were he in the place of a slave with no wages for his work, no praise for well doing, no motive for toil but the lash—he would try every possible scheme by which to escape labor. I say I have no doubt of this; the reason is, that there are not, under the whole heavens, a set of men who cultivate such an intense dread of labor as do the slaveholders. The charge of laziness against the slave is ever on their lips, and is the standing apology for every species of cruelty and brutality. These men literally "bind heavy burdens, grievous to be borne, and lay them on men's shoulders; but they, themselves, will not move them with one of their fingers."

My kind readers shall have, in the next chapter—what they were led, perhaps, to expect to find in this—namely: an account of my partial disenthrallment from the tyranny of Covey, and the marked change which it brought about.

CHAPTER XVII. The Last Flogging

A SLEEPLESS NIGHT—RETURN TO COVEY'S—PURSUED BY COVEY—THE CHASE DEFEATED—VENGEANCE POSTPONED—MUSINGS IN THE WOODS—THE ALTERNATIVE—DEPLORABLE SPECTACLE—NIGHT IN THE WOODS—EXPECTED ATTACK—ACCOSTED BY SANDY, A FRIEND, NOT A HUNTER—SANDY'S HOSPITALITY—THE "ASH CAKE" SUPPER—THE INTERVIEW WITH SANDY—HIS ADVICE—SANDY A CONJURER AS WELL AS A CHRISTIAN—THE MAGIC ROOT— STRANGE
MEETING WITH COVEY—HIS MANNER—COVEY'S SUNDAY FACE—MY DEFENSIVE
RESOLVE—THE FIGHT—THE VICTORY, AND ITS RESULTS.

Sleep itself does not always come to the relief of the weary in body, and the broken in spirit; especially when past troubles only foreshadow coming disasters. The last hope had been extinguished. My master, who I did not venture to hope would protect me as a man, had even now refused to protect me as his property; and had cast me back, covered with reproaches and bruises, into the hands of a stranger to that mercy which was the soul of the religion he professed. May the reader never spend such a night as that allotted to me, previous to the morning which was to herald my return to the den of horrors from which I had made a temporary escape.

I remained all night—sleep I did not—at St. Michael's; and in the morning (Saturday) I started off, according to the order of Master Thomas, feeling that I had no friend on earth, and doubting if I had one in heaven. I reached Covey's about nine o'clock; and just as I stepped into the field, before I had reached the house, Covey, true to his snakish habits, darted out at me from a fence corner, in which he had secreted himself, for the purpose of securing me. He was amply provided with a cowskin and a rope; and he evidently intended to tie me up, and to wreak his vengeance on me to the fullest extent. I should have been an easy prey, had he succeeded in getting his hands upon me, for I had taken no refreshment since noon on Friday; and this, together with the pelting, excitement, and the loss of blood, had reduced my strength. I, however, darted back into the woods, before the ferocious hound could get hold of me, and buried myself in a thicket, where he lost sight of me. The corn-field afforded me cover, in getting to the woods. But for the tall corn, Covey would have overtaken me, and made me his captive. He seemed very much chagrined that he did not catch me, and gave up the chase, very reluctantly; for I could see his angry movements, toward the house from which he had sallied, on his foray.

Well, now I am clear of Covey, and of his wrathful lash, for present. I am in the wood, buried in its somber gloom, and hushed in its solemn silence; hid from all human eyes; shut in with nature and nature's God, and absent from all human contrivances. Here was a good place to pray; to pray for help for deliverance—a prayer I had often made before. But how could I pray? Covey could pray—Capt. Auld could pray—I would fain pray; but doubts (arising partly from my own neglect of the means of grace, and partly from the sham religion which everywhere prevailed, cast in my mind a doubt upon all religion, and led me to the conviction that prayers were unavailing and delusive) prevented my embracing the opportunity, as a religious one. Life, in itself, had almost become burdensome to me. All my outward relations were against me; I must stay here and starve (I was already hungry) or go home to Covey's, and have my flesh torn to pieces, and my spirit humbled under the cruel lash of Covey. This was the painful alternative presented to me. The day was long and irksome. My physical condition was deplorable. I was weak, from the toils of the previous day, and from the want of food and rest; and had been so little concerned about my appearance, that I had not yet washed the blood from my garments. I was an object of horror, even to myself. Life, in Baltimore, when most oppressive, was a paradise to this. What had I done, what had my parents done, that such a life as this should be mine? That day, in the woods, I would have exchanged my manhood for the brutehood of an ox.

Night came. I was still in the woods, unresolved what to do. Hunger had not yet pinched me to the point of going home, and I laid myself down in the leaves to rest; for I had been watching for hunters all day, but not being molested during the day, I expected no disturbance during the night. I had come to the conclusion that Covey relied upon hunger to drive me home; and in this I was quite correct—the facts showed that he had made no effort to catch me, since morning.

During the night, I heard the step of a man in the woods. He was coming toward the place where I lay. A person lying still has the advantage over one walking in the woods, in the day time, and this advantage is much greater at night. I was not able to engage in a physical struggle, and I had recourse to the common resort of the weak. I hid myself in the leaves to prevent discovery. But, as the night rambler in the woods drew nearer, I found him to be a friend, not an enemy; it was a slave of Mr. William Groomes, of Easton, a kind hearted fellow, named "Sandy." Sandy lived with Mr. Kemp that year, about four miles from St. Michael's. He, like myself had been hired out by the year; but, unlike myself, had not been hired out to be broken. Sandy was the husband of a free woman, who lived in the lower part of "Potpie Neck," and he was now on his way through the woods, to see her, and to spend the Sabbath with her. As soon as I had ascertained that the disturber of my solitude was not an enemy, but the good-hearted Sandy—a man as famous among the slaves of the neighborhood for his good nature, as for his good sense I came out from my hiding place, and made myself known to him. I explained the circumstances of the past two days, which had driven me to the woods, and he deeply compassionated my distress. It was a bold thing for him to shelter me, and I could not ask him to do so; for, had I been found in his hut, he would have suffered the penalty of thirty-nine lashes on his bare back, if not something worse. But Sandy was too generous to permit the fear of punishment to prevent his relieving a brother bondman from hunger and exposure; and, therefore, on his own motion, I accompanied him to his home, or rather to the home of his wife—for the house and lot were hers. His wife was called up—for it was now about midnight—a fire was made, some Indian meal was soon mixed with salt and water, and an ash cake was baked in a hurry to relieve my hunger. Sandy's wife was not behind him in kindness—both seemed to esteem it a privilege to succor me; for, although I was hated by Covey and by my master, I was loved by the colored people, because they thought I was hated for my knowledge, and persecuted because I was feared. I was the only slave now in that region who could read and write. There had been one other man, belonging to Mr. Hugh Hamilton, who could read (his name was "Jim"), but he, poor fellow, had, shortly after my coming into the neighborhood, been sold off to the far south. I saw Jim ironed, in the cart, to be carried to Easton for sale—pinioned like a yearling for the slaughter. My knowledge was now the pride of my brother slaves; and, no doubt, Sandy felt something of the general interest in me on that account. The supper was soon ready, and though I have feasted since, with honorables, lord mayors and aldermen, over the sea, my supper on ash cake and cold water, with Sandy, was the meal, of all my life, most sweet to my taste, and now most vivid in my memory.

Supper over, Sandy and I went into a discussion of what was possible for me, under the perils and hardships which now overshadowed my path. The question was, must I go back to Covey, or must I now tempt to run away? Upon a careful survey, the latter was found to be impossible; for I was on a narrow neck of land, every avenue from which would bring me in sight of pursuers. There was the Chesapeake bay to the right, and "Pot-pie" river to the left, and St. Michael's and its neighborhood occupying the only space through which there was any retreat.

I found Sandy an old advisor. He was not only a religious man, but he professed to believe in a system for which I have no name. He was a genuine African, and had inherited some of the so-called magical powers, said to be possessed by African and eastern nations. He told me that he could help me; that, in those very woods, there was an herb, which in the morning might be found, possessing all the powers required for my protection (I put his thoughts in my own language); and that, if I would take his advice, he would procure me the root of the herb of which he spoke. He told me further, that if I would take that root and wear it on my right side, it would be impossible for Covey to strike me a blow; that with this root about my person, no white man could whip me. He said he had carried it for years, and that he had fully tested its virtues. He had never received a blow from a slaveholder since he carried it; and he never expected to receive one, for he always meant to carry that root as a protection. He knew Covey well, for Mrs. Covey was the daughter of Mr. Kemp; and he (Sandy) had heard of the barbarous treatment to which I was subjected, and he wanted to do something for me.

Now all this talk about the root, was to me, very absurd and ridiculous, if not positively sinful. I at first rejected the idea that the simple carrying a root on my right side (a root, by the way, over which I walked every time I went into the woods) could possess any such magic power as he ascribed to it, and I was, therefore, not disposed to cumber my pocket with it. I had a positive aversion to all pretenders to "divination." It was beneath one of my intelligence to countenance such dealings with the devil, as this power implied. But, with all my learning—it was really precious little—Sandy was more than a match for me. "My book learning," he said, "had not kept Covey off me" (a powerful argument just then) and he entreated me, with flashing eyes, to try this. If it did me no good, it could do me no harm, and it would cost me nothing, any way. Sandy was so earnest, and so confident of the good qualities of this weed, that, to please him, rather than from any conviction of its excellence, I was induced to take it. He had been to me the good Samaritan, and had, almost providentially, found me, and helped me when I could not help myself; how did I know but that the hand of the Lord was in it? With thoughts of this sort, I took the roots from Sandy, and put them in my right hand pocket. This was, of course, Sunday morning. Sandy now urged me to go home, with all speed, and to walk up bravely to the house, as though nothing had happened. I saw in Sandy too deep an insight into human nature, with all his superstition, not to have some respect for his advice; and perhaps, too, a slight gleam or shadow of his superstition had fallen upon me. At any rate, I started off toward Covey's, as directed by Sandy. Having, the previous night, poured my griefs into Sandy's ears, and got him enlisted in my behalf, having made his wife a sharer in my sorrows, and having, also, become well refreshed by sleep and food, I moved off, quite courageously, toward the much dreaded Covey's. Singularly enough, just as I entered his yard gate, I met him and his wife, dressed in their Sunday best—looking as smiling as angels—on their way to church. The manner of Covey astonished me. There was something really benignant in his countenance. He spoke to me as never before; told me that the pigs had got into the lot, and he wished me to drive them out; inquired how I was, and seemed an altered man. This extraordinary conduct of Covey, really made me begin to think that Sandy's herb had more virtue in it than I, in my pride, had been willing to allow; and, had the day been other than Sunday, I should have attributed Covey's altered manner solely to the magic power of the root. I suspected, however, that the Sabbath, and not the root, was the real explanation of Covey's manner. His religion hindered him from breaking the Sabbath, but not from breaking my skin. He had more respect for the day than for the man, for whom the day was mercifully given; for while he would cut and slash my body during the week, he would not hesitate, on Sunday, to teach me the value of my soul, or the way of life and salvation by Jesus Christ. All went well with me till Monday morning; and then, whether the root had lost its virtue, or whether my tormentor had gone deeper into the black art than myself (as was sometimes said of him), or whether he had obtained a special indulgence, for his faithful Sabbath day's worship, it is not necessary for me to know, or to inform the reader; but, this I may say—the pious and benignant smile which graced Covey's face on Sunday, wholly disappeared on Monday. Long before daylight, I was called up to go and feed, rub, and curry the horses. I obeyed the call, and would have so obeyed it, had it been made at an earilier(sic) hour, for I had brought my mind to a firm resolve, during that Sunday's reflection, viz: to obey every order, however unreasonable, if it were possible, and, if Mr. Covey should then undertake to beat me, to defend and protect myself to the best of my ability. My religious views on the subject of resisting my master, had suffered a serious shock, by the savage persecution to which I had been subjected, and my hands were no longer tied by my religion. Master Thomas's indifference had served the last link. I had now to this extent "backslidden" from this point in the slave's religious creed; and I soon had occasion to make my fallen state known to my Sunday-pious brother, Covey.

Whilst I was obeying his order to feed and get the horses ready for the field, and when in the act of going up the stable loft for the purpose of throwing down some blades, Covey sneaked into the stable, in his peculiar snake-like way, and seizing me suddenly by the leg, he brought me to the stable floor, giving my newly mended body a fearful jar. I now forgot my roots, and remembered my pledge to stand up in my own defense. The brute was endeavoring skillfully to get a slip-knot on my legs, before I could draw up my feet. As soon as I found what he was up to, I gave a sudden spring (my two day's rest had been of much service to me,) and by that means, no doubt, he was able to bring me to the floor so heavily. He was defeated in his plan of tying me. While down, he seemed to think he had me very securely in his power. He little thought he was—as the rowdies say—"in" for a "rough and tumble" fight; but such was the fact. Whence came the daring spirit necessary to grapple with a man who, eight-and-forty hours before, could, with his slightest word have made me tremble like a leaf in a storm, I do not know; at any rate, I was resolved to fight, and, what was better still, I was actually hard at it. The fighting madness had come upon me, and I found my strong fingers firmly attached to the throat of my cowardly tormentor; as heedless of consequences, at the moment, as though we stood as equals before the law. The very color of the man was forgotten. I felt as supple as a cat, and was ready for the snakish creature at every turn. Every blow of his was parried, though I dealt no blows in turn. I was strictly on the defensive, preventing him from injuring me, rather than trying to injure him. I flung him on the ground several times, when he meant to have hurled me there. I held him so firmly by the throat, that his blood followed my nails. He held me, and I held him.

All was fair, thus far, and the contest was about equal. My resistance was entirely unexpected, and Covey was taken all aback by it, for he trembled in every limb. "Are you going to resist, you scoundrel?" said he. To which, I returned a polite "Yes sir;" steadily gazing my interrogator in the eye, to meet the first approach or dawning of the blow, which I expected my answer would call forth. But, the conflict did not long remain thus equal. Covey soon cried out lustily for help; not that I was obtaining any marked advantage over him, or was injuring him, but because he was gaining none over me, and was not able, single handed, to conquer me. He called for his cousin Hughs, to come to his assistance, and now the scene was changed. I was compelled to give blows, as well as to parry them; and, since I was, in any case, to suffer for resistance, I felt (as the musty proverb goes) that "I might as well be hanged for an old sheep as a lamb." I was still defensive toward Covey, but aggressive toward Hughs; and, at the first approach of the latter, I dealt a blow, in my desperation, which fairly sickened my youthful assailant. He went off, bending over with pain, and manifesting no disposition to come within my reach again. The poor fellow was in the act of trying to catch and tie my right hand, and while flattering himself with success, I gave him the kick which sent him staggering away in pain, at the same time that I held Covey with a firm hand.

Taken completely by surprise, Covey seemed to have lost his usual strength and coolness. He was frightened, and stood puffing and blowing, seemingly unable to command words or blows. When he saw that poor Hughes was standing half bent with pain—his courage quite gone the cowardly tyrant asked if I "meant to persist in my resistance." I told him "I did mean to resist, come what might;" that I had been by him treated like a brute, during the last six months; and that I should stand it no longer. With that, he gave me a shake, and attempted to drag me toward a stick of wood, that was lying just outside the stable door. He meant to knock me down with it; but, just as he leaned over to get the stick, I seized him with both hands by the collar, and, with a vigorous and sudden snatch, I brought my assailant harmlessly, his full length, on the not overclean ground—for we were now in the cow yard. He had selected the place for the fight, and it was but right that he should have all the advantges(sic) of his own selection.

By this time, Bill, the hiredman, came home. He had been to Mr. Hemsley's, to spend the Sunday with his nominal wife, and was coming home on Monday morning, to go to work. Covey and I had been skirmishing from before daybreak, till now, that the sun was almost shooting his beams over the eastern woods, and we were still at it. I could not see where the matter was to terminate. He evidently was afraid to let me go, lest I should again make off to the woods; otherwise, he would probably have obtained arms from the house, to frighten me. Holding me, Covey called upon Bill for assistance. The scene here, had something comic about it. "Bill," who knew precisely what Covey wished him to do, affected ignorance, and pretended he did not know what to do. "What shall I do, Mr. Covey," said Bill. "Take hold of him—take hold of him!" said Covey. With a toss of his head, peculiar to Bill, he said, "indeed, Mr. Covey I want to go to work." "This is your work," said Covey; "take hold of him." Bill replied, with spirit, "My master hired me here, to work, and not to help you whip Frederick." It was now my turn to speak. "Bill," said I, "don't put your hands on me." To which he replied,

"My GOD! Frederick, I ain't goin' to tech ye," and Bill walked off, leaving Covey and myself to settle our matters as best we might.

But, my present advantage was threatened when I saw Caroline (the slave-woman of Covey) coming to the cow yard to milk, for she was a powerful woman, and could have mastered me very easily, exhausted as I now was. As soon as she came into the yard, Covey attempted to rally her to his aid. Strangely—and, I may add, fortunately—Caroline was in no humor to take a hand in any such sport. We were all in open rebellion, that morning. Caroline answered the command of her master to "take hold of me," precisely as Bill had answered, but in her, it was at greater peril so to answer; she was the slave of Covey, and he could do what he pleased with her. It was not so with Bill, and Bill knew it. Samuel Harris, to whom Bill belonged, did not allow his slaves to be beaten, unless they were guilty of some crime which the law would punish. But, poor Caroline, like myself, was at the mercy of the merciless Covey; nor did she escape the dire effects of her refusal. He gave her several sharp blows.

Covey at length (two hours had elapsed) gave up the contest. Letting me go, he said—puffing and blowing at a great rate—"Now, you scoundrel, go to your work; I would not have whipped you half so much as I have had you not resisted." The fact was, he had not whipped me at all. He had not, in all the scuffle, drawn a single drop of blood from me. I had drawn blood from him; and, even without this satisfaction, I should have been victorious, because my aim had not been to injure him, but to prevent his injuring me.

During the whole six months that I lived with Covey, after this transaction, he never laid on me the weight of his finger in anger. He would, occasionally, say he did not want to have to get hold of me again—a declaration which I had no difficulty in believing; and I had a secret feeling, which answered, "You need not wish to get hold of me again, for you will be likely to come off worse in a second fight than you did in the first."

Well, my dear reader, this battle with Mr. Covey—undignified as it was, and as I fear my narration of it is—was the turning point in my "life as a slave." It rekindled in my breast the smouldering embers of liberty; it brought up my Baltimore dreams, and revived a sense of my own manhood. I was a changed being after that fight. I was nothing before; I WAS A MAN NOW. It recalled to life my crushed self-respect and my self-confidence, and inspired me with a renewed determination to be A FREEMAN. A man, without force, is without the essential dignity of humanity. Human nature is so constituted, that it cannot honor a helpless man, although it can pity him; and even this it cannot do long, if the signs of power do not arise. He can only understand the effect of this combat on my spirit, who has himself incurred something, hazarded something, in repelling the unjust and cruel aggressions of a tyrant. Covey was a tyrant, and a cowardly one, withal. After resisting him, I felt as I had never felt before. It was a resurrection from the dark and pestiferous tomb of slavery, to the heaven of comparative freedom. I was no longer a servile coward, trembling under the frown of a brother worm of the dust, but, my long-cowed spirit was roused to an attitude of manly independence. I had reached the point, at which I was not afraid to die. This spirit made me a freeman in fact, while I remained a slave in form. When a slave cannot be flogged he is more than half free. He has a domain as broad as his own manly heart to defend, and he is really "a power on earth." While slaves prefer their lives, with flogging, to instant death, they will always find Christians enough, like unto Covey, to accommodate that preference. From this time, until that of my escape from slavery, I was never fairly whipped. Several attempts were made to whip me, but they were always unsuccessful. Bruises I did get, as I shall hereafter inform the reader; but the case I have been describing, was the end of the brutification to which slavery had subjected me.

The reader will be glad to know why, after I had so grievously offended Mr. Covey, he did not have me taken in hand by the authorities; indeed, why the law of Maryland, which assigns hanging to the slave who resists his master, was not put in force against me; at any rate, why I was not taken up, as is usual in such cases, and publicly whipped, for an example to other slaves, and as a means of deterring me from committing the same offense again. I confess, that the easy manner in which I got off, for a long time, a surprise to me, and I cannot, even now, fully explain the cause.

The only explanation I can venture to suggest, is the fact, that Covey was, probably, ashamed to have it known and confessed that he had been mastered by a boy of sixteen. Mr. Covey enjoyed the unbounded and very valuable reputation, of being a first rate overseer and Negro breaker. By means of this reputation, he was able to procure his hands for very trifling compensation, and with very great ease. His interest and his pride mutually suggested the wisdom of passing the matter by, in silence. The story that he had undertaken to whip a lad, and had been resisted, was, of itself, sufficient to damage him; for his bearing should, in the estimation of slaveholders, be of that imperial order that should make such an occurrence impossible. I judge from these circumstances, that Covey deemed it best to give me the go-by. It is, perhaps, not altogether creditable to my natural temper, that, after this conflict with Mr. Covey, I did, at times, purposely aim to provoke him to an attack, by refusing to keep with the other hands in the field, but I could never bully him to another battle. I had made up my mind to do him serious damage, if he ever again attempted to lay violent hands on me.

> Hereditary bondmen, know ye not
> Who would be free, themselves must strike the blow?

CHAPTER XVIII. New Relations and Duties

CHANGE OF MASTERS—BENEFITS DERIVED BY THE CHANGE—FAME OF THE FIGHT
WITH COVEY—RECKLESS UNCONCERN—MY ABHORRENCE OF SLAVERY—ABILITY
TO READ A CAUSE OF PREJUDICE—THE HOLIDAYS—HOW SPENT—SHARP HIT AT
SLAVERY—EFFECTS OF HOLIDAYS—A DEVICE OF SLAVERY—DIFFERENCE BETWEEN
COVEY AND FREELAND—AN IRRELIGIOUS MASTER PREFERRED TO A RELIGIOUS
ONE—CATALOGUE OF FLOGGABLE OFFENSES—HARD LIFE AT COVEY'S
USEFUL—IMPROVED CONDITION NOT FOLLOWED BY CONTENTMENT—CONGENIAL
SOCIETY AT FREELAND'S—SABBATH SCHOOL INSTITUTED—SECRECY
NECESSARY—AFFECTIONATE RELATIONS OF TUTOR AND PUPILS—CONFIDENCE
AND FRIENDSHIP AMONG SLAVES—I DECLINE PUBLISHING PARTICULARS OF
CONVERSATIONS WITH MY FRIENDS—SLAVERY THE INVITER OF VENGEANCE.

My term of actual service to Mr. Edward Covey ended on Christmas day, 1834. I gladly left the snakish Covey, although he was now as gentle as a lamb. My home for the year 1835 was already secured—my next master was already selected. There is always more or less excitement about the matter of changing hands, but I had become somewhat reckless. I cared very little into whose hands I fell—I meant to fight my way. Despite of Covey, too, the report got abroad, that I was hard to whip; that I was guilty of kicking back; that though generally a good tempered Negro, I sometimes "got the devil in me." These sayings were rife in Talbot county, and they distinguished me among my servile brethren. Slaves, generally, will fight each other, and die at each other's hands; but there are few who are not held in awe by a white man. Trained from the cradle up, to think and feel that their masters are superior, and invested with a sort of sacredness, there are few who can outgrow or rise above the control which that sentiment exercises. I had now got free from it, and the thing was known. One bad sheep will spoil a whole flock. Among the slaves, I was a bad sheep. I hated slavery, slaveholders, and all pertaining to them; and I did not fail to inspire others with the same feeling, wherever and whenever opportunity was presented. This made me a marked lad among the slaves, and a suspected one among the slaveholders. A knowledge of my ability to read and write, got pretty widely spread, which was very much against me.

The days between Christmas day and New Year's, are allowed the slaves as holidays. During these days, all regular work was suspended, and there was nothing to do but to keep fires, and look after the stock. This time was regarded as our own, by the grace of our masters, and we, therefore used it, or abused it, as we pleased. Those who had families at a distance, were now expected to visit them, and to spend with them the entire week. The younger slaves, or the unmarried ones, were expected to see to the cattle, and attend to incidental duties at home. The holidays were variously spent. The sober, thinking and industrious ones of our number, would employ themselves in manufacturing corn brooms, mats, horse collars and baskets, and some of these were very well made. Another class spent their time in hunting opossums, coons, rabbits, and other game. But the majority spent the holidays in sports, ball playing, wrestling, boxing, running foot races, dancing, and drinking whisky; and this latter mode of spending the time was generally most agreeable to their masters. A slave who would work during the holidays, was thought, by his master, undeserving of holidays. Such an one had rejected the favor of his master. There was, in this simple act of continued work, an accusation against slaves; and a slave could not help thinking, that if he made three dollars during the holidays, he might make three hundred during the year. Not to be drunk during the holidays, was disgraceful; and he was esteemed a lazy and improvident man, who could not afford to drink whisky during Christmas.

The fiddling, dancing and "jubilee beating," was going on in all directions. This latter performance is strictly southern. It supplies the place of a violin, or of other musical instruments, and is played so easily, that almost every farm has its "Juba" beater. The performer improvises as he beats, and sings his merry songs, so ordering the words as to have them fall pat with the movement of his hands. Among a mass of nonsense and wild frolic, once in a while a sharp hit is given to the meanness of slaveholders. Take the following, for an example:

> We raise de wheat,
> Dey gib us de corn;
> We bake de bread,
> Dey gib us de cruss;
> We sif de meal,
> Dey gib us de huss;
> We peal de meat,
> Dey gib us de skin,
> And dat's de way
> Dey takes us in.
> We skim de pot,
> Dey gib us the liquor,
> And say dat's good enough for nigger.
>> Walk over! walk over!
> Tom butter and de fat;
>> Poor nigger you can't get over dat;
>>> Walk over!

This is not a bad summary of the palpable injustice and fraud of slavery, giving—as it does—to the lazy and idle, the comforts which God designed should be given solely to the honest laborer. But to the holiday's.

Judging from my own observation and experience, I believe these holidays to be among the most effective means, in the hands of slaveholders, of keeping down the spirit of insurrection among the slaves.

To enslave men, successfully and safely, it is necessary to have their minds occupied with thoughts and aspirations short of the liberty of which they are deprived. A certain degree of attainable good must be kept before them. These holidays serve the purpose of keeping the minds of the slaves occupied with prospective pleasure, within the limits of slavery. The young man can go wooing; the married man can visit his wife; the father and mother can see their children; the industrious and money loving can make a few dollars; the great wrestler can win laurels; the young people can meet, and enjoy each other's society; the drunken man can get plenty of whisky; and the religious man can hold prayer meetings, preach, pray and exhort during the holidays. Before the holidays, these are pleasures in prospect; after the holidays, they become pleasures of memory, and they serve to keep out thoughts and wishes of a more dangerous character. Were slaveholders at once to abandon the practice of allowing their slaves these liberties, periodically, and to keep them, the year round, closely confined to the narrow circle of their homes, I doubt not that the south would blaze with insurrections. These holidays are conductors or safety valves to carry off the explosive elements inseparable from the human mind, when reduced to the condition of slavery. But for these, the rigors of bondage would become too severe for endurance, and the slave would be forced up to dangerous desperation. Woe to the slaveholder when he undertakes to hinder or to prevent the operation of these electric conductors. A succession of earthquakes would be less destructive, than the insurrectionary fires which would be sure to burst forth in different parts of the south, from such interference.

Thus, the holidays, became part and parcel of the gross fraud, wrongs and inhumanity of slavery. Ostensibly, they are institutions of benevolence, designed to mitigate the rigors of slave life, but, practically, they are a fraud, instituted by human selfishness, the better to secure the ends of injustice and oppression. The slave's happiness is not the end sought, but, rather, the master's safety. It is not from a generous unconcern for the slave's labor that this cessation from labor is allowed, but from a prudent regard to the safety of the slave system. I am strengthened in this opinion, by the fact, that most slaveholders like to have their slaves spend the holidays in such a manner as to be of no real benefit to the slaves. It is plain, that everything like rational enjoyment among the slaves, is frowned upon; and only those wild and low sports, peculiar to semi-civilized people, are encouraged. All the license allowed, appears to have no other object than to disgust the slaves with their temporary freedom, and to make them as glad to return to their work, as they were to leave it. By plunging them into exhausting depths of drunkenness and dissipation, this effect is almost certain to follow. I have known slaveholders resort to cunning tricks, with a view of getting their slaves deplorably drunk. A usual plan is, to make bets on a slave, that he can drink more whisky than any other; and so to induce a rivalry among them, for the mastery in this degradation. The scenes, brought about in this way, were often scandalous and loathsome in the extreme. Whole multitudes might be found stretched out in brutal drunkenness, at once helpless and disgusting. Thus, when the slave asks for a few hours of virtuous freedom, his cunning master takes advantage of his ignorance, and cheers him with a dose of vicious and revolting dissipation, artfully labeled with the name of LIBERTY. We were induced to drink, I among the rest, and when the holidays were over, we all staggered up from our filth and wallowing, took a long breath, and went away to our various fields of work; feeling, upon the whole, rather glad to go from that which our masters artfully deceived us into the belief was freedom, back again to the arms of slavery. It was not what we had taken it to be, nor what it might have been, had it not been abused by us. It was about as well to be a slave to master, as to be a slave to rum and whisky. I am the more induced to take this view of the holiday system, adopted by slaveholders, from what I know of their treatment of slaves, in regard to other things. It is the commonest thing for them to try to disgust their slaves with what they do not want them to have, or to enjoy. A slave, for instance, likes molasses; he steals some; to cure him of the taste for it, his master, in many cases, will go away to town, and buy a large quantity of the poorest quality, and set it before his slave, and, with whip in hand, compel him to eat it, until the poor fellow is made to sicken at the very thought of molasses. The same course is often adopted to cure slaves of the disagreeable and inconvenient practice of asking for more food, when their allowance has failed them. The same disgusting process works well, too, in other things, but I need not cite them. When a slave is drunk, the slaveholder has no fear that he will plan an insurrection; no fear that he will escape to the north. It is the sober, thinking slave who is dangerous, and needs the vigilance of his master, to keep him a slave. But, to proceed with my narrative.

On the first of January, 1835, I proceeded from St. Michael's to Mr. William Freeland's, my new home. Mr. Freeland lived only three miles from St. Michael's, on an old worn out farm, which required much labor to restore it to anything like a self-supporting establishment.

I was not long in finding Mr. Freeland to be a very different man from Mr. Covey. Though not rich, Mr. Freeland was what may be called a well-bred southern gentleman, as different from Covey, as a well-trained and hardened Negro breaker is from the best specimen of the first families of the south. Though Freeland was a slaveholder, and shared many of the vices of his class, he seemed alive to the sentiment of honor. He had some sense of justice, and some feelings of humanity. He was fretful, impulsive and passionate, but I must do him the justice to say, he was free from the mean and selfish characteristics which distinguished the creature from which I had now, happily, escaped. He was open, frank, imperative, and practiced no concealments, disdaining to play the spy. In all this, he was the opposite of the crafty Covey. Among the many advantages gained in my change from Covey's to Freeland's—startling as the statement may be—was the fact that the latter gentleman made no profession of religion. I assert most unhesitatingly, that the religion of the south—as I have observed it and proved it— is a mere covering for the most horrid crimes; the justifier of the most appalling barbarity; a sanctifier of the most hateful frauds; and a secure shelter, under which the darkest, foulest, grossest, and most infernal abominations fester and flourish. Were I again to be reduced to the condition of a slave, next to that calamity, I should regard the fact of being the slave of a religious slaveholder, the greatest that could befall me. For all slaveholders with whom I have ever met, religious slaveholders are the worst. I have found them, almost invariably, the vilest, meanest and basest of their class. Exceptions there may be, but this is true of religious slaveholders, as a class. It is not for me to explain the fact. Others may do that; I simply state it as a fact, and leave the theological, and psychological inquiry, which it raises, to be decided by others more competent than myself. Religious slaveholders, like religious persecutors, are ever extreme in their malice and violence. Very near my new home, on an adjoining farm, there lived the Rev. Daniel Weeden, who was both pious and cruel after the real Covey pattern. Mr. Weeden was a local preacher of the Protestant Methodist persuasion, and a most zealous supporter of the ordinances of religion, generally. This Weeden owned a woman called "Ceal," who was a standing proof of his mercilessness. Poor Ceal's back, always scantily clothed, was kept literally raw, by the lash of this religious man and gospel minister. The most notoriously wicked man—so called in distinction from church members—could hire hands more easily than this brute. When sent out to find a home, a slave would never enter the gates of the preacher Weeden, while a sinful sinner needed a hand. Be have ill, or behave well, it was the known maxim of Weeden, that it is the duty of a master to use the lash. If, for no other reason, he contended that this was essential to remind a slave of his condition, and of his master's authority. The good slave must be whipped, to be kept good, and the bad slave must be whipped, to be made good. Such was Weeden's theory, and such was his practice. The back of his slave-woman will, in the judgment, be the swiftest witness against him.

While I am stating particular cases, I might as well immortalize another of my neighbors, by calling him by name, and putting him in print. He did not think that a "chiel" was near, "taking notes," and will, doubtless, feel quite angry at having his character touched off in the ragged style of a slave's pen. I beg to introduce the reader to REV. RIGBY HOPKINS. Mr. Hopkins resides between Easton and St. Michael's, in Talbot county, Maryland. The severity of this man made him a perfect terror to the slaves of his neighborhood. The peculiar feature of his government, was, his system of whipping slaves, as he said, in advance of deserving it. He always managed to have one or two slaves to whip on Monday morning, so as to start his hands to their work, under the inspiration of a new assurance on Monday, that his preaching about kindness, mercy, brotherly love, and the like, on Sunday, did not interfere with, or prevent him from establishing his authority, by the cowskin. He seemed to wish to assure them, that his tears over poor, lost and ruined sinners, and his pity for them, did not reach to the blacks who tilled his fields. This saintly Hopkins used to boast, that he was the best hand to manage a Negro in the county. He whipped for the smallest offenses, by way of preventing the commission of large ones.

The reader might imagine a difficulty in finding faults enough for such frequent whipping. But this is because you have no idea how easy a matter it is to offend a man who is on the look-out for offenses. The man, unaccustomed to slaveholding, would be astonished to observe how many foggable offenses there are in the slaveholder's catalogue of crimes; and how easy it is to commit any one of them, even when the slave least intends it. A slaveholder, bent on finding fault, will hatch up a dozen a day, if he chooses to do so, and each one of these shall be of a punishable description. A mere look, word, or motion, a mistake, accident, or want of power, are all matters for which a slave may be whipped at any time. Does a slave look dissatisfied with his condition? It is said, that he has the devil in him, and it must be whipped out. Does he answer loudly, when spoken to by his master, with an air of self-consciousness? Then, must he be taken down a button-hole lower, by the lash, well laid on. Does he forget, and omit to pull off his hat, when approaching a white person? Then, he must, or may be, whipped for his bad manners. Does he ever venture to vindicate his conduct, when harshly and unjustly accused? Then, he is guilty of impudence, one of the greatest crimes in the social catalogue of southern society. To allow a slave to escape punishment, who has impudently attempted to exculpate himself from unjust charges, preferred against him by some white person, is to be guilty of great dereliction of duty. Does a slave ever venture to suggest a better way of doing a thing, no matter what? He is, altogether, too officious—wise above what is written—and he deserves, even if he does not get, a flogging for his presumption. Does he, while plowing, break a plow, or while hoeing, break a hoe, or while chopping, break an ax? No matter what were the imperfections of the implement broken, or the natural liabilities for breaking, the slave can be whipped for carelessness. The reverend slaveholder could always find something of this sort, to justify him in using the lash several times during the week. Hopkins—like Covey and Weeden—were shunned by slaves who had the privilege (as many had) of finding their own masters at the end of each year; and yet, there was not a man in all that section of country, who made a louder profession of religion, than did MR. RIGBY HOPKINS.

But, to continue the thread of my story, through my experience when at Mr. William Freeland's.

My poor, weather-beaten bark now reached smoother water, and gentler breezes. My stormy life at Covey's had been of service to me. The things that would have seemed very hard, had I gone direct to Mr. Freeland's, from the home of Master Thomas, were now (after the hardships at Covey's) "trifles light as air." I was still a field hand, and had come to prefer the severe labor of the field, to the enervating duties of a house servant. I had become large and strong; and had begun to take pride in the fact, that I could do as much hard work as some of the older men. There is much rivalry among slaves, at times, as to which can do the most work, and masters generally seek to promote such rivalry. But some of us were too wise to race with each other very long. Such racing, we had the sagacity to see, was not likely to pay. We had our times for measuring each other's strength, but we knew too much to keep up the competition so long as to produce an extraordinary day's work. We knew that if, by extraordinary exertion, a large quantity of work was done in one day, the fact, becoming known to the master, might lead him to require the same amount every day. This thought was enough to bring us to a dead halt when over so much excited for the race.

At Mr. Freeland's, my condition was every way improved. I was no longer the poor scape-goat that I was when at Covey's, where every wrong thing done was saddled upon me, and where other slaves were whipped over my shoulders. Mr. Freeland was too just a man thus to impose upon me, or upon any one else.

It is quite usual to make one slave the object of especial abuse, and to beat him often, with a view to its effect upon others, rather than with any expectation that the slave whipped will be improved by it, but the man with whom I now was, could descend to no such meanness and wickedness. Every man here was held individually responsible for his own conduct.

This was a vast improvement on the rule at Covey's. There, I was the general pack horse. Bill Smith was protected, by a positive prohibition made by his rich master, and the command of the rich slaveholder is LAW to the poor one; Hughes was favored, because of his relationship to Covey; and the hands hired temporarily, escaped flogging, except as they got it over my poor shoulders. Of course, this comparison refers to the time when Covey could whip me. Mr. Freeland, like Mr. Covey, gave his hands enough to eat, but, unlike Mr. Covey, he gave them time to take their meals; he worked us hard during the day, but gave us the night for rest—another advantage to be set to the credit of the sinner, as against that of the saint. We were seldom in the field after dark in the evening, or before sunrise in the morning. Our implements of husbandry were of the most improved pattern, and much superior to those used at Covey's.

Nothwithstanding the improved condition which was now mine, and the many advantages I had gained by my new home, and my new master, I was still restless and discontented. I was about as hard to please by a master, as a master is by slave. The freedom from bodily torture and unceasing labor, had given my mind an increased sensibility, and imparted to it greater activity. I was not yet exactly in right relations. "How be it, that was not first which is spiritual, but that which is natural, and afterward that which is spiritual." When entombed at Covey's, shrouded in darkness and physical wretchedness, temporal wellbeing was the grand desideratum; but, temporal wants supplied, the spirit puts in its claims. Beat and cuff your slave, keep him hungry and spiritless, and he will follow the chain of his master like a dog; but, feed and clothe him well—work him moderately—surround him with physical comfort—and dreams of freedom intrude. Give him a bad master, and he aspires to a good master; give him a good master, and he wishes to become his own master. Such is human nature. You may hurl a man so low, beneath the level of his kind, that he loses all just ideas of his natural position;] but elevate him a little, and the clear conception of rights arises to life and power, and leads him onward. Thus elevated, a little, at Freeland's, the dreams called into being by that good man, Father Lawson, when in Baltimore, began to visit me; and shoots from the tree of liberty began to put forth tender buds, and dim hopes of the future began to dawn.

I found myself in congenial society, at Mr. Freeland's. There were Henry Harris, John Harris, Handy Caldwell, and Sandy Jenkins. 6

Henry and John were brothers, and belonged to Mr. Freeland. They were both remarkably bright and intelligent, though neither of them could read. Now for mischief! I had not been long at Freeland's before I was up to my old tricks. I early began to address my companions on the subject of education, and the advantages of intelligence over ignorance, and, as far as I dared, I tried to show the agency of ignorance in keeping men in slavery. Webster's spelling book and the Columbian Orator were looked into again. As summer came on, and the long Sabbath days stretched themselves over our idleness, I became uneasy, and wanted a Sabbath school, in which to exercise my gifts, and to impart the little knowledge of letters which I possessed, to my brother slaves. A house was hardly necessary in the summer time; I could hold my school under the shade of an old oak tree, as well as any where else. The thing was, to get the scholars, and to have them thoroughly imbued with the desire to learn. Two such boys were quickly secured, in Henry and John, and from them the contagion spread. I was not long bringing around me twenty or thirty young men, who enrolled themselves, gladly, in my

Sabbath school, and were willing to meet me regularly, under the trees or elsewhere, for the purpose of learning to read. It was surprising with what ease they provided themselves with spelling books. These were mostly the cast off books of their young masters or mistresses. I taught, at first, on our own farm. All were impressed with the necessity of keeping the matter as private as possible, for the fate of the St. Michael's attempt was notorious, and fresh in the minds of all. Our pious masters, at St. Michael's, must not know that a few of their dusky brothers were learning to read the word of God, lest they should come down upon us with the lash and chain. We might have met to drink whisky, to wrestle, fight, and to do other unseemly things, with no fear of interruption from the saints or sinners of St. Michael's.

But, to meet for the purpose of improving the mind and heart, by learning to read the sacred scriptures, was esteemed a most dangerous nuisance, to be instantly stopped. The slaveholders of St. Michael's, like slaveholders elsewhere, would always prefer to see the slaves engaged in degrading sports, rather than to see them acting like moral and accountable beings.

Had any one asked a religious white man, in St. Michael's, twenty years ago, the names of three men in that town, whose lives were most after the pattern of our Lord and Master, Jesus Christ, the first three would have been as follows:

GARRISON WEST, Class Leader.

WRIGHT FAIRBANKS, Class Leader.

THOMAS AULD, Class Leader.

And yet, these were men who ferociously rushed in upon my Sabbath school, at St. Michael's, armed with mob-like missiles, and I must say, I thought him a Christian, until he took part in bloody by the lash. This same Garrison West was my class leader, and I must say, I thought him a Christian, until he took part in breaking up my school. He led me no more after that. The plea for this outrage was then, as it is now and at all times—the danger to good order. If the slaves learnt to read, they would learn something else, and something worse. The peace of slavery would be disturbed; slave rule would be endangered. I leave the reader to characterize a system which is endangered by such causes. I do not dispute the soundness of the reasoning. It is perfectly sound; and, if slavery be right, Sabbath schools for teaching slaves to read the bible are wrong, and ought to be put down. These Christian class leaders were, to this extent, consistent. They had settled the question, that slavery is right, and, by that standard, they determined that Sabbath schools are wrong. To be sure, they were Protestant, and held to the great Protestant right of every man to "search the scriptures" for himself; but, then, to all general rules, there are exceptions. How convenient! What crimes may not be committed under the doctrine of the last remark. But, my dear, class leading Methodist brethren, did not condescend to give me a reason for breaking up the Sabbath school at St. Michael's; it was enough that they had determined upon its destruction. I am, however, digressing.

After getting the school cleverly into operation, the second time holding it in the woods, behind the barn, and in the shade of trees—I succeeded in inducing a free colored man, who lived several miles from our house, to permit me to hold my school in a room at his house. He, very kindly, gave me this liberty; but he incurred much peril in doing so, for the assemblage was an unlawful one. I shall not mention, here, the name of this man; for it might, even now, subject him to persecution, although the offenses were committed more than twenty years ago. I had, at one time, more than forty scholars, all of the right sort; and many of them succeeded in learning to read. I have met several slaves from Maryland, who were once my scholars; and who obtained their freedom, I doubt not, partly in consequence of the ideas imparted to them in that school. I have had various employments during my short life; but I look back to none with more satisfaction, than to that afforded by my Sunday school. An attachment, deep and lasting, sprung up between me and my persecuted pupils, which made parting from them intensely grievous; and, when I think that most of these dear souls are yet shut up in this abject thralldom, I am overwhelmed with grief.

Besides my Sunday school, I devoted three evenings a week to my fellow slaves, during the winter. Let the reader reflect upon the fact, that, in this christian country, men and women are hiding from professors of religion, in barns, in the woods and fields, in order to learn to read the holy bible. Those dear souls, who came to my Sabbath school, came not because it was popular or reputable to attend such a place, for they came under the liability of having forty stripes laid on their naked backs. Every moment they spend in my school, they were under this terrible liability; and, in this respect, I was sharer with them. Their minds had been cramped and starved by their cruel masters; the light of education had been completely excluded; and their hard earnings had been taken to educate their master's children. I felt a delight in circumventing the tyrants, and in blessing the victims of their curses.

The year at Mr. Freeland's passed off very smoothly, to outward seeming. Not a blow was given me during the whole year. To the credit of Mr. Freeland—irreligious though he was—it must be stated, that he was the best master I ever had, until I became my own master, and assumed for myself, as I had a right to do, the responsibility of my own existence and the exercise of my own powers. For much of the happiness—or absence of misery—with which I passed this year with Mr. Freeland, I am indebted to the genial temper and ardent friendship of my brother slaves. They were, every one of them, manly, generous and brave, yes; I say they were brave, and I will add, fine looking. It is seldom the lot of mortals to have truer and better friends than were the slaves on this farm. It is not uncommon to charge slaves with great treachery toward each other, and to believe them incapable of confiding in each other; but I must say, that I never loved, esteemed, or confided in men, more than I did in these. They were as true as steel, and no band of brothers could have been more loving. There were no mean advantages taken of each other, as is sometimes the case where slaves are situated as we were; no tattling; no giving each other bad names to Mr. Freeland; and no elevating one at the expense of the other. We never undertook to do any thing, of any importance, which was likely to affect each other, without mutual consultation. We were generally a unit, and moved together. Thoughts and sentiments were exchanged between us, which might well be called very incendiary, by oppressors and tyrants; and perhaps the time has not even now come, when it is safe to unfold all the flying suggestions which arise in the minds of intelligent slaves. Several of my friends and brothers, if yet alive, are still in some part of the house of bondage; and though twenty years have passed away, the suspicious malice of slavery might punish them for even listening to my thoughts.

The slaveholder, kind or cruel, is a slaveholder still—the every hour violator of the just and inalienable rights of man; and he is, therefore, every hour silently whetting the knife of vengeance for his own throat. He never lisps a syllable in commendation of the fathers of this republic, nor denounces any attempted oppression of himself, without inviting the knife to his own throat, and asserting the rights of rebellion for his own slaves.

The year is ended, and we are now in the midst of the Christmas holidays, which are kept this year as last, according to the general description previously given.

CHAPTER XIX. The Run-Away Plot

NEW YEAR'S THOUGHTS AND MEDITATIONS—AGAIN BOUGHT BY FREELAND—NO
AMBITION TO BE A SLAVE—KINDNESS NO COMPENSATION FOR SLAVERY—INCIPIENT
STEPS TOWARD ESCAPE—CONSIDERATIONS LEADING THERETO—IRRECONCILABLE
HOSTILITY TO SLAVERY—SOLEMN VOW TAKEN—PLAN DIVULGED TO THE
SLAVES—Columbian Orator—SCHEME GAINS FAVOR, DESPITE PRO-SLAVERY

PREACHING—DANGER OF DISCOVERY—SKILL OF SLAVEHOLDERS IN READING THE MINDS OF THEIR SLAVES—SUSPICION AND COERCION—HYMNS WITH DOUBLE MEANING—VALUE, IN DOLLARS, OF OUR COMPANY—PRELIMINARY CONSULTATION—PASS-WORD—CONFLICTS OF HOPE AND FEAR—DIFFICULTIES TO BE OVERCOME—IGNORANCE OF GEOGRAPHY—SURVEY OF IMAGINARY DIFFICULTIES—EFFECT ON OUR MINDS—PATRICK HENRY—SANDY BECOMES A DREAMER—ROUTE TO THE NORTH LAID OUT—OBJECTIONS CONSIDERED—FRAUDS PRACTICED ON FREEMEN—PASSES WRITTEN—ANXIETIES AS THE TIME DREW NEAR—DREAD OF FAILURE—APPEALS TO COMRADES—STRANGE PRESENTIMENT—COINCIDENCE—THE BETRAYAL DISCOVERED—THE MANNER OF ARRESTING US—RESISTANCE MADE BY HENRY HARRIS—ITS EFFECT—THE UNIQUE SPEECH OF MRS. FREELAND—OUR SAD PROCESSION TO PRISON—BRUTAL JEERS BY THE MULTITUDE ALONG THE ROAD—PASSES EATEN—THE DENIAL—SANDY TOO WELL LOVED TO BE SUSPECTED—DRAGGED BEHIND HORSES—THE JAIL A RELIEF—A NEW SET OF TORMENTORS—SLAVE-TRADERS—JOHN, CHARLES AND HENRY RELEASED—ALONE IN PRISON—I AM TAKEN OUT, AND SENT TO BALTIMORE.

I am now at the beginning of the year 1836, a time favorable for serious thoughts. The mind naturally occupies itself with the mysteries of life in all its phases—the ideal, the real and the actual. Sober people look both ways at the beginning of the year, surveying the errors of the past, and providing against possible errors of the future. I, too, was thus exercised. I had little pleasure in retrospect, and the prospect was not very brilliant. "Notwithstanding," thought I, "the many resolutions and prayers I have made, in behalf of freedom, I am, this first day of the year 1836, still a slave, still wandering in the depths of spirit-devouring thralldom. My faculties and powers of body and soul are not my own, but are the property of a fellow mortal, in no sense superior to me, except that he has the physical power to compel me to be owned and controlled by him. By the combined physical force of the community, I am his slave—a slave for life." With thoughts like these, I was perplexed and chafed; they rendered me gloomy and disconsolate. The anguish of my mind may not be written.

At the close of the year 1835, Mr. Freeland, my temporary master, had bought me of Capt. Thomas Auld, for the year 1836. His promptness in securing my services, would have been flattering to my vanity, had I been ambitious to win the reputation of being a valuable slave. Even as it was, I felt a slight degree of complacency at the circumstance. It showed he was as well pleased with me as a slave, as I was with him as a master. I have already intimated my regard for Mr. Freeland, and I may say here, in addressing northern readers—where is no selfish motive for speaking in praise of a slaveholder—that Mr. Freeland was a man of many excellent qualities, and to me quite preferable to any master I ever had.

But the kindness of the slavemaster only gilds the chain of slavery, and detracts nothing from its weight or power. The thought that men are made for other and better uses than slavery, thrives best under the gentle treatment of a kind master. But the grim visage of slavery can assume no smiles which can fascinate the partially enlightened slave, into a forgetfulness of his bondage, nor of the desirableness of liberty.

I was not through the first month of this, my second year with the kind and gentlemanly Mr. Freeland, before I was earnestly considering and advising plans for gaining that freedom, which, when I was but a mere child, I had ascertained to be the natural and inborn right of every member of the human family. The desire for this freedom had been benumbed, while I was under the brutalizing dominion of Covey; and it had been postponed, and rendered inoperative, by my truly pleasant Sunday school engagements with my friends, during the year 1835, at Mr. Freeland's. It had, however, never entirely subsided. I hated slavery, always, and the desire for freedom only needed a favorable breeze, to fan it into a blaze, at any moment. The thought of only being a creature of the present and the past, troubled me, and I longed to have a future—a future with hope in it. To be shut up entirely to the past and present, is abhorrent to the human mind; it is to the soul—whose life and happiness is unceasing progress—what the prison is to the body; a blight and mildew, a hell of horrors. The dawning of this, another year, awakened me from my temporary slumber, and roused into life my latent, but long cherished aspirations for freedom. I was now not only ashamed to be contented in slavery, but ashamed to seem to be contented, and in my present favorable condition, under the mild rule of Mr. F., I am not sure that some kind reader will not condemn me for being over ambitious, and greatly wanting in proper humility, when I say the truth, that I now drove from me all thoughts of making the best of my lot, and welcomed only such thoughts as led me away from the house of bondage. The intense desires, now felt, to be free, quickened by my present favorable circumstances, brought me to the determination to act, as well as to think and speak. Accordingly, at the beginning of this year 1836, I took upon me a solemn vow, that the year which had now dawned upon me should not close, without witnessing an earnest attempt, on my part, to gain my liberty. This vow only bound me to make my escape individually; but the year spent with Mr. Freeland had attached me, as with "hooks of steel," to my brother slaves. The most affectionate and confiding friendship existed between us; and I felt it my duty to give them an opportunity to share in my virtuous determination by frankly disclosing to them my plans and purposes. Toward Henry and John Harris, I felt a friendship as strong as one man can feel for another; for I could have died with and for them. To them, therefore, with a suitable degree of caution, I began to disclose my sentiments and plans; sounding them, the while on the subject of running away, provided a good chance should offer. I scarcely need tell the reader, that I did my very best to imbue the minds of my dear friends with my own views and feelings. Thoroughly awakened, now, and with a definite vow upon me, all my little reading, which had any bearing on the subject of human rights, was rendered available in my communications with my friends. That (to me) gem of a book, the Columbian Orator, with its eloquent orations and spicy dialogues, denouncing oppression and slavery—telling of what had been dared, done and suffered by men, to obtain the inestimable boon of liberty—was still fresh in my memory, and whirled into the ranks of my speech with the aptitude of well trained soldiers, going through the drill. The fact is, I here began my public speaking. I canvassed, with Henry and John, the subject of slavery, and dashed against it the condemning brand of God's eternal justice, which it every hour violates. My fellow servants were neither indifferent, dull, nor inapt. Our feelings were more alike than our opinions. All, however, were ready to act, when a feasible plan should be proposed. "Show us how the thing is to be done," said they, "and all is clear."

We were all, except Sandy, quite free from slaveholding priestcraft. It was in vain that we had been taught from the pulpit at St. Michael's, the duty of obedience to our masters; to recognize God as the author of our enslavement; to regard running away an offense, alike against God and man; to deem our enslavement a merciful and beneficial arrangement; to esteem our condition, in this country, a paradise to that from which we had been snatched in Africa; to consider our hard hands and dark color as God's mark of displeasure, and as pointing us out as the proper subjects of slavery; that the relation of master and slave was one of reciprocal benefits; that our work was not more serviceable to our masters, than our master's thinking was serviceable to us. I say, it was in vain that the pulpit of St. Michael's had constantly inculcated these plausible doctrine. Nature laughed them to scorn. For my own part, I had now become altogether too big for my chains. Father Lawson's solemn words, of what I ought to be, and might be, in the providence of God, had not fallen dead on my soul. I was fast verging toward manhood, and the prophecies of my childhood were still unfulfilled. The thought, that year after year had passed away, and my resolutions to run away had failed and faded—that I was still a slave, and a slave, too, with chances for gaining my freedom diminished and still diminishing—was not a matter to be slept over easily; nor did I easily sleep over it.

But here came a new trouble. Thoughts and purposes so incendiary as those I now cherished, could not agitate the mind long, without danger of making themselves manifest to scrutinizing and unfriendly beholders. I had reason to fear that my sable face might prove altogether too transparent for the safe concealment of my hazardous enterprise. Plans of greater moment have leaked through stone walls, and revealed their projectors. But, here was no stone wall to hide my purpose. I would have given my poor, tell tale face for the immoveable countenance of an Indian, for it was far from being proof against the daily, searching glances of those with whom I met.

It is the interest and business of slaveholders to study human nature, with a view to practical results, and many of them attain astonishing proficiency in discerning the thoughts and emotions of slaves. They have to deal not with earth, wood, or stone, but with men; and, by every regard they have for their safety and prosperity, they must study to know the material on which they are at work. So much intellect as the slaveholder has around him, requires watching. Their safety depends upon their vigilance. Conscious of the injustice and wrong they are every hour perpetrating, and knowing what they themselves would do if made the victims of such wrongs, they are looking out for the first signs of the dread retribution of justice. They watch, therefore, with skilled and practiced eyes, and have learned to read, with great accuracy, the state of mind and heart of the slaves, through his sable face. These uneasy sinners are quick to inquire into the matter, where the slave is concerned. Unusual sobriety, apparent abstraction, sullenness and indifference—indeed, any mood out of the common way—afford ground for suspicion and inquiry. Often relying on their superior position and wisdom, they hector and torture the slave into a confession, by affecting to know the truth of their accusations. "You have got the devil in you," say they, "and we will whip him out of you." I have often been put thus to the torture, on bare suspicion. This system has its disadvantages as well as their opposite. The slave is sometimes whipped into the confession of offenses which he never committed. The reader will see that the good old rule—"a man is to be held innocent until proved to be guilty"—does not hold good on the slave plantation. Suspicion and torture are the approved methods of getting at the truth, here. It was necessary for me, therefore, to keep a watch over my deportment, lest the enemy should get the better of me.

But with all our caution and studied reserve, I am not sure that Mr. Freeland did not suspect that all was not right with us. It did seem that he watched us more narrowly, after the plan of escape had been conceived and discussed amongst us. Men seldom see themselves as others see them; and while, to ourselves, everything connected with our contemplated escape appeared concealed, Mr. Freeland may have, with the peculiar prescience of a slaveholder, mastered the huge thought which was disturbing our peace in slavery.

I am the more inclined to think that he suspected us, because, prudent as we were, as I now look back, I can see that we did many silly things, very well calculated to awaken suspicion. We were, at times, remarkably buoyant, singing hymns and making joyous exclamations, almost as triumphant in their tone as if we reached a land of freedom and safety. A keen observer might have detected in our repeated singing of

> O Canaan, sweet Canaan,
> I am bound for the land of Canaan,

something more than a hope of reaching heaven. We meant to reach the north—and the north was our Canaan.

> I thought I heard them say,
> There were lions in the way,
> I don't expect to Star
>   Much longer here.

> Run to Jesus—shun the danger—
> I don't expect to stay
>   Much longer here.

was a favorite air, and had a double meaning. In the lips of some, it meant the expectation of a speedy summons to a world of spirits; but, in the lips of our company, it simply meant, a speedy pilgrimage toward a free state, and deliverance from all the evils and dangers of slavery.

I had succeeded in winning to my (what slaveholders would call wicked) scheme, a company of five young men, the very flower of the neighborhood, each one of whom would have commanded one thousand dollars in the home market. At New Orleans, they would have brought fifteen hundred dollars a piece, and, perhaps, more. The names of our party were as follows: Henry Harris; John Harris, brother to Henry; Sandy Jenkins, of root memory; Charles Roberts, and Henry Bailey. I was the youngest, but one, of the party. I had, however, the advantage of them all, in experience, and in a knowledge of letters. This gave me great influence over them. Perhaps not one of them, left to himself, would have dreamed of escape as a possible thing. Not one of them was self-moved in the matter. They all wanted to be free; but the serious thought of running away, had not entered into their minds, until I won them to the undertaking. They all were tolerably well off—for slaves—and had dim hopes of being set free, some day, by their masters. If any one is to blame for disturbing the quiet of the slaves and slave-masters of the neighborhood of St. Michael's, I am the man. I claim to be the instigator of the high crime (as the slaveholders regard it) and I kept life in it, until life could be kept in it no longer.

Pending the time of our contemplated departure out of our Egypt, we met often by night, and on every Sunday. At these meetings we talked the matter over; told our hopes and fears, and the difficulties discovered or imagined; and, like men of sense, we counted the cost of the enterprise to which we were committing ourselves.

These meetings must have resembled, on a small scale, the meetings of revolutionary conspirators, in their primary condition. We were plotting against our (so called) lawful rulers; with this difference that we sought our own good, and not the harm of our enemies. We did not seek to overthrow them, but to escape from them. As for Mr. Freeland, we all liked him, and would have gladly remained with him, as freeman. LIBERTY was our aim; and we had now come to think that we had a right to liberty, against every obstacle even against the lives of our enslavers.

We had several words, expressive of things, important to us, which we understood, but which, even if distinctly heard by an outsider, would convey no certain meaning. I have reasons for suppressing these pass-words, which the reader will easily divine. I hated the secrecy; but where slavery is powerful, and liberty is weak, the latter is driven to concealment or to destruction.

The prospect was not always a bright one. At times, we were almost tempted to abandon the enterprise, and to get back to that comparative peace of mind, which even a man under the gallows might feel, when all hope of escape had vanished. Quiet bondage was felt to be better than the doubts, fears and uncertainties, which now so sadly perplexed and disturbed us.

The infirmities of humanity, generally, were represented in our little band. We were confident, bold and determined, at times; and, again, doubting, timid and wavering; whistling, like the boy in the graveyard, to keep away the spirits.

To look at the map, and observe the proximity of Eastern Shore, Maryland, to Delaware and Pennsylvania, it may seem to the reader quite absurd, to regard the proposed escape as a formidable undertaking. But to understand, some one has said a man must stand under. The real distance was great enough, but the imagined distance was, to our ignorance, even greater. Every slaveholder seeks to impress his slave with a belief in the boundlessness of slave territory, and of his own almost illimitable power. We all had vague and indistinct notions of the geography of the country.

The distance, however, is not the chief trouble. The nearer are the lines of a slave state and the borders of a free one, the greater the peril. Hired kidnappers infest these borders. Then, too, we knew that merely reaching a free state did not free us; that, wherever caught, we could be returned to slavery. We could see no spot on this side the ocean, where we could be free. We had heard of Canada, the real Canaan of the American bondmen, simply as a country to which the wild goose and the swan repaired at the end of winter, to escape the heat of summer, but not as the home of man. I knew something of theology, but nothing of geography. I really did not, at that time, know that there was a state of New York, or a state of Massachusetts. I had heard of Pennsylvania, Delaware and New Jersey, and all the southern states, but was ignorant of the free states, generally. New York city was our northern limit, and to go there, and be forever harassed with the liability of being hunted down and returned to slavery—with the certainty of being treated ten times worse than we had ever been treated before was a prospect far from delightful, and it might well cause some hesitation about engaging in the enterprise. The case, sometimes, to our excited visions, stood thus: At every gate through which we had to pass, we saw a watchman; at every ferry, a guard; on every bridge, a sentinel; and in every wood, a patrol or slave-hunter. We were hemmed in on every side. The good to be sought, and the evil to be shunned, were flung in the balance, and weighed against each other. On the one hand, there stood slavery; a stern reality, glaring frightfully upon us, with the blood of millions in his polluted skirts—terrible to behold—greedily devouring our hard earnings and feeding himself upon our flesh. Here was the evil from which to escape. On the other hand, far away, back in the hazy distance, where all forms seemed but shadows, under the flickering light of the north star—behind some craggy hill or snow-covered mountain—stood a doubtful freedom, half frozen, beckoning us to her icy domain. This was the good to be sought. The inequality was as great as that between certainty and uncertainty. This, in itself, was enough to stagger us; but when we came to survey the untrodden road, and conjecture the many possible difficulties, we were appalled, and at times, as I have said, were upon the point of giving over the struggle altogether.

The reader can have little idea of the phantoms of trouble which flit, in such circumstances, before the uneducated mind of the slave. Upon either side, we saw grim death assuming a variety of horrid shapes. Now, it was starvation, causing us, in a strange and friendless land, to eat our own flesh. Now, we were contending with the waves (for our journey was in part by water) and were drowned. Now, we were hunted by dogs, and overtaken and torn to pieces by their merciless fangs. We were stung by scorpions—chased by wild beasts—bitten by snakes; and, worst of all, after having succeeded in swimming rivers—encountering wild beasts— sleeping in the woods—suffering hunger, cold, heat and nakedness—we supposed ourselves to be overtaken by hired kidnappers, who, in the name of the law, and for their thrice accursed reward, would, perchance, fire upon us—kill some, wound others, and capture all. This dark picture, drawn by ignorance and fear, at times greatly shook our determination, and not unfrequently caused us to

>Rather bear those ills we had
>Than fly to others which we knew not of.

I am not disposed to magnify this circumstance in my experience, and yet I think I shall seem to be so disposed, to the reader. No man can tell the intense agony which is felt by the slave, when wavering on the point of making his escape. All that he has is at stake; and even that which he has not, is at stake, also. The life which he has, may be lost, and the liberty which he seeks, may not be gained.

Patrick Henry, to a listening senate, thrilled by his magic eloquence, and ready to stand by him in his boldest flights, could say, GIVE ME LIBERTY OR GIVE ME DEATH, and this saying was a sublime one, even for a freeman; but, incomparably more sublime, is the same sentiment, when practically asserted by men accustomed to the lash and chain—men whose sensibilities must have become more or less deadened by their bondage. With us it was a doubtful liberty, at best, that we sought; and a certain, lingering death in the rice swamps and sugar fields, if we failed. Life is not lightly regarded by men of sane minds. It is precious, alike to the pauper and to the prince—to the slave, and to his master; and yet, I believe there was not one among us, who would not rather have been shot down, than pass away life in hopeless bondage.

In the progress of our preparations, Sandy, the root man, became troubled. He began to have dreams, and some of them were very distressing. One of these, which happened on a Friday night, was, to him, of great significance; and I am quite ready to confess, that I felt somewhat damped by it myself. He said, "I dreamed, last night, that I was roused from sleep, by strange noises, like the voices of a swarm of angry birds, that caused a roar as they passed, which fell upon my ear like a coming gale over the tops of the trees. Looking up to see what it could mean," said Sandy, "I saw you, Frederick, in the claws of a huge bird, surrounded by a large number of birds, of all colors and sizes. These were all picking at you, while you, with your arms, seemed to be trying to protect your eyes. Passing over me, the birds flew in a south-westerly direction, and I watched them until they were clean out of sight. Now, I saw this as plainly as I now see you; and furder, honey, watch de Friday night dream; dare is sumpon in it, shose you born; dare is, indeed, honey."

I confess I did not like this dream; but I threw off concern about it, by attributing it to the general excitement and perturbation consequent upon our contemplated plan of escape. I could not, however, shake off its effect at once. I felt that it boded me no good. Sandy was unusually emphatic and oracular, and his manner had much to do with the impression made upon me.

The plan of escape which I recommended, and to which my comrades assented, was to take a large canoe, owned by Mr. Hamilton, and, on the Saturday night previous to the Easter holidays, launch out into the Chesapeake bay, and paddle for its head—a distance of seventy miles with all our might. Our course, on reaching this point, was, to turn the canoe adrift, and bend our steps toward the north star, till we reached a free state.

There were several objections to this plan. One was, the danger from gales on the bay. In rough weather, the waters of the Chesapeake are much agitated, and there is danger, in a canoe, of being swamped by the waves. Another objection was, that the canoe would soon be missed; the absent persons would, at once, be suspected of having taken it; and we should be pursued by some of the fast sailing bay craft out of St. Michael's. Then, again, if we reached the head of the bay, and turned the canoe adrift, she might prove a guide to our track, and bring the land hunters after us.

These and other objections were set aside, by the stronger ones which could be urged against every other plan that could then be suggested. On the water, we had a chance of being regarded as fishermen, in the service of a master. On the other hand, by taking the land route, through the counties adjoining Delaware, we should be subjected to all manner of interruptions, and many very disagreeable questions, which might give us serious trouble. Any white man is authorized to stop a man of color, on any road, and examine him, and arrest him, if he so desires.

By this arrangement, many abuses (considered such even by slaveholders) occur. Cases have been known, where freemen have been called upon to show their free papers, by a pack of ruffians—and, on the presentation of the papers, the ruffians have torn them up, and seized their victim, and sold him to a life of endless bondage.

The week before our intended start, I wrote a pass for each of our party, giving them permission to visit Baltimore, during the Easter holidays. The pass ran after this manner:

This is to certify, that I, the undersigned, have given the
bearer, my servant, John, full liberty to go to Baltimore, to
spend the Easter holidays.

W.H.

Near St. Michael's, Talbot county, Maryland

Although we were not going to Baltimore, and were intending to land east of North Point, in the direction where I had seen the Philadelphia steamers go, these passes might be made useful to us in the lower part of the bay, while steering toward Baltimore. These were not, however, to be shown by us, until all other answers failed to satisfy the inquirer. We were all fully alive to the importance of being calm and self-possessed, when accosted, if accosted we should be; and we more times than one rehearsed to each other how we should behave in the hour of trial. These were long, tedious days and nights. The suspense was painful, in the extreme. To balance probabilities, where life and liberty hang on the result, requires steady nerves. I panted for action, and was glad when the day, at the close of which we were to start, dawned upon us. Sleeping, the night before, was out of the question. I probably felt more deeply than any of my companions, because I was the instigator of the movement. The responsibility of the whole enterprise rested on my shoulders. The glory of success, and the shame and confusion of failure, could not be matters of indifference to me. Our food was prepared; our clothes were packed up; we were all ready to go, and impatient for Saturday morning—considering that the last morning of our bondage.

I cannot describe the tempest and tumult of my brain, that morning. The reader will please to bear in mind, that, in a slave state, an unsuccessful runaway is not only subjected to cruel torture, and sold away to the far south, but he is frequently execrated by the other slaves. He is charged with making the condition of the other slaves intolerable, by laying them all under the suspicion of their masters—subjecting them to greater vigilance, and imposing greater limitations on their privileges. I dreaded murmurs from this quarter. It is difficult, too, for a slavemaster to believe that slaves escaping have not been aided in their flight by some one of their fellow slaves. When, therefore, a slave is missing, every slave on the place is closely examined as to his knowledge of the undertaking; and they are sometimes even tortured, to make them disclose what they are suspected of knowing of such escape.

Our anxiety grew more and more intense, as the time of our intended departure for the north drew nigh. It was truly felt to be a matter of life and death with us; and we fully intended to fight as well as run, if necessity should occur for that extremity. But the trial hour was not yet to come. It was easy to resolve, but not so easy to act. I expected there might be some drawing back, at the last. It was natural that there should be; therefore, during the intervening time, I lost no opportunity to explain away difficulties, to remove doubts, to dispel fears, and to inspire all with firmness. It was too late to look back; and now was the time to go forward. Like most other men, we had done the talking part of our work, long and well; and the time had come to act as if we were in earnest, and meant to be as true in action as in words. I did not forget to appeal to the pride of my comrades, by telling them that, if after having solemnly promised to go, as they had done, they now failed to make the attempt, they would, in effect, brand themselves with cowardice, and might as well sit down, fold their arms, and acknowledge themselves as fit only to be slaves. This detestable character, all were unwilling to assume. Every man except Sandy (he, much to our regret, withdrew) stood firm; and at our last meeting we pledged ourselves afresh, and in the most solemn manner, that, at the time appointed, we would certainly start on our long journey for a free country. This meeting was in the middle of the week, at the end of which we were to start.

Early that morning we went, as usual, to the field, but with hearts that beat quickly and anxiously. Any one intimately acquainted with us, might have seen that all was not well with us, and that some monster lingered in our thoughts. Our work that morning was the same as it had been for several days past—drawing out and spreading manure. While thus engaged, I had a sudden presentiment, which flashed upon me like lightning in a dark night, revealing to the lonely traveler the gulf before, and the enemy behind. I instantly turned to Sandy Jenkins, who was near me, and said to him, "Sandy, we are betrayed; something has just told me so." I felt as sure of it, as if the officers were there in sight. Sandy said, "Man, dat is strange; but I feel just as you do." If my mother—then long in her grave—had appeared before me, and told me that we were betrayed, I could not, at that moment, have felt more certain of the fact.

In a few minutes after this, the long, low and distant notes of the horn summoned us from the field to breakfast. I felt as one may be supposed to feel before being led forth to be executed for some great offense. I wanted no breakfast; but I went with the other slaves toward the house, for form's sake. My feelings were not disturbed as to the right of running away; on that point I had no trouble, whatever. My anxiety arose from a sense of the consequences of failure.

In thirty minutes after that vivid presentiment came the apprehended crash. On reaching the house, for breakfast, and glancing my eye toward the lane gate, the worst was at once made known. The lane gate off Mr. Freeland's house, is nearly a half mile from the door, and shaded by the heavy wood which bordered the main road. I was, however, able to descry four white men, and two colored men, approaching. The white men were on horseback, and the colored men were walking behind, and seemed to be tied. "It is all over with us," thought I, "we are surely betrayed." I now became composed, or at least comparatively so, and calmly awaited the result. I watched the ill-omened company, till I saw them enter the gate. Successful flight was impossible, and I made up my mind to stand, and meet the evil, whatever it might be; for I was not without a slight hope that things might turn differently from what I at first expected. In a few moments, in came Mr. William Hamilton, riding very rapidly, and evidently much excited. He was in the habit of riding very slowly, and was seldom known to gallop his horse. This time, his horse was nearly at full speed, causing the dust to roll thick behind him. Mr. Hamilton, though one of the most resolute men in the whole neighborhood, was, nevertheless, a remarkably mild spoken man; and, even when greatly excited, his language was cool and circumspect. He came to the door, and inquired if Mr. Freeland was in. I told him that Mr. Freeland was at the barn. Off the old gentleman rode, toward the barn, with unwonted speed. Mary, the cook, was at a loss to know what was the matter, and I did not profess any skill in making her understand. I knew she would have united, as readily as any one, in cursing me for bringing trouble into the family; so I held my peace, leaving matters to develop themselves, without my assistance. In a few moments, Mr. Hamilton and Mr. Freeland came down from the barn to the house; and, just as they made their appearance in the front yard, three men (who proved to be constables) came dashing into the lane, on horseback, as if summoned by a sign requiring quick work. A few seconds brought them into the front yard, where they hastily dismounted, and tied their horses. This done, they joined Mr. Freeland and Mr. Hamilton, who were standing a short distance from the kitchen. A few moments were spent, as if in consulting how to proceed, and then the whole party walked up to the kitchen door. There was now no one in the kitchen but myself and John Harris. Henry and Sandy were yet at the barn. Mr. Freeland came inside the kitchen door, and with an agitated voice, called me by name, and told me to come forward; that there was some gentlemen who wished to see me. I stepped toward them, at the door, and asked what they wanted, when the constables grabbed me, and told me that I had better not resist; that I had been in a scrape, or was said to have been in one; that they were merely going to take me where I could be examined; that they were going to carry me to St. Michael's, to have me brought before my master. They further said, that, in case the evidence against me was not true, I should be acquitted. I was now firmly tied, and completely at the mercy of my captors. Resistance was idle. They were five in number, armed to the very teeth. When they had secured me, they next turned to John Harris, and, in a few moments, succeeded in tying him as firmly as they had already tied me. They next turned toward Henry Harris, who had now returned from the barn. "Cross your hands," said the constables, to Henry. "I won't" said Henry, in a voice so firm and clear, and in a manner so determined, as for a moment to arrest all proceedings. "Won't you cross your hands?" said Tom Graham, the constable. "No I won't," said Henry, with increasing emphasis. Mr. Hamilton, Mr. Freeland, and the officers, now came near to Henry. Two of the constables drew out their shining pistols, and swore by the name of God, that he should cross his hands, or they would shoot him down. Each of these hired ruffians now cocked their pistols, and, with fingers apparently on the triggers, presented their deadly weapons to the breast of the unarmed slave, saying, at the same time, if he did not cross his hands, they would "blow his d—d heart out of him."

"Shoot! shoot me!" said Henry. "You can't kill me but once. Shoot!—shoot! and be d—d. I won't be tied." This, the brave fellow said in a voice as defiant and heroic in its tone, as was the language itself; and, at the moment of saying this, with the pistols at his very breast, he quickly raised his arms, and dashed them from the puny hands of his assassins, the weapons flying in opposite directions. Now came the struggle. All hands was now rushed upon the brave fellow, and, after beating him for some time, they succeeded in overpowering and tying him. Henry put me to shame; he fought, and fought bravely. John and I had made no resistance. The fact is, I never see much use in fighting, unless there is a reasonable probability of whipping somebody. Yet there was something almost providential in the resistance made by the gallant Henry. But for that resistance, every soul of us would have been hurried off to the far south. Just a moment previous to the trouble with Henry, Mr. Hamilton mildly said—and this gave me the unmistakable clue to the cause of our arrest—"Perhaps we had now better make a search for those protections, which we understand Frederick has written for himself and the rest." Had these passes been found, they would have been point blank proof against us, and would have confirmed all the statements of our betrayer. Thanks to the resistance of Henry, the excitement produced by the scuffle drew all attention in that direction, and I succeeded in flinging my pass, unobserved, into the fire. The confusion attendant upon the scuffle, and the apprehension of further trouble, perhaps, led our captors to forego, for the present, any search for "those protections" which Frederick was said to have written for his companions; so we were not yet convicted of the purpose to run away; and it was evident that there was some doubt, on the part of all, whether we had been guilty of such a purpose.

Just as we were all completely tied, and about ready to start toward St. Michael's, and thence to jail, Mrs. Betsey Freeland (mother to William, who was very much attached—after the southern fashion—to Henry and John, they having been reared from childhood in her house) came to the kitchen door, with her hands full of biscuits—for we had not had time to take our breakfast that morning—and divided them between Henry and John. This done, the lady made the following parting address to me, looking and pointing her bony finger at me. "You devil! you yellow devil! It was you that put it into the heads of Henry and John to run away. But for you, you long legged yellow devil, Henry and John would never have thought of running away." I gave the lady a look, which called forth a scream of mingled wrath and terror, as she slammed the kitchen door, and went in, leaving me, with the rest, in hands as harsh as her own broken voice.

Could the kind reader have been quietly riding along the main road to or from Easton, that morning, his eye would have met a painful sight. He would have seen five young men, guilty of no crime, save that of preferring liberty to a life of bondage, drawn along the public highway—firmly bound together—tramping through dust and heat, bare-footed and bare-headed—fastened to three strong horses, whose riders were armed to the teeth, with pistols and daggers—on their way to prison, like felons, and suffering every possible insult from the crowds of idle, vulgar people, who clustered around, and heartlessly made their failure the occasion for all manner of ribaldry and sport. As I looked upon this crowd of vile persons, and saw myself and friends thus assailed and persecuted, I could not help seeing the fulfillment of Sandy's dream. I was in the hands of moral vultures, and firmly held in their sharp talons, and was hurried away toward Easton, in a south-easterly direction, amid the jeers of new birds of the same feather, through every neighborhood we passed. It seemed to me (and this shows the good understanding between the slaveholders and their allies) that every body we met knew the cause of our arrest, and were out, awaiting our passing by, to feast their vindictive eyes on our misery and to gloat over our ruin. Some said, I ought to be hanged, and others, I ought to be burnt, others, I ought to have the "hide" taken from my back; while no one gave us a kind word or sympathizing look, except the poor slaves, who were lifting their heavy hoes, and who cautiously glanced at us through the post-and-rail fences, behind which they were at work. Our sufferings, that morning, can be more easily imagined than described. Our hopes were all blasted, at a blow. The cruel injustice, the victorious crime, and the helplessness of innocence, led me to ask, in my ignorance and weakness "Where now is the God of justice and mercy? And why have these wicked men the power thus to trample upon our rights, and to insult our feelings?" And yet, in the next moment, came the consoling thought, "The day of oppressor will come at last." Of one thing I could be glad—not one of my dear friends, upon whom I had brought this great calamity, either by word or look, reproached me for having led them into it. We were a band of brothers, and never dearer to each other than now. The thought which gave us the most pain, was the probable separation which would now take place, in case we were sold off to the far south, as we were likely to be. While the constables were looking forward, Henry and I, being fastened together, could occasionally exchange a word, without being observed by the kidnappers who had us in charge. "What shall I do with my pass?" said Henry. "Eat it with your biscuit," said I; "it won't do to tear it up." We were now near St. Michael's. The direction concerning the passes was passed around, and executed. "Own nothing!" said I. "Own nothing!" was passed around and enjoined, and assented to. Our confidence in each other was unshaken; and we were quite resolved to succeed or fail together—as much after the calamity which had befallen us, as before.

On reaching St. Michael's, we underwent a sort of examination at my master's store, and it was evident to my mind, that Master Thomas suspected the truthfulness of the evidence upon which they had acted in arresting us; and that he only affected, to some extent, the positiveness with which he asserted our guilt. There was nothing said by any of our company, which could, in any manner, prejudice our cause; and there was hope, yet, that we should be able to return to our homes—if for nothing else, at least to find out the guilty man or woman who had betrayed us.

To this end, we all denied that we had been guilty of intended flight. Master Thomas said that the evidence he had of our intention to run away, was strong enough to hang us, in a case of murder. "But," said I, "the cases are not equal. If murder were committed, some one must have committed it—the thing is done! In our case, nothing has been done! We have not run away. Where is the evidence against us? We were quietly at our work." I talked thus, with unusual freedom, to bring out the evidence against us, for we all wanted, above all things, to know the guilty wretch who had betrayed us, that we might have something tangible upon which to pour the execrations. From something which dropped, in the course of the talk, it appeared that there was but one witness against us—and that that witness could not be produced. Master Thomas would not tell us who his informant was; but we suspected, and suspected one person only. Several circumstances seemed to point SANDY out, as our betrayer. His entire knowledge of our plans his participation in them—his withdrawal from us—his dream, and his simultaneous presentiment that we were betrayed—the taking us, and the leaving him—were calculated to turn suspicion toward him; and yet, we could not suspect him. We all loved him too well to think it possible that he could have betrayed us. So we rolled the guilt on other shoulders.

We were literally dragged, that morning, behind horses, a distance of fifteen miles, and placed in the Easton jail. We were glad to reach the end of our journey, for our pathway had been the scene of insult and mortification. Such is the power of public opinion, that it is hard, even for the innocent, to feel the happy consolations of innocence, when they fall under the maledictions of this power. How could we regard ourselves as in the right, when all about us denounced us as criminals, and had the power and the disposition to treat us as such.

In jail, we were placed under the care of Mr. Joseph Graham, the sheriff of the county. Henry, and John, and myself, were placed in one room, and Henry Baily and Charles Roberts, in another, by themselves. This separation was intended to deprive us of the advantage of concert, and to prevent trouble in jail.

Once shut up, a new set of tormentors came upon us. A swarm of imps, in human shape the slave-traders, deputy slave-traders, and agents of slave-traders—that gather in every country town of the state, watching for chances to buy human flesh (as buzzards to eat carrion) flocked in upon us, to ascertain if our masters had placed us in jail to be sold. Such a set of debased and villainous creatures, I never saw before, and hope never to see again. I felt myself surrounded as by a pack of fiends, fresh from perdition. They laughed, leered, and grinned at us; saying, "Ah! boys, we've got you, havn't we? So you were about to make your escape? Where were you going to?" After taunting us, and peering at us, as long as they liked, they one by one subjected us to an examination, with a view to ascertain our value; feeling our arms and legs, and shaking us by the shoulders to see if we were sound and healthy; impudently asking us, "how we would like to have them for masters?" To such questions, we were, very much to their annoyance, quite dumb, disdaining to answer them. For one, I detested the whisky-bloated gamblers in human flesh; and I believe I was as much detested by them in turn. One fellow told me, "if he had me, he would cut the devil out of me pretty quick." These Negro buyers are very offensive to the genteel southern Christian public. They are looked upon, in respectable Maryland society, as necessary, but detestable characters. As a class, they are hardened ruffians, made such by nature and by occupation. Their ears are made quite familiar with the agonizing cry of outraged and woe-smitten humanity. Their eyes are forever open to human misery. They walk amid desecrated affections, insulted virtue, and blasted hopes. They have grown intimate with vice and blood; they gloat over the wildest illustrations of their soul-damning and earth-polluting business, and are moral pests. Yes; they are a legitimate fruit of slavery; and it is a puzzle to make out a case of greater villainy for them, than for the slaveholders, who make such a class possible. They are mere hucksters of the surplus slave produce of Maryland and Virginia coarse, cruel, and swaggering bullies, whose very breathing is of blasphemy and blood.

Aside from these slave-buyers, who infested the prison, from time to time, our quarters were much more comfortable than we had any right to expect they would be. Our allowance of food was small and coarse, but our room was the best in the jail—neat and spacious, and with nothing about it necessarily reminding us of being in prison, but its heavy locks and bolts and the black, iron lattice-work at the windows. We were prisoners of state, compared with most slaves who are put into that Easton jail. But the place was not one of contentment. Bolts, bars and grated windows are not acceptable to freedom-loving people of any color. The suspense, too, was painful. Every step on the stairway was listened to, in the hope that the comer would cast a ray of light on our fate. We would have given the hair off our heads for half a dozen words with one of the waiters in Sol. Lowe's hotel. Such waiters were in the way of hearing, at the table, the probable course of things. We could see them flitting about in their white jackets in front of this hotel, but could speak to none of them.

Soon after the holidays were over, contrary to all our expectations, Messrs. Hamilton and Freeland came up to Easton; not to make a bargain with the "Georgia traders," nor to send us up to Austin Woldfolk, as is usual in the case of run-away salves, but to release Charles, Henry Harris, Henry Baily and John Harris, from prison, and this, too, without the infliction of a single blow. I was now left entirely alone in prison. The innocent had been taken, and the guilty left. My friends were separated from me, and apparently forever. This circumstance caused me more pain than any other incident connected with our capture and imprisonment. Thirty-nine lashes on my naked and bleeding back, would have been joyfully borne, in preference to this separation from these, the friends of my youth. And yet, I could not but feel that I was the victim of something like justice. Why should these young men, who were led into this scheme by me, suffer as much as the instigator? I felt glad that they were leased from prison, and from the dread prospect of a life (or death I should rather say) in the rice swamps. It is due to the noble Henry, to say, that he seemed almost as reluctant to leave the prison with me in it, as he was to be tied and dragged to prison. But he and the rest knew that we should, in all the likelihoods of the case, be separated, in the event of being sold; and since we were now completely in the hands of our owners, we all concluded it would be best to go peaceably home.

Not until this last separation, dear reader, had I touched those profounder depths of desolation, which it is the lot of slaves often to reach. I was solitary in the world, and alone within the walls of a stone prison, left to a fate of life-long misery. I had hoped and expected much, for months before, but my hopes and expectations were now withered and blasted. The ever dreaded slave life in Georgia, Louisiana and Alabama—from which escape is next to impossible now, in my loneliness, stared me in the face. The possibility of ever becoming anything but an abject slave, a mere machine in the hands of an owner, had now fled, and it seemed to me it had fled forever. A life of living death, beset with the innumerable horrors of the cotton field, and the sugar plantation, seemed to be my doom. The fiends, who rushed into the prison when we were first put there, continued to visit me, and to ply me with questions and with their tantalizing remarks. I was insulted, but helpless; keenly alive to the demands of justice and liberty, but with no means of asserting them. To talk to those imps about justice and mercy, would have been as absurd as to reason with bears and tigers. Lead and steel are the only arguments that they understand.

After remaining in this life of misery and despair about a week, which, by the way, seemed a month, Master Thomas, very much to my surprise, and greatly to my relief, came to the prison, and took me out, for the purpose, as he said, of sending me to Alabama, with a friend of his, who would emancipate me at the end of eight years. I was glad enough to get out of prison; but I had no faith in the story that this friend of Capt. Auld would emancipate me, at the end of the time indicated. Besides, I never had heard of his having a friend in Alabama, and I took the announcement, simply as an easy and comfortable method of shipping me off to the far south. There was a little scandal, too, connected with the idea of one Christian selling another to the Georgia traders, while it was deemed every way proper for them to sell to others. I thought this friend in Alabama was an invention, to meet this difficulty, for Master Thomas was quite jealous of his Christian reputation, however unconcerned he might be about his real Christian character. In these remarks, however, it is possible that I do Master Thomas Auld injustice. He certainly did not exhaust his power upon me, in the case, but acted, upon the whole, very generously, considering the nature of my offense. He had the power and the provocation to send me, without reserve, into the very everglades of Florida, beyond the remotest hope of emancipation; and his refusal to exercise that power, must be set down to his credit.

After lingering about St. Michael's a few days, and no friend from Alabama making his appearance, to take me there, Master Thomas decided to send me back again to Baltimore, to live with his brother Hugh, with whom he was now at peace; possibly he became so by his profession of religion, at the camp-meeting in the Bay Side. Master Thomas told me that he wished me to go to Baltimore, and learn a trade; and that, if I behaved myself properly, he would emancipate me at twenty-five! Thanks for this one beam of hope in the future. The promise had but one fault; it seemed too good to be true.

CHAPTER XX. Apprenticeship Life

NOTHING LOST BY THE ATTEMPT TO RUN AWAY—COMRADES IN THEIR OLD HOMES—REASONS FOR SENDING ME AWAY—RETURN TO BALTIMORE—CONTRAST
BETWEEN TOMMY AND THAT OF HIS COLORED COMPANION—TRIALS IN GARDINER'S
SHIP YARD—DESPERATE FIGHT—ITS CAUSES—CONFLICT BETWEEN WHITE AND BLACK
LABOR—DESCRIPTION OF THE OUTRAGE—COLORED TESTIMONY NOTHING—CONDUCT OF
MASTER HUGH—SPIRIT OF SLAVERY IN BALTIMORE—MY CONDITION

IMPROVES—NEW
ASSOCIATIONS—SLAVEHOLDER'S RIGHT TO TAKE HIS WAGES—HOW TO MAKE A
CONTENTED SLAVE.

Well! dear reader, I am not, as you may have already inferred, a loser by the general upstir, described in the foregoing chapter. The little domestic revolution, notwithstanding the sudden snub it got by the treachery of somebody—I dare not say or think who—did not, after all, end so disastrously, as when in the iron cage at Easton, I conceived it would. The prospect, from that point, did look about as dark as any that ever cast its gloom over the vision of the anxious, out-looking, human spirit. "All is well that ends well." My affectionate comrades, Henry and John Harris, are still with Mr. William Freeland. Charles Roberts and Henry Baily are safe at their homes. I have not, therefore, any thing to regret on their account. Their masters have mercifully forgiven them, probably on the ground suggested in the spirited little speech of Mrs. Freeland, made to me just before leaving for the jail—namely: that they had been allured into the wicked scheme of making their escape, by me; and that, but for me, they would never have dreamed of a thing so shocking! My friends had nothing to regret, either; for while they were watched more closely on account of what had happened, they were, doubtless, treated more kindly than before, and got new assurances that they would be legally emancipated, some day, provided their behavior should make them deserving, from that time forward. Not a blow, as I learned, was struck any one of them. As for Master William Freeland, good, unsuspecting soul, he did not believe that we were intending to run away at all. Having given—as he thought—no occasion to his boys to leave him, he could not think it probable that they had entertained a design so grievous. This, however, was not the view taken of the matter by "Mas' Billy," as we used to call the soft spoken, but crafty and resolute Mr. William Hamilton. He had no doubt that the crime had been meditated; and regarding me as the instigator of it, he frankly told Master Thomas that he must remove me from that neighborhood, or he would shoot me down. He would not have one so dangerous as "Frederick" tampering with his slaves. William Hamilton was not a man whose threat might be safely disregarded. I have no doubt that he would have proved as good as his word, had the warning given not been promptly taken. He was furious at the thought of such a piece of high-handed theft, as we were about to perpetrate the stealing of our own bodies and souls! The feasibility of the plan, too, could the first steps have been taken, was marvelously plain. Besides, this was a new idea, this use of the bay. Slaves escaping, until now, had taken to the woods; they had never dreamed of profaning and abusing the waters of the noble Chesapeake, by making them the highway from slavery to freedom. Here was a broad road of destruction to slavery, which, before, had been looked upon as a wall of security by slaveholders. But Master Billy could not get Mr. Freeland to see matters precisely as he did; nor could he get Master Thomas so excited as he was himself. The latter—I must say it to his credit—showed much humane feeling in his part of the transaction, and atoned for much that had been harsh, cruel and unreasonable in his former treatment of me and others. His clemency was quite unusual and unlooked for. "Cousin Tom" told me that while I was in jail, Master Thomas was very unhappy; and that the night before his going up to release me, he had walked the floor nearly all night, evincing great distress; that very tempting offers had been made to him, by the Negro-traders, but he had rejected them all, saying that money could not tempt him to sell me to the far south. All this I can easily believe, for he seemed quite reluctant to send me away, at all. He told me that he only consented to do so, because of the very strong prejudice against me in the neighborhood, and that he feared for my safety if I remained there.

Thus, after three years spent in the country, roughing it in the field, and experiencing all sorts of hardships, I was again permitted to return to Baltimore, the very place, of all others, short of a free state, where I most desired to live. The three years spent in the country, had made some difference in me, and in the household of Master Hugh. "Little Tommy" was no longer little Tommy; and I was not the slender lad who had left for the Eastern Shore just three years before. The loving relations between me and Mas' Tommy were broken up. He was no longer dependent on me for protection, but felt himself a man, with other and more suitable associates. In childhood, he scarcely considered me inferior to himself certainly, as good as any other boy with whom he played; but the time had come when his friend must become his slave. So we were cold, and we parted. It was a sad thing to me, that, loving each other as we had done, we must now take different roads. To him, a thousand avenues were open.

Education had made him acquainted with all the treasures of the world, and liberty had flung open the gates thereunto; but I, who had attended him seven years, and had watched over him with the care of a big brother, fighting his battles in the street, and shielding him from harm, to an extent which had induced his mother to say, "Oh! Tommy is always safe, when he is with Freddy," must be confined to a single condition. He could grow, and become a MAN; I could grow, though I could not become a man, but must remain, all my life, a minor—a mere boy. Thomas Auld, Junior, obtained a situation on board the brig "Tweed," and went to sea. I know not what has become of him; he certainly has my good wishes for his welfare and prosperity. There were few persons to whom I was more sincerely attached than to him, and there are few in the world I would be more pleased to meet.

Very soon after I went to Baltimore to live, Master Hugh succeeded in getting me hired to Mr. William Gardiner, an extensive ship builder on Fell's Point. I was placed here to learn to calk, a trade of which I already had some knowledge, gained while in Mr. Hugh Auld's ship-yard, when he was a master builder. Gardiner's, however, proved a very unfavorable place for the accomplishment of that object. Mr. Gardiner was, that season, engaged in building two large man-of-war vessels, professedly for the Mexican government. These vessels were to be launched in the month of July, of that year, and, in failure thereof, Mr. G. would forfeit a very considerable sum of money. So, when I entered the ship-yard, all was hurry and driving. There were in the yard about one hundred men; of these about seventy or eighty were regular carpenters—privileged men. Speaking of my condition here I wrote, years ago—and I have now no reason to vary the picture as follows:

There was no time to learn any thing. Every man had to do that which he knew how to do. In entering the ship-yard, my orders from Mr. Gardiner were, to do whatever the carpenters commanded me to do. This was placing me at the beck and call of about seventy-five men. I was to regard all these as masters. Their word was to be my law. My situation was a most trying one. At times I needed a dozen pair of hands. I was called a dozen ways in the space of a single minute. Three or four voices would strike my ear at the same moment. It was—"Fred., come help me to cant this timber here." "Fred., come carry this timber yonder."—"Fred., bring that roller here."—"Fred., go get a fresh can of water."—"Fred., come help saw off the end of this timber."—"Fred., go quick and get the crow bar."—"Fred., hold on the end of this fall."—"Fred., go to the blacksmith's shop, and get a new punch."—
"Hurra, Fred.! run and bring me a cold chisel."—"I say, Fred., bear a hand, and get up a fire as quick as lightning under that steam-box."—"Halloo, nigger! come, turn this grindstone."—"Come, come! move, move! and bowse this timber forward."—"I say, darkey, blast your eyes, why don't you heat up some pitch?"—"Halloo! halloo! halloo!" (Three voices at the same time.) "Come here!—Go there!—Hold on where you are! D—n you, if you move, I'll knock your brains out!"

Such, dear reader, is a glance at the school which was mine, during, the first eight months of my stay at Baltimore. At the end of the eight months, Master Hugh refused longer to allow me to remain with Mr. Gardiner. The circumstance which led to his taking me away, was a brutal outrage, committed upon me by the white apprentices of the ship-yard. The fight was a desperate one, and I came out of it most shockingly mangled. I was cut and bruised in sundry places, and my left eye was nearly knocked out of its socket. The facts, leading to this barbarous outrage upon me, illustrate a phase of slavery destined to become an important element in the overthrow of the slave system, and I may, therefore state them with some minuteness. That phase is this: the conflict of slavery with the interests of the white mechanics and laborers of the south. In the country, this conflict is not so apparent; but, in cities, such as Baltimore, Richmond, New Orleans, Mobile, &c., it is seen pretty clearly. The slaveholders, with a craftiness peculiar to themselves, by encouraging the enmity of the poor, laboring white man against the blacks, succeeds in making the said white man almost as much a slave as the black slave himself. The difference between the white slave, and the black slave, is this: the latter belongs to one slaveholder, and the former belongs to all the slaveholders, collectively. The white slave has taken from him, by indirection, what the black slave has taken from him, directly, and without ceremony. Both are plundered, and by the same plunderers. The slave is robbed, by his master, of all his earnings, above what is required for his bare physical necessities; and the white man is robbed by the slave system, of the just results of his labor, because he is flung into competition with a class of laborers who work without wages. The competition, and its injurious consequences, will, one day, array the nonslaveholding white people of the slave states, against the slave system, and make them the most effective workers against the great evil. At present, the slaveholders blind them to this competition, by keeping alive their prejudice against the slaves, as men—not against them as slaves. They appeal to their pride, often denouncing emancipation, as tending to place the white man, on an equality with Negroes, and, by this means, they succeed in drawing off the minds of the poor whites from the real fact, that, by the rich slave-master, they are already regarded as but a single remove from equality with the slave. The impression is cunningly made, that slavery is the only power that can prevent the laboring white man from falling to the level of the slave's poverty and degradation. To make this enmity deep and broad, between the slave and the poor white man, the latter is allowed to abuse and whip the former, without hinderance. But—as I have suggested—this state of facts prevails mostly in the country. In the city of Baltimore, there are not unfrequent murmurs, that educating the slaves to be mechanics may, in the end, give slavemasters power to dispense with the services of the poor white man altogether. But, with characteristic dread of offending the slaveholders, these poor, white mechanics in Mr. Gardiner's ship-yard—instead of applying the natural, honest remedy for the apprehended evil, and objecting at once to work there by the side of slaves—made a cowardly attack upon the free colored mechanics, saying they were eating the bread which should be eaten by American freemen, and swearing that they would not work with them. The feeling was, really, against having their labor brought into competition with that of the colored people at all; but it was too much to strike directly at the interest of the slaveholders; and, therefore proving their servility and cowardice they dealt their blows on the poor, colored freeman, and aimed to prevent him from serving himself, in the evening of life, with the trade with which he had served his master, during the more vigorous portion of his days. Had they succeeded in driving the black freemen out of the ship-yard, they would have determined also upon the removal of the black slaves. The feeling was very bitter toward all colored people in Baltimore, about this time (1836), and they—free and slave suffered all manner of insult and wrong.

Until a very little before I went there, white and black ship carpenters worked side by side, in the ship yards of Mr. Gardiner, Mr. Duncan, Mr. Walter Price, and Mr. Robb. Nobody seemed to see any impropriety in it. To outward seeming, all hands were well satisfied. Some of the blacks were first rate workmen, and were given jobs requiring highest skill. All at once, however, the white carpenters knocked off, and swore that they would no longer work on the same stage with free Negroes. Taking advantage of the heavy contract resting upon Mr. Gardiner, to have the war vessels for Mexico ready to launch in July, and of the difficulty of getting other hands at that season of the year, they swore they would not strike another blow for him, unless he would discharge his free colored workmen.

Now, although this movement did not extend to me, in form, it did reach me, in fact. The spirit which it awakened was one of malice and bitterness, toward colored people generally, and I suffered with the rest, and suffered severely. My fellow apprentices very soon began to feel it to be degrading to work with me. They began to put on high looks, and to talk contemptuously and maliciously of "the Niggers;" saying, that "they would take the country," that "they ought to be killed." Encouraged by the cowardly workmen, who, knowing me to be a slave, made no issue with Mr. Gardiner about my being there, these young men did their utmost to make it impossible for me to stay. They seldom called me to do any thing, without coupling the call with a curse, and Edward North, the biggest in every thing, rascality included, ventured to strike me, whereupon I picked him up, and threw him into the dock. Whenever any of them struck me, I struck back again, regardless of consequences. I could manage any of them singly, and, while I could keep them from combining, I succeeded very well. In the conflict which ended my stay at Mr. Gardiner's, I was beset by four of them at once—Ned North, Ned Hays, Bill Stewart, and Tom Humphreys. Two of them were as large as myself, and they came near killing me, in broad day light. The attack was made suddenly, and simultaneously. One came in front, armed with a brick; there was one at each side, and one behind, and they closed up around me. I was struck on all sides; and, while I was attending to those in front, I received a blow on my head, from behind, dealt with a heavy hand-spike. I was completely stunned by the blow, and fell, heavily, on the ground, among the timbers. Taking advantage of my fall, they rushed upon me, and began to pound me with their fists. I let them lay on, for a while, after I came to myself, with a view of gaining strength. They did me little damage, so far; but, finally, getting tired of that sport, I gave a sudden surge, and, despite their weight, I rose to my hands and knees. Just as I did this, one of their number (I know not which) planted a blow with his boot in my left eye, which, for a time, seemed to have burst my eyeball. When they saw my eye completely closed, my face covered with blood, and I staggering under the stunning blows they had given me, they left me. As soon as I gathered sufficient strength, I picked up the hand-spike, and, madly enough, attempted to pursue them; but here the carpenters interfered, and compelled me to give up my frenzied pursuit. It was impossible to stand against so many.

Dear reader, you can hardly believe the statement, but it is true, and, therefore, I write it down: not fewer than fifty white men stood by, and saw this brutal and shameless outrage committed, and not a man of them all interposed a single word of mercy. There were four against one, and that one's face was beaten and battered most horribly, and no one said, "that is enough;" but some cried out, "Kill him—kill him—kill the d—d nigger! knock his brains out—he struck a white person." I mention this inhuman outcry, to show the character of the men, and the spirit of the times, at Gardiner's ship yard, and, indeed, in Baltimore generally, in 1836. As I look back to this period, I am almost amazed that I was not murdered outright, in that ship yard, so murderous was the spirit which prevailed there. On two occasions, while there, I came near losing my life. I was driving bolts in the hold, through the keelson, with Hays. In its course, the bolt bent. Hays cursed me, and said that it was my blow which bent the bolt. I denied this, and charged it upon him. In a fit of rage he seized an adze, and darted toward me. I met him with a maul, and parried his blow, or I should have then lost my life. A son of old Tom Lanman (the latter's double murder I have elsewhere charged upon him), in the spirit of his miserable father, made an assault upon me, but the blow with his maul missed me. After the united assault of North, Stewart, Hays and Humphreys, finding that the carpenters were as bitter toward me as the apprentices, and that the latter were probably set on by the former, I found my only chances for life was in flight. I succeeded in getting away, without an additional blow. To strike a white man, was death, by Lynch law, in Gardiner's ship yard; nor was there much of any other law toward colored people, at that time, in any other part of Maryland. The whole sentiment of Baltimore was murderous.

After making my escape from the ship yard, I went straight home, and related the story of the outrage to Master Hugh Auld; and it is due to him to say, that his conduct—though he was not a religious man—was every way more humane than that of his brother, Thomas, when I went to the latter in a somewhat similar plight, from the hands of "Brother Edward Covey." He listened attentively to my narration of the circumstances leading to the ruffianly outrage, and gave many proofs of his strong indignation at what was done. Hugh was a rough, but manly-hearted fellow, and, at this time, his best nature showed itself.

The heart of my once almost over-kind mistress, Sophia, was again melted in pity toward me. My puffed-out eye, and my scarred and blood-covered face, moved the dear lady to tears. She kindly drew a chair by me, and with friendly, consoling words, she took water, and washed the blood from my face. No mother's hand could have been more tender than hers. She bound up my head, and covered my wounded eye with a lean piece of fresh beef. It was almost compensation for the murderous assault, and my suffering, that it furnished and occasion for the manifestation, once more, of the orignally(sic) characteristic kindness of my mistress. Her affectionate heart was not yet dead, though much hardened by time and by circumstances.

As for Master Hugh's part, as I have said, he was furious about it; and he gave expression to his fury in the usual forms of speech in that locality. He poured curses on the heads of the whole ship yard company, and swore that he would have satisfaction for the outrage. His indignation was really strong and healthy; but, unfortunately, it resulted from the thought that his rights of property, in my person, had not been respected, more than from any sense of the outrage committed on me as a man. I inferred as much as this, from the fact that he could, himself, beat and mangle when it suited him to do so. Bent on having satisfaction, as he said, just as soon as I got a little the better of my bruises, Master Hugh took me to Esquire Watson's office, on Bond street, Fell's Point, with a view to procuring the arrest of those who had assaulted me. He related the outrage to the magistrate, as I had related it to him, and seemed to expect that a warrant would, at once, be issued for the arrest of the lawless ruffians. Mr. Watson heard it all, and instead of drawing up his warrant, he inquired.—

"Mr. Auld, who saw this assault of which you speak?"

"It was done, sir, in the presence of a ship yard full of hands."

"Sir," said Watson, "I am sorry, but I cannot move in this matter except upon the oath of white witnesses."

"But here's the boy; look at his head and face," said the excited Master Hugh; "they show what has been done."

But Watson insisted that he was not authorized to do anything, unless white witnesses of the transaction would come forward, and testify to what had taken place. He could issue no warrant on my word, against white persons; and, if I had been killed in the presence of a thousand blacks, their testimony, combined would have been insufficient to arrest a single murderer. Master Hugh, for once, was compelled to say, that this state of things was too bad; and he left the office of the magistrate, disgusted.

Of course, it was impossible to get any white man to testify against my assailants. The carpenters saw what was done; but the actors were but the agents of their malice, and only what the carpenters sanctioned. They had cried, with one accord, "Kill the nigger!" "Kill the nigger!" Even those who may have pitied me, if any such were among them, lacked the moral courage to come and volunteer their evidence. The slightest manifestation of sympathy or justice toward a person of color, was denounced as abolitionism; and the name of abolitionist, subjected its bearer to frightful liabilities. "D—n abolitionists," and "Kill the niggers," were the watch-words of the foul-mouthed ruffians of those days. Nothing was done, and probably there would not have been any thing done, had I been killed in the affray. The laws and the morals of the Christian city of Baltimore, afforded no protection to the sable denizens of that city.

Master Hugh, on finding he could get no redress for the cruel wrong, withdrew me from the employment of Mr. Gardiner, and took me into his own family, Mrs. Auld kindly taking care of me, and dressing my wounds, until they were healed, and I was ready to go again to work. While I was on the Eastern Shore, Master Hugh had met with reverses, which overthrew his business; and he had given up ship building in his own yard, on the City Block, and was now acting as foreman of Mr. Walter Price. The best he could now do for me, was to take me into Mr. Price's yard, and afford me the facilities there, for completing the trade which I had began to learn at Gardiner's. Here I rapidly became expert in the use of my calking tools; and, in the course of a single year, I was able to command the highest wages paid to journeymen calkers in Baltimore.

The reader will observe that I was now of some pecuniary value to my master. During the busy season, I was bringing six and seven dollars per week. I have, sometimes, brought him as much as nine dollars a week, for the wages were a dollar and a half per day.

After learning to calk, I sought my own employment, made my own contracts, and collected my own earnings; giving Master Hugh no trouble in any part of the transactions to which I was a party.

Here, then, were better days for the Eastern Shore slave. I was now free from the vexatious assalts(sic) of the apprentices at Mr. Gardiner's; and free from the perils of plantation life, and once more in a favorable condition to increase my little stock of education, which had been at a dead stand since my removal from Baltimore. I had, on the Eastern Shore, been only a teacher, when in company with other slaves, but now there were colored persons who could instruct me. Many of the young calkers could read, write and cipher. Some of them had high notions about mental improvement; and the free ones, on Fell's Point, organized what they called the "East Baltimore Mental Improvement Society." To this society, notwithstanding it was intended that only free persons should attach themselves, I was admitted, and was, several times, assigned a prominent part in its debates. I owe much to the society of these young men.

The reader already knows enough of the ill effects of good treatment on a slave, to anticipate what was now the case in my improved condition. It was not long before I began to show signs of disquiet with slavery, and to look around for means to get out of that condition by the shortest route. I was living among free men; and was, in all respects, equal to them by nature and by attainments. Why should I be a slave? There was no reason why I should be the thrall of any man.

Besides, I was now getting—as I have said—a dollar and fifty cents per day. I contracted for it, worked for it, earned it, collected it; it was paid to me, and it was rightfully my own; and yet, upon every returning Saturday night, this money—my own hard earnings, every cent of it—was demanded of me, and taken from me by Master Hugh. He did not earn it; he had no hand in earning it; why, then, should he have it? I owed him nothing. He had given me no schooling, and I had received from him only my food and raiment; and for these, my services were supposed to pay, from the first. The right to take my earnings, was the right of the robber. He had the power to compel me to give him the fruits of my labor, and this power was his only right in the case. I became more and more dissatisfied with this state of things; and, in so becoming, I only gave proof of the same human nature which every reader of this chapter in my life—slaveholder, or nonslaveholder—is conscious of possessing.

To make a contented slave, you must make a thoughtless one. It is necessary to darken his moral and mental vision, and, as far as possible, to annihilate his power of reason. He must be able to detect no inconsistencies in slavery. The man that takes his earnings, must be able to convince him that he has a perfect right to do so. It must not depend upon mere force; the slave must know no Higher Law than his master's will. The whole relationship must not only demonstrate, to his mind, its necessity, but its absolute rightfulness. If there be one crevice through which a single drop can fall, it will certainly rust off the slave's chain.

CHAPTER XXI. My Escape from Slavery

CLOSING INCIDENTS OF "MY LIFE AS A SLAVE"—REASONS WHY FULL PARTICULARS
OF THE MANNER OF MY ESCAPE WILL NOT BE GIVEN—CRAFTINESS AND MALICE OF

SLAVEHOLDERS—SUSPICION OF AIDING A SLAVE'S ESCAPE ABOUT AS DANGEROUS AS POSITIVE EVIDENCE—WANT OF WISDOM SHOWN IN PUBLISHING DETAILS OF THE ESCAPE OF THE FUGITIVES—PUBLISHED ACCOUNTS REACH THE MASTERS, NOT THE SLAVES—SLAVEHOLDERS STIMULATED TO GREATER WATCHFULNESS—MY CONDITION—DISCONTENT—SUSPICIONS IMPLIED BY MASTER HUGH'S MANNER, WHEN RECEIVING MY WAGES—HIS OCCASIONAL GENEROSITY!—DIFFICULTIES IN THE WAY OF ESCAPE—EVERY AVENUE GUARDED—PLAN TO OBTAIN MONEY—I AM ALLOWED TO HIRE MY TIME—A GLEAM OF HOPE—ATTENDS CAMP-MEETING, WITHOUT PERMISSION—ANGER OF MASTER HUGH THEREAT—THE RESULT—MY PLANS OF ESCAPE ACCELERATED THERBY—THE DAY FOR MY DEPARTURE FIXED—HARASSED BY DOUBTS AND FEARS—PAINFUL THOUGHTS OF SEPARATION FROM FRIENDS—THE ATTEMPT MADE—ITS SUCCESS.

I will now make the kind reader acquainted with the closing incidents of my "Life as a Slave," having already trenched upon the limit allotted to my "Life as a Freeman." Before, however, proceeding with this narration, it is, perhaps, proper that I should frankly state, in advance, my intention to withhold a part of the(sic) connected with my escape from slavery. There are reasons for this suppression, which I trust the reader will deem altogether valid. It may be easily conceived, that a full and complete statement of all facts pertaining to the flight of a bondman, might implicate and embarrass some who may have, wittingly or unwittingly, assisted him; and no one can wish me to involve any man or woman who has befriended me, even in the liability of embarrassment or trouble.

Keen is the scent of the slaveholder; like the fangs of the rattlesnake, his malice retains its poison long; and, although it is now nearly seventeen years since I made my escape, it is well to be careful, in dealing with the circumstances relating to it. Were I to give but a shadowy outline of the process adopted, with characteristic aptitude, the crafty and malicious among the slaveholders might, possibly, hit upon the track I pursued, and involve some one in suspicion which, in a slave state, is about as bad as positive evidence. The colored man, there, must not only shun evil, but shun the very appearance of evil, or be condemned as a criminal. A slaveholding community has a peculiar taste for ferreting out offenses against the slave system, justice there being more sensitive in its regard for the peculiar rights of this system, than for any other interest or institution. By stringing together a train of events and circumstances, even if I were not very explicit, the means of escape might be ascertained, and, possibly, those means be rendered, thereafter, no longer available to the liberty-seeking children of bondage I have left behind me. No antislavery man can wish me to do anything favoring such results, and no slaveholding reader has any right to expect the impartment of such information.

While, therefore, it would afford me pleasure, and perhaps would materially add to the interest of my story, were I at liberty to gratify a curiosity which I know to exist in the minds of many, as to the manner of my escape, I must deprive myself of this pleasure, and the curious of the gratification, which such a statement of facts would afford. I would allow myself to suffer under the greatest imputations that evil minded men might suggest, rather than exculpate myself by explanation, and thereby run the hazards of closing the slightest avenue by which a brother in suffering might clear himself of the chains and fetters of slavery.

The practice of publishing every new invention by which a slave is known to have escaped from slavery, has neither wisdom nor necessity to sustain it. Had not Henry Box Brown and his friends attracted slaveholding attention to the manner of his escape, we might have had a thousand Box Browns per annum. The singularly original plan adopted by William and Ellen Crafts, perished with the first using, because every slaveholder in the land was apprised of it. The salt water slave who hung in the guards of a steamer, being washed three days and three nights—like another Jonah—by the waves of the sea, has, by the publicity given to the circumstance, set a spy on the guards of every steamer departing from southern ports.

I have never approved of the very public manner, in which some of our western friends have conducted what they call the "Under-ground Railroad," but which, I think, by their open declarations, has been made, most emphatically, the "Upper-ground Railroad." Its stations are far better known to the slaveholders than to the slaves. I honor those good men and women for their noble daring, in willingly subjecting themselves to persecution, by openly avowing their participation in the escape of slaves; nevertheless, the good resulting from such avowals, is of a very questionable character. It may kindle an enthusiasm, very pleasant to inhale; but that is of no practical benefit to themselves, nor to the slaves escaping. Nothing is more evident, than that such disclosures are a positive evil to the slaves remaining, and seeking to escape. In publishing such accounts, the anti-slavery man addresses the slaveholder, not the slave; he stimulates the former to greater watchfulness, and adds to his facilities for capturing his slave. We owe something to the slaves, south of Mason and Dixon's line, as well as to those north of it; and, in discharging the duty of aiding the latter, on their way to freedom, we should be careful to do nothing which would be likely to hinder the former, in making their escape from slavery. Such is my detestation of slavery, that I would keep the merciless slaveholder profoundly ignorant of the means of flight adopted by the slave. He should be left to imagine himself surrounded by myriads of invisible tormentors, ever ready to snatch, from his infernal grasp, his trembling prey. In pursuing his victim, let him be left to feel his way in the dark; let shades of darkness, commensurate with his crime, shut every ray of light from his pathway; and let him be made to feel that, that, at every step he takes, with the hellish purpose of reducing a brother man to slavery, he is running the frightful risk of having his hot brains dashed out by an invisible hand.

But, enough of this. I will now proceed to the statement of those facts, connected with my escape, for which I am alone responsible, and for which no one can be made to suffer but myself.

My condition in the year (1838) of my escape, was, comparatively, a free and easy one, so far, at least, as the wants of the physical man were concerned; but the reader will bear in mind, that my troubles from the beginning, have been less physical than mental, and he will thus be prepared to find, after what is narrated in the previous chapters, that slave life was adding nothing to its charms for me, as I grew older, and became better acquainted with it. The practice, from week to week, of openly robbing me of all my earnings, kept the nature and character of slavery constantly before me. I could be robbed by indirection, but this was too open and barefaced to be endured. I could see no reason why I should, at the end of each week, pour the reward of my honest toil into the purse of any man. The thought itself vexed me, and the manner in which Master Hugh received my wages, vexed me more than the original wrong. Carefully counting the money and rolling it out, dollar by dollar, he would look me in the face, as if he would search my heart as well as my pocket, and reproachfully ask me, "Is that all?"—implying that I had, perhaps, kept back part of my wages; or, if not so, the demand was made, possibly, to make me feel, that, after all, I was an "unprofitable servant." Draining me of the last cent of my hard earnings, he would, however, occasionally— when I brought home an extra large sum—dole out to me a sixpence or a shilling, with a view, perhaps, of kindling up my gratitude; but this practice had the opposite effect—it was an admission of my right to the whole sum. The fact, that he gave me any part of my wages, was proof that he suspected that I had a right to the whole of them. I always felt uncomfortable, after having received anything in this way, for I feared that the giving me a few cents, might, possibly, ease his conscience, and make him feel himself a pretty honorable robber, after all! Held to a strict account, and kept under a close watch—the old suspicion of my running away not having been entirely removed—escape from slavery, even in Baltimore, was very difficult. The railroad from Baltimore to Philadelphia was under regulations so stringent, that even free colored travelers were almost excluded. They must have free papers; they must be measured and carefully examined, before they were allowed to enter the cars; they only went in the day time, even when so examined. The steamboats were under regulations equally stringent. All the great turnpikes, leading northward, were beset with kidnappers, a class of men who watched the newspapers for advertisements for runaway slaves, making their living by the accursed reward of slave hunting.

My discontent grew upon me, and I was on the look-out for means of escape. With money, I could easily have managed the matter, and, therefore, I hit upon the plan of soliciting the privilege of hiring my time. It is quite common, in Baltimore, to allow slaves this privilege, and it is the practice, also, in New Orleans. A slave who is considered trustworthy, can, by paying his master a definite sum regularly, at the end of each week, dispose of his time as he likes. It so happened that I was not in very good odor, and I was far from being a trustworthy slave. Nevertheless, I watched my opportunity when Master Thomas came to Baltimore (for I was still his property, Hugh only acted as his agent) in the spring of 1838, to purchase his spring supply of goods, and applied to him, directly, for the much-coveted privilege of hiring my time. This request Master Thomas unhesitatingly refused to grant; and he charged me, with some sternness, with inventing this stratagem to make my escape. He told me, "I could go nowhere but he could catch me; and, in the event of my running away, I might be assured he should spare no pains in his efforts to recapture me." He recounted, with a good deal of eloquence, the many kind offices he had done me, and exhorted me to be contented and obedient. "Lay out no plans for the future," said he. "If you behave yourself properly, I will take care of you." Now, kind and considerate as this offer was, it failed to soothe me into repose. In spite of Master Thomas, and, I may say, in spite of myself, also, I continued to think, and worse still, to think almost exclusively about the injustice and wickedness of slavery. No effort of mine or of his could silence this trouble-giving thought, or change my purpose to run away.

About two months after applying to Master Thomas for the privilege of hiring my time, I applied to Master Hugh for the same liberty, supposing him to be unacquainted with the fact that I had made a similar application to Master Thomas, and had been refused. My boldness in making this request, fairly astounded him at the first. He gazed at me in amazement. But I had many good reasons for pressing the matter; and, after listening to them awhile, he did not absolutely refuse, but told me he would think of it. Here, then, was a gleam of hope. Once master of my own time, I felt sure that I could make, over and above my obligation to him, a dollar or two every week. Some slaves have made enough, in this way, to purchase their freedom. It is a sharp spur to industry; and some of the most enterprising colored men in Baltimore hire themselves in this way. After mature reflection—as I must suppose it was Master Hugh granted me the privilege in question, on the following terms: I was to be allowed all my time; to make all bargains for work; to find my own employment, and to collect my own wages; and, in return for this liberty, I was required, or obliged, to pay him three dollars at the end of each week, and to board and clothe myself, and buy my own calking tools. A failure in any of these particulars would put an end to my privilege. This was a hard bargain. The wear and tear of clothing, the losing and breaking of tools, and the expense of board, made it necessary for me to earn at least six dollars per week, to keep even with the world. All who are acquainted with calking, know how uncertain and irregular that employment is. It can be done to advantage only in dry weather, for it is useless to put wet oakum into a seam. Rain or shine, however, work or no work, at the end of each week the money must be forthcoming.

Master Hugh seemed to be very much pleased, for a time, with this arrangement; and well he might be, for it was decidedly in his favor. It relieved him of all anxiety concerning me. His money was sure. He had armed my love of liberty with a lash and a driver, far more efficient than any I had before known; and, while he derived all the benefits of slaveholding by the arrangement, without its evils, I endured all the evils of being a slave, and yet suffered all the care and anxiety of a responsible freeman. "Nevertheless," thought I, "it is a valuable privilege another step in my career toward freedom." It was something even to be permitted to stagger under the disadvantages of liberty, and I was determined to hold on to the newly gained footing, by all proper industry. I was ready to work by night as well as by day; and being in the enjoyment of excellent health, I was able not only to meet my current expenses, but also to lay by a small sum at the end of each week. All went on thus, from the month of May till August; then—for reasons which will become apparent as I proceed—my much valued liberty was wrested from me.

During the week previous to this (to me) calamitous event, I had made arrangements with a few young friends, to accompany them, on Saturday night, to a camp-meeting, held about twelve miles from Baltimore. On the evening of our intended start for the camp-ground, something occurred in the ship yard where I was at work, which detained me unusually late, and compelled me either to disappoint my young friends, or to neglect carrying my weekly dues to Master Hugh. Knowing that I had the money, and could hand it to him on another day, I decided to go to camp-meeting, and to pay him the three dollars, for the past week, on my return. Once on the camp-ground, I was induced to remain one day longer than I had intended, when I left home. But, as soon as I returned, I went straight to his house on Fell street, to hand him his (my) money. Unhappily, the fatal mistake had been committed. I found him exceedingly angry. He exhibited all the signs of apprehension and wrath, which a slaveholder may be surmised to exhibit on the supposed escape of a favorite slave. "You rascal! I have a great mind to give you a severe whipping. How dare you go out of the city without first asking and obtaining my permission?" "Sir," said I, "I hired my time and paid you the price you asked for it. I did not know that it was any part of the bargain that I should ask you when or where I should go."

"You did not know, you rascal! You are bound to show yourself here every Saturday night." After reflecting, a few moments, he became somewhat cooled down; but, evidently greatly troubled, he said, "Now, you scoundrel! you have done for yourself; you shall hire your time no longer. The next thing I shall hear of, will be your running away. Bring home your tools and your clothes, at once. I'll teach you how to go off in this way."

Thus ended my partial freedom. I could hire my time no longer; and I obeyed my master's orders at once. The little taste of liberty which I had had—although as the reader will have seen, it was far from being unalloyed—by no means enhanced my contentment with slavery. Punished thus by Master Hugh, it was now my turn to punish him. "Since," thought I, "you will make a slave of me, I will await your orders in all things;" and, instead of going to look for work on Monday morning, as I had formerly done, I remained at home during the entire week, without the performance of a single stroke of work. Saturday night came, and he called upon me, as usual, for my wages. I, of course, told him I had done no work, and had no wages. Here we were at the point of coming to blows. His wrath had been accumulating during the whole week; for he evidently saw that I was making no effort to get work, but was most aggravatingly awaiting his orders, in all things. As I look back to this behavior of mine, I scarcely know what possessed me, thus to trifle with those who had such unlimited power to bless or to blast me. Master Hugh raved and swore his determination to "get hold of me;" but, wisely for him, and happily for me, his wrath only employed those very harmless, impalpable missiles, which roll from a limber tongue. In my desperation, I had fully made up my mind to measure strength with Master Hugh, in case he should undertake to execute his threats. I am glad there was no necessity for this; for resistance to him could not have ended so happily for me, as it did in the case of Covey. He was not a man to be safely resisted by a slave; and I freely own, that in my conduct toward him, in this instance, there was more folly than wisdom. Master Hugh closed his reproofs, by telling me that, hereafter, I need give myself no uneasiness about getting work; that he "would, himself, see to getting work for me, and enough of it, at that." This threat I confess had some terror in it; and, on thinking the matter over, during the Sunday, I resolved, not only to save him the trouble of getting me work, but that, upon the third day of September, I would attempt to make my escape from slavery. The refusal to allow me to hire my time, therefore, hastened the period of flight. I had three weeks, now, in which to prepare for my journey.

Once resolved, I felt a certain degree of repose, and on Monday, instead of waiting for Master Hugh to seek employment for me, I was up by break of day, and off to the ship yard of Mr. Butler, on the City Block, near the draw-bridge. I was a favorite with Mr. B., and, young as I was, I had served as his foreman on the float stage, at calking. Of course, I easily obtained work, and, at the end of the week—which by the way was exceedingly fine I brought Master Hugh nearly nine dollars. The effect of this mark of returning good sense, on my part, was excellent. He was very much pleased; he took the money, commended me, and told me I might have done the same thing the week before. It is a blessed thing that the tyrant may not always know the thoughts and purposes of his victim. Master Hugh little knew what my plans were. The going to camp-meeting without asking his permission—the insolent answers made to his reproaches—the sulky deportment the week after being deprived of the privilege of hiring my time—had awakened in him the suspicion that I might be cherishing disloyal purposes. My object, therefore, in working steadily, was to remove suspicion, and in this I succeeded admirably. He probably thought I was never better satisfied with my condition, than at the very time I was planning my escape. The second week passed, and again I carried him my full week's wages—nine dollars; and so well pleased was he, that he gave me TWENTY-FIVE CENTS! and "bade me make good use of it!" I told him I would, for one of the uses to which I meant to put it, was to pay my fare on the underground railroad.

Things without went on as usual; but I was passing through the same internal excitement and anxiety which I had experienced two years and a half before. The failure, in that instance, was not calculated to increase my confidence in the success of this, my second attempt; and I knew that a second failure could not leave me where my first did—I must either get to the far north, or be sent to the far south. Besides the exercise of mind from this state of facts, I had the painful sensation of being about to separate from a circle of honest and warm hearted friends, in Baltimore. The thought of such a separation, where the hope of ever meeting again is excluded, and where there can be no correspondence, is very painful. It is my opinion, that thousands would escape from slavery who now remain there, but for the strong cords of affection that bind them to their families, relatives and friends. The daughter is hindered from escaping, by the love she bears her mother, and the father, by the love he bears his children; and so, to the end of the chapter. I had no relations in Baltimore, and I saw no probability of ever living in the neighborhood of sisters and brothers; but the thought of leaving my friends, was among the strongest obstacles to my running away. The last two days of the week— Friday and Saturday—were spent mostly in collecting my things together, for my journey. Having worked four days that week, for my master, I handed him six dollars, on Saturday night. I seldom spent my Sundays at home; and, for fear that something might be discovered in my conduct, I kept up my custom, and absented myself all day. On Monday, the third day of September, 1838, in accordance with my resolution, I bade farewell to the city of Baltimore, and to that slavery which had been my abhorrence from childhood.

How I got away—in what direction I traveled—whether by land or by water; whether with or without assistance—must, for reasons already mentioned, remain unexplained.

LIFE as a FREEMAN

CHAPTER XXII. Liberty Attained

TRANSITION FROM SLAVERY TO FREEDOM—A WANDERER IN NEW YORK—FEELINGS
ON REACHING THAT CITY—AN OLD ACQUAINTANCE MET—UNFAVORABLE
IMPRESSIONS—LONELINESS AND INSECURITY—APOLOGY FOR SLAVES WHO RETURN
TO THEIR MASTERS—COMPELLED TO TELL MY CONDITION—SUCCORED BY A
SAILOR—DAVID RUGGLES—THE UNDERGROUND RAILROAD—MARRIAGE—BAGGAGE TAKEN
FROM ME—KINDNESS OF NATHAN JOHNSON—MY CHANGE OF NAME—DARK NOTIONS OF
NORTHERN CIVILIZATION—THE CONTRAST—COLORED PEOPLE IN NEW BEDFORD—AN
INCIDENT ILLUSTRATING THEIR SPIRIT—A COMMON LABORER—DENIED WORK AT
MY TRADE—THE FIRST WINTER AT THE NORTH—REPULSE AT THE DOORS OF THE
CHURCH—SANCTIFIED HATE—THE Liberator AND ITS EDITOR.

There is no necessity for any extended notice of the incidents of this part of my life. There is nothing very striking or peculiar about my career as a freeman, when viewed apart from my life as a slave. The relation subsisting between my early experience and that which I am now about to narrate, is, perhaps, my best apology for adding another chapter to this book.

Disappearing from the kind reader, in a flying cloud or balloon (pardon the figure), driven by the wind, and knowing not where I should land—whether in slavery or in freedom—it is proper that I should remove, at once, all anxiety, by frankly making known where I alighted. The flight was a bold and perilous one; but here I am, in the great city of New York, safe and sound, without loss of blood or bone. In less than a week after leaving Baltimore, I was walking amid the hurrying throng, and gazing upon the dazzling wonders of Broadway. The dreams of my childhood and the purposes of my manhood were now fulfilled. A free state around me, and a free earth under my feet! What a moment was this to me! A whole year was pressed into a single day. A new world burst upon my agitated vision. I have often been asked, by kind friends to whom I have told my story, how I felt when first I found myself beyond the limits of slavery; and I must say here, as I have often said to them, there is scarcely anything about which I could not give a more satisfactory answer. It was a moment of joyous excitement, which no words can describe. In a letter to a friend, written soon after reaching New York. I said I felt as one might be supposed to feel, on escaping from a den of hungry lions. But, in a moment like that, sensations are too intense and too rapid for words. Anguish and grief, like darkness and rain, may be described, but joy and gladness, like the rainbow of promise, defy alike the pen and pencil.

For ten or fifteen years I had been dragging a heavy chain, with a huge block attached to it, cumbering my every motion. I had felt myself doomed to drag this chain and this block through life. All efforts, before, to separate myself from the hateful encumbrance, had only seemed to rivet me the more firmly to it. Baffled and discouraged at times, I had asked myself the question, May not this, after all, be God's work? May He not, for wise ends, have doomed me to this lot? A contest had been going on in my mind for years, between the clear consciousness of right and the plausible errors of superstition; between the wisdom of manly courage, and the foolish weakness of timidity. The contest was now ended; the chain was severed; God and right stood vindicated. I was A FREEMAN, and the voice of peace and joy thrilled my heart.

Free and joyous, however, as I was, joy was not the only sensation I experienced. It was like the quick blaze, beautiful at the first, but which subsiding, leaves the building charred and desolate. I was soon taught that I was still in an enemy's land. A sense of loneliness and insecurity oppressed me sadly. I had been but a few hours in New York, before I was met in the streets by a fugitive slave, well known to me, and the information I got from him respecting New York, did nothing to lessen my apprehension of danger. The fugitive in question was "Allender's Jake," in Baltimore; but, said he, I am "WILLIAM DIXON," in New York! I knew Jake well, and knew when Tolly Allender and Mr. Price (for the latter employed Master Hugh as his foreman, in his shipyard on Fell's Point) made an attempt to recapture Jake, and failed. Jake told me all about his circumstances, and how narrowly he escaped being taken back to slavery; that the city was now full of southerners, returning from the springs; that the black people in New York were not to be trusted; that there were hired men on the lookout for fugitives from slavery, and who, for a few dollars, would betray me into the hands of the slave-catchers; that I must trust no man with my secret; that I must not think of going either on the wharves to work, or to a boarding-house to board; and, worse still, this same Jake told me it was not in his power to help me. He seemed, even while cautioning me, to be fearing lest, after all, I might be a party to a second attempt to recapture him. Under the inspiration of this thought, I must suppose it was, he gave signs of a wish to get rid of me, and soon left me his whitewash brush in hand—as he said, for his work. He was soon lost to sight among the throng, and I was alone again, an easy prey to the kidnappers, if any should happen to be on my track.

New York, seventeen years ago, was less a place of safety for a runaway slave than now, and all know how unsafe it now is, under the new fugitive slave bill. I was much troubled. I had very little money enough to buy me a few loaves of bread, but not enough to pay board, outside a lumber yard. I saw the wisdom of keeping away from the ship yards, for if Master Hugh pursued me, he would naturally expect to find me looking for work among the calkers. For a time, every door seemed closed against me. A sense of my loneliness and helplessness crept over me, and covered me with something bordering on despair. In the midst of thousands of my fellowmen, and yet a perfect stranger! In the midst of human brothers, and yet more fearful of them than of hungry wolves! I was without home, without friends, without work, without money, and without any definite knowledge of which way to go, or where to look for succor.

Some apology can easily be made for the few slaves who have, after making good their escape, turned back to slavery, preferring the actual rule of their masters, to the life of loneliness, apprehension, hunger, and anxiety, which meets them on their first arrival in a free state. It is difficult for a freeman to enter into the feelings of such fugitives. He cannot see things in the same light with the slave, because he does not, and cannot, look from the same point from which the slave does. "Why do you tremble," he says to the slave "you are in a free state;" but the difficulty is, in realizing that he is in a free state, the slave might reply. A freeman cannot understand why the slave-master's shadow is bigger, to the slave, than the might and majesty of a free state; but when he reflects that the slave knows more about the slavery of his master than he does of the might and majesty of the free state, he has the explanation. The slave has been all his life learning the power of his master—being trained to dread his approach—and only a few hours learning the power of the state. The master is to him a stern and flinty reality, but the state is little more than a dream. He has been accustomed to regard every white man as the friend of his master, and every colored man as more or less under the control of his master's friends—the white people. It takes stout nerves to stand up, in such circumstances. A man, homeless, shelterless, breadless, friendless, and moneyless, is not in a condition to assume a very proud or joyous tone; and in just this condition was I, while wandering about the streets of New York city and lodging, at least one night, among the barrels on one of its wharves. I was not only free from slavery, but I was free from home, as well. The reader will easily see that I had something more than the simple fact of being free to think of, in this extremity.

I kept my secret as long as I could, and at last was forced to go in search of an honest man—a man sufficiently human not to betray me into the hands of slave-catchers. I was not a bad reader of the human face, nor long in selecting the right man, when once compelled to disclose the facts of my condition to some one.

I found my man in the person of one who said his name was Stewart. He was a sailor, warm-hearted and generous, and he listened to my story with a brother's interest. I told him I was running for my freedom—knew not where to go—money almost gone—was hungry—thought it unsafe to go the shipyards for work, and needed a friend. Stewart promptly put me in the way of getting out of my trouble. He took me to his house, and went in search of the late David Ruggles, who was then the secretary of the New York Vigilance Committee, and a very active man in all anti-slavery works. Once in the hands of Mr. Ruggles, I was comparatively safe. I was hidden with Mr. Ruggles several days. In the meantime, my intended wife, Anna, came on from Baltimore—to whom I had written, informing her of my safe arrival at New York—and, in the presence of Mrs. Mitchell and Mr. Ruggles, we were married, by Rev. James W. C. Pennington.

Mr. Ruggles 7 was the first officer on the under-ground railroad with whom I met after reaching the north, and, indeed, the first of whom I ever heard anything. Learning that I was a calker by trade, he promptly decided that New Bedford was the proper place to send me. "Many ships," said he, "are there fitted out for the whaling business, and you may there find work at your trade, and make a good living." Thus, in one fortnight after my flight from Maryland, I was safe in New Bedford, regularly entered upon the exercise of the rights, responsibilities, and duties of a freeman.

I may mention a little circumstance which annoyed me on reaching New Bedford. I had not a cent of money, and lacked two dollars toward paying our fare from Newport, and our baggage not very costly—was taken by the stage driver, and held until I could raise the money to redeem it. This difficulty was soon surmounted. Mr. Nathan Johnson, to whom we had a line from Mr. Ruggles, not only received us kindly and hospitably, but, on being informed about our baggage, promptly loaned me two dollars with which to redeem my little property. I shall ever be deeply grateful, both to Mr. and Mrs. Nathan Johnson, for the lively interest they were pleased to take in me, in this hour of my extremest need. They not only gave myself and wife bread and shelter, but taught us how to begin to secure those benefits for ourselves. Long may they live, and may blessings attend them in this life and in that which is to come!

Once initiated into the new life of freedom, and assured by Mr. Johnson that New Bedford was a safe place, the comparatively unimportant matter, as to what should be my name, came up for considertion(sic). It was necessary to have a name in my new relations. The name given me by my beloved mother was no less pretentious than "Frederick Augustus Washington Bailey." I had, however, before leaving Maryland, dispensed with the Augustus Washington, and retained the name Frederick Bailey. Between Baltimore and New Bedford, however, I had several different names, the better to avoid being overhauled by the hunters, which I had good reason to believe would be put on my track. Among honest men an honest man may well be content with one name, and to acknowledge it at all times and in all places; but toward fugitives, Americans are not honest. When I arrived at New Bedford, my name was Johnson; and finding that the Johnson family in New Bedford were already quite numerous— sufficiently so to produce some confusion in attempts to distinguish one from another—there was the more reason for making another change in my name. In fact, "Johnson" had been assumed by nearly every slave who had arrived in New Bedford from Maryland, and this, much to the annoyance of the original "Johnsons" (of whom there were many) in that place. Mine host, unwilling to have another of his own name added to the community in this unauthorized way, after I spent a night and a day at his house, gave me my present name. He had been reading the "Lady of the Lake," and was pleased to regard me as a suitable person to wear this, one of Scotland's many famous names. Considering the noble hospitality and manly character of Nathan Johnson, I have felt that he, better than I, illustrated the virtues of the great Scottish chief. Sure I am, that had any slave-catcher entered his domicile, with a view to molest any one of his household, he would have shown himself like him of the "stalwart hand."

The reader will be amused at my ignorance, when I tell the notions I had of the state of northern wealth, enterprise, and civilization. Of wealth and refinement, I supposed the north had none. My Columbian Orator, which was almost my only book, had not done much to enlighten me concerning northern society. The impressions I had received were all wide of the truth. New Bedford, especially, took me by surprise, in the solid wealth and grandeur there exhibited. I had formed my notions respecting the social condition of the free states, by what I had seen and known of free, white, non-slaveholding people in the slave states. Regarding slavery as the basis of wealth, I fancied that no people could become very wealthy without slavery. A free white man, holding no slaves, in the country, I had known to be the most ignorant and poverty-stricken of men, and the laugh ing stock even of slaves themselves—called generally by them, in derision, "poor white trash." Like the non-slaveholders at the south, in holding no slaves, I suppose the northern people like them, also, in poverty and degradation. Judge, then, of my amazement and joy, when I found—as I did find—the very laboring population of New Bedford living in better houses, more elegantly furnished—surrounded by more comfort and refinement—than a majority of the slaveholders on the Eastern Shore of Maryland. There was my friend, Mr. Johnson, himself a colored man (who at the south would have been regarded as a proper marketable commodity), who lived in a better house—dined at a richer board—was the owner of more books—the reader of more newspapers—was more conversant with the political and social condition of this nation and the world—than nine-tenths of all the slaveholders of Talbot county, Maryland. Yet Mr. Johnson was a working man, and his hands were hardened by honest toil. Here, then, was something for observation and study. Whence the difference? The explanation was soon furnished, in the superiority of mind over simple brute force. Many pages might be given to the contrast, and in explanation of its causes. But an incident or two will suffice to show the reader as to how the mystery gradually vanished before me.

My first afternoon, on reaching New Bedford, was spent in visiting the wharves and viewing the shipping. The sight of the broad brim and the plain, Quaker dress, which met me at every turn, greatly increased my sense of freedom and security. "I am among the Quakers," thought I, "and am safe." Lying at the wharves and riding in the stream, were full-rigged ships of finest model, ready to start on whaling voyages. Upon the right and the left, I was walled in by large granite-fronted warehouses, crowded with the good things of this world. On the wharves, I saw industry without bustle, labor without noise, and heavy toil without the whip. There was no loud singing, as in southern ports, where ships are loading or unloading—no loud cursing or swearing—but everything went on as smoothly as the works of a well adjusted machine. How different was all this from the nosily fierce and clumsily absurd manner of labor-life in Baltimore and St. Michael's! One of the first incidents which illustrated the superior mental character of northern labor over that of the south, was the manner of unloading a ship's cargo of oil. In a southern port, twenty or thirty hands would have been employed to do what five or six did here, with the aid of a single ox attached to the end of a fall. Main strength, unassisted by skill, is slavery's method of labor. An old ox, worth eighty dollars, was doing, in New Bedford, what would have required fifteen thousand dollars worth of human bones and muscles to have performed in a southern port. I found that everything was done here with a scrupulous regard to economy, both in regard to men and things, time and strength. The maid servant, instead of spending at least a tenth part of her time in bringing and carrying water, as in Baltimore, had the pump at her elbow. The wood was dry, and snugly piled away for winter. Woodhouses, in-door pumps, sinks, drains, self-shutting gates, washing machines, pounding barrels, were all new things, and told me that I was among a thoughtful and sensible people. To the ship-repairing dock I went, and saw the same wise prudence. The carpenters struck where they aimed, and the calkers wasted no blows in idle flourishes of the mallet. I learned that men went from New Bedford to Baltimore, and bought old ships, and brought them here to repair, and made them better and more valuable than they ever were before. Men talked here of going whaling on a four years' voyage with more coolness than sailors where I came from talked of going a four months' voyage.

I now find that I could have landed in no part of the United States, where I should have found a more striking and gratifying contrast to the condition of the free people of color in Baltimore, than I found here in New Bedford. No colored man is really free in a slaveholding state. He wears the badge of bondage while nominally free, and is often subjected to hardships to which the slave is a stranger; but here in New Bedford, it was my good fortune to see a pretty near approach to freedom on the part of the colored people. I was taken all aback when Mr. Johnson—who lost no time in making me acquainted with the fact—told me that there was nothing in the constitution of Massachusetts to prevent a colored man from holding any office in the state. There, in New Bedford, the black man's children—although anti-slavery was then far from popular—went to school side by side with the white children, and apparently without objection from any quarter. To make me at home, Mr. Johnson assured me that no slaveholder could take a slave from New Bedford; that there were men there who would lay down their lives, before such an outrage could be perpetrated. The colored people themselves were of the best metal, and would fight for liberty to the death.

Soon after my arrival in New Bedford, I was told the following story, which was said to illustrate the spirit of the colored people in that goodly town: A colored man and a fugitive slave happened to have a little quarrel, and the former was heard to threaten the latter with informing his master of his whereabouts. As soon as this threat became known, a notice was read from the desk of what was then the only colored church in the place, stating that business of importance was to be then and there transacted. Special measures had been taken to secure the attendance of the would-be Judas, and had proved successful. Accordingly, at the hour appointed, the people came, and the betrayer also. All the usual formalities of public meetings were scrupulously gone through, even to the offering prayer for Divine direction in the duties of the occasion. The president himself performed this part of the ceremony, and I was told that he was unusually fervent. Yet, at the close of his prayer, the old man (one of the numerous family of Johnsons) rose from his knees, deliberately surveyed his audience, and then said, in a tone of solemn resolution, "Well, friends, we have got him here, and I would now recommend that you young men should just take him outside the door and kill him." With this, a large body of the congregation, who well understood the business they had come there to transact, made a rush at the villain, and doubtless would have killed him, had he not availed himself of an open sash, and made good his escape. He has never shown his head in New Bedford since that time. This little incident is perfectly characteristic of the spirit of the colored people in New Bedford. A slave could not be taken from that town seventeen years ago, any more than he could be so taken away now. The reason is, that the colored people in that city are educated up to the point of fighting for their freedom, as well as speaking for it.

Once assured of my safety in New Bedford, I put on the habiliments of a common laborer, and went on the wharf in search of work. I had no notion of living on the honest and generous sympathy of my colored brother, Johnson, or that of the abolitionists. My cry was like that of Hood's laborer, "Oh! only give me work." Happily for me, I was not long in searching. I found employment, the third day after my arrival in New Bedford, in stowing a sloop with a load of oil for the New York market. It was new, hard, and dirty work, even for a calker, but I went at it with a glad heart and a willing hand. I was now my own master—a tremendous fact—and the rapturous excitement with which I seized the job, may not easily be understood, except by some one with an experience like mine. The thoughts—"I can work! I can work for a living; I am not afraid of work; I have no Master Hugh to rob me of my earnings"—placed me in a state of independence, beyond seeking friendship or support of any man. That day's work I considered the real starting point of something like a new existence. Having finished this job and got my pay for the same, I went next in pursuit of a job at calking. It so happened that Mr. Rodney French, late mayor of the city of New Bedford, had a ship fitting out for sea, and to which there was a large job of calking and coppering to be done. I applied to that noblehearted man for employment, and he promptly told me to go to work; but going on the float-stage for the purpose, I was informed that every white man would leave the ship if I struck a blow upon her. "Well, well," thought I, "this is a hardship, but yet not a very serious one for me." The difference between the wages of a calker and that of a common day laborer, was an hundred per cent in favor of the former; but then I was free, and free to work, though not at my trade. I now prepared myself to do anything which came to hand in the way of turning an honest penny; sawed wood—dug cellars—shoveled coal—swept chimneys with Uncle Lucas Debuty—rolled oil casks on the wharves—helped to load and unload vessels—worked in Ricketson's candle works—in Richmond's brass foundery, and elsewhere; and thus supported myself and family for three years.

The first winter was unusually severe, in consequence of the high prices of food; but even during that winter we probably suffered less than many who had been free all their lives. During the hardest of the winter, I hired out for nine dolars(sic) a month; and out of this rented two rooms for nine dollars per quarter, and supplied my wife—who was unable to work—with food and some necessary articles of furniture. We were closely pinched to bring our wants within our means; but the jail stood over the way, and I had a wholesome dread of the consequences of running in debt. This winter past, and I was up with the times—got plenty of work—got well paid for it—and felt that I had not done a foolish thing to leave Master Hugh and Master Thomas. I was now living in a new world, and was wide awake to its advantages. I early began to attend the meetings of the colored people of New Bedford, and to take part in them. I was somewhat amazed to see colored men drawing up resolutions and offering them for consideration. Several colored young men of New Bedford, at that period, gave promise of great usefulness. They were educated, and possessed what seemed to me, at the time, very superior talents. Some of them have been cut down by death, and others have removed to different parts of the world, and some remain there now, and justify, in their present activities, my early impressions of them.

Among my first concerns on reaching New Bedford, was to become united with the church, for I had never given up, in reality, my religious faith. I had become lukewarm and in a backslidden state, but I was still convinced that it was my duty to join the Methodist church. I was not then aware of the powerful influence of that religious body in favor of the enslavement of my race, nor did I see how the northern churches could be responsible for the conduct of southern churches; neither did I fully understand how it could be my duty to remain separate from the church, because bad men were connected with it. The slaveholding church, with its Coveys, Weedens, Aulds, and Hopkins, I could see through at once, but I could not see how Elm Street church, in New Bedford, could be regarded as sanctioning the Christianity of these characters in the church at St. Michael's. I therefore resolved to join the Methodist church in New Bedford, and to enjoy the spiritual advantage of public worship. The minister of the Elm Street Methodist church, was the Rev. Mr. Bonney; and although I was not allowed a seat in the body of the house, and was proscribed on account of my color, regarding this proscription simply as an accommodation of the uncoverted congregation who had not yet been won to Christ and his brotherhood, I was willing thus to be proscribed, lest sinners should be driven away form the saving power of the gospel. Once converted, I thought they would be sure to treat me as a man and a brother. "Surely," thought I, "these Christian people have none of this feeling against color. They, at least, have renounced this unholy feeling." Judge, then, dear reader, of my astonishment and mortification, when I found, as soon I did find, all my charitable assumptions at fault.

An opportunity was soon afforded me for ascertaining the exact position of Elm Street church on that subject. I had a chance of seeing the religious part of the congregation by themselves; and although they disowned, in effect, their black brothers and sisters, before the world, I did think that where none but the saints were assembled, and no offense could be given to the wicked, and the gospel could not be "blamed," they would certainly recognize us as children of the same Father, and heirs of the same salvation, on equal terms with themselves.

The occasion to which I refer, was the sacrament of the Lord's Supper, that most sacred and most solemn of all the ordinances of the Christian church. Mr. Bonney had preached a very solemn and searching discourse, which really proved him to be acquainted with the inmost secrets(sic) of the human heart. At the close of his discourse, the congregation was dismissed, and the church remained to partake of the sacrament. I remained to see, as I thought, this holy sacrament celebrated in the spirit of its great Founder.

There were only about a half dozen colored members attached to the Elm Street church, at this time. After the congregation was dismissed, these descended from the gallery, and took a seat against the wall most distant from the altar. Brother Bonney was very animated, and sung very sweetly, "Salvation 'tis a joyful sound," and soon began to administer the sacrament. I was anxious to observe the bearing of the colored members, and the result was most humiliating. During the whole ceremony, they looked like sheep without a shepherd. The white members went forward to the altar by the bench full; and when it was evident that all the whites had been served with the bread and wine, Brother Bonney—pious Brother Bonney—after a long pause, as if inquiring whether all the whites members had been served, and fully assuring himself on that important point, then raised his voice to an unnatural pitch, and looking to the corner where his black sheep seemed penned, beckoned with his hand, exclaiming, "Come forward, colored friends! come forward! You, too, have an interest in the blood of Christ. God is no respecter of persons. Come forward, and take this holy sacrament to your comfort." The colored members poor, slavish souls went forward, as invited. I went out, and have never been in that church since, although I honestly went there with a view to joining that body. I found it impossible to respect the religious profession of any who were under the dominion of this wicked prejudice, and I could not, therefore, feel that in joining them, I was joining a Christian church, at all. I tried other churches in New Bedford, with the same result, and finally, I attached myself to a small body of colored Methodists, known as the Zion Methodists. Favored with the affection and confidence of the members of this humble communion, I was soon made a classleader and a local preacher among them. Many seasons of peace and joy I experienced among them, the remembrance of which is still precious, although I could not see it to be my duty to remain with that body, when I found that it consented to the same spirit which held my brethren in chains.

In four or five months after reaching New Bedford, there came a young man to me, with a copy of the Liberator, the paper edited by WILLIAM LLOYD GARRISON, and published by ISAAC KNAPP, and asked me to subscribe for it. I told him I had but just escaped from slavery, and was of course very poor, and remarked further, that I was unable to pay for it then; the agent, however, very willingly took me as a subscriber, and appeared to be much pleased with securing my name to his list. From this time I was brought in contact with the mind of William Lloyd Garrison. His paper took its place with me next to the bible.

The Liberator was a paper after my own heart. It detested slavery exposed hypocrisy and wickedness in high places—made no truce with the traffickers in the bodies and souls of men; it preached human brotherhood, denounced oppression, and, with all the solemnity of God's word, demanded the complete emancipation of my race. I not only liked—I loved this paper, and its editor. He seemed a match for all the oponents(sic) of emancipation, whether they spoke in the name of the law, or the gospel. His words were few, full of holy fire, and straight to the point. Learning to love him, through his paper, I was prepared to be pleased with his presence. Something of a hero worshiper, by nature, here was one, on first sight, to excite my love and reverence.

Seventeen years ago, few men possessed a more heavenly countenance than William Lloyd Garrison, and few men evinced a more genuine or a more exalted piety. The bible was his text book—held sacred, as the word of the Eternal Father—sinless perfection—complete submission to insults and injuries—literal obedience to the injunction, if smitten on one side to turn the other also. Not only was Sunday a Sabbath, but all days were Sabbaths, and to be kept holy. All sectarism false and mischievous—the regenerated, throughout the world, members of one body, and the HEAD Christ Jesus. Prejudice against color was rebellion against God. Of all men beneath the sky, the slaves, because most neglected and despised, were nearest and dearest to his great heart. Those ministers who defended slavery from the bible, were of their "father the devil"; and those churches which fellowshiped slaveholders as Christians, were synagogues of Satan, and our nation was a nation of liars. Never loud or noisy—calm and serene as a summer sky, and as pure. "You are the man, the Moses, raised up by God, to deliver his modern Israel from bondage," was the spontaneous feeling of my heart, as I sat away back in the hall and listened to his mighty words; mighty in truth—mighty in their simple earnestness.

I had not long been a reader of the Liberator, and listener to its editor, before I got a clear apprehension of the principles of the anti-slavery movement. I had already the spirit of the movement, and only needed to understand its principles and measures. These I got from the Liberator, and from those who believed in that paper. My acquaintance with the movement increased my hope for the ultimate freedom of my race, and I united with it from a sense of delight, as well as duty.

Every week the Liberator came, and every week I made myself master of its contents. All the anti-slavery meetings held in New Bedford I promptly attended, my heart burning at every true utterance against the slave system, and every rebuke of its friends and supporters. Thus passed the first three years of my residence in New Bedford. I had not then dreamed of the posibility(sic) of my becoming a public advocate of the cause so deeply imbedded in my heart. It was enough for me to listen—to receive and applaud the great words of others, and only whisper in private, among the white laborers on the wharves, and elsewhere, the truths which burned in my breast.

CHAPTER XXIII. Introduced to the Abolitionists

FIRST SPEECH AT NANTUCKET—MUCH SENSATION—EXTRAORDINARY SPEECH OF
MR. GARRISON—AUTHOR BECOMES A PUBLIC LECTURER—FOURTEEN YEARS EXPERIENCE—YOUTHFUL ENTHUSIASM—A BRAND NEW FACT—MATTER OF MY AUTHOR'S
SPEECH—COULD NOT FOLLOW THE PROGRAMME—FUGITIVE SLAVESHIP DOUBTED—TO
SETTLE ALL DOUBT I WRITE MY EXPERIENCE OF SLAVERY—DANGER OF RECAPTURE
INCREASED.

In the summer of 1841, a grand anti-slavery convention was held in Nantucket, under the auspices of Mr. Garrison and his friends. Until now, I had taken no holiday since my escape from slavery. Having worked very hard that spring and summer, in Richmond's brass foundery—sometimes working all night as well as all day—and needing a day or two of rest, I attended this convention, never supposing that I should take part in the proceedings. Indeed, I was not aware that any one connected with the convention even so much as knew my name. I was, however, quite mistaken. Mr. William C. Coffin, a prominent abolitionst(sic) in those days of trial, had heard me speaking to my colored friends, in the little school house on Second street, New Bedford, where we worshiped. He sought me out in the crowd, and invited me to say a few words to the convention. Thus sought out, and thus invited, I was induced to speak out the feelings inspired by the occasion, and the fresh recollection of the scenes through which I had passed as a slave. My speech on this occasion is about the only one I ever made, of which I do not remember a single connected sentence. It was with the utmost difficulty that I could stand erect, or that I could command and articulate two words without hesitation and stammering. I trembled in every limb. I am not sure that my embarrassment was not the most effective part of my speech, if speech it could be called. At any rate, this is about the only part of my performance that I now distinctly remember. But excited and convulsed as I was, the audience, though remarkably quiet before, became as much excited as myself. Mr. Garrison followed me, taking me as his text; and now, whether I had made an eloquent speech in behalf of freedom or not, his was one never to be forgotten by those who heard it. Those who had heard Mr. Garrison oftenest, and had known him longest, were astonished. It was an effort of unequaled power, sweeping down, like a very tornado, every opposing barrier, whether of sentiment or opinion. For a moment, he possessed that almost fabulous inspiration, often referred to but seldom attained, in which a public meeting is transformed, as it were, into a single individuality—the orator wielding a thousand heads and hearts at once, and by the simple majesty of his all controlling thought, converting his hearers into the express image of his own soul. That night there were at least one thousand Garrisonians in Nantucket! A(sic) the close of this great meeting, I was duly waited on by Mr. John A. Collins—then the general agent of the Massachusetts anti-slavery society—and urgently solicited by him to become an agent of that society, and to publicly advocate its anti-slavery principles. I was reluctant to take the proffered position. I had not been quite three years from slavery—was honestly distrustful of my ability—wished to be excused; publicity exposed me to discovery and arrest by my master; and other objections came up, but Mr. Collins was not to be put off, and I finally consented to go out for three months, for I supposed that I should have got to the end of my story and my usefulness, in that length of time.

Here opened upon me a new life a life for which I had had no preparation. I was a "graduate from the peculiar institution," Mr. Collins used to say, when introducing me, "with my diploma written on my back!" The three years of my freedom had been spent in the hard school of adversity. My hands had been furnished by nature with something like a solid leather coating, and I had bravely marked out for myself a life of rough labor, suited to the hardness of my hands, as a means of supporting myself and rearing my children.

Now what shall I say of this fourteen years' experience as a public advocate of the cause of my enslaved brothers and sisters? The time is but as a speck, yet large enough to justify a pause for retrospection—and a pause it must only be.

Young, ardent, and hopeful, I entered upon this new life in the full gush of unsuspecting enthusiasm. The cause was good; the men engaged in it were good; the means to attain its triumph, good; Heaven's blessing must attend all, and freedom must soon be given to the pining millions under a ruthless bondage. My whole heart went with the holy cause, and my most fervent prayer to the Almighty Disposer of the hearts of men, were continually offered for its early triumph. "Who or what," thought I, "can withstand a cause so good, so holy, so indescribably glorious. The God of Israel is with us. The might of the Eternal is on our side. Now let but the truth be spoken, and a nation will start forth at the sound!" In this enthusiastic spirit, I dropped into the ranks of freedom's friends, and went forth to the battle. For a time I was made to forget that my skin was dark and my hair crisped. For a time I regretted that I could not have shared the hardships and dangers endured by the earlier workers for the slave's release. I soon, however, found that my enthusiasm had been extravagant; that hardships and dangers were not yet passed; and that the life now before me, had shadows as well as sunbeams.

Among the first duties assigned me, on entering the ranks, was to travel, in company with Mr. George Foster, to secure subscribers to the Anti-slavery Standard and the Liberator. With him I traveled and lectured through the eastern counties of Massachusetts. Much interest was awakened—large meetings assembled. Many came, no doubt, from curiosity to hear what a Negro could say in his own cause. I was generally introduced as a "chattel"—a"thing"—a piece of southern "property"—the chairman assuring the audience that it could speak. Fugitive slaves, at that time, were not so plentiful as now; and as a fugitive slave lecturer, I had the advantage of being a "brand new fact"—the first one out. Up to that time, a colored man was deemed a fool who confessed himself a runaway slave, not only because of the danger to which he exposed himself of being retaken, but because it was a confession of a very low origin! Some of my colored friends in New Bedford thought very badly of my wisdom for thus exposing and degrading myself. The only precaution I took, at the beginning, to prevent Master Thomas from knowing where I was, and what I was about, was the withholding my former name, my master's name, and the name of the state and county from which I came. During the first three or four months, my speeches were almost exclusively made up of narrations of my own personal experience as a slave. "Let us have the facts," said the people. So also said Friend George Foster, who always wished to pin me down to my simple narrative. "Give us the facts," said Collins, "we will take care of the philosophy." Just here arose some embarrassment. It was impossible for me to repeat the same old story month after month, and to keep up my interest in it. It was new to the people, it is true, but it was an old story to me; and to go through with it night after night, was a task altogether too mechanical for my nature. "Tell your story, Frederick," would whisper my then revered friend, William Lloyd Garrison, as I stepped upon the platform. I could not always obey, for I was now reading and thinking. New views of the subject were presented to my mind. It did not entirely satisfy me to narrate wrongs; I felt like denouncing them. I could not always curb my moral indignation for the perpetrators of slaveholding villainy, long enough for a circumstantial statement of the facts which I felt almost everybody must know. Besides, I was growing, and needed room. "People won't believe you ever was a slave, Frederick, if you keep on this way," said Friend Foster. "Be yourself," said Collins, "and tell your story." It was said to me, "Better have a little of the plantation manner of speech than not; 'tis not best that you seem too learned." These excellent friends were actuated by the best of motives, and were not altogether wrong in their advice; and still I must speak just the word that seemed to me the word to be spoken by me.

At last the apprehended trouble came. People doubted if I had ever been a slave. They said I did not talk like a slave, look like a slave, nor act like a slave, and that they believed I had never been south of Mason and Dixon's line. "He don't tell us where he came from—what his master's name was—how he got away—nor the story of his experience. Besides, he is educated, and is, in this, a contradiction of all the facts we have concerning the ignorance of the slaves." Thus, I was in a pretty fair way to be denounced as an impostor. The committee of the Massachusetts anti-slavery society knew all the facts in my case, and agreed with me in the prudence of keeping them private. They, therefore, never doubted my being a genuine fugitive; but going down the aisles of the churches in which I spoke, and hearing the free spoken Yankees saying, repeatedly, "He's never been a slave, I'll warrant ye," I resolved to dispel all doubt, at no distant day, by such a revelation of facts as could not be made by any other than a genuine fugitive.

In a little less than four years, therefore, after becoming a public lecturer, I was induced to write out the leading facts connected with my experience in slavery, giving names of persons, places, and dates—thus putting it in the power of any who doubted, to ascertain the truth or falsehood of my story of being a fugitive slave. This statement soon became known in Maryland, and I had reason to believe that an effort would be made to recapture me.

It is not probable that any open attempt to secure me as a slave could have succeeded, further than the obtainment, by my master, of the money value of my bones and sinews. Fortunately for me, in the four years of my labors in the abolition cause, I had gained many friends, who would have suffered themselves to be taxed to almost any extent to save me from slavery. It was felt that I had committed the double offense of running away, and exposing the secrets and crimes of slavery and slaveholders. There was a double motive for seeking my reenslavement—avarice and vengeance; and while, as I have said, there was little probability of successful recapture, if attempted openly, I was constantly in danger of being spirited away, at a moment when my friends could render me no assistance. In traveling about from place to place—often alone I was much exposed to this sort of attack. Any one cherishing the design to betray me, could easily do so, by simply tracing my whereabouts through the anti-slavery journals, for my meetings and movements were promptly made known in advance. My true friends, Mr. Garrison and Mr. Phillips, had no faith in the power of Massachusetts to protect me in my right to liberty. Public sentiment and the law, in their opinion, would hand me over to the tormentors. Mr. Phillips, especially, considered me in danger, and said, when I showed him the manuscript of my story, if in my place, he would throw it into the fire. Thus, the reader will observe, the settling of one difficulty only opened the way for another; and that though I had reached a free state, and had attained position for public usefulness, I ws(sic) still tormented with the liability of losing my liberty. How this liability was dispelled, will be related, with other incidents, in the next chapter.

CHAPTER XXIV. Twenty-One Months in Great Britain

GOOD ARISING OUT OF UNPROPITIOUS EVENTS—DENIED CABIN PASSAGE—PROSCRIPTION TURNED TO GOOD ACCOUNT—THE HUTCHINSON FAMILY—THE
MOB ON BOARD THE "CAMBRIA"—HAPPY INTRODUCTION TO THE BRITISH PUBLIC—LETTER ADDRESSED TO WILLIAM LLOYD GARRISON—TIME AND LABORS WHILE ABROAD—FREEDOM PURCHASED—MRS. HENRY RICHARDSON—FREE
PAPERS—ABOLITIONISTS DISPLEASED WITH THE RANSOM—HOW MY ENERGIES
WERE DIRECTED—RECEPTION SPEECH IN LONDON—CHARACTER OF THE SPEECH
DEFENDED—CIRCUMSTANCES EXPLAINED—CAUSES CONTRIBUTING TO THE SUCCESS OF
MY MISSION—FREE CHURCH OF SCOTLAND—TESTIMONIAL.

The allotments of Providence, when coupled with trouble and anxiety, often conceal from finite vision the wisdom and goodness in which they are sent; and, frequently, what seemed a harsh and invidious dispensation, is converted by after experience into a happy and beneficial arrangement. Thus, the painful liability to be returned again to slavery, which haunted me by day, and troubled my dreams by night, proved to be a necessary step in the path of knowledge and usefulness. The writing of my pamphlet, in the spring of 1845, endangered my liberty, and led me to seek a refuge from republican slavery in monarchical England. A rude, uncultivated fugitive slave was driven, by stern necessity, to that country to which young American gentlemen go to increase their stock of knowledge, to seek pleasure, to have their rough, democratic manners softened by contact with English aristocratic refinement. On applying for a passage to England, on board the "Cambria", of the Cunard line, my friend, James N.

Buffum, of Lynn, Massachusetts, was informed that I could not be received on board as a cabin passenger. American prejudice against color triumphed over British liberality and civilization, and erected a color test and condition for crossing the sea in the cabin of a British vessel. The insult was keenly felt by my white friends, but to me, it was common, expected, and therefore, a thing of no great consequence, whether I went in the cabin or in the steerage. Moreover, I felt that if I could not go into the first cabin, first-cabin passengers could come into the second cabin, and the result justified my anticipations to the fullest extent. Indeed, I soon found myself an object of more general interest than I wished to be; and so far from being degraded by being placed in the second cabin, that part of the ship became the scene of as much pleasure and refinement, during the voyage, as the cabin itself. The Hutchinson Family, celebrated vocalists—fellow-passengers—often came to my rude forecastle deck, and sung their sweetest songs, enlivening the place with eloquent music, as well as spirited conversation, during the voyage. In two days after leaving Boston, one part of the ship was about as free to me as another. My fellow-passengers not only visited me, but invited me to visit them, on the saloon deck. My visits there, however, were but seldom. I preferred to live within my privileges, and keep upon my own premises. I found this quite as much in accordance with good policy, as with my own feelings. The effect was, that with the majority of the passengers, all color distinctions were flung to the winds, and I found myself treated with every mark of respect, from the beginning to the end of the voyage, except in a single instance; and in that, I came near being mobbed, for complying with an invitation given me by the passengers, and the captain of the "Cambria," to deliver a lecture on slavery. Our New Orleans and Georgia passengers were pleased to regard my lecture as an insult offered to them, and swore I should not speak. They went so far as to threaten to throw me overboard, and but for the firmness of Captain Judkins, probably would have (under the inspiration of slavery and brandy) attempted to put their threats into execution. I have no space to describe this scene, although its tragic and comic peculiarities are well worth describing. An end was put to the melee, by the captain's calling the ship's company to put the salt water mobocrats in irons. At this determined order, the gentlemen of the lash scampered, and for the rest of the voyage conducted themselves very decorously.

This incident of the voyage, in two days after landing at Liverpool, brought me at once before the British public, and that by no act of my own. The gentlemen so promptly snubbed in their meditated violence, flew to the press to justify their conduct, and to denounce me as a worthless and insolent Negro. This course was even less wise than the conduct it was intended to sustain; for, besides awakening something like a national interest in me, and securing me an audience, it brought out counter statements, and threw the blame upon themselves, which they had sought to fasten upon me and the gallant captain of the ship.

Some notion may be formed of the difference in my feelings and circumstances, while abroad, from the following extract from one of a series of letters addressed by me to Mr. Garrison, and published in the Liberator. It was written on the first day of January, 1846:

MY DEAR FRIEND GARRISON: Up to this time, I have given no direct expression of the views, feelings, and opinions which I have formed, respecting the character and condition of the people of this land. I have refrained thus, purposely. I wish to speak advisedly, and in order to do this, I have waited till, I trust, experience has brought my opinions to an intelligent maturity. I have been thus careful, not because I think what I say will have much effect in shaping the opinions of the world, but because whatever of influence I may possess, whether little or much, I wish it to go in the right direction, and according to truth. I hardly need say that, in speaking of Ireland, I shall be influenced by no prejudices in favor of America. I think my circumstances all forbid that. I have no end to serve, no creed to uphold, no government to defend; and as to nation, I belong to none. I have no protection at home, or resting-place abroad. The land of my birth welcomes me to her shores only as a slave, and spurns with contempt the idea of treating me differently; so that I am an outcast from the society of my childhood, and an outlaw in the land of my birth. "I am a stranger with thee, and a sojourner, as all my fathers were." That men should be patriotic, is to me perfectly natural; and as a philosophical fact, I am able to give it an intellectual recognition. But no further can I go. If ever I had any patriotism, or any capacity for the feeling, it was whipped out of me long since, by the lash of the American soul-drivers.

In thinking of America, I sometimes find myself admiring her bright blue sky, her grand old woods, her fertile fields, her beautiful rivers, her mighty lakes, and star-crowned mountains. But my rapture is soon checked, my joy is soon turned to mourning. When I remember that all is cursed with the infernal spirit of slaveholding, robbery, and wrong; when I remember that with the waters of her noblest rivers, the tears of my brethren are borne to the ocean, disregarded and forgotten, and that her most fertile fields drink daily of the warm blood of my outraged sisters; I am filled with unutterable loathing, and led to reproach myself that anything could fall from my lips in praise of such a land. America will not allow her children to love her. She seems bent on compelling those who would be her warmest friends, to be her worst enemies. May God give her repentance, before it is too late, is the ardent prayer of my heart. I will continue to pray, labor, and wait, believing that she cannot always be insensible to the dictates of justice, or deaf to the voice of humanity.

My opportunities for learning the character and condition of the people of this land have been very great. I have traveled almost from the Hill of Howth to the Giant's Causeway, and from the Giant's Causway, to Cape Clear. During these travels, I have met with much in the chara@@ and condition of the people to approve, and much to condemn; much that @@thrilled me with pleasure, and very much that has filled me with pain. I @@ @@t, in this letter, attempt to give any description of those scenes which have given me pain. This I will do hereafter. I have enough, and more than your subscribers will be disposed to read at one time, of the bright side of the picture. I can truly say, I have spent some of the happiest moments of my life since landing in this country. I seem to have undergone a transformation. I live a new life. The warm and generous cooperation extended to me by the friends of my despised race; the prompt and liberal manner with which the press has rendered me its aid; the glorious enthusiasm with which thousands have flocked to hear the cruel wrongs of my down-trodden and long-enslaved fellow-countrymen portrayed; the deep sympathy for the slave, and the strong abhorrence of the slaveholder, everywhere evinced; the cordiality with which members and ministers of various religious bodies, and of various shades of religious opinion, have embraced me, and lent me their aid; the kind of hospitality constantly proffered to me by persons of the highest rank in society; the spirit of freedom that seems to animate all with whom I come in contact, and the entire absence of everything that looked like prejudice against me, on account of the color of my skin—contrasted so strongly with my long and bitter experience in the United States, that I look with wonder and amazement on the transition. In the southern part of the United States, I was a slave, thought of and spoken of as property; in the language of the LAW, "held, taken, reputed, and adjudged to be a chattel in the hands of my owners and possessors, and their executors, administrators, and assigns, to all intents, constructions, and purposes whatsoever." (Brev. Digest, 224). In the northern states, a fugitive slave, liable to be hunted at any moment, like a felon, and to be hurled into the terrible jaws of slavery—doomed by an inveterate prejudice against color to insult and outrage on every hand (Massachusetts out of the question)—denied the privileges and courtesies common to others in the use of the most humble means of conveyance—shut out from the cabins on steamboats—refused admission to respectable hotels—caricatured, scorned, scoffed, mocked, and maltreated with impunity by any one (no matter how black his heart), so he has a white skin. But now behold the change! Eleven days and a half gone, and I have crossed three thousand miles of the perilous deep. Instead of a democratic government, I am under a monarchical government. Instead of the bright, blue sky of America, I am covered with the soft, grey fog of the Emerald Isle. I breathe, and lo! the chattel becomes a man. I gaze around in vain for one who will question my equal humanity, claim me as his slave, or offer me an insult. I employ a cab—I am seated beside white people—I reach the hotel—I enter the same door—I am shown into the same parlor—I dine at the same table and no one is offended. No delicate nose grows deformed in my presence. I find no difficulty here in obtaining admission into any place of worship, instruction, or amusement, on equal terms with people as white as any I ever saw in the United States. I meet nothing to remind me of my complexion. I find myself regarded and treated at every turn with the kindness and deference paid to white people. When I go to church, I am met by no upturned nose and scornful lip to tell me, "We don't allow niggers in here!"

I remember, about two years ago, there was in Boston, near the south-west corner of Boston Common, a menagerie. I had long desired to see such a collection as I understood was being exhibited there. Never having had an opportunity while a slave, I resolved to seize this, my first, since my escape. I went, and as I approached the entrance to gain admission, I was met and told by the door-keeper, in a harsh and contemptuous tone, "We don't allow niggers in here." I also remember attending a revival meeting in the Rev. Henry Jackson's meeting-house, at New Bedford, and going up the broad aisle to find a seat, I was met by a good deacon, who told me, in a pious tone, "We don't allow niggers in here!" Soon after my arrival in New Bedford, from the south, I had a strong desire to attend the Lyceum, but was told, "They don't allow niggers in here!" While passing from New York to Boston, on the steamer Massachusetts, on the night of the 9th of December, 1843, when chilled almost through with the cold, I went into the cabin to get a little warm. I was soon touched upon the shoulder, and told, "We don't allow niggers in here!" On arriving in Boston, from an anti-slavery tour, hungry and tired, I went into an eating-house, near my friend, Mr. Campbell's to get some refreshments. I was met by a lad in a white apron, "We don't allow niggers in here!" A week or two before leaving the United States, I had a meeting appointed at Weymouth, the home of that glorious band of true abolitionists, the Weston family, and others. On attempting to take a seat in the omnibus to that place, I was told by the driver (and I never shall forget his fiendish hate). "I don't allow niggers in here!" Thank heaven for the respite I now enjoy! I had been in Dublin but a few days, when a gentleman of great respectability kindly offered to conduct me through all the public buildings of that beautiful city; and a little afterward, I found myself dining with the lord mayor of Dublin. What a pity there was not some American democratic Christian at the door of his splendid mansion, to bark out at my approach, "They don't allow niggers in here!" The truth is, the people here know nothing of the republican Negro hate prevalent in our glorious land. They measure and esteem men according to their moral and intellectual worth, and not according to the color of their skin. Whatever may be said of the aristocracies here, there is none based on the color of a man's skin. This species of aristocracy belongs preeminently to "the land of the free, and the home of the brave." I have never found it abroad, in any but Americans. It sticks to them wherever they go. They find it almost as hard to get rid of, as to get rid of their skins.

The second day after my arrival at Liverpool, in company with my friend, Buffum, and several other friends, I went to Eaton Hall, the residence of the Marquis of Westminster, one of the most splendid buildings in England. On approaching the door, I found several of our American passengers, who came out with us in the "Cambria," waiting for admission, as but one party was allowed in the house at a time. We all had to wait till the company within came out. And of all the faces, expressive of chagrin, those of the Americans were preeminent. They looked as sour as vinegar, and as bitter as gall, when they found I was to be admitted on equal terms with themselves. When the door was opened, I walked in, on an equal footing with my white fellow-citizens, and from all I could see, I had as much attention paid me by the servants that showed us through the house, as any with a paler skin. As I walked through the building, the statuary did not fall down, the pictures did not leap from their places, the doors did not refuse to open, and the servants did not say, "We don't allow niggers in here!"

A happy new-year to you, and all the friends of freedom.

My time and labors, while abroad were divided between England, Ireland, Scotland, and Wales. Upon this experience alone, I might write a book twice the size of this, My Bondage and My Freedom. I visited and lectured in nearly all the large towns and cities in the United Kingdom, and enjoyed many favorable opportunities for observation and information. But books on England are abundant, and the public may, therefore, dismiss any fear that I am meditating another infliction in that line; though, in truth, I should like much to write a book on those countries, if for nothing else, to make grateful mention of the many dear friends, whose benevolent actions toward me are ineffaceably stamped upon my memory, and warmly treasured in my heart. To these friends I owe my freedom in the United States. On their own motion, without any solicitation from me (Mrs. Henry Richardson, a clever lady, remarkable for her devotion to every good work, taking the lead), they raised a fund sufficient to purchase my freedom, and actually paid it over, and placed the papers 8 of my manumission in my hands, before they would tolerate the idea of my returning to this, my native country. To this commercial transaction I owe my exemption from the democratic operation of the Fugitive Slave Bill of 1850. But for this, I might at any time become a victim of this most cruel and scandalous enactment, and be doomed to end my life, as I began it, a slave. The sum paid for my freedom was one hundred and fifty pounds sterling.

Some of my uncompromising anti-slavery friends in this country failed to see the wisdom of this arrangement, and were not pleased that I consented to it, even by my silence. They thought it a violation of anti-slavery principles—conceding a right of property in man—and a wasteful expenditure of money. On the other hand, viewing it simply in the light of a ransom, or as money extorted by a robber, and my liberty of more value than one hundred and fifty pounds sterling, I could not see either a violation of the laws of morality, or those of economy, in the transaction.

It is true, I was not in the possession of my claimants, and could have easily remained in England, for the same friends who had so generously purchased my freedom, would have assisted me in establishing myself in that country. To this, however, I could not consent. I felt that I had a duty to perform—and that was, to labor and suffer with the oppressed in my native land. Considering, therefore, all the circumstances—the fugitive slave bill included—I think the very best thing was done in letting Master Hugh have the hundred and fifty pounds sterling, and leaving me free to return to my appropriate field of labor. Had I been a private person, having no other relations or duties than those of a personal and family nature, I should never have consented to the payment of so large a sum for the privilege of living securely under our glorious republican form of government. I could have remained in England, or have gone to some other country; and perhaps I could even have lived unobserved in this. But to this I could not consent. I had already become some what notorious, and withal quite as unpopular as notorious; and I was, therefore, much exposed to arrest and recapture.

The main object to which my labors in Great Britain were directed, was the concentration of the moral and religious sentiment of its people against American slavery. England is often charged with having established slavery in the United States, and if there were no other justification than this, for appealing to her people to lend their moral aid for the abolition of slavery, I should be justified. My speeches in Great Britain were wholly extemporaneous, and I may not always have been so guarded in my expressions, as I otherwise should have been. I was ten years younger then than now, and only seven years from slavery. I cannot give the reader a better idea of the nature of my discourses, than by republishing one of them, delivered in Finsbury chapel, London, to an audience of about two thousand persons, and which was published in the London Universe, at the time. 9

Those in the United States who may regard this speech as being harsh in its spirit and unjust in its statements, because delivered before an audience supposed to be anti-republican in their principles and feelings, may view the matter differently, when they learn that the case supposed did not exist. It so happened that the great mass of the people in England who attended and patronized my anti-slavery meetings, were, in truth, about as good republicans as the mass of Americans, and with this decided advantage over the latter—they are lovers of republicanism for all men, for black men as well as for white men. They are the people who sympathize with Louis Kossuth and Mazzini, and with the oppressed and enslaved, of every color and nation, the world over. They constitute the democratic element in British politics, and are as much opposed to the union of church and state as we, in America, are to such an union. At the meeting where this speech was delivered, Joseph Sturge—a world-wide philanthropist, and a member of the society of Friends—presided, and addressed the meeting. George William Alexander, another Friend, who has spent more than an Ameriacn(sic) fortune in promoting the anti-slavery cause in different sections of the world, was on the platform; and also Dr. Campbell (now of the British Banner) who combines all the humane tenderness of Melanchthon, with the directness and boldness of Luther. He is in the very front ranks of non-conformists, and looks with no unfriendly eye upon America. George Thompson, too, was there; and America will yet own that he did a true man's work in relighting the rapidly dying-out fire of true republicanism in the American heart, and be ashamed of the treatment he met at her hands. Coming generations in this country will applaud the spirit of this much abused republican friend of freedom. There were others of note seated on the platform, who would gladly ingraft upon English institutions all that is purely republican in the institutions of America. Nothing, therefore, must be set down against this speech on the score that it was delivered in the presence of those who cannot appreciate the many excellent things belonging to our system of government, and with a view to stir up prejudice against republican institutions.

Again, let it also be remembered—for it is the simple truth—that neither in this speech, nor in any other which I delivered in England, did I ever allow myself to address Englishmen as against Americans. I took my stand on the high ground of human brotherhood, and spoke to Englishmen as men, in behalf of men. Slavery is a crime, not against Englishmen, but against God, and all the members of the human family; and it belongs to the whole human family to seek its suppression. In a letter to Mr. Greeley, of the New York Tribune, written while abroad, I said:

I am, nevertheless aware that the wisdom of exposing the sins of one nation in the ear of another, has been seriously questioned by good and clear-sighted people, both on this and on your side of the Atlantic. And the thought is not without weight on my own mind. I am satisfied that there are many evils which can be best removed by confining our efforts to the immediate locality where such evils exist. This, however, is by no means the case with the system of slavery. It is such a giant sin—such a monstrous aggregation of iniquity—so hardening to the human heart—so destructive to the moral sense, and so well calculated to beget a character, in every one around it, favorable to its own continuance,—that I feel not only at liberty, but abundantly justified, in appealing to the whole world to aid in its removal. But, even if I had—as has been often charged—labored to bring American institutions generally into disrepute, and had not confined my labors strictly within the limits of humanity and morality, I should not have been without illustrious examples to support me. Driven into semi-exile by civil and barbarous laws, and by a system which cannot be thought of without a shudder, I was fully justified in turning, if possible, the tide of the moral universe against the heaven-daring outrage.

Four circumstances greatly assisted me in getting the question of American slavery before the British public. First, the mob on board the "Cambria," already referred to, which was a sort of national announcement of my arrival in England. Secondly, the highly reprehensible course pursued by the Free Church of Scotland, in soliciting, receiving, and retaining money in its sustentation fund for supporting the gospel in Scotland, which was evidently the ill-gotten gain of slaveholders and slave-traders. Third, the great Evangelical Alliance—or rather the attempt to form such an alliance, which should include slaveholders of a certain description—added immensely to the interest felt in the slavery question. About the same time, there was the World's Temperance Convention, where I had the misfortune to come in collision with sundry American doctors of divinity—Dr. Cox among the number—with whom I had a small controversy.

It has happened to me—as it has happened to most other men engaged in a good cause—often to be more indebted to my enemies than to my own skill or to the assistance of my friends, for whatever success has attended my labors. Great surprise was expressed by American newspapers, north and south, during my stay in Great Britain, that a person so illiterate and insignificant as myself could awaken an interest so marked in England. These papers were not the only parties surprised. I was myself not far behind them in surprise. But the very contempt and scorn, the systematic and extravagant disparagement of which I was the object, served, perhaps, to magnify my few merits, and to render me of some account, whether deserving or not. A man is sometimes made great, by the greatness of the abuse a portion of mankind may think proper to heap upon him. Whether I was of as much consequence as the English papers made me out to be, or not, it was easily seen, in England, that I could not be the ignorant and worthless creature, some of the American papers would have them believe I was. Men, in their senses, do not take bowie-knives to kill mosquitoes, nor pistols to shoot flies; and the American passengers who thought proper to get up a mob to silence me, on board the "Cambria," took the most effective method of telling the British public that I had something to say.

But to the second circumstance, namely, the position of the Free Church of Scotland, with the great Doctors Chalmers, Cunningham, and Candlish at its head. That church, with its leaders, put it out of the power of the Scotch people to ask the old question, which we in the north have often most wickedly asked—"What have we to do with slavery?" That church had taken the price of blood into its treasury, with which to build free churches, and to pay free church ministers for preaching the gospel; and, worse still, when honest John Murray, of Bowlien Bay—now gone to his reward in heaven—with William Smeal, Andrew Paton, Frederick Card, and other sterling anti-slavery men in Glasgow, denounced the transaction as disgraceful and shocking to the religious sentiment of Scotland, this church, through its leading divines, instead of repenting and seeking to mend the mistake into which it had fallen, made it a flagrant sin, by undertaking to defend, in the name of God and the bible, the principle not only of taking the money of slave-dealers to build churches, but of holding fellowship with the holders and traffickers in human flesh. This, the reader will see, brought up the whole question of slavery, and opened the way to its full discussion, without any agency of mine. I have never seen a people more deeply moved than were the people of Scotland, on this very question. Public meeting succeeded public meeting. Speech after speech, pamphlet after pamphlet, editorial after editorial, sermon after sermon, soon lashed the conscientious Scotch people into a perfect furore. "SEND BACK THE MONEY!" was indignantly cried out, from Greenock to Edinburgh, and from Edinburgh to Aberdeen. George Thompson, of London, Henry C. Wright, of the United States, James N. Buffum, of Lynn, Massachusetts, and myself were on the anti-slavery side; and Doctors Chalmers, Cunningham, and Candlish on the other. In a conflict where the latter could have had even the show of right, the truth, in our hands as against them, must have been driven to the wall; and while I believe we were able to carry the conscience of the country against the action of the Free Church, the battle, it must be confessed, was a hard-fought one. Abler defenders of the doctrine of fellowshiping slaveholders as christians, have not been met with. In defending this doctrine, it was necessary to deny that slavery is a sin. If driven from this position, they were compelled to deny that slaveholders were responsible for the sin; and if driven from both these positions, they must deny that it is a sin in such a sense, and that slaveholders are sinners in such a sense, as to make it wrong, in the circumstances in which they were placed, to recognize them as Christians. Dr. Cunningham was the most powerful debater on the slavery side of the question; Mr. Thompson was the ablest on the anti-slavery side. A scene occurred between these two men, a parallel to which I think I never witnessed before, and I know I never have since. The scene was caused by a single exclamation on the part of Mr. Thompson.

The general assembly of the Free Church was in progress at] Cannon Mills, Edinburgh. The building would hold about twenty-five hundred persons; and on this occasion it was densely packed, notice having been given that Doctors Cunningham and Candlish would speak, that day, in defense of the relations of the Free Church of Scotland to slavery in America. Messrs. Thompson, Buffum, myself, and a few anti-slavery friends, attended, but sat at such a distance, and in such a position, that, perhaps we were not observed from the platform. The excitement was intense, having been greatly increased by a series of meetings held by Messrs. Thompson, Wright, Buffum, and myself, in the most splendid hall in that most beautiful city, just previous to the meetings of the general assembly. "SEND BACK THE MONEY!" stared at us from every street corner; "SEND BACK THE MONEY!" in large capitals, adorned the broad flags of the pavement; "SEND BACK THE MONEY!" was the chorus of the popular street songs; "SEND BACK THE MONEY!" was the heading of leading editorials in the daily newspapers. This day, at Cannon Mills, the great doctors of the church were to give an answer to this loud and stern demand. Men of all parties and all sects were most eager to hear. Something great was expected. The occasion was great, the men great, and great speeches were expected from them.

In addition to the outside pressure upon Doctors Cunningham and Candlish, there was wavering in their own ranks. The conscience of the church itself was not at ease. A dissatisfaction with the position of the church touching slavery, was sensibly manifest among the members, and something must be done to counteract this untoward influence. The great Dr. Chalmers was in feeble health, at the time. His most potent eloquence could not now be summoned to Cannon Mills, as formerly. He whose voice was able to rend asunder and dash down the granite walls of the established church of Scotland, and to lead a host in solemn procession from it, as from a doomed city, was now old and enfeebled. Besides, he had said his word on this very question; and his word had not silenced the clamor without, nor stilled the anxious heavings within. The occasion was momentous, and felt to be so. The church was in a perilous condition. A change of some sort must take place in her condition, or she must go to pieces. To stand where she did, was impossible. The whole weight of the matter fell on Cunningham and Candlish. No shoulders in the church were broader than theirs; and I must say, badly as I detest the principles laid down and defended by them, I was compelled to acknowledge the vast mental endowments of the men. Cunningham rose; and his rising was the signal for almost tumultous applause. You will say this was scarcely in keeping with the solemnity of the occasion, but to me it served to increase its grandeur and gravity. The applause, though tumultuous, was not joyous. It seemed to me, as it thundered up from the vast audience, like the fall of an immense shaft, flung from shoulders already galled by its crushing weight. It was like saying, "Doctor, we have borne this burden long enough, and willingly fling it upon you. Since it was you who brought it upon us, take it now, and do what you will with it, for we are too weary to bear it.

Doctor Cunningham proceeded with his speech, abounding in logic, learning, and eloquence, and apparently bearing down all opposition; but at the moment—the fatal moment—when he was just bringing all his arguments to a point, and that point being, that neither Jesus Christ nor his holy apostles regarded slaveholding as a sin, George Thompson, in a clear, sonorous, but rebuking voice, broke the deep stillness of the audience, exclaiming, HEAR! HEAR! HEAR! The effect of this simple and common exclamation is almost incredible. It was as if a granite wall had been suddenly flung up against the advancing current of a mighty river. For a moment, speaker and audience were brought to a dead silence. Both the doctor and his hearers seemed appalled by the audacity, as well as the fitness of the rebuke. At length a shout went up to the cry of "Put him out!" Happily, no one attempted to execute this cowardly order, and the doctor proceeded with his discourse. Not, however, as before, did the learned doctor proceed. The exclamation of Thompson must have reechoed itself a thousand times in his memory, during the remainder of his speech, for the doctor never recovered from the blow. The deed was done, however; the pillars of the church—the proud, Free Church of Scotland— were committed and the humility of repentance was absent. The Free Church held on to the blood-stained money, and continued to justify itself in its position—and of course to apologize for slavery—and does so till this day. She lost a glorious opportunity for giving her voice, her vote, and her example to the cause of humanity; and to-day she is staggering under the curse of the enslaved, whose blood is in her skirts. The people of Scotland are, to this day, deeply grieved at the course pursued by the Free Church, and would hail, as a relief from a deep and blighting shame, the "sending back the money" to the slaveholders from whom it was gathered.

One good result followed the conduct of the Free Church; it furnished an occasion for making the people of Scotland thoroughly acquainted with the character of slavery, and for arraying against the system the moral and religious sentiment of that country. Therefore, while we did not succeed in accomplishing the specific object of our mission, namely—procure the sending back of the money—we were amply justified by the good which really did result from our labors.

Next comes the Evangelical Alliance. This was an attempt to form a union of all evangelical Christians throughout the world. Sixty or seventy American divines attended, and some of them went there merely to weave a world-wide garment with which to clothe evangelical slaveholders. Foremost among these divines, was the Rev. Samuel Hanson Cox, moderator of the New School Presbyterian General Assembly. He and his friends spared no pains to secure a platform broad enough to hold American slaveholders, and in this partly succeeded. But the question of slavery is too large a question to be finally disposed of, even by the Evangelical Alliance. We appealed from the judgment of the Alliance, to the judgment of the people of Great Britain, and with the happiest effect. This controversy with the Alliance might be made the subject of extended remark, but I must forbear, except to say, that this effort to shield the Christian character of slaveholders greatly served to open a way to the British ear for anti-slavery discussion, and that it was well improved.

The fourth and last circumstance that assisted me in getting before the British public, was an attempt on the part of certain doctors of divinity to silence me on the platform of the World's Temperance Convention. Here I was brought into point blank collison with Rev. Dr. Cox, who made me the subject not only of bitter remark in the convention, but also of a long denunciatory letter published in the New York Evangelist and other American papers. I replied to the doctor as well as I could, and was successful in getting a respectful hearing before the British public, who are by nature and practice ardent lovers of fair play, especially in a conflict between the weak and the strong.

Thus did circumstances favor me, and favor the cause of which I strove to be the advocate. After such distinguished notice, the public in both countries was compelled to attach some importance to my labors. By the very ill usage I received at the hands of Dr. Cox and his party, by the mob on board the "Cambria," by the attacks made upon me in the American newspapers, and by the aspersions cast upon me through the organs of the Free Church of Scotland, I became one of that class of men, who, for the moment, at least, "have greatness forced upon them." People became the more anxious to hear for themselves, and to judge for themselves, of the truth which I had to unfold. While, therefore, it is by no means easy for a stranger to get fairly before the British public, it was my lot to accomplish it in the easiest manner possible.

Having continued in Great Britain and Ireland nearly two years, and being about to return to America—not as I left it, a slave, but a freeman—leading friends of the cause of emancipation in that country intimated their intention to make me a testimonial, not only on grounds of personal regard to myself, but also to the cause to which they were so ardently devoted. How far any such thing could have succeeded, I do not know; but many reasons led me to prefer that my friends should simply give me the means of obtaining a printing press and printing materials, to enable me to start a paper, devoted to the interests of my enslaved and oppressed people. I told them that perhaps the greatest hinderance to the adoption of abolition principles by the people of the United States, was the low estimate, everywhere in that country, placed upon the Negro, as a man; that because of his assumed natural inferiority, people reconciled themselves to his enslavement and oppression, as things inevitable, if not desirable. The grand thing to be done, therefore, was to change the estimation in which the colored people of the United States were held; to remove the prejudice which depreciated and depressed them; to prove them worthy of a higher consideration; to disprove their alleged inferiority, and demonstrate their capacity for a more exalted civilization than slavery and prejudice had assigned to them. I further stated, that, in my judgment, a tolerably well conducted press, in the hands of persons of the despised race, by calling out the mental energies of the race itself; by making them acquainted with their own latent powers; by enkindling among them the hope that for them there is a future; by developing their moral power; by combining and reflecting their talents—would prove a most powerful means of removing prejudice, and of awakening an interest in them. I further informed them—and at that time the statement was true—that there was not, in the United States, a single newspaper regularly published by the colored people; that many attempts had been made to establish such papers; but that, up to that time, they had all failed. These views I laid before my friends. The result was, nearly two thousand five hundred dollars were speedily raised toward starting my paper. For this prompt and generous assistance, rendered upon my bare suggestion, without any personal efforts on my part, I shall never cease to feel deeply grateful; and the thought of fulfilling the noble expectations of the dear friends who gave me this evidence of their confidence, will never cease to be a motive for persevering exertion.

Proposing to leave England, and turning my face toward America, in the spring of 1847, I was met, on the threshold, with something which painfully reminded me of the kind of life which awaited me in my native land. For the first time in the many months spent abroad, I was met with proscription on account of my color. A few weeks before departing from England, while in London, I was careful to purchase a ticket, and secure a berth for returning home, in the "Cambria"—the steamer in which I left the United States—paying therefor the round sum of forty pounds and nineteen shillings sterling. This was first cabin fare. But on going aboard the Cambria, I found that the Liverpool agent had ordered my berth to be given to another, and had forbidden my entering the saloon! This contemptible conduct met with stern rebuke from the British press. For, upon the point of leaving England, I took occasion to expose the disgusting tyranny, in the columns of the London Times. That journal, and other leading journals throughout the United Kingdom, held up the outrage to unmitigated condemnation. So good an opportunity for calling out a full expression of British sentiment on the subject, had not before occurred, and it was most fully embraced. The result was, that Mr. Cunard came out in a letter to the public journals, assuring them of his regret at the outrage, and promising that the like should never occur again on board his steamers; and the like, we believe, has never since occurred on board the steamships of the Cunard line.

It is not very pleasant to be made the subject of such insults; but if all such necessarily resulted as this one did, I should be very happy to bear, patiently, many more than I have borne, of the same sort. Albeit, the lash of proscription, to a man accustomed to equal social position, even for a time, as I was, has a sting for the soul hardly less severe than that which bites the flesh and draws the blood from the back of the plantation slave. It was rather hard, after having enjoyed nearly two years of equal social privileges in England, often dining with gentlemen of great literary, social, political, and religious eminence never, during the whole time, having met with a single word, look, or gesture, which gave me the slightest reason to think my color was an offense to anybody—now to be cooped up in the stern of the "Cambria," and denied the right to enter the saloon, lest my dark presence should be deemed an offense to some of my democratic fellow-passengers. The reader will easily imagine what must have been my feelings.

CHAPTER XXV. Various Incidents

NEWSPAPER ENTERPRISE—UNEXPECTED OPPOSITION—THE OBJECTIONS TO IT—THEIR
PLAUSIBILITY ADMITTED—MOTIVES FOR COMING TO ROCHESTER—DISCIPLE OF MR.
GARRISON—CHANGE OF OPINION—CAUSES LEADING TO IT—THE CONSEQUENCES OF
THE CHANGE—PREJUDICE AGAINST COLOR—AMUSING CONDESCENSION—"JIM CROW
CARS"—COLLISIONS WITH CONDUCTORS AND BRAKEMEN—TRAINS ORDERED NOT TO
STOP AT LYNN—AMUSING DOMESTIC SCENE—SEPARATE TABLES FOR MASTER AND
MAN—PREJUDICE UNNATURAL—ILLUSTRATIONS—IN HIGH COMPANY—ELEVATION OF
THE FREE PEOPLE OF COLOR—PLEDGE FOR THE FUTURE.

I have now given the reader an imperfect sketch of nine years' experience in freedom—three years as a common laborer on the wharves of New Bedford, four years as a lecturer in New England, and two years of semi-exile in Great Britain and Ireland. A single ray of light remains to be flung upon my life during the last eight years, and my story will be done.

A trial awaited me on my return from England to the United States, for which I was but very imperfectly prepared. My plans for my then future usefulness as an anti-slavery advocate were all settled. My friends in England had resolved to raise a given sum to purchase for me a press and printing materials; and I already saw myself wielding my pen, as well as my voice, in the great work of renovating the public mind, and building up a public sentiment which should, at least, send slavery and oppression to the grave, and restore to "liberty and the pursuit of happiness" the people with whom I had suffered, both as a slave and as a freeman. Intimation had reached my friends in Boston of what I intended to do, before my arrival, and I was prepared to find them favorably disposed toward my much cherished enterprise. In this I was mistaken. I found them very earnestly opposed to the idea of my starting a paper, and for several reasons. First, the paper was not needed; secondly, it would interfere with my usefulness as a lecturer; thirdly, I was better fitted to speak than to write; fourthly, the paper could not succeed. This opposition, from a quarter so highly esteemed, and to which I had been accustomed to look for advice and direction, caused me not only to hesitate, but inclined me to abandon the enterprise. All previous attempts to establish such a journal having failed, I felt that probably I should but add another to the list of failures, and thus contribute another proof of the mental and moral deficiencies of my race. Very much that was said to me in respect to my imperfect literary acquirements, I felt to be most painfully true. The unsuccessful projectors of all the previous colored newspapers were my superiors in point of education, and if they failed, how could I hope for success? Yet I did hope for success, and persisted in the undertaking. Some of my English friends greatly encouraged me to go forward, and I shall never cease to be grateful for their words of cheer and generous deeds.

I can easily pardon those who have denounced me as ambitious and presumptuous, in view of my persistence in this enterprise. I was but nine years from slavery. In point of mental experience, I was but nine years old. That one, in such circumstances, should aspire to establish a printing press, among an educated people, might well be considered, if not ambitious, quite silly. My American friends looked at me with astonishment! "A wood-sawyer" offering himself to the public as an editor! A slave, brought up in the very depths of ignorance, assuming to instruct the highly civilized people of the north in the principles of liberty, justice, and humanity! The thing looked absurd. Nevertheless, I persevered. I felt that the want of education, great as it was, could be overcome by study, and that knowledge would come by experience; and further (which was perhaps the most controlling consideration). I thought that an intelligent public, knowing my early history, would easily pardon a large share of the deficiencies which I was sure that my paper would exhibit. The most distressing thing, however, was the offense which I was about to give my Boston friends, by what seemed to them a reckless disregard of their sage advice. I am not sure that I was not under the influence of something like a slavish adoration of my Boston friends, and I labored hard to convince them of the wisdom of my undertaking, but without success. Indeed, I never expect to succeed, although time has answered all their original objections. The paper has been successful. It is a large sheet, costing eighty dollars per week—has three thousand subscribers—has been published regularly nearly eight years—and bids fair to stand eight years longer. At any rate, the eight years to come are as full of promise as were the eight that are past.

It is not to be concealed, however, that the maintenance of such a journal, under the circumstances, has been a work of much difficulty; and could all the perplexity, anxiety, and trouble attending it, have been clearly foreseen, I might have shrunk from the undertaking. As it is, I rejoice in having engaged in the enterprise, and count it joy to have been able to suffer, in many ways, for its success, and for the success of the cause to which it has been faithfully devoted. I look upon the time, money, and labor bestowed upon it, as being amply rewarded, in the development of my own mental and moral energies, and in the corresponding development of my deeply injured and oppressed people.

From motives of peace, instead of issuing my paper in Boston, among my New England friends, I came to Rochester, western New York, among strangers, where the circulation of my paper could not interfere with the local circulation of the Liberator and the Standard; for at that time I was, on the anti-slavery question, a faithful disciple of William Lloyd Garrison, and fully committed to his doctrine touching the pro-slavery character of the constitution of the United States, and the non-voting principle, of which he is the known and distinguished advocate. With Mr. Garrison, I held it to be the first duty of the non-slaveholding states to dissolve the union with the slaveholding states; and hence my cry, like his, was, "No union with slaveholders." With these views, I came into western New York; and during the first four years of my labor here, I advocated them with pen and tongue, according to the best of my ability.

About four years ago, upon a reconsideration of the whole subject, I became convinced that there was no necessity for dissolving the "union between the northern and southern states;" that to seek this dissolution was no part of my duty as an abolitionist; that to abstain from voting, was to refuse to exercise a legitimate and powerful means for abolishing slavery; and that the constitution of the United States not only contained no guarantees in favor of slavery, but, on the contrary, it is, in its letter and spirit, an anti-slavery instrument, demanding the abolition of slavery as a condition of its own existence, as the supreme law of the land.

Here was a radical change in my opinions, and in the action logically resulting from that change. To those with whom I had been in agreement and in sympathy, I was now in opposition. What they held to be a great and important truth, I now looked upon as a dangerous error. A very painful, and yet a very natural, thing now happened. Those who could not see any honest reasons for changing their views, as I had done, could not easily see any such reasons for my change, and the common punishment of apostates was mine.

The opinions first entertained were naturally derived and honestly entertained, and I trust that my present opinions have the same claims to respect. Brought directly, when I escaped from slavery, into contact with a class of abolitionists regarding the constitution as a slaveholding instrument, and finding their views supported by the united and entire history of every department of the government, it is not strange that I assumed the constitution to be just what their interpretation made it. I was bound, not only by their superior knowledge, to take their opinions as the true ones, in respect to the subject, but also because I had no means of showing their unsoundness. But for the responsibility of conducting a public journal, and the necessity imposed upon me of meeting opposite views from abolitionists in this state, I should in all probability have remained as firm in my disunion views as any other disciple of William Lloyd Garrison.

My new circumstances compelled me to re-think the whole subject, and to study, with some care, not only the just and proper rules of legal interpretation, but the origin, design, nature, rights, powers, and duties of civil government, and also the relations which human beings sustain to it. By such a course of thought and reading, I was conducted to the conclusion that the constitution of the United States—inaugurated "to form a more perfect union, establish justice, insure domestic tranquillity, provide for the common defense, promote the general welfare, and secure the blessing of liberty"—could not well have been designed at the same time to maintain and perpetuate a system of rapine and murder, like slavery; especially, as not one word can be found in the constitution to authorize such a belief. Then, again, if the declared purposes of an instrument are to govern the meaning of all its parts and details, as they clearly should, the constitution of our country is our warrant for the abolition of slavery in every state in the American Union. I mean, however, not to argue, but simply to state my views. It would require very many pages of a volume like this, to set forth the arguments demonstrating the unconstitutionality and the complete illegality of slavery in our land; and as my experience, and not my arguments, is within the scope and contemplation of this volume, I omit the latter and proceed with the former.

I will now ask the kind reader to go back a little in my story, while I bring up a thread left behind for convenience sake, but which, small as it is, cannot be properly omitted altogether; and that thread is American prejudice against color, and its varied illustrations in my own experience.

When I first went among the abolitionists of New England, and began to travel, I found this prejudice very strong and very annoying. The abolitionists themselves were not entirely free from it, and I could see that they were nobly struggling against it. In their eagerness, sometimes, to show their contempt for the feeling, they proved that they had not entirely recovered from it; often illustrating the saying, in their conduct, that a man may "stand up so straight as to lean backward." When it was said to me, "Mr. Douglass, I will walk to meeting with you; I am not afraid of a black man," I could not help thinking—seeing nothing very frightful in my appearance—"And why should you be?" The children at the north had all been educated to believe that if they were bad, the old black man—not the old devil—would get them; and it was evidence of some courage, for any so educated to get the better of their fears. The custom of providing separate cars for the accommodation of colored travelers, was established on nearly all the railroads of New England, a dozen years ago. Regarding this custom as fostering the spirit of caste, I made it a rule to seat myself in the cars for the accommodation of passengers generally. Thus seated, I was sure to be called upon to betake myself to the "Jim Crow car." Refusing to obey, I was often dragged out of my seat, beaten, and severely bruised, by conductors and brakemen. Attempting to start from Lynn, one day, for Newburyport, on the Eastern railroad, I went, as my custom was, into one of the best railroad carriages on the road. The seats were very luxuriant and beautiful. I was soon waited upon by the conductor, and ordered out; whereupon I demanded the reason for my invidious removal. After a good deal of parleying, I was told that it was because I was black. This I denied, and appealed to the company to sustain my denial; but they were evidently unwilling to commit themselves, on a point so delicate, and requiring such nice powers of discrimination, for they remained as dumb as death. I was soon waited on by half a dozen fellows of the baser sort (just such as would volunteer to take a bull-dog out of a meeting-house in time of public worship), and told that I must move out of that seat, and if I did not, they would drag me out. I refused to move, and they clutched me, head, neck, and shoulders. But, in anticipation of the stretching to which I was about to be subjected, I had interwoven myself among the seats. In dragging me out, on this occasion, it must have cost the company twenty-five or thirty dollars, for I tore up seats and all. So great was the excitement in Lynn, on the subject, that the superintendent, Mr. Stephen A. Chase, ordered the trains to run through

Lynn without stopping, while I remained in that town; and this ridiculous farce was enacted. For several days the trains went dashing through Lynn without stopping. At the same time that they excluded a free colored man from their cars, this same company allowed slaves, in company with their masters and mistresses, to ride unmolested.

After many battles with the railroad conductors, and being roughly handled in not a few instances, proscription was at last abandoned; and the "Jim Crow car"—set up for the degradation of colored people—is nowhere found in New England. This result was not brought about without the intervention of the people, and the threatened enactment of a law compelling railroad companies to respect the rights of travelers. Hon. Charles Francis Adams performed signal service in the Massachusetts legislature, in bringing this reformation; and to him the colored citizens of that state are deeply indebted.

Although often annoyed, and sometimes outraged, by this prejudice against color, I am indebted to it for many passages of quiet amusement. A half-cured subject of it is sometimes driven into awkward straits, especially if he happens to get a genuine specimen of the race into his house.

In the summer of 1843, I was traveling and lecturing, in company with William A. White, Esq., through the state of Indiana. Anti-slavery friends were not very abundant in Indiana, at that time, and beds were not more plentiful than friends. We often slept out, in preference to sleeping in the houses, at some points. At the close of one of our meetings, we were invited home with a kindly-disposed old farmer, who, in the generous enthusiasm of the moment, seemed to have forgotten that he had but one spare bed, and that his guests were an ill-matched pair. All went on pretty well, till near bed time, when signs of uneasiness began to show themselves, among the unsophisticated sons and daughters. White is remarkably fine looking, and very evidently a born gentleman; the idea of putting us in the same bed was hardly to be tolerated; and yet, there we were, and but the one bed for us, and that, by the way, was in the same room occupied by the other members of the family. White, as well as I, perceived the difficulty, for yonder slept the old folks, there the sons, and a little farther along slept the daughters; and but one other bed remained. Who should have this bed, was the puzzling question. There was some whispering between the old folks, some confused looks among the young, as the time for going to bed approached. After witnessing the confusion as long as I liked, I relieved the kindly-disposed family by playfully saying, "Friend White, having got entirely rid of my prejudice against color, I think, as a proof of it, I must allow you to sleep with me to-night." White kept up the joke, by seeming to esteem himself the favored party, and thus the difficulty was removed. If we went to a hotel, and called for dinner, the landlord was sure to set one table for White and another for me, always taking him to be master, and me the servant. Large eyes were generally made when the order was given to remove the dishes from my table to that of White's. In those days, it was thought strange that a white man and a colored man could dine peaceably at the same table, and in some parts the strangeness of such a sight has not entirely subsided.

Some people will have it that there is a natural, an inherent, and an invincible repugnance in the breast of the white race toward dark-colored people; and some very intelligent colored men think that their proscription is owing solely to the color which nature has given them. They hold that they are rated according to their color, and that it is impossible for white people ever to look upon dark races of men, or men belonging to the African race, with other than feelings of aversion. My experience, both serious and mirthful, combats this conclusion. Leaving out of sight, for a moment, grave facts, to this point, I will state one or two, which illustrate a very interesting feature of American character as well as American prejudice. Riding from Boston to Albany, a few years ago, I found myself in a large car, well filled with passengers. The seat next to me was about the only vacant one. At every stopping place we took in new passengers, all of whom, on reaching the seat next to me, cast a disdainful glance upon it, and passed to another car, leaving me in the full enjoyment of a hole form. For a time, I did not know but that my riding there was prejudicial to the interest of the railroad company. A circumstance occurred, however, which gave me an elevated position at once. Among the passengers on this train was Gov. George N. Briggs. I was not acquainted with him, and had no idea that I was known to him, however, I was, for upon observing me, the governor left his place, and making his way toward me, respectfully asked the privilege of a seat by my side; and upon introducing himself, we entered into a conversation very pleasant and instructive to me. The despised seat now became honored. His excellency had removed all the prejudice against sitting by the side of a Negro; and upon his leaving it, as he did, on reaching Pittsfield, there were at least one dozen applicants for the place. The governor had, without changing my skin a single shade, made the place respectable which before was despicable.

A similar incident happened to me once on the Boston and New Bedford railroad, and the leading party to it has since been governor of the state of Massachusetts. I allude to Col. John Henry Clifford. Lest the reader may fancy I am aiming to elevate myself, by claiming too much intimacy with great men, I must state that my only acquaintance with Col. Clifford was formed while I was his hired servant, during the first winter of my escape from slavery. I owe it him to say, that in that relation I found him always kind and gentlemanly. But to the incident. I entered a car at Boston, for New Bedford, which, with the exception of a single seat was full, and found I must occupy this, or stand up, during the journey. Having no mind to do this, I stepped up to the man having the next seat, and who had a few parcels on the seat, and gently asked leave to take a seat by his side. My fellow-passenger gave me a look made up of reproach and indignation, and asked me why I should come to that particular seat. I assured him, in the gentlest manner, that of all others this was the seat for me. Finding that I was actually about to sit down, he sang out, "O! stop, stop! and let me get out!" Suiting the action to the word, up the agitated man got, and sauntered to the other end of the car, and was compelled to stand for most of the way thereafter. Halfway to New Bedford, or more, Col. Clifford, recognizing me, left his seat, and not having seen me before since I had ceased to wait on him (in everything except hard arguments against his pro-slavery position), apparently forgetful of his rank, manifested, in greeting me, something of the feeling of an old friend. This demonstration was not lost on the gentleman whose dignity I had, an hour before, most seriously offended. Col. Clifford was known to be about the most aristocratic gentleman in Bristol county; and it was evidently thought that I must be somebody, else I should not have been thus noticed, by a person so distinguished. Sure enough, after Col. Clifford left me, I found myself surrounded with friends; and among the number, my offended friend stood nearest, and with an apology for his rudeness, which I could not resist, although it was one of the lamest ever offered. With such facts as these before me—and I have many of them—I am inclined to think that pride and fashion have much to do with the treatment commonly extended to colored people in the United States. I once heard a very plain man say (and he was cross-eyed, and awkwardly flung together in other respects) that he should be a handsome man when public opinion shall be changed.

Since I have been editing and publishing a journal devoted to the cause of liberty and progress, I have had my mind more directed to the condition and circumstances of the free colored people than when I was the agent of an abolition society. The result has been a corresponding change in the disposition of my time and labors. I have felt it to be a part of my mission— under a gracious Providence to impress my sable brothers in this country with the conviction that, notwithstanding the ten thousand discouragements and the powerful hinderances, which beset their existence in this country—notwithstanding the blood-written history of Africa, and her children, from whom we have descended, or the clouds and darkness (whose stillness and gloom are made only more awful by wrathful thunder and lightning) now overshadowing them—progress is yet possible, and bright skies shall yet shine upon their pathway; and that "Ethiopia shall yet reach forth her hand unto God."

Believing that one of the best means of emancipating the slaves of the south is to improve and elevate the character of the free colored people of the north I shall labor in the future, as I have labored in the past, to promote the moral, social, religious, and intellectual elevation of the free colored people; never forgetting my own humble orgin(sic), nor refusing, while Heaven lends me ability, to use my voice, my pen, or my vote, to advocate the great and primary work of the universal and unconditional emancipation of my entire race.

RECEPTION SPEECH. At Finsbury Chapel, Moorfields, England, May 12,

Footnote 10

1846

Mr. Douglass rose amid loud cheers, and said: I feel exceedingly glad of the opportunity now afforded me of presenting the claims of my brethren in bonds in the United States, to so many in London and from various parts of Britain, who have assembled here on the present occasion. I have nothing to commend me to your consideration in the way of learning, nothing in the way of education, to entitle me to your attention; and you are aware that slavery is a very bad school for rearing teachers of morality and religion. Twenty-one years of my life have been spent in slavery—personal slavery—surrounded by degrading influences, such as can exist nowhere beyond the pale of slavery; and it will not be strange, if under such circumstances, I should betray, in what I have to say to you, a deficiency of that refinement which is seldom or ever found, except among persons that have experienced superior advantages to those which I have enjoyed. But I will take it for granted that you know something about the degrading influences of slavery, and that you will not expect great things from me this evening, but simply such facts as I may be able to advance immediately in connection with my own experience of slavery.

Now, what is this system of slavery? This is the subject of my lecture this evening—what is the character of this institution? I am about to answer the inquiry, what is American slavery? I do this the more readily, since I have found persons in this country who have identified the term slavery with that which I think it is not, and in some instances, I have feared, in so doing, have rather (unwittingly, I know) detracted much from the horror with which the term slavery is contemplated. It is common in this country to distinguish every bad thing by the name of slavery. Intemperance is slavery; to be deprived of the right to vote is slavery, says one; to have to work hard is slavery, says another; and I do not know but that if we should let them go on, they would say that to eat when we are hungry, to walk when we desire to have exercise, or to minister to our necessities, or have necessities at all, is slavery. I do not wish for a moment to detract from the horror with which the evil of intemperance is contemplated—not at all; nor do I wish to throw the slightest obstruction in the way of any political freedom that any class of persons in this country may desire to obtain. But I am here to say that I think the term slavery is sometimes abused by identifying it with that which it is not. Slavery in the United States is the granting of that power by which one man exercises and enforces a right of property in the body and soul of another. The condition of a slave is simply that of the brute beast. He is a piece of property—a marketable commodity, in the language of the law, to be bought or sold at the will and caprice of the master who claims him to be his property; he is spoken of, thought of, and treated as property. His own good, his conscience, his intellect, his affections, are all set aside by the master. The will and the wishes of the master are the law of the slave. He is as much a piece of property as a horse. If he is fed, he is fed because he is property. If he is clothed, it is with a view to the increase of his value as property. Whatever of comfort is necessary to him for his body or soul that is inconsistent with his being property, is carefully wrested from him, not only by public opinion, but by the law of the country. He is carefully deprived of everything that tends in the slightest degree to detract from his value as property. He is deprived of education. God has given him an intellect; the slaveholder declares it shall not be cultivated. If his moral perception leads him in a course contrary to his value as property, the slaveholder declares he shall not exercise it. The marriage institution cannot exist among slaves, and one-sixth of the population of democratic America is denied its privileges by the law of the land. What is to be thought of a nation boasting of its liberty, boasting of its humanity, boasting of its Christianity, boasting of its love of justice and purity, and yet having within its own borders three millions of persons denied by law the right of marriage?—what must be the condition of that people? I need not lift up the veil by giving you any experience of my own. Every one that can put two ideas together, must see the most fearful results from such a state of things as I have just mentioned. If any of these three millions find for themselves companions, and prove themselves honest, upright, virtuous persons to each other, yet in these cases—few as I am bound to confess they are—the virtuous live in constant apprehension of being torn asunder by the merciless men-stealers that claim them as their property. This is American slavery; no marriage—no education—the light of the gospel shut out from the dark mind of the bondman—and he forbidden by law to learn to read. If a mother shall teach her children to read, the law in Louisiana proclaims that she may be hanged by the neck. If the father attempt to give his son a knowledge of letters, he may be punished by the whip in one instance, and in another be killed, at the discretion of the court. Three millions of people shut out from the light of knowledge! It is easy for you to conceive the evil that must result from such a state of things.

I now come to the physical evils of slavery. I do not wish to dwell at length upon these, but it seems right to speak of them, not so much to influence your minds on this question, as to let the slaveholders of America know that the curtain which conceals their crimes is being lifted abroad; that we are opening the dark cell, and leading the people into the horrible recesses of what they are pleased to call their domestic institution. We want them to know that a knowledge of their whippings, their scourgings, their brandings, their chainings, is not confined to their plantations, but that some Negro of theirs has broken loose from his chains—has burst through the dark incrustation of slavery, and is now exposing their deeds of deep damnation to the gaze of the christian people of England.

The slaveholders resort to all kinds of cruelty. If I were disposed, I have matter enough to interest you on this question for five or six evenings, but I will not dwell at length upon these cruelties. Suffice it to say, that all of the peculiar modes of torture that were resorted to in the West India islands, are resorted to, I believe, even more frequently, in the United States of America. Starvation, the bloody whip, the chain, the gag, the thumb-screw, cat-hauling, the cat-o'-nine-tails, the dungeon, the blood-hound, are all in requisition to keep the slave in his condition as a slave in the United States. If any one has a doubt upon this point, I would ask him to read the chapter on slavery in Dickens's Notes on America. If any man has a doubt upon it, I have here the "testimony of a thousand witnesses," which I can give at any length, all going to prove the truth of my statement. The blood-hound is regularly trained in the United States, and advertisements are to be found in the southern papers of the Union, from persons advertising themselves as blood-hound trainers, and offering to hunt down slaves at fifteen dollars a piece, recommending their hounds as the fleetest in the neighborhood, never known to fail. Advertisements are from time to time inserted, stating that slaves have escaped with iron collars about their necks, with bands of iron about their feet, marked with the lash, branded with red-hot irons, the initials of their master's name burned into their flesh; and the masters advertise the fact of their being thus branded with their own signature, thereby proving to the world, that, however damning it may appear to non-slavers, such practices are not regarded discreditable among the slaveholders themselves. Why, I believe if a man should brand his horse in this country—burn the initials of his name into any of his cattle, and publish the ferocious deed here—that the united execrations of Christians in Britain would descend upon him. Yet in the United States, human beings are thus branded. As Whittier says—

   ... Our countrymen in chains,
    The whip on woman's shrinking flesh,

Our soil yet reddening with the stains
Caught from her scourgings warm and fresh.

The slave-dealer boldly publishes his infamous acts to the world. Of all things that have been said of slavery to which exception has been taken by slaveholders, this, the charge of cruelty, stands foremost, and yet there is no charge capable of clearer demonstration, than that of the most barbarous inhumanity on the part of the slaveholders toward their slaves. And all this is necessary; it is necessary to resort to these cruelties, in order to make the slave a slave, and to keep him a slave. Why, my experience all goes to prove the truth of what you will call a marvelous proposition, that the better you treat a slave, the more you destroy his value as a slave, and enhance the probability of his eluding the grasp of the slaveholder; the more kindly you treat him, the more wretched you make him, while you keep him in the condition of a slave. My experience, I say, confirms the truth of this proposition. When I was treated exceedingly ill; when my back was being scourged daily; when I was whipped within an inch of my life—life was all I cared for. "Spare my life," was my continual prayer. When I was looking for the blow about to be inflicted upon my head, I was not thinking of my liberty; it was my life. But, as soon as the blow was not to be feared, then came the longing for liberty. If a slave has a bad master, his ambition is to get a better; when he gets a better, he aspires to have the best; and when he gets the best, he aspires to be his own master. But the slave must be brutalized to keep him as a slave. The slaveholder feels this necessity. I admit this necessity. If it be right to hold slaves at all, it is right to hold them in the only way in which they can be held; and this can be done only by shutting out the light of education from their minds, and brutalizing their persons. The whip, the chain, the gag, the thumb-screw, the blood-hound, the stocks, and all the other bloody paraphernalia of the slave system, are indispensably necessary to the relation of master and slave. The slave must be subjected to these, or he ceases to be a slave. Let him know that the whip is burned; that the fetters have been turned to some useful and profitable employment; that the chain is no longer for his limbs; that the blood-hound is no longer to be put upon his track; that his master's authority over him is no longer to be enforced by taking his life—and immediately he walks out from the house of bondage and asserts his freedom as a man. The slaveholder finds it necessary to have these implements to keep the slave in bondage; finds it necessary to be able to say, "Unless you do so and so; unless you do as I bid you—I will take away your life!"

Some of the most awful scenes of cruelty are constantly taking place in the middle states of the Union. We have in those states what are called the slave-breeding states. Allow me to speak plainly. Although it is harrowing to your feelings, it is necessary that the facts of the case should be stated. We have in the United States slave-breeding states. The very state from which the minister from our court to yours comes, is one of these states—Maryland, where men, women, and children are reared for the market, just as horses, sheep, and swine are raised for the market. Slave-rearing is there looked upon as a legitimate trade; the law sanctions it, public opinion upholds it, the church does not condemn it. It goes on in all its bloody horrors, sustained by the auctioneer's block. If you would see the cruelties of this system, hear the following narrative. Not long since the following scene occurred. A slave-woman and a slaveman had united themselves as man and wife in the absence of any law to protect them as man and wife. They had lived together by the permission, not by right, of their master, and they had reared a family. The master found it expedient, and for his interest, to sell them. He did not ask them their wishes in regard to the matter at all; they were not consulted. The man and woman were brought to the auctioneer's block, under the sound of the hammer. The cry was raised, "Here goes; who bids cash?" Think of it—a man and wife to be sold! The woman was placed on the auctioneer's block; her limbs, as is customary, were brutally exposed to the purchasers, who examined her with all the freedom with which they would examine a horse. There stood the husband, powerless; no right to his wife; the master's right preeminent. She was sold. He was next brought to the auctioneer's block. His eyes followed his wife in the distance; and he looked beseechingly, imploringly, to the man that had bought his wife, to buy him also. But he was at length bid off to another person. He was about to be separated forever from her he loved. No word of his, no work of his, could save him from this separation. He asked permission of his new master to go and take the hand of his wife at parting. It was denied him. In the agony of his soul he rushed from the man who had just bought him, that he might take a farewell of his wife; but his way was obstructed, he was struck over the head with a loaded whip, and was held for a moment; but his agony was too great. When he was let go, he fell a corpse at the feet of his master. His heart was broken. Such scenes are the everyday fruits of American slavery. Some two years since, the Hon. Seth. M. Gates, an anti-slavery gentleman of the state of New York, a representative in the congress of the United States, told me he saw with his own eyes the following circumstances. In the national District of Columbia, over which the star-spangled emblem is constantly waving, where orators are ever holding forth on the subject of American liberty, American democracy, American republicanism, there are two slave prisons. When going across a bridge, leading to one of these prisons, he saw a young woman run out, bare-footed and bare-headed, and with very little clothing on. She was running with all speed to the bridge he was approaching. His eye was fixed upon her, and he stopped to see what was the matter. He had not paused long before he saw three men run out after her. He now knew what the nature of the case was; a slave escaping from her chains—a young woman, a sister—escaping from the bondage in which she had been held. She made her way to the bridge, but had not reached, ere from the Virginia side there came two slaveholders. As soon as they saw them, her pursuers called out, "Stop her!" True to their Virginian instincts, they came to the rescue of their brother kidnappers, across the bridge. The poor girl now saw that there was no chance for her. It was a trying time. She knew if she went back, she must be a slave forever—she must be dragged down to the scenes of pollution which the slaveholders continually provide for most of the poor, sinking, wretched young women, whom they call their property. She formed her resolution; and just as those who were about to take her, were going to put hands upon her, to drag her back, she leaped over the balustrades of the bridge, and down she went to rise no more. She chose death, rather than to go back into the hands of those christian slaveholders from whom she had escaped. Can it be possible that such things as these exist in the United States? Are not these the exceptions? Are any such scenes as this general? Are not such deeds condemned by the law and denounced by public opinion? Let me read to you a few of the laws of the slaveholding states of America. I think no better exposure of slavery can be made than is made by the laws of the states in which slavery exists. I prefer reading the laws to making any statement in confirmation of what I have said myself; for the slaveholders cannot object to this testimony, since it is the calm, the cool, the deliberate enactment of their wisest heads, of their most clear-sighted, their own constituted representatives. "If more than seven slaves together are found in any road without a white person, twenty lashes a piece; for visiting a plantation without a written pass, ten lashes; for letting loose a boat from where it is made fast, thirty-nine lashes for the first offense; and for the second, shall have cut off from his head one ear; for keeping or carrying a club, thirty-nine lashes; for having any article for sale, without a ticket from his master, ten lashes; for traveling in any other than the most usual and accustomed road, when going alone to any place, forty lashes; for traveling in the night without a pass, forty lashes." I am afraid you do not understand the awful character of these lashes. You must bring it before your mind. A human being in a perfect state of nudity, tied hand and foot to a stake, and a strong man standing behind with a heavy whip, knotted at the end, each blow cutting into the flesh, and leaving the warm blood dripping to the feet; and for these trifles. "For being found in another person's negro-quarters, forty lashes; for hunting with dogs in the woods, thirty lashes; for being on horseback without the written permission of his master, twenty-five lashes; for riding or going abroad in the night, or riding horses in the day time, without leave, a slave may be whipped, cropped, or branded in the cheek with the letter R. or otherwise punished, such punishment not extending to life, or so as to render him unfit for labor." The laws referred to, may be found by consulting Brevard's Digest; Haywood's Manual; Virginia

Revised Code; Prince's Digest; Missouri Laws; Mississippi Revised Code. A man, for going to visit his brethren, without the permission of his master—and in many instances he may not have that permission; his master, from caprice or other reasons, may not be willing to allow it—may be caught on his way, dragged to a post, the branding-iron heated, and the name of his master or the letter R branded into his cheek or on his forehead. They treat slaves thus, on the principle that they must punish for light offenses, in order to prevent the commission of larger ones. I wish you to mark that in the single state of Virginia there are seventy-one crimes for which a colored man may be executed; while there are only three of these crimes, which, when committed by a white man, will subject him to that punishment. There are many of these crimes which if the white man did not commit, he would be regarded as a scoundrel and a coward. In the state of Maryland, there is a law to this effect: that if a slave shall strike his master, he may be hanged, his head severed from his body, his body quartered, and his head and quarters set up in the most prominent places in the neighborhood. If a colored woman, in the defense of her own virtue, in defense of her own person, should shield herself from the brutal attacks of her tyrannical master, or make the slightest resistance, she may be killed on the spot. No law whatever will bring the guilty man to justice for the crime.

But you will ask me, can these things be possible in a land professing Christianity? Yes, they are so; and this is not the worst. No; a darker feature is yet to be presented than the mere existence of these facts. I have to inform you that the religion of the southern states, at this time, is the great supporter, the great sanctioner of the bloody atrocities to which I have referred. While America is printing tracts and bibles; sending missionaries abroad to convert the heathen; expending her money in various ways for the promotion of the gospel in foreign lands—the slave not only lies forgotten, uncared for, but is trampled under foot by the very churches of the land. What have we in America? Why, we have slavery made part of the religion of the land. Yes, the pulpit there stands up as the great defender of this cursed institution, as it is called. Ministers of religion come forward and torture the hallowed pages of inspired wisdom to sanction the bloody deed. They stand forth as the foremost, the strongest defenders of this "institution." As a proof of this, I need not do more than state the general fact, that slavery has existed under the droppings of the sanctuary of the south for the last two hundred years, and there has not been any war between the religion and the slavery of the south. Whips, chains, gags, and thumb-screws have all lain under the droppings of the sanctuary, and instead of rusting from off the limbs of the bondman, those droppings have served to preserve them in all their strength. Instead of preaching the gospel against this tyranny, rebuke, and wrong, ministers of religion have sought, by all and every means, to throw in the back-ground whatever in the bible could be construed into opposition to slavery, and to bring forward that which they could torture into its support. This I conceive to be the darkest feature of slavery, and the most difficult to attack, because it is identified with religion, and exposes those who denounce it to the charge of infidelity. Yes, those with whom I have been laboring, namely, the old organization anti-slavery society of America, have been again and again stigmatized as infidels, and for what reason? Why, solely in consequence of the faithfulness of their attacks upon the slaveholding religion of the southern states, and the northern religion that sympathizes with it. I have found it difficult to speak on this matter without persons coming forward and saying, "Douglass, are you not afraid of injuring the cause of Christ? You do not desire to do so, we know; but are you not undermining religion?" This has been said to me again and again, even since I came to this country, but I cannot be induced to leave off these exposures. I love the religion of our blessed Savior. I love that religion that comes from above, in the "wisdom of God," which is first pure, then peaceable, gentle, and easy to be entreated, full of mercy and good fruits, without partiality and without hypocrisy. I love that religion that sends its votaries to bind up the wounds of him that has fallen among thieves. I love that religion that makes it the duty of its disciples to visit the father less and the widow in their affliction. I love that religion that is based upon the glorious principle, of love to God and love to man; which makes its followers do unto others as they themselves would be done by. If you demand liberty to yourself, it says, grant it to your neighbors. If you claim a right to think for yourself, it says, allow your neighbors the same right. If you claim to act for yourself, it says, allow your neighbors the same right. It is because I love this religion that I hate the slaveholding, the woman-whipping, the mind-darkening, the soul-destroying religion that exists in the southern states of America. It is because I regard the one as good, and pure, and holy, that I cannot but regard the other as bad, corrupt, and wicked. Loving the one I must hate the other; holding to the one I must reject the other.

I may be asked, why I am so anxious to bring this subject before the British public—why I do not confine my efforts to the United States? My answer is, first, that slavery is the common enemy of mankind, and all mankind should be made acquainted with its abominable character. My next answer is, that the slave is a man, and, as such, is entitled to your sympathy as a brother. All the feelings, all the susceptibilities, all the capacities, which you have, he has. He is a part of the human family. He has been the prey—the common prey—of Christendom for the last three hundred years, and it is but right, it is but just, it is but proper, that his wrongs should be known throughout the world. I have another reason for bringing this matter before the British public, and it is this: slavery is a system of wrong, so blinding to all around, so hardening to the heart, so corrupting to the morals, so deleterious to religion, so sapping to all the principles of justice in its immediate vicinity, that the community surrounding it lack the moral stamina necessary to its removal. It is a system of such gigantic evil, so strong, so overwhelming in its power, that no one nation is equal to its removal. It requires the humanity of Christianity, the morality of the world to remove it. Hence, I call upon the people of Britain to look at this matter, and to exert the influence I am about to show they possess, for the removal of slavery from America. I can appeal to them, as strongly by their regard for the slaveholder as for the slave, to labor in this cause. I am here, because you have an influence on America that no other nation can have. You have been drawn together by the power of steam to a marvelous extent; the distance between London and Boston is now reduced to some twelve or fourteen days, so that the denunciations against slavery, uttered in London this week, may be heard in a fortnight in the streets of Boston, and reverberating amidst the hills of Massachusetts. There is nothing said here against slavery that will not be recorded in the United States. I am here, also, because the slaveholders do not want me to be here; they would rather that I were not here. I have adopted a maxim laid down by Napoleon, never to occupy ground which the enemy would like me to occupy. The slaveholders would much rather have me, if I will denounce slavery, denounce it in the northern states, where their friends and supporters are, who will stand by and mob me for denouncing it. They feel something as the man felt, when he uttered his prayer, in which he made out a most horrible case for himself, and one of his neighbors touched him and said, "My friend, I always had the opinion of you that you have now expressed for yourself—that you are a very great sinner." Coming from himself, it was all very well, but coming from a stranger it was rather cutting. The slaveholders felt that when slavery was denounced among themselves, it was not so bad; but let one of the slaves get loose, let him summon the people of Britain, and make known to them the conduct of the slaveholders toward their slaves, and it cuts them to the quick, and produces a sensation such as would be produced by nothing else. The power I exert now is something like the power that is exerted by the man at the end of the lever; my influence now is just in proportion to the distance that I am from the United States. My exposure of slavery abroad will tell more upon the hearts and consciences of slaveholders, than if I was attacking them in America; for almost every paper that I now receive from the United States, comes teeming with statements about this fugitive Negro, calling him a "glib-tongued scoundrel," and saying that he is running out against the institutions and people of America. I deny the charge that I am saying a word against the institutions of America, or the people, as such. What I have to say is against slavery and slaveholders. I feel at liberty to speak on this subject. I have on my back the marks of the lash; I have four sisters and one brother now under the galling chain. I feel it my duty to cry aloud and spare not. I am not averse to having the good opinion of my fellow creatures. I am not averse to being kindly regarded by all men; but I am bound, even at the hazard of making a large class of religionists in this country hate me, oppose me, and malign me as they have done—I am bound by the prayers, and tears, and entreaties of three millions of kneeling bondsmen, to have no compromise with men who are in any shape or form connected with the slaveholders of America. I expose slavery in this country, because to expose it is to kill it. Slavery is one of those monsters of darkness to whom the light of truth is death. Expose slavery, and it dies. Light is to slavery what the heat of the sun is to the root of a tree; it must die under it. All the slaveholder asks of me is silence. He does not ask me to go abroad and preach in favor of slavery; he does not ask any one to do that. He would not say that slavery is a good thing, but the best under the circumstances. The slaveholders want total darkness on the subject. They want the hatchway shut down, that the monster may crawl in his den of darkness, crushing human hopes and happiness, destroying the bondman at will, and having no one to reprove or rebuke him. Slavery shrinks from the light; it hateth the light, neither cometh to the light, lest its deeds should be reproved. To tear off the mask from this abominable system, to expose it to the light of heaven, aye, to the heat of the sun, that it may burn and wither it out of existence, is my object in coming to this country. I want the slaveholder surrounded, as by a wall of anti-slavery fire, so that he may see the condemnation of himself and his system glaring down in letters of light. I want him to feel that he has no sympathy in England, Scotland, or Ireland; that he has none in Canada, none in Mexico, none among the poor wild Indians; that the voice of the civilized, aye, and savage world is against him. I would have condemnation blaze down upon him in every direction, till, stunned and overwhelmed with shame and confusion, he is compelled to let go the grasp he holds upon the persons of his victims, and restore them to their long-lost rights.

Dr. Campbell's Reply

From Rev. Dr. Campbell's brilliant reply we extract the following: FREDERICK DOUGLASS, "the beast of burden," the portion of "goods and chattels," the representative of three millions of men, has been raised up! Shall I say the man? If there is a man on earth, he is a man. My blood boiled within me when I heard his address tonight, and thought that he had left behind him three millions of such men.
We must see more of this man; we must have more of this man. One would have taken a voyage round the globe some forty years back—especially since the introduction of steam—to have heard such an exposure of slavery from the lips of a slave. It will be an era in the individual history of the present assembly. Our children—our boys and girls—I have tonight seen the delightful sympathy of their hearts evinced by their heaving breasts, while their eyes sparkled with wonder and admiration, that this black man—this slave—had so much logic, so much wit, so much fancy, so much eloquence. He was something more than a man, according to their little notions. Then, I say, we must hear him again. We have got a purpose to accomplish. He has appealed to the pulpit of England. The English pulpit is with him. He has appealed to the press of England; the press of England is conducted by English hearts, and that press will do him justice. About ten days hence, and his second master, who may well prize "such a piece of goods," will have the pleasure of reading his burning words, and his first master will bless himself that he has got quit of him. We have to create public opinion, or rather, not to create it, for it is created already; but we have to foster it; and when tonight I heard those magnificent words—the words of Curran, by which my heart, from boyhood, has ofttimes been deeply moved—I rejoice to think that they embody an instinct of an

Englishman's nature. I heard, with inexpressible delight, how they told on this mighty mass of the citizens of the metropolis.

Britain has now no slaves; we can therefore talk to the other nations now, as we could not have talked a dozen years ago. I want the whole of the London ministry to meet Douglass. For as his appeal is to England, and throughout England, I should rejoice in the idea of churchmen and dissenters merging all sectional distinctions in this cause. Let us have a public breakfast. Let the ministers meet him; let them hear him; let them grasp his hand; and let him enlist their sympathies on behalf of the slave. Let him inspire them with abhorrence of the man-stealer— the slaveholder. No slaveholding American shall ever my cross my door. No slaveholding or slavery-supporting minister shall ever pollute my pulpit. While I have a tongue to speak, or a hand to write, I will, to the utmost of my power, oppose these slaveholding men. We must have Douglass amongst us to aid in fostering public opinion.

The great conflict with slavery must now take place in America; and while they are adding other slave states to the Union, our business is to step forward and help the abolitionists there. It is a pleasing circumstance that such a body of men has risen in America, and whilst we hurl our thunders against her slavers, let us make a distinction between those who advocate slavery and those who oppose it. George Thompson has been there. This man, Frederick Douglass, has been there, and has been compelled to flee. I wish, when he first set foot on our shores, he had made a solemn vow, and said, "Now that I am free, and in the sanctuary of freedom, I will never return till I have seen the emancipation of my country completed." He wants to surround these men, the slaveholders, as by a wall of fire; and he himself may do much toward kindling it. Let him travel over the island—east, west, north, and south—everywhere diffusing knowledge and awakening principle, till the whole nation become a body of petitioners to America. He will, he must, do it. He must for a season make England his home. He must send for his wife. He must send for his children. I want to see the sons and daughters of such a sire. We, too, must do something for him and them worthy of the English name. I do not like the idea of a man of such mental dimensions, such moral courage, and all but incomparable talent, having his own small wants, and the wants of a distant wife and children, supplied by the poor profits of his publication, the sketch of his life. Let the pamphlet be bought by tens of thousands. But we will do something more for him, shall we not?

It only remains that we pass a resolution of thanks to Frederick Douglass, the slave that was, the man that is! He that was covered with chains, and that is now being covered with glory, and whom we will send back a gentleman.

LETTER TO HIS OLD MASTER. To My Old Master, Thomas Auld

Footnote 11

SIR—The long and intimate, though by no means friendly, relation which unhappily subsisted between you and myself, leads me to hope that you will easily account for the great liberty which I now take in addressing you in this open and public manner. The same fact may remove any disagreeable surprise which you may experience on again finding your name coupled with mine, in any other way than in an advertisement, accurately describing my person, and offering a large sum for my arrest. In thus dragging you again before the public, I am aware that I shall subject myself to no inconsiderable amount of censure. I shall probably be charged with an unwarrantable, if not a wanton and reckless disregard of the rights and properties of private life. There are those north as well as south who entertain a much higher respect for rights which are merely conventional, than they do for rights which are personal and essential. Not a few there are in our country, who, while they have no scruples against robbing the laborer of the hard earned results of his patient industry, will be shocked by the extremely indelicate manner of bringing your name before the public. Believing this to be the case, and wishing to meet every reasonable or plausible objection to my conduct, I will frankly state the ground upon which I justfy(sic) myself in this instance, as well as on former occasions when I have thought proper to mention your name in public. All will agree that a man guilty of theft, robbery, or murder, has forfeited the right to concealment and private life; that the community have a right to subject such persons to the most complete exposure. However much they may desire retirement, and aim to conceal themselves and their movements from the popular gaze, the public have a right to ferret them out, and bring their conduct before the proper tribunals of the country for investigation. Sir, you will undoubtedly make the proper application of these generally admitted principles, and will easily see the light in which you are regarded by me; I will not therefore manifest ill temper, by calling you hard names. I know you to be a man of some intelligence, and can readily determine the precise estimate which I entertain of your character. I may therefore indulge in language which may seem to others indirect and ambiguous, and yet be quite well understood by yourself.

I have selected this day on which to address you, because it is the anniversary of my emancipation; and knowing no better way, I am led to this as the best mode of celebrating that truly important events. Just ten years ago this beautiful September morning, yon bright sun beheld me a slave—a poor degraded chattel—trembling at the sound of your voice, lamenting that I was a man, and wishing myself a brute. The hopes which I had treasured up for weeks of a safe and successful escape from your grasp, were powerfully confronted at this last hour by dark clouds of doubt and fear, making my person shake and my bosom to heave with the heavy contest between hope and fear. I have no words to describe to you the deep agony of soul which I experienced on that never-to-be-forgotten morning—for I left by daylight. I was making a leap in the dark. The probabilities, so far as I could by reason determine them, were stoutly against the undertaking. The preliminaries and precautions I had adopted previously, all worked badly. I was like one going to war without weapons—ten chances of defeat to one of victory. One in whom I had confided, and one who had promised me assistance, appalled by fear at the trial hour, deserted me, thus leaving the responsibility of success or failure solely with myself. You, sir, can never know my feelings. As I look back to them, I can scarcely realize that I have passed through a scene so trying. Trying, however, as they were, and gloomy as was the prospect, thanks be to the Most High, who is ever the God of the oppressed, at the moment which was to determine my whole earthly career, His grace was sufficient; my mind was made up. I embraced the golden opportunity, took the morning tide at the flood, and a free man, young, active, and strong, is the result.

I have often thought I should like to explain to you the grounds upon which I have justified myself in running away from you. I am almost ashamed to do so now, for by this time you may have discovered them yourself. I will, however, glance at them. When yet but a child about six years old, I imbibed the determination to run away. The very first mental effort that I now remember on my part, was an attempt to solve the mystery—why am I a slave? and with this question my youthful mind was troubled for many days, pressing upon me more heavily at times than others. When I saw the slave-driver whip a slave-woman, cut the blood out of her neck, and heard her piteous cries, I went away into the corner of the fence, wept and pondered over the mystery. I had, through some medium, I know not what, got some idea of God, the Creator of all mankind, the black and the white, and that he had made the blacks to serve the whites as slaves. How he could do this and be good, I could not tell. I was not satisfied with this theory, which made God responsible for slavery, for it pained me greatly, and I have wept over it long and often. At one time, your first wife, Mrs. Lucretia, heard me sighing and saw me shedding tears, and asked of me the matter, but I was afraid to tell her. I was puzzled with this question, till one night while sitting in the kitchen, I heard some of the old slaves talking of their parents having been stolen from Africa by white men, and were sold here as slaves.

The whole mystery was solved at once. Very soon after this, my Aunt Jinny and Uncle Noah ran away, and the great noise made about it by your father-in-law, made me for the first time acquainted with the fact, that there were free states as well as slave states. From that time, I resolved that I would some day run away. The morality of the act I dispose of as follows: I am myself; you are yourself; we are two distinct persons, equal persons. What you are, I am. You are a man, and so am I. God created both, and made us separate beings. I am not by nature bond to you, or you to me. Nature does not make your existence depend upon me, or mine to depend upon yours. I cannot walk upon your legs, or you upon mine. I cannot breathe for you, or you for me; I must breathe for myself, and you for yourself. We are distinct persons, and are each equally provided with faculties necessary to our individual existence. In leaving you, I took nothing but what belonged to me, and in no way lessened your means for obtaining an honest living. Your faculties remained yours, and mine became useful to their rightful owner. I therefore see no wrong in any part of the transaction. It is true, I went off secretly; but that was more your fault than mine. Had I let you into the secret, you would have defeated the enterprise entirely; but for this, I should have been really glad to have made you acquainted with my intentions to leave.

You may perhaps want to know how I like my present condition. I am free to say, I greatly prefer it to that which I occupied in Maryland. I am, however, by no means prejudiced against the state as such. Its geography, climate, fertility, and products, are such as to make it a very desirable abode for any man; and but for the existence of slavery there, it is not impossible that I might again take up my abode in that state. It is not that I love Maryland less, but freedom more. You will be surprised to learn that people at the north labor under the strange delusion that if the slaves were emancipated at the south, they would flock to the north. So far from this being the case, in that event, you would see many old and familiar faces back again to the south. The fact is, there are few here who would not return to the south in the event of emancipation. We want to live in the land of our birth, and to lay our bones by the side of our fathers; and nothing short of an intense love of personal freedom keeps us from the south. For the sake of this, most of us would live on a crust of bread and a cup of cold water.

Since I left you, I have had a rich experience. I have occupied stations which I never dreamed of when a slave. Three out of the ten years since I left you, I spent as a common laborer on the wharves of New Bedford, Massachusetts. It was there I earned my first free dollar. It was mine. I could spend it as I pleased. I could buy hams or herring with it, without asking any odds of anybody. That was a precious dollar to me. You remember when I used to make seven, or eight, or even nine dollars a week in Baltimore, you would take every cent of it from me every Saturday night, saying that I belonged to you, and my earnings also. I never liked this conduct on your part—to say the best, I thought it a little mean. I would not have served you so. But let that pass. I was a little awkward about counting money in New England fashion when I first landed in New Bedford. I came near betraying myself several times. I caught myself saying phip, for fourpence; and at one time a man actually charged me with being a runaway, whereupon I was silly enough to become one by running away from him, for I was greatly afraid he might adopt measures to get me again into slavery, a condition I then dreaded more than death.

I soon learned, however, to count money, as well as to make it, and got on swimmingly. I married soon after leaving you; in fact, I was engaged to be married before I left you; and instead of finding my companion a burden, she was truly a helpmate. She went to live at service, and I to work on the wharf, and though we toiled hard the first winter, we never lived more happily. After remaining in New Bedford for three years, I met with William Lloyd Garrison, a person of whom you have possibly heard, as he is pretty generally known among slaveholders. He put it into my head that I might make myself serviceable to the cause of the slave, by devoting a portion of my time to telling my own sorrows, and those of other slaves, which had come under my observation. This was the commencement of a higher state of existence than any to which I had ever aspired. I was thrown into society the most pure, enlightened, and benevolent, that the country affords. Among these I have never forgotten you, but have invariably made you the topic of conversation—thus giving you all the notoriety I could do. I need not tell you that the opinion formed of you in these circles is far from being favorable. They have little respect for your honesty, and less for your religion.

But I was going on to relate to you something of my interesting experience. I had not long enjoyed the excellent society to which I have referred, before the light of its excellence exerted a beneficial influence on my mind and heart. Much of my early dislike of white persons was removed, and their manners, habits, and customs, so entirely unlike what I had been used to in the kitchen-quarters on the plantations of the south, fairly charmed me, and gave me a strong disrelish for the coarse and degrading customs of my former condition. I therefore made an effort so to improve my mind and deportment, as to be somewhat fitted to the station to which I seemed almost providentially called. The transition from degradation to respectability was indeed great, and to get from one to the other without carrying some marks of one's former condition, is truly a difficult matter. I would not have you think that I am now entirely clear of all plantation peculiarities, but my friends here, while they entertain the strongest dislike to them, regard me with that charity to which my past life somewhat entitles me, so that my condition in this respect is exceedingly pleasant. So far as my domestic affairs are concerned, I can boast of as comfortable a dwelling as your own. I have an industrious and neat companion, and four dear children—the oldest a girl of nine years, and three fine boys, the oldest eight, the next six, and the youngest four years old. The three oldest are now going regularly to school—two can read and write, and the other can spell, with tolerable correctness, words of two syllables. Dear fellows! they are all in comfortable beds, and are sound asleep, perfectly secure under my own roof. There are no slaveholders here to rend my heart by snatching them from my arms, or blast a mother's dearest hopes by tearing them from her bosom. These dear children are ours—not to work up into rice, sugar, and tobacco, but to watch over, regard, and protect, and to rear them up in the nurture and admonition of the gospel—to train them up in the paths of wisdom and virtue, and, as far as we can, to make them useful to the world and to themselves. Oh! sir, a slaveholder never appears to me so completely an agent of hell, as when I think of and look upon my dear children. It is then that my feelings rise above my control. I meant to have said more with respect to my own prosperity and happiness, but thoughts and feel ings which this recital has quickened, unfit me to proceed further in that direction. The grim horrors of slavery rise in all their ghastly terror before me; the wails of millions pierce my heart and chill my blood. I remember the chain, the gag, the bloody whip; the death-like gloom overshadowing the broken spirit of the fettered bondman; the appalling liability of his being torn away from wife and children, and sold like a beast in the market. Say not that this is a picture of fancy. You well know that I wear stripes on my back, inflicted by your direction; and that you, while we were brothers in the same church, caused this right hand, with which I am now penning this letter, to be closely tied to my left, and my person dragged, at the pistol's mouth, fifteen miles, from the Bay Side to Easton, to be sold like a beast in the market, for the alleged crime of intending to escape from your possession. All this, and more, you remember, and know to be perfectly true, not only of yourself, but of nearly all of the slaveholders around you.

At this moment, you are probably the guilty holder of at least three of my own dear sisters, and my only brother, in bondage. These you regard as your property. They are recorded on your ledger, or perhaps have been sold to human flesh-mongers, with a view to filling our own ever-hungry purse. Sir, I desire to know how and where these dear sisters are. Have you sold them? or are they still in your possession? What has become of them? are they living or dead? And my dear old grandmother, whom you turned out like an old horse to die in the woods—is she still alive? Write and let me know all about them. If my grandmother be still alive, she is of no service to you, for by this time she must be nearly eighty years old—too old to be cared for by one to whom she has ceased to be of service; send her to me at Rochester, or bring her to Philadelphia, and it shall be the crowning happiness of my life to take care of her in her old age. Oh! she was to me a mother and a father, so far as hard toil for my comfort could make her such. Send me my grandmother! that I may watch over and take care of her in her old age. And my sisters—let me know all about them. I would write to them, and learn all I want to know of them, without disturbing you in any way, but that, through your unrighteous conduct, they have been entirely deprived of the power to read and write. You have kept them in utter ignorance, and have therefore robbed them of the sweet enjoyments of writing or receiving letters from absent friends and relatives. Your wickedness and cruelty, committed in this respect on your fellow-creatures, are greater than all the stripes you have laid upon my back or theirs. It is an outrage upon the soul, a war upon the immortal spirit, and one for which you must give account at the bar of our common Father and Creator.

The responsibility which you have assumed in this regard is truly awful, and how you could stagger under it these many years is marvelous. Your mind must have become darkened, your heart hardened, your conscience seared and petrified, or you would have long since thrown off the accursed load, and sought relief at the hands of a sin-forgiving God. How, let me ask, would you look upon me, were I, some dark night, in company with a band of hardened villains, to enter the precincts of your elegant dwelling, and seize the person of your own lovely daughter, Amanda, and carry her off from your family, friends, and all the loved ones of her youth—make her my slave—compel her to work, and I take her wages—place her name on my ledger as property—disregard her personal rights—fetter the powers of her immortal soul by denying her the right and privilege of learning to read and write—feed her coarsely— clothe her scantily, and whip her on the naked back occasionally; more, and still more horrible, leave her unprotected—a degraded victim to the brutal lust of fiendish overseers, who would pollute, blight, and blast her fair soul—rob her of all dignity—destroy her virtue, and annihilate in her person all the graces that adorn the character of virtuous womanhood? I ask, how would you regard me, if such were my conduct? Oh! the vocabulary of the damned would not afford a word sufficiently infernal to express your idea of my God-provoking wickedness. Yet, sir, your treatment of my beloved sisters is in all essential points precisely like the case I have now supposed. Damning as would be such a deed on my part, it would be no more so than that which you have committed against me and my sisters.

I will now bring this letter to a close; you shall hear from me again unless you let me hear from you. I intend to make use of you as a weapon with which to assail the system of slavery—as a means of concentrating public attention on the system, and deepening the horror of trafficking in the souls and bodies of men. I shall make use of you as a means of exposing the character of the American church and clergy—and as a means of bringing this guilty nation, with yourself, to repentance. In doing this, I entertain no malice toward you personally. There is no roof under which you would be more safe than mine, and there is nothing in my house which you might need for your comfort, which I would not readily grant. Indeed, I should esteem it a privilege to set you an example as to how mankind ought to treat each other.

I am your fellow-man, but not your slave.

THE NATURE OF SLAVERY. Extract from a Lecture on Slavery, at Rochester,

December 1, 1850

More than twenty years of my life were consumed in a state of slavery. My childhood was environed by the baneful peculiarities of the slave system. I grew up to manhood in the presence of this hydra headed monster—not as a master—not as an idle spectator—not as the guest of the slaveholder—but as A SLAVE, eating the bread and drinking the cup of slavery with the most degraded of my brother-bondmen, and sharing with them all the painful conditions of their wretched lot. In consideration of these facts, I feel that I have a right to speak, and to speak strongly. Yet, my friends, I feel bound to speak truly.

Goading as have been the cruelties to which I have been subjected—bitter as have been the trials through which I have passed—exasperating as have been, and still are, the indignities offered to my manhood—I find in them no excuse for the slightest departure from truth in dealing with any branch of this subject.

First of all, I will state, as well as I can, the legal and social relation of master and slave. A master is one—to speak in the vocabulary of the southern states—who claims and exercises a right of property in the person of a fellow-man. This he does with the force of the law and the sanction of southern religion. The law gives the master absolute power over the slave. He may work him, flog him, hire him out, sell him, and, in certain contingencies, kill him, with perfect impunity. The slave is a human being, divested of all rights—reduced to the level of a brute—a mere "chattel" in the eye of the law—placed beyond the circle of human brotherhood—cut off from his kind—his name, which the "recording angel" may have enrolled in heaven, among the blest, is impiously inserted in a master's ledger, with horses, sheep, and swine. In law, the slave has no wife, no children, no country, and no home. He can own nothing, possess nothing, acquire nothing, but what must belong to another. To eat the fruit of his own toil, to clothe his person with the work of his own hands, is considered stealing. He toils that another may reap the fruit; he is industrious that another may live in idleness; he eats unbolted meal that another may eat the bread of fine flour; he labors in chains at home, under a burning sun and biting lash, that another may ride in ease and splendor abroad; he lives in ignorance that another may be educated; he is abused that another may be exalted; he rests his toil-worn limbs on the cold, damp ground that another may repose on the softest pillow; he is clad in coarse and tattered raiment that another may be arrayed in purple and fine linen; he is sheltered only by the wretched hovel that a master may dwell in a magnificent mansion; and to this condition he is bound down as by an arm of iron.

From this monstrous relation there springs an unceasing stream of most revolting cruelties. The very accompaniments of the slave system stamp it as the offspring of hell itself. To ensure good behavior, the slaveholder relies on the whip; to induce proper humility, he relies on the whip; to rebuke what he is pleased to term insolence, he relies on the whip; to supply the place of wages as an incentive to toil, he relies on the whip; to bind down the spirit of the slave, to imbrute and destroy his manhood, he relies on the whip, the chain, the gag, the thumb-screw, the pillory, the bowie knife the pistol, and the blood-hound. These are the necessary and unvarying accompaniments of the system. Wherever slavery is found, these horrid instruments are also found. Whether on the coast of Africa, among the savage tribes, or in South Carolina, among the refined and civilized, slavery is the same, and its accompaniments one and the same. It makes no difference whether the slaveholder worships the God of the Christians, or is a follower of Mahomet, he is the minister of the same cruelty, and the author of the same misery. Slavery is always slavery; always the same foul, haggard, and damning scourge, whether found in the eastern or in the western hemisphere.

There is a still deeper shade to be given to this picture. The physical cruelties are indeed sufficiently harassing and revolting; but they are as a few grains of sand on the sea shore, or a few drops of water in the great ocean, compared with the stupendous wrongs which it inflicts upon the mental, moral, and religious nature of its hapless victims. It is only when we contemplate the slave as a moral and intellectual being, that we can adequately comprehend the unparalleled enormity of slavery, and the intense criminality of the slaveholder. I have said that the slave was a man. "What a piece of work is man! How noble in reason! How infinite in faculties! In form and moving how express and admirable! In action how like an angel! In apprehension how like a God! The beauty of the world! The paragon of animals!"

The slave is a man, "the image of God," but "a little lower than the angels;" possessing a soul, eternal and indestructible; capable of endless happiness, or immeasurable woe; a creature of hopes and fears, of affections and passions, of joys and sorrows, and he is endowed with those mysterious powers by which man soars above the things of time and sense, and grasps, with undying tenacity, the elevating and sublimely glorious idea of a God. It is such a being that is smitten and blasted. The first work of slavery is to mar and deface those characteristics of its victims which distinguish men from things, and persons from property. Its first aim is to destroy all sense of high moral and religious responsibility. It reduces man to a mere machine. It cuts him off from his Maker, it hides from him the laws of God, and leaves him to grope his way from time to eternity in the dark, under the arbitrary and despotic control of a frail, depraved, and sinful fellow-man. As the serpent-charmer of India is compelled to extract the deadly teeth of his venomous prey before he is able to handle him with impunity, so the slaveholder must strike down the conscience of the slave before he can obtain the entire mastery over his victim.

It is, then, the first business of the enslaver of men to blunt, deaden, and destroy the central principle of human responsibility. Conscience is, to the individual soul, and to society, what the law of gravitation is to the universe. It holds society together; it is the basis of all trust and confidence; it is the pillar of all moral rectitude. Without it, suspicion would take the place of trust; vice would be more than a match for virtue; men would prey upon each other, like the wild beasts of the desert; and earth would become a hell.

Nor is slavery more adverse to the conscience than it is to the mind. This is shown by the fact, that in every state of the American Union, where slavery exists, except the state of Kentucky, there are laws absolutely prohibitory of education among the slaves. The crime of teaching a slave to read is punishable with severe fines and imprisonment, and, in some instances, with death itself.

Nor are the laws respecting this matter a dead letter. Cases may occur in which they are disregarded, and a few instances may be found where slaves may have learned to read; but such are isolated cases, and only prove the rule. The great mass of slaveholders look upon education among the slaves as utterly subversive of the slave system. I well remember when my mistress first announced to my master that she had dis covered that I could read. His face colored at once with surprise and chagrin. He said that "I was ruined, and my value as a slave destroyed; that a slave should know nothing but to obey his master; that to give a negro an inch would lead him to take an ell; that having learned how to read, I would soon want to know how to write; and that by-and-by I would be running away." I think my audience will bear witness to the correctness of this philosophy, and to the literal fulfillment of this prophecy.

It is perfectly well understood at the south, that to educate a slave is to make him discontened(sic) with slavery, and to invest him with a power which shall open to him the treasures of freedom; and since the object of the slaveholder is to maintain complete authority over his slave, his constant vigilance is exercised to prevent everything which militates against, or endangers, the stability of his authority. Education being among the menacing influences, and, perhaps, the most dangerous, is, therefore, the most cautiously guarded against.

It is true that we do not often hear of the enforcement of the law, punishing as a crime the teaching of slaves to read, but this is not because of a want of disposition to enforce it. The true reason or explanation of the matter is this: there is the greatest unanimity of opinion among the white population in the south in favor of the policy of keeping the slave in ignorance. There is, perhaps, another reason why the law against education is so seldom violated. The slave is too poor to be able to offer a temptation sufficiently strong to induce a white man to violate it; and it is not to be supposed that in a community where the moral and religious sentiment is in favor of slavery, many martyrs will be found sacrificing their liberty and lives by violating those prohibitory enactments.

As a general rule, then, darkness reigns over the abodes of the enslaved, and "how great is that darkness!"

We are sometimes told of the contentment of the slaves, and are entertained with vivid pictures of their happiness. We are told that they often dance and sing; that their masters frequently give them wherewith to make merry; in fine, that they have little of which to complain. I admit that the slave does sometimes sing, dance, and appear to be merry. But what does this prove? It only proves to my mind, that though slavery is armed with a thousand stings, it is not able entirely to kill the elastic spirit of the bondman. That spirit will rise and walk abroad, despite of whips and chains, and extract from the cup of nature occasional drops of joy and gladness. No thanks to the slaveholder, nor to slavery, that the vivacious captive may sometimes dance in his chains; his very mirth in such circumstances stands before God as an accusing angel against his enslaver.

It is often said, by the opponents of the anti-slavery cause, that the condition of the people of Ireland is more deplorable than that of the American slaves. Far be it from me to underrate the sufferings of the Irish people. They have been long oppressed; and the same heart that prompts me to plead the cause of the American bondman, makes it impossible for me not to sympathize with the oppressed of all lands. Yet I must say that there is no analogy between the two cases. The Irishman is poor, but he is not a slave. He may be in rags, but he is not a slave. He is still the master of his own body, and can say with the poet, "The hand of Douglass is his own." "The world is all before him, where to choose;" and poor as may be my opinion of the British parliament, I cannot believe that it will ever sink to such a depth of infamy as to pass a law for the recapture of fugitive Irishmen! The shame and scandal of kidnapping will long remain wholly monopolized by the American congress. The Irishman has not only the liberty to emigrate from his country, but he has liberty at home. He can write, and speak, and cooperate for the attainment of his rights and the redress of his wrongs.

The multitude can assemble upon all the green hills and fertile plains of the Emerald Isle; they can pour out their grievances, and proclaim their wants without molestation; and the press, that "swift-winged messenger," can bear the tidings of their doings to the extreme bounds of the civilized world. They have their "Conciliation Hall," on the banks of the Liffey, their reform clubs, and their newspapers; they pass resolutions, send forth addresses, and enjoy the right of petition. But how is it with the American slave? Where may he assemble? Where is his Conciliation Hall? Where are his newspapers? Where is his right of petition? Where is his freedom of speech? his liberty of the press? and his right of locomotion? He is said to be happy; happy men can speak. But ask the slave what is his condition—what his state of mind—what he thinks of enslavement? and you had as well address your inquiries to the silent dead. There comes no voice from the enslaved. We are left to gather his feelings by imagining what ours would be, were our souls in his soul's stead.

If there were no other fact descriptive of slavery, than that the slave is dumb, this alone would be sufficient to mark the slave system as a grand aggregation of human horrors.

Most who are present, will have observed that leading men in this country have been putting forth their skill to secure quiet to the nation. A system of measures to promote this object was adopted a few months ago in congress. The result of those measures is known. Instead of quiet, they have produced alarm; instead of peace, they have brought us war; and so it must ever be.

While this nation is guilty of the enslavement of three millions of innocent men and women, it is as idle to think of having a sound and lasting peace, as it is to think there is no God to take cognizance of the affairs of men. There can be no peace to the wicked while slavery continues in the land. It will be condemned; and while it is condemned there will be agitation. Nature must cease to be nature; men must become monsters; humanity must be transformed; Christianity must be exterminated; all ideas of justice and the laws of eternal goodness must be utterly blotted out from the human soul—ere a system so foul and infernal can escape condemnation, or this guilty republic can have a sound, enduring peace.

INHUMANITY OF SLAVERY. Extract from A Lecture on Slavery, at Rochester,

December 8, 1850

The relation of master and slave has been called patriarchal, and only second in benignity and tenderness to that of the parent and child. This representation is doubtless believed by many northern people; and this may account, in part, for the lack of interest which we find among persons whom we are bound to believe to be honest and humane. What, then, are the facts? Here I will not quote my own experience in slavery; for this you might call one-sided testimony. I will not cite the declarations of abolitionists; for these you might pronounce exaggerations. I will not rely upon advertisements cut from newspapers; for these you might call isolated cases. But I will refer you to the laws adopted by the legislatures of the slave states. I give you such evidence, because it cannot be invalidated nor denied. I hold in my hand sundry extracts from the slave codes of our country, from which I will quote. * * * Now, if the foregoing be an indication of kindness, what is cruelty? If this be parental affection, what is bitter malignity? A more atrocious and blood-thirsty string of laws could not well be conceived of. And yet I am bound to say that they fall short of indicating the horrible cruelties constantly practiced in the slave states.

I admit that there are individual slaveholders less cruel and barbarous than is allowed by law; but these form the exception. The majority of slaveholders find it necessary, to insure obedience, at times, to avail themselves of the utmost extent of the law, and many go beyond it. If kindness were the rule, we should not see advertisements filling the columns of almost every southern newspaper, offering large rewards for fugitive slaves, and describing them as being branded with irons, loaded with chains, and scarred by the whip. One of the most telling testimonies against the pretended kindness of slaveholders, is the fact that uncounted numbers of fugitives are now inhabiting the Dismal Swamp, preferring the untamed wilderness to their cultivated homes—choosing rather to encounter hunger and thirst, and to roam with the wild beasts of the forest, running the hazard of being hunted and shot down, than to submit to the authority of kind masters.

I tell you, my friends, humanity is never driven to such an unnatural course of life, without great wrong. The slave finds more of the milk of human kindness in the bosom of the savage Indian, than in the heart of his Christian master. He leaves the man of the bible, and takes refuge with the man of the tomahawk. He rushes from the praying slaveholder into the paws of the bear. He quits the homes of men for the haunts of wolves. He prefers to encounter a life of trial, however bitter, or death, however terrible, to dragging out his existence under the dominion of these kind masters.

The apologists for slavery often speak of the abuses of slavery; and they tell us that they are as much opposed to those abuses as we are; and that they would go as far to correct those abuses and to ameliorate the condition of the slave as anybody. The answer to that view is, that slavery is itself an abuse; that it lives by abuse; and dies by the absence of abuse. Grant that slavery is right; grant that the relations of master and slave may innocently exist; and there is not a single outrage which was ever committed against the slave but what finds an apology in the very necessity of the case. As we said by a slaveholder (the Rev. A. G. Few) to the Methodist conference, "If the relation be right, the means to maintain it are also right;" for without those means slavery could not exist. Remove the dreadful scourge—the plaited thong—the galling fetter—the accursed chain—and let the slaveholder rely solely upon moral and religious power, by which to secure obedience to his orders, and how long do you suppose a slave would remain on his plantation? The case only needs to be stated; it carries its own refutation with it.

Absolute and arbitrary power can never be maintained by one man over the body and soul of another man, without brutal chastisement and enormous cruelty.

To talk of kindness entering into a relation in which one party is robbed of wife, of children, of his hard earnings, of home, of friends, of society, of knowledge, and of all that makes this life desirable, is most absurd, wicked, and preposterous.

I have shown that slavery is wicked—wicked, in that it violates the great law of liberty, written on every human heart—wicked, in that it violates the first command of the decalogue—wicked, in that it fosters the most disgusting licentiousness—wicked, in that it mars and defaces the image of God by cruel and barbarous inflictions—wicked, in that it contravenes the laws of eternal justice, and tramples in the dust all the humane and heavenly precepts of the New Testament.

The evils resulting from this huge system of iniquity are not confined to the states south of Mason and Dixon's line. Its noxious influence can easily be traced throughout our northern borders. It comes even as far north as the state of New York. Traces of it may be seen even in Rochester; and travelers have told me it casts its gloomy shadows across the lake, approaching the very shores of Queen Victoria's dominions.

The presence of slavery may be explained by—as it is the explanation of—the mobocratic violence which lately disgraced New York, and which still more recently disgraced the city of Boston. These violent demonstrations, these outrageous invasions of human rights, faintly indicate the presence and power of slavery here. It is a significant fact, that while meetings for almost any purpose under heaven may be held unmolested in the city of Boston, that in the same city, a meeting cannot be peaceably held for the purpose of preaching the doctrine of the American Declaration of Independence, "that all men are created equal." The pestiferous breath of slavery taints the whole moral atmosphere of the north, and enervates the moral energies of the whole people.

The moment a foreigner ventures upon our soil, and utters a natural repugnance to oppression, that moment he is made to feel that there is little sympathy in this land for him. If he were greeted with smiles before, he meets with frowns now; and it shall go well with him if he be not subjected to that peculiarly fining method of showing fealty to slavery, the assaults of a mob.

Now, will any man tell me that such a state of things is natural, and that such conduct on the part of the people of the north, springs from a consciousness of rectitude? No! every fibre of the human heart unites in detestation of tyranny, and it is only when the human mind has become familiarized with slavery, is accustomed to its injustice, and corrupted by its selfishness, that it fails to record its abhorrence of slavery, and does not exult in the triumphs of liberty.

The northern people have been long connected with slavery; they have been linked to a decaying corpse, which has destroyed the moral health. The union of the government; the union of the north and south, in the political parties; the union in the religious organizations of the land, have all served to deaden the moral sense of the northern people, and to impregnate them with sentiments and ideas forever in conflict with what as a nation we call genius of American institutions. Rightly viewed, this is an alarming fact, and ought to rally all that is pure, just, and holy in one determined effort to crush the monster of corruption, and to scatter "its guilty profits" to the winds. In a high moral sense, as well as in a national sense, the whole American people are responsible for slavery, and must share, in its guilt and shame, with the most obdurate men-stealers of the south.

While slavery exists, and the union of these states endures, every American citizen must bear the chagrin of hearing his country branded before the world as a nation of liars and hypocrites; and behold his cherished flag pointed at with the utmost scorn and derision. Even now an American abroad is pointed out in the crowd, as coming from a land where men gain their fortunes by "the blood of souls," from a land of slave markets, of blood-hounds, and slave-hunters; and, in some circles, such a man is shunned altogether, as a moral pest. Is it not time, then, for every American to awake, and inquire into his duty with respect to this subject? Wendell Phillips—the eloquent New England orator—on his return from Europe, in 1842, said, "As I stood upon the shores of Genoa, and saw floating on the placid waters of the Mediterranean, the beautiful American war ship Ohio, with her masts tapering proportionately aloft, and an eastern sun reflecting her noble form upon the sparkling waters, attracting the gaze of the multitude, my first impulse was of pride, to think myself an American; but when I thought that the first time that gallant ship would gird on her gorgeous apparel, and wake from beneath her sides her dormant thunders, it would be in defense of the African slave trade, I blushed in utter shame for my country."

Let me say again, slavery is alike the sin and the shame of the American people; it is a blot upon the American name, and the only national reproach which need make an American hang his head in shame, in the presence of monarchical governments.

With this gigantic evil in the land, we are constantly told to look at home; if we say ought against crowned heads, we are pointed to our enslaved millions; if we talk of sending missionaries and bibles abroad, we are pointed to three millions now lying in worse than heathen darkness; if we express a word of sympathy for Kossuth and his Hungarian fugitive brethren, we are pointed to that horrible and hell-black enactment, "the fugitive slave bill." Slavery blunts the edge of all our rebukes of tyranny abroad—the criticisms that we make upon other nations, only call forth ridicule, contempt, and scorn. In a word, we are made a reproach and a by-word to a mocking earth, and we must continue to be so made, so long as slavery continues to pollute our soil.

We have heard much of late of the virtue of patriotism, the love of country, &c., and this sentiment, so natural and so strong, has been impiously appealed to, by all the powers of human selfishness, to cherish the viper which is stinging our national life away. In its name, we have been called upon to deepen our infamy before the world, to rivet the fetter more firmly on the limbs of the enslaved, and to become utterly insensible to the voice of human woe that is wafted to us on every southern gale. We have been called upon, in its name, to desecrate our whole land by the footprints of slave-hunters, and even to engage ourselves in the horrible business of kidnapping.

I, too, would invoke the spirit of patriotism; not in a narrow and restricted sense, but, I trust, with a broad and manly signification; not to cover up our national sins, but to inspire us with sincere repentance; not to hide our shame from the the(sic) world's gaze, but utterly to abolish the cause of that shame; not to explain away our gross inconsistencies as a nation, but to remove the hateful, jarring, and incongruous elements from the land; not to sustain an egregious wrong, but to unite all our energies in the grand effort to remedy that wrong.

I would invoke the spirit of patriotism, in the name of the law of the living God, natural and revealed, and in the full belief that "righteousness exalteth a nation, while sin is a reproach to any people." "He that walketh righteously, and speaketh uprightly; he that despiseth the gain of oppressions, that shaketh his hands from the holding of bribes, he shall dwell on high, his place of defense shall be the munitions of rocks, bread shall be given him, his water shall be sure."

We have not only heard much lately of patriotism, and of its aid being invoked on the side of slavery and injustice, but the very prosperity of this people has been called in to deafen them to the voice of duty, and to lead them onward in the pathway of sin. Thus has the blessing of God been converted into a curse. In the spirit of genuine patriotism, I warn the American people, by all that is just and honorable, to BEWARE!

I warn them that, strong, proud, and prosperous though we be, there is a power above us that can "bring down high looks; at the breath of whose mouth our wealth may take wings; and before whom every knee shall bow;" and who can tell how soon the avenging angel may pass over our land, and the sable bondmen now in chains, may become the instruments of our nation's chastisement! Without appealing to any higher feeling, I would warn the American people, and the American government, to be wise in their day and generation. I exhort them to remember the history of other nations; and I remind them that America cannot always sit "as a queen," in peace and repose; that prouder and stronger governments than this have been shattered by the bolts of a just God; that the time may come when those they now despise and hate, may be needed; when those whom they now compel by oppression to be enemies, may be wanted as friends. What has been, may be again. There is a point beyond which human endurance cannot go. The crushed worm may yet turn under the heel of the oppressor. I warn them, then, with all solemnity, and in the name of retributive justice, to look to their ways; for in an evil hour, those sable arms that have, for the last two centuries, been engaged in cultivating and adorning the fair fields of our country, may yet become the instruments of terror, desolation, and death, throughout our borders.

It was the sage of the Old Dominion that said—while speaking of the possibility of a conflict between the slaves and the slaveholders—"God has no attribute that could take sides with the oppressor in such a contest. I tremble for my country when I reflect that God is just, and that his justice cannot sleep forever." Such is the warning voice of Thomas Jefferson; and every day's experience since its utterance until now, confirms its wisdom, and commends its truth.

WHAT TO THE SLAVE IS THE FOURTH OF JULY?. Extract from an Oration, at

Rochester, July 5, 1852

Fellow-Citizens—Pardon me, and allow me to ask, why am I called upon to speak here to-day? What have I, or those I represent, to do with your national independence? Are the great principles of political freedom and of natural justice, embodied in that Declaration of Independence, extended to us? and am I, therefore, called upon to bring our humble offering to the national altar, and to confess the benefits, and express devout gratitude for the blessings, resulting from your independence to us?

Would to God, both for your sakes and ours, that an affirmative answer could be truthfully returned to these questions! Then would my task be light, and my burden easy and delightful. For who is there so cold that a nation's sympathy could not warm him? Who so obdurate and dead to the claims of gratitude, that would not thankfully acknowledge such priceless benefits? Who so stolid and selfish, that would not give his voice to swell the hallelujahs of a nation's jubilee, when the chains of servitude had been torn from his limbs? I am not that man. In a case like that, the dumb might eloquently speak, and the "lame man leap as an hart."

But, such is not the state of the case. I say it with a sad sense of the disparity between us. I am not included within the pale of this glorious anniversary! Your high independence only reveals the immeasurable distance between us. The blessings in which you this day rejoice, are not enjoyed in common. The rich inheritance of justice, liberty, prosperity, and independence, bequeathed by your fathers, is shared by you, not by me. The sunlight that brought life and healing to you, has brought stripes and death to me. This Fourth of July is yours, not mine. You may rejoice, I must mourn. To drag a man in fetters into the grand illuminated temple of liberty, and call upon him to join you in joyous anthems, were inhuman mockery and sacrilegious irony. Do you mean, citizens, to mock me, by asking me to speak to-day? If so, there is a parallel to your conduct. And let me warn you that it is dangerous to copy the example of a nation whose crimes, towering up to heaven, were thrown down by the breath of the Almighty, burying that nation in irrecoverable ruin! I can to-day take up the plaintive lament of a peeled and woe-smitten people.

"By the rivers of Babylon, there we sat down. Yea! we wept when we remembered Zion. We hanged our harps upon the willows in the midst thereof. For there, they that carried us away captive, required of us a song; and they who wasted us required of us mirth, saying, Sing us one of the songs of Zion. How can we sing the Lord's song in a strange land? If I forget thee, O Jerusalem, let my right hand forget her cunning. If I do not remember thee, let my tongue cleave to the roof of my mouth."

Fellow-citizens, above your national, tumultous joy, I hear the mournful wail of millions, whose chains, heavy and grievous yesterday, are to-day rendered more intolerable by the jubilant shouts that reach them. If I do forget, if I do not faithfully remember those bleeding children of sorrow this day, "may my right hand forget her cunning, and may my tongue cleave to the roof of my mouth!" To forget them, to pass lightly over their wrongs, and to chime in with the popular theme, would be treason most scandalous and shocking, and would make me a reproach before God and the world. My subject, then, fellow-citizens, is AMERICAN SLAVERY. I shall see this day and its popular characteristics from the slave's point of view. Standing there, identified with the American bondman, making his wrongs mine, I do not hesitate to declare, with all my soul, that the character and conduct of this nation never looked blacker to me than on this Fourth of July. Whether we turn to the declarations of the past, or to the professions of the present, the conduct of the nation seems equally hideous and revolting. America is false to the past, false to the present, and solemnly binds herself to be false to the future. Standing with God and the crushed and bleeding slave on this occasion, I will, in the name of humanity which is outraged, in the name of liberty which is fettered, in the name of the constitution and the bible, which are disregarded and trampled upon, dare to call in question and to denounce, with all the emphasis I can command, everything that serves to perpetuate slavery—the great sin and shame of America! "I will not equivocate; I will not excuse;" I will use the severest language I can command; and yet not one word shall escape me that any man, whose judgment is not blinded by prejudice, or who is not at heart a slaveholder, shall not confess to be right and just.

But I fancy I hear some one of my audience say, it is just in this circumstance that you and your brother abolitionists fail to make a favorable impression on the public mind. Would you argue more, and denounce less, would you persuade more and rebuke less, your cause would be much more likely to succeed. But, I submit, where all is plain there is nothing to be argued. What point in the anti-slavery creed would you have me argue? On what branch of the subject do the people of this country need light? Must I undertake to prove that the slave is a man? That point is conceded already. Nobody doubts it. The slaveholders themselves acknowledge it in the enactment of laws for their government. They acknowledge it when they punish disobedience on the part of the slave. There are seventy-two crimes in the state of Virginia, which, if committed by a black man (no matter how ignorant he be), subject him to the punishment of death; while only two of these same crimes will subject a white man to the like punishment. What is this but the acknowledgement that the slave is a moral, intellectual, and responsible being. The manhood of the slave is conceded. It is admitted in the fact that southern statute books are covered with enactments forbidding, under severe fines and penalties, the teaching of the slave to read or write. When you can point to any such laws, in reference to the beasts of the field, then I may consent to argue the manhood of the slave. When the dogs in your streets, when the fowls of the air, when the cattle on your hills, when the fish of the sea, and the reptiles that crawl, shall be unable to distinguish the slave from a brute, then will I argue with you that the slave is a man!

For the present, it is enough to affirm the equal manhood of the Negro race. Is it not astonishing that, while we are plowing, planting, and reaping, using all kinds of mechanical tools, erecting houses, constructing bridges, building ships, working in metals of brass, iron, copper, silver, and gold; that, while we are reading, writing, and cyphering, acting as clerks, merchants, and secretaries, having among us lawyers, doctors, ministers, poets, authors, editors, orators, and teachers; that, while we are engaged in all manner of enterprises common to other men—digging gold in California, capturing the whale in the Pacific, feeding sheep and cattle on the hillside, living, moving, acting, thinking, planning, living in families as husbands, wives, and children, and, above all, confessing and worshiping the Christian's God, and looking hopefully for life and immortality beyond the grave—we are called upon to prove that we are men!

Would you have me argue that man is entitled to liberty? that he is the rightful owner of his own body? You have already declared it. Must I argue the wrongfulness of slavery? Is that a question for republicans? Is it to be settled by the rules of logic and argumentation, as a matter beset with great difficulty, involving a doubtful application of the principle of justice, hard to be understood? How should I look to-day in the presence of Americans, dividing and subdividing a discourse, to show that men have a natural right to freedom, speaking of it relatively and positively, negatively and affirmatively? To do so, would be to make myself ridiculous, and to offer an insult to your understanding. There is not a man beneath the canopy of heaven that does not know that slavery is wrong for him.

What! am I to argue that it is wrong to make men brutes, to rob them of their liberty, to work them without wages, to keep them ignorant of their relations to their fellow-men, to beat them with sticks, to flay their flesh with the lash, to load their limbs with irons, to hunt them with dogs, to sell them at auction, to sunder their families, to knock out their teeth, to burn their flesh, to starve them into obedience and submission to their masters? Must I argue that a system, thus marked with blood and stained with pollution, is wrong? No; I will not. I have better employment for my time and strength than such arguments would imply.

What, then, remains to be argued? Is it that slavery is not divine; that God did not establish it; that our doctors of divinity are mistaken? There is blasphemy in the thought. That which is inhuman cannot be divine. Who can reason on such a proposition! They that can, may! I cannot. The time for such argument is past.

At a time like this, scorching irony, not convincing argument, is needed. Oh! had I the ability, and could I reach the nation's ear, I would to-day pour out a fiery stream of biting ridicule, blasting reproach, withering sarcasm, and stern rebuke. For it is not light that is needed, but fire; it is not the gentle shower, but thunder. We need the storm, the whirlwind, and the earthquake. The feeling of the nation must be quickened; the conscience of the nation must be roused; the propriety of the nation must be startled; the hypocrisy of the nation must be exposed; and its crimes against God and man must be proclaimed and denounced.

What to the American slave is your Fourth of July? I answer, a day that reveals to him, more than all other days in the year, the gross injustice and cruelty to which he is the constant victim. To him, your celebration is a sham; your boasted liberty, an unholy license; your national greatness, swelling vanity; your sounds of rejoicing are empty and heartless; your denunciations of tyrants, brass-fronted impudence; your shouts of liberty and equality, hollow mockery; your prayers and hymns, your sermons and thanksgivings, with all your religious parade and solemnity, are to him mere bombast, fraud, deception, impiety, and hypocrisy—a thin veil to cover up crimes which would disgrace a nation of savages. There is not a nation on the earth guilty of practices more shocking and bloody, than are the people of these United States, at this very hour.

Go where you may, search where you will, roam through all the monarchies and despotisms of the old world, travel through South America, search out every abuse, and when you have found the last, lay your facts by the side of the every-day practices of this nation, and you will say with me, that, for revolting barbarity and shameless hypocrisy, America reigns without a rival.

THE INTERNAL SLAVE TRADE. Extract from an Oration, at Rochester, July

5, 1852

Take the American slave trade, which, we are told by the papers, is especially prosperous just now. Ex-senator Benton tells us that the price of men was never higher than now. He mentions the fact to show that slavery is in no danger. This trade is one of the peculiarities of American institutions. It is carried on in all the large towns and cities in one-half of this confederacy; and millions are pocketed every year by dealers in this horrid traffic. In several states this trade is a chief source of wealth. It is called (in contradistinction to the foreign slave trade) "the internal slave trade." It is, probably, called so, too, in order to divert from it the horror with which the foreign slave trade is contemplated. That trade has long since been denounced by this government as piracy. It has been denounced with burning words, from the high places of the nation, as an execrable traffic. To arrest it, to put an end to it, this nation keeps a squadron, at immense cost, on the coast of Africa. Everywhere in this country, it is safe to speak of this foreign slave trade as a most inhuman traffic, opposed alike to the laws of God and of man. The duty to extirpate and destroy it is admitted even by our doctors of divinity. In order to put an end to it, some of these last have consented that their colored brethren (nominally free) should leave this country, and establish themselves on the western coast of Africa. It is, however, a notable fact, that, while so much execration is poured out by Americans, upon those engaged in the foreign slave trade, the men engaged in the slave trade between the states pass without condemnation, and their business is deemed honorable.

Behold the practical operation of this internal slave trade—the American slave trade sustained by American politics and American religion! Here you will see men and women reared like swine for the market. You know what is a swine-drover? I will show you a man-drover. They inhabit all our southern states. They perambulate the country, and crowd the highways of the nation with droves of human stock. You will see one of these human-flesh-jobbers, armed with pistol, whip, and bowie-knife, driving a company of a hundred men, women, and children, from the Potomac to the slave market at New Orleans. These wretched people are to be sold singly, or in lots, to suit purchasers. They are food for the cotton-field and the deadly sugar-mill. Mark the sad procession as it moves wearily along, and the inhuman wretch who drives them. Hear his savage yells and his blood-chilling oaths, as he hurries on his affrighted captives. There, see the old man, with locks thinned and gray. Cast one glance, if you please, upon that young mother, whose shoulders are bare to the scorching sun, her briny tears falling on the brow of the babe in her arms. See, too, that girl of thirteen, weeping, yes, weeping, as she thinks of the mother from whom she has been torn. The drove moves tardily. Heat and sorrow have nearly consumed their strength. Suddenly you hear a quick snap, like the discharge of a rifle; the fetters clank, and the chain rattles simultaneously; your ears are saluted with a scream that seems to have torn its way to the center of your soul. The crack you heard was the sound of the slave whip; the scream you heard was from the woman you saw with the babe. Her speed had faltered under the weight of her child and her chains; that gash on her shoulder tells her to move on. Follow this drove to New Orleans. Attend the auction; see men examined like horses; see the forms of women rudely and brutally exposed to the shocking gaze of American slave-buyers. See this drove sold and separated forever; and never forget the deep, sad sobs that arose from that scattered multitude. Tell me, citizens, where, under the sun, can you witness a spectacle more fiendish and shocking. Yet this is but a glance at the American slave trade, as it exists at this moment, in the ruling part of the United States. I was born amid such sights and scenes. To me the American slave trade is a terrible reality. When a child, my soul was often pierced with a sense of its horrors. I lived on Philpot street, Fell's Point, Baltimore, and have watched from the wharves the slave ships in the basin, anchored from the shore, with their cargoes of human flesh, waiting for favorable winds to waft them down the Chesapeake. There was, at that time, a grand slave mart kept at the head of Pratt street, by Austin Woldfolk. His agents were sent into every town and county in Maryland, announcing their arrival through the papers, and on flaming hand-bills, headed, "cash for negroes." These men were generally well dressed, and very captivating in their manners; ever ready to drink, to treat, and to gamble. The fate of many a slave has depended upon the turn of a single card; and many a child has been snatched from the arms of its mothers by bargains arranged in a state of brutal drunkenness.

The flesh-mongers gather up their victims by dozens, and drive them, chained, to the general depot at Baltimore. When a sufficient number have been collected here, a ship is chartered, for the purpose of conveying the forlorn crew to Mobile or to New Orleans. From the slave-prison to the ship, they are usually driven in the darkness of night; for since the anti-slavery agitation a certain caution is observed.

In the deep, still darkness of midnight, I have been often aroused by the dead, heavy footsteps and the piteous cries of the chained gangs that passed our door. The anguish of my boyish heart was intense; and I was often consoled, when speaking to my mistress in the morning, to hear her say that the custom was very wicked; that she hated to hear the rattle of the chains, and the heart-rending cries. I was glad to find one who sympathized with me in my horror. Fellow citizens, this murderous traffic is to-day in active operation in this boasted republic. In the solitude of my spirit, I see clouds of dust raised on the highways of the south; I see the bleeding footsteps; I hear the doleful wail of fettered humanity, on the way to the slave markets, where the victims are to be sold like horses, sheep, and swine, knocked off to the highest bidder. There I see the tenderest ties ruthlessly broken, to gratify the lust, caprice, and rapacity of the buyers and sellers of men. My soul sickens at the sight.

Is this the land your fathers loved?
The freedom which they toiled to win?
Is this the earth whereon they moved?
Are these the graves they slumber in?

But a still more inhuman, disgraceful, and scandalous state of things remains to be presented. By an act of the American congress, not yet two years old, slavery has been nationalized in its most horrible and revolting form. By that act, Mason and Dixon's line has been obliterated; New York has become as Virginia; and the power to hold, hunt, and sell men, women, and children as slaves, remains no longer a mere state institution, but is now an institution of the whole United States. The power is coextensive with the star-spangled banner and American christianity. Where these go, may also go the merciless slave-hunter. Where these are, man is not sacred. He is a bird for the sportsman's gun. By that most foul and fiendish of all human decrees, the liberty and person of every man are put in peril. Your broad republican domain is a hunting-ground for men. Not for thieves and robbers, enemies of society, merely, but for men guilty of no crime. Your law-makers have commanded all good citizens to engage in this hellish sport. Your president, your secretary of state, your lords, nobles, and ecclesiastics, enforce as a duty you owe to your free and glorious country and to your God, that you do this accursed thing. Not fewer than forty Americans have within the past two years been hunted down, and without a moment's warning, hurried away in chains, and consigned to slavery and excruciating torture. Some of these have had wives and children dependent on them for bread; but of this no account was made. The right of the hunter to his prey, stands superior to the right of marriage, and to all rights in this republic, the rights of God included! For black men there are neither law, justice, humanity, nor religion. The fugitive slave law makes MERCY TO THEM A CRIME; and bribes the judge who tries them. An American judge GETS TEN DOLLARS FOR EVERY VICTIM HE CONSIGNS to slavery, and five, when he fails to do so. The oath of an(sic) two villains is sufficient, under this hell-black enactment, to send the most pious and exemplary black man into the remorseless jaws of slavery! His own testimony is nothing. He can bring no witnesses for himself. The minister of American justice is bound by the law to hear but one side, and that side is the side of the oppressor. Let this damning fact be perpetually told. Let it be thundered around the world, that, in tyrant-killing, king hating, people-loving, democratic, Christian America, the seats of justice are filled with judges, who hold their office under an open and palpable bribe, and are bound, in deciding in the case of a man's liberty, to hear only his accusers!

In glaring violation of justice, in shameless disregard of the forms of administering law, in cunning arrangement to entrap the defenseless, and in diabolical intent, this fugitive slave law stands alone in the annals of tyrannical legislation. I doubt if there be another nation on the globe having the brass and the baseness to put such a law on the statute-book. If any man in this assembly thinks differently from me in this matter, and feels able to disprove my statements, I will gladly confront him at any suitable time and place he may select.

THE SLAVERY PARTY. Extract from a Speech Delivered before the A. A. S.

Society, in New York, May, 1853.

Sir, it is evident that there is in this country a purely slavery party—a party which exists for no other earthly purpose but to promote the interests of slavery. The presence of this party is felt everywhere in the republic. It is known by no particular name, and has assumed no definite shape; but its branches reach far and wide in the church and in the state. This shapeless and nameless party is not intangible in other and more important respects. That party, sir, has determined upon a fixed, definite, and comprehensive policy toward the whole colored population of the United States. What that policy is, it becomes us as abolitionists, and especially does it become the colored people themselves, to consider and to understand fully. We ought to know who our enemies are, where they are, and what are their objects and measures. Well, sir, here is my version of it—not original with me—but mine because I hold it to be true.

I understand this policy to comprehend five cardinal objects. They are these: 1st. The complete suppression of all anti-slavery discussion. 2d. The expatriation of the entire free people of color from the United States. 3d. The unending perpetuation of slavery in this republic. 4th. The nationalization of slavery to the extent of making slavery respected in every state of the Union. 5th. The extension of slavery over Mexico and the entire South American states.

Sir, these objects are forcibly presented to us in the stern logic of passing events; in the facts which are and have been passing around us during the last three years. The country has been and is now dividing on these grand issues. In their magnitude, these issues cast all others into the shade, depriving them of all life and vitality. Old party ties are broken. Like is finding its like on either side of these great issues, and the great battle is at hand. For the present, the best representative of the slavery party in politics is the democratic party. Its great head for the present is President Pierce, whose boast it was, before his election, that his whole life had been consistent with the interests of slavery, that he is above reproach on that score. In his inaugural address, he reassures the south on this point. Well, the head of the slave power being in power, it is natural that the pro slavery elements should cluster around the administration, and this is rapidly being done. A fraternization is going on. The stringent protectionists and the free-traders strike hands. The supporters of Fillmore are becoming the supporters of Pierce. The silver-gray whig shakes hands with the hunker democrat; the former only differing from the latter in name. They are of one heart, one mind, and the union is natural and perhaps inevitable. Both hate Negroes; both hate progress; both hate the "higher law;" both hate William H. Seward; both hate the free democratic party; and upon this hateful basis they are forming a union of hatred. "Pilate and Herod are thus made friends." Even the central organ of the whig party is extending its beggar hand for a morsel from the table of slavery democracy, and when spurned from the feast by the more deserving, it pockets the insult; when kicked on one side it turns the other, and preseveres in its importunities. The fact is, that paper comprehends the demands of the times; it understands the age and its issues; it wisely sees that slavery and freedom are the great antagonistic forces in the country, and it goes to its own side. Silver grays and hunkers all understand this. They are, therefore, rapidly sinking all other questions to nothing, compared with the increasing demands of slavery. They are collecting, arranging, and consolidating their forces for the accomplishment of their appointed work. The keystone to the arch of this grand union of the slavery party of the United States, is the compromise of 1850. In that compromise we have all the objects of our slaveholding policy specified. It is, sir, favorable to this view of the designs of the slave power, that both the whig and the democratic party bent lower, sunk deeper, and strained harder, in their conventions, preparatory to the late presidential election, to meet the demands of the slavery party than at any previous time in their history. Never did parties come before the northern people with propositions of such undisguised contempt for the moral sentiment and the religious ideas of that people. They virtually asked them to unite in a war upon free speech, and upon conscience, and to drive the Almighty presence from the councils of the nation. Resting their platforms upon the fugitive slave bill, they boldly asked the people for political power to execute the horrible and hell-black provisions of that bill. The history of that election reveals, with great clearness, the extent to which slavery has shot its leprous distillment through the life-blood of the nation. The party most thoroughly opposed to the cause of justice and humanity, triumphed; while the party suspected of a leaning toward liberty, was overwhelmingly defeated, some say annihilated.

But here is a still more important fact, illustrating the designs of the slave power. It is a fact full of meaning, that no sooner did the democratic slavery party come into power, than a system of legislation was presented to the legislatures of the northern states, designed to put the states in harmony with the fugitive slave law, and the malignant bearing of the national government toward the colored inhabitants of the country. This whole movement on the part of the states, bears the evidence of having one origin, emanating from one head, and urged forward by one power. It was simultaneous, uniform, and general, and looked to one end. It was intended to put thorns under feet already bleeding; to crush a people already bowed down; to enslave a people already but half free; in a word, it was intended to discourage, dishearten, and drive the free colored people out of the country. In looking at the recent black law of Illinois, one is struck dumb with its enormity. It would seem that the men who enacted that law, had not only banished from their minds all sense of justice, but all sense of shame. It coolly proposes to sell the bodies and souls of the blacks to increase the intelligence and refinement of the whites; to rob every black stranger who ventures among them, to increase their literary fund.

While this is going on in the states, a pro-slavery, political board of health is established at Washington. Senators Hale, Chase, and Sumner are robbed of a part of their senatorial dignity and consequence as representing sovereign states, because they have refused to be inoculated with the slavery virus. Among the services which a senator is expected by his state to perform, are many that can only be done efficiently on committees; and, in saying to these honorable senators, you shall not serve on the committees of this body, the slavery party took the responsibility of robbing and insulting the states that sent them. It is an attempt at Washington to decide for the states who shall be sent to the senate. Sir, it strikes me that this aggression on the part of the slave power did not meet at the hands of the proscribed senators the rebuke which we had a right to expect would be administered. It seems to me that an opportunity was lost, that the great principle of senatorial equality was left undefended, at a time when its vindication was sternly demanded. But it is not to the purpose of my present statement to criticise the conduct of our friends. I am persuaded that much ought to be left to the discretion of anti slavery men in congress, and charges of recreancy should never be made but on the most sufficient grounds. For, of all the places in the world where an anti-slavery man needs the confidence and encouragement of friends, I take Washington to be that place.

Let me now call attention to the social influences which are operating and cooperating with the slavery party of the country, designed to contribute to one or all of the grand objects aimed at by that party. We see here the black man attacked in his vital interests; prejudice and hate are excited against him; enmity is stirred up between him and other laborers. The Irish people, warm-hearted, generous, and sympathizing with the oppressed everywhere, when they stand upon their own green island, are instantly taught, on arriving in this Christian country, to hate and despise the colored people. They are taught to believe that we eat the bread which of right belongs to them. The cruel lie is told the Irish, that our adversity is essential to their prosperity. Sir, the Irish-American will find out his mistake one day. He will find that in assuming our avocation he also has assumed our degradation. But for the present we are sufferers. The old employments by which we have heretofore gained our livelihood, are gradually, and it may be inevitably, passing into other hands. Every hour sees us elbowed out of some employment to make room perhaps for some newly-arrived emigrants, whose hunger and color are thought to give them a title to especial favor. White men are becoming house-servants, cooks, and stewards, common laborers, and flunkeys to our gentry, and, for aught I see, they adjust themselves to their stations with all becoming obsequiousness. This fact proves that if we cannot rise to the whites, the whites can fall to us. Now, sir, look once more. While the colored people are thus elbowed out of employment; while the enmity of emigrants is being excited against us; while state after state enacts laws against us; while we are hunted down, like wild game, and oppressed with a general feeling of insecurity—the American colonization society—that old offender against the best interests and slanderer of the colored people—awakens to new life, and vigorously presses its scheme upon the consideration of the people and the government. New papers are started—some for the north and some for the south—and each in its tone adapting itself to its latitude. Government, state and national, is called upon for appropriations to enable the society to send us out of the country by steam! They want steamers to carry letters and Negroes to Africa. Evidently, this society looks upon our "extremity as its opportunity," and we may expect that it will use the occasion well. They do not deplore, but glory, in our misfortunes.

But, sir, I must hasten. I have thus briefly given my view of one aspect of the present condition and future prospects of the colored people of the United States. And what I have said is far from encouraging to my afflicted people. I have seen the cloud gather upon the sable brows of some who hear me. I confess the case looks black enough. Sir, I am not a hopeful man. I think I am apt even to undercalculate the benefits of the future. Yet, sir, in this seemingly desperate case, I do not despair for my people. There is a bright side to almost every picture of this kind; and ours is no exception to the general rule. If the influences against us are strong, those for us are also strong. To the inquiry, will our enemies prevail in the execution of their designs. In my God and in my soul, I believe they will not. Let us look at the first object sought for by the slavery party of the country, viz: the suppression of anti slavery discussion. They desire to suppress discussion on this subject, with a view to the peace of the slaveholder and the security of slavery. Now, sir, neither the principle nor the subordinate objects here declared, can be at all gained by the slave power, and for this reason: It involves the proposition to padlock the lips of the whites, in order to secure the fetters on the limbs of the blacks. The right of speech, precious and priceless, cannot, will not, be surrendered to slavery. Its suppression is asked for, as I have said, to give peace and security to slaveholders. Sir, that thing cannot be done. God has interposed an insuperable obstacle to any such result. "There can be no peace, saith my God, to the wicked." Suppose it were possible to put down this discussion, what would it avail the guilty slaveholder, pillowed as he is upon heaving bosoms of ruined souls? He could not have a peaceful spirit. If every anti-slavery tongue in the nation were silent—every anti-slavery organization dissolved—every anti-slavery press demolished—every anti slavery periodical, paper, book, pamphlet, or what not, were searched out, gathered, deliberately burned to ashes, and their ashes given to the four winds of heaven, still, still the slaveholder could have "no peace." In every pulsation of his heart, in every throb of his life, in every glance of his eye, in the breeze that soothes, and in the thunder that startles, would be waked up an accuser, whose cause is, "Thou art, verily, guilty concerning thy brother."

THE ANTI-SLAVERY MOVEMENT. Extracts from a Lecture before Various

Anti-Slavery Bodies, in the Winter of 1855.

A grand movement on the part of mankind, in any direction, or for any purpose, moral or political, is an interesting fact, fit and proper to be studied. It is such, not only for those who eagerly participate in it, but also for those who stand aloof from it—even for those by whom it is opposed. I take the anti-slavery movement to be such an one, and a movement as sublime and glorious in its character, as it is holy and beneficent in the ends it aims to accomplish. At this moment, I deem it safe to say, it is properly engrossing more minds in this country than any other subject now before the American people. The late John C. Calhoun—one of the mightiest men that ever stood up in the American senate—did not deem it beneath him; and he probably studied it as deeply, though not as honestly, as Gerrit Smith, or William Lloyd Garrison. He evinced the greatest familiarity with the subject; and the greatest efforts of his last years in the senate had direct reference to this movement. His eagle eye watched every new development connected with it; and he was ever prompt to inform the south of every important step in its progress. He never allowed himself to make light of it; but always spoke of it and treated it as a matter of grave import; and in this he showed himself a master of the mental, moral, and religious constitution of human society. Daniel Webster, too, in the better days of his life, before he gave his assent to the fugitive slave bill, and trampled upon all his earlier and better convictions—when his eye was yet single—he clearly comprehended the nature of the elements involved in this movement; and in his own majestic eloquence, warned the south, and the country, to have a care how they attempted to put it down. He is an illustration that it is easier to give, than to take, good advice. To these two men—the greatest men to whom the nation has yet given birth—may be traced the two great facts of the present—the south triumphant, and the north humbled. Their names may stand thus—Calhoun and domination—Webster and degradation. Yet again. If to the enemies of liberty this subject is one of engrossing interest, vastly more so should it be such to freedom's friends. The latter, it leads to the gates of all valuable knowledge—philanthropic, ethical, and religious; for it brings them to the study of man, wonderfully and fearfully made—the proper study of man through all time—the open book, in which are the records of time and eternity.

Of the existence and power of the anti-slavery movement, as a fact, you need no evidence. The nation has seen its face, and felt the controlling pressure of its hand. You have seen it moving in all directions, and in all weathers, and in all places, appearing most where desired least, and pressing hardest where most resisted. No place is exempt. The quiet prayer meeting, and the stormy halls of national debate, share its presence alike. It is a common intruder, and of course has the name of being ungentlemanly. Brethren who had long sung, in the most affectionate fervor, and with the greatest sense of security,

    Together let us sweetly live—together let us die,

have been suddenly and violently separated by it, and ranged in hostile attitude toward each other. The Methodist, one of the most powerful religious organizations of this country, has been rent asunder, and its strongest bolts of denominational brotherhood started at a single surge. It has changed the tone of the northern pulpit, and modified that of the press. A celebrated divine, who, four years ago, was for flinging his own mother, or brother, into the remorseless jaws of the monster slavery, lest he should swallow up the Union, now recognizes anti-slavery as a characteristic of future civilization. Signs and wonders follow this movement; and the fact just stated is one of them. Party ties are loosened by it; and men are compelled to take sides for or against it, whether they will or not. Come from where he may, or come for what he may, he is compelled to show his hand. What is this mighty force? What is its history? and what is its destiny? Is it ancient or modern, transient or permanent? Has it turned aside, like a stranger and a sojourner, to tarry for a night? or has it come to rest with us forever? Excellent chances are here for speculation; and some of them are quite profound. We might, for instance, proceed to inquire not only into the philosophy of the anti-slavery movement, but into the philosophy of the law, in obedience to which that movement started into existence. We might demand to know what is that law or power, which, at different times, disposes the minds of men to this or that particular object—now for peace, and now for war—now for free dom, and now for slavery; but this profound question I leave to the abolitionists of the superior class to answer. The speculations which must precede such answer, would afford, perhaps, about the same satisfaction as the learned theories which have rained down upon the world, from time to time, as to the origin of evil. I shall, therefore, avoid water in which I cannot swim, and deal with anti-slavery as a fact, like any other fact in the history of mankind, capable of being described and understood, both as to its internal forces, and its external phases and relations.

[After an eloquent, a full, and highly interesting exposition of the nature, character, and history of the anti-slavery movement, from the insertion of which want of space precludes us, he concluded in the following happy manner.]

Present organizations may perish, but the cause will go on. That cause has a life, distinct and independent of the organizations patched up from time to time to carry it forward. Looked at, apart from the bones and sinews and body, it is a thing immortal. It is the very essence of justice, liberty, and love. The moral life of human society, it cannot die while conscience, honor, and humanity remain. If but one be filled with it, the cause lives. Its incarnation in any one individual man, leaves the whole world a priesthood, occupying the highest moral eminence even that of disinterested benevolence. Whoso has ascended his height, and has the grace to stand there, has the world at his feet, and is the world's teacher, as of divine right. He may set in judgment on the age, upon the civilization of the age, and upon the religion of the age; for he has a test, a sure and certain test, by which to try all institutions, and to measure all men. I say, he may do this, but this is not the chief business for which he is qualified. The great work to which he is called is not that of judgment. Like the Prince of Peace, he may say, if I judge, I judge righteous judgment; still mainly, like him, he may say, this is not his work. The man who has thoroughly embraced the principles of justice, love, and liberty, like the true preacher of Christianity, is less anxious to reproach the world of its sins, than to win it to repentance. His great work on earth is to exemplify, and to illustrate, and to ingraft those principles upon the living and practical understandings of all men within the reach of his influence. This is his work; long or short his years, many or few his adherents, powerful or weak his instrumentalities, through good report, or through bad report, this is his work. It is to snatch from the bosom of nature the latent facts of each individual man's experience, and with steady hand to hold them up fresh and glowing, enforcing, with all his power, their acknowledgment and practical adoption. If there be but one such man in the land, no matter what becomes of abolition societies and parties, there will be an anti-slavery cause, and an anti-slavery movement. Fortunately for that cause, and fortunately for him by whom it is espoused, it requires no extraordinary amount of talent to preach it or to receive it when preached. The grand secret of its power is, that each of its principles is easily rendered appreciable to the faculty of reason in man, and that the most unenlightened conscience has no difficulty in deciding on which side to register its testimony. It can call its preachers from among the fishermen, and raise them to power. In every human breast, it has an advocate which can be silent only when the heart is dead. It comes home to every man's understanding, and appeals directly to every man's conscience. A man that does not recognize and approve for himself the rights and privileges contended for, in behalf of the American slave, has not yet been found. In whatever else men may differ, they are alike in the apprehension of their natural and personal rights. The difference between abolitionists and those by whom they are opposed, is not as to principles. All are agreed in respect to these. The manner of applying them is the point of difference.

The slaveholder himself, the daily robber of his equal brother, discourses eloquently as to the excellency of justice, and the man who employs a brutal driver to flay the flesh of his negroes, is not offended when kindness and humanity are commended. Every time the abolitionist speaks of justice, the anti-abolitionist assents says, yes, I wish the world were filled with a disposition to render to every man what is rightfully due him; I should then get what is due me. That's right; let us have justice. By all means, let us have justice. Every time the abolitionist speaks in honor of human liberty, he touches a chord in the heart of the anti-abolitionist, which responds in harmonious vibrations. Liberty—yes, that is evidently my right, and let him beware who attempts to invade or abridge that right. Every time he speaks of love, of human brotherhood, and the reciprocal duties of man and man, the anti-abolitionist assents—says, yes, all right—all true—we cannot have such ideas too often, or too fully expressed. So he says, and so he feels, and only shows thereby that he is a man as well as an anti-abolitionist. You have only to keep out of sight the manner of applying your principles, to get them endorsed every time. Contemplating himself, he sees truth with absolute clearness and distinctness. He only blunders when asked to lose sight of himself. In his own cause he can beat a Boston lawyer, but he is dumb when asked to plead the cause of others. He knows very well whatsoever he would have done unto himself, but is quite in doubt as to having the same thing done unto others. It is just here, that lions spring up in the path of duty, and the battle once fought in heaven is refought on the earth. So it is, so hath it ever been, and so must it ever be, when the claims of justice and mercy make their demand at the door of human selfishness. Nevertheless, there is that within which ever pleads for the right and the just.

In conclusion, I have taken a sober view of the present anti-slavery movement. I am sober, but not hopeless. There is no denying, for it is everywhere admitted, that the anti-slavery question is the great moral and social question now before the American people. A state of things has gradually been developed, by which that question has become the first thing in order. It must be met. Herein is my hope. The great idea of impartial liberty is now fairly before the American people. Anti-slavery is no longer a thing to be prevented. The time for prevention is past. This is great gain. When the movement was younger and weaker—when it wrought in a Boston garret to human apprehension, it might have been silently put out of the way. Things are different now. It has grown too large—its friends are too numerous—its facilities too abundant—its ramifications too extended—its power too omnipotent, to be snuffed out by the contingencies of infancy. A thousand strong men might be struck down, and its ranks still be invincible. One flash from the heart-supplied intellect of Harriet Beecher Stowe could light a million camp fires in front of the embattled host of slavery, which not all the waters of the Mississippi, mingled as they are with blood, could extinguish. The present will be looked to by after coming generations, as the age of anti-slavery literature—when supply on the gallop could not keep pace with the ever growing demand—when a picture of a Negro on the cover was a help to the sale of a book—when conservative lyceums and other American literary associations began first to select their orators for distinguished occasions from the ranks of the previously despised abolitionists. If the anti-slavery movement shall fail now, it will not be from outward opposition, but from inward decay. Its auxiliaries are everywhere. Scholars, authors, orators, poets, and statesmen give it their aid. The most brilliant of American poets volunteer in its service. Whittier speaks in burning verse to more than thirty thousand, in the National Era. Your own Longfellow whispers, in every hour of trial and disappointment, "labor and wait." James Russell Lowell is reminding us that "men are more than institutions." Pierpont cheers the heart of the pilgrim in search of liberty, by singing the praises of "the north star." Bryant, too, is with us; and though chained to the car of party, and dragged on amidst a whirl of political excitement, he snatches a moment for letting drop a smiling verse of sympathy for the man in chains. The poets are with us. It would seem almost absurd to say it, considering the use that has been made of them, that we have allies in the Ethiopian songs; those songs that constitute our national music, and without which we have no national music. They are heart songs, and the finest feelings of human nature are expressed in them. "Lucy Neal," "Old Kentucky Home," and "Uncle Ned," can make the heart sad as well as merry, and can call forth a tear as well as a smile. They awaken the sympathies for the slave, in which antislavery principles take root, grow, and flourish. In addition to authors, poets, and scholars at home, the moral sense of the civilized world is with us. England, France, and Germany, the three great lights of modern civilization, are with us, and every American traveler learns to regret the existence of slavery in his country. The growth of intelligence, the influence of commerce, steam, wind, and lightning are our allies. It would be easy to amplify this summary, and to swell the vast conglomeration of our material forces; but there is a deeper and truer method of measuring the power of our cause, and of comprehending its vitality. This is to be found in its accordance with the best elements of human nature. It is beyond the power of slavery to annihilate affinities recognized and established by the Almighty. The slave is bound to mankind by the powerful and inextricable net-work of human brotherhood. His voice is the voice of a man, and his cry is the cry of a man in distress, and man must cease to be man before he can become insensible to that cry. It is the righteous of the cause—the humanity of the cause—which constitutes its potency. As one genuine bankbill is worth more than a thousand counterfeits, so is one man, with right on his side, worth more than a thousand in the wrong. "One may chase a thousand, and put ten thousand to flight." It is, therefore, upon the goodness of our cause, more than upon all other auxiliaries, that we depend for its final triumph.

Another source of congratulations is the fact that, amid all the efforts made by the church, the government, and the people at large, to stay the onward progress of this movement, its course has been onward, steady, straight, unshaken, and unchecked from the beginning. Slavery has gained victories large and numerous; but never as against this movement—against a temporizing policy, and against northern timidity, the slave power has been victorious; but against the spread and prevalence in the country, of a spirit of resistance to its aggression, and of sentiments favorable to its entire overthrow, it has yet accomplished nothing. Every measure, yet devised and executed, having for its object the suppression of anti-slavery, has been as idle and fruitless as pouring oil to extinguish fire. A general rejoicing took place on the passage of "the compromise measures" of 1850. Those measures were called peace measures, and were afterward termed by both the great parties of the country, as well as by leading statesmen, a final settlement of the whole question of slavery; but experience has laughed to scorn the wisdom of pro-slavery statesmen; and their final settlement of agitation seems to be the final revival, on a broader and grander scale than ever before, of the question which they vainly attempted to suppress forever. The fugitive slave bill has especially been of positive service to the anti-slavery movement. It has illustrated before all the people the horrible character of slavery toward the slave, in hunting him down in a free state, and tearing him away from wife and children, thus setting its claims higher than marriage or parental claims. It has revealed the arrogant and overbearing spirit of the slave states toward the free states; despising their principles—shocking their feelings of humanity, not only by bringing before them the abominations of slavery, but by attempting to make them parties to the crime. It has called into exercise among the colored people, the hunted ones, a spirit of manly resistance well calculated to surround them with a bulwark of sympathy and respect hitherto unknown. For men are always disposed to respect and defend rights, when the victims of oppression stand up manfully for themselves.

There is another element of power added to the anti-slavery movement, of great importance; it is the conviction, becoming every day more general and universal, that slavery must be abolished at the south, or it will demoralize and destroy liberty at the north. It is the nature of slavery to beget a state of things all around it favorable to its own continuance. This fact, connected with the system of bondage, is beginning to be more fully realized. The slave-holder is not satisfied to associate with men in the church or in the state, unless he can thereby stain them with the blood of his slaves. To be a slave-holder is to be a propagandist from necessity; for slavery can only live by keeping down the under-growth morality which nature supplies. Every new-born white babe comes armed from the Eternal presence, to make war on slavery. The heart of pity, which would melt in due time over the brutal chastisements it sees inflicted on the helpless, must be hardened. And this work goes on every day in the year, and every hour in the day.

What is done at home is being done also abroad here in the north. And even now the question may be asked, have we at this moment a single free state in the Union? The alarm at this point will become more general. The slave power must go on in its career of exactions. Give, give, will be its cry, till the timidity which concedes shall give place to courage, which shall resist. Such is the voice of experience, such has been the past, such is the present, and such will be that future, which, so sure as man is man, will come. Here I leave the subject; and I leave off where I began, consoling myself and congratulating the friends of freedom upon the fact that the anti-slavery cause is not a new thing under the sun; not some moral delusion which a few years' experience may dispel. It has appeared among men in all ages, and summoned its advocates from all ranks. Its foundations are laid in the deepest and holiest convictions, and from whatever soul the demon, selfishness, is expelled, there will this cause take up its abode. Old as the everlasting hills; immovable as the throne of God; and certain as the purposes of eternal power, against all hinderances, and against all delays, and despite all the mutations of human instrumentalities, it is the faith of my soul, that this anti-slavery cause will triumph.

FOOTNOTES

1 .[Letter, Introduction to Life of Frederick Douglass, Boston, 1841.]
2. [One of these ladies, impelled by the same noble spirit which carried Miss Nightingale to Scutari, has devoted her time, her untiring energies, to a great extent her means, and her high literary abilities, to the advancement and support of Frederick Douglass' Paper, the only organ of the downtrodden, edited and published by one of themselves, in the United States.]
3.[Mr. Stephen Myers, of Albany, deserves mention as one of the most persevering among the colored editorial fraternity.]
4 .[The German physiologists have even discovered vegetable matter—starch—in the human body. See Med. Chirurgical Rev., Oct., 1854, p. 339.]
5 .[Mr. Wm. H. Topp, of Albany.]
6 .[This is the same man who gave me the roots to prevent my being whipped by Mr. Covey. He was "a clever soul." We used frequently to talk about the fight with Covey, and as often as we did so, he would claim my success as the result of the roots which he gave me. This superstition is very common among the more ignorant slaves. A slave seldom dies, but that his death is attributed to trickery.]
7 .[He was a whole-souled man, fully imbued with a love of his afflicted and hunted people, and took pleasure in being to me, as was his wont, "Eyes to the blind, and legs to the lame." This brave and devoted man suffered much from the persecutions common to all who have been prominent benefactors. He at last became blind, and needed a friend to guide him, even as he had been a guide to others. Even in his blindness, he exhibited his manly character. In search of health, he became a physician. When hope of gaining is(sic) own was gone, he had hope for others. Believing in hydropathy, he established, at Northampton, Massachusetts, a

large "Water Cure," and became one of the most successful of all engaged in that mode of treatment.]

8 .[The following is a copy of these curious papers, both of my transfer from Thomas to Hugh Auld, and from Hugh to myself:

"Know all men by these Presents, That I, Thomas Auld, of Talbot county, and state of Maryland, for and in consideration of the sum of one hundred dollars, current money, to me paid by Hugh Auld, of the city of Baltimore, in the said state, at and before the sealing and delivery of these presents, the receipt whereof, I, the said Thomas Auld, do hereby acknowledge, have granted, bargained, and sold, and by these presents do grant, bargain, and sell unto the said Hugh Auld, his executors, administrators, and assigns, ONE NEGRO MAN, by the name of FREDERICK BAILY, or DOUGLASS, as he callls(sic) himself—he is now about twenty-eight years of age—to have and to hold the said negro man for life. And I, the said Thomas Auld, for myself my heirs, executors, and administrators, all and singular, the said FREDERICK BAILY alias DOUGLASS, unto the said Hugh Auld, his executors, administrators, and assigns against me, the said Thomas Auld, my executors, and administrators, and against ali and every other person or persons whatsoever, shall and will warrant and forever defend by these presents. In witness whereof, I set my hand and seal, this thirteenth day of November, eighteen hundred and forty-six.

THOMAS AULD

"Signed, sealed, and delivered in presence of Wrightson Jones.

"JOHN C. LEAS.

The authenticity of this bill of sale is attested by N. Harrington, a justice of the peace of the state of Maryland, and for the county of Talbot, dated same day as above.

"To all whom it may concern: Be it known, that I, Hugh Auld, of the city of Baltimore, in Baltimore county, in the state of Maryland, for divers good causes and considerations, me thereunto moving, have released from slavery, liberated, manumitted, and set free, and by these presents do hereby release from slavery, liberate, manumit, and set free, MY NEGRO MAN, named FREDERICK BAILY, otherwise called DOUGLASS, being of the age of twenty-eight years, or thereabouts, and able to work and gain a sufficient livelihood and maintenance; and him the said negro man named FREDERICK BAILY, otherwise called FREDERICK DOUGLASS, I do declare to be henceforth free, manumitted, and discharged from all manner of servitude to me, my executors, and administrators forever.

"In witness whereof, I, the said Hugh Auld, have hereunto set my hand and seal the fifth of December, in the year one thousand eight hundred and forty-six.

Hugh Auld

"Sealed and delivered in presence of T. Hanson Belt.

"JAMES N. S. T. WRIGHT"]

9 .[See Appendix to this volume, page 317.]

10 .[Mr. Douglass' published speeches alone, would fill two volumes of the size of this. Our space will only permit the insertion of the extracts which follow; and which, for originality of thought, beauty and force of expression, and for impassioned, indignatory eloquence, have seldom been equaled.]

11 .[It is not often that chattels address their owners. The following letter is unique; and probably the only specimen of the kind extant. It was written while in England.]

Narrative of the Life of Frederick Douglass

PREFACE

In the month of August, 1841, I attended an anti-slavery convention in Nantucket, at which it was my happiness to become acquainted with FREDERICK DOUGLASS, the writer of the following Narrative. He was a stranger to nearly every member of that body; but, having recently made his escape from the southern prison-house of bondage, and feeling his curiosity excited to ascertain the principles and measures of the abolitionists,—of whom he had heard a somewhat vague description while he was a slave,—he was induced to give his attendance, on the occasion alluded to, though at that time a resident in New Bedford. Fortunate, most fortunate occurrence!—fortunate for the millions of his manacled brethren, yet panting for deliverance from their awful thraldom!—fortunate for the cause of negro emancipation, and of universal liberty!—fortunate for the land of his birth, which he has already done so much to save and bless!—fortunate for a large circle of friends and acquaintances, whose sympathy and affection he has strongly secured by the many sufferings he has endured, by his virtuous traits of character, by his ever-abiding remembrance of those who are in bonds, as being bound with them!—fortunate for the multitudes, in various parts of our republic, whose minds he has enlightened on the subject of slavery, and who have been melted to tears by his pathos, or roused to virtuous indignation by his stirring eloquence against the enslavers of men!—fortunate for himself, as it at once brought him into the field of public usefulness, "gave the world assurance of a MAN," quickened the slumbering energies of his soul, and consecrated him to the great work of breaking the rod of the oppressor, and letting the oppressed go free!

I shall never forget his first speech at the convention—the extraordinary emotion it excited in my own mind—the powerful impression it created upon a crowded auditory, completely taken by surprise—the applause which followed from the beginning to the end of his felicitous remarks. I think I never hated slavery so intensely as at that moment; certainly, my perception of the enormous outrage which is inflicted by it, on the godlike nature of its victims, was rendered far more clear than ever. There stood one, in physical proportion and stature commanding and exact—in intellect richly endowed—in natural eloquence a prodigy—in soul manifestly "created but a little lower than the angels"—yet a slave, ay, a fugitive slave,—trembling for his safety, hardly daring to believe that on the American soil, a single white person could be found who would befriend him at all hazards, for the love of God and humanity! Capable of high attainments as an intellectual and moral being—needing nothing but a comparatively small amount of cultivation to make him an ornament to society and a blessing to his race—by the law of the land, by the voice of the people, by the terms of the slave code, he was only a piece of property, a beast of burden, a chattel personal, nevertheless! A beloved friend from New Bedford prevailed on Mr. DOUGLASS to address the convention: He came forward to the platform with a hesitancy and embarrassment, necessarily the attendants of a sensitive mind in such a novel position. After apologizing for his ignorance, and reminding the audience that slavery was a poor school for the human intellect and heart, he proceeded to narrate some of the facts in his own history as a slave, and in the course of his speech gave utterance to many noble thoughts and thrilling reflections. As soon as he had taken his seat, filled with hope and admiration, I rose, and declared that PATRICK HENRY, of revolutionary fame, never made a speech more eloquent in the cause of liberty, than the one we had just listened to from the lips of that hunted fugitive. So I believed at that time—such is my belief now. I reminded the audience of the peril which surrounded this self-emancipated young man at the North,—even in Massachusetts, on the soil of the Pilgrim Fathers, among the descendants of revolutionary sires; and I appealed to them, whether they would ever allow him to be carried back into slavery,—law or no law, constitution or no constitution. The response was unanimous and in thunder-tones—"NO!" "Will you succor and protect him as a brother-man—a resident of the old Bay State?" "YES!" shouted the whole mass, with an energy so startling, that the ruthless tyrants south of Mason and Dixon's line might almost have heard the mighty burst of feeling, and recognized it as the pledge of an invincible determination, on the part of those who gave it, never to betray him that wanders, but to hide the outcast, and firmly to abide the consequences.

It was at once deeply impressed upon my mind, that, if Mr. DOUGLASS could be persuaded to consecrate his time and talents to the promotion of the anti-slavery enterprise, a powerful impetus would be given to it, and a stunning blow at the same time inflicted on northern prejudice against a colored complexion. I therefore endeavored to instil hope and courage into his mind, in order that he might dare to engage in a vocation so anomalous and responsible for a person in his situation; and I was seconded in this effort by warm-hearted friends, especially by the late General Agent of the Massachusetts Anti-Slavery Society, Mr. JOHN A. COLLINS, whose judgment in this instance entirely coincided with my own. At first, he could give no encouragement; with unfeigned diffidence, he expressed his conviction that he was not adequate to the performance of so great a task; the path marked out was wholly an untrodden one; he was sincerely apprehensive that he should do more harm than good. After much deliberation, however, he consented to make a trial; and ever since that period, he has acted as a lecturing agent, under the auspices either of the American or the Massachusetts Anti-Slavery Society. In labors he has been most abundant; and his success in combating prejudice, in gaining proselytes, in agitating the public mind, has far surpassed the most sanguine expectations that were raised at the commencement of his brilliant career. He has borne himself with gentleness and meekness, yet with true manliness of character. As a public speaker, he excels in pathos, wit, comparison, imitation, strength of reasoning, and fluency of language. There is in him that union of head and heart, which is indispensable to an enlightenment of the heads and a winning of the hearts of others. May his strength continue to be equal to his day! May he continue to "grow in grace, and in the knowledge of God," that he may be increasingly serviceable in the cause of bleeding humanity, whether at home or abroad!

It is certainly a very remarkable fact, that one of the most efficient advocates of the slave population, now before the public, is a fugitive slave, in the person of FREDERICK DOUGLASS; and that the free colored population of the United States are as ably represented by one of their own number, in the person of CHARLES LENOX REMOND, whose eloquent appeals have extorted the highest applause of multitudes on both sides of the Atlantic. Let the calumniators of the colored race despise themselves for their baseness and illiberality of spirit, and henceforth cease to talk of the natural inferiority of those who require nothing but time and opportunity to attain to the highest point of human excellence.

It may, perhaps, be fairly questioned, whether any other portion of the population of the earth could have endured the privations, sufferings and horrors of slavery, without having become more degraded in the scale of humanity than the slaves of African descent. Nothing has been left undone to cripple their intellects, darken their minds, debase their moral nature, obliterate all traces of their relationship to mankind; and yet how wonderfully they have sustained the mighty load of a most frightful bondage, under which they have been groaning for centuries! To illustrate the effect of slavery on the white man,—to show that he has no powers of endurance, in such a condition, superior to those of his black brother,—DANIEL O'CONNELL, the distinguished advocate of universal emancipation, and the mightiest champion of prostrate but not conquered Ireland, relates the following anecdote in a speech delivered by him in the Conciliation Hall, Dublin, before the Loyal National Repeal Association, March 31, 1845. "No matter," said Mr. O'CONNELL, "under what specious term it may disguise itself, slavery is still hideous. It has a natural, an inevitable tendency to brutalize every noble faculty of man. An American sailor, who was cast away on the shore of Africa, where he was kept in slavery for three years, was, at the expiration of that period, found to be imbruted and stultified—he had lost all reasoning power; and having forgotten his native language, could only utter some savage gibberish between Arabic and English, which nobody could understand, and which even he himself found difficulty in pronouncing. So much for the humanizing influence of THE DOMESTIC INSTITUTION!" Admitting this to have been an extraordinary case of mental deterioration, it proves at least that the white slave can sink as low in the scale of humanity as the black one.

Mr. DOUGLASS has very properly chosen to write his own Narrative, in his own style, and according to the best of his ability, rather than to employ some one else. It is, therefore, entirely his own production; and, considering how long and dark was the career he had to run as a slave,—how few have been his opportunities to improve his mind since he broke his iron fetters,—it is, in my judgment, highly creditable to his head and heart. He who can peruse it without a tearful eye, a heaving breast, an afflicted spirit,—without being filled with an unutterable abhorrence of slavery and all its abettors, and animated with a determination to seek the immediate overthrow of that execrable system,—without trembling for the fate of this country in the hands of a righteous God, who is ever on the side of the oppressed, and whose arm is not shortened that it cannot save,—must have a flinty heart, and be qualified to act the part of a trafficker "in slaves and the souls of men." I am confident that it is essentially true in all its statements; that nothing has been set down in malice, nothing exaggerated, nothing drawn from the imagination; that it comes short of the reality, rather than overstates a single fact in regard to SLAVERY AS IT IS. The experience of FREDERICK DOUGLASS, as a slave, was not a peculiar one; his lot was not especially a hard one; his case may be regarded as a very fair specimen of the treatment of slaves in Maryland, in which State it is conceded that they are better fed and less cruelly treated than in Georgia, Alabama, or Louisiana. Many have suffered incomparably more, while very few on the plantations have suffered less, than himself. Yet how deplorable was his situation! what terrible chastisements were inflicted upon his person! what still more shocking outrages were perpetrated upon his mind! with all his noble powers and sublime aspirations, how like a brute was he treated, even by those professing to have the same mind in them that was in Christ Jesus! to what dreadful liabilities was he continually subjected! how destitute of friendly counsel and aid, even in his greatest extremities! how heavy was the midnight of woe which shrouded in blackness the last ray of hope, and filled the future with terror and gloom! what longings after freedom took possession of his breast, and how his misery augmented, in proportion as he grew reflective and intelligent,—thus demonstrating that a happy slave is an extinct man! how he thought, reasoned, felt, under the lash of the driver, with the chains upon his limbs! what perils he encountered in his endeavors to escape from his horrible doom! and how signal have been his deliverance and preservation in the midst of a nation of pitiless enemies!

This Narrative contains many affecting incidents, many passages of great eloquence and power; but I think the most thrilling one of them all is the description DOUGLASS gives of his feelings, as he stood soliloquizing respecting his fate, and the chances of his one day being a freeman, on the banks of the Chesapeake Bay—viewing the receding vessels as they flew with their white wings before the breeze, and apostrophizing them as animated by the living spirit of freedom. Who can read that passage, and be insensible to its pathos and sublimity? Compressed into it is a whole Alexandrian library of thought, feeling, and sentiment—all that can, all that need be urged, in the form of expostulation, entreaty, rebuke, against that crime of crimes,—making man the property of his fellow-man! O, how accursed is that system, which entombs the godlike mind of man, defaces the divine image, reduces those who by creation were crowned with glory and honor to a level with four-footed beasts, and exalts the dealer in human flesh above all that is called God! Why should its existence be prolonged one hour? Is it not evil, only evil, and that continually? What does its presence imply but the absence of all fear of God, all regard for man, on the part of the people of the United States? Heaven speed its eternal overthrow!

So profoundly ignorant of the nature of slavery are many persons, that they are stubbornly incredulous whenever they read or listen to any recital of the cruelties which are daily inflicted on its victims. They do not deny that the slaves are held as property; but that terrible fact seems to convey to their minds no idea of injustice, exposure to outrage, or savage barbarity. Tell them of cruel scourgings, of mutilations and brandings, of scenes of pollution and blood, of the banishment of all light and knowledge, and they affect to be greatly indignant at such enormous exaggerations, such wholesale misstatements, such abominable libels on the character of the southern planters! As if all these direful outrages were not the natural results of slavery! As if it were less cruel to reduce a human being to the condition of a thing, than to give him a severe flagellation, or to deprive him of necessary food and clothing! As if whips, chains, thumb-screws, paddles, blood-hounds, overseers, drivers, patrols, were not all indispensable to keep the slaves down, and to give protection to their ruthless oppressors! As if, when the marriage institution is abolished, concubinage, adultery, and incest, must not necessarily abound; when all the rights of humanity are annihilated, any barrier remains to protect the victim from the fury of the spoiler; when absolute power is assumed over life and liberty, it will not be wielded with destructive sway! Skeptics of this character abound in society. In some few instances, their incredulity arises from a want of reflection; but, generally, it indicates a hatred of the light, a desire to shield slavery from the assaults of its foes, a contempt of the colored race, whether bond or free. Such will try to discredit the shocking tales of slaveholding cruelty which are recorded in this truthful Narrative; but they will labor in vain. Mr. DOUGLASS has frankly disclosed the place of his birth, the names of those who claimed ownership in his body and soul, and the names also of those who committed the crimes which he has alleged against them. His statements, therefore, may easily be disproved, if they are untrue.

In the course of his Narrative, he relates two instances of murderous cruelty,—in one of which a planter deliberately shot a slave belonging to a neighboring plantation, who had unintentionally gotten within his lordly domain in quest of fish; and in the other, an overseer blew out the brains of a slave who had fled to a stream of water to escape a bloody scourging. Mr. DOUGLASS states that in neither of these instances was any thing done by way of legal arrest or judicial investigation. The Baltimore American, of March 17, 1845, relates a similar case of atrocity, perpetrated with similar impunity—as follows:—"Shooting a slave.—We learn, upon the authority of a letter from Charles county, Maryland, received by a gentleman of this city, that a young man, named Matthews, a nephew of General Matthews, and whose father, it is believed, holds an office at Washington, killed one of the slaves upon his father's farm by shooting him. The letter states that young Matthews had been left in charge of the farm; that he gave an order to the servant, which was disobeyed, when he proceeded to the house, obtained a gun, and, returning, shot the servant. He immediately, the letter continues, fled to his father's residence, where he still remains unmolested."—Let it never be forgotten, that no slaveholder or overseer can be convicted of any outrage perpetrated on the person of a slave, however diabolical it may be, on the testimony of colored witnesses, whether bond or free. By the slave code, they are adjudged to be as incompetent to testify against a white man, as though they were indeed a part of the brute creation. Hence, there is no legal protection in fact, whatever there may be in form, for the slave population; and any amount of cruelty may be inflicted on them with impunity. Is it possible for the human mind to conceive of a more horrible state of society?

The effect of a religious profession on the conduct of southern masters is vividly described in the following Narrative, and shown to be any thing but salutary. In the nature of the case, it must be in the highest degree pernicious. The testimony of Mr. DOUGLASS, on this point, is sustained by a cloud of witnesses, whose veracity is unimpeachable. "A slaveholder's profession of Christianity is a palpable imposture. He is a felon of the highest grade. He is a man-stealer. It is of no importance what you put in the other scale."

Reader! are you with the man-stealers in sympathy and purpose, or on the side of their down-trodden victims? If with the former, then are you the foe of God and man. If with the latter,

what are you prepared to do and dare in their behalf? Be faithful, be vigilant, be untiring in your efforts to break every yoke, and let the oppressed go free. Come what may—cost what it may—inscribe on the banner which you unfurl to the breeze, as your religious and political motto—"NO COMPROMISE WITH SLAVERY! NO UNION WITH SLAVEHOLDERS!"
WM. LLOYD GARRISON BOSTON,
May 1, 1845.

LETTER FROM WENDELL PHILLIPS, ESQ.

BOSTON, APRIL 22, 1845.

My Dear Friend:
You remember the old fable of "The Man and the Lion," where the lion complained that he should not be so misrepresented "when the lions wrote history."
I am glad the time has come when the "lions write history." We have been left long enough to gather the character of slavery from the involuntary evidence of the masters. One might, indeed, rest sufficiently satisfied with what, it is evident, must be, in general, the results of such a relation, without seeking farther to find whether they have followed in every instance. Indeed, those who stare at the half-peck of corn a week, and love to count the lashes on the slave's back, are seldom the "stuff" out of which reformers and abolitionists are to be made. I remember that, in 1838, many were waiting for the results of the West India experiment, before they could come into our ranks. Those "results" have come long ago; but, alas! few of that number have come with them, as converts. A man must be disposed to judge of emancipation by other tests than whether it has increased the produce of sugar,—and to hate slavery for other reasons than because it starves men and whips women,—before he is ready to lay the first stone of his anti-slavery life.
I was glad to learn, in your story, how early the most neglected of God's children waken to a sense of their rights, and of the injustice done them. Experience is a keen teacher; and long before you had mastered your A B C, or knew where the "white sails" of the Chesapeake were bound, you began, I see, to gauge the wretchedness of the slave, not by his hunger and want, not by his lashes and toil, but by the cruel and blighting death which gathers over his soul. In connection with this, there is one circumstance which makes your recollections peculiarly valuable, and renders your early insight the more remarkable. You come from that part of the country where we are told slavery appears with its fairest features. Let us hear, then, what it is at its best estate—gaze on its bright side, if it has one; and then imagination may task her powers to add dark lines to the picture, as she travels southward to that (for the colored man) Valley of the Shadow of Death, where the Mississippi sweeps along.
Again, we have known you long, and can put the most entire confidence in your truth, candor, and sincerity. Every one who has heard you speak has felt, and, I am confident, every one who reads your book will feel, persuaded that you give them a fair specimen of the whole truth. No one-sided portrait,—no wholesale complaints,—but strict justice done, whenever individual kindliness has neutralized, for a moment, the deadly system with which it was strangely allied. You have been with us, too, some years, and can fairly compare the twilight of rights, which your race enjoy at the North, with that "noon of night" under which they labor south of Mason and Dixon's line. Tell us whether, after all, the half-free colored man of Massachusetts is worse off than the pampered slave of the rice swamps!
In reading your life, no one can say that we have unfairly picked out some rare specimens of cruelty. We know that the bitter drops, which even you have drained from the cup, are no

incidental aggravations, no individual ills, but such as must mingle always and necessarily in the lot of every slave. They are the essential ingredients, not the occasional results, of the system.

After all, I shall read your book with trembling for you. Some years ago, when you were beginning to tell me your real name and birthplace, you may remember I stopped you, and preferred to remain ignorant of all. With the exception of a vague description, so I continued, till the other day, when you read me your memoirs. I hardly knew, at the time, whether to thank you or not for the sight of them, when I reflected that it was still dangerous, in Massachusetts, for honest men to tell their names! They say the fathers, in 1776, signed the Declaration of Independence with the halter about their necks. You, too, publish your declaration of freedom with danger compassing you around. In all the broad lands which the Constitution of the United States overshadows, there is no single spot,—however narrow or desolate,—where a fugitive slave can plant himself and say, "I am safe." The whole armory of Northern Law has no shield for you. I am free to say that, in your place, I should throw the MS. into the fire.

You, perhaps, may tell your story in safety, endeared as you are to so many warm hearts by rare gifts, and a still rarer devotion of them to the service of others. But it will be owing only to your labors, and the fearless efforts of those who, trampling the laws and Constitution of the country under their feet, are determined that they will "hide the outcast," and that their hearths shall be, spite of the law, an asylum for the oppressed, if, some time or other, the humblest may stand in our streets, and bear witness in safety against the cruelties of which he has been the victim.

Yet it is sad to think, that these very throbbing hearts which welcome your story, and form your best safeguard in telling it, are all beating contrary to the "statute in such case made and provided." Go on, my dear friend, till you, and those who, like you, have been saved, so as by fire, from the dark prison-house, shall stereotype these free, illegal pulses into statutes; and New England, cutting loose from a blood-stained Union, shall glory in being the house of refuge for the oppressed,—till we no longer merely "hide the outcast," or make a merit of standing idly by while he is hunted in our midst; but, consecrating anew the soil of the Pilgrims as an asylum for the oppressed, proclaim our WELCOME to the slave so loudly, that the tones shall reach every hut in the Carolinas, and make the broken-hearted bondman leap up at the thought of old Massachusetts.

God speed the day!

Till then, and ever,

Yours truly,

WENDELL PHILLIPS

FREDERICK DOUGLASS.

Frederick Douglass was born in slavery as Frederick Augustus Washington Bailey near Easton in Talbot County, Maryland. He was not sure of the exact year of his birth, but he knew that it was 1817 or 1818. As a young boy he was sent to Baltimore, to be a house servant, where he learned to read and write, with the assistance of his master's wife. In 1838 he escaped from slavery and went to New York City, where he married Anna Murray, a free colored woman whom he had met in Baltimore. Soon thereafter he changed his name to Frederick Douglass. In 1841 he addressed a convention of the Massachusetts Anti-Slavery Society in Nantucket and so greatly impressed the group that they immediately employed him as an agent. He was such an impressive orator that numerous persons doubted if he had ever been a slave, so he wrote NARRATIVE OF THE LIFE OF FREDERICK DOUGLASS. During the Civil War he assisted in the recruiting of colored men for the 54th and 55th Massachusetts Regiments and consistently argued for the emancipation of slaves. After the war he was active in securing and protecting the rights of the freemen. In his later years, at different times, he was secretary of the Santo Domingo Commission, marshall and recorder of deeds of the District of Columbia, and United States Minister to Haiti. His other autobiographical works are MY BONDAGE AND MY FREEDOM and LIFE AND TIMES OF FREDERICK DOUGLASS, published in 1855 and 1881 respectively. He died in 1895.

CHAPTER I

I was born in Tuckahoe, near Hillsborough, and about twelve miles from Easton, in Talbot county, Maryland. I have no accurate knowledge of my age, never having seen any authentic record containing it. By far the larger part of the slaves know as little of their ages as horses know of theirs, and it is the wish of most masters within my knowledge to keep their slaves thus ignorant. I do not remember to have ever met a slave who could tell of his birthday. They seldom come nearer to it than planting-time, harvest-time, cherry-time, spring-time, or fall-time. A want of information concerning my own was a source of unhappiness to me even during childhood. The white children could tell their ages. I could not tell why I ought to be deprived of the same privilege. I was not allowed to make any inquiries of my master concerning it. He deemed all such inquiries on the part of a slave improper and impertinent, and evidence of a restless spirit. The nearest estimate I can give makes me now between twenty-seven and twenty-eight years of age. I come to this, from hearing my master say, some time during 1835, I was about seventeen years old.
My mother was named Harriet Bailey. She was the daughter of Isaac and Betsey Bailey, both colored, and quite dark. My mother was of a darker complexion than either my grandmother or grandfather.
My father was a white man. He was admitted to be such by all I ever heard speak of my parentage. The opinion was also whispered that my master was my father; but of the correctness of this opinion, I know nothing; the means of knowing was withheld from me. My mother and I were separated when I was but an infant—before I knew her as my mother. It is a common custom, in the part of Maryland from which I ran away, to part children from their mothers at a very early age. Frequently, before the child has reached its twelfth month, its mother is taken from it, and hired out on some farm a considerable distance off, and the child is placed under the care of an old woman, too old for field labor. For what this separation is done, I do not know, unless it be to hinder the development of the child's affection toward its mother, and to blunt and destroy the natural affection of the mother for the child. This is the inevitable result.
I never saw my mother, to know her as such, more than four or five times in my life; and each of these times was very short in duration, and at night. She was hired by a Mr. Stewart, who lived about twelve miles from my home. She made her journeys to see me in the night, travelling the whole distance on foot, after the performance of her day's work. She was a field hand, and a whipping is the penalty of not being in the field at sunrise, unless a slave has special permission from his or her master to the contrary—a permission which they seldom get, and one that gives to him that gives it the proud name of being a kind master. I do not recollect of ever seeing my mother by the light of day. She was with me in the night. She would lie down with me, and get me to sleep, but long before I waked she was gone. Very little communication ever took place between us. Death soon ended what little we could have

while she lived, and with it her hardships and suffering. She died when I was about seven years old, on one of my master's farms, near Lee's Mill. I was not allowed to be present during her illness, at her death, or burial. She was gone long before I knew any thing about it. Never having enjoyed, to any considerable extent, her soothing presence, her tender and watchful care, I received the tidings of her death with much the same emotions I should have probably felt at the death of a stranger.

Called thus suddenly away, she left me without the slightest intimation of who my father was. The whisper that my master was my father, may or may not be true; and, true or false, it is of but little consequence to my purpose whilst the fact remains, in all its glaring odiousness, that slaveholders have ordained, and by law established, that the children of slave women shall in all cases follow the condition of their mothers; and this is done too obviously to administer to their own lusts, and make a gratification of their wicked desires profitable as well as pleasurable; for by this cunning arrangement, the slaveholder, in cases not a few, sustains to his slaves the double relation of master and father.

I know of such cases; and it is worthy of remark that such slaves invariably suffer greater hardships, and have more to contend with, than others. They are, in the first place, a constant offence to their mistress. She is ever disposed to find fault with them; they can seldom do any thing to please her; she is never better pleased than when she sees them under the lash, especially when she suspects her husband of showing to his mulatto children favors which he withholds from his black slaves. The master is frequently compelled to sell this class of his slaves, out of deference to the feelings of his white wife; and, cruel as the deed may strike any one to be, for a man to sell his own children to human flesh-mongers, it is often the dictate of humanity for him to do so; for, unless he does this, he must not only whip them himself, but must stand by and see one white son tie up his brother, of but few shades darker complexion than himself, and ply the gory lash to his naked back; and if he lisp one word of disapproval, it is set down to his parental partiality, and only makes a bad matter worse, both for himself and the slave whom he would protect and defend.

Every year brings with it multitudes of this class of slaves. It was doubtless in consequence of a knowledge of this fact, that one great statesman of the south predicted the downfall of slavery by the inevitable laws of population. Whether this prophecy is ever fulfilled or not, it is nevertheless plain that a very different-looking class of people are springing up at the south, and are now held in slavery, from those originally brought to this country from Africa; and if their increase do no other good, it will do away the force of the argument, that God cursed Ham, and therefore American slavery is right. If the lineal descendants of Ham are alone to be scripturally enslaved, it is certain that slavery at the south must soon become unscriptural; for thousands are ushered into the world, annually, who, like myself, owe their existence to white fathers, and those fathers most frequently their own masters.

I have had two masters. My first master's name was Anthony. I do not remember his first name. He was generally called Captain Anthony—a title which, I presume, he acquired by sailing a craft on the Chesapeake Bay. He was not considered a rich slaveholder. He owned two or three farms, and about thirty slaves. His farms and slaves were under the care of an overseer. The overseer's name was Plummer. Mr. Plummer was a miserable drunkard, a profane swearer, and a savage monster. He always went armed with a cowskin and a heavy cudgel. I have known him to cut and slash the women's heads so horribly, that even master would be enraged at his cruelty, and would threaten to whip him if he did not mind himself. Master, however, was not a humane slaveholder. It required extraordinary barbarity on the part of an overseer to affect him. He was a cruel man, hardened by a long life of slaveholding. He would at times seem to take great pleasure in whipping a slave. I have often been awakened at the dawn of day by the most heart-rending shrieks of an own aunt of mine, whom he used to tie up to a joist, and whip upon her naked back till she was literally covered with blood. No words, no tears, no prayers, from his gory victim, seemed to move his iron heart from its bloody purpose. The louder she screamed, the harder he whipped; and where the blood ran fastest, there he whipped longest. He would whip her to make her scream, and whip her to make her hush; and not until overcome by fatigue, would he cease to swing the blood-clotted cowskin. I remember the first time I ever witnessed this horrible exhibition. I was quite a child, but I well remember it. I never shall forget it whilst I remember any thing. It was the first of a long series of such outrages, of which I was doomed to be a witness and a participant. It struck me with awful force. It was the blood-stained gate, the entrance to the hell of slavery, through which I was about to pass. It was a most terrible spectacle. I wish I could commit to paper the feelings with which I beheld it.

This occurrence took place very soon after I went to live with my old master, and under the following circumstances. Aunt Hester went out one night,—where or for what I do not know,—and happened to be absent when my master desired her presence. He had ordered her not to go out evenings, and warned her that she must never let him catch her in company with a young man, who was paying attention to her belonging to Colonel Lloyd. The young man's name was Ned Roberts, generally called Lloyd's Ned. Why master was so careful of her, may be safely left to conjecture. She was a woman of noble form, and of graceful proportions, having very few equals, and fewer superiors, in personal appearance, among the colored or white women of our neighborhood.

Aunt Hester had not only disobeyed his orders in going out, but had been found in company with Lloyd's Ned; which circumstance, I found, from what he said while whipping her, was the chief offence. Had he been a man of pure morals himself, he might have been thought interested in protecting the innocence of my aunt; but those who knew him will not suspect him of any such virtue. Before he commenced whipping Aunt Hester, he took her into the kitchen, and stripped her from neck to waist, leaving her neck, shoulders, and back, entirely naked. He then told her to cross her hands, calling her at the same time a d——d b——h. After crossing her hands, he tied them with a strong rope, and led her to a stool under a large hook in the joist, put in for the purpose. He made her get upon the stool, and tied her hands to the hook. She now stood fair for his infernal purpose. Her arms were stretched up at their full length, so that she stood upon the ends of her toes. He then said to her, "Now, you d——d b——h, I'll learn you how to disobey my orders!" and after rolling up his sleeves, he commenced to lay on the heavy cowskin, and soon the warm, red blood (amid heart-rending shrieks from her, and horrid oaths from him) came dripping to the floor. I was so terrified and horror-stricken at the sight, that I hid myself in a closet, and dared not venture out till long after the bloody transaction was over. I expected it would be my turn next. It was all new to me. I had never seen any thing like it before. I had always lived with my grandmother on the outskirts of the plantation, where she was put to raise the children of the younger women. I had therefore been, until now, out of the way of the bloody scenes that often occurred on the plantation.

CHAPTER II

My master's family consisted of two sons, Andrew and Richard; one daughter, Lucretia, and her husband, Captain Thomas Auld. They lived in one house, upon the home plantation of Colonel Edward Lloyd. My master was Colonel Lloyd's clerk and superintendent. He was what might be called the overseer of the overseers. I spent two years of childhood on this plantation in my old master's family. It was here that I witnessed the bloody transaction recorded in the first chapter; and as I received my first impressions of slavery on this plantation, I will give some description of it, and of slavery as it there existed. The plantation is about twelve miles north of Easton, in Talbot county, and is situated on the border of Miles River. The principal products raised upon it were tobacco, corn, and wheat. These were raised in great abundance; so that, with the products of this and the other farms belonging to him, he was able to keep in almost constant employment a large sloop, in carrying them to market at Baltimore. This sloop was named Sally Lloyd, in honor of one of the colonel's daughters. My master's son-in-law, Captain Auld, was master of the vessel; she was otherwise manned by the colonel's own slaves. Their names were Peter, Isaac, Rich, and Jake. These were esteemed very highly by the other slaves, and looked upon as the privileged ones of the plantation; for it was no small affair, in the eyes of the slaves, to be allowed to see Baltimore.

Colonel Lloyd kept from three to four hundred slaves on his home plantation, and owned a large number more on the neighboring farms belonging to him. The names of the farms nearest to the home plantation were Wye Town and New Design. "Wye Town" was under the overseership of a man named Noah Willis. New Design was under the overseership of a Mr. Townsend. The overseers of these, and all the rest of the farms, numbering over twenty, received advice and direction from the managers of the home plantation. This was the great business place. It was the seat of government for the whole twenty farms. All disputes among the overseers were settled here. If a slave was convicted of any high misdemeanor, became unmanageable, or evinced a determination to run away, he was brought immediately here, severely whipped, put on board the sloop, carried to Baltimore, and sold to Austin Woolfolk, or some other slave-trader, as a warning to the slaves remaining.

Here, too, the slaves of all the other farms received their monthly allowance of food, and their yearly clothing. The men and women slaves received, as their monthly allowance of food, eight pounds of pork, or its equivalent in fish, and one bushel of corn meal. Their yearly clothing consisted of two coarse linen shirts, one pair of linen trousers, like the shirts, one jacket, one pair of trousers for winter, made of coarse negro cloth, one pair of stockings, and one pair of shoes; the whole of which could not have cost more than seven dollars. The allowance of the slave children was given to their mothers, or the old women having the care of them. The children unable to work in the field had neither shoes, stockings, jackets, nor trousers, given to them; their clothing consisted of two coarse linen shirts per year. When these failed them, they went naked until the next allowance-day. Children from seven to ten years old, of both sexes, almost naked, might be seen at all seasons of the year.

There were no beds given the slaves, unless one coarse blanket be considered such, and none but the men and women had these. This, however, is not considered a very great privation. They find less difficulty from the want of beds, than from the want of time to sleep; for when their day's work in the field is done, the most of them having their washing, mending, and cooking to do, and having few or none of the ordinary facilities for doing either of these, very many of their sleeping hours are consumed in preparing for the field the coming day; and when this is done, old and young, male and female, married and single, drop down side by side, on one common bed,—the cold, damp floor,—each covering himself or herself with their miserable blankets; and here they sleep till they are summoned to the field by the driver's horn. At the sound of this, all must rise, and be off to the field. There must be no halting; every one must be at his or her post; and woe betides them who hear not this morning summons to the field; for if they are not awakened by the sense of hearing, they are by the sense of feeling: no age nor sex finds any favor. Mr. Severe, the overseer, used to stand by the door of the quarter, armed with a large hickory stick and heavy cowskin, ready to whip any one who was so unfortunate as not to hear, or, from any other cause, was prevented from being ready to start for the field at the sound of the horn.

Mr. Severe was rightly named: he was a cruel man. I have seen him whip a woman, causing the blood to run half an hour at the time; and this, too, in the midst of her crying children, pleading for their mother's release. He seemed to take pleasure in manifesting his fiendish barbarity. Added to his cruelty, he was a profane swearer. It was enough to chill the blood and stiffen the hair of an ordinary man to hear him talk. Scarce a sentence escaped him but that was commenced or concluded by some horrid oath. The field was the place to witness his cruelty and profanity. His presence made it both the field of blood and of blasphemy. From the rising till the going down of the sun, he was cursing, raving, cutting, and slashing among the slaves of the field, in the most frightful manner. His career was short. He died very soon after I went to Colonel Lloyd's; and he died as he lived, uttering, with his dying groans, bitter curses and horrid oaths. His death was regarded by the slaves as the result of a merciful providence. Mr. Severe's place was filled by a Mr. Hopkins. He was a very different man. He was less cruel, less profane, and made less noise, than Mr. Severe. His course was characterized by no extraordinary demonstrations of cruelty. He whipped, but seemed to take no pleasure in it. He was called by the slaves a good overseer.

The home plantation of Colonel Lloyd wore the appearance of a country village. All the mechanical operations for all the farms were performed here. The shoemaking and mending, the blacksmithing, cartwrighting, coopering, weaving, and grain-grinding, were all performed by the slaves on the home plantation. The whole place wore a business-like aspect very unlike the neighboring farms. The number of houses, too, conspired to give it advantage over the neighboring farms. It was called by the slaves the Great House Farm. Few privileges were esteemed higher, by the slaves of the out-farms, than that of being selected to do errands at the Great House Farm. It was associated in their minds with greatness. A representative could not be prouder of his election to a seat in the American Congress, than a slave on one of the out-farms would be of his election to do errands at the Great House Farm. They regarded it as evidence of great confidence reposed in them by their overseers; and it was on this account, as well as a constant desire to be out of the field from under the driver's lash, that they esteemed it a high privilege, one worth careful living for. He was called the smartest and most trusty fellow, who had this honor conferred upon him the most frequently. The competitors for this office sought as diligently to please their overseers, as the office-seekers in the political parties seek to please and deceive the people. The same traits of character might be seen in Colonel Lloyd's slaves, as are seen in the slaves of the political parties.

The slaves selected to go to the Great House Farm, for the monthly allowance for themselves and their fellow-slaves, were peculiarly enthusiastic. While on their way, they would make the dense old woods, for miles around, reverberate with their wild songs, revealing at once the highest joy and the deepest sadness. They would compose and sing as they went along, consulting neither time nor tune. The thought that came up, came out—if not in the word, in the sound;—and as frequently in the one as in the other. They would sometimes sing the most pathetic sentiment in the most rapturous tone, and the most rapturous sentiment in the most pathetic tone. Into all of their songs they would manage to weave something of the Great House Farm. Especially would they do this, when leaving home. They would then sing most exultingly the following words:—

"I am going away to the Great House Farm!

O, yea! O, yea! O!"

This they would sing, as a chorus, to words which to many would seem unmeaning jargon, but which, nevertheless, were full of meaning to themselves. I have sometimes thought that the mere hearing of those songs would do more to impress some minds with the horrible character of slavery, than the reading of whole volumes of philosophy on the subject could do.

I did not, when a slave, understand the deep meaning of those rude and apparently incoherent songs. I was myself within the circle; so that I neither saw nor heard as those without might see and hear. They told a tale of woe which was then altogether beyond my feeble comprehension; they were tones loud, long, and deep; they breathed the prayer and complaint of souls boiling over with the bitterest anguish. Every tone was a testimony against slavery, and a prayer to God for deliverance from chains. The hearing of those wild notes always depressed my spirit, and filled me with ineffable sadness. I have frequently found myself in tears while hearing them. The mere recurrence to those songs, even now, afflicts me; and while I am writing these lines, an expression of feeling has already found its way down my cheek. To those songs I trace my first glimmering conception of the dehumanizing character of slavery. I can never get rid of that conception. Those songs still follow me, to deepen my hatred of slavery, and quicken my sympathies for my brethren in bonds. If any one wishes to be impressed with the soul-killing effects of slavery, let him go to Colonel Lloyd's plantation, and, on allowance-day, place himself in the deep pine woods, and there let him, in silence, analyze the sounds that shall pass through the chambers of his soul,—and if he is not thus impressed, it will only be because "there is no flesh in his obdurate heart."

I have often been utterly astonished, since I came to the north, to find persons who could speak of the singing, among slaves, as evidence of their contentment and happiness. It is impossible to conceive of a greater mistake. Slaves sing most when they are most unhappy. The songs of the slave represent the sorrows of his heart; and he is relieved by them, only as an aching heart is relieved by its tears. At least, such is my experience. I have often sung to drown my sorrow, but seldom to express my happiness. Crying for joy, and singing for joy, were alike uncommon to me while in the jaws of slavery. The singing of a man cast away upon a desolate island might be as appropriately considered as evidence of contentment and happiness, as the singing of a slave; the songs of the one and of the other are prompted by the same emotion.

CHAPTER III

Colonel Lloyd kept a large and finely cultivated garden, which afforded almost constant employment for four men, besides the chief gardener, (Mr. M'Durmond.) This garden was probably the greatest attraction of the place. During the summer months, people came from far and near—from Baltimore, Easton, and Annapolis—to see it. It abounded in fruits of almost every description, from the hardy apple of the north to the delicate orange of the south. This garden was not the least source of trouble on the plantation. Its excellent fruit was quite a temptation to the hungry swarms of boys, as well as the older slaves, belonging to the colonel, few of whom had the virtue or the vice to resist it. Scarcely a day passed, during the summer, but that some slave had to take the lash for stealing fruit. The colonel had to resort to all kinds of stratagems to keep his slaves out of the garden. The last and most successful one was that of tarring his fence all around; after which, if a slave was caught with any tar upon his person, it was deemed sufficient proof that he had either been into the garden, or had tried to get in. In either case, he was severely whipped by the chief gardener. This plan worked well; the slaves became as fearful of tar as of the lash. They seemed to realize the impossibility of touching TAR without being defiled.

The colonel also kept a splendid riding equipage. His stable and carriage-house presented the appearance of some of our large city livery establishments. His horses were of the finest form and noblest blood. His carriage-house contained three splendid coaches, three or four gigs, besides dearborns and barouches of the most fashionable style.

This establishment was under the care of two slaves—old Barney and young Barney—father and son. To attend to this establishment was their sole work. But it was by no means an easy employment; for in nothing was Colonel Lloyd more particular than in the management of his horses. The slightest inattention to these was unpardonable, and was visited upon those, under whose care they were placed, with the severest punishment; no excuse could shield them, if the colonel only suspected any want of attention to his horses—a supposition which he frequently indulged, and one which, of course, made the office of old and young Barney a very trying one. They never knew when they were safe from punishment. They were frequently whipped when least deserving, and escaped whipping when most deserving it. Every thing depended upon the looks of the horses, and the state of Colonel Lloyd's own mind when his horses were brought to him for use. If a horse did not move fast enough, or hold his head high enough, it was owing to some fault of his keepers. It was painful to stand near the stable-door, and hear the various complaints against the keepers when a horse was taken out for use. "This horse has not had proper attention. He has not been sufficiently rubbed and curried, or he has not been properly fed; his food was too wet or too dry; he got it too soon or too late; he was too hot or too cold; he had too much hay, and not enough of grain; or he had too much grain, and not enough of hay; instead of old Barney's attending to the horse, he had very improperly left it to his son." To all these complaints, no matter how unjust, the slave must answer never a word. Colonel Lloyd could not brook any contradiction from a slave. When he spoke, a slave must stand, listen, and tremble; and such was literally the case. I have seen Colonel Lloyd make old Barney, a man between fifty and sixty years of age, uncover his bald head, kneel down upon the cold, damp ground, and receive upon his naked and toil-worn shoulders more than thirty lashes at the time. Colonel Lloyd had three sons—Edward, Murray, and Daniel,—and three sons-in-law, Mr. Winder, Mr. Nicholson, and Mr. Lowndes. All of these lived at the Great House Farm, and enjoyed the luxury of whipping the servants when they pleased, from old Barney down to William Wilkes, the coach-driver. I have seen Winder make one of the house-servants stand off from him a suitable distance to be touched with the end of his whip, and at every stroke raise great ridges upon his back.

To describe the wealth of Colonel Lloyd would be almost equal to describing the riches of Job. He kept from ten to fifteen house-servants. He was said to own a thousand slaves, and I think this estimate quite within the truth. Colonel Lloyd owned so many that he did not know them when he saw them; nor did all the slaves of the out-farms know him. It is reported of him, that, while riding along the road one day, he met a colored man, and addressed him in the usual manner of speaking to colored people on the public highways of the south: "Well, boy, whom do you belong to?" "To Colonel Lloyd," replied the slave. "Well, does the colonel treat you well?" "No, sir," was the ready reply. "What, does he work you too hard?" "Yes, sir." "Well, don't he give you enough to eat?" "Yes, sir, he gives me enough, such as it is."

The colonel, after ascertaining where the slave belonged, rode on; the man also went on about his business, not dreaming that he had been conversing with his master. He thought, said, and heard nothing more of the matter, until two or three weeks afterwards. The poor man was then informed by his overseer that, for having found fault with his master, he was now to be sold to a Georgia trader. He was immediately chained and handcuffed; and thus, without a moment's warning, he was snatched away, and forever sundered, from his family and friends, by a hand more unrelenting than death. This is the penalty of telling the truth, of telling the simple truth, in answer to a series of plain questions.

It is partly in consequence of such facts, that slaves, when inquired of as to their condition and the character of their masters, almost universally say they are contented, and that their masters are kind. The slaveholders have been known to send in spies among their slaves, to ascertain their views and feelings in regard to their condition. The frequency of this has had the effect to establish among the slaves the maxim, that a still tongue makes a wise head. They suppress the truth rather than take the consequences of telling it, and in so doing prove themselves a part of the human family. If they have any thing to say of their masters, it is generally in their masters' favor, especially when speaking to an untried man. I have been frequently asked, when a slave, if I had a kind master, and do not remember ever to have given a negative answer; nor did I, in pursuing this course, consider myself as uttering what was absolutely false; for I always measured the kindness of my master by the standard of kindness set up among slaveholders around us. Moreover, slaves are like other people, and imbibe prejudices quite common to others. They think their own better than that of others. Many, under the influence of this prejudice, think their own masters are better than the masters of other slaves; and this, too, in some cases, when the very reverse is true. Indeed, it is not uncommon for slaves even to fall out and quarrel among themselves about the relative goodness of their masters, each contending for the superior goodness of his own over that of the others. At the very same time, they mutually execrate their masters when viewed separately. It was so on our plantation. When Colonel Lloyd's slaves met the slaves of Jacob Jepson, they seldom parted without a quarrel about their masters; Colonel Lloyd's slaves contending that he was the richest, and Mr. Jepson's slaves that he was the smartest, and most of a man. Colonel Lloyd's slaves would boast his ability to buy and sell Jacob Jepson. Mr. Jepson's slaves would boast his ability to whip Colonel Lloyd. These quarrels would almost always end in a fight between the parties, and those that whipped were supposed to have gained the point at issue. They seemed to think that the greatness of their masters was transferable to themselves. It was considered as being bad enough to be a slave; but to be a poor man's slave was deemed a disgrace indeed!

CHAPTER IV

Mr. Hopkins remained but a short time in the office of overseer. Why his career was so short, I do not know, but suppose he lacked the necessary severity to suit Colonel Lloyd. Mr. Hopkins was succeeded by Mr. Austin Gore, a man possessing, in an eminent degree, all those traits of character indispensable to what is called a first-rate overseer. Mr. Gore had served Colonel Lloyd, in the capacity of overseer, upon one of the out-farms, and had shown himself worthy of the high station of overseer upon the home or Great House Farm.

Mr. Gore was proud, ambitious, and persevering. He was artful, cruel, and obdurate. He was just the man for such a place, and it was just the place for such a man. It afforded scope for the full exercise of all his powers, and he seemed to be perfectly at home in it. He was one of those who could torture the slightest look, word, or gesture, on the part of the slave, into impudence, and would treat it accordingly. There must be no answering back to him; no explanation was allowed a slave, showing himself to have been wrongfully accused. Mr. Gore acted fully up to the maxim laid down by slaveholders,—"It is better that a dozen slaves should suffer under the lash, than that the overseer should be convicted, in the presence of the slaves, of having been at fault." No matter how innocent a slave might be—it availed him nothing, when accused by Mr. Gore of any misdemeanor. To be accused was to be convicted, and to be convicted was to be punished; the one always following the other with immutable certainty. To escape punishment was to escape accusation; and few slaves had the fortune to do either, under the overseership of Mr. Gore. He was just proud enough to demand the most debasing homage of the slave, and quite servile enough to crouch, himself, at the feet of the master. He was ambitious enough to be contented with nothing short of the highest rank of overseers, and persevering enough to reach the height of his ambition. He was cruel enough to inflict the severest punishment, artful enough to descend to the lowest trickery, and obdurate enough to be insensible to the voice of a reproving conscience. He was, of all the overseers, the most dreaded by the slaves. His presence was painful; his eye flashed confusion; and seldom was his sharp, shrill voice heard, without producing horror and trembling in their ranks.

Mr. Gore was a grave man, and, though a young man, he indulged in no jokes, said no funny words, seldom smiled. His words were in perfect keeping with his looks, and his looks were in perfect keeping with his words. Overseers will sometimes indulge in a witty word, even with the slaves; not so with Mr. Gore. He spoke but to command, and commanded but to be obeyed; he dealt sparingly with his words, and bountifully with his whip, never using the former where the latter would answer as well. When he whipped, he seemed to do so from a sense of duty, and feared no consequences. He did nothing reluctantly, no matter how disagreeable; always at his post, never inconsistent. He never promised but to fulfil. He was, in a word, a man of the most inflexible firmness and stone-like coolness.

His savage barbarity was equalled only by the consummate coolness with which he committed the grossest and most savage deeds upon the slaves under his charge. Mr. Gore once undertook to whip one of Colonel Lloyd's slaves, by the name of Demby. He had given Demby but few stripes, when, to get rid of the scourging, he ran and plunged himself into a creek, and stood there at the depth of his shoulders, refusing to come out. Mr. Gore told him that he would give him three calls, and that, if he did not come out at the third call, he would shoot him. The first call was given. Demby made no response, but stood his ground. The second and third calls were given with the same result. Mr. Gore then, without consultation or deliberation with any one, not even giving Demby an additional call, raised his musket to his face, taking deadly aim at his standing victim, and in an instant poor Demby was no more. His mangled body sank out of sight, and blood and brains marked the water where he had stood.

A thrill of horror flashed through every soul upon the plantation, excepting Mr. Gore. He alone seemed cool and collected. He was asked by Colonel Lloyd and my old master, why he resorted to this extraordinary expedient. His reply was, (as well as I can remember,) that Demby had become unmanageable. He was setting a dangerous example to the other slaves,— one which, if suffered to pass without some such demonstration on his part, would finally lead to the total subversion of all rule and order upon the plantation. He argued that if one slave refused to be corrected, and escaped with his life, the other slaves would soon copy the example; the result of which would be, the freedom of the slaves, and the enslavement of the whites. Mr. Gore's defence was satisfactory. He was continued in his station as overseer upon the home plantation. His fame as an overseer went abroad. His horrid crime was not even submitted to judicial investigation. It was committed in the presence of slaves, and they of course could neither institute a suit, nor testify against him; and thus the guilty perpetrator of one of the bloodiest and most foul murders goes unwhipped of justice, and uncensured by the community in which he lives. Mr. Gore lived in St. Michael's, Talbot county, Maryland, when I left there; and if he is still alive, he very probably lives there now; and if so, he is now, as he was then, as highly esteemed and as much respected as though his guilty soul had not been stained with his brother's blood.

I speak advisedly when I say this,—that killing a slave, or any colored person, in Talbot county, Maryland, is not treated as a crime, either by the courts or the community. Mr. Thomas Lanman, of St. Michael's, killed two slaves, one of whom he killed with a hatchet, by knocking his brains out. He used to boast of the commission of the awful and bloody deed. I have heard him do so laughingly, saying, among other things, that he was the only benefactor of his country in the company, and that when others would do as much as he had done, we should be relieved of "the d——d niggers."

The wife of Mr. Giles Hicks, living but a short distance from where I used to live, murdered my wife's cousin, a young girl between fifteen and sixteen years of age, mangling her person in the most horrible manner, breaking her nose and breastbone with a stick, so that the poor girl expired in a few hours afterward. She was immediately buried, but had not been in her untimely grave but a few hours before she was taken up and examined by the coroner, who decided that she had come to her death by severe beating. The offence for which this girl was thus murdered was this:—She had been set that night to mind Mrs. Hicks's baby, and during the night she fell asleep, and the baby cried. She, having lost her rest for several nights previous, did not hear the crying. They were both in the room with Mrs. Hicks. Mrs. Hicks, finding the girl slow to move, jumped from her bed, seized an oak stick of wood by the fireplace, and with it broke the girl's nose and breastbone, and thus ended her life. I will not say that this most horrid murder produced no sensation in the community. It did produce sensation, but not enough to bring the murderess to punishment. There was a warrant issued for her arrest, but it was never served. Thus she escaped not only punishment, but even the pain of being arraigned before a court for her horrid crime.

Whilst I am detailing bloody deeds which took place during my stay on Colonel Lloyd's plantation, I will briefly narrate another, which occurred about the same time as the murder of Demby by Mr. Gore.

Colonel Lloyd's slaves were in the habit of spending a part of their nights and Sundays in fishing for oysters, and in this way made up the deficiency of their scanty allowance. An old man belonging to Colonel Lloyd, while thus engaged, happened to get beyond the limits of Colonel Lloyd's, and on the premises of Mr. Beal Bondly. At this trespass, Mr. Bondly took offence, and with his musket came down to the shore, and blew its deadly contents into the poor old man.

Mr. Bondly came over to see Colonel Lloyd the next day, whether to pay him for his property, or to justify himself in what he had done, I know not. At any rate, this whole fiendish transaction was soon hushed up. There was very little said about it at all, and nothing done. It was a common saying, even among little white boys, that it was worth a half-cent to kill a "nigger," and a half-cent to bury one.

CHAPTER V

As to my own treatment while I lived on Colonel Lloyd's plantation, it was very similar to that of the other slave children. I was not old enough to work in the field, and there being little else than field work to do, I had a great deal of leisure time. The most I had to do was to drive up the cows at evening, keep the fowls out of the garden, keep the front yard clean, and run of errands for my old master's daughter, Mrs. Lucretia Auld. The most of my leisure time I spent in helping Master Daniel Lloyd in finding his birds, after he had shot them. My connection with Master Daniel was of some advantage to me. He became quite attached to me, and was a sort of protector of me. He would not allow the older boys to impose upon me, and would divide his cakes with me.

I was seldom whipped by my old master, and suffered little from any thing else than hunger and cold. I suffered much from hunger, but much more from cold. In hottest summer and coldest winter, I was kept almost naked—no shoes, no stockings, no jacket, no trousers, nothing on but a coarse tow linen shirt, reaching only to my knees. I had no bed. I must have perished with cold, but that, the coldest nights, I used to steal a bag which was used for carrying corn to the mill. I would crawl into this bag, and there sleep on the cold, damp, clay floor, with my head in and feet out. My feet have been so cracked with the frost, that the pen with which I am writing might be laid in the gashes.

We were not regularly allowanced. Our food was coarse corn meal boiled. This was called MUSH. It was put into a large wooden tray or trough, and set down upon the ground. The children were then called, like so many pigs, and like so many pigs they would come and devour the mush; some with oyster-shells, others with pieces of shingle, some with naked hands, and none with spoons. He that ate fastest got most; he that was strongest secured the best place; and few left the trough satisfied.

I was probably between seven and eight years old when I left Colonel Lloyd's plantation. I left it with joy. I shall never forget the ecstasy with which I received the intelligence that my old master (Anthony) had determined to let me go to Baltimore, to live with Mr. Hugh Auld, brother to my old master's son-in-law, Captain Thomas Auld. I received this information about three days before my departure. They were three of the happiest days I ever enjoyed. I spent the most part of all these three days in the creek, washing off the plantation scurf, and preparing myself for my departure.

The pride of appearance which this would indicate was not my own. I spent the time in washing, not so much because I wished to, but because Mrs. Lucretia had told me I must get all the dead skin off my feet and knees before I could go to Baltimore; for the people in Baltimore were very cleanly, and would laugh at me if I looked dirty. Besides, she was going to give me a pair of trousers, which I should not put on unless I got all the dirt off me. The thought of owning a pair of trousers was great indeed! It was almost a sufficient motive, not only to make me take off what would be called by pig-drovers the mange, but the skin itself. I went at it in good earnest, working for the first time with the hope of reward.

The ties that ordinarily bind children to their homes were all suspended in my case. I found no severe trial in my departure. My home was charmless; it was not home to me; on parting from it, I could not feel that I was leaving any thing which I could have enjoyed by staying. My mother was dead, my grandmother lived far off, so that I seldom saw her. I had two sisters and one brother, that lived in the same house with me; but the early separation of us from our mother had well nigh blotted the fact of our relationship from our memories. I looked for home elsewhere, and was confident of finding none which I should relish less than the one which I was leaving. If, however, I found in my new home hardship, hunger, whipping, and nakedness, I had the consolation that I should not have escaped any one of them by staying. Having already had more than a taste of them in the house of my old master, and having endured them there, I very naturally inferred my ability to endure them elsewhere, and especially at Baltimore; for I had something of the feeling about Baltimore that is expressed in the proverb, that "being hanged in England is preferable to dying a natural death in Ireland." I had the strongest desire to see Baltimore. Cousin Tom, though not fluent in speech, had inspired me with that desire by his eloquent description of the place. I could never point out any thing at the Great House, no matter how beautiful or powerful, but that he had seen something at Baltimore far exceeding, both in beauty and strength, the object which I pointed out to him. Even the Great House itself, with all its pictures, was far inferior to many buildings in Baltimore. So strong was my desire, that I thought a gratification of it would fully compensate for whatever loss of comforts I should sustain by the exchange. I left without a regret, and with the highest hopes of future happiness.

We sailed out of Miles River for Baltimore on a Saturday morning. I remember only the day of the week, for at that time I had no knowledge of the days of the month, nor the months of the year. On setting sail, I walked aft, and gave to Colonel Lloyd's plantation what I hoped would be the last look. I then placed myself in the bows of the sloop, and there spent the remainder of the day in looking ahead, interesting myself in what was in the distance rather than in things near by or behind.

In the afternoon of that day, we reached Annapolis, the capital of the State. We stopped but a few moments, so that I had no time to go on shore. It was the first large town that I had ever seen, and though it would look small compared with some of our New England factory villages, I thought it a wonderful place for its size—more imposing even than the Great House Farm!

We arrived at Baltimore early on Sunday morning, landing at Smith's Wharf, not far from Bowley's Wharf. We had on board the sloop a large flock of sheep; and after aiding in driving them to the slaughterhouse of Mr. Curtis on Louden Slater's Hill, I was conducted by Rich, one of the hands belonging on board of the sloop, to my new home in Alliciana Street, near Mr. Gardner's ship-yard, on Fells Point.

Mr. and Mrs. Auld were both at home, and met me at the door with their little son Thomas, to take care of whom I had been given. And here I saw what I had never seen before; it was a white face beaming with the most kindly emotions; it was the face of my new mistress, Sophia Auld. I wish I could describe the rapture that flashed through my soul as I beheld it. It was a new and strange sight to me, brightening up my pathway with the light of happiness. Little Thomas was told, there was his Freddy,—and I was told to take care of little Thomas; and thus I entered upon the duties of my new home with the most cheering prospect ahead.

I look upon my departure from Colonel Lloyd's plantation as one of the most interesting events of my life. It is possible, and even quite probable, that but for the mere circumstance of being removed from that plantation to Baltimore, I should have to-day, instead of being here seated by my own table, in the enjoyment of freedom and the happiness of home, writing this Narrative, been confined in the galling chains of slavery. Going to live at Baltimore laid the foundation, and opened the gateway, to all my subsequent prosperity. I have ever regarded it as the first plain manifestation of that kind providence which has ever since attended me, and marked my life with so many favors. I regarded the selection of myself as being somewhat remarkable. There were a number of slave children that might have been sent from the plantation to Baltimore. There were those younger, those older, and those of the same age. I was chosen from among them all, and was the first, last, and only choice.

I may be deemed superstitious, and even egotistical, in regarding this event as a special interposition of divine Providence in my favor. But I should be false to the earliest sentiments of my soul, if I suppressed the opinion. I prefer to be true to myself, even at the hazard of incurring the ridicule of others, rather than to be false, and incur my own abhorrence. From my earliest recollection, I date the entertainment of a deep conviction that slavery would not always be able to hold me within its foul embrace; and in the darkest hours of my career in slavery, this living word of faith and spirit of hope departed not from me, but remained like ministering angels to cheer me through the gloom. This good spirit was from God, and to him I offer thanksgiving and praise.

CHAPTER VI

My new mistress proved to be all she appeared when I first met her at the door,—a woman of the kindest heart and finest feelings. She had never had a slave under her control previously to myself, and prior to her marriage she had been dependent upon her own industry for a living. She was by trade a weaver; and by constant application to her business, she had been in a good degree preserved from the blighting and dehumanizing effects of slavery. I was utterly astonished at her goodness. I scarcely knew how to behave towards her. She was entirely unlike any other white woman I had ever seen. I could not approach her as I was accustomed to approach other white ladies. My early instruction was all out of place. The crouching servility, usually so acceptable a quality in a slave, did not answer when manifested toward her. Her favor was not gained by it; she seemed to be disturbed by it. She did not deem it impudent or unmannerly for a slave to look her in the face. The meanest slave was put fully at ease in her presence, and none left without feeling better for having seen her. Her face was made of heavenly smiles, and her voice of tranquil music.

But, alas! this kind heart had but a short time to remain such. The fatal poison of irresponsible power was already in her hands, and soon commenced its infernal work. That cheerful eye, under the influence of slavery, soon became red with rage; that voice, made all of sweet accord, changed to one of harsh and horrid discord; and that angelic face gave place to that of a demon.

Very soon after I went to live with Mr. and Mrs. Auld, she very kindly commenced to teach me the A, B, C. After I had learned this, she assisted me in learning to spell words of three or four letters. Just at this point of my progress, Mr. Auld found out what was going on, and at once forbade Mrs. Auld to instruct me further, telling her, among other things, that it was unlawful, as well as unsafe, to teach a slave to read. To use his own words, further, he said, "If you give a nigger an inch, he will take an ell. A nigger should know nothing but to obey his master—to do as he is told to do. Learning would spoil the best nigger in the world. Now," said he, "if you teach that nigger (speaking of myself) how to read, there would be no keeping him. It would forever unfit him to be a slave. He would at once become unmanageable, and of no value to his master. As to himself, it could do him no good, but a great deal of harm. It would make him discontented and unhappy." These words sank deep into my heart, stirred up sentiments within that lay slumbering, and called into existence an entirely new train of thought. It was a new and special revelation, explaining dark and mysterious things, with which my youthful understanding had struggled, but struggled in vain. I now understood what had been to me a most perplexing difficulty—to wit, the white man's power to enslave the black man. It was a grand achievement, and I prized it highly. From that moment, I understood the pathway from slavery to freedom. It was just what I wanted, and I got it at a time when I the least expected it. Whilst I was saddened by the thought of losing the aid of my kind mistress, I was gladdened by the invaluable instruction which, by the merest accident, I had gained from my master. Though conscious of the difficulty of learning without a teacher, I set out with high hope, and a fixed purpose, at whatever cost of trouble, to learn how to read. The very decided manner with which he spoke, and strove to impress his wife with the evil consequences of giving me instruction, served to convince me that he was deeply sensible of the truths he was uttering. It gave me the best assurance that I might rely with the utmost confidence on the results which, he said, would flow from teaching me to read. What he most dreaded, that I most desired. What he most loved, that I most hated. That which to him was a great evil, to be carefully shunned, was to me a great good, to be diligently sought; and the argument which he so warmly urged, against my learning to read, only served to inspire me with a desire and determination to learn. In learning to read, I owe almost as much to the bitter opposition of my master, as to the kindly aid of my mistress. I acknowledge the benefit of both.

I had resided but a short time in Baltimore before I observed a marked difference, in the treatment of slaves, from that which I had witnessed in the country. A city slave is almost a freeman, compared with a slave on the plantation. He is much better fed and clothed, and enjoys privileges altogether unknown to the slave on the plantation. There is a vestige of decency, a sense of shame, that does much to curb and check those outbreaks of atrocious cruelty so commonly enacted upon the plantation. He is a desperate slaveholder, who will shock the humanity of his non-slaveholding neighbors with the cries of his lacerated slave. Few are willing to incur the odium attaching to the reputation of being a cruel master; and above all things, they would not be known as not giving a slave enough to eat. Every city slaveholder is anxious to have it known of him, that he feeds his slaves well; and it is due to them to say, that most of them do give their slaves enough to eat. There are, however, some painful exceptions to this rule. Directly opposite to us, on Philpot Street, lived Mr. Thomas Hamilton. He owned two slaves. Their names were Henrietta and Mary. Henrietta was about twenty-two years of age, Mary was about fourteen; and of all the mangled and emaciated creatures I ever looked upon, these two were the most so. His heart must be harder than stone, that could look upon these unmoved. The head, neck, and shoulders of Mary were literally cut to pieces. I have frequently felt her head, and found it nearly covered with festering sores, caused by the lash of her cruel mistress. I do not know that her master ever whipped her, but I have been an eye-witness to the cruelty of Mrs. Hamilton. I used to be in Mr. Hamilton's house nearly every day. Mrs. Hamilton used to sit in a large chair in the middle of the room, with a heavy cowskin always by her side, and scarce an hour passed during the day but was marked by the blood of one of these slaves. The girls seldom passed her without her saying, "Move faster, you black gip!" at the same time giving them a blow with the cowskin over the head or shoulders, often drawing the blood. She would then say, "Take that, you black gip!" continuing, "If you don't move faster, I'll move you!" Added to the cruel lashings to which these slaves were subjected, they were kept nearly half-starved. They seldom knew what it was to eat a full meal. I have seen Mary contending with the pigs for the offal thrown into the street. So much was Mary kicked and cut to pieces, that she was oftener called "pecked" than by her name.

CHAPTER VII

I lived in Master Hugh's family about seven years. During this time, I succeeded in learning to read and write. In accomplishing this, I was compelled to resort to various stratagems. I had no regular teacher. My mistress, who had kindly commenced to instruct me, had, in compliance with the advice and direction of her husband, not only ceased to instruct, but had set her face against my being instructed by any one else. It is due, however, to my mistress to say of her, that she did not adopt this course of treatment immediately. She at first lacked the depravity indispensable to shutting me up in mental darkness. It was at least necessary for her to have some training in the exercise of irresponsible power, to make her equal to the task of treating me as though I were a brute.

My mistress was, as I have said, a kind and tender-hearted woman; and in the simplicity of her soul she commenced, when I first went to live with her, to treat me as she supposed one human being ought to treat another. In entering upon the duties of a slaveholder, she did not seem to perceive that I sustained to her the relation of a mere chattel, and that for her to treat me as a human being was not only wrong, but dangerously so. Slavery proved as injurious to her as it did to me. When I went there, she was a pious, warm, and tender-hearted woman. There was no sorrow or suffering for which she had not a tear. She had bread for the hungry, clothes for the naked, and comfort for every mourner that came within her reach. Slavery soon proved its ability to divest her of these heavenly qualities. Under its influence, the tender heart became stone, and the lamblike disposition gave way to one of tiger-like fierceness. The first step in her downward course was in her ceasing to instruct me. She now commenced to practise her husband's precepts. She finally became even more violent in her opposition than her husband himself. She was not satisfied with simply doing as well as he had commanded; she seemed anxious to do better. Nothing seemed to make her more angry than to see me with a newspaper. She seemed to think that here lay the danger. I have had her rush at me with a face made all up of fury, and snatch from me a newspaper, in a manner that fully revealed her apprehension. She was an apt woman; and a little experience soon demonstrated, to her satisfaction, that education and slavery were incompatible with each other.

From this time I was most narrowly watched. If I was in a separate room any considerable length of time, I was sure to be suspected of having a book, and was at once called to give an account of myself. All this, however, was too late. The first step had been taken. Mistress, in teaching me the alphabet, had given me the inch, and no precaution could prevent me from taking the ell.

The plan which I adopted, and the one by which I was most successful, was that of making friends of all the little white boys whom I met in the street. As many of these as I could, I converted into teachers. With their kindly aid, obtained at different times and in different places, I finally succeeded in learning to read. When I was sent of errands, I always took my book with me, and by going one part of my errand quickly, I found time to get a lesson before my return. I used also to carry bread with me, enough of which was always in the house, and to which I was always welcome; for I was much better off in this regard than many of the poor white children in our neighborhood. This bread I used to bestow upon the hungry little urchins, who, in return, would give me that more valuable bread of knowledge. I am strongly tempted to give the names of two or three of those little boys, as a testimonial of the gratitude and affection I bear them; but prudence forbids;—not that it would injure me, but it might embarrass them; for it is almost an unpardonable offence to teach slaves to read in this Christian country. It is enough to say of the dear little fellows, that they lived on Philpot Street, very near Durgin and Bailey's ship-yard. I used to talk this matter of slavery over with them. I would sometimes say to them, I wished I could be as free as they would be when they got to be men. "You will be free as soon as you are twenty-one, but I am a slave for life! Have not I as good a right to be free as you have?" These words used to trouble them; they would express for me the liveliest sympathy, and console me with the hope that something would occur by which I might be free.

I was now about twelve years old, and the thought of being a slave for life began to bear heavily upon my heart. Just about this time, I got hold of a book entitled "The Columbian Orator." Every opportunity I got, I used to read this book. Among much of other interesting matter, I found in it a dialogue between a master and his slave. The slave was represented as having run away from his master three times. The dialogue represented the conversation which took place between them, when the slave was retaken the third time. In this dialogue, the whole argument in behalf of slavery was brought forward by the master, all of which was disposed of by the slave. The slave was made to say some very smart as well as impressive things in reply to his master—things which had the desired though unexpected effect; for the conversation resulted in the voluntary emancipation of the slave on the part of the master. In the same book, I met with one of Sheridan's mighty speeches on and in behalf of Catholic emancipation. These were choice documents to me. I read them over and over again with unabated interest. They gave tongue to interesting thoughts of my own soul, which had frequently flashed through my mind, and died away for want of utterance. The moral which I gained from the dialogue was the power of truth over the conscience of even a slaveholder. What I got from Sheridan was a bold denunciation of slavery, and a powerful vindication of human rights. The reading of these documents enabled me to utter my thoughts, and to meet the arguments brought forward to sustain slavery; but while they relieved me of one difficulty, they brought on another even more painful than the one of which I was relieved. The more I read, the more I was led to abhor and detest my enslavers. I could regard them in no other light than a band of successful robbers, who had left their homes, and gone to Africa, and stolen us from our homes, and in a strange land reduced us to slavery. I loathed them as being the meanest as well as the most wicked of men. As I read and contemplated the subject, behold! that very discontentment which Master Hugh had predicted would follow my learning to read had already come, to torment and sting my soul to unutterable anguish. As I writhed under it, I would at times feel that learning to read had been a curse rather than a blessing. It had given me a view of my wretched condition, without the remedy. It opened my eyes to the horrible pit, but to no ladder upon which to get out. In moments of agony, I envied my fellow-slaves for their stupidity. I have often wished myself a beast. I preferred the condition of the meanest reptile to my own. Any thing, no matter what, to get rid of thinking! It was this everlasting thinking of my condition that tormented me. There was no getting rid of it. It was pressed upon me by every object within sight or hearing, animate or inanimate. The silver trump of freedom had roused my soul to eternal wakefulness. Freedom now appeared, to disappear no more forever. It was heard in every sound, and seen in every thing. It was ever present to torment me with a sense of my wretched condition. I saw nothing without seeing it, I heard nothing without hearing it, and felt nothing without feeling it. It looked from every star, it smiled in every calm, breathed in every wind, and moved in every storm.

I often found myself regretting my own existence, and wishing myself dead; and but for the hope of being free, I have no doubt but that I should have killed myself, or done something for which I should have been killed. While in this state of mind, I was eager to hear any one speak of slavery. I was a ready listener. Every little while, I could hear something about the abolitionists. It was some time before I found what the word meant. It was always used in such connections as to make it an interesting word to me. If a slave ran away and succeeded in getting clear, or if a slave killed his master, set fire to a barn, or did any thing very wrong in the mind of a slaveholder, it was spoken of as the fruit of abolition. Hearing the word in this connection very often, I set about learning what it meant. The dictionary afforded me little or no help. I found it was "the act of abolishing;" but then I did not know what was to be abolished. Here I was perplexed. I did not dare to ask any one about its meaning, for I was satisfied that it was something they wanted me to know very little about. After a patient waiting, I got one of our city papers, containing an account of the number of petitions from the north, praying for the abolition of slavery in the District of Columbia, and of the slave trade between the States. From this time I understood the words abolition and abolitionist, and always drew near when that word was spoken, expecting to hear something of importance to myself and fellow-slaves. The light broke in upon me by degrees. I went one day down on the wharf of Mr. Waters; and seeing two Irishmen unloading a scow of stone, I went, unasked, and helped them. When we had finished, one of them came to me and asked me if I were a slave. I told him I was. He asked, "Are ye a slave for life?" I told him that I was. The good Irishman seemed to be deeply affected by the statement. He said to the other that it was a pity so fine a little fellow as myself should be a slave for life. He said it was a shame to hold me. They both advised me to run away to the north; that I should find friends there, and that I should be free. I pretended not to be interested in what they said, and treated them as if I did not understand them; for I feared they might be treacherous. White men have been known to encourage slaves to escape, and then, to get the reward, catch them and return them to their masters. I was afraid that these seemingly good men might use me so; but I nevertheless remembered their advice, and from that time I resolved to run away. I looked forward to a time at which it would be safe for me to escape. I was too young to think of doing so immediately; besides, I wished to learn how to write, as I might have occasion to write my own pass. I consoled myself with the hope that I should one day find a good chance. Meanwhile, I would learn to write.

The idea as to how I might learn to write was suggested to me by being in Durgin and Bailey's ship-yard, and frequently seeing the ship carpenters, after hewing, and getting a piece of timber ready for use, write on the timber the name of that part of the ship for which it was intended. When a piece of timber was intended for the larboard side, it would be marked thus—"L." When a piece was for the starboard side, it would be marked thus—"S." A piece for the larboard side forward, would be marked thus—"L. F." When a piece was for starboard side forward, it would be marked thus—"S. F." For larboard aft, it would be marked thus—"L. A." For starboard aft, it would be marked thus—"S. A." I soon learned the names of these letters, and for what they were intended when placed upon a piece of timber in the ship-yard. I immediately commenced copying them, and in a short time was able to make the four letters named. After that, when I met with any boy who I knew could write, I would tell him I could write as well as he. The next word would be, "I don't believe you. Let me see you try it." I would then make the letters which I had been so fortunate as to learn, and ask him to beat that. In this way I got a good many lessons in writing, which it is quite possible I should never have gotten in any other way. During this time, my copy-book was the board fence, brick wall, and pavement; my pen and ink was a lump of chalk. With these, I learned mainly how to write. I then commenced and continued copying the Italics in Webster's Spelling Book, until I could make them all without looking on the book. By this time, my little Master Thomas had gone to school, and learned how to write, and had written over a number of copy-books. These had been brought home, and shown to some of our near neighbors, and then laid aside. My mistress used to go to class meeting at the Wilk Street meetinghouse every Monday afternoon, and leave me to take care of the house. When left thus, I used to spend the time in writing in the spaces left in Master Thomas's copy-book, copying what he had written. I continued to do this until I could write a hand very similar to that of Master Thomas. Thus, after a long, tedious effort for years, I finally succeeded in learning how to write.

CHAPTER VIII

In a very short time after I went to live at Baltimore, my old master's youngest son Richard died; and in about three years and six months after his death, my old master, Captain Anthony, died, leaving only his son, Andrew, and daughter, Lucretia, to share his estate. He died while on a visit to see his daughter at Hillsborough. Cut off thus unexpectedly, he left no will as to the disposal of his property. It was therefore necessary to have a valuation of the property, that it might be equally divided between Mrs. Lucretia and Master Andrew. I was immediately sent for, to be valued with the other property. Here again my feelings rose up in detestation of slavery. I had now a new conception of my degraded condition. Prior to this, I had become, if not insensible to my lot, at least partly so. I left Baltimore with a young heart overborne with sadness, and a soul full of apprehension. I took passage with Captain Rowe, in the schooner Wild Cat, and, after a sail of about twenty-four hours, I found myself near the place of my birth. I had now been absent from it almost, if not quite, five years. I, however, remembered the place very well. I was only about five years old when I left it, to go and live with my old master on Colonel Lloyd's plantation; so that I was now between ten and eleven years old. We were all ranked together at the valuation. Men and women, old and young, married and single, were ranked with horses, sheep, and swine. There were horses and men, cattle and women, pigs and children, all holding the same rank in the scale of being, and were all subjected to the same narrow examination. Silvery-headed age and sprightly youth, maids and matrons, had to undergo the same indelicate inspection. At this moment, I saw more clearly than ever the brutalizing effects of slavery upon both slave and slaveholder.

After the valuation, then came the division. I have no language to express the high excitement and deep anxiety which were felt among us poor slaves during this time. Our fate for life was now to be decided. we had no more voice in that decision than the brutes among whom we were ranked. A single word from the white men was enough—against all our wishes, prayers, and entreaties—to sunder forever the dearest friends, dearest kindred, and strongest ties known to human beings. In addition to the pain of separation, there was the horrid dread of falling into the hands of Master Andrew. He was known to us all as being a most cruel wretch,—a common drunkard, who had, by his reckless mismanagement and profligate dissipation, already wasted a large portion of his father's property. We all felt that we might as well be sold at once to the Georgia traders, as to pass into his hands; for we knew that that would be our inevitable condition,—a condition held by us all in the utmost horror and dread.

I suffered more anxiety than most of my fellow-slaves. I had known what it was to be kindly treated; they had known nothing of the kind. They had seen little or nothing of the world. They were in very deed men and women of sorrow, and acquainted with grief. Their backs had been made familiar with the bloody lash, so that they had become callous; mine was yet tender; for while at Baltimore I got few whippings, and few slaves could boast of a kinder master and mistress than myself; and the thought of passing out of their hands into those of Master Andrew—a man who, but a few days before, to give me a sample of his bloody disposition, took my little brother by the throat, threw him on the ground, and with the heel of his boot stamped upon his head till the blood gushed from his nose and ears—was well calculated to make me anxious as to my fate. After he had committed this savage outrage upon my brother, he turned to me, and said that was the way he meant to serve me one of these days,—meaning, I suppose, when I came into his possession.

Thanks to a kind Providence, I fell to the portion of Mrs. Lucretia, and was sent immediately back to Baltimore, to live again in the family of Master Hugh. Their joy at my return equalled their sorrow at my departure. It was a glad day to me. I had escaped a worse than lion's jaws. I was absent from Baltimore, for the purpose of valuation and division, just about one month, and it seemed to have been six.

Very soon after my return to Baltimore, my mistress, Lucretia, died, leaving her husband and one child, Amanda; and in a very short time after her death, Master Andrew died. Now all the property of my old master, slaves included, was in the hands of strangers,—strangers who had had nothing to do with accumulating it. Not a slave was left free. All remained slaves, from the youngest to the oldest. If any one thing in my experience, more than another, served to deepen my conviction of the infernal character of slavery, and to fill me with unutterable loathing of slaveholders, it was their base ingratitude to my poor old grandmother. She had served my old master faithfully from youth to old age. She had been the source of all his wealth; she had peopled his plantation with slaves; she had become a great grandmother in his service. She had rocked him in infancy, attended him in childhood, served him through life, and at his death wiped from his icy brow the cold death-sweat, and closed his eyes forever. She was nevertheless left a slave—a slave for life—a slave in the hands of strangers; and in their hands she saw her children, her grandchildren, and her great-grandchildren, divided, like so many sheep, without being gratified with the small privilege of a single word, as to their or her own destiny. And, to cap the climax of their base ingratitude and fiendish barbarity, my grandmother, who was now very old, having outlived my old master and all his children, having seen the beginning and end of all of them, and her present owners finding she was of but little value, her frame already racked with the pains of old age, and complete helplessness fast stealing over her once active limbs, they took her to the woods, built her a little hut, put up a little mud-chimney, and then made her welcome to the privilege of supporting herself there in perfect loneliness; thus virtually turning her out to die! If my poor old grandmother now lives, she lives to suffer in utter loneliness; she lives to remember and mourn over the loss of children, the loss of grandchildren, and the loss of great-grandchildren. They are, in the language of the slave's poet, Whittier,—

"Gone, gone, sold and gone
To the rice swamp dank and lone,
Where the slave-whip ceaseless swings,
Where the noisome insect stings,
Where the fever-demon strews
Poison with the falling dews,
Where the sickly sunbeams glare
Through the hot and misty air:—
Gone, gone, sold and gone
To the rice swamp dank and lone,
From Virginia hills and waters—
Woe is me, my stolen daughters!"

The hearth is desolate. The children, the unconscious children, who once sang and danced in her presence, are gone. She gropes her way, in the darkness of age, for a drink of water. Instead of the voices of her children, she hears by day the moans of the dove, and by night the screams of the hideous owl. All is gloom. The grave is at the door. And now, when weighed down by the pains and aches of old age, when the head inclines to the feet, when the beginning and ending of human existence meet, and helpless infancy and painful old age combine together—at this time, this most needful time, the time for the exercise of that tenderness and affection which children only can exercise towards a declining parent—my poor old grandmother, the devoted mother of twelve children, is left all alone, in yonder little hut, before a few dim embers. She stands—she sits—she staggers—she falls—she groans—she dies—and there are none of her children or grandchildren present, to wipe from her wrinkled brow the cold sweat of death, or to place beneath the sod her fallen remains. Will not a righteous God visit for these things?

In about two years after the death of Mrs. Lucretia, Master Thomas married his second wife. Her name was Rowena Hamilton. She was the eldest daughter of Mr. William Hamilton. Master now lived in St. Michael's. Not long after his marriage, a misunderstanding took place between himself and Master Hugh; and as a means of punishing his brother, he took me from him to live with himself at St. Michael's. Here I underwent another most painful separation. It, however, was not so severe as the one I dreaded at the division of property; for, during this interval, a great change had taken place in Master Hugh and his once kind and affectionate wife. The influence of brandy upon him, and of slavery upon her, had effected a disastrous change in the characters of both; so that, as far as they were concerned, I thought I had little to lose by the change. But it was not to them that I was attached. It was to those little Baltimore boys that I felt the strongest attachment. I had received many good lessons from them, and was still receiving them, and the thought of leaving them was painful indeed. I was leaving, too, without the hope of ever being allowed to return. Master Thomas had said he would never let me return again. The barrier betwixt himself and brother he considered impassable.

I then had to regret that I did not at least make the attempt to carry out my resolution to run away; for the chances of success are tenfold greater from the city than from the country. I sailed from Baltimore for St. Michael's in the sloop Amanda, Captain Edward Dodson. On my passage, I paid particular attention to the direction which the steamboats took to go to Philadelphia. I found, instead of going down, on reaching North Point they went up the bay, in a north-easterly direction. I deemed this knowledge of the utmost importance. My determination to run away was again revived. I resolved to wait only so long as the offering of a favorable opportunity. When that came, I was determined to be off.

CHAPTER IX

I have now reached a period of my life when I can give dates. I left Baltimore, and went to live with Master Thomas Auld, at St. Michael's, in March, 1832. It was now more than seven years since I lived with him in the family of my old master, on Colonel Lloyd's plantation. We of course were now almost entire strangers to each other. He was to me a new master, and I to him a new slave. I was ignorant of his temper and disposition; he was equally so of mine. A very short time, however, brought us into full acquaintance with each other. I was made acquainted with his wife not less than with himself. They were well matched, being equally mean and cruel. I was now, for the first time during a space of more than seven years, made to feel the painful gnawings of hunger—a something which I had not experienced before since I left Colonel Lloyd's plantation. It went hard enough with me then, when I could look back to no period at which I had enjoyed a sufficiency. It was tenfold harder after living in Master Hugh's family, where I had always had enough to eat, and of that which was good. I have said Master Thomas was a mean man. He was so. Not to give a slave enough to eat, is regarded as the most aggravated development of meanness even among slaveholders. The rule is, no matter how coarse the food, only let there be enough of it. This is the theory; and in the part of Maryland from which I came, it is the general practice,—though there are many exceptions. Master Thomas gave us neither coarse nor fine food. There were four slaves of us in the kitchen—my sister Eliza, my aunt Priscilla, Henny, and myself; and we were allowed less than a half of a bushel of corn-meal per week, and very little else, either in the shape of meat or vegetables. It was not enough for us to subsist upon. We were therefore reduced to the wretched necessity of living at the expense of our neighbors. This we did by begging and stealing, whichever came handy in the time of need, the one being considered as legitimate as the other. A great many times have we poor creatures been nearly perishing with hunger, when food in abundance lay mouldering in the safe and smoke-house, and our pious mistress was aware of the fact; and yet that mistress and her husband would kneel every morning, and pray that God would bless them in basket and store!

Bad as all slaveholders are, we seldom meet one destitute of every element of character commanding respect. My master was one of this rare sort. I do not know of one single noble act ever performed by him. The leading trait in his character was meanness; and if there were any other element in his nature, it was made subject to this. He was mean; and, like most other mean men, he lacked the ability to conceal his meanness. Captain Auld was not born a slaveholder. He had been a poor man, master only of a Bay craft. He came into possession of all his slaves by marriage; and of all men, adopted slaveholders are the worst. He was cruel, but cowardly. He commanded without firmness. In the enforcement of his rules, he was at times rigid, and at times lax. At times, he spoke to his slaves with the firmness of Napoleon and the fury of a demon; at other times, he might well be mistaken for an inquirer who had lost his way. He did nothing of himself. He might have passed for a lion, but for his ears. In all things noble which he attempted, his own meanness shone most conspicuous. His airs, words, and actions, were the airs, words, and actions of born slaveholders, and, being assumed, were awkward enough. He was not even a good imitator. He possessed all the disposition to deceive, but wanted the power. Having no resources within himself, he was compelled to be the copyist of many, and being such, he was forever the victim of inconsistency; and of consequence he was an object of contempt, and was held as such even by his slaves. The luxury of having slaves of his own to wait upon him was something new and unprepared for. He was a slaveholder without the ability to hold slaves. He found himself incapable of managing his slaves either by force, fear, or fraud. We seldom called him "master;" we generally called him "Captain Auld," and were hardly disposed to title him at all. I doubt not that our conduct had much to do with making him appear awkward, and of consequence fretful. Our want of reverence for him must have perplexed him greatly. He wished to have us call him master, but lacked the firmness necessary to command us to do so. His wife used to insist upon our calling him so, but to no purpose. In August, 1832, my master attended a Methodist camp-meeting held in the Bay-side, Talbot county, and there experienced religion. I indulged a faint hope that his conversion would lead him to emancipate his slaves, and that, if he did not do this, it would, at any rate, make him more kind and humane. I was disappointed in both these respects. It neither made him to be humane to his slaves, nor to emancipate them. If it had any effect on his character, it made him more cruel and hateful in all his ways; for I believe him to have been a much worse man after his conversion than before. Prior to his conversion, he relied upon his own depravity to shield and sustain him in his savage barbarity; but after his conversion, he found religious sanction and support for his slaveholding cruelty. He made the greatest pretensions to piety. His house was the house of prayer. He prayed morning, noon, and night. He very soon distinguished himself among his brethren, and was soon made a class-leader and exhorter. His activity in revivals was great, and he proved himself an instrument in the hands of the church in converting many souls. His house was the preachers' home. They used to take great pleasure in coming there to put up; for while he starved us, he stuffed them. We have had three or four preachers there at a time. The names of those who used to come most frequently while I lived there, were Mr. Storks, Mr. Ewery, Mr. Humphry, and Mr. Hickey. I have also seen Mr. George Cookman at our house. We slaves loved Mr. Cookman. We believed him to be a good man. We thought him instrumental in getting Mr. Samuel Harrison, a very rich slaveholder, to emancipate his slaves; and by some means got the impression that he was laboring to effect the emancipation of all the slaves. When he was at our house, we were sure to be called in to prayers. When the others were there, we were sometimes called in and sometimes not. Mr. Cookman took more notice of us than either of the other ministers. He could not come among us without betraying his sympathy for us, and, stupid as we were, we had the sagacity to see it.

While I lived with my master in St. Michael's, there was a white young man, a Mr. Wilson, who proposed to keep a Sabbath school for the instruction of such slaves as might be disposed to learn to read the New Testament. We met but three times, when Mr. West and Mr. Fairbanks, both class-leaders, with many others, came upon us with sticks and other missiles, drove us off, and forbade us to meet again. Thus ended our little Sabbath school in the pious town of St. Michael's.

I have said my master found religious sanction for his cruelty. As an example, I will state one of many facts going to prove the charge. I have seen him tie up a lame young woman, and whip her with a heavy cowskin upon her naked shoulders, causing the warm red blood to drip; and, in justification of the bloody deed, he would quote this passage of Scripture—"He that knoweth his master's will, and doeth it not, shall be beaten with many stripes."

Master would keep this lacerated young woman tied up in this horrid situation four or five hours at a time. I have known him to tie her up early in the morning, and whip her before breakfast; leave her, go to his store, return at dinner, and whip her again, cutting her in the places already made raw with his cruel lash. The secret of master's cruelty toward "Henny" is found in the fact of her being almost helpless. When quite a child, she fell into the fire, and burned herself horribly. Her hands were so burnt that she never got the use of them. She could do very little but bear heavy burdens. She was to master a bill of expense; and as he was a mean man, she was a constant offence to him. He seemed desirous of getting the poor girl out of existence. He gave her away once to his sister; but, being a poor gift, she was not disposed to keep her. Finally, my benevolent master, to use his own words, "set her adrift to take care of herself." Here was a recently-converted man, holding on upon the mother, and at the same time turning out her helpless child, to starve and die! Master Thomas was one of the many pious slaveholders who hold slaves for the very charitable purpose of taking care of them. My master and myself had quite a number of differences. He found me unsuitable to his purpose. My city life, he said, had had a very pernicious effect upon me. It had almost ruined me for every good purpose, and fitted me for every thing which was bad. One of my greatest faults was that of letting his horse run away, and go down to his father-inlaw's farm, which was about five miles from St. Michael's. I would then have to go after it. My reason for this kind of carelessness, or carefulness, was, that I could always get something to eat when I went there. Master William Hamilton, my master's father-in-law, always gave his slaves enough to eat. I never left there hungry, no matter how great the need of my speedy return. Master Thomas at length said he would stand it no longer. I had lived with him nine months, during which time he had given me a number of severe whippings, all to no good purpose. He resolved to put me out, as he said, to be broken; and, for this purpose, he let me for one year to a man named Edward Covey. Mr. Covey was a poor man, a farm-renter. He rented the place upon which he lived, as also the hands with which he tilled it. Mr. Covey had acquired a very high reputation for breaking young slaves, and this reputation was of immense value to him. It enabled him to get his farm tilled with much less expense to himself than he could have had it done without such a reputation. Some slaveholders thought it not much loss to allow Mr. Covey to have their slaves one year, for the sake of the training to which they were subjected, without any other compensation. He could hire young help with great ease, in consequence of this reputation. Added to the natural good qualities of Mr. Covey, he was a professor of religion—a pious soul—a member and a class-leader in the Methodist church. All of this added weight to his reputation as a "nigger-breaker." I was aware of all the facts, having been made acquainted with them by a young man who had lived there. I nevertheless made the change gladly; for I was sure of getting enough to eat, which is not the smallest consideration to a hungry man.

CHAPTER X

I had left Master Thomas's house, and went to live with Mr. Covey, on the 1st of January, 1833. I was now, for the first time in my life, a field hand. In my new employment, I found myself even more awkward than a country boy appeared to be in a large city. I had been at my new home but one week before Mr. Covey gave me a very severe whipping, cutting my back, causing the blood to run, and raising ridges on my flesh as large as my little finger. The details of this affair are as follows: Mr. Covey sent me, very early in the morning of one of our coldest days in the month of January, to the woods, to get a load of wood. He gave me a team of unbroken oxen. He told me which was the in-hand ox, and which the off-hand one. He then tied the end of a large rope around the horns of the in-hand ox, and gave me the other end of it, and told me, if the oxen started to run, that I must hold on upon the rope. I had never driven oxen before, and of course I was very awkward. I, however, succeeded in getting to the edge of the woods with little difficulty; but I had got a very few rods into the woods, when the oxen took fright, and started full tilt, carrying the cart against trees, and over stumps, in the most frightful manner. I expected every moment that my brains would be dashed out against the trees. After running thus for a considerable distance, they finally upset the cart, dashing it with great force against a tree, and threw themselves into a dense thicket. How I escaped death, I do not know. There I was, entirely alone, in a thick wood, in a place new to me. My cart was upset and shattered, my oxen were entangled among the young trees, and there was none to help me. After a long spell of effort, I succeeded in getting my cart righted, my oxen disentangled, and again yoked to the cart. I now proceeded with my team to the place where I had, the day before, been chopping wood, and loaded my cart pretty heavily, thinking in this way to tame my oxen. I then proceeded on my way home. I had now consumed one half of the day. I got out of the woods safely, and now felt out of danger. I stopped my oxen to open the woods gate; and just as I did so, before I could get hold of my ox-rope, the oxen again started, rushed through the gate, catching it between the wheel and the body of the cart, tearing it to pieces, and coming within a few inches of crushing me against the gate-post. Thus twice, in one short day, I escaped death by the merest chance. On my return, I told Mr. Covey what had happened, and how it happened. He ordered me to return to the woods again immediately. I did so, and he followed on after me. Just as I got into the woods, he came up and told me to stop my cart, and that he would teach me how to trifle away my time, and break gates. He then went to a large gum-tree, and with his axe cut three large switches, and, after trimming them up neatly with his pocketknife, he ordered me to take off my clothes. I made him no answer, but stood with my clothes on. He repeated his order. I still made him no answer, nor did I move to strip myself. Upon this he rushed at me with the fierceness of a tiger, tore off my clothes, and lashed me till he had worn out his switches, cutting me so savagely as to leave the marks visible for a long time after. This whipping was the first of a number just like it, and for similar offences.

I lived with Mr. Covey one year. During the first six months, of that year, scarce a week passed without his whipping me. I was seldom free from a sore back. My awkwardness was almost always his excuse for whipping me. We were worked fully up to the point of endurance. Long before day we were up, our horses fed, and by the first approach of day we were off to the field with our hoes and ploughing teams. Mr. Covey gave us enough to eat, but scarce time to eat it. We were often in less than five minutes taking our meals. We were often in the field from the first approach of day till its last lingering ray had left us; and at saving-fodder time, midnight often caught us in the field binding blades.

Covey would be out with us. The way he used to stand it, was this. He would spend the most of his afternoons in bed. He would then come out fresh in the evening, ready to urge us on with his words, example, and frequently with the whip. Mr. Covey was one of the few slaveholders who could and did work with his hands. He was a hard-working man. He knew by himself just what a man or a boy could do. There was no deceiving him. His work went on in his absence almost as well as in his presence; and he had the faculty of making us feel that he was ever present with us. This he did by surprising us. He seldom approached the spot where we were at work openly, if he could do it secretly. He always aimed at taking us by surprise. Such was his cunning, that we used to call him, among ourselves, "the snake." When we were at work in the cornfield, he would sometimes crawl on his hands and knees to avoid detection, and all at once he would rise nearly in our midst, and scream out, "Ha, ha! Come, come! Dash on, dash on!" This being his mode of attack, it was never safe to stop a single minute. His comings were like a thief in the night. He appeared to us as being ever at hand. He was under every tree, behind every stump, in every bush, and at every window, on the plantation. He would sometimes mount his horse, as if bound to St. Michael's, a distance of seven miles, and in half an hour afterwards you would see him coiled up in the corner of the wood-fence, watching every motion of the slaves. He would, for this purpose, leave his horse tied up in the woods. Again, he would sometimes walk up to us, and give us orders as though he was upon the point of starting on a long journey, turn his back upon us, and make as though he was going to the house to get ready; and, before he would get half way thither, he would turn short and crawl into a fence-corner, or behind some tree, and there watch us till the going down of the sun.

Mr. Covey's FORTE consisted in his power to deceive. His life was devoted to planning and perpetrating the grossest deceptions. Every thing he possessed in the shape of learning or religion, he made conform to his disposition to deceive. He seemed to think himself equal to deceiving the Almighty. He would make a short prayer in the morning, and a long prayer at night; and, strange as it may seem, few men would at times appear more devotional than he. The exercises of his family devotions were always commenced with singing; and, as he was a very poor singer himself, the duty of raising the hymn generally came upon me. He would read his hymn, and nod at me to commence. I would at times do so; at others, I would not. My non-compliance would almost always produce much confusion. To show himself independent of me, he would start and stagger through with his hymn in the most discordant manner. In this state of mind, he prayed with more than ordinary spirit. Poor man! such was his disposition, and success at deceiving, I do verily believe that he sometimes deceived himself into the solemn belief, that he was a sincere worshipper of the most high God; and this, too, at a time when he may be said to have been guilty of compelling his woman slave to commit the sin of adultery. The facts in the case are these: Mr. Covey was a poor man; he was just commencing in life; he was only able to buy one slave; and, shocking as is the fact, he bought her, as he said, for A BREEDER. This woman was named Caroline. Mr. Covey bought her from Mr. Thomas Lowe, about six miles from St. Michael's. She was a large, able-bodied woman, about twenty years old. She had already given birth to one child, which proved her to be just what he wanted. After buying her, he hired a married man of Mr. Samuel Harrison, to live with him one year; and him he used to fasten up with her every night! The result was, that, at the end of the year, the miserable woman gave birth to twins. At this result Mr. Covey seemed to be highly pleased, both with the man and the wretched woman. Such was his joy, and that of his wife, that nothing they could do for Caroline during her confinement was too good, or too hard, to be done. The children were regarded as being quite an addition to his wealth.

If at any one time of my life more than another, I was made to drink the bitterest dregs of slavery, that time was during the first six months of my stay with Mr. Covey. We were worked in all weathers. It was never too hot or too cold; it could never rain, blow, hail, or snow, too hard for us to work in the field. Work, work, work, was scarcely more the order of the day than of the night. The longest days were too short for him, and the shortest nights too long for him. I was somewhat unmanageable when I first went there, but a few months of this discipline tamed me. Mr. Covey succeeded in breaking me. I was broken in body, soul, and spirit. My natural elasticity was crushed, my intellect languished, the disposition to read departed, the cheerful spark that lingered about my eye died; the dark night of slavery closed in upon me; and behold a man transformed into a brute!

Sunday was my only leisure time. I spent this in a sort of beast-like stupor, between sleep and wake, under some large tree. At times I would rise up, a flash of energetic freedom would dart through my soul, accompanied with a faint beam of hope, that flickered for a moment, and then vanished. I sank down again, mourning over my wretched condition. I was sometimes prompted to take my life, and that of Covey, but was prevented by a combination of hope and fear. My sufferings on this plantation seem now like a dream rather than a stern reality.

Our house stood within a few rods of the Chesapeake Bay, whose broad bosom was ever white with sails from every quarter of the habitable globe. Those beautiful vessels, robed in purest white, so delightful to the eye of freemen, were to me so many shrouded ghosts, to terrify and torment me with thoughts of my wretched condition. I have often, in the deep stillness of a summer's Sabbath, stood all alone upon the lofty banks of that noble bay, and traced, with saddened heart and tearful eye, the countless number of sails moving off to the mighty ocean. The sight of these always affected me powerfully. My thoughts would compel utterance; and there, with no audience but the Almighty, I would pour out my soul's complaint, in my rude way, with an apostrophe to the moving multitude of ships:—

"You are loosed from your moorings, and are free; I am fast in my chains, and am a slave! You move merrily before the gentle gale, and I sadly before the bloody whip! You are freedom's swift-winged angels, that fly round the world; I am confined in bands of iron! O that I were free! O, that I were on one of your gallant decks, and under your protecting wing! Alas! betwixt me and you, the turbid waters roll. Go on, go on. O that I could also go! Could I but swim! If I could fly! O, why was I born a man, of whom to make a brute! The glad ship is gone; she hides in the dim distance. I am left in the hottest hell of unending slavery. O God, save me! God, deliver me! Let me be free! Is there any God? Why am I a slave? I will run away. I will not stand it. Get caught, or get clear, I'll try it. I had as well die with ague as the fever. I have only one life to lose. I had as well be killed running as die standing. Only think of it; one hundred miles straight north, and I am free! Try it? Yes! God helping me, I will. It cannot be that I shall live and die a slave. I will take to the water. This very bay shall yet bear me into freedom. The steamboats steered in a north-east course from North Point. I will do the same; and when I get to the head of the bay, I will turn my canoe adrift, and walk straight through Delaware into Pennsylvania. When I get there, I shall not be required to have a pass; I can travel without being disturbed. Let but the first opportunity offer, and, come what will, I am off. Meanwhile, I will try to bear up under the yoke. I am not the only slave in the world. Why should I fret? I can bear as much as any of them. Besides, I am but a boy, and all boys are bound to some one. It may be that my misery in slavery will only increase my happiness when I get free. There is a better day coming."

Thus I used to think, and thus I used to speak to myself; goaded almost to madness at one moment, and at the next reconciling myself to my wretched lot.

I have already intimated that my condition was much worse, during the first six months of my stay at Mr. Covey's, than in the last six. The circumstances leading to the change in Mr. Covey's course toward me form an epoch in my humble history. You have seen how a man was made a slave; you shall see how a slave was made a man. On one of the hottest days of the month of August, 1833, Bill Smith, William Hughes, a slave named Eli, and myself, were engaged in fanning wheat. Hughes was clearing the fanned wheat from before the fan. Eli was turning, Smith was feeding, and I was carrying wheat to the fan. The work was simple, requiring strength rather than intellect; yet, to one entirely unused to such work, it came very hard. About three o'clock of that day, I broke down; my strength failed me; I was seized with a violent aching of the head, attended with extreme dizziness; I trembled in every limb. Finding what was coming, I nerved myself up, feeling it would never do to stop work. I stood as long as I could stagger to the hopper with grain. When I could stand no longer, I fell, and felt as if held down by an immense weight. The fan of course stopped; every one had his own work to do; and no one could do the work of the other, and have his own go on at the same time.

Mr. Covey was at the house, about one hundred yards from the treading-yard where we were fanning. On hearing the fan stop, he left immediately, and came to the spot where we were. He hastily inquired what the matter was. Bill answered that I was sick, and there was no one to bring wheat to the fan. I had by this time crawled away under the side of the post and rail-fence by which the yard was enclosed, hoping to find relief by getting out of the sun. He then asked where I was. He was told by one of the hands. He came to the spot, and, after looking at me awhile, asked me what was the matter. I told him as well as I could, for I scarce had strength to speak. He then gave me a savage kick in the side, and told me to get up. I tried to do so, but fell back in the attempt. He gave me another kick, and again told me to rise. I again tried, and succeeded in gaining my feet; but, stooping to get the tub with which I was feeding the fan, I again staggered and fell. While down in this situation, Mr. Covey took up the hickory slat with which Hughes had been striking off the half-bushel measure, and with it gave me a heavy blow upon the head, making a large wound, and the blood ran freely; and with this again told me to get up. I made no effort to comply, having now made up my mind to let him do his worst. In a short time after receiving this blow, my head grew better. Mr. Covey had now left me to my fate. At this moment I resolved, for the first time, to go to my master, enter a complaint, and ask his protection. In order to do this, I must that afternoon walk seven miles; and this, under the circumstances, was truly a severe undertaking. I was exceedingly feeble; made so as much by the kicks and blows which I received, as by the severe fit of sickness to which I had been subjected. I, however, watched my chance, while Covey was looking in an opposite direction, and started for St. Michael's. I succeeded in getting a considerable distance on my way to the woods, when Covey discovered me, and called after me to come back, threatening what he would do if I did not come. I disregarded both his calls and his threats, and made my way to the woods as fast as my feeble state would allow; and thinking I might be overhauled by him if I kept the road, I walked through the woods, keeping far enough from the road to avoid detection, and near enough to prevent losing my way. I had not gone far before my little strength again failed me. I could go no farther. I fell down, and lay for a considerable time. The blood was yet oozing from the wound on my head. For a time I thought I should bleed to death; and think now that I should have done so, but that the blood so matted my hair as to stop the wound. After lying there about three quarters of an hour, I nerved myself up again, and started on my way, through bogs and briers, barefooted and bareheaded, tearing my feet sometimes at nearly every step; and after a journey of about seven miles, occupying some five hours to perform it, I arrived at master's store. I then presented an appearance enough to affect any but a heart of iron. From the crown of my head to my feet, I was covered with blood. My hair was all clotted with dust and blood; my shirt was stiff with blood. I suppose I looked like a man who had escaped a den of wild beasts, and barely escaped them. In this state I appeared before my master, humbly entreating him to interpose his authority for my protection. I told him all the circumstances as well as I could, and it seemed, as I spoke, at times to affect him. He would then walk the floor, and seek to justify Covey by saying he expected I deserved it. He asked me what I wanted. I told him, to let me get a new home; that as sure as I lived with Mr. Covey again, I should live with but to die with him; that Covey would surely kill me; he was in a fair way for it. Master Thomas ridiculed the idea that there was any danger of Mr. Covey's killing me, and said that he knew Mr. Covey; that he was a good man, and that he could not think of taking me from him; that, should he do so, he would lose the whole year's wages; that I belonged to Mr. Covey for one year, and that I must go back to him, come what might; and that I must not trouble him with any more stories, or that he would himself GET HOLD OF ME. After threatening me thus, he gave me a very large dose of salts, telling me that I might remain in St. Michael's that night, (it being quite late,) but that I must be off back to Mr. Covey's early in the morning; and that if I did not, he would get hold of me, which meant that he would whip me. I remained all night, and, according to his orders, I started off to Covey's in the morning, (Saturday morning,) wearied in body and broken in spirit. I got no supper that night, or breakfast that morning. I reached Covey's about nine o'clock; and just as I was getting over the fence that divided Mrs. Kemp's fields from ours, out ran Covey with his cowskin, to give me another whipping. Before he could reach me, I succeeded in getting to the cornfield; and as the corn was very high, it afforded me the means of hiding. He seemed very angry, and searched for me a long time. My behavior was altogether unaccountable. He finally gave up the chase, thinking, I suppose, that I must come home for something to eat; he would give himself no further trouble in looking for me. I spent that day mostly in the woods, having the alternative before me,—to go home and be whipped to death, or stay in the woods and be starved to death. That night, I fell in with Sandy Jenkins, a slave with whom I was somewhat acquainted. Sandy had a free wife who lived about four miles from Mr. Covey's; and it being Saturday, he was on his way to see her. I told him my circumstances, and he very kindly invited me to go home with him. I went home with him, and talked this whole matter over, and got his advice as to what course it was best for me to pursue. I found Sandy an old adviser. He told me, with great solemnity, I must go back to Covey; but that before I went, I must go with him into another part of the woods, where there was a certain root, which, if I would take some of it with me, carrying it always on my right side, would render it impossible for Mr. Covey, or any other white man, to whip me. He said he had carried it for years; and since he had done so, he had never received a blow, and never expected to while he carried it. I at first rejected the idea, that the simple carrying of a root in my pocket would have any such effect as he had said, and was not disposed to take it; but Sandy impressed the necessity with much earnestness, telling me it could do no harm, if it did no good. To please him, I at length took the root, and, according to his direction, carried it upon my right side. This was Sunday morning. I immediately started for home; and upon entering the yard gate, out came Mr. Covey on his way to meeting. He spoke to me very kindly, bade me drive the pigs from a lot near by, and passed on towards the church. Now, this singular conduct of Mr. Covey really made me begin to think that there was something in the ROOT which Sandy had given me; and had it been on any other day than Sunday, I could have attributed the conduct to no other cause than the influence of that root; and as it was, I was half inclined to think the root to be something more than I at first had taken it to be. All went well till Monday morning. On this morning, the virtue of the ROOT was fully tested. Long before daylight, I was called to go and rub, curry, and feed, the horses. I obeyed, and was glad to obey. But whilst thus engaged, whilst in the act of throwing down some blades from the loft, Mr. Covey entered the stable with a long rope; and just as I was half out of the loft, he caught hold of my legs, and was about tying me. As soon as I found what he was up to, I gave a sudden spring, and as I did so, he holding to my legs, I was brought sprawling on the stable floor. Mr. Covey seemed now to think he had me, and could do what he pleased; but at this moment—from whence came the spirit I don't know—I resolved to fight; and, suiting my action to the resolution, I seized Covey hard by the throat; and as I did so, I rose. He held on to me, and I to him. My resistance was so entirely unexpected that Covey seemed taken all aback. He trembled like a leaf. This gave me assurance, and I held him uneasy, causing the blood to run where I touched him with the ends of my fingers. Mr. Covey soon called out to Hughes for help. Hughes came, and, while Covey held me, attempted to tie my right hand. While he was in the act of doing so, I watched my chance, and gave him a heavy kick close under the ribs. This kick fairly sickened Hughes, so that he left me in the hands of Mr. Covey. This kick had the effect of not only weakening Hughes, but Covey also. When he saw Hughes bending over with pain, his courage quailed. He asked me if I meant to persist in my resistance. I told him I did, come what might; that he had used me like a brute for six months, and that I was determined to be used so no longer. With that, he strove to drag me to a stick that was lying just out of the stable door. He meant to knock me down. But just as he was leaning over to get the stick, I seized him with both hands by his collar, and brought him by a sudden snatch to the ground. By this time, Bill came. Covey called upon him for assistance. Bill wanted to know what he could do. Covey said, "Take hold of him, take hold of him!" Bill said his master hired him out to work, and not to help to whip me; so he left Covey and myself to fight our own battle out. We were at it for nearly two hours. Covey at length let me go, puffing and blowing at a great rate, saying that if I had not resisted, he would not have whipped me half so much. The truth was, that he had not whipped me at all. I considered him as getting entirely the worst end of the bargain; for he had drawn no blood from me, but I had from him. The whole six months afterwards, that I spent with Mr. Covey, he never laid the weight of his finger upon me in anger. He would occasionally say, he didn't want to get hold of me again. "No," thought I, "you need not; for you will come off worse than you did before." This battle with Mr. Covey was the turning-point in my career as a slave. It rekindled the few expiring embers of freedom, and revived within me a sense of my own manhood. It recalled the departed self-confidence, and inspired me again with a determination to be free. The gratification afforded by the triumph was a full compensation for whatever else might follow, even death itself. He only can understand the deep satisfaction which I experienced, who has himself repelled by force the bloody arm of slavery. I felt as I never felt before. It was a glorious resurrection, from the tomb of slavery, to the heaven of freedom. My long-crushed spirit rose, cowardice departed, bold defiance took its place; and I now resolved that, however long I might remain a slave in form, the day had passed forever when I could be a slave in fact. I did not hesitate to let it be known of me, that the white man who expected to succeed in whipping, must also succeed in killing me.

From this time I was never again what might be called fairly whipped, though I remained a slave four years afterwards. I had several fights, but was never whipped.

It was for a long time a matter of surprise to me why Mr. Covey did not immediately have me taken by the constable to the whipping-post, and there regularly whipped for the crime of raising my hand against a white man in defence of myself. And the only explanation I can now think of does not entirely satisfy me; but such as it is, I will give it. Mr. Covey enjoyed the most unbounded reputation for being a first-rate overseer and negro-breaker. It was of considerable importance to him. That reputation was at stake; and had he sent me—a boy about sixteen years old—to the public whipping-post, his reputation would have been lost; so, to save his reputation, he suffered me to go unpunished.

My term of actual service to Mr. Edward Covey ended on Christmas day, 1833. The days between Christmas and New Year's day are allowed as holidays; and, accordingly, we were not required to perform any labor, more than to feed and take care of the stock. This time we regarded as our own, by the grace of our masters; and we therefore used or abused it nearly as we pleased. Those of us who had families at a distance, were generally allowed to spend the whole six days in their society. This time, however, was spent in various ways. The staid, sober, thinking and industrious ones of our number would employ themselves in making corn-brooms, mats, horse-collars, and baskets; and another class of us would spend the time in hunting opossums, hares, and coons. But by far the larger part engaged in such sports and merriments as playing ball, wrestling, running foot-races, fiddling, dancing, and drinking whisky; and this latter mode of spending the time was by far the most agreeable to the feelings of our masters. A slave who would work during the holidays was considered by our masters as scarcely deserving them. He was regarded as one who rejected the favor of his master. It was deemed a disgrace not to get drunk at Christmas; and he was regarded as lazy indeed, who had not provided himself with the necessary means, during the year, to get whisky enough to last him through Christmas.

From what I know of the effect of these holidays upon the slave, I believe them to be among the most effective means in the hands of the slaveholder in keeping down the spirit of insurrection. Were the slaveholders at once to abandon this practice, I have not the slightest doubt it would lead to an immediate insurrection among the slaves. These holidays serve as conductors, or safety-valves, to carry off the rebellious spirit of enslaved humanity. But for these, the slave would be forced up to the wildest desperation; and woe betide the slaveholder, the day he ventures to remove or hinder the operation of those conductors! I warn him that, in such an event, a spirit will go forth in their midst, more to be dreaded than the most appalling earthquake.

The holidays are part and parcel of the gross fraud, wrong, and inhumanity of slavery. They are professedly a custom established by the benevolence of the slaveholders; but I undertake to say, it is the result of selfishness, and one of the grossest frauds committed upon the down-trodden slave. They do not give the slaves this time because they would not like to have their work during its continuance, but because they know it would be unsafe to deprive them of it. This will be seen by the fact, that the slaveholders like to have their slaves spend those days just in such a manner as to make them as glad of their ending as of their beginning. Their object seems to be, to disgust their slaves with freedom, by plunging them into the lowest depths of dissipation. For instance, the slaveholders not only like to see the slave drink of his own accord, but will adopt various plans to make him drunk. One plan is, to make bets on their slaves, as to who can drink the most whisky without getting drunk; and in this way they succeed in getting whole multitudes to drink to excess. Thus, when the slave asks for virtuous freedom, the cunning slaveholder, knowing his ignorance, cheats him with a dose of vicious dissipation, artfully labelled with the name of liberty. The most of us used to drink it down, and the result was just what might be supposed; many of us were led to think that there was little to choose between liberty and slavery. We felt, and very properly too, that we had almost as well be slaves to man as to rum. So, when the holidays ended, we staggered up from the filth of our wallowing, took a long breath, and marched to the field,—feeling, upon the whole, rather glad to go, from what our master had deceived us into a belief was freedom, back to the arms of slavery.

I have said that this mode of treatment is a part of the whole system of fraud and inhumanity of slavery. It is so. The mode here adopted to disgust the slave with freedom, by allowing him to see only the abuse of it, is carried out in other things. For instance, a slave loves molasses; he steals some. His master, in many cases, goes off to town, and buys a large quantity; he returns, takes his whip, and commands the slave to eat the molasses, until the poor fellow is made sick at the very mention of it. The same mode is sometimes adopted to make the slaves refrain from asking for more food than their regular allowance. A slave runs through his allowance, and applies for more. His master is enraged at him; but, not willing to send him off without food, gives him more than is necessary, and compels him to eat it within a given time. Then, if he complains that he cannot eat it, he is said to be satisfied neither full nor fasting, and is whipped for being hard to please! I have an abundance of such illustrations of the same principle, drawn from my own observation, but think the cases I have cited sufficient. The practice is a very common one.

On the first of January, 1834, I left Mr. Covey, and went to live with Mr. William Freeland, who lived about three miles from St. Michael's. I soon found Mr. Freeland a very different man from Mr. Covey. Though not rich, he was what would be called an educated southern gentleman. Mr. Covey, as I have shown, was a well-trained negro-breaker and slave-driver. The former (slaveholder though he was) seemed to possess some regard for honor, some reverence for justice, and some respect for humanity. The latter seemed totally insensible to all such sentiments. Mr. Freeland had many of the faults peculiar to slaveholders, such as being very passionate and fretful; but I must do him the justice to say, that he was exceedingly free from those degrading vices to which Mr. Covey was constantly addicted. The one was open and frank, and we always knew where to find him. The other was a most artful deceiver, and could be understood only by such as were skilful enough to detect his cunningly-devised frauds. Another advantage I gained in my new master was, he made no pretensions to, or profession of, religion; and this, in my opinion, was truly a great advantage. I assert most unhesitatingly, that the religion of the south is a mere covering for the most horrid crimes,—a justifier of the most appalling barbarity,—a sanctifier of the most hateful frauds,—and a dark shelter under, which the darkest, foulest, grossest, and most infernal deeds of slaveholders find the strongest protection. Were I to be again reduced to the chains of slavery, next to that enslavement, I should regard being the slave of a religious master the greatest calamity that could befall me. For of all slaveholders with whom I have ever met, religious slaveholders are the worst. I have ever found them the meanest and basest, the most cruel and cowardly, of all others. It was my unhappy lot not only to belong to a religious slaveholder, but to live in a community of such religionists. Very near Mr. Freeland lived the Rev. Daniel Weeden, and in the same neighborhood lived the Rev. Rigby Hopkins. These were members and ministers in the Reformed Methodist Church. Mr. Weeden owned, among others, a woman slave, whose name I have forgotten. This woman's back, for weeks, was kept literally raw, made so by the lash of this merciless, religious wretch. He used to hire hands. His maxim was, Behave well or behave ill, it is the duty of a master occasionally to whip a slave, to remind him of his master's authority. Such was his theory, and such his practice.

Mr. Hopkins was even worse than Mr. Weeden. His chief boast was his ability to manage slaves. The peculiar feature of his government was that of whipping slaves in advance of deserving it. He always managed to have one or more of his slaves to whip every Monday morning. He did this to alarm their fears, and strike terror into those who escaped. His plan was to whip for the smallest offences, to prevent the commission of large ones. Mr. Hopkins could always find some excuse for whipping a slave. It would astonish one, unaccustomed to a slaveholding life, to see with what wonderful ease a slaveholder can find things, of which to make occasion to whip a slave. A mere look, word, or motion,—a mistake, accident, or want of power,—are all matters for which a slave may be whipped at any time. Does a slave look dissatisfied? It is said, he has the devil in him, and it must be whipped out. Does he speak loudly when spoken to by his master? Then he is getting high-minded, and should be taken down a button-hole lower. Does he forget to pull off his hat at the approach of a white person? Then he is wanting in reverence, and should be whipped for it. Does he ever venture to vindicate his conduct, when censured for it? Then he is guilty of impudence,—one of the greatest crimes of which a slave can be guilty. Does he ever venture to suggest a different mode of doing things from that pointed out by his master? He is indeed presumptuous, and getting above himself; and nothing less than a flogging will do for him. Does he, while ploughing, break a plough,—or, while hoeing, break a hoe? It is owing to his carelessness, and for it a slave must always be whipped. Mr. Hopkins could always find something of this sort to justify the use of the lash, and he seldom failed to embrace such opportunities. There was not a man in the whole county, with whom the slaves who had the getting their own home, would not prefer to live, rather than with this Rev. Mr. Hopkins. And yet there was not a man any where round, who made higher professions of religion, or was more active in revivals,—more attentive to the class, love-feast, prayer and preaching meetings, or more devotional in his family,—that prayed earlier, later, louder, and longer,—than this same reverend slave-driver, Rigby Hopkins.

But to return to Mr. Freeland, and to my experience while in his employment. He, like Mr. Covey, gave us enough to eat; but, unlike Mr. Covey, he also gave us sufficient time to take our meals. He worked us hard, but always between sunrise and sunset. He required a good deal of work to be done, but gave us good tools with which to work. His farm was large, but he employed hands enough to work it, and with ease, compared with many of his neighbors. My treatment, while in his employment, was heavenly, compared with what I experienced at the hands of Mr. Edward Covey.

Mr. Freeland was himself the owner of but two slaves. Their names were Henry Harris and John Harris. The rest of his hands he hired. These consisted of myself, Sandy Jenkins,* and Handy Caldwell.

> *This is the same man who gave me the roots to prevent my
> being whipped by Mr. Covey. He was "a clever soul." We used
> frequently to talk about the fight with Covey, and as often
> as we did so, he would claim my success as the result of the
> roots which he gave me. This superstition is very common
> among the more ignorant slaves. A slave seldom dies but that
> his death is attributed to trickery.

Henry and John were quite intelligent, and in a very little while after I went there, I succeeded in creating in them a strong desire to learn how to read. This desire soon sprang up in the others also. They very soon mustered up some old spelling-books, and nothing would do but that I must keep a Sabbath school. I agreed to do so, and accordingly devoted my Sundays to teaching these my loved fellow-slaves how to read. Neither of them knew his letters when I went there. Some of the slaves of the neighboring farms found what was going on, and also availed themselves of this little opportunity to learn to read. It was understood, among all who came, that there must be as little display about it as possible. It was necessary to keep our religious masters at St. Michael's unacquainted with the fact, that, instead of spending the Sabbath in wrestling, boxing, and drinking whisky, we were trying to learn how to read the will of God; for they had much rather see us engaged in those degrading sports, than to see us behaving like intellectual, moral, and accountable beings. My blood boils as I think of the bloody manner in which Messrs. Wright Fairbanks and Garrison West, both class-leaders, in connection with many others, rushed in upon us with sticks and stones, and broke up our virtuous little Sabbath school, at St. Michael's—all calling themselves Christians! humble followers of the Lord Jesus Christ! But I am again digressing.

I held my Sabbath school at the house of a free colored man, whose name I deem it imprudent to mention; for should it be known, it might embarrass him greatly, though the crime of holding the school was committed ten years ago. I had at one time over forty scholars, and those of the right sort, ardently desiring to learn. They were of all ages, though mostly men and women. I look back to those Sundays with an amount of pleasure not to be expressed. They were great days to my soul. The work of instructing my dear fellow-slaves was the sweetest engagement with which I was ever blessed. We loved each other, and to leave them at the close of the Sabbath was a severe cross indeed. When I think that these precious souls are to-day shut up in the prison-house of slavery, my feelings overcome me, and I am almost ready to ask, "Does a righteous God govern the universe? and for what does he hold the thunders in his right hand, if not to smite the oppressor, and deliver the spoiled out of the hand of the spoiler?" These dear souls came not to Sabbath school because it was popular to do so, nor did I teach them because it was reputable to be thus engaged. Every moment they spent in that school, they were liable to be taken up, and given thirty-nine lashes. They came because they wished to learn. Their minds had been starved by their cruel masters. They had been shut up in mental darkness. I taught them, because it was the delight of my soul to be doing something that looked like bettering the condition of my race. I kept up my school nearly the whole year I lived with Mr. Freeland; and, beside my Sabbath school, I devoted three evenings in the week, during the winter, to teaching the slaves at home. And I have the happiness to know, that several of those who came to Sabbath school learned how to read; and that one, at least, is now free through my agency.

The year passed off smoothly. It seemed only about half as long as the year which preceded it. I went through it without receiving a single blow. I will give Mr. Freeland the credit of being the best master I ever had, till I became my own master. For the ease with which I passed the year, I was, however, somewhat indebted to the society of my fellow-slaves. They were noble souls; they not only possessed loving hearts, but brave ones. We were linked and interlinked with each other. I loved them with a love stronger than any thing I have experienced since. It is sometimes said that we slaves do not love and confide in each other. In answer to this assertion, I can say, I never loved any or confided in any people more than my fellow-slaves, and especially those with whom I lived at Mr. Freeland's. I believe we would have died for each other. We never undertook to do any thing, of any importance, without a mutual consultation. We never moved separately. We were one; and as much so by our tempers and dispositions, as by the mutual hardships to which we were necessarily subjected by our condition as slaves.

At the close of the year 1834, Mr. Freeland again hired me of my master, for the year 1835. But, by this time, I began to want to live upon free land as well as with Freeland; and I was no longer content, therefore, to live with him or any other slaveholder. I began, with the commencement of the year, to prepare myself for a final struggle, which should decide my fate one way or the other. My tendency was upward. I was fast approaching manhood, and year after year had passed, and I was still a slave. These thoughts roused me—I must do something. I therefore resolved that 1835 should not pass without witnessing an attempt, on my part, to secure my liberty. But I was not willing to cherish this determination alone. My fellow-slaves were dear to me. I was anxious to have them participate with me in this, my life-giving determination. I therefore, though with great prudence, commenced early to ascertain their views and feelings in regard to their condition, and to imbue their minds with thoughts of freedom. I bent myself to devising ways and means for our escape, and meanwhile strove, on all fitting occasions, to impress them with the gross fraud and inhumanity of slavery. I went first to Henry, next to John, then to the others. I found, in them all, warm hearts and noble spirits. They were ready to hear, and ready to act when a feasible plan should be proposed. This was what I wanted. I talked to them of our want of manhood, if we submitted to our enslavement without at least one noble effort to be free. We met often, and consulted frequently, and told our hopes and fears, recounted the difficulties, real and imagined, which we should be called on to meet. At times we were almost disposed to give up, and try to content ourselves with our wretched lot; at others, we were firm and unbending in our determination to go. Whenever we suggested any plan, there was shrinking—the odds were fearful. Our path was beset with the greatest obstacles; and if we succeeded in gaining the end of it, our right to be free was yet questionable—we were yet liable to be returned to bondage. We could see no spot, this side of the ocean, where we could be free. We knew nothing about Canada. Our knowledge of the north did not extend farther than New York; and to go there, and be forever harassed with the frightful liability of being returned to slavery—with the certainty of being treated tenfold worse than before—the thought was truly a horrible one, and one which it was not easy to overcome. The case sometimes stood thus: At every gate through which we were to pass, we saw a watchman—at every ferry a guard—on every bridge a sentinel—and in every wood a patrol. We were hemmed in upon every side. Here were the difficulties, real or imagined—the good to be sought, and the evil to be shunned. On the one hand, there stood slavery, a stern reality, glaring frightfully upon us,—its robes already crimsoned with the blood of millions, and even now feasting itself greedily upon our own flesh. On the other hand, away back in the dim distance, under the flickering light of the north star, behind some craggy hill or snow-covered mountain, stood a doubtful freedom—half frozen—beckoning us to come and share its hospitality. This in itself was sometimes enough to stagger us; but when we permitted ourselves to survey the road, we were frequently appalled. Upon either side we saw grim death, assuming the most horrid shapes. Now it was starvation, causing us to eat our own flesh;—now we were contending with the waves, and were drowned;—now we were overtaken, and torn to pieces by the fangs of the terrible bloodhound. We were stung by scorpions, chased by wild beasts, bitten by snakes, and finally, after having nearly reached the desired spot,—after swimming rivers, encountering wild beasts, sleeping in the woods, suffering hunger and nakedness,—we were overtaken by our pursuers, and, in our resistance, we were shot dead upon the spot! I say, this picture sometimes appalled us, and made us

"rather bear those ills we had,
   Than fly to others, that we knew not of."

In coming to a fixed determination to run away, we did more than Patrick Henry, when he resolved upon liberty or death. With us it was a doubtful liberty at most, and almost certain death if we failed. For my part, I should prefer death to hopeless bondage.

Sandy, one of our number, gave up the notion, but still encouraged us. Our company then consisted of Henry Harris, John Harris, Henry Bailey, Charles Roberts, and myself. Henry Bailey was my uncle, and belonged to my master. Charles married my aunt: he belonged to my master's father-in-law, Mr. William Hamilton.

The plan we finally concluded upon was, to get a large canoe belonging to Mr. Hamilton, and upon the Saturday night previous to Easter holidays, paddle directly up the Chesapeake Bay. On our arrival at the head of the bay, a distance of seventy or eighty miles from where we lived, it was our purpose to turn our canoe adrift, and follow the guidance of the north star till we got beyond the limits of Maryland. Our reason for taking the water route was, that we were less liable to be suspected as runaways; we hoped to be regarded as fishermen; whereas, if we should take the land route, we should be subjected to interruptions of almost every kind. Any one having a white face, and being so disposed, could stop us, and subject us to examination. The week before our intended start, I wrote several protections, one for each of us. As well as I can remember, they were in the following words, to wit:—

"This is to certify that I, the undersigned, have given the bearer, my servant, full liberty to go to Baltimore, and spend the Easter holidays. Written with mine own hand, &c., 1835.

"WILLIAM HAMILTON,

"Near St. Michael's, in Talbot county, Maryland."

We were not going to Baltimore; but, in going up the bay, we went toward Baltimore, and these protections were only intended to protect us while on the bay.

As the time drew near for our departure, our anxiety became more and more intense. It was truly a matter of life and death with us. The strength of our determination was about to be fully tested. At this time, I was very active in explaining every difficulty, removing every doubt, dispelling every fear, and inspiring all with the firmness indispensable to success in our undertaking; assuring them that half was gained the instant we made the move; we had talked long enough; we were now ready to move; if not now, we never should be; and if we did not intend to move now, we had as well fold our arms, sit down, and acknowledge ourselves fit only to be slaves. This, none of us were prepared to acknowledge. Every man stood firm; and at our last meeting, we pledged ourselves afresh, in the most solemn manner, that, at the time appointed, we would certainly start in pursuit of freedom. This was in the middle of the week, at the end of which we were to be off. We went, as usual, to our several fields of labor, but with bosoms highly agitated with thoughts of our truly hazardous undertaking. We tried to conceal our feelings as much as possible; and I think we succeeded very well.

After a painful waiting, the Saturday morning, whose night was to witness our departure, came. I hailed it with joy, bring what of sadness it might. Friday night was a sleepless one for me. I probably felt more anxious than the rest, because I was, by common consent, at the head of the whole affair. The responsibility of success or failure lay heavily upon me. The glory of the one, and the confusion of the other, were alike mine. The first two hours of that morning were such as I never experienced before, and hope never to again. Early in the morning, we went, as usual, to the field. We were spreading manure; and all at once, while thus engaged, I was overwhelmed with an indescribable feeling, in the fulness of which I turned to Sandy, who was near by, and said, "We are betrayed!" "Well," said he, "that thought has this moment struck me." We said no more. I was never more certain of any thing.

The horn was blown as usual, and we went up from the field to the house for breakfast. I went for the form, more than for want of any thing to eat that morning. Just as I got to the house, in looking out at the lane gate, I saw four white men, with two colored men. The white men were on horseback, and the colored ones were walking behind, as if tied. I watched them a few moments till they got up to our lane gate. Here they halted, and tied the colored men to the gate-post. I was not yet certain as to what the matter was. In a few moments, in rode Mr. Hamilton, with a speed betokening great excitement. He came to the door, and inquired if Master William was in. He was told he was at the barn. Mr. Hamilton, without dismounting, rode up to the barn with extraordinary speed. In a few moments, he and Mr. Freeland returned to the house. By this time, the three constables rode up, and in great haste dismounted, tied their horses, and met Master William and Mr. Hamilton returning from the barn; and after talking awhile, they all walked up to the kitchen door. There was no one in the kitchen but myself and John. Henry and Sandy were up at the barn. Mr. Freeland put his head in at the door, and called me by name, saying, there were some gentlemen at the door who wished to see me. I stepped to the door, and inquired what they wanted. They at once seized me, and, without giving me any satisfaction, tied me—lashing my hands closely together. I insisted upon knowing what the matter was. They at length said, that they had learned I had been in a "scrape," and that I was to be examined before my master; and if their information proved false, I should not be hurt.

In a few moments, they succeeded in tying John. They then turned to Henry, who had by this time returned, and commanded him to cross his hands. "I won't!" said Henry, in a firm tone, indicating his readiness to meet the consequences of his refusal. "Won't you?" said Tom Graham, the constable. "No, I won't!" said Henry, in a still stronger tone. With this, two of the constables pulled out their shining pistols, and swore, by their Creator, that they would make him cross his hands or kill him. Each cocked his pistol, and, with fingers on the trigger, walked up to Henry, saying, at the same time, if he did not cross his hands, they would blow his damned heart out. "Shoot me, shoot me!" said Henry; "you can't kill me but once. Shoot, shoot,—and be damned! I won't be tied!" This he said in a tone of loud defiance; and at the same time, with a motion as quick as lightning, he with one single stroke dashed the pistols from the hand of each constable. As he did this, all hands fell upon him, and, after beating him some time, they finally overpowered him, and got him tied.

During the scuffle, I managed, I know not how, to get my pass out, and, without being discovered, put it into the fire. We were all now tied; and just as we were to leave for Easton jail, Betsy Freeland, mother of William Freeland, came to the door with her hands full of biscuits, and divided them between Henry and John. She then delivered herself of a speech, to the following effect:—addressing herself to me, she said, "You devil! You yellow devil! it was you that put it into the heads of Henry and John to run away. But for you, you long-legged mulatto devil! Henry nor John would never have thought of such a thing." I made no reply, and was immediately hurried off towards St. Michael's. Just a moment previous to the scuffle with Henry, Mr. Hamilton suggested the propriety of making a search for the protections which he had understood Frederick had written for himself and the rest. But, just at the moment he was about carrying his proposal into effect, his aid was needed in helping to tie Henry; and the excitement attending the scuffle caused them either to forget, or to deem it unsafe, under the circumstances, to search. So we were not yet convicted of the intention to run away.

When we got about half way to St. Michael's, while the constables having us in charge were looking ahead, Henry inquired of me what he should do with his pass. I told him to eat it with his biscuit, and own nothing; and we passed the word around, "Own nothing;" and "Own nothing!" said we all. Our confidence in each other was unshaken. We were resolved to succeed or fail together, after the calamity had befallen us as much as before. We were now prepared for any thing. We were to be dragged that morning fifteen miles behind horses, and then to be placed in the Easton jail. When we reached St. Michael's, we underwent a sort of examination. We all denied that we ever intended to run away. We did this more to bring out the evidence against us, than from any hope of getting clear of being sold; for, as I have said, we were ready for that. The fact was, we cared but little where we went, so we went together. Our greatest concern was about separation. We dreaded that more than any thing this side of death. We found the evidence against us to be the testimony of one person; our master would not tell who it was; but we came to a unanimous decision among ourselves as to who their informant was. We were sent off to the jail at Easton. When we got there, we were delivered up to the sheriff, Mr. Joseph Graham, and by him placed in jail. Henry, John, and myself, were placed in one room together—Charles, and Henry Bailey, in another. Their object in separating us was to hinder concert.

We had been in jail scarcely twenty minutes, when a swarm of slave traders, and agents for slave traders, flocked into jail to look at us, and to ascertain if we were for sale. Such a set of beings I never saw before! I felt myself surrounded by so many fiends from perdition. A band of pirates never looked more like their father, the devil. They laughed and grinned over us, saying, "Ah, my boys! we have got you, haven't we?" And after taunting us in various ways, they one by one went into an examination of us, with intent to ascertain our value. They would impudently ask us if we would not like to have them for our masters. We would make them no answer, and leave them to find out as best they could. Then they would curse and swear at us, telling us that they could take the devil out of us in a very little while, if we were only in their hands.

While in jail, we found ourselves in much more comfortable quarters than we expected when we went there. We did not get much to eat, nor that which was very good; but we had a good clean room, from the windows of which we could see what was going on in the street, which was very much better than though we had been placed in one of the dark, damp cells. Upon the whole, we got along very well, so far as the jail and its keeper were concerned. Immediately after the holidays were over, contrary to all our expectations, Mr. Hamilton and Mr. Freeland came up to Easton, and took Charles, the two Henrys, and John, out of jail, and carried them home, leaving me alone. I regarded this separation as a final one. It caused me more pain than any thing else in the whole transaction. I was ready for any thing rather than separation. I supposed that they had consulted together, and had decided that, as I was the whole cause of the intention of the others to run away, it was hard to make the innocent suffer with the guilty; and that they had, therefore, concluded to take the others home, and sell me, as a warning to the others that remained. It is due to the noble Henry to say, he seemed almost as reluctant at leaving the prison as at leaving home to come to the prison. But we knew we should, in all probability, be separated, if we were sold; and since he was in their hands, he concluded to go peaceably home.

I was now left to my fate. I was all alone, and within the walls of a stone prison. But a few days before, and I was full of hope. I expected to have been safe in a land of freedom; but now I was covered with gloom, sunk down to the utmost despair. I thought the possibility of freedom was gone. I was kept in this way about one week, at the end of which, Captain Auld, my master, to my surprise and utter astonishment, came up, and took me out, with the intention of sending me, with a gentleman of his acquaintance, into Alabama. But, from some cause or other, he did not send me to Alabama, but concluded to send me back to Baltimore, to live again with his brother Hugh, and to learn a trade.

Thus, after an absence of three years and one month, I was once more permitted to return to my old home at Baltimore. My master sent me away, because there existed against me a very great prejudice in the community, and he feared I might be killed.

In a few weeks after I went to Baltimore, Master Hugh hired me to Mr. William Gardner, an extensive ship-builder, on Fell's Point. I was put there to learn how to calk. It, however, proved a very unfavorable place for the accomplishment of this object. Mr. Gardner was engaged that spring in building two large man-of-war brigs, professedly for the Mexican government. The vessels were to be launched in the July of that year, and in failure thereof, Mr. Gardner was to lose a considerable sum; so that when I entered, all was hurry. There was no time to learn any thing. Every man had to do that which he knew how to do. In entering the shipyard, my orders from Mr. Gardner were, to do whatever the carpenters commanded me to do. This was placing me at the beck and call of about seventy-five men. I was to regard all these as masters. Their word was to be my law. My situation was a most trying one. At times I needed a dozen pair of hands. I was called a dozen ways in the space of a single minute. Three or four voices would strike my ear at the same moment. It was—"Fred., come help me to cant this timber here."—"Fred., come carry this timber yonder."—"Fred., bring that roller here."—"Fred., go get a fresh can of water."—"Fred., come help saw off the end of this timber."—"Fred., go quick, and get the crowbar."—"Fred., hold on the end of this fall."—"Fred., go to the blacksmith's shop, and get a new punch."—"Hurra, Fred! run and bring me a cold chisel."—"I say, Fred., bear a hand, and get up a fire as quick as lightning under that steam-box."—"Halloo, nigger! come, turn this grindstone."—"Come, come! move, move! and BOWSE this timber forward."—"I say, darky, blast your eyes, why don't you heat up some pitch?"—"Halloo! halloo! halloo!" (Three voices at the same time.) "Come here!—Go there!—Hold on where you are! Damn you, if you move, I'll knock your brains out!"

This was my school for eight months; and I might have remained there longer, but for a most horrid fight I had with four of the white apprentices, in which my left eye was nearly knocked out, and I was horribly mangled in other respects. The facts in the case were these: Until a very little while after I went there, white and black ship-carpenters worked side by side, and no one seemed to see any impropriety in it. All hands seemed to be very well satisfied. Many of the black carpenters were freemen. Things seemed to be going on very well. All at once, the white carpenters knocked off, and said they would not work with free colored workmen. Their reason for this, as alleged, was, that if free colored carpenters were encouraged, they would soon take the trade into their own hands, and poor white men would be thrown out of employment. They therefore felt called upon at once to put a stop to it. And, taking advantage of Mr. Gardner's necessities, they broke off, swearing they would work no longer, unless he would discharge his black carpenters. Now, though this did not extend to me in form, it did reach me in fact. My fellow-apprentices very soon began to feel it degrading to them to work with me. They began to put on airs, and talk about the "niggers" taking the country, saying we all ought to be killed; and, being encouraged by the journeymen, they commenced making my condition as hard as they could, by hectoring me around, and sometimes striking me. I, of course, kept the vow I made after the fight with Mr. Covey, and struck back again, regardless of consequences; and while I kept them from combining, I succeeded very well; for I could whip the whole of them, taking them separately. They, however, at length combined, and came upon me, armed with sticks, stones, and heavy handspikes. One came in front with a half brick. There was one at each side of me, and one behind me. While I was attending to those in front, and on either side, the one behind ran up with the handspike, and struck me a heavy blow upon the head. It stunned me. I fell, and with this they all ran upon me, and fell to beating me with their fists. I let them lay on for a while, gathering strength. In an instant, I gave a sudden surge, and rose to my hands and knees. Just as I did that, one of their number gave me, with his heavy boot, a powerful kick in the left eye. My eyeball seemed to have burst. When they saw my eye closed, and badly swollen, they left me. With this I seized the handspike, and for a time pursued them. But here the carpenters interfered, and I thought I might as well give it up. It was impossible to stand my hand against so many. All this took place in sight of not less than fifty white ship-carpenters, and not one interposed a friendly word; but some cried, "Kill the damned nigger! Kill him! kill him! He struck a white person." I found my only chance for life was in flight. I succeeded in getting away without an additional blow, and barely so; for to strike a white man is death by Lynch law,—and that was the law in Mr. Gardner's ship-yard; nor is there much of any other out of Mr. Gardner's ship-yard.

I went directly home, and told the story of my wrongs to Master Hugh; and I am happy to say of him, irreligious as he was, his conduct was heavenly, compared with that of his brother Thomas under similar circumstances. He listened attentively to my narration of the circumstances leading to the savage outrage, and gave many proofs of his strong indignation at it. The heart of my once overkind mistress was again melted into pity. My puffed-out eye and blood-covered face moved her to tears. She took a chair by me, washed the blood from my face, and, with a mother's tenderness, bound up my head, covering the wounded eye with a lean piece of fresh beef. It was almost compensation for my suffering to witness, once more, a manifestation of kindness from this, my once affectionate old mistress. Master Hugh was very much enraged. He gave expression to his feelings by pouring out curses upon the heads of those who did the deed. As soon as I got a little the better of my bruises, he took me with him to Esquire Watson's, on Bond Street, to see what could be done about the matter. Mr. Watson inquired who saw the assault committed. Master Hugh told him it was done in Mr. Gardner's ship-yard at midday, where there were a large company of men at work. "As to that," he said, "the deed was done, and there was no question as to who did it." His answer was, he could do nothing in the case, unless some white man would come forward and testify. He could issue no warrant on my word. If I had been killed in the presence of a thousand colored people, their testimony combined would have been insufficient to have arrested one of the murderers. Master Hugh, for once, was compelled to say this state of things was too bad. Of course, it was impossible to get any white man to volunteer his testimony in my behalf, and against the white young men. Even those who may have sympathized with me were not prepared to do this. It required a degree of courage unknown to them to do so; for just at that time, the slightest manifestation of humanity toward a colored person was denounced as abolitionism, and that name subjected its bearer to frightful liabilities. The watchwords of the bloody-minded in that region, and in those days, were, "Damn the abolitionists!" and "Damn the niggers!" There was nothing done, and probably nothing would have been done if I had been killed. Such was, and such remains, the state of things in the Christian city of Baltimore.

Master Hugh, finding he could get no redress, refused to let me go back again to Mr. Gardner. He kept me himself, and his wife dressed my wound till I was again restored to health. He then took me into the ship-yard of which he was foreman, in the employment of Mr. Walter Price. There I was immediately set to calking, and very soon learned the art of using my mallet and irons. In the course of one year from the time I left Mr. Gardner's, I was able to command the highest wages given to the most experienced calkers. I was now of some importance to my master. I was bringing him from six to seven dollars per week. I sometimes brought him nine dollars per week: my wages were a dollar and a half a day. After learning how to calk, I sought my own employment, made my own contracts, and collected the money which I earned. My pathway became much more smooth than before; my condition was now much more comfortable. When I could get no calking to do, I did nothing. During these leisure times, those old notions about freedom would steal over me again. When in Mr. Gardner's employment, I was kept in such a perpetual whirl of excitement, I could think of nothing, scarcely, but my life; and in thinking of my life, I almost forgot my liberty. I have observed this in my experience of slavery,—that whenever my condition was improved, instead of its increasing my contentment, it only increased my desire to be free, and set me to thinking of plans to gain my freedom. I have found that, to make a contented slave, it is necessary to make a thoughtless one. It is necessary to darken his moral and mental vision, and, as far as possible, to annihilate the power of reason. He must be able to detect no inconsistencies in slavery; he must be made to feel that slavery is right; and he can be brought to that only when he ceases to be a man.

I was now getting, as I have said, one dollar and fifty cents per day. I contracted for it; I earned it; it was paid to me; it was rightfully my own; yet, upon each returning Saturday night, I was compelled to deliver every cent of that money to Master Hugh. And why? Not because he earned it,—not because he had any hand in earning it,—not because I owed it to him,—nor because he possessed the slightest shadow of a right to it; but solely because he had the power to compel me to give it up. The right of the grim-visaged pirate upon the high seas is exactly the same.

CHAPTER XI

I now come to that part of my life during which I planned, and finally succeeded in making, my escape from slavery. But before narrating any of the peculiar circumstances, I deem it proper to make known my intention not to state all the facts connected with the transaction. My reasons for pursuing this course may be understood from the following: First, were I to give a minute statement of all the facts, it is not only possible, but quite probable, that others would thereby be involved in the most embarrassing difficulties. Secondly, such a statement would most undoubtedly induce greater vigilance on the part of slaveholders than has existed heretofore among them; which would, of course, be the means of guarding a door whereby some dear brother bondman might escape his galling chains. I deeply regret the necessity that impels me to suppress any thing of importance connected with my experience in slavery. It would afford me great pleasure indeed, as well as materially add to the interest of my narrative, were I at liberty to gratify a curiosity, which I know exists in the minds of many, by an accurate statement of all the facts pertaining to my most fortunate escape. But I must deprive myself of this pleasure, and the curious of the gratification which such a statement would afford. I would allow myself to suffer under the greatest imputations which evil-minded men might suggest, rather than exculpate myself, and thereby run the hazard of closing the slightest avenue by which a brother slave might clear himself of the chains and fetters of slavery.

I have never approved of the very public manner in which some of our western friends have conducted what they call the underground railroad, but which I think, by their open declarations, has been made most emphatically the upper-ground railroad. I honor those good men and women for their noble daring, and applaud them for willingly subjecting themselves to bloody persecution, by openly avowing their participation in the escape of slaves. I, however, can see very little good resulting from such a course, either to themselves or the slaves escaping; while, upon the other hand, I see and feel assured that those open declarations are a positive evil to the slaves remaining, who are seeking to escape. They do nothing towards enlightening the slave, whilst they do much towards enlightening the master. They stimulate him to greater watchfulness, and enhance his power to capture his slave. We owe something to the slave south of the line as well as to those north of it; and in aiding the latter on their way to freedom, we should be careful to do nothing which would be likely to hinder the former from escaping from slavery. I would keep the merciless slaveholder profoundly ignorant of the means of flight adopted by the slave. I would leave him to imagine himself surrounded by myriads of invisible tormentors, ever ready to snatch from his infernal grasp his trembling prey. Let him be left to feel his way in the dark; let darkness commensurate with his crime hover over him; and let him feel that at every step he takes, in pursuit of the flying bondman, he is running the frightful risk of having his hot brains dashed out by an invisible agency. Let us render the tyrant no aid; let us not hold the light by which he can trace the footprints of our flying brother. But enough of this. I will now proceed to the statement of those facts, connected with my escape, for which I am alone responsible, and for which no one can be made to suffer but myself.

In the early part of the year 1838, I became quite restless. I could see no reason why I should, at the end of each week, pour the reward of my toil into the purse of my master. When I carried to him my weekly wages, he would, after counting the money, look me in the face with a robber-like fierceness, and ask, "Is this all?" He was satisfied with nothing less than the last cent. He would, however, when I made him six dollars, sometimes give me six cents, to encourage me. It had the opposite effect. I regarded it as a sort of admission of my right to the whole. The fact that he gave me any part of my wages was proof, to my mind, that he believed me entitled to the whole of them. I always felt worse for having received any thing; for I feared that the giving me a few cents would ease his conscience, and make him feel himself to be a pretty honorable sort of robber. My discontent grew upon me. I was ever on the look-out for means of escape; and, finding no direct means, I determined to try to hire my time, with a view of getting money with which to make my escape. In the spring of 1838, when Master Thomas came to Baltimore to purchase his spring goods, I got an opportunity, and applied to him to allow me to hire my time. He unhesitatingly refused my request, and told me this was another stratagem by which to escape. He told me I could go nowhere but that he could get me; and that, in the event of my running away, he should spare no pains in his efforts to catch me. He exhorted me to content myself, and be obedient. He told me, if I would be happy, I must lay out no plans for the future. He said, if I behaved myself properly, he would take care of me. Indeed, he advised me to complete thoughtlessness of the future, and taught me to depend solely upon him for happiness. He seemed to see fully the pressing necessity of setting aside my intellectual nature, in order to contentment in slavery. But in spite of him, and even in spite of myself, I continued to think, and to think about the injustice of my enslavement, and the means of escape.

About two months after this, I applied to Master Hugh for the privilege of hiring my time. He was not acquainted with the fact that I had applied to Master Thomas, and had been refused. He too, at first, seemed disposed to refuse; but, after some reflection, he granted me the privilege, and proposed the following terms: I was to be allowed all my time, make all contracts with those for whom I worked, and find my own employment; and, in return for this liberty, I was to pay him three dollars at the end of each week; find myself in calking tools, and in board and clothing. My board was two dollars and a half per week. This, with the wear and tear of clothing and calking tools, made my regular expenses about six dollars per week. This amount I was compelled to make up, or relinquish the privilege of hiring my time. Rain or shine, work or no work, at the end of each week the money must be forthcoming, or I must give up my privilege. This arrangement, it will be perceived, was decidedly in my master's favor. It relieved him of all need of looking after me. His money was sure. He received all the benefits of slaveholding without its evils; while I endured all the evils of a slave, and suffered all the care and anxiety of a freeman. I found it a hard bargain. But, hard as it was, I thought it better than the old mode of getting along. It was a step towards freedom to be allowed to bear the responsibilities of a freeman, and I was determined to hold on upon it. I bent myself to the work of making money. I was ready to work at night as well as day, and by the most untiring perseverance and industry, I made enough to meet my expenses, and lay up a little money every week. I went on thus from May till August. Master Hugh then refused to allow me to hire my time longer. The ground for his refusal was a failure on my part, one Saturday night, to pay him for my week's time. This failure was occasioned by my attending a camp meeting about ten miles from Baltimore. During the week, I had entered into an engagement with a number of young friends to start from Baltimore to the camp ground early Saturday evening; and being detained by my employer, I was unable to get down to Master Hugh's without disappointing the company. I knew that Master Hugh was in no special need of the money that night. I therefore decided to go to camp meeting, and upon my return pay him the three dollars. I staid at the camp meeting one day longer than I intended when I left. But as soon as I returned, I called upon him to pay him what I considered his due. I found him very angry; he could scarce restrain his wrath. He said he had a great mind to give me a severe whipping. He wished to know how I dared go out of the city without asking his permission. I told him I hired my time and while I paid him the price which he asked for it, I did not know that I was bound to ask him when and where I should go. This reply troubled him; and, after reflecting a few moments, he turned to me, and said I should hire my time no longer; that the next thing he should know of, I would be running away. Upon the same plea, he told me to bring my tools and clothing home forthwith. I did so; but instead of seeking work, as I had been accustomed to do previously to hiring my time, I spent the whole week without the performance of a single stroke of work. I did this in retaliation. Saturday night, he called upon me as usual for my week's wages. I told him I had no wages; I had done no work that week. Here we were upon the point of coming to blows. He raved, and swore his determination to get hold of me. I did not allow myself a single word; but was resolved, if he laid the weight of his hand upon me, it should be blow for blow. He did not strike me, but told me that he would find me in constant employment in future. I thought the matter over during the next day, Sunday, and finally resolved upon the third day of September, as the day upon which I would make a second attempt to secure my freedom. I now had three weeks during which to prepare for my journey. Early on Monday morning, before Master Hugh had time to make any engagement for me, I went out and got employment of Mr. Butler, at his ship-yard near the drawbridge, upon what is called the City Block, thus making it unnecessary for him to seek employment for me. At the end of the week, I brought him between eight and nine dollars. He seemed very well pleased, and asked why I did not do the same the week before. He little knew what my plans were. My object in working steadily was to remove any suspicion he might entertain of my intent to run away; and in this I succeeded admirably. I suppose he thought I was never better satisfied with my condition than at the very time during which I was planning my escape. The second week passed, and again I carried him my full wages; and so well pleased was he, that he gave me twenty-five cents, (quite a large sum for a slaveholder to give a slave,) and bade me to make a good use of it. I told him I would.

Things went on without very smoothly indeed, but within there was trouble. It is impossible for me to describe my feelings as the time of my contemplated start drew near. I had a number of warmhearted friends in Baltimore,—friends that I loved almost as I did my life,—and the thought of being separated from them forever was painful beyond expression. It is my opinion that thousands would escape from slavery, who now remain, but for the strong cords of affection that bind them to their friends. The thought of leaving my friends was decidedly the most painful thought with which I had to contend. The love of them was my tender point, and shook my decision more than all things else. Besides the pain of separation, the dread and apprehension of a failure exceeded what I had experienced at my first attempt. The appalling defeat I then sustained returned to torment me. I felt assured that, if I failed in this attempt, my case would be a hopeless one—it would seal my fate as a slave forever. I could not hope to get off with any thing less than the severest punishment, and being placed beyond the means of escape. It required no very vivid imagination to depict the most frightful scenes through which I should have to pass, in case I failed. The wretchedness of slavery, and the blessedness of freedom, were perpetually before me. It was life and death with me. But I remained firm, and, according to my resolution, on the third day of September, 1838, I left my chains, and succeeded in reaching New York without the slightest interruption of any kind. How I did so,—what means I adopted,—what direction I travelled, and by what mode of conveyance,—I must leave unexplained, for the reasons before mentioned.

I have been frequently asked how I felt when I found myself in a free State. I have never been able to answer the question with any satisfaction to myself. It was a moment of the highest excitement I ever experienced. I suppose I felt as one may imagine the unarmed mariner to feel when he is rescued by a friendly man-of-war from the pursuit of a pirate. In writing to a dear friend, immediately after my arrival at New York, I said I felt like one who had escaped a den of hungry lions. This state of mind, however, very soon subsided; and I was again seized with a feeling of great insecurity and loneliness. I was yet liable to be taken back, and subjected to all the tortures of slavery. This in itself was enough to damp the ardor of my enthusiasm. But the loneliness overcame me. There I was in the midst of thousands, and yet a perfect stranger; without home and without friends, in the midst of thousands of my own brethren—children of a common Father, and yet I dared not to unfold to any one of them my sad condition. I was afraid to speak to any one for fear of speaking to the wrong one, and thereby falling into the hands of money-loving kidnappers, whose business it was to lie in wait for the panting fugitive, as the ferocious beasts of the forest lie in wait for their prey. The motto which I adopted when I started from slavery was this—"Trust no man!" I saw in every white man an enemy, and in almost every colored man cause for distrust. It was a most painful situation; and, to understand it, one must needs experience it, or imagine himself in similar circumstances. Let him be a fugitive slave in a strange land—a land given up to be the hunting-ground for slaveholders—whose inhabitants are legalized kidnappers—where he is every moment subjected to the terrible liability of being seized upon by his fellowmen, as the hideous crocodile seizes upon his prey!—I say, let him place himself in my situation—without home or friends—without money or credit—wanting shelter, and no one to give it—wanting bread, and no money to buy it,—and at the same time let him feel that he is pursued by merciless men-hunters, and in total darkness as to what to do, where to go, or where to stay,—perfectly helpless both as to the means of defence and means of escape,—in the midst of plenty, yet suffering the terrible gnawings of hunger,—in the midst of houses, yet having no home,—among fellow-men, yet feeling as if in the midst of wild beasts, whose greediness to swallow up the trembling and half-famished fugitive is only equalled by that with which the monsters of the deep swallow up the helpless fish upon which they subsist,—I say, let him be placed in this most trying situation,—the situation in which I was placed,—then, and not till then, will he fully appreciate the hardships of, and know how to sympathize with, the toil-worn and whip-scarred fugitive slave.

Thank Heaven, I remained but a short time in this distressed situation. I was relieved from it by the humane hand of Mr. DAVID RUGGLES, whose vigilance, kindness, and perseverance, I shall never forget. I am glad of an opportunity to express, as far as words can, the love and gratitude I bear him. Mr. Ruggles is now afflicted with blindness, and is himself in need of the same kind offices which he was once so forward in the performance of toward others. I had been in New York but a few days, when Mr. Ruggles sought me out, and very kindly took me to his boarding-house at the corner of Church and Lespenard Streets. Mr. Ruggles was then very deeply engaged in the memorable Darg case, as well as attending to a number of other fugitive slaves, devising ways and means for their successful escape; and, though watched and hemmed in on almost every side, he seemed to be more than a match for his enemies.

Very soon after I went to Mr. Ruggles, he wished to know of me where I wanted to go; as he deemed it unsafe for me to remain in New York. I told him I was a calker, and should like to go where I could get work. I thought of going to Canada; but he decided against it, and in favor of my going to New Bedford, thinking I should be able to get work there at my trade. At this time, Anna,* my intended wife, came on; for I wrote to her immediately after my arrival at New York, (notwithstanding my homeless, houseless, and helpless condition,) informing her of my successful flight, and wishing her to come on forthwith. In a few days after her arrival, Mr. Ruggles called in the Rev. J. W. C. Pennington, who, in the presence of Mr. Ruggles, Mrs. Michaels, and two or three others, performed the marriage ceremony, and gave us a certificate, of which the following is an exact copy:—

"This may certify, that I joined together in holy matrimony Frederick Johnson** and Anna Murray, as man and wife, in the presence of Mr. David Ruggles and Mrs. Michaels.

"JAMES W. C. PENNINGTON
"NEW YORK, SEPT. 15, 1838"

*She was free.

**I had changed my name from Frederick BAILEY to that of JOHNSON.

Upon receiving this certificate, and a five-dollar bill from Mr. Ruggles, I shouldered one part of our baggage, and Anna took up the other, and we set out forthwith to take passage on board of the steamboat John W. Richmond for Newport, on our way to New Bedford. Mr. Ruggles gave me a letter to a Mr. Shaw in Newport, and told me, in case my money did not serve me to New Bedford, to stop in Newport and obtain further assistance; but upon our arrival at Newport, we were so anxious to get to a place of safety, that, notwithstanding we lacked the necessary money to pay our fare, we decided to take seats in the stage, and promise to pay when we got to New Bedford. We were encouraged to do this by two excellent gentlemen, residents of New Bedford, whose names I afterward ascertained to be Joseph Ricketson and William C. Taber. They seemed at once to understand our circumstances, and gave us such assurance of their friendliness as put us fully at ease in their presence.

It was good indeed to meet with such friends, at such a time. Upon reaching New Bedford, we were directed to the house of Mr. Nathan Johnson, by whom we were kindly received, and hospitably provided for. Both Mr. and Mrs. Johnson took a deep and lively interest in our welfare. They proved themselves quite worthy of the name of abolitionists. When the stage-driver found us unable to pay our fare, he held on upon our baggage as security for the debt. I had but to mention the fact to Mr. Johnson, and he forthwith advanced the money.

We now began to feel a degree of safety, and to prepare ourselves for the duties and responsibilities of a life of freedom. On the morning after our arrival at New Bedford, while at the breakfast-table, the question arose as to what name I should be called by. The name given me by my mother was, "Frederick Augustus Washington Bailey." I, however, had dispensed with the two middle names long before I left Maryland so that I was generally known by the name of "Frederick Bailey." I started from Baltimore bearing the name of "Stanley." When I got to New York, I again changed my name to "Frederick Johnson," and thought that would be the last change. But when I got to New Bedford, I found it necessary again to change my name. The reason of this necessity was, that there were so many Johnsons in New Bedford, it was already quite difficult to distinguish between them. I gave Mr. Johnson the privilege of choosing me a name, but told him he must not take from me the name of "Frederick." I must hold on to that, to preserve a sense of my identity. Mr. Johnson had just been reading the "Lady of the Lake," and at once suggested that my name be "Douglass." From that time until now I have been called "Frederick Douglass;" and as I am more widely known by that name than by either of the others, I shall continue to use it as my own.

I was quite disappointed at the general appearance of things in New Bedford. The impression which I had received respecting the character and condition of the people of the north, I found to be singularly erroneous. I had very strangely supposed, while in slavery, that few of the comforts, and scarcely any of the luxuries, of life were enjoyed at the north, compared with what were enjoyed by the slaveholders of the south. I probably came to this conclusion from the fact that northern people owned no slaves. I supposed that they were about upon a level with the non-slaveholding population of the south. I knew they were exceedingly poor, and I had been accustomed to regard their poverty as the necessary consequence of their being non-slaveholders. I had somehow imbibed the opinion that, in the absence of slaves, there could be no wealth, and very little refinement. And upon coming to the north, I expected to meet with a rough, hard-handed, and uncultivated population, living in the most Spartan-like simplicity, knowing nothing of the ease, luxury, pomp, and grandeur of southern slaveholders. Such being my conjectures, any one acquainted with the appearance of New Bedford may very readily infer how palpably I must have seen my mistake.

In the afternoon of the day when I reached New Bedford, I visited the wharves, to take a view of the shipping. Here I found myself surrounded with the strongest proofs of wealth. Lying at the wharves, and riding in the stream, I saw many ships of the finest model, in the best order, and of the largest size. Upon the right and left, I was walled in by granite warehouses of the widest dimensions, stowed to their utmost capacity with the necessaries and comforts of life. Added to this, almost every body seemed to be at work, but noiselessly so, compared with what I had been accustomed to in Baltimore. There were no loud songs heard from those engaged in loading and unloading ships. I heard no deep oaths or horrid curses on the laborer. I saw no whipping of men; but all seemed to go smoothly on. Every man appeared to understand his work, and went at it with a sober, yet cheerful earnestness, which betokened the deep interest which he felt in what he was doing, as well as a sense of his own dignity as a man. To me this looked exceedingly strange. From the wharves I strolled around and over the town, gazing with wonder and admiration at the splendid churches, beautiful dwellings, and finely-cultivated gardens; evincing an amount of wealth, comfort, taste, and refinement, such as I had never seen in any part of slaveholding Maryland.

Every thing looked clean, new, and beautiful. I saw few or no dilapidated houses, with poverty-stricken inmates; no half-naked children and barefooted women, such as I had been accustomed to see in Hillsborough, Easton, St. Michael's, and Baltimore. The people looked more able, stronger, healthier, and happier, than those of Maryland. I was for once made glad by a view of extreme wealth, without being saddened by seeing extreme poverty. But the most astonishing as well as the most interesting thing to me was the condition of the colored people, a great many of whom, like myself, had escaped thither as a refuge from the hunters of men. I found many, who had not been seven years out of their chains, living in finer houses, and evidently enjoying more of the comforts of life, than the average of slaveholders in Maryland.

I will venture to assert, that my friend Mr. Nathan Johnson (of whom I can say with a grateful heart, "I was hungry, and he gave me meat; I was thirsty, and he gave me drink; I was a stranger, and he took me in") lived in a neater house; dined at a better table; took, paid for, and read, more newspapers; better understood the moral, religious, and political character of the nation,—than nine tenths of the slaveholders in Talbot county Maryland. Yet Mr. Johnson was a working man. His hands were hardened by toil, and not his alone, but those also of Mrs. Johnson. I found the colored people much more spirited than I had supposed they would be. I found among them a determination to protect each other from the blood-thirsty kidnapper, at all hazards. Soon after my arrival, I was told of a circumstance which illustrated their spirit. A colored man and a fugitive slave were on unfriendly terms. The former was heard to threaten the latter with informing his master of his whereabouts. Straightway a meeting was called among the colored people, under the stereotyped notice, "Business of importance!" The betrayer was invited to attend. The people came at the appointed hour, and organized the meeting by appointing a very religious old gentleman as president, who, I believe, made a prayer, after which he addressed the meeting as follows: "Friends, we have got him here, and I would recommend that you young men just take him outside the door, and kill him!" With this, a number of them bolted at him; but they were intercepted by some more timid than themselves, and the betrayer escaped their vengeance, and has not been seen in New Bedford since. I believe there have been no more such threats, and should there be hereafter, I doubt not that death would be the consequence.

I found employment, the third day after my arrival, in stowing a sloop with a load of oil. It was new, dirty, and hard work for me; but I went at it with a glad heart and a willing hand. I was now my own master. It was a happy moment, the rapture of which can be understood only by those who have been slaves. It was the first work, the reward of which was to be entirely my own. There was no Master Hugh standing ready, the moment I earned the money, to rob me of it. I worked that day with a pleasure I had never before experienced. I was at work for myself and newly-married wife. It was to me the starting-point of a new existence. When I got through with that job, I went in pursuit of a job of calking; but such was the strength of prejudice against color, among the white calkers, that they refused to work with me, and of course I could get no employment.*

    * I am told that colored persons can now get employment at calking in New Bedford—a result of anti-slavery effort.

Finding my trade of no immediate benefit, I threw off my calking habiliments, and prepared myself to do any kind of work I could get to do. Mr. Johnson kindly let me have his wood-horse and saw, and I very soon found myself a plenty of work. There was no work too hard—none too dirty. I was ready to saw wood, shovel coal, carry wood, sweep the chimney, or roll oil casks,—all of which I did for nearly three years in New Bedford, before I became known to the anti-slavery world.

In about four months after I went to New Bedford, there came a young man to me, and inquired if I did not wish to take the "Liberator." I told him I did; but, just having made my escape from slavery, I remarked that I was unable to pay for it then. I, however, finally became a subscriber to it. The paper came, and I read it from week to week with such feelings as it would be quite idle for me to attempt to describe. The paper became my meat and my drink. My soul was set all on fire. Its sympathy for my brethren in bonds—its scathing denunciations of slaveholders—its faithful exposures of slavery—and its powerful attacks upon the upholders of the institution—sent a thrill of joy through my soul, such as I had never felt before!

I had not long been a reader of the "Liberator," before I got a pretty correct idea of the principles, measures and spirit of the anti-slavery reform. I took right hold of the cause. I could do but little; but what I could, I did with a joyful heart, and never felt happier than when in an anti-slavery meeting. I seldom had much to say at the meetings, because what I wanted to say was said so much better by others. But, while attending an anti-slavery convention at

Nantucket, on the 11th of August, 1841, I felt strongly moved to speak, and was at the same time much urged to do so by Mr. William C. Coffin, a gentleman who had heard me speak in the colored people's meeting at New Bedford. It was a severe cross, and I took it up reluctantly. The truth was, I felt myself a slave, and the idea of speaking to white people weighed me down. I spoke but a few moments, when I felt a degree of freedom, and said what I desired with considerable ease. From that time until now, I have been engaged in pleading the cause of my brethren—with what success, and with what devotion, I leave those acquainted with my labors to decide.

APPENDIX

I find, since reading over the foregoing Narrative, that I have, in several instances, spoken in such a tone and manner, respecting religion, as may possibly lead those unacquainted with my religious views to suppose me an opponent of all religion. To remove the liability of such misapprehension, I deem it proper to append the following brief explanation. What I have said respecting and against religion, I mean strictly to apply to the slaveholding religion of this land, and with no possible reference to Christianity proper; for, between the Christianity of this land, and the Christianity of Christ, I recognize the widest possible difference—so wide, that to receive the one as good, pure, and holy, is of necessity to reject the other as bad, corrupt, and wicked. To be the friend of the one, is of necessity to be the enemy of the other. I love the pure, peaceable, and impartial Christianity of Christ: I therefore hate the corrupt, slaveholding, women-whipping, cradle-plundering, partial and hypocritical Christianity of this land. Indeed, I can see no reason, but the most deceitful one, for calling the religion of this land Christianity. I look upon it as the climax of all misnomers, the boldest of all frauds, and the grossest of all libels. Never was there a clearer case of "stealing the livery of the court of heaven to serve the devil in." I am filled with unutterable loathing when I contemplate the religious pomp and show, together with the horrible inconsistencies, which every where surround me. We have men-stealers for ministers, women-whippers for missionaries, and cradle-plunderers for church members. The man who wields the blood-clotted cowskin during the week fills the pulpit on Sunday, and claims to be a minister of the meek and lowly Jesus. The man who robs me of my earnings at the end of each week meets me as a class-leader on Sunday morning, to show me the way of life, and the path of salvation. He who sells my sister, for purposes of prostitution, stands forth as the pious advocate of purity. He who proclaims it a religious duty to read the Bible denies me the right of learning to read the name of the God who made me. He who is the religious advocate of marriage robs whole millions of its sacred influence, and leaves them to the ravages of wholesale pollution. The warm defender of the sacredness of the family relation is the same that scatters whole families,—sundering husbands and wives, parents and children, sisters and brothers,—leaving the hut vacant, and the hearth desolate. We see the thief preaching against theft, and the adulterer against adultery. We have men sold to build churches, women sold to support the gospel, and babes sold to purchase Bibles for the POOR HEATHEN! ALL FOR THE GLORY OF GOD AND THE GOOD OF SOULS! The slave auctioneer's bell and the church-going bell chime in with each other, and the bitter cries of the heart-broken slave are drowned in the religious shouts of his pious master. Revivals of religion and revivals in the slave-trade go hand in hand together. The slave prison and the church stand near each other. The clanking of fetters and the rattling of chains in the prison, and the pious psalm and solemn prayer in the church, may be heard at the same time. The dealers in the bodies and souls of men erect their stand in the presence of the pulpit, and they mutually help each other. The dealer gives his blood-stained gold to support the pulpit, and the pulpit, in return, covers his infernal business with the garb of Christianity. Here we have religion and robbery the allies of each other—devils dressed in angels' robes, and hell presenting the semblance of paradise.

"Just God! and these are they,
Who minister at thine altar, God of right!
Men who their hands, with prayer and blessing, lay
On Israel's ark of light.

"What! preach, and kidnap men?
Give thanks, and rob thy own afflicted poor?
Talk of thy glorious liberty, and then
Bolt hard the captive's door?

"What! servants of thy own
Merciful Son, who came to seek and save
The homeless and the outcast, fettering down
The tasked and plundered slave!

"Pilate and Herod friends!
Chief priests and rulers, as of old, combine!
Just God and holy! is that church which lends
Strength to the spoiler thine?"

The Christianity of America is a Christianity, of whose votaries it may be as truly said, as it was of the ancient scribes and Pharisees, "They bind heavy burdens, and grievous to be borne, and lay them on men's shoulders, but they themselves will not move them with one of their fingers. All their works they do for to be seen of men.—They love the uppermost rooms at feasts, and the chief seats in the synagogues, ... and to be called of men, Rabbi, Rabbi.—But woe unto you, scribes and Pharisees, hypocrites! for ye shut up the kingdom of heaven against men; for ye neither go in yourselves, neither suffer ye them that are entering to go in. Ye devour widows' houses, and for a pretence make long prayers; therefore ye shall receive the greater damnation. Ye compass sea and land to make one proselyte, and when he is made, ye make him twofold more the child of hell than yourselves.—Woe unto you, scribes and Pharisees, hypocrites! for ye pay tithe of mint, and anise, and cumin, and have omitted the weightier matters of the law, judgment, mercy, and faith; these ought ye to have done, and not to leave the other undone. Ye blind guides! which strain at a gnat, and swallow a camel. Woe unto you, scribes and Pharisees, hypocrites! for ye make clean the outside of the cup and of the platter; but within, they are full of extortion and excess.—Woe unto you, scribes and Pharisees, hypocrites! for ye are like unto whited sepulchres, which indeed appear beautiful outward, but are within full of dead men's bones, and of all uncleanness. Even so ye also outwardly appear righteous unto men, but within ye are full of hypocrisy and iniquity."

Dark and terrible as is this picture, I hold it to be strictly true of the overwhelming mass of professed Christians in America. They strain at a gnat, and swallow a camel. Could any thing be more true of our churches? They would be shocked at the proposition of fellowshipping a SHEEP-stealer; and at the same time they hug to their communion a MAN-stealer, and brand me with being an infidel, if I find fault with them for it. They attend with Pharisaical strictness to the outward forms of religion, and at the same time neglect the weightier matters of the law, judgment, mercy, and faith. They are always ready to sacrifice, but seldom to show mercy. They are they who are represented as professing to love God whom they have not seen, whilst they hate their brother whom they have seen. They love the heathen on the other side of the globe. They can pray for him, pay money to have the Bible put into his hand, and missionaries to instruct him; while they despise and totally neglect the heathen at their own doors. Such is, very briefly, my view of the religion of this land; and to avoid any misunderstanding, growing out of the use of general terms, I mean by the religion of this land, that which is revealed in the words, deeds, and actions, of those bodies, north and south, calling themselves Christian churches, and yet in union with slaveholders. It is against religion, as presented by these bodies, that I have felt it my duty to testify.

I conclude these remarks by copying the following portrait of the religion of the south, (which is, by communion and fellowship, the religion of the north,) which I soberly affirm is "true to the life," and without caricature or the slightest exaggeration. It is said to have been drawn, several years before the present anti-slavery agitation began, by a northern Methodist preacher, who, while residing at the south, had an opportunity to see slaveholding morals, manners, and piety, with his own eyes. "Shall I not visit for these things? saith the Lord. Shall not my soul be avenged on such a nation as this?"

A PARODY

"Come, saints and sinners, hear me tell
How pious priests whip Jack and Nell,
And women buy and children sell,
And preach all sinners down to hell,
And sing of heavenly union.

"They'll bleat and baa, dona like goats,
Gorge down black sheep, and strain at motes,
Array their backs in fine black coats,
Then seize their negroes by their throats,
And choke, for heavenly union.

"They'll church you if you sip a dram,
And damn you if you steal a lamb;
Yet rob old Tony, Doll, and Sam,
Of human rights, and bread and ham;
Kidnapper's heavenly union.

"They'll loudly talk of Christ's reward,
And bind his image with a cord,
And scold, and swing the lash abhorred,
And sell their brother in the Lord
To handcuffed heavenly union.

"They'll read and sing a sacred song,
And make a prayer both loud and long,
And teach the right and do the wrong,
Hailing the brother, sister throng,
With words of heavenly union.

"We wonder how such saints can sing,
Or praise the Lord upon the wing,
Who roar, and scold, and whip, and sting,
And to their slaves and mammon cling,
In guilty conscience union.

"They'll raise tobacco, corn, and rye,

And drive, and thieve, and cheat, and lie,
And lay up treasures in the sky,
By making switch and cowskin fly,
In hope of heavenly union.

"They'll crack old Tony on the skull,
And preach and roar like Bashan bull,
Or braying ass, of mischief full,
Then seize old Jacob by the wool,
And pull for heavenly union.

"A roaring, ranting, sleek man-thief,
Who lived on mutton, veal, and beef,
Yet never would afford relief
To needy, sable sons of grief,
Was big with heavenly union.

"'Love not the world,' the preacher said,
And winked his eye, and shook his head;
He seized on Tom, and Dick, and Ned,
Cut short their meat, and clothes, and bread,
Yet still loved heavenly union.

"Another preacher whining spoke
Of One whose heart for sinners broke:
He tied old Nanny to an oak,
And drew the blood at every stroke,
And prayed for heavenly union.

"Two others oped their iron jaws,
And waved their children-stealing paws;
There sat their children in gewgaws;
By stinting negroes' backs and maws,
They kept up heavenly union.

"All good from Jack another takes,
And entertains their flirts and rakes,
Who dress as sleek as glossy snakes,
And cram their mouths with sweetened cakes;
And this goes down for union."

Sincerely and earnestly hoping that this little book may do something toward throwing light on the American slave system, and hastening the glad day of deliverance to the millions of my brethren in bonds—faithfully relying upon the power of truth, love, and justice, for success in my humble efforts—and solemnly pledging my self anew to the sacred cause,—I subscribe myself,

FREDERICK DOUGLASS LYNN,
Mass., April 28, 1845.
THE END

MY ESCAPE FROM SLAVERY

In the first narrative of my experience in slavery, written nearly forty years ago, and in various writings since, I have given the public what I considered very good reasons for withholding the manner of my escape. In substance these reasons were, first, that such publication at any time during the existence of slavery might be used by the master against the slave, and prevent the future escape of any who might adopt the same means that I did. The second reason was, if possible, still more binding to silence: the publication of details would certainly have put in peril the persons and property of those who assisted. Murder itself was not more sternly and certainly punished in the State of Maryland than that of aiding and abetting the escape of a slave. Many colored men, for no other crime than that of giving aid to a fugitive slave, have, like Charles T. Torrey, perished in prison. The abolition of slavery in my native State and throughout the country, and the lapse of time, render the caution hitherto observed no longer necessary. But even since the abolition of slavery, I have sometimes thought it well enough to baffle curiosity by saying that while slavery existed there were good reasons for not telling the manner of my escape, and since slavery had ceased to exist, there was no reason for telling it. I shall now, however, cease to avail myself of this formula, and, as far as I can, endeavor to satisfy this very natural curiosity. I should, perhaps, have yielded to that feeling sooner, had there been anything very heroic or thrilling in the incidents connected with my escape, for I am sorry to say I have nothing of that sort to tell; and yet the courage that could risk betrayal and the bravery which was ready to encounter death, if need be, in pursuit of freedom, were essential features in the undertaking. My success was due to address rather than courage, to good luck rather than bravery. My means of escape were provided for me by the very men who were making laws to hold and bind me more securely in slavery.

It was the custom in the State of Maryland to require the free colored people to have what were called free papers. These instruments they were required to renew very often, and by charging a fee for this writing, considerable sums from time to time were collected by the State. In these papers the name, age, color, height, and form of the freeman were described, together with any scars or other marks upon his person which could assist in his identification. This device in some measure defeated itself—since more than one man could be found to answer the same general description. Hence many slaves could escape by personating the owner of one set of papers; and this was often done as follows: A slave, nearly or sufficiently answering the description set forth in the papers, would borrow or hire them till by means of them he could escape to a free State, and then, by mail or otherwise, would return them to the owner. The operation was a hazardous one for the lender as well as for the borrower. A failure on the part of the fugitive to send back the papers would imperil his benefactor, and the discovery of the papers in possession of the wrong man would imperil both the fugitive and his friend. It was, therefore, an act of supreme trust on the part of a freeman of color thus to put in jeopardy his own liberty that another might be free. It was, however, not unfrequently bravely done, and was seldom discovered. I was not so fortunate as to resemble any of my free acquaintances sufficiently to answer the description of their papers. But I had a friend—a sailor—who owned a sailor's protection, which answered somewhat the purpose of free papers—describing his person, and certifying to the fact that he was a free American sailor. The instrument had at its head the American eagle, which gave it the appearance at once of an authorized document. This protection, when in my hands, did not describe its bearer very accurately. Indeed, it called for a man much darker than myself, and close examination of it would have caused my arrest at the start.

In order to avoid this fatal scrutiny on the part of railroad officials, I arranged with Isaac Rolls, a Baltimore hackman, to bring my baggage to the Philadelphia train just on the moment of starting, and jumped upon the car myself when the train was in motion. Had I gone into the station and offered to purchase a ticket, I should have been instantly and carefully examined, and undoubtedly arrested. In choosing this plan I considered the jostle of the train, and the natural haste of the conductor, in a train crowded with passengers, and relied upon my skill and address in playing the sailor, as described in my protection, to do the rest. One element in my favor was the kind feeling which prevailed in Baltimore and other sea-ports at the time, toward "those who go down to the sea in ships." "Free trade and sailors' rights" just then expressed the sentiment of the country. In my clothing I was rigged out in sailor style. I had on a red shirt and a tarpaulin hat, and a black cravat tied in sailor fashion carelessly and loosely about my neck. My knowledge of ships and sailor's talk came much to my assistance, for I knew a ship from stem to stern, and from keelson to cross-trees, and could talk sailor like an "old salt." I was well on the way to Havre de Grace before the conductor came into the negro car to collect tickets and examine the papers of his black passengers. This was a critical moment in the drama. My whole future depended upon the decision of this conductor. Agitated though I was while this ceremony was proceeding, still, externally, at least, I was apparently calm and self-possessed. He went on with his duty—examining several colored passengers before reaching me. He was somewhat harsh in tome and peremptory in manner until he reached me, when, strange enough, and to my surprise and relief, his whole manner changed. Seeing that I did not readily produce my free papers, as the other colored persons in the car had done, he said to me, in friendly contrast with his bearing toward the others:

"I suppose you have your free papers?"

To which I answered:

"No sir; I never carry my free papers to sea with me."

"But you have something to show that you are a freeman, haven't you?"

"Yes, sir," I answered; "I have a paper with the American Eagle on it, and that will carry me around the world."

With this I drew from my deep sailor's pocket my seaman's protection, as before described. The merest glance at the paper satisfied him, and he took my fare and went on about his business. This moment of time was one of the most anxious I ever experienced. Had the conductor looked closely at the paper, he could not have failed to discover that it called for a very different-looking person from myself, and in that case it would have been his duty to arrest me on the instant, and send me back to Baltimore from the first station. When he left me with the assurance that I was all right, though much relieved, I realized that I was still in great danger: I was still in Maryland, and subject to arrest at any moment. I saw on the train several persons who would have known me in any other clothes, and I feared they might recognize me, even in my sailor "rig," and report me to the conductor, who would then subject me to a closer examination, which I knew well would be fatal to me.

Though I was not a murderer fleeing from justice, I felt perhaps quite as miserable as such a criminal. The train was moving at a very high rate of speed for that epoch of railroad travel, but to my anxious mind it was moving far too slowly. Minutes were hours, and hours were days during this part of my flight. After Maryland, I was to pass through Delaware—another slave State, where slave-catchers generally awaited their prey, for it was not in the interior of the State, but on its borders, that these human hounds were most vigilant and active. The border lines between slavery and freedom were the dangerous ones for the fugitives. The heart of no fox or deer, with hungry hounds on his trail in full chase, could have beaten more anxiously or noisily than did mine from the time I left Baltimore till I reached Philadelphia. The passage of the Susquehanna River at Havre de Grace was at that time made by ferry-boat, on board of which I met a young colored man by the name of Nichols, who came very near betraying me. He was a "hand" on the boat, but, instead of minding his business, he insisted upon knowing me, and asking me dangerous questions as to where I was going, when I was coming back, etc. I got away from my old and inconvenient acquaintance as soon as I could decently do so, and went to another part of the boat. Once across the river, I encountered a new danger. Only a few days before, I had been at work on a revenue cutter, in Mr. Price's ship-yard in Baltimore, under the care of Captain McGowan. On the meeting at this point of the two trains, the one going south stopped on the track just opposite to the one going north, and it so happened that this Captain McGowan sat at a window where he could see me very distinctly, and would certainly have recognized me had he looked at me but for a second. Fortunately, in the hurry of the moment, he did not see me; and the trains soon passed each other on their respective ways. But this was not my only hair-breadth escape. A German blacksmith whom I knew well was on the train with me, and looked at me very intently, as if he thought he had seen me somewhere before in his travels. I really believe he knew me, but had no heart to betray me. At any rate, he saw me escaping and held his peace.

The last point of imminent danger, and the one I dreaded most, was Wilmington. Here we left the train and took the steam-boat for Philadelphia. In making the change here I again apprehended arrest, but no one disturbed me, and I was soon on the broad and beautiful Delaware, speeding away to the Quaker City. On reaching Philadelphia in the afternoon, I inquired of a colored man how I could get on to New York. He directed me to the William-street depot, and thither I went, taking the train that night. I reached New York Tuesday morning, having completed the journey in less than twenty-four hours.

My free life began on the third of September, 1838. On the morning of the fourth of that month, after an anxious and most perilous but safe journey, I found myself in the big city of New York, a FREE MAN—one more added to the mighty throng which, like the confused waves of the troubled sea, surged to and fro between the lofty walls of Broadway. Though dazzled with the wonders which met me on every hand, my thoughts could not be much withdrawn from my strange situation. For the moment, the dreams of my youth and the hopes of my manhood were completely fulfilled. The bonds that had held me to "old master" were broken. No man now had a right to call me his slave or assert mastery over me. I was in the rough and tumble of an outdoor world, to take my chance with the rest of its busy number. I have often been asked how I felt when first I found myself on free soil. There is scarcely anything in my experience about which I could not give a more satisfactory answer. A new world had opened upon me. If life is more than breath and the "quick round of blood," I lived more in that one day than in a year of my slave life. It was a time of joyous excitement which words can but tamely describe. In a letter written to a friend soon after reaching New York, I said: "I felt as one might feel upon escape from a den of hungry lions." Anguish and grief, like darkness and rain, may be depicted; but gladness and joy, like the rainbow, defy the skill of pen or pencil. During ten or fifteen years I had been, as it were, dragging a heavy chain which no strength of mine could break; I was not only a slave, but a slave for life. I might become a husband, a father, an aged man, but through all, from birth to death, from the cradle to the grave, I had felt myself doomed. All efforts I had previously made to secure my freedom had not only failed, but had seemed only to rivet my fetters the more firmly, and to render my escape more difficult. Baffled, entangled, and discouraged, I had at times asked myself the question, May not my condition after all be God's work, and ordered for a wise purpose, and if so, Is not submission my duty? A contest had in fact been going on in my mind for a long time, between the clear consciousness of right and the plausible make-shifts of theology and superstition. The one held me an abject slave—a prisoner for life, punished for some transgression in which I had no lot nor part; and the other counseled me to manly endeavor to secure my freedom. This contest was now ended; my chains were broken, and the victory brought me unspeakable joy.

But my gladness was short-lived, for I was not yet out of the reach and power of the slave-holders. I soon found that New York was not quite so free or so safe a refuge as I had supposed, and a sense of loneliness and insecurity again oppressed me most sadly. I chanced to meet on the street, a few hours after my landing, a fugitive slave whom I had once known well in slavery. The information received from him alarmed me. The fugitive in question was known in Baltimore as "Allender's Jake," but in New York he wore the more respectable name of "William Dixon." Jake, in law, was the property of Doctor Allender, and Tolly Allender, the son of the doctor, had once made an effort to recapture MR. DIXON, but had failed for want of evidence to support his claim. Jake told me the circumstances of this attempt, and how narrowly he escaped being sent back to slavery and torture. He told me that New York was then full of Southerners returning from the Northern watering-places; that the colored people of New York were not to be trusted; that there were hired men of my own color who would betray me for a few dollars; that there were hired men ever on the lookout for fugitives; that I must trust no man with my secret; that I must not think of going either upon the wharves or into any colored boarding-house, for all such places were closely watched; that he was himself unable to help me; and, in fact, he seemed while speaking to me to fear lest I myself might be a spy and a betrayer. Under this apprehension, as I suppose, he showed signs of wishing to be rid of me, and with whitewash brush in hand, in search of work, he soon disappeared.

This picture, given by poor "Jake," of New York, was a damper to my enthusiasm. My little store of money would soon be exhausted, and since it would be unsafe for me to go on the wharves for work, and I had no introductions elsewhere, the prospect for me was far from cheerful. I saw the wisdom of keeping away from the ship-yards, for, if pursued, as I felt certain I should be, Mr. Auld, my "master," would naturally seek me there among the calkers. Every door seemed closed against me. I was in the midst of an ocean of my fellow-men, and yet a perfect stranger to every one. I was without home, without acquaintance, without money, without credit, without work, and without any definite knowledge as to what course to take, or where to look for succor. In such an extremity, a man had something besides his new-born freedom to think of. While wandering about the streets of New York, and lodging at least one night among the barrels on one of the wharves, I was indeed free—from slavery, but free from food and shelter as well. I kept my secret to myself as long as I could, but I was compelled at last to seek some one who would befriend me without taking advantage of my destitution to betray me. Such a person I found in a sailor named Stuart, a warm-hearted and generous fellow, who, from his humble home on Centre street, saw me standing on the opposite sidewalk, near the Tombs prison. As he approached me, I ventured a remark to him which at once enlisted his interest in me. He took me to his home to spend the night, and in the morning went with me to Mr. David Ruggles, the secretary of the New York Vigilance Committee, a co-worker with Isaac T. Hopper, Lewis and Arthur Tappan, Theodore S. Wright, Samuel Cornish, Thomas Downing, Philip A. Bell, and other true men of their time. All these (save Mr. Bell, who still lives, and is editor and publisher of a paper called the "Elevator," in San Francisco) have finished their work on earth. Once in the hands of these brave and wise men, I felt comparatively safe. With Mr. Ruggles, on the corner of Lispenard and Church streets, I was hidden several days, during which time my intended wife came on from Baltimore at my call, to share the burdens of life with me. She was a free woman, and came at once on getting the good news of my safety. We were married by Rev. J. W. C. Pennington, then a well-known and respected Presbyterian minister. I had no money with which to pay the marriage fee, but he seemed well pleased with our thanks.

Mr. Ruggles was the first officer on the "Underground Railroad" whom I met after coming North, and was, indeed, the only one with whom I had anything to do till I became such an officer myself. Learning that my trade was that of a calker, he promptly decided that the best place for me was in New Bedford, Mass. He told me that many ships for whaling voyages were fitted out there, and that I might there find work at my trade and make a good living. So, on the day of the marriage ceremony, we took our little luggage to the steamer John W. Richmond, which, at that time, was one of the line running between New York and Newport, R. I. Forty-three years ago colored travelers were not permitted in the cabin, nor allowed abaft the paddle-wheels of a steam vessel. They were compelled, whatever the weather might be,—whether cold or hot, wet or dry,—to spend the night on deck. Unjust as this regulation was, it did not trouble us much; we had fared much harder before. We arrived at Newport the next morning, and soon after an old fashioned stage-coach, with "New Bedford" in large yellow letters on its sides, came down to the wharf. I had not money enough to pay our fare, and stood hesitating what to do. Fortunately for us, there were two Quaker gentlemen who were about to take passage on the stage,—Friends William C. Taber and Joseph Ricketson,—who at once discerned our true situation, and, in a peculiarly quiet way, addressing me, Mr. Taber said: "Thee get in." I never obeyed an order with more alacrity, and we were soon on our way to our new home. When we reached "Stone Bridge" the passengers alighted for breakfast, and paid their fares to the driver. We took no breakfast, and, when asked for our fares, I told the driver I would make it right with him when we reached New Bedford. I expected some objection to this on his part, but he made none. When, however, we reached New Bedford, he took our baggage, including three music-books,—two of them collections by Dyer, and one by Shaw,—and held them until I was able to redeem them by paying to him the amount due for our rides. This was soon done, for Mr. Nathan Johnson not only received me kindly and hospitably, but, on being informed about our baggage, at once loaned me the two dollars with which to square accounts with the stage-driver. Mr. and Mrs. Nathan Johnson reached a good old age, and now rest from their labors. I am under many grateful obligations to them. They not only "took me in when a stranger" and "fed me when hungry," but taught me how to make an honest living. Thus, in a fortnight after my flight from Maryland, I was safe in New Bedford, a citizen of the grand old commonwealth of Massachusetts.

Once initiated into my new life of freedom and assured by Mr. Johnson that I need not fear recapture in that city, a comparatively unimportant question arose as to the name by which I should be known thereafter in my new relation as a free man. The name given me by my dear mother was no less pretentious and long than Frederick Augustus Washington Bailey. I had, however, while living in Maryland, dispensed with the Augustus Washington, and retained only Frederick Bailey. Between Baltimore and New Bedford, the better to conceal myself from the slave-hunters, I had parted with Bailey and called myself Johnson; but in New Bedford I found that the Johnson family was already so numerous as to cause some confusion in distinguishing them, hence a change in this name seemed desirable. Nathan Johnson, mine host, placed great emphasis upon this necessity, and wished me to allow him to select a name for me. I consented, and he called me by my present name—the one by which I have been known for three and forty years—Frederick Douglass. Mr. Johnson had just been reading the "Lady of the Lake," and so pleased was he with its great character that he wished me to bear his name. Since reading that charming poem myself, I have often thought that, considering the noble hospitality and manly character of Nathan Johnson—black man though he was—he, far more than I, illustrated the virtues of the Douglas of Scotland. Sure am I that, if any slave-catcher had entered his domicile with a view to my recapture, Johnson would have shown himself like him of the "stalwart hand."

The reader may be surprised at the impressions I had in some way conceived of the social and material condition of the people at the North. I had no proper idea of the wealth, refinement, enterprise, and high civilization of this section of the country. My "Columbian Orator," almost my only book, had done nothing to enlighten me concerning Northern society. I had been taught that slavery was the bottom fact of all wealth. With this foundation idea, I came naturally to the conclusion that poverty must be the general condition of the people of the free States. In the country from which I came, a white man holding no slaves was usually an ignorant and poverty-stricken man, and men of this class were contemptuously called "poor white trash." Hence I supposed that, since the non-slave-holders at the South were ignorant, poor, and degraded as a class, the non-slave-holders at the North must be in a similar condition. I could have landed in no part of the United States where I should have found a more striking and gratifying contrast, not only to life generally in the South, but in the condition of the colored people there, than in New Bedford. I was amazed when Mr. Johnson told me that there was nothing in the laws or constitution of Massachusetts that would prevent a colored man from being governor of the State, if the people should see fit to elect him. There, too, the black man's children attended the public schools with the white man's children, and apparently without objection from any quarter. To impress me with my security from recapture and return to slavery, Mr. Johnson assured me that no slave-holder could take a slave out of New Bedford; that there were men there who would lay down their lives to save me from such a fate.

The fifth day after my arrival, I put on the clothes of a common laborer, and went upon the wharves in search of work. On my way down Union street I saw a large pile of coal in front of the house of Rev. Ephraim Peabody, the Unitarian minister. I went to the kitchen door and asked the privilege of bringing in and putting away this coal. "What will you charge?" said the lady. "I will leave that to you, madam." "You may put it away," she said. I was not long in accomplishing the job, when the dear lady put into my hand TWO SILVER HALF-DOLLARS. To understand the emotion which swelled my heart as I clasped this money, realizing that I had no master who could take it from me,—THAT IT WAS MINE—THAT MY HANDS WERE MY OWN, and could earn more of the precious coin,—one must have been in some sense himself a slave. My next job was stowing a sloop at Uncle Gid. Howland's wharf with a cargo of oil for New York. I was not only a freeman, but a free working-man, and no "master" stood ready at the end of the week to seize my hard earnings.

The season was growing late and work was plenty. Ships were being fitted out for whaling, and much wood was used in storing them. The sawing this wood was considered a good job. With the help of old Friend Johnson (blessings on his memory) I got a saw and "buck," and went at it. When I went into a store to buy a cord with which to brace up my saw in the frame, I asked for a "fip's" worth of cord. The man behind the counter looked rather sharply at me, and said with equal sharpness, "You don't belong about here." I was alarmed, and thought I had betrayed myself. A fip in Maryland was six and a quarter cents, called fourpence in Massachusetts. But no harm came from the "fi'penny-bit" blunder, and I confidently and cheerfully went to work with my saw and buck. It was new business to me, but I never did better work, or more of it, in the same space of time on the plantation for Covey, the negro-breaker, than I did for myself in these earliest years of my freedom.

Notwithstanding the just and humane sentiment of New Bedford three and forty years ago, the place was not entirely free from race and color prejudice. The good influence of the Roaches, Rodmans, Arnolds, Grinnells, and Robesons did not pervade all classes of its people. The test of the real civilization of the community came when I applied for work at my trade, and then my repulse was emphatic and decisive. It so happened that Mr. Rodney French, a wealthy and enterprising citizen, distinguished as an anti-slavery man, was fitting out a vessel for a whaling voyage, upon which there was a heavy job of calking and coppering to be done. I had some skill in both branches, and applied to Mr. French for work. He, generous man that he was, told me he would employ me, and I might go at once to the vessel. I obeyed him, but upon reaching the float-stage, where others [sic] calkers were at work, I was told that every white man would leave the ship, in her unfinished condition, if I struck a blow at my trade upon her. This uncivil, inhuman, and selfish treatment was not so shocking and scandalous in my eyes at the time as it now appears to me. Slavery had inured me to hardships that made ordinary trouble sit lightly upon me. Could I have worked at my trade I could have earned two dollars a day, but as a common laborer I received but one dollar. The difference was of great importance to me, but if I could not get two dollars, I was glad to get one; and so I went to work for Mr. French as a common laborer. The consciousness that I was free—no longer a slave—kept me cheerful under this, and many similar proscriptions, which I was destined to meet in New Bedford and elsewhere on the free soil of Massachusetts. For instance, though colored children attended the schools, and were treated kindly by their teachers, the New Bedford Lyceum refused, till several years after my residence in that city, to allow any colored person to attend the lectures delivered in its hall. Not until such men as Charles Sumner, Theodore Parker, Ralph Waldo Emerson, and Horace Mann refused to lecture in their course while there was such a restriction, was it abandoned.

Becoming satisfied that I could not rely on my trade in New Bedford to give me a living, I prepared myself to do any kind of work that came to hand. I sawed wood, shoveled coal, dug cellars, moved rubbish from back yards, worked on the wharves, loaded and unloaded vessels, and scoured their cabins.

I afterward got steady work at the brass-foundry owned by Mr. Richmond. My duty here was to blow the bellows, swing the crane, and empty the flasks in which castings were made; and at times this was hot and heavy work. The articles produced here were mostly for ship work, and in the busy season the foundry was in operation night and day. I have often worked two nights and every working day of the week. My foreman, Mr. Cobb, was a good man, and more than once protected me from abuse that one or more of the hands was disposed to throw upon me. While in this situation I had little time for mental improvement. Hard work, night and day, over a furnace hot enough to keep the metal running like water, was more favorable to action than thought; yet here I often nailed a newspaper to the post near my bellows, and read while I was performing the up and down motion of the heavy beam by which the bellows was inflated and discharged. It was the pursuit of knowledge under difficulties, and I look back to it now, after so many years, with some complacency and a little wonder that I could have been so earnest and persevering in any pursuit other than for my daily bread. I certainly saw nothing in the conduct of those around to inspire me with such interest: they were all devoted exclusively to what their hands found to do. I am glad to be able to say that, during my engagement in this foundry, no complaint was ever made against me that I did not do my work, and do it well. The bellows which I worked by main strength was, after I left, moved by a steam-engine.

Douglass, Frederick. "Reconstruction."
Atlantic Monthly 18 (1866): 761-765.

Abolition Fanaticism in New York

FLAMING
ABOLITION SPEECH
DELIVERED BY THE RUNAWAY SLAVE,
FREDERICK DOUGLASS,
At the Anniversary of the American Anti-Slavery Society,
IN THE TABERNACLE, NEW YORK, MAY 11, 1847.

The following Report will show to Marylanders, how a runaway slave talks, when he reaches the Abolition regions of the country. This presumptive negro was even present at the London World's Temperance Convention, last year; and in spite of all the efforts of the American Delegates to prevent it, he palmed off his Abolition bombast upon an audience of 7000 persons! Of this high-handed measure he now makes his boast in New-York, one of the hot-beds of Abolitionism. The Report is given exactly as published in the New-York Tribune. The reader will make his own comments.

Mr. Douglass was introduced to the audience by Wm. Lloyd Garrison, Esq., President of the American Anti-Slavery Society, and, upon taking the platform, was greeted with enthusiastic and long-continued applause by the vast concourse which filled the spacious Tabernacle to overflowing. As soon as the audience became silent, Mr. D. with, at first, a slight degree of embarrassment, addressed them as follows:

"I am very glad to be here. I am very glad to be present at this Anniversary—glad again to mingle my voice with those with whom I have stood identified, with those with whom I have labored, for the last seven years, for the purpose of undoing the burdens of my brethren, and hastening the day of their emancipation.

I do not doubt but that a large portion of this audience will be disappointed, both by the manner and the matter of what I shall this day set forth. The extraordinary and unmerited eulogies which have been showered upon me, here and elsewhere, have done much to create expectations which, I am well aware, I can never hope to gratify. I am here, a simple man, knowing what I have experienced in Slavery, knowing it to be a bad system, and desiring, by all Christian means, to seek its overthrow. I am not here to please you with an eloquent speech, with a refined and logical address, but to speak to you the sober truths of a heart overborne with gratitude to God that we have in this land, cursed as it is with Slavery, so noble a band to second my efforts and the efforts of others in the noble work of undoing the Yoke of Bondage, with which the majority of the States of this Union are now unfortunately cursed.

Since the last time I had the pleasure of mingling my voice with the voices of my friends on this platform, many interesting and even trying events have occurred to me. I have experienced, within the last eighteen or twenty months, many incidents, all of which it would be interesting to communicate to you; but many of these I shall be compelled to pass over at this time, and confine my remarks to giving a general outline of the manner and spirit with which I have been hailed abroad, and welcomed at the different places which I have visited during my absence of twenty months.

You are aware, doubtless, that my object in going from this country, was to get beyond the reach of the clutch of the man who claimed to own me as his property. I had written a book giving a history of that portion of my life spent in the gall and bitterness and degradation of

Slavery, and in which I also identified my oppressors as the perpetrators of some of the most atrocious crimes. This had deeply incensed them against me, and stirred up within them the purpose of revenge, and my whereabouts being known, I believed it necessary for me, if I would preserve my liberty, to leave the shores of America, and take up my abode in some other land, at least until the excitement occasioned by the publication of my Narrative had subsided. I went to England, Monarchical England, to get rid of Democratic Slavery, and I must confess that, at the very threshold, I was satisfied that I had gone to the right place. Say what you will of England—of the degradation—of the poverty—and there is much of it there—say what you will of the oppression and suffering going on in England at this time, there is Liberty there—there is Freedom there, not only for the white man, but for the black man also. The instant I stepped upon the shore, and looked into the faces of the crowd around me, I saw in every man a recognition of my manhood, and an absence, a perfect absence, of everything like that disgusting hate with which we are pursued in this country. [Cheers.] I looked around in vain to see in any man's face a token of the slightest aversion to me on account of my complexion. Even the cabmen demeaned themselves to me as they did to other men, and the very dogs and pigs of old England treated me as a man! I cannot, however, my friends, dwell upon this anti-Prejudice, or rather the many illustrations of the absence of Prejudice against Color in England—but will proceed, at once, to defend the Right and Duty of invoking English aid and English sympathy for the overthrow of American Slavery, for the education of Colored Americans, and to forward in every way, the interests of humanity; inasmuch as the right of appealing to England for aid in overthrowing Slavery in this country, has been called in question, in public meetings and by the press, in this city.

I cannot agree with my friend Mr. Garrison in relation to my love and attachment to this land. I have no love for America, as such; I have no patriotism. I have no country. What country have I? The Institutions of this country do not know me—do not recognize me as a man. I am not thought of, spoken of, in any direction, out of the Anti-Slavery ranks, as a man. I am not thought of or spoken of, except as a piece of property belonging to some Christian Slaveholder, and all the Religious and Political Institutions of this Country alike pronounce me a Slave and a chattel. Now, in such a country as this I cannot have patriotism. The only thing that links me to this land is my family, and the painful consciousness that here there are 3,000,000 of my fellow creatures groaning beneath the iron rod of the worst despotism that could be devised even in Pandemonium,—that here are men and brethren who are identified with me by their complexion, identified with me by their hatred of Slavery, identified with me by their love and aspirations for Liberty, identified with me by the stripes upon their backs, their inhuman wrongs and cruel sufferings. This, and this only, attaches me to this land, and brings me here to plead with you, and with this country at large, for the disenthrallment of my oppressed countrymen, and to overthrow this system of Slavery which is crushing them to the earth. How can I love a country that dooms 3,000,000 of my brethren, some of them my own kindred, my own brothers, my own sisters, who are now clanking the chains of Slavery upon the plains of the South, whose warm blood is now making fat the soil of Maryland and of Alabama, and over whose crushed spirits rolls the dark shadow of Oppression, shutting out and extinguishing forever the cheering rays of that bright Sun of Liberty, lighted in the souls of all God's children by the omnipotent hand of Deity itself? How can I, I say, love a country thus cursed, thus bedewed with the blood of my brethren? A Country, the Church of which, and the Government of which, and the Constitution of which are in favor of supporting and perpetuating this monstrous system of injustice and blood? I have not, I cannot have, any love for this country, as such, or for its Constitution. I desire to see it overthrown as speedily as possible and its Constitution shivered in a thousand fragments, rather than this foul curse should continue to remain as now. [Hisses and cheers.]

In all this, my friends, let me make myself understood. I do not hate America as against

England, or against any other country or land. I love Humanity all over the globe. I am anxious to see Righteousness prevail in all directions. I am anxious to see Slavery overthrown here; but, I never appealed to Englishmen in a manner calculated to awaken feelings of hatred or disgust, or to inflame their prejudices toward America as a nation, or in a manner provocative of national jealousy or ill-will; but I always appealed to their conscience—to the higher and nobler feelings of the people of that country, to enlist them in this cause. I always appealed to their manhood, that which preceded their being Englishmen, (to quote an expression of my friend Phillips,) I appealed to them as men, and I had a right to do so. They are men, and the Slave is a man, and we have a right to call upon all men to assist in breaking his bonds, let them be born when and live where they may.

But it is asked, 'What good will this do?' or 'What good has it done?' 'Have you not irritated, have you not annoyed your American friends and the American people rather than done them good?' I admit that we have irritated them. They deserve to be irritated. I am anxious to irritate the American people on this question. As it is in physics, so in morals, there are cases which demand irritation and counter-irritation. The conscience of the American public needs this irritation, and I would blister it all over from centre to circumference, until it gives signs of a purer and a better life than it is now manifesting to the world.

But why expose the sins of one nation in the eyes of another? Why attempt to bring one people under the odium of another people? There is much force in this question. I admit that there are sins in almost every country which can be best removed by means confined exclusively to their immediate locality. But such evils and such sins pre-suppose the existence of a moral power in their immediate locality sufficient to accomplish the work of renovation. But, where, pray, can we go to find moral power in this nation sufficient to overthrow Slavery? To what institution, to what party shall we apply for aid? I say we admit that there are evils which can be best removed by influences confined to their immediate locality. But in regard to American Slavery it is not so. It is such a giant crime, so darkening to the soul, so blinding in its moral influence, so well calculated to blast and corrupt all the humane principles of our nature, so well adapted to infuse its own accursed spirit into all around it, that the people among whom it exists have not the moral power to abolish it. Shall we go to the Church for this influence? We have heard its character described. Shall we go to Politicians or Political Parties? Have they the moral power necessary to accomplish this mighty task? They have not. What are they doing at this moment? Voting supplies for Slavery—voting supplies for the extension, the stability, the perpetuation of Slavery in this land. What is the press doing? The same. The pulpit? Almost the same. I do not flatter myself that there is moral power in the land sufficient to overthrow Slavery, and I welcome the aid of England. And that aid will come. The growing intercourse between England and this country, by means of steam navigation, the relaxation of the protective system in various countries in Europe, gives us an opportunity to bring in the aid, the moral and Christian aid of those living on the other side of the Atlantic. We welcome it in the language of the resolution. We entreat our British friends to continue to send their remonstrances across the deep against Slavery in this land. And these remonstrances will have a powerful effect here. Sir, the Americans may tell of their ability, and I have no doubt they have it, to keep back the invader's hosts, to repulse the strongest force that its enemies may send against this country. It may boast, and rightly boast of its capacity to build its ramparts so high that no foe can hope to scale them—to render them so impregnable as to defy the assaults of the world. But, sir, there is one thing it cannot resist, come from what quarter it may. It cannot resist TRUTH. You cannot build your forts so strong, nor your ramparts so high, nor arm yourselves so powerfully, as to be able to withstand the overwhelming MORAL SENTIMENT against Slavery now flowing into this land. For example: Prejudice against Color is continually becoming weaker in this land; and why? Because the whole European Continent denounces this sentiment as unworthy a lodgment in the breast of an enlightened community. And the American abroad dares not now, even in a public conveyance, to lift his voice in defence of this disgusting prejudice.

I do not mean to say that there are no practices abroad which deserve to receive an influence, favorable to their extermination, from America. I am most glad to know that Democratic Freedom—not the bastard Democracy which, while loud in its protestations of regard for Liberty and Equality, builds up Slavery, and, in the name of Freedom fights the battles of Despotism—is making great strides in Europe. We see, abroad, in England especially, happy indications of the progress of American principles. A little while ago England was cursed by a Corn monopoly—by that giant monopoly which snatched from the mouths of the famishing Poor the bread which you sent from this land. The community—the people of England demanded its destruction, and they have triumphed! We have aided them, and they aid us, and the mission of the two nations, henceforth, is to serve each other.

Sir, it is said that, when abroad, I misrepresented my country on this question. I am not aware of any misrepresentation. I stated facts and facts only. A gentleman of your own City, Rev. Dr. Cox, has taken particular pains to stigmatize me as having introduced the subject of Slavery illegitimately into the World's Temperance Convention. But what was the fact? I went to that Convention, not as a Delegate—I went into it by the invitation of a Committee of the Convention. I suppose most of you know the circumstances, but I wish to say one word in relation to the spirit and the principle which animated me at that meeting. I went into it at the invitation of the Committee, and spoke not only at their urgent request, but by public announcement. I stood on the platform on the evening referred to, and heard some eight or ten Americans address the 7,000 people assembled in that vast Hall. I heard them speak of the Temperance movement in the land. I heard them eulogize the Temperance Societies in the highest terms, calling on England to follow their example (and England may follow them with advantage to herself;) but I heard no reference made to the 3,000,000 of people in this country who are denied the privilege, not only of Temperance, but of all other Societies. I heard not a word of the American Slaves, who, if seven of them were found together at a Temperance meeting or any other place, would be scourged and beaten by their cruel tyrants. Yes, nine-and-thirty lashes is the penalty required to be inflicted by the law if any of the Slaves get together in a number exceeding seven, for any purpose, however peaceable or laudable. And while these American gentlemen were extending their hands to me, and saying, 'How do you do, Mr. Douglass? I am most happy to meet you here,' &c. &c. I knew that, in America, they would not have touched me with a pair of tongues. I felt, therefore, that that was the place and the time to call to remembrance the 3,000,000 of Slaves, whom I aspired to represent on that occasion. I did so, not maliciously, but with a desire, only, to subserve the best interests of my race. I besought the American Delegates who had at first responded to my speech with shouts of applause, when they should arrive at home, to extend the borders of their Temperance Societies, so as to include the 500,000 Colored People in the Northern States of the Union. I also called to mind the facts in relation to the mob that occurred in the City of Philadelphia in the year 1842. I stated these facts to show to the British public how difficult it is for a colored man in this country to do anything to elevate himself or his race from the state of degradation in which they are plunged; how difficult it is for him to be virtuous or temperate, or anything but a menial, an outcast. You all remember the circumstances of the mob to which I have alluded. A number of intelligent, philanthropic, manly colored men, desirous of snatching their colored brethren from the fangs of intemperance, formed themselves into a procession and walked through the streets of Philadelphia with appropriate banners, and badges, and mottoes. I stated the fact that that procession was not allowed to proceed far, in the City of Philadelphia—the American City of Brotherly Love, the city of all others loudest in its boasts of freedom and liberty—before these noble-minded men were assaulted by the citizens, their banners torn in shreds and themselves trampled in the dust, and inhumanly beaten, and all their bright and fond hopes and anticipations in behalf of their friends and their race blasted by the wanton cruelty of their white fellow citizens. And all this was done for no other reason than that they had presumed to walk through the streets with Temperance banners and badges, like human beings.

The statement of this fact caused the whole Convention to break forth in one general expression of intense disgust at such atrocious and inhuman conduct. This disturbed the composure of some of our American representatives, who, in serious alarm, caught hold of the skirts of my coat, and attempted to make me desist from my exposition of the situation of the colored race in this country. There was one Doctor of Divinity there—the ugliest man that I ever saw in my life—who almost tore the skirts of my coat off, so vehement was he in his friendly attempts to induce me to yield the floor. But fortunately the audience came to my rescue, and demanded that I should go on, and I did go on, and, I trust, discharged my duty to my brethren in bonds and the cause of Human Liberty, in a manner not altogether unworthy the occasion.

I have been accused of dragging the question of Slavery into the Convention. I had a right to do so. It was the World's Convention—not the Convention of any sect or number of sects—not the convention of any particular Nation—not a man's nor a woman's Convention, not a black man's nor a white man's Convention, but the World's Convention, the convention of ALL, black as well as white, bond as well as free. And I stood there, as I thought, a representative of 3,000,000 of men whom I had left in rags and wretchedness to be devoured by the accursed Institution which stands by them, as with a drawn sword, ever ready to fall upon their devoted and defenceless heads. I felt, as I said to Dr. Cox, that it was demanded of me by Conscience, to speak out boldly in behalf of those whom I had left behind. [Cheers.] And, sir, (I think I may say this, without subjecting myself to the charge of egotism) I deem it very fortunate for the friends of the Slave, that Mr. Garrison and myself were there just at that time. Sir, the Churches in this country have long repined at the position of the Churches in England on the subject of Slavery. They have sought many opportunities to do away the prejudices of the English Churches against American Slavery. Why, sir, at this time there were not far from Seventy Ministers of the Gospel from Christian America, in England, pouring their leprous pro-slavery distilment into the ears of the people of that country, and by their prayers, their conversation and their public speeches, seeking to darken the British mind on the subject of Slavery, and to create in the English public the same cruel and heartless apathy that prevails in this country in relation to the Slave, his wrongs and his rights. I knew them by their continuous slandering of my race, and at this time, and under these circumstances, I deemed it a happy interposition of God, in behalf of my oppressed, and misrepresented, and slandered people, that one of their number should be able to break his chains and burst up through the dark incrustations of malice and hate and degradation which had been thrown over them, and stand before the British public to open to them the secrets of the prison-house of bondage in America. [Cheers.] Sir, the Slave sends no Delegates to the Evangelical Alliance. [Cheers.] The Slave sends no Delegates to the World's Temperance Convention. Why? Because chains are upon his arms, and fetters fast bind his limbs. He must be driven out to be sold at auction by some Christian Slaveholder, and the money for which his soul is bartered must be appropriated to spread the Gospel among the Heathen.

Sir, I feel it is good to be here. There is always work to be done. Slavery is everywhere. Slavery goes out in the Cambria and comes back in the Cambria. Slavery was in the Evangelical Alliance, looking saintly in the person of Rev. Doctor Smythe; it was in the World's Temperance Convention, in the person of Rev. Mr. Kirk. Dr. Marsh went about saying, in so many words, that the unfortunate Slaveholders in America were so peculiarly situated, so environed by uncontrollable circumstances that they could not liberate their slaves;

that if they were to emancipate them they would be, in many instances, cast into prison. Sir, it did me good to go around on the heels of this gentleman. I was glad to follow him around for the sake of my country, for the country is not, after all, so bad as Rev. Dr. Marsh represented it to be. My fellow countrymen, what think ye he said of you, on the other side of the Atlantic? He said you were not only pro-Slavery, but that you actually aided the Slaveholder in holding his Slaves securely in his grasp; that, in fact, you compelled him to be a Slaveholder. This I deny. You are not so bad as that. You do not compel the Slaveholder to be a Slaveholder.

And Rev. Doctor Cox, too, talked a great deal over there, and among other things, he said that 'many Slave-holders—dear Christian men!—were sincerely anxious to get rid of their slaves;' and to show how difficult it is for them to get rid of their human chattels, he put the following case: A man living in a State, the laws of which compel all persons emancipating their slaves to remove them beyond its limits, wishes to liberate his slaves; but he is too poor to transport them beyond the confines of the State in which he resides; therefore he cannot emancipate them—he is necessarily a slaveholder. But, sir, there was one fact, which I happened, fortunately, to have on hand just at that time, which completely neutralized this very affecting statement of the Doctor's. It so happens that Messrs. Gerrit Smith and Arthur Tappan have advertised for the especial benefit of this afflicted class of Slaveholders, that they have set apart the sum of $10,000, to be appropriated in aiding them to remove their emancipated Slaves beyond the jurisdiction of the State, and that the money would be forthcoming on application being made for it; but no such application was ever made. This shows that however truthful the statements of these gentlemen may be concerning the things of the world to come, they are lamentably reckless in their statements concerning things appertaining to this world. I do not mean to say that they would designedly tell that which is false; but they did make the statements which I have ascribed to them.

And Doct. Cox and others charge me with having stirred up warlike feeling while abroad. This charge, also, I deny. The whole of my arguments and the whole of my appeals, while I was abroad, were in favor of any thing else than war. I embraced every opportunity to propagate the principles of Peace while I was in Great Britain. I confess, honestly, that were I not a Peace man, were I a believer in fighting at all, I should have gone through England, saying to Englishmen, as Englishmen, 'There are 3,000,000 of men across the Atlantic who are whipped, scourged, robbed of themselves, denied every privilege, denied the right to read the Word of the God who made them, trampled under foot, denied all the rights of human beings; go to their rescue; shoulder your muskets, buckle on your knapsacks, and in the invincible cause of Human Rights and Universal Liberty, go forth, and the laurels which you shall win will be as fadeless and as imperishable as the eternal aspirations of the human soul after that Freedom which every being made after God's image instinctively feels is his birthright.' This would have been my course had I been a war man. That such was not my course, I appeal to my whole career while abroad to determine.

Weapons of war we have cast from the battle:
Truth is our armor—our watchword is Love;
Hushed be the sword, and the musketry's rattle,
All our equipments are drawn from above.
Praise then the God of Truth,
Hoary age and ruddy youth.
Long may our rally be
Love, Light and Liberty;
Ever our banner the banner of Peace."
Mr. Douglass took his seat in the midst of the most enthusiastic and overwhelming applause in which the whole of the vast assembly appeared heartily to join.

John Brown

INTRODUCTION.

In substance, this address, now for the first time published, was prepared several years ago, and has been delivered in many parts of the North. Its publication now in pamphlet form is due to its delivery at Harper's Ferry, W. Va., on Decoration day, 1881, and to the fact that the proceeds from the sale of it are to be used toward the endowment of a John Brown Professorship in Storer College, Harper's Ferry—an institution mainly devoted to the education of colored youth.

That such an address could be delivered at such a place, at such a time, is strikingly significant, and illustrates the rapid, vast and wonderful changes through which the American people have been passing since 1859. Twenty years ago Frederick Douglass and others were mobbed in the city of Boston, and driven from Tremont Temple for uttering sentiments concerning John Brown similar to those contained in this address. Yet now he goes freely to the very spot where John Brown committed the offense which caused all Virginia to clamor for his life, and without reserve or qualification, commends him as a hero and martyr in the cause of liberty. This incident is rendered all the more significant by the fact that Hon. Andrew Hunter, of Charlestown,—the District Attorney who prosecuted John Brown and secured his execution,—sat on the platform directly behind Mr. Douglass during the delivery of the entire address and at the close of it shook hands with him, and congratulated him, and invited him to Charlestown (where John Brown was hanged), adding that if Robert E. Lee were living, he would give him his hand also.

ADDRESS.

Not to fan the flame of sectional animosity now happily in the process of rapid and I hope permanent extinction; not to revive and keep alive a sense of shame and remorse for a great national crime, which has brought its own punishment, in loss of treasure, tears and blood; not to recount the long list of wrongs, inflicted on my race during more than two hundred years of merciless bondage; nor yet to draw, from the labyrinths of far-off centuries, incidents and achievements wherewith to rouse your passions, and enkindle your enthusiasm, but to pay a just debt long due, to vindicate in some degree a great historical character, of our own time and country, one with whom I was myself well acquainted, and whose friendship and confidence it was my good fortune to share, and to give you such recollections, impressions and facts, as I can, of a grand, brave and good old man, and especially to promote a better understanding of the raid upon Harper's Ferry of which he was the chief, is the object of this address.

In all the thirty years' conflict with slavery, if we except the late tremendous war, there is no subject which in its interest and importance will be remembered longer, or will form a more thrilling chapter in American history than this strange, wild, bloody and mournful drama. The story of it is still fresh in the minds of many who now hear me, but for the sake of those who may have forgotten its details, and in order to have our subject in its entire range more fully and clearly before us at the outset, I will briefly state the facts in that extraordinary transaction.

On the night of the 16th of October, 1859, there appeared near the confluence of the Potomac and Shenandoah rivers, a party of nineteen men—fourteen white and five colored. They were not only armed themselves, but had brought with them a large supply of arms for such persons as might join them. These men invaded Harper's Ferry, disarmed the watchman, took possession of the arsenal, rifle-factory, armory and other government property at that place, arrested and made prisoners nearly all the prominent citizens of the neighborhood, collected about fifty slaves, put bayonets into the hands of such as were able and willing to fight for their liberty, killed three men, proclaimed general emancipation, held the ground more than thirty hours, were subsequently overpowered and nearly all killed, wounded or captured, by a body of United States troops, under command of Colonel Robert E. Lee, since famous as the rebel Gen. Lee. Three out of the nineteen invaders were captured whilst fighting, and one of these was Captain John Brown, the man who originated, planned and commanded the expedition. At the time of his capture Capt. Brown was supposed to be mortally wounded, as he had several ugly gashes and bayonet wounds on his head and body; and apprehending that he might speedily die, or that he might be rescued by his friends, and thus the opportunity of making him a signal example of slave-holding vengeance would be lost, his captors hurried him to Charlestown two miles further within the border of Virginia, placed him in prison strongly guarded by troops, and before his wounds were healed he was brought into court, subjected to a nominal trial, convicted of high treason and inciting slaves to insurrection, and was executed. His corpse was given to his woe-stricken widow, and she, assisted by Anti-slavery friends, caused it to be borne to North Elba, Essex County, N. Y., and there his dust now reposes, amid the silent, solemn and snowy grandeur of the Adirondacks.

Such is the story; with no line softened or hardened to my inclining. It certainly is not a story to please, but to pain. It is not a story to increase our sense of social safety and security, but to fill the imagination with wild and troubled fancies of doubt and danger. It was a sudden and startling surprise to the people of Harper's Ferry, and it is not easy to conceive of a situation more abundant in all the elements of horror and consternation. They had retired as usual to rest, with no suspicion that an enemy lurked in the surrounding darkness. They had quietly and trustingly given themselves up to "tired Nature's sweet restorer, balmy sleep," and while thus all unconscious of danger, they were roused from their peaceful slumbers by the sharp crack of the invader's rifle, and felt the keen-edged sword of war at their throats, three of their number being already slain.

Every feeling of the human heart was naturally outraged at this occurrence, and hence at the moment the air was full of denunciation and execration. So intense was this feeling, that few ventured to whisper a word of apology. But happily reason has her voice as well as feeling, and though slower in deciding, her judgments are broader, deeper, clearer and more enduring. It is not easy to reconcile human feeling to the shedding of blood for any purpose, unless indeed in the excitement which the shedding of blood itself occasions. The knife is to feeling always an offence. Even when in the hands of a skillful surgeon, it refuses consent to the operation long after reason has demonstrated its necessity. It even pleads the cause of the known murderer on the day of his execution, and calls society half criminal when, in cold blood, it takes life as a protection of itself from crime. Let no word be said against this holy feeling; more than to law and government are we indebted to this tender sentiment of regard for human life for the safety with which we walk the streets by day and sleep secure in our beds at night. It is nature's grand police, vigilant and faithful, sentineled in the soul, guarding against violence to peace and life. But whilst so much is freely accorded to feeling in the economy of human welfare, something more than feeling is necessary to grapple with a fact so grim and significant as was this raid. Viewed apart and alone, as a transaction separate and distinct from its antecedents and bearings, it takes rank with the most cold-blooded and atrocious wrongs ever perpetrated; but just here is the trouble—this raid on Harper's Ferry, no more than Sherman's march to the sea can consent to be thus viewed alone.

There is, in the world's government, a force which has in all ages been recognized, sometimes as Nemesis, sometimes as the judgment of God and sometimes as retributive justice; but under whatever name, all history attests the wisdom and beneficence of its chastisements, and men become reconciled to the agents through whom it operates, and have extolled them as heroes, benefactors and demigods.

To the broad vision of a true philosophy, nothing in this world stands alone. Everything is a necessary part of everything else. The margin of chance is narrowed by every extension of reason and knowledge, and nothing comes unbidden to the feast of human experience. The universe, of which we are a part, is continually proving itself a stupendous whole, a system of law and order, eternal and perfect: Every seed bears fruit after its kind, and nothing is reaped which was not sowed. The distance between seed time and harvest, in the moral world, may not be quite so well defined or as clearly intelligible as in the physical, but there is a seed time, and there is a harvest time, and though ages may intervene, and neither he who ploughed nor he who sowed may reap in person, yet the harvest nevertheless will surely come; and as in the physical world there are century plants, so it may be in the moral world, and their fruitage is as certain in the one as in the other. The bloody harvest of Harper's Ferry was ripened by the heat and moisture of merciless bondage of more than two hundred years. That startling cry of alarm on the banks of the Potomac was but the answering back of the avenging angel to the midnight invasions of Christian slave-traders on the sleeping hamlets of Africa. The history of the African slave-trade furnishes many illustrations far more cruel and bloody.

Viewed thus broadly our subject is worthy of thoughtful and dispassionate consideration. It invites the study of the poet, scholar, philosopher and statesman. What the masters in natural science have done for man in the physical world, the masters of social science may yet do for him in the moral world. Science now tells us when storms are in the sky, and when and where their violence will be most felt. Why may we not yet know with equal certainty when storms are in the moral sky, and how to avoid their desolating force? But I can invite you to no such profound discussions. I am not the man, nor is this the occasion for such philosophical enquiry. Mine is the word of grateful memory to an old friend; to tell you what I knew of him—what I knew of his inner life—of what he did and what he attempted, and thus if possible to make the mainspring of his actions manifest and thereby give you a clearer view of his character and services.

It is said that next in value to the performance of great deeds ourselves, is the capacity to appreciate such when performed by others; to more than this I do not presume. Allow me one other personal word before I proceed. In the minds of some of the American people I was myself credited with an important agency in the John Brown raid. Governor Henry A. Wise was manifestly of that opinion. He was at the pains of having Mr. Buchanan send his Marshals to Rochester to invite me to accompany them to Virginia. Fortunately I left town several hours previous to their arrival.

What ground there was for this distinguished consideration shall duly appear in the natural course of this lecture. I wish however to say just here that there was no foundation whatever for the charge that I in any wise urged or instigated John Brown to his dangerous work. I rejoice that it is my good fortune to have seen, not only the end of slavery, but to see the day when the whole truth can be told about this matter without prejudice to either the living or the dead. I shall however allow myself little prominence in these disclosures. Your interests, like mine, are in the all-commanding figure of the story, and to him I consecrate the hour. His zeal in the cause of my race was far greater than mine—it was as the burning sun to my taper light—mine was bounded by time, his stretched away to the boundless shores of eternity. I could live for the slave, but he could die for him. The crown of martyrdom is high, far beyond the reach of ordinary mortals, and yet happily no special greatness or superior moral excellence is necessary to discern and in some measure appreciate a truly great soul. Cold, calculating and unspiritual as most of us are, we are not wholly insensible to real greatness; and when we are brought in contact with a man of commanding mold, towering high and alone above the millions, free from all conventional fetters, true to his own moral convictions, a "law unto himself," ready to suffer misconstruction, ignoring torture and death for what he believes to be right, we are compelled to do him homage.

In the stately shadow, in the sublime presence of such a soul I find myself standing to-night; and how to do it reverence, how to do it justice, how to honor the dead with due regard to the living, has been a matter of most anxious solicitude.

Much has been said of John Brown, much that is wise and beautiful, but in looking over what may be called the John Brown literature, I have been little assisted with material, and even less encouraged with any hope of success in treating the subject. Scholarship, genius and devotion have hastened with poetry and eloquence, story and song to this simple altar of human virtue, and have retired dissatisfied and distressed with the thinness and poverty of their offerings, as I shall with mine.

The difficulty in doing justice to the life and character of such a man is not altogether due to the quality of the zeal, or of the ability brought to the work, nor yet to any imperfections in the qualities of the man himself; the state of the moral atmosphere about us has much to do with it. The fault is not in our eyes, nor yet in the object, if under a murky sky we fail to discover the object. Wonderfully tenacious is the taint of a great wrong. The evil, as well as "the good that men do, lives after them." Slavery is indeed gone; but its long, black shadow yet falls broad and large over the face of the whole country. It is the old truth oft repeated, and never more fitly than now, "a prophet is without honor in his own country and among his own people." Though more than twenty years have rolled between us and the Harper's Ferry raid, though since then the armies of the nation have found it necessary to do on a large scale what John Brown attempted to do on a small one, and the great captain who fought his way through slavery has filled with honor the Presidential chair, we yet stand too near the days of slavery, and the life and times of John Brown, to see clearly the true martyr and hero that he was and rightly to estimate the value of the man and his works. Like the great and good of all ages— the men born in advance of their times, the men whose bleeding footprints attest the immense cost of reform, and show us the long and dreary spaces, between the luminous points in the progress of mankind,—this our noblest American hero must wait the polishing wheels of after-coming centuries to make his glory more manifest, and his worth more generally acknowledged. Such instances are abundant and familiar. If we go back four and twenty centuries, to the stately city of Athens, and search among her architectural splendor and her miracles of art for the Socrates of to-day, and as he stands in history, we shall find ourselves perplexed and disappointed. In Jerusalem Jesus himself was only the "carpenter's son"—a young man wonderfully destitute of worldly prudence—a pestilent fellow, "inexcusably and perpetually interfering in the world's business,"—"upsetting the tables of the money-changers"—preaching sedition, opposing the good old religion—"making himself greater than Abraham," and at the same time "keeping company" with very low people; but behold the change! He was a great miracle-worker, in his day, but time has worked for him a greater miracle than all his miracles, for now his name stands for all that is desirable in government, noble in life, orderly and beautiful in society. That which time has done for other great men of his class, that will time certainly do for John Brown. The brightest gems shine at first with subdued light, and the strongest characters are subject to the same limitations. Under the influence of adverse education and hereditary bias, few things are more difficult than to render impartial justice. Men hold up their hands to Heaven, and swear they will do justice, but what are oaths against prejudice and against inclination! In the face of high-sounding professions and affirmations we know well how hard it is for a Turk to do justice to a Christian, or for a

Christian to do justice to a Jew. How hard for an Englishman to do justice to an Irishman, for an Irishman to do justice to an Englishman, harder still for an American tainted by slavery to do justice to the Negro or the Negro's friends. "John Brown," said the late Wm. H. Seward, "was justly hanged." "John Brown," said the late John A. Andrew, "was right." It is easy to perceive the sources of these two opposite judgments: the one was the verdict of slave-holding and panic-stricken Virginia, the other was the verdict of the best heart and brain of free old Massachusetts. One was the heated judgment of the passing and passionate hour, and the other was the calm, clear, unimpeachable judgment of the broad, illimitable future.

There is, however, one aspect of the present subject quite worthy of notice, for it makes the hero of Harper's Ferry in some degree an exception to the general rules to which I have just now adverted. Despite the hold which slavery had at that time on the country, despite the popular prejudice against the Negro, despite the shock which the first alarm occasioned, almost from the first John Brown received a large measure of sympathy and appreciation. New England recognized in him the spirit which brought the pilgrims to Plymouth rock and hailed him as a martyr and saint. True he had broken the law, true he had struck for a despised people, true he had crept upon his foe stealthily, like a wolf upon the fold, and had dealt his blow in the dark whilst his enemy slept, but with all this and more to disturb the moral sense, men discerned in him the greatest and best qualities known to human nature, and pronounced him "good." Many consented to his death, and then went home and taught their children to sing his praise as one whose "soul is marching on" through the realms of endless bliss. One element in explanation of this somewhat anomalous circumstance will probably be found in the troubled times which immediately succeeded, for "when judgments are abroad in the world, men learn righteousness."

The country had before this learned the value of Brown's heroic character. He had shown boundless courage and skill in dealing with the enemies of liberty in Kansas. With men so few, and means so small, and odds against him so great, no captain ever surpassed him in achievements, some of which seem almost beyond belief. With only eight men in that bitter war, he met, fought and captured Henry Clay Pate, with twenty-five well armed and mounted men. In this memorable encounter, he selected his ground so wisely, handled his men so skillfully, and attacked the enemy so vigorously, that they could neither run nor fight, and were therefore compelled to surrender to a force less than one-third their own. With just thirty men on another important occasion during the same border war, he met and vanquished four hundred Missourians under the command of Gen. Read. These men had come into the territory under an oath never to return to their homes till they had stamped out the last vestige of free State spirit in Kansas; but a brush with old Brown took this high conceit out of them, and they were glad to get off upon any terms, without stopping to stipulate. With less than one hundred men to defend the town of Lawrence, he offered to lead them and give battle to fourteen hundred men on the banks of the Waukerusia river, and was much vexed when his offer was refused by Gen. Jim Lane and others to whom the defense of the town was confided. Before leaving Kansas, he went into the border of Missouri, and liberated a dozen slaves in a single night, and, in spite of slave laws and marshals, he brought these people through a half dozen States, and landed them safely in Canada. With eighteen men this man shook the whole social fabric of Virginia. With eighteen men he overpowered a town of nearly three thousand souls. With these eighteen men he held that large community firmly in his grasp for thirty long hours. With these eighteen men he rallied in a single night fifty slaves to his standard, and made prisoners of an equal number of the slave-holding class. With these eighteen men he defied the power and bravery of a dozen of the best militia companies that Virginia could send against him. Now, when slavery struck, as it certainly did strike, at the life of the country, it was not the fault of John Brown that our rulers did not at first know how to deal with it. He had already shown us the weak side of the rebellion, had shown us where to strike and how. It was not from lack of native courage that Virginia submitted for thirty long hours and at last was relieved only by Federal troops; but because the attack was made on the side of her conscience and thus armed her against herself. She beheld at her side the sullen brow of a black Ireland. When John Brown proclaimed emancipation to the slaves of Maryland and Virginia he added to his war power the force of a moral earthquake. Virginia felt all her strong-ribbed mountains to shake under the heavy tread of armed insurgents. Of his army of nineteen her conscience made an army of nineteen hundred.

Another feature of the times, worthy of notice, was the effect of this blow upon the country at large. At the first moment we were stunned and bewildered. Slavery had so benumbed the moral sense of the nation, that it never suspected the possibility of an explosion like this, and it was difficult for Captain Brown to get himself taken for what he really was. Few could seem to comprehend that freedom to the slaves was his only object. If you will go back with me to that time you will find that the most curious and contradictory versions of the affair were industriously circulated, and those which were the least rational and true seemed to command the readiest belief. In the view of some, it assumed tremendous proportions. To such it was nothing less than a wide-sweeping rebellion to overthrow the existing government, and construct another upon its ruins, with Brown for its President and Commander-in-Chief; the proof of this was found in the old man's carpet-bag in the shape of a constitution for a new Republic, an instrument which in reality had been executed to govern the conduct of his men in the mountains. Smaller and meaner natures saw in it nothing higher than a purpose to plunder. To them John Brown and his men were a gang of desperate robbers, who had learned by some means that government had sent a large sum of money to Harper's Ferry to pay off the workmen in its employ there, and they had gone thence to fill their pockets from this money. The fact is, that outside of a few friends, scattered in different parts of the country, and the slave-holders of Virginia, few persons understood the significance of the hour. That a man might do something very audacious and desperate for money, power or fame, was to the general apprehension quite possible; but, in face of plainly-written law, in face of constitutional guarantees protecting each State against domestic violence, in face of a nation of forty million of people, that nineteen men could invade a great State to liberate a despised and hated race, was to the average intellect and conscience, too monstrous for belief. In this respect the vision of Virginia was clearer than that of the nation. Conscious of her guilt and therefore full of suspicion, sleeping on pistols for pillows, startled at every unusual sound, constantly fearing and expecting a repetition of the Nat Turner insurrection, she at once understood the meaning, if not the magnitude of the affair. It was this understanding which caused her to raise the lusty and imploring cry to the Federal government for help, and it was not till he who struck the blow had fully explained his motives and object, that the incredulous nation in any wise comprehended the true spirit of the raid, or of its commander. Fortunate for his memory, fortunate for the brave men associated with him, fortunate for the truth of history, John Brown survived the saber gashes, bayonet wounds and bullet holes, and was able, though covered with blood, to tell his own story and make his own defense. Had he with all his men, as might have been the case, gone down in the shock of battle, the world would have had no true basis for its judgment, and one of the most heroic efforts ever witnessed in behalf of liberty would have been confounded with base and selfish purposes. When, like savages, the Wises, the Vallandinghams, the Washingtons, the Stuarts and others stood around the fallen and bleeding hero, and sought by torturing questions to wring from his supposed dying lips some word by which to soil the sublime undertaking, by implicating Gerrit Smith, Joshua R. Giddings, Dr. S. G. Howe, G. L. Stearns, Edwin Morton, Frank Sanborn, and other prominent Anti-slavery men, the brave old man, not only avowed his object to be the emancipation of the slaves, but serenely and proudly announced himself as solely responsible for all that had happened. Though some thought of his own life might at such a moment have seemed natural and excusable, he showed none, and scornfully rejected the idea that he acted as the agent or instrument of any man or set of men. He admitted that he had friends and sympathizers, but to his own head he invited all the bolts of slave-holding wrath and fury, and welcomed them to do their worst. His manly courage and self-forgetful nobleness were not lost upon the crowd about him, nor upon the country. They drew applause from his bitterest enemies. Said Henry A. Wise, "He is the gamest man I ever met." "He was kind and humane to his prisoners," said Col. Lewis Washington.

To the outward eye of men, John Brown was a criminal, but to their inward eye he was a just man and true. His deeds might be disowned, but the spirit which made those deeds possible was worthy highest honor. It has been often asked, why did not Virginia spare the life of this man? why did she not avail herself of this grand opportunity to add to her other glory that of a lofty magnanimity? Had they spared the good old man's life—had they said to him, "You see we have you in our power, and could easily take your life, but we have no desire to hurt you in any way; you have committed a terrible crime against society; you have invaded us at midnight and attacked a sleeping community, but we recognize you as a fanatic, and in some sense instigated by others; and on this ground and others, we release you. Go about your business, and tell those who sent you that we can afford to be magnanimous to our enemies." I say, had Virginia held some such language as this to John Brown, she would have inflicted a heavy blow on the whole Northern abolition movement, one which only the omnipotence of truth and the force of truth could have overcome. I have no doubt Gov. Wise would have done so gladly, but, alas, he was the executive of a State which thought she could not afford such magnanimity. She had that within her bosom which could more safely tolerate the presence of a criminal than a saint, a highway robber than a moral hero. All her hills and valleys were studded with material for a disastrous conflagration, and one spark of the dauntless spirit of Brown might set the whole State in flames. A sense of this appalling liability put an end to every noble consideration. His death was a foregone conclusion, and his trial was simply one of form.

Honor to the brave young Col. Hoyt who hastened from Massachusetts to defend his friend's life at the peril of his own; but there would have been no hope of success had he been allowed to plead the case. He might have surpassed Choate or Webster in power—a thousand physicians might have sworn that Capt. Brown was insane, it would have been all to no purpose; neither eloquence nor testimony could have prevailed. Slavery was the idol of Virginia, and pardon and life to Brown meant condemnation and death to slavery. He had practically illustrated a truth stranger than fiction,—a truth higher than Virginia had ever known,—a truth more noble and beautiful than Jefferson ever wrote. He had evinced a conception of the sacredness and value of liberty which transcended in sublimity that of her own Patrick Henry and made even his fire-flashing sentiment of "Liberty or Death" seem dark and tame and selfish. Henry loved liberty for himself, but this man loved liberty for all men, and for those most despised and scorned, as well as for those most esteemed and honored. Just here was the true glory of John Brown's mission. It was not for his own freedom that he was thus ready to lay down his life, for with Paul he could say, "I was born free." No chain had bound his ankle, no yoke had galled his neck. History has no better illustration of pure, disinterested benevolence. It was not Caucasian for Caucasian—white man for white man; not rich man for rich man, but Caucasian for Ethiopian—white man for black man—rich man for poor man—the man admitted and respected, for the man despised and rejected. "I want you to understand, gentlemen," he said to his persecutors, "that I respect the rights of the poorest and weakest of the colored people, oppressed by the slave system, as I do those of the most wealthy and powerful." In this we have the key to the whole life and career of the man. Than in this sentiment humanity has nothing more touching, reason nothing more noble, imagination nothing more sublime; and if we could reduce all the religions of the world to one essence we could find in it nothing more divine. It is much to be regretted that some great artist, in sympathy with the spirit of the occasion, had not been present when these and similar words were spoken. The situation was thrilling. An old man in the center of an excited and angry crowd, far away from home, in an enemy's country—with no friend near—overpowered, defeated, wounded, bleeding—covered with reproaches—his brave companions nearly all dead—his two faithful sons stark and cold by his side—reading his death-warrant in his fast-oozing blood and increasing weakness as in the faces of all around him—yet calm, collected, brave, with a heart for any fate—using his supposed dying moments to explain his course and vindicate his cause: such a subject would have been at once an inspiration and a power for one of the grandest historical pictures ever painted....

With John Brown, as with every other man fit to die for a cause, the hour of his physical weakness was the hour of his moral strength—the hour of his defeat was the hour of his triumph—the moment of his capture was the crowning victory of his life. With the Alleghany mountains for his pulpit, the country for his church and the whole civilized world for his audience, he was a thousand times more effective as a preacher than as a warrior, and the consciousness of this fact was the secret of his amazing complacency. Mighty with the sword of steel, he was mightier with the sword of the truth, and with this sword he literally swept the horizon. He was more than a match for all the Wises, Masons, Vallandinghams and Washingtons, who could rise against him. They could kill him, but they could not answer him.

In studying the character and works of a great man, it is always desirable to learn in what he is distinguished from others, and what have been the causes of this difference. Such men as he whom we are now considering, come on to the theater of life only at long intervals. It is not always easy to explain the exact and logical causes that produce them, or the subtle influences which sustain them, at the immense heights where we sometimes find them; but we know that the hour and the man are seldom far apart, and that here, as elsewhere, the demand may in some mysterious way, regulate the supply. A great iniquity, hoary with age, proud and defiant, tainting the whole moral atmosphere of the country, subjecting both church and state to its control, demanded the startling shock which John Brown seemed especially inspired to give it.

Apart from this mission there was nothing very remarkable about him. He was a wool-dealer, and a good judge of wool, as a wool-dealer ought to be. In all visible respects he was a man like unto other men. No outward sign of Kansas or Harper's Ferry was about him. As I knew him, he was an even-tempered man, neither morose, malicious nor misanthropic, but kind, amiable, courteous, and gentle in his intercourse with men. His words were few, well chosen and forcible. He was a good business man, and a good neighbor. A good friend, a good citizen, a good husband and father: a man apparently in every way calculated to make a smooth and pleasant path for himself through the world. He loved society, he loved little children, he liked music, and was fond of animals. To no one was the world more beautiful or life more sweet. How then as I have said shall we explain his apparent indifference to life? I can find but one answer, and that is, his intense hatred to oppression. I have talked with many men, but I remember none, who seemed so deeply excited upon the subject of slavery as he. He would walk the room in agitation at mention of the word. He saw the evil through no mist or haze, but in a light of infinite brightness, which left no line of its ten thousand horrors out of sight. Law, religion, learning, were interposed in its behalf in vain. His law in regard to it was that which Lord Brougham described, as "the law above all the enactments of human codes, the same in all time, the same throughout the world—the law unchangeable and eternal—the law written by the finger of God on the human heart—that law by which property in man is, and ever must remain, a wild and guilty phantasy."

Against truth and right, legislative enactments were to his mind mere cobwebs—the pompous emptiness of human pride—the pitiful outbreathings of human nothingness. He used to say "whenever there is a right thing to be done, there is a 'thus saith the Lord' that it shall be done."

It must be admitted that Brown assumed tremendous responsibility in making war upon the peaceful people of Harper's Ferry, but it must be remembered also that in his eye a slave-holding community could not be peaceable, but was, in the nature of the case, in one incessant state of war. To him such a community was not more sacred than a band of robbers: it was the right of any one to assault it by day or night. He saw no hope that slavery would ever be abolished by moral or political means: "he knew," he said, "the proud and hard hearts of the slave-holders, and that they never would consent to give up their slaves, till they felt a big stick about their heads."

It was five years before this event at Harper's Ferry, while the conflict between freedom and slavery was waxing hotter and hotter with every hour, that the blundering statesmanship of the National Government repealed the Missouri compromise, and thus launched the territory of Kansas as a prize to be battled for between the North and the South. The remarkable part taken in this contest by Brown has been already referred to, and it doubtless helped to prepare him for the final tragedy, and though it did not by any means originate the plan, it confirmed him in it and hastened its execution.

During his four years' service in Kansas it was my good fortune to see him often. On his trips to and from the territory he sometimes stopped several days at my house, and at one time several weeks. It was on this last occasion that liberty had been victorious in Kansas, and he felt that he must hereafter devote himself to what he considered his larger work. It was the theme of all his conversation, filling his nights with dreams and his days with visions. An incident of his boyhood may explain, in some measure, the intense abhorrence he felt to slavery. He had for some reason been sent into the State of Kentucky, where he made the acquaintance of a slave boy, about his own age, of whom he became very fond. For some petty offense this boy was one day subjected to a brutal beating. The blows were dealt with an iron shovel and fell fast and furiously upon his slender body. Born in a free State and unaccustomed to such scenes of cruelty, young Brown's pure and sensitive soul revolted at the shocking spectacle and at that early age he swore eternal hatred to slavery. After years never obliterated the impression, and he found in this early experience an argument against contempt for small things. It is true that the boy is the father of the man. From the acorn comes the oak. The impression of a horse's foot in the sand suggested the art of printing. The fall of an apple intimated the law of gravitation. A word dropped in the woods of Vincennes, by royal hunters, gave Europe and the world a "William the Silent," and a thirty years' war. The beating of a Hebrew bondsman, by an Egyptian, created a Moses, and the infliction of a similar outrage on a helpless slave boy in our own land may have caused, forty years afterwards, a John Brown and a Harper's Ferry Raid.

Most of us can remember some event or incident which has at some time come to us, and made itself a permanent part of our lives. Such an incident came to me in the year 1847. I had then the honor of spending a day and a night under the roof of a man, whose character and conversation made a very deep impression on my mind and heart; and as the circumstance does not lie entirely out of the range of our present observations, you will pardon for a moment a seeming digression. The name of the person alluded to had been several times mentioned to me, in a tone that made me curious to see him and to make his acquaintance. He was a merchant, and our first meeting was at his store—a substantial brick building, giving evidence of a flourishing business. After a few minutes' detention here, long enough for me to observe the neatness and order of the place, I was conducted by him to his residence where I was kindly received by his family as an expected guest. I was a little disappointed at the appearance of this man's house, for after seeing his fine store, I was prepared to see a fine residence; but this logic was entirely contradicted by the facts. The house was a small, wooden one, on a back street in a neighborhood of laboring men and mechanics, respectable enough, but not just the spot where one would expect to find the home of a successful merchant. Plain as was the outside, the inside was plainer. Its furniture might have pleased a Spartan. It would take longer to tell what was not in it, than what was; no sofas, no cushions, no curtains, no carpets, no easy rocking chairs inviting to enervation or rest or repose. My first meal passed under the misnomer of tea. It was none of your tea and toast sort, but potatoes and cabbage, and beef soup; such a meal as a man might relish after following the plough all day, or after performing a forced march of a dozen miles over rough ground in frosty weather. Innocent of paint, veneering, varnish or tablecloth, the table announced itself unmistakably and honestly pine and of the plainest workmanship. No hired help passed from kitchen to dining room, staring in amazement at the colored man at the white man's table. The mother, daughters and sons did the serving, and did it well. I heard no apology for doing their own work; they went through it, as if used to it, untouched by any thought of degradation or impropriety. Supper over, the boys helped to clear the table and wash the dishes. This style of housekeeping struck me as a little odd. I mention it because household management is worthy of thought. A house is more than brick and mortar, wood or paint; this to me at least was. In its plainness it was a truthful reflection of its inmates: no disguises, no illusions, no make-believes here, but stern truth and solid purpose breathed in all its arrangements. I was not long in company with the master of this house before I discovered that he was indeed the master of it, and likely to become mine too, if I staid long with him. He fulfilled St. Paul's idea of the head of the family—his wife believed in him, and his children observed him with reverence. Whenever he spoke, his words commanded earnest attention. His arguments which I ventured at some points to oppose, seemed to convince all, his appeals touched all, and his will impressed all. Certainly I never felt myself in the presence of a stronger religious influence than while in this house. "God and duty, God and duty," run like a thread of gold through all his utterances, and his family supplied a ready "Amen." In person he was lean and sinewy, of the best New England mould, built for times of trouble, fitted to grapple with the flintiest hardships. Clad in plain American woolen, shod in boots of cowhide leather, and wearing a cravat of the same substantial material, under six feet high, less than one hundred and fifty lbs. in weight, aged about fifty, he presented a figure straight and symmetrical as a mountain pine. His bearing was singularly impressive. His head was not large, but compact and high. His hair was coarse, strong, slightly gray and closely trimmed and grew close to his forehead. His face was smoothly shaved and revealed a strong square mouth, supported by a broad and prominent chin. His eyes were clear and grey, and in conversation they alternated with tears and fire. When on the street, he moved with a long springing, race-horse step, absorbed by his own reflections, neither seeking nor shunning observation. Such was the man whose name I heard uttered in whispers—such was the house in which he lived—such were his family and household management—and such was Captain John Brown.

He said to me at this meeting, that he had invited me to his house for the especial purpose of laying before me his plan for the speedy emancipation of my race. He seemed to apprehend opposition on my part as he opened the subject and touched my vanity by saying, that he had observed my course at home and abroad, and wanted my co-operation. He said he had been for the last thirty years looking for colored men to whom he could safely reveal his secret, and had almost despaired, at times, of finding such, but that now he was encouraged for he saw heads rising up in all directions, to whom he thought he could with safety impart his plan. As this plan then lay in his mind it was very simple, and had much to commend it. It did not, as was supposed by many, contemplate a general rising among the slaves, and a general slaughter of the slave masters (an insurrection he thought would only defeat the object), but it did contemplate the creating of an armed force which should act in the very heart of the South. He was not averse to the shedding of blood, and thought the practice of carrying arms would be a good one for the colored people to adopt, as it would give them a sense of manhood. No people he said could have self-respect or be respected who would not fight for their freedom. He called my attention to a large map of the U. States, and pointed out to me the far-reaching Alleghanies, stretching away from the borders of New York into the Southern States. "These mountains," he said, "are the basis of my plan. God has given the strength of these hills to freedom; they were placed here to aid the emancipation of your race; they are full of natural forts, where one man for defense would be equal to a hundred for attack; they are also full of good hiding places where a large number of men could be concealed and baffle and elude pursuit for a long time. I know these mountains well and could take a body of men into them and keep them there in spite of all the efforts of Virginia to dislodge me, and drive me out. I would take at first about twenty-five picked men and begin on a small scale, supply them arms and ammunition, post them in squads of fives on a line of twenty-five miles, these squads to busy themselves for a time in gathering recruits from the surrounding farms, seeking and selecting the most restless and daring." He saw that in this part of the work the utmost care must be used to guard against treachery and disclosure; only the most conscientious and skillful should be sent on this perilous duty. With care and enterprise he thought he could soon gather a force of one hundred hardy men, men who would be content to lead the free and adventurous life to which he proposed to train them. When once properly drilled and each had found the place for which he was best suited, they would begin work in earnest; they would run off the slaves in large numbers, retain the strong and brave ones in the mountains, and send the weak and timid ones to the North by the underground Rail-road; his operations would be enlarged with increasing numbers and would not be confined to one locality. Slave-holders should in some cases be approached at midnight and told to give up their slaves and to let them have their best horses to ride away upon. Slavery was a state of war, he said, to which the slaves were unwilling parties and consequently they had a right to anything necessary to their peace and freedom. He would shed no blood and would avoid a fight except in self-defense, when he would of course do his best. He believed this movement would weaken slavery in two ways—first by making slave property insecure, it would become undesirable; and secondly it would keep the anti-slavery agitation alive and public attention fixed upon it, and thus lead to the adoption of measures to abolish the evil altogether. He held that there was need of something startling to prevent the agitation of the question from dying out; that slavery had come near being abolished in Virginia by the Nat. Turner insurrection, and he thought his method would speedily put an end to it, both in Maryland and Virginia. The trouble was to get the right men to start with and money enough to equip them. He had adopted the simple and economical mode of living to which I have referred with a view to save money for this purpose. This was said in no boastful tone, for he felt that he had delayed already too long and had no room to boast either his zeal or his self-denial.

From 8 o'clock in the evening till 3 in the morning, Capt. Brown and I sat face to face, he arguing in favor of his plan, and I finding all the objections I could against it. Now mark! this meeting of ours was full twelve years before the strike at Harper's Ferry. He had been watching and waiting all that time for suitable heads to rise or "pop up" as he said among the sable millions in whom he could confide; hence forty years had passed between his thought and his act. Forty years, though not a long time in the life of a nation, is a long time in the life of a man; and here forty long years, this man was struggling with this one idea; like Moses he was forty years in the wilderness. Youth, manhood, middle age had come and gone; two marriages had been consummated, twenty children had called him father; and through all the storms and vicissitudes of busy life, this one thought, like the angel in the burning bush, had confronted him with its blazing light, bidding him on to his work. Like Moses he had made excuses, and as with Moses his excuses were overruled. Nothing should postpone further what was to him a divine command, the performance of which seemed to him his only apology for existence. He often said to me, though life was sweet to him, he would willingly lay it down for the freedom of my people; and on one occasion he added, that he had already lived about as long as most men, since he had slept less, and if he should now lay down his life the loss would not be great, for in fact he knew no better use for it. During his last visit to us in Rochester there appeared in the newspapers a touching story connected with the horrors of the Sepoy War in British India. A Scotch missionary and his family were in the hands of the enemy, and were to be massacred the next morning. During the night, when they had given up every hope of rescue, suddenly the wife insisted that relief would come. Placing her ear close to the ground she declared she heard the Slogan—the Scotch war song. For long hours in the night no member of the family could hear the advancing music but herself. "Dinna ye hear it? Dinna ye hear it?" she would say, but they could not hear it. As the morning slowly dawned a Scotch regiment was found encamped indeed about them, and they were saved from the threatened slaughter. This circumstance, coming at such a time, gave Capt. Brown a new word of cheer. He would come to the table in the morning his countenance fairly illuminated, saying that he had heard the Slogan, and he would add, "Dinna ye hear it? Dinna ye hear it?" Alas! like the Scotch missionary I was obliged to say "No." Two weeks prior to the meditated attack, Capt. Brown summoned me to meet him in an old stone quarry on the Conecochequi river, near the town of Chambersburgh, Penn. His arms and ammunition were stored in that town and were to be moved on to Harper's Ferry. In company with Shields Green I obeyed the summons, and prompt to the hour we met the dear old man, with Kagi, his secretary, at the appointed place. Our meeting was in some sense a council of war. We spent the Saturday and succeeding Sunday in conference on the question, whether the desperate step should then be taken, or the old plan as already described should be carried out. He was for boldly striking Harper's Ferry at once and running the risk of getting into the mountains afterwards. I was for avoiding Harper's Ferry altogether. Shields Green and Mr. Kagi remained silent listeners throughout. It is needless to repeat here what was said, after what has happened. Suffice it, that after all I could say, I saw that my old friend had resolved on his course and that it was idle to parley. I told him finally that it was impossible for me to join him. I could see Harper's Ferry only as a trap of steel, and ourselves in the wrong side of it. He regretted my decision and we parted.

Thus far, I have spoken exclusively of Capt. Brown. Let me say a word or two of his brave and devoted men, and first of Shields Green. He was a fugitive slave from Charleston, South Carolina, and had attested his love of liberty by escaping from slavery and making his way through many dangers to Rochester, where he had lived in my family, and where he met the man with whom he went to the scaffold. I said to him, as I was about to leave, "Now Shields, you have heard our discussion. If in view of it, you do not wish to stay, you have but to say so, and you can go back with me." He answered, "I b'l'eve I'll go wid de old man;" and go with him he did, into the fight, and to the gallows, and bore himself as grandly as any of the number. At the moment when Capt. Brown was surrounded, and all chance of escape was cut off, Green was in the mountains and could have made his escape as Osborne Anderson did, but when asked to do so, he made the same answer he did at Chambersburgh, "I b'l'eve I'll go down wid de ole man." When in prison at Charlestown, and he was not allowed to see his old friend, his fidelity to him was in no wise weakened, and no complaint against Brown could be extorted from him by those who talked with him.

If a monument should be erected to the memory of John Brown, as there ought to be, the form and name of Shields Green should have a conspicuous place upon it. It is a remarkable fact, that in this small company of men, but one showed any sign of weakness or regret for what he did or attempted to do. Poor Cook broke down and sought to save his life by representing that he had been deceived, and allured by false promises. But Stephens, Hazlett and Green went to their doom like the heroes they were, without a murmur, without a regret, believing alike in their captain and their cause.

For the disastrous termination of this invasion, several causes have been assigned. It has been said that Capt. Brown found it necessary to strike before he was ready; that men had promised to join him from the North who failed to arrive; that the cowardly negroes did not rally to his support as he expected, but the true cause as stated by himself, contradicts all these theories, and from his statement there is no appeal. Among the questions put to him by Mr. Vallandingham after his capture were the following: "Did you expect a general uprising of the slaves in case of your success?" To this he answered, "No, sir, nor did I wish it. I expected to gather strength from time to time and then to set them free." "Did you expect to hold possession here until then?" Answer, "Well, probably I had quite a different idea. I do not know as I ought to reveal my plans. I am here wounded and a prisoner because I foolishly permitted myself to be so. You overstate your strength when you suppose I could have been taken if I had not allowed it. I was too tardy after commencing the open attack in delaying my movements through Monday night and up to the time of the arrival of government troops. It was all because of my desire to spare the feelings of my prisoners and their families."

But the question is, Did John Brown fail? He certainly did fail to get out of Harper's Ferry before being beaten down by United States soldiers; he did fail to save his own life, and to lead a liberating army into the mountains of Virginia. But he did not go to Harper's Ferry to save his life. The true question is, Did John Brown draw his sword against slavery and thereby lose his life in vain? and to this I answer ten thousand times, No! No man fails, or can fail who so grandly gives himself and all he has to a righteous cause. No man, who in his hour of extremest need, when on his way to meet an ignominious death, could so forget himself as to stop and kiss a little child, one of the hated race for whom he was about to die, could by any possibility fail. Did John Brown fail? Ask Henry A. Wise in whose house less than two years after, a school for the emancipated slaves was taught. Did John Brown fail? Ask James M. Mason, the author of the inhuman fugitive slave bill, who was cooped up in Fort Warren, as a traitor less than two years from the time that he stood over the prostrate body of John Brown. Did John Brown fail? Ask Clement C. Vallandingham, one other of the inquisitorial party; for he too went down in the tremendous whirlpool created by the powerful hand of this bold invader. If John Brown did not end the war that ended slavery, he did at least begin the war that ended slavery. If we look over the dates, places and men, for which this honor is claimed, we shall find that not Carolina, but Virginia—not Fort Sumpter, but Harper's Ferry and the arsenal—not Col. Anderson, but John Brown, began the war that ended American slavery and made this a free Republic. Until this blow was struck, the prospect for freedom was dim, shadowy and uncertain. The irrepressible conflict was one of words, votes and compromises. When John Brown stretched forth his arm the sky was cleared. The time for compromises was gone—the armed hosts of freedom stood face to face over the chasm of a broken Union—and the clash of arms was at hand. The South staked all upon getting possession of the Federal Government, and failing to do that, drew the sword of rebellion and thus made her own, and not Brown's, the lost cause of the century.

THE COLOR LINE.

Few evils are less accessible to the force of reason, or more tenacious of life and power, than a long-standing prejudice. It is a moral disorder, which creates the conditions necessary to its own existence, and fortifies itself by refusing all contradiction. It paints a hateful picture according to its own diseased imagination, and distorts the features of the fancied original to suit the portrait. As those who believe in the visibility of ghosts can easily see them, so it is always easy to see repulsive qualities in those we despise and hate.

Prejudice of race has at some time in their history afflicted all nations. "I am more holy than thou" is the boast of races, as well as that of the Pharisee. Long after the Norman invasion and the decline of Norman power, long after the sturdy Saxon had shaken off the dust of his humiliation and was grandly asserting his great qualities in all directions, the descendants of the invaders continued to regard their Saxon brothers as made of coarser clay than themselves, and were not well pleased when one of the former subject race came between the sun and their nobility. Having seen the Saxon a menial, a hostler, and a common drudge, oppressed and dejected for centuries, it was easy to invest him with all sorts of odious peculiarities, and to deny him all manly predicates. Though eight hundred years have passed away since Norman power entered England, and the Saxon has for centuries been giving his learning, his literature, his language, and his laws to the world more successfully than any other people on the globe, men in that country still boast their Norman origin and Norman perfections. This superstition of former greatness serves to fill out the shriveled sides of a meaningless race-pride which holds over after its power has vanished. With a very different lesson from the one this paper is designed to impress, the great Daniel Webster once told the people of Massachusetts (whose prejudices in the particular instance referred to were right) that they "had conquered the sea, and had conquered the land," but that "it remained for them to conquer their prejudices." At one time we are told that the people in some of the towns of Yorkshire cherished a prejudice so strong and violent against strangers and foreigners that one who ventured to pass through their streets would be pelted with stones.

Of all the races and varieties of men which have suffered from this feeling, the colored people of this country have endured most. They can resort to no disguises which will enable them to escape its deadly aim. They carry in front the evidence which marks them for persecution. They stand at the extreme point of difference from the Caucasian race, and their African origin can be instantly recognized, though they may be several removes from the typical African race. They may remonstrate like Shylock -- "Hath not a Jew eyes? hath not a Jew hands, organs, dimensions, senses, affections, passions? fed with the same food, hurt with the same weapons, subject to the same diseases, healed by the same means, warmed and cooled by the same summer and winter, as a Christian is?" -- but such eloquence is unavailing. They are negroes -- and that is enough, in the eye of this unreasoning prejudice, to justify indignity and violence. In nearly every department of American life they are confronted by this insidious influence. It fills the air. It meets them at the workshop and factory, when they apply for work. It meets them at the church, at the hotel, at the ballot-box, and worst of all, it meets them in the jury-box. Without crime or offense against law or gospel, the colored man is the Jean Valjean of American society. He has escaped from the galleys, and hence all presumptions are against him. The workshop denies him work, and the inn denies him shelter; the ballot-box a fair vote, and the jury-box a fair trial. He has ceased to be the slave of society. He may not now be bought and sold like a beast in the market, but he is the trammeled victim of a prejudice, well calculated to repress his manly ambition, paralyze his energies, and make him a dejected and spiritless man, if not a sullen enemy to society, fit to prey upon life and property and to make trouble generally.

When this evil spirit is judge, jury, and prosecutor, nothing less than overwhelming evidence is sufficient to overcome the force of unfavorable presumptions.

Everything against the person with the hated color is promptly taken for granted; while everything in his favor is received with suspicion and doubt.

A boy of this color is found in his bed tied, mutilated, and bleeding, when forthwith all ordinary experience is set aside, and he is presumed to have been guilty of the outrage upon himself; weeks and months he is kept on trial for the offense, and every effort is made to entangle the poor fellow in the confused meshes of expert testimony (the least trustworthy of all evidence). This same spirit, which promptly assumes everything against us, just as readily denies or explains away everything in our favor. We are not, as a race, even permitted to appropriate the virtues and achievements of our individual representatives. Manliness, capacity, learning, laudable ambition, heroic service, by any of our number, are easily placed to the credit of the superior race. One drop of Teutonic blood is enough to account for all good and great qualities occasionally coupled with a colored skin; and on the other hand, one drop of negro blood, though in the veins of a man of Teutonic whiteness, is enough of which to predicate all offensive and ignoble qualities. In presence of this spirit, if a crime is committed, and the criminal is not positively known, a suspicious-looking colored man is sure to have been seen in the neighborhood. If an unarmed colored man is shot down and dies in his tracks, a jury, under the influence of this spirit, does not hesitate to find the murdered man the real criminal, and the murderer innocent.

Now let us examine this subject a little more closely. It is claimed that this wonder-working prejudice -- this moral magic that can change virtue into vice, and innocence to crime; which makes the dead man the murderer, and holds the living homicide harmless -- is a natural, instinctive, and invincible attribute of the white race, and one that cannot be eradicated; that even evolution itself cannot carry us beyond or above it. Alas for this poor suffering world (for four-fifths of mankind are colored), if this claim be true! In that case men are forever doomed to injustice, oppression, hate, and strife; and the religious sentiment of the world, with its grand idea of human brotherhood, its "peace on earth and good-will to men," and its golden rule, must be voted a dream, a delusion, and a snare. But is this color prejudice the natural and inevitable thing it claims to be? If it is so, then it is utterly idle to write against it, preach, pray, or legislate against it, or pass constitutional amendments against it. Nature will have her course, and one might as well preach and pray to a horse against running, to a fish against swimming, or to a bird against flying. Fortunately, however, there is good ground for calling in question this high pretension of a vulgar and wicked prepossession.

If I could talk with all my white fellow-countrymen on this subject, I would say to them, in the language of Scripture: "Come and let us reason together." Now, without being too elementary and formal, it may be stated here that there are at least seven points which candid men will be likely to admit, but which, if admitted, will prove fatal to the popular thought and practice of the times.

First. If what we call prejudice against color be natural, *i.e.*, a part of human nature itself, it follows that it must be co-extensive with human nature, and will and must manifest itself whenever and wherever the two races are brought into contact. It would not vary with either latitude, longitude, or altitude; but like fire and gunpowder, whenever brought together, there would be an explosion of contempt, aversion, and hatred.

Secondly. If it can be shown that there is anywhere on the globe any considerable country where the contact of the African and Caucasian is not distinguished by this explosion of race-wrath, there is reason to doubt that the prejudice is an ineradicable part of human nature.

Thirdly. If this so-called natural, instinctive prejudice can be satisfactorily accounted for by facts and considerations wholly apart from the color features of the respective races, thus placing it among the things subject to human volition and control, we may venture to deny the claim set up for it in the name of human nature.

Fourthly. If any considerable number of white people have overcome this prejudice in themselves, have cast it out as an unworthy sentiment, and have survived the operation, the fact shows that this prejudice is not at any rate a vital part of human nature, and may be eliminated from the race without harm.

Fifthly. If this prejudice shall, after all, prove to be, in its essence and in its natural manifestation, simply a prejudice against condition, and not against race or color, and that it disappears when this or that condition is absent, then the argument drawn from the nature of the Caucasian race falls to the ground.

Sixthly. If prejudice of race and color is only natural in the sense that ignorance, superstition, bigotry, and vice are natural, then it has no better defense than they, and should be despised and put away from human relations as an enemy to the peace, good order, and happiness of human society.

Seventhly. If, still further, this averson* to the negro arises out of the fact that he is as we see him, poor, spiritless, ignorant, and degraded, then whatever is humane, noble, and superior, in the mind of the superior and more fortunate race, will desire that all arbitrary barriers against his manhood, intelligence, and elevation shall be removed, and a fair chance in the race of life be given him.

The first of these propositions does not require discussion. It commends itself to the understanding at once. Natural qualities are common and universal, and do not change essentially on the mountain or in the valley. I come therefore to the second point -- the existence of countries where this malignant prejudice, as we know it in America, does not prevail; where character, not color, is the passport to consideration; where the right of the black man to be a man, and a man among men, is not questioned; where he may, without offense, even presume to be a gentleman. That there are such countries in the world there is ample evidence. Intelligent and observing travelers, having no theory to support, men whose testimony would be received without question in respect of any other matter, and should not be questioned in this, tell us that they find no color prejudice in Europe, except among Americans who reside there. In England and on the Continent, the colored man is no more an object of hate than any other person. He mingles with the multitude unquestioned, without offense given or received. During the two years which the writer spent abroad, though he was much in society, and was sometimes in the company of lords and ladies, he does not remember one word, look, or gesture that indicated the slightest aversion to him on account of color. His experience was not in this respect exceptional or singular. Messrs. Remond, Ward, Garnet, Brown, Pennington, Crummell, and Bruce, all of them colored, and some of them black, bear the same testimony. If what these gentleman say (and it can be corroborated by a thousand witnesses) is true there is no prejudice against color in England, save as it is carried there by Americans -- carried there as a moral disease from an infected country. It is American, not European; local, not general; limited, not universal, and must be ascribed to artificial conditions, and not to any fixed and universal law of nature.

The third point is: Can this prejudice against color, as it is called, be accounted for by circumstances outside and independent of race or color? If it can be thus explained, an incubus may be removed from the breasts of both the white and the black people of this country, as well as from that large intermediate population which has sprung up between these alleged irreconcilable extremes. It will help us to see that it is not necessary that the Ethiopian shall change his skin, nor needful that the white man shall change the essential elements of his nature, in order that mutual respect and consideration may exist between the two races.

Now it is easy to explain the conditions outside of race or color from which may spring feelings akin to those which we call prejudice. A man without the ability or the disposition to pay a just debt does not feel at ease in the presence of his creditor. He does not want to meet him on the street, or in the market-place. Such meeting makes him uncomfortable. He would rather find fault with the bill than pay the debt, and the creditor himself will soon develop in the eyes of the debtor qualities not altogether to his taste.

Some one has well said, we may easily forgive those who injure us, but it is hard to forgive those whom we injure. The greatest injury this side of death, which one human being can inflict on another, is to enslave him, to blot out his personality, degrade his manhood, and sink him to the condition of a beast of burden; and just this has been done here during more than two centuries. No other people under heaven, of whatever type or endowments, could have been so enslaved without falling into contempt and scorn on the part of those enslaving them. Their slavery would itself stamp them with odious features, and give their oppressors arguments in favor of oppression. Besides the long years of wrong and injury inflicted upon the colored race in this country, and the effect of these wrongs upon that race, morally, intellectually, and physically, corrupting their morals, darkening their minds, and twisting their bodies and limbs out of all approach to symmetry, there has been a mountain of gold -- uncounted millions of dollars -- resting upon them with crushing weight. During all the years of their bondage, the slave master had a direct interest in discrediting the personality of those he held as property. Every man who had a thousand dollars so invested had a thousand reasons for painting the black man as fit only for slavery. Having made him the companion of horses and mules, he naturally sought to justify himself by assuming that the negro was not much better than a mule. The holders of twenty hundred million dollars' worth of property in human chattels procured the means of influencing press, pulpit, and politician, and through these instrumentalities they belittled our virtues and magnified our vices, and have made us odious in the eyes of the world. Slavery had the power at one time to make and unmake Presidents, to construe the law, dictate the policy, set the fashion in national manners and customs, interpret the Bible, and control the church; and, naturally enough, the old masters set themselves up as much too high as they set the manhood of the negro too low. Out of the depths of slavery has come this prejudice and this color line. It is broad enough and black enough to explain all the malign influences which assail the newly emancipated millions to-day. In reply to this argument it will perhaps be said that the negro has no slavery now to contend with, and that having been free during the last sixteen years, he ought by this time to have contradicted the degrading qualities which slavery formerly ascribed to him. All very true as to the letter, but utterly false as to the spirit. Slavery is indeed gone, but its shadow still lingers over the country and poisons more or less the moral atmosphere of all sections of the republic. The money motive for assailing the negro which slavery represented is indeed absent, but love of power and dominion, strengthened by two centuries of irresponsible power, still remains.

Having now shown how slavery created and sustained this prejudice against race and color, and the powerful motive for its creation, the other four points made against it need not be discussed in detail and at length, but may only be referred to in a general way.

If what is called the instinctive aversion of the white race for the colored, when analyzed, is seen to be the same as that which men feel or have felt toward other objects wholly apart from color; if it should be the same as that sometimes exhibited by the haughty and rich to the humble and poor, the same as the Brahmin feels toward the lower caste, the same as the Norman felt toward the Saxon, the same as that cherished by the Turk against Christians, the same as Christians have felt toward the Jews, the same as that which murders a Christian in Wallachia, calls him a "dog" in Constantinople, oppresses and persecutes a Jew in Berlin, hunts down a socialist in St. Petersburg, drives a Hebrew from an hotel at Saratoga, that scorns the Irishman in London, the same as Catholics once felt for Protestants, the same as that which insults, abuses, and kills the Chinaman on the Pacific slope -- then may we well enough affirm that this prejudice really has nothing whatever to do with race or color, and that it has its motive and mainspring in some other source with which the mere facts of color and race have nothing to do.

After all, some very well informed and very well meaning people will read what I have now said, and what seems to me so just and reasonable, and will still insist that the color of the negro has something to do with the feeling entertained toward him; that the white man naturally shudders at the thought of contact with one who is black -- that the impulse is one which he can neither resist nor control. Let us see if this conclusion is a sound one. An argument is unsound when it proves too little or too much, or when it proves nothing. If color is an offense, it is so, entirely apart from the manhood it envelops. There must be something in color of itself to kindle rage and inflame hate, and render the white man generally uncomfortable. If the white man were really so constituted that color were, in itself, a torment to him, this grand old earth of ours would be no place for him. Colored objects confront him here at every point of the compass. If he should shrink and shudder every time he sees anything dark, he would have little time for anything else. He would require a colorless world to live in -- a world where flowers, fields, and floods should all be of snowy whiteness; where rivers, lakes, and oceans should all be white; where all the men, and women, and children should be white; where all the fish of the sea, all the birds of the air, all the "cattle upon a thousand hills," should be white; where the heavens above and the earth beneath should be white, and where day and night should not be divided by light and darkness, but the world should be one eternal scene of light. In such a white world, the entrance of a black man would be hailed with joy by the inhabitants. Anybody or anything would be welcome that would break the oppressive and tormenting monotony of the all-prevailing white.

In the abstract, there is no prejudice against color. No man shrinks from another because he is clothed in a suit of black, nor offended with his boots because they are black. We are told by those who have resided there that a white man in Africa comes to think that ebony is about the proper color for man. Good old Thomas Whitson -- a noble old Quaker -- a man of rather odd appearance -- used to say that even he would be handsome if he could change public opinion.

Aside from the curious contrast to himself, the white child feels nothing on the first sight of a colored man. Curiosity is the only feeling. The office of color in the color line is a very plain and subordinate one. It simply advertises the objects of oppression, insult, and persecution. It is not the maddening liquor, but the black letters on the sign telling the world where it may be had. It is not the hated Quaker, but the broad brim and the plain coat. It is not the hateful Cain, but the mark by which he is known. The color is innocent enough, but things with which it is coupled make it hated. Slavery, ignorance, stupidity, servility, poverty, dependence, are undesirable conditions. When these shall cease to be coupled with color, there will be no color line drawn. It may help in this direction to observe a few of the inconsistencies of the color-line feeling, for it is neither uniform in its operations nor consistent in its principles. Its contradictions in the latter respect would be amusing if the feeling itself were not so deserving of unqualified abhorrence. Our Californian brothers, of Hibernian descent, hate the Chinaman, and kill him, and when asked why they do so, their answer is that a Chinaman is so industrious he will do all the work, and can live by wages upon which other people would starve. When the same people and others are asked why they hate the colored people, the answer is that they are indolent and wasteful, and cannot take care of themselves. Statesmen of the South will tell you that the negro is too ignorant and stupid properly to exercise the elective franchise, and yet his greatest offense is that he acts with the only party intelligent enough in the eyes of the nation to legislate for the country. In one breath they tell us that the negro is so weak in intellect, and so destitute of manhood, that he is but the echo of designing white men, and yet in another they will virtually tell you that the negro is so clear in his moral perceptions, so firm in purpose, so steadfast in his convictions, that he cannot be persuaded by arguments or intimidated by threats, and that nothing but the shot-gun can restrain him from voting for the men and measures he approves. They shrink back in horror from contact with the negro as a man and a gentleman, but like him very well as a barber, waiter, coachman, or cook. As a slave, he could ride anywhere, side by side with his white master, but as a freeman, he must be thrust into the smoking-car. As a slave, he could go into the first cabin; as a freeman, he was not allowed abaft the wheel. Formerly it was said he was incapable of learning, and at the same time it was a crime against the State for any man to teach him to read. To-day he is said to be originally and permanently inferior to the white race, and yet wild apprehensions are expressed lest six millions of this inferior race will somehow or other manage to rule over thirty-five millions of the superior race. If inconsistency can prove the hollowness of anything, certainly the emptiness of this pretense that color has any terrors is easily shown. The trouble is that most men, and especially mean men, want to have something under them. The rich man would have the poor man, the white would have the black, the Irish would have the negro, and the negro must have a dog, if he can get nothing higher in the scale of intelligence to dominate. This feeling is one of the vanities which enlightenment will dispel. A good but simple-minded Abolitionist said to me that he was not ashamed to walk with me down Broadway arm-in-arm, in open daylight, and evidently thought he was saying something that must be very pleasing to my self-importance, but it occurred to me, at the moment, this man does not dream of any reason why I might be ashamed to walk arm-in-arm with him through Broadway in open daylight. Riding in a stage-coach from Concord, New Hampshire, to Vergennes, Vermont, many years ago, I found myself on very pleasant terms with all the passengers through the night, but the morning light came to me as it comes to the stars; I was as Dr. Beecher says he was at the first fire he witnessed, when a bucket of cold water was poured down his back -- "the fire was not put out, but he was." The fact is, the higher the colored man rises in the scale of society, the less prejudice does he meet.

The writer has met and mingled freely with the leading great men of his time, -- at home and abroad, in public halls and private houses, on the platform and at the fireside, -- and can remember no instance when among such men has he been made to feel himself an object of aversion. Men who are really great are too great to be small. This was gloriously true of the late Abraham Lincoln, William H. Seward, Salmon P. Chase, Henry Wilson, John P. Hale, Lewis Tappan, Edmund Quincy, Joshua R. Giddings, Gerrit Smith, and Charles Sumner, and many others among the dead. Good taste will not permit me now to speak of the living, except to say that the number of those who rise superior to prejudice is great and increasing. Let those who wish to see what is to be the future of America, as relates to races and race relations, attend, as I have attended, during the administration of President Hayes, the grand diplomatic receptions at the executive mansion, and see there, as I have seen, in its splendid east room, the wealth, culture, refinement, and beauty of the nation assembled, and with it the eminent representatives of other nations, -- the swarthy Turk with his "fez," the Englishman shining with gold, the German, the Frenchman, the Spaniard, the Japanese, the Chinaman, the

Caucasian, the Mongolian, the Sandwich Islander, and the negro, -- all moving about freely, each respecting the rights and dignity of the other, and neither receiving nor giving offense.

"Then let us pray that come it may,
As come it will for a' that,
That sense and worth, o'er a' the earth,
May bear the gree, and a' that;
"That man to man, the world o'er,
Shall brothers be, for a' that."

FREDERICK DOUGLASS.

THE HEROIC SLAVE.

PART I.

Oh! child of grief, why weepest thou?
   Why droops thy sad and mournful brow?
Why is thy look so like despair ?
   What deep, sad sorrow lingers there?

The State of Virginia is famous in American annals for the multitudinous array of her statesmen and heroes. She has been dignified by some the mother of statesmen. History has not been sparing in recording their names, or in blazoning their deeds. Her high position in this respect, has given her an enviable distinction among her sister States. With Virginia for his birth-place, even a man of ordinary parts, on account of the general partiality for her sons, easily rises to eminent stations. Men, not great enough to attract special attention in their native States, have, like a certain distinguished citizen in the State of New York, sighed and repined that they were not born in Virginia. Yet not all the great ones of the Old Dominion have, by the fact of their birth-place, escaped undeserved obscurity. By some strange neglect, *one* of the truest, manliest, and bravest of her children, -- one who, in after years, will, I think, command the pen of genius to set his merits forth, holds now no higher place in the records of that grand old Commonwealth than is held by a horse or an ox. Let those account for it who can, but there stands the fact, that a man who loved liberty as well as did Patrick Henry, -- who deserved it as much as Thomas Jefferson, -- and who fought for it with a valor as high, an arm as strong, and against odds as great, as he who led all the armies of the American colonies through the great war for freedom and independence, lives now only in the chattel records of his native State.

Glimpses of this great character are all that can now be presented. He is brought to view only by a few transient incidents, and these afford but partial satisfaction. Like a guiding star on a stormy night, he is seen through the parted clouds and the howling tempests; or, like the gray peak of a menacing rock on a perilous coast, he is seen by the quivering flash of angry lightning, and he again disappears covered with mystery.

Curiously, earnestly, anxiously we peer into the dark, and wish even for the blinding flash, or the light of northern skies to reveal him. But alas! he is still enveloped in darkness, and we return from the pursuit like a wearied and disheartened mother, (after a tedious and unsuccessful search for a lost child,) who returns weighed down with disappointment and sorrow. Speaking of marks, traces, possibles, and probabilities, we come before our readers.

In the spring of 1835, on a Sabbath morning, within hearing of the solemn peals of the church bells at a distant village, a Northern traveller through the State of Virginia drew up his horse to drink at a sparkling brook, near the edge of a dark pine forest. While his weary and thirsty steed drew in the grateful water, the rider caught the sound of a human voice, apparently engaged in earnest conversation.

Following the direction of the sound, he descried, among the tall pines, the man whose voice had arrested his attention. "To whom can he be speaking?" thought the traveller. "He seems to be alone." The circumstance interested him much, and he became intensely curious to know what thoughts and feelings, or, it might be, high aspirations, guided those rich and mellow accents. Tieing his horse at a short distance from the brook, he stealthily drew near the solitary speaker; and, concealing himself by the side of a huge fallen tree, he distinctly heard the following soliloquy: --

"What, then, is life to me? it is aimless and worthless, and worse than worthless. Those birds, perched on yon swinging boughs, in friendly conclave, sounding forth their merry notes in seeming worship of the rising sun, though liable to the sportsman's fowling-piece, are still my superiors. They *live free*, though they may die slaves. They fly where they list by day, and retire in freedom at night. But what is freedom to me, or I to it? I am a *slave*, -- born a slave, an abject slave, -- even before I made part of this breathing world, the scourge was platted for my back; the fetters were forged for my limbs. How mean a thing am I. That accursed and crawling snake, that miserable reptile, that has just glided into its slimy home, is freer and better off than I. He escaped my blow, and is safe. But here am I, a man, -- yes, *a man*! -- with thoughts and wishes, with powers and faculties as far as angel's flight above that hated reptile, -- yet he is my superior, and scorns to own me as his master, or to stop to take my blows. When he saw my uplifted arm, he darted beyond my reach, and turned to give me battle. I dare not do as much as that. I neither run nor fight, but do meanly stand, answering each heavy blow of a cruel master with doleful wails and piteous cries. I am galled with irons; but even these are more tolerable than the consciousness, the *galling* consciousness of cowardice and indecision. Can it be that I *dare* not run away? *Perish the thought*, I *dare* do any thing which may be done by another. When that young man struggled with the waves *for life*, and others stood back appalled in helpless horror, did I not plunge in, forgetful of life, to save his? The raging bull from whom all others fled, pale with fright, did I not keep at bay with a single pitchfork? Could a coward do that? *No*, -- *no*, -- I wrong myself, -- I am no coward. *Liberty* I will have, or die in the attempt to gain it. This working that others may in idleness! This cringing submission to insolence and curses! This living under the constant dread and apprehension of being sold and transferred, like a mere brute, is *too*much for me. I will stand it no longer. What others have done, I will do. These trusty legs, or these sinewy arms shall place me among the free. Tom escaped; so can I. The North Star will not be less kind to me than to him. I will follow it. I will at least make the trial. I have nothing to lose. If I am caught, I shall only be a slave. If I am shot, I shall only lose a life which is a burden and a curse. If I get clear, (as something tells me I shall,) liberty, the inalienable birth-right of every man, precious and priceless, will be mine. My resolution is fixed. *I shall be free.*"

At these words the traveller raised his head cautiously and noiselessly, and caught, from his hiding-place, a full view of the unsuspecting speaker. Madison (for that was the name of our hero) was standing erect, a smile of satisfaction rippled upon his expressive countenance, like that which plays upon the face of one who has but just solved a difficult problem, or vanquished a malignant foe; for at that moment he was free, at least in spirit. The future gleamed brightly before him, and his fetters lay broken at his feet. His air was triumphant.

Madison was of manly form. Tall, symmetrical, round, and strong. In his movements he seemed to combine, with the strength of the lion, a lion's elasticity. His torn sleeves disclosed arms like polished iron. His face was "black, but comely." His eye, lit with emotion, kept guard under a brow as dark and as glossy as the raven's wing. His whole appearance betokened Herculean strength: yet there was nothing savage or forbidding in his aspect. A child might play in his arms, or dance on his shoulders. A giant's strength, but not a giant's heart was in him. His broad mouth and nose spoke only of good nature and kindness. But his voice, that unfailing index of the soul, though full and melodious, had that in it which could terrify as well as charm. He was just the man you would choose when hardships were to be endured, or danger to be encountered, -- intelligent and brave. He had the head to conceive, and the hand to execute. In a word, he was one to be sought as a friend, but to be dreaded as an enemy.

As our traveller gazed upon him, he almost trembled at the thought of his dangerous intrusion. Still he could not quit the place. He had long desired to sound the mysterious depths of the thoughts and feelings of a slave. He was not, therefore, disposed to allow so providential an opportunity to pass unimproved. He resolved to hear more; so he listened again for those mellow and mournful accents which, he says, made such an impression upon him as can never be erased. He did not have to wait long. There came another gush from the same full fountain; now bitter, and now sweet. Scathing denunciations of the cruelty and injustice of slavery; heart-touching narrations of his own personal suffering, intermingled with prayers to the God of the oppressed for help and deliverance, were followed by presentations of the dangers and difficulties of escape, and formed the burden of his eloquent utterances; but his high resolution clung to him, -- for he ended each speech by an emphatic declaration of his purpose to be free. It seemed that the very repetition of this, imparted a glow to his countenance. The hope of freedom seemed to sweeten, for a season, the bitter cup of slavery, and to make it, for a time, tolerable; for when in the very whirlwind of anguish, -- when his heart's cord seemed screwed up to snapping tension, hope sprung up and soothed his troubled spirit. Fitfully he would exclaim, "How can I leave her? Poor thing! what can she do when I am gone? Oh! oh! 'tis impossible that I can leave poor Susan!"

A brief pause intervened. Our traveller raised his head, and saw again the sorrow-smitten slave. His eye was fixed upon the ground. The strong man staggered under a heavy load. Recovering himself, he argued thus aloud: "All is uncertain here. To-morrow's sun may not rise before I am sold, and separated from her I love. What, then, could I do for her? I should be in more hopeless slavery, and she no nearer to liberty, -- whereas if I were free, -- my arms my own, -- I might devise the means to rescue her."

This said, Madison cast around a searching glance, as if the thought of being overheard had flashed across his mind. He said no more, but, with measured steps, walked away, and was lost to the eye of our traveller amidst the wildering woods.

Long after Madison had left the ground, Mr. Listwell (our traveller) remained in motionless silence, meditating on the extraordinary revelations to which he had listened. He seemed fastened to the spot, and stood half hoping, half fearing the return of the sable preacher to his solitary temple. The speech of Madison rung through the chambers of his soul, and vibrated through his entire frame. "Here is indeed a man," thought he, "of rare endowments, -- a child of God, -- guilty of no crime but the color of his skin, hiding away from the face of humanity, and pouring out his thoughts and feelings, his hopes and resolutions to the lonely woods; to him those distant church bells have no grateful music. He shuns the church, the altar, and the great congregation of christian worshippers, and wanders away to the gloomy forest, to utter in the vacant air complaints and griefs, which the religion of his times and his country can neither console nor relieve. Goaded almost to madness by the sense of the injustice done him, he resorts hither to give vent to his pent up feelings, and to debate with himself the feasibility of plans, plans of his own invention, for his own deliverance. From this hour I am an abolitionist. I have seen enough and heard enough, and I shall go to my home in Ohio resolved to atone for my past indifference to this ill-starred race, by making such exertions as I shall be able to do, for the speedy emancipation of every slave in the land.

PART II.

"The gaudy, blabbling and remorseful day
Is crept into the bosom of the sea;
And now loud-howlig wolves arouse the jades
That drag the tragic melancholy night;
Who with their drowsy, slow, and flagging wings
Clip dead men's graves, and from their misty jaws
Breathe foul contagions, darkness in the air."
Shakspeare.

Five years after the foregoing singular occurence, in the winter of 1840, Mr. and Mrs. Listwell sat together by the fireside of their own happy home in the State of Ohio. The children were all gone to bed. A single lamp burnt brightly on the centre-table. All was still and comfortable within; but the night was cold and dark; a heavy wind sighed and moaned sorrowfully around the house and barn, occasionally bringing against the clattering windows a stray leaf from the large oak trees that embowered their dwelling. It was a night for strange noises and for strange fancies. A whole wilderness of thought might pass through one's mind during such an evening. The smouldering embers, partaking of the spirit of the restless night, became fruitful of varied and fantastic pictures, and revived man bygone scenes and old impressions. The happy pair seemed to sit in silent fascination, gazing on the fire. Suddenly this *reverie* was interrupted by a heavy growl. Ordinarily such an occurrence would have scarcely provoked a single word, or excited the least apprehension. But there are certain seasons when the slightest sound sends a jar through all the subtle chambers of the mind; and such a season was this. The happy pair started up, as if some sudden danger had come upon them. The growl was from their trusty watch-dog.

"What can it mean? certainly no one can be out on such a night as this," said Mrs. Listwell.

"The wind has deceived the dog, my dear; he has mistaken the noise of falling branches, brought down by the wind, for that of the footsteps of persons coming to the house. I have several times to-night thought that I heard the sound of footsteps. I am sure, however, that it was but the wind. Friends would not be likely to come out at such an hour, or such a night; and thieves are too lazy and self-indulgent to expose themselves to this biting frost; but should there be any one about, our brave old Monte, who is on the lookout, will not be slow in sounding the alarm."

Saying this they quietly left the window, whither they had gone to learn the cause of the menacing growl, and re-seated themselves by the fire, as if reluctant to leave the slowly expiring embers, although the hour was late. A few minutes only intervened after resuming their seats, when again their sober meditations were disturbed. Their faithful dog now growled and barked furiously, as if assailed by an advancing foe. Simultaneously the good couple arose, and stood in mute expectation. The contest without seemed fierce and violent. It was, however, soon over, -- the barking ceased, for, with true canine instinct, Monte quickly discovered that a friend, not an enemy of the family, was coming to the house, and instead of rushing to repel the supposed intruder, he was now at the door, whimpering and dancing for the admission of himself and his newly made friend.

Mr. Listwell knew by this movement that all was well; he advanced and opened the door, and saw by the light that streamed out into the darkness, a tall man advancing slowly towards the house, with a stick in one hand, and a small bundle in the other. "It is a traveller," thought he, "who has missed his way, and is coming to inquire the road. I am glad we did not go to bed earlier, -- I have felt all the evening as if somebody would be here to-night."

The man had now halted a short distance from the door, and looked prepared alike for flight or battle. "Come in, sir, don't be alarmed, you have probably lost your way."

Slightly hesitating, the traveller walked in; not, however, without regarding his host with a scrutinizing glance. "No, sir," said he "I have come to ask you a greater favor."

Instantly Mr. Listwell exclaimed, (as the recollection of the Virginia forest scene flashed upon him,) "Oh, sir, I know not your name, but I have seen your face, and heard your voice before. I am glad to see you. *I know all.* You are flying for your liberty, -- be seated, -- be seated, -- banish all fear. You are safe under my roof."

This recognition, so unexpected, rather disconcerted and disquieted the noble fugitive. The timidity and suspicion of persons escaping from slavery are easily awakened, and often what is intended to dispel the one, and to allay the other, has precisely the opposite effect. It was so in this case. Quickly observing the unhappy impression made by his words and action, Mr. Listwell assumed a more quiet and inquiring aspect, and finally succeeded in removing the apprehensions which his very natural and generous salutation had aroused.

Thus assured, the stranger said, "Sir, you have rightly guessed, I am, indeed, a fugitive from slavery. My name is Madison, -- Madison Washington my mother used to call me. I am on my way to Canada, where I learn that persons of my color are protected in all the rights of men; and my object in calling upon you was, to beg the privilege of resting my weary limbs for the night in your barn. It was my purpose to have continued my journey till morning; but the piercing cold, and the frowning darkness compelled me to seek shelter; and, seeing a light through the lattice of your window, I was encouraged to come here to beg the privilege named. You will do me a great favor by affording me shelter for the night."

"A resting-place, indeed, sir, you shall have; not, however, in my barn, but in the best room of my house. Consider yourself, if you please, under the roof of a friend; for such I am to you, and to all your deeply injured race."

While this introductory conversation was going on, the kind lady had revived the fire, and was diligently preparing supper; for she, not less than her husband, felt for the sorrows of the oppressed and hunted ones of earth, and was always glad of an opportunity to do them a service. A bountiful repast was quickly prepared, and the hungry and toil-worn bondman was cordially invited to partake thereof. Gratefully he acknowledged the favor of his benevolent benefactress; but appeared scarcely to understand what such hospitality could mean. It was the first time in his life that he had met so humane and friendly a greeting at the hands of persons whose color was unlike his own; yet it was impossible for him to doubt the charitableness of his new friends, or the genuineness of the welcome so freely given; and he therefore, with many thanks, took his seat at the table with Mr. and Mrs. Listwell, who, desirous to make him feel at home, took a cup of tea themselves, while urging upon Madison the best that the house could afford.

Supper over, all doubts and apprehensions banished, the three drew around the blazing fire, and a conversation commenced which lasted till long after midnight.

"Now," said Madison to Mr. Listwell, "I was a little surprised and alarmed when I came in, by what you said; do tell me, sir, *why* you thought you had seen my face before, and by what you knew me to be a fugitive from slavery; for I am sure that I never was before in this neighborhood, and I certainly sought to conceal what I supposed to be the manner of a fugitive slave."

Mr. Listwell at once frankly disclosed the secret; describing the place where he first saw him; rehearsing the language which he (Madison) had used; referring to the effect which his manner and speech had made upon him; declaring the resolution he there formed to be an abolitionist; telling how often he had spoken of the circumstance, and the deep concern he had ever since felt to know what had become of him; and whether he had carried out the purpose to make his escape, as in the woods he declared he would do.

"Ever since that morning," said Mr. Listwell, "you have seldom been absent from my mind, and though now I did not dare to hope that I should ever see you again, I have often wished that such might be my fortune; for, from that hour, your face seemed to be daguerreotyped on my memory."

Madison looked quite astonished, and felt amazed at the narration to which he had listened. After recovering himself he said, "I well remember that morning, and the bitter anguish that wrung my heart; I will state the occasion of it. I had, on the previous Saturday, suffered a cruel lashing; had been tied tip to the limb of a tree, with my feet chained together, and a heavy iron bar placed between my ankles. Thus suspended, I received on my naked back forty stripes, and was kept in this distressing position three or four hours, and was then let down, only to have my torture increased; for my bleeding back, gashed by the cow-skin, was washed by the overseer with old brine, partly to augment my suffering, and partly, as he said, to prevent inflammation. My crime was that I had stayed longer at the mill, the day previous, than it was thought I ought to have done, which, I assured my master and the overseer, was no fault of mine; but no excuses were allowed. 'Hold your tongue, you impudent rascal,' met my every explanation. Slave-holders are so imperious when their passions are excited, as to construe every word of the slave into insolence. I could do nothing but submit to the agonizing infliction. Smarting still from the wounds, as well as from the consciousness of being whipt for no cause, I took advantage of the absence of my master, who had gone to church, to spend the time in the woods, and brood over my wretched lot. Oh, sir, I remember it well, and can never forget it."

"But this was five years ago; where have you been since?"

"I will try to tell you," said Madison. "Just four weeks after that Sabbath morning, I gathered up the few rags of clothing I had, and started, as I supposed, for the North and for freedom. I must not stop to describe my feelings on taking this step. It seemed like taking a leap into the dark. The thought of leaving my poor wife and two little children caused me indescribable anguish; but consoling myself with the reflection that once free, I could, possibly, devise ways and means to gain their freedom also, I nerved myself up to make the attempt. I started, but ill-luck attended me; for after being out a whole week, strange to say, I still found myself on my master's grounds; the third night after being out, a season of clouds and rain set in, wholly preventing me from seeing the North Star, which I had trusted as my guide, not dreaming that clouds might intervene between us.

"This circumstance was fatal to my project, for in losing my star, I lost my way; so when I supposed I was far towards the North, and had almost gained my freedom, I discovered myself at the very point from which I had started. It was a severe trial, for I arrived at home in great destitution; my feet were sore, and in travelling in the dark, I had dashed my foot against a stump, and started a nail, and lamed myself. I was wet and cold; one week had exhausted all my stores; and when I landed on my master's plantation, with all my work to do over again, -- hungry, tired, lame, and bewildered, -- I almost cursed the day that I was born. In this extremity I approached the quarters. I did so stealthily, although in my desperation I hardly cared whether I was discovered or not. Peeping through the rents of the quarters, I saw my fellow-slaves seated by a warm fire, merrily passing away the time, as though their hearts knew no sorrow. Although I envied their seeming contentment, all wretched as I was, I despised the cowardly acquiescence in their own degradation which it implied, and felt a kind of pride and glory in my own desperate lot. I dared not enter the quarters, -- for where there is seeming contentment with slavery, there is certain treachery to freedom. I proceeded towards the great house, in the hope of catching a glimpse of my poor wife, whom I knew might be trusted with my secrets even on the scaffold. Just as I reached the fence which divided the field from the garden, I saw a woman in the yard, who in the darkness I took to be my wife; but a nearer approach told me it was not she. I was about to speak; had I done so, I would not have been here this night; for an alarm would have been sounded, and the hunters been put on my track. Here were hunger, cold, thirst, disappointment, and chagrin, confronted only by the dim hope of liberty. I tremble to think of that dreadful hour. To face the deadly cannon's mouth in warm blood unterrified, is, I think, a small achievement, compared with a conflict like this with gaunt starvation. The gnawings of hunger conquers by degrees, till all that a man has he would give in exchange for a single crust of bread. Thank God, I was not quite reduced to this extremity.

"Happily for me, before the fatal moment of utter despair, my good wife made her appearance in the yard. It was she; I knew her step. All was well now. I was, however, afraid to speak lest I should frighten her. Yet speak I did; and, to my great joy, my voice was known. Our meeting can be more easily imagined than described. For a time hunger, thirst, weariness, and lameness were forgotten. But it was soon necessary for her to return to the house. She being a house-servant, her absence from the kitchen, if discovered, might have excited suspicion. Our parting was like tearing the flesh from my bones; yet it was the part of wisdom for her to go. She left me with the purpose of meeting me at midnight in the very forest where you last saw me. She knew the place well, as one of my melancholy resorts, and could easily find it, though the night was dark.

"I hastened away, therefore, and concealed myself, to await the arrival of my good angel. As I lay there among the leaves, I was strongly tempted to return again to the house of my master and give myself up; but remembering my solemn pledge on that memorable Sunday morning, I was able to linger out the two long hours between ten and midnight. I may well call them long hours. I have endured much hardship; I have encountered many perils; but the anxiety of those two hours, was the bitterest I ever experienced. True to her word, my wife came laden with provisions, and we sat down on the side of a log, at that dark and lonesome hour of the night. I cannot say we talked; our feelings were too great for that; yet we came to an understanding that I should make the woods my home, for if I gave myself up, I should be whipped and sold away; and if I started for the North, I should leave a wife doubly dear to me. We mutually determined, therefore, that I should remain in the vicinity. In the dismal swamps I lived, sir, five long years, -- a cave for my home during the day. I wandered about at night with the wolf and the bear, -- sustained by the promise that my good Susan would meet me in the pine woods at least once a week. This promise was redeemed, I assure you, to the letter, greatly to my relief. I had partly become contented with my mode of life, and had made up my mind to spend my days there; but the wilderness that sheltererd me thus long took fire, and refused longer to be my hiding-place.

"I will not harrow up your feelings by portraying the terrific scene of this awful conflagration. There is nothing to which I can liken it. It was horribly and indescribably grand.

The whole world seemed on fire, and it appeared to me that the day of judgment had come; that the burning bowels of the earth had burst forth, and that the end of all things was at hand. Bears and wolves, scorched from their mysterious hiding-places in the earth, and all the wild inhabitants of the untrodden forest, filled with a common dismay, ran forth, yelling, howling, bewildered amidst the smoke and flame. The very heavens seemed to rain down fire through the towering trees; it was by the merest chance that I escaped the devouring element. Running before it, and stopping occasionally to take breath, I looked back to behold its frightful ravages, and to drink in its savage magnificence. It was awful, thrilling, solemn, beyond compare. When aided by the fitful wind, the merciless tempest of fire swept on, sparkling, creaking, cracking, curling, roaring, out-doing in its dreadful splendor a thousand thunderstorms at once. From tree to tree it leaped, swallowing them up in its lurid, baleful glare; and leaving them leafless, limbless, charred, and lifeless behind. The scene was overwhelming, stunning, -- nothing was spared, -- cattle, tame and wild, herds of swine and of deer, wild beasts of every name and kind, -- huge night-birds, bats, and owls, that had retired to their homes in lofty tree-tops to rest, perished in that fiery storm. The long-winged buzzard, and croaking raven mingled their dismal cries with those of the countless myriads of small birds that rose up to the skies, and were lost to the sight in clouds of smoke and flame. Oh, I shudder when I think of it! Many a poor wandering fugitive, who, like myself, had sought among wild beasts the mercy denied by our fellow men, saw, in helpless consternation, his dwelling-place and city of refuge reduced to ashes forever. It was this grand conflagration that drove me hither; I ran alike from fire and from slavery."

After a slight pause, (for both speaker and hearers were deeply moved by the above recital,) Mr. Listwell, addressing Madison, said, "If it does not weary you too much, do tell us something of your journeyings since this disastrous burning, -- we are deeply interested in everything which can throw light on the hardships of persons escaping from slavery; we could hear you talk all night; are there no incidents that you could relate of your travels hither? or are they such that you do not like to mention them."

"For the most part, sir, my course has been uninterrupted; and, considering the circumstances, at times even pleasant. I have suffered little for want of food; but I need not tell you how I got it. Your moral code may differ from mine, as your customs and usages are different. The fact is, sir, during my flight, I felt myself robbed by society of all my just rights; that I was in an enemy's land, who sought both my life and my liberty. They had transformed me into a brute; made merchandise of my body, and, for all the purposes of my flight, turned day into night, -- and guided by my own necessities, and in contempt of their conventionalities, I did not scruple to take bread where I could get it."

"And just there you were right," said Mr. Listwell; "I once had doubts on this point myself, but a conversation with Gerrit Smith, (a man, by the way, that I wish you could see, for he is a devoted friend of your race, and I know he would receive you gladly,) put an end to all my doubts on this point. But do not let me interrupt you."

"I had but one narrow escape during my whole journey, " said Madison.

"Do let us hear of it," said Mr. Listwell.

"Two weeks ago," continued Madison, "after travelling all night, I was overtaken by daybreak, in what seemed to me an almost interminable wood. I deemed it unsafe to go farther, and, as usual, I looked around for a suitable tree in which to spend the day. I liked one with a bushy top, and found one just to my mind. Up I climbed, and hiding myself as well I could, I, with this strap, (pulling one out of his old coat-pocket,) lashed myself to a bough, and flattered myself that I should get a *good night's* sleep that day; but in this I was soon disappointed. I had scarcely got fastened to my natural hammock, when I heard the voices of a number of persons, apparently approaching the part of the woods where I was. Upon my word, sir, I dreaded more these human voices than I should have done those of wild beasts. I was at a loss to know what to do. If I descended, I should probably be discovered by the men; and if they had dogs I should, doubtless, be *'treed.'* It was an anxious moment, but hardships and dangers have been the accompaniments of my life; and have, perhaps, imparted to me a certain hardness of character, which, to some extent, adapts me to them. In my present predicament, I decided to hold my place in the tree-top, and abide the consequences. But here I must disappoint you; for the men, who were all colored, halted at least a hundred yards from me, and began with their axes, in right good earnest, to attack the trees. The sound of their laughing axes was like the report of as many well-charged pistols. By and by there came down at least a dozen trees with a terrible crash. They leaped upon the fallen trees with an air of victory. I could see no dog with them, and felt myself comparatively safe, though I could not forget the possibility that some freak or fancy might bring the axe a little nearer my dwelling than comported with my safety.

"There was no sleep for me that day, and I wished for night. You may imagine that the thought of having the tree attacked under me was far from agreeable, and that it very easily kept me on the look-out. The day was not without diversion. The men at work seemed to be a gay set; and they would often make the woods resound with that uncontrolled laughter for which we, as a race, are remarkable. I held my place in the tree till sunset, -- saw the men put on their jackets to be off. I observed that all left the ground except one, whom I saw sitting on the side of a stump, with his head bowed, and his eyes apparently fixed on the ground. I became interested in him. After sitting in the position to which I have alluded ten or fifteen minutes, he left the stump, walked directly towards the tree in which I was secreted, and halted almost under the same. He stood for a moment and looked around, deliberately and reverently took off his hat, by which I saw that I saw that he was a man in the evening of life, slightly bald and quite gray. After laying down his hat carefully, he knelt and prayed aloud, and such a prayer, the most fervent, earnest, and solemn, to which I think I ever listened. After reverently addressing the Almighty, as the all-wise, all-good, and the common Father of all mankind, he besought God for grace, for strength, to bear up under, and to endure, as a good soldier, all the hardships and trials which beset the journey of life, and to enable him to live in a manner which accorded with the gospel of Christ. His soul now broke out in humble supplication for deliverance from bondage. 'O thou,' said he, 'that hearest the raven's cry, take pity on poor me! O deliver me! O deliver me! in mercy, O God, deliver me from the chains and manifold hardships of slavery! With thee, O Father, all things are possible. Thou canst stand and measure the earth. Thou hast beheld and drove asunder the nations, -- all power is in thy hand, -- thou didst say of old, "I have seen the affliction of my people, and am come to deliver them," -- Oh look down upon our afflictions, and have mercy upon us.' But I cannot repeat his prayer, nor can I give you an idea of its deep pathos. I had given but little attention to religion, and had but little faith in it; yet, as the old man prayed, I felt almost like coming down and kneel by his side, and mingle my broken complaint with his.

He had already gained my confidence; as how could it be otherwise? I knew enough of religion to know that the man who prays in secret is far more likely to be sincere than he who loves to pray standing in the street, or in the great congregation. When he arose from his knees, like another Zacheus, I came down from the tree. He seemed a little alarmed at first, but I told him my story, and the good man embraced me in his arms, and assured me of his sympathy.

"I was now about out of provisions, and thought I might safely ask him to help me replenish my store. He said he had no money; but if he had, he would freely give it me. I told him I had *one dollar*; it was all the money I had in the world. I gave it to him, and asked him to purchase some crackers and cheese, and to kindly bring me the balance; that I would remain in or near that place, and would come to him on his return, if he would whistle. He was gone only about an hour. Meanwhile, from some cause or other, I know not what, (but as you shall see very wisely,) I changed my place. On his return I started to meet him; but it seemed as if the shadow of approaching danger fell upon my spirit, and checked my progress. In a very few minutes, closely on the heels of the old man, I distinctly saw *fourteen men*, with something like guns in their hands."

"Oh! the old wretch!" exclaimed Mrs. Listwell "he had betrayed you, had he?"

"I think not," said Madison, "I cannot believe that the old man was to blame. He probably went into a store, asked for the articles for which I sent, and presented the bill I gave him; and it is so unusual for slaves in the country to have money, that fact, doubtless, excited suspicion, and gave rise to inquiry. I can easily believe that the truthfulness of the old man's character compelled him to disclose the facts; and thus were these blood-thirsty men put on my track. Of course I did not present myself ; but hugged my hiding-place securely. If discovered and attacked, I resolved to sell my life as dearly as possible.

"After searching about the woods silently for a time, the whole company gathered around the old man; one charged him with lying, and called him an old villain; said he was a thief; charged him with stealing money; said if he did not instantly tell where he got it, they would take the shirt from his old back, and give him thirty-nine lashes.

"'I did *not* steal the money,' said the old man, 'it was given me, as I told you at the store; and if the man who gave it me is not here, it is not my fault.'

"'Hush! you lying old rascal; we'll make you smart for it. You shall not leave this spot until you have told where you got that money.'

"They now took hold of him, and began to strip him; while others went to get sticks with which to beat him. I felt, at the moment, like rushing out in the midst of them; but considering that the old man would be whipped the more for having aided a fugitive slave, and that, perhaps, in the *melée* he might be killed outright, I disobeyed this impulse. They tied him to a tree, and began to whip him. My own flesh crept at every blow, and I seem to hear the old man's piteous cries even now. They laid thirty-nine lashes on his bare back, and were going to repeat that number, when one of the company besought his comrades to desist. 'You'll kill the d -- d old scoundrel! You've already whipt a dollar's worth out of him, even if he stole it!' 'O yes,' said another, 'let him down. He'll never tell us another lie, I'll warrant ye!' With this, one of the company untied the old man, and bid him go about his business.

"The old man left, but the company remained as much as an hour, scouring the woods. Round and round they went, turning up the underbrush, and peering about like so many bloodhounds. Two or three times they came within six feet of where I lay. I tell you I held my stick with a firmer grasp than I did in coming up to your house tonight. I expected to level one of them at least. Fortunately, however, I eluded their pursuit, and they left me alone in the woods.

"My last dollar was now gone, and you may well suppose I felt the loss of it; but the thought of being once again free to pursue my journey, prevented that depression which a sense of destitution causes; so swinging my little bundle on my back, I caught a glimpse of the *Great Bear* (which ever points the way to my beloved star,) and I started again on my journey. What I lost in money I made up at a hen-roost that same night, upon which I fortunately came."

"But you did 'nt eat your food raw? How did you cook it?" said Mrs. Listwell.

"O no, Madam," said Madison, turning to his little bundle: -- "I had the means of cooking." Here he took out of his bundle an old-fashioned tinder-box, and taking up a piece of a file, which he brought with him, he struck it with a heavy flint, and brought out at least a dozen sparks at once. "I have had this old box," said he, "more than five years. It is the *only* property saved from the fire in the dismal swamp. It has done me good service. It has given me the means of broiling many a chicken!"

It seemed quite a relief to Mrs. Listwell to know that Madison had, at least, lived upon cooked food. Women have a perfect horror of eating uncooked food. By this time thoughts of what was best to be done about getting Madison to Canada, began to trouble Mr. Listwell; for the laws of Ohio were very stringent against any one who should aid, or who were found aiding a slave to escape through that State. A citizen, for the simple act of taking a fugitive slave in his carriage, had just been stripped of all his property, and thrown penniless upon the world. Notwithstanding this, Mr. Listwell was determined to see Madison safely on his way to Canada. "Give yourself no uneasiness," said he to Madison, "for if it cost my farm, I shall see you safely out of the States, and on your way to a land of liberty. Thank God that there *such* a land so near us! You will spend to-morrow with us, and to-morrow night I will take you in my carriage to the Lake. Once upon that, and you are safe."

"Thank you! thank you," said the fugitive; "I will commit myself to your care."

For the *first* time during *five* years, Madison enjoyed the luxury of resting his limbs on a comfortable bed, and inside a human habitation. Looking at the white sheets, he said to Mr. Listwell, "What, sir! you don't mean that I shall sleep in that bed?"

"'Oh yes, oh yes."

After Mr. Listwell left the room, Madison said he really hesitated whether or not he should lie on the floor; for that was *far* more comfortable and inviting than any bed to which he had been used.

We pass over the thoughts and feelings, the hopes and fears, the plans and purposes, that revolved in the mind of Madison during the day that he was secreted at the house of Mr. Listwell. The reader will be content to know that nothing occurred to endanger his liberty, or to excite alarm. Many were the little attentions bestowed upon him in his quiet retreat and hiding-place. In the evening, Mr. Listwell, after treating Madison to a new suit of winter clothes, and replenishing his exhausted purse with five dollars, all in silver, brought out his two-horse wagon, well provided with buffaloes, and silently started off with him to Cleveland. They arrived there without interruption, a few minutes before sunrise the next morning. Fortunately the steamer Admiral lay at the wharf, and was to start for Canada at nine o'clock. Here the last anticipated danger was surmounted. It was feared that just at this point the hunters of men might be on the look-out, and, possibly, pounce upon their victim. Mr. Listwell saw the captain of the boat; cautiously sounded him on the matter of carrying liberty-loving passengers, before he introduced his precious charge. This done, Madison was conducted on board. With usual generosity this true subject of the emancipating queen welcomed Madison, and assured him that he should be safely landed in Canada, free of charge. Madison now felt himself no more a piece of merchandise, but a passenger, and, like any other passenger, going about his business, carrying with him what belonged to him, and nothing which rightfully belonged to anybody else.

Wrapped in his new winter suit, snug and comfortable, a pocket full of silver, safe from his pursuers, embarked for a free country, Madison gave every sign of sincere gratitude, and bade his kind benefactor farewell, with such a grip of the hand as bespoke a heart full of honest manliness, and a soul that knew how to appreciate kindness. It need scarcely be said that Mr. Listwell was deeply moved by the gratitude and friendship he had excited in a nature so noble as that of the fugitive. He went to his home that day with a joy and gratification which knew no bounds. He had done something "to deliver the spoiled out of the hands of the spoiler," he had given bread to the hungry, and clothes to the naked; he had befriended a man to whom the laws of his country forbade all friendship, -- and in proportion to the odds against his righteous deed, was the delightful satisfaction that gladdened his heart. On reaching home, he exclaimed, "*He is safe, -- he is safe, -- he is safe,*" -- and the cup of his joy was shared by his excellent lady. The following letter was received from Madison a few days after.

"WINDSOR, CANADA WEST, DEC. 16, 1840.

My dear Friend, -- for such you truly are: --
Madison is out of the woods at last; I nestle in the mane of the British lion, protected by his mighty paw from the talons and the beak of the American eagle. I AM FREE, and breathe an atmosphere too pure for *slaves*, slave-hunters, or slave-holders. My heart is full. As many thanks to you, sir, and to your kind lady, as there are pebbles on the shores of Lake Erie; and may the blessing of God rest upon you both. You will never be forgotten by your profoundly grateful friend,

MADISON WASHINGTON."

PART III.

-- His head was with his heart,
    And that was far away!
Childe Harold.

Just upon the edge of the great road. from Petersburg, Virginia, to Richmond, and only about fifteen miles from the latter place, there stands a somewhat ancient and famous public tavern, quite notorious in its better days, as being the grand resort for most of the leading gamblers, horse-racers, cock-fighters, and slave-traders from all the country round about. This old rookery, the nucleus of all sorts of birds, mostly those of ill omen, has, like everything else peculiar to Virginia, lost much of its ancient consequence and splendor; yet it keeps up some appearance of gaiety and high life, and is still frequented, even by respectable travellers, who are unacquainted with its past history and present condition. Its fine old portico looks well at a distance, and gives the building an air of grandeur. A nearer view, however, does little to sustain this pretension. The house is large, and its style imposing, but time and dissipation, unfailing in their results, have made ineffaceable marks upon it, and it must, in the common course of events, soon be numbered with the things that were. The gloomy mantle of ruin is, already, outspread to envelop it, and its remains, even but now remind one of a human skull, after the flesh has mingled with the earth. Old hats and rags fill the places in the upper windows once occupied by large panes of glass, and the moulding boards along the roofing have dropped off from their places, leaving holes and crevices in the rented wall for bats and swallows to build their nests in. The platform of the portico, which fronts the highway is a rickety affair, its planks are loose, and in some places entirely gone, leaving effective mantraps in their stead for nocturnal ramblers. The wooden pillars, which once supported it, but which now hang as encumbrances, are all rotten, and tremble with the touch. A part of the stable, a fine old structure in its day, which has given comfortable shelter to hundreds of the noblest steeds of "the Old Dominion" at once, was blown down many years ago, and never has been, and probably never will be, rebuilt. The doors of the barn are in wretched condition; they will shut with a little human strength to help their worn out hinges, but not otherwise. The side of the great building seen from the road is much discolored in sundry places by slops poured from the upper windows, rendering it unsightly and offensive in other respects. Three or four great dogs, looking as dull and gloomy as the mansion itself, lie stretched out along the door-sills under the portico; and double the number of loafers, some of them completely rum-ripe, and others ripening, dispose themselves like so many sentinels about the front of the house. These latter understand the science of scraping acquaintance to perfection. They know every-body, and almost every-body knows them. Of course, as their title implies, they have no regular employment. They are (to use an expressive phrase) *hangers on*, or still better, they are what sailors would denominate *holders-on to the slack, in every-body's mess, and in nobody's watch*. They are, however, as good as the newspaper for the events of the day, and they sell their knowledge almost as cheap. Money they seldom have; yet they always have capital the most reliable. They make their way with a succeeding traveller by intelligence gained from a preceding one. All the great names of Virginia they know by heart, and have seen their owners often. The history of the house is folded in their lips, and they rattle off stories in connection with it, equal to the guides at Dryburgh Abbey. He must be a shrewd man, and well skilled in the art of evasion, who gets out of the hands of these fellows without being at the expense of a treat.

It was at this old tavern, while on a second visit to the State of Virginia in 1841, that Mr. Listwell, unacquainted with the fame of the place, turned aside, about sunset, to pass the night. Riding up to the house, he had scarcely dismounted, when one of the half dozen bar-room fraternity met and addressed him in a manner exceedingly bland and accommodating.

"Fine evening, sir."

"Very fine," said Mr. Listwell. "This is a tavern, I believe?"

"O yes, sir, yes; although you may think it looks a little the worse for wear, it was once as good a house as any in Virginy. I make no doubt if ye spend the night here, you'll think it a good house yet; for there aint a more accommodating man in the country than you'll find the landlord."

Listwell. "The most I want is a good bed for myself, and a full manger for my horse. If I get these, I shall be quite satisfied."

Loafer. "Well, I alloys like to hear a gentleman talk for his horse; and just becase the horse can't talk for itself. A man that don't care about his beast, and don't look arter it when he's travelling, aint much in my eye anyhow. Now, sir, I likes a horse, and I'll guarantee your horse will be taken good care on here. That old stable, for all you see it looks so shabby now, once sheltered the great *Eclipse,* when he run here agin *Batchelor* and *Jumping Jemmy.* Them was fast horses, but he beat 'em both."

Listwell. "Indeed."

Loafer. "Well, I rather reckon you've travelled a right smart distance to-day, from the look of your horse?"

Listwell. "Forty miles only."

Loafer. "Well! I'll be darned if that aint a pretty good *only.* Mister, that beast of yours is a singed cat, I warrant you. I never see'd a creature like that that was'nt good on the road. You've come about forty miles, then?"

Listwell. "Yes, yes, and a pretty good pace at that."

Loafer. "You're somewhat in a hurry, then, I make no doubt? I reckon I could guess if I would, what you're going to Richmond for? It would'nt be much of a guess either; for it's rumored hereabouts, that there's to be the greatest sale of niggers at Richmond to-morrow that has taken place there in a long time; and I'll be bound you're a going there to have a hand in it."

Listwell. "Why, you must think, then, that there's money to be made at that business?"

Loafer. "Well, 'pon my honor, sir, I never made any that way myself; but it stands to reason that it's a money making business; for almost all other business in Virginia is dropped to engage in this. One thing is sartain, I never see'd a nigger-buyer yet that had 'nt a plenty of money, and he was 'nt as free with it as water. I has known one on 'em to treat as high as twenty times in a night; and, ginerally speaking, they's men of edication, and knows all about the government. The fact is, sir, I alloys like to hear 'em talk, bekase I alloys can learn something from them."

Listwell. "What may I call your name, sir?"

Loafer. "Well, now, they calls me Wilkes. I'm known all around by the gentlemen that comes here. They all knows old Wilkes."

Listwell. "Well, Wilkes, you seem to be acquainted here, and I see you have a strong liking for a horse. Be so good as to speak a kind word for mine to the hostler to-night, and you'll not lose anything by it."

Loafer. "Well, sir, I see you don't say much, but you I've got an insight into things. It's alloys wise to get the good will of them that's acquainted about a tavern; for a man don't know when he goes into a house what may happen, or how much he may need a friend. Here the loafer gave Mr. Listwell a significant grin, which expressed a sort of triumphant pleasure at having, as he supposed, by his tact succeeded in placing so fine appearing a gentleman under obligations to him. The pleasure, however, was mutual; for there was something so insinuating in the glance of this loquacious customer, that Mr. Listwell was very glad to get quit of him, and to do so more successfully, he ordered his supper to be brought to him in his private room, private to the eye, but not to the ear. This room was directly over the bar, and the plastering being off, nothing but pine boards and naked laths separated him from the disagreeable company below, -- he could easily hear what was said in the bar-room, and was rather glad of the advantage it afforded, for, as you shall see, it furnished him important hints as to the manner and deportment he should assume during his stay at that tavern.

Mr. Listwell says he had got into his room but a few moments, when he heard the officious Wilkes below, in a tone of disappointment, exclaim, "Whar's that gentleman?" Wilkes was evidently expecting to meet with his friend at the bar-room, on his return, and had no doubt of his doing the handsome thing. "He has gone to his room," answered the landlord, "and has ordered his supper to be brought to him."

Here some one shouted out, "Who is he, Wilkes? Where's he going?"

"Well, now, I'll be hanged if I know; but I'm willing to make any man a bet of this old hat agin a five dollar bill, that that gent is as full of money as a dog is of fleas. He's going down to Richmond to buy niggers, I make no doubt. He's no fool, I warrant ye."

"Well, he acts d -- d strange," said another, "anyhow. I likes to see a man, when he comes up to a tavern, to come straight into the bar-room, and show that he's a man among men. Nobody was going to bite him."

"Now, I don't blame him a bit for not coming in here. That man knows his business, and means to take care on his money," answered Wilkes.

"Wilkes, you 're a fool. You only say that, becase you hope to get a few coppers out on him."

"You only measure my corn by your half-bushel, I won't say that you're only mad becase I got the chance of speaking to him first."

"O Wilkes! you're known here. You'll praise up any body that will give you a copper; besides, 'tis my opinion that that fellow who took his long slab-sides up stairs, for all the world just like a half-scared woman, afraid to look honest men in the face, is a *Northerner,* and as mean as dish-water."

"Now what will you bet of that," said Wilkes.

The speaker said, "I make no bets with you, 'kase you can get that fellow up stairs there to say anything."

"Well," said Wilkes, "I am willing to bet any man in the company that *that* gentleman is a *nigger*-buyer. He did 'nt tell me so right down, but I reckon I knows enough about men to give a pretty clean guess as to what they are arter."

The dispute as to *who* Mr. Listwell was, what his business, where he was going, etc., was kept up with much animation for some time, and more than once threatened a serious disturbance of the peace. Wilkes had his friends as well as his opponents. After this sharp debate, the company amused themselves by drinking whiskey, and telling stories. The latter consisting of quarrels, fights, *rencontres,* and duels, in which distinguished persons of that neighborhood, and frequenters of that house, had been actors. Some of these stories were frightful enough, and were told, too, with a relish which bespoke the pleasure of the parties with the horrid scenes they portrayed. It would not be proper here to give the reader any idea of the vulgarity and dark profanity which rolled, as "a sweet morsel," under these corrupt tongues. A more brutal set of creatures, perhaps, never congregated.

Disgusted, and a little alarmed withal, Mr. Listwell, who was not accustomed to such entertainment, at length retired, but not to sleep. He was *too* much wrought upon by what he had heard to rest quietly, and what snatches of sleep he got, were interrupted by dreams which were anything than pleasant. At eleven o'clock, there seemed to be several hundreds of persons crowding into the house. A loud and confused clamour, cursing and cracking of whips, and the noise of chains startled him from his bed; for a moment he would have given the half of his farm in Ohio to have been at home. This uproar was kept up with undulating course, till near morning. There was loud laughing, -- loud singing, -- loud cursing, -- and yet there seemed to be weeping and mourning in the midst of all. Mr. Listwell said he had heard enough during the forepart of the night to convince him that a buyer of men and women stood the best chance of being respected. And he, therefore, thought it best to say nothing which might undo the favorable opinion that had been formed of him in the bar-room by at least one of the fraternity that swarmed about it. While he would not avow himself a purchaser of slaves, he deemed it not prudent to disavow it. He felt that he might, properly, refuse to cast such a pearl before parties which, to him, were worse than swine. To reveal himself, and to impart a knowledge of his real character and sentiments would, to say the least, be imparting intelligence with the certainty of seeing it and himself both abused. Mr. Listwell confesses, that this reasoning did not altogether satisfy his conscience, for, hating slavery as he did, and regarding it to be the immediate duty of every man to cry out against it, "without compromise and without concealment," it was hard for him to admit to himself the possibility of circumstances wherein a man might, properly, hold his tongue on the subject. Having as little of the spirit of a martyr as Erasmus, he concluded, like the latter, that it was wiser to trust the mercy of God for his soul, than the humanity of slave-traders for his body. Bodily fear, not conscientious scruples, prevailed.

In this spirit he rose early in the morning, manifesting no surprise at what he had heard during the night. His quondam friend was soon at his elbow, boring him with all sorts of questions. All, however, directed to find out his character, buiness, residence, purposes, and destination. With the most perfect appearance of good nature and carelessness, Mr. Listwell evaded these meddlesome inquiries, and turned conversation to general topics, leaving himself and all that specially pertained to him, out of discussion. Disengaging himself from their troublesome companionship, he made his way towards an old bowling-alley, which was connected with the house, and which, like all the rest, was in very bad repair.

On reaching the alley Mr. Listwell saw, for the first time in his life, a slave-gang on their way to market. A sad sight truly. Here were one hundred and thirty human beings, -- children of a common Creator -- guilty of no crime -- men and women, with hearts, minds, and deathless spirits, chained and fettered, and bound for the market, in a christian country, -- in a country boasting of its liberty, independence, and high civilization! Humanity converted into merchandise, and linked in iron bands, with no regard to decency or humanity! All sizes, ages, and sexes, mothers, fathers, daughters, brothers, sisters, -- all huddled together, on their way to market to be sold and separated from home, and from each other forever. And all to fill the pockets of men too lazy to work for an honest living, and who gain their fortune by plundering the helpless, and trafficking in the souls and sinews of men. As he gazed upon this revolting and heart-rending scene, our informant said he almost doubted the existence of a God of justice! And he stood wondering that the earth did not open and swallow up such wickedness.

In the midst of these reflections, and while running his eye up and down the fettered ranks, he met the glance of one whose face he thought he had seen before. To be resolved, he moved towards the spot. It was MADISON WASHINGTON! Here was a scene for the pencil! Had Mr. Listwell been confronted by one risen from the dead, he could not have been more appalled. He was completely stunned. A thunderbolt could not have struck him more dumb. He stood, for a few moments, as motionless as one petrified; collecting himself, he at length exclaimed, "*Madison! is that you?*"

The noble fugitive, but little less astonished than himself, answered cheerily, "O yes, sir, they 've got me again."

Thoughtless of consequences for the moment, Mr. Listwell ran up to his old friend, placing his hands upon his shoulders, and looked him in the face! Speechless they stood gazing at each other as if to be doubly resolved that there was no mistake about the matter, till Madison motioned his friend away, intimating a fear lest the keepers should find him there, and suspect him of tampering with the slaves.

"They will soon be out to look after us. You can come when they go to breakfast, and I will tell you all."

Pleased with this arrangement, Mr. Listwell passed out of the alley; but only just in time to save himself, for, while near the door, he observed three men making their way to the alley. The thought occurred to him to await their arrival, as the best means of diverting the ever ready suspicions of the guilty.

While the scene between Mr. Listwell and his friend Madison was going on, the other slaves stood as mute spectators, -- at a loss to know what all this could mean. As he left, he heard the man chained to Madison ask, "Who is that gentleman?"

"He is a friend of mine. I cannot tell you now. Suffice it to say he is a friend. You shall hear more of him before long, but mark me! whatever shall pass between that gentleman and me, in your hearing, I pray you will say nothing about it. We are all chained here together, -- ours is a common lot; and that gentleman is not less *your* friend than *mine.*" At these words, all mysterious as they were, the unhappy company gave signs of satisfaction and hope. It seems that Madison, by that mesmeric power which is the invariable accompaniment of genius, had already won the confidence of the gang, and was a sort of general-in-chief among them.

By this time the keepers arrived. A horrid trio, well fitted for their demoniacal work. Their uncombed hair came down over foreheads "*villainously low,*" and with eyes, mouths, and noses to match. "Hallo! hallo!" they growled out as they entered. "Are you all there!"

"All here," said Madison.

"Well, well, that's right! your journey will soon be over. You'll be in Richmond by eleven to-day, and then you'll have an easy time on it."

"I say, gal, what in the devil are you crying about?" said one of them. I 'll give you something to cry about, if you don't mind." This was said to a girl, apparently not more than twelve years old, who had been weeping bitterly. She had, probably, left behind her a loving mother, affectionate sisters, brothers, and friends, and her tears were but the natural expression of her sorrow, and the only solace. But the dealers in human flesh have *no* respect for such sorrow. They look upon it as a protest against their cruel injustice, and they are prompt to punish it.

This is a puzzle not easily solved. *How* came he here? what can I do for him? may I not even now be in some way compromised in this affair? were thoughts that troubled Mr. Listwell, and made him eager for the promised opportunity of speaking to Madison.

The bell now sounded for breakfast, and keepers and drivers, with pistols and bowie-knives gleaming from their belts, hurried in, as if to get the best places. Taking the chance now afforded, Mr. Listwell hastened back to the bowling-alley. Reaching Madison, he said, "Now *do* tell me all about the matter. Do you know me?"

"Oh, yes," said Madison, "I know you well, and shall never forget you nor that cold and dreary night you gave me shelter. I must be short," he continued, "for they'll soon be out again. This, then, is the story in brief. On reaching Canada, and getting over the excitement of making my escape, sir, my thoughts turned to my poor wife, who had well deserved my love by her virtuous fidelity and undying affection for me. I could not bear the thought of leaving her in the cruel jaws of slavery, without making an effort to rescue her. First, I tried to get money to buy her; but oh! the process was *too slow*. I despaired of accomplishing it. She was in all my thoughts by day, and my dreams by night. At times I could almost hear her voice, saying, 'O Madison! Madison! will you then leave me here? can you leave me here to die? No! no! you will come! you will come!' I was wretched. I lost my appetite. I could neither work, eat, nor sleep, till I resolved to hazard my own liberty, to gain that of my wife! But I must be short. Six weeks ago I reached my old master's place. I laid about the neighborhood nearly a week, watching my chance, and, finally, I ventured upon the desperate attempt to reach my poor wife's room by means of a ladder. I reached the window, but the noise in raising it frightened my wife, and she screamed and fainted. I took her in my arms, and was descending the ladder, when the dogs began to bark furiously, and before I could get to the woods the white folks were roused. The cool night air soon restored my wife, and she readily recognized me. We made the best of our way to the woods, but it was now *too* late, -- the dogs were after us as though they would have torn us to pieces. It was all over with me now! My old master and his two sons ran out with loaded rifles, and before we were out of gunshot, our ears were assailed with '*Stop! stop! or be shot down*.' Nevertheless we ran on. Seeing that we gave no heed to their calls, they fired, and my poor wife fell by my side dead, while I received but a slight flesh wound. I now became desperate, and stood my ground, and awaited their attack over her dead body. They rushed upon me, with their rifles in hand. I parried their blows, and fought them 'till I was knocked down and overpowered."

"Oh! it was madness to have returned," said Mr. Listwell.

"Sir, I could not be free with the galling thought that my poor wife was still a slave. With her in slavery, my body, not my spirit, was free. I was taken to the house, -- chained to a ring-bolt, -- my wounds dressed. I was kept there three days. All the slaves, for miles around, were brought to see me. Many slave-holders came with their slaves, using me as proof of the completeness of their power, and of the impossibility of slaves getting away. I was taunted, jeered at, and berated by them, in a manner that pierced me to the soul.

Thank God, I was able to smother my rage, and to bear it all with seeming composure. After my wounds were nearly healed, I was taken to a tree and stripped, and I received sixty lashes on my naked back. A few days after, I was sold to a slave-trader, and placed in this gang for the New Orleans market."

"Do you think your master would sell you to me?"

"O no, sir! I was sold on condition of my being taken South. Their motive is revenge."

"Then, then," said Mr. Listwell, "I fear I can do nothing for you. Put your trust in God, and bear your sad lot with the manly fortitude which becomes a man. I shall see you at Richmond, but don't recognize me." Saying this, Mr. Listwell handed Madison ten dollars; said a few words to the other slaves; received their hearty "God bless you," and made his way to the house.

Fearful of exciting suspicion by too long delay, our friend went to the breakfast table, with the air of one who half reproved the greediness of those who rushed in at the sound of the bell. A cup of coffee was all that he could manage. His feelings were too bitter and excited, and his heart was too full with the fate of poor Madison (whom he loved as well as admired) to relish his breakfast; and although he sat long after the company had left the table, he really did little more than change the position of his knife and fork. The strangeness of meeting again one whom he had met on two several occasions before, under extraordinary circumstances, was well calculated to suggest the idea that a supernatural power, a wakeful providence, or an inexorable fate, had linked their destiny together; and that no efforts of his could disentangle him from the mysterious web of circumstances which enfolded him.

On leaving the table, Mr. Listwell nerved himself up and walked firmly into the bar-room. He was at once greeted again by that talkative chatter-box, Mr. Wilkes.

"Them's a likely set of niggers in the alley there," said Wilkes.

"Yes, they're fine looking fellows, one of them I should like to purchase, and for him I would be willing to give a handsome sum."

Turning to one of his comrades, and with a grin of victory, Wilkes said, "Aha, Bill, did you hear that? I told you I know'd that gentleman wanted to buy niggers, and would bid as high as any purchaser in the market."

"Come, come," said Listwell, "don't be too loud in your praise, you are old enough to know that prices rise when purchasers are plenty."

"That's a fact," said Wilkes, "I see you knows the ropes -- and there's not a man in old Virginy whom I'd rather help to make a good bargain than you, sir.

"Mr. Listwell here threw a dollar at Wilkes, (which the latter caught with a dexterous hand,) saying, "Take that for your kind good will."

Wilkes held up the dollar to his right eye, with a grin of victory, and turned to the morose grumbler in the corner who had questioned the liberality of a man of whom he knew nothing.

Mr. Listwell now stood as well with the company as any other occupant of the bar-room.

We pass over the hurry and bustle, the brutal vociferations of the slave-drivers in getting their unhappy gang in motion for Richmond; and we need not narrate every application of the lash to those who faltered in the journey. Mr. Listwell followed the train at a long distance, with a sad heart; and on reaching Richmond, left his horse at a hotel, and made his way to the wharf in the direction of which he saw the slave-coffle driven. He was just in time to see the whole company embark for New Orleans. The thought struck him that, while mixing with the multitude, he might do his friend Madison one last service, and he stept into a hardware store and purchased three strong *files*. These he took with him, and standing near the small boat, which lay in waiting to bear the company by parcels to the side of the brig that lay in the stream, he managed, as Madison passed him, to slip the files into his pocket, and at once darted back among the crowd.

All the company now on board, the imperious voice of the captain sounded, and instantly a dozen hardy seamen were in the rigging, hurrying aloft to unfurl the broad canvas of our Baltimore built American Slaver. The sailors hung about the ropes, like so many black cats, now in the round-tops, now in the cross-trees, now on the yard-arms; all was bluster and activity. Soon the broad fore topsail, the royal and top gallant sail were spread to the breeze. Round went the heavy windlass, clank, clank went the fall-bit, -- the anchors weighed, jibs, mainsails, and topsails hauled to the wind, and the long, low, black slaver, with her cargo of human flesh, careened and moved forward to the sea.

Mr. Listwell stood on the shore, and watched the slaver till the last speck of her upper sails faded from sight, and announced the limit of human vision. "Farewell! farewell! brave and true man! God grant that brighter skies may smile upon your future than have yet looked down upon your thorny pathway."

Saying this to himself, our friend lost no time in completing his business, and in making his way homewards, gladly shaking off from his feet the dust of Old Virginia.

PART IV.

Oh, where's the slave so lowly
Condemn'd to chains unholy,
Who could he burst
His bonds at first
Would pine beneath them slowly ?
Moore.

-- Know ye not
Who would be free, *themselves* must strike the blow.
Childe Harold.

What a world of inconsistency, as well as of wickedness, is suggested by the smooth and gliding phrase, AMERICAN SLAVE TRADE; and how strange and perverse is that moral sentiment which loathes, execrates, and brands as piracy and as deserving of death the carrying away into captivity men, women, and children from the *African coast*; but which is neither shocked nor disturbed by a similar traffic, carried on with the same motives and purposes, and characterized by even *more* odious peculiarities on the coast of our MODEL

REPUBLIC. We execrate and hang the wretch guilty of this crime on the coast of Guinea, while we respect and applaud the guilty participators in this murderous business on enlightened shores of the Chesapeake. The inconsistency is so flagrant and glaring, that it would seem to cast a doubt on the doctrine of the innate moral sense of mankind.

Just two months after the sailing of the Virginia slave brig, which the reader has seen move off to sea so proudly with her human cargo for the New Orleans market, there chanced to meet, in the Marine Coffee-house at Richmond, a company of *ocean birds*, when the following conversation, which throws some light on the subsequent history, not only of Madison Washington, but of the hundred and thirty human beings with whom we last saw him chained.

"I say, shipmate, you had rather rough weather on your late passage to Orleans?" said Jack Williams, a regular old salt, tauntingly, to a trim, compact, manly looking person, who proved to be the first mate of the slave brig in question.

"Foul play, as well as foul weather," replied the firmly knit personage, evidently but little inclined to enter upon a subject which terminated so ingloriously to the captain and officers of the American slaver.

"Well, betwixt you and me," said Williams, that whole affair on board of the Creole was miserably and disgracefully managed. Those black rascals got the upper hand of ye altogether; and, in my opinion, the whole disaster was the result of ignorance of the real character of darkies in general. With half a dozen *resolute* white men, (I say it not boastingly,) I could have had the rascals in irons in ten minutes, not because I'm so strong, but I know how to manage 'em. With my back against the *caboose*, I could, myself, have flogged a dozen of them; and had I been on board, by every monster of the deep, every black devil of 'em all would have had his neck stretched from the yard-arm. Ye made a mistake in yer manner of fighting 'em. All that is needed in dealing with a set of rebellious *darkies*, is to show that yer not afraid of 'em. For my own part, I would not honor a dozen niggers by pointing a gun at one on 'em, -- a good stout whip, or a stiff rope's end, is better than all the guns at Old Point to quell a *nigger* insurrection. Why, sir, to take a gun to a *nigger* is the best way you can select to tell him you are afraid of him, and the best way of inviting his attack."

This speech made quite a sensation among the company, and a part of them indicated solicitude for the answer which might be made to it. Our first mate replied, "Mr. Williams, all that you've now said sounds very well *here* on shore, where, perhaps, you have studied negro character. I do not profess to understand the subject as well as yourself; but it strikes me, you apply the same rule in dissimilar cases. It is quite easy to talk of flogging niggers here on land, where you have the sympathy of the community, and the whole physical force of the government, State and national, at your command; and where, if a negro shall lift his hand against a white man, the white community, with one accord, are ready to unite in shooting him down. I say, in such circumstances, it's easy to talk of flogging negroes and of negro cowardice ; but, sir, I deny that the negro is, naturally, a coward, or that your theory of managing slaves will stand the test of *salt* water. It may do very well for an overseer, a contemptible hireling, to take advantage of fears already in existence, and which his presence has no power to inspire; to swagger about whip in hand, and discourse on the timidity and cowardice of negroes; for they have a smooth sea and a fair wind. It is one thing to manage a company of slaves on a Virginia plantation, and quite another thing to quell an insurrection on the lonely billows of the Atlantic, where every breeze speaks of courage and liberty. For the negro to act cowardly on shore, may be to act wisely; and I've some doubts whether *you*, Mr. Williams, would find it very convenient were you a slave in Algiers, to raise your hand against the bayonets of a whole government."

"By George, shipmate," said Williams, you're coming rather *too* near. Either I've fallen very low in your estimation, or your notions of negro courage have got up a button-hole too high. Now I more than ever wish I'd been on board of that luckless craft. I'd have given ye practical evidence of the truth of my theory. I don't doubt there's some difference in being at sea. But a nigger's a nigger, on sea or land; and is a coward, find him where you will; a drop of blood from one on 'em will skeer a hundred. A knock on the nose, or a kick on the shin, will tame the wildest *'darkey'* you can fetch me. I say again, and will stand by it, I could, with half a dozen good men, put the whole nineteen on 'em in irons, and have carried them safe to New Orleans too. Mind, I don't blame you, but I do say, and every gentleman here will bear me out in it, that the fault was somewhere, or them niggers would never have got off as they have done. For my part I feel ashamed to have the idea go abroad, that a ship load of slaves can't be safely taken from Richmond to New Orleans. I should like, merely to redeem the character of Virginia sailors, to take charge of a ship load on 'em to-morrow."

Williams went on in this strain, occasionally casting an imploring glance at the company for applause for his wit, and sympathy for his contempt of negro courage. He had, evidently, however, waked up the wrong passenger; for besides being in the right, his opponent carried that in his eye which marked him a man not to be trifled with.

"Well, Sir," said the sturdy mate, "you can select your own method for distinguishing yourself; -- the path of ambition in this direction is quite open to you in Virginia, and I've no doubt that you will be highly appreciated and compensated for all your valiant achievements in that line; but for myself, while I do not profess to be a giant, I have resolved never to set my foot on the deck of a slave ship, either as officer, or common sailor again; I have got enough of it."

"Indeed! indeed!" exclaimed Williams, derisively.

"Yes, *indeed*," echoed the mate; "but don't misunderstand me. It is not the high value that I set upon my life that makes me say what I have said; yet I'm resolved never to endanger my life again in a cause which my conscience does not approve. I dare say *here* what many men *feel*, but *dare not speak*, that this whole slave-trading business is a disgrace and scandal to Old Virginia."

"Hold! hold on! shipmate," said Williams, I hardly thought you'd have shown your colors so soon, -- I'll be hanged if you're not as good an abolitionist as Garrison himself."

The mate now rose from his chair, manifesting some excitement. "What do you mean, sir," said he, in a commanding tone. "*That man does not live who shall offer me an insult with impunity.*"

The effect of the words was marked; and the company clustered around. Williams, in an apologetic tone, said, "Shipmate! keep your temper. I mean't no insult. We all know that Tom Grant is no coward, and what I said about your being an abolitionist was simply this: you *might* have put down them black mutineers and murderers, but your conscience held you back."

"In that, too," said Grant, "you were mistaken. I did all that any man with equal strength and presence of mind could have done. The fact is, Mr. Williams, you underrate the courage as well as the skill of these negroes, and further, you do not seem to have been correctly informed about the case in hand at all."

"All I know about it is," said Williams, "that on the ninth day after you left Richmond, a dozen or two of the niggers ye had on board, came on deck and took the ship from, you; -- had her steered into a British port, where, by the by, every wooly head of them went ashore and was free. Now I take this to be a discreditable piece of business, and one demanding explanation."

"There are a great many discreditable things in the world," said Grant. For a ship to go down under a calm sky is, upon the first flush of it, disgraceful either to sailors or caulkers. But when we learn, that by some mysterious disturbance in nature, the waters parted beneath, and swallowed the ship up, we lose our indignation and disgust in lamentation of the disaster, and in awe of the Power which controls the elements."

"Very true, very true," said Williams, "I should be very glad to have an explanation which would relieve the affair of its present discreditable features. I have desired to see you ever since you got home, and to learn from you a full statement of the facts in the case. To me the whole thing seems unaccountable. I cannot see how a dozen or two of ignorant negroes, not one of whom had ever been to sea before, and all of them were closely ironed between decks, should be able to get their fetters off, rush out of the hatchway in open daylight, kill two white men, the one the captain and the other their master, and then carry the ship into a British port, where every '*darkey*' of them was set free. There must have been great carelessness, or cowardice somewhere!"

The company which had listened in silence during most of this discussion, now became much excited. One said, I agree with Williams; and several said the thing looks black enough. After the temporary tumultuous exclamations had subsided, --

"I see," said Grant, "how you regard this case, and how difficult it will be for me to render our ship's company blameless in your eyes. Nevertheless, I will state the fact precisely as they came under my own observation. Mr. Williams speaks of 'ignorant negroes,' and, as a general rule, they are ignorant; but had he been on board the *Creole* as I was, he would have seen cause to admit that there are exceptions to this general rule. The leader of the mutiny in question was just as shrewd a fellow as ever I met in my life, and was as well fitted to lead in a dangerous enterprise as any one white man in ten thousand. The name of this man, strange to say, (ominous of greatness,) was MADISON WASHINGTON. In the short time he had been on board, he had secured the confidence of every officer. The negroes fairly worshipped him. His manner and bearing were such, that no one could suspect him of a murderous purpose. The only feeling with which we regarded him was, that he was a powerful, good-disposed negro. He seldom spake to to any one, and when he did speak, it was with the utmost propriety. His words were well chosen, and his pronunciation equal to that of any schoolmaster. It was a mystery to us *where* he got his knowledge of language; but as little was said to him, none of us knew the extent of his intelligence and ability till it was too late. It seems he brought three files with him on board, and must have gone to work upon his fetters the first night out; and he must have worked well at that; for on the day of the rising, he got the irons *off eighteen* besides himself.

"The attack began just about twilight in the evening. Apprehending a squall, I had commanded the second mate to order all hands on deck, to take in sail. A few minutes before this I had seen Madison's head above the hatchway, looking out upon the white-capped waves at the leeward. I think I never saw him look more good-natured. I stood just about midship, on the larboard side. The captain was pacing the quarter-deck on the starboard side, in company with Mr. Jameson, the owner of most of the slaves on board. Both were armed. I had just told the men to lay aloft, and was looking to see my orders obeyed, when I heard the discharge of a pistol on the starboard side; and turning suddenly around, the very deck seemed covered with fiends from the pit. The nineteen negroes were all on deck, with their broken fetters in their hands, rushing in all directions. I put my hand quickly in my pocket to draw out my jack-knife; but before I could draw it, I was knocked senseless to the deck. When I came to myself, (which I did in a few minutes, I suppose, for it was yet quite light,) there was not a white man on deck. The sailors were all aloft in the rigging, and dared not come down. Captain Clarke and Mr. Jameson lay stretched on the quarter-deck, -- both dying, -- while Madison himself stood at the helm unhurt.

"I was completely weakened by the loss of blood, and had not recovered from the stunning blow which felled me to the deck; but it was a little too much for me, even in my prostrate condition, to see our good brig commanded by a *black murderer*. So I called out to the men to come down and take the ship, or die in the attempt. Suiting the action to the word, I started aft. You murderous villain, said I, to the imp at the helm, and rushed upon him to deal him a blow, when he pushed me back with his strong, black arm, as though I had been a boy of twelve. I looked around for the men. They were still in the rigging. Not one had come down. I started towards Madison again. The rascal now told me to stand back. 'Sir,' said he, 'your life is in my hands. I could have killed you a dozen times over during this last half hour, and could kill you now. You call me a *black murderer*. I am not a murderer. God is my witness that LIBERTY, not *malice*, is the motive for this night's work. I have done no more to those dead men yonder, than they would have done to me in like circumstances. We have struck for our freedom, and if a true man's heart be in you, you will honor us for the deed. We have done that which you applaud your fathers for doing, and if we are murderers, *so were they*.'

"I felt little disposition to reply to this impudent speech. By heaven, it disarmed me. The fellow loomed up before me. I forgot his blackness in the dignity of his manner, and the eloquence of his speech. It seemed as if the souls of both the great dead (whose names he bore) had entered him. To the sailors in the rigging he said: 'Men! the battle is over, -- your captain is dead. I have complete command of this vessel. All resistance to my authority will be in vain. My men have won their liberty, with no other weapons but their own BROKEN FETTERS. We are nineteen in number. We do not thirst for your blood, we demand only our rightful freedom. Do not flatter yourselves that I am ignorant of chart or compass. I know both. We are now only about sixty miles from Nassau. Come down, and do your duty. Land us in Nassau, and not a hair of your heads shall be hurt.'

"I shouted, *Stay where you are, men*, -- when a sturdy black fellow ran at me with a handspike, and would have split my head open, but for the interference of Madison, who darted between me
and the blow. 'I know what you are up to,' said the latter to me. 'You want to navigate this brig into a slave port, where you would have us all hanged; but you'll miss it; before this brig shall touch a slave-cursed shore while I am on board, I will myself put a match to the magazine, and blow her, and be blown with her, into a thousand fragments. Now I have saved your life twice within these last twenty minutes, -- for, when you lay helpless on deck, my men were about to kill you. I held them in check. And if you now (seeing I am your friend and not your enemy) persist in your resistance to my authority, I give you fair warning YOU SHALL DIE.'

"Saying this to me, he cast a glance into the rigging where the terror-stricken sailors were clinging, like so many frightened monkeys, and commanded them to come down, in a tone from which there was no appeal; for four men stood by with muskets in hand, ready at the word of command to shoot them down.

"I now became satisfied that resistance was out of the question; that my best policy was to put the brig into Nassau, and secure the assistance of the American consul at that port. I felt sure that the authorities would enable us to secure the murderers, and bring them to trial.

"By this time the apprehended squall had burst upon us. The wind howled furiously, -- the ocean was white with foam, which, on account of the darkness, we could see only by the quick flashes of lightning that darted occasionally from the angry sky. All was alarm and confusion. Hideous cries came up from the slave women. Above the roaring billows a succession of heavy thunder rolled along, swelling the terrific din. Owing to the great darkness, and a sudden shift of the wind, we found ourselves in the trough of the sea. When shipping a heavy sea over the starboard bow, the bodies of the captain and Mr. Jameson were washed overboard. For awhile we had dearer interests to look after than slave property. A more savage thunder-gust never swept the ocean. Our brig rolled and creaked as if every bolt would be started, and every thread of oakum would be pressed out of the seams. To the pumps! to the pumps! I cried, but not a sailor would quit his grasp. Fortunately this squall soon passed over, or we must have been food for sharks.

"During all the storm, Madison stood firmly at the helm, -- his keen eye fixed upon the binnacle. He was not indifferent to the dreadful hurricane; yet he met it with the equanimity of an old sailor. He was silent but not agitated. The first words he uttered after the storm had slightly subsided, were characteristic of the man. 'Mr. mate, you cannot write the bloody laws of slavery on those restless billows. The ocean, if not the land, is free.' I confess, gentlemen, I felt myself in the presence of a superior man; one who, had he been a white man, I would have followed willingly and gladly in any honorable enterprise. Our difference of color was the only ground for difference of action. It was not that his principles were wrong in the abstract; for they are the principles of 1776. But I could not bring myself to recognize their application to one whom I deemed my inferior.

"But to my story. What happened now is soon told. Two hours after the frightful tempest had spent itself, we were plump at the wharf in Nassau. I sent two of our men immediately to our consul with a statement of facts, requesting his interference in our behalf. What he did, or whither he did anything, I don't know; but, by order of the authorities, a company of *black* soldiers came on board, for the purpose, as they said, of protecting the property. These impudent rascals, when I called on them to assist me in keeping the slaves on board, sheltered themselves adroitly under their instructions only to protect property, -- and said they did not recognize *persons as property.* I told them that by the laws of Virginia and the laws of the United States, the slaves on board were as much property as the barrels of flour in the hold. At this the stupid blockheads showed their *ivory*, rolled up their white eyes in horror, as if the idea of putting men on a footing with merchandise were revolting to their humanity. When these instructions were understood among the negroes, it was impossible for us to keep them on board. They deliberately gathered up their baggage before our eyes, and, against our remonstrances, poured through the gangway, -- formed themselves into a procession on the wharf, -- bid farewell to all on board, and, uttering the wildest shouts of exultation, they marched, amidst the deafening cheers of a multitude of sympathizing spectators, under the triumphant leadership of their heroic chief and deliverer, MADISON WASHINGTON."

The Life and Times of Frederick Douglass

FIRST PART: LIFE AS A SLAVE

CHAPTER I: BIRTH AND PARENTAGE.

Place of birth—Description of country—Its inhabitants—Genealogical trees—Method of counting time in slave districts—Date of birth—Names of grandparents—Their cabin—Home with them—Slave practice of separating mothers from their children—Recollections of his mother—Who was his father?

IN Talbot County, Eastern Shore, State of Maryland, near Easton, the County town, there is a small district of country, thinly populated, and remarkable for nothing that I know of more than for the worn-out, sandy, desert-like appearance of its soil, the general dilapidation of its farms and fences, the indigent and spiritless character of its inhabitants, and the prevalence of ague and fever. It was in this dull, flat, and unthrifty district or neighbourhood, bordered by the Choptank river, among the laziest and muddiest of streams, surrounded by a white population of the lowest order, indolent and drunken to a proverb, and among slaves who, in point of ignorance and indolence, were fully in accord with their surroundings, that I, without any fault of my own, was born, and spent the first years of my childhood.

The reader must not expect me to say much of my family. Genealogical trees did not flourish among slaves. A person of some consequence in civilized society, sometimes designated as father, was literally unknown to slave law and slave practice. I never met with a slave in that part of the country who could tell me with any certainty how old he was. Few at that time knew anything of the months of the year, or of the days of the month. They measured the ages of their children by spring-time, winter-time, harvest-time, planting-time, and the like. Masters allowed no questions to be put to them by slaves concerning their ages. Such questions were regarded by the masters as evidence of an impudent curiosity. From certain events, however, the dates of which I have since learned, I suppose myself to have been born in February, 1817.

My first experience of life, as I now remember it, and I remember it but hazily, began in the family of my grandmother and grandfather, Betsey and Isaac Bailey. They were considered old settlers in the neighbourhood, and from certain circumstances I infer that my grandmother, especially, was held in high esteem, far higher than was the lot of most coloured persons in that region. She was a good nurse, and a capital hand at making nets used for catching shad and herring, and was, withal, somewhat famous as a fisherwoman. I have known her to be in the water waist deep, for hours, seine-hauling. She was a gardener as well as a fisher-woman, and remarkable for her success in keeping her seedling sweet potatoes through the months of winter, and easily got the reputation of being born to "good luck." In planting time Grandmother Betsey was sent for in all directions, simply to place the seedling potatoes in the hills or drills; for superstition had it that her touch was needed to make them grow. This reputation was full of advantage to her and her grandchildren, for a good crop, after her planting for the neighbours, brought her a share of the harvest.

Whether because she was too old for field service, or because she had so faithfully discharged the duties of her station in early life, I know not, but she enjoyed the privilege of living in a cabin separate from the slave quarters, having only the charge of the young children and the burden of her own support imposed upon her. She esteemed it great good fortune to live there, and took much comfort in having the children. The practice of separating mothers from their children and hiring them out at distances too great to admit of their meeting, save at long intervals, was a marked feature of the cruelty and barbarity of the slave system, which always and everywhere sought to reduce man to a level with the brute. It had no interest in recognizing or preserving any of the ties that bind families together or to their homes.

My grandmother's five daughters were hired out in this way, and my only recollections of my own mother are of a few hasty visits made in the night on foot, after the daily tasks were over, and when she was under the necessity of returning in time to respond to the driver's call to the field in the early morning. These little glimpses of my mother, obtained under such circumstances and against such odds, meagre as they were, are ineffaceably stamped upon my memory. She was tall and finely proportioned, of dark glossy complexion, with regular features and amongst the slaves was remarkably sedate and dignified. There is, in "Prichard's Natural History of Man," the head of a figure, the features of which so resemble my mother's, that I often recur to it with something of the feeling which I suppose others experience when looking upon the likenesses of their own dear departed ones.

Of my father I know nothing. Slavery had no recognition of fathers, as none of families. That the mother was a slave was enough for its deadly purpose. By its law the child followed the condition of its mother. The father might be a freeman and the child a slave. The father might be a white man, glorying in the purity of his Anglo-Saxon blood, and his child ranked with the blackest slaves. Father he might be, and not be husband, and could sell his own child without incurring reproach, if in its veins coursed one drop of African blood.

CHAPTER II: REMOVAL FROM GRANDMOTHER'S.

Early home—Its charms—Ignorance of "old master"—His gradual perception of the truth concerning him—His relations to Col. Edward Lloyd—Removal to "old master's" home—His journey thence—His separation from his grandmother—His grief.

LIVING thus with my grandmother, whose kindness and love stood in place of my mother's, it was some time before I knew myself to be a slave. I knew many other things before I knew that. Her little cabin had to me the attractions of a palace. Its fence railed floor—which was equally floor and bedstead—up stairs, and its clay floor down stairs, its dirt, and straw chimney and windowless sides, and that most curious piece of workmanship, the ladder stairway, and the hole so strangely dug in front of the fire-place, beneath which grandmamma placed her sweet potatoes, to keep them from frost in winter, were full of interest to my childish observation. The squirrels, as they skipped the fences, climbed the trees or gathered their nuts, were an unceasing delight to me. There, too, right at the side of the hut, stood the old well, with its stately and skyward-pointing beam, so aptly placed between the limbs of what had once been a tree, and so nicely balanced, that I could move it up and down with only one hand, and could get a drink myself without calling for help. Nor were these all the attractions of the place. At a little distance stood Mr. Lee's mill, where the people came in large numbers to get their corn ground. I can never tell the many things thought and felt, as I sat on the bank and watched that mill, and the turning of its ponderous wheel. The mill-pond, too, had its charms; and with my pin-hook and thread line I could get amusing nibbles if I could catch no fish.

It was not long, however, before I began to learn the sad fact that this house of my childhood belonged not to my dear old grandmother, but to some one I had never seen, and who lived a great distance off. I learned, too, the sadder fact, that not only the home and lot, but that grandmother herself and all the little children around her, belonged to a mysterious personage, called by grandmother, with every mark of reverence, "Old Master." Thus early, did clouds and shadows begin to fall upon my path.

I learned that this old master, whose name seemed ever to be mentioned with fear and shuddering, only allowed the little children to live with grandmother for a limited time, and that as soon as they were big enough they were promptly taken away to live with the said old master. These were distressing revelations indeed. My grandmother was all the world to me, and the thought of being separated from her was a most unwelcome suggestion to my affections and hopes. This mysterious old master was really a man of some consequence. He owned several farms in Tuckahoe, was the chief clerk and butler on the home plantation of Colonel Lloyd, had overseers as well as slaves on his own farms, and gave directions to the overseers on the farms owned by Colonel Lloyd. Captain Aaron Anthony, for such was the name and title of my old master, lived on Colonel Lloyd's plantation, which was situated on the Wye river, and which was one of the largest, most fertile, and best appointed in the State.

About this plantation and this old master I was most eager to know everything which could be known; and, unhappily for me, all the information I could get concerning him increased my dread of being separated from my grandmother and grandfather. I wished it was possible I could remain small all my life, knowing that the sooner I grew large the shorter would be my time to remain with them, Everything about the cabin became doubly dear, and I was sure there could be no other spot equal to it on earth. But the time came when I must go and my grandmother, knowing my fears, in pity for them, kindly kept me ignorant of the dreaded moment up to the morning, a beautiful summer morning, when we were to start, and indeed, during the whole journey, which, child, as I was, I remember as well as if it were yesterday, she kept the unwelcome truth hidden from me. The distance from Tuckahoe to Colonel Lloyd's, where my old master lived, was full twelve miles, and the walk was quite a severe test of the endurance of my young legs. The journey would have proved too severe for me, but that my dear old grandmother—blessings on her memory!—afforded occasional relief by "toteing" me on her shoulder. Advanced in years as she was, as was evident from the more than one gray hair which peeped from between the ample and graceful folds of her newly and smoothly ironed bandana turban, grandmother was yet a woman of power and spirit. She was remarkably straight in figure, elastic and muscular in movement. I seemed hardly to be a burden to her. She would have "toted" me farther, but I felt myself too much of a man to allow it. Yet while I walked I was not independent of her. She often found me holding her skirts lest something should come out of the woods and eat me up. Several old logs and stumps imposed upon me, and got themselves taken for enormous animals. I could plainly see their legs, eyes, ears, and teeth, till I got close enough to see that the eyes were knots washed with rain, and the legs were broken limbs, and the ears and teeth only such because of the point from which they were seen.

As the day advanced the heat increased, and it was not until the afternoon that we reached the much dreaded end of the journey. Here I found myself in the midst of a group of children of all sizes and of many colours, black, brown, copper coloured, and nearly white. I had not seen so many children before. As a new comer I was an object of special interest. After laughing and yelling around me and playing all sorts of wild tricks they asked me to go out and play with them. This I refused to do. Grandmamma looked sad, and I could not help feeling that our being there boded no good to me. She was soon to lose another object of affection, as she had lost many before. Affectionately patting me on the head she told me to be a good boy and go out to play with the children. They are "kin to you," she said, "go and play with them." She pointed out to me my brother Perry, my sisters, Sarah and Eliza. I had never seen them before, and though I had sometimes heard of them and felt a curious interest in them, I really did not understand what they were to me or I to them. Brothers and sisters we were by blood, but slavery had made us strangers. They were already initiated into the mysteries of old master's domicile, and they seemed to look upon me with a certain degree of compassion. I really wanted to play with them, but they were strangers to me, and I was full of fear that my grandmother might leave for home without taking me with her. Entreated to do so, however, and that, too, by my dear grandmother, I went to the back part of the house to play with them and the other children. Play, however, I did not, but stood with my back against the wall witnessing the playing of the others. At last, while standing there, one of the children, who had been in the kitchen, ran up to me in a sort of roguish glee, exclaiming, "Fed, Fed, grandmamma gone!" I could not believe it. Yet, fearing the worst, I ran into the kitchen to see for myself, and lo! she was indeed gone, and was now far away and "clean" out of sight. I need not tell all that happened now. Almost heart-broken at the discovery, I fell upon the ground and wept a boy's bitter tears, refusing to be comforted. My brother gave me peaches and pears to quiet me, but I promptly threw them on the ground. I had never been deceived before, and something of resentment at this, mingled with my grief at parting with my grandmother.

It was now late in the afternoon. The day had been an exciting and wearisome one, and, I know not how, but I suppose I sobbed myself to sleep, and its balm was never more welcome to any wounded soul than to mine. The reader may be surprised that I relate so minutely an incident apparently so trivial and which must have occurred when I was less than seven years old, but as I wish to give a faithful history of my experience in slavery, I cannot withold a circumstance which at the time affected me so deeply, and which I still remember so vividly. Besides, this was my first introduction to the realities of the slave system.

CHAPTER III: TROUBLES OF CHILDHOOD.

Col. Lloyd's plantation—Aunt Katy—Her cruelty and ill-nature—Capt. Anthony's partiality to Aunt Katy—Allowance of food—Hunger—Unexpected rescue by his mother—The reproof of Aunt Katy—Sleep—A slavemother's love—His inheritance—His mother's acquirements—Her death.

ONCE established on the home plantation of Col. Lloyd—I was with the children there, left to the tender mercies of Aunt Katy, a slave woman who was to my master, what he was to Col. Lloyd. Disposing of us in classes or sizes, he left to Aunt Katy all the minor details concerning our management. She was a woman who never allowed herself to act greatly within the limits of delegated power, no matter how broad that authority might be. Ambitious of old master's favour, ill-tempered and cruel by nature, she found in her present position an ample field for the exercise of her ill-omened qualities. She had a strong hold upon old master, for she was a first-rate cook, and very industrious. She was therefore greatly favoured by him—and as one mark of his favour she was the only mother who was permitted to retain her children around her, and even to these, her own children, she was often fiendish in her brutality. Cruel, however, as she sometimes was to her own children, she was not destitute of maternal feeling, and in her instinct to satisfy their demands for food, she was often guilty of starving me and the other children. Want of food was my chief trouble during my first summer here. Captain Anthony, instead of allowing a given quantity of food to each slave, committed the allowance for all to Aunt Katy, to be divided by her, after cooking, amongst us. The allowance consisted of coarse corn meal, not very abundant, and which by passing through Aunt Katy's hands, became more slender still for some of us. I have often been so pinched with hunger, as to dispute with old "Nep" the dog, for the crumbs which fell from the kitchen table. Many times have I followed with eager step, the waiting-girl when she shook the table-cloth, to get the crumbs and small bones flung out for the dogs and cats. It was a great thing to have the privilege of dipping a piece of bread into the water in which meat had been boiled—and the skin taken from the rusty bacon was a positive luxury. With this description of the domestic arrangements of my new home, I may here recount a circumstance which is deeply impressed on my memory, as affording a bright gleam of a slave-mother's love, and the earnestness of a mother's care. I had offended Aunt Katy. I do not remember in what way, for my offences were numerous in that quarter, greatly depending upon her moods as to their heinousness; and she had adopted her usual mode of punishing me: namely, making me go all day without food. For the first hour or two after dinner time, I succeeded pretty well in keeping up my spirits; but as the day wore away, I found it quite impossible to do so any longer. Sundown came, but no bread; and in its stead came the threat from Aunt Katy, with a scowl well suited to its terrible import, that she would starve the life out of me. Brandishing her knife, she chopped off the heavy slices of bread for the other children, and put the loaf away, muttering all the while her savage designs upon myself. Against this disappointment, for I was expecting that her heart would relent at last, I made an extra effort to maintain my dignity; but when I saw the other children around me with satisfied faces, I could stand it no longer. I went out behind the kitchen wall and cried like a fine fellow. When wearied with this, I returned to the kitchen, sat by the fire and brooded over my hard lot. I was too hungry to sleep. While I sat in the corner, I caught sight of an ear of Indian corn upon an upper shelf. I watched my chance and got it; and shelling off a few grains, I put it back again. These grams I quickly put into the hot ashes to roast. I did this at the risk of getting a brutal thumping, for Aunt Katy could beat as well as starve me. My corn was not long in roasting, and I eagerly pulled it from the ashes, and placed it upon a stool in a clever little pile. I began to help myself, when who but my own dear mother should come in. The scene which followed is beyond my power to describe. The friendless and hungry boy, in his extremest need, found himself in the strong protecting arms of his mother. I have before spoken of my mother's dignified and impressive manner. I shall never forget the indescribable expression of her countenance when I told her that Aunt Katy had said she would starve the life out of me, There was deep and tender pity in her glance at me, and a fiery indignation at Aunt Katy at the same moment, and while she took the corn from me, and gave in its stead a large ginger cake, she read Aunt Katy a lecture which was never forgotten. That night I learned as I had never learned before, that I was not only a child, but somebody's child. I was grander upon my mother's knee than a king upon his throne. But my triumph was short. I dropped off to sleep, and waked in the morning to find my mother gone and myself at the mercy again of the virago in my master's kitchen, whose fiery wrath was my constant dread.

My mother had walked twelve miles to see me, and had the same distance to travel over again before the morning sunrise. I do not remember ever seeing her again. Her death soon ended the little communication that had existed between us, and with it, I believe, a life full of weariness and heartfelt sorrow. To me it has ever been a grief that I knew my mother so little, and have so few of her words treasured in my remembrance. I have since learned that she was the only one of all the coloured people of Tuckahoe who could read. How she acquired this knowledge I know not, for Tuckahoe was the last place in the world where she would have been likely to find facilities for learning. I can therefore fondly and proudly ascribe to her, an earnest love of knowledge.

That a field-hand should learn to read in any slave State is remarkable, but the achievements of my mother, considering the place and circumstances, were very extraordinary. In view of this fact, I am happy to attribute any love of letters I may have, not to my presumed Anglo-Saxon paternity, but to the native genius of my sable, unprotected, and uncultivated mother—a woman who belonged to a race whose mental endowments are still disparaged and despised.

CHAPTER IV: A GENERAL SURVEY OF THE SLAVE PLANTATION.

Home Plantation of Colonel Lloyd—Its Isolation—Its Industries—The Slave Rule—Power of Overseers—Finds some enjoyment—Natural Scenery—Sloop "Sally Lloyd"—Wind Mill—Slave Quarter—"Old Master's" House—Stables, Store-Houses, &c., &c.—The Great House—Its Surroundings—Lloyd—Burial-Place—Superstition of Slaves—Colonel Lloyd's Wealth—Negro Politeness—Doctor Copper—Captain Anthony—His Family—Master Daniel Lloyd—His Brothers—Social Etiquette.

IT was generally supposed that slavery in the State of Maryland existed in its mildest form, and that it was totally divested of those harsh and terrible peculiarities which characterized the slave system in the Southern and South Western States of the American Union. The ground of this opinion was the contiguity of the free States, and the influence of their moral, religious, and humane sentiments. Public opinion was, indeed, a measurable restraint upon the cruelty and barbarity of masters, overseers, and slave-drivers, whenever and wherever it could reach them; but there were certain secluded and out of the way places, even in the State of Maryland, fifty years ago, seldom visited by a single ray of healthy public sentiment, where slavery, wrapt in its own congenial darkness, could and did develop all its malign and shocking characteristics, where it could be indecent without shame, cruel without shuddering, and murderous without apprehension or fear of exposure or punishment. Just such a secluded, dark, and out of the way place, was the home plantation of Colonel Edward Lloyd, in Talbot county, eastern shore of Maryland. It was far away from all the great thoroughfares of travel and commerce, and proximate to no town or village. There was neither school-house nor town-house in its neighbourhood. The school-house was unnecessary, for there were no children to go to school. The children and grand children of Col. Lloyd were taught in the house by a private tutor, a Mr. Page from Greenfield, Massachusetts, a tall, gaunt, sapling of a man, remarkably dignified, thoughful, and reticent, and who did not speak a dozen words to a slave in a whole year. The overseer's children went off somewhere in the State to school, and therefore could bring no foreign or dangerous influence from abroad to embarrass the natural operation of the slave system of the place. Not even the commonest mechanics, from whom there might have been an occasional outburst of honest and telling indignation at cruelty and wrong on other plantations, were white men here. Its whole public was made up of and divided into three classes, slaveholders, slaves, and overseers. Its blacksmiths, wheelrights, shoemakers, weavers, and coopers, were slaves. Not even commerce, selfish and indifferent to moral considerations as it usually is, was permitted within its secluded precints. Whether with a view of guarding against the escape of its secrets, I know not, but it is a fact, that every leaf and grain of the products of this plantation and those of the neighbouring farms, belonging to Col. Lloyd, were transported to Baltimore in his own vessels, every man and boy on board of which, except the captain, were owned by him as his property. In return everything brought to the plantation came through the same channel. To make this isolation more apparent it may be stated that the adjoining estates to Col. Lloyd's were owned and occupied by friends of his, who were as deeply interested as himself in maintaining the slave system in all its rigour. These were the Tilgmans, the Goldboroughs, the Lockermans, the Pacas, the Skinners, Gibsons, and others of lesser affluence and standing.

The fact is, public opinion in such a quarter, the reader must see, was not likely to be very efficient in protecting the slave from cruelty. To be a restraint upon abuses of this nature, opinion must emanate from humane and virtuous communities, and to no such opinion or influence was Col. Lloyd's plantation exposed. It was a little nation by itself, having its own language, its own rules, regulations, and customs, The troubles and controversies arising here were not settled by the civil power of the State. The overseer was the important dignitary. He was generally accuser, judge, jury, advocate, and executioner. The criminal was always dumb—and no slave was allowed to testify, other than against his brother slave.

There were, of course, no conflicting rights of property, for all the people were the property of one man, and they could themselves own no property. Religion and politics were largely excluded. One class of the population was too high to be reached by the common preacher, and the other class was too low in condition and ignorance to be much cared for by religious teachers, and yet some religious ideas did enter this dark corner.

This, however, is not the only view which the place presented. Though civilisation was in many respects shut out, nature could not be. Though separated from the rest of the world, though public opinion, as I have said, could seldom penetrate its dark domain, though the whole place was stamped with its own peculiar iron-like individuality, and though crimes, high-handed and atrocious, could be committed there with strange and shocking impunity, it was to outward seeming, a most strikingly interesting place, full of life, activity and spirit, and presented a very favourable contrast to the indolent monotony and languor of Tuckahoe. It resembled in some respects descriptions I have since read of the old baronial domains of Europe. Keen as was my regret, and great as was my sorrow, at leaving my old home, I was not long in adapting myself to my new one. A man's troubles are always half disposed of when he finds endurance the only alternative. I found myself there; there was no getting away; and naught remained for me but to make the best of it. There were plenty of children to play with, and plenty of pleasant resorts for boys of my age and older. The little tendrils of affection so rudely broken from the darling objects in and around my grandmother's home, gradually began to extend and twine themselves around the new surroundings. There for the first time I saw a large windmill, with its wide-sweeping white wings, a commanding object to a child's eye. This was situated on what was called Long Point—a tract of land dividing Miles river from the Wye. I spent many hours watching the wings of this wondrous mill. In the river, or what was called the "Swash," at a short distance from the shore, quietly lying at anchor, with her small row boat dancing at her stern, was a large sloop, the Sally Lloyd, called by that name in honour of the favourite daughter of the Colonel. These two objects, the sloop and mill, as I remember, awakened thoughts, ideas, and wondering. Then there were a great many houses, human habitations full of the mysteries of life at every stage of it. There was the little red house up the road, occupied by Mr. Seveir, the overseer; a little nearer to my old master's stood a long, low, rough building literally alive with slaves of all ages, sexes, conditions, sizes, and colours. This was called the long quarter. Perched upon a hill east of our house, was a tall dilapidated old brick building, the architectural dimensions of which proclaimed its creation for a different purpose, now occupied by slaves, in a similar manner to the long quarters. Besides these, there were numerous other slave houses and huts, scattered around in the neighbourhood, every nook and corner of which were completely occupied.

Old master's house, a long brick building, plain but substantial, was centrally located, and was an independent establishment. Besides these houses there were barns, stables, store-houses, tobacco-houses, blacksmith shops, wheelwright shops, cooper shops; but above all there stood the grandest building my young eyes had ever beheld, called by every one on the plantation the great house. This was occupied by Col. Lloyd and his family. It was surrounded by numerous and variously shaped out-buildings. There were kitchens, wash-houses, dairies, summer-houses, green-houses, hen-houses, turkey-houses, pigeon-houses, and arbours of many sizes and devices, all neatly painted or whitewashed—interspersed with grand old trees, ornamental and primitive, which afforded delightful shade in summer, and imparted to the scene a high degree of stately beauty. The great house itself was a large white wooden building with wings on three sides of it. In front a broad portico extended the entire length of the building, supported by a long range of columns, which gave to the Colonel's home an air of great dignity and grandeur. It was a treat to my young and gradually opening mind to behold this elaborate exhibition of wealth, power, and beauty.

The carriage entrance to the house was by a large gate, more than a quarter of a mile distant. The intermediate space was a beautiful lawn, very neatly kept and cared for. It was dotted thickly over with trees and flowers. The road or lane from the gate to the great house was richly paved with white pebbles from the beach, and in its course formed a complete circle around the lawn. Outside this select enclosure were parks, as about the residences of the English nobility, where rabbits, deer, and other wild game might be seen peering and playing about, with "none to molest them or make them afraid." The tops of the stately poplars were often covered with red-winged blackbirds, making all nature vocal with the joyous life and beauty of their wild, warbling notes. These all belonged to me as well as to Col. Edward Lloyd, and, whether they did or not, I greatly enjoyed them. Not far from the great house were the stately mansions of the dead Lloyds—a place of sombre aspect. Vast tombs, embowered beneath the weeping willow and the fir tree, told of the generations of the family, as well as their wealth. Superstition was rife among the slaves about this family burying-ground. Strange sights had been seen by some of the older slaves, and I was often compelled to hear stories of shrouded ghosts, riding on great black horses, and of balls of fire which had been seen to fly there at midnight, and of startling and dreadful sounds that had been repeatedly heard. Slaves knew enough of the orthodox theology at the time, to consign all bad slaveholders to hell, and they often fancied such persons wishing themselves back again to wield the lash. Tales of sights and sounds strange and terrible, connected with the huge black tombs, were a great security to the grounds about them, for few of the slaves had the courage to approach them during the day time. It was a dark, gloomy and forbidding place, and it was difficult to feel that the spirits of the sleeping dust there deposited reigned with the blest in the realms of eternal peace.

Here was transacted the business of twenty or thirty different farms, which, with the slaves upon them, numbering, in all, not less than a thousand, all belonged to Col. Lloyd. Each farm was under the management of an overseer, whose word was law.

Mr. Lloyd at this time was very rich. His slaves alone, numbering as I have said not less than a thousand, were an immense fortune, and though scarcely a month passed without the sale of one or more lots to the Georgia traders, there was no apparent diminution in the number of his human stock. The selling of any to the State of Georgia was a sore and mournful event to those left behind, as well as to the victims themselves.

The reader has already been informed of the handicrafts carried on here by the slaves. "Uncle" Toney was the blacksmith, "Uncle" Harry the cartwright, and "Uncle" Abel was the shoemaker, and these had assistants in their several departments. These mechanics are called "Uncles" by all the younger slaves, not because they really sustained that relationship to any, but according to plantation etiquette as a mark of respect, due from the younger to the older slaves. Strange and even ridiculous as it may seem, among a people so uncultivated and with so many stern trials to look in the face, there is not to be found among any people a more rigid enforcement of the law of respect to elders than is maintained among them. I set this down as partly constitutional with the coloured race and partly conventional. There is no better material in the world for making a gentleman than is furnished in the African.

Among other slave notabilities, I found here one called by everybody, white and colored, "Uncle" Isaac Copper. It was seldom that a slave, however venerable, was honoured with a surname in Maryland, and so completely has the south shaped the manners of the north in this respect that their right to such honor is tardily admitted even now. It goes sadly against the grain to address and treat a negro as one would address and treat a white man. But once in a while, even in a slave state, a negro had a surname fastened to him by common consent. This was the case with "Uncle" Isaac Copper. Where the "Uncle" was dropped, he was called Doctor Copper. He was both our Doctor of Medicine and our Doctor of Divinity. When he took his degree I am unable to say, but he was too well established in his profession to permit question as to his native skill, or attainments. One qualification he certainly had. He was a confirmed cripple, wholly unable to work, and was worth nothing for sale in the market. Though lame, he was no sluggard. He made his crutches do him good service, and was always on the alert looking up the sick, and such as were supposed to need his aid and counsel. His remedial prescriptions embraced four articles. For diseases of the body, Epsom salts and castor oil; for those of the soul, the "Lord's prayer," and a few stout hickory switches.

I was early sent to Doctor Isaac Copper, with twenty or thirty other children, to learn the Lord's prayer. The old man was seated on a huge three-legged oaken stool, armed with several large hickory switches, and from the point where he sat, lame as he was, he could reach every boy in the room. After standing a while to learn what was expected of us, he commanded us to kneel down. This done, he told us to say everything he said. "Our Father"—this we repeated after him with promptness and uniformity—"who art in Heaven," was less promptly and uniformly repeated, and the old gentleman paused in the prayer to give us a short lecture, and to use his switches on our backs.

Everybody in the South seemed to want the privilege of whipping somebody else. "Uncle" Isaac, though a good old man, shared the common passion of his time and country. I cannot say I was much edified by attendance upon his ministry. There was even at that time something a little inconsistent and laughable, in my mind, in the blending of prayer with punishment. I was not long in my new home before I found that the dread I had conceived of Captain Anthony was in a measure groundless. Instead of leaping out from some hiding place and destroying me, he hardly seemed to notice my presence. He probably thought as little of my arrival there, as of an additional pig to his stock. He was the chief agent of his employer. The overseers of all the farms composing the Lloyd estate, were in some sort under him. The Colonel himself seldom addressed an overseer, or allowed himself to be addressed by one. To Captain Anthony, therefore, was committed the head-ship of all the farms. He carried the keys of all the store-houses, weighed and measured the allowances of each slave, at the end of each month; superintended the storing of all goods brought to the store-house; dealt out the raw material to the different handicraftsmen, shipped the grain, tobacco, and all other saleable produce of the numerous farms to Baltimore, and had a general oversight of all the workshops of the place. In addition to all this he was frequently called abroad to Easton and elsewhere in the discharge of his numerous duties as chief agent of the estate.

The family of Captain Anthony consisted of two sons—Andrew and Richard, his daughter Lucretia and her newly-married husband, Captain Thomas Auld. In the kitchen were Aunt Katy, Aunt Esther, and ten or a dozen children, most of them older than myself. Captain Anthony was not considered a rich slave-holder, though he was pretty well off in the world. He owned about thirty slaves and three farms in the Tuckahoe district. The more valuable part of his property was in slaves, of whom he sold one every year, which brought him in seven or eight hundred dollars, besides his yearly salary and other revenue from his lands.

I have been often asked during the earlier part of my free life at the North, how I happened to have so little of the slave accent in my speech. The mystery is in some measure explained by my association with Daniel Lloyd, the youngest son of Colonel Edward Lloyd. The law of compensation holds here as well as elsewhere. While this lad could not associate with ignorance without sharing its shade, he could not give his black playmates his company without giving them his superior intelligence as well. Without knowing this, or caring about it at the time, I, for some cause or other, was attracted to him and was much his companion.

I had little to do with the older brothers of Daniel—Edward and Murray. They were grown up and were fine looking men. Edward was especially esteemed by the slave children and by me among the rest, not that he ever said anything to us or for us which could be called particularly kind. It was enough for us that he never looked or acted scornfully towards us. The idea of rank and station was rigidly maintained on this estate. The family of Captain Anthony never visited the great house, and the Lloyds never came to our house. Equal non-intercourse was observed between Captain Anthony's family and the family of Mr. Seveir, the overseer.

Such, kind readers, was the community and such the place in which my earliest and most lasting impressions of the workings of slavery were received—of which impressions you will learn more in the after chapters of this book.

CHAPTER V: A SLAVEHOLDER'S CHARACTER.

Increasing acquaintance with old Master—Evils of unresisted passion—Apparent tenderness—A man of trouble—Custom of muttering to himself—Brutal outrage—A drunken overseer—Slaveholder's impatience—Wisdom of appeal—A base and selfish attempt to break up a courtship.

ALTHOUGH my old master, Captain Anthony, gave me, at the first of my coming to him from my grandmother's, very little attention, and although that little was of a remarkably mild and gentle description, a few months only were sufficient to convince me that mildness and gentleness were not the prevailing or governing traits of his character. These excellent qualities were displayed only occasionally. He could, when it suited him, appear to be literally insensible to the claims of humanity. He could not only be deaf to the appeals of the helpless against the aggressor, but he could himself commit outrages deep, dark, and nameless. Yet he was not by nature worse than other men. Had he been brought up in a free state, surrounded by the full restraints of civilized society—restraints which are necessary to the freedom of all its members, alike and equally, Captain Anthony might have been as humane a man as are members of such society generally. A man's character always takes its hue, more or less, from the form and colour of things about him. The slaveholder, as well as the slave, was the victim of the slave system. Under the whole heavens there could be no relation more unfavourable to the development of honourable character than that sustained by the slaveholder to the slave. Reason is imprisoned here and passions run wild. Could the reader have seen Captain Anthony gently leading me by the hand, as he sometimes did, patting me on the head, speaking to me in soft, caressing tones and calling me his little Indian boy, he would have deemed him a kind-hearted old man, and really almost fatherly to the slave boy. But the pleasant moods of a slaveholder are transient and fitful. They neither come either nor remain long. The temper of the old man was subject to special trials, but since these trials were never borne patiently, they added little to his natural stock of patience. Aside from his troubles with his slaves and those of Mr. Lloyd's, he made the impression upon me of being an unhappy man. Even to my child's eye he wore a troubled and at times a haggard aspect. His strange movements excited my curiosity and awakened my compassion. He seldom walked alone without muttering to himself, and he occasionally stormed about as if defying an army of invisible foes. Most of his leisure was spent in walking around, cursing and gesticulating as if possessed by a demon. He was evidently a wretched man, at war with his own soul and all the world around him. To be overheard by the children disturbed him very little. He made no more of our presence than that of the ducks and geese he met on the green. But when his gestures were most violent, ending with a threatening shake of the head and a sharp snap of his middle finger and thumb, I deemed it wise to keep at a safe distance from him.

One of the first circumstances that opened my eyes to the cruelties and wickedness of slavery and its hardening influences upon my old master, was his refusal to interpose his authority to protect and shield a young woman, a cousin of mine, who had been most cruelly abused and beaten by his overseer in Tuckahoe. This overseer, a Mr. Plummer, was like most of his class, little less than a human brute; and in addition to his general profligacy and repulsive coarseness, he was a miserable drunkard, a man not fit to have the management of a drove of mules. In one of his moments of drunken madness he committed the outrage which brought the young woman in question down to my old master's for protection. The poor girl, on her arrival at our house, presented a most pitiable appearance. She had left in haste and without preparation, and probably without the knowledge of Mr. Plummer. She had travelled twelve miles, bare-footed, bare-necked, and bare-headed. Her neck and shoulders were covered with scars newly made, and not content with marring her neck and shoulders with the cowhide, the cowardly wretch had dealt her a blow on the head with a hickory club, which cut a horrible gash and left her face literally covered with blood. In this condition the poor young woman came down to implore protection at the hands of my old master. I expected to see him boil over with rage at the revolting deed, and to hear him fill the air with curses upon the brutal Plummer; but I was disappointed. He sternly told her in an angry tone, "She deserved every bit of it, and if she did not go home instantly he would himself take the remaining skin from her neck and back." Thus the poor girl was compelled to return without redress, and perhaps to receive an additional flogging for daring to appeal to authority higher than that of the overseer.

I did not at that time understand the philosophy of this treatment of my cousin. I think I now understand it. This treatment was a part of the system, rather than a part of the man. To have encouraged appeals of this kind would have occasioned much loss of time, and left the overseer powerless to enforce obedience. Nevertheless, when a slave had nerve enough to go straight to his master, with a well-founded complaint against an overseer, though he might be repelled and have even that of which he complained at the time repeated, and though he might be beaten by his master as well as by the overseer, for his temerity, in the end, the policy of complaining was generally vindicated by the relaxed rigour of the overseer's treatment. The latter became more careful and less disposed to use the lash upon such slaves thereafter.

The overseer very naturally disliked to have the ear of the master disturbed by complaints, and either for this reason or because of advice privately given him by his employer, he generally modified the rigor of his rule after complaints of this kind had been made against him. For some cause or other the slaves, no matter how often they were repulsed by their masters, were ever disposed to regard them with less abhorrence than the overseer. And yet these masters would often go beyond their overseers in wanton cruelty. They wielded the lash without any sense of responsibility. They could cripple or kill without fear of consequences. I have seen my old master in a tempest of wrath, full of pride, hatred, jealousy, and revenge, when he seemed a very fiend.

The circumstances which I am about to narrate, and which gave rise to this fearful tempest of passion, were not singular, but very common in our slave-holding community.

The reader will have noticed that among the names of slaves, Esther is mentioned. This was a young woman who possessed that which was ever a curse to the slave girl—namely, personal beauty. She was tall, light-coloured, well-formed, and made a fine appearance. Esther was courted by "Ned Roberts," the son of a favourite slave of Colonel Lloyd, who was as fine-looking a young man as Esther was a woman. Some slaveholders would have been glad to have promoted the marriage of two such persons, but for some reason, Captain Anthony disapproved of their courtship. He strictly ordered her to quit the company of young Roberts, telling her that he would punish her severely if he ever found her again in his company. But it was impossible to keep this couple apart. Meet they would, and meet they did. Had Mr. Anthony been himself a man of honour, his motives in this matter might have appeared more favourably. As it was, they appeared as abhorrent as they were contemptible. It was one of the damning characteristics of slavery, that it robbed its victims of every earthly incentive to a holy life. The fear of God and the hope of heaven were sufficient to sustain many slave women amidst the snares and dangers of their strange lot; but they were ever at the mercy of the power, passion, and caprice of their owners. Slavery provided no means for the honourable perpetuation of the race. Yet despite of this destitution there were many men and women among the slaves who were true and faithful to each other through life.

But to the case in hand. Abhorred and circumvented as he was, Captain Anthony, having the power was determined on revenge. I happened to see its shocking execution, and shall never forget the scene. It was early in the morning, when all was still, and before any of the family in the house or kitchen had risen. I was, in fact, awakened by the heart-rending shrieks and piteous cries of poor Esther. My sleeping-place was on the dirt floor of a little rough closet which opened into the kitchen, and through the cracks in its unplaned boards I could distinctly see and hear what was going on, without being seen. Esther's wrists were firmly tied, and the twisted rope was fastened to a strong iron staple in a heavy wooden beam above, near the fireplace. Here she stood on a bench, her arms tightly drawn above her head. Her back and shoulders were perfectly bare. Behind her stood old master, with cowhide in hand, pursuing his barbarous work with all manner of harsh, coarse, and tantalizing epithets. He was cruelly deliberate, and protracted the torture as one who was delighted with the agony of his victim. Again and again he drew the hateful scourge through his hand, adjusting it with a view of dealing the most pain-giving blow his strength and skill could inflict. Poor Esther had never before been severely whipped. Her shoulders were plump and tender. Each blow, vigorously laid on, brought screams from her as well as blood. "Have mercy! Oh, mercy!" she cried. "I won't do so no more." But her piercing cries seemed only to increase his fury. The whole scene, with all its attendants, was revolting and shocking to the last degree, and when the motives for the brutal castigation are known, language has no power to convey a just sense of its dreadful criminality. After laying on I dare not say how many stripes, old master untied his suffering victim. When let down she could scarcely stand. From my heart I pitied her, and child as I was, and new to such scenes, the shock was tremendous. I was terrified, hushed, stunned, and bewildered. The scene here described was often repeated, for Edward and Esther continued to meet, notwithstanding all efforts to prevent their meeting.

CHAPTER VI: A CHILD'S REASONING

Early reflections on slavery—Aunt Jennie and Uncle Noah—Presentiment of one day becoming a freeman—Conflict between an overseer and a slave woman. Advantage of resistance—Death of an overseer—Colonel Lloyd's plantation home—Monthly distribution of food—Singing of Slaves—An explanation—The slave's food and clothing—Naked children—Life in the quarter—Sleeping places—Not beds—Deprivation of sleep—Care of nursing babies—Ash cake—Contrast.

THE incidents in the foregoing chapter led me thus early to enquire into the origin and nature of slavery. Why am I a slave? Why are some people slaves and others masters? These were perplexing questions and very troublesome to my childhood. I was told by some one very early that "God up in the sky" had made all things, and had made black people to be slaves and white people to be masters. I was told too, that God was good and that He knew what was best for everybody. This was, however, less satisfactory than the first statement. It came point blank against all my notions of goodness. The case of Aunt Esther was in my mind. Besides, I could not tell how anybody could know that God made black people to be slaves. Then I found, too, that there were puzzling exceptions to this theory of slavery, in the fact that all black people were not slaves, and all white people were not masters. An incident occurred about this time that made a deep impression on my mind. One of the men slaves of Captain Anthony and my aunt Jennie ran away. A great noise was made about it. Old master was furious. He said he would follow them and catch them and bring them back, but he never did it, and somebody told me that Uncle Noah and Aunt Jennie had gone to the Free States and were free. Besides this occurrence, which brought much light to my mind on the subject, there were several slaves on Mr. Lloyd's place who remembered being brought from Africa. There were others that told me that their fathers and mothers were stolen from Africa.

This to me was important knowledge, but not such as to make me feel very easy in my slave condition. The success of Aunt Jennie and Uncle Noah in getting away from slavery was, I think, the first fact that made me seriously think of escape for myself. I could not have been more than seven or eight years old at the time of this occurrence, but young as I was, I was already a fugitive from slavery in spirit and purpose.

Up to the time of the brutal treatment of my Aunt Esther, already narrated, and the shocking plight in which I had seen my cousin from Tuckahoe, my attention had not been especially directed to the grosser and more revolting features of slavery. I had, of course, heard of whippings and savage mutilation of slaves by brutal overseers, but happily for me I had always been out of the way of such occurrences. My play time was spent outside of the corn and tobacco fields, where the overseers and slaves were brought together and in conflict. But after the case of my Aunt Esther I saw others of the same disgusting and shocking nature. The one of these which agitated and distressed me most, was the whipping of a woman, not belonging to my old master, but to Col. Lloyd.

The charge against her was very common and very indefinite, namely, "impudence." This crime could be committed by a slave in a hundred different ways, and depended much upon the temper and caprice of the overseer as to whether it was committed at all. He could create the offence whenever it pleased him. A look, a word, a gesture, accidental or intentional, never failed to be taken as "impudence" when he was in the right mood for such an offence. In this case there were all the necessary conditions for the commission of the crime charged. The offender was nearly white, to begin with; she was the wife of a favourite hand on board of Mr. Lloyd's sloop, and was besides the mother of five sprightly children. Vigorous and spirited woman that she was, a wife and a mother, she had a predominating share of the blood of the master running in her veins. Nellie, for that was her name, had all the qualities essential to "impudence" to a slave overseer. My attention was called to the scene of the castigation by the loud screams and curses that proceeded from the direction of it. When I came near the parties engaged in the struggle, the overseer had hold of Nellie, endeavouring with his whole strength to drag her to a tree against her resistance. Both his and her faces were bleeding, for the woman was doing her best. Three of her children were present, and though quite small, from seven to ten years old I should think, they gallantly took the side of their mother against the overseer, and pelted him with stones and epithets. Amid the screams of the children "Let my mammy go! Let my mammy go!" the hoarse voice of the maddened overseer was heard in terrible oaths that he would teach her how to give a white man "impudence." The blood on his face and on hers attested her skill in the use of her nails, and his dogged determination to conquer. His purpose was to tie her up to a tree and give her, in slave-holding parlance, a "genteel flogging;" and he evidently had not expected the stern and protracted resistance he was meeting, or the strength and skill needed to its execution. There were times when she seemed likely to get the better of the brute, but he finally overpowered her, and succeeded in getting her arms firmly tied to the tree towards which he had been dragging her. The victim was now at the mercy of his merciless lash. What followed I need not here describe. The cries of the now helpless woman, while undergoing the terrible infliction, were mingled with the hoarse curses of the overseer and the wild cries of her distracted children. When the poor woman was untied, her back was covered with blood. She was whipped, terribly whipped, but she was not subdued, and continued to denounce the overseer, and pour upon him every vile epithet she could think of. Such floggings are seldom repeated by overseers on the same persons. They preferred to whip those who were the most easily whipped. The doctrine that submission to violence is the best cure for violence did not hold good as between slaves and overseers. He was whipped oftener who was whipped easiest. That slave who had the courage to stand up for himself against the overseer, although he might have many hard stripes at first, became, while legally a slave, virtually, a freeman. "You can shoot me," said a slave to Rigby Hopkins, "but you can't whip me," and the result was he was neither whipped nor shot. I do not know that Mr. Sevier ever attempted to whip Nellie again. He probably never did, for not long after he was taken sick and died. It was commonly said that his death-bed was a wretched one, and that the ruling passion being strong in death, he died flourishing the slave whip, and with horrid oaths upon his lips. Such a death-bed scene may only have been the imagining of the slaves. One thing is certain, that when he was in health his profanity was enough to chill the blood of an ordinary man. Nature, or habit had given to his face an expression of uncommon savageness. Tobacco and rage had ground his teeth short, and nearly every sentence that he uttered was commenced or completed with an oath. Hated for his cruelty, despised for his cowardice, he went to his grave lamented by nobody on the place outside of his own house, if, indeed, he was even lamented there.

In Mr. James Hopkins, the succeeding overseer, we had a different and a better man, as good perhaps as any man could be in the position of a slave overseer. Though he sometimes wielded the lash, it was evident that he took no pleasure in it and did it with much reluctance. He stayed but a short time here, and his removal from the position was much regretted by the slaves generally. Of the successor of Mr. Hopkins I shall have something to say at another time and in another place.

For the present we will attend to a further description of the business-like aspect of Colonel Lloyd's "Great House" farm. There was always much bustle and noise there on the two days at the end of each month; for then the slaves belonging to the different branches of this great estate assembled there by their representatives to obtain their monthly allowances of corn-meal and pork. These were gala days for the slaves of the out-lying farms, and there was much rivalry among them as to who should be elected to go up to the Great House farm for the "Allowances;" and indeed, to attend to any other business at this great place, to them the capitol of a little nation. Its beauty and grandeur, its immense wealth, its numerous population, and the fact that Uncles Harry, Peter, and Jake, the sailors on board the sloop, usually kept trinkets on sale, which they bought in Baltimore to sell to their less fortunate fellow servants, made a visit to the Great House farm a high privilege, and eagerly sought. It was valued, too, as a mark of distinction and confidence; but probably, the chief motive among the competitors for the office was the opportunity it afforded to shake off the monotony of the field, and to get beyond the overseer's eye and lash. Once on the road with an ox team, and seated on the tongue of the cart, with no overseer to look after him, he felt himself comparatively free.

Slaves were expected to sing as well as to work. A silent slave was not liked either by masters, or by overseers. "Make a noise there! make a noise there!" and "bear a hand," were words usually addressed to slaves when they were silent. This, and the natural disposition of the negro to make a noise in the world, may account for the almost constant singing among them when at work. There was generally more or less singing among the teamsters at all times. It was a means of telling the overseer, in the distance, where they were, and what they were about. But on the allowance days those commissioned to the Great House farm were peculiarly vocal. While on the way, they would make the grand old woods for miles around reverberate with their wild and plaintive notes. They were indeed both merry and sad. Child as I was, these wild songs greatly depressed my spirits. Nowhere outside of dear old Ireland, in the days of want and famine, have I heard sounds so mournful.

In all these slave songs there was ever some expression of praise of the Great House farm—something that would please the pride of the Lloyds.

- I am going away to the Great House farm,

- O, yea! O, yea! O, yea!

- My old master is a good old master,

- O, yea! O, yea! O, yea!

These words would be sung over and over again, with others, improvised as they went along—jargon, perhaps, to the reader, but full of meaning to the singers. I have sometimes thought, that the mere hearing of these songs would have done more to impress the good people of the North with the soul-crushing character of slavery, than whole volumes exposing the physical cruelties of the slave system; for the heart has no language like song. Many years ago, when recollecting my experience in this respect, I wrote of these slave songs in the following strain:—

"I did not, when a slave, fully understand the deep meaning of those rude and apparently incoherent songs. I was, myself, within the circle, so that I could then neither hear nor see as those without might see and hear. They breathed the prayer and complaint of souls overflowing with the bitterest anguish. They depressed my spirits and filled my heart with ineffable sadness."

The remark in the olden time was not unfrequently made, that slaves were the most contented and happy labourers in the world, and their dancing and singing were referred to in proof of this alleged fact; but it was a great mistake to suppose them happy because they sometimes made those joyful noises. The songs of the slaves represented their sorrows, rather than their joys. Like tears, they were a relief to their aching hearts. It is not inconsistent with the constitution of the human mind, that it avails itself of one and the same method for expressing opposite emotions. Sorrow and desolation have their songs, as well as joy and peace.

It was the boast of slaveholders that their slaves enjoyed more of the physical comforts of life than the peasantry of any country in the world. My experience contradicts this. The men and the women slaves on Col. Lloyd's farm received as their monthly allowance of food, eight pounds of pickled pork, or its equivalent in fish. The pork was often tainted, and the fish were of the poorest quality. With their pork or fish, they had given them one bushel of Indian meal, unbolted, of which quite fifteen per cent. was more fit for pigs than for men. With this, one pint of salt was given, and this was the entire monthly allowance of a full-grown slave, working constantly in the open field from morning till night every day in the month except Sunday. There is no kind of work which really requires a better supply of food to prevent physical exhaustion than the field work of a slave. The yearly allowance of clothing was not more ample than the supply of food. It consisted of two tow-linen shirts, one pair of trousers of the same coarse material, for summer, and a woollen pair of trowsers and a woollen jacket for winter, with one pair of yarn stockings and a pair of the coarsest description. Children under ten years old had neither shoes, stockings, jackets, nor trousers. They had two coarse tow-linen shirts per year, and when these were worn out they went naked till the next allowance day—and this was the condition of the little girls as well as the boys. As to beds, they had none. One coarse blanket was given them, and this only to the men and women. The children stuck themselves in holes and corners about the quarters, often in the corners of huge chimneys, with their feet in the ashes to keep them warm. The want of beds, however, was not considered a great privation by the field hands. Time to sleep was of far greater importance. For when the day's work was done most of them had their washing, mending, and cooking to do, and having few or no facilities for doing such things, very many of their needed sleeping hours were consumed in necessary preparations for the labours of the coming day. The sleeping apartments, if they could have been properly called such, had little regard to comfort or decency. Old and young, male and female, married and single, dropped down upon the common clay floor, each covered up with his or her blanket, their only protection from cold or exposure. The night, however, was shortened at both ends. The slaves worked often as long as they could see, and were late in cooking and mending for the coming day, and at the first gray streak of the morning they were summoned to the field by the overseer's horn. They were whipped for over-sleeping more than for any other fault. Neither age nor sex found any favour. The overseer stood at the quarter door, armed with stick and whip, ready to deal heavy blows upon any who might be a little behind time. When the horn was blown there was a rush for the door, for the hindermost one was sure to get a blow from the overseer. Young mothers who worked in the field were allowed an hour about ten o'clock in the morning to go home to nurse their children. This was when they were not required to take them to the field with them, and leave them upon "turning row," or in the corner of the fences.

As a general rule the slaves did not come to their quarters to take their meals, but took their ash-cake—called thus because baked in the ashes—and piece of pork, or their salt herrings, where they were at work.

But let us now leave the rough usage of the field, where vulgar coarseness and brutal cruelty flourished as rank as weeds in the tropics, where a vile wretch, in the shape of a man, rides, walks, and struts about, with whip in hand, dealing heavy blows and leaving deep gashes on the flesh of men and women, and turn our attention to the less repulsive slave life as it existed in the home of my childhood. Some idea of the splendour of that place sixty years ago has already been given. The contrast between the condition of the slaves and that of their masters was marvellously sharp and striking. There were pride, pomp, and luxury on the one hand, servility, dejection, and misery on the other.

CHAPTER VII: LUXURIES AT THE GREAT HOUSE.

Contrasts—Great House luxuries—Its hospitality—Entertainments—Faultfinding—Shameful humiliation of an old and faithful coachman—William Wilks—Curious incident—Expressed satisfaction not always genuine—Reasons for suppressing the truth.

THE close-fisted stinginess that fed the poor slave on coarse corn-meal and tainted meat, that clothed him in trashy tow-linen, and hurried him on to toil through the field in all weathers, with wind and rain beating through his tattered garments, that scarcely gave even the young slave-mother time to nurse her infant in the fence-corner, wholly vanished on approaching the sacred precincts of the "Great House" itself. There, the scriptural phrase descriptive of the wealthy found exact illustration. The highly-favoured inmates of the mansion were literally arrayed in "purple and fine linen, and fared sumptuously every day." The table of the house groaned under the blood-bought luxuries gathered with pains-taking care at home and abroad. Fields, forests, rivers, and seas were made tributary. Immense wealth and its lavish expenditure filled the Great House with all that could please the eye, or tempt the taste. Fish, flesh, and fowl were there in profusion. Chickens of all breeds; ducks of all kinds, wild and tame, the common and the huge Muscovite; Guinea fowls, turkeys, geese, and pea-fowls were fat, and fattening for the destined vortex. There the graceful swan, the mongrels, the black-necked wild goose, partridges, quails, pheasants, and pigeons, choice water-fowl, with all their strange varieties, were caught in the huge net. Beef, veal, mutton, and venison, of the most select kinds and quality, rolled in bounteous profusion to this grand consumer. The teeming riches of Chesapeake Bay, its rock-perch, drums, crocus, trout, oysters, crabs, and terrapin were drawn thither to adorn the glittering table. The dairy, too, the finest then on the eastern shore of Maryland, supplied by cattle of the best English stock, imported for the express purpose, poured its rich donations of fragrant cheese, golden butter, and delicious cream to heighten the attractions of the gorgeous, unending round of feasting. Nor were the fruits of the earth overlooked. The fertile garden, many acres in size, constituting a separate establishment distinct from the common farm, with its scientific gardener direct from Scotland, a Mr. McDermott, and four men under his direction, was not behind, either in the abundance or in the delicacy of its contributions. The tender asparagus, the crispy celery, and the delicate cauliflower, egg plants, beets, lettuce, parsnips, peas, and French beans, early and late, radishes, cantelopes, melons of all kinds; and the fruits of all climes and of every description, from the hardy apples of the North to the lemon and orange of the South, culminated at this point. Here were gathered figs, raisins, almonds, and grapes from Spain, wines and brandies from France, teas of various flavour from China, and rich aromatic coffee from Java, all conspiring to swell the tide of high life, where pride and indolence lounged in magnificence and satiety.

Behind the tall-backed and elaborately wrought chairs stood the servants, fifteen in number, carefully selected, not only with a view to their capacity and adeptness, but with especial regard to their personal appearance, their graceful agility, and pleasing address. Some of these servants, armed with fans, wafted reviving breezes to the over-heated brows of the alabaster ladies, whilst others watched with eager eye and fawn-like step, anticipating and supplying wants before they were sufficiently formed to be announced by word or sign.

These servants constituted a sort of black aristocracy. They resembled the field hands in nothing except their colour, and in this they held the advantage of a velvet-like glossiness, rich and beautiful. The hair, too, showed the same advantage. The delicately-formed coloured maid rustled in the scarcely-worn silk of her young mistress, while the servant men were equally well attired from the overflowing wardrobe of their young masters, so that in dress, as well as in form and feature, in manner and speech, in tastes and habits, the distance between these favoured few and the sorrow and hunger-smitten multitudes of the quarter and the field was immense.

In the stables and carriage-houses were to be found the same evidences of pride and luxurious extravagance. Here were three splendid coaches, soft within and lustrous without. Here, too, were gigs, phaetons, barouches, sulkeys, and sleighs. Here were saddles and harness, beautifully wrought and richly mounted. No less than thirty-five horses of the best approved blood, both for speed and beauty, were kept only for pleasure. The care of these horses constituted the entire occupation of two men, one or the other of them being always in the stable to answer any call which might be made from the Great House, Over the way from the stable was a house built expressly for the hounds, a pack of twenty-five or thirty, the fare for which would have made glad the hearts of a dozen slaves. Horses and hounds, however, were not the only consumers of the slave's toil. The hospitality practised at the Lloyd's, would have astonished and charmed many a health-seeking divine or merchant from the North. Viewed from his table, and not from the field, Colonel Lloyd was, indeed, a model of generous hospitality. His house was literally a hotel for weeks, during the summer months. At these times, especially, the air was freighted with the rich fumes of baking, boiling, roasting, and broiling. It was something to me that I could share these odours with the winds, even if the meats themselves were under a more stringent monopoly. In master Daniel I had a friend at court, who would sometimes give me a cake, and who kept me well informed as to their guests and their entertainments. Viewed from Col. Lloyd's table, who could have said that his slaves were not well clad and well cared for? Who would have said they did not glory in being the slaves of such a master? Who but a fanatic could have seen any cause for sympathy for either master or slave? Alas, this immense wealth, this gilded splendour, this profusion of luxury, this exemption from toil, this life of ease, this sea of plenty were not the pearly gates they seemed to a world of happiness aud sweet content. The poor slave, on his hard pine plank, scantily covered with his thin blanket, slept more soundly than the feverish voluptuary who reclined upon his downy pillow. Food to the indolent is poison, not sustenance. Lurking beneath the rich and tempting viands were invisible spirits of evil, which filled the self-deluded gourmandizer with aches and pains, passions uncontrollable, fierce tempers, dyspepsia, rheumatism, lumbago, and gout, and of these the Lloyds had a full share.

I had many opportunities of witnessing the restless discontent and capricious irritation of the Lloyds. My fondness for horses attracted me to the stables much of the time. The two men in charge of this establishment were old and young Barney—father and son. Old Barney was a fine looking, portly old man of a brownish complexion, and a respectful and dignified bearing. He was much devoted to his profession, and held his office as an honourable one. He was a farrier as well as an ostler, and could bleed, remove lampers from their mouths, and administer medicine to horses. No one on the farm knew so well as old Barney what to do with a sick horse; but his office was not an enviable one, and his gifts and acquirements were of little advantage to him. In nothing was Col. Lloyd more unreasonable and exacting than in respect to the management of his horses. Any supposed inattention to these animals was sure to be visited with degrading punishment. His horses and dogs fared better than his men. Their beds were far softer and cleaner than those of his human cattle. No excuse could shield old Barney if the Colonel only suspected something wrong about his horses, and consequently he was often punished when faultless. It was painful to hear the unreasonable and fretful scoldings administered by Col. Lloyd, his son Murray, and his sons-in-law, to this poor man. Three of the daughters of Col. Lloyd were married, and they with their husbands remained at the great house a portion of the year, and enjoyed the luxury of whipping the servants when they pleased. A horse was seldom brought out of the stable to which no objection could be raised. "There was dust in his hair;" "there was a twist in his reins;" "his foretop was not combed;" "his mane did not lie straight;" "his head did not look well;" "his fetlocks had not been properly trimmed." Something was always wrong. However groundless the complaint, Barney must stand, hat in hand, lips sealed, never answering a word in explanation or excuse. In a free State, a master thus complaining without cause, might be told by his ostler: "Sir, I am sorry I cannot please you, but since I have done the best I can and fail to do so, your remedy is to dismiss me." But here the ostler must listen and tremblingly abide his master's behest. One of the most heart-saddening and humiliating scenes I ever witnessed was the whipping of old

Barney by Col. Lloyd. These two men were both advanced in years; there were the silver locks of the master, and the bald and toil-worn brow of the slave—superior and inferior here, powerful and weak here, but equals before God. "Uncover your head," said the imperious master; he was obeyed. "Take off your jacket, you old rascal?" and off came Barney's jacket. "Down on your knees!" down knelt the old man, his shoulders bare, his bald head glistening in the sunshine, and his aged knees on the cold, damp ground. In this humble and debasing attitude, that master, to whom he had devoted the best years and the best strength of his life, came forward and laid on thirty lashes with his horse-whip. The old man made no resistance, but bore it patiently, answering each blow with only a shrug of the shoulders and a groan. I do not think that the physical suffering from this infliction was severe, for the whip was a light riding-whip; but the spectacle of an aged man—a husband and a father—humbly kneeling before his fellow-man, shocked me at the time; and since I have grown older, few of the features of slavery have impressed me with a deeper sense of its injustice and barbarity than this exciting scene. I owe it to the truth, however, to say that this was the first and last time I ever saw a slave compelled to kneel to receive a whipping.

Another incident, illustrating a phase of slavery to which I have referred in another connection, I may here mention. Besides two other coachmen, Col. Lloyd owned one named William Wilks, and his was one of the exceptional cases where a slave possessed a surname, and was recognised by it, by both coloured and white people. Wilks was a very fine-looking man. He was about as white as any one on the plantation, and in form and feature bore a very striking resemblance to Murray Lloyd. It was whispered and generally believed that William Wilks was a son of Col. Lloyd, by a highly favoured slave-woman, who was still on the plantation. There were many reasons for believing this whisper, not only from his personal appearance, but from the undeniable freedom which he enjoyed over all others, and his apparent consciousness of being something more than a slave to his master. It was notorious too, that William had a deadly enemy in Murray Lloyd, whom he so much resembled, and that the latter greatly worried his father with importunities to sell William. Indeed, he gave his father no rest, until he did sell him to Austin Woldfolk, the great slavetrader at that time. Before selling him, however, he tried to make things smooth by giving William a whipping, but it proved a failure. It was a compromise, and like most such, defeated itself,—for soon after Col. Lloyd atoned to William for the abuse, by giving him a gold watch and chain. Another fact somewhat curious was, that though sold to the remorseless Woldfolk, taken in irons to Baltimore, and cast into prison, with a view to being sent to the South, William outbid all his purchasers, paid for himself, and afterwards resided in Baltimore. How this was accomplished was a great mystery at the time, explained only on the supposition that the hand which had bestowed the gold watch and chain, had also supplied the purchase-money, but I have since learned that this was not the true explanation. Wilks had many friends in Baltimore and Annapolis, and they united to save him from a fate which was the one of all others most dreaded by the slaves. Practical amalgamation was however so common at the South, and so many circumstances pointed in that direction, that there was little reason to doubt that William Wilks was the son of Edward Lloyd.

The real feelings and opinions of the slaves were not much known or respected by their masters. The distance between the two was too great to admit of such knowledge; and in this respect Col. Lloyd was no exception to the rule. His slaves were so numerous he did not know them when he saw them. Nor, indeed, did all his slaves know him. It is reported of him, that riding along the road one day he met a coloured man, and addressed him in what was the usual way of speaking to coloured people on the public highways of the South: "Well, boy, who do you belong to?" "To Col. Lloyd," replied the slave. "Well, does the Colonel treat you well?" "No, sir," was the ready reply. "What, does he work you hard?" "Yes, sir." "Well, don't he give you enough to eat?" "Yes, sir, he gives me enough to eat, such as it is." The Colonel rode on; the slave also went on about his business, not dreaming that he had been conversing with his master. He thought and said nothing of the matter, until two or three weeks afterwards, he was informed by the overseer that for having found fault with his master, he was now to be sold to a Georgia trader. He was immediately chained and handcuffed; and thus without a moment's warning, he was snatched away, and forever sundered from his family and friends by a hand as unrelenting as that of death. This was the penalty of telling the simple truth, in answer to a series of plain questions. It was partly in consequence of such facts, that slaves, when inquired of as to their condition and the character of their masters, would almost invariably say that they were contented and their masters kind. Slaveholders are known to have sent spies among their slaves to ascertain if possible their views and feelings in regard to their condition; hence the maxim established among them, that "a still tongue makes a wise head." They would suppress the truth rather than take the consequence of telling it, and in so doing they proved themselves a part of the human family. I was frequently asked if I had a kind master, and I do not remember ever to have given a negative reply. I did not consider myself as uttering that which was strictly untrue, for I always measured the kindness of my master by the standard of kindness set by the slaveholders around us.

CHAPTER VIII: CHARACTERISTICS OF OVERSEERS.

Austin Gore—Sketch of his character—Overseers as a class—Their peculiar characteristics— The marked individuality of Austin Gore—His sense of duty—Murder of poor Denby— Sensation—How Gore made his peace with Colonel Lloyd—Other horrible murders—No laws for the protection of slaves could possibly be enforced.

THE comparatively moderate rule of Mr. Hopkins as overseer on Col. Lloyd's plantation was succeeded by that of another whose name was Austin Gore. I hardly know how to bring this man fitly before the reader, for under him there was more suffering from violence and bloodshed than had, according to the older slaves, ever been experienced before at that place. He was an overseer, and possessed the peculiar characteristics of his class, yet to call him merely an overseer would not give one a fair conception of the man. I speak of overseers as a class, for they were such. They were as distinct from the slave-holding gentry of the South as are the fish-women of Paris, and the coal-heavers of London, distinct from other grades of society. They constituted a separate fraternity at the South. They were arranged and classified by that great law of attraction which determines the sphere and affinities of men; which ordains that men whose malign and brutal propensities preponderate over their moral and intellectual endowments shall naturally fall into those employments which promise the largest gratification to those predominating instincts or propensities. The office of overseer took this raw material of vulgarity and brutality, and stamped it as a distinct class in Southern life. But in this class, as in all other classes, there were sometimes persons of marked individuality, yet with a general resemblance to the mass. Mr. Gore was one of those to whom a general characterization would do no manner of justice. He was an overseer, but he was something more. With the malign and tyrannical qualities of an overseer he combined something of the lawful master. He had the artfulness and mean ambition of his class, without its disgusting swagger and noisy bravado. There was an easy air of independence about him; a calm self-possession; at the same time a sternness of glance which might well daunt less timid hearts than those of poor slaves, accustomed from childhood to cower before a driver's lash. He was one of those overseers who could torture the slightest word or look into "impudence," and he had the nerve not only to resent but to punish promptly and severely. There could be no answering back. Guilty or not guilty, to be accused was to be sure of a flogging. His very presence was fearful, and I shunned him as I would have shunned a rattlesnake. His piercing black eyes and sharp, shrill voice ever awakened sensations of dread. Other overseers, how brutal soever they might be, would sometimes seek to gain favour with the slaves, by indulging in a little pleasantry; but Gore never said a funny thing, or perpetrated a joke. He was always cold, distant, and unapproachable—the overseer on Col. Edward Lloyd's plantation—and needed no higher pleasure than the performance of the duties of his office. When he used the lash, it was from a sense of duty, without fear of consequences. There was a stern will, an iron-like reality about him, which would easily have made him chief of a band of pirates, had his environments been favourable to such a sphere. Among many other deeds of shocking cruelty committed by him was the murder of a young coloured man named Bill Denby. He was a powerful fellow, full of animal spirits, and one of the most valuable of Col. Lloyd's slaves. In some way—I know not what—he offended this Mr. Austin Gore, and in accordance with the usual custom the latter undertook to flog him. He had given him but few stripes when Digby broke away from him, plunged into the creek, and standing there with the water up to his neck refused to come out; whereupon, for this refusal, Gore shot him dead; It is said that Gore gave Denby three calls to come out, telling him if he did not obey the last call he should shoot him. When the last call was given Denby still stood his ground, and Gore, without further parley, or without making any further effort to induce obedience, raised his gun deliberately to his face, took deadly aim at his standing victim, and with one click of the gun the mangled body sank out of sight, and only his warm red blood marked the place where he had stood.

This fiendish murder produced, as it could not help doing, a tremendous sensation. The slaves were panic-stricken, and howled with alarm. The atrocity roused my old master, and he spoke out in reprobation of it. Both he and Colonel Lloyd arraigned Gore for his cruelty; but he, calm and collected, as though nothing unusual had happened, declared that Denby had become unmanageable; that he set a dangerous example to the other slaves, and that unless some such prompt measure was resorted to, there would be an end to all rule and order on the plantation. That convenient covert for all manner of villainy and outrage, that cowardly alarm-cry, that the slaves would "take the place," was pleaded, just as it had been in thousands of similar cases. Gore's defence was evidently considered satisfactory, for he was continued in his office, without being subjected to a judicial investigation. The murder was committed in the presence of slaves only, and they, being slaves, could neither institute a suit nor testify against the murderer. Mr. Gore lived in St. Michaels, Talbot Co., Maryland, and I have no reason to doubt, from what I know to have been the moral sentiment of the place, that he was as highly esteemed and as much respected as though his guilty soul had not been stained with innocent blood.

I speak advisedly when I say that killing a slave, or any colored person, in Talbot Co., Maryland, was not treated as a crime, either by the courts or the community. Mr. Thomas Lanman, ship carpenter of St. Michael's, killed two slaves, one of whom he butchered with a hatchet, by knocking his brains out. He used to boast of having committed the awful and bloody deed. I have heard him do so laughingly, declaring himself a benefactor of his country, and that "when others would do as much as he had done, they would be rid of the d—d niggers."

Another notorious fact which I may state was the murder of a young girl between fifteen and sixteen years of age, by her mistress, Mrs. Giles Hicks, who lived but a short distance from Colonel Lloyd's. This wicked woman, in the paroxysm of her wrath, not content with killing her victim, literally mangled her face, and broke her breast-bone. Wild and infuriated as she was, she took the precaution to cause the burial of the girl; but, the facts of the case getting abroad, the remains were disinterred, and a coroner's jury assembled, who, after due deliberation, decided that "the girl had come to her death from severe beating." The offence for which this girl was thus hurried out of the world was this, she had been set that night, and several preceding nights, to mind Mrs. Hicks' baby, and having fallen into a sound sleep, the crying of the baby did not wake her, as it did its mother. The tardiness of the girl excited Mrs. Hicks, who, after calling her many times, seized a piece of fire-wood from the fire-place, and pounded in her skull and breast-bone till death ensued. I will not say that this murder most foul produced no sensation. It did produce a sensation. A warrant was issued for the arrest of Mrs. Hicks, but incredible to tell, for some reason or other, that warrant was never served, and she not only escaped condign punishment, but also the pain and mortification of being arraigned before a court of justice.

While I am detailing the bloody deeds that took place during my stay on Colonel Lloyd's plantation, I will briefly narrate another dark transaction, which occurred about the time of the murder of Denby.

On the side of the river Wye, opposite Colonel Lloyd's, there lived a Mr. Beal Bondley, a wealthy slaveholder. In the direction of his land, and near the shore, there was an excellent oyster fishing-ground, and to this some of Lloyd's slaves occasionally resorted in their little canoes at night, with a view of making up the deficiency of their scanty allowance of food by the oysters that they could easily get there. Mr. Bondley took it into his head to regard this as a trespass, and while an old man slave was engaged in catching a few of the many millions of oysters that lined the bottom of the creek, to satisfy his hunger, the rascally Bondley, lying in ambush, without the slightest warning, discharged the contents of his musket into the back of the poor old man. As good fortune would have it, the shot did not prove fatal, and Mr. Bondley came over, the next day, to see Colonel Lloyd about it. What happened between them I know not, but there was little said about it and nothing publicly done. One of the commonest sayings to which my ears early became accustomed, was that it was "worth but half a cent to kill a nigger, and half a cent to bury one." While I heard of numerous murders committed by slaveholders on the eastern shore of Maryland, I never knew a solitary instance where a slaveholder was either hung or imprisoned for having murdered a slave. The usual pretext for such crimes was that the slave had offered resistance. Should a slave, when assaulted, but raise his hand in self-defence, the white assaulting party was fully justified by Southern law, and Southern public opinion, in shooting the slave down, and for this there was no redress.

CHAPTER IX: CHANGE OF LOCATION.

Miss Lucretia—Her kindness—How it was manifested—"Ike"—A battle with him—Miss Lucretia's balsam—Bread—How it was obtained—Gleams of sunlight amidst the general darkness—Suffering from cold—How we took our meal mush—Preparations for going to Baltimore—Delight at the change—Cousin Tom's opinion of Baltimore—Arrival there—Kind reception—Mr. and Mrs. Hugh Auld—Their son Tommy—My relations to them—My duties—A turning-point in my life.

I HAVE nothing cruel or shocking to relate of my own personal experience while I remained on Colonel Lloyd's plantation, at the home of my old master. An occasional cuff from Aunt Katy, and a regular whipping from old master, such as any heedless and mischievous boy might get from his father, is all that I have to say of this sort. I was not old enough to work in the field, and there being little else than field-work to perform, I had much leisure. The most I had to do was to drive up the cows in the evening, to keep the front-yard clean, and to perform small errands for my young mistress, Lucretia Auld. I had reasons for thinking this lady was very kindly disposed towards me, and although I was not often the object of her attention, I constantly regarded her as my friend, and was always glad when it was my privilege to do her a service. In a family where there was so much that was harsh and indifferent, the slightest word or look of kindness was of great value. Miss Lucretia—as we all continued to call her long after her marriage—had bestowed on me such looks and words as taught me that she pitied me, if she did not love me. She sometimes gave me a piece of bread and butter, an article not set down in our bill of fare, but an extra ration aside from both Aunt Katy and old master, and given as I believed solely out of the tender regard she had for me. Then too, I one day got into the wars with Uncle Abel's son "Ike," and had got sadly worsted; the little rascal struck me directly in the forehead with a sharp piece of cinder, fused with iron, from the old blacksmith's forge, which made a cross in my forehead very plainly to be seen even now. The gash bled very freely, and I roared and betook myself home. The cold-hearted Aunt Katy paid no attention either to my wound or my roaring, except to tell me it "served me right; and I had no business with Ike; it would do me good; I would now keep away from 'dem Lloyd niggers.' " Miss Lucretia in this state of the case came forward, and called me into the parlour, an extra privilege of itself, and without using toward me any of the hard and reproachful epithets of Aunt Katy, quietly acted the good Samaritan. With her own soft hand she washed the blood from my head and face, brought her own bottle of balsam, and with the balsam wetted a nice piece of white linen and bound up my head. The balsam was not more healing to the wound in my head, than her kindness was healing to the wounds in my spirit, induced by the unfeeling words of Aunt Katy. After this Miss Lucretia was yet more my friend. I felt her to be such; and I have no doubt that the simple act of binding up my head did much to awaken in her heart an interest in my welfare. It is quite true that this interest seldom showed itself in anything more than in giving me a piece of bread and butter, but this was a great favour on a slave plantation, and I was the only one of the children to whom such attention was paid. When very severely pinched with hunger, I had the habit of singing, which the good lady very soon came to understand, and when she heard me singing under her window, I was very apt to be paid for my music. Thus I had two friends, both at important points,—Mas'r Daniel at the great house, and Miss Lucretia at home. From Mas'r Daniel I got protection from the bigger boys, and from Miss Lucretia I got bread by singing when I was hungry, and sympathy when I was abused by the termagant in the kitchen. For such friendship I was deeply grateful, and bitter as are my recollections of slavery, it is true pleasure to recall any instances of kindness, any sunbeams of humane treatment, which found way to my soul, through the iron grating of my house of bondage. Such beams seem all the brighter from the general darkness into which they penetrate, and the impression they make there is vividly distinct.

As before intimated, I received no severe treatment from the hands of my master, but the insufficiency of both food and clothing was a serious trial to me, especially from the lack of clothing. In hottest summer and coldest winter, I was kept almost in a state of nudity. My only clothing—a little coarse sack-cloth or tow-linen sort of shirt, scarcely reaching to my knees, was worn night and day and changed once a week. In the day time I could protect myself by keeping on the sunny side of the house, or in stormy weather, in the corner of the kitchen chimney. But the great difficulty was to keep warm during the night. The pigs in the pen had leaves, and the horses in the stable had straw, but the children had no beds. They lodged anywhere in the ample kitchen. I slept generally in a little closet, without even a blanket to cover me. In very cold weather I sometimes got down the bag in which corn was carried to the mill, and crawled into that. Sleeping there with my head in and my feet out, I was partly protected, though never comfortable. My feet have been so cracked with the frost that the pen with which I am writing might be laid in the gashes. Our corn meal mush, which was our only regular if not all-sufficing diet, when sufficiently cooled from the cooking, was placed in a large tray or trough. This was set down on the floor of the kitchen, or out of doors on the ground, and the children were called like so many pigs, and like so many pigs would come, some with oyster-shells, some with pieces of shingle, but none with spoons, and literally devour the mush. He who could eat fastest got most, and he that was strongest got the best place, but few left the trough really satisfied. I was the most unlucky of all, for Aunt Katy had no good feeling for me, and if I pushed the children, or if they told her of anything unfavourable of me, she always believed the worst, and was sure to whip me.

As I grew older and more thoughtful, I became more and more filled with a sense of my wretchedness. The unkindness of Aunt Katy, the hunger and cold I suffered, and the terrible reports of wrongs and outrages which came to my ear, together with what I almost daily witnessed, led me to wish I had never been born. I used to contrast my condition with that of the black-birds, whose wild and sweet songs made me fancy them so happy. Their apparent joy only deepened the shades of my sorrow. There are thoughtful days in the lives of children—at least there were in mine—when they grapple with all the great primary subjects of knowledge, and reach in a moment conclusions which no subsequent experience can shake. I was just as well aware of the unjust, unnatural, and murderous character of slavery, when nine years old, as I am now. Without any appeal to books, to laws, or to authorities of any kind, to regard God as "Our Father," condemned slavery as a crime.

I was in this unhappy state when I received from Miss Lucretia the joyful intelligence that my old master had determined to let me go to Baltimore to live with Mr. Hugh Auld, a brother to Mr. Thomas Auld, Miss Lucretia's husband. I shall never forget the ecstacy with which I received this information, three days before the time set for my departure. They were the three happiest days I had ever known. I spent the largest part of them in the creek, washing off the plantation scurf, and thus preparing for my new home. Miss Lucretia took a lively interest in getting me ready. She told me I must get all the dead skin off my feet and knees, for the people in Baltimore were very cleanly, and would laugh at me if I looked dirty; and besides she was intending to give me a pair of trowsers, but which I could not put on unless I got all the dirt off. This was a warning which I was bound to heed, for the thought of owning and wearing a pair of trowsers was great indeed. So I went at it in good earnest, working for the first time in my life in the hope of reward. I was greatly excited, and could hardly consent to sleep lest I should be left. The ties that ordinarily bind children to their homes, had no existence in my case, and in thinking of a home elsewhere, I was confident of finding none that I should relish less than the one I was leaving, If I should meet with hardship, hunger, and nakedness, I had known them all before, and I could endure them elsewhere, especially in Baltimore, for I had something of the feeling about that city which is expressed in the saying that "being hanged in England is better than dying a natural death in Ireland." I had the strongest desire to see Baltimore. My cousin Tom, a boy two or three years older than I, had been there, and, though not fluent in speech,—he stuttered immoderately,—he had inspired me with that desire by his eloquent descriptions of the place. Tom was sometimes cabin-boy on board the sloop "Sally Lloyd," which Capt. Thomas Auld commanded, and when he came home from Baltimore he was always a sort of hero among us, at least till his trip to Baltimore was forgotten. I could never tell him anything, or point out anything that struck me as beautiful or powerful, but he had seen something in Baltimore far surpassing it. Even the "great house," with all its pictures within, and pillars without, he had the hardihood to say, "was nothing to Baltimore." He bought a trumpet, worth sixpence, and brought it home; told what he had seen in the windows of the stores; that he had heard shooting-crackers, and seen soldiers; that he had seen a steamboat; that there were ships in Baltimore that could carry four such sloops as the "Sally Lloyd." He said a great deal about the Market house; of the ringing of the bells; and of many other things which roused my curiosity very much, and indeed which brightened my hopes of happiness in my new home. We sailed out of Miles River for Baltimore early on Saturday morning. I remember only the day of the week, for at that time I had no knowledge of the days of the month, nor indeed of the months of the year. On setting sail I walked aft and gave to Col. Lloyd's plantation what I hoped would be the last look I should give to it, or to any place like it. After taking this last view, I quitted the quarter-deck, made my way to the bow of the boat, and spent the remainder of the day in looking ahead; interesting myself in what was in the distance, rather than in what was near by, or behind. The vessels sweeping along the bay were objects full of interest to me. The broad bay opened like a shoreless ocean on my boyish vision, filling me with wonder and admiration.

Late in the afternoon we reached Annapolis, stopping there not long enough to admit of going ashore. It was the first large town I had ever seen, and though it was inferior to many a factory village in New England, my feelings on seeing it were excited to a pitch very little below that reached by travellers at the first view of Rome. The dome of the State house was especially imposing, and surpassed in grandeur the appearance of the "great house" I had left behind. So the great world was opening upon me, and I was eagerly acquainting myself with its multifarious lessons.

We arrived in Baltimore on Sunday morning, and landed at Smith's wharf, not far from Bowly's wharf. We had on board a large flock of sheep, for the Baltimore market; and after assisting in driving them to the slaughter house of Mr. Curtiss on Loudon Slater's hill, I was conducted by Rich—one of the hands belonging to the sloop—to my new home on Alliciana street, near Gardiner's ship-yard, on Fell's point. Mr. and Mrs. Hugh Auld, my new master and mistress, were both at home and met me at the door with their rosy-cheeked little son Thomas, to take care of whom was to constitute my further occupation. In fact it was to "little Tommy," rather than to his parents, that old master made a present of me, and, though there were no legal form or arrangement entered into, I have no doubt that Mr. and Mrs. Auld felt that in due time I should be the legal property of their bright-eyed and beloved boy Tommy. I was struck with the appearance especially of my new mistress. Her face was lighted with the kindliest emotions; and the reflex influence of her countenance, as well as the tenderness with which she seemed to regard me, while asking me sundry little questions, greatly delighted me, and lit up, to my fancy, the pathway of my future. Little Thomas was affectionately told by his mother, that "there was his Freddy," and that "Freddy would take care of him;" and I was told to "be kind to little Tommy," an injunction I scarcely needed, for I had already fallen in love with the dear boy. With these little ceremonies I was initiated into my new home, and entered upon my peculiar duties, then unconscious of a cloud to dim its broad horizon.

I may say here, that I regard my removal from Col. Lloyd's plantation as one of the most interesting and fortunate events of my life. Viewing it in the light of human likelihoods, it is quite probable that but for the mere circumstance of being thus removed, before the rigors of slavery had fully fastened upon me; before my young spirit had been crushed under the iron control of the slave-driver, I might have continued in slavery until emancipated by the war.

CHAPTER X: LEARNING TO READ.

City annoyances—Plantation regrets—My mistress—Her history—Her kindness—My master—His sourness—My comforts—Increased sensitiveness—My occupation—Learning to read—Baneful effects of slaveholding on my dear, good mistress—Mr. Hugh forbids Mrs. Sophia to teach me further—Clouds gather on my bright prospects—Master Auld's exposition of the Philosophy of Slavery—City slaves—Country slaves—Contrasts—Exceptions—Mr. Hamilton's two slaves—Mrs. Hamilton's cruel treatment of them—Piteous aspect presented by them—No power to come between the slave and slaveholder.

ESTABLISHED in my new home in Baltimore, I was not very long in perceiving that in picturing to myself what was to be my life there, my imagination had painted only the bright side; and that the reality had its dark shades as well as its light ones. The open country, which had been so much to me, was all shut out. Walled in on every side by towering brick buildings, the heat of the summer was intolerable to me, and the hard brick pavements almost blistered my feet. If I ventured out to the streets, new and strange objects glared upon me at every step, and startling sounds greeted my ears from all directions. My country eyes and ears were confused and bewildered. Troops of hostile boys pounced upon me at every corner. They chased me, and called me "Eastern-Shore man," till really I almost wished myself back on the Eastern Shore. My new mistress happily proved to be all she had seemed, and in her presence I easily forgot all the outside annoyances. Mrs. Sophia was naturally of an excellent disposition—kind, gentle, and cheerful. The supercilious contempt for the rights and feelings of others, and the petulance and bad humour which generally characterized slaveholding ladies, were all quite absent from her manner and bearing toward me. She had never been a slaveholder—a thing then quite unusual at the South—but had depended almost entirely upon her own industry for a living. To this fact the dear lady no doubt owed the excellent preservation of her natural goodness of heart, for slavery could change a saint into a sinner, and an angel into a demon. I hardly knew how to behave towards "Miss Sophia," as I used to call Mrs. Hugh Auld. I could not approach her even, as I had formerly approached Mrs. Thomas Auld. Why should I hang down my head, and speak with bated breath, when there was no pride to scorn me, no coldness to repel me, and no hatred to inspire me with fear? I therefore soon came to regard her as something more akin to a mother than a slaveholding mistress. So far from deeming it impudent in a slave to look her straight in the face, she seemed ever to say, "look up, child; don't be afraid." The sailors belonging to the sloop esteemed it a great privilege to be the bearers of parcels or messages to her, for whenever they came, they were sure of a most kind and pleasant reception. If little Thomas was her son, and her most dearly loved child, she made me something like his half-brother in her affections. If dear Tommy was exalted to a place on his mother's knee, "Feddy" was honoured by a place at the mother's side. Nor did the slave-boy lack the caressing strokes of her gentle hand, soothing him into the consciousness that, though motherless, he was not friendless. Mrs. Auld was not only kindhearted, but remarkably pious; frequent in her attendance at public worship, much given to reading the Bible, and to chanting hymns of praise when alone. Mr. Hugh was altogether a different character. He cared very little about religion; knew more of the world, and was more a part of the world, than his wife. He set out doubtless to be, as the world goes, a respectable man, and to get on by becoming a successful ship-builder, in that city of ship-building. This was his ambition, and it fully occupied him. I was of course of very little consequence to him, and when he smiled upon me, as he sometimes did, the smile was borrowed from his lovely wife, and like all borrowed light, was transient, and vanished with the source whence it was derived. Though I must, in truth, characterize Master Hugh as a sour man of forbidding appearance, it is due to him to acknowledge that he was never cruel to me, according to the notion of cruelty in Maryland. During the first year or two, he left me almost exclusively to the management of his wife. She was my law-giver. In hands so tender as hers, and in the absence of the cruelties of the plantation, I became both physically and mentally much more sensitive, and a frown from my mistress caused me far more suffering than Aunt Katy's hardest cuffs. Instead of the cold, damp floor of my old master's kitchen, I was on carpets; for the corn bag in winter, I had a good straw bed, well furnished with covers; for the coarse corn meal in the morning, I had good bread and mush occasionally; for my old tow-linen shirt, I had good clean clothes. I was really well off. My employment was to run errands, and to take care of Tommy; to prevent his getting in the way of carriages, and to keep him out of harm's way generally. So for a time everything went well. I say for a time, because the fatal poison of irresponsible power, and the natural influence of slave customs, were not very long in making their impression on the gentle and loving disposition of my excellent mistress. She regarded me at first as a child, like any other. This was the natural and spontaneous thought; afterwards, when she came to consider me as property, our relations to each other were changed, but a nature so noble as hers could not instantly become perverted, and it took several years before the sweetness of her temper was wholly lost.

The frequent hearing of my mistress reading the Bible aloud, for she often read aloud when her husband was absent, awakened my curiosity in respect to this mystery of reading, and roused in me the desire to learn. Up to this time I had known nothing whatever of this wonderful art, and my ignorance and inexperience of what it could do for me, as well as my confidence in my mistress, emboldened me to ask her to teach me to read. With an unconsciousness and inexperience equal to my own, she readily consented, and in an incredibly short time, by her kind assistance, I had mastered the alphabet and could spell words of three or four letters. My mistress seemed almost as proud of my progress as if I had been her own child, and supposing that her husband would be as well pleased, she made no secret of what she was doing for me. Indeed, she exultingly told him of the aptness of her pupil, and of her intention to persevere in teaching me, as she felt it her duty to do, at least to read the Bible. And here arose the first dark cloud over my Baltimore prospects, the precursor of chilling blasts and drenching storms. Master Hugh was astounded beyond measure, and probably for the first time, proceeded to unfold to his wife the true philosophy of the slave system, and the peculiar rules necessary in the nature of the case to be observed in the management of human chattels. Of course he forbade her to give me any further instruction, telling her in the first place that to do so was unlawful, as it was also unsafe, "for," said he, "if you give a nigger an inch he will take an ell. Learning will spoil the best nigger in the world. If he learns to read the Bible it will for ever unfit him to be a slave. He should know nothing but the will of his master, and learn to obey it. As to himself, learning will do him no good, but a great deal of harm, making him disconsolate and unhappy. If you teach him how to read, he'll want to know how to write, and this accomplished, he'll be running away with himself." Such was the tenor of Master Hugh's oracular exposition; and it must be confessed that he very clearly comprehended the nature and the requirements of the relation of master and slave. His discourse was the first decidedly antislavery lecture to which it had been my lot to listen. Mrs. Auld evidently felt the force of what he said, and like an obedient wife, began to shape her course in the direction indicated by him. The effect of his words on me was neither slight nor transitory. His iron sentences, cold and harsh, sunk like heavy weights deep into my heart, and stirred up within me a rebellion not soon to be allayed. This was a new and special revelation, dispelling a painful mystery against which my youthful understanding had struggled, and struggled in vain, to wit, the white man's power to perpetuate the enslavement of the black man. "Very well," thought I. "Knowledge unfits a child to be a slave." I instinctively assented to the proposition, and from that moment I understood the direct pathway from slavery to freedom, It was just what I needed, and it came to me at a time and from a source whence I least expected it. Of course I was greatly saddened at the thought of losing the assistance of my kind mistress, but the information so instantly derived, to some extent compensated me for the loss I had sustained in this direction. Wise as Mr. Auld was, he underrated my comprehension, and had little idea of the use to which I was capable of putting the impressive lesson he was giving to his wife. He wanted me to be a slave; I had already voted against that on the home plantation of Col. Lloyd. That which he most loved I most hated; and the very determination which he expressed to keep me in ignorance, only rendered me the more resolute to seek intelligence. In learning to read, therefore, I am not sure that I do not owe quite as much to the opposition of my master as to the kindly assistance of my amiable mistress. I acknowledge the benefit rendered me by the one, and by the other, believing that but for my mistress I might have grown up in ignorance.

CHAPTER XI: GROWING IN KNOWLEDGE.

My mistress—Her slaveholding duties—The effects on her originally noble nature—The conflict in her mind—She opposes my learning to read—Too late—She had given me the "inch," I was resolved to take the "ell"—How I pursued my study to read—My tutors—What progress I made—Slavery—What I heard said about it—Thirteen years old—Columbian orator—Dialogue Speeches—Sheridan—Pitt—Lords Chatham and Fox—Knowledge increasing—Liberty—Singing—Sadness—Unhappiness of Mrs. Sophia—My hatred of slavery—One Upas tree overshadows us all.

I LIVED in the family of Mr. Auld, at Baltimore, seven years, during which time, as the almanac makers say of the weather, my condition was variable. The most interesting feature of my history here, was my learning to read and write under somewhat marked disadvantages. In attaining this knowledge I was compelled to resort to indirections by no means congenial to my nature, and which were really humiliating to my sense of candour and uprightness. My mistress, checked in her benevolent designs toward me, not only ceased instructing me herself, but set her face as a flint against my learning to read by any means. It is due to her to say, however, that she did not adopt this course in all its stringency at first. She either thought it unnecessary, or she lacked the depravity needed to make herself forget at once my human nature. She was, as I have said, naturally a kind and tender-hearted woman, and in the humanity of her heart and the simplicity of her mind, she set out, when I first went to live with her, to treat me as she supposed one human being ought to treat another.

Nature never intended that men and women should be either slaves or slaveholders, and nothing but rigid training, long persisted in, can perfect the character of the one or the other. Mrs. Auld was singularly deficient in the qualities of a slave-holder. It was no easy matter for her to think or to feel that the curly-headed boy, who stood by her side, and even leaned on her lap, who was loved by little Tommy, and who loved little Tommy in turn, sustained to her only the relation of a chattel. I was more than that; she felt me to be more than that. I could talk and sing; I could laugh and weep; I could reason and remember; I could love and hate. I was human, and she, dear lady, knew and felt me to be so. How could she then treat me as a brute, without a mighty struggle with all the noblest powers of her soul? That struggle came, and the will and power of the husband was victorious. Her noble soul was overcome, and he who wrought the wrong was injured in the fall, no less than the rest of the household. When I went into that household, it was the abode of happiness and contentment. The wife and mistress there was a model of affection and tenderness. Her fervent piety and watchful uprightness made it impossible to see her without thinking and feeling, "that woman is a Christian." There was no sorrow nor suffering for which she had not a tear, and there was no innocent joy for which she had not a smile. She had bread for the hungry, clothes for the naked, and comfort for every mourner who came within her reach. But slavery soon proved its ability to divest her of these excellent qualities, and her home of its early happiness. Conscience cannot stand much violence. Once thoroughly injured, who is he who can repair the damage? If it be broken toward the slave on Sunday, it will be toward the master on Monday. It cannot long endure such shocks. It must stand unharmed, or it does not stand at all. As my condition in the family waxed bad, that of the family waxed no better. The first step in the wrong direction was the violence done to nature and to conscience, in arresting the benevolence that would have enlightened my young mind. In ceasing to instruct me, my mistress had to seek to justify herself to herself; and once consenting to take sides in such a debate, she was compelled to hold her position. One needs little knowledge of moral philosophy to see where she inevitably landed. She finally became even more violent in her opposition to my learning to read, than was Mr. Auld himself. Nothing now appeared to make her more angry than seeing me, seated in some nook or corner, quietly reading a book or newspaper. She would rush at me with the utmost fury, and snatch the book or paper from my hand, with something of the wrath and consternation which a traitor might be supposed to feel on being discovered in a plot by some dangerous spy. The conviction once thoroughly established in her mind, that education and slavery were incompatible with each other, I was most narrowly watched in all my movements. If I remained in a separate room from the family for any considerable time, I was sure to be suspected of having a book, and was at once called to give an account of myself. But this was too late: the first and never-to-be-retraced step had been taken. Teaching me the alphabet had been the "inch" given, I was now waiting only for the opportunity to "take the ell."

Filled with the determination to learn to read at any cost, I hit upon many expedients to accomplish that much desired end. The plan which I mainly adopted, and the one which was most successful, was that of using my young white playmates, whom I met in the streets, as teachers. I used to carry almost constantly a copy of Webster's spelling-book in my pocket, and when sent on errands, or when play-time was allowed me, I would step aside with my young friends and take a lesson in spelling. I am greatly indebted to these boys—Gustavus Dorgan, Joseph Bailey, Charles Farity, and William Cosdry.

Although slavery was a delicate subject, and very cautiously talked about among grown-up people in Maryland, I frequently talked about it, and that very freely, with the white boys. I would sometimes say to them, while seated on a curbstone or a cellar door, "I wish I could be free, as you will be when you get to be men." "You will be free, you know, as soon as you are twenty-one, and can go where you like, but I am a slave for life. Have I not as good a right to be free as you have?" Words like these, I observed, always troubled them; and I had no small satisfaction in drawing out from them, as I occasionally did, that fresh and bitter condemnation of slavery which ever springs from natures unseared and unperverted. Of all consciences, let me have those to deal with, which have not been seared and bewildered with the cares and perplexities of life. I do not remember ever to have met with a boy while I was in slavery, who defended the system; but I do remember many times, when I was consoled by them, and by them encouraged to hope that something would yet occur by which I would be made free. Over and over again, they have told me that "they believed I had as good a right to be free as they had," and that "they did not believe God ever made any one to be a slave." It is easily seen that such little conversations with my playfellows had no tendency to weaken my love of liberty, nor to render me contented as a slave.

When I was about thirteen years old, and had succeeded in learning to read, every increase of knowledge, especially anything respecting the Free States, was an additional weight to the almost intolerable burden of my thought—"I am a slave for life." To my bondage I could see no end. It was a terrible reality, and I shall never be able to tell how sadly that thought chafed my young spirit. Fortunately, or unfortunately, I had earned a little money in blacking boots for some gentlemen, with which I purchased of Mr. Knight, on Thames street, what was then a very popular school-book, viz., "The Columbian Orator," for which I paid fifty cents. I was led to buy this book by hearing some little boys say they were going to learn some pieces out of it for recitation. This volume was indeed a rich treasure, and every opportunity afforded me, for a time, was spent in diligently perusing it. Among much other interesting matter, that which I read again and again, with unflagging satisfaction, was a short dialogue between a master and his slave. The slave is represented as having been recaptured in a second attempt to run away; and the master opens the dialogue with an upbraiding speech, charging the slave with ingratitude, and demanding to know what he has to say in his own defence. Thus upbraided, and thus called upon to reply, the slave rejoins that he knows how little anything that he can say will avail, seeing that he is completely in the hands of his owner; and with noble resolution, calmly says, "I submit to my fate." Touched by the slave's answer, the master insists upon his further speaking, and recapitulates the many acts of kindness which he has performed toward the slave, and tells him he is permitted to speak for himself. Thus invited, the quondam slave makes a spirited defence of himself, and thereafter the whole argument for and against slavery is brought out. The master is vanquished at every turn in the argument, and appreciating the fact, he generously and meekly emancipates the slave, with his best wishes for his prosperity. It is unnecessary to say that a dialogue with such an origin and such an end, read by me when every nerve of my being was in revolt at my own condition as a slave, affected me most powerfully. I could not help feeling that the day might yet come, when the well-directed answers made by the slave to the master, in this instance, would find a counterpart in my own experience. This however, was not all the fanaticism which I found in the Columbian Orator. I met there one of Sheridan's mighty speeches, on the subject of Catholic Emancipation, Lord Chatham's speech on the American War, and speeches by the great William Pitt, and by Fox. These were all choice documents to me, and I read them over and over again, with an interest ever increasing, because it was ever gaining in intelligence; for the more I read them the better I understood them. The reading of these speeches added much to my limited stock of language, and enabled me to give tongue to many interesting thoughts which had often flashed through my mind and died away for want of words in which to give them utterance. The mighty power and heart-searching directness of truth penetrating the heart of a slave-holder, compelling him to yield up his earthly interests to the claims of eternal justice, were finely illustrated in the dialogue; and from the speeches of Sheridan I got a bold and powerful denunciation of oppression and a most brilliant vindication of the rights of man. Here was indeed a noble acquisition. If I had ever wavered under the consideration that the Almighty, in some way, had ordained slavery, and willed my enslavement for His own glory, I wavered no longer. I had now penetrated to the secret of all slavery and all oppression, and had ascertained their true foundation to be in the pride, the power, and the avarice of man. With a book in my hand so redolent of the principles of liberty, with a perception of my own human nature, and the facts of my past and present experience, I was equal to a contest with the religious advocates of slavery, whether white or black,—for blindness in this matter was not confined to the white people. I have met many good religious coloured people at the South, who were under the delusion that God required them to submit to slavery, and to wear their chains with meekness and humility. I could entertain no such nonsense as this; and I quite lost my patience when I found a coloured man weak enough to believe such stuff. Nevertheless, eager as I was to partake of the tree of knowledge, its fruits were bitter as well as sweet. "Slaveholders," thought I, "are only a band of successful robbers, who, leaving their own homes, went into Africa for the purpose of stealing and reducing my people to slavery." I loathed them as the meanest and the most wicked of men. And as I read, behold! the very discontent so graphically predicted by Master Hugh had already come upon me. I was no longer the light-hearted gleesome boy, full of mirth and play, as when I landed in Baltimore. Light had penetrated the moral dungeon where I had lain, and I saw the bloody whip for my back, and the iron chain for my feet, and my good, kind master, he was the author of my situation. The revelation haunted me, stung me, and made me gloomy and miserable. As I writhed under the sting and torment of this knowledge, I almost envied my fellow slaves their stupid indifference. It opened my eyes to the horrible pit, and revealed the teeth of the frightful dragon that was ready to pounce upon me; but alas, it opened no way for my escape. I wished myself a beast, a bird, anything rather than a slave. I was wretched and gloomy beyond my ability to describe. This everlasting thinking distressed and tormented me; and yet there was no getting rid of this subject of my thoughts. Liberty, as the inestimable birthright of every man, converted every object into an asserter of this right. I heard it in every sound, and saw it in every object. It was ever present to torment me with a sense of my wretchedness. The more beautiful and charming the smiles of nature, the more horrible and desolate my condition. I saw nothing without seeing it, and I heard nothing without hearing it. I do not exaggerate when I say it looked at me in every star, it smiled in every calm, breathed in every wind, and moved in every storm. I have no doubt that my state of mind had something to do with the change in treatment which my mistress adopted towards me. I can easily believe that my leaden, downcast, and disconsolate look was very offensive to her. Poor lady! She did not understand my trouble, and I could not tell her. Could I have made her acquainted with the real state of my mind and given her the reason for it, it might have been well for both of us. As it was, her abuse fell upon me like the blows of the false prophet upon his ass; she did not know that an angel stood in the way. Nature made us friends, but slavery had made us enemies. My interests were in a direction opposite to hers, and we both had our private thoughts and plans. She aimed to keep me ignorant, and I resolved to know, although knowledge only increased my misery. My feelings were not the result of any marked cruelty in the treatment I received; they sprang from the consideration of my being a slave at all. It was slavery, not its mere incidents I hated. I had been cheated. I saw through the attempt to keep me in ignorance. I saw that slaveholders would have gladly made me believe that they were merely acting under the authority of God in making a slave of me and in making slaves of others, and I felt to them as to robbers and deceivers. The feeding and clothing me well could not atone for taking my liberty from me. The smiles of my mistress could not remove the deep sorrow that dwelt in my young bosom. Indeed, these came in time but to deepen my sorrow. She had changed, and the reader will see that I had changed, too. We were both victims to the same overshadowing evil, she as mistress, I as slave. I will not censure her harshly.

CHAPTER XII: RELIGIOUS NATURE AWAKENED.

Abolitionists spoken of—Eagerness to know the meaning of word—Consults the dictionary—Incendiary information—The enigma solved—"Nat Turner" insurrection—Cholera—Religion—Methodist minister—Religious impressions—Father Lawson—His character and occupation—His influence over me—Our mutual attachment—New hopes and aspirations—Heavenly light—Two Irishmen on wharf—Conversation with them—Learning to write—My aims.

IN the unhappy state of mind described in the foregoing chapter, regretting my very existence because doomed to a life of bondage, so goaded and so wretched as to be even tempted at times to take my own life, I was most keenly sensitive to know any and everything possible that had any relation to the subject of slavery. I was all ears, all eyes, whenever the words slave or slavery dropped from the lips of any white person, and the occasions became more and more frequent when these words became leading ones in high social debate at our house. Very often I would overhear Master Hugh, or some of his company, speak with much warmth of the "abolitionists." Who or what the abolitionists were, I was totally ignorant. I found, however, that whoever or whatever they might be, they were most cordially hated and abused by slaveholders of every grade. I very soon discovered, too, that slavery was, in some sort, under consideration whenever the abolitionists were alluded to. This made the term a very interesting one to me. If a slave had made good his escape from slavery, it was generally alleged that he had been persuaded and assisted to do so by the abolitionists. If a slave killed his master, or struck down his overseer, or set fire to his master's dwelling, or committed any violence or crime out of the common way, it was certain to be said that such a crime was the legitimate fruits of the abolition movement. Hearing such charges often repeated, I, naturally enough, received the impression that abolition—whatever else it might be—was not unfriendly to the slave, nor very friendly to the slaveholder. I therefore set about finding out, if possible, who and what the abolitionists were, and why they were so obnoxious to the slaveholders. The dictionary offered me very little help. It taught me that abolition was "the act of abolishing;" but it left me in ignorance at the very point where I most wanted information, and that was, as to the thing to be abolished. A city newspaper—the "Baltimore American"—gave me the incendiary information denied me by the dictionary. In its columns I found that on a certain day a vast number of petitions and memorials had been presented to Congress, praying for the abolition of slavery in the District of Columbia, and for the abolition of the slave trade between the States of the Union. This was enough. The vindictive bitterness, the marked caution, the studied reserve, and the ambiguity practised by our white folks when alluding to this subject, was now fully explained. Ever after that, when I heard the word abolition, I felt the matter one of a personal concern, and I drew near to listen whenever I could do so, without seeming too solicitous and prying. There was HOPE in those words. Ever and anon, too, I could see some terrible denunciation of slavery in our papers,—copied from abolition papers at the North,—and the injustice of such denunciation commented on. These I read with avidity. I had a deep satisfaction in the thought that the rascality of slaveholders was not concealed from the eyes of the world, and that I was not alone in abhorring the cruelty and brutality of slavery. A still deeper train of thought was stirred. I saw that there was fear as well as rage in the manner of speaking of the abolitionists, and from this I inferred that they must have some power in the country, and I felt that they might perhaps succeed in their designs. When I met with a slave to whom I deemed it safe to talk on the subject, I would impart to him so much of the mystery as I had been able to penetrate. Thus the light of this grand movement broke in upon my mind by degrees; and I must say that, ignorant as I was of the philosophy of that movement, I believed in it from the first, and I believed in it partly because I saw that it alarmed the consciences of the slaveholders. The insurrection of Nat. Turner had been quelled, but the alarm and terror which it occasioned had not subsided. The cholera was then on its way to this country, and I remember thinking that God was angry with the white people because of their slaveholding wickedness, and therefore his judgments were abroad in the land. Of course it was impossible for me not to hope much for the abolition movement when I saw it supported by the Almighty, and armed with Death.

Previously to my contemplation of the anti-slavery movement and its probable results, my mind had been seriously awakened to the subject of religion. I was not more than thirteen years old when, in my loneliness and destitution, I longed for some one to whom I could go, as to a father and protector. The preaching of a white Methodist minister, named Hanson, was the means of causing me to feel that in God I had such a friend. He taught that all men, great and small, bond and free, were sinners in the sight of God; that they were but natural rebels against his government; and that they must repent of their sins, and be reconciled to God through Christ. I cannot say that I had a very distinct notion of what was required of me, but one thing I did know well: I was wretched and had no means of making myself otherwise. I consulted a good coloured man named Charles Lawson, and in tones of holy affection he told me to pray, and to "cast all my care upon God." This I sought to do; and though for weeks I was a poor, broken-hearted mourner, travelling through doubts and fears, I finally found my burden lightened, and my heart relieved. I loved all mankind, slaveholders not excepted, though I abhorred slavery more than ever. I saw the world in a new light, and my great concern was to have everybody converted. My desire to learn increased, and especially did I want a thorough acquaintance with the contents of the Bible. I have gathered scattered pages of the Bible from the filthy street-gutters, and washed and dried them, that in moments of leisure I might get a word or two of wisdom from them. While thus religiously seeking knowledge, I became acquainted with a good old coloured man named Lawson. This man not only prayed three times a day, but he prayed as he walked through the streets, at his work, on his dray— everywhere. His life was a life of prayer, and his words when he spoke to any one, were about a better world. Uncle Lawson lived near Master Hugh's house, and, becoming deeply attached to him, I went often with him to prayer-meeting, and spent much of my leisure time with him on Sunday. The old man could read a little, and I was a great help to him in making out the hard words, for I was a better reader than he. I could teach him "the letter," but he could teach me "the spirit," and refreshing times we had together, in singing and praying. These meetings went on for a long time without the knowledge of Master Hugh or my mistress. Both knew, however, I had become religious, and seemed to respect my conscientious piety. My mistress was still a professor of religion, and belonged to class. Her leader was no less a person than Rev. Beverly Waugh, the presiding elder, and afterwards one of the bishops of the Methodist Episcopal church.

In view of the cares and anxieties incident to the life she was leading, and especially in view of the separation from religious associations to which she was subjected, my mistress had, as I have before stated, become lukewarm, and needed to be looked up by her leader. This often brought Mr. Waugh to our house, and gave me an opportunity to hear him extort and pray. But my chief instructor in religious matters was Uncle Lawson. He was my spiritual father and I loved him intensely, and was at his house every chance I could get. This pleasure, however, was not long unquestioned, Master Hugh became averse to our intimacy, and threatened to whip me if I ever went there again. I now felt myself persecuted by a wicked man, and I would go. The good old man had told me that the "Lord had a great work for me to do," and I must prepare to do it; that he had been shown that I must preach the gospel. His words made a very deep impression upon me, and I verily felt that some work was before me, though I could not see how I could ever engage in its performance. "The good Lord would bring it to pass in His own time," he said, and I must go on reading and studying the scriptures. This advice and these suggestions were not without their influence on my character and destiny. He fanned my already intense love of knowledge into a flame by assuring me that I was to be a useful man in the world. When I would say to him, "How can these things be? and what can I do?" his simple reply was, "Trust in the Lord." When I would tell him, "I am a slave, and a slave for life, how can I do anything?" he would quietly answer, "The Lord can make you free, my dear; all things are possible with Him; only have faith in God. 'Ask, and it shall be given you.' If you want liberty, ask the Lord for it infaith,and he will give it to you."

Thus assured and thus cheered on, under the inspiration of hope, I worked and prayed with a light heart, believing that my life was under the guidance of a wisdom higher than my own. With all other blessings sought at the mercy seat, I always prayed that God would, of His great mercy and in His own good time, deliver me from my bondage.

I went one day to the wharf of Mr. Waters, and seeing two Irishmen unloading a scow of stone or ballast, I went on board, unasked, and helped them. When we had finished the work, one of the men came to me, aside, and asked me a number of questions, and among them if I were a slave? I told him "I was a slave for life." The good Irishman gave a shrug, and seemed deeply affected. He said it was a pity so fine a little fellow as I was should be a slave for life. They both had much to say about the matter, and expressed the deepest sympathy with me, and the most decided hatred of slavery. They went so far as to tell me that I ought to run away and go to the North; that I should find friends there, and that I should be as free as anybody. I pretended not to be interested in what they said, for I feared they might be treacherous. White men were not unfrequently known to encourage slaves to escape, and then, to get the reward, they would kidnap them and return them to their masters. While I mainly inclined to the notion that these men were honest and meant me no ill, I feared it might be otherwise. I nevertheless remembered their words and their advice, and looked forward to an escape to the North as a possible means of gaining the liberty for which my heart panted. It was not my enslavement at the then present time which most affected me; the being a slave for life was the saddest thought. I was too young to think of running away immediately; besides I wished to learn to write before going, as I might have occasion to write my own pass. I now not only had the hope of freedom, but a foreshadowing of the means by which I might some day gain that inestimable boon. Meanwhile, I resolved to add to my educational attainments the art of writing.

After this manner I began to learn to write. I was much in the ship-yards—Master Hugh's, and that of Durgan & Bailey—and I observed that the carpenters after hewing and getting ready a piece of timber to use, wrote on it the initials of the name of that part of the ship for which it was intended. When, for instance, a piece of timber was ready for the starboard side, it was marked with a capital "S." A piece for the larboard side was marked "L.;" larboard-forward was marked "L. F.;" larboard-aft was marked "L. A.;" starboard-aft "S. A.;" and starboard-forward "S. F." I soon learned these letters, and for what they were placed on the timbers.

My work now was to keep fire under the steam-box, and to watch the ship-yard while the carpenters were gone to dinner. This interval gave me a fine opportunity for copying the letters named. I soon astonished myself at the ease with which I made the letters, and the thought was soon present, "If I can make four letters, I can make more." Having made these readily and easily, when I met boys about the Bethel church or on any of our play-grounds, I entered the lists with them in the art of writing, and would make the letters which I had been so fortunate as to learn, and ask them to "beat that if they could." With play-mates for my teachers, fences and pavements for my copybooks, and chalk for my pen and ink, I learned to write. I however adopted, afterwards, various methods for improving my hand. The most successful was copying the italics in Webster's spelling-book until I could make them all without looking on the book. By this time my little "Master Tommy" had grown to be a big boy, and had written over a number of copy-books and brought them home. They had been shown to the neighbours, had elicited due praise, and had been laid carefully away. Spending part of my time both at the ship-yard and the house, I was often the keeper of the latter as of the former. When my mistress left me in charge of the house I had a grand time. I got Master Tommy's copy-books and a pen and ink, and in the ample space between the lines I wrote other lines as nearly like his as possible. The process was a tedious one, and I ran the risk of getting a flogging for marking the highly-prized copy-books of the eldest son. In addition to these opportunities, sleeping as I did in the kitchen loft, a room seldom visited by any of the family, I contrived to get a flour-barrel up there and a chair, and upon the head of that barrel I have written, or endeavoured to write, copying from the Bible and the Methodist hymn-book, and other books which I had accumulated, till late at night, and when all the family were in bed and asleep. I was supported in my endeavours by renewed advice and by holy promises from the good father Lawson, with whom I continued to meet, and pray, and read the Scriptures. Although Master Hugh was aware of these meetings, I must say, to his credit, that he never executed his threats to whip me for having thus innocently employed my leisure time.

CHAPTER XIII: THE VICISSITUDES OF SLAVE LIFE.

Death of old Master's son Richard, speedily followed by that of old Master—Valuation and division of all the property, including the slaves—Sent for, to come to Hillsborough to be valued and divided—Sad prospects and grief—Parting—Slaves have no voice in deciding their own destinies—General dread of falling into Master Andrew's hands—His drunkenness—Good fortune in falling to Miss Lucretia—She allows my return to Baltimore—Joy at Master Hugh's—Death of Miss Lucretia—Master Thomas Auld's second marriage—The new wife unlike the old—Again removed from Master Hugh's—Reasons for regret—Plan of escape.

I MUST now ask the reader to go back with me a little in point of time, in my humble story, and notice another circumstance that entered into my slavery experience, and which, doubtless, has had a share in deepening my horror of slavery, and my hostility toward those men and measures that practically uphold the slave system.

It has already been observed that though I was, after my removal from Col. Lloyd's plantation, in form the slave of Master Hugh Auld, I was in fact and in law the slave of my old master, Capt. Anthony. Very well. In a very short time after I went to Baltimore my old master's youngest son, Richard, died; and in three years and six months after, my old master himself died, leaving only his daughter Lucretia and his son Andrew to share the estate. The old man died while on a visit to his daughter in Hillsborough, where Capt. Auld and Mrs. Lucretia now lived. Master Thomas having given up the command of Col. Lloyd's sloop was now keeping store in that town.

Cut off thus unexpectedly, Capt. Anthony died intestate, and his property must be equally divided between his two children, Andrew and Lucretia.

The valuation and division of slaves among contending heirs was a most important incident in slave life. The characters and tendencies of the heirs were generally well understood by the slaves who were to be divided, and all had their aversions and their preferences. But neither their aversions nor their preferences availed anything.

On the death of old master, I was immediately sent for to be valued and divided with the other property. Personally, my concern was mainly about my possible removal from the home of Master Hugh, for up to this time there had no dark clouds arisen to darken the sky of that happy abode. It was a sad day to me when I left for the Eastern Shore, to be valued and divided, as it was for my dear mistress and teacher, and for little Tommy. We all three wept bitterly, for we were parting, and it might be we were parting for ever. No one could tell amongst which pile of chattels I might be flung. Thus early, I got a foretaste of that painful uncertainty which in one form or another was ever obtruding itself in the pathway of the slave. It furnished me a new insight into the unnatural power to which I was subjected. Sickness, adversity, and death may interfere with the plans and purposes of all, but the slave had the added danger of changing homes, in the separations unknown to other men. Then, too, there was the intensified degradation of the spectacle. What an assemblage! Men and women, young and old, married and single; moral and thinking human beings, in open contempt of their humanity, levelled at a blow with horses, sheep, horned cattle, and swine. Horses and men, cattle and women, pigs and children—all holding the same rank in the scale of social existence, and all subjected to the same narrow inspection, to ascertain their value in gold and silver—the only standard of worth applied by slaveholders to their slaves. Personality swallowed up in the sordid idea of property! Manhood lost in chattel-hood!

The valuation over, then came the division and apportionment. Our destiny was to be fixed for life, and we had no more voice in the decision of the question than the oxen and cows that stood chewing at the hay-mow. One word of the appraisers, against all preferences and prayers, could rend asunder all the ties of friendship and affection, even to separating husbands and wives, parents and children. We were all appalled before that power which, to human seeming, could bless or blast us in a moment. Added to this dread of separation, most painful to the majority of the slaves, we all had a decided horror of falling into the hands of Master Andrew, who was distinguished for his cruelty and intemperance.

Slaves had a great dread, very naturally, of falling into the hands of drunken owners. Master Andrew was a confirmed sot, and had already, by his profligate dissipation, wasted a large portion of his father's property. To fall into his hands, therefore, was considered as the first step toward being sold away to the far South. He would no doubt spend his fortune in a few years, it was thought, and his farms and slaves would be sold at public auction, and the slaves hurried away to the cotton-fields and rice-swamps of the burning South. This was cause of deep consternation.

The people of the North, and free people generally, I think, have less attachment to the places where they are born and brought up, than had the slaves. Their freedom to come and go, to be here or there, as they list, prevents any extravagant attachment to any one particular place. On the other hand, the slave was a fixture; he had no choice, no goal, but was pegged down to one single spot, and must take root there or nowhere. The idea of removal elsewhere came, generally, in shape of a threat, and in punishment for crime. It was therefore attended with fear and dread. The enthusiasm which animates the bosoms of young freemen, when they contemplate a life in the far West, or in some distant country, where they expect to rise to wealth and distinction, could have no place in the thoughts of the slave; nor could those from whom they separated know anything of that cheerfulness with which friends and relations yield each other up, when they feel that it is good for the departing one that he is removed from his native place. Then, too, there is correspondence and the hope of reunion, but with the slaves all these mitigating circumstances were wanting. There was no improvement in condition probable—no correspondence possible—no reunion attainable. His going out into the world was like a living man going into the tomb, who, with open eyes, sees himself buried out of sight and hearing of wife, children, and friends of kindred tie.

In contemplating the likelihoods and possibilities of our circumstances, I probably suffered more than most of my fellow-servants. I had known what it was to experience kind and even tender treatment; they had known nothing of the sort. Life to them had been rough and thorny, as well as dark. They had—most of them—lived on my old master's farm in Tuckahoe, and had felt the rigours of Mr. Plummer's rule. He had written his character on the living parchment of most of their backs, and left them seamed and callous; my back, thanks to my early removal to Baltimore, was yet tender. I had left a kind mistress in tears when we parted, and the probability of never seeing her again, trembling in the balance as it were, could not fail to excite in me alarm and agony. The thought of becoming the slave of Andrew Anthony—who but a few days before the division had in my presence seized my brother Perry by the throat, dashed him on the ground, and with the heel of his boot stamped him on the head, until the blood gushed from his nose and ears—was terrible! This fiendish proceeding had no better apology than the fact that Perry had gone to play when Master Andrew wanted him for some trifling service. After inflicting this cruel treatment on my brother, observing me, as I looked at him in astonishment, he said: "That's the way I'll serve you, one of these days"; meaning, probably, when I should come into his possession. This threat, the reader may well suppose, was not very tranquillizing to my feelings.

At last, the anxiety and suspense were ended; and ended, thanks to a kind Providence, in accordance with my wishes. I fell to the portion of Mrs. Lucretia, the dear lady who bound up my head in her father's kitchen, and shielded me from the maledictions of Aunt Katy.

Captain Thomas Auld and Mrs. Lucretia at once decided on my return to Baltimore. They knew how warmly Mrs. Hugh Auld was attached to me, and how delighted Tommy would be to see me, and withal, having no immediate use for me, they willingly concluded this arrangement.

I need not stop to narrate my joy on finding myself back in Baltimore. I was just one month absent, but the time seemed fully six months.

I had returned to Baltimore but a short time when the tidings reached me that my kind friend, Mrs. Lucretia, was dead. She left one child, a daughter, named Amanda, of whom I shall speak again. Shortly after the death of Mrs. Lucretia, Master Andrew died, leaving a wife and one child. Thus the whole family of Anthonys, as it existed when I went to Col. Lloyd's place, was swept away during the first five years' time of my residence at Master Hugh Auld's in Baltimore.

No especial alteration took place in the condition of the slaves, in consequence of these deaths, yet I could not help the feeling that I was less secure now that Mrs. Lucretia was gone. While she lived, I felt that I had a strong friend to plead for me in any emergency.

In a little book which I published six years after my escape from slavery, entitled "Narrative of Frederick Douglass,"—when the distance between the past then described, and the present was not so great as it is now,—speaking of these changes in my master's family, and their results, I used this language: "Now all the property of my old master, slaves included, was in the hands of strangers—strangers who had nothing to do in accumulating it. Not a slave was left free. All remained slaves, from the youngest to the oldest. If any one thing in my experience, more than another, has served to deepen my conviction of the infernal character of slavery, and to fill me with unutterable loathing of slaveholders, it was their base ingratitude to my poor old grandmother. She had served my old master faithfully from youth to old age. She had been the source of all his wealth; she had peopled his plantation with slaves; she had become a great-grandmother in his service. She had rocked him in his infancy, attended him in his childhood, served him through life, and at his death wiped from his icy brow the cold death-sweat, and closed his eyes for ever. She was nevertheless a slave—a slave for life—a slave in the hands of strangers; and in their hands she saw her children, her grand-children, and her great-grand-children, divided like so many sheep, without being gratified with the small privilege of a single word as to their or her own destiny. And to cap the climax of their base ingratitude, my grandmother, who was now very old, having outlived my old master and all his children, having seen the beginning and end of them, and her present owner—his grand-son—finding she was of but little value—her frame already racked with the pains of old age, and complete helplessness fast stealing over her once active limbs—took her to the woods, built her a little hut with a mud chimney, and then gave her the bounteous privilege of supporting herself there in utter loneliness; thus virtually turning her out to die. If my poor, dear old grandmother now lives, she lives to remember and mourn over the loss of children, the loss of grand-children, and the loss of great-grand-children. They are, in the language of Whittier, the slave's poet:

-

  o 'Gone, gone, sold and gone,

  o To the rice-swamp dank and lone:

  o Where the slave-whip ceaseless swings,

  o Where the noisome insect stings,

  o Where the fever-demon strews

  o Poison with the falling dews,

  o Where the sickly sunbeams glare

  o Through the hot and misty air:—

-

  o Gone, gone, sold and gone,

  o To the rice-swamp, dank and lone,

o   From Virginia's hills and waters—

o   Woe is me, my stolen daughters!'

The hearth is desolate. The unconscious children who once sang and danced in her presence are gone. She gropes her way, in the darkness of age, for a drink of water. Instead of the voices of her children, she hears by day the moans of the dove, and by night the screams of the hideous owl. All is gloom. The grave is at the door; and now, weighed down by the pains and aches of old age, when the head inclines to the feet, when the beginning and ending of human existence meet, and helpless infancy, and painful old age combine together; at this time,—this most needed time for the exercise of that tenderness and affection which children only can bestow on a declining parent,—my poor old grandmother, the devoted mother of twelve children, is left all alone, in yonder little hut, before a few dim cinders."

Two years after the death of Mrs. Lucretia, Master Thomas married his second wife. Her name was Rowena Hamilton, the eldest daughter of Mr. William Hamilton, a rich slaveholder on the Eastern Shore of Maryland, who lived about five miles from St. Michaels, the then place of Master Thomas Auld's residence.

Not long after his marriage, Master Thomas had a misunderstanding with Master Hugh, and as a means of punishing him, he ordered him to send me home. As the ground of the misunderstanding will serve to illustrate the character of Southern chivalry and Southern humanity, fifty years ago, I will relate it.

Among the children of my Aunt Milly, was a daughter named Henny. When quite a child, Henny had fallen into the fire and had burnt her hands so badly that they were of very little use to her. Her fingers were drawn almost into the palms of her hands. She could make out to do something, but she was considered hardly worth the having—of little more value than a horse with a broken leg. This unprofitable piece of property, ill-shapen and disfigured, Captain Auld sent off to Baltimore.

After giving poor Henny a fair trial, Master Hugh and his wife came to the conclusion that they had no use for the poor cripple, and they sent her back to Master Thomas. This the latter took as an act of ingratitude on the part of his brother, and as a mark of his displeasure, he required him to send me immediately to St. Michaels, saying, "if he cannot keep Hen., he shan't have Fred."

Here was another shock to my nerves, another breaking up of plans, and another severance of my religious and social alliances. I was now a big boy. I had become quite useful to several young coloured men, who had made me their teacher. I had taught some of them to read, and was accustomed to spend many of my leisure hours with them. Our attachment was strong, and I greatly dreaded the separation. But regrets with slaves were unavailing: my wishes were nothing; my happiness was the sport of my master.

My regrets at leaving Baltimore now, were not for the same reasons as when I before left the city to be valued and handed over to a new owner.

A change had taken place, both in Master Hugh and in his once pious and affectionate wife. The influence of brandy and bad company on him, and of slavery and social isolation on her, had wrought disastrously upon the characters of both. Thomas was no longer "little Tommy," but was a big boy, and had learned to assume the airs of his class towards me. My condition, therefore, in the house of Master Hugh was not by any means so comfortable as in former years. My attachments were now outside of our family: They were fixed upon those to whom I imparted instruction, and to those little white boys, from whom I received instruction. There, too, was my dear old father, the pious Lawson, who was in all the Christian graces the very counterpart of "Uncle Tom"—the resemblance so perfect that he might have been the original of Mrs. Stowe's Christian hero. The thought of leaving these dear friends greatly troubled me, for I was going without the hope of ever returning again; the feud being most bitter, and apparently wholly irreconcilable.

In addition to the pain of parting from friends, as I supposed, for ever, I had the added grief of neglected chances of escape to brood over. I had put off running away until I was now to be placed where opportunities for escape would be much more difficult, and less frequent.

As we sailed down the Chesapeake bay, on board the sloop Amanda, to St. Michaels, and were passed by the steamers playing between Baltimore and Philadelphia, I formed many a plan for my future, beginning and ending in the same determination—yet to find some way of escape from slavery.

CHAPTER XIV: EXPERIENCE IN ST. MICHAELS.

St. Michaels and its inhabitants—Captain Auld—His new wife—Sufferings from hunger—Forced to steal—Argument in vindication thereof—Southern camp-meeting—What Captain Auld did there—Hopes—Suspicions—The result—Faith and works at variance—Position in the church—Poor Cousin Henny—Methodist preachers—Their disregard of the slaves—One exception—Sabbath-school—How and by whom broken up—Sad change in my prospects—Covey, the negro-breaker.

ST. MICHAELS, the village in which was now my new home, compared favourably with villages in slave States generally, at this time—1833. There were a few comfortable dwellings in it, but the place as a whole wore a dull, slovenly, enterprise-forsaken, aspect. The mass of the buildings were of wood; they had never enjoyed the artificial adornment of paint, and time and storms had worn off the bright colour of the wood, leaving them almost as black as buildings charred by a conflagration.

St. Michaels had, in former years, enjoyed some reputation as a ship-building community, but that business had almost entirely given place to oyster-fishing for the Baltimore and Philadelphia markets, a course of life highly unfavourable to morals, industry, and manners. Miles River was broad, and its oyster-fishing grounds were extensive, and the fishermen were out often all day and a part of the night, during autumn, winter, and spring. This exposure was an excuse for carrying with them, in considerable quantities, spirituous liquors, the then supposed best antidote for cold. Each canoe was supplied with its jug of rum, and tippling among this class of the citizens became general. This drinking habit, in an ignorant population, fostered coarseness, vulgarity, and an indolent disregard for the social improvement of the place, so that it was admitted by the few sober thinking people who remained there, that St. Michaels was an unsaintly, as well as unsightly place.

I went to St. Michaels to live in March, 1833. I know the year, because it was the one succeeding the first cholera in Baltimore, and it was also the year of that strange phenomenon, when the heavens seemed about to part with its starry train. I witnessed this gorgeous spectacle, and was awe-struck. The air seemed filled with bright descending messengers from the sky. It was about daybreak when I saw this sublime scene. I was not without the suggestion that it might be the harbinger of the coming of the Son of Man; and in my then state of mind I was prepared to hail Him as my friend and deliverer. I had read that the "stars shall fall from heaven," and they were now falling. I was suffering very much in my mind. It did seem that every time the young tendrils of my affection became attached they were rudely broken by some unnatural outside power; and I was looking away to heaven for the rest denied me on earth.

But to my story. It was now more than seven years since I had lived with Master Thomas Auld, in the family of my old master, Capt. Anthony, on the home plantation of Col. Lloyd. As I knew him then it was as the husband of old master's daughter; I had now to know him as my master. All my lessons concerning his temper and disposition, and the best methods of pleasing him, were yet to be learned. Slave-holders, however, were not very ceremonious in approaching a slave, and my ignorance of the new material in the shape of a master was but transient. Nor was my new mistress long in making known her animus. Unlike Miss Lucretia, whom I remembered with the tenderness which departed blessings leave, Mrs. Rowena Auld was cold and cruel, as her husband was stingy, and possessed the power to make him as cruel as herself, while she could easily descend to the level of his meanness.

As long as I had lived in Mr. Hugh Auld's family, whatever changes had come over them, there had been always a bountiful supply of food; and now, for the first time in seven years, I realized the pitiless pinchings of hunger. So wretchedly starved were we, that we were compelled to live at the expense of our neighbours, or to steal from the home larder. This was a hard thing to do; but after much reflection I reasoned myself into the conviction that there was no other way to do, and that after all there was no wrong in it. Considering that my labour and person were the property of Master Thomas, and that I was deprived of the necessaries of life—necessaries obtained by my own labour, it was easy to deduce the right to supply myself with what was my own. It was simply appropriating what was my own to the use of my master, since the health and strength derived from such food were exerted in his service. To be sure this was stealing, according to the law and gospel I heard from the pulpit; but I had begun to attach less importance to what dropped from that quarter on such points. It was not always convenient to steal from master, and the same reason why I might innocently steal from him did not seem to justify me in stealing from others. In the case of my master it was a question of removal—the taking his meat out of one tub and putting it into another; the ownership of the meat was not affected by the transaction. At first he owned it in the tub, and last he owned it in me. His meat-house was not always open. There was a strict watch kept at that point, and the key was carried in Mrs. Auld's pocket. We were oftentimes severely pinched with hunger, when meat and bread were mouldering under lock and key. This was so, when she knew we were nearly half starved; and yet with saintly air would she kneel with her husband and pray each morning that a merciful God would "bless them in basket and store, and save them at last in His kingdom." But I proceed with my argument.

It was necessary that the right to steal from others should be established; and this could only rest upon a wider range of generalization than that which supposed the right to steal from my master. It was some time before I arrived at this clear right. To give some idea of my train of reasoning, I will state the case as I laid it out in my mind. "I am," I thought, "not only the slave of Master Thomas, but I am the slave of society at large. Society at large has bound itself, in form and in fact, to assist Master Thomas in robbing me of my rightful liberty, and of the just reward of my labour; therefore, whatever rights I have against Master Thomas I have equally against those confederated with him in robbing me of liberty. As society has marked me out as privileged plunder, on the principle of self-preservation, I am justified in plundering in turn. Since each slave belongs to all, all must therefore belong to each." I reasoned further, "that within the bounds of his just earnings the slave was fully justified in helping himself to the gold and silver, and the best apparel of his master, or that of any other slave-holder; and that such taking was not stealing, in any just sense of the word."

The morality of free society could have no application to slave society. Slaveholders made it almost impossible for the slave to commit any crime, known either to the laws of God or to the laws of man. If he stole he but took his own; if he killed his master, he only imitated the heroes of the Revolution. Slaveholders I held to be individually and collectively responsible for all the evils which grew out of the horrid relation, and I believed they would be so held in the sight of God. To make a man a slave was to rob him of moral responsibility. Freedom of choice is the essence of all accountability; but my kind readers are probably less concerned about what were my opinions than about that which more nearly touched my personal experience, albeit my opinions have, in some sort, been the outgrowth of my experience.

When I lived with Capt. Auld I thought him incapable of a noble action. His leading characteristic was intense selfishness. I think he was fully aware of this fact himself, and often tried to conceal it. Capt. Auld was not a born slave-holder—not a birthright member of the slave-holding oligarchy. He was only a slaveholder by marriage-right; and of all slave-holders these were by far the most exacting. There was in him all the love of domination, the pride of mastery, and the swagger of authority; but his rule lacked the vital element of consistency. He could be cruel: but his methods of showing it were cowardly, and evinced his meanness, rather than his spirit. His commands were strong, his enforcements weak.

Slaves were not insensible to the whole-souled qualities of a generous, dashing slave-holder, who was fearless of consequences, and they preferred a master of this bold and daring kind, even with the risk of being shot down for impudence, to the fretful little soul who never used the lash but at the suggestion of a love of gain.

Slaves, too, readily distinguished between the birthright bearing of the original slaveholder, and the assumed attributes of the accidental slaveholder; and while they could have no respect for either, they despised the latter more than the former.

The luxury of having slaves to wait upon him was new to Master Thomas, and for it he was wholly unprepared. He was a slave-holder, without the ability to hold or manage his slaves. Failing to command their respect, both himself and wife were ever on the alert lest some indignity should be offered them by the slaves.

It was in the month of August, 1833, when I had become almost desperate under the treatment of Master Thomas, and entertained more strongly than ever the oft-repeated determination to run away,—a circumstance occurred which seemed to promise brighter and better days for us all. At a Methodist camp-meeting, held in the Bay side, a famous place for camp-meetings, about eight miles from St. Michaels, Master Thomas came out with a profession of religion. He had long been an object of interest to the church, and to the ministers, as I had seen by the repeated visits and lengthy exhortations of the latter. He was a fish quite worth catching, for he had money and standing. In the community of St. Michaels he was equal to the best citizen. He was strictly temperate, and there was little to do for him, to give the appearance of piety, and to make him a pillar of the church. Well, the camp meeting continued a week; people gathered from all parts of the country, and two steamboats came loaded from Baltimore. The ground was happily chosen; seats were arranged; a stand erected; a rude altar fenced in, fronting the preacher's stand, with straw in it, making a soft kneeling-place for the accommodation of mourners. This place would have held at least one hundred persons. In front and on the sides of the preacher's stand, and outside the long rows of seats, rose the first class of stately tents, each vieing with the other in strength, neatness, and capacity for accommodation, Behind this first circle of tents, was another less imposing, which reached round the camp ground to the speaker's stand. Outside this second class of tents were covered wagons, ox-carts, and vehicles of every shape and size. These served as tents to their owners. Outside of these, huge fires were burning in all directions, where roasting and boiling and frying were going on, for the benefit of those who were attending to their spiritual welfare within the circle. Behind the preacher's stand, a narrow space was marked out for the use of the coloured people. There were no seats provided for this class of persons, and if the preachers addressed them at all, it was in an aside. After the preaching was over, at every service, an invitation was given to mourners to come forward into the pen; and in some cases, ministers went out to persuade men and women to come in. By one of these ministers, Master Thomas was persuaded to go inside the pen. I was deeply interested in that matter, and followed; and, though coloured people were not allowed either in the pen or in front of the preacher's stand, I ventured to take my stand at a sort of half-way place between the blacks and whites, where I could distinctly see the movements of the mourners, and especially the progress of Master Thomas. "If he has got religion," thought I, "he will emancipate his slaves; or, if he should not do as much as this, he will at any rate behave towards us more kindly, and feed us more generously than he has heretofore done." Appealing to my own religious experience, and judging my master by what was true in my own case, I could not regard him as soundly converted, unless some such good results followed his profession of religion. But in my expectations I was doubly disappointed: Master Thomas was Master Thomas still. The fruits of his righteousness were to show themselves in no such way as I had anticipated. His conversion was not to change his relation toward men—at any rate not toward black men—but toward God. My faith I confess was not great. There was something in his appearance that, in my mind, cast a doubt over his conversion. Standing where I did, I could see his every movement. I watched very narrowly while he remained in the pen; and although I saw that his face was extremely red, and his hair dishevelled, and though I heard him groan, and saw a stray tear halting on his cheek, as if inquiring, "which way shall I go?"—I could not wholly confide in the genuineness of the conversion. The hesitating behaviour of that tear-drop, and its loneliness, distressed me, and cast a doubt upon the whole transaction, of which it was a part. But people said, "Capt. Auld has come through," and it was for me to hope for the best. I was bound to do this in charity, for I, too, was religious, and had been in the church full three years, although now I was not more than sixteen years old. Slave-owners might sometimes have confidence in the piety of some of their slaves, but the slaves seldom had confidence in the piety of their masters. "He can't go to heaven without blood on his skirts," was a settled point in the creed of every slave, which rose superior to all teaching to the contrary, and stood for ever as a fixed fact. The highest evidence the slaveholder could give the slave of his acceptance with God, was the emancipation of his slaves. This was proof to us that he was willing to give up all to God, and for the sake of God; and not to do this was, in our estimation, an evidence of hard-heartedness, and was wholly inconsistent with the idea of genuine conversion. I had read somewhere in the Methodist Discipline, the following question and answer: "Question—What shall be done for the extirpation of slavery?" "Answer—We declare that we are as much as ever convinced of the great evil of slavery; therefore no slaveholder shall be eligible to any official office in our church." These words sounded in my ears for a long time, and encouraged me to hope. But as I have before said, I was doomed to disappointment. Master Thomas seemed to be aware of my hopes and expectations concerning him. I have thought before now that he looked at me in answer to my glances, as much as to say, "I will teach you, young man, that though I have parted with my sins, I have not parted with my sense. I shall hold my slaves, and go to heaven too."

There was always a scarcity of good nature about the man; but now his whole countenance was soured all over with the seemings of piety and he became more rigid and stringent in his exactions. If religion had any effect at all on him, it made him more cruel and hateful in all his ways. Do I judge him harshly? God forbid. Capt. Auld made the greatest professions of piety. His house was literally a house of prayer. In the morning and in the evening loud prayers and hymns were heard there, in which both himself and wife joined: yet no more nor better meal was distributed at the quarters, no more attention was paid to the moral welfare of the kitchen, and nothing was done to make us feel that the heart of Master Thomas was one whit better than it was before he went into the little pen, opposite the preacher's stand on the camp-ground. Our hopes, too, founded on the discipline, soon vanished; for he was taken into the church at once, and before he was out of his term of probation, he lead in class. He quite distinguished himself among the brethren as a fervent exhorter. His progress was almost as rapid as the growth of the fabled Jack and the beanstalk. No man was more active in revivals, nor would go more miles to assist in carrying them on, and in getting outsiders interested in religion. His house, being one of the holiest in St. Michaels, became the "preachers' home." They evidently liked to share his hospitality; for while he starved us, he stuffed them—three or four of these "ambassadors" being there not unfrequently at a time—all living on the fat of the land, while we in the kitchen were worse than hungry. Not often did we get a smile of recognition from these holy men. They seemed about as unconcerned about our getting to heaven, as about our getting out of slavery. To this general charge, I must make one exception—the Reverend George Cookman. Unlike Rev. Messrs. Storks, Ewry, Nicky, Humphrey, and Cooper, all of whom were on the St. Michaels circuit, he kindly took an interest in our temporal and spiritual welfare. Our souls and our bodies were alike sacred in his sight, and he really had a good deal of genuine anti-slavery feeling mingled with his colonization ideas. There was not a slave in our neighbourhood who did not love and venerate Mr. Cookman. It was pretty generally believed that he had been instrumental in bringing one of the largest slaveholders in the neighbourhood—Mr. Samuel Harrison—to emancipate all his slaves; and the general impression about Mr. Cookman was, that whenever he met slaveholders, he laboured faithfully with them, as a religious duty, to induce them to liberate their bondsmen. When this good man was at our house, we were all sure to be called in to prayers in the morning; and he was not slow in making enquiries as to the state of our minds, nor in giving us a word of exhortation and of encouragement. Great was the sorrow of all the slaves when this faithful preacher of the gospel was removed from the circuit. He was an eloquent preacher, and possessed what few ministers, south of Mason and Dixon's line, possessed or dared to show—viz., a warm and philanthropic heart. This Mr. Cookman was an Englishman by birth, and perished on board the ill-fated steamship "President," while on his way to England.

But to return to my experience with Master Thomas after his conversion. In Baltimore I could occasionally get into a Sabbath-school, amongst the free children, and receive lessons with the rest; but having learned to read and write already, I was more a teacher than a scholar, even there. When, however, I went back to the Eastern shore and was at the house of Master Thomas, I was not allowed either to teach or to be taught. The whole community, with but one exception among the whites, frowned upon everything like imparting instruction, either to slaves or to free coloured persons. That single exception, a pious young man named Wilson, asked me one day if I would like to assist him in teaching a little Sabbath-school, at the house of a free coloured man named James Mitchell. The idea was to me a delightful one, and I told him I would gladly devote as much of my Sabbaths as I could command to that most laudable work. Mr. Wilson soon mustered up a dozen old spelling-books and a few testaments, and we commenced operations, with some twenty scholars in our school. Here, thought I, is something worth living for; here is a chance for usefulness. The first Sunday passed delightfully, and I spent the week after, very joyously. I could not go to Baltimore, where I and the little company of young friends who had been so much to me there, and from whom I felt parted for ever, but I could make a little Baltimore here. At our second meeting I learned there were some objections to the existence of our school; and sure enough we had scarcely got to work—good work, simply teaching a few coloured children how to read the gospel of the Son of God—when in rushed a mob, headed by two class-leaders, Mr. Wright Fairbanks and Mr. Garrison West, and with them Master Thomas. They were armed with sticks and other missiles, and drove us off, commanding us never to meet for such a purpose again. One of this pious crew told me that as for me, I wanted to be another Nat. Turner, and if I did not look out I should get as many balls in me as Nat. did into him. Thus ended the Sabbath-school; and the reader will not be surprised that this conduct, on the part of class-leaders and professedly holy men, did not serve to strengthen my religious convictions. The cloud over my St. Michaels home grew heavier and blacker than ever.

It was not merely the agency of Master Thomas in breaking up our Sabbath-school, that shook my confidence in the power of that kind of Southern religion to make men wiser or better, but I saw in him all the cruelty and meanness after his conversion which he had exhibited before. His cruelty and meanness were especially displayed in his treatment of my unfortunate cousin Henny, whose lameness made her a burden to him. I have seen him tie up this lame and maimed woman and whip her in a manner most brutal and shocking; and then with blood-chilling blasphemy he would quote the passage of Scripture, "That servant which knew his lord's will and prepared not himself, neither did according to his will, shall be beaten with many stripes." He would keep this lacerated woman tied up by her wrists to a bolt in the joist, three, four, and five hours at a time. He would tie her up early in the morning, whip her with a cowskin before breakfast, leave her tied up, go to his store, and returning to dinner repeat the same castigation, laying on the rugged lash on flesh already raw by repeated blows. He seemed desirous to get the poor girl out of existence, or at any rate off his hands. In proof of this, he afterwards gave her away to his sister Sarah—Mrs. Cline—but as in the case of Mr. Hugh, Henny was soon returned on his hands. Finally, upon a pretence that he could do nothing for her, I use his own words, he "set her adrift to take care of herself." Here was a recently converted man, holding with tight grasp the well-framed and able-bodied slaves left him by old master—the persons who in freedom could have taken care of themselves; yet turning loose the only cripple among them, virtually to starve and die. No doubt, had Master Thomas been asked by some pious Northern brother, why he held slaves? his reply would have been precisely that which many another slaveholder has returned to the same enquiry, viz., "I hold my slaves for their own good."

The many differences springing up between Master Thomas and myself, owing to the clear perception I had of his character, and the boldness with which I defended myself against his capricious complaints, led him to declare that I was unsuited to his wants; that my city life had affected me perniciously; that in fact it had almost ruined me for every good purpose, and had fitted me for everything bad. One of my greatest faults, or offences, was that of letting his horse get away and go down to the farm which belonged to his father-in-law. The animal had a liking for that farm with which I fully sympathized. Whenever I let it out it would go dashing down the road to Mr. Hamilton's as if going on a grand frolic. My horse gone, of course I must go after it. The explanation of our mutual attachment to the place is the same—the horse found good pasturage, and I found there plenty of bread. Mr. Hamilton had his faults, but starving his slaves was not one of them. He gave food in abundance, and of excellent quality. In Mr. Hamilton's cook—Aunt Mary—I found a generous and considerate friend. She never allowed me to go there without giving me bread enough to make good the deficiencies of a day or two. Master Thomas at last resolved to endure my behaviour no longer; he could keep neither me nor his horse, we liked so well to be at his father-in-law's farm. I had now lived with him nearly nine months, and he had given me a number of severe whippings, without any visible improvement in my character or conduct, and now he was resolved to put me out, as he said, "to be broken."

There was, in the Bay-side, very near the camp-ground where my master received his religious impressions, a man named Edward Covey, who enjoyed the reputation of being a first-rate hand at breaking young negroes. This Covey was a poor man, a farm renter; and his reputation for being a good hand to break in slaves was of immense pecuniary advantage to him, since it enabled him to get his farm tilled at very little expense, compared with what it would have cost him otherwise. Some slaveholders thought it an advantage to let Mr. Covey have the government of their slaves a year or two, almost free of charge, for the sake of the excellent training they had under his management. Like some horse-breakers noted for their skill, who ride the best horses in the country without expense, Mr. Covey could have under him the most fiery bloods of the neighbourhood, for the reward of returning them to their owners well broken. Added to the natural fitness of Mr. Covey for the duties of his profession, he was said "to enjoy religion," and he was as strict in the cultivation of piety as he was in the cultivation of his farm. I was made aware of these traits in his character by some who had been under his hand, and while I could not look foward to going to him with any degree of pleasure, I was glad to get away from St. Michaels. I believed I should get enough to eat at Covey's, even if I suffered in other respects, and this to a hungry man is not a prospect to be regarded with indifference.

CHAPTER XV: COVEY, THE NEGRO BREAKER.

Journey to Covey's—Meditations by the way—Covey's house—Family—Awkwardness as a field hand—A cruel beating—Why given—Description of Covey—First attempt at driving oxen—Hair-breadth escape—Ox and man alike property—Hard labor more effective than the whip for breaking down the spirit—Cunning and trickery of Covey—Family worship—Shocking and indecent contempt for chastity—Great mental agitation—Anguish beyond description.

THE morning of January 1, 1834, with its chilling wind and pinching frost, quite in harmony with the winter in my own mind, found me, with my little bundle of clothing on the end of a stick swung across my shoulder, on the main road bending my way toward's Covey's, whither I had been imperiously ordered by Master Thomas. He had been as good as his word, and had committed me without reserve to the mastery of that hard man. Eight or ten years had now passed since I had been taken from my grandmother's cabin in Tuckahoe; and these years, for the most part, I had spent in Baltimore, where, as the reader has already seen, I was treated with comparative tenderness. I was now about to sound profounder depths in slave life. My new master was notorious for his fierce and savage disposition, and my only consolation in going to live with him was the certainty of finding him precisely as represented by common fame. There was neither joy in my heart nor elasticity in my frame as I started for the tyrant's home. Starvation made me glad to leave Thomas Auld's, and the cruel lash made me dread to go to Covey's. Escape, however, was impossible; so, heavy and sad, I paced the seven miles which lay between his house and St. Michaels, thinking much by the solitary way of my adverse condition. But thinking was all I could do. Like a fish in a net, allowed to play for a time, I was now drawn rapidly to the shore, secured at all points. "I am," thought I, "but the sport of a power which makes no account either of my welfare or my happiness. By a law which I can comprehend, but cannot evade or resist, I am ruthlessly snatched from the hearth of a fond grandmother and hurried away to the home of a mysterious old master; again I am removed from there to a master in Baltimore; thence I am snatched away to the eastern shore to be valued with the beasts of the field, and with them to be divided and set apart for a possessor; then I am sent back to Baltimore, and by the time I have formed new attachments and have begun to hope that no more rude shocks shall touch me, a difference arises between brothers, and I am again broken up and sent to St. Michaels; and now from the latter place I am footing my way to the home of another master, where I am given to understand that like a wild young working animal I am to be broken to the yoke of a bitter and life-long bondage." With thoughts and reflections like these, I came in sight of a small wood-coloured building, about a mile from the main road, which, from the description I had received at starting, I easily recognized as my new home. The Chesapeake bay, upon the jutting banks of which the little wood-coloured house was standing, was white with foam raised by the heavy north-west wind; Poplar Island, covered with a thick black pine forest, standing out amid this half ocean; and Keat Point, stretching its sandy, desert-like shores out into the foam-crested bay, were all in sight, and served to deepen the wild and desolate scene.

The good clothes I had brought with me from Baltimore were now worn thin, and had not been replaced; for Master Thomas was as little careful to provide against cold as hunger. Met here by a north wind, sweeping through an open space of forty miles, I was glad to make any port, and, therefore, I speedily pressed on to the wood-coloured house. The family consisted of Mr. and Mrs. Covey; Mrs. Kemp, a broken-backed woman, sister to Mrs. Covey; William Hughes, cousin to Mr. Covey; Caroline, the cook; Bill Smith, a hired man, and myself. Bill Smith, Bill Hughes, and myself were the working force of the farm, which comprised three or four hundred acres. I was now for the first time in my life to be a field-hand; and in my new employment I found myself even more awkward than a green country boy may be supposed to be upon his first entrance into the bewildering scenes of city life; and my awkwardness gave me much trouble. Strange and unnatural as it may seem, I had been in my new home but three days before Mr. Covey, my brother in the Methodist church, gave me a bitter foretaste of what was in reserve for me. I presume he thought that since he had but a single year in which to complete his work, the sooner he began the better. Perhaps he thought by coming to blows at once we should mutually understand better our relations to each other. But to whatever motive, direct or indirect, the cause may be referred, I had not been in his possession three whole days before he subjected me to a most brutal chastisement. Under his heavy blows blood flowed freely, and wales were left on my back as large as my little finger. The sores from this flogging continued for weeks, for they were kept open by the rough and coarse cloth which I wore for shirting. The occasion and details of this first chapter of my experience as a field-hand must be told, that the reader may see how unreasonable, as well as how cruel, my new master, Covey, was. The whole thing I found to be characteristic of the man, and I was probably treated no worse by him than scores of lads who had previously been committed to him, for reasons similar to those which induced my master to place me with him. But here are the facts connected with the affair, precisely as they occurred.

On one of the coldest mornings of the whole month of January, 1834, I was ordered at daybreak to get a load of wood from a forest about two miles from the house. In order to perform this work, Mr. Covey gave me a pair of unbroken oxen, for it seemed that his breaking abilities had not been turned in that direction. In due form, and with all proper ceremony, I was introduced to this huge yoke of unbroken oxen, and was carefully made to understand which was "Buck," and which was "Darby,"—which was the "in hand," and which was the "off hand" ox. The master of this important ceremony was no less a person than Mr. Covey himself; and the introduction was the first of the kind I had ever had.

My life, hitherto, had been quite away from horned cattle, and I had no knowledge of the art of managing them. What was meant by the "in ox," as against the "off ox," when both were equally fastened to one cart, and under one yoke, I could not very easily divine; and the difference implied by the names, and the peculiar duties of each, were alike Greek to me. Why was not the "off ox" called the "in ox?" Where and what is the reason for this distinction in names, when there is none in the things themselves? After initiating me into the use of the "whoa," "back," "gee," "hither,"—the entire language spoken between oxen and driver,—Mr. Covey took a rope about ten feet long and one inch thick, and placed one end of it around the horns of the "in hand ox," and gave the other end to me, telling me that if the oxen started to run away, as the scamp knew they would, I must hold on to the rope and stop them. I need not tell any one who is acquainted with either the strength or the disposition of an untamed ox, that this order was about as unreasonable as a command to shoulder a mad bull. I had never driven oxen before, and I was as awkward a driver as it is possible to conceive. I could not plead my ignorance to Mr. Covey; there was that in his manner which forbade any reply. Cold, distant, morose, with a face wearing all the marks of captious pride and malicious sternness, he repelled all advances. He was not a large man—not more than five feet ten inches in height, I should think; short-necked, round-shouldered, of quick and wiry motion, of thin and wolfish visage, with a pair of small, greenish-gray eyes, set well back under a forehead without dignity, and which were constantly in motion, expressing his passions rather than his thoughts in looks, but denying them utterance in words. The creature presented an appearance altogether ferocious and sinister, disagreeable and forbidding, in the extreme. When he spoke, it was from the corner of his mouth, and in a sort of light growl, like a dog, when an attempt is made to take a bone from him. I already believed him a worse fellow than he had been represented to be. With his directions, and without stopping to question, I started for the woods, quite anxious to perform my first exploit in driving in a creditable manner. The distance from the house to the wood's gate—a full mile, I should think—was passed over with little difficulty: for, although the animals ran, I was fleet enough in the open field to keep pace with them, especially as they pulled me along at the end of the rope; but on reaching the woods, I was speedily thrown into a distressing plight. The animals took fright, and started off ferociously into the woods, carrying the cart full tilt against trees, over stumps, and dashing from side to side in a manner altogether frightful. As I held the rope I expected every moment to be crushed between the cart and the huge trees, among which they were so furiously dashing. After running thus for several minutes, my oxen were finally brought to a stand by a tree, against which they dashed themselves with great violence, upsetting the cart, and entangling themselves among sundry young saplings. By the shock the body of the cart was flung in one direction and the wheels and tongue in another, and all in the greatest confusion. There I was, all alone in a thick wood to which I was a stranger; my cart upset and shattered, my oxen entangled, wild, and enraged, and I, poor soul, but a green hand to set all this disorder right. I knew no more of oxen than the ox-driver is supposed to know of wisdom.

After standing a few minutes, surveying the damage, and not without a presentiment that this trouble would draw after it others even more distressing, I took one end of the cart body and, by an extra outlay of strength, I lifted it toward the axle-tree, from which it had been violently flung; and after much pulling and straining, I succeeded in getting the body of the cart in its place. This was an important step out of the difficulty, and its performance increased my courage for the work which remained to be done. The cart was provided with an axe, a tool with which I had become pretty well acquainted in the ship-yard at Baltimore. With this I cut down the saplings by which my oxen were entangled, and again pursued my journey, with my heart in my mouth, lest the oxen should again take it into their senseless heads to cut up a caper. But their spree was over for the present, and the rascals now moved off as soberly as though their behaviour had been natural and exemplary. On reaching the part of the forest where I had been the day before chopping wood, I filled the cart with a heavy load, as a security against another runaway. But the neck of an ox is equal in strength to iron: it defies ordinary burdens. Tame and docile to a proverb when well trained, the ox is the most sullen and intractable of animals when but half-broken to the yoke. I saw in my own situation several points of similarity with that of the oxen. They were property: so was I. Covey was to break me—I was to break them. Break and be broken was the order.

Half of the day was already gone and I had not yet turned my face homeward. It required only two days' experience and observation to teach me that no such apparent waste of time would be lightly overlooked by Covey. I therefore hurried toward home; but in reaching the lane gate I met the crowning disaster of the day. This gate was a fair specimen of Southern handicraft. There were two huge posts eighteen inches in diameter, rough hewed and square, and the heavy gate was so hung on one of these that it opened only about half the proper distance. On arriving here it was necessary for me to let go the end of the rope on the horns of the "in hand ox"; and now as soon as the gate was open and I let go of it to get the rope again, off went my oxen, making nothing of their load, full tilt; and in so doing they caught the huge gate between the wheel and the cart body, literally crushing it to splinters, and coming only within a few inches of subjecting me to a similar crushing, for I was just in advance of the wheel when it struck the left gate post. With these two hair-breadth escapes I thought I could successfully explain to Mr. Covey the delay, and avert punishment—I was not without a faint hope of being commended for the stern resolution which I had displayed in accomplishing the difficult task—a task which I afterwards learned even Covey himself would not have undertaken without first driving the oxen for some time in the open field, preparatory to their going to the woods. But in this I was disappointed. On coming to him his countenance assumed an aspect of rigid displeasure, and as I gave him a history of the casualties of my trip, his wolfish face, with his greenish eyes, became intensely ferocious. "Go back to the woods again," he said, muttering something else about wasting time. I hastily obeyed, but I had not gone far on my way when I saw him coming after me. My oxen now behaved themselves with singular propriety, contrasting their present conduct to my representation of their former antics. I almost wished, now that Covey was coming, they would do something in keeping with the character I had given them; but no, they had already had their spree, and they could afford now to be extra good, readily obeying orders, and seeming to understand them quite as well as I did myself. On reaching the woods my tormentor, who seemed all the time to be remarking to himself upon the good behaviour of the oxen, came up to me and ordered me to stop the cart, accompanying the same with the threat that he would now teach me how to break gates and idle away my time when he sent me to the woods. Suiting the action to the words, Covey paced off, in his own wiry fashion, to a large gum tree, the young shoots of which are generally used for ox goads, they being exceedingly tough. Three of these goads, from four to six feet long, he cut off and trimmed up with his large jack-knife. This done, he ordered me to take off my clothes. To this unreasonable order I made no reply, but in my apparent unconsciousness and inattention to this command I indicated very plainly a stern determination to do no such thing. "If you will beat me," thought I, "you shall do so over my clothes." After many threats, which made no impression on me, he rushed at me with something of the savage fierceness of a wolf, tore off the few and thinly worn clothes I had on, and proceeded to wear out on my back the heavy goads which he had cut from the gum tree. This flogging was the first of a series of floggings, and though very severe, it was no less so than many which came after it, and these for offences far lighter than the gate-breaking.

I remained with Mr. Covey one year—I cannot say I lived with him,—and during the first six months that I was there I was whipped, either with sticks or cow-skins, every week. Aching bones and a sore back were my constant companions. Frequently as the lash was used, Mr. Covey thought less of it as a means of breaking down my spirit than that of hard and continued labour. He worked me steadily up to the point of my powers of endurance. From the dawn of day in the morning till the darkness was complete in the evening I was kept at hard work in the field or the woods. At certain seasons of the year we were all kept in the field till eleven and twelve o'clock at night. At these times Covey would attend us in the field and urge us on with words or blows, as it seemed best to him. He had, in his life, been an overseer, and he well understood the business of slave-driving. There was no deceiving him. He knew just what a man or boy could do, and he held both to strict account. When he pleased he would work himself like a very Turk, making everything fly before him. It was, however, scarcely necessary for Mr. Covey to be really present in the field to have his work go on industriously. He had the faculty of making us feel that he was always present. By a series of adroitly managed surprises which he practised, I was prepared to expect him at any moment. His plan was never to approach the spot where his hands were at work in an open, manly, and direct manner. No thief was ever more artful in his devices than this man Covey. He would creep and crawl in ditches and gullies, hide behind stumps and bushes, and practice so much of the cunning of the serpent, that Bill Smith and I, between ourselves, never called him by any other name than "the snake." We fancied that in his eyes and his gait we could see a snakish resemblance. One half of his proficiency in the art of negro-breaking consisted, I should think, in this species of cunning. We were never secure. He could see or hear us nearly all the time. He was to us behind every stump, tree, bush, and fence on the plantation. He carried this kind of trickery so far that he would sometimes mount his horse and make believe he was going to St. Michaels, and in thirty minutes afterwards you might find his horse tied in the woods, and the snake-like Covey lying flat in the ditch with his head lifted above its edge, or in a fence-corner, watching every movement of the slaves. I have known him walk up to us and give us special orders as to our work in advance, as if he were leaving home with a view to being absent several days, and before he got half way to the house he would avail himself of our inattention to his movements to turn short on his heel, conceal himself behind a fence-corner, or a tree, and watch us until the going down of the sun. Mean and contemptible as is all this, it is in keeping with the character which the life of a slave-holder was calculated to produce. There was no earthly inducement in the slave's condition to incite him to labour faithfully. The fear of punishment was the sole motive of any sort of industry with him. Knowing this fact as the slaveholder did, and judging the slave by himself, he naturally concluded that the slave would be idle whenever the cause for this fear was absent. Hence all sorts of petty deceptions were practised to inspire fear.

But with Mr. Covey trickery was natural. Everything in the shape of learning or religion which he possessed was made to conform to this semi-lying propensity. He did not seem conscious that the practice had anything unmanly, base, or contemptible about it. It was a part of an important system with him, essential to the relation of master and slave. I thought I saw, in his very religious devotions, this controlling element of his character. A long prayer at night made up for a short prayer in the morning, and few men could seem more devotional than he, when he had nothing else to do.

Mr. Covey was not content with the cold style of family worship adopted in the cold latitudes, which begin and end with a simple prayer. No! the voice of praise as well as of prayer must be heard in his house night and morning. At first I was called upon to bear some part in these exercises; but the repeated floggings given me turned the whole thing into mockery. He was a poor singer, and mainly relied on me for raising the hymn for the family, and when I failed to do so he was thrown into much confusion. I do not think he ever abused me on account of these vexations. His religion was a thing altogether apart from his worldly concerns. He knew nothing of it as a holy principle directing and controlling his daily life, making the latter conform to the requirements of the Gospel. One or two facts will illustrate his character better than a volume of generalities.

I have already implied that Mr. Edward Covey was a poor man. He was, in fact, just commencing to lay the foundation of his fortune, as fortune was regarded in a slave state. The first condition of wealth and respectability there being the ownership of human property, every nerve was strained by the poor man to obtain it, with little regard sometimes as to the means. In pursuit of this object, pious as Mr. Covey was, he proved himself as unscrupulous and base as the worst of his neighbours. In the beginning he was only able—as he said—"to buy one slave"; and scandalous and shocking as is the fact, he boasted that he bought her simply "as a breeder." But the worst of this is not told in this naked statement. This young woman, Caroline was her name, was virtually compelled by Covey to abandon herself to the object for which he had purchased her; and the result was the birth of twins at the end of the year. At this addition to his human stock Covey and his wife were ecstatic with joy. No one dreamed of reproaching the woman, or of finding fault with the hired man, Bill Smith, the father of the children, for Mr. Covey himself had locked the two up together every night, thus inviting the result.

But I will pursue this revolting subject no farther. No better illustration of the unchaste, demoralizing, and debasing character of slavery can be found, than is furnished in the fact that this professedly Christian slave-holder, amidst all his prayers and hymns, was shamelessly and boastfully encouraging and actually compelling, in his own house, undisguised and unmitigated unchastity, as a means of increasing his stock. It was the system of slavery which made this allowable, and which no more condemned the slaveholder for buying a slave-woman and devoting her to this life, than for buying a cow and raising stock from her; and the same rules were observed, with a view to increasing the number and quality of the one, as of the other.

If at any one time in my life, more than another, I was made to drink the bitterest dregs of slavery, that time was during the first six months of my stay with this man Covey. We were worked in all weathers. It was never too hot, nor too cold; it could never rain, blow, snow, nor hail too hard to prevent us from working in the field. Work, work, work, was scarcely more the order of the day than of the night. The longest days were too short for him, and the shortest nights were too long for him. I was somewhat unmanageable at the first, but a few months of this discipline tamed me. Mr. Covey succeeded in breaking me—in body, soul, and spirit. My natural elasticity was crushed; my intellect languished; the disposition to read departed, the cheerful spark that lingered about my eye died out; the dark night of slavery closed in upon me, and beheld a man transformed to a brute.

Sunday was my only leisure time. I spent this in a sort of beast-like stupor, between sleeping and waking under some large tree. At times I would rise up, a flash of energetic freedom would dart through my soul, accompanied with a faint beam of hope that flickered for a moment, and then vanished. I sank down again, mourning over my wretched condition. I was sometimes tempted to take my life and that of Covey, but was prevented by a combination of hope and fear. My sufferings, as I remember them now, seem like a dream rather than a stern real reality.

Our house stood within a few rods of the Chesapeake Bay, whose broad bosom was ever white with sails from every quarter of the habitable globe. Those beautiful vessels, robed in white, and so delightful to the eyes of freemen, were to me so many shrouded ghosts, to terrify and torment me with thoughts of my wretched condition. I have often, in the deep stillness of a summer's Sabbath, stood all alone upon the banks of that noble bay, and traced, with saddened heart and tearful eye, the countless number of sails moving off to the mighty ocean. The sight of these always affected me powerfully. My thoughts would compel utterance; and there, with no audience but the Almighty, I would pour out my soul's complaint in my rude way with an apostrophe to the moving multitude of ships:—

"You are loosed from your moorings, and free. I am fast in my chains, and am a slave! You move merrily before the gentle gale, and I sadly before the bloody whip. You are freedom's swift-winged angels, that fly around the world; I am confined in bonds of iron. O, that I were free! O, that I were on one of your gallant decks, and under your protecting wing! Alas! betwixt me and you the turbid waters roll. Go on, go on; O, that I could also go! Could I but swim! If I could fly! O, why was I born a man, of whom to make a brute? The glad ship is gone: she hides in the dim distance. I am left in the hell of unending slavery. O, God, save me! God, deliver me! Let me be free!—Is there any God? Why am I a slave? I will run away. I will not stand it. Get caught or get clear, I'll try it. I may as well die with ague as with fever. I have only one life to lose. I may as well be killed running as die standing. Only think of it: one hundred miles north, and I am free! Try it? Yes! God helping me, I will. It cannot be that I shall live and die a slave. I will take to the water. This very day shall yet bear me into freedom. The steamboats steer in a northeast course from North Point; I will do the same; and when I get to the head of the bay, I will turn my canoe adrift, and walk straight through Delaware into Pennsylvania. When I get there I shall not be required to have a pass: I will travel there without being disturbed. Let but the first opportunity offer, and come what will, I am off. Meanwhile I will try the yoke. I am not the only slave in the world. Why should I fret? I can bear as much as any of them. Besides, I am but a boy yet, and all boys are bound out to some one. It may be that my misery in slavery will only increase my happiness when I get free. There is a better day coming."

I shall never be able to narrate half the mental experience through which it was my lot to pass, during my stay at Covey's. I was completely wrecked, changed, and bewildered; goaded almost to madness at one time, and at another, reconciling myself to my wretched condition. All the kindness I had received at Baltimore, all my former hopes and aspirations for usefulness in the world, and even the happy moments spent in the exercises of religion, contrasted with my then present lot, served but to increase my anguish.

I suffered bodily as well as mentally. I had neither sufficient time in which to eat, nor to sleep, except on Sundays. The overwork, and the brutal chastisement of which I was the victim, combined with that ever-gnawing and soul-devouring thought—"I am a slave—a slave for life—a slave with no rational ground to hope for freedom"—rendered me a living embodiment of mental and physical wretchedness.

CHAPTER XVI: ANOTHER PRESSURE OF THE TYRANT'S VICE.

Experience at Covey's summed up—First six months severer than the remaining six—Preliminaries to the change—Reasons for narrating the circumstances—Scene in the treading-yard—Taken ill—Escapes to St. Michaels—The pursuit—Suffering in the woods—Talk with Master Thomas—His beating—Driven back to Covey's—The slaves never sick—Natural to expect them to feign sickness—Laziness of slaveholders.

THE reader has but to repeat, in his mind, once a week the scene in the woods, where Covey subjected me to his merciless lash, to have a true idea of my bitter experience during the first six months of the breaking process through which he carried me. I have no heart to repeat each separate transaction. Such a narration would fill a volume much larger than the present one. I aim only to give the reader a truthful impression of my slave-life without unnecessarily affecting him with harrowing details.

As I have intimated, my hardships were much greater during the first six months of my stay at Covey's than during the remainder of the year, and as the change in my condition was owing to causes which may help the reader to a better understanding of human nature, when subjected to the terrible extremities of slavery, I will narrate the circumstances of this change, although I may seem thereby to applaud my own courage.

The reader has seen me humbled, degraded, broken down, enslaved, and brutalized; and understands how it was done; now let us see the converse of all this, and how it was brought about; and this will take us through the year 1834.

On one of the hottest days in the month of August, of the year just mentioned, had the reader been passing through Covey's farm, he might have seen me at work in what was called the "treading-yard"—a yard upon which wheat was trodden out from the straw by the horses' feet. I was there at work feeding the "fan," or rather bringing wheat to the fan, while Bill Smith was feeding. Our force consisted of Bill Hughes, Bill Smith, and a slave by the name of Eli, the latter having been hired for the occasion. The work was simple, and required strength and activity, rather than any skill or intelligence; and yet to one entirely unused to such work, it came very hard. The heat was intense and overpowering, and there was much hurry to get the wheat trodden out that day through the fan; since if that work was done an hour before sundown, the hands would have, according to a promise of Covey, that hour added to their night's rest. I was not behind any of them in the wish to complete the day's work before sundown, and hence I struggled with all my might to get it forward. The promise of one hour's repose on a week day was sufficient to quicken my pace, and to spur me on to extra endeavour. Besides, we had all planned to go fishing, and I certainly wished to have a hand in that. But I was disappointed, and the day turned out to be one of the bitterest I ever experienced. About three o'clock, while the sun was pouring down his burning rays, and not a breeze was stirring, I broke down; my strength failed me; I was seized with a violent aching of the head, attended with extreme dizziness, and trembling in every limb. Finding what was coming, and feeling it would never do to stop work, I nerved myself up, and staggered on, until I fell by the side of the wheat fan, with a feeling that the earth had fallen in upon me. This brought the entire work to a dead stand. There was work for four: each one had his part to perform, and each part depended on the other, so that when one stopped, all were compelled to stop. Covey, who had become my dread, was at the house, about a hundred yards from where I was fanning, and instantly upon hearing the fan stop he came down to the treading-yard to inquire into the cause of the stopping. Bill Smith told him I was sick, and that I was unable longer to bring wheat to the fan.

I had by this time crawled away under the side of a post-and-rail fence in the shade, and was exceedingly ill. The intense heat of the sun, the heavy dust rising from the fan, the stooping to take up the wheat from the yard, together with the hurrying to get through, had caused a rush of blood to my head. In this condition Covey, finding out where I was, came to me; and after standing over me a while he asked me what the matter was. I told him as well as I could, for it was with difficulty that I could speak. He gave me a savage kick in the side which jarred my whole frame, and commanded me to get up. The monster had obtained complete control over me, and if he had commanded me to do any possible thing I should, in my then state of mind, have endeavoured to comply. I made an effort to rise, but fell back in the attempt before gaining my feet. He gave me another heavy kick, and again told me to rise. I again tried, and succeeded in standing up; but upon stooping to get the tub with which I was feeding the fan I again staggered and fell to the ground; and I must have so fallen had I been sure that a hundred bullets would have pierced me through as the consequence. While down in this sad condition, and perfectly helpless, the merciless negro-breaker took up the hickory slab with which Hughes had been striking off the wheat to a level with the sides of the half-bushel measure—a very hard weapon—and with the edge of it he dealt me a heavy blow on my head, which made a large gash and caused the blood to run freely, saying at the same time, "If you have the headache I'll cure you." This done, he ordered me again to rise; but I made no effort to do so, for I had now made up my mind that it was useless, and that the heartless villain might do his worst, he could but kill me and that might put me out of my misery. Finding me unable to rise, or rather despairing of my doing so, Covey left me, with a view to getting on with the work without me. I was bleeding very freely, and my face was soon covered with my warm blood. Cruel and merciless as was the motive that dealt that blow, the wound was a fortunate one for me. Bleeding was never more efficacious. The pain in my head speedily abated, and I was soon able to rise. Covey had, as I have said, left me to my fate, and the question was, shall I return to my work, or shall I find my way to St. Michaels and make Captain Auld acquainted with the atrocious cruelty of his brother Covey and beseech him to get me another master? Remembering the object he had in view in placing me under the management of Covey, and further his cruel treatment of my poor crippled cousin Henny, and his meanness in the matter of feeding and clothing his slaves, there was little ground to hope for a favourable reception at the hands of Captain Thomas Auld. Nevertheless, I resolved to go straight to him, thinking that, if not animated by motives of humanity, he might be induced to interfere on my behalf from selfish considerations. "He cannot," I thought, "allow his property to be thus bruised and battered, marred and defaced, and I will go to him about the matter." In order to get to St. Michaels by the most favourable and direct road I must walk seven miles, and this, in my sad condition, was no easy performance. I had already lost much blood, I was exhausted by over exertion, my sides were sore from the heavy blows planted there by the stout boots of Mr. Covey, and I was in every way in an unfavourable plight for the journey. I, however, watched my chance, while the cruel and cunning Covey was looking in an opposite direction, and started off across the field for St. Michaels. This was a daring step. If it failed it would only exasperate Covey, and increase the rigours of my bondage during the remainder of my term of service under him; but the step was taken, and I must go forward. I succeeded in getting nearly half way across the broad field towards the woods, when Covey observed me. I was still bleeding, and the exertion of running had started the blood afresh. "Come back! Come back!" he vociferated, with threats of what he would do if I did not return instantly. But disregarding his calls and threats, I pressed on towards the woods as fast as my feeble state would allow. Seeing no signs of my stopping he caused his horse to be brought out and saddled, as if he intended to pursue me. The race was now to be an unequal one, and thinking I might be overhauled by him if I kept the main road I walked nearly the whole distance in the woods, keeping far enough from the road to avoid detection and pursuit. But I had not gone far before my little strength again failed me, and I was obliged to lie down. The blood was still oozing from the wound in my head, and for a time I suffered more than I can describe. There I was in the deep woods, sick and emaciated, pursued by a wretch whose character for revolting cruelty beggars all opprobrious speech, bleeding and almost bloodless. I was not without the fear of bleeding to death. The thought of dying in the woods all alone, and of being torn in pieces by the buzzards, had not yet been rendered tolerable by my many troubles and hardships, and I was glad when the shade of the trees and the cool evening breeze combined with my matted hair to stop the flow of blood. After lying there about three quarters of an hour brooding over the singular and mournful lot to which I was doomed, my mind passing over the whole scale or circle of belief and unbelief, from faith in the over-ruling Providence of God to the blackest atheism, I again took up my journey toward St. Michaels, more weary and sad than on the morning when I left Thomas Auld's for the home of Covey. I was bare-footed, bare-headed, and in my shirt sleeves. The way was through briars and bogs, and I tore my feet often during the journey. I was full five hours in going the seven or eight miles; partly because of the difficulties of the way, and partly because of the feebleness induced by my illness, bruises, and loss of blood.

On gaining my master's store, I presented an appearance of wretchedness and woe calculated to move any but a heart of stone. From the crown of my head to the sole of my feet there were marks of blood. My hair was all clotted with dust and blood, and the back of my shirt was literally stiff with the same. Briars and thorns had scarred and torn my feet and legs. Had I escaped from a den of tigers, I could not have looked worse. In this plight I appeared before my professedly Christian master, humbly to invoke the interposition of his power and authority, to protect me from further abuse and violence. During the latter part of my tedious journey, I had begun to hope that my master would now show himself in a nobler light than I had before seen him. But I was disappointed. I had jumped from a sinking ship into the sea; I had fled from a tiger to something worse. I told him all the circumstances, as well as I could: how I was endeavouring to please Covey; how hard I was at work in the present instance; how unwillingly I sank down under the heat, toil, and pain; the brutal manner in which Covey had kicked me in the side, the gash cut in my head; my hesitation about troubling him, Capt. Auld, with complaints; but that now I felt it would not be best longer to conceal from him the outrages committed on me from time to time. At first Master Thomas seemed somewhat affected by the story of my wrongs, but he soon repressed whatever feeling he may have had, and became as cold and hard as iron. It was impossible, at first, as I stood before him, to seem indifferent. I distinctly saw his human nature asserting its conviction against the slave system, which made cases like mine possible; but, as I have said, humanity fell before the systematic tyranny of slavery. He first walked the floor, apparently much agitated by my story, and the spectacle I presented; but soon it was his turn to talk. He began moderately by finding excuses for Covey, and ended with a full justification of him, and a passionate condemnation of me. He had no doubt I deserved the flogging. He did not believe I was sick; I was only endeavouring to get rid of work. My dizziness was laziness, and Covey did right to flog me as he had done. After thus fairly annihilating me, and arousing himself by his eloquence, he fiercely demanded what I wished him to do in the case! With such a knockdown to all my hopes, and feeling as I did my entire subjection to his power, I had very little heart to reply. I must not assert my innocence of the allegations he had piled up against me, for that would be impudence. The guilt of a slave was always and everywhere presumed, and the innocence of the slaveholder, or employer, was always asserted. The word of the slave against this presumption was generally treated as impudence, worthy of punishment. "Do you dare to contradict me, you rascal?" was a final silencer of counter-statements from the lips of a slave. Calming down a little, in view of my silence and hesitation, and perhaps a little touched at my forlorn and miserable appearance, he enquired again, what I wanted him to do? Thus invited a second time, I told him I wished him to allow me to get a new home, and to find a new master; that as sure as I went back to live again with Mr. Covey, I should be killed by him; that he would never forgive my coming home with complaints; that since I had lived with him he had almost crushed my spirit, and I believed he would ruin me for future service, and that my life was not safe in his hands. This Master Thomas, my brother in the church, regarded as "nonsense." There was no danger that Mr. Covey would kill me; he was a good man, industrious, and religious; and he would not think of removing me from that home; "besides," said he—and this I found was the most distressing thought of all to him—"if you should leave Covey now that your year is but half expired, I should lose your wages for the entire year. You belong to Mr. Covey for one year, and you must go back to him, come what will; and you must not trouble me with any more stories; and if you don't go immediately home, I'll get hold of you myself." This was just what I expected when I found he had prejudged the case against me. "But, sir," I said, "I am sick and tired, and I cannot get home to night." At this he somewhat relented, and finally allowed me to stay the night, but said I must be off early in the morning, and concluded his directions by making me swallow a huge dose of Epsom salts, which was about the only medicine ever administered to slaves.

It was quite natural for Master Thomas to presume I was feigning sickness to escape work, for he probably thought that were he in the place of a slave, with no wages for his work, no praise for well doing, no motive for toil but the lash, he would try every possible scheme by which to escape labour. I say I have no doubt of this; the reason is that there were not, under the whole heavens, a set of men who cultivated such a dread of labour as did the slave-holders. The charge of laziness against the slaves was ever on their lips, and was the standing apology for every species of cruelty and brutality. These men did, indeed, literally "bind heavy burdens, grievous to be borne, and laid them upon men's shoulder's, but they themselves would not move them with one of their fingers."

CHAPTER XVII: THE LAST FLOGGING.

A sleepless night—Return to Covey's—Punished by him—The chase defeated—Vengeance postponed—Musings in the woods—The alternative—Deplorable spectacle—Night in the woods—Expected attack—Accosted by Sandy—A friend, not a master—Sandy's hospitality—The ash-cake supper—Interview with Sandy—His advice—Sandy a conjurer as well as a Christian—The magic root—Strange meeting with Covey—His manner—Covey's Sunday face—Defensive resolve—The fight—The victory, and its results.

SLEEP does not always come to the relief of the weary in body and broken in spirit; especially is it so when past troubles only foreshadow coming disasters. My last hope had been extinguished. My master, whom I did not venture to hope would protect me as aman, had now refused to protect me as his property, and had cast me back, covered with reproaches and bruises, into the hands of one who was a stranger to that mercy which is the soul of the religion he professed. May the reader never know what it is to spend such a night as that was to me, which heralded my return to the den of horrors from which I had made a temporary escape.

I remained—sleep I did not—all night at St. Michaels, and in the morning I started off, obedient to the order of Master Thomas, feeling that I had no friend on earth, and doubting if I had one in heaven. I reached Covey's about nine o'clock; and just as I stepped into the field, before I had reached the house, true to his snakish habits, Covey darted out at me from a fence corner, in which he had secreted himself for the purpose of securing me. He was provided with a cowskin and a rope, and he evidently intended to tie me up, and wreak his vengeance on me to the fullest extent. I should have been an easy prey had he succeeded in getting his hands upon me, for I had taken no refreshment since the previous noon; and this, with the other trying circumstances had greatly reduced my strength. I, however, darted back into the woods before the ferocious hound could reach me, and buried myself in a thicket, where he lost sight of me. The cornfield afforded me shelter in getting to the woods. But for the tall corn, Covey would have overtaken me, and made me his captive. He was much chagrined that he did not, and gave up the chase very reluctantly, as I could see by his angry movements as he returned to the house.

Well, now I am clear of Covey and his lash, for a little time. I am in the wood, buried in its sombre gloom, and hushed in its solemn silence; hidden from all human eyes, shut in with nature, and with nature's God, and absent from all human contrivances. Here was a good place to pray; to pray for help, for deliverance—a prayer I had often made before. But how could I pray? Covey could pray—Captain Auld could pray. I would fain pray; but doubts arising, partly from my neglect of the means of grace, and partly from the sham religion which everywhere prevailed, cast in my mind a doubt upon all religion, and led me to the conviction that prayers were unavailing and delusive.

Life in itself had almost become burdensome to me. All my outward relations were against me; I must stay here and starve, or go home to Covey's and have my flesh torn to pieces and my spirit humbled under the cruel lash of Covey. These were the alternatives before me. The day was long and irksome. I was weak from the toils of the previous day, and from want of food and sleep, and I had been so little concerned about my appearance that I had not yet washed the blood from my garments. I was an object of horror, even to myself. Life in Baltimore, when most oppressive, was a paradise to this. What had I done, what had my parents done, that such a life as this should be mine? That day, in the woods, I would have exchanged my manhood for the brutehood of an ox.

Night came. I was still in the woods, and still unresolved what to do. Hunger had not yet pinched me to the point of going home, and I laid myself down in the leaves to rest; for I had been watching for hunters all day, but not being molested by them during the day, I expected no disturbance from them during the night. I had come to the conclusion that Covey relied upon hunger to drive me home, and in this I was quite correct, for he made no effort to catch me after the morning.

During the night I heard the step of a man in the woods. He was coming toward the place where I lay. A person laying still has the advantage over one walking in the woods in the day-time, and this advantage is much greater at night. I was not able to engage in physical struggle, and I had recourse to the common resort of the weak. I hid myself in the leaves to prevent discovery. But as the night rambler in the woods drew nearer I found him to be a friend, not an enemy, a slave of Mr. William Groomes, of Easton, a kind-hearted fellow named "Sandy." Sandy lived with Mr. Kemp that year, about four miles from St. Michaels. He, like myself, had been hired out that year, but unlike myself had not been hired out to be broken. He was the husband of a free woman who lived in the lower part of "Poppie Neck," and he was now on his way through the woods to see her and spend the Sabbath with her.

As soon as I had ascertained that the disturber of my solitude was not an enemy, but the good-hearted Sandy—a man as famous among the slaves of the neighbourhood for his good nature as for his good sense—I came out from my hiding-place and made myself known to him. I explained the circumstances of the past two days which had driven me to the woods, and he deeply compassionated my distress. It was a bold thing for him to shelter me, and I could not ask him to do so, for had I been found in his hut he would have suffered the penalty of thirty-nine lashes on his bare back, if not something worse. But Sandy was too generous to permit the fear of punishment to prevent his relieving a brother bondman from hunger and exposure, and therefore, on his own motion, I accompanied him home to his wife—for the house and lot were hers, as she was a free woman. It was about midnight, but his wife was called up, a fire was made, some Indian meal was soon mixed with salt and water, and an ash-cake was baked in a hurry, to relieve my hunger. Sandy's wife was not behind him in kindness; both seemed to esteem it a privilege to succour me, for although I was hated by Covey and by my master, I was loved by the coloured people, because they thought I was hated for my knowledge, and persecuted because I was feared. I was the only slave in that region who could read or write. There had been one other man, belonging to Mr. Hugh Hamilton, who could read, but he, poor fellow, had shortly after coming into the neighbourhood been sold off to the far South, I saw him ironed, in the cart, to be carried to Easton for sale, pinioned like a yearling for the slaughter. My knowledge was now the pride of my brother slaves, and no doubt Sandy felt something of the general interest in me on that account. The supper was soon ready, and though I have since feasted with honourables, lord mayors, and aldermen over the sea, my supper on ash-cake and cold water, with Sandy, was the meal of all my life most sweet to my taste, and now most vivid to my memory.

Supper over, Sandy and I went to a discussion of what was possible for me, under the perils and hardships which overshadowed my path. The question was, must I go back to Covey, or must I attempt to run away? Upon a careful survey the latter was found to be impossible; for I was on a narrow neck of land, every avenue from which would bring me in sight of pursuers.

There was Chesapeake Bay to the right, and "Pot-pie" river to the left, and St. Michaels and its neighbourhood occupied the only space through which there was any retreat.

I found Sandy an old adviser. He was not only a religious man, but he professed to believe in a system for which I have no name. He was a genuine African, and had inherited some of the so-called magical powers said to be possessed by the eastern nations. He told me that he could help me; that in those very woods there was an herb which in the morning might be found, possessing all the powers required for my protection—I put his words in my own language— and that if I would take his advice he would procure me the root of the herb of which he spoke. He told me, further, that if I would take that root and wear it on my right side it would be impossible for Covey to strike me a blow; that with this root about my person no white man could whip me. He said he had carried it for years, and that he had fully tested its virtues. He had never received a blow from a slave-holder since he had carried it, and he never expected to receive one, for he meant always to carry that root for protection. He knew Covey well, for Mrs. Covey was the daughter of Mrs. Kemp; and he, Sandy, had heard of the barbarous treatment to which I had been subjected, and he wanted to do something for me.

Now all this talk about the root was to me very absurd and ridiculous, if not positively sinful. I at first rejected the idea that the simple carrying a root on my right side—a root, by the way, over which I walked every time I went into the woods—could posess any such magic power as he ascribed to it, and I was, therefore, not disposed to cumber my pocket with it. I had a positive aversion to all pretenders to "divination." It was beneath one of my intelligence to countenance such dealings with the devil as this power implied. But with all my learning—it was really precious—Sandy was more than a match for me. "My book-learning," he said, "had not kept Covey off me"—a powerful argument just then—and he entreated me, with flashing eyes, to try this. If it did me no good it could do me no harm, and it would cost me nothing any way. Sandy was so earnest and so confident of the good qualities of this weed that, to please him, I was induced to take it. He had been to me the good Samaritan, and had, almost providentially, found me and helped me when I could not help myself; how did I know but that the hand of the Lord was in it? With thoughts of this sort I took the root from Sandy and put them in my right hand pocket.

This was Sunday morning. Sandy now urged me to go home with all speed, and to walk up bravely to the house, as though nothing had happened. I saw in Sandy too deep an insight into human nature, with all his superstition, not to have some respect for his advice; and perhaps, too, a slight gleam or shadow of his superstition had fallen on me. At any rate, I started off toward Covey's as directed. Having, the previous night, poured my griefs into Sandy's ears and enlisted him in my behalf, having made his wife a sharer in my sorrows, and having also become well refreshed by sleep and food, I moved off quite courageously toward the dreaded Covey's. Singularly enough, just as I entered the yard gate I met him and his wife, dressed in their Sunday best, looking as smiling as angels, on their way to church. His manner perfectly astonished me. There was something really benignant in his countenance. He spoke to me as never before, told me that the pigs had got into the lot and he wished me to go and drive them out; inquired how I was, and seemed an altered man. This extraordinary conduct really made me begin to think that Sandy's herb had more virtue in it than I, in my pride, had been willing to allow, and had the day been other than Sunday I should have attributed Covey's altered manner solely to the power of the root. I suspected, however, that the Sabbath, not the root, was the real explanation of the change. His religion hindered him from breaking the Sabbath, but not from breaking my skin on any other day than Sunday. He had more respect for the day than for the man for whom the day was mercifully given; for while he would cut and slash my body during the week, he would on Sunday teach me the value of my soul, and the way of life and salvation by Jesus Christ.

All went well with me till Monday morning; and then, whether the root had lost its virtue, or whether my tormenter had gone deeper into the black art than I had—as was sometimes said of him,—or whether he had obtained a special indulgence for his faithful Sunday's worship, it is not necessary for me to know or to inform the reader; but this much I may say, the pious and benignant smile which graced the face of Covey on Sunday wholly disappeared on Monday.

Long before daylight I was called up to feed, rub, and curry the horses. I obeyed the call, as I should have done had it been made at an earlier hour, for I had brought my mind to a firm resolve during that Sunday's reflection to obey every order, however unreasonable, if it were possible, and if Mr. Covey should then undertake to beat me to defend and protect myself to the best of my ability. My religious views on the subject of resisting my master had suffered a serious shock by the savage persecution to which I had been subjected, and my hands were no longer tied by my religion. Master Thomas's indifference had severed the last link. I had backslidden from this point in the slaves' religious creed, and I soon had occasion to make my fallen state known to my Sunday-pious brother, Covey.

While I was obeying his order to feed and get the horses ready for the field, and when I was in the act of going up the stable loft, for the purpose of throwing down some blades, Covey sneaked into the stable, in his peculiar way, and seizing me suddenly by the leg, he brought me to the stable-floor, giving my newly-mended body a terrible jar. I now forgot all about my roots, and remembered my pledge to stand up in my own defence. The brute was skilfully endeavouring to get a slip-knot on my legs, before I could draw up my feet. As soon as I found what he was up to, I gave a sudden spring—my two days' rest had been of much service to me—and by that means, no doubt, he was able to bring me to the floor so heavily. He was defeated in his plan of tying me. While down, he seemed to think he had me very securely in his power. He little thought he was—as the rowdies say—"in" for a "rough and tumble" fight: but such was the fact. Whence came the daring spirit necessary to grapple with a man, who eight-and-forty hours before, could, with his slightest word, have made me tremble like a leaf in a storm, I do not know; at any rate I was resolved to fight, and what was better still, I actually was hard at it. The fighting madness had come upon me, and I found my strong fingers firmly attached to the throat of the tyrant, as heedless of consequences, at the moment, as if we stood as equals before the law. The very colour of the man was forgotten, I felt supple as a cat, and was ready for him at every turn. Every blow of his was parried, though I dealt no blows in return. I was strictly on the defensive, preventing him from injuring me, rather than trying to injure him. I flung him on to the ground several times when he meant to have hurled me there. I held him so firmly by the throat that his blood followed my nails. He held me, and I held him.

All was fair thus far, and the contest was about equal. My resistance was entirely unexpected, and Covey was taken all aback by it, and he trembled in every limb. "Are you going to resist, you scoundrel?" said he. To which I returned a polite "yes, sir," steadily gazing my interrogator in the eye, to meet the first approach or dawning of the blow which I expected my answer would call forth. But the conflict did not long remain equal. Covey soon cried lustily for help; not that I was obtaining any marked advantage over him, or was injuring him, but because he was gaining none over me, and was not able, single-handed, to conquer me. He called for his cousin Hughes to come to his assistance, and now the scene was changed. I was compelled to give blows, as well as to parry them, and since I was in any case to suffer for resistance, I felt—as the musty proverb goes—that I "might as well be hanged for an old sheep as a lamb." I was still defensive toward Covey, but aggressive toward Hughes, on whom at his first approach, I dealt a blow which fairly sickened him. He went off, bending over with pain, and manifesting no disposition to come again within my reach. The poor fellow was in the act of trying to catch and tie my right hand, and while flattering himself with success, I gave him a kick which sent him staggering away in pain, at the same time that I held Covey with a firm hand.

Taken completely by surprise, Covey seemed to have lost his usual strength and coolness. He was frightened, and stood puffing and blowing, seemingly unable to command words or blows. When he saw that Hughes was standing half bent with pain, his courage quite gone, the cowardly tyrant asked if I "meant to persist in my resistance." I told him I "did mean to resist, come what might; that I had been treated like a brute during the last six months, and that I should stand it no longer." With that he gave me a shake, and attempted to drag me toward a stick of wood that was lying just outside the stable door. He meant to knock me down with it, but just as he leaned over to get the stick, I seized him with both hands, by the collar, and with a vigorous and sudden snatch, I brought my assailant harmlessly, his full length, on the not over clean ground, for we were now in the cow-yard. He had selected the place for the fight, and it was but right that he should have the advantages of his own selection.

By this time Bill, the hired man, came home. He had been to Mr. Helmsley's to spend Sunday with his nominal wife. Covey and I had been at skirmishing from before daybreak till now, and the sun was now shooting his beams almost over the eastern woods, and we were still at it. I could not see where the matter was to terminate. He evidently was afraid to let me go, lest I should again make off to the woods, otherwise he would probably have obtained arms from the house to frighten me. Holding me, he called upon Bill to assist him. The scene here had something comic about it. Bill, who knew precisely what Covey wished him to do, affected ignorance, and pretended he did not know what to do. "What shall I do, Master Covey?" said Bill. "Take hold of him!—take hold of him!" said Covey. With a toss of his head, peculiar to Bill, he said, "indeed Master Covey, I want to go to work." "This is your work," said Covey; "take hold of him." Bill replied, with spirit: "My master hired me to work, and not to help you whip Frederick." It was my turn to speak. "Bill," said I, "don't put your hands on me." To which he replied: "My God, Frederick, I ain't goin' to tech ye;" and Bill walked off, leaving Covey and myself to settle our differences as best we might.

But my present advantage was threatened when I saw Caroline—the slave woman of Covey—coming to the cow-shed to milk, for she was a powerful woman, and could have mastered me easily, exhausted as I was.

As soon as she came near, Covey attempted to rally her to his aid. Strangely and fortunately, Caroline was in no humour to take a hand in any such sport. We were all in open rebellion that morning. Caroline answered the command of her master "to take hold of me," precisely as Bill had done, but in her it was at far greater peril, for she was the slave of Covey, and he could do what he pleased with her. It was not so with Bill, and Bill knew it. Samuel Harris, to whom Bill belonged, did not allow his slaves to be beaten, unless they were guilty of some crime which the law would punish. But poor Caroline, like myself, was at the mercy of the merciless Covey, nor did she escape the dire effects of her refusal: he gave her several sharp blows.

At length, after two hours had elapsed, the contest was given over. Letting go of me, puffing and blowing at a great rate, Covey said; "Now, you scoundrel, go to your work; I would not have whipped you half as hard if you had not resisted." The fact was, he had not whipped me at all. He had not, in all the scuffle, drawn a single drop of blood from me. I had drawn blood from him, and should even without this satisfaction have been victorious, because my aim had not been to injure him, but to prevent his injuring me.

During the whole six months I lived with Covey after this transaction, he never again laid the weight of his finger on me in anger. He would occasionally say he did not want to have to get hold of me again—a declaration which I had no difficulty in believing; and I had a secret feeling which answered, "you had better not wish to get hold of me again, for you will be likely to come off worse in a second fight than you did in the first."

Well, my dear reader, this battle with Mr. Covey, undignified as it was, and as I fear my narration of it is, was the turning point in my "life as a slave." It rekindled in my breast the smouldering embers of liberty; it brought up my Baltimore dreams, and revived a sense of my own manhood. I was a changed being after that fight. I was nothing before; I was a man now. It recalled to life my crushed self-respect, and my self-confidence, and inspired me with a renewed determination to be a free man. A man without force is without the essential dignity of humanity. Human nature is so constituted, that it cannot honour a helpless man, though it can pity him, and even this it cannot do long if signs of power do not arise.

He only can understand the effect of this combat on my spirit, who has himself incurred something, hazarded something, in repelling the unjust and cruel aggressions of a tyrant. Covey was a tyrant and a cowardly one withal. After resisting him, I felt as I never felt before. It was a resurrection from the dark and pestiferous tomb of slavery, to the heaven of comparative freedom. I was no longer a servile coward, trembling under the frown of a brother worm of the dust, but my long-cowed spirit was roused to an attitude of independence. I had reached the point at which I was not afraid to die. This spirit made me a freeman in fact, though I still remained a slave in form. When a slave cannot be flogged, he is more than half free. He has a domain as broad as his own manly heart to defend, and he is really "a power on the earth." From this time until my escape from slavery, I was never fairly whipped. Several attempts were made, but they were always unsuccessful. Bruises I did get, but the instance I have described was the end of that brutification to which slavery had subjected me.

The reader may like to know why, after I had so grievously offended Mr. Covey, he did not have me taken in hand by the authorities; indeed, why the law of Maryland, which assigned hanging to the slave who resisted his master, was not put in force against me; at any rate why I was not taken up, as was usual in such cases, and publicly whipped, as an example to other slaves, and as a means of deterring me from committing the same offence again. I confess that the easy manner in which I got off was always a surprise to me, and even now I cannot fully explain the cause, though the probability is that Covey was ashamed to have it known that he had been mastered by a boy of sixteen. He enjoyed the unbounded and very valuable reputation of being a first-rate overseer and negro-breaker, and by means of this reputation he was able to procure his hands at very trifling compensation and with very great ease. His interest and his pride would mutually suggest the wisdom of passing the matter by in silence. The story that he had undertaken to whip a lad and had been resisted, would of itself be damaging to him in the estimation of slave-holders.

It is perhaps not altogether creditable to my natural temper that after this conflict with Mr. Covey I did, at times, purposely aim to provoke him to an attack, by refusing to keep with the other hands in the field, but I could never bully him to another battle. I was determined on doing him serious damage if he ever again attempted to lay violent hands on me.

- "Hereditary bondmen know ye not

- Who would be free, themselves must strike the blow?"

CHAPTER XVIII: NEW RELATIONS AND DUTIES.

Change of masters—Benefits derived by change—Fame of the fight with Covey—Reckless unconcern—Abhorrence of slavery—Ability to read a cause of prejudice—The holidays—How spent—Sharp hit at slavery—Effects of holidays—Difference between Covey and Freeland—An irreligious master preferred to a religious one—Hard life at Covey's useful—Improved condition does not bring contentment—Congenial society at Freeland's—Sabbath-school—Secrecy necessary—Affectionate relations of tutor and pupils—Confidence and friendship among slaves—Slavery the inviter of vengeance.

MY term of service with Edward Covey expired on Christmas day, 1834. I gladly enough left him, although he was by this time as gentle as a lamb. My home for the year 1835 was already secured, my next master selected. There was always more or less excitement about the changing of hands, but I had become somewhat reckless and cared little into whose hands I fell, determined to fight my way. The report got abroad that I was hard to whip, that I was guilty of kicking back, that though generally a good-natured negro, I sometimes "got the devil in me." These sayings were rife in Talbot County, and they distinguished me among my servile brethren. Slaves would sometimes fight with each other, and even die at each other's hands, but there were very few who were not held in awe by a white man. Trained from the cradle to think and feel that their masters were superior, and invested with a sort of sacredness, there were few who could rise above the control which that sentiment exercised. I had freed myself from it, and the thing was known. One bad sheep will spoil a whole flock. I was a bad sheep. I hated slavery, slave-holders, and all pertaining to them; and I did not fail to inspire others with the same feeling wherever and whenever opportunity was presented. This made me a marked lad among the slaves, and a suspected one among slave-holders, A knowledge of my ability to read and write got pretty widely spread, which was very much against me.

The days between Christmas and New Year's day were allowed the slaves as holidays. During these days all regular work was suspended, and there was nothing to do but keep fires and look after the stock. We regarded this time as our own by the grace of our masters, and we therefore used it or abused it as we pleased. Those who had families at a distance were expected to visit them and spend with them the entire week. The younger slaves or the unmarried ones were expected to see to the cattle, and to attend to incidental duties at home. The holidays were variously spent. The sober, thinking, industrious ones would employ themselves in manufacturing corn brooms, mats, horse collars, and baskets, and some of these were very well made. Another class spent their time in hunting opossums, coons, rabbits, and other game. But the majority spent the holidays in sports, ball-playing, wrestling, boxing, running foot-races, dancing, and drinking whiskey; and this latter mode was generally most agreeable to their masters. A slave who would work during the holidays was thought by his master undeserving of holidays. There was in this simple act of continued work an accusation against slaves, and a slave could not help thinking that if he made three dollars during the holidays he might make three hundred during the year. Not to be drunk during the holidays was disgraceful.

The fiddling, dancing, and "jubilee beating" was carried on in all directions. This latter performance was strictly southern. It supplied the place of violin, or of other musical instruments, and was played so easily that almost every farm had its "Juba" beater. The performer improvised as he beat the instument, marking the words as he sang so as to have them fall pat with the movement of his hands. Among a mass of nonsense and wild frolic, once in a while a sharp hit was given to the meanness of slave-holders. Take the following for example:

- We raise de wheat,

- Dey gib us de corn;

- We bake de bread,

- Dey gib us de crust;

- We sif de meal,

- Dey gib us de huss;

•

- We peel de meat,

- Dey gib us de skin;

- And dat's de way

- Dey take us in;

- We skim de pot,

- Dey give us de liquor,

- And say dat's good enough for nigger.

•

- Walk over! walk over!

- Your butter and de fat;

- Poor nigger you can't get over dat.

- Walk over—

This is not a summary of the palpable injustice and fraud of slavery, giving, as it does, to the lazy and idle the comforts which God designed should be given solely to the honest labourer. But to the holidays. Judging from my own observation and experience, I believe those holidays were among the most effective means in the hands of slave-holders of keeping down the spirit of insurrection among the slaves.

To enslave men successfully and safely it is necessary to keep their minds occupied with thoughts and aspirations short of the liberty of which they are deprived. A certain degree of attainable good must be kept before them. These holidays served the purpose of keeping the minds of the slaves occupied with prospective pleasure within the limits of slavery. The young man could go wooing, the married man to see his wife, the father and mother to see their children, the industrious and money-loving could make a few dollars, the great wrestler could win laurels, the young people meet and enjoy each other's society, the drunken man could get plenty of whiskey, and the religious man could hold prayer-meetings, preach, pray, and exhort.

Before the holidays there were pleasures in prospect; after the holidays they were pleasures of memory, and they served to keep out thoughts and wishes of a more dangerous character. These holidays were also conductors or safety-valves, to carry off the explosive elements inseparable from the human mind when reduced to the condition of slavery. But for these the rigours of bondage would have become too severe for endurance, and the slave would have been forced to dangerous desperation.

Thus they became a part and parcel of the gross wrongs and inhumanity of slavery. Ostensibly they were institutions of benevolence designed to mitigate the rigours of slave life, but practically they were a fraud instituted by human selfishness, the better to secure the ends of injustice and oppression. The slave's happiness was not the end sought, but the master's safety. It was not from a generous unconcern for the slave's labour, but from a prudent regard for the slave system. I am strengthened in this opinion from the fact that most slave-holders liked to have their slaves spend the holidays in such a manner as to be of no real benefit to them. Everything like rational enjoyment was frowned upon, and only those wild and low sports peculiar to semi-civilized people were encouraged. The licence allowed appeared to have no other object than to disgust the slaves with their temporary freedom, and to make them as glad to return to their work as they were to leave it. I have known slave-holders resort to cunning tricks, with a view of getting their slaves deplorably drunk. The usual plan was to make bets on a slave that he could drink more whiskey than any other, and so induce a rivalry among them for the mastery in this degradation. The scenes brought about in this way were often scandalous and loathsome in the extreme. Whole multitudes might be found stretched out in brutal drunkenness, at once helpless and disgusting. Thus, when the slave asked for hours of "virtuous liberty," his cunning master took advantage of his ignorance and cheered him with a dose of vicious and revolting dissipation artfully labelled with the name of "liberty."

We were induced to drink, I among the rest, and when the holidays were over we all staggered up from our filth, and wallowing, took a long breath, and went away to our various fields of work, feeling, upon the whole, rather glad to go from that which our masters had artfully deceived us into the belief was freedom, back again to the arms of slavery. It was not what we had taken it to be, nor what it would have been, had it not been abused by us. It was about as well to be a slave to a master, as to be a slave to whiskey and rum. When the slave was drunk the slave-holder had no fear that he would escape to the North. It was the sober, thoughtful slave who was dangerous, and needed the vigilance of his master to keep him a slave.

On the first of January, 1835, I proceeded from St. Michaels to Mr. William Freeland's—my new home. Mr. Freeland lived only three miles from St. Michaels, on an old, worn-out farm, which required much labour to render it anything like a self-supporting establishment.

I found Mr. Freeland a different man from Covey. Though not rich, he was what might have been called a well-bred Southern gentleman. Though a slave-holder and sharing in common with them many of the vices of his class, he seemed alive to the sentiment of honour, and had also some sense of justice, and some feelings of humanity. He was fretful, impulsive, and passionate, but free from the mean and selfish characteristics which distinguished the creature from whom I had happily escaped. Mr. Freeland was open, frank, imperative, and practised no concealments, and disdained to play the spy; in all these qualities he was the opposite of Covey.

My poor weather-beaten bark now reached smoother water and gentler breezes. My stormy life at Covey's had been of service to me. The things that would have seemed very hard had I gone direct to Mr. Freeland's from the home of Master Thomas were now "trifles light as air."

I was still a field hand, and had come to prefer the severe labour of the field to the enervating duties of a house servant. I had become large and strong, and had begun to take pride in the fact that I could do as much hard work as some of the older men. There was much rivalry among slaves at times as to which could do the most work, and masters generally sought to promote such rivalry. But some of us were too wise to race with each other very long. Such racing, we had the sagacity to see, was not likely to pay. We had our times for measuring each other's strength, but we knew too much to keep up the competition so long as to produce an extraordinary day's work. We knew that if by extraordinary exertion a large quantity of work was done in one day, on its becoming known to the master, it might lead him to require the same amount every day. This thought was enough to bring us to a dead halt when ever so much excited in the race.

At Mr. Freeland's my condition was every way improved. I was no longer the scapegoat that I was when at Covey's, where every wrong thing done was saddled upon me, and where other slaves were whipped over my shoulders. Bill Smith was protected by a positive prohibition, made by his rich master,—and the command of the rich slave-holder was law to the poor one. Hughes was favoured by his relationship to Covey, and the hands hired temporarily escaped flogging. I was the general pack horse; but Mr. Freeland held every man individually responsible for his own conduct. Mr. Freeland, like Mr. Covey, gave his hands enough to eat, but, unlike Mr. Covey, he gave them time to take their meals. He worked us hard during the day, but gave us the night for rest. We were seldom in the field after dark in the evening, or before sunrise in the morning, Our implements of husbandry were of the most improved pattern, and much superior to those used at Covey's.

Notwithstanding all the improvement in my relations, notwithstanding the many advantages I had gained by my new home and my new master, I was still restless and discontented. I was about as hard to please with a master as a master is with a slave. The freedom from bodily torture and unceasing labour had given my mind an increased sensibility, and imparted to it greater activity. I was not yet exactly in right relations. "Howbeit, that was not first which is spiritual, but that which is natural, and afterward that which is spiritual." When entombed at Covey's, shrouded in darkness and physical wretchedness, temporal well-being was the grand desideratum; but, temporal wants supplied, the spirit puts in its claim. Beat and cuff your slave, keep him hungry and spiritless, and he will follow the lead of his master like a dog; but feed and clothe him well, work him moderately, surround him with physical comfort, and dreams of freedom intrude. Give him a bad master, and he wishes for a good master; give him a good master and he aspires to become his own master. Such is human nature. You may place a man so far beneath the level of his kind, that he loses all just ideas of his natural position, but elevate him a little, and the clear conception of rights rises to life and power, and leads him onward. Thus, elevated a little at Freeland's, the dreams called into being by that good man, Father Lawson, when in Baltimore, began to visit me again; shoots from the tree of liberty began to put forth buds, and dim hopes of the future began to dawn.

I found myself in congenial society. There were Henry Harris, John Harris, Handy Caldwell, and Sandy Jenkins, this last of the root-preventive memory.

Henry and John Harris were brothers, and belonged to Mr. Freeland. They were both remarkably bright and intelligent, though neither of them could read. Now for my mischief! I had not been long there before I was up to my old tricks. I began to address my companions on the subject of education, and the advantages of intelligence over ignorance, and, as far as I dared, I tried to show the agency of ignorance in keeping men in slavery. Webster's spelling book and the Columbian Orator were looked into again. As summer came on, and the long Sabbath days stretched themselves over our idleness, I became uneasy, and wanted a Sabbath-school, wherein to exercise my gifts, and to impart the little knowledge I possessed to my brother slaves. A house was hardly necessary in the summer time; I could hold my school under the shade of an old oak as well as anywhere else. The thing was to get the scholars, and to have them thoroughly imbued with the desire to learn. Two such boys were quickly found in Henry and John, and from them the contagion spread. I was not long in bringing around me twenty or thirty young men, who enrolled themselves gladly in my Sabbath-school, and were willing to meet me regularly under the trees or elsewhere, for the purpose of learning to read. It was surprising with what ease they provided themselves with spelling-books. These were mostly the cast-off books of their young masters or mistresses. I taught at first on our own farm. All were impressed with the necessity of keeping the matter as private as possible, for the fate of the St. Michaels attempt was still fresh in the minds of all. Our pious masters at St. Michaels must not know that a few of their dusky brothers were learning to read the Word of God, lest they should come down upon us with the lash and chain. We might have met to drink whiskey, to wrestle, fight, and to do other unseemly things, with no fear of interruption from the saints or the sinners of St. Michaels. But to meet for the purpose of improving the mind and heart, by learning to read the sacred Scriptures, was a nuisance to be instantly stopped. The slave-holders there, like slave-holders elsewhere, preferred to see the slaves engaged in degrading sports, rather than acting like moral and accountable beings. Had any one asked a religious white man in St. Michaels at that time the names of three men in that town whose lives were most after the pattern of our Lord and Master Jesus Christ, the reply would have been: Garrison West, class-leader, Wright Fairbanks, and Thomas Auld, both also class-leaders; and yet these men ferociously rushed in upon my Sabbath-school, armed with mob-like missiles, and forbade our meeting again on pain of having our backs subjected to the bloody lash. This same Garrison West was my class-leader, and I had thought him a Christian until he took part in breaking up my school. He led me no more after that.

The plea for this outrage was then, as it is always, the tyrant's plea of necessity. If the slaves learned to read they would learn something more and something worse. The peace of slavery would be disturbed; slave rule would be endangered. I do not dispute the soundness of the reasoning. If slavery were right, Sabbath-schools for teaching slaves to read were wrong, and ought to have been put down. These Christian class-leaders were, to this extent, consistent. They had settled the question that slavery was right, and by that standard they determined that Sabbath-schools were wrong. To be sure they were Protestants, and held to the great protestant right of every man to "search the Scriptures" for himself; but then, to all general rules there are exceptions. How convenient! What crimes may not be committed under such ruling! But my dear class-leading Methodist brethren did not condescend to give me a reason for breaking up the school at St. Michaels; they had determined its destruction, and that was enough. However, I am digressing.

After getting the school nicely started a second time, holding it in the woods behind the barn, and in the shade of trees, I succeeded in inducing a free coloured man who lived several miles from our house to permit me to hold my school in a room at his house. He incurred much peril in doing so, for the assemblage was an unlawful one. I had at one time more than forty scholars, all of the right sort, and many of them succeeded in learning to read. I have had various employments during my life, but I look to none with more satisfaction. An attachment, deep and permanent, sprung up between me and my persecuted pupils, which made my parting from then intensely painful.

Besides my Sunday-school, I devoted three evenings a week to my other fellow slaves during the winter. Those dear souls who came to my Sabbath-school came not because it was popular or reputable to do so, for they came with a liability of having forty stripes laid on their naked backs. In this Christian country men and women were obliged to hide in barns and woods and trees from professing Christians, in order to learn to read the Holy Bible. Their minds had been cramped and starved by their cruel masters; the light of education had been completely excluded, and their hard earnings had been taken to educate their master's children. I felt a delight in circumventing the tyrants, and in blessing the victims of their curses.

The year at Mr. Freeland's passed off very smoothly, to outward seeming. Not a blow was given me during the whole year. To the credit of Mr. Freeland, irreligious though he were, it must be stated that he was the best master I ever had until I became my own master and assumed for myself, as I had a right to do, the responsibility of my own existence and the exercise of my own powers.

For much of the happiness, or absence of misery, with which I passed this year, I am indebted to the genial temper and ardent friendship of my brother slaves. They were every one of them manly, generous, and brave; yes, I say they were brave, and I will add fine looking. It is seldom the lot of any to have truer and better friends than were the slaves on this farm. It was not uncommon to charge slaves with great treachery toward each other, but I must say I never loved, esteemed, or confided in men more than I did in these. They were as true as steel, and no band of brothers could be more loving. There were no mean advantages taken of each other, no tattling, no giving each other bad names to Mr. Freeland, and no elevating one at the expense of the other. We never undertook anything of any importance which was likely to affect each other without mutual consultation. We were generally a unit, and moved together. Thoughts and sentiments were exchanged between us which might well have been considered incendiary had they been known by our masters. The slave-holder, were he kind or cruel, was a slave-holder still, the every-hourviolator of the just and inalienable rights of man, and he was therefore every hour silently but surely whetting the knife of vengeance for his own throat. He never lisped a syllable in commendation of the fathers of this republic without inviting the sword, and asserting the right of rebellion for his own slaves.

CHAPER XIX: THE RUNAWAY PLOT.

New Year's thoughts and meditations—Again hired by Freeland—Kindness no compensation for slavery—Incipient steps toward escape—Considerations leading thereto—Hostility to slavery—Solemn vow taken—Plan divulged to slaves—Columbian Orator again—Scheme gains favour—Danger of discovery—Skill of slave-holders—Suspicion and coercion—Hymns with double meaning—Consultation—Pass-word—Hope and fear—Ignorance of Geography—Imaginary difficulties—Patrick Henry—Sandy, a dreamer—Route to the North mapped out—Objections—Frauds—Passes—Anxieties—Fear of failure—Strange presentiment—Coincidence—Betrayal—Arrests—Resistance—Mrs. Freeland—Prison— Brutal jests—Passes eaten—Denial—Sandy—Dragged behind horses—Slave-traders—Alone in prison—Sent to Baltimore.

I AM now at the beginning of the year—1836—when the mind naturally occupies itself with the mysteries of life in all its phases—the ideal, the real, and the actual. Sober people look both ways at the begining of a new year, surveying the errors of the past, and providing against the possible errors of the future. I, too, was thus exercised. I had little pleasure in retrospect, and the future prospect was not brilliant. "Notwithstanding," thought I, "the many resolutions and prayers I have made in behalf of freedom, I am, this first day of the year 1836, still a slave, still wandering in the depths of a miserable bondage. My faculties and powers of body and soul are not my own, but are the property of a fellow-mortal in no sense superior to me, except that he has the physical power to compel me to be owned and controlled by him. By the combined physical force of the community I am his slave—a slave for life." With thoughts like these I was chafed and perplexed, and they rendered me gloomy and disconsolate. The anguish of my mind cannot be written.

At the close of the year, Mr. Freeland renewed the purchase of my services from Mr. Auld for the coming year. His promptness in doing so would have been flattering to my vanity had I been ambitious to win the reputation of being a valuable slave. Even as it was, I felt a slight degree of complacency at the circumstance. It showed him to be as well pleased with me as a slave as I with him as a master. But the kindness of the slave-master only gilded the chain, it detracted nothing from its weight or strength. The thought that men are made for other and better uses than slavery throve best under the gentle treatment of a kind master. Its grim visage could assume no smiles able to fascinate the partially enlightened slave into a forgetfulness of his bondage, or of the desirableness of liberty.

I was not through the first month of my second year with the kind and gentlemanly Mr. Freeland, before I was earnestly considering and devising plans for gaining that freedom, which, when I was but a mere child, I had ascertained to be the natural and inborn right of every member of the human family. The desire for this freedom had been benumbed while I was under the brutalizing dominion of Covey, and it had been postponed and rendered inoperative by my truely pleasant Sunday-school engagements with my friends during the year at Mr. Freeland's. It had, however, never entirely subsided. I hated slavery always, and my desire for freedom needed only a favourable breeze to fan it into a blaze at at any moment. The thought of being only a creature of the present and the past troubled me, and I longed to have a future—a future with hope in it. To be shut up entirely to the past and present is to the soul whose life and happiness is unceasing progress—what the prison is to the body—a blight and mildew, a hell of horrors. The dawning of this, another year, awakened me from my temporary slumber, and roused into life my latent but long-cherished aspirations for freedom. I became not only ashamed to be contented in slavery, but ashamed to seem to be contented, and in my present favourable condition under the mild rule of Mr. Freeland, I am not sure that some kind reader will not condemn me for being over ambitious, and greatly wanting in humility, when I say the truth, that I now drove from me all thoughts of making the best of my lot, and welcomed only such thoughts as led me away from the house of bondage. The intensity of my desire to be free, quickened by my present favourable circumstances, brought me to the determination to act as well as to think and speak. Accordingly, at the beginning of this year 1836, I took upon me a solemn vow, that the year which had just now dawned upon me should not close without witnessing an earnest attempt, on my part, to gain my liberty, This vow only bound me to make good my own individual escape, but my friendship for my brother-slaves was so affectionate and confiding that I felt it my duty, as well as my pleasure, to give them an opportunity to share in my determination. Toward Harry and John Harris I felt a friendship as strong as one man can feel for another, for I could have died with and for them. To them, therefore, with suitable caution, I began to disclose my sentiments and plans, sounding them the while on the subject of running away, provided a good chance should offer. I need not say that I did my very best to imbue the minds of my dear friends with my own views and feelings. Thoroughly awakened now, and with a definite vow upon me, all my little reading which had any bearing on the subject of human rights was rendered available in my communications with my friends. That gem of a book, the Columbian Orator, with its eloquent orations and spicy dialogues denouncing oppression and slavery—telling what had been dared, done, and suffered by men, to obtain the inestimable boon of liberty, was still fresh in my memory, and whirled into the ranks of my speech with the aptitude of well-trained soldiers going through the drill. I here began my public speaking. I canvassed with Henry and John the subject of slavery, and dashed against it the condemning brand of God's eternal justice. My fellow-servants were neither indifferent, dull, nor inapt. Our feelings were more alike than our opinions. All, however, were ready to act when a feasible plan should be proposed. "Show us how the thing is to be done," said they, "and all else is clear."

We were all, except Sandy, quite clear from slave-holding priestcraft. It was in vain that we had been taught from the pulpit at St. Michaels the duty of obedience to our masters; to recognise God as the author of our enslavement; to regard running away as an offence, alike against God and man; to deem our enslavement a merciful and beneficial arrangement; to esteem our condition in this country a paradise to that from which we had been snatched in Africa; to consider our hard hands and dark colour as God's displeasure, and as pointing us out as the proper subjects of slavery; that the relation of master and slave was one of reciprocal benefits; that our work was not more servicable to our masters than our masters' thinking was to us. I say it was in vain that the pulpit of St. Michaels had constantly inculcated these plausible doctrines. Nature laughed them to scorn. For my part, I had become altogether too big for my chains. Father Lawson's solemn words of what I ought to be, and what I might be in the providence of God, had not fallen dead on my soul. I was fast verging toward manhood, and the prophecies of my childhood were still unfulfilled. The thought that year after year had passed away, and my best resolutions to run away had failed and faded, that I was still a slave, with chances for gaining my freedom diminished and still diminishing—was not a matter to be slept over easily. But here came a trouble. Such thoughts and purposes as I now cherished could not agitate the mind long, without making themselves manifest to scrutinizing and unfriendly observers. I had reason to fear that my sable face might prove altogether too transparent for the safe concealment of my hazardous enterprise. Plans of great moment have leaked through stone walls, and revealed their projectors. But here was no stone wall to hide my purpose. I would have given my poor tell-tale face for the immovable countenance of an Indian, for it was far from proof against the daily searching glances of those whom I met.

It was the interest and business of slaveholders to study human nature, and the slave nature in particular, with a view to practical results; and many of them attained astonishing proficiency in this direction. They had to deal not with earth, wood, and stone, but with men; and by every regard they had for their own safety and prosperity, they had need to know the material on which they were to work. So much intellect as slaveholders had round them required watching. Their safety depended on their vigilance. Conscious of the injustice and wrong they were every hour perpetrating, and knowing what they themselves would do if they were victims of such wrongs, they were constantly looking out for the first signs of the dread retribution. They watched, therefore, with skilled and practised eyes, and learned to read, with great accuracy, the state of mind and heart of the slave through his sable face. Unusual sobriety, apparent abstraction, sullenness, or indifference,—indeed, any mood out of the common way,—afforded ground for suspicion and inquiry. Relying on their superior position and wisdom, they would often hector the slave into a confession by affecting to know the truth of their accusations. "You have got the devil in you, and we'll whip him out of you," they would say. I have often been put thus to the torture on bare suspicion. This system had its disadvantages as well as its opposite—the slave being sometimes whipped into the confession of offences which he never committed. It will be seen that the good old rule, "A man is to be held innocent until proved to be guilty," did not hold good on the slave plantation. Suspicion and torture were the approved methods of getting at the truth there. It was necessary, therefore, for me to keep a watch over my deportment, lest the enemy should get the better of me. But with all our caution and studied reserve, I am not sure that Mr. Freeland did not suspect that all was not right with us. It did seem that he watched us more narrowly after the plan of escape had been conceived and discussed amongst us. Men seldom see themselves as others see them; and while to ourselves everything connected with our contemplated escape appeared concealed, Mr. Freeland may, with the peculiar prescience of a slaveholder, have mastered the huge thought which was disturbing our peace. As I now look back, I am the more inclined to think he suspected us, because, prudent as we were, I can see that we did many silly things very well calculated to awaken suspicion. We were at times remarkably buoyant, singing hymns, and making joyous exclamations, almost as triumphant in their tone as if we had reached a land of freedom and safety. A keen observer might have detected in our repeated singing of

- "O Canaan, sweet Canaan,

- I am bound for the land of Canaan,

something more than a hope of reaching heaven. We meant to reach the North, and the North was our Canaan.

- "I thought I heard them say

- There were lions in the way,

- I don't expect to stay

- Much longer here.

- Run to Jesus, shun the danger—

- I don't expect to stay

- Much longer here,"

was a favourite air, and had a double meaning. In the lips of some, it meant the expectation of a speedy summons to a world of spirits; but in the lips of our company, it simply meant a speedy pilgrimage to a free State, and deliverance from all the evils and dangers of slavery.

I had succeeded in winning to my scheme a company of five young men, the very flower of the neighbourhood, each one of whom would have commanded one thousand dollars in the home market. At New Orleans they would have brought fifteen hundred dollars apiece, and perhaps more. Their names were as follows: Henry Harris, John Harris, Sandy Jenkins, Charles Roberts, and Henry Bailey. I was the youngest but one of the party. I had, however, the advantage of them all in experience, and in a knowledge of letters. This gave me a great influence over them. Perhaps not one of them, left to himself, would have dreamed of escape as a possible thing. They all wanted to be free, but the serious thought of running away had not entered into their minds until I won them to the undertaking. They all were tolerably well off—for slaves—and had dim hopes of being set free some day by their masters. If any one is to blame for disturbing the quiet of the slaves and slave-masters of the neighbourhood of St. Michaels, I am the man. I claim to be the instigator of the high crime—as slaveholders regarded it,—and I kept life in it till life could be kept in it no longer.

Pending the time of our contemplated departure out of our Egypt, we met often by night, and on every Sunday. At these meetings we talked the matter over, told our hopes and fears, and the difficulties discovered or imagined; and like men of sense, we counted the cost of the enterprise to which we were committing ourselves. These meetings must have resembled, on a small scale, the meetings of the revolutionary conspirators in their primary condition. We were plotting against our, so-called lawful rulers, with this difference—we sought our own good, and not the harm of our enemies. We did not seek to overthrow them, but to escape from them.

As for Mr. Freeland, we all liked him, and would gladly have remained with him as free men. Liberty was our aim, and we had now come to think that we had a right to it against every obstacle, even against the lives of our enslavers.

We had several words, expressive of things important to us, which we understood, but which, even if distinctly heard by an outsider, would have conveyed no certain meaning. I hated this secresy, but where slavery was powerful, and liberty weak, the latter was driven to concealment to escape destruction.

The prospect was not always bright. At times we were almost tempted to abandon the enterprise, and try to get back to that comparative peace of mind which even a man under the gallows might feel, when all hope of escape had vanished. We were confident, bold, and determined at times, and again, doubting, timid, and wavering, whistling, like the boy in the grave-yard, to keep away the spirits.

To look at the map and observe the proximity of Eastern shore, Maryland, to Delaware and Pennsylvania, it may seem to the reader quite absurd to regard the proposed escape as a formidable undertaking. But to understand, some one has said, a man must stand under. The real distance was great enough, but the imagined distance was, to our ignorance, much greater. Slaveholders sought to impress their slaves with a belief in the boundlessness of slave territory, and of their own limitless power. Our notions of the geography of the country were very vague and indistinct. The distance, however, was not the chief trouble, for the nearer the lines of a slave State to the borders of a free State, the greater was the trouble. Hired kidnappers infested the borders. Then, too, we knew that merely reaching a free State did not free us, that whereever caught we could be returned to slavery. We knew of no spot this side the ocean where we could be safe. We had heard of Canada, then the only real Canaan of the American bondsman, simply as a country to which the wild goose and the swan repaired at the end of winter to escape the heat of summer, but not as the home of man. I knew something of Theology, but nothing of Geography. I really did not know that there was a State of New York or a State of Massachusetts. I had heard of Pennsylvania, Delaware, and New Jersey, and all the Southern States, but was utterly ignorant of the Free States. New York City was our northern limit, and to go there and to be for ever harassed with the liability of being hunted down and returned to slavery, with the certainty of being treated ten times worse than ever before, was a prospect which might well cause some hesitation. The case sometimes, to our excited visions, stood thus: At every gate through which we had to pass we saw a watchman; at every ferry a guard; on every bridge a sentinel, and in every wood a patrol or slave-hunter. We were hemmed in on every side. The good to be sought and the evil to be shunned, were flung in the balance and weighed against each other. On the one hand stood slavery, a stern reality glaring frightfully upon us, with the blood of millions in its polluted skirts, terrible to behold, greedily devouring our hard earnings and feeding itself upon our flesh. This was the evil from which to escape. On the other hand, far away, back in the hazy distance, where all forms seemed but shadows under the flickering light of the north star, behind the craggy hill or snow capped mountain, stood a doubtful freedom, half frozen, beckoning us to her icy domain. This was the good to be sought. The inequality was as great as that between certainty and uncertainty. This in itself was enough to stagger us; but when we came to survey the untrodden road and conjecture the many possible difficulties, we were appalled, and at times, as I have said, were upon the point of giving over the struggle altogether. The reader can have little idea of the phantoms which would flit, in such circumstances, before the uneducated mind of the slave. Upon either side we saw grim death, assuming a variety of horrid shapes. Now it was starvation, causing us, in a strange and friendless land, to eat our own flesh. Now we were contending with the waves and were drowned. Now we were hunted by dogs and overtaken, and torn to pieces by their merciless fangs. We were stung by scorpions, chased by wild beasts, bitten by snakes, and worst of all, after having succeeded in swimming rivers, encountering wild beasts, sleeping in the woods, suffering hunger, cold, heat, and nakedness, overtaken by hired kidnappers, who in the name of law and for the thrice-cursed reward, would, perchance, fire upon us, kill some, wound others, and capture all. This dark picture, drawn by ignorance and fear, at times greatly shook our determination, and not unfrequently caused us to

- "Rather bear the ills we had,

- Than flee to others which we knew not of."

I am not disposed to magnify this circumstance in my experience, and yet I think I shall seem to be so disposed to the reader, but no man can tell the intense agony which was felt by the slave when wavering on the point of making his escape. All that he has is at stake, and even that which he has not, is at stake also. The life which he has may be lost, and the liberty which he seeks may not be gained.

Patrick Henry, to a listening senate which was thrilled by his magic eloquence and ready to stand by him in his boldest flights, could say, "Give me liberty or give me death," and this saying was a sublime one, even for a free man; but incomparably more sublime is the same sentiment when practically asserted by men accustomed to the lash and chain, men whose sensibilities must have become more or less deadened by their bondage. With us it was a doubtful liberty, at best, that we sought, and a certain lingering death in the rice-swamps and sugar-fields if we failed. Life is not lightly regarded by men of sane minds. It is precious both to the pauper and to the prince, to the slave and to his master; and yet I believe there was not one among us who would not rather have been shot down than pass away life in hopeless bondage.

In the progress of our preparations Sandy, the root man, became troubled. He began to have distressing dreams. One of these, which happened on a Friday night, was to him of great significance, and I am quite ready to confess that I felt somewhat damped by it myself. He said, "I dreamed last night that I was roused from sleep by strange noises like the noises of a swarm of angry birds that caused a roar as they passed, and which fell upon my ear like a coming gale over the tops of the trees. Looking up to see what it could mean I saw you, Frederick, in the claws of a huge bird, surrounded by a large number of birds of all colours and sizes. These were all pecking at you, while you, with your arms, seemed to be trying to protect your eyes. Passing over me, the birds flew in a south-westerly direction, and I watched them until they were clean out of sight. Now I saw this as plainly as I now see you; and furder, honey, watch de Friday night dream; dare is sumpon in it shose you born; dare is indeed, honey." I did not like the dream, but I showed no concern, attributing it to the general excitement and perturbation consequent upon our contemplated plan to escape. I could not, however, shake off its effect at once. I felt that it boded no good. Sandy was unusually emphatic and oracular, and his manner had much to do with the impression made upon me.

The plan which I recommended, and to which my comrades consented, for our escape, was to take a large canoe owned by Mr. Hamilton, and on the Saturday night previous to the Easter holidays launch out into the Chesapeake bay and paddle for its head, a distance of seventy miles, with all our might. On reaching this point we were to turn the canoe adrift and bend our steps toward the north star till we reached a Free State.

There were several objections to this plan. In rough weather the waters of the Chesapeake are much agitated, and there would be danger, in a canoe, of being swamped by the waves.

Another objection was that the canoe would soon be missed, the absent slaves would at once be suspected of having taken it, and we should be pursued by some of the fast-sailing craft out of St. Michaels. Then again, if we reached the head of the bay and turned the canoe adrift, she might prove a guide to our track and bring the hunters after us.

These and other objections were set aside by the stronger ones, which could be urged against every other plan that could then be suggested. On the water we had a chance of being regarded as fishermen, in the service of a master. On the other hand, by taking the land route, through the counties adjoining Delaware, we should be subjected to all manner of interruptions, and many disagreeable questions, which might give us serious trouble. Any white man if he pleased, was authorised to stop a man of colour on any road, and examine and arrest him. By this arrangement many abuses, considered such even by slaveholders, occurred. Cases have been known where freemen, being called upon to show their free papers by a pack of ruffians, and on the presentation of the papers, the ruffians have torn them up, and seized the victim and sold him to a life of endless bondage.

The week before our intended start, I wrote a pass for each of our party, giving them permission to visit Baltimore during the Easter holidays. The pass ran after this manner:

"This is to certify that I, the undersigned, have given the bearer, my servant John, full liberty to go to Baltimore to spend the Easter holidays.

w. h.

• Near St. Michaels, Talbot Co., Md."

Although we were now going to Baltimore, and were intending to land east of North Point, in the direction I had seen the Philadelphia steamers go, these passes might be useful to us in the lower part of the bay, while steering towards Baltimore. These were not, however, to be shown by us, until all other answers failed to satisfy the inquirers. We were all fully alive to the importance of being calm and self-possessed when accosted, if accosted we should be; and we more than once rehearsed to each other how we should behave in the hour of trial.

Those were long, tedious days and nights. The suspense was painful in the extreme. To balance probabilities, where life and liberty hang on the result, requires steady nerves. I panted for action, and was glad when the day, at the close of which we were to start, dawned upon us. Sleeping the night before, was out of the question. I probably felt more deeply than any of my companions, because I was the instigator of the movement. The responsibility of the whole enterprise rested on my shoulders. The glory of success, and the shame and confusion of failure, could not be matters of indifference to me. Our food was prepared, our clothes were packed; we were all ready to go, and impatient for Saturday morning—considering that the last of our bondage.

I cannot describe the tempest and tumult of my brain that morning. The reader will please bear in mind that in a slave State an unsuccesful runaway was not only subject to cruel torture, and sold away to the far South, but he was frequently execrated by the other slaves. He was charged with making the condition of the other slaves intolerable, by laying them all under the suspicion of their masters—subjecting them to greater vigilance, and imposing greater limitations on their privileges. I dreaded murmurs from this quarter. It was difficult, too, for a slave-master to believe that slaves escaping had not been aided in their flight by some one of their fellow-slaves. When, therefore, a slave was missing, every slave on the place was closely examined as to his knowledge of the undertaking.

Our anxiety grew more and more intense, as the time of our intended departure drew nigh. It was truly felt to be a matter of life and death with us, and we fully intended to fight, as well as run, if necessity should arise for that extremity. But the trial hour had not yet come. It was easy to resolve, but not so easy to act. I expected there might be some drawing back at the last; it was natural there should be; therefore, during the intervening time, I lost no opportunity to explain away difficulties, remove doubts, dispel fears, and inspire all with firmness. It was too late to look back, and now was the time to go forward. I appealed to the pride of my comrades by telling them, that, if after having solemnly promised to go, as they had done, they now failed to make the attempt, they would in effect brand themselves with cowardice, and might well sit down, fold their arms, and acknowledge themselves fit only to be slaves. This detestable character all were unwilling to assume. Every man except Sandy—he, much to our regret, withdrew—stood firm, and at our last meeting we pledged ourselves afresh, and in the most solemn manner, that at the time appointed we would certainly start on our long journey for a free country. This meeting was in the middle of the week, at the end of which we were to start.

Early on the appointed morning we went as usual to the field, but with hearts that beat quickly and anxiously. Any one intimately acquainted with us might have seen that all was not well with us, and that some monster lingered in our thoughts. Our work that morning was the same as it had been for several days past—drawing out and spreading manure. While thus engaged, I had a sudden presentiment, which flashed upon me like lightning in a dark night, revealing to the lonely traveller the gulf before, and the enemy behind. I instantly turned to Sandy Jenkins, who was near me, and said: "Sandy, we are betrayed' something has just told me so." I felt as sure of it as if the officers were in sight. Sandy said: "Man, dat is strange; but I feel just as you do." If my mother—then long in her grave—had appeared before me and told me that we were betrayed, I could not at that moment have felt more certain of the fact.

In a few minutes after this, the long, low, and distant notes of the horn summoned us from the field to breakfast. I felt as one may be supposed to feel before being led forth to be executed for some great offence. I wanted no breakfast, but I went with the other slaves towards the house for form's sake, My feelings were not disturbed as to the right of running away; on that point I had no misgiving whatever, but from a sense of the consequences of failure.

In thirty minutes after that vivid impression, came the apprehended crash. On reaching the house, and glancing my eye toward the lane gate, the worst was at once made known. The lane gate to Mr. Freeland's house was nearly half a mile from the door, and much shaded by the heavy wood which bordered the main road. I was, however, able to descry four white men and two coloured men approaching. The white men were on horseback, and the coloured men were walking behind, and seemed to be tied. "It is indeed all over with us; we are surely betrayed," I thought to myself. I became composed, or at least comparatively so, and calmly awaited the result. I watched the ill-omened company entering the gate. Successful flight was impossible, and I made up my mind to stand and meet the evil, whatever it might be, for I was not altogether without a slight hope that things might turn out differently from what I had at first feared. In a few moments in came Mr. William Hamilton, riding very rapidly and evidently much excited. He was in the habit of riding very slowly, and was seldom known to gallop his horse. This time his horse was nearly at full speed, causing the dust to roll thick behind him. Mr. Hamilton, though one of the most resolute men in the whole neighbourhood, was, nevertheless, a remarkably mild-spoken man, and, even when greatly excited, his language was cool and circumspect. He came to the door, and inquired if Mr. Freeland was in. I told him that Mr. Freeland was at the barn. Off the old gentleman rode towards the barn, with unwonted speed. In a few moments Mr. Hamilton and Mr. Freeland came down from the barn to the house, and just as they made their appearance in the front-yard, three men, who proved to be constables, came dashing into the lane on horse-back, as if summoned by a sign requiring quick work. A few seconds brought them into the front-yard, where they hastily dismounted and tied their horses. This done they joined Mr. Freeland and Mr. Hamilton, who were standing a short distance from the kitchen. A few moments were spent as if in consulting how to proceed, and then the whole party walked up to the kitchen door. There was now no one in the kitchen but myself and John Harris; Henry and Sandy were yet in the barn. Mr. Freeland came inside the kitchen door, and with an agitated voice called me by name, and told me to come forward, that there were some gentlemen who wished to see me. I stepped towards them at the door, and asked what they wanted, when the constables grabbed me, and told me I had better not resist; that I had been in a scrape, or was said to have been in one; that they were merely going to take me where I could be examined; that they would have me brought before my master at St. Michaels, and if the evidence against me was not proved true, I should be acquitted. I was now firmly tied, and completely at the mercy of my captors. Resistance was idle. They were five in number, armed to the teeth. When they had secured me, they turned to John Harris, and in a few moments succeeded in tying him as firmly as they had tied me. They next turned toward Henry Harris, who had now returned from the barn. "Cross your hands," said the constable to Henry. "I won't," said Henry, in a voice so firm and clear, and in a manner so determined, as for a moment to arrest all proceedings. "Won't you cross your hands?" said Tom Graham, the constable. "No, I won't," said Henry, with increasing emphasis. Mr. Hamilton, Mr. Freeland, and the officers now came near to Henry. Two of the constables drew out their shining pistols, and swore, by the name of God, that he should cross his hands or they would shoot him down. Each of these hired ruffians now cocked their pistols, and, with fingers apparently on the triggers, presented their deadly weapons to the breast of the unarmed slave, saying, if he did not cross his hands, they would "blow his d—d heart out of him." "Shoot me, shoot me," said Henry; "you can't kill me but once. Shoot, shoot, and be demned! I won't be tied!" This the brave fellow said in a voice as defiant and heroic in its tones as was the language itself; and at the moment of saying this, with the pistol at his very breast, he quickly raised his arms, and dashed them from the puny hands of his assassins, the weapons flying in all directions. Now came the struggle. All hands rushed upon the brave fellow, and after beating him for some time they succeeded in overpowering and tying him. Henry put me to shame; he fought, and fought bravely. John and I had made no resistance. The fact is, I never saw much use in fighting where there was no reasonable probability of whipping anybody. Yet there was something almost providential in the resistance made by Henry. But for that resistance every soul of us would have been hurried off to the far South. Just a moment previous to the trouble with Henry, Mr. Hamilton mildly said,—and this gave me the unmistakable clue to the cause of our arrest,—"Perhaps we had now better make a search for those protections, which we understand Frederick has written for himself and the rest." Had these passes been found, they would have been point-blank proof against us, and would have confirmed all the statements of our betrayer. Thanks to the resistance of Henry, the excitement produced by the scuffle drew all attention in that direction, and I succeeded in flinging my pass, unobserved, into the fire. The confusion attendant on the scuffle, and the apprehension of still further trouble, perhaps, led our captors to forego, for the time, any search for "those protections which Frederick was said to have written for his companions;" so we were not yet convicted of the purpose to run away, and it was evident that there was some doubt on the part of all whether we had been guilty of such purpose.

Just as we were all completely tied, and about ready to start toward St. Michaels, and thence to gaol, Mrs. Betsey Freeland, mother to William, who was much attached, after the Southern fashion, to Henry and John, they having been reared from childhood in her house, came to the kitchen door with her hands full of biscuits, for we had not had our breakfast that morning, and divided them between Henry and John. This done, the lady made the following parting address to me, pointing her bony finger at me: "You devil, you yellow devil! It was you who put it into the heads of Henry and John to run away. But for you, you long-legged yellow devil, Henry and John would never have thought of running away." I gave the lady a look which called forth from her a scream of mingled wrath and terror, as she slammed the kitchen door and went in, leaving me, with the rest, in hands as harsh as her own broken voice.

Could the kind reader have been riding along the main road to or from Easton that morning, his eye would have met a painful sight. He would have seen five young men, guilty of no crime save that of preferring liberty to slavery, drawn along the public highway—firmly bound together, tramping through dust and heat, bare-footed and bare-headed—fastened to three strong horses, whose riders were armed with pistols and daggers, on their way to prison like felons, and suffering every possible insult from the crowds of idle, vulgar people, who clustered round, and heart-lessly made their failure to escape, the occasion for all manner of ribaldry and sport. As I looked upon this crowd of vile persons, and saw myself and friends thus assailed and persecuted, I could not help seeing the fulfilment of Sandy's dream. I was in the hands of moral vultures, and held in their sharp talons, and was being hurried away towards Easton, in a south-easterly direction, amid the jeers of new birds of the same feather, through every neighbourhood we passed. It seemed to me that everybody was out, and knew the cause of our arrest, and awaited our passing in order to feast their vindictive eyes on our misery.

Some said "I ought to be hanged;" and others, "I ought to be burned;" others, "I ought to have the 'hide' taken off my back;" while no one gave us a kind word or sympathizing look, except the poor slaves who were lifting their heavy hoes, and who cautiously glanced at us through the post and rail fences, behind which they were at work. Our sufferings that morning can be more easily imagined than described. Our hopes were all blasted at one blow. The cruel injustice, the victorious crime, and the helplessness of innocence, led me to ask in my ignorance and weakness. Where is now the God of justice and mercy? and why have these wicked men the power thus to trample upon our rights, and to insult our feelings? and yet in the next moment came the consoling thought, "the day of the oppressor will come at last." Of one thing I could be glad: not one of my dear friends upon whom I had brought this great calamity, either by word or look, reproached me for having led them into it. We were a band of brothers, and never dearer to each other than now. The thought which gave us the most pain, was the probable separation which would now take place in case we were sold off to the far South, as we were likely to be. While the constables were looking forward. Henry and I, being fastened together, could occasionally exchange a word without being observed by the kidnappers who had us in charge. "What shall I do with my pass?" said Henry. "Eat it with your biscuit," said I; "it won't do to tear it up." We were now near St. Michaels. The direction concerning the passes was passed around, and executed. "Own nothing," said I. "Own nothing" was passed round, enjoined, and assented to. Our confidence in each other was unshaken, and we were quite resolved to succeed or fail together, as much after the calamity which had befallen us as before.

On reaching St. Michaels we underwent a sort of examination at my master's store, and it was evident to my mind that Master Thomas suspected the truthfulness of the evidence upon which they had acted in arresting us, and that he only affected, to some extent, the positiveness with which he asserted our guilt. There was nothing said by any of our company, which could, in any manner, prejudice our cause, and there was hope yet that we should be able to return to our homes, if for nothing else, at least to find out the guilty man or woman who betrayed us.

To this end we all denied that we had been guilty of intended flight. Master Thomas said that the evidence he had of our intention to run away was strong enough to hang us in a case of murder. "But," said I, "the cases are not equal; if murder were committed,—the thing is done!

but we have not run away. Where is the evidence against us? We were quietly at our work." I talked thus, with unusual freedom, to bring out the evidence against us, for we all wanted, above all things, to know who had betrayed us, that we might have something tangible on which to pour our execrations. From something which dropped, in the course of the talk, it appeared that there was but one witness against us, and that that witness could not be produced. Master Thomas would not tell us who his informant was, but we suspected, and suspected one person only. Several circumstances seemed to point Sandy out as our betrayer. His entire knowledge of our plans, his participation in them, his withdrawal from us, his dream, and his simultaneous presentiment that we were betrayed, the taking us and the leaving him, were calculated to turn suspicion towards him, and yet we could not suspect him. We all loved him too well to think it possible that he could have betrayed us. So we rolled the guilt on other shoulders.

We were literally dragged, that morning, behind horses, a distance of fifteen miles, and placed in the Easton gaol. We were glad to reach the end of our journey, for our pathway had been full of insult and mortification. Such is the power of public opinion that it is hard, even for the innocent, to feel the happy consolations of innocence when they fall under the maledictions of this power. How could we regard ourselves as in the right, when all about us denounced us as criminals, and had the power and the disposition to treat us as such.

In gaol we were placed under the care of Mr. Joseph Graham, the sheriff of the county. Henry and John and myself were placed in one room, and Henry Bailey and Charles Roberts in another by themselves. This separation was intended to deprive us of the advantage of concert, and to prevent trouble in gaol.

Once shut up, a new set of tormentors came upon us. A swarm of imps in human shape,—the slave-traders and agents of slave-traders—who gathered in every country town of the state, watching for chances to buy human flesh, as buzzards watch for carrion, flocked in upon us to ascertain if our masters had placed us in gaol to be sold. Such a set of debased and villainous creatures I never saw before, and hope never to see again. I felt as if surrounded by a pack of fiends fresh from perdition. They laughed, leered, and grinned at us, saying, "Ah, boys, we have got you, haven't we? So you were about to make your escape? Where were you going to?" After taunting us in this way as long as they liked, they one by one subjected us to an examination, with a view to ascertaining our value, feeling our arms and legs and shaking us by the shoulders, to see if we were sound and healthy, impudently asking us, "how we would like to have them for masters?" To such questions we were quite dumb, much to their annoyance. One fellow told me, "if he had me he would cut the devil out of me pretty quick."

These negro-buyers were very offensive to the genteel Southern Christian public. They were looked upon in respectable Maryland society as necessary but detestable characters. As a class, they were hardened ruffians, made such by nature and by occupation. Yes, they were the legitimate fruit of slavery, and were second in villainy only to the slaveholders themselves, who made such a class possible. They were mere hucksters of the slave produce of Maryland and Virginia—coarse, cruel, and swaggering bullies, whose very breathing was of blasphemy and blood.

Aside from these slave-buyers who infested the prison from time to time, our quarters were much more comfortable than we had any right to expect them to be. Our allowance of food was small and coarse, but our room was the best in the gaol—neat and spacious, and with nothing about it necessarily reminding us of being in prison but its heavy locks and bolts and the black iron lattice work at the windows. We were prisoners of state compared with most slaves who were put into the Easton gaol. But the place was not one of contentment. Bolts, bars, and grated windows are not acceptable to freedom-loving people of any colour. The suspense, too, was painful. Every step on the stairway was listened to, in the hope that the comer would cast a ray of light on our fate. We would have given the hair of our heads for half a dozen words with one of the waiters in Sol. Lowe's hotel. Such waiters were in the way of hearing, at the table, the probable course of things. We could see them flitting about in their white jackets in front of this hotel, but could speak to none of them.

Soon after the holidays were over, contrary to all our expectations, Messrs. Hamilton and Freeland came up to Easton; not to make a bargain with the "Georgia traders," nor to send us up to Austin Woldfolk, as was usual in the case of runaway-slaves, but to release Charles, Henry Harris, Henry Bailey, and John Harris from prison, and this, too, without the infliction of a single blow. I was left alone in prison. The innocent had been taken, and the guilty left. My friends were separated from me, and apparently for ever. This circumstance caused me more pain than any other incident connected with our capture and imprisonment. Thirty-nine lashes on my naked and bleeding back would have been joyfully borne, in preference to this separation from these, the friends of my youth. And yet I could not but feel that I was the victim of something like justice. Why should these young men, who were led into this scheme by me, suffer as much as the instigator? I felt glad that they were released from prison, and from the dread prospect of a life, or death I should rather say, in the rice-swamps. It is due to the noble Henry to say that he was almost as reluctant to leave the prison with me in it as he had been to be tied and dragged to prison. But we all knew that we should, in all the likelihoods of the case, be separated, in the event of being sold; and since we were completely in the hands of our owners, they concluded it would be the best to go peaceably home.

Not until this last separation, dear reader, had I touched those profounder depths of desolation which it is the lot of slaves often to reach. I was solitary and alone, within the walls of a stone prison, left to a fate of life-long misery. I had hoped and expected much, for months before; but my hopes and expectations were now withered and blasted. The ever dreaded slave life in Georgia, Louisiana, and Alabama,—from which escape was next to impossible—now in my loneliness stared me in the face. The possibility of ever becoming anything but an abject slave, a mere machine in the hands of an owner, had now fled, and it seemed to me it had fled for ever. A life of living death, beset with the innumerable horrors of the cotton-field and the sugar-plantation, seemed to be my doom. The fiends who rushed into the prison when we were first put there, continued to visit me and ply me with questions and tantalizing remarks. I was insulted, but helpless; keenly alive to the demands of justice and liberty, but with no means of asserting them. To talk to those imps about justice or mercy would have been as absurd as to reason with bears and tigers. Lead and steel were the only arguments that they were capable of appreciating, as the events of the subsequent years have proved.

After remaining in this life of misery and despair about a week, which seemed a month, Master Thomas, very much to my surprise, and greatly to my relief, came to the prison and took me out for the purpose, as he said, of sending me to Alabama with a friend of his, who would emancipate me at the end of eight years. I was glad enough to get out of prison, but I had no faith in the story that his friend would emancipate me. Besides, I had never heard of his having a friend in Alabama, and I took the announcement simply as an easy and comfortable method of shipping me off to the far South. There was a little scandal, too, connected with the idea of one Christian selling another to the Georgia traders, while it was deemed every way proper for them to sell to others. I thought this friend in Alabama was an invention to meet this difficulty, for Master Thomas was quite jealous of his religious reputation, however unconcerned he might have been about his real Christian character. In these remarks it is possible I did him injustice. He certainly did not exert his power over me as he might have done in the case, but acted, upon the whole, very generously, considering the nature of my offence. He had the power and the provocation to send me, without reserve, into the very everglades of Florida, beyond the remotest hope of emancipation; and his refusal to exercise that power must be set down to his credit.

After lingering about St. Michaels a few days, and no friend from Alabama appearing, Master Thomas decided to send me back again to Baltimore, to live with his brother Hugh, with whom he was now at peace; possibly he became so by his profession of religion at the camp-meeting in the Bay side. Master Thomas told me he wished me to go to Baltimore and learn a trade; and that if I behaved myself properly he would emancipate me at twenty-five. Thanks for this one beam of hope in the future. The promise had but one fault—it seemed too good to be true.

CHAPTER XX: APPRENTICESHIP LIFE.

Nothing lost by my attempt to run away—Comrades at home—Reasons for sending me away—Return to Baltimore—Tommy changed—Caulking in Gardiner's ship yard—Desperate fight—Its causes—Conflict between white and black labour—Outrage—Testimony—Master Hugh—Slavery in Baltimore—My condition improves—New associations—Slaveholder's right to the slave's wages—How to make a discontented slave.

OUR little domestic revolution, notwithstanding the sudden snub it got by the treachery of somebody, did not, after all, end so disastrously as when in the iron cage at Easton I conceived it would. The prospect from that point did look about as dark as any that ever cast its gloom over the vision of an anxious, out-looking human spirit. "All's well that ends well!" My affectionate friends, Henry and John Harris, were still with Mr. Freeland. Charles Roberts and Henry Bailey were safe at their homes. I had not, therefore, anything to regret on their account. Their masters had mercifully forgiven them, probably on the ground suggested in the spirited little speech of Mrs. Freeland made to me just before leaving for the gaol. My friends had nothing to regret either: for while they were watched more closely, they were doubtless treated more kindly than before, and got new assurances that they should some day be legally emancipated, provided their behaviour from that time forward should make them deserving. Not a blow did any one of them receive. As for Master Freeland, good soul, he did not believe we were intending to run away at all. Having given—as he thought—no occasion to his boys to leave him, he could not think it possible that they had entertained a design so grievous.

This, however, was not the view taken of the matter by "Mars'r Billy," as we used to call the soft-spoken, but crafty and resolute Mr. William Hamilton. He had no doubt that the crime had been meditated, and regarding me as the instigator of it, he frankly told Master Thomas that he must remove me from that neighbourhood or he would shoot me. He would not have one so dangerous as "Frederick" tampering with his slaves. William Hamilton was not a man whose threat might be safely disregarded. I have no doubt he would have proved as good as his word, had the warning given been disregarded. He was furious at the thought of such a piece of high-handed theft as we were about to perpetrate—the stealing of our own bodies and souls. The feasibility of the plan, too, could the first steps have been taken, was marvellously plain. Besides, this was a new idea, this use of the Bay. Slaves escaping, until now, had taken to the woods; they had never dreamed of profaning or abusing the waters of the noble Chesapeake, by making them the highway from slavery to freedom. Here was a broad road leading to the destruction of slavery, which hitherto had been looked upon as a wall of security by the slaveholders. But Master Billy could not get Mr. Freeland to see matters precisely as he did, nor could he get Master Thomas, excited as he was. The latter, I must say it to his credit, showed much humane feeling, and atoned for much that had been harsh, cruel, and unreasonable in his former treatment of me and of others. My "Cousin Tom" told me that while I was in gaol Master Thomas was very unhappy, and that the night before his going up to release me he had walked the floor nearly all night, evincing great distress; that very tempting offers had been made to him by the negro-traders, but he had rejected them all, saying that money could not tempt him to sell me to the far South. I can easily believe all this, for he seemed quite reluctant to send me away at all. He told me that he only consented to do so because of the very strong prejudice against me in the neighbourhood, and that he feared for my safety if I remained there.

Thus after three years spent in the country, roughing it in the fields, and experiencing all sorts of hardships, I was again permitted to return to Baltimore, the very place of all others, short of a Free State, where I most desired to live. The three years spent in the country had made some difference in me, and in the household of Master Hugh. "Little Tommy" was no longer little Tommy; and I was not the slender lad who had left the Eastern Shore just three years before. The loving relations between Master Tommy and myself were broken up. He was no longer dependent on me for protection, but felt himself a man, with other and more suitable associates. In childhood he had considered me scarcely inferior to himself,—certainly quite as good as any other boy with whom he played—but the time had come when his friend must be his slave. So we were cold to each other, and parted. It was a sad thing to me, that loving each other as we had done, we must now take different roads. To him, a thousand avenues were open. Education had made him acquainted with all the treasures of the world, and liberty had flung open the gates thereunto; but I, who had attended him seven years, had watched over him with the care of a big brother, fighting his battles in the street, and shielding him from harm to an extent which induced his mother to say, "Oh, Tommy is always safe when he is with Freddy"—I must be confined to a single condition. He had grown and become a man; I, though grown to the stature of manhood, must all my life remain a minor—a mere boy. Thomas Auld, junior, obtained a situation on board the brig Tweed, and went to sea. I have since heard of his death. There were few persons to whom I was more sincerely attached, than to him.

Very soon after I went to Baltimore to live, Master Hugh succeeded in getting me hired to Mr. William Gardiner, an extensive ship-builder on Fell's Point. I was placed there to learn to caulk; a trade of which I already had some knowledge, gained while in Mr. Hugh Auld's ship-yard. Gardiner's, however, proved a very unfavourable place for the accomplishment of the desired object. Mr. Gardiner was that season engaged in building two large man-of-war vessels, professedly for the Mexican government. These vessels were to be launched in the month of July of that year, and in failure thereof, Mr. Gardiner would forfeit a very considerable sum of money. So when I entered the ship-yard, all was hurry and driving. There were in the yard about one hundred men; of these, seventy or eighty were regular carpenters— privileged men. There was no time for a raw hand to learn anything. Every man had to do that which he knew how to do, and in entering the yard, Mr. Gardiner had directed me to do whatever the carpenters told me to do. This was placing me at the beck and call of about seventy-five men. I was to regard all these as my masters. Their word was to be my law. My situation was a trying one. I was called a dozen ways in the space of a single minute. I needed a dozen pairs of hands. Three or four voices would strike my ear at the same moment. It was "Fred, come help me to cant this timber here,"—"Fred, come carry this timber yonder,"— "Fred, bring that roller here,"—"Fred, go get a fresh can of water,"—"Fred, come help saw off the end of this timber,"—"Fred, go quick and get the crow-bar,"—"Fred, hold on the end of this fall,"—"Fred, go to the blacksmith's shop and get a new punch,"—"Halloo, Fred! run and bring me a cold-chisel,"—"I say, Fred, bear a hand, and get up a fire under the steam-box as quick as lightning,"—"Hullo, nigger! come turn this grindstone,"—"Come, come; move, move! and bowse this timber forward,"—"I say, darkey, blast your eyes! why don't you heat up some pitch?"—"Halloo! halloo! halloo! (three voices at the same time)"—"Come here; go there; hold on where you are. D—n you, if you move I'll knock your brains out!" Such, my dear reader, is a glance at the school which was mine, during the first eight months of my stay at Gardiner's ship-yard. At the end of eight months Master Hugh refused longer to allow me to remain with Gardiner. The circumstances which led to this refusal was the committing of an outrage upon me, by the white apprentices of the ship-yard. The fight was a desperate one, and I came out of it shockingly mangled. I was cut and bruised in sundry places, and my left eye was nearly knocked out of its socket. The facts which led to this brutal outrage upon me, illustrate a phase of slavery which was destined to become an important element in the overthrow of the slave system, and I may therefore state them with some minuteness. That phase was this—the conflict of slavery with the interests of white mechanics and labourers. In the country this conflict was not so apparent; but in cities, such as Baltimore, Richmond, New Orleans, Mobile, etc., it was seen pretty clearly. The slaveholders, with a craftiness peculiar to themselves, by encouraging the enmity of the poor labouring white man against the blacks, succeeded in making the said white man almost as much a slave as the black slave himself. The difference between the white slave and the black slave was this: the latter belonged to one slaveholder, and the former belonged to the slaveholders collectively. The white slave had taken from him by indirection what the black slave had taken from him directly and without ceremony. Both were plundered, and by the same plunderers. The slave was robbed by his master of all his earnings, above what was required for his bare physical necessities, and the white labouring man was robbed by the slave system of the just results of his labour, because he was flung into competition with a class of labourers who worked without wages. The slave-holders blinded them to this competition by keeping alive their prejudice against the slaves as men—not against them as slaves. They appealed to their pride, often denouncing emancipation as tending to place the white working man on an equality with negroes, and by this means they succeeded in drawing off the minds of the poor whites from the real fact, that, by the rich slave-master, they were already regarded as but a single remove from equality with the slave. The impression was cunningly made, that slavery was the only power that could prevent the labouring white man from falling to the level of the slave's poverty and degradation. To make this enmity deep and broad between the slave and the poor white man, the latter was allowed to abuse and whip the former without hindrance. But, as I have said, this state of affairs prevailed mostly in the country. In the city of Baltimore, there were not unfrequent murmurs that educating slaves to be mechanics might, in the end, give slave-masters power to dispose altogether with the services of the poor white man. But with characteristic dread of offending the slave-holders, these poor white mechanics in Mr. Gardiner's ship-yard, instead of applying the natural, honest remedy for the apprehended evil, and objecting at once to work there by the side of slaves, made a cowardly attack upon the free coloured mechanics, saying they were eating the bread which should be eaten by American freemen, and swearing that they would not work with them. The feeling was really against having their labour brought into competition with that of the coloured freeman, and aimed to prevent him from serving himself, in the evening of life, with the trade with which he had served his master, during the more vigorous portion of his days. Had they succeeded in driving the black freemen out of the ship-yard, they would have determined also upon the removal of the black slaves. The feeling was very bitter toward all coloured people in Baltimore about this time, 1836, and they—free and slave—suffered all manner of insult and wrong.

Until a very little time before I went there, white and black carpenters worked side by side in the ship-yards of Mr. Gardiner, Mr. Duncan, Mr. Walter Price, and Mr. Robb. Nobody seemed to see any impropriety in it. Some of the blacks were first rate workmen, and were given jobs requiring the highest skill. All at once, however, the white carpenters knocked off, and swore that they would no longer work on the same stage with negroes. Taking advantage of the heavy contract resting upon Mr. Gardiner to have the vessels for Mexico ready to launch in July, and of the difficulty of getting other hands at that season of the year, they swore they would not strike another blow for him, unless he would discharge his free coloured workmen. Now, although this movement did not extend to me in form, it did reach me in fact. The spirit which it awakened was one of malice and bitterness toward coloured people generally, and I suffered with the rest, and suffered severely. My fellow-apprentices very soon began to feel it to be degrading to work with me. They began to put on high looks, and to talk contemptuously and maliciously of "the niggers," saying that they would take the "country," that they "ought to be killed." Encouraged by workmen who, knowing me to be a slave, made no issue with Mr. Gardiner about my being there, these young men did their utmost to make it impossible for me to stay. They seldom called me to do anything, without coupling the call with a curse, and Edward North, the biggest in everything, rascality included, ventured to strike me, whereupon I picked him up and threw him into the dock. Whenever any of them struck me, I struck back at them, regardless of consequences. I could manage any of them singly, and so long as I could keep them from combining I got on pretty well. In the conflict which ended my stay at Mr. Gardiner's, I was beset by four of them at once—Ned North, Ned Hays, Bill Stewart, and Tom Humphreys. Two of them were as big as myself, and they came near killing me in broad daylight. One came in front, armed with a brick; there was one at each side and one behind, and they closed up all around me. I was struck on all sides; and while I was attending to those in front, I received a blow on my head from behind, dealt with a heavy hand-spike. I was completely stunned by the blow, and fell heavily on the ground among the timbers. Taking advantage of my fall they rushed upon me and began to pound me with their fists. I let them lay on for a while after I came to myself, with a view of gaining strength. They did me little damage so far; but finally getting tired of that sport I gave a sudden surge, and despite their weight I rose to my hands and knees. Just as I did this one of their number planted a blow with his boot in my left eye, which for a time seemed to have burst my eye-ball. When they saw my eye completely closed, my face covered with blood, and I staggering under the stunning blows they had given me, they left me. As soon as I gathered strength I picked up the hand-spike and madly enough attempted to pursue them; but here the carpenters interfered, and compelled me to give up my pursuit. It was impossible to stand against so many.

Dear reader, you can hardly believe the statement, but it is true, and therefore I write it down: no fewer than fifty white men stood by and saw this brutal and shameful outrage committed, and not a man of them all interposed a single word of mercy. There were four against one, and that one's face was beaten and battered most horribly, and no one said "that is enough;" but some cried out, "Kill him! kill him! kill the d—n nigger! knock his brains out! he struck a white person!" I mention this inhuman outcry to show the character of the men and the spirit of the times at Gardiner's ship-yard; and, indeed, in Baltimore generally, in 1836. As I look back to the period, I am almost amazed that I was not murdered outright, so reckless was the spirit which prevailed there. On two other occasions while there I came near losing my life, on one of which I was driving bolts in the hold through the keelson with Hays. In its course the bolt bent. Hays cursed me, and said that it was my blow which bent the bolt. I denied this, and charged it upon him. In a fit of rage he seized an adze and darted towards me. I met him with a maul, and parried his blow, or I should have lost my life.

After the united attack of North, Stewart, Hays, and Humphreys, finding that the carpenters were as bitter toward me as the apprentices, and that the latter were probably set on by the former, I found my only chance for life was in flight. I succeeded in getting away without an additional blow. To strike a white man was death by lynch law, in Gardiner's ship-yard; nor was there much of any other law toward the coloured people at that time, in any other part of Maryland.

After making my escape from the ship-yard I went straight home and related my story to Master Hugh; and to his credit I say it, that his conduct, though he was not a religious man, was every way more humane than that of his brother Thomas, when I went to him in a somewhat similar plight, from the hands of his "Brother Edward Covey." Master Hugh listened attentively to my narration of the circumstances leading to the ruffianly assault, and gave many evidence of his strong indignation at what was done. He was a rough but manly-hearted fellow, and at this time his best nature showed itself.

The heart of my once kind mistress Sophia was again melted in pity toward me. My puffed-out eye and my scarred and blood-covered face moved the dear lady to tears. She kindly drew a chair by me, and with friendly and consoling words, she took water and washed the blood from my face. No mother's hand could have been more tender than hers. She bound up my head and covered my wounded eye with a lean piece of fresh beef. It was almost compensation for all I had suffered, that it occasioned the manifestation once more of the originally characteristic kindness of my mistress. Her affectionate heart was not yet dead, though much hardened by time and circumstances.

As for Master Hugh he was furious, and gave expression to his feelings in the forms of speech usual in that locality. He poured curses on the whole of the ship-yard company, and swore that he would have satisfaction. His indignation was really strong and healthy; but unfortunately it resulted from the thought that his rights of property, in my person, had not been respected; more than from any sense of the outrage perpetrated upon me as a man. I had reason to think this from the fact that he could himself beat and mangle, when it suited him to do so.

Bent on having satisfaction, as he said, just as soon as I got a little the better of my bruises, Master Hugh took me to Esquire Watson's office on Bond Street, Fell's Point, with a view of procuring the arrest of those who had assaulted me. He related the outrage to the magistrate as I had related it to him, and seemed to expect that a warrant would at once be issued for the arrest of the lawless ruffians. Mr. Watson heard all he had to say, then coolly inquired—"Mr. Auld, who saw this assault of which you speak?" "It was done, sir, in the presence of a shipyard full of hands." "Sir," said Mr. Watson, "I am sorry, but I cannot move in this matter, except upon the oath of white witnesses." "But here's the boy; look at his head and face," said the excited Master Hugh; "they show what has been done." But Watson insisted that he was not authorized to do anything, unless white witnesses of the transaction would come forward and testify to what had taken place. He could issue no warrant on my word, against white persons, if I had been killed in the presence of a thousand blacks; their testimony combined would have been insufficient to condemn a single murderer. Master Hugh was compelled to say, for once, that this state of things was too bad, and he left the office of the magistrate disgusted.

Of course it was impossible to get any white man to testify against my assailants. The carpenters saw what was done; but the actors were but the agents of their malice, and did only what the carpenters sanctioned. They had cried with one accord, "Kill the nigger! kill the nigger!" Even those who may have pitied me, if any such were among them, lacked the moral courage to volunteer their evidence. The slightest show of sympathy or justice toward a person of colour was denounced as abolitionism; and the name of abolitionist subjected its hearer to frightful liabilities. "D—n abolitionists," and "kill the niggers," were the watch-words of the foul-mouthed ruffians of those days. Nothing was done, and probably there would not have been, had I been killed in the affray. The laws and the morals of the Christian city of Baltimore afforded no protection to the sable denizens of that city.

Master Hugh, on finding he could get no redress for the cruel wrong, withdrew me from the employment of Mr. Gardiner, and took me into his own family, Mrs. Auld kindly taking care of me and dressing my wounds until they were healed, and I was ready to go to work again.

While I was on the Eastern Shore, Master Hugh had met with reverses which overthrew his business; and he had given up shipbuilding in his own yard, on the City Block, and was now acting as foreman of Mr. Walter Price. The best he could do for me was to take me into Mr. Price's yard, and afford me the facilities there for completing the trade which I began to learn at Gardiner's. Here I rapidly became expert in the use of caulker's tools, and in the course of a single year, I was able to command the highest wages paid to journeymen caulkers in Baltimore.

The reader will observe that I was now of some pecuniary value to my master. During the busy season I was bringing six or seven dollars per week. I have sometimes brought him as much as nine dollars a week, for the wages were a dollar and a half per day.

After learning to caulk, I sought my own employment, made my own contracts, and collected my own earnings—giving Master Hugh no trouble in any part of the transactions to which I was a party.

Here, then, were better days for the Eastern Shore slave. I was free from the vexatious assaults of the apprentices at Mr. Gardiner's, and free from the perils of plantation life, and once more in favourable condition to increase my little stock of education, which had been at a dead stand since my removal from Baltimore. I had on the Eastern Shore been only a teacher, when in company with other slaves, but now there were coloured persons here who could instruct me. Many of the young caulkers could read, write, and cipher. Some of them had high notions about mental improvement, and the free ones on Fell's Point organized what they called the "East Baltimore Mental Improvement Society." To this society, notwithstanding it was intended that only free persons should attach themselves, I was admitted, and was several times assigned a prominent part in its debates. I owe much to the society of these young men.

The reader already knows enough of the ill effects of good treatment on a slave, to anticipate what was now the case in my improved condition. It was not long before I began to show signs of disquiet with slavery, and to look around for means to get out of it by the shortest route. I was living among freemen, and was in all respects equal to them by nature and attainments. Why should I be a slave? There was no reason why I should be the thrall of any man. Besides, I was now getting, as I have said, a dollar and fifty cents per day. I contracted for it, worked for it, collected it; it was paid to me, and it was rightfully my own; and yet upon every returning Saturday night, this money—my own hard earnings, every cent of it—was demanded of me, and taken from me, by Master Hugh. He did not earn it; he had no hand in earning it; why, then, should he have it? I owed him nothing. He had given me no schooling, and I had received from him only my food and raiment; and for these my services were supposed to pay from the first. The right to take my earnings was the right of the robber. He had the power to compel me to give him the fruits of my labour, and this power was the only right in the case. I became more and more dissatisfied with this state of things, and in so becoming, I only gave proof of the same human nature which every reader of this chapter in my life—slaveholder, or non-slaveholder—is conscious of possessing.

To make a contented slave, you must make a thoughtless one. It is necessary to darken his moral and mental vision, and, as far as possible, annihilate his power of reason. He must be able to detect no inconsistencies in slavery. The man who takes his earnings must be able to convince him that he has a perfect right to do so. It must not depend upon mere force: the slave must know no higher law than his master's will. The whole relationship must not only demonstrate to his mind its necessity, but its absolute rightfulness. If there be one crevice through which a single drop can fall, it will certainly rust off the slave's chain.

CHAPTER XXI: ESCAPE FROM SLAVERY.

Closing incidents in my "Life as a Slave"—Discontent—Suspicions—Master's generosity—Difficulties in the way of escape—Plan to obtain money—Allowed to hire my time—A gleam of hope—Attend Camp-meeting—Anger of Master Hugh—The result—Plans of escape—Day for departure fixed—Harassing doubts and fears—Painful thoughts of separation from friends.

MY condition during the year of my escape, "1838," was comparatively a free and easy one, so far, at least, as the wants of the physical man were concerned; but the reader will bear in mind that my troubles from the beginning had been less physical than mental, and he will thus be prepared to find slave life was adding nothing to its charms for me as I grew older, and became more and more acquainted with it. The practice from week to week of openly robbing me of all my earnings, kept the nature and character of slavery constantly before me. I could be robbed by indirection, but this was too open and barefaced to be endured. I could see no reason why I should, at the end of each week, pour the reward of my honest toil into the purse of my master. My obligation to do this vexed me, and the manner in which Master Hugh received my wages vexed me yet more. Carefully counting the money, and rolling it out dollar by dollar, he would look me in the face as if he would search my heart as well as my pocket, and reproachfully ask me, "Is that all?"—implying that I had perhaps kept back part of my wages; or, if not so, the demand was made possibly to make me feel that, after all, I was an "unprofitable servant." Draining me of the last cent of my hard earnings, he would, however, occasionally, when I brought home an extra large sum, dole out to me a sixpence or a shilling, with a view, perhaps, of enkindling my gratitude. But it had the opposite effect; it was an admission of my right to the whole sum. The fact that he gave me any part of my wages, was proof that he suspected I had a right to the whole of them; and I always felt uncomfortable after having received anything in this way, lest his giving me a few cents might possibly ease his conscience, and make him feel himself to be a pretty honourable robber, after all.

Held to a strict account, and kept under a close watch,—the old suspicion of my running away not having been entirely removed,—to accomplish my escape seemed a very difficult thing. The railroad from Baltimore to Philadelphia was under regulations so stringent, that even free coloured travellers were almost excluded. They must have free papers; they must be measured, and carefully examined, before they could enter the cars, and could go only in the day time, even when so examined. The steamboats were under regulations equally stringent. And still more, and worse than all, all the great turnpikes leading Northward, were beset with kidnappers; a class of men who watched the newspapers for advertisements for runaway slaves, thus making their living by the accursed reward of slave-hunting.

My discontent grew upon me, and I was on the constant look-out for means to get away. With money I could easily have managed the matter, and from this consideration I hit upon the plan of soliciting the privilege of hiring my time. It was quite common in Baltimore to allow slaves this privilege, and was the practice also in New Orleans. A slave who was considered trustworthy could, by paying his master a definite sum regularly, at the end of each week, dispose of his time as he liked. It so happened that I was not in very good odour, and I was far from being a trustworthy slave. Nevertheless, I watched my opportunity when Master Thomas came to Baltimore—for I was still his property, Hugh only acting as his agent—in the spring of 1838, to purchase his spring supply of goods, and applied to him directly for the much-coveted privilege of hiring my time. This request Master Thomas unhesitatingly refused to grant; and he charged me, with some sternness, with inventing this stratagem to make my escape. He told me I could go nowhere but he would catch me; and, in the event of my running away, I might be assured he should spare no pains in his efforts to recapture me. He recounted, with a good deal of eloquence, the many kind offices he had done me, and exhorted me to be contented and obedient. "Lay out no plans for the future," said he; "If you behave yourself properly, I will take care of you." Now, kind and considerate as this offer was, it failed to soothe me into repose. In spite of all Master Thomas had said, and in spite of my own efforts to the contrary, the injustice and wickedness of slavery was always uppermost in my thoughts, strengthening my purpose to make my escape at the earliest moment possible.

About two months after applying to Master Thomas for the privilege of hiring my time, I applied to Master Hugh for the same liberty, supposing him to be unacquainted with the fact, that I had made a similar application to Master Thomas, and had been refused. My boldness in making this request fairly astounded him at first. He gazed at me in amazement. But I had many good reasons for pressing the matter, and, after listening to them awhile, he did not absolutely refuse, but told me he would think of it. There was hope for me in this. Once master of my own time, I felt sure that I could make over and above my obligation to him—a dollar or two every week. Some slaves had made enough in this way to purchase their freedom. It was a sharp spur to their industry; and some of the most enterprising coloured men in Baltimore hired themselves in that way.

After mature reflection, as I suppose it was, Master Hugh granted me the privilege in question, on the following terms: I was to be allowed all my time; to make all bargains for work, and to collect my own wages; and in return for this liberty, I was required or obliged to pay him three dollars at the end of each week, and to board and clothe myself, and buy my own caulking tools. A failure in any of these particulars would put an end to the privilege. This was a hard bargain. The wear and tear of clothing, the losing and breaking of tools, and the expense of board made it necessary for me to earn at least six dollars per week to keep even with the world. All who are acquainted with caulking know how uncertain and irregular that employment is. It can be done to advantage only in dry weather, for it is useless to put wet oakum into a ship's seam. Rain or shine, however, work or no work, at the end of each week the money must be forthcoming.

Master Hugh seemed much pleased with this arrangement for a time; and well he might be, for it was decidedly in his favour. It relieved him of all anxiety concerning me. His money was sure. He had armed my love of liberty with a lash and a driver far more efficient than any I had before known; and while he derived all the benefits of slaveholding by the arrangement, without its evils, I endured all the evils of being a slave, and yet suffered all the care and anxiety of a responsible freeman. "Nevertheless," thought I, "it is a valuable privilege—another step in my career toward freedom." It was something, even to be permitted to stagger under the disadvantages of liberty, and I was determined to hold on to the newly-gained footing by all proper industry. I was ready to work by night as by day, and being in the possession of excellent health, I was not only able to meet my current expenses, but also to lay by a small sum at the end of each week. All went on thus from the month of May till August; then, for reasons which will become apparent as I proceed, my much-valued liberty was wrested from me.

During the week previous to this calamitous event, I had made arrangements with a few young friends to accompany them on Saturday night to a camp-meeting, to be held about twelve miles from Baltimore. On the evening of our intended start for the camp-ground, something occurred in the ship-yard where I was at work, which detained me unusually late, and compelled me either to disappoint my friends, or to neglect carrying my weekly dues to Master Hugh. Knowing that I had the money and could hand it to him on another day, I decided to go to camp-meeting, and to pay him the three dollars for the past week on my return. Once on the camp-ground, I was induced to remain one day longer than I had intended when I left home. But as soon as I returned I went directly to his home in Fell Street, to hand him his (my) money. Unhappily the fatal mistake had been made. I found him exceedingly angry. He exhibited all the signs of apprehension and wrath which a slaveholder might be surmised to exhibit on the supposed escape of a favourite slave. "You rascal! I have a great mind to give you a sound whipping. How dare you go out of the city without first asking and obtaining my permission?" "Sir," I said, "I hired my time and paid you the price you asked for it. I did not know that it was any part of the bargain that I should ask you when or where I should go." "You did not know, you rascal! You are bound to show yourself here every Saturday night." After reflecting a few moments, he became somewhat cooled down; but evidently greatly troubled, and said: "Now, you scoundrel, you have done for yourself; you shall hire your time no longer. The next thing I shall hear of, will be your running away. Bring home your tools at once. I'll teach you how to go off in this way."

Thus ended my partial freedom. I could hire my time no longer; and I obeyed my master's orders at once. The little taste of liberty which I had had—although as it will be seen, that taste was far from being unalloyed—by no means enhanced my contentment with slavery. Punished by Master Hugh, it was now my turn to punish him. "Since," thought I, "you will make a slave of me, I will await your order in all things." So, instead of going to look for work on Monday morning, as I had formerly done, I remained at home during the entire week, without the performance of a single stroke of work. Saturday night came, and he called upon me as usual for my wages. I, of course, told him I had done no work, and had no wages. Here we were at the point of coming to blows. His wrath had been accumulating during the whole week; for he evidently saw that I was making no effort to get work, but was most aggravatingly awaiting his orders in all things. As I look back to this behaviour of mine, I scarcely know what possessed me, thus to trifle with one who had such unlimited power to bless or blast me. Master Hugh raved, and swore he would "get hold of me," but wisely for him, and happily for me, his wrath employed only those harmless, impalpable missiles which roll from a limber tongue. In my desperation I had fully made up my mind to measure strength with him, in case he should attempt to execute his threats. I am glad there was no occasion for this, for resistance to him could not have ended so happily for me, as it did in the case of Covey. Master Hugh was not a man to be safely resisted by a slave; and I freely own that in my conduct toward him, in this instance, there was more folly than wisdom. He closed his reproof, by telling me that hereafter I need give myself no uneasiness about getting work; he "would himself see to getting work for me, and enough of it at that." This threat, I confess, had some terror in it, and on thinking the matter over during the Sunday, I resolved not only to save him the trouble of getting me work, but that on the third day of September I would attempt to make my escape. His refusal to allow me to hire my time therefore hastened the period of my flight. I had three weeks in which to prepare for my journey.

Once resolved, I felt a certain degree of repose, and on Monday morning, instead of waiting for Master Hugh to seek employment for me, I was up by break of day, and off to the ship-yard of Mr. Butler, on the City Block, near the draw-bridge. I was a favourite with Mr. Butler, and, young as I was, I had served as his foreman, on the float-stage, at caulking. Of course I easily obtained work, and at the end of the week, which, by the way, was exceedingly fine, I brought Master Hugh nine dollars. The effect of this mark of returning good sense on my part, was excellent. He was very much pleased; he took the money, commended me, and told me I might have done the same thing the week before. It is a blessed thing that the tyrant may not always know the thoughts and purposes of his victim. Master Hugh little knew my plans. The going to camp-meeting without asking his permission, the insolent answers to his reproaches, the sulky deportment of the week, after being deprived of the privilege of hiring my time, had awakened the suspicion that I might be cherishing disloyal purposes. My object, therefore, in working steadily, was to remove suspicion; and in this I succeeded admirably, He probably thought I was never better satisfied with my condition than at the very time I was planning my escape. The second week passed, and I again carried him my full week's wages—nine dollars; and so well pleased was he that he gave me twenty-five cents! and bade me "make good use of it." I told him I would do so; for one of the uses to which I intended to put it was to pay my fare on the "underground railroad."

Things without went on as usual; but I was passing through the same internal excitement and anxiety which I had experienced two years and a half before. The failure in that instance was not calculated to increase my confidence in the success of this, my second attempt; and I knew that a second failure could not leave me where my first did. I must either get to the far North or be sent to the far South. Besides the exercise of mind from this state of facts, I had the painful sensation of being about to separate from a circle of honest and warm-hearted friends. The thought of such a separation, where the hope of ever meeting again was excluded, and where there could be no correspondence was very painful. It is my opinion that thousands more would have escaped from slavery but for the strong affection which bound them to their families, relatives, and friends. The daughter was hindered by the love she bore her mother, and the father by the love he bore his wife and children, and so on to the end of the chapter. I had no relations in Baltimore, and I saw no probability of ever living in the neighbourhood of sisters and brothers; but the thought of leaving my friends was the strongest obstacle to my running away. The last two days of the week, Friday and Saturday, were spent mostly in collecting my things together for my journey. Having worked four days that week for my master, I handed him six dollars on Saturday night. I seldom spent my Sundays at home, and for fear that something might be discovered in my conduct, I kept up my custom and absented myself all day. On Monday, the third day of September, 1838, in accordance with my resolution, I bade farewell to the city of Baltimore, and to that slavery which had been my abhorrence from childhood.

SECOND PART: ESCAPE FROM SLAVERY.

CHAPTER I: ESCAPE FROM SLAVERY.

Reasons for not having revealed the manner of escape—Nothing of romance in the method—Danger—Free Papers—Unjust tax—Protection papers—"Free trade and sailors' rights"—American eagle—Railroad train—Unobserving conductor—Capt. McGowan—Honest German—Fears—Safe arrival in Philadelphia—Ditto in New York.

IN the first narrative of my experience in slavery, written nearly forty years ago, and in various writings since, I have given the public what I considered very good reasons for withholding the manner of my escape. In substance these reasons were, first, that such publication at any time during the existence of slavery might be used by the master against the slave, and prevent the future escape of any who might adopt the same means that I did. The second reason was, if possible, still more binding to silence—for publication of details would certainly have put in peril the persons and property of those who assisted. Murder itself was not more sternly and certainly punished in the State of Maryland, than that of aiding and abetting the escape of a slave. Many coloured men, for no other crime than that of giving aid to a fugitive slave, have, like Charles T. Torrey, perished in prison. The abolition of slavery in my native state and throughout the country, and the lapse of time, render the caution hitherto observed no longer necessary. But even since the abolition of slavery, I have sometimes thought it well enough to baffle curiosity, by saying that while slavery existed there were good reasons for not telling the manner of my escape, and since slavery had ceased to exist, there was no reason for telling it. I shall now, however, cease to avail myself of this formula, and as far as I can, endeavour to satisfy this very natural curiosity. I should perhaps have yielded to that feeling sooner, had there been anything very heroic or thrilling in the incidents connected with my escape, but I am sorry to say I have nothing of that sort to tell; and yet, the courage that could risk betrayal, and the bravery which was ready to encounter death, if need be, in pursuit of freedom, were essential features in the undertaking. My success was due to address rather than courage; to good luck rather than bravery. My means of escape were provided for me by the very men who were making laws to hold and bind me more securely in slavery. It was the custom in the State of Maryland to require the free coloured people to have what were called free papers. This instrument they were required to renew very often, and by charging a fee for this writing, considerable sums, from time to time, were collected by the State. In these papers the name, age, colour, height, and form of the free man were described, together with any scars or other marks upon his person, which could assist in his identification. This device of slaveholding ingenuity, like other devices of wickedness, in some measure defeated itself—since more than one man could be found to answer the same general description. Hence many slaves could escape by personating the owner of one set of papers; and this was often done as follows: A slave nearly or sufficiently answering the description set forth in papers, would borrow or hire them till he could by their means escape to a free State, and then, by mail or otherwise, return them to the owner. The operation was a hazardous one for the lender as well as the borrower. A failure on the part of the fugitive to send back the papers would imperil his benefactor, and the discovery of the papers in possession of the wrong man, would imperil both the fugitive and his friend. It was, therefore, an act of supreme trust on the part of a freeman of colour thus to put in jeopardy his own liberty, that another might be free. It was, however, not unfrequently bravely done, and was seldom discovered. I was not so fortunate to sufficiently resemble any of my free acquaintances as to answer the description of their papers. But I had one friend—a sailor—who owned a sailor's protection, which answered somewhat the purpose of free papers—describing his person, and certifying to the fact that he was a free American sailor. The instrument had at its head the American eagle, which gave it the appearance at once of an authorized document. This protection did not, when in my hands, describe its bearer very accurately. Indeed, it called for a man much darker than myself, and close examination of it would have caused my arrest at the start. In order to avoid this fatal scrutiny on the part of the railroad official, I had arranged with Isaac Rolls, a hackman, to bring my baggage to the train just on the moment of its starting, and I jumped upon the car myself when the train was already in motion. Had I gone into the station and offered to purchase a ticket, I should have been instantly and carefully examined, and undoubtedly arrested. In choosing this plan upon which to act, I considered the jostle of the train, and the natural haste of the conductor, in a train crowded with passengers, and relied upon my skill and address in playing the sailor as described in my protection, to do the rest. One element in my favour, was the kind feeling which prevailed in Baltimore and other seaports at the time, towards "those who go down to the sea in ships." "Free trade and sailors' rights" expressed the sentiment of the country just then. In my clothing, I was rigged out in sailor style. I had on a red shirt and a tarpaulin hat and black cravat, tied in sailor fashion, carelessly and loosely about my neck. My knowledge of ships and sailor's talk came much to my assistance, for I knew a ship from stem to stern, and from keelson to cross-trees, and could talk sailor like an "old salt." On sped the train, and I was well on the way to Havre de Grace before the conductor came into the negro car to collect tickets and examine the papers of his black passengers. This was a critical moment in the drama. My whole future depended upon the decision of this conductor. Agitated I was while this ceremony was proceeding, but still externally, at least, I was apparently calm and self-possessed. He went on with his duty— examining several coloured passengers before reaching me. He was somewhat harsh in tone, and peremptory in manner until he reached me, when, strangely enough, and to my surprise and relief, his whole manner changed. Seeing that I did not readily produce my free papers, as the other coloured persons in the car had done, he said to me, in a friendly contrast with that observed towards the others: "I suppose you have your free papers?" To which I answered: "No, sir; I never carry my free papers to sea with me." "But you have something to show that you are a free man, have you not?" "Yes, sir," I answered; "I have a paper with the American eagle on it, and that will carry me round the world." With this I drew from my deep sailor's pocket my seaman's protection, as before described. The merest glance at the paper satisfied him, and he took my fare and went on about his business. This moment of time was one of the most anxious I ever experienced. Had the conductor looked closely at the paper, he could not have failed to discover that it called for a very different looking person from myself, and in that case, it would have been his duty to arrest me on that instant, and send me back to Baltimore from the first station. When he left me with the assurance that I was all right, though much relieved, I realised that I was still in great danger. I was still in Maryland, and subject to arrest at any moment. I saw on the train several persons who would have known me in any other clothes, and I feared they might recognise me, even in my sailor "rig," and report me to the conductor, who would then subject me to a closer examination, which I knew well would be fatal to me.

Though I was not a murderer fleeing from justice, I felt perhaps quite as miserable as such a criminal. The train was moving at a very high rate of speed for that time of railroad travel, but to my anxious mind, it was moving far too slowly. Minutes were hours, and hours were days, during this part of my flight. After Maryland, I was to pass through Delaware—another slave State, where slave-catchers generally awaited their prey, for it was not in the interior of the State, but on its borders, that these human hounds were most vigilant and active. The border lines between slavery and freedom were the dangerous ones, for the fugitives. The heart of no fox or deer, with hungry hounds on his trail in full chase, could have beaten more anxiously or noisily than did mine, from the time I left Baltimore till I reached Philadelphia. The passage of the Susquehanna river at Havre de Grace was made by ferry boat at that time, on board of which I met a young coloured man by the name of Nichols, who came very near betraying me. He was a "hand" on the boat, but instead of minding his business, he insisted upon knowing me, and asking me dangerous questions as to where I was going, and when I was coming back, &c. I got away from my old and inconvenient acquaintance as soon as I could decently do so, and went to another part of the boat. Once across the river I encountered a new danger. Only a few days before, I had been at work on a revenue-cutter, in Mr. Price's ship-yard, under the care of Captain McGowan. On the meeting at this point of the two trains, the one going South stopped on the track just opposite to the one going North, and it so happened that this Captain McGowan sat at a window where he could see me very distinctly, and would certainly have recognised me had he looked at me but for a second. Fortunately, in the hurry of the moment, he did not see me; and the trains soon passed each other on their respective ways. But this was not my only hair-breadth escape. A German blacksmith whom I knew well, was on the train with me, and looked at me very intently, as if he thought he had seen me somewhere before in his travels. I really believe he knew me, but had no heart to betray me. At any rate he saw me escaping and held his peace.

The last point of imminent danger, and the one I dreaded most, was Wilmington. Here we left the train, and took the steamboat for Philadelphia. In making the change here I again apprehended arrest, but no one disturbed me, and I was soon on the broad and beautiful Delaware, speeding away to the Quaker City. On reaching Philadelphia in the afternoon, I inquired of a coloured man how I could get on to New York. He directed me to the William Street depôt, and thither I went, taking the train that night. I reached New York on Tuesday morning, having completed the journey in less than twenty-four hours. Such is briefly the manner of my escape from slavery—and the end of my experience as a slave. Other chapters will tell the story of my life as a freeman.

CHAPTER II: LIFE AS A FREEMAN.

Loneliness and Insecurity—"Allender's Jake"—Succoured by a Sailor—David Ruggles—Marriage—Steamer J. W. Richmond—Stage to New Bedford—Arrival there—Driver's detention of baggage—Nathan Johnson—Change of Name—Why called "Douglas"—Obtaining work—The Liberator and its Editor.

MY free life began on the third of September, 1838. On the morning of the 4th of that month, after an anxious and most perilous, but safe journey, I found myself in the big city of New York, a free man; one more added to the mighty throng which, like the confused waves of the troubled sea, surged to and fro between the lofty walls of Broadway. Though dazzled with the wonders which met me on every hand, my thoughts could not be much withdrawn from my strange situation. For the moment, the dreams of my youth, and the hopes of my manhood, were completely fulfilled. The bonds that had held me to "old master" were broken. No man now had a right to call me his slave, or assert mastery over me. I was in the rough and tumble of an out-door world, to take my chance with the rest of its busy number. I have often been asked how I felt, when first I found myself on free soil; and my readers may share the same curiosity. There is scarcely anything in my experience about which I could not give a more satisfactory answer. A new world had opened upon me. If life is more than breath, and the "quick round of blood," I lived more in one day than in a year of my slave life. It was a time of joyous excitement which words can but tamely describe. In a letter written to a friend soon after reaching New York, I said: "I felt as one might feel, upon escape from a den of hungry lions." Anguish and grief, like darkness and rain, may be depicted; but gladness and joy, like the rainbow, defy the skill of pen or pencil. During ten or fifteen years I had, as it were, been dragging a heavy chain, which no strength of mine could break; I was not only a slave, but a slave for life. I might become a husband, a father, an aged man, but through all, from birth to death, from the cradle to the grave, I had felt myself doomed. All efforts I had previously made to secure my freedom, had not only failed, but had seemed only to rivet my fetters the more firmly, and to render my escape more difficult. Baffled, entangled, and discouraged, I had at times asked myself the question: may not my condition after all be God's work, and ordered for a wise purpose, and if so, was not submission my duty? A contest had in fact been going on in my mind for a long time, between the clear consciousness of right, and the plausible make-shifts of theology and superstition. The one held me an abject slave—a prisoner for life, punished for some transgression in which I had no lot or part; and the other counselled me to manly endeavour to secure my freedom. This contest was now ended my chains were broken, and the victory brought me unspeakable joy. But my gladness was short lived, for I was not yet out of the reach and power of the slave-holders. I soon found that New York was not quite so free, or so safe a refuge as I had supposed, and a sense of loneliness and insecurity, again oppressed me most sadly. I chanced to meet on the street, a few hours after my landing, a fugitive slave, whom I had once known well in slavery. The information received from him alarmed me. The fugitive in question was known in Baltimore as "Allender's Jake," but in New York he bore the more respectable name of "William Dixon."

Jake, in law, was the property of Doctor Allender, and Tolly Allender, the son of the doctor, had once made an effort to recapture Mr. Dixon, but had failed for want of evidence to support his claim. Jake told me the circumstances of this attempt, and how narrowly he escaped being sent back to slavery and torture. He told me that New York was then full of Southerners returning from the watering places North; that the coloured people of New York were not to be trusted; that there were hired men of my own colour who would betray me for a few dollars; that there were hired men ever on the look-out for fugitives; that I must trust no man with my secret; that I must not think of going either upon the wharves, or into any coloured boarding-house, for all such places were closely watched; that he was himself unable to help me; and, in fact, he seemed while speaking to me to fear lest I myself might be a spy, and a betrayer. Under this apprehension, as I suppose, he showed signs of wishing to be rid of me, and with whitewash-brush in hand, in search of work, he soon disappeared. This picture, given by poor "Jake," of New York, was a damper to my enthusiasm. My little store of money would soon be exhausted, and since it would be unsafe for me to go on the wharves for work, and I had no introductions elsewhere, the prospect for me was far from cheerful. I saw the wisdom of keeping away from the ship-yards, for, if pursued, as I felt certain I should be, Mr. Auld would naturally seek me there, among the caulkers. Every door seemed closed against me. I was in the midst of an ocean of my fellow-men, and yet a perfect stranger to every one. I was without home, without aquaintance, without money, without credit, without work, and without any definite knowledge as to what course to take, or where to look for succour. In such an extremity, a man has something beside his new-born freedom to think of. While wandering about the streets of New York, and lodging at least one night among the barrels on one of the wharves, I was indeed free from slavery—but free from food and shelter as well. I kept my secret to myself as long as I could, but was compelled at last to seek some one who would befriend me, without taking advantage of my destitution to betray me. Such an one I found in a sailor named Stuart, a warm-hearted and generous fellow, who from his humble home on Centre Street, saw me standing on the opposite sidewalk, near "The Tombs." As he approached me, I ventured a remark to him which at once enlisted his interest in me. He took me to his home to spend the night, and in the morning went with me to Mr. David Ruggles, the secretary of the New York Vigilance Committee, a co-worker with Isaac T. Hopper, Lewis and Arthur Tappan, Theodore S. Wright, Samuel Cornish, Thomas Downing, Phillip A. Bell, and other true men of their time. All these "save Mr. Bell, who still lives, and is editor and publisher of a paper called the Elevator, in San Francisco," have finished their work on earth. Once in the hands of these brave and wise men, I felt comparatively safe. With Mr. Ruggles, on the corner of Lispenard and Church Streets, I was hidden several days, during which time my intended wife came on from Baltimore at my call, to share the burdens of life with me. She was a free woman, and came at once on getting the good news of my safety. We were married by Rev. J. W. C. Pennington, then a well-known and respected Presbyterian minister. I had no money with which to pay the marriage fee, but he seemed well pleased with our thanks.

Mr. Ruggles was the first officer on the underground railroad with whom I met after coming North; and was indeed the only one with whom I had anything to do, till I became such an officer myself. Learning that my trade was that of a caulker, he promptly decided that the best place for me was in New Bedford, Mass. He told me that many ships for whaling voyages were fitted out there, and that I might there find work at my trade, and make a good living. So on the day of the marriage ceremony, we took our little luggage to the steamer "John W. Richmond," which at that time was one of the line running between New York and Newport, R. I. Forty-three years ago coloured travellers were not permitted in the cabin, nor allowed abaft the paddle-wheels of a steam vessel. They were compelled, whatever the weather might be, whether cold or hot, wet or dry, to spend the night on deck. Unjust as this regulation was, it did not trouble us much. We had fared much harder before. We arrived at Newport the next morning, and soon after an old-fashioned stage-coach with "New Bedford" in large yellow letters on its sides, came down to the wharf. I had not money enough to pay our fare, and stood hesitating to know what to do. Fortunately for us, there were two Quaker gentlemen who were about to take passage on the stage,—Friends William C. Taber and Joseph Ricketson,—who at once discerned our true situation, and in a peculiarly quiet way, addressing me, Mr. Taber said: "Thee get in." I never obeyed an order with more alacrity, and we were soon on our way to our new home. When we reached "Stone Bridge" the passengers alighted for breakfast, and paid their fares to the driver. We took no breakfast, and when asked for our fares I told the driver I would make it right with him when we reached New Bedford. I expected some objection to this on his part, but he made none. When, however, we reached New Bedford he took our baggage, including three music books,—two of them collections by Dyer, and one by Shaw,—and held them until I was able to redeem them by paying to him the sums due for our rides. This was soon done, for Mr. Nathan Johnson not only received me kindly, and hospitably, but, on being informed about our baggage, at once loaned me the two dollars with which to square accounts with the stage-driver. Mr. and Mrs. Nathan Johnson reached a good old age, and now rest from their labours. I am under many grateful obligations to them. They not only "took me in when a stranger," and "fed me when hungry," but taught me how to make an honest living.

Thus, in a fortnight after my flight from Maryland, I was safe in New Bedford,—a citizen of the grand old commonwealth of Massachusetts.

Once initiated into my new life of freedom, and assured by Mr. Johnson that I need not fear recapture in that city, a comparatively unimportant question arose, as to the name by which I should be known thereafter, in my new relation as a free man. The name given me by my dear mother was no less pretentious and long than Frederick Augustus Washington Bailey. I had, however, while living in Maryland dispensed with the Augustus Washington, and retained only Frederick Bailey. Between Baltimore and New Bedford, the better to conceal myself from the slave-hunters, I had parted with Bailey and called myself Johnson; but finding that in New Bedford the Johnson family was already so numerous, as to cause some confusion in distinguishing one from another, a change in this name seemed desirable. Nathan Johnson, mine host, was emphatic as to this necessity, and wished me to allow him to select a name for me. I consented, and he called me by my present name, the one by which I have been known for three and forty years,—Frederick Douglass. Mr. Johnson had just been reading the "Lady of the Lake," and so pleased was he with its great character, that he wished me to bear his name. Since reading that charming poem myself, I have often thought that, considering the noble hospitality and manly character of Nathan Johnson, black man though he was, he, far more than I, illustrated the virtues of the Douglas of Scotland. Sure am I that if any slave-catcher had entered his domicile with a view to my recapture, Johnson would have been like him of the "stalwart hand."

The reader may be surprised,—living in Baltimore as I had done for many years—when I tell the honest truth of the impressions I had in some way conceived of the social and material condition of the people at the North. I had no proper idea of the wealth, refinement, enterprise, and high civilization of this section of the country. My Columbian Orator, almost my only book, had done nothing to enlighten me concerning Northern society. I had been taught that slavery was the bottom-fact of all wealth. With this foundation idea, I came naturally to the conclusion, that poverty must be the general condition of the people of the free States. A white man holding no slaves in the country from which I came, was usually an ignorant and poverty-stricken man. Men of this class were contemptuously called "poor white trash." Hence I supposed, that since the non-slaveholders at the South were ignorant, poor, and degraded as a class, the non-slaveholders at the North, must be in a similar condition. New Bedford therefore, which at that time was really the richest city in the Union, in proportion to its population, took me greatly by surprise, in the evidences it gave, of its solid wealth and grandeur. I found that even the labouring classes lived in better houses, that their houses were more elegantly furnished, and were more abundantly supplied with conveniences and comforts, than the houses of many who owned slaves on the Eastern Shore of Maryland. This was true, not only of the white people of that city, but it was so of my friend, Mr. Johnson. He lived in a nicer house, dined at a more ample board, was the owner of more books, the reader of more newspapers, was more conversant with the moral, social, and political condition of the country and the world, than nine-tenths of the slaveholders in all Talbot county. I was not long in finding the cause of the difference in these respects, between the people of the North and South. It was the superiority of educated mind over mere brute force. I will not detain the reader by extended illustrations as to how my understanding was enlightened on this subject. On the wharves of New Bedford I received my first light. I saw there industry without bustle, labour without noise, toil—honest, earnest, and exhaustive, without the whip. There was no loud singing or hallooing, as at the wharves of Southern ports when ships were loading or unloading; no loud cursing or quarrelling; everything went on as smoothly as well-oiled machinery. One of the first incidents which impressed me with the superior mental character of labour in the North, over that of the South, was in the manner of loading and unloading vessels. In a Southern port twenty or thirty hands would be employed to do what five or six men, with the help of one ox, would do at the wharf in New Bedford. Main strength—human muscle—unassisted by intelligent skill, was slavery's method of labour. With a capital of about sixty dollars, in the shape of a good-natured old ox, attached to the end of a stout rope, New Bedford did the work of ten or twelve thousand dollars, represented in the bones and muscles of slaves, and did it far better. In a word, I found everything managed with a much more scrupulous regard to economy, both of men and things, time and strength, than in the country from which I had come. Instead of going a hundred yards to the spring, the maid-servant had a well or pump at her elbow. The wood used for fuel was kept dry, and snugly piled away for winter. Here were sinks, drains, self-shutting gates, pounding-barrels, washing-machines, wringing-machines, and a hundred other contrivances for saving time and money. The ship-repairing docks showed the same thoughtful wisdom as was seen elsewhere. Everybody seemed in earnest. The carpenter struck the nail on its head, and the caulkers wasted no strength in idle flourishes of their mallets. Ships brought here for repairs, were made stronger and better than when new. I could have landed in no part of the United States where I should have found a more striking and gratifying contrast, not only to life generally in the South, but in the condition of the coloured people, than in New Bedford. No coloured man was really free, while residing in a slave State. He was ever more or less subject to the condition of his slave brother. In his colour was his badge of bondage. I saw in New Bedford the nearest approach to freedom and equality that I had ever seen. I was amazed when Mr. Johnson told me that there was nothing in the laws or constitution of Massachusetts, that would prevent a coloured man from being governor of the State, if the people should see fit to elect him. There too the black man's children attended the same public schools with the white man's children, and apparently without objection from any quarter. To impress me with my security from recapture, and return to slavery, Mr. Johnson assured me that no slaveholder could take a slave out of New Bedford; that there were men there who would lay down their lives to save me from such a fate. A threat was once made by a coloured man, to inform a Southern master where his runaway slave could be found. As soon as this threat became known to the coloured people, they were furious. A notice was read from the pulpit of the Third Christian church—coloured—for a public meeting, when important business would be transacted—not stating what the important business was. In the meantime special measures had been taken to secure the attendance of the would-be Judas, and these had proved successful, for when the hour of meeting arrived, ignorant of the object for which they were called together, the offender was promptly in attendance. All the usual formalities were gone through, the prayer, appointments of president, secretaries, etc. Then the president, with an air of great solemnity, rose and said: "Well, friends and brethren, we have got him here, and I would recommend that you young men should take him outside the door and kill him." This was enough; there was a rush for the villain, who would probably have been killed but for his escape by an open window. He was never seen again in New Bedford.

The fifth day after my arrival I put on the clothes of a common labourer, and went upon the wharves in search of work. On my way down Union Street, I saw a large pile of coal in front of the house of the Rev. Ephraim Peabody, the Unitarian minister. I went to the kitchen door, and asked the privilege of bringing in and putting away this coal. "What will you charge?" said the lady. "I will leave that to you, madam." "You may put it away," she said. I was not long in accomplishing the job, when the dear lady put into my hand two silver half-dollars. To understand the emotion which swelled my heart as I clasped this money, realizing that I had no master who could take it from me—that it was mine—that my hands were my own, and could earn more of the precious coin—one must have been in some sense himself a slave. My next job was stowing a sloop, at Uncle Gid. Howland's wharf, with a cargo of oil for New York. I was not only a freeman, but a free-working man, and no Master Hugh stood ready at the end of the week to seize my hard earnings.

The season was growing late and work was plenty. Ships were being fitted out for whaling, and much wood was used in storing them. The sawing of this wood was considered a good job. With the help of old Friend Johnson—blessings on his memory! I got a "saw" and "buck," and went at it. When I went into a store to buy a cord with which to brace up my saw in the frame, I asked for a "fip's" worth of cord. The man behind the counter looked rather sharply at me, and said with equal sharpness, "You don't belong about here." I was alarmed, and thought I had betrayed myself. A fip in Maryland was six and a quarter cents, called fourpence in Massachusetts, But no harm came, except my fear, from the "fipenny-bit" blunder, and I confidently and cheerfully went to work with my saw and buck. It was new business to me, but I never did better work, or more of it in the same space of time for Covey, the negro-breaker, than I did for myself in these earliest years of my freedom.

Notwithstanding the just and humane sentiment of New Bedford three and forty years ago, the place was not entirely free from race and colour prejudice. The good influence of the Roaches, Rodmans, Arnolds, Grinnells, and Robesons did not pervade all classes of its people. The test of the real civilisation of the community came when I applied for work at my trade, and then my repulse was emphatic and decisive. It so happened that Mr. Rodney French, a wealthy and enterprising citizen, distinguished as an anti-slavery man, was fitting out a vessel for a whaling voyage, upon which there was a heavy job of caulking and coppering to be done. I had some skill in both branches, and applied to Mr. French for work. He, generous man that he was, told me he would employ me, and I might go at once to the vessel. I obeyed him, but upon reaching the float-stage, where other caulkers were at work, I was told that every white man would leave the ship in her unfinished condition, if I struck a blow at my trade upon her. This uncivil, inhuman, and selfish treatment was not so shocking and scandalous in my eyes at the time as it now appears to me. Slavery had inured me to hardships that made ordinary trouble sit lightly upon me. Could I have worked at my trade, I could have earned two dollars a day, but as a common labourer, I received but one dollar. The difference was of great importance to me, but if I could not get two dollars, I was glad to get one; and so I went to work for Mr. French as a common labourer. The consciousness that I was free—no longer a slave—kept me cheerful under this, and many similar proscriptions, which I was destined to meet in New Bedford, and elsewhere on the free soil of Massachusetts. For instance, though white and coloured children attended the same schools, and were treated kindly by their teachers, the New Bedford Lyceum refused, till several years after my residence in that city, to allow any coloured person to attend the lectures delivered in its hall. Not until such men as Hon. Chas.

Sumner, Theodore Parker, Ralph W. Emerson, and Horace Mann refused to lecture in their course while there was such a restriction, was it abandoned.

Becoming satisfied that I could not rely on my trade in New Bedford to give me a living, I prepared myself to do any kind of work that came to hand. I sawed wood, shovelled coal, dug cellars, moved rubbish from back-yards, worked on the wharves, loaded and unloaded vessels, and scoured their cabins.

This was an uncertain and unsatisfactory mode of life, for it kept me too much of the time in search of work. Fortunately it was not to last long. One of the gentlemen of whom I have spoken as being in company with Mr. Taber on the Newport wharf, when he said to me "thee get in," was Mr. Joseph Ricketson; and he was the proprietor of a large candle-works in the south part of the city. In this "candle-works" as it was called, though no candles were manufactured there, by the kindness of Mr. Ricketson, I found what is of the utmost importance to a young man just starting in life—constant employment and regular wages. My work in this oil refinery required good wind and muscle. Large casks of oil were to be moved from place to place, and much heavy lifting to be done. Happily I was not deficient in the requisite qualities. Young, twenty-one years old, strong, and active, and ambitious to do my full share, I soon made myself useful, and, I think, was liked by the men who worked with me, though they were all white. I was retained here as long as there was anything for me to do; when I went again to the wharves, and obtained work as a labourer on two vessels which belonged to Mr. George Howland, and which were being repaired and fitted up for whaling. My employer was a man of great industry: a hard driver, but a good paymaster, and I got on well with him. I was not only fortunate in finding work with Mr. Howland, but in my work-fellows. I have seldom met three working-men more intelligent than were John Briggs, Abraham Rodman, and Solomon Pennington, who laboured with me on the "Java" and "Golconda." They were sober, thoughtful, and upright, thoroughly imbued with the spirit of liberty, and I am much indebted to them, for many valuable ideas and impressions. They taught me that all coloured men were not light-hearted triflers, incapable of serious thought or effort. My next place of work, was at the brass-foundry owned by Mr. Richmond. My duty here was to blow the bellows, swing the crane, and empty the flasks in which castings were made; and at times this was hot and heavy work. The articles produced here were mostly for ship work, and in the busy season, the foundry was in operation night and day. I have often worked two nights and each working day of the week. My foreman, Mr. Cobb, was a good man, and more than once protected me from abuse that one or more of the hands was disposed to throw upon me. While in this situation I had little time for mental improvement. Hard work, night and day, over a furnace hot enough to keep the metal running like water, was more favourable to action than thought; yet here, I often nailed a newspaper to the post near my bellows, and read while I was performing the up and down motion of the heavy beam, by which the bellows was inflated and discharged. It was the pursuit of knowledge under difficulties, and I look back to it now, after so many years, with some complacency and a little wonder, that I could have been so earnest and persevering in any pursuit, other than for my daily bread. I certainly saw nothing in the conduct of those around to inspire me with such interest: they were all devoted exclusively to what their hands found to do. I am glad to be able to say that during my engagement in this foundry, no complaint was ever made against me, that I did not do my work, and do it well. The bellows which I worked by main strength was, after I left, moved by a steam engine.

I had been living four or five months in New Bedford when there came a young man to me with a copy of the Liberator, the paper edited by William Lloyd Garrison, and published by Isaac Knapp, and asked me to subscribe for it. I told him I had but just escaped from slavery, and was of course very poor, and had no money then to pay for it. He was very willing to take me as a subscriber, notwithstanding, and from this time I was brought into contact with the mind of Mr. Garrison, and his paper took a place in my heart, second only to the Bible. It detested slavery, and made no truce with the traffickers in the bodies and souls of men. It preached human brotherhood; it exposed hypocrisy and wickedness in high places; it denounced oppression, and with all the solemnity of "Thus saith the Lord," demanded the complete emancipation of my race. I loved this paper and its editor. He seemed to me, an all-sufficient match for every opponent, whether they spoke in the name of the law, or the gospel. His words were full of holy fire, and straight to the point. Something of a heroworshipper by nature, here was one to excite my admiration and reverence.

Soon after becoming a reader of the Liberator, it was my privilege to listen to a lecture in Liberty Hall, by Mr. Garrison, its editor. He was then a young man, of a singularly pleasing countenance, and earnest and impressive manner. On this occasion he announced nearly all his heresies. His Bible was his text book—held sacred as the very word of the Eternal Father. He believed in sinless perfection, complete submission to insults and injuries, and literal obedience to the injunction "if smitten on one cheek, to turn the other also." Not only was Sunday a Sabbath, but all days were Sabbaths, and to be kept holy. All sectarianism was false and mischievous—the regenerated throughout the world, being members of one body, and the head Christ Jesus. Prejudice against colour, was rebellion against God. Of all men beneath the sky, the slaves—because most neglected and despised—were nearest and dearest to His great heart. Those ministers who defended slavery from the Bible, were of their "father, the devil;" and those churches which fellowshipped slaveholders as Christians, were synagogues of Satan, and our nation was a nation of liars. He was never loud and noisy, but calm and serene as a summer sky, and as pure. "You are the man—the Moses, raised up by God, to deliver his modern Israel from bondage," was the spontaneous feeling of my heart, as I sat away back in the hall and listened to his mighty words,—mighty in truth,—mighty in their simple earnestness. I had not long been a reader of the Liberator, and a listener to its editor, before I got a clear comprehension of the principles of the anti-slavery movement. I had already its spirit, and only needed to understand its principles and measures, and as I became acquainted with these my hope for the ultimate freedom of my race increased. Every week the Liberator came, and every week I made myself master of its contents. All the anti-slavery meetings held in New Bedford I promptly attended, my heart bounding at every true utterance against the slave system, and every rebuke of it by its friends and supporters. Thus passed the first three years of my free life. I had not then dreamed of the possibility of my becoming a public advocate of the cause so deeply imbedded in my heart. It was enough for me to listen, to receive, and applaud the great words of others, and only whisper in private, among the white labourers on the wharves and elsewhere, the truths which burned in my heart.

CHAPTER III: INTRODUCED TO THE ABOLITIONISTS.

Anti-Slavery Convention at Nantucket—First Speech—Much Sensation—Extraordinary Speech of Mr. Garrison—Anti-Slavery Agency—Youthful Enthusiasm—Fugitive Slaveship Doubted—Experience in Slavery Written—Danger of Recapture.

IN the summer of 1841, a grand anti-slavery convention was held in Nantucket, under the auspices of Mr. Garrison and his friends. I had taken no holiday since establishing myself in New Bedford, and feeling the need of a little rest, I determined on attending the meeting, though I had no thought of taking part in any of its proceedings. Indeed, I was not aware that any one connected with the convention so much as knew my name. Mr. William C. Coffin, a prominent abolitionist in those days of trial, had heard me speaking to my coloured friends in the little schoolhouse on Second street, where we worshipped, He sought me out in the crowd, and invited me to say a few words to the convention. Thus sought out, and thus invited, I was induced to express the feelings inspired by the occasion, and the fresh recollection of the scenes through which I had passed as a slave. It was with the utmost difficulty that I could stand erect, or that I could command and articulate two words without hesitation or stammering. I trembled in every limb. I am not sure that my embarrassment was not the most effective part of my speech, if speech it could be called. At any rate, this is about the only part of my performance that I now distinctly remember. The audience sympathised with me at once, and from having been remarkably quiet, became much excited. Mr. Garrison followed me, taking me as his text, and now, whether I had made an eloquent plea in behalf of freedom, or not, his was one, never to be forgotten. Those who had heard him oftenest, and had known him longest, were astonished at his masterly effort. For the time, he possessed that almost fabulous inspiration, often referred to, but seldom attained, by which a public meeting is transformed, as it were, into a single individuality, the orator swaying a thousand heads and hearts at once, and by the simple majesty of his all-controlling thought, converting his hearers into the express image of his own soul. That night there were at least a thousand Garrisonians in Nantucket!

At the close of this great meeting, I was duly waited on by Mr. John A. Collins, then the general agent of the Massachusetts Anti-Slavery Society, and urgently solicited by him to become an Agent of that society, and publicly advocate its principles. I was reluctant to take the proffered position. I had not been quite three years from slavery and was honestly distrustful of my ability, and I wished to be excused. Besides, publicity might discover me to my master, and many other objections presented themselves. But Mr. Collins was not to be refused, and I finally consented to go out for three months, supposing I should, in that length of time, come to the end of my story and my consequent usefulness.

Here opened for me a new life—a life for which I had had no preparation. Mr. Collins used to say, when introducing me to an audience, I was a "graduate from the peculiar institution, with my diploma written on my back." The three years of my freedom had been spent in the hard school of adversity. My hands seemed to be furnished with something like a leather coating, and I had marked out for myself a life of rough labour, suited to the hardness of my hands, as a means of supporting my family and rearing my children.

Young, ardent, and hopeful, I entered upon this new life in the full gush of unsuspecting enthusiasm. The cause was good, the men engaged in it were good, the means to attain its triumph, good. Heaven's blessing must attend all, and freedom must soon be given to the millions pining under a ruthless bondage. My whole heart went with the holy cause, and my most fervent prayer to the Almighty Disposer of the hearts of men, was continually offered for its early triumph. In this enthusiastic spirit I dropped into the ranks of freedom's friends, and went forth to the battle. For a time, I was made to forget that my skin was dark and my hair crisped. For a time, I regretted that I could not have shared the hardships and dangers endured by the earlier workers for the slave's release. I found, however, full soon, that my enthusiasm had been extravagant, that hardships and dangers were not all over, and that the life now before me had its shadows also, as well as its sunbeams.

Among the first duties assigned me on entering the ranks, was to travel in company with Mr. George Foster to secure subscribers to the Anti-Slavery Standard and the Liberator. With him I travelled and lectured through the eastern counties of Massachusetts. Much interest was awakened—large meetings assembled. Many came, no doubt from curiosity, to hear what a negro could say in his own cause. I was generally introduced as a "chattel,"—a "thing"—a piece of Southern property—the chairman assuring the audience that it could speak. Fugitive slaves were rare then, and as a fugitive slave Lecturer, I had the advantage of being a "bran new fact"—the first one out. Up to that time, a coloured man was deemed a fool who confessed himself a runaway slave, not only because of the danger to which he exposed himself of being retaken, but because it was a confession of a very low origin. Some of my coloured friends in New Bedford thought very badly of my wisdom, in thus exposing and degrading myself. The only precaution I took at the beginning, to prevent Master Thomas from knowing where I was and what I was about, was the withholding my former name, my master's name, and the name of the State and county from which I came, During the first three or four months, my speeches were almost exclusively made up of narrations of my own personal experience as a slave. "Let us have the facts," said the people. So also said friend George Foster, who always wished to pin me down to my simple narrative. "Give us the facts," said Collins, "we will take care of the philosophy." Just here arose some embarrassment. It was impossible for me to repeat the same old story, month after month, and to keep up my interest in it. It was new to the people, it is true, but it was an old story to me; and to go through with it night after night, was a task altogether too mechanical for my nature, "Tell your story, Frederick," would whisper my revered friend, Mr. Garrison, as I stepped upon the platform. I could not always follow the injunction, for I was now reading and thinking. New views of the subject were being presented to my mind. It did not entirely satisfy me to narrate wrongs; I felt like denouncing them. I could not always curb my moral indignation for the perpetrators of slaveholding villainy, long enough for a circumstantial statement of the facts, which I felt almost sure everybody must know. Besides, I was growing, and needed room. "People won't believe you ever were a slave, Frederick, if you keep on this way," said friend Foster. "Be yourself," said Collins, "and tell your story." "Better have a little of the plantation speech than not," it was said to me; "it is not best that you seem too learned." These excellent friends were actuated by the best of motives, and were not altogether wrong in their advice; and still, I must speak just the word that seemed to me the word to be spoken by me.

At last the apprehended trouble came. People doubted if I had ever been a slave. They said I did not talk like a slave, look like a slave, nor act like a slave, and that they believed I had never been south of Mason and Dixon's line. "He don't tell us where he came from—what his master's name was, nor how he got away; besides, he is educated, and is, in this, a contradiction of all the facts we have concerning the ignorance of the slaves." Thus I was in a pretty fair way to be denounced as an impostor. The committee of the Massachusetts Anti-Slavery knew all the facts in my case, and agreed with me thus far in the prudence of keeping them private; but going down the aisles of the churches in which my meetings were held, and hearing the out-spoken Yankees repeatedly saying, "He's never been a slave, I'll warrant you," I resolved to dispel all doubt at no distant day, by such a revelation of facts as could not be made by any other than a genuine fugitive. In a little less than four years, therefore, after becoming a public lecturer, I was induced to write out the leading facts connected with my experience in slavery, giving names of persons, places, and dates—thus putting it in the power of any who doubted, to ascertain the truth or falsehood of my story. This statement soon became known in Maryland, and I had reason to believe that an effort would be made to recapture me.

It is not probable that any open attempt to secure me as a slave could have succeeded, further than the obtainment by my master, of the money value of my bones and sinews. Fortunately for me, in the four years of my labours in the abolition cause, I had gained many friends, who would have suffered themselves to be taxed to almost any extent to save me from slavery. It was felt that I had committed the double offence of running away and of exposing the secrets and crimes of slavery and slaveholders. There was a double motive for seeking my re-enslavement—avarice and vengeance; and while, as I have said, there was little probability of successful recapture, if attempted openly, I was constantly in danger of being spirited away, at a moment when my friends could render me no assistance. In travelling about from place to place, often alone, I was much exposed to this sort of attack. Any one cherishing the design to betray me, could easily do so, by simply tracking my whereabouts through the anti-slavery journals, for my movements and meetings were made known through these in advance. My friends, Mr. Garrison and Mr. Phillips, had no faith in the power of Massachusetts to protect me in my right to liberty. Public sentiment and the law, in their opinion, would hand me over to the tormentors. Mr. Phillips especially considered me in danger, and said, when I showed him the manuscript of my story, if in my place, he would "throw it into the fire." Thus, the reader will observe, that overcoming one difficulty only opened the way for another; and that though I had reached a free State, and had attained a position for public usefulness, I was still under the liability of losing all I had gained.

CHAPTER IV: RECOLLECTIONS OF OLD FRIENDS.

Work in Rhode Island—Dorr War—Recollections of Old Friends—Further labours in Rhode Island and elsewhere in New England.

IN the State of Rhode Island, under the leadership of Thomas W. Dorr, an effort was made in 1841 to set aside the old colonial charter, under which that State had lived and flourished since the Revolution, and to replace it with a new constitution having such improvements as it was thought that time and experience had shown to be wise and necessary. This new constitution was especially framed to enlarge the basis of representation so far as the white people of the State were concerned—to abolish an odious property qualification, and to confine the right of suffrage to white male citizens only. Mr. Dorr was himself a well-meaning man, and, after his fashion, a man of broad and progressive views, quite in advance of the party with which he acted. To gain their support, he consented to this restriction to a class, of a right which ought to be enjoyed by all citizens. In this he consulted policy rather than right, and at last shared the fate of all compromisers and trimmers, for he was disastrously defeated. The prospective features of his constitution shocked the sense of right, and roused the moral indignation of the abolitionists of the State, a class which would otherwise have gladly co-operated with him, at the same time that it did nothing to win support from the conservative class which clung to the old charter. Anti-slavery men wanted a new constitution, but they did not want a defective instrument, which required reform at the start. The result was that such men as William M. Chase, Thomas Davis, George L. Clark, Asa Fairbanks, Alphonso Janes, and others, of Providence; the Perry brothers of Westerly; John Brown and C. C. Eldridge of East Greenwich; Daniel Mitchell, William Adams, and Robert Shove of Pawtucket; Peleg Clark, Caleb Kelton, G. J. Adams, and the Anthonys and Goulds of Coventry and vicinity; Edward Norris of Woonsocket; and other abolitionists of the State, decided that the time had come, when the people of Rhode Island might be taught a more comprehensive gospel of human rights than had gotten itself into this Dorr constitution. The public mind was awake, and one class of its people at least, was ready to work with us to the extent of seeking to defeat the proposed constitution, though their reasons for such work were far different from ours. Stephen S. Foster, Parker Pillsbury, Abby Kelley, James Monroe, and myself, were called into the State to advocate equal rights, as against this narrow and proscriptive constitution. The work to which we were invited was not free from difficulty. The majority of the people were evidently with the new constitution; even the word white in it chimed well with the popular prejudice against the coloured race, and at the first, helped to make the movement popular. On the other hand, all the arguments which the Dorr men could urge against a property qualification for suffrage were equally cogent against a colour qualification, and this was our advantage. But the contest was intensely bitter and exciting. We were as usual denounced as intermeddlers—carpet-bagger had not come into use at that time—and were told to mind our own business, and the like;—a mode of defence common to men when called to account for mean and discreditable conduct. Stephen S. Foster, Parker Pillsbury, and the rest of us were not the kind of men to be ordered off by that sort of opposition. We cared nothing for the Dorr party on the one hand, nor the "law and order party" on the other. What we wanted, and what we laboured to obtain, was a constitution free from the narrow, selfish, and senseless limitation of the word white. Naturally enough when we said a strong and striking word against the Dorr Constitution, the conservatives were pleased and applauded, while the Dorr men were disgusted and indignant. Foster and Pillsbury were like the rest of us, young, strong, and at their best in this contest. The splendid vehemence of the one, and the weird and terrible denunciations of the other, never failed to stir up mob-ocratic wrath wherever they spoke. Foster especially, was effective in this line, His theory was that he must make converts or mobs. If neither came, he charged it either to his want of skill or his unfaithfulness. I was much with Mr. Foster during the tour in Rhode Island, and though at times he seemed to me extravagant and needlessly offensive in his manner of presenting his ideas, yet take him for all in all, he was one of the most impressive advocates the cause of the American slave ever had. No white man ever made the black man's cause more completely his own. Abby Kelley, since Abby Kelley Foster, was perhaps the most successful of any of us. Her youth and simple Quaker beauty, combined with her wonderful earnestness, her large knowledge and great logical power, bore down all opposition in the end, wherever she spoke, though she had been pelted with foul eggs, and no less foul words, from the noisy mobs which attended us.

Monroe and I were less aggressive than either of our co-workers, and of course did not provoke the same resistance. He at least, had the eloquence that charms, and the skill that disarms. I think that our labours in Rhode Island during this Dorr excitement did more to abolitionise the State than any previous, or subsequent work. It was the "tide taken at the flood." One effect of these labours was to induce the old "Law and Order" party, when it set about making its new constitution, to avoid the narrow folly of the Dorrites, and make a constitution which should not abridge any man's rights on account of race or colour. Such a constitution was finally adopted.

Owing perhaps to my efficiency in this campaign I was, for a while, employed in farther labours in Rhode Island by the State Anti-Slavery Society, and made there many friends to my cause as well as to myself. As a class, the abolitionists of this State partook of the spirit of its founder. They had their own opinions, were independent, and called no man master. I have reason to remember them most gratefully. They received me as a man and a brother, when I was new from the house of bondage, and had few of the graces derived from free and refined society. They took me with earnest hand to their homes and hearths, and made me feel that though I wore the burnished livery of the sun, I was still a countryman and kinsman of whom they were never ashamed. I can never forget the Clarks, Keltons, Chaces, Browns, Adams, Greenes, Sissons, Eldredges, Mitchells, Shoves, Anthonys, Applins, Janes, Goulds, and Fairbanks, and many others.

While thus remembering the noble anti-slavery men and women of Rhode Island, I do not forget that I suffered much rough usage within her borders. It was, like all the Northern States at that time, under the influence of slave power, and often showed a proscription and persecuting spirit, especially upon its railways, steamboats, and public-houses. The Stonington route was a "hard road" for a coloured man "to travel" in that day. I was several times dragged from the cars for the crime of being coloured. On the Sound, between New York and Stonington, there were the same proscriptions which I have before named, as enforced on the steamboats running between New York and Newport. No coloured man was allowed abaft the wheel, and in all seasons of the year, in heat or cold, wet or dry, the deck was his only place. If I would lie down at night, I must do so upon the freight on deck, and this in cold weather was not a very comfortable bed. When travelling in company with my white friends I always urged them to leave me, and go into the cabin and take their comfortable berths. I saw no reason why they should be miserable because I was. Some of them took my advice very readily. I confess, however, that while I was entirely honest in urging them to go, and saw no principle that should bind them to stay and suffer with me, I always felt a little nearer to those who did not take my advice, and persisted in sharing my hardships with me.

There is something in the world above fixed rules and the logic of right and wrong, and there is some foundation for recognising works, which may be called works of supererogation. Wendell Phillips, James Monroe, and William White, were always dear to me for their nice feeling on this point. I have known James Monroe to pull his coat about him, crawl upon the cotton bales between decks, and pass the night with me, without a murmur. Wendell Phillips would never go into a first-class car while I was forced into what was called the Jim Crow car. True men they were, who could accept welcome at no man's table where I was refused. I speak of these gentlemen, not as singular or exceptional cases, but as representatives of a large class of the early workers for the abolition of slavery. As a general rule, there was little difficulty in obtaining suitable places in New England after 1840, where I could plead the cause of my people. The abolitionists had passed the Red Sea of mobs, and had conquered the right of a respectful hearing. I, however, found several towns in which the people closed their doors, and refused to entertain the subject. Notably among these was Hartford, Conn., and Grafton, Mass. In the former place, Messrs. Garrison, Hudson, Foster, Abby Kelley, and myself, determined to hold our meetings under the open sky, which we did in a little court under the eaves of the "sanctuary," where the Rev. Dr. Hawes ministered, with much satisfaction to ourselves, and I think with advantage to our cause. In Grafton I was alone, and there was neither house, hall, church, nor market-place, in which I could speak to the people; but determined to speak, I went to the hotel and borrowed a dinner bell, with which in hand, I passed through the principal streets, ringing the bell and crying out, "Notice! Frederick Douglas, recently a slave, will lecture on American Slavery, on Grafton Common, this evening at 7 o'clock. Those who would like to hear of the workings of slavery, by one of the slaves, are respectfully invited to attend." This notice brought out a large audience, after which the largest church in the town was open to me. Only in one instance was I compelled to pursue this course thereafter, and that was in Manchester, N.H., and my labours there were followed by similar results. When people found that I would be heard, they saw it was the part of wisdom to open the way for me.

My treatment in the use of public conveyances about these times was extremely rough, especially on the "Eastern Railroad, from Boston to Portland." On that road, as on many others, there was a mean, dirty, and uncomfortable car set apart for coloured travellers, called the "Jim Crow" car. Regarding this as the fruit of slaveholding prejudice, and being determined to fight the spirit of slavery wherever I might find it, I resolved to avoid this car, though it sometimes required some courage to do so. The coloured people generally accepted the situation, and complained of me as making matters worse, rather than better, by refusing to submit to this proscription. I, however, persisted, and sometimes was soundly beaten by conductor and brakeman. On one occasion, six of these "fellows of the baser sort," under the direction of the conductor, set out to eject me from my seat. As usual, I had purchased a first-class ticket, and paid the required sum for it, and on the requirement of the conductor to leave, refused to do so, when he called on these men "to snake me out." They attempted to obey with an air which plainly told me they relished the job. They, however, found me much attached to my seat, and in removing me I tore away two or three of the surrounding ones, on which I held with a firm grasp, and did the car no service in some other respects. I was strong and muscular, and the seats were not then so firmly attached or of as solid make as now. The result was that Stephen A. Chase, superintendent of the road, ordered all passenger trains to pass through Lynn, where I then lived, without stopping. This was a great inconvenience to the people, large numbers of whom did business in Boston, and at other points of the road. Led on, however, by James N. Buffum, Jonathan Buffum, Christopher Robinson, William Bassett, and others, the people of Lynn stood bravely by me, and denounced the railroad management in emphatic terms. Mr. Chase made reply that a railroad corporation was neither a religious nor reformatory body; that the road was run for the accommodation of the public, and that it required the exclusion of coloured people from its cars. With an air of triumph he told us that we ought not to expect a railroad company to be better than the Evangelical Church, and that until the churches abolished the "negro pew," we ought not to expect the railroad company to abolish the negro car. This argument was certainly good enough as against the Church, but good for nothing as against the demands of justice and equality. My old and dear friend, J. N. Buffum, made a point against the company that they "often allowed dogs and monkeys to ride in first-class cars, and yet excluded a man like Frederick Douglass!" In a very few years this barbarous practice was put away, and I think there have been no instances of such exclusion during the past thirty years; and coloured people now, everywhere in New England, ride upon equal terms with other passengers.

CHAPTER V: ONE HUNDRED CONVENTIONS.

Anti-slavery Conventions held in parts of New England, and in some of the Middle and Western States—Mobs, Incidents, &c.

THE year 1843 was one of remarkable anti-slavery activity. The New England Anti-Slavery Society at its annual meeting, held in the spring of that year, resolved, under the auspices of Mr. Garrison and his friends, to hold a series of one hundred conventions. The territory embraced in this plan for creating anti-slavery sentiment included New Hampshire. Vermont, New York, Ohio, Indiana, and Pennsylvania. I had the honour to be chosen one of the agents to assist in these proposed conventions, and I never entered upon any work with more heart and hope. All that the American people needed, I thought, was light. Could they know slavery as I knew it, they would hasten to the work of its extinction. The corps of speakers who were to be associated with me in carrying on these conventions were Messrs. George Bradburn, John A. Collins, James Monroe, William A. White, Charles L. Remond, and Sydney Howard Gay. They were all masters of the subject, and some of them able and eloquent orators. It was a piece of great good fortune to me, only a few years from slavery as I was, to be brought into contact with such men. It was a real campaign, and required nearly six months for its accomplishment.

Those who only know the State of Vermont as it is to-day, can hardly understand, and must wonder that there was need for anti-slavery effort within its borders forty years ago. Our first convention was held in Middlebury, its chief seat of learning, and the home of William Slade, who was for years the co-worker with John Quincy Adams in Congress; and yet in this town the opposition to our anti-slavery convention was intensely bitter and violent. The only man of note in the town whom I now remember as giving us sympathy or welcome was Mr. Edward Barber, who was a man of courage as well as ability, and did his best to make our convention a success. In advance of our arrival, the college students had very industriously and mischievously placarded the town with violent aspersions of our characters, and the grossest misrepresentations of our principles, measures, and objects. I was described as an escaped convict from the State Prison, and the other speakers were assailed not less slanderously. Few people attended our meeting, and apparently little was accomplished by it. In the neighbouring town of Ferrisburgh the case was different and more favourable. The way had been prepared for us by such stalwart anti-slavery workers as Orson S. Murray, Charles C. Burleigh, Rowland T. Robinson and others. Upon the whole, however, the several towns visited showed that Vermont was surprisingly under the influence of the slave power. Her proud boast that no slave had ever been delivered up to his master within her borders did not hinder her hatred of anti-slavery. What was true of the Green Mountain State in this respect, was most discouragingly true of New York, the State next visited. All along the Erie canal, from Albany to Buffalo, there was apathy, indifference, aversion, and sometimes mob-ocratic spirit evinced. Even Syracuse, afterwards the home of the humane Samuel J. May, and the scene of the "Jerry rescue," where Gerrit Smith, Beriah Greene, William Goodell, Alvin Stewart, and other able men afterwards taught their noblest lessons, would not at that time furnish us with church, market, house, or hall in which to hold our meetings. Discovering this state of things, some of our number were disposed to turn their backs upon the town, and shake its dust from their feet, but of these, I am glad to say, I was not one. I had somewhere read of a command to go into the hedges and highways and compel men to come in. Mr. Stephen Smith, under whose hospitable roof we were made at home, thought as I did. It would be easy to silence anti-slavery agitation if refusing its agents the use of halls and churches could effect that result. The house of our friend Smith stood on the south-west corner of the park, which was well covered with young trees, too small to furnish shade or shelter, but better than none. Taking my stand under a small tree, in the south-east corner of this park, I began to speak in the morning to an audience of five persons, and before the close of the afternoon meeting I had before me not less than five hundred. In the evening I was waited upon by the officers of the Congregational church, who tendered the use of an old wooden building, which they had deserted for a better, but still owned; and here our convention was continued during three days. I believe there has been no trouble to find places in Syracuse in which to hold anti-slavery meetings since. I never go there without endeavouring to see that tree, which, like the cause it sheltered, has grown large and strong and imposing.

I believe my first offence against our Anti-Slavery Israel, was committed during these Syracuse meetings. It was on this wise: Our general agent, John A. Collins, had recently returned from England full of communistic ideas, which ideas would do away with individual property, and have all things in common. He had arranged a corps of speakers of his communistic persuasion, consisting of John O. Wattles, Nathaniel Whiting, and John Orvis to follow our anti-slavery conventions, and while our meeting was in progress in Syracuse, a meeting, as the reader will observe, obtained under much difficulty, Mr. Collins came in with his new friends and doctrines, and proposed to adjourn our anti-slavery discussions and take up the subject of communism. To this I ventured to object. I held that it was imposing an additional burden of unpopularity on our cause, and an act of bad faith with the people, who paid the salary of Mr. Collins, and were responsible for these hundred conventions. Strange to say, my course in this matter did not meet the approval of Mrs. W. H. Chapman, an influential member of the board of managers of the Massachusetts Anti-Slavery Society, and called out a sharp reprimand from her, for my insubordination to my superiors. This was a strange and distressing revelation to me, and one of which I was not soon relieved. I thought I had only done my duty, and I think so still. The chief reason for the reprimand was the use which the liberty party papers would make of my seeming rebellion against the commanders of our Anti-Slavery Army.

In the growing city of Rochester we had in every way a better reception. Abolitionists of all shades of opinion were broad enough to give the Garrisonians, for such we were, a hearing. Samuel D. Porter and the Avery family, though they belonged to the Gerrit Smith, Myron Holly, and William Goodell school, were not so narrow as to refuse us the use of their church for the convention. They heard our moral suasion arguments, and in a manly way met us in debate. We were opposed to carrying the anti-slavery cause to the ballot-box, and they believed in carrying it there. They looked at slavery as a creature of law; we regarded it as a creature of public opinion. It is surprising how small the difference appears as I look back to it, over the space of forty years; yet at the time, this difference was immense.

During our stay at Rochester we were hospitably entertained by Isaac and Amy Post, two people of all-bounding benevolence, the truest and best of Long Island, and Elias Hicks, Quakers. They were not more amiable than brave, for they never seemed to ask, What will the world say? but walked straight forward in what seemed to them the line of duty, please or offend whomsoever it might. Many a poor fugitive slave found shelter under their roof, when such shelter was hard to find elsewhere, and I mention them here in the warmth and fulness of earnest gratitude.

Pleased with our success in Rochester, we—that is Mr. Bradburn and myself—made our way to Buffalo, then a rising city of steamboats, bustle, and business. Buffalo was too busy to attend to such matters as we had in hand. Our friend, Mr. Marsh, had been able to secure for our convention only an old dilapidated and deserted room, formerly used as a post-office. We went at the time appointed, and found seated a few cabmen in their coarse, every-day clothes, whips in hand, while their teams were standing on the street waiting for a job. Friend Bradburn looked around upon this unpromising audience, and turned upon his heel, saying he would not speak to "such a set of ragamuffins," and took the first steamer to Cleveland, the home of his brother Charles, and left me to "do" Buffalo alone. For nearly a week I spoke every day in this old post-office, to audiences constantly increasing in numbers and respectability, till the Baptist church was thrown open to me; and when this became too small, I went on Sunday into the open Park and addressed an assembly of four or five thousand persons. After this my coloured friends, Charles L. Remond, Henry Highland Garnett, Theodore S. Wright, Amos G. Beaman, Charles M. Ray, and other well-known coloured men, held a convention here, and then Remond and myself left for our next meeting in Chester county, Ohio. This was held in a great shed, built by the abolitionists, of whom Dr. Abram Brook and Valentine Nicholson were the most noted, for this special purpose. Thousands gathered here and were addressed by Bradburn, White, Monroe, Remond, Gay, and myself. The influence of this meeting was deep and wide-spread. It would be tedious to tell of all, or a small part of all that was interesting and illustrative of the difficulties encountered by the early advocates of anti-slavery in connection with this campaign, and hence I leave this part of it at once.

From Ohio we divided our forces and went into Indiana. At our first meeting we were mobbed, and some of us got our good clothes spoiled by evil-smelling eggs. This was at Richmond, where Henry Clay had been recently invited to the high seat of the Quaker meeting-house, just after his gross abuse of Mr. Mendenhall, because of his presenting him a respectful petition, asking him to emancipate his slaves. At Pendleton this mob-ocratic spirit was even more pronounced. It was found impossible to obtain a building in which to hold our convention, and our friends, Dr. Fussell and others, erected a platform in the woods, where quite a large audience assembled. Mr. Bradburn, Mr. White, and myself were in attendance. As soon as we began to speak, a mob of about sixty of the roughest characters I ever looked upon ordered us, through its leaders, to "be silent," threatening us, if we were not, with violence. We attempted to dissuade them, but they had not come to parley but to fight, and were well armed. They tore down the platform on which we stood, assaulted Mr. White, knocking out several of his teeth; dealt a heavy blow on William A. White, striking him on the back part of the head, badly cutting his scalp and felling him to the ground. Undertaking to fight my way through the crowd with a stick which I caught up in the mélée, I attracted the fury of the mob, which laid me prostrate on the ground under a torrent of blows. Leaving me thus, with my right hand broken, and in a state of unconsciousness, the mob-ocrats hastily mounted their horses and rode to Andersonville, where most of them resided. I was soon raised up and revived by Neal Hardy, a kind-hearted member of the Society of Friends, and carried by him in his wagon about three miles in the country to his home, where I was tenderly nursed and bandaged by good Mrs. Hardy, till I was again on my feet, but as the bones broken were not properly set my hand has never recovered its natural strength and dexterity. We lingered long in Indiana, and the good effects of our labours there are felt at this day. I have lately visited Pendleton, now one of the best Republican towns in the State, and looked again upon the spot where I was beaten down, and have again taken by the hand some of the witnesses of that scene, amongst whom was the kind, good lady—Mrs. Hardy—who, so like the good Samaritan of old, bound up my wounds, and cared for me so kindly. A complete history of these hundred conventions would fill a volume far larger than the one in which this simple reference is to find a place. It would be a grateful duty to speak of the noble young men, who forsook ease and pleasure, as did White, Gay, and Monroe, and endured all manner of privations in the cause of the enslaved and down-trodden of my race. Gay, Monroe, and myself, are the only ones who participated as agents in the one hundred conventions who now survive. Mr. Monroe was for many years consul to Brazil, and has since been a faithful member of Congress from the Oberlin District, Ohio, and has filled other important positions in his State. Mr. Gay was managing editor of the National Anti-Slavery Standard, and afterwards of the New York Tribune, and still later of the New York Evening Post.

CHAPTER VI: IMPRESSIONS ABROAD.

Danger to be averted—A refuge sought abroad—Voyage on the Steamship Cambria—Refusal of first-class passage—Attractions of the forecastle-deck—Hutchinson family—Invited to make a speech—Southerners feel insulted—Captain threatens to put them in irons—Experiences abroad—Attentions received—Impressions of different members of Parliament, and of other public men—Contrast with Life in America—Kindness of friends—Their purchase of my person, and the gift of the same to myself—My return.

AS I have before intimated, the publishing of my "Narrative" was regarded by my friends with mingled feelings of satisfaction and apprehension. They were glad to have the doubts and insinuations which the advocates and apologists of slavery had made against me, proved to the world to be false, but they had many fears lest this very proof should endanger my safety, and make it necessary for me to leave a position which in a signal manner had opened before me, and one in which I had thus far been efficient in assisting and arousing the moral sentiment of the community against a system which had deprived me, in common with my fellow-slaves, of all the attributes of manhood.

I became myself painfully alive to the liability which surrounded me, and which might at any moment scatter all my proud hopes, and return me to a doom worse than death. It was thus I was led to seek a refuge in monarchical England, from the dangers of Republican slavery. A rude, uncultivated fugitive slave, I was driven to that country to which American young gentlemen go to increase their stock of knowledge—to seek pleasure, and to have their rough democratic manners softened by contact with English aristocratic refinement.

My friend, James N. Buffum, of Lynn, Mass., who was to accompany me, applied on board the steamer "Cambria," of the Cunard line, for tickets, and was told that I could not be received as a cabin passenger. American prejudice against colour had triumphed over British liberality and civilisation, and had erected a colour test as condition for crossing the sea in the cabin of a British vessel.

The insult was keenly felt by my white friends, but to me such insults were so frequent, and expected, that it was of no great consequence whether I went into the cabin or into the steerage. Moreover, I felt that if I could not go into the first cabin, first cabin passengers could come into the second cabin, and in this thought I was not mistaken, as I soon found myself an object of more general interest than I wished to be, and, so far from being degraded by being placed in the second cabin, that part of the ship became the scene of as much pleasure and refinement as the cabin itself. The Hutchinson family from New Hampshire—sweet singers of anti-slavery songs, and the "good time coming"—were fellow-passengers, and often came to my rude forecastle-deck and sang their sweetest songs, making the place eloquent with music and alive with spirited conversation. They not only visited me, but invited me to visit them; and in two days after leaving Boston one part of the ship was about as free to me as another. My visits there, however, were but seldom. I preferred to live within my privileges, and keep upon my own premises. This course was quite as much in accord with good policy as with my own feelings. The effect was, that with the majority of the passengers all colour distinctions were flung to the winds, and I found myself treated with every mark of respect from the beginning to the end of the voyage, except in one single instance; and in that I came near being mobbed for complying with an invitation given me by the passengers and the captain of the "Cambria" to deliver a lecture on slavery. There were several young men—passengers from Georgia and New Orleans; and they were pleased to regard my lecture as an insult offered to them, and swore I should not speak. They went so far as to threaten to throw me overboard, and but for the firmness of Captain Judkins, they would probably, under the inspiration of slavery and brandy, have attempted to put their threats into execution. I have no space to describe this scene, although its tragic and comic features are well worth description. An end was put to the mêlée by the captain's call to the ship's company to put the salt-water mob-ocrats in irons, at which determined order the gentlemen of the lash scampered, and for the remainder of the voyage conducted themselves very decorously.

This incident of the voyage brought me, within two days after landing at Liverpool, before the British public. The gentlemen so promptly withheld in their attempted violence toward me, flew to the press to justify their conduct, and to denounce me as a worthless and insolent negro. This course was even less wise than the conduct it was intended to sustain; for, besides awakening something like a national interest in me, and securing me an audience, it brought out counter statements, and threw the blame upon themselves, which they had sought to fasten upon me and the gallant captain of the ship.

My visit to England did much for me every way. Not the least among the many advantages derived from it was the opportunity it afforded me of becoming acquainted with educated people, and of seeing and hearing many of the most distinguished men of that country. My friend, Mr. Wendell Phillips, knowing something of my appreciation of orators and oratory, had said to me before leaving Boston: "Although Americans are generally better speakers than Englishmen, you will find in England individual orators superior to the best of ours." I do not know that Mr. Phillips was quite just to himself in this remark, for I found in England few, if any, superior to him in the gift of speech. When I went to England that country was in the midst of a tremendous agitation. The people were divided by two great questions of "Repeal:"—the repeal of the corn laws, and the repeal of the union between England and Ireland.

Debate ran high in Parliament, and among the people everywhere, especially concerning the corn laws. Two powerful interests of the country confronted each other: one venerable from age, and the other young, stalwart, and growing. Both strove for ascendancy. Conservatism united for retaining the corn laws, while the rising power of commerce and manufactures demanded repeal. It was interest against interest, but something more and deeper: for, while there was an aggrandizement of the landed aristocracy on the one side, there was famine and pestilence on the other. Of the anti-corn law movement, Richard Cobden and John Bright, both then members of Parliament, were the leaders. They were the rising statesmen of England, and possessed a very friendly disposition toward America. Mr. Bright, who is now the Right Honourable John Bright, and occupies a high place in the British Cabinet, was friendly to the loyal and progressive spirit which abolished our slavery and saved our country from dismemberment. I have seen and heard both of these great men, and if I may be allowed so much egotism, I may say I was acquainted with both of them. I was, besides, a welcome guest at the house of Mr. Bright, in Rochdale, and treated as a friend and brother among his brothers and sisters. Messrs. Cobden and Bright were well-matched leaders. One was in large measure the complement of the other. They were spoken of usually as Cobden and Bright, but there was no reason, except that Cobden was the elder of the two, why their names might not have been reversed.

They were about equally fitted for their respective parts in the great movement of which they were the distinguished leaders, and neither was likely to encroach upon the work of the other. The contrast was quite marked in their persons as well as in their oratory. The powerful speeches of the one, as they travelled together over the country, heightened the effect of the speeches of the other, so that their difference was as effective for good, as was their agreement. Mr. Cobden—for an Englishman—was lean, tall, and slightly sallow, and might have been taken for an American or Frenchman. Mr. Bright was, in the broadest sense, an Englishman, abounding in all the physical perfections peculiar to his countrymen—full, round, and ruddy. Cobden had dark eyes and hair, a well-formed head, high above his shoulders, and, when sitting quiet, had a look of sadness and fatigue. In the House of Commons, he often sat with one hand supporting his head. Bright appeared the very opposite in this and other respects. His eyes were blue, his hair light, his head massive, and firmly set upon his shoulders, suggesting immense energy and determination. In his oratory Mr. Cobden was cool, candid, deliberate, straight-forward, yet at times slightly hesitating. Bright, on the other hand, was fervid, fluent, rapid; always ready in thought or word. Mr. Cobden was full of facts and figures, dealing in statistics by the hour. Mr. Bright was full of wit, knowledge, and pathos, and possessed amazing power of expression. One spoke to the cold, calculating side of the British nation, which asks "if the new idea will pay?" The other spoke to the infinite side of human nature—the side which asks, first of all, "is it right? is it just? is it humane?" Wherever these two great men appeared, the people assembled in thousands. They could, at an hour's notice, pack the Town Hall of Birmingham, which would hold seven thousand persons, or the Free Trade Hall in Manchester, and Covent Garden Theatre, London, each of which was capable of holding eight thousand.

One of the first attentions shown me by these gentlemen, was to make me welcome at the Free Trade Club in London.

I was not long in England before a crisis was reached in the anti-corn law movement. The announcement that Sir Robert Peel, then Prime Minister of England, had become a convert to the views of Messrs. Cobden and Bright, came upon the country with startling effect, and formed the turning point in the anticorn law question. Sir Robert had been the strong defence of the landed aristocracy of England, and his defection left them without a competent leader, and just here came the opportunity for Mr. Benjamin Disraeli the Hebrew—since Lord Beaconsfield. To him it was in public affairs, the "tide which led on to fortune." With a bitterness unsurpassed, he had been denounced by Daniel O'Connell as a lineal descendant of the thief on the cross. But now his time had come, and he was not the man to permit it to pass unimproved. For the first time, it seems, he conceived the idea of placing himself at the head of a great party, and thus become the chief defender of the landed aristocracy. The way was plain. He was to transcend all others in effective denunciation of Sir Robert Peel, and surpass all others in zeal. His ability was equal to the situation, and the world knows the result of his ambition. I watched him narrowly when I saw him in the House of Commons, but I saw and heard nothing there that foreshadowed the immense space he at last came to fill in the mind of his country and the world. He had nothing of the grace and warmth of Peel in debate, and his speeches were better in print than when listened to,—yet when he spoke, all eyes were fixed, and all ears attent. Despite all his ability and power, however, as the defender of the landed interests in England, his cause was already lost. The increasing power of the anti-corn law league—the burden of the tax upon bread, the cry of distress coming from famine-stricken Ireland, and the adhesion of Peel to the views of Cobden and Bright, made the repeal of the corn laws speedy and certain.

The repeal of the union between England and Ireland was not so fortunate. It is still, under one name or another, the cherished hope and aspiration of her sons. It stands little better or stronger than it did six-and-thirty years ago, when its greatest advocate, Daniel O'Connell, welcomed me to Ireland, and to "Conciliation Hall," and where I first had a specimen of his truly wondrous eloquence. Until I heard this man, I had thought that the story of his oratory and power were greatly exaggerated. I did not see how a man could speak to twenty or thirty thousand people at one time, and be heard by any considerable number of them; but the mystery was solved when I saw his vast person, and heard his musical voice. His eloquence came down upon the vast assembly like a summer thunder-shower upon a dusty road. He could stir the multitude at will, to a tempest of wrath, or reduce it to the silence with which a mother leaves the cradle-side of her sleeping babe. Such tenderness—such pathos—such world-embracing love! and, on the other hand, such indignation—such fiery and thunderous denunciation, and such wit and humour, I never heard surpassed, if equalled, at home or abroad. He held Ireland within the grasp of his strong hand, and could lead it whithersoever he would, for Ireland believed in him and loved him, as she has loved and believed in no leader since. In Dublin, when he had been absent from that city a few weeks, I saw him followed through Sackville Street by a multitude of little boys and girls, shouting in loving accents: "There goes Dan! there goes Dan!" while he looked at the ragged and shoeless crowd with the kindly air of a loving parent returning to his gleeful children. He was called "The Liberator," and not without cause; for, though he failed to effect the repeal of the union between England and Ireland, he fought out the battle of Catholic emancipation, and was clearly the friend of liberty the world over. In introducing me to an immense audience in Conciliation Hall, he playfully called me the "Black O'Connell of the United States;" nor did he let the occasion pass without his usual word of denunciation of our slave system. O. A. Brownson had then recently become a Catholic, and taking advantage of his new Catholic audience, in "Brownson's Review," had charged O'Connell with attacking American institutions. In reply, Mr. O'Connell said: "I am charged with attacking American institutions, as slavery is called; I am not ashamed of this attack. My sympathy is not confined to the narrow limits of my own green Ireland, my spirit walks abroad upon sea and land, and wherever there is oppression, I hate the oppressor, and wherever the tyrant rears his head, I will deal my bolts upon it; and wherever there is sorrow and suffering, there is my spirit to succour and relieve." No transatlantic statesman bore a testimony more marked and telling against the crime and curse of slavery, than did Daniel O'Connell. He would shake the hand of no slaveholder, nor allow himself to be introduced to one, if he knew him to be such. When the friends of repeal in the Southern States sent him money with which to carry on his work, he, with ineffable scorn, refused the bribe, and sent back what he considered the blood-stained offering, saying he would "never purchase the freedom of Ireland with the price of slaves."

It was not long after my seeing Mr. O'Connell that his health broke down, and his career ended in death. I felt that a great champion of freedom had fallen, and that the cause of the American slave, not less than the cause of his country, had met with a great loss. All the more was this felt, when I saw the kind of men who came to the front when the voice of O'Connell was no longen heard in Ireland. He was succeeded by the Duffys, Mitchells, Meagher, and others,—men who loved liberty for themselves and their country, but were utterly destitute of sympathy with the cause of liberty in countries other than their own. One of the first utterances of John Mitchell on reaching the United States, from his exile and bondage, was a wish for a "slave plantation. well stocked with slaves."

Besides hearing Cobden, Bright, Peel, Disraeli, O'Connell, Lord John Russell, and other Parliamentary debaters, it was my good fortune to hear Lord Brougham when nearly at his best. He was then a little over sixty, and that for a British statesman is not considered old; and in his case there were thirty years of life still before him. He struck me as the most wonderful speaker of them all. How he was ever reported I cannot imagine. Listening to him, was like standing near the track of a railway train, drawn by a locomotive at the rate of forty miles an hour. You were riveted to the spot, charmed with the sublime spectacle of speed and power, but could give no description of the carriages, nor of the passengers at the windows. There was so much to see and hear, and so little time left the beholder and hearer to note particulars, that when this strange man sat down, you felt like one who had hastily passed through the wildering wonders of a world's exhibition. On the occasion of my listening to him, his speech was on the postal relations of England with the outside world, and he seemed to have a perfect knowledge of the postal arrangements of every nation in Europe, and, indeed, in the whole universe. He possessed the great advantage, so valuable to a Parliamentary debater, of being able to make all interruptions serve the purposes of his thought and speech, and carried on a dialogue with several persons without interrupting the rapid current of his reasoning. I had more curiosity to hear this man than any other in England, and he more than fulfilled my expectations.

While in England, I saw few literary celebrities, except William and Mary Howitt, and Sir John Bowering. I was invited to breakfast by the latter in company with Wm. Lloyd Garrison, and spent a delightful morning with him, chiefly as a listener to their conversation. Sir John was a poet, a statesman, and a diplomat, and had represented England as minister to China. He was full of interesting information, and had a charming way of imparting his knowledge. The conversation was about slavery, and about China, and as my knowledge was very slender about the "Flowery Kingdom," and its people, I was greatly interested in Sir John's description of the ideas and manners prevailing among them. According to him, the doctrine of substitution was carried so far in that country that men sometimes procured others to suffer even the penalty of death in their stead. Justice seemed not intent upon the punishment of the actual criminal, if only somebody was punished when the law was violated.

William and Mary Howitt were among the kindliest people I ever met. Their interest in America, and their well-known testimonies against slavery, made me feel much at home with them at their house in that part of London known as Clapham. Whilst stopping there, I met the Swedish poet and author—Hans Christian Andersen. He, like myself, was a guest, spending a few days. I saw but little of him, though under the same roof. He was singular in his appearance, and equally singular in his silence. His mind seemed to me all the while turned inwardly. He walked about the beautiful garden as one might in a dream. The Howitts had translated his works into English, and could of course address him in his own language. Possibly his bad English and my destitution of Swedish, may account for the fact of our mutual silence, and yet I observed he was much the same towards every one. Mr. and Mrs. Howitt were indefatigable writers. Two more industrious and kind-hearted people did not breathe. With all their literary work, they always had time to devote to strangers, and to all benevolent efforts, to ameliorate the condition of the poor and needy. Quakers though they were, they took deep interest in the Hutchinsons—Judson, John, Asa, and Abby, who were much at their house during my stay there. Mrs. Howitt not inaptly styled them a "Band of young apostles." They sang for the oppressed and the poor—for liberty and humanity.

Whilst in Edinburgh, so famous for its beauty, its educational institutions, its literary men, and its history, I had a very intense desire gratified—and that was to see and converse with George Combe, the eminent mental philosopher, and author of "Combe's Constitution of Man," a book which had been placed in my hands a few years before by Dr. Pelig Clark, of Rhode Island, the reading of which had relieved my path of many shadows. In company with George Thompson, James N. Buffum, and William L. Garrison, I had the honour to be invited by Mr. Combe to breakfast, and the occasion was one of the most delightful I met in dear old Scotland. Of course in the presence of such men, my part was a very subordinate one. I was a listener. Mr. Combe did the most of the talking, and did it so well, that nobody felt like interposing a word, except so far as to draw him on. He discussed the corn laws, and the proposal to reduce the hours of labour. He looked at all political and social questions through his peculiar mental science. His manner was remarkably quiet, and he spoke as not expecting opposition to his views. Phrenology explained everything to him, from the finite to the infinite, I look back to the morning spent with this singularly clear-headed man with much satisfaction.

It would detain the reader too long, and make this volume too large, to tell of the many kindnesses shown me while abroad, or even to mention all the great and noteworthy persons who gave me a friendly hand and a cordial welcome; but there is one other, now long gone to his rest, of whom a few words must be spoken, and that one was Thomas Clarkson—the last of the noble line of Englishmen who inaugurated the anti-slavery movement for England and the civilized world—the life-long friend and co-worker with Granville Sharpe, William Wilberforce, Thomas Fowell Buxton, and other leaders in that great reform which has nearly put an end to slavery in all parts of the globe. As in the case of George Combe, I went to see Mr. Clarkson in company with Messrs. Garrison and Thompson. They had by note advised him of our coming, and had received one in reply, bidding us welcome. We found the venerable object of our visit seated at a table, where he had been busily writing a letter to America against slavery; for, though in his eighty-seventh year, he continued to write. When we were presented to him, he rose to receive us. The scene was impressive. It was the meeting of two centuries. Garrison, Thompson, and myself were young men. After shaking hands with my two distinguished friends, and giving them welcome, he took one of my hands in both of his, and, in a tremulous voice, said, "God bless you, Frederick Douglass! I have given sixty years of my life to the emancipation of your people, and if I had sixty years more they should all be given to the same cause." Our stay was short with this great-hearted old man, He was feeble, and our presence greatly excited him, and we left the house with something of the feeling with which friends take final leave of a beloved friend at the edge of the grave.

Some notion may be formed of the difference in my feelings and circumstances while abroad, from an extract from one of a series of letters addressed by me to Mr. Garrison, and published in the Liberator. It was written on the 1st day of January, 1846.

"My Dear Friend Garrison,—

"Up to this time, I have given no direct expression of the views, feelings, and opinions which I have formed respecting the character and condition of the people of this land. I have refrained thus purposely. I wish to speak advisedly, and, in order to do this, I have waited till, I trust, experience has brought my opinion to an intelligent maturity. I have been thus careful, not because I think what I say will have much effect in shaping the opinions of the world, but because what influence I may possess, whether little or much, I wish to go in the right direction, and according to truth. I hardly need say that in speaking of Ireland, I shall be influenced by no prejudices in favour of America. I think my circumstances all forbid that. I have no end to serve, no creed to uphold, no government to defend; and as to nation, I belong to none. I have no protection at home, or resting-place abroad. The land of my birth welcomes me to her shores only as a slave, and spurns with contempt the idea of treating me differently; so that I am an outcast from the society of my childhood, and an outlaw in the land of my birth. 'I am a stranger with thee and a sojourner, as all my fathers were.' That men should be patriotic, is to me perfectly natural; and as a philosophical fact, I am able to give it an intellectual recognition. But no further can I go. If ever I had any patriotism, or any capacity for the feeling, it was whipped out of me long since by the lash of the American soul-drivers. In thinking of America, I sometimes find myself admiring her bright blue sky, her grand old woods, her fertile fields, her beautiful rivers, her mighty lakes, and star-crowned mountains. But my rapture is soon checked—my joy is soon turned to mourning. When I remember that all is cursed with the infernal spirit of slaveholding, robbery, and wrong; when I remember that with the waters of her noblest rivers, the tears of my brethren are borne to the ocean, disregarded and forgotten, and that her most fertile fields drink daily of the warm blood of my outraged sisters, I am filled with unutterable loathing, and led to reproach myself that anything could fall from my lips in praise of such a land. America will not allow her children to love her. She seems bent on compelling those who would be her warmest friends, to be her worst enemies. May God give her repentance before it is too late, is the ardent prayer of my heart. I will continue to pray, labour, and wait, believing that she cannot always be insensible to the dictates of justice, or deaf to the voice of humanity. My opportunities for learning the character and condition of the people of this land have been very great. I have travelled from the Hill of Howth to the Giant's Causeway, and from the Giant's Causeway to Cape Clear. During these travels I have met with much in the character and condition of the people to approve, and much to condemn; much that has thrilled me with pleasure, and much that has filled me with pain. I will not, in this letter, attempt to give any description of those scenes which give me pain. This I will do hereafter. I have enough, and more than your subscribers will be disposed to read at one time, of the bright side of the picture. I can truly say I have spent some of the happiest days of my life since landing in this country. I seem to have undergone a transformation. I live a new life. The warm and generous co-operation extended to me by the friends of my despised race; the prompt and liberal manner with which the Press has rendered me its aid; the glorious enthusiasm with which thousands have flocked to hear the cruel wrongs of my down-trodden and long-enslaved fellow countrymen pourtrayed; the deep sympathy for the slave, and the strong abhorrence of the slaveholder everywhere evinced; the cordiality with which members and ministers of various religious bodies, and of various shades of religious opinion have embraced me and lent me their aid; the kind hospitality constantly proffered me by persons of the highest rank in society; the spirit of freedom that seems to animate all with whom I come in contact, and the entire absence of everything that looks like prejudice against me, on account of the colour of my skin, contrasts so strongly with my long and bitter experience in the United States, that I look with wonder and amazement on the transition. In the Southern part of the United States, I was a slave— thought of and spoken of as property; in the language of law, 'held, taken, reputed, and adjudged to be a chattel in the hands of my owners and possessors, and their executors, administrators, and assigns, to all intents, constructions, and purposes, whatsoever.' (Brev. Digest., 224.) In the Northern States, a fugitive slave, liable to be hunted at any moment like a felon, and to be hurled into the terrible jaws of slavery—doomed by an inveterate prejudice against colour, to insult and outrage on every hand—Massachusetts out of the question— denied the privileges and courtesies common to others in the use of the most humble means of conveyance—shut out from the cabins on steamboats, refused admission to respectable hotels, caricatured, scorned, scoffed, mocked, and maltreated with impunity by any one—no matter how black his heart—so he has a white skin. But now behold the change! Eleven days and a half gone, and I have crossed three thousand miles of perilous deep. Instead of a democratic government, I am under a monarchical government. Instead of the bright, blue sky of America, I am covered with the soft, gray fog of the Emerald Isle. I breathe, and lo! the chattel becomes a man! I gaze around in vain for one who will question my equal humanity, claim me as a slave, or offer me an insult. I employ a cab—I am seated beside white people—I reach the hotel—I enter the same door—I am shown into the same parlour—I dine at the same table— and no one is offended. No delicate nose grows deformed in my presence. I find no difficulty here in obtaining admission into any place of worship, instruction, or amusement, on equal terms, with people as white as any I ever saw in the United States. I meet nothing to remind me of my complexion. I find myself regarded and treated at every turn with the kindness and deference paid to white people. When I go to church I am met by no upturned nose and scornful lip, to tell me—'We don't allow niggers in here.' "

I remember about two years ago there was in Boston, near the south-west corner of Boston Common, a menagerie. I had long desired to see such a collection as I understood was being exhibited there. Never having had an opportunity while a slave, I resolved to seize this, and as I approached the entrance to gain admission, I was told by the door-keeper, in a harsh and contemptuous tone, "We don't allow niggers in here." I also remember attending a revival meeting in the Rev. Henry Jackson's meeting-house, at New Bedford, and going up the broad aisle for a seat, I was met by a good deacon, who told me, in a pious tone, "We don't allow niggers in here." Soon after my arrival in New Bedford, from the South, I had a strong desire to attend the Lyceum, but was told, "They don't allow niggers there." While passing from New York to Boston on the steamer "Massachusetts," on the night of the 9th of December, 1843, when chilled almost through with the cold, I went into the cabin to get a little warm. I was soon touched upon the shoulder, and told, "We don't allow niggers in here." A week or two before leaving the United States, I had a meeting appointed at Weymouth, the house of that glorious band of true abolitionists—the Weston family and others. On attempting to take a seat in the omnibus to that place, I was told by the driver—and I never shall forget his fiendish hate—"I don't allow niggers in here." Thank heaven for the respite I now enjoy! I had been in Dublin but a few days when a gentleman of great respectability kindly offered to conduct me through all the public buildings of that beautiful city, and soon afterwards I was invited by the Lord Mayor to dine with him. What a pity there was not some democratic Christian at the door of his splendid mansion to bark out at me approach, "They don't allow niggers in here!" The truth is, the people here know nothing of the republican negro-hate prevalent in our glorious land. They measure and esteem men according to their moral and intellectual worth, and not according to the colour of their skin. Whatever may be said of the aristocracies here, there is none based on the colour of a man's skin. This species of aristocracy belongs pre-eminently to "the land of the free, and the home of the brave." I have never found it abroad in any but Americans. It sticks to them wherever they go. They find it almost as hard to get rid of as to get rid of their skins.

The second day after my arrival in Liverpool, in company with my friend Buffum, and several other friends, I went to Eaton Hall, the residence of the Marquis of Westminster, one of the most splendid buildings in England. On approaching the door, I found several of our American passengers who came out with us in the "Cambria," waiting for admission, as but one party was allowed in the house at a time. We all had to wait till the company within came out, and of all the faces expressive of chagrin, those of the Americans were pre-eminent. They looked as sour as vinegar, and as bitter as gall, when they found I was to be admitted on equal terms with themselves. When the door was opened, I walked in on a footing with my white fellow-citizens, and, from all I could see, I had as much attention paid me by the servants who showed us through the house, as any with a paler skin. As I walked through the building, the statuary did not fall down, the pictures did not leap from their places, the doors did not refuse to open, and the servants did not say, "We don't allow niggers in here."

My time and labours while abroad were divided between England, Ireland, Scotland, and Wales. Upon this experience alone I might fill a volume. Amongst the few incidents which space will permit me to mention, and one which attracted much attention and provoked much discussion in America, was a brief statement made by me in the World's Temperance Convention, held in Covent Garden Theatre, London, August 7, 1846. The United States was largely represented in this convention by eminent divines, mostly doctors of divinity. They had come to England for the double purpose of attending the World's Evangelical Alliance, and the World's Temperance Convention. In the former these ministers were endeavouring to procure endorsement for the Christian character of slaveholders; and, naturally enough, they were adverse to the exposure of slaveholding practices. It was not pleasant to them to see one of the slaves running at large in England, and telling the other side of the story. The Rev. Samuel Hanson Cox, D.D., of Brooklyn, N. Y., was especially disturbed at my presence and speech in the Temperance Convention. I will give here, first, the reverend gentleman's version of the occasion in a letter from him as it appeared in the New York Evangelist, the organ of his denomination. After a description of the place, Covent Garden Theatre, and the speakers, he says:

"They all advocated the same cause, showed a glorious unity of thought and feeling, and the effect was constantly raised—the moral scene was superb and glorious—when Frederick Douglass, the coloured abolition agitator and ultraist, came to the platform, and so spake, à la mode, as to ruin the influence of almost all that preceded! He lugged in anti-slavery, or abolition, no doubt prompted to it by some of the politic ones, who can use him to do what they would not themselves adventure to do in person. He is supposed to have been well paid for the abomination.

"What a perversion, an abuse, an iniquity against the law of reciprocal righteousness, to call thousands together, and get them, some certain ones, to seem conspicuous and devoted for one sole and grand object, and then all at once, with obliquity, open an avalanche on them for some imputed evil or monstrosity, for which, whatever be the wound or injury inflicted, they were both too fatigued and hurried with surprise, and too straightened for time to be properly prepared. I say it is a streak of meanness! It is abominable! On this occasion Mr. Douglass allowed himself to denounce America and all its temperance societies together, as a grinding community of the enemies of his people; said evil, with no alloy of good, concerning the whole of us, was perfectly indiscriminate in his severities; talked of the American delegates, and to them, as if he had been our schoolmaster, and we his docile and devoted pupils, and launched his revengeful missiles at our country without one palliative, and as if not a Christian or a true anti-slavery man lived in the whole of the United States. The fact is, the man has been petted, and flattered, and used, and paid by certain abolitionists, not unknown to us, of the ne plus ultra stamp, till he forgets himself; and, though he may gratify his own impulses, and those of old Adam in others, yet sure I am that all this is just the way to ruin his own influence, to defeat his own object, and to do mischief—not good—to the very cause he professes to love. With the single exception of one cold-hearted parricide, whose character I abhor, and whom I will not name, and who has, I fear, no feeling of true patriotism or piety within him, all the delegates from our country were together wounded and indignant. No wonder at it. I write freely. It was not done in a corner. It was inspired, I believe, from beneath, and not from above. It was adapted to re-kindle on both sides of the Atlantic the flames of national exasperation and war. And this is the game which Mr. Frederick Douglass and his silly patrons are playing in England and in Scotland, and wherever they can find 'some mischief still for idle hands to do.' I came here his sympathizing friend; I am such no more, as I know him. My own opinion is increasing that this spirit must be exorcised out of England and America before any substantial good can be effected for the cause of the slave. It is adapted only to make bad worse, and to inflame the passions of indignant millions to an incurable resentment. None but an ignoramus or a madman could think that this way was that of the inspired apostles of the son of God. It may gratify the feelings of a self-deceived and malignant few, but it will do no good in any direction—least of all to the poor slave! It is short-sighted, impulsive, partisan, reckless, and tending only to sanguinary ends. None of this with men of sense and principle.

"We all wanted to reply, but it was too late; the whole theatre seemed taken with the spirit of the Ephesian uproar; they were furious and boisterous in the extreme, and Mr. Kirk could hardly obtain a moment, though many were desirous in his behalf to say a few words, as he did, very calmly and properly, that the cause of temperance was not at all responsible for slavery, and had no connection with it.

Now, to show the reader what ground there was for this tirade from the pen of this eminent divine, and how easily Americans parted with their candour and self-possession when slavery was mentioned adversely, I will give here the head and front of my offence. Let it be borne in mind that this was a world's convention of the friends of temperance. It was not an American or a white man's convention but one composed of men of all nations and races; and as such, the convention had the right to know all about the temperance cause in every part of the world, and especially to know what hindrances were interposed in any part of the world, to its progress. I was perfectly in order in speaking precisely as I did. I was neither an "intruder," nor "out of order." I had been invited and advertised to speak by the same committee that invited Doctors Beecher, Cox, Patton, Kirk, Marsh, and others, and my speech was perfectly within the limits of good order, as the following report will show:

"Mr. Chairman—Ladies and Gentlemen:—

"I am not a delegate to this convention. Those who would have been most likely to elect me as a delegate could not, because they are to-night held in abject slavery in the United States. Sir, I regret that I cannot fully unite with the American delegates in their patriotic eulogies of America, and American temperance societies. I cannot do so for this good reason: there are at this moment three millions of the American population, by slavery and prejudice, placed entirely beyond the pale of American temperance societies. The three million slaves are completely excluded by slavery, and four hundred thousand free coloured people are almost as completely excluded by an inveterate prejudice against them, on account of their colour. [Cries of shame! shame!]

"I do not say these things to wound the feelings of the American delegates. I simply mention them in their presence and before this audience, that, seeing how you regard this hatred and neglect of the coloured people, they may be inclined on their return home to enlarge the field of their temperance operations, and embrace within the scope of their influence, my long-neglected race. [Great cheering, and some confusion on the platform.] Sir, to give you some idea of the difficulties and obstacles in the way of the temperance reformation of the coloured population in the United States, allow me to state a few facts.

"About the year 1840, a few intelligent, sober, and benevolent coloured gentlemen in Philadelphia, being acquainted with the appalling ravages of intemperance among a numerous class of coloured people in that city, and, finding themselves neglected and excluded from white societies, organized societies among themselves, appointed committees, sent out agents, built temperance halls, and were earnestly and successfully rescuing many from the fangs of intemperance.

"The cause went nobly on till August 1, 1842, the day when England gave liberty to eight hundred thousand souls in the West Indies. The coloured temperance societies selected this day to march in procession through the city, in the hope that such a demonstration would have the effect of bringing others into their ranks. They formed their procession, unfurled their teetotal banners, and proceeded to the accomplishment of their purpose. It was a delightful sight. But, sir, they had not proceeded down two streets before they were brutally assailed by a ruthless mob; their banner was torn down, and trampled in the dust, their ranks broken up, their persons beaten and pelted with stones and brickbats. One of their churches was burned to the ground, and their best temperance hall utterly demolished." ["Shame! shame! shame!" from the audience—great confusion, and cries of "Sit down" from the American delegates on the platform.]

In the midst of this commotion, the chairman tapped me on the shoulder, and, whispering, informed me that the fifteen minutes allotted to each speaker had expired; whereupon the vast audience simultaneously shouted: "Don't interrupt!" "don't dictate!" "go on!" "go on!" "Douglass!" "Douglass!" This continued several minutes, when I proceeded as follows. "Kind friends, I beg to assure you that the chairman has not in the slightest degree sought to alter any sentiment which I am anxious to express on this occasion. He was simply reminding me that the time allotted for me to speak had expired. I do not wish to occupy one moment more than is allotted to other speakers. Thanking your for your kind indulgence, I will take my seat." Proceeding to do so again, "there were cries of "Go on!" "go on!" with which I complied for a few minutes, but without saying anything more that particularly related to the coloured people of America. I did not allow the letter of Dr. Cox to go unanswered through the American journals, but promptly exposed its unfairness. That letter is too long for insertion here. A part of it was published in the Evangelist, and in many other papers, both in America and in England. Our eminent divine made no rejoinder, and his silence was regarded at the time as an admission of defeat.

Another interesting circumstance connected with my visit to England, was the position of the Free Church of Scotland with the great Doctors Chalmers, Cunningham, and Candlish at its head. That church had settled for itself the question which was frequently asked by the opponents of abolition at home—"What have we to do with slavery?" by accepting contributions from slaveholders; i.e., receiving the price of blood into its treasury, with which to build churches and pay ministers for preaching the gospel; and worse than this, when honest John Murray of Bowlein Bay, with William Smeal, Andrew Paton, Frederick Card, and other sterling anti-slavery men in Glasgow, denounced the transaction as disgraceful, and shocking to the religious sentiment of Scotland, this Church, through its leading divines, instead of repenting and seeking to amend the mistake into which it had fallen, caused that mistake to become a flagrant sin by undertaking to defend, in the name of God and the Bible, the principle not only of taking the money of slave-dealers to build churches and thus extend the gospel, but of holding fellowship with the traffickers in human flesh. This, the reader will see, brought up the whole question of slavery, and opened the way to its full discussion. I have never seen a people more deeply moved than were the people of Scotland on this very question. Public meeting succeeded public meeting, speech after speech, pamphlet after pamphlet, editorial after editorial, sermon after sermon, lashed the concientious Scotch people into a perfect furore. "Send back the money!" was indignantly shouted from Greenock to Edinburgh, and from Edinburgh to Aberdeen. George Thompson of London, Henry C. Wright, J. N. Buffum, and myself from America, were of course, on the anti-slavery side, and Chalmers, Cunningham, and Cavendish, on the other. Dr. Cunningham was the most powerful debater on the slavery side of the question, Mr. Thompson the ablest on the anti-slavery side. A scene occurred between these two men, a parallel to which I think I have never witnessed before or since. It was caused by a single exclamation on the part of Mr. Thompson, and was on this wise:

The general assembly of the Free Church was in progress at Cannon Mills, Edinburgh. The building would hold twenty-five hundred persons, and on this occasion was densely packed, notice having been given that Doctors Cunningham and Candlish would speak that day in defence of the relations of the Free Church of Scotland to slavery in America. Messrs. Thompson, Buffum, myself and a few other anti-slavery friends attended, but sat at such distance and in such position as not to be observed from the platform. The excitement was intense, having been greatly increased by a series of meetings held by myself and friends, in the most splendid hall in that most beautiful city, just previous to this meeting of the general assembly. "Send back the money!" in large capitals, stared from every street corner; "Send back the money!" adorned the broad flags of the pavement; "Send back the money!" was the chorus of the popular street-song; "Send back the money!" was the heading of leading editorials in the daily newspapers. This day, at Cannon Mills, the great doctors of the church were to give an answer to this loud and stern demand. Men of all parties and sects were most eager to hear. Something great was expected. The occasion was great, the men were great, and great speeches were expected from them.

In addition to the outward pressure there was wavering within. The conscience of the Church itself was not at ease. A dissatisfaction with the position of the Church touching slavery was sensibly manifest among the members, and something must be done to counteract this untoward influence. The great Dr. Chalmers was in feeble health at the time, so his most potent eloquence could not now be summoned to Cannon Mills, as formerly. He whose voice had been so powerful as to rend asunder and dash down the granite walls of the Established Church of Scotland, and to lead a host in solemn procession from it as from a doomed city, was now old and enfeebled. Besides, he had said his word on this very question, and it had not silenced the clamour without nor stilled the anxious heavings within. The occasion was momentous, and felt to be so. The Church was in a perilous condition. A change of some sort must take place, or she must go to pieces. To stand where she did was impossible. The whole weight of the matter fell on Cunningham and Candlish. No shoulders in the Church were broader than theirs; and I must say, badly as I detested the principles laid down and defended by them, I was compelled to acknowledge the vast mental endowments of the men.

Cunningham rose, and his rising was the signal for tumultuous applause. It may be said that this was scarcely in keeping with the solemnity of the occasion, but to me it served to increase its grandeur and gravity. The applause, though tumultuous, was not joyous. It seemed to me, as it thundered up from the vast audience, like the fall of an immense shaft, flung from shoulders already galled by its crushing weight. It was like saying "Doctor, we have borne this burden long enough, and willingly fling it upon you. Since it was you who brought it upon us, take it now and do what you will with it, for we are too weary to bear it."

The Doctor proceeded with his speech—abounding in logic, learning, and eloquence, and apparently bearing down all opposition; but at the moment—the fatal moment—when he was just bringing all his arguments to a point—that point being that "neither Jesus Christ nor His holy apostles regarded slaveholding as a sin"—George Thompson, in a clear, sonorous, but rebuking voice, broke the deep stillness of the audience, exclaiming "Hear! Hear! Hear!" The effect of this simple and common exclamation is almost incredible. It was as if a granite wall had been suddenly flung up against the advancing current of a mighty river. For a moment speaker and audience were brought to a dead silence. Both the Doctor and his hearers seemed appalled by the audacity, as well as the fitness of the rebuke. At length a shout went up to the cry of "Put him out!" Happily no one attempted to execute this cowardly order, and the discourse went on; but not as before. The exclamation of Thompson must have re-echoed a thousand times in the memory of the Doctor, who, during the remainder of his speech, was utterly unable to recover from the blow. The deed was done, however; the pillars of the

Church—the proud Free Church of Scotland—were committed, and the humility of repentance was absent. The Free Church held on to the blood-stained money, and continued to justify itself in its position.

One good result followed the conduct of the Free Church: it furnished an occasion for making the people thoroughly acquainted with the character of slavery, and for arraying against it the moral and religious sentiment of that country; therefore, while we did not procure the sending back of the money, we were amply justified, by the good which really did result from our labours.

I must add one word in regard to the Evangelical Alliance. This was an attempt to form a union of all Evangelical Christians throughout the world, and which held its first session in London, in the year 1846, at the time of the World's Temperance Convention there. Some sixty or seventy ministers from America attended this convention, the object of some of them being to weave a world-wide garment with which to clothe evangelical slaveholders; and in this they partially succeeded. But the question of slavery was too large a question to be finally disposed of by the Evangelical Alliance, and from its judgment we appealed to the judgment of the people of Great Britain, with the happiest effect—this effort of our countrymen to shield the character of slaveholders serving to open a way to the British ear for antislavery discussion.

I may mention here an incident somewhat amusing and instructive, as it serves to illustrate how easily Americans could set aside their notoriously inveterate prejudice against colour, when it stood in the way of their wishes, or when in an atmosphere which made their prejudice unpopular and un-Christian.

At the entrance to the House of Commons I had one day been conversing for a few moments with Lord Morpeth, and just as I was parting from him I felt an emphatic push against my arm, and, looking around, I saw at my elbow the Rev. Dr. Kirk of Boston. "Introduce me to Lord Morpeth," he said. "Certainly," said I, and introduced him; not without remembering, however, that the amiable Doctor would scarcely have asked such a favour of a coloured man at home.

The object of my labours in Great Britain was the concentration of the moral and religious sentiment of its people against American slavery. To this end, I visited and lectured in nearly all the large towns and cities in the United Kingdom, and enjoyed many favourable opportunities for observation and information. I should like to write a book on those countries, if for nothing else, to make grateful mention of the many dear friends whose benevolent actions towards me are ineffaceably stamped upon my memory, and warmly treasured in my heart. To these friends, I owe my freedom in the United States.

Mrs. Ellen Richardson, an excellent member of the society of friends, assisted by her sister-in-law, Mrs. Henry Richardson,—a lady devoted to every good word and work—the friend of the Indian and the African, conceived the plan of raising a fund to effect my ransom from slavery. They corresponded with Hon. Walter Forward of Pennsylvania, and through him, ascertained that Captain Auld would take one hundred and fifty pounds sterling for me; and this sum they promptly raised, and paid for my liberation; placing the papers of my manumission in my hands, before they would tolerate the idea of my return to my native land. To this commercial transaction, to this blood-money, I owe my immunity from the operation of the fugitive slave law of 1793, and also from that of 1850. The whole affair speaks for itself, and needs no comment now that slavery has ceased to exist in the United States, and is not likely ever again to be revived.

Some of my uncompromising anti-slavery friends in America failed to see the wisdom of this commercial transaction, and were not pleased that I consented to it, even by my silence. They thought it a violation of anti-slavery principles, conceding the right of property in man, and a wasteful expenditure of money. For myself, viewing it simply in the light of a ransom, or as money extorted by a robber, and my liberty being of more value to me than one hundred and fifty pounds sterling, I could not see either a violation of the laws of morality or of economy. It is true, I was not in the possession of my claimants, and could have remained in England, for my friends would have generously assisted me in establishing myself there. To this I could not consent. I felt it my duty to labour and suffer with my oppressed people in my native land. Considering all the circumstances, the Fugitive Slave Bill included, I think now as then, that the very best thing was done in letting Master Hugh have the money, and thus leaving me free to return to my appropriate field of labour. Had I been a private person, with no relations or duties other than those of a personal and family nature, I should not have consented to the payment of so large a sum, for the privilege of living securely under our glorious republican (?) form of government. I could have lived elsewhere, or perhaps might have been unobserved even in the United States; but I had become somewhat notorious and withal quite as unpopular in some directions as notorious, and I was therefore, much exposed to arrest and capture.*

Having remained abroad nearly two years, and being about to return to America, not as I left it—a slave—but a freeman, prominent friends of the cause of emancipation intimated their intention to present me with a testimonial, both on grounds of personal regard for me, and also of the cause to which they were so ardently devoted. How such a project would have succeeded I do not know, but many reasons led me to prefer that my friends should simply give me the means of obtaining a printing press and materials, to enable me to start a paper, advocating the interests of my enslaved and oppressed people. I told them that perhaps the greatest hindrance to the adoption of abolition principles by the people of the United States was the low estimate everywhere in that country placed upon the negro as a man; that because of his assumed natural inferiority, people reconciled themselves to his enslavement and oppression, as being inevitable if not desirable. The grand thing to be done, therefore, was to change this estimation, by disproving his inferiority and demonstrating his capacity for a more exalted civilization than slavery and prejudice had assigned him. In my judgment, a tolerably well-conducted press in the hands of persons of the despised race, would, by calling out and making them acquainted with their own latent powers, by enkindling their hope of a future, and developing their moral force, prove a most powerful means of removing prejudice and awakening an interest in them. At that time there was not a single newspaper regularly published by the coloured people in the country, though many attempts had been made to establish such, and had from one cause or another failed. These views I laid before my friends. The result was, that nearly two thousand five hundred dollars were speedily raised towards my establishing such a paper as I had indicated. For this prompt and generous assistance, rendered upon my bare suggestion, without any personal effort on my part, I shall never cease to feel deeply grateful, and the thought of fulfilling the expectations of the dear friends who had given me this evidence of their confidence, was an abiding inspiration for persevering exertion.

Proposing to leave England, and turning my face towards America in the spring of 1847, I was painfully reminded of the kind of life which awaited me on my arrival. For the first time in the many months spent abroad, I met with proscription on account of my colour. While in London I had purchased a ticket, and secured a berth, for returning home in the "Cambria"—the steamer in which I had come from thence—and paid therefor the round sum of forty pounds, nineteen shillings sterling. This was first cabin fare; but on going on board I found that the Liverpool agent had ordered my berth to be given to another, and forbidden my entering the saloon. It was rather hard after having enjoyed for so long a time equal social privileges, after dining with persons of great literary, social, political, and religious eminence, and never, during the whole time, having met with a single word, look, or gesture, which gave the slightest reason to think my colour was an offence to anybody—now to be cooped up in the stern of the "Cambria," and denied the right to enter the saloon, lest my presence should disturb some democratic fellow-passenger. The reader can easily imagine what must have been my feelings under such an indignity.

This contemptible conduct met with stern rebuke from the British Press. The London Times, and other leading journals throughout the United Kingdom, held up the outrage to unmitigated condemnation. So good an opportunity for calling out British sentiment on the subject had not before occurred, and it was fully embraced. The result was, that Mr. Cunard came out with a letter expressive of his regret, and promising that the like indignity should never occur again on his steamers; which promise, I believe, has been faithfully kept.

CHAPTER VII: TRIUMPHS AND TRIALS.

New experiences—Painful disagreement of opinion with old friends—Final decision to publish my paper in Rochester—Its fortunes—Change in my own views regarding the Constitution of the United States—Fidelity to conviction—Loss of old friends—Support of new ones—Loss of house, etc., by fire—Triumphs and trials—Underground railroad—Incidents.

PREPARED as I was to meet with many trials and perplexities on reaching home, one of which I little dreamed was awaiting me. My plans for future usefulness, as indicated in the last chapter, were all settled, and in imagination I already saw myself wielding my pen as well as my voice in the great work of renovating the public mind, and building up a public sentiment, which should send slavery to the grave, and restore to "liberty and the pursuit of happiness" the people with whom I had suffered.

My friends in Boston had been informed of what I was intending, and I expected to find them favourably disposed towards my cherished enterprise. In this I was mistaken. They had many reasons against it. First, no such paper was needed; secondly, it would interfere with my usefulness as a lecturer; thirdly, I was better fitted to speak than to write; fourthly, the paper could not succeed. This opposition from a quarter so highly esteemed, and to which I had been accustomed to look for advice and direction, caused me not only to hesitate, but inclined me to abandon the undertaking. All previous attempts to establish such a journal having failed, I feared lest I should but add another to the list, and thus contribute another proof of the mental deficiencies of my race. Very much that was said of me in respect to my imperfect literary attainments, I felt to be most painfully true. The unsuccessful projectors of all former attempts had been my superiors in point of education, and if they had failed how could I hope for success? Yet I did hope for success, and persisted in the undertaking, encouraged by my English friends to go forward.

I can easily pardon those who saw in my persistence, an unwarrantable ambition and presumption. I was but nine years escaped from slavery. In many phases of mental experience I was but nine years old. That one under such circumstances should aspire to establish a printing press, surrounded by an educated people, might well be considered unpractical if not ambitious. My American friends looked at me with astonishment. "A wood-sawyer" offering himself to the public as an editor! A slave, brought up in the depths of ignorance, assuming to instruct the highly civilized people of the North in the principles of liberty, justice, and humanity! The thing looked absurd. Nevertheless I persevered. I felt that the want of education, great as it was, could be overcome by study, and that wisdom would come by experience; and further, what was perhaps the most controlling consideration, I thought that an intelligent public, knowing my early history, would easily pardon the many deficiencies which I well knew my paper must exhibit. The most distressing part of it all, was the offence which I saw I must give my friends of the old anti-slavery organization, by what seemed to them a reckless disregard of their opinion and advice. I am not sure that I was not under the influence of something like a slavish adoration of these good people, and I laboured hard to convince them that my way of thinking about the matter was the right one, but without success.

From motives of peace, instead of issuing my paper in Boston, among New England friends, I went to Rochester, N.Y., among strangers, where the local circulation of my paper—"The North Star"—would not interfere with that of the Liberator, or the Anti-Slave Standard; for I was then a faithful disciple of Wm. Lloyd Garrison, and fully committed to his doctrine touching the pro-slavery character of the Constitution of the United States, also the non-voting principle, of which he was the known and distinguished advocate. With him, I held it to be the first duty of the non-slaveholding States to dissolve the union with the slaveholding States, and hence my cry, like his, was "No union with slaveholders." With these views I came into western New York, and during the first four years of my labours there, I advocated them with pen and tongue, to the best of my ability. After a time, a careful reconsideration of the subject convinced me that there was no necessity for dissolving the "union between the Northern and Southern States;" that to seek this dissolution was no part of my duty as an abolitionist; that to abstain from voting was to refuse to exercise a legitimate and powerful means for abolishing slavery; and that the Constitution of the United States not only contained no guarantees in favour of slavery, but on the contrary, was in its letter and spirit an anti-slavery instrument, demanding the abolition of slavery as a condition of its own existence, as the supreme law of the land.

This radical change in my opinions produced a corresponding change in my action. To those with whom I had been in agreement and in sympathy, I came to be in opposition. What they held to be a great and important truth, I now looked upon as a dangerous error. A very natural, but to me a very painful thing, now happened. Those who could not see any honest reasons for changing their views, as I had done, could not easily see any such reasons for my change, and the common punishment of apostates was mine.

My first opinions were naturally derived and honestly entertained. Brought directly, when I escaped from slavery, into contact with abolitionists who regarded the Constitution as a slaveholding instrument, and finding their views supported by the united and entire history of every department of the Government, it is not strange that I assumed the Constitution to be just what these friends made it seem to be. I was bound not only by their superior knowledge to take their opinions in respect to this subject, as the true ones, but also because I had no means of showing their unsoundness. But for the responsibility of conducting a public journal, and the necessity imposed upon me of meeting opposite views from abolitionists outside of New England, I should in all probability have remained firm in my disunion views. My new circumstances compelled me to re-think the whole subject, and study with some care not only the just and proper rules of legal interpretation, but the origin, design, nature, rights, powers, and duties of civil governments, and also the relations which human beings sustain to it. By such a course of thought and reading I was conducted to the conclusion that the Constitution of the United States—inaugurated "to form a more perfect union, establish justice, insure domestic tranquillity, provide for the common defence, promote the general welfare, and secure the blessings of liberty"—could not well have been designed at the same time to maintain and perpetuate a system of rapine and murder, like slavery, especially as not one word can be found in the Constitution to authorize such a belief. Then, again, if the declared purposes of an instrument are to govern the meaning of all its parts and details, as they clearly should, the Constitution of our country is our warrant for the abolition of slavery in every State of the Union. It would require much time and space to set forth the arguments which demonstrated to my mind the unconstitutionality of slavery; but being convinced of the fact, my duty was plain upon this point in the further conduct of my paper. The North Star was a large sheet, published weekly, at a cost of $80 per week, and an average circulation of 3,000 subscribers. There were many times, when in my experience as editor and publisher, I was very hard pressed for money, but by one means or another I succeeded so well as to keep my pecuniary engagements, and to keep my anti-slavery banner steadily flying during all the conflict from the autumn of 1847 till the union of the States was assured, and emancipation was a fact accomplished. I had friends abroad as well as at home who helped me liberally. I can never be too grateful to the Rev. Russell Lunt Carpenter and to Mrs. Carpenter, for the moral and material aid they tendered me through all the vicissitudes of my paper enterprise. But to no one person was I more indebted for substantial assistance than to Mrs. Julia Griffiths Crofts. She came to my relief when my paper had nearly absorbed all my means, and was heavily in debt, and when I had mortgaged my house to raise money to meet current expenses; and by her energetic and effective management, in a single year enabled me to extend the circulation of my paper from 2,000 to 4,000 copies, pay off the debts and lift the mortgage from my house. Her industry was equal to her devotion. She seemed to rise with every emergency, and her resources appeared inexhaustible. I shall never cease to remember with sincere gratitude the assistance rendered me by this noble lady, and I mention her here in the desire in some humble measure to "give honour to whom honour is due." During the first three or four years my paper was published under the name of The North Star. It was subsequently changed to Frederick Douglass' Paper in order to distinguish it from the many papers with "Stars" in their titles. There were "North Stars," "Morning Stars," "Evening Stars," and I know not how many other stars in the newspaper firmament, and some confusion arose naturally enough in distinguishing between them; for this reason, and also because some of these stars were older than my star I felt that mine, not theirs, ought to be the one to "go out."

Of course there were moral forces operating against me in Rochester, as well as material ones. There were those who regarded the publication of a "Negro paper" in that beautiful city as a blemish and a misfortune. The New York Herald, true to the spirit of the times, counselled the people of the place to throw my printing press into Lake Ontario, and to banish me to Canada; and while they were not quite prepared for this violence, it was plain that many of them did not well relish my presence amongst them. This feeling, however, wore away gradually, as the people knew more of me and my works. I lectured every Sunday evening during an entire winter in the beautiful Corinthian Hall, then owned by Wm. R. Reynolds, Esq., who though he was not an abolitionist, was a lover of fair-play, and was willing to allow me to be heard. If in these lectures I did not make abolitionists. I did succeed in making tolerant and moral atmosphere in Rochester; so much so, indeed, that I came to feel as much at home there as I had ever done in the most friendly parts of New England. I had been at work there with my paper but a few years before coloured travellers told me that they felt the influence of my labours when they came within fifty miles. I did not rely alone upon what I could do by the paper, but would write all day, then take a train to Victor, Farmington, Canandaigua, Geneva, Waterloo, Batavia, or Buffalo, or elsewhere, and speak in the evening, returning home afterwards or early in the morning, to be again at my desk writing or mailing papers. There were times when I almost thought my Boston friends were right in dissuading me from my newspaper project. But looking back to those nights and days of toil and thought, compelled often to do work for which I had no educational preparation, I have come to think that, under the circumstances it was the best school possible for me. It obliged me to think and read, it taught me to express my thoughts clearly, and was perhaps better han any other course I could have adopted. Besides, it made it necessary for me to lean upon myself, and not upon the heads of our anti-slavery church;—to be a principal, and not an agent. I had an audience to speak to every week, and must say something worth their hearing, or cease to speak altogether. There is nothing like the lash and sting of necessity to make a man work, and my paper furnished this motive power. More than one gentleman from the South, when stopping at Niagara, came to see me, that they might know for themselves if I could indeed write, having, as they said, believed it impossible that an uneducated fugitive slave could write the articles attributed to me. I found it hard to get credit in some quarters either for what I wrote or what I said. While there was nothing very profound or learned in either, the low estimate of Negro possibilities induced the belief that both my editorials and my speeches were written by white persons. I doubt if this scepticism does not still linger in the minds of some of my democratic fellow-citizens.

The 2nd of June, 1872, brought me a very grievous loss. My house in Rochester was burned to the ground, and among other other things of value, twelve volumes of my paper, covering the period from 1848 to 1860, was devoured by the flames. I have never been able to replace them, and the loss is immeasurable. Only a few weeks before, I had been invited to send these bound volumes to the library of Harvard University, where they would have been preserved in a fire-proof building, and the result of my procrastination attests the wisdom of more than one proverb. Outside the years embraced in the late tremendous war, there has been no period, more pregnant with great events, or better suited to call out the best mental and moral energies of men, than that covered by these lost volumes. If I have at any time said or written that which is worth remembering or repeating, I must have said such things between the years 1848 and 1860, and my paper was a chronicle of most of what I said during that time. Within that space we had the great Free Soil Convention at Buffalo, the nomination of Martin Van Buren, the Fugitive Slave Law, the 7th March Speech by Daniel Webster, the Dred Scott decision, the repeal of the Missouri Compromise, the Kansas Nebraska Bill, the border war in Kansas, the John Brown raid upon Harper's Ferry, and a part of the War against the Rebellion, with much else, well calculated to fire the souls of men having one spark of Liberty and Patriotism within them. I have only fragments now, of all the work accomplished during these twelve years, and must cover this chasm, as best I can, from memory and the incidental items which I am able to glean from various sources. Two volumes of the North Star have been kindly supplied me, by my friend, Marshall Pierce, of Saco, Me. He had these carefully preserved and bound in one cover and sent to me in Washington. He was one of the most systematically careful men of all my anti-slavery friends, for I doubt if another entire volume of the paper exists.

One important branch of my anti-slavery work in Rochester, in addition to that of speaking and writing against slavery, must not be forgotten or omitted. My position gave me the chance of hitting that old enemy some telling blows, in another direction than these. I was on the southern border of Lake Ontario, and the Queen's Dominions were right over the way—and my prominence as an abolitionist, and as the editor of an anti-slavery paper, naturally made me the station master and conductor of the underground railroad passing through this goodly city. Secrecy and concealment were necessary conditions to the successful operation of this railroad, and hence its prefix "underground." My agency was all the more exciting and interesting, because not altogether free from danger. I could take no step in it without exposing myself to fine and imprisonment, for these were the penalties imposed by the Fugitive Slave Law, for feeding, harbouring, or otherwise assisting a slave to escape from his master; but in face of this fact, I can say, I never did more congenial, attractive, fascinating, and satisfactory work. True, as a means of destroying slavery, it was like an attempt to bail out the ocean with a teaspoon, but the thought that there was one less slave, and one more freeman,—having myself been a slave, and a fugitive slave—brought to my heart unspeakable joy. On one occasion I had eleven fugitives at the same time under my roof, and it was necessary for them to remain with me, until I could collect sufficient money to get them on to Canada. It was the largest number I ever had at any one time, and I had some difficulty in providing so many with food and shelter, but as may well be imagined, they were not very fastidious in either direction, and were well content with very plain food, and a strip of carpet on the floor for a bed, or a place on the straw in the barn loft.

The underground railroad had many branches; but that one with which I was connected had its main stations in Baltimore, Wilmington, Philadelphia, New York, Albany, Syracuse, Rochester, and St. Catharines, Canada. It is not necessary to tell who were the principal agents in Baltimore, Thomas Garrett was the agent in Wilmington; Melloe McKim, William Still, Robert Purvis, Edward M. Davis, and others did the work in Philadelphia; David Ruggles, Isaac T. Hooper, Napolian, and others, in New York City; the Misses Mott and Stephen Myers, were forwarders from Albany; Revs. Samuel J. May and J. W. Loguen, were the agents in Syracuse; and J. P. Morris and myself received and despatched passengers from Rochester to Canada, where they were received by the Rev. Hiram Wilson. When a party arrived in Rochester, it was the business of Mr. Morris and myself to raise funds with which to pay their passages to St. Catharines, and it is due to truth to state, that we seldom called in vain upon whig or democrat for help. Men were better than their theology, and truer to humanity, than to their politics, or their offices.

On one occasion while a slave master was in the office of a United States commissioner, procuring the papers necessary for the arrest and rendition of three young men who had escaped from Maryland, one of whom was under my roof at the time, another at Farmington, and the other at work on the farm of Asa Anthony just a little outside the city limits, the law partner of the commissioner, then a distinguished democrat, sought me out, and told me what was going on in his office, and urged me by all means to get these young men out of the way of their pursuers and claimants. Of course no time was to be lost. A swift horseman was despatched to Farmington, eighteen miles distant, another to Asa Anthony's farm about three miles, and another to my house on the south side of the city, and before the papers could be served, all three of the young men were on the free waves of Lake Ontario, bound to Canada. In writing to their old master, they had dated their letter at Rochester, though they had taken the precaution to send it to Canada to be mailed, but this blunder in the date had betrayed their whereabouts, so that the hunters were at once on their tracks.

So numerous were the fugitives passing through Rochester, that I was obliged at last to appeal to my British friends for the means of sending them on their way, and when Mr. and Mrs. Carpenter and Mrs. Crofts took the matter in hand, I had never any further trouble in that respect. When slavery was abolished I wrote to Mrs. Carpenter, congratulating her that she was relieved of the work of raising funds for such purposes, and the characteristic reply of that lady was that she had been very glad to do what she had done, and had no wish for relief.

My pathway was not entirely free from thorns in Rochester, and the wounds and pains inflicted by them were perhaps much less easily born, because of my exemption from such annoyances while in England. Men can in time become accustomed to almost anything, even to being insulted and ostracised, but such treatment comes hard at first, and when to some extent unlooked for. The vulgar prejudice against colour, so common to Americans, met me in several disagreeable forms. A seminary for young ladies and misses, under the auspices of Miss Tracy, was near my house in Alexander Street, and desirous of having my daughter educated like the daughters of other men, I applied to Miss Tracy for her admission to her school. All seemed fair, and the child was duly sent to "Tracy Seminary," and I went about my business happy in the thought that she was in the way of a refined and Christian education. Several weeks elapsed before I knew how completely I was mistaken. The little girl came home to me one day and told me she was lonely in that school; that she was in fact kept in solitary confinement; that she was not allowed to be in the room with the other girls, nor to go into the yard when they went out; that she was kept in a room by herself and not permitted to be seen nor heard by the others. No man with the feeling of a parent could be less than moved by such a revelation, and I confess that I was shocked, grieved, and indignant. I went at once to Miss Tracy to ascertain if what I had heard was true, and was coolly told it was, and the miserable plea was offered that it would have injured her school if she had done otherwise. I told her she should have told me so at the beginning, but I did not believe that any girl in the school would be opposed to the presence of my daughter, and that I should be glad to have the question submitted to them. She consented to this, and to the credit of the young ladies, not one made objection. Not satisfied with this verdict of the natural and uncorrupted sense of justice and humanity of these young ladies, Miss Tracy insisted that the parents must be consulted, and if one of them objected she should not admit my child to the same apartment and privileges of the other pupils. One parent only had the cruelty to object, and he was Mr. Horatio G. Warner, a democratic editor, and upon his adverse conclusion, my daughter was excluded from "Tracy Seminary." Of course Miss Tracy was a devout Christian lady after the fashion of the time and locality, in good and regular standing in the Church.

My troubles attending the education of my children were not to end here. They were not allowed in the public school in the district in which I lived, owned property, and paid taxes, but were compelled, if they went to a public school, to go over to the other side of the city, to an inferior coloured school. I hardly need say that I was not prepared to submit tamely to this proscription, any more than I had been to submit to slavery, so I had them taught at home for a while, by Miss Thayer. Meanwhile I went to the people with the question and created considerable agitation. I sought and obtained a hearing before the Board of Education, and after repeated efforts with voice and pen, the doors of the public schools were opened and coloured children were permitted to attend them in common with others.

There were barriers erected against coloured people in most other places of instruction and amusements in the city, and until I went there, they were imposed without any apparent sense of injustice or wrong, and submitted to in silence; but, one by one, they have gradually been removed, and coloured people now enter freely all places of public resort without hindrance or observation. This change has not been wholly effected by me. From the first, I was cheered on and supported in my demands for equal rights by such respectable citizens as Isaac Post, Wm. Hallowell, Samuel D. Porter, Wm. C. Bloss, Benj. Fish, Asa Anthony, and many other good and true men of Rochester.

Notwithstanding what I have said of the adverse feeling exhibited by some of its citizens at my selection of Rochester as the place to establish my paper, and the trouble in educational matters just referred to, that selection was in many respects very fortunate. The city was, and still is, the centre of a various, intelligent, enterprising, liberal, and growing population. The surrounding country is remarkable for its fertility; and the city itself possesses one of the finest water-powers in the world. It is on the line of the New York Central railroad—a line that with its connections, spans the whole country. Its people were industrious and in comfortable circumstances; not so rich as to be indifferent to the claims of humanity, and not so poor as to be unable to help any good cause which commanded the approval of their judgment.

The ground had been measurably prepared for me by the labours of others—notably by the Hon. Myron Holley, whose monument of enduring marble now stands in the beautiful cemetery at Mount Hope, upon an eminence befitting his noble character. I know of no place in the Union where I could have been located at the time with less resistance, or received a larger measure of sympathy and co-operation; and I now look back upon my life and labours there with unalloyed satisfaction, and having spent a quarter of a century among its people, I shall always feel more at home there than any where else in the United States.

CHAPTER VIII: JOHN BROWN AND MRS. STOWE.

My first meeting with Capt. John Brown—The Free-Soil Movement—Coloured Convention—Uncle Tom's Cabin—Industrial school for coloured people—Letter to Mrs. H. B. Stowe.

ABOUT the time I began my enterprise in Rochester, I chanced to spend a night and a day under the roof of a man whose character and conversation, and whose objects and aims in life made a very deep impression upon my mind and heart. His name had been mentioned to me by several prominent coloured men. among whom were the Rev. Henry Highland Garnet and J. W. Loguen. In speaking of him their voices would drop to a whisper, and what they said of him made me very eager to see and know him. Fortunately I was invited to see him in his own house. At the time to which I now refer, this man was a respectable merchant in a populous and thriving city, and our first place of meeting was at his store. This was a substantial brick building, in a prominent, busy street. A glance at the interior, as well as at the massive walls without, gave me the impression that the owner must be a man of considerable wealth. From this store I was conducted to his house, where I was kindly received as an expected guest. My welcome was all I could have asked. Every member of the family, young and old, seemed glad to see me, and I was made much at home in a very little while. I was, however, a little disappointed with the appearance of the house and with its location. After seeing the fine store, I was prepared to see a fine residence, in an eligible locality, but this conclusion was completely dispelled by actual observation. In fact, the house was neither commodious nor elegant, nor its situation desirable, It was a small wooden building, in a back street, in a neighbourhood chiefly occupied by labouring men and mechanics; respectable enough to be sure, but not quite the place, I thought, where one would look for the residence of a flourishing and successful merchant. Plain as was the outside of this man's house, the inside was plainer. Its furniture would have satisfied a Spartan. It would take longer to tell what was not in this house than what was in it. There was an air of plainness about it which almost suggested destitution. My first meal passed under the misnomer of tea, though there was nothing about it resembling the usual significance of that term. It consisted of beef soup, cabbage, and potatoes; a meal such as a man might relish after following the plough all day, or performing a forced march of a dozen miles over a rough road in frosty weather. Innocent of paint, veneering, varnish, or table-cloth, the table announced itself unmistakably of pine and of the plainest workmanship. There was no hired help visible. The mother, daughters, and sons did the serving, and did it well. They were evidently used to it, and had no thought of any impropriety or degradation in being their own servants. It is said that a house in some measure reflects the character of its occupants; this one certainly did. In it there were no disguises, no illusions, no make believes. Everything implied stern truth, solid purpose, and rigid economy. I was not long in company with the master of this house before I discovered that he was indeed the master of it, and was likely to become mine too if I stayed long enough with him. He fulfilled St. Paul's idea of the head of the family. His wife believed in him, and his children observed him with reverence. Whenever he spoke his words commanded earnest attention. His arguments, which I ventured at some points to oppose, seemed to convince all; his appeals touched all, and his will impressed all. Certainly I never felt myself in the presence of a stronger religious influence than while in this man's house.

In person he was lean, strong, and sinewy, of the best New England mould, built for times of trouble, fitted to grapple with the flintiest hardships. Clad in plain American woollen, shod in boots of cowhide leather, and wearing a cravat of the same substantial material, under six feet high, less than 150 pounds in weight, aged about fifty, he presented a figure, straight and symmetrical as a mountain pine. His bearing was singularly impressive. His head was not large, but compact and high. His hair was coarse, strong, slightly gray and closely trimmed, and grew low on his forehead. His face was smoothly shaved, and revealed a strong square mouth, supported by a broad and prominent chin. His eyes were bluish gray, and in conversation they were full of light and fire. When in the street, he moved with a long, springing race-horse step, absorbed by his own reflections, neither seeking nor shunning observation. Such was the man, whose name I had heard in whispers, such was the spirit of his house and family, such was the house in which he lived, and such was Captain John Brown, whose name has now passed into history, as one of the most marked characters, and greatest heroes known to American fame.

After the strong meal already described, Captain Brown cautiously approached the subject which he wished to bring to my attention; for he seemed to apprehend opposition to his views. He denounced slavery in look and language fierce and bitter, thought that slaveholders had forfeited their right to live, that the slaves had the right to gain their liberty in any way they could, did not believe that moral suasion would ever liberate the slave, or that political action would abolish the system. He said that he had long had a plan which could accomplish this end, and he had invited me to his house to lay that plan before me. He said he had been for some time looking for coloured men to whom he could safely reveal his secret, and at times he had almost despaired of finding such men, but that now he was encouraged, for he saw heads of such, rising up in all directions. He had observed my course at home and abroad, and he wanted my co-operation. His plan as it then lay in his mind, had much to commend it. It did not, as some suppose, contemplate a general rising among the slaves, and a general slaughter of the slave masters. An insurrection he thought would only defeat the object, but his plan did contemplate the creating of an armed force, which should act in the very heart of the South. He was not averse to the shedding of blood, and thought the practice of carrying arms would be a good one for the coloured people to adopt, as it would give them a sense of their manhood. No people, he said, could have self-respect, or be respected, who would not fight for their freedom. He called my attention to a map of the United States, and pointed out to me the far-reaching Alleghanies, which stretch away from the borders of New York, into the Southern States. "These mountains," he said, "are the basis of my plan. God has given the strength of the hills to freedom, they were placed here for the emancipation of the negro race; they are full of natural forts, where one man for defence will be equal to a hundred for attack; they are full also of good hiding places, where large numbers of brave men could be concealed, and baffle and elude pursuit for a long time. I know these mountains well, and could take a body of men into them and keep them there, despite all the efforts of Virginia to dislodge them. The true object to be sought is first of all to destroy the money value of slave property; and that can only be done by rendering such property insecure. My plan then is to take at first about twenty-five picked men, and begin on a small scale; supply them with arms and ammunition, post them in squads of fives on a line of twenty-five miles, the most persuasive and judicious of whom shall go down to the fields from time to time, as opportunity offers, and induce the slaves to join them, seeking and selecting the most restless and daring."

He saw that in this part of the work the utmost care must be used to avoid treachery and disclosure. Only the most conscientious and skilful should be sent on this perilous duty; with care and enterprise he thought he could soon gather a force of one hundred hardy men, men who would be content to lead the free and adventurous life in which he proposed to train them; when these were properly drilled, and each man had found the place for which he was best suited, they would begin work in earnest; they would run off the slaves in large numbers, retain the brave and strong ones in the mountains, and send the weak and timid to the North by the underground railroad; his operations would be enlarged with increasing numbers, and would not be confined to one locality.

When I asked him how he would support these men, he said emphatically, he would subsist them upon the enemy. Slavery was a state of war, and the slave had a right to anything necessary to his freedom. But, said I, "suppose you succeed in running off a few slaves, and thus impress the Virginia slaveholders with a sense of insecurity in their slaves, the effect will be only to make them sell their slaves further South." "That," said he, "will be first what I want to do; then I would follow them up. If we could drive slavery out of one county, it would be a great gain; it would weaken the system throughout the State." "But they would employ bloodhounds to hunt you out of the mountains." "That they might attempt," said he, "but the chances are, we should whip them, and when we should have whipped one squad, they would be careful how they pursued." "But you might be surrounded and cut off from your provisions or means of subsistence." He thought that could not be done so that they could not cut their way out; but even if the worst came, he could but be killed; and he had no better use for his life than to lay it down in the cause of the slave. When I suggested that we might convert the slaveholders, he became much excited, and said that could never be;—"he knew their proud hearts, and that they would never be induced to give up their slaves, until they felt a big stick about their heads." He observed, that I might have noticed the simple manner in which he lived, adding that he had adopted this method in order to save money to carry out his purposes. This was said in no boastful tone, for he felt that he had delayed already too long, and had no room to boast either his zeal or his self-denial. Had some men made such display of rigid virtue, I should have rejected it, as affected, false, and hypocritical, but in John Brown, I felt it to be real as iron or granite. From this night spent with John Brown in Springfield, Mass., 1847, while I continued to write and speak against slavery, I became all the same less hopeful of its peaceful abolition. My utterances became more and more tinged by the colour of this man's strong impressions. Speaking at an anti-slavery convention in Salem, Ohio, I expressed the apprehension that slavery could only be destroyed by bloodshed, when I was suddenly and sharply interrupted by my good old friend, Sojourner Truth, with the question, "Frederick, is God dead?" "No," I answered, and "because God is not dead slavery can only end in blood." My quaint old sister was of the Garrison school of non-resistants, and was shocked at my sanguinary doctrine, but she too became an advocate of the sword, when the war for the maintenance of the Union was declared.

In 1848 it was my privilege to attend, and in some measure, to participate in, the famous Free-Soil Convention held in Buffalo, New York. It was a vast and variegated assemblage, composed of persons from all sections of the North, and may be said to have formed a new departure in the history of forces organized to resist the growing and aggressive demands of slavery and the slave power. Until this Buffalo Convention, anti-slavery agencies had been mainly directed to the work of changing public sentiment, by exposing through the press and on the platform, the nature of the slave system. Anti-slavery thus far had only been sheet lightning; the Buffalo Convention sought to make it a thunderbolt. It is true the Liberty party, a political organisation, had been in existence since 1840, when it cast seven thousand votes for James G. Birney, a former slaveholder, but who, in obedience to an enlightened conscience, had nobly emancipated his slaves, and was now devoting his time and talents to the overthrow of slavery. It is true that this little party of brave men had increased their numbers at one time to sixty thousand voters. It, however, had now apparently reached its culminating point, and was no longer able to attract to itself and combine all the available elements of the North, capable of being marshalled against the growing and aggressive measures and aims of the slave power. There were many in the old Whig party known as Conscience Whigs; and in the Democratic party known as Barnburners and Free Democrats, who were anti-slavery in sentiment and utterly opposed to the extension of the slave system to territory hitherto uncursed by its presence; but who, nevertheless, were not willing to join the Liberty party. It was held to be deficient in numbers, and wanting in prestige. Its fate was the fate of all pioneers. The work it had been required to perform had exposed it to assaults from all sides, and it wore on its front the ugly marks of conflict. It was unpopular from its very fidelity to the cause of liberty and justice. No wonder that some of its members, such as Gerrit Smith, William Goodell, Beriah Green, and Julius Lemoyne refused to quit the old for the new. They felt that the Free-Soil party was a step backward, a lowering of the standard, that the people should come to them, not they to the people. The party which had been good enough for them ought to be good enough for all others. Events, however, over-ruled this reasoning. The conviction became general that the time had come for a new organisation, which should embrace all who were in any manner opposed to slavery and the slave power, and this Buffalo Free-Soil Convention was the result of that conviction. It is easy to say that this or that measure would have been wiser and better than the one adopted. But any measure is vindicated by its necessity and its results. It was impossible for the mountain to go to Mahomet, or for the Free-Soil element to go to the old Liberty party, so the latter went to the former. "All is well that ends well." This Buffalo Convention of Free-Soilers, however low was their standard, did lay the foundation of a grand superstructure. It was a powerful link in the chain of events by which the slave system has been abolished, the slave emancipated, and the country saved from dismemberment.

It is nothing against the actors in this new movement that they did not see the end from the beginning; that they did not at first take the high ground that further on in the conflict their successors felt themselves called upon to take; or that their Free-Soil party, like the old Liberty party, was ultimately required to step aside and make room for the great Republican party. In all this, and more, it illustrates the experience of reform in all ages, and conforms to the laws of human progress—Measures change, principles never.

I was not the only coloured man well known to the country who was present at this convention. Samuel Ringold Ward, Henry Highland Garnet, Charles L. Remond, and Henry Bibb, were there, and made speeches which were received with surprise and gratification by the thousands there assembled. As a coloured man I felt greatly encouraged and strengthened in my cause while listening to these men—in the presence of the ablest men of the Caucasian race. Mr. Ward especially attracted attention at that convention. As an orator and thinker he was vastly superior, I thought, to any of us, and being perfectly black and of unmixed African descent, the splendours of his intellect went directly to the glory of his race. In depth of thought, fluency of speech, readiness of wit, logical exactness, and general intelligence, Samuel R. Ward has left no successor among the coloured men amongst us, and it was a sad day for our cause when he was laid low in the soil of a foreign country.

After the Free Soil party, with "Free Soil," "Free Labour," "Free States," "Free Speech," and "Free Men," on its banners, had defeated the almost permanently victorious Democratic party under the leadership of so able and popular a standard-bearer as General Lewis Cass, Mr. Calhoun, and other Southern statesmen were more than ever alarmed at the rapid increase of anti-slavery feeling in the North, and devoted their energies, more and more, to the work of devising means to stay the torrents and tie up the storm. They were not ignorant of whereunto this sentiment would grow if unsubjected and unextinguished. Hence they became fierce and furious in debate, and more extravagant than ever in their demands for additional safeguards to their system of robbery and murder. Assuming that the Constitution guaranteed their rights of property in their fellow-men, they held it to be in open violation of the Constitution for any American citizen in any part of the United States to speak, write, or act, against this right. But this shallow logic they plainly saw could do them no good unless they could obtain further safeguards for slavery. In order to effect this, the idea was suggested of so changing the

Constitution that there should be two instead of one President of the United States—one from the North and the other from the South—and that no measure should become a law without the assent of both. But this device was so utterly impracticable that it soon dropped out of sight, and it is mentioned here only to show the desperation of slaveholders to prop up their system of barbarism, against which the sentiment of the North was being directed with destructive skill and effect. They clamoured for more slave States, more power in the Senate and House of Representatives, and insisted upon the suppression of free speech. At the end of two years, in 1850, when Clay and Calhoun, two of the ablest leaders the South ever had, were still in the Senate, we had an attempt at a settlement of differences between the North and South which our legislators meant to be final. What those measures were I need not here enumerate, except to say that chief among them was the "Fugitive Slave Bill," framed by James M. Mason of Virginia, and supported by Daniel Webster of Massachusetts; a bill, undoubtedly more designed to involve the North in complicity with slavery and deaden its moral sentiment, than to procure the return of fugitives to their so-called owners. For a time this design did not altogether fail. Letters, speeches, and pamphlets literally rained down upon the people of the North, reminding them of their constitutional duty to hunt down and return to bondage runaway slaves. In this the preachers were not much behind the press and the politicians, especially that class of preachers known as Doctors of Divinity. A long list of these came forward with their Bibles to show that neither Christ nor His holy apostles objected to returning fugitives to slavery. Now, that this evil day is past, a sight of those sermons would, I doubt not, bring the red blush of shame to the cheeks of many.

Living as I then did in Rochester, on the borders of Canada, I was compelled to see the terribly distressing effects of this cruel enactment. Fugitive slaves, who had lived for many years safely and securely in Western New York and elsewhere, some of whom had by industry and economy saved money and bought little homes for themselves and their children, were suddenly alarmed, and compelled to flee to Canada for safety as from an enemy's land—a doomed city—and take up a dismal march to a new abode, empty-handed, among strangers. My old friend Ward, of whom I have just now spoken, found it necessary to give up the contest and flee to Canada, and thousands followed his example. Bishop Daniel A. Payne, of the African Methodist Episcopal Church, came to me about this time to consult me as to whether it was best to stand our ground or flee to Canada. I told him I could not desert my post until I saw I could not hold it, adding that I did not wish to leave while Garnet and Ward remained. "Why," said he, "Ward, Ward, he is already gone. I saw him crossing from Detroit to Windsor." I asked him if he was going to stay, and he answered, "Yes; we are whipped, we are whipped! and we might as well retreat in order." This was indeed a stunning blow. This man had power to do more to defeat this inhuman enactment than any other coloured man in the land, for no other could bring such brain power to bear against it. I felt like a besieged city at the news that its defenders had fallen at its gates.

The hardships imposed by this atrocious and shameless law were cruel and shocking, and yet only a few of all the fugitives of the Northern States were returned to slavery under its infamously wicked provisions. As a means of recapturing their runaway property in human flesh the law was an utter failure. Its efficiency was destroyed by its enormity. Its chief effect was to produce alarm and terror among the class subject to its operation, and this it did most effectually and distressingly. Even coloured people who had been free all their lives felt themselves very insecure in their freedom, for under this law, the oaths of any two villains were sufficient to consign a free man to slavery for life. While the law was a terror to the free, it was a still greater terror to the escaped bondman. To him there was no peace. Asleep or awake, at work or at rest, in church or market, he was liable to surprise and capture. By the law the judge got ten dollars a head for all he could consign to slavery, and only five dollars apiece for any which he might adjudge free. Although I was now myself free, I was not without apprehension. My purchase was of doubtful validity, having been bought when out of the possession of my owner, and when he must take what was given or take nothing. It was a question, whether my claimant could be stopped by such a sale, from asserting certain or supposable equitable rights in my body and soul. From rumours that reached me my house was guarded by my friends several nights, when kidnappers, had they come, would have got anything but a cool reception, for there would have been "blows to take as well as blows to give." Happily this reign of terror did not continue long. Despite the efforts of Daniel Webster and Millard Fillmore and our Doctors of Divinity, the law fell rapidly into disrepute. The rescue of Shadrack, resulting in the death of one of the kidnappers, in Boston, the cases of Simms and Anthony Burns, in the same place, created the deepest feeling against the law and its upholders. But the thing which more than all else destroyed the fugitive slave law was the resistance made to it by the fugitives themselves. A decided check was given to the execution of the law at Christiana, Penn., where three coloured men, being pursued by Mr. Gorsuch and his son, slew the father, wounded the son, drove away the officers, and made their escape to my house in Rochester. The work of getting these men safely into Canada was a delicate one. They were not only fugitives from slavery but charged with murder, and officers were in pursuit of them. There was no time for delay. I could not look upon them as murderers. To me, they were heroic defenders of the just rights of man against man-stealers and murderers. So I fed them, and sheltered them in my house. Had they been pursued then and there, my home would have been stained with blood, for these men who had already tasted blood were well armed and prepared to sell their lives at the expense of the lives and limbs of their probable assailants. What they had already done at Christiana, and the cool determination which showed very plainly, especially in Parker, for that was the name of the leader, left no doubt on my mind that their courage was genuine and that their deeds would equal their words. The situation was critical and dangerous. The telegraph had that day announced their deeds at Christiana, their escape, and that the mountains of Pennsylvania were being searched for the murderers. These men had reached me simultaneously with this news in the New York papers. Immediately after the occurrence at Christiana, they, instead of going into the mountains, were placed on a train which brought them to Rochester. They were thus almost in advance of the lightning, and much in advance of probable pursuit, unless the telegraph had already raised agents here. The hours they spent at my house were therefore hours of anxiety as well as activity. I dispatched my friend Miss Julia Griffiths to the landing three miles away on the Genesee River to ascertain if a steamer would leave that night for any port in Canada, and remained at home myself to guard my tired, dust-covered, and sleeping guests, for they had been harassed and travelling for two days and nights, and needed rest. Happily for us the suspense was not long, for it turned out, that that very night a steamer was to leave for Toronto, Canada.

This fact, however, did not end my anxiety. There was danger that between my house and the landing or at the landing itself we might meet with trouble. Indeed the landing was the place where trouble was likely to occur, if at all. As patiently as I could, I waited for the shades of night to come on, and then put the men in my "Democrat carriage," and started for the landing on the Genesee. It was an exciting ride, and somewhat speedy withal. We reached the boat at least fifteen minutes before the time of its departure, and that without remark or molestation. But those fifteen minutes seemed much longer than usual. I remained on board till the order to haul in the gang-way was given; I shook hands with my friends, received from Parker the revolver that fell from the hand of Gorsuch when he died, presented now as a token of gratitude and a memento of the battle for Liberty at Christiana, and I returned to my home with a sense of relief which I cannot stop here to describe. This affair, at Christiana, and the Jerry Rescue of Syracuse, inflicted fatal wounds on the Fugitive Slave Bill. It became thereafter almost a dead letter, for slaveholders found that not only did it fail to put them in possession of their slaves, but that the attempt to enforce it brought odium upon themselves and weakened the slave system.

In the midst of these fugitive slave troubles came the book known as "Uncle Tom's Cabin," a work of marvellous depth and power. Nothing could have better suited the moral and humane requirements of the hour. Its effect was amazing, instantaneous, and universal. No book on the subject of slavery had so generally and favourably touched the American heart. It combined all the power and pathos of preceding publications of the kind, and was hailed by many as an inspired production. Mrs. Stowe at once became an object of interest and admiration. She made fortune and fame at home, and awakened a deep interest abroad. Eminent persons in England roused to anti-slavery enthusiasm by her "Uncle Tom's Cabin," invited her to visit that country, and promised to give her a testimonial. Mrs. Stowe accepted the invitation and the proffered testimonial. Before sailing for England, however, she invited me from Rochester, N. Y., to spend a day at her house in Andover, Mass. Delighted with an opportunity to become personally acquainted with the gifted authoress, I lost no time in making my way to Andover. I was received at her home with genuine cordiality. There was no contradiction between the authoress and her book. Mrs. Stowe appeared in conversation equally as well as she appeared in her writings. She made to me a nice little speech in announcing her object in sending for me. "I have invited you here, she said, "because I wish to confer with you as to what can be done with the free coloured people of the country. I am going to England, and expect to have a considerable sum of money placed in my hands, and I intend to use it in some way, for the permanent improvement of the free coloured people, and especially for that class which has become free by their own exertions. In what way I can do this most successfully is the subject I wish to talk with you about. In any event I desire to have some monument raised after 'Uncle Tom's Cabin,' which shall show that it produced more than transient influence." She said several plans had been suggested, among others an educational institution pure and simple, but that she thought favourably of the establishment of an industrial school; and she desired me to express my views as to what I thought would be the best plan to help the free coloured people. I was not slow to tell Mrs. Stowe all I knew and had thought on the subject. As to a purely educational institution, I agreed with her that it did not meet our necessities. I argued against expending money in that way. I was also opposed to an ordinary industrial school where pupils should merely earn the means of obtaining an education in books. There were such schools, already. What I thought of as best was rather a series of workshops, where coloured people could learn some of the handicrafts, learn to work in iron, wood, and leather, and where a plain English education could also be taught. I argued that the want of money was the root of all evil to the coloured people. They were shut out from all lucrative employments and compelled to be merely barbers, waiters, coachmen and the like, at wages so low that they could lay up little or nothing. Their poverty kept them ignorant, and their ignorance kept them degraded. We needed more to learn how to make a good living, than to learn Latin and Greek. After listening to me at considerable length, she was good enough to tell me that she favoured my views, and would devote the money she expected to receive abroad to meeting the want I had described as the most important; by establishing an institution in which coloured youth should learn trades as well as to read, write, and count. When about to leave Andover, Mrs. Stowe asked me to put my views on the subject in the form of a letter, so that she could take it to England with her and show it to her friends there, that they might see to what their contributions were to be devoted. I acceded to her request, and wrote her the following letter for the purpose named:—

Rochester, March 8, 1853.

My Dear Mrs. Stowe:

You kindly informed me, when at your house a fortnight ago, that you designed to do something which would permanently contribute to the improvement and elevation of the free coloured people in the United States. You especially expressed interest in such of this class as had become free by their own exertions, and desired most of all to be of service to them. In what manner and by what means you can assist this class most successfully, is the subject upon which you have done me the honour to ask my opinion. . . . I assert then that poverty, ignorance and degradation are the combined evils; or in other words, these constitute the social disease of the free coloured people of the United States.

To deliver them from this triple malady, is to improve and elevate them, by which I mean, simply to put them on an equal footing with their white fellow countrymen in the sacred right to "Life, Liberty, and the pursuit of happiness." I am for no fancied or artificial elevation, but only ask fair play. How shall this be obtained? I answer, first, not by establishing for our use high schools and colleges. Such institutions are, in my judgment, beyond our immediate occasions and are not adapted to our present most pressing wants. High schools and colleges are excellent institutions, and will in due season be greatly subservient to our progress; but they are the result, as well as they are the demand of a point of progress, which we as a people have not yet attained. Accustomed as we have been, to the rougher and harder modes of living, and of gaining a livelihood, we cannot, and we ought not to hope that in a single leap from our low condition, we can reach that of Ministers, Lawyers, Doctors, Editors, Merchants, etc. These will doubtless be attained by us; but this will only be, when we have patiently and laboriously, and I may add successfully, mastered and passed through the intermediate gradations of agriculture and the mechanical arts. Besides, there are—and perhaps this is a better reason for my view of the case—numerous institutions of learning in this country, already thrown open to coloured youth. To my thinking, there are quite as many facilities now afforded to the coloured people, as they can spare the time from the sterner duties of life, to avail themselves of. In their present condition of poverty, they cannot spare their sons and daughters two or three years at boarding-schools or colleges, to say nothing of finding the means to sustain them while at such institutions. I take it, therefore, that we are well provided for in this respect; and that it may be fairly inferred from the fact, that the facilities for our education, so far as schools and colleges in the Free States are concerned, will increase quite in proportion with our future wants. Colleges have been open to coloured youth in this country during the last dozen years. Yet few comparatively, have acquired a classical education; and even this few have found themselves educated far above a living condition, there being no methods by which they could turn their learning to account. Several of this latter class have entered the ministry; but you need not be told that an educated people is needed to sustain an educated ministry. There must be a certain amount of cultivation among the people, to sustain such a ministry. At present we have not that cultivation amongst us; and therefore, we value in the preacher, strong lungs, rather than high learning. I do not say, that educated ministers are not needed amongst us, far from it! I wish there were more of them! but to increase their number, is not the largest benefit you can bestow upon us.

We have two or three coloured lawyers in this country; and I rejoice in the fact; for it affords very gratifying evidence of our progress. Yet it must be confessed, that in point of success, our lawyers are as great failures as our ministers, White people will not employ them to the obvious embarrassment of their causes, and the blacks, taking their cue from the whites, have not sufficient confidence in their abilities to employ them. Hence educated coloured men, among the coloured people, are at a very great discount. It would seem that education and emigration go together with us, for as soon as a man rises amongst us, capable, by his genius and learning, to do us great service, just so soon he finds that he can serve himself better by going elsewhere. In proof of this, I might instance the Russwurms, the Garnets, the Wards, the Crummells and others, all men of superior ability and attainments, and capable of removing mountains of prejudice against their race, by their simple presence in the country; but these gentlemen, finding themselves embarrassed here by the peculiar disadvantages to which I have referred, disadvantages in part growing out of their education, being repelled by ignorance on the one hand, and prejudice on the other, and having no taste to continue a contest against such odds, they have sought more congenial climes, where they can live more peaceable and quiet lives. I regret their election, but I cannot blame them, for with an equal amount of education and the hard lot which was theirs, I might follow their example. . . .

There is little reason to hope that any considerable number of the free coloured people will ever be induced to leave this country, even if such a thing were desirable. This black man— unlike the Indian—loves civilization. He does not make very great progress in civilization himself but he likes to be in the midst of it, and prefers to share its most galling evils, to encountering barbarism. Then the love of the country, the dread of isolation, the lack of adventurous spirit, and the thought of seeming to desert their "brethren in bonds," are a powerful check upon all schemes of colonization, which look to the removal of the coloured people, without the slaves. The truth is, dear madam, we are here, and here we are likely to remain. Individuals emigrate—nations never. We have grown up with this republic, and I see nothing in her character, or even in the character of the American people as yet, which compels the belief that we must leave the United States. If then, we are to remain here, the question for the wise and good is precisely that you have submitted to me—namely: What can be done to improve the condition of the free people of colour in the United States? The plan which I humbly submit in answer to this inquiry—and in the hope that it may find favour with you, and with the many friends of humanity who honour, love, and co-operate with you—is the establishment in Rochester, N. Y., or in some other part of the United States equally favourable to such an enterprise, of an Industrial College in which shall be taught several important branches of the mechanical arts. This college to be opened to coloured youth. I will pass over the details of such an institution as I propose. . . . . Never having had a day's schooling in all my life I may not be expected to map out the details of a plan so comprehensive as that involved in the idea of a college. I repeat, then, I leave the organisation and administration to the superior wisdom of yourself and the friends who second your noble efforts. The argument in favour of an Industrial College—a college to be conducted by the best men—and the best workmen which the mechanical arts can afford, a college where coloured youth can be instructed to use their hands, as well as their heads, where they can be put into possession of the means of getting a living whether their lot in after life may be cast among civilized or uncivilized men; whether they choose to stay here, or prefer to return to the land of their fathers—is briefly this. Prejudice against the free coloured people in the United States has shown itself nowhere so invincible as among mechanics. The farmer and the professional man cherish no feeling so bitter as that cherished by these. The latter would starve us out of the country entirely. At this moment I can more easily get my son into a lawyer's office to learn law than I can into a blacksmith's shop to blow the bellows and to wield the sledge-hammer. Denied the means of learning useful trades we are pressed into the narrowest limits to obtain a livelihood. In times past we have been the hewers of wood and the drawers of water for American society, and we once enjoyed a monopoly in menial enjoyments, but this is so no longer. Even these enjoyments are rapidly passing away out of our hands. The fact is—every day begins with the lesson, and ends with the lesson—that coloured men must learn trades, and must find new employment, new modes of usefulness to society, or that they must decay under the pressing wants to which their condition is rapidly bringing them.

We must become mechanics; we must build as well as live in houses; we must make as well as use furniture, we must construct bridges as well as pass over them, before we can properly live or be respected by our fellow men. We need mechanics as well as ministers. We need workers in iron, clay, and leather. We have orators, authors, and other professional men, but these reach only a certain class, and get respect for our race in certain select circles. To live here as we ought we must fasten ourselves to our countrymen through their every day cardinal wants. We must not only be able to black boots, but to make them. At present we are unknown in the Northern States as mechanics. We give no proof of genius or skill at the county, State, or national fairs. We are unknown at any of the great exhibitions of the industry of our fellow-citizens, and being unknown we are unconsidered.

The fact that we make no show of our ability is held conclusive of our inability to make any, hence all the indifference and contempt with which incapacity is regarded, fall upon us, and that too, when we have had no means of disproving the infamous opinion of our natural inferiority. I have during the last dozen years denied before the Americans that we are an inferior race, but this has been done by arguments based upon admitted principles rather than by the presentation of facts. Now, firmly believing, as I do, that there are skill, invention, power, industy, and real mechanical genius, among the coloured people, which will bear favourable testimony for them, and which only need the means to develop them, I am decidedly in favour of the establishment of such a college as I have mentioned. The benefits of such an institution would not be confined to the Northern States, nor to the free coloured people. They would extend over the whole Union. The slave not less than the freeman would be benefited by such an institution. It must be confessed that the most powerful argument now used by the Southern slaveholder, and the one most soothing to his conscience, is that derived from the low condition of the free coloured people of the North. I have long felt that too little attention has been given by our truest friends in this country to removing this stumbling block out of the way of the slave's liberation.

The most telling, the most killing refutation of slavery, is the presentation of an industrious, enterprising, thrifty, and intelligent free black population. Such a population I believe would rise in the Northern States under the fostering care of such a college as that supposed.

To show that we are capable of becoming mechanics I might adduce any amount of testimony; but dear madam, I need not ring the changes on such a proposition. There is no question in the mind of any unprejudiced person that the negro is capable of making a good mechanic. Indeed, even those who cherish the bitterest feelings towards us have admitted that the apprehension that negroes might be employed in their stead, dictated the policy of excluding them from trades altogether. But I will not dwell upon this point as I fear I have already trespassed too long upon your precious time, and written more than I ought to expect you to read. Allow me to say in conclusion, that I believe every intelligent coloured man in America will approve and rejoice at the establishment of some such institution as that now suggested. There are many respectable coloured men, fathers of large familes, having boys nearly grown up, whose minds are tossed by day and by night with the anxious enquiry, "what shall I do with my boys?" Such an institution would meet the wants of such persons. Then, too, the establishment of such an institution would be in character with the eminently practical philanthropy of your trans-Atlantic friends. America could scarcely object to it as an attempt to agitate the public mind on the subject of slavery, or to dissolve the Union. It could not be tortured into a cause for hard words by the American people, but the noble and good of all classes would see in the effort an excellent motive, a benevolent object, temperately, wisely, and practically manifested.

Wishing, you, dear madam, renewed health, a pleasant passage, and safe return to your native land.

I am most truly, your grateful friend,

Frederick Douglass.

Mrs. H. B. Stowe.

I was not only requested to write the foregoing letter for the purpose indicated, but I was also asked, with admirable foresight, to see and ascertain, as far as possible, the views of the free coloured people themselves in respect to the proposed measure for their benefit. This I was able to do in July, 1853, at the largest and most enlightened coloured convention that, up to that time, had ever assembled in the country. This convention warmly approved the plan of a manual labour school, as already described, and expressed high appreciation of the wisdom and benevolence of Mrs. Stowe. This convention was held in Rochester, N. Y., and will long be remembered there for the surprise and gratification it caused our friends in that city. They were not looking for such an exhibition of enlightened zeal and ability as were there displayed in speeches, addresses, and resolutions; and in the conduct of the business for which it had assembled. Its proceedings attracted wide-spread attention at home and abroad.

While Mrs. Stowe was abroad, she was attacked by the proslavery press of the United States so persistently and vigorously, for receiving money for her own private use, that the Rev. Henry Ward Beecher felt called upon to notice and reply to them in the columns of the New York Independent, of which he was then the editor. He denied that Mrs. Stowe was gathering British gold for herself; and referred her assailants to me, if they would learn what she intended to do with the money. In answer to her maligners, I denounced their accusations as groundless, and assured the public through the columns of my paper, that the testimonial then being raised in England by Mrs. Stowe, would be sacredly devoted to the establishment of an industrial school for coloured youth. This announcement was circulated by other journals, and the attacks ceased. Nobody could well object to such an application of money, received from any source, at home or abroad. After her return to this country, I called again on Mrs. Stowe, and was much disappointed to learn from her that she had reconsidered her plan for the industrial school. I have never been able to see any force in the reasons for this change. It is enough, however, to say that they were sufficient for her, and that she no doubt acted conscientiously, though her change of purpose was a great disappointment, and placed me in an awkward position before the coloured people of this country, as well as to friends abroad, to whom I had given assurances that the money would be appropriated in the manner I have described.

CHAPTER IX: INCREASING DEMANDS OF THE SLAVE POWER.

Increased demands of slavery—War in Kansas—John Brown's raid—His capture and execution—My escape to England from United States marshals.

NOTWITHSTANDING the natural tendency of the human mind to weary of an old story, and to turn away from chronic abuses for which it sees no remedy, the anti-slavery agitation for thirty long years—from 1830 to 1860—was sustained with ever increasing intensity and power. This was not entirely due to the extraordinary zeal and ability of the anti-slavery agitators themselves; for with all their admitted ardour and eloquence, they could have done very little without the aid rendered them, unwittingly, by the aggressive character of slavery itself. It was in the nature of the system never to rest in obscurity, although that condition was in a high degree essential to its security. It was for ever forcing itself into prominence. Unconscious, apparently, of its own deformity, it omitted no occasion for inviting disgust by seeking approval and admiration. It was noisiest when it should have been most silent, and unobtrusive. One of its defenders, when asked what would satisfy him as a slaveholder, said, "he never would be satisfied until he could call the roll of his slaves in the shadow of Bunker Hill monument." Every effort made to put down agitation only served to impart to it new strength and vigour. Of this class was the "gag rule," attempted and partially enforced in

Congress—the attempted suppression of the right of petition—the mob-ocratic demonstrations against the exercise of free speech—the display of pistols, bludgeons, and plantation manners in the Congress of the nation—the demand, shamelessly made by our Government upon England, for the return of slaves who had won their liberty by their valour on the high seas—the bill for the recapture of runaway slaves—the annexation of Texas for the avowed purpose of increasing the number of slave States, and thus increasing the power of slavery in the union—the war with Mexico—the fillibustering expeditions against Cuba and Central America—the cold-blooded decision of Chief Justice Taney in the Dred Scott case, wherein he states, as it were, a historical fact, that "negroes are deemed to have no rights which white men are bound to respect"—the perfidious repeal of the Missouri compromise, when all its advantages to the South had been gained and appropriated, and when nothing had been gained by the North—the armed and bloody attempt to force slavery upon the virgin soil of Kansas—the efforts of both of the great political parties to drive from place and power every man suspected of ideas and principles hostile to slavery—the rude attacks made upon Giddings, Hale, Chase, Wilson, Wm. H. Seward, and Charles Sumner—the effort to degrade these brave men, and drive them from positions of prominence—the summary manner in which Virginia hanged John Brown;—in a word, whatever was done or attempted, with a view to the support and security of slavery, only served as fuel to the fire, and heated the furnace of agitation to a higher degree than any before attained. This was true up to the moment when the nation found it necessary to gird on the sword for the salvation of the country and the destruction of slavery.

At no time during all the ten years preceding the war, was the public mind at rest. Mr. Clay's compromise measures in 1850, whereby all the troubles of the country about slavery were to be "in the deep bosom of the ocean buried," was hardly dry on the pages of the statute book before the whole land was rocked with rumoured agitation, and for one, I did my best, by pen and voice, and by ceaseless activity to keep it alive and vigorous. Later on, in 1854, we had the Missouri compromise, which removed the only grand legal barrier against the spread of slavery over all the territory of the United States. From this time there was no pause, no repose. Everybody, however dull, could see that this was a phase of the slavery question which was not to be slighted or ignored. The people of the North had been accustomed to ask, in a tone of cruel indifference, "What have we to do with slavery?" and now no laboured speech was required in answer. Slaveholding aggression settled this question for us. The presence of slavery in a territory would certainly exclude the sons and daughters of the Free States more effectually than statutes or yellow fever. Those who cared nothing for the slave, and were willing to tolerate slavery inside the slave States, were nevertheless not quite prepared to find themselves and their children excluded from the common inheritance of the nation. It is not surprising therefore, that the public mind of the North was easily kept intensely alive on this subject, nor that in 1856 an alarming expression of feeling on this point was seen in the large vote given for John C. Fremont and William L. Dayton for President and Vice-President of the United States. Until this last uprising of the North against the slave power the anti-slavery movement was largely retained in the hands of the original abolitionists, whose most prominent leaders have already been mentioned elsewhere in this volume. After 1856 a mightier arm and a more numerous host was raised against it; the agitation becoming broader and deeper. The times at this point illustrated the principle of tension and compression, action and reaction. The more open, flagrant, and impudent the slave power, the more firmly it was confronted by the rising anti-slavery spirit of the North. No one act did more to rouse the North to a comprehension of the infernal and barbarous spirit of slavery and its determination to "rule or ruin," than the cowardly and brutal assault made in the American Senate upon Charles Sumner, by Preston S. Brooks, a member of Congress from South Carolina. Shocking and scandalous as was this attack, the spirit in which the deed was received and commended by the community, was still more disgraceful. Southern ladies even applauded the armed bully for his murderous assault upon an unarmed Northern senator, because of words spoken in debate! This, more than all else, told the thoughtful people of the North the kind of civilization to which they were linked, and how plainly it foreshadowed a conflict on a larger scale.

As a measure of agitation, the repeal of the Missouri Compromise alluded to, was perhaps the most effective. It was that which brought Abraham Lincoln into prominence, and into conflict with Stephen A. Douglas—who was the author of that measure—and compelled the Western States to take a deeper interest than they ever had done before in the whole question. Pregnant words were now spoken on the side of freedom, words which went straight to the heart of the nation. It was Mr. Lincoln who told the American people at this crisis that the "Union could not long endure half slave and half free; that they must be all one or the other, and that the public mind could find no resting place but in the belief in the ultimate extinction of slavery." These were not the words of an abolitionist—branded a fanatic, and carried away by an enthusiastic devotion to the Negro—but the calm, cool, deliberate utterance of a statesman, comprehensive enough to take in the welfare of the whole country. No wonder that the friends of freedom saw in this plain man of Illinois the proper standard-bearer of all the moral and political forces which could be united and wielded against the slave power. In a few simple words he had embodied the thought of the loyal nation, and indicated the character fit to lead and guide the country amid perils present and to come.

The South was not far behind the North in recognising Abraham Lincoln as the natural leader of the rising political sentiment of the country against slavery; and it was equally quick in its efforts to counteract and destroy his influence. Its papers teemed with the bitterest invectives against the "backwoodsman of Illinois," the "flat-boatman," the "rail-splitter," the "third-rate lawyer," and much else and worse.

Preceding the repeal of the Missouri Compromise, I gave at the anniversary of the American Anti-Slavery Society in New York, the following picture of the state of the anti-slavery conflict as it then existed.

"It is evident that there is in this country a purely slavery party, a party which exists for no other earthly purpose but to promote the interest of slavery. It is known by no particular name, and has assumed no definite shape, but its branches reach far and wide in Church and State. This shapeless and nameless party is not intangible in other and more important respects. It has a fixed, definite, and comprehensive policy towards the whole free coloured population of the United States. I understand that policy to comprehend: first, the complete suppression of all anti-slavery discussion, second, the expulsion of the entire free coloured people of the United States; third, the nationalization of slavery; fourth, guarantees for the endless perpetuation of slavery and its extension over Mexico and Central America. Sir, these objects are forcibly presented to us in the stern logic of passing events, and in all the facts that have been before us during the last three years. The country has been and is dividing on these grand issues. Old party ties are broken. Like is finding its like on both sides of these issues, and the great battle is at hand. For the present the best representation of the slavery party is the Democratic party. Its great head for the present is President Pierce, whose boast it was before his election, that his whole life had been consistent with the interests of slavery—that he is above reproach on that score. In his inaugural address he reassures the South on this point, so that there shall be no misapprehension. Well, the head of the slave power being in power, it is natural that the proslavery elements should cluster around his administration, and that is rapidly being done. The stringent protectionist and the free-trader strike hands. The supporters of Fillmore are becoming the supporters of Pierce. Silver Gray Whigs shake hands with Hunker Democrats, the former only differing from the latter in name. They are in fact of one heart and one mind, and the union is natural and perhaps inevitable. Pilate and Herod made friends. The keystone to the arch of this grand union of forces of the slave party is the so-called Compromise of 1850. In that measure we have all the objects of our slaveholding policy specified. It is, sir, favourable to this view of the situation, that the Whig party and the Democratic party bent lower, sunk deeper, and strained harder in their conventions, preparatory to the late Presidential election to meet the demands of slavery. Never did parties come before the Northern people with propositions of such undisguised contempt for the moral sentiment and religious ideas of that people. They dared to ask them to unite with them in a war upon free speech, upon conscience, and to drive the Almighty presence from the councils of the nation. Resting their platforms upon the Fugitive Slave Bill they have boldly asked this people for political power to execute its horrible and hell-black provisions. The history of that election reveals with great clearness, the extent to which slavery has "shot its leprous distilment" through the life blood of the nation. The party most thoroughly opposed to the cause of justice and humanity triumphed, while the party only suspected of leaning toward those principles was overwhelmingly defeated, and some say annihilated. But here is a still more important fact, which still better discloses the designs of the slave power. It is a fact full of meaning, that no sooner did the Democratic party come into power than a system of legislation was presented to all the legislatures of the Northern States designed to put those States in harmony with the Fugitive Slave Law, and with the malignant spirit evinced by the national government towards the free coloured inhabitants of the country. The whole movement on the part of the States bears unmistakable evidence of having one origin, of emanating from one head and urged forward by one power. It was simultaneous, uniform and general, and looked only to one end. It was intended to put thorns under feet already bleeding; to crush a people already bowed down; to enslave a people already but half free; in a word, it was intended and well calculated to discourage, dishearten, and if possible to drive the whole free coloured people out of the country. In looking at the black law then recently enacted in the State of Illinois one is struck dumb by its enormity. It would seem that the men who passed that law, had not only successfully banished from their minds all sense of justice, but all sense of shame as well: these law codes propose to sell the bodies and souls of the blacks to provide the means of intelligence and refinement for the whites; to rob every black stranger who ventures among them to increase their educational fund.

"While this kind of legislation is going on in the States a pro-slavery political board of health is being established at Washington. Senators Hale, Chase, and Sumner are robbed of their senatorial rights and dignity as representatives of sovereign states, because they have refused to be inoculated with the pro-slavery virus of the times. Among the services which a senator is expected to perform, are many that can only be done efficiently as members of important committees, and the slave power in the Senate in saying to these honourable senators, you shall not serve on the committees of this body, took the responsibility of insulting and robbing the States which had sent them there. It is an attempt at Washington to decide for the States who the States shall send to the Senate. Sir, it strikes me that this aggression on the part of the slave power did not meet at the hands of the proscribed and insulted senators the rebuke which they had a right to expect from them. It seems to me that a great opportunity was lost, that the great principle of senatorial equality was left undefended at a time when its vindication was sternly demanded. But it is not to the purpose of my present statement to criticise the conduct of friends. Much should be left to the discretion of anti-slavery men in Congress. Charges of recreancy should never be made but on the most sufficient grounds. For of all places in the world where an anti-slavery man needs the confidence and encouragement of his friends, I take Washington—the citadel of slavery—to be that place.

"Let attention now be called to the social influences operating and cooperating with the slave power at the time, designed to promote all its malign objects. We see here the black man attacked in his most vital interests: prejudice and hate are systematically excited against him. The wrath of other labourers is stirred up against him. The Irish, who at home readily sympathise with the oppressed everywhere, are instantly taught when they step upon our soil to hate and despise the negro. They are taught to believe that he eats the bread that belongs to them. The cruel lie is told them, that we deprive them of labour and receive the money which would otherwise make its way into their pockets. Sir, the Irish-American will find out his mistake one day. He will find that in assuming our avocation, he has also assumed our degradation. But for the present we are the sufferers. Our old employments, by which we have been accustomed to gain a livelihood are gradually slipping from our hands; every hour sees us elbowed out of some employment to make room for some newly-arrived emigrant from the Emerald Isle, whose hunger and colour entitle him to special favour. These white men are becoming house-servants, cooks, stewards, waiters, and flunkies. For aught I see they adjust themselves to their stations with all proper humility. If they cannot rise to the dignity of white men, they show that they can fall to the degradation of black men. But now, sir, look once more' While the coloured people are thus elbowed out of employment; while a ceaseless enmity in the Irish is excited against us; while State after State enacts laws against us; while we are being hunted down like wild beasts; while we are oppressed with the sense of increasing insecurity, the American Colonization Society, with hypocrisy written on its brow, comes to the front, awakens new life, and vigorously presses its scheme for our expatriation upon the attention of the American people. Papers have been started in the North and the South to promote this long cherished object—to get rid of the negro, who is presumed to be a standing menace to slavery. Each of these papers is adapted to the latitude in which it is published, but each and all are united in calling upon the Government for appropriations to enable the Colonization Society to send us out of the country by steam. Evidently this society looks upon our extremity as their opportunity, and whenever the elements are stirred against us, they are stimulated to unusual activity. They do not deplore our misfortunes, but rather rejoice in them, since they prove that the two races cannot flourish on the same soil. But, sir, I must hasten. I have thus briefly given my view of one aspect of the present position and future prospects of the coloured people of the United States. And what I have said is far from encouraging to my afflicted people. I have seen the cloud gather upon the sable brows of some who hear me. I confess the case looks bad enough. Sir, I am not a hopeful man. I think I am apt to undercalculate the benefits of the future. Yet, sir, in this seemingly desperate case, I do not despair for my people. There is a bright side to almost every picture, and ours is no exception to the general rule. If the influences against us are strong, those for us are also strong. To the inquiry, will our enemies prevail in the execution of their designs—in my God, and in my soul, I believe they will not. Let us look at the first object sought for by the slavery party of the country, viz., the suppression of the anti-slavery discussion. They desire to suppress discussion on this subject, with a view to the peace of the slaveholder and the security of slavery Now, sir, neither the principle nor the subordinate objects, here declared, can be at all gained by the slave power, and for this reason: it involves the proposition to padlock the lips of the whites, in order to secure the fetters on the limbs of the blacks. The right of speech, precious and priceless, cannot—will not—be surrendered to slavery. Its suppression is asked for, as I have said, to give peace and security to slaveholders. Sir, that thing cannot be done. God has interposed an insuperable obstacle to any such result. "There can be no peace, saith my God, to the wicked." Suppose it were possible to put down this discussion, what would it avail the guilty slaveholder, pillowed as he is upon the heaving bosoms of ruined souls? He could not have a peaceful spirit. If every anti-slavery tongue in the nation were silent—every anti-slavery organization dissolved—every anti-slavery periodical, paper, pamphlet, book, or what not, searched out, burned to ashes, and their ashes given to the four winds of heaven, still, still the slaveholder could have no peace. In every pulsation of the heart, in every throb of his life, in every glance of his eye, in the breeze that soothes, and in the thunder that startles, would be waked up an accuser, whose cause is 'thou art verily guilty concerning thy brother.' "

This is no fancy sketch of the times indicated. The situation during all the administration of President Pierce was only less threatening and stormy than that under the administration of James Buchanan. One sowed, the other reaped. One was the wind, the other was the whirlwind. Intoxicated by their success in repealing the Missouri compromise—in divesting the native-born coloured man of American citizenship—in harnessing both the Whig and Democratic parties to the car of slavery, and in holding continued possession of the national government, the propagandists of slavery threw off all disguises, abandoned all semblance of moderation, and very naturally and inevitably proceeded under Mr. Buchanan, to avail themselves of all the advantages of their victories. Having legislated out of existence the great national wall, erected in the better days of the Republic, against the spread of slavery, and against the increase of its power—having blotted out all distinction, as they thought, between freedom and slavery in the law, theretofore, governing the territories of the United States, and having left the whole question of the legislation or prohibition of slavery to be decided by the people of a territory, the next thing in order was to fill up the territory of Kansas—the one likely to be first organised—with a people friendly to slavery, and to keep out all such as were opposed to making that territory a Free State. Here was an open invitation to a fierce and bitter strife; and the history of the times shows how promptly that invitation was accepted by both classes to which it was given, and the scenes of lawless violence and blood that followed.

All advantages were at first on the side of those who were for making Kansas a slave State. The moral force of the repeal of the Missouri Compromise was with them; the strength of the triumphant Democratic party was with them; the power and patronage of the Federal government was with them; the various governors, sent out under the territorial government, were with them; and, above all, the proximity of the territory to the slave State of Missouri favoured them and all their designs. Those who opposed the making Kansas a slave State, for the most part were far away from the battle-ground, residing chiefly in New England, more than a thousand miles from the eastern border of the territory, and their direct way of entering it was through a country violently hostile to them. With such odds against them, and only an idea—though a grand one—to support them, it will ever be a wonder that they succeeded in making Kansas a Free State. It is not my purpose to write particularly of this or of any other phase of the conflict with slavery, but simply to indicate the nature of the struggle, and the successive steps leading to the final result. The important point to me, as one desiring to see the slave power crippled, slavery limited and abolished, was the effect of this Kansas battle upon the moral sentiment of the North: how it made abolitionists before they themselves became aware of it, and how it rekindled the zeal, stimulated the activity, and strengthened the faith of our old anti-slavery forces. "Draw on me for £200 per month while the conflict lasts," said the great-hearted Gerritt Smith. George L. Stearns poured out his thousands, and anti-slavery men of smaller means were proportionally liberal. H. W. Beecher shouted the right word at the head of a mighty column; Sumner in the Senate spoke as no man had ever spoken there before. Lewis Tappan representing one class of the old opponents of slavery, and William L. Garrison the other, lost sight of their former differences, and bent all their energies to the freedom of Kansas. But these and others were merely generators of anti-slavery force. The men who went to Kansas with the purpose of making it a Free State, were the heroes and martyrs. One of the leaders in this holy crusade for freedom, with whom I was brought into near relations, was John Brown, whose person, house, and purposes I have already described. This brave old man and his sons were amongst the first to hear and heed the trumpet of freedom calling them to battle. What they did and suffered, what they sought and gained, and by what means, are matters of history, and need not be repeated here.

When it became evident, as it soon did, that the war for and against slavery in Kansas was not to be decided by the peaceful means of words and ballots, but swords and bullets were to be employed on both sides, Captain John Brown felt that now, after long years of waiting, his hour had come; and never did man meet the perilous requirements of any occasion more cheerfully, courageously, and disinterestedly than he. I met him often during this struggle, and saw deeper into his soul than when I met him in Springfield seven or eight years before, and all I saw of him gave me a more favourable impression of the man, and inspired me with a higher respect for his character. In his repeated visits to the East to obtain necessary arms and supplies, he often did me the honour of spending hours and days with me at Rochester. On more than one occasion I got up meetings and solicited aid to be used by him for the cause, and I may say without boasting that my efforts in this respect were not entirely fruitless. Deeply interested as "Ossawatamie Brown" was in Kansas he never lost sight of what he called his greater work—the liberation of all the slaves in the United States. But for the then present he saw his way to the great end through Kansas. It would be a grateful task to tell of his exploits in the border struggle, how he met persecution with persecution, war with war, strategy with strategy, assassination and house-burning with signal and terrible retaliation, till even the blood-thirsty propagandists of slavery were compelled to cry for quarter. The horrors wrought by his iron hand cannot be contemplated without a shudder, but it is the shudder which one feels at the execution of a murderer. The amputation of a limb is a severe trial to feeling, but necessity is a full justification of it to reason. To call out a murderer at midnight, and without note or warning, judge or jury, run him through with a sword, was a terrible remedy for a terrible malady. The question was not merely which class should prevail in Kansas, but whether free-state men should live there at all. The border ruffians from Missouri had openly declared their purpose not only to make Kansas a slave State, but that they would make it impossible for free-state men to live there. They burned their towns, burned their farm-houses, and by assassination spread terror among them until many of the free-state settlers were compelled to escape for their lives. John Brown was therefore the logical result of slaveholding persecutions. Until the lives of tyrants and murderers shall become more precious in the sight of men than justice and liberty, John Brown will need no defender. In dealing with the ferocious enemies of the free-state cause in Kansas he not only showed boundless courage but eminent military skill. With men so few and odds against him so great, few captains ever surpassed him in achievements, some of which seem too disproportionate for belief, and yet no voice has called them in question. With only eight men he met, fought, whipped, and captured Henry Clay Pate with twenty-five well-armed and well-mounted men. In this battle he selected his ground so wisely, handled his men so skilfully, and attacked his enemies so vigorously, that they could neither run nor fight, and were therefore compelled to surrender to a force less than one-third their own. With just thirty men on another memorable occasion he met and vanquished 400 Missourians under the command of General Read. These men had come into the territory under an oath never to return to their homes in Missouri till they had stamped out the last vestige of the free-state spirit in Kansas. But a brush with old Brown instantly took this high conceit out of them, and they were glad to get home upon any terms, without stopping to stipulate. With less than 100 men to defend the town of Lawrence, he offered to lead them and give battle to 1,400 men on the banks of the Waukerusia river, and was much vexed when his offer was refused by General Jim Lane and others, to whom the defence of the place was committed. Before leaving Kansas he went into the border of Missouri, and liberated a dozen slaves in a single night, and despite of slave laws and marshals, he brought these people through half a dozen States and landed them safe in Canada. The successful efforts of the North in making Kansas a Free State, despite all the sophistical doctrines and the sanguinary measures of the South to make it a slave State, exercised a potent influence upon subsequent political forces and events in the then near future. It is interesting to note the facility with which the statesmanship of a section of the country adapted its convictions to changed conditions. When it was found that the doctrine of popular sovereignty—first I think invented by General Cass, and afterwards adopted by Stephen A. Douglas—failed to make Kansas a slave State, and could not be safely trusted in other emergencies, Southern statesmen promptly abandoned and reprobated that doctrine, and took what they considered firmer ground. They lost faith in the rights, powers, and wisdom of the people, and took refuge in the Constitution, Henceforth the favourite doctrine of the South was that the people of a territory had no voice in the matter of slavery whatever; that the Constitution of the United States, of its own force and effect, carried slavery safely into any territory of the United States and protected the system there until it ceased to be a territory and became a State. The practical operation of this doctrine would be to make all the future new States slaveholding States, for slavery once planted and nursed for years in a territory would easily strengthen itself against the evil day and defy eradication. This doctrine was in some sense supported by Chief Justice Taney, in the infamous Dred Scott decision. This new ground, however, was destined to bring misfortune to its inventors, for it divided for a time the Democratic party, one faction of it going with John C. Breckenridge and the other espousing the cause of Stephen A. Douglas; the one held firmly to the doctrine that the United States Constitution, without any legislation, territorial, national, or otherwise, by its own, force and effect, carried slavery into all the territories of the United States; the other held that the people of a territory had the right to admit slavery or reject slavery, as in their judgment they might deem best. Now, while this war of words—this conflict of doctrines—was in progress, the portentous shadow of a stupendous civil war became more and more visible. Bitter complaints were raised by the slaveholders that they were about to be despoiled of their proper share in territory won by a common valour, or bought by a common treasure. The North, on the other hand, or rather a large and growing party at the North, insisted that the complaint was unreasonable and groundless; that nothing properly considered as property was excluded or meant to be excluded from the territories; that Southern men could settle in any territory of the United States with some kinds of property, and on the same footing and with the same protection as citizens of the North; that men and women are not property in the same sense as houses, lands, horses, sheep, and swine are property, and that the fathers of the Republic neither intended the extension nor the perpetuity of slavery; that liberty is national, and slavery is sectional. From 1856 to 1860 the whole land rocked with this great controversy. When the explosive force of this controversy had already weakened the bolts of the American Union; when the agitation of the public mind was at its topmost height; when the two sections were at their extreme points of difference; when comprehending the perilous situation, such statesmen of the North as William H. Seward sought to allay the rising storm by soft persuasive speech, and when all hope of compromise had nearly vanished, as if to banish even the last glimmer of hope for peace between the sections, John Brown came upon the scene. On the night of the 16th of October, 1859, there appeared near the confluence of the Potomac and Shenandoah rivers, a party of nineteen men—fourteen white and five coloured. They were not only armed themselves, but they brought with them a large supply of arms for such persons as might join them. These men invaded the town of Harper's Ferry, disarmed the watchman, took possession of the arsenal, rifle factory, armoury, and other Government property at that place, arrested and made prisoners of nearly all the prominent citizens in the neighbourhood, collected about fifty slaves, put bayonets into the hands of such as were able and willing to fight for their liberty, killed three men, proclaimed general emancipation, held the ground more than thirty hours, were subsequently overpowered and nearly all killed, wounded, or captured by a body of United States troops under command of Col. Robert E. Lee, since famous as the rebel General Lee. Three out of the nineteen invaders were captured while fighting, and one of them was Capt. John Brown—the man who originated, planned, and commanded the expedition. At the time of his capture Capt. Brown was supposed to be mortally wounded, as he had several ugly gashes and bayonet wounds on his head and body, and apprehending that he might speedily die, or that he might be rescued by his friends, and thus the opportunity to make him a signal example of slaveholding vengeance, would be lost, his captors hurried him to Charlestown, ten miles further within the border of Virginia, placed him in prison strongly guarded by troops, and before his wounds were healed he was brought into court.

[The preliminary examination of Brown took place at Charlestown, Virginia He protested against the unfairness of being so hastily charged, and denounced the whole proceedings as a mockery of justice. His conviction was a foregone conclusion, as the conviction of any man must be, who is taken in the very act of breaking the laws. He had challenged the strength of Virginia, and indeed of all the Southern States, and of the Federation itself. He had defied ordinances which he knew to exist, and roused the passions and fears of men. It was not to be expected that the slave-owners would show him any mercy. They had power on theirside, and legal right; and, however great one's admiration of the motives which influenced this man, it is impossible not to see that a slave-insurrection, had it been really brought about, would have proved the most disastrous method of settling the great difficulty that could possibly have been devised. Brown was warmly supported by the Abolitionists; but, even in the North, more temperate politicians deplored the error he had committed, and saw that there was no reasonable hope of his being spared. The case was handed over to the grand jury, and the trial took place on the 27th of October. The prisoner requested time to prepare his defence, the assistance of counsel from the Free States, and liberty of communicating with the other prisoners, but most of these demands were refused, and the trial was pushed on with cruel and indecent haste. Virginia was frightened and vindictive, and, as an excuse for not granting any delay, it was urged that the women of the State were harassed by alarm and anxiety as long as their husbands were away from home, and that the jurymen desired to return to them. When Brown was brought into court, he was so weak, owing to the wounds he had received, that he could not stand upon his feet, but lay full-length upon a bed; yet the fears of his enemies were even then predominant. The Governor of Virginia, Mr. Wise, is stated to have remarked at Richmond, before the members of the Legislature, that Brown was a murderer, and ought to be hanged. As it was one of the prerogatives of the Governor to grant pardons, after convictions which might appear to him not strictly in accordance with justice, it was a monstrous outrage on propriety to give utterance to such an opinion while the case was yet awaiting trial. But the remark was only of a piece with the whole procedure. The prisoner was, indeed, furnished with counsel by the court, but the gentlemen to whom the duty of defending him was assigned, had no time for preparing their speeches, for calling witnesses, or for examining the law of the case. He was supplied with no list of witnesses, for the prosecution, nor had he any knowledge of who they were to be, until they were produced in court. Brown himself had sent for counsel to the Northern States, but on arriving, they were so exhausted by their long and hurried journey that they asked for a short delay, which was denied them. All this while, the prisoner lay on his pallet, sick, feverish, and half-conscious, knowing little of the methods by which his conviction was to be secured, but feeling certain from the first that conviction was inevitable. A verdict of guilty, on the 31st of October, was followed by sentence of death, and the execution was fixed for the 2nd of December. The decision was appealed against, but ultimately confirmed. On hearing the verdict and the sentence of the judge, Brown said, "Gentlemen, make an end of slavery, or slavery will make an end of you." It was an utterance in the spirit of prophecy.

As the fatal day approached, the feeling of apprehension on the part of the Virginians became still more intense. Governor Wise ordered out a large military force, to overawe any attempt at rescue that might be made. It was also proposed to establish martial law; but this was not done. Brown expressed entire resignation to his fate, and money was liberally contributed in the Northern and Western States to support his family. At eleven o'clock on the morning of the 2nd of December, the prisoner was brought out of gaol. Before leaving, he bade adieu to his fellow-prisoners, and was very affectionate to all excepting his principal assistant, a man named Cook, whom he charged with having deceived and misled him respecting the support he was to receive from the slaves. Brown, it appears, had been led to believe that they were ripe for insurrection; but, whether from fear, or from actual disinclination, this seems not to have been the case. Cook denied the charge, but otherwise said very little. When asked whether he was ready, Brown replied, "I am always ready," and it was the simple truth. His arms were pinioned, and, wearing a black slouched hat, and the same clothes in which he had appeared at the trial, he proceeded to the door, apparently calm and cheerful. As he stepped out into the open air he saw a negro woman with her child in her arms he paused for a moment, and kissed the infant tenderly. Another black woman exclaimed, "God bless you, old man! I wish I could help you, but I cannot." Six companies of infantry, and one troop of horse, were drawn up in front of the gaol; close by was a waggon, containing a coffin. After talking with some persons whom he knew, Brown seated himself in the waggon, and looked at the soldiers gathered about him. The vehicle then moved off, flanked by two files of riflemen in close order. The field where the gallows had been erected was also in full possession of the military. Pickets were stationed at various localities, and the spectators were kept back at the point of the bayonet, to prevent all possibility of a rescue. When Brown had mounted the gallows, and the cap had been put on his head, together with the rope around his neck, the executioner asked him to step forward on to the trap. He replied, "You must lead me—I cannot see." All was now ready on the scaffold itself, but, owing to some fear on the part of the authorities, the soldiers were marched and counter-marched, frequently changing their positions as if in the face of an enemy. This lasted ten minutes, and the executioner asked the unfortunate man if he was not tired "No," answered Brown, "not tired, but don't keep me waiting longer than is necessary." At length the fatal act was completed; but Brown was a strong man, and the pulse did not entirely cease, until after thirty-five minutes. His companions were executed in March, 1860.

It was a curious feature in the case that the criminal had expressed a desire that no religious ceremony should be performed over his body by "ministers who consent to or approve of the enslavement of their fellow-creatures." He said he should prefer to be accompanied to the scaffold by a dozen slave-children and a good old slave-mother, with their appeal to God for blessings on his soul, rather than have all the eloquence of the whole clergy of the commonwealth combined.—Ed.]

His corpse was given up to his woe-stricken widow, and she, assisted by anti-slavery friends, caused it to be borne to North Elba, Essex county, N.Y., and there his dust now reposes amid the silent, solemn, and snowy grandeurs of the Adirondacks. This raid upon Harper's Ferry was as the last straw to the camel's back. What in the tone of Southern sentiment had been fierce before, became furious and uncontrollable now. A scream for vengeance came up from all sections of the slave States, and from great multitudes in the North. All who were supposed to have been any way connected with John Brown were to be hunted down and surrendered to the tender mercies of slaveholding and panic-stricken Virginia, and there to be tried after the fashion of John Brown, and of course to be summarily executed.

On the evening when the news came that John Brown had taken and was then holding the town of Harper's Ferry, it so happened that I was speaking to a large audience in National Hall, Philadelphia. The announcement came upon us with the startling effect of an earthquake. It was something to make the boldest hold his breath. I saw at once that my old friend had attempted what he had long ago resolved to do, and I felt certain that the result must be his capture and destruction. As I expected, the next day brought the news that with two or three men he had fortified and was holding a small engine house, but that he was surrounded by a body of Virginia militia, who thus far had not ventured to capture the insurgents, but that escape was impossible. A few hours later, and word came that Colonel Robert E. Lee, with a company of United States troops had made a breach in Capt. Brown's fort, and had captured him alive, though mortally wounded. His carpet bag had been secured by Governor Wise, and it was found to contain numerous letters and documents which directly implicated Gerritt Smith, Joshua R. Giddings, Samuel G. Howe, Frank P. Sanborn, and myself. This intelligence was soon followed by a telegram saying that we were all to be arrested. Knowing that I was then in Philadelphia, stopping with my friend, Thomas J. Dorsey, Mr. John Horn, the telegraph operator, came to me and with others urged me to leave the city by the first train, as it was known through the newspapers that I was then in Philadelphia, and officers might even then be on my track. To me there was nothing improbable in all this. My friends for the most part were appalled at the thought of my being arrested then and there, or while on my way across the ferry from Walnut Street wharf to Camden, for there was where I felt sure the arrest would be made, and asked some of them to go so far as this with me merely to see what might occur, but upon one ground or another they all thought it best not to be found in my company at such a time, except dear old Franklin Turner—a true man. The truth is, that in the excitement which prevailed, my friends had reason to fear that the very fact that they were with me would be a sufficient reason for their arrest with me. The delay in the departure of the steamer seemed unusually long to me, for I confess I was seized with a desire to reach a more Northern latitude. My friend Frank did not leave my side till "all ashore" was ordered and the paddles began to move. I reached New York at night, still under the apprehension of arrest at any moment, but no signs of such event being made, I went at once to the Barclay Street Ferry, took the boat across the river and went direct to Washington Street, Hoboken, the home of Mrs. Marks, where I spent the night, and I may add without undue profession of timidity, an anxious night. The morning papers brought no relief, for they announced that the Government would spare no pains in ferretting out and bringing to punishment all who were connected with the Harper's Ferry outrage, and that papers as well as persons would be searched for. I was now somewhat uneasy from the fact that sundry letters and a constitution written by John Brown were locked up in my desk in Rochester. In order to prevent these papers from falling into the hands of the government of Virginia, I got my friend Miss Ottilia Assing to write by my dictation the following telegram to B. F. Blackall, the telegraph operator in Rochester, a friend and frequent visitor at my house, who would readily understand the meaning of the dispatch:

"B. F. Blackall, Esq.,

"Tell Lewis—my eldest son—to secure all the important papers in my high desk."

I did not sign my name, and the result showed that I had rightly judged that Mr. Blackall would understand and promptly attend to the request. The mark of the chisel with which the desk was opened is still on the drawer, and is one of the traces of the John Brown raid. Having taken measures to secure my papers the trouble was to know just what to do with myself. To stay at Hoboken was out of the question, and to go to Rochester was to all appearance to go into the hands of the hunters, for they would naturally seek me at my home if they sought me at all. I, however, resolved to go home and risk my safety there. I felt sure that once in the city I could not be easily taken from there without a preliminary hearing upon the requisition, and not then, if the people could be made aware of what was in progress. But how to get to Rochester became a serious question. It would not do to go to New York city and take the train, for that city was not less incensed against the John Brown conspirators than many parts of the South. The course hit upon by my friends, Mr. Johnson and Miss Assing, was to take me at night in a private conveyance from Hoboken to Paterson, where I could take the Erie railroad for home. This plan was carried out and I reached home in safety, but had been there but a few moments when I was called upon by Samuel D. Porter, Esq., and my neighbour, Lieutenant-Governor Selden, who informed me that the Governor of the State would certainly surrender me on a proper requisition from the Governor of Virginia, and that while the people of Rochester would not permit me to be taken South, yet in order to avoid collision with the Government and consequent bloodshed, they advised me to quit the country, which I did— going to Canada. Governor Wise, in the meantime, being advised that I had left Rochester for the State of Michigan, made requisition on the Governor of that State for my surrender to Virginia.

The following letter from Governor Wise to President James Buchanan—which since the war was sent me by B. J. Lossing, the historian—will show by what means the Governor of Virginia meant to get me in his power, and that my apprehensions of arrest were not altogether groundless:—

[Confidential.]

Richmond, Va., Nov. 13, 1859.

To His Excellency, James Buchanan, President of the United States, and to the Honourable Postmaster-General of the United States:

Gentlemen—I have information such as has caused me, upon proper affidavits, to make requisition upon the Executive of Michigan for the delivery up of the person of Frederick Douglass, a negro man, supposed now to be in Michigan, charged with murder, robbery, and inciting servile insurrection in the State of Virginia. My agents for the arrest and reclamation of the person so charged are Benjamin M. Morris and William N. Kelly. The latter has the requisition, and will wait on you to the end of obtaining nominal authority as post-office agents. They need be very secretive in this matter, and some pretext for travelling through the dangerous section for the execution of the laws in this behalf, and some protection against obtrusive, unruly, or lawless, violence. If it be proper so to do, will the Postmaster-General be pleased to give to Mr. Kelly, for each of these men, a permit and authority to act as detectives for the postoffice department, without pay, but to pass and repass without question, delay, or hindrance?

Respectfully submitted by your obedient servant,

Henry A. Wise.

There is no reason to doubt that James Buchanan afforded Governor Wise all the aid and co-operation for which he was asked. I have been informed that several United States marshals were in Rochester in search of me within six hours after my departure. I do not know that I can do better at this stage of my story than to insert the following letter, written by me to the Rochester Democrat and American:

Canada West, Oct. 31st, 1859.

Mr. Editor:

I notice that the telegraph makes Mr. Cook—one of the unfortunate insurgents at Harper's Ferry, and now a prisoner in the hands of the thing calling itself the Government of Virginia, but which in fact is but an organised conspiracy by one party of the people against another and weaker—denounce me as a coward, and assert that I promised to be present in person at the Harper's Ferry Insurrection. This is certainly a very grave impeachment, whether viewed in its bearings upon friends or upon foes, and you will not think it strange that I should take a somewhat serious notice of it. Having no acquaintance whatever with Mr. Cook, and never having exchanged a word with him about the Harper's Ferry Insurrection, I am disposed to doubt if he could have used the language concerning me, which the wires attribute to him. The lightning when speaking for itself, is among the most direct, reliable, and truthful of things;

but when speaking of the terror-stricken slaveholders at Harper's Ferry, it has been made the swiftest of liars. Under its nimble and trembling fingers it magnifies 17 men into 700 and has since filled the columns of the New York Herald for days with its interminable contradictions. But assuming that it has told only the simple truth as to the sayings of Mr. Cook in this instance, I have this answer to make to my accuser: Mr. Cook may be perfectly right in denouncing me as a coward; I have not one word to say in defence or vindication of my character for courage: I have always been more distinguished for running than fighting, and tried by the Harper's-Ferry-Insurrection test, I am most miserably deficient in courage, even more so than Cook, when he deserted his brave old captain and fled to the mountains. To this extent Mr. Cook is entirely right, and will meet no contradiction from me, or from anybody else. But wholly, grievously and most unaccountably wrong is Mr. Cook when he asserts that I promised to be present in person at the Harper's Ferry Insurrection. Of whatever other imprudence and indiscretion I may have been guilty, I have never made a promise so rash and wild as this. The taking of Harper's Ferry was a measure never encouraged by my word or by my vote. At any time or place, my wisdom or my cowardice, has not only kept me from Harper's Ferry, but has equally kept me from making any promise to go there. I desire to be quite emphatic here, for of all guilty men, he is the guiltiest who lures his fellowmen to an undertaking of this sort, under promise of assistance which he afterwards fails to render. I therefore declare that there is no man living, and no man dead, who if living, could truthfully say that I ever promised him, or anybody else, either conditionally, or otherwise, that I would be present in person at the Harper's Ferry Insurrection. My field of labour for the abolition of slavery has not extended to an attack upon the United States Arsenal. In the teeth of the documents already published, and of those which may hereafter be published, I affirm that no man connected with that insurrection, from its noble and heroic leader down, can connect my name with a single broken promise of any sort whatever. So much I deem it proper to say negatively. The time for a full statement of what I know, and of all I know, of this desperate but sublimely disinterested effort to emancipate the slaves of Maryland and Virginia from their cruel task-masters, has not yet come, and may never come. In the denial which I have now made, my motive is more a respectful consideration for the opinions of the slave's friends than from my fear of being made an accomplice in the general conspiracy against slavery, when there is a reasonable hope for success. Men who live by robbing their fellowmen of their labour and liberty have forfeited their right to know anything of the thoughts, feelings, or purposes of those whom they rob and plunder. They have by the single act of slaveholding, voluntarily placed themselves beyond the laws of justice and honour, and have become only fitted for companionship with thieves and pirates—the common enemies of God and of all mankind. While it shall be considered right to protect oneself against thieves, burglars, robbers, and assassins, and to slay a wild beast in the act of devouring his human prey, it can never be wrong for the imbruted and whipscarred slaves, or their friends, to hunt, harass, and even strike down the traffickers in human flesh. If anybody is disposed to think less of me on account of this sentiment, or because I may have had a knowledge of what was about to occur, and did not assume the base and detestable character of an informer, he is a man whose good or bad opinion of me may be equally repugnant and despicable.

Entertaining these sentiments, I may be asked why I did not join John Brown—the noble old hero whose one right hand has shaken the foundation of the American Union, and whose ghost will haunt the bed-chambers of all the born and unborn slaveholders of Virginia through all generations, filling them with alarm and consternation. My answer to this has already been given—at least impliedly given—"The tools to those who can use them!" Let every man work for the abolition of slavery in his own way. I would help all and hinder none. My position in regard to the Harper's Ferry Insurrection may be easily inferred from these remarks, and I shall be glad if those papers which have spoken of me in connection with it, would find room for this brief statement. I have no apology for keeping out of the way of those gentlemanly

United States Marshals, who are said to have paid Rochester a somewhat protracted visit lately, with a view to an interview with me. A government recognising the validity of the Dred Scott decision, at such a time as this is not likely to have any very charitable feelings towards me, and if I am to meet its representatives I prefer to do so at least upon equal terms. If I have committed any offence against society I have done so on the soil of the State of New York, and I should be perfectly willing to be arraigned there before an impartial jury; but I have quite insuperable objections to being caught by the hounds of Mr. Buchanan, and "bagged" by Gov. Wise. For this appears to be the arrangement. Buchanan does the fighting and hunting, and Wise "bags" the game. Some reflections may be made upon my leaving on a tour to England just at this time. I have only to say that my going to that country has been rather delayed than hastened by the insurrection at Harper's Ferry. All know that I had intended to leave here in the first week in November.

Frederick Douglass."

CHAPTER X: THE BEGINNING OF THE END.

My connection with John Brown—To and from England—Presidential contest—Election of Abraham Lincoln.

WHAT was my connection with John Brown, and what I knew of his scheme for the capture of Harper's Ferry, I may now proceed to state. From the time of my visit to him at Springfield, Mass., in 1847, our relations were friendly and confidential. I never passed through Springfield without calling on him, and he never came to Rochester without calling on me. He often stopped over night with me, when we talked over the feasibility of his plan for destroying the value of slave property, and the motive for holding slaves in the border States. That plan, as already intimated elsewhere, was to take twenty or twenty-five discreet and trustworthy men into the mountains of Virginia and Maryland, and station them in squads of five, about five miles apart, on a line of twenty-five miles; each squad to co-operate with all, and all with each. They were to have selected for them, secure and comfortable retreats in the fastnesses of the mountains, where they could easily defend themselves in case of attack. They were to subsist upon the country roundabout. They were to be well armed, but were to avoid battle or violence, unless compelled by pursuit or in self-defence. In that case, they were to make it as costly as possible to the assailing party, whether that party should be soldiers or citizens. He further proposed to have a number of stations from the line of Pennsylvania to the Canada border, where such slaves as he might, through his men, induce to run away, should be supplied with food and shelter, and be forwarded from one station to another till they should reach a place of safety either in Canada or the Northern States. He proposed to add to his force in the mountains any courageous and intelligent fugitives who might be willing to remain and endure the hardships and brave the dangers of this mountain life. These, he thought, if properly selected, on account of their knowledge of the surrounding country, could be made valuable auxiliaries. The work of going into the valley of Virginia and persuading the slaves to flee to the mountains, was to be committed to the most courageous and judicious man connected with each squad.

Hating slavery as I did, and making its abolition the object of my life, I was ready to welcome any new mode of attack upon the slave system which gave any promise of success. I readily saw that this plan could be made very effective in rendering slave property in Maryland and Virginia valueless by rendering it insecure. Men do not like to buy runaway horses, nor to invest their money in a species of property likely to take legs and walk off with itself. In the worst case, too, if the plan should fail, and John Brown should be driven from the mountains, a new fact would be developed by which the nation would be kept awake to the existence of slavery. Hence, I assented to this, John Brown's scheme or plan for running off slaves.

To set this plan in operation, money and men, arms and ammunition, food and clothing, were needed; and these, from the nature of the enterprise, were not easily obtained, and nothing was immediately done. Captain Brown, too, notwithstanding his rigid economy, was poor, and was unable to arm and equip men for the dangerous life he had mapped out. So the work lingered till after the Kansas trouble was over, and freedom was a fact accomplished in that Territory. This left him with arms and men, for the men who had been with him in Kansas, believed in him, and would follow him in any humane but dangerous enterprise he might undertake.

After the close of his Kansas work, Captain Brown came to my house in Rochester, and said he desired to stop with me several weeks; "but," he added, "I will not stay unless you will allow me to pay board." Knowing that he was no trifler and meant all he said, and desirous of retaining him under my roof, I charged three dollars a week. While here, he spent most of his time in correspondence. He wrote often to George L. Stearns of Boston, Gerrit Smith of Peterboro, N. Y., and many others, and received many letters in return. When he was not writing letters, he was writing and revising a constitution which he meant to put in operation by the men who should go with him into the mountains. He said that to avoid anarchy and confusion, there should be a regularly constituted government, to which each man who came with him should be sworn to honour and support. I have a copy of this constitution in Captain Brown's own handwriting, as prepared by himself at my house.

He called his friends from Chatham, Canada, to come together that he might lay his constitution before them, for their approval and adoption. His whole time and thought were given to this subject. It was the first thing in the morning and last thing at night, till I confess it began to be something of a bore to me. Once in a while, he would say he could, with a few resolute men, capture Harper's Ferry, and supply himself with arms belonging to the Government at that place, but he never announced his intention to do so. It was, however, very evidently passing in his mind as a thing he might do. I paid but little attention to such remarks, though I never doubted that he thought just what he said. Soon after his coming to me, he asked me to get for him two smoothly planed boards, upon which he could illustrate, with a pair of dividers, by a drawing, the plan of fortification which he meant to adopt in the mountains.

These forts were to be so arranged as to connect one with the other, by secret passages, so that if one was carried, another could easily be fallen back upon, and be the means of dealing death to the enemy at the very moment when he might think himself victorious. I was less interested in these drawings than my children were, but they showed that the old man had an eye to the means as well as to the end, and was giving his best thought to the work he was about to take in hand.

While at my house, John Brown made the acquaintance of a coloured man, who called himself by different names—sometimes "Emperor," at other times, "Shields Green." He was a fugitive slave, who had made his escape from Charlestown, South Carolina, a State from which a slave found it no easy matter to run away. But Shields Green was not one to shrink from hardships or dangers. He was a man of few words, and his speech was singularly broken; but his courage and self-respect made him quite a dignified character. John Brown saw at once what "stuff" Green "was made of," and confided to him his plans and purposes. Green easily believed in Brown, and promised to go with him whenever he should be ready to move. About three weeks before the raid on Harper's Ferry, John Brown wrote to me, informing me that a beginning in his work would soon be made, and that before going forward he wanted to see me, and appointed an old stone quarry near Chambersburg, Penn., as our place of meeting. Mr. Kagi, his secretary, would be there, and they wished me to bring any money I could command, and Shields Green along with me. In the same letter, he said that his "mining tools" and stores were then at Chambersburg, and that he would be there to remove them. I obeyed the old man's summons. Taking Shields, we passed through New York City, where we called upon the Rev. James Glocester and his wife, and told them where and for what we were going, and that our old friend needed money. Mrs. Glocester gave me ten dollars, and asked me to hand the same to John Brown, with her best wishes.

When I reached Chambersburg, a good deal of surprise was expressed, for I was instantly recognised, that I should come there unannounced, and I was pressed to make a speech to them, with which invitation I readily complied. Meanwhile, I called upon Mr. Henry Watson, a simple-minded and warm-hearted man, to whom Captain Brown had imparted the secret of my visit, to show me the road to the appointed rendezvous. Watson was very busy in his barber's shop, but he dropped all and put me on the right track. I approached the old quarry very cautiously, for John Brown was generally well armed, and regarded strangers with suspicion. He was there under the ban of the Government, and heavy rewards were offered for his arrest, for offences said to have been committed in Kansas. He was passing under the name of John Smith. As I came near, he regarded me rather suspiciously, but soon recognized me, and received me cordially. He had in his hand when I met him, a fishing tackle, with which he had apparently been fishing in a stream hard by; but I saw no fish, and did not suppose that he cared much for his "fisherman's luck." The fishing was simply a disguise, and was certainly a good one. He looked every way like a man of the neighbourhood, and as much at home as any of the farmers around there. His hat was old, and storm-beaten, and his clothing was about the colour of the stone quarry itself—his then present dwelling-place.

His face wore an anxious expression, and he was much worn by thought and exposure. I felt that I was on a dangerous mission, and was as little desirous of discovery as himself, though no reward had been offered for me.

We—Mr. Kagi, Captain Brown, Shields Green, and myself, sat down among the rocks and talked over the enterprise which was about to be undertaken, The taking of Harper's Ferry, of which Captain Brown had merely hinted before, was now declared as his settled purpose, and he wanted to know what I thought of it. I at once opposed the measure with all the arguments at my command. To me, such a measure would be fatal to running off slaves, as was the original plan, and fatal to all engaged in doing so. It would be an attack upon the Federal Government, and would array the whole country against us. Captain Brown did most of the talking on the other side of the question. He did not at all object to rousing the nation; it seemed to him that something startling was just what the nation needed. He had completely renounced his old plan, and thought that the capture of Harper's Ferry would serve as notice to the slaves that their friends had come, and as a trumpet, to rally them to his standard. He described the place as to its means of defence, and how impossible it would be to dislodge him if once in possession. Of course, I was no match for him in such matters, but I told him, and these were my words, that all his arguments, and all his descriptions of the place, convinced me that he was going into a perfect steel-trap, and that once in he would never get out alive; that he would be surrounded at once and escape would be impossible. He was not to be shaken by anything I could say, but treated my views respectfully, replying that even if surrounded he would find means for cutting his way out; but that would not be forced upon him; he should have a number of the best citizens of the neighbourhood as his prisoners at the start, and that holding them as hostages, he should be able if worse came to worse, to dictate terms of egress from the town. I looked at him with some astonishment, that he could rest upon a reed so weak and broken, and told him that Virginia would blow him and his hostages sky-high, rather than that he should hold Harper's Ferry an hour. Our talk was long and earnest; we spent the most of Saturday and a part of Sunday in this debate—Brown for Harper's Ferry, and I against it; he for striking a blow which should instantly rouse the country, and I for the policy of gradually and unaccountably drawing off the slaves to the mountains, as at first suggested and proposed by him. When I found that he had fully made up his mind and could not be dissuaded, I turned to Shields Green and told him he heard what Captain Brown had said; his old plan was changed, and that I should return home, and if he wished to go with me he could do so. Captain Brown urged us both to go with him, but I could not do so, and could but feel that he was about to rivet the fetters more firmly than ever on the limbs of the enslaved. In parting he put his arms around me in a manner more than friendly, and said: "Come with me, Douglass, I will defend you with my life. I want you for a special purpose. When I strike, the bees will begin to swarm, and I shall want you to help hive them." But my discretion or my cowardice made me proof against the dear old man's eloquence—perhaps it was something of both which determined my course. When about to leave I asked Green what he had decided to do, and was surprised by his coolly saying in his broken way, "I b'leve I'll go wid de ole man." Here we separated; they to go to Harper's Ferry, I to Rochester. There has been some difference of opinion as to the propriety of my course in thus leaving my friend. Some have thought that I ought to have gone with him, but I have no reproaches for myself on this point, and since I have been assailed only by coloured men who kept even farther from this brave and heroic man than I did, I shall not trouble myself about their criticisms. They compliment me in assuming that I should perform greater deeds than themselves.

Such then was my connection with John Brown, and it may be asked if this is all, why should I have objected to being sent to Virginia to be tried for the offence charged. The explanation is not difficult. I knew if my enemies could not prove me guilty of the offence of being with John Brown they could prove that I was Frederick Douglass; they could prove that I was in correspondence and conspiracy with Brown against slavery; they could prove that I brought Shields Green, one of the bravest of his soldiers, all the way from Rochester to him at Chambersburg; they could prove that I brought money to aid him, and in what was then the state of the public mind I could not hope to make a jury of Virginia believe I did not go the whole length which he went, or that I was not one of his supporters, and I knew that all Virginia, were I once in her clutches, would say "let him be hanged." Before I had left Canada for England, Jeremiah Anderson, one of Brown's men, who was present and took part in the raid but escaped by the mountains, joined me, and he told me that he and Shields Green were sent out on special duty as soon as the capture of the arsenal, etc., was effected. Their business was to bring in the slaves from the surrounding country, and hence they were on the outside when Brown was surrounded. I said to him, "Why then did not Shields come with you?" "Well," he said, "I told him to come; that we could do nothing more, but he simply said he must go down to de ole man." Anderson further told me that Captain Brown was careful to keep his plans from his men, and that there was much opposition among them when they found what were the precise movements determined upon; but they were an oath-bound company, and like good soldiers were agreed to follow their captain wherever he might lead.

On the 12th of November, 1859, I took passage from Quebec on board the steamer "Scotia," Captain Thompson, of the Allan line. My going to England was not at first suggested by my connection with John Brown, but the fact that I was now in danger of arrest on the ground of complicity with him, made what I had intended a pleasure a necessity, for though in Canada, and under British law, it was not impossible that I might be kidnapped and taken to Virginia. England had given me shelter and protection when the slavehounds were on my track fourteen years before, and her gates were still open to me now that I was pursued in the name of Virginian justice. I could but feel that I was going into exile, perhaps for life. Slavery seemed to be at the very top of its power; the national government, with all its powers and appliances, were in its hands, and it bade fair to wield them for many years to come. Nobody could then see that in the short space of four years this power would be broken and the slave system destroyed. So I started on my voyage with feelings far from cheerful. No one who has not himself been compelled to leave his home and country to go into permanent banishment, can well imagine the state of mind and heart which such a condition brings. The voyage out was by the North Passage, and at this season, as usual, it was cold, dark, and stormy. Before quitting the coast of Labrador, we had four degrees below zero. Although I had crossed the Atlantic twice before, I had not experienced such unfriendly weather as during the most of this voyage. Our great ship was dashed about upon the surface of the sea as though she had been the smallest "dug-out." It seemed to tax all the seamanship of our captain to keep her in manageable condition; but after battling with the waves on an angry ocean during fourteen long days, I gratefully found myself upon the soil of Great Britain, beyond the reach of Buchanan's power and Virginia's prisons. On reaching Liverpool, I learned that England was nearly as much alive to what had happened at Harper's Ferry as the United States, and I was immediately called upon in different parts of the country to speak on the subject of slavery, and especially to give some account of the men who had thus flung away their lives in a desperate attempt to free the slaves. My own relation to the affair was a subject of much interest, as was the fact of my presence there being in some sense to elude the demands of Governor Wise, who having learned that I was not in Michigan, but was on a British steamer bound for England, publicly declared that "could he overtake that vessel, he would take me from her deck at any cost."

While in England, and wishing to visit France, I wrote to Mr. George M. Dallas, the American minister at the British court, to obtain a passport. The attempt upon the life of Napoleon III. about that time, and the suspicion that the conspiracy against him had been hatched in England, made the French government very strict in the enforcement of its passport system. I might possibly have been permitted to visit that country without a certificate of my citizenship, but wishing to leave nothing to chance, I applied to the only competent authority; but, true to the traditions of the Democratic party—true to the slaveholding policy of his country—true to the decision of the United States Supreme Court, and true, perhaps, to the petty meanness of his own nature, Mr. George M. Dallas, the Democratic American minister, refused to grant me a passport, on the ground that I was not a citizen of the United States, I did not beg or remonstrate with this dignitary further, but simply addressed a note to the French minister in London, asking for a permit to visit France, and that paper came without delay. I mention this, not to be-little the civilization of my native country, but as a part of the story of my life. I could have born this denial with more serenity, could I have foreseen what has since happened, but, under the circumstances, it was a galling disappointment.

I had at this time been about six months out of the United States. My time had been chiefly occupied in speaking on slavery, and other subjects, in different parts of England and Scotland, meeting and enjoying the while the society of many of the kind friends whose acquaintance I had made during my visit to those countries fourteen years before. Much of the excitement caused by the Harper's Ferry Insurrection had subsided, both at home and abroad, and I should have now gratified a long-cherished desire to visit France, and avail myself, for that purpose, of the permit so promptly and civilly given by the French minister, had not news reached me from home of the death of my beloved daughter Annie, the light and life of my house. Deeply distressed by this bereavement, and acting upon the impulse of the moment, regardless of the peril, I at once resolved to return home, and took the first outgoing steamer for Portland, Maine. After a rough passage of seventeen days, I reached home by way of Canada, and remained in my house nearly a month before the knowledge got abroad that I was again in America. Great changes had now taken place in the public mind touching the John

Brown Raid. Virginia had satisfied her thirst for blood. She had executed all the raiders who had fallen into her hands. She had not given Captain Brown the benefit of a reasonable doubt, but hurried him to the scaffold in panic-stricken haste. She had made herself ridiculous by her fright, and despisable by her fury. Emerson's prediction that Brown's gallows would become like the Cross, was already being fulfilled. The old hero, in the trial hour, had behaved so grandly that men regarded him not as a murderer, but as a martyr. All over the North men were singing the John Brown song. His body was in the dust, but his soul was marching on. His defeat was already assuming the form and pressure of victory, and his death was giving new life and power to the principles of justice and liberty. He had spoken great words in the face of death and the champions of slavery. He had quailed before neither. What he had lost by the sword, he had more than gained by the truth. Had he wavered, had he retreated or apologized, the case had been different. He did not even ask that the cup of death might pass from him. To his own soul he was right, and neither "principalities nor powers, life nor death, things present nor things to come," could shake his dauntless spirit, or move him from his ground. He may not have stooped on his way to the gallows to kiss a little coloured child, as it is reported he did, but the act would have been in keeping with the tender heart, as well as with the heroic spirit of the man. Those who looked for confession heard only the voice of rebuke and warning.

Early after the insurrection at Harper's Ferry, an investigating committee was appointed by Congress, and a "drag-net" was spread all over the country, in the hope of inculpating many distinguished persons. They had imprisoned Thaddeus Hyatt, who denied their right to interrogate him, and had called many witnesses before them, as if the judicial power of the nation had been confided to their committee, and not the Supreme Court of the United States. But Captain Brown implicated nobody. Upon his own head he invited all the bolts of slaveholding vengeance. He said that he, and he alone, was responsible for all that had happened. He had many friends, but no instigators. In all their efforts this committee signally failed, and soon after my arrival home, they gave up the search, and asked to be discharged, not having half fulfilled the duty for which they were appointed.

I have never been able to account satisfactorily for the sudden abandonment of this investigation on any other ground than that the men engaged in it expected soon to be in rebellion themselves, and that, not a rebellion for liberty like that of John Brown, but a rebellion for slavery; and that they saw that by using their senatorial power in search of rebels they might be whetting a knife for their own throats. At any rate the country was soon relieved of the congressional drag-net, and was now engaged in the heat and turmoil of a presidential canvass—a canvass which had no parallel, involving as it did the question of peace or war, the integrity or the dismemberment of the Republic; and I may add, the maintenance or destruction of slavery. In some of the Southern States the people were already organizing and arming to be ready for an apprehended contest, and with this work on their hands they had no time to spare for those they had wished to convict as instigators of the raid, however desirous they might have been to do so under other circumstances, for they had parted with none of their hate. As showing their feeling towards me, I may state, that a coloured man appeared about this time in Knoxville, Ten., and was beset by a furious crowd with knives and bludgeons, because he was supposed to be Fred. Douglass. But, however perilous it would have been for me to have shown myself in any Southern State, there was no especial danger for me in the North.

Though disappointed in my tour on the Continent, and called home by one of the saddest events that can afflict the domestic circle, my presence here was fortunate, since it enabled me to participate in the most important and memorable presidential canvass ever witnessed in the United States, and to labour for the election of a man who in the order of events was destined to do a greater service to his country and to mankind, than any man who had gone before him in the presidential office. It is something to couple one's name with great occasions, and it was a great thing to me to be permitted to bear some humble part in this, the greatest that had thus far come to the American people. It was a great thing to achieve American independence when we numbered three millions, but it was a greater thing to save the country from dismemberment and ruin when it numbered thirty millions. He alone of all our Presidents was to have the opportunity to destroy slavery, and to lift into manhood millions of his countrymen hitherto held as chattels and numbered with the beasts of the field.

The presidential canvass of 1860 was three sided, and each side had its distinctive doctrine as to the question of slavery and slavery extension. We had three candidates in the field. Stephen A. Douglas was the standard-bearer of what may be called the Western faction of the old divided Democratic party, and John C. Breckenridge was the standard-bearer of the Southern or slaveholding faction of that party. Abraham Lincoln represented the then young, growing, and united Republican party. The lines between these parties and candidates were about as distinctly and clearly drawn as political lines are capable of being drawn. The name of Douglas stood for territorial sovereignty, or in other words, for the right of the people of a territory to admit or exclude, to establish or abolish, slavery, as to them might seem best. The doctrine of Breckenridge was that slaveholders were entitled to carry their slaves into any territory of the United States and to hold them there, with or without the consent of the people of the territory; that the Constitution of its own force carried slavery, and protected it, into any territory open for settlement in the United States. To both these parties, factions, and doctrines, Abraham Lincoln and the Republican party stood opposed. They held that the Federal Government had the right and the power to exclude slavery from the territories of the United States, and that that right and power ought to be exercised to the extent of confining slavery inside the slave States, with a view to its ultimate extinction. The position of Mr. Douglas gave him a splendid pretext for the display of a species of oratory of which he was a distinguished master. He alone of the three candidates took the stump, as the preacher of popular sovereignty, called in derision at the time "Squatter" sovereignty. This doctrine, if not the times, gave him a chance to play fast and loose, and blow hot and cold, as occasion might require. In the South and among slaveholders he could say, "My great principle of popular sovereignty does not and was not intended by me to prevent the extension of slavery; on the contrary, it gives you the right to take your slaves into the territories and secure legislation legalizing slavery; it denies to the Federal Government all right of interference against you, and hence is eminently favourable to your interests." When among people known to be indifferent, he could say, "I do not care whether slavery is voted up or voted down in the territory," but when addressing the known opponents of the extension of slavery, he could say that the people of the territories were in no danger of having slavery forced upon them since they could keep it out by adverse legislation. Had he made these representations before railroads, electric wires, phonography, and newspapers had become the powerful auxiliaries they have done, Mr. Douglas might have gained many votes, but they were of little avail now. The South was too sagacious to leave slavery to the chance of defeat in a fair vote by the people of a territory. Of all property, none could less afford to take such a risk, for no property can require more strongly favouring conditions for its existence. Not only the intelligence of the slave, but the instincts of humanity, must be barred by positive law, hence Breckenridge and his friends erected the flinty walls of the Constitution and the Supreme Court for the protection of slavery at the outset. Against both Douglas and Breckenridge, Abraham Lincoln proposed his grand historic doctrine of the power and duty of the National Government to prevent the spread and perpetuity of slavery. Into this contest I threw myself, with firmer faith and more ardent hope than ever before, and what I could do by pen or voice was done with a will. The most remarkable and memorable feature of this canvass, was that it was prosecuted under the portentous shadow of a threat. Leading public men of the South had with the vehemence of fiery purpose, given it out in advance that in case of their failure to elect their candidate—Mr. C. Breckenridge—they would proceed to take the slaveholding States out of the Union, and that in no event whatever would they submit to the rule of Abraham Lincoln. To many of the peaceloving friends of the Union, this was a fearful announcement, and it doubtless cost the Republican candidate many votes. By many others, however, it was deemed a mere bravado—sound and fury signifying nothing. With a third class its effect was very different. They were tired of the rule-or-ruin intimidation adopted by the South, and felt then, if never before, that they had quailed before it too often and too long. It came as an insult and a challenge in one, and imperatively called upon them for independence, self-assertion, and resentment. Had Southern men puzzled their brains to find the most effective means to array against slavery and slaveholding manners the solid opposition of the North, they could not have hit upon any expedient better suited to that end, than was this threat. It was not only unfair, but insolent, and more like an address to cowardly slaves than to independent freemen; it had in it the meanness of the horse-jockey, who, on entering a race, proposes, if beaten, to run off with the stakes. In all my speeches made during this canvass, I did not fail to take advantage of this Southern bluster and bullying.

As I have said, this Southern threat lost many votes, but it gained more than would have covered the loss. It frightened the timid, but stimulated the brave; and the result was—the triumphant election of Abraham Lincoln.

Then came the question, what will the South do about it? Will she eat her bold words, and submit to the verdict of the people, or proceed to the execution of the programme she had marked out for herself prior to the election? The inquiry was an anxious one, and the blood of the North stood still, waiting for the response. It had not to wait long, for the trumpet of war was soon sounded, and the tramp of armed men was heard in that region. During all the winter of 1860 notes of preparation for a tremendous conflict came to us from that quarter on every wind. Still the warning was not taken. Few of the North could really believe that this insolent display of arms would end in anything more substantial than dust and smoke.

The shameful and shocking course of President Buchanan and his Cabinet towards this rising rebellion against the Government which each and all of them had solemnly sworn to "support, defend, and maintain"—that the treasury was emptied, that the army was scattered, that our ships of war were sent out of the way, that our forts and arsenals in the South were weakened and crippled—purposely left an easy prey to the prospective insurgents—that one after another the States were allowed to secede, that these rebel measures were largely encouraged by the doctrine of Mr. Buchanan, that he found no power in the constitution to coerce a State, are all matters of history, and need only the briefest mention here.

To arrest this tide of secession and revolution which was sweeping over the South, the Southern papers, which still had some dread of the consequences likely to ensue from the course marked out before the election, proposed as a means for promoting conciliation and satisfaction, that "each Northern State, through her legislature, or in convention assembled, should repeal all laws passed for the injury of the constitutional rights of the South—meaning thereby, all laws passed for the protection of personal liberty;—that they should pass laws for the easy and prompt execution of the Fugitive Slave Law; that they should pass other laws imposing penalties on all malefactors who should hereafter assist or encourage the escape of fugitive slaves; also, laws declaring and protecting the right of slaveholders to travel and sojourn in Northern States, accompanied by their slaves; also, that they should instruct their representatives and senators in Congress, to repeal the law prohibiting the sale of slaves in the district of Columbia, and pass laws sufficient for the full protection of slave property in the territories of the Union."

It may, indeed, be well regretted that there was a class of men in the North willing to patch up a peace with this rampant spirit of disunion, by compliance with these offensive, scandalous, and humiliating terms; and to do so without any guarantee that the South would then be pacified; rather with the certainty, learned by past experience, that it would by no means promote this end. I confess to a feeling allied to satisfaction at the prospect of a conflict between the North and the South. Standing outside the pale of American humanity, denied citizenship, unable to call the land of my birth my country, and adjudged by the Supreme Court of the United States to have no rights which white men were bound to respect, and longing for the end of the bondage of my people, I was ready for any political upheaval which should bring about a change in the existing condition of things. Whether the war of words would or would not end in blows was for a time a matter of doubt; and when it became certain that the South was wholly in earnest, and meant at all hazards to execute its threats of disruption, a visible change in the sentiments of the North was apparent.

The reaction from the glorious assertion of freedom and independence on the part of the North in the triumphant election of Abraham Lincoln, was a painful and humiliating development of its weakness. It seemed as if all that had been gained in the canvass was about to be surrendered to the vanquished; that the South, though beaten at the polls, was to be victorious and have everything its own way in the final result. During all the intervening months, from November to the ensuing March, the drift of Northern sentiment was towards compromise. To smooth the way for this, most of the Northern legislatures repealed their personal liberty bills, as they were supposed to embarrass the surrender of fugitive slaves to their claimants. The feeling everywhere seemed to be that something must be done to convince the South that the election of Mr. Lincoln meant no harm to slavery or the slave power, that the North was sound on the question of the right of the master to hold and hunt his slave as long as he pleased, and that even the right to hold slaves in the Territories should be submitted to the Supreme Court, which would probably decide in favour of the most extravagant demands of the slave States. The Northern Press took a more conservative tone towards the slavery propagandists, and a corresponding tone of bitterness towards anti-slavery men and measures. It came to be a no uncommon thing to hear men denouncing South Carolina and Massachusetts in the same breath, and in the same measure of disapproval. The old pro-slavery spirit which, in 1835, mobbed anti-slavery prayer-meetings, and dragged William Lloyd Garrison through the streets of Boston with a halter about his neck, was revived. From Massachusetts to Missouri, anti-slavery meetings were ruthlessly assailed and broken up. With others, I was roughly handled by a mob headed by one of the wealthiest men of that city, in Tremont Temple, Boston. The talk was that the blood of some abolitionist must be shed to appease the wrath of the offended South, and to restore peaceful relations between the two sections of the country. A howling mob followed Wendell Phillips for three days whenever he appeared on the pavements of his native city, because of his ability and prominence in the propagation of anti-slavery opinions.

While this humiliating reaction was going on in the North, various devices were suggested and pressed at Washington, to bring about peace and reconciliation. Committees were appointed to listen to Southern grievances, and, if possible, devise means of redress for such as might be alleged. Some of these peace propositions would have been shocking to the last degree to the moral sense of the North, had not fear for the safety of the Union overwhelmed all moral conviction. Such men as William H. Seward, Charles Francis Adams, Henry B. Anthony, Joshua R. Giddings, and others—men whose courage had been equal to all other emergencies—bent before this Southern storm, and were ready to purchase peace at any price. Those who had stimulated the courage of the North before the election, and had shouted "Who's afraid?" were now shaking in their shoes with apprehension and dread. One was for passing laws in the Northern States for the better protection of slave-hunters, and for the greater efficiency of the Fugitive Slave Bill. Another was for enacting laws to punish the invasion of the slave States, and others were for so altering the Constitution of the United States that the Federal Government should never abolish slavery while any one State should object to such a measure. Everything that could be demanded by insatiable pride and selfishness on the part of the slaveholding South, or could be surrendered by abject fear and servility on the part of the North, had able and eloquent advocates,

Happily for the cause of human freedom, and for the final unity of the American nation, the South was mad, and would listen to no concessions. They would neither accept the terms offered, nor offer others to be accepted. They had made up their minds that under a given contingency they would secede from the Union and thus dismember the Republic. That contingency had happened, and they should execute their threat. Mr. Ireson, of Georgia, expressed the ruling sentiment of his section when he told the Northern peacemakers that if the people of the South were given a blank sheet of paper upon which to write their own terms on which they would remain in the Union, they would not stay. They had come to hate everything which had the prefix "Free"—free soil, free states, free territories, free schools, free speech, and freedom generally, and they would have no more such prefixes. This haughty, unreasonable, and unreasoning attitude of the imperious South saved the slave and saved the nation. Had the South accepted our concessions and remained in the Union the slave power would in all probability have continued to rule; the North would have become utterly demoralized; the hands on the dial-plate of American civilization would have been reversed, and the slave would have been dragging his hateful chains to-day wherever the American flag floats to the breeze. Those who may wish to see to what depths of humility and self-abasement a noble people can be brought under the sentiment of fear, will find no chapter of history more instructive than that which treats of the events in official circles in Washington during the space between the months of November, 1859, and March, 1860.

CHAPTER XI.: SECESSION AND WAR.

Recruiting of the 54th and 55th Coloured Regiments—Visit to President Lincoln and Secretary Stanton—Promised a Commission as Adjutant General to General Thomas—Disappointment.

THE cowardly and disgraceful reaction, from a courageous and manly assertion of right principles, as described in the foregoing pages, continued surprisingly long after secession and war were commenced. The patience and forbearance of the loyal people of the North were amazing. Speaking of this feature of the situation in Corinthian Hall, Rochester, at the time, I said:—

We, the people of the North, are a charitable people, and in the excess of this feeling we were disposed to put the very best construction upon the strange behaviour of our Southern brethren. We hoped that all would yet go well. We thought that South Carolina might secede; it was entirely like her to do so. She had talked extravagantly about going out of the Union, and it was natural that she should do something extravagant and startling if for nothing else, to make a show of consistency. Georgia, too, we thought might possible secede. But strangely enough we thought and felt quite sure that these twin rebellious States would stand alone and unsupported in infamy and impotency; that they would soon tire of their isolation, repent of their folly, and come back to their places in the Union. Traitors withdrew from the Cabinet, from the House of Representatives, and from the Senate, and hastened to their several States to 'fire the Southern heart,' and to fan the hot flames of treason at home. Still we doubted if anything serious would come of it. We treated it as a bubble on the wave—a nine days' wonder. Calm and thoughtful men ourselves, we relied upon the sober second thought of the Southern people. Even the capture of a fort, a shot at one of our ships—an insult to the national flag—caused only a momentary feeling of indignation and resentment. We could not but believe that there existed in the South a latent and powerful Union sentiment which would assert itself at last. Though loyal soldiers had been fired upon in the streets of Baltimore; though loyal blood had stained the pavements, of that beautiful city, and the National Government was warned to send no troops through Baltimore to the defence of the National Capital, we could not be made to believe that the border States would plunge madly into the bloody vortex of rebellion.

"But this confidence, patience, and forbearance could not last for ever. Those blissful illusions of hope were in a measure dispelled when the batteries of Charlestown harbour were opened upon the starving garrison at Fort Sumpter. For the moment the Northern lamb was transformed into a lion, and his roar was terrible. But he only showed his teeth, and clearly had no wish to use them. We preferred to fight with dollars and not daggers. 'The fewer battles the better,' was the hopeful motto at Washington. 'Peace in sixty days,' was held out by the astute Secretary of State. In fact, there was at the North no disposition to fight; no spirit of hate; no comprehension of the stupendous character and dimensions of the rebellion, and no proper appreciation of its inherent wickedness. Treason had shot its poisonous roots deeper, and had spread its death-dealing branches further than any Northern calculation had covered. Thus while rebels were waging a barbarous war, marshalling savage Indians to join them in slaughter; while rifled cannon balls were battering down the walls of our forts, and the iron-clad hand of monarchical power was being invoked to assist in the destruction of our government and the dismemberment of our country, while a tremendous rebel ram was sinking our fleet and threatening the cities of our coast, we were still dreaming of peace. This infatuation, this blindness to the significance of passing events can only be accounted for by the rapid passage of these events, and by the fact of the habitual leniency and good-will cherished by the North towards the South Our very lack of preparation for the conflict disposed us to look for some other way than the way of blood out of the difficulty. Treason had largely infected both army and navy. Floyd had scattered our arms, Cobb had depleted our treasury, and Buchanan had poisoned the political thought of the times by his doctrines of anti-coercion. It was in such a condition of things as this that Abraham Lincoln, compelled from fear of assassination to enter the capital in disguise, was inaugurated and issued his proclamation for the 'repossession of the forts, places, and property which had been seized from the Union,' and his call upon the militia of the several States to the number of 75,000 men—a paper which showed how little even he comprehended the work then before the loyal nation. It was perhaps better for the country and for mankind that the good man could not know the end from the beginning. Had he foreseen the thousands who must sink into bloody graves; the mountains of debt to be laid on the breast of the nation; the terrible hardships and sufferings involved in the contest; and his own death by an assassin's hand, he too might have adopted the weak sentiment of those who said 'erring sisters, depart in peace.' "

From the first, I, for one, saw in this war the end of slavery and truth requires me to say that my interest in the success of the North was largely due to this belief. True it is that this faith was many times shaken by passing events, but never destroyed. When Secretary Seward instructed our ministers to say to the Governments to which they were accredited, that, "terminate however it might, the status of no class of the people of the United States would be changed by the rebellion—that the slaves would be slaves still, and that the masters would be masters still"—when General McClellan and General Butler warned the slaves in advance that if any attempt was made by them to gain their freedom, it would be suppressed with an iron hand—when the Government persistently refused to employ coloured troops—when the emancipation proclamation of General John C. Freemont in Missouri was withdrawn—when slaves were being returned from our lines to their masters—when Union soldiers were stationed about the farm houses of Virginia to guard and protect the master in holding his slaves—when Union soldiers made themselves more active in kicking coloured men out of their camps than in shooting rebels—when even Mr. Lincoln could tell the poor negro that "he was the cause of the war," I still believed, and spoke as I believed, all over the North, that the mission of the war was the liberation of the slave, as well as the salvation of the Union; and hence from the first I reproached the North that they fought the rebels with only one hand, when they might strike effectually with two—that they fought with their soft white hand while they kept their black iron hand chained and helpless behind them—that they fought the effect while they protected the cause, and that the Union cause would never prosper till the war assumed an anti-slavery attitude, and the negro was enlisted on the loyal side. In every way possible, in the columns of my paper and on the platform, by letters to friends, at home and abroad, I did all that I could to impress this conviction upon the country. But nations seldom listen to advice from individuals, however reasonable. They are taught less by theories than by facts and events. There was much that could be said against making the war an abolition war—much that seemed wise and patriotic. "Make the war an abolition war," we were told, "and you drive the border States into the rebellion, and thus add power to the enemy, and increase the number you will have to meet on the battle-field. You will exasperate and intensify Southern feeling, making it more desperate, and put far away the day of peace between the two sections." "Employ the arm of the negro, and the loyal men of the North will throw down their arms and go home." "This is the white man's country, and the white man's war." "It would inflict an intolerable wound upon the pride and spirit of white soldiers of the Union, to see the negro in the United States uniform. Besides, if you make the negro a soldier, you cannot depend on his courage: a crack of his old master's whip would send him scampering in terror from the field." And so it was, that custom, pride, prejudice, and the old-time respect for Southern feeling, held back the Government from an anti-slavery policy, and from arming the negro. Meanwhile the rebellion availed itself of the negro most effectively. He was not only the stomach of the rebellion, by supplying its commissary department, but he built its forts, and dug its entrenchments, and performed other duties of its camp, which left the rebel soldier more free to fight the loyal army than he could otherwise have been. It was the cotton and corn of the negro that made the rebellion sack stand on end, and caused a continuance of the war, "Destroy these," was the burden of all my utterances during this part of the struggle, "and you cripple and destroy the rebellion." It is surprising how long and bitterly the Government resisted and rejected this view of the situation. The abolition heart of the North ached over the delay, and uttered its bitter complaints, but the administration remained blind and dumb. Bull's Run, Ball's Bluff, Big Bethel, Fredericksburg, and the Peninsula disasters were the only teachers whose authority was of sufficient importance to excite the attention or respect of our rulers, and they were even slow in being taught by these. An important point was gained, however, when General B. F. Butler, at Fortress Monroe, announced the policy of treating the slaves as "contrabands," to be made useful to the Union cause, and was sustained therein at Washington, and sentiments of a similar nature were expressed on the floor of Congress by Hon. A. G. Riddle of Ohio. A grand accession was made to this view of the case when the Hon. Simon Cameron, then Secretary of War, gave it his earnest support, and General David Hunter put the measure into practical operation in South Carolina. General Phelps from Vermont, in command at Carrollton, La., also advocated the same plan, though under discouragements which cost him his command. And many and grievous disasters on flood and field were needed to educate the loyal nation and President Lincoln up to the realization of the necessity, not to say justice, of this position, and many devices, intermediate steps, and make-shifts were suggested to smooth the way for the ultimate policy of freeing the slave, and arming the freedman.

When at last the truth began to dawn upon the administration, that the negro might be made useful to loyalty, as well as to treason, to the Union as well as to the Confederacy, it then considered in what way it could employ him, which would in the least shock and offend the popular prejudice against him. He was already in the army as a waiter, and in that capacity there was no objection to him, and so it was thought that as this was the case, the feeling which tolerated him as a waiter would not seriously object if he should be admitted to the army as a labourer, especially as no one cared to have a monopoly of digging and toiling in trenches under a Southern sun. This was the first step in employing negroes in the United States service. The second step was to give them a peculiar costume which should distinguish them from soldiers, and yet mark them as a part of the loyal force. As the eyes of the loyal administration still further opened, it was proposed to give these labourers something better than spades and shovels with which to defend themselves in cases of emergency. Still later it was proposed to make them soldiers, but soldiers without the blue uniform—soldiers with a mark upon them to show that they were inferior to other soldiers; soldiers with a badge of degradation upon them. However, once in the army as a labourer, once there with a red shirt on his back and a pistol in his belt, the negro was not long in appearing on the field as a soldier. But still he was not to be a soldier in the sense, and on an equal footing, with white soldiers. It was given out that he was not to be employed in the open field with white troops, under the inspiration of doing battle and winning victories for the Union cause, and in the face and teeth of his old masters; but that he should be made to garrison forts in yellow fever and otherwise unhealthy localities of the South, to save the health of white soldiers, and in order to keep up the distinction further, the black soldiers were to have only half the wages of the white soldiers, and were to be commanded entirely by white commissioned officers. While of course I was deeply pained and saddened by the estimate thus put upon my race, and grieved at the slowness of heart which marked the conduct of the loyal government, I was not discouraged, and urged every man who could to enlist; to get an eagle on his button, a musket on his shoulder, and the star-spangled banner over his head. Hence, as soon as Governor Andrew of Massachusetts received permission from Mr. Lincoln to raise two coloured regiments, the 54th and 55th, I wrote the following address to the coloured citizens of the North. It appeared in my paper, then being published in Rochester, and was copied in the leading journals:—

MEN OF COLOUR, TO ARMS.

"When first the rebel cannon shattered the walls of Sumpter and drove away its starving garrison, I predicted that the war then and there inaugurated would not be fought out entirely by white men. Every month's experience during these dreary years has confirmed that opinion. A war undertaken and brazenly carried on for the perpetual enslavement of coloured men, calls logically and loudly for coloured men to help and suppress it. Only a moderate share of sagacity was needed to see that the arm of the slave was the best defence against the arm of the slaveholder. Hence with every reverse to the national arms, with every exulting shout of victory raised by the slaveholding rebels, I have implored the imperilled nation to unchain against her foes, her powerful black hand. Slowly and reluctantly that appeal is beginning to be heeded. Stop not now to complain that it was not heeded sooner. It may or it may not have been best that it should not. This is not the time to discuss that question. Leave it to the future. When the war is over, the country saved, peace established, and the black man's rights secured, as they will be, history with an impartial hand, will dispose of that and sundry other questions. Action! Action! not criticism, is the plain duty of this hour. Words are now useful only as they stimulate to blows. The office of speech now is only to point out when, where, and how to strike to the best advantage. There is no time to delay. The tide is at its flood that leads on to fortune. From East to West, from North to South, the sky is written all over 'now or never.' Liberty won by white men would lose half its lustre. 'Who would be free, themselves must strike the blow.' 'Better even die free, than to live slaves.' This is the sentiment of every brave coloured man amongst us. There are weak and cowardly men in all nations. We have them amongst us. They tell you this is the 'white man's war,' that you will be no 'better off after than before the war,' that the getting of you into the army is to 'sacrifice you on the first opportunity.' Believe them not, cowards themselves, they do not wish to have their cowardice shamed by your brave example. Leave them to their timidity, or to whatever motive may hold them back. I have not thought lightly of the words I am now addressing you. The counsel I give comes of close observation of the great struggle now in progress, and of the deep conviction that this is your hour and mine. In good earnest then, and after the best deliberation, I now for the first time during this war, feel at liberty to call and counsel you to arms. By every consideration which binds you to your enslaved fellow-countrymen, and the peace and welfare of your country; by every aspiration which you cherish for the freedom and equality of yourselves and your children; by all the ties of blood and identity which makes us one with the brave black men now fighting our battles in Louisiana and South Carolina, I urge you to fly to arms and smite with death the power that would bury the Government and your liberty in the same hopeless grave. I wish I could tell you that the State of New York calls you to this high honour. For the moment her constituted authorities are silent on the subject. They will speak by-and-bye, and doubtless on the right side; but we are not compelled to wait for her. We can get at the throat of treason and slavery through the State of Massachusetts. She was first in the War of Independence; first to break the chains of her slaves first to make the black man equal before the law; first to admit coloured children to her common schools, and she was first to answer with her blood the alarm cry of the nation, when its capital was menaced by rebels. You know her patriotic governor, and you know Charles Sumner. I need not add more.

Massachusetts now welcomes you to arms as soldiers. She has but a small coloured population from which to recruit. She has full leave of the general government to send one regiment to the war, and she has undertaken to do it. Go quickly and help fill up the first coloured regiment from the North. I am authorized to assure you that you will receive the same wages, the same rations the same equipments, the same protection, the same treatment, and the same bounty, secured to white soldiers. You will be led by able and skilful officers, men who will take especial pride in your efficiency and success. They will be quick to accord to you all the honour you shall merit by your valour, and see that your rights and feelings are respected by other soldiers. I have assured myself on these points, and can speak with authority. More than twenty years of unswerving devotion to our common cause may give me some humble claim to be trusted at this momentous crisis. I will not argue. To do so implies hesitation and doubt, and you do not hesitate. You do not doubt. The day dawns, the morning star is bright upon the horizon! The iron gate of our prison stands half open. One gallant rush from the North will fling it wide open, while four millions of our brothers and sisters shall march out into liberty. The chance is now given you to end in a day the bondage of centuries, and to rise in one bound from social degradation to the plane of common equality with all other varieties of men. Remember Denmark Vesey of Charlestown; remember Nathaniel Turner of South Hampton; remember Shields Green and Copeland, who followed noble John Brown, and fell as glorious martyrs for the cause of the slave. Remember that in a contest with oppression, the Almighty has no attribute which can take sides with oppressors. The case is before you. This is our golden opportunity. Let us accept it, and for ever wipe out the dark reproaches unsparingly hurled against us by our enemies. Let us win for ourselves the gratitude of our country, and the best blessings of our posterity through all time. The nucleus of this first regiment is now in camp at Readville, a short distance from Boston. I will undertake to forward to Boston all persons adjudged fit to be mustered into the regiment, who shall apply to me at any time within the next two weeks.

Rochester, March 2, 1863."

Immediately after authority had been given by President Lincoln to Governor John A. Andrew of Massachusetts to raise and equip two regiments of coloured men for the war, I received a letter from George L. Stearns, of Boston, a noble worker for freedom in Kansas, and a warm friend of John Brown, earnestly entreating me to assist in raising the required number of men. It was presumed that by my labours in the anti-slavery cause, I had gained some influence with the coloured men of the country, and that they would listen to me in this emergency; which supposition, I am happy to say, was supported by the results. There were fewer coloured people in Massachusetts then now, and it was necessary in order to make up the full quota of these regiments, to recruit for them in other Northern States. The nominal conditions on which coloured men were asked to enlist, were not satisfactory to me or them; but assurances from Governor Andrew that they would in the end be made just and equal, together with my faith in the logic of events, and my conviction that the wise thing to do, was for the coloured man to get into the army by any door open to him, no matter how narrow, made me accept with alacrity the work to which I was invited. The raising of these two regiments—the 54th and 55th—and their splendid behaviour in South and North Carolina was the beginning of great things for the coloured people of the whole country; and not the least satisfaction I now have in contemplating my humble part in raising them, is the fact that my two sons, Charles and Lewis, were the two first in the State of New York to enlist in them. The 54th was not long in the field before it proved itself gallant and strong, worthy to rank with the most courageous of its white companions in arms. Its assault upon Fort Wagner, in which it was so fearfully cut to pieces, and lost nearly half its officers, including its beloved and trusted commander, Col. Shaw, at once gave it a name and a fame throughout the country. In that terrible battle, under the wing of night, more cavils in respect of the quality of negro manhood were set at rest than could have been during a century of ordinary life and observation. After that assault we heard no more of sending negroes to garrison forts and arsenals, to fight miasma, yellow fever, and small-pox. Talk of his ability to meet the foe in the open field, and of his equal fitness with the white man to stop a bullet, then began to prevail. From this time, and the fact ought to be remembered, the coloured troops were called upon to occupy positions which required the courage, steadiness, and endurance of veterans, and even their enemies were obliged to admit that they proved themselves worthy of the confidence reposed in them. After the 54th and 55th Massachusetts coloured regiments were placed in the field, and one of them had distinguished itself with so much credit in the hour of trial, the desire to send more such troops to the front became pretty general. Pennsylvania proposed to raise ten regiments. I was again called upon by my friend Mr. Stearns to assist in raising these regiments, and I set about the work with full purpose of heart, using every argument of which I was capable, to persuade every coloured man able to bear arms to rally around the flag, and help to save the country and save the race. It was during this time that the attitude of the Government at Washington caused me deep sadness and discouragement, and forced me in a measure to suspend my efforts in that direction. I had assured coloured men that once in the Union Army they would be put upon an equal footing with other soldiers; that they would be paid, promoted, and exchanged as prisoners of war, Jeff Davis' threat that they would be treated as felons to the contrary notwithstanding. But thus far, the Government had not kept its promise, nor the promise made for it. The following letter which I find published in my paper of the same date will show the course I felt it my duty to take under the circumstances:—

"Rochester, August 1st, 1863.

"Major George L. Stearns:

"My Dear Sir—

Having declined to attend the meeting to promote enlistments, appointed for me at Pittsburgh, in present circumstances, I owe you a word of explanation. I have hitherto deemed it a duty, as it certainly has been a pleasure, to co-operate with you in the work of raising coloured troops in the Free States to fight the battles of the Republic against slaveholding rebels and traitors. Upon the first call you gave me to this work I responded with alacrity. I saw, or thought I saw a ray of light, brightening the future of my whole race as well as that of our war-troubled country, in arousing coloured men to fight for the nation's life. I continue to believe in the black man's arm, and still have some hope in the integrity of our rulers. Nevertheless I must for the present leave to others the work of persuading coloured men to join the Union Army. I owe it to my long-abused People, and especially to those already in the army, to expose their wrongs and plead their cause. I cannot do that in connection with recruiting. When I plead for recruits I want to do it with all my heart, without qualification. I cannot do that now. The impression settles upon me that coloured men have much over-rated the enlightenment, justice, and generosity of our rulers at Washington. In my humble way I have contributed somewhat to that false estimate. You know that when the idea of raising coloured troops was first suggested, the special duty to be assigned them, was the garrisoning of forts and arsenals in certain warm, unhealthy, and miasmetic localities in the South. They were thought to be better adapted to that service than white troops. White troops trained to war, brave and daring, were to take fortifications, and the blacks were to hold them from falling again into the hands of the rebels. Three advantages were to arise out of this wise division of labour: 1st, the spirit and pride of white troops was not to waste itself in dull monotonous inactivity in fort life; their arms were to be kept bright by constant use. 2nd, The health of white troops was to be preserved. 3rd, Black troops were to have the advantage of sound military training and to be otherwise useful at the same time that they should be tolerably secure from capture by the rebels, who early avowed their determination to enslave and slaughter them in defiance of the laws of war. Two out of the three advantages were to accrue to the white troops. Thus far, however, I believe that no such duty as holding fortifications has been committed to coloured troops. They have done far other and more important work than holding fortifications. I have no special complaint to make at this point, and I simply mention it to strengthen the statement, that from the beginning of this business it was the confident belief among both the coloured and white friends of coloured enlistments that President Lincoln as commander-in-chief of the army and navy, would certainly see to it that his coloured troops should be so handled and disposed of as to be but little exposed to capture by the rebels, and that, if so exposed, as they have repeatedly been from the first, the President possesses both the disposition and the means for compelling the rebels to respect the rights of such as might fall into their hands. The piratical proclamation of Jefferson Davis, announcing slavery and assassination to coloured prisoners was before the country and the world. But men had faith in Mr. Lincoln and his advisers. He was silent to be sure, but charity suggested that being a man of action rather than words he only waited for a case in which he should be required to act. This faith in the man enabled us to speak with warmth and effect in urging enlistments among coloured men. That faith, my dear sir, is now nearly gone. Various occasions have arisen during the last six months for the exercise of his power in behalf of the coloured men in his service, But no word comes to us from the War Department, sternly assuring the rebel chief that inquisition shall yet be made for innocent blood. No word of retaliation when a black man is slain by a rebel in cold blood. No word was said when free men from Massachusetts were caught and sold into slavery in Texas. No word is said when brave black men who, according to the testimony of both friend and foe, fought like heroes to plant the star-spangled banner on the blazing parapets of Fort Wagner, and in doing so were captured, some mutilated and killed, and others sold into slavery. The same crushing silence reigns over this scandalous outrage as over that of the slaughtered teamsters at Murfreesboro; the same as over that at Milliken's Bend and Vicksburg. I am free to say, my dear sir, that the case looks as if the confiding coloured soldiers had been betrayed into bloody hands by the Government in whose defence they were heroically fighting. I know what you will say to this: you will say 'wait a little longer, and after all, the best way to have justice done to your people is to get them into the army as fast as you can.' You may be right in this; my argument has been the same, but have we not already waited, and have we not already shown the highest qualities of soldiers, and on this account deserve the protection of the Government for which we are fighting? Can any case stronger than that before Charlestown ever arise? If the President is ever to demand justice and humanity, for black soldiers, is not this the time for him to do it? How many 54th's must be cut to pieces, its mutilated prisoners killed, and its living prisoners sold into slavery, to be tortured to death by inches, before Mr. Lincoln shall say, 'Hold, enough!'

You know the 54th. To you, more than to any man, belongs the credit of raising that regiment. Think of its noble and brave officers literally hacked to pieces, while many of its rank and file have been sold into slavery worse than death, and pardon me, if I hesitate about assisting in raising a fourth regiment until the President shall give the same protection to them as to white soldiers.

With warm and sincere regards,

Frederick Douglass."

"Since writing the foregoing letter, which we have now put upon record, we have received assurances from Major Stearns that the Government of the United States is already taking measures which will secure the captured coloured soldiers at Charlestown and elsewhere the same protection against slavery and cruelty extended to white soldiers. What ought to have been done at the beginning, comes late, but it comes. The poor coloured soldiers have purchased interference dearly. It really seems that nothing of justice, liberty, or humanity can come to us except through tears and blood."

THE BLACK MAN AT THE WHITE HOUSE.

My efforts to secure just and fair treatment for the coloured soldiers did not stop at letters and speeches. At the suggestion of my friend, Major Stearns, to whom the foregoing letter was addressed, I was induced to go to Washington and lay the complaints of my people before President Lincoln and the Secretary of War; and to urge upon them such action as should secure to the coloured troops then fighting for the country a reasonable degree of fair play. I need not say that at the time I undertook this mission it required much more nerve than a similar one would require now. The distance then between the black man and the white American citizen, was immeasurable. I was an ex-slave, identified with a despised race; and yet I was to meet the most exalted person in this great Republic. It was altogether an unwelcome duty, and one from which I would gladly have been excused. I could not know what kind of a reception would be accorded me. I might be told to go home and mind my own business, and leave such questions as I had come to discuss to be managed by the men wisely chosen by the American people to deal with them, or I might be refused an interview altogether. Nevertheless, I felt bound to go; and my acquaintance with Senators Charles Sumner, Henry Wilson, Samuel Pomeroy, Secretary Salmon, P. Chase, Secretary William H. Seward, and Assistant Secretary of War Charles A. Dana, encouraged me to hope at least for a civil reception. My confidence was fully justified in the result. I shall never forget my first interview with this great man. I was accompanied to the executive mansion and introduced to President Lincoln by Senator Pomeroy. The room in which he received visitors was the one now used by the president's secretaries. I entered it with a moderate estimate of my own consequence, and yet there I was to talk with, and even to advise, the head man of a great nation. Happily for me, there was no vain pomp and ceremony about him. I was never more quickly or more completely put at ease in the presence of a great man, than in that of Abraham Lincoln. He was seated, when I entered, in a low arm chair, with his feet extended on the floor, surrounded by a large number of documents, and several busy secretaries. The room bore the marks of business, and the persons in it, the President included, appeared to be much over-worked and tired. Long lines of care were already deeply written on Mr. Lincoln's brow, and his strong face, full of earnestness, lighted up as soon as my name was mentioned. As I approached and was introduced to him, he rose and extended his hand, and bade me welcome. I at once felt myself in the presence of an honest man—one whom I could love, honour, and trust without reserve or doubt. Proceeding to tell him who I was, and what I was doing, he promptly, but kindly, stopped me, saying: "I know who you are, Mr. Douglass; Mr. Seward has told me all about you. Sit down. I am glad to see you." I then told him the object of my visit: that I was assisting to raise coloured troops; that several months before I had been very successful in getting men to enlist, but that now it was not easy to induce the coloured men to enter the service, because there was a feeling among them that the Government did not deal fairly with them in several respects. Mr. Lincoln asked me to state particulars. I replied that there were three particulars which I wished to bring to his attention. First, that coloured soldiers ought to receive the same wages as those paid to white soldiers. Second, that coloured soldiers ought to receive the same protection when taken prisoners, and be exchanged as readily, and on the same terms, as any other prisoners, and if Jefferson Davis should shoot or hang coloured soldiers in cold blood, the United States Government should retaliate in kind and degree without delay upon Confederate prisoners in its hands. Third, when coloured soldiers, seeking the "bubble-reputation at the cannon's mouth," performed great and uncommon service on the battle-field, they should be rewarded by distinction and promotion, precisely as white soldiers are rewarded for like services.

Mr. Lincoln listened with patience and silence to all I had to say. He was serious and even troubled by what I had said, and by what he had evidently thought himself before upon the same points. He impressed me with the solid gravity of his character, by his silent listening, not less than by his earnest reply to my words.

He began by saying that the employment of coloured troops at all was a great gain to the coloured people; that the measure could not have been successfully adopted at the beginning of the war; that the wisdom of making coloured men soldiers was still doubted; that their enlistment was a serious offence to popular prejudice; that they had larger motives for being soldiers than white men; that they ought to be willing to enter the service upon any conditions; that the fact that they were not to receive the same pay as white soldiers, seemed a necessary concession to smooth the way to their employment at all as soldiers; but that ultimately they would receive the same. On the second point, in respect to equal protection, he said the case was more difficult. Retaliation was a terrible remedy, and one which it was very difficult to apply; one which if once begun, there was no telling where it would end; that if he could get hold of the confederate soldiers who had been guilty of treating coloured soldiers as felons, he could easily retaliate, but the thought of hanging men for a crime perpetrated by others, was revolting to his feelings. He thought that the rebels themselves would stop such barbarous warfare, and less evil would be done if retaliation were not resorted to. That he had already received information that coloured soldiers were being treated as prisoners of war. In all this I saw the tender heart of the man rather than the stern warrior and commander-in-chief of the American army and navy, and while I could not agree with him, I could not but respect his humane spirit.

On the third point he appeared to have less difficulty, though he did not absolutely commit himself. He simply said that he would sign any commission to coloured soldiers whom his Secretary of War should commend to him. Though I was not entirely satisfied with his views, I was so well satisfied with the man and with the educating tendency of the conflict, that I determined to go on with the recruiting.

From the President, I went to see Secretary Stanton. The manner of no two men could be more widely different. I was introduced by Assistant Secretary Dana, whom I had known many years before at "Brook Farm," Mass., and afterwards as managing editor of the New York Tribune. Every line in Mr. Stanton's face told me that my communication with him must be brief, clear, and to the point; that he might turn his back upon me as a bore at any moment; that politeness was not one of his weaknesses. His first glance was that of a man who says, "Well, what do you want? I have no time to waste upon you or anybody else, and I shall waste none. Speak quick, or I shall leave you." The man and the place seemed alike busy. Seeing I had no time to lose, I hastily went over the ground I had gone over with President Lincoln. As I ended, I was surprised by seeing a changed man before me. Contempt and suspicion, and brusqueness, had all disappeared from his face and manner, and for a few minutes he made the best defence that I had then heard from anybody of the treatment of coloured soldiers by the Government. I was not satisfied, yet I left in the full belief that the true course to the black man's freedom and citizenship was over the battle-field, and that my business was to get every black man I could into the Union armies. Both the President and Secretary of War assured me that justice would ultimately be done to my race, and I gave full faith and credit to their promise. On assuring Mr. Stanton of my willingness to take a commission, he said he would make me assistant adjutant to General Thomas, who was then recruiting and organizing troops in the Mississippi Valley. He asked me how soon I could be ready. I told him in two weeks, and that my commission might be sent me to Rochester. For some reason, however, my commission never came. The Government, I fear, was still clinging to the idea that positions of honour in the service should be occupied by white men, and that it would not do to inaugurate just then the policy of perfect equality. I wrote to the department for my commission, but was simply told to report to General Thomas. This was so different from what I expected, and from what I had been promised, that I wrote to Secretary Stanton that I would report to General Thomas on receipt of my commission, but it did not come, and I did not go to the Mississippi Valley as I had fondly hoped. I knew too much of camp life and the value of shoulder straps in the army to go into the service without some visible mark of my rank. I have no doubt that Mr. Stanton, in the moment of our meeting, meant all he said, but thinking the matter over, he felt that the time had not then come for a step so radical and aggressive. Meanwhile, my three sons were in the service; Lewis and Charles, as already named, in the Massachusetts regiments, and Frederick recruiting coloured troops in the Mississippi Valley.

CHAPTER XII: HOPE FOR THE NATION.

Proclamation of emancipation—Its reception in Boston—Objections brought against it—Its effect on the country—Interview with President Lincoln—New York riots—Re-election of Mr. Lincoln—His inauguration, and inaugural speech—Vice-President Johnson—Presidential reception—The fall of Richmond—Fanueil Hall—The assassination—Condolence.

THE first of January, 1863, was a memorable day in the progress of American liberty and civilization. It was the turning-point in the conflict between freedom and slavery. A death-blow was then given to the slaveholding rebellion. Until then the Federal arm had been more than tolerant to that relic of barbarism. It had defended it inside the Slave States; it had countermanded the emancipation policy of John C. Fremont in Missouri; it had returned slaves to their so-called owners; and had threatened that any attempt on the part of the slaves to gain their freedom by insurrection, or otherwise, would be put down with an iron hand; it had even refused to allow the Hutchinson family to sing their anti-slavery songs in the camps of the army of the Potomac; it had surrounded the houses of slave-holders with bayonets for their protection; and through its Secretary of War, William H. Seward, had given notice to the world that, "however the war for the Union might terminate, no change would be made in the relation of master and slave." Upon this pro-slavery platform the war against the rebellion had been waged during more than two years. It had not been a war of conquest, but rather a war of conciliation. McClellan, in command of the army, had been trying, apparently, to put down the rebellion without hurting the rebels, certainly without hurting slavery, and the Government had seemed to co-operate with him in both respects. Charles Sumner, William Lloyd Garrison, Wendell Phillips, Gerrit Smith, and the whole anti-slavery phalanx at the North, had denounced this policy, and had besought Mr. Lincoln to adopt an opposite one, but in vain. Generals in the field, and councils in the Cabinet, had persisted in advancing this policy through defeats and disasters, even to the verge of ruin. We fought the rebellion, but not its cause. The key to the situation was the four million of slaves; yet the slave who loved us, was hated, and the slave-holder who hated us, was loved. We kissed the hand that smote us, and spurned the hand that helped us. When the means of victory were before us—within our grasp—we went in search of the means of defeat. And now, on this 1st day of January, 1863, the formal and solemn announcement was made that thereafter the Government would be found on the side of emancipation. This proclamation changed everything. It gave a new direction to the councils of the Cabinet, and to the conduct of the national arms. I shall leave to the statesman, the philosopher, and historian, the more comprehensive discussion of this document, and only tell how it touched me, and those in like condition with me at the time. I was in Boston, and its reception there may indicate the importance attached to it elsewhere. An immense assembly convened in Tremont Temple to await the first flash of the electric wires announcing the "new departure." Two years of war prosecuted in the interests of slavery, had made free speech possible in Boston, and we now met together to receive and celebrate the first utterance of the long-hoped-for proclamation, if it came, and if it did not come, to speak our minds freely; for, in view of the past, it was by no means certain that it would come. The occasion, therefore, was one of both hope and fear. Our ship was on the open sea, tossed by a terrible storm; wave after wave was passing over us, and every hour was fraught with increasing peril. Whether we should survive or perish, depended in large measure upon the coming of this proclamation. At least so we felt. Although the conditions on which Mr. Lincoln had promised to withhold it, had not been complied with, yet, from many considerations, there was room to doubt and fear. Mr. Lincoln was known to be a man of tender heart, and boundless patience; no man could tell to what length he might go, or might refrain from going in the direction of peace and reconciliation. Hitherto, he had not shown himself a man of heroic measures, and, properly enough, this step belonged to that class. It must be the end of all compromises with slavery—a declaration that thereafter the war was to be conducted on a new principle, with a new aim. It would be a full and fair assertion that the Government would neither trifle, nor be trifled with any longer. But would it come? On the side of doubt, it was said that Mr. Lincoln's kindly nature might cause him to relent at the last moment; that Mrs. Lincoln, coming from an old slaveholding family, would influence him to delay, and give the slaveholders one other chance.* Every moment of waiting chilled our hopes, and strengthened our fears. A line of messengers was established between the telegraph office and the platform of Tremont Temple, and the time was occupied with brief speeches from Hon. Thomas Russell of Plymouth, Miss Anna E. Dickinson (a lady of marvellous eloquence), Rev. Mr. Grimes, J. Sella Martin, William Wells Brown, and myself. But speaking or listening to speeches was not the thing for which the people had come together. The time for argument was passed. It was not logic, but the trump of jubilee, which everybody wanted to hear. We were waiting and listening as for a bolt from the sky, which should rend the fetters of four million of slaves; we were watching, as it were, by the dim light of the stars, for the dawn of a new day; we were longing for the answer to the agonizing prayers of centuries. Remembering those in bonds as bound with them, we wanted to join in the shout for freedom, and in the anthem of the redeemed.

Eight, nine, ten o'clock came and went, and still no word. A visible shadow seemed falling on the expecting throng, which the confident utterances of the speakers sought in vain to dispel. At last, when patience was well-nigh exhausted, and suspense was becoming agony, a man—I think it was Judge Russell—with hasty step advanced through the crowd, and with a face fairly illuminated with the news he bore, exclaimed in tones that thrilled all hearts, "It is coming!" "It is on the wires!!" The effect of this announcement was startling beyond description, and the scene was wild and grand. Joy and gladness exhausted all forms of expression from shouts of praise, to sobs and tears. My old friend Rue, a coloured preacher, a man of wonderful vocal power, expressed the heartfelt emotion of the hour, when he led all voices in the anthem, "Sound the loud timbrel o'er Egypt's dark sea, Jehovah hath triumphed, his people are free." About twelve o'clock, seeing there was no disposition to retire from the hall, which must be vacated, my friend Grimes—of blessed memory—rose and moved that the meeting adjourn to the Twelfth Baptist Church, of which he was pastor, and soon that church was packed from doors to pulpit, and this meeting did not break up till near the dawn of day. It was one of the most affecting and thrilling occasions I ever witnessed, and a worthy celebration of the first step on the part of the nation in its departure from the thraldom of ages.

There was evidently no disposition on the part of this meeting to criticise the proclamation; nor was there with any one at first. At the moment we saw only its anti-slavery side. But further and more critical examination showed it to be extremely defective. It was not a proclamation of "liberty throughout all the land, unto all the inhabitants thereof," such as we had hoped it would be; but was one marked by discriminations and reservations. Its operation was confined within certain geographical and military lines. It only abolished slavery where it did not exist, and left it intact where it did exist. It was a measure apparently inspired by the law motive of military necessity, and by so far as it was so, it would become inoperative and useless when military necessity should cease. There was much said in this line, and much that was narrow and erroneous. For my own part, I took the proclamation, first and last, for a little more than it purported; and saw in its spirit, a life and power far beyond its letter. Its meaning to me was the entire abolition of slavery, wherever the evil could be reached by the Federal arm, and I saw that its moral power would extend much further. It was in my estimation an immense gain to have the War for the Union committed to the extinction of Slavery, even from a military necessity. It is not a bad thing to have individuals or nations do right though they do so from selfish motives. I approved the one-spur-wisdom of "Paddy" who thought if he could get one side of his horse to go, he could trust the speed of the other side.

The effect of the proclamation abroad was highly beneficial to the loyal cause. Disinterested parties could now see in it a benevolent character. It was no longer a mere strife for territory and dominion, but a contest of civilization against barbarism.

The Proclamation itself was like Mr. Lincoln throughout. It was framed with a view to the least harm and the most good possible in the circumstances, and with especial consideration of the latter. It was thoughtful, cautious, and well guarded at all points. While he hated slavery, and really desired its destruction, he always proceeded against it in a manner the least likely to shock or drive from him any who were truly in sympathy with the preservation of the Union, but who were not friendly to emancipation. For this he kept up the distinction between loyal and disloyal slaveholders, and discriminated in favour of the one, as against the other. In a word, in all that he did, or attempted, he made it manifest that the one great and all commanding object with him, was the peace and preservation of the Union, and that this was the motive and main spring of all his measures. His wisdom and moderation at this point were for a season useful to the loyal cause in the border States, but it may be fairly questioned, whether it did not chill the Union ardour of the loyal people of the North in some degree, and diminish, rather than increase, the sum of our power against the rebellion: for moderate, cautious and guarded as was this proclamation, it created a howl of indignation and wrath amongst the rebels and their allies. The old cry was raised by the copperhead organs of "an abolition war," and a pretext was thus found for an excuse for refusing to enlist, and for marshalling all the negro prejudice of the North on the rebel side. Men could say they were willing to fight for the Union, but that they were not willing to fight for the freedom of the negroes; and thus it was made difficult to procure enlistments or to enforce the draft. This was especially true of New York, where there was a large Irish population. The attempt to enforce the draft in that city was met by mobs, riot, and bloodshed. There is perhaps no darker chapter in the whole history of the war, than this cowardly and bloody uprising in July, 1863. For three days and nights New York was in the hands of a ferocious mob, and there was not sufficient power in the government of the country or of the city itself, to stay the hands of violence, and the effusion of blood. Though this mob was nominally against the draft which had been ordered, it poured out its fiercest wrath upon the coloured people and their friends. It spared neither age nor sex; it hanged negroes simply because they were negroes; it murdered women in their homes, and burned their homes over their heads; it dashed out the brains of young children against the lamp posts; it burned the coloured orphan asylum, a noble charity on the corner of Fifth Avenue, and scarce allowing time for the helpless two hundred children to make good their escape, plundered the building of every valuable piece of furniture; and coloured men, women, and children were forced to seek concealment in cellars or garrets, or wheresoever else it could be found, until this high carnival of crime and reign of terror should pass away.

In connection with Geo. L. Stearns, Thomas Webster, and Col. Wagner, I had been at Camp William Penn, Philadelphia, assisting in the work of filling up the coloured regiments, and was on my way home from there, just as these events were transpiring in New York. I was met by a friend at Newark, who informed me of this condition of things. I, however, pressed on my way to the Chambers-street station of the Hudson River Railroad in safety, the mob being in the upper part of the city, fortunately for me, for not only my colour, but my known activity in procuring enlistments would have made me especially obnoxious to its murderous spirit. This was not the first time I had been in imminent peril in New York city. My arrival there, after my escape from slavery, was full of danger. My passage through its borders after the attack of John Brown on Harper's Ferry was scarcely less safe. I had encountered Isaiah Rynders and his gang of ruffians in the old Broadway Tabernacle at our anti-slavery anniversary meeting, and I knew something of the crazy temper of such crowds; but this anti-draft—anti-negro mob was something more and something worse—it was a part of the rebel force, without the rebel uniform, but with all its deadly hate; it was the fire of the enemy opened in the rear of the loyal army. Such men as Franklin Pierce and Horatio Seymour had done much in their utterances to encourage resistance to the drafts. Seymour was then Governor of the State of New York, and while the mob was doing its deadly work he addressed them as "My friends," telling them to desist then, while he could arrange at Washington to have the draft arrested. Had Governor Seymour been loyal to his country, and to his country's cause, in this her moment of need, he would have burned his tongue with a red hot iron sooner than allow it to call these thugs, thieves, and murderers his "friends."

My interviews with President Lincoln and his able Secretary, before narrated, greatly increased my confidence in the anti-slavery integrity of the Government, although I confess I was greatly disappointed at my failure to receive the commission promised me by Secretary Stanton. I, however, faithfully believed, and loudly proclaimed my belief, that the rebellion would be suppressed, the Union preserved, the slaves emancipated, and the coloured soldiers would in the end have justice done them. This confidence was immeasurably strengthened when I saw Gen. George B. McClellan relieved from the command of the army of the Potomac, and Gen. U. S. Grant placed at its head, and in command of all the armies of the

United States. My confidence in Gen. Grant was not entirely due to the brilliant military successes achieved by him, but there was a moral as well as military basis for my faith in him. He had shown his single mindedness and superiority to popular prejudice by his prompt co-operation with President Lincoln in his policy of employing coloured troops, and his order commanding his soldiers to treat such troops with due respect. In this way he proved himself to be not only a wise general, but a great man—one who could adjust himself to new conditions, and adopt the lessons taught by the events of the hour. This quality in General Grant was and is made all the more conspicuous and striking in contrast with his West Point education and his former political associations; for neither West Point nor the Democratic party have been good schools in which to learn justice and fair play to the negro.

It was when General Grant was fighting his way through the Wilderness to Richmond, on the "line" he meant to pursue "if it took all summer," and every reverse to his arms was made the occasion for a fresh demand for peace without emancipation, that President Lincoln did me the honor to invite me to the Executive Mansion for a conference on the situation. I need not say I went most gladly. The main subject on which he wished to confer with me was as to the means most desirable to be employed outside the army to induce the slaves in the rebel States to come within the Federal lines. The increasing opposition to the war, in the North, and the mad cry against it, because it was being made an abolition war, alarmed Mr. Lincoln, and make him apprehensive that a peace might be forced upon him which would leave still in slavery all who had not come within our lines. What he wanted was to make his proclamation as effective as possible in the event of such a peace. He said in a regretful tone, "The slaves are not coming so rapidly and so numerously to us as I hoped." I replied that the slaveholders knew how to keep such things from their slaves, and probably very few knew of his proclamation, "Well," he said, "I want you to set about devising some means for making them acquainted with it, and for bringing them into our lines." He spoke with great earnestness and much solicitude, and seemed troubled by the attitude of Mr. Greeley, and the growing impatience there was being manifested through the North at the war. He said he was being accused of protracting the war beyond its legitimate object, and of failing to make peace, when he might have done so to advantage. He was afraid of what might come of all these complaints, but was persuaded that no solid and lasting peace could come, short of absolute submission on the part of the rebels, and he was not for giving them rest by futile conferences at Niagara Falls, or elsewhere, with unauthorised persons. He saw the danger of premature peace, and, like a thoughtful and sagacious man as he was, he wished to provide means of rendering such consummation as harmless as possible. I was the more impressed by this benevolent consideration because he before said, in answer to the peace clamour, that his object was to save the Union, and to do so with or without slavery. What he said on this day showed a deeper moral conviction against slavery than I had even seen before in anything spoken or written by him. I listened with the deepest interest and profoundest satisfaction, and, at his suggestion, agreed to undertake the organizing a band of scouts, composed of coloured men, whose business should be somewhat after the original plan of John Brown, to go into the rebel States, beyond the lines of our armies, and carry the news of emancipation, and urge the slaves to come within our boundaries.

This plan, however, was very soon rendered unnecessary by the success of the war in the Wilderness and elsewhere, and by its termination in the complete abolition of slavery.

I refer to this conversation because I think it is evidence conclusive on Mr. Lincoln's part that the proclamation, so far as least as he was concerned, was not effected merely as a "necessity."

An incident occurred during this interview which illustrates the character of this great man, though the mention of it may savour a little of vanity on my part. While in conversation with him his secretary twice announced "Governor Buckingham of Connecticut:" one of the noblest and most patriotic of the loyal Governors. Mr. Lincoln said, "Tell Governor Buckingham to wait, for I want to have a long talk with my friend Frederick Douglass." I interposed, and begged him to see the Governor at once, as I could wait; but no, he persisted he wanted to talk with me, and Governor Buckingham could wait. This was probably the first time in the history of this Republic when its chief magistrate found occasion or disposition to exercise such an act of impartiality between persons so widely different in their positions and supposed claims upon his attention. From the manner of the Governor, when he was finally admitted, I inferred that he was as well satisfied with what Mr. Lincoln had done, or had omitted to do, as I was.

I have often said elsewhere what I wish to repeat here, that Mr. Lincoln was not only a great President, but a great man—too great to be small in anything. In his company I was never in any way reminded of my humble origin, or of my unpopular colour. While I am, as it may seem, bragging of the kind consideration which I have reason to believe that Mr. Lincoln entertained towards me, I may mention one thing more. At the door of my friend John A. Gray, where I was stopping in Washington, I found, one afternoon, the carriage of Secretary Dole, and a messenger from President Lincoln with an invitation for me to take tea with him at the Soldiers' Home, where he then passed his nights, riding out after the business of the day was over at the Executive Mansion. Unfortunately, I had an engagement to speak that evening, and having made it one of the rules of my conduct in life never to break an engagement, if possible to keep it, I felt obliged to decline the honour. I have often regretted that I did not make this an exception to my general rule. Could I have known that no such opportunity would come to me again, I should have justified myself in disappointing a large audience for the sake of such a visit with Abraham Lincoln.

It is due perhaps to myself to say here that I did not take Mr. Lincoln's attentions as due to my merits or personal qualities. While I have no doubt that Messrs. Seaward and Chase had spoken well of me to him, and the fact of my having been a slave, and gained my freedom, and of having picked up some sort of an education, and being in some sense a "self-made man," and having made myself useful as an advocate of the claims of my people, gave me favour in his eyes; yet I am quite sure that the main thing which gave me consideration with him was my well-known relation to the coloured people of the Republic, and especially the help which that relation enabled me to give to the work of suppressing the rebellion and of placing the Union on a firmer basis than it ever had or could have sustained in the days of slavery.

So long as there was any hope whatsoever of the success of rebellion, there was of course a corresponding fear that a new lease of life would be granted to slavery. The proclamation of Fremont in Missouri, the letter of Phelps in the Department of the Gulf, the enlistment of coloured troops by General Hunter, the "Contraband" letter of General B. F. Butler, the soldierly qualities surprisingly displayed by coloured soldiers in the terrific battles of Port Hudson, Vicksburg, Morris Island, and elsewhere, the Emancipation Proclamation by Abraham Lincoln had given slavery many and deadly wounds, yet it was in fact only wounded and crippled, not disabled and killed. With this condition of national affairs came the summer of 1864, and with it the revived Democratic party, with the story in its mouth that the war was a failure, and with General George B. McClellan, the greatest failure of the war, as its candidate for the Presidency. It is needless to say that the success of such a party, on such a platform, with such a candidate at such a time, would have been a fatal calamity. All that had been done towards suppressing the rebellion and abolishing slavery would have proved of no avail, and the final settlement between the two sections of the Republic, touching slavery and the right of secession, would have been left to tear and rend the country again at no distant future.

It was said that this Democratic party, which, under Mr. Buchanan, had betrayed the Government into the hands of secession and treason, was the only party which could restore the country to peace and union. No doubt it would have "patched up" a peace, but it would have been a peace more to be dreaded than war. So at least I felt and worked. When we were thus asked to exchange Abraham Lincoln for McClellan—a successful Union President for an unsuccessful Union General—a party earnestly endeavouring to save the Union, torn and rent by a gigantic rebellion, I thought with Mr. Lincoln, that it was not wise to "swap horses while crossing a stream." Regarding, as I did, the continuance of the war to the complete suppression of the rebellion, and the retention in office of President Lincoln as essential to the total destruction of slavery, I certainly exerted myself to the uttermost, in my small way, to secure his re-election. This most important object was not attained, however, by speeches, letters, or other electioneering appliances. The staggering blows dealt upon the rebellion that year by the armies under Grant and Sherman, and his own great character, ground all opposition to dust, and made his election sure, even before the question reached the polls. Since William the Silent, who was the soul of the mighty war for religious liberty against Spain and the Spanish inquisition, no leader of men has been loved and trusted in such generous measure as Abraham Lincoln. His election silenced, in a good degree, the discontent felt at the length of the war, and the complaints of its being an Abolition war. Every victory of our arms, on flood and field, was a rebuke to McClellan and the Democratic party, and an endorsement of Abraham Lincoln for President, and his new policy. It was my good fortune to be present at his inauguration in March, and to hear on that occasion his remarkable inaugural address. On the night previous I took tea with Chief Justice Chase, and assisted his beloved daughter, Mrs. Sprague, in placing over her honoured father's shoulders the new robe, then being made, in which he was to administer the oath of office to the re-elected President. There was a dignity and grandeur about the Chief Justice which marked him as one born great. He had known me in early anti-slavery days, and had conquered his race-prejudice, if he ever had any; at any rate, he had welcomed me to his home and his table, when to do so was a strange thing in Washington; and the fact was by no means an insignificant one.

The inauguration, like the election, was a most important event. Four years before, after Mr. Lincoln's first election, the pro-slavery spirit determined against his inauguration, and it no doubt would have accomplished its purpose had he attempted to pass openly and recognised through Baltimore. There was murder in the air then, and there was murder in the air now. His first inauguration arrested the fall of the Republic, and the second was to restore it to enduring foundations. At the time of the second inauguration the rebellion was apparently vigorous, defiant, and formidable; but in reality weak, dejected, and desperate. It had reached that verge of madness when it had called upon the negro for help to fight against the freedom which he so longed to find, for the bondage he would escape—against Lincoln the Emancipator for Davis the enslaver. But desperation discards logic as well as law, and the South was desperate. Sherman was marching to the sea, and Virginia with its rebel capital was in the firm grip of Ulysses S. Grant. To those who knew the situation it was evident that unless some startling change was made the confederacy had but a short time to live, and that time full of misery. This condition of things made the air at Washington dark and lowering. The friends of the Confederate cause here were neither few nor insignificant. They were among the rich and influential. A wink or a nod from such men might unchain the hand of violence and set order and law at defiance. To those who saw beneath the surface it was clearly perceived that there was danger abroad; and as the procession passed down Pennsylvania Avenue, I for one felt an instinctive apprehension that at any moment a short from some assassin in the crowd might end the glittering pageant, and throw the country into the depths of anarchy. I did not then know, what has since become history, that the plot was already formed and its execution contemplated for that very day, which though several weeks delayed, at last accomplished its deadly work. Reaching the Capitol, I took my place in the crowd where I could see the

Presidential procession as it came upon the east portico, and where I could hear and see all that took place. There was no such throng as that which celebrated the inauguration of President Garfield, nor that of President Rutherford B. Hayes. The whole proceeding was wonderfully quiet, earnest, and solemn. From the oath, as administered by Chief Justice Chase, to the brief but weighty address delivered by Mr. Lincoln, there was a leaden stillness about the crowd. The address sounded more like a sermon than a state paper. In the fewest words possible it referred to the condition of the country four years before, on his first accession to the presidency—to the causes of the war, and the reasons on both sides for which it had been waged. "Neither party," he said, "expected for the war the magnitude or the duration which it had already attained. Neither anticipated that the cause of the conflict might cease with or even before the conflict itself should cease. Each looked for an easier triumph, and a result less fundamental and astounding." Then in a few short sentences, admitting the conviction that slavery had been the "offence which, in the providence of God, must needs come, and the war as the woe due to those by whom the offence came," he asked if there can be "discerned in this, any departure from those Divine attributes which the believers in a loving God always ascribe to Him? Fondly do we hope," he continued, "fervently do we pray that this mighty scourge of war may speedily pass away. Yet if God wills that it continue until all the wealth piled by the bondman's two hundred and fifty years of unrequited toil shall be sunk, and until every drop of blood drawn with the lash shall be paid by another drawn with the sword, as was said three thousand years ago, so still it must be said, 'The judgments of the Lord are true and righteous altogether.'

"With malice towards none, with charity for all, with firmness in the right, as God gives us to see the right, let us strive to finish the work we are in, and bind up the nation's wounds, to care for him who shall have borne the battle, and for his widow and his orphans, to do all which may achieve and cherish a just and lasting peace among ourselves and with all nations."

I know not how many times, and before how many people I have quoted these solemn words of our martyred President; they struck me at the time, and have seemed to me ever since to contain more vital substance than I have ever seen compressed into a space so narrow; yet on this memorable occasion when I clapped my hands in gladness and thanksgiving at their utterance, I saw in the faces of many about me expressions of widely different emotion.

On this inauguration day, while waiting for the opening of the ceremonies, I made a discovery in regard to the Vice-President—Andrew Johnson. There are moments in the lives of most men, when the doors of their souls are open, and unconsciously to themselves, their true characters may be read by the observant eye. It was at such an instant I caught a glimpse of the real nature of this man, which all subsequent developments proved true. I was standing in the crowd by the side of Mrs. Thomas J. Dorsey, when Mr. Lincoln touched Mr. Johnson, and pointed me out to him. The first expression which came to his face, and which I think was the true index of his heart, was one of bitter contempt and aversion. Seeing that I observed him, he tried to assume a more friendly appearance; but it was too late; it was useless to close the door when all within had been seen. His first glance was the frown of the man, the second was the bland and sickly smile of the demagogue. I turned to Mrs. Dorsey and said, "Whatever Andrew Johnson may be, he certainly is no friend of our race."

No stronger contrast could well be presented between two men than between President Lincoln and Vice-President Johnson on this day. Mr. Lincoln was like one who was treading the hard and thorny path of duty and self-denial; Mr. Johnson was like one just from a drunken debauch. The face of the one was full of manly humility, although at the topmost height of power and pride, the other was full of pomp and swaggering vanity. The fact was though it was yet early in the day, Mr. Johnson was drunk.

In the evening of the day of the inauguration, another new experience awaited me. The usual reception was given at the executive mansion, and though no coloured persons had ever ventured to present themselves on such occasions, it seemed, now that freedom had become the law of the Republic, now that coloured men were on the battle-field mingling their blood with that of white men in one common effort to save the country, it was not too great an assumption for a coloured man to offer his congratulations to the President with those of other citizens. I decided to go, and sought in vain for some one of my own colour to accompany me. It is never an agreeable experience to go where there can be any doubt of welcome, and my coloured friends had too often realised discomfiture from this cause to be willing to subject themselves to such unhappiness; they wished me to go, as my New England coloured friends, in the long ago, liked very well to have me take passage on the first-class cars, and be hauled out and pounded by rough-handed brakesmen, to make way for them. It was plain, then, that some one must lead the way, and that if the coloured man would have his rights, he must take them; and now, though it was plainly quite the thing for me to attend President Lincoln's reception, "they all with one accord began to make excuse." It was finally arranged that Mrs. Dorsey should bear me company, so together we joined in the grand procession of citizens from all parts of the country, and moved slowly towards the executive mansion. I had for some time looked upon myself as a man, but now in this multitude of the élite of the land, I felt myself a man among men. I regret to be obliged to say, however, that this comfortable assurance was not of long duration, for on reaching the door, two policemen stationed there took me rudely by the arm and ordered me to stand back, for their directions were to admit no persons of my colour. The reader need not be told that this was a disagreeable set-back. But once in the battle, I did not think it well to submit to repulse. I told the officers I was quite sure there must be some mistake, for no such order could have emanated from President Lincoln; and if he knew I was at the door he would desire my admission. They then, to put an end to the parley, as I suppose, for we were obstructing the door way, and were not easily pushed aside, assumed an air of politeness, and offered to conduct me in. We followed their lead, and soon found ourselves walking some planks out of a window, which had been arranged as a temporary passage for the exit of visitors. We halted as soon as we saw the trick, and I said to the officers. "You have deceived me. I shall not go out of this building till I have seen President Lincoln." At this moment a gentleman who was passing in, recognized me, and I said to him: "Be so kind as to say to Mr. Lincoln that Frederick Douglass is detained by officers at the door." It was not long before Mrs. Dorsey and I walked into the spacious East Room, amid a scene of elegance such as in this country I had never witnessed before. Like a mountain pine high above all others, Mr. Lincoln stood, in his grand simplicity, and home-like beauty. Recognising me, even before I reached him, he exclaimed, so that all around could hear him, "Here comes my friend Douglass." Taking me by the hand, he said, "I am glad to see you. I saw you in the crowd to-day, listening to my inaugural address; how did you like it?" I said, "Mr. Lincoln, I must not detain you with my poor opinion, when there are thousands waiting to shake hands with you." "No, no," he said, "you must stop a little, Douglass; there is no man in the country whose opinion I value more than yours. I want to know what you think of it?" I replied, "Mr. Lincoln, that was a sacred effort." "I am glad you liked it!" he said, and I passed on, feeling that any man, however distinguished, might well regard himself honoured by such expressions, from such a man.

It came out that the officers at the White House had received no orders from Mr. Lincoln, or from any one else. They were simply complying with an old custom, the outgrowth of slavery, as dogs will sometimes rub their necks, long after their collars are removed, thinking they are still there. My coloured friends were well pleased with what had seemed to them a doubtful experiment, and I believe were encouraged by its success to follow my example. I have found in my experience that the way to break down an unreasonable custom, is to contradict it in practice. To be sure in pursuing this course I have had to contend not merely with the white race, but with the black. The one has condemned me for my presumption in daring to associate with them, and the other for pushing myself where they take it for granted I am not wanted. I am pained to think that the latter objection springs largely from a consciousness of inferiority, for as colours alone can have nothing against each other, and the conditions of human association are founded upon character rather than colour, character depending upon mind and morals, there can be nothing blameworthy in people thus equal, meeting each other on the plane of civil or social rights.

A series of important events followed soon after the second inauguration of Mr. Lincoln, conspicuous amongst which was the fall of Richmond. The strongest endeavour, and the best generalship of the rebellion was employed to hold that place, and when it fell, the pride, prestige, and power of the rebellion fell with it, never to rise again. The news of this great event found me again in Boston. The enthusiasm of that loyal city cannot be easily described. As usual, when anything touches the great heart of Boston, Faneuil Hall became vocal and eloquent. This Hall is an immense building, and its history is correspondingly great. It has been the theatre of much patriotic declamation from the days of the "Revolution" and before; as it has, since my day, been the scene where the strongest efforts of the most popular orators of Massachusetts have been made. Here Webster the great "expounder" addressed the "sea of upturned faces." Here Choate, the wonderful Boston barrister, by his weird, electric eloquence, enchained his thousands; here Everett charmed with his classic periods the flower of Boston aristocracy; and here, too, Charles Sumner, Horace Mann, John A. Andrew, and Wendell Phillips, the last superior to most, and equal to any, have for forty years spoken their great words for justice, liberty, and humanity, sometimes in the calm and sunshine of unruffled peace, but oftener in the tempest and whirlwind of mob-ocratic violence. It was here that Mr. Phillips made his famous speech in denunciation of the murder of Elijah P. Lovejoy in 1837, which changed the whole current of his life and made him pre-eminently the leader of anti-slavery thought in New England. Here too Theodore Parker, whose early death not only Boston, but the lovers of liberty throughout the world, still mourn, gave utterance to his deep and life-giving thoughts in words of fulness and power. But I set out to speak of the meeting, which was held there in celebration of the fall of Richmond, for it was a meeting as remarkable for its composition, as for its occasion. Among the speakers by whom it was addressed, and who gave voice to the patriotic sentiments which filled and overflowed each loyal heart, were the Hon. Henry Wilson, and the Hon. Robert C. Winthrop. It would be difficult to find two public men more distinctly opposite than these. If any one may properly boast an aristocratic descent, or if there be any value or worth in that boast, Robert C. Winthrop may without undue presumption, avail himself of it. He was born in the midst of wealth and luxury, and never felt the flint of hardship or the grip of poverty. Just the opposite to this was the experience of Henry Wilson. The son of common people, wealth and education had done little for him; but he had in him a true heart, with a world of common sense; and these with industry, good habits, and perseverance, had carried him further and lifted him higher, than the brilliant man with whom he formed such a striking contrast. Winthrop, before the war, like many others of his class, had resisted the anti-slavery current of his State, had sided largely with the demands of the slave power, had abandoned many of his old Whig friends, when they went for Free Soil and Free Men in 1848, and had gone into the Democratic party.

During the war he was too good to be a rebel sympathizer, and not quite good enough to become as Wilson was—a power in the Union cause. Wilson had risen to eminence by his devotion to liberal ideas, while Winthrop had sunken almost to obscurity from his indifference to such ideas. But now either himself or his friends, most likely the latter, thought that the time had come when some word implying interest in the loyal cause should fall from his lips. It was not so much the need of the Union, as the need of himself, that he should speak; the time when the Union needed him, and all others, was when the slaveholding rebellion raised its defiant head, not when as now, that head was in the dust and ashes of defeat and destruction. But the beloved Winthrop, the proud representative of what Daniel Webster once called the "solid men of Boston," had great need to speak now. It had been no fault of the loyal cause that he had not spoken sooner. Its "gates, like those of Heaven, stood open night and day." If he did not come in, it was his own fault. Regiment after regiment, brigade after brigade, had passed over Boston Common to endure the perils and hardships of war; Governor Andrew had poured out his soul, and exhausted his wonderful powers of speech in patriotic words to the brave departing sons of old Massachusetts, and a word from Winthrop would have gone far to nerve up those young soldiers going forth to lay down their lives for the life of the Republic; but no word came. Yet now in the last quarter of the eleventh hour, when the day's work was nearly done, Robert C. Winthrop was seen standing upon the same platform with the veteran Henry Wilson. He was there in all his native grace and dignity, elegantly and aristocratically clothed, his whole bearing marking his social sphere as widely different from many present. Happily for his good name, and for those who shall bear it when he is no longer among the living, he was found even at the last hour, in the right place—in old Faneuil Hall—side by side with plain Henry Wilson—the shoemaker senator. But this was not the only contrast on that platform on that day. It was my strange fortune to follow Mr. Winthrop on this interesting occasion. I remembered him as the guest of John H. Clifford of New Bedford, afterwards Governor of Massachusetts, when twenty-five years before, I had been only a few months from slavery—I was behind his chair as waiter, and was even then charmed by his elegant conversation—and now after this lapse of time, I found myself no longer behind the chair of this princely man, but announced to succeed him in the order of speakers, before that brilliant audience. I was not insensible to the contrast in our history and positions, and was curious to observe if it effected him, and how. To his credit, I am happy to say, he bore himself grandly throughout. His speech was fully up to the enthusiasm of the hour, and the great audience greeted his utterances with merited applause. I need not speak of the speeches of Henry Wilson and others, nor of my own. The meeting was in every way a remarkable expression of popular feeling, created by a great and important event.

After the fall of Richmond, the collapse of the rebellion was not long delayed, though it did not perish without adding to its long list of atrocities, one which sent a thrill of horror throughout the civilized world, in the assassination of Abraham Lincoln a man so amiable, so kind, humane, and honest, that one is at a loss to know how he could have had an enemy on earth. The details of his "taking off" are too familiar to be more than mentioned here. The assassination of James Abraham Garfield has made us all too painfully familiar with the shock and sensation produced by the hell-black crime, to make any description necessary. The curious will note, that the Christian name of both men is the same, and that both were remarkable for their kind qualities, and for having risen by their own energies from among the people, and that both were victims of assassins at the beginning of a presidential term.

Mr. Lincoln had reason to look forward to a peaceful and happy term of office. To all appearance, we were on the eve of a restoration of the Union, and a solid and lasting peace. He had served one term as President of the Disunited States, he was now for the first time to be President of the United States. Heavy had been his burden, hard had been his toil, bitter had been his trials, and terrible had been his anxiety; but the future seemed now bright and full of hope. Richmond had fallen, Grant had General Lee and the army of Virginia firmly in his clutch; Sherman had fought and found his way from the banks of the great river to the shores of the sea, leaving the two ends of the rebellion squirming and twisting in agony, like the severed parts of a serpent, doomed to inevitable death; and now there was but a little time longer for the good President to bear his burden, and be the target of reproach. His accusers, in whose opinion he was always too fast or too slow, too weak or too strong, too conciliatory or too aggressive, would soon become his admirers; it was soon to be seen that he had conducted the affairs of the nation with singular wisdom, and with absolute fidelity to the great trust confided to him. A country, redeemed and regenerated from the foulest crime against human nature that ever saw the sun! What a bright vision of peace, prosperity, and happiness must have come to that tired and overworked brain, and weary spirit. Men used to talk of his jokes, and he no doubt indulged in them, but I seemed never to have the faculty of calling them to the surface. I saw him oftener than many who have reported him, but I never saw any levity in him. He always impressed me as a strong, earnest man, having no time or disposition to trifle; grappling the work he had in hand with all his might. The expression of his face was a blending of suffering with patience and fortitude. Men called him homely, and homely he was; but it was manifestly a human homeliness, for there was nothing of the tiger or other wild animal about him. His eyes had in them the tenderness of motherhood, and his mouth and other features the highest perfection of a genuine manhood. His picture, by Marshall, now before me in my study, corresponds well with the impression I have of him. But, alas! what are all good and great qualities; what are human hopes and human happiness to the revengeful hand of an assassin? What are sweet dreams of peace; what are visions of the future? A simple leaden bullet, and a few grains of powder, in the shortest limit of time, are sufficient to blast and ruin all that is precious in human existence, not alone of the murdered, but of the murderer. I write this in the deep gloom flung over my spirit by the cruel, wanton, and cold-blooded assassination of Abraham Garfield, as well as that of Abraham Lincoln.

I was in Rochester, N.Y., where I then resided, when news of the death of Mr. Lincoln was received. Our citizens, not knowing what else to do in the agony of the hour, betook themselves to the City Hall. Though all hearts ached for utterance, few felt like speaking. We were stunned and overwhelmed by a crime and calamity hitherto unknown to our country and our government. The hour was hardly one for speech, for no speech could rise to the level of feeling. Doctor Robinson, then of Rochester University, but now of Brown University, Providence, R. I., was prevailed upon to take the stand, and made one of the most touching and eloquent speeches I ever heard. At the close of his address, I was called upon, and spoke out of the fulness of my heart, and, happily, I gave expression to so much of the soul of the people present, that my voice was several times utterly silenced by the sympathetic tumult of the great audience. I had resided long in Rochester, and had made many speeches there which had more or less touched the hearts of my hearers, but never till this day was I brought into such close accord with them. We shared in common a terrible calamity, and this "touch of nature, made us," more than countrymen, it made us "kin."

CHAPTER XIII: VAST CHANGES.

Satisfaction and anxiety—New fields of labour opening—Lyceums and colleges soliciting addresses—Literary attractions—Pecuniary gain—Still pleading for human rights—President Andy Johnson—Coloured delegation—Their reply to him—National Loyalist Convention, 1866, and its procession—Not wanted—Meeting with an old friend—Joy and surprise—The old master's welcome, and Miss Amanda's friendship—Enfranchisement discussed—Its accomplishment—The negro a citizen.

WHEN the war for the union was substantially ended, and peace had dawned upon the land, as was the case almost immediately after the tragic death of President Lincoln; when the gigantic system of American slavery which had defied the march of time, resisted all the appeals and arguments of the abolitionists, and the humane testimonies of good men of every generation during two hundred and fifty years, was finally abolished and for ever prohibited by the organic law of the land; a strange and, perhaps, perverse feeling came over me. My great and exceeding joy over these stupendous achievements, especially over the abolition of slavery—which had been the deepest desire and the great labour of my life,—was slightly tinged with a feeling of sadness.

I felt I had reached the end of the noblest and best part of my life; my school was broken up, my church disbanded, and the beloved congregation dispersed, never to come together again. The anti-slavery platform had performed its work, and my voice was no longer needed. "Othello's occupation was gone." The great happiness of meeting with my fellow-workers was now to be among the things of memory. Then, too, some thought of my personal future came in. Like Daniel Webster, when asked by his friends to leave John Tyler's Cabinet, I naturally inquired: "where shall I go?" I was still in the midst of my years, and had something of life before me, and as the minister, urged by my old friend George Bradburn to preach anti-slavery, when to do so was unpopular, said, "It is necessary for ministers to live," I felt it was necessary for me to live, and to live honestly. But where should I go, and what should I do? I could not now take hold of life as I did when I first landed in New Bedford, twenty-five years before; I could not go to the wharf of either Gideon or George Howland, to Richmond's brass foundry, or Richeton's candle and oil works, load and unload vessels, or even ask Governor Clifford for a place as a servant. Rolling oil casks and shovelling coal were all well enough when I was younger, immediately after getting out of slavery. Doing this was a step up, rather than a step down; but all these avocations had had their day for me, and I had had my day for them. My public life and labours had unfitted me for the pursuits of my earlier years, and yet had not prepared me for more congenial and higher employment. Outside the question of slavery, my thoughts had not been much directed, and I could hardly hope to make myself useful in any other cause than that to which I had given the best twenty-five years of my life. A man in the situation I found myself, has not only to divest himself of the old, which is never easily done, but to adjust himself to the new, which is still more difficult. Delivering lectures under various names, John B. Gough says, "whatever may be the title, my lecture is always on Temperance;" and such is apt to be the case with any man who has devoted his time and thoughts to one subject for any considerable length of time. But what should I do? was the question. I had a few thousand dollars—a great convenience, and one not generally so highly prized by my people as it ought to be—saved from the sale of "my bondage and my freedom," and the proceeds of my lectures at home and abroad. With this sum I thought of following the noble example of my old friends Stephen and Abby Kelley Foster, purchase a little farm and settle myself down to earn an honest living by tilling the soil. My children were all grown up, and ought to be able to take care of themselves. This question, however, was soon decided for me. I had after all acquired—a very unusual thing—a little more knowledge and aptitude fitting me for the new condition of things than I knew, and had a deeper hold upon public attention than I had supposed. Invitations began to pour in upon me from colleges, Lyceums, and literary societies, offering me one hundred, and even two hundred dollars for a single lecture.

I had some time before, prepared a lecture on "Self-made men," and also one upon Ethnology, with a special reference to Africa. The latter had cost me much labour, though as I now look back upon it, it was a very defective production. I wrote it at the instance of my friend Doctor M. B. Anderson, President of Rochester University, himself a distinguished Ethnologist, a deep thinker and scholar. I had been invited by one of the literary societies of Western Reserve College—then at Hudson, but recently removed to Cleveland, Ohio—to address it on "Commencement Day;" and never having spoken on such an occasion, never, indeed, having been inside of a school-house for the purpose of an education, I hesitated about accepting the invitation, and finally called upon Prof. Henry Wayland, son of the great Doctor Wayland of Brown University, and on Doctor Anderson, and asked their advice whether I ought to accept.

Both gentlemen advised me to do so. They knew me, and evidently thought well of my ability, But the puzzling question now was, what shall I say if I go there? It won't do to give them an old-fashioned anti-slavery discourse. I learned afterwards that such a discourse was precisely what they needed, though not what they wished; for the faculty, including the President, was in great distress because I, a coloured man, had been invited, and because of the reproach this circumstance might bring upon the College. But what shall I talk about? became the difficult question. I finally hit upon the one before mentioned. I had read, when in England a few years before, with great interest, parts of Doctor Pritchard's "Natural History of Man," a large volume marvellously calm and philosophical in its discussion of the science of the origin of the races, and was thus in the line of my then convictions. I sought this valuable book at once in our bookstores, but could not obtain it anywhere in this country. I sent to England, where I paid the sum of seven and a half dollars for it. In addition to this valuable work, President Anderson kindly gave me a little book entitled, "Man and his Migrations," by Dr. R. G. Latham, and loaned me the large work of Dr. Morton, the famous Archæologist, and that of Messrs. Nott and Glidden, the latter written evidently to degrade the negro and support the then prevalent Calhoun doctrine of the rightfulness of slavery. With these books, and occasional suggestions from Dr. Anderson and Professor Wayland, I set about preparing my "Commencement address." For many days and nights I toiled, and succeeded at last in getting something together in due form. Written orations had not been in my line. I had usually depended upon my unsystematized knowledge, and the inspiration of the hour and the occasion; but I had now got the "scholar bee in my bonnet," and supposed that inasmuch as I was to speak to college professors and students, I must at least, make a show of some familiarity with letters. It proved, as to its immediate effect, a great mistake; for my carefully studied and written address, full of learned quotations, fell dead at my feet, while a few remarks I made extemporaneously at collation, were enthusiastically received. Nevertheless, the reading and labour expended were of much value to me. They were needed steps preparatory to the work upon which I was about to enter. If they failed at the beginning, they helped to success in the end. My lecture on "The Races of Men" was seldom called for, but that on "Self-made Men" was in great demand, especially through the West. I found that the success of a lecturer depends more upon the quality of his stock in store, than the amount. My friend, Wendell Phillips,—for such I esteem him,—who has said more cheering words to me, and in vindication of my race, than any man now living, has delivered his famous lecture on the "Lost Arts" during the last forty years; and I doubt if among all his lectures, and he has many, there is one in such requisition as this. When Daniel O'Connell was asked why he did not make a new speech, he playfully replied, that "it would take Ireland twenty years to learn his old ones." Upon some such consideration as this, I adhered pretty closely to my old lecture on "Self-made Men," retouching and shading it a little from time to time as occasion seemed to require.

Here, then, was a new vocation before me, full of advantages, mentally and pecuniarily. When in the employment of the American Anti-Slavery Society, my salary was about four hundred and fifty dollars a year, and I felt I was well paid for my services; but I could now make from fifty to a hundred dollars a night, and have the satisfaction, too, that I was in some small measure helping to lift my race into consideration: for no man who lives at all, lives unto himself; he either helps or hinders all who are in anywise connected with him. I never rise to speak before an American audience without something of the feeling that my failure or success will bring blame or benefit to my whole race. But my activities were not now confined entirely to lectures before Lyceums. Though slavery was abolished, the wrongs of my people were not ended. Though they were not slaves they were not yet quite free. No man can be truly free, whose liberty is dependent upon the thought, feeling, and action of others; and who has himself no means in his own hands for guarding, protecting, defending, and maintaining that liberty. Yet the negro, after his emancipation, was precisely in this state of destitution. The law, on the side of freedom, is of great advantage only where there is power to make that law respected. I know no class of my fellowmen, however just, enlightened, and humane, which can be wisely and safely trusted absolutely with the liberties of any other class. Protestants are excellent people, but it would not be wise for Catholics to depend entirely upon them to look after their rights and interests. Catholics are a pretty good sort of people—though there is a soul-shuddering history behind them,—yet no enlightened Protestant would commit his liberty to their care and keeping. And yet the Government had left the freedmen in a worse condition than either of these. It felt that it had done enough for them. It had made them free, and henceforth they must make their own way in the world, or as the slang phrase has it, "Root, pig, or die;" yet they had none of the conditions for self-preservation or self-protection. They were free from the individual master, but the slaves of society. They had neither property, money, nor friends. They were free from the old plantation, but they had nothing but the dusty road under their feet. They were free from the old quarter that once gave them shelter, but slaves to the rains of summer and the frosts of winter. They were in a word, literally turned loose, naked, hungry, and destitute to the open sky, The first feeling towards them by the old master classes, was full of bitterness and wrath. They resented their emancipation as an act of hostility towards themselves, and since they could not punish the emancipator, they felt like punishing the objects which that act had emancipated. Hence they drove them off the old plantation, and told them they were no longer wanted there. They not only hated them because they had been freed as a punishment to them, but because they felt that they had been robbed of their labour. An element of still greater bitterness came into their hearts: the freedmen had been the friends of the Government, and many of them had borne arms against their masters during the war. The thought of paying cash for labour that they could formerly extort by the lash did not in anywise improve their disposition to the emancipated slaves, or improve their own condition. Now, since poverty has, and can have no chance against wealth, the landless against the land owner, the ignorant against the intelligent, the freedmen were powerless. They had nothing left them but a slavery-distorted and diseased body, and lame and twisted limbs with which to fight the battle of life. I, therefore, soon found that the negro had still a cause, and that he needed my voice and pen with others to plead for it. The American Anti-Slavery Society, under the lead of Mr. Garrison, had disbanded, its newspapers were discontinued, its agents were withdrawn from the field, and all systematic efforts by abolitionists were abandoned. Many of the society, Mr. Phillips and myself amongst the number, differed from Mr. Garrison as to the wisdom of this course. I felt that the work of the Society was not done, that it had not fulfilled its mission, which was not merely to emancipate, but to elevate the enslaved class; but against Mr. Garrison's leadership, and amid the surprise and joy occasioned by the emancipation, it was impossible to keep the association alive; and the cause of the freedmen was left mainly to individual effort, and to hastily extemporized societies of ephemeral character, brought together under benevolent impulse, but having no history behind them, and being new to the work, they were not as effective for good as the old society would have been, had it followed up its work and kept its old instrumentalities in operation.

From the first I saw no chance of bettering the condition of the freedman, until he should cease to be merely a freedman, and should become a citizen. I insisted that there was no safety for him, nor for anybody else in America, outside the American Government: that to guard, protect, and maintain his liberty, the freedman should have the ballot; that the liberties of the American people were dependent upon the Ballot-box, the Jury-box, and the Cartridge-box, that without these no class of people could live and flourish in this country; and this was now the word for the hour with me, and the word to which the people of the North willingly listened when I spoke. Hence, regarding as I did, the elective franchise as the one great power by which all civil rights are obtained, enjoyed, and maintained under our form of government, and the one without which freedom to any class is delusive if not impossible, I set myself to work with whatever force and energy I possessed to secure this power for the recently emancipated millions.

The demand for the ballot was such a vast advance upon the former objects proclaimed by the friends of the coloured race, that it startled and struck men as preposterous and wholly inadmissible. Anti-slavery men themselves were not united as to the wisdom of such demand. Mr. Garrison himself, though foremost for the abolition of slavery, was not yet quite ready to join this advanced movement. In this respect he was in the rear of Mr. Phillips; who saw not only the justice, but the wisdom and necessity of the measure. To his credit it may be said, that he gave the full strength of his character and eloquence to its adoption. While Mr. Garrison thought it too much to ask, Mr. Phillips thought it too little. While the one thought it might be postponed to the future, the other thought it ought to be done at once. But Mr. Garrison was not a man to lag far in the rear of truth and right, and he soon came to see with the rest of us that the ballot was essential to the freedom of the freemen. A man's head will not long remain wrong, when his heart is right. The applause awarded to Mr. Garrison by the Conservatives, for his moderation both in respect of his views on this question, and the disbandment of the American Anti-Slavery Society must have disturbed him. He was at any rate soon found on the right side of the suffrage question.

The enfranchisement of the freedmen was resisted on many grounds, but mainly these two: first the tendency of the measure to bring the freedmen into conflict with the old master class, and the white people of the South generally. Secondly, their unfitness, by reason of their ignorance, servility, and degradation, to exercise so great a power as the ballot, over the destinies of this great nation.

These reasons against the measure, which were supposed to be unanswerable, were in some senses the most powerful arguments in its favour. The argument that the possession of the suffrage would be likely to bring the negro into conflict with the old master-class of the South, had its main force in the admission that the interests of the two classes antagonized each other and that the maintenance of the one would prove inimical to the other. It resolved itself into this, if the negro had the means of protecting his civil rights, those who had formerly denied him these rights would be offended and would make war upon him. Experience has shown, in a measure, the correctness of this position. The old master was offended to find the negro whom he lately possessed the right to enslave and flog to toil, casting a ballot equal to his own; and he resorted to all sorts of meanness, violence, and crime to dispossess him of the enjoyment of this point of equality. In this respect the exercise of the right of suffrage by the negro has been attended with the evil, which the opponents of the measure predicted, and they could say "I told you so," but immeasurably and intolerably greater would have been the evil consequences resulting from the denial to one class, of this natural means of protection, and granting it to the other, and the hostile class. It would have been, to have committed the lamb to the care of the wolf—the arming of one class and disarming the other—protecting one interest, and destroying the other—making the rich strong, and the poor weak—the white man a tyrant, and the black man a slave. The very fact, therefore, that the old master-classes of the South felt that their interests were opposed to those of the freedmen, instead of being a reason against their enfranchisement, was the most powerful one in its favour. Until it shall be safe to leave the lamb in the hold of the lion, the labourer in the power of the capitalist, the poor in the hands of the rich, it will not be safe to leave a newly emancipated people completely in the power of their former masters, especially when such masters have not ceased to be such from enlightened moral convictions, but by irresistible force. Then on the part of the Government itself, had it denied this great right to the freedmen, it would have been another proof that "Republics are ungrateful." It would have been rewarding its enemies, and punishing its friends—embracing its foes, and spurning its allies,—setting a premium on treason, and degrading loyalty. As to the second point, viz. the negro's ignorance and degradation, there was no disputing either. It was the nature of slavery, from whose depths he had arisen, to make him so, and it would have kept him so. It was the policy of the system to keep him both ignorant and degraded, the better and more safely to defraud him of his hard earnings; and this argument never staggered me. The ballot in the hands of the negro was necessary to open the door of the school-house, and to unlock the treasures of knowledge to him. Granting all that was said of his ignorance, I used to say, "if the negro knows enough to fight for his country, he knows enough to vote; if he knows enough to pay taxes for the support of the Government, he knows enough to vote; if he knows as much when sober, as an Irishman knows when drunk, he knows enough to vote."

And now, while I am not blind to the evils which have thus far attended the enfranchisement of the coloured people, I hold that the evils from which we escaped, and the good we have derived from that act, amply vindicate its wisdom. The evils it brought are in their nature temporary, and the good is permanent. The one is comparatively small, the other absolutely great. The young child has staggered on to his little legs, and he has sometimes fallen and hurt his head in the fall, but then he has learned to walk. The boy in the water came near drowning, but then he has learned to swim. Great changes in the relations of mankind can never come, without evils analagous to those which have attended the emancipation and enfranchisement of the coloured people of the United States. I am less amazed at these evils, than by the rapidity with which they are subsiding, and not more astonished at the facility with which the former slave has become a free man, than at the rapid adjustment of the master-class to the new situation.

Unlike the movement for the abolition of slavery, the success of the effort for the enfranchisement of the freedmen was not long delayed. It is another illustration of how one advance in pursuance of a right principle, prepares and makes easy the way to another. The way of transgression is a bottomless pit, one step in that direction invites the next, and the end is never reached; and it is the same with the path of righteous obedience. Two hundred years ago, the pious Dr. Godwin dared affirm that it was "not a sin to baptize a negro," and won for him the rite of baptism. It was a small concession to his manhood; but it was strongly resisted by the slaveholders of Jamaica, and Virginia. In this they were logical in their argument, but they were not logical in their object. They saw plainly, that to concede the negro's right to baptism was to receive him into the Christian Church, and make him a brother in Christ; and hence they opposed the first step sternly and bitterly. So long as they could keep him beyond the circle of human brotherhood, they could scourge him to toil, as a beast of burden, with a good Christian conscience, and without reproach. "What!" said they, "baptize a negro? preposterous!" Nevertheless the negro was baptized and admitted to Church fellowship; and though for a long time his soul belonged to God, his body to his master, and he, poor fellow, had nothing left for himself, he is at last not only baptized, but emancipated and enfranchised.

In this achievemeut, an interview with President Andrew Johnson, on the 7th of February, 1866, by a delegation consisting of George T. Downing, Lewis H. Douglass, Wm. E. Matthews, John Jones, John F. Cook, Joseph E. Otis, A. W. Ross, William Whipper, John M. Brown, Alexander Dunlop, and myself, will take its place in history as one of the first steps. What was said on that occasion brought the whole question, virtually, before the American people. Until that interview, the country was not fully aware of the intentions and policy of President Johnson on the subject of reconstruction, especially in respect of the newly emancipated class of the South. After having heard the brief addresses made to him by Mr. Downing and myself, he occupied at least three-quarters of an hour in what seemed a set speech, and refused to listen to any reply on our part, although solicited to grant a few moments for that purpose. Seeing the advantage that Mr. Johnson would have over us in getting his speech paraded before the country in the morning papers, the members of the delegation met on the evening of that day, and instructed me to prepare a brief reply which should go out to the country simultaneously with the President's speech to us. Since this reply indicates the points of difference between the President and ourselves, I produce it here as a part of the history of the times, it being concurred in by all the members of the delegation.

Both the speech and the reply were commented upon very extensively.

Mr. President. In consideration of a delicate sense of propriety, as well as your own repeated intimations of indisposition to discuss, or listen to a reply to the views and opinions you were pleased to express to us in your elaborate speech to-day, the undersigned would respectfully take this method of replying thereto. Believing as we do that the views and opinions you expressed in that address are entirely unsound and prejudicial to the highest interests of our race as well as our country at large, we cannot do other than expose the same, and, as far as may be in our power, arrest their dangerous influence. It is not necessary at this time to call attention to more than two or three features of your remarkable address:

1. The first point to which we feel especially bound to take exception, is your attempt to found a policy opposed to our enfranchisement, upon the alleged ground of an existing hostility on the part of the former slaves toward the poor white people of the South. We admit the existence of this hostility, and hold that it is entirely reciprocal. But you obviously commit an error by drawing an argument from an incident of slavery, and making it a basis for a policy adapted to a state of freedom. The hostility between the whites and blacks of the South is easily explained. It has its root and sap in the relation of slavery, and was incited on both sides by the cunning of the slave masters. Those masters secured their ascendancy over both the poor whites and blacks by putting enmity between them.

They divided both to conquer each. There was no earthly reason why the blacks should not hate and dread the poor whites when in a state of slavery, for it was from this class that their masters received their slave catchers, slave drivers, and overseers. They were the men called in upon all occasions by the masters, whenever any fiendish outrage was to be committed upon the slave. Now, sir, you cannot but perceive that the cause of this hatred removed, the effect must be removed also. Slavery is abolished. The cause of this antagonism is removed, and you must see that it is altogether illogical, and "putting new wine into old bottles," to legislate from slaveholding and slave driving premises, for a people whom you have repeatedly declared your purpose to maintain in freedom.

2. Besides, even if it were true, as you allege, that the hostility of the blacks towards the poor whites must necessarily project itself into a state of freedom, and that this enmity between the two races is even more intense in a state of freedom than in a state of slavery, in the name of Heaven, we reverently ask you how you can, in view of your professed desire to promote the welfare of the black man, deprive him of all means of defence, and clothe him whom you regard as his enemy in the panoply of political power? Can it be that you recommend a policy which would arm the strong and cast down the defenceless? Can you, by any possibility of reasoning, regard this as just, fair, or wise? Experience proves that those are most abused who can be abused with the greatest impunity. Men are whipped oftenest who are whipped easiest. Peace between races is not to be secured by degrading one race and exalting another, by giving power to one race and withholding it from another, but, by maintaining a state of equal justice between all classes. First pure, then peaceable.

3. On the colonization theory you were pleased to broach, very much could be said. It is impossible to suppose, in view of the usefulness of the black man in time of peace as a

labourer in the South, and in time of war as a soldier in the North, and the growing respect for his rights among the people, and his increasing adaptation to a high state of civilization in his native land, there can ever come a time when he can be removed from this country without a terrible shock to its prosperity and peace. Besides, the worst enemy of a nation could not cast upon its fair name a greater infamy than to admit that negroes could be tolerated among them in a state of the most degrading slavery and oppression, and must be cast away, driven into exile, for no other cause than having been freed from their chains.

Washington, February 7th, 1866.

From this time onward, the question of suffrage for the freedmen, was not allowed to rest. The rapidity with which it gained strength, was something quite marvellous and surprising even to its advocates. Senator Charles Sumner soon took up the subject in the Senate and treated it in his usually able and exhaustive manner. It was a great treat to listen to his argument, running through two days, abounding as it did, in eloquence, learning, and conclusive reasoning. A committee of the Senate had reported a proposition giving to the States lately in rebellion in so many words complete option as to the enfranchisement of their coloured citizens; only coupling with that proposition the condition, that to such States as chose to enfranchise such citizens, the basis of their representation in Congress should be proportionately increased; or, in other words, only three-fifths of the coloured citizens should be counted in the basis of representation in States where coloured citizens were not allowed to vote, while in the States granting suffrage to coloured citizens, the entire coloured people should be counted in the basis of representation. Against this proposition, myself and associates addressed to the Senate of the United States the following memorial:

"To the Honourable the Senate of the United States:

"The undersigned, being a delegation representing the coloured people of the several States, and now sojourning in Washington, charged with the duty to look after the best interests of the recently emancipated, would most respectfully, but earnestly, pray your honourable body to favour no amendment of the Constitution of the United States which would grant any one or all of the States of this Union to disfranchise any class of citizens on the ground of race or colour, for any consideration whatever. They would further respectfully represent that the Constitution as adopted by the fathers of the Republic in 1789, evidently contemplated the result which has now happened, to wit, the abolition of slavery. The men who framed it, and those who adopted it, framed and adopted it for the people, and the whole people—coloured men being at that time legal voters in most of the States. In that instrument, as it now stands, there is not a sentence nor a syllable conveying any shadow of right or authority by which any State may make colour or race a disqualification for the exercise of the right of suffrage; and the undersigned will regard as a real calamity the introduction of any words, expressly or by implication, giving any State or States such power, and we respectfully submit that if the amendment now pending before your honourable body shall be adopted, it will enable any State to deprive any class of citizens of the elective franchise, notwithstanding it was obviously framed with a view to affect the question of negro suffrage only.

"For these, and other reasons, the undersigned respectfully pray that the amendment to the Constitution, recently passed by the House, and now before your body, be not adopted. And as in duty bound, etc."

It was the opinion of Senator Wm. Pitt Fessenden, Senator Henry Wilson, and many others, that the measure here memorialized against, would, if incorporated into the Constitution, certainly bring about the enfranchisement of the whole coloured population of the South. It was held by them to be an inducement to the States to make suffrage universal, since the basis of representation would be enlarged or contracted, according as suffrage should be extended or limited; but the judgment of these leaders was not the judgment of Senator Sumner, Senator Wade, Yates, Howe, and others, or of the coloured people. Yet, weak as this measure was, it encountered the united opposition of Democratic senators. On that side, the Hon. Thomas H. Hendricks of Indiana, took the lead in appealing to popular prejudice against the negro. He contended that among other objectionable and insufferable results that would flow from its adoption would be, that a negro would ultimately be a member of the United States Senate. I never shall forget the ineffable scorn and indignation with which Mr. Hendricks deplored the possibility of such an event. In less, however, than a decade from that debate, Senators Revels and Bruce, both coloured men, have fulfilled the startling prophecy of the Indiana senator. It was not, however, by the half-way measure, which he was opposing for its radicalism, but by the fourteenth and fifteenth amendments, that these gentlemen reached their honourable positions.

In defeating the option proposed to be given to the States, to extend or deny suffrage to their coloured population, much credit is due to the delegation already named as visiting President Johnson. That delegation made it their business to personally see and urge upon leading Republican statesmen the wisdom and duty of impartial suffrage. Day after day, Mr. Downing and myself saw and conversed with those members of the Senate, whose advocacy of the suffrage would be likely to insure its success.

The second marked step in effecting the enfranchisement of the negro, was made at the "National Loyalist's Convention," held at Philadelphia in September, 1866. This body was composed of delegates from the South, North, and West. Its object was to diffuse clear views of the situation of affairs in the South, and to indicate the principles deemed advisable by it to be observed in the reconstruction of society in the Southern States.

This Convention was, as its history shows, numerously attended by the ablest and most influential men from all sections of the country, and its deliberations participated in, by them.

The policy foreshadowed by Andrew Johnson, who, by the grace of the assassin's bullet, was then in Abraham Lincoln's seat, a policy based upon the idea that the rebel States were never out of the Union, and hence had forfeited no rights which his pardon could not restore—gave importance to this Convention, more than anything which was then occurring in the South; for through the treachery of this bold, bad man, we seemed then about to lose nearly all that had been gained by the war.

I was residing in Rochester at the time, and was duly elected as a delegate from that city to attend this Convention. The honour was a surprise and a gratification to me. It was unprecedented for a city of over sixty thousand white citizens and only about two hundred coloured residents, to elect a coloured man to represent them in a national political convention, and the announcement of it gave a shock to the country, of no inconsiderable violence. Many Republicans, with every feeling of respect for me personally were unable to see the wisdom of such a course. They dreaded the clamour of social equality and amalgamation which would be raised against the party, in consequence of this startling innovation. They, dear fellows, found it much more agreeable to talk of the principles of liberty as glittering generalities, than to reduce those principles to practice.

When the train on which I was going to the convention reached Harrisburgh, it met and was attached to another from the West, crowded with Western and Southern delegates on the way to the Convention, and among them were several loyal Governors, chief among whom was the loyal Governor of Indiana, Oliver P. Morton, a man of Websterian mould in all that appertained to mental power. When my presence became known to these gentlemen, a consultation was immediately held among them, upon the question as to what it was best to do with me. It seems strange now, in view of all the progress which has been made, that such a question could arise. But the circumstances of the times made me the Jonah of the Republican ship, and responsible for the contrary winds and misbehaving weather. Before we reached Lancaster, on our eastward bound trip, I was duly waited upon by a committee of my brother delegates, which had been appointed by other honourable delegates, to represent to me the undesirableness of my attendance upon the National Loyalist's Convention. The spokesman of these sub-delegates was a gentleman from New Orleans, with a very French name, which has now escaped me, but which I wish I could recall, that I might credit him with a high degree of politeness and the gift of eloquence. He began by telling me that he knew my history and my works, that he entertained a very high respect for me, that both himself and the gentlemen who sent him, as well as those who accompanied him, regarded me with admiration; that there was not among them the remotest objection to sitting in the Convention with me, but their personal wishes in the matter they felt should be set aside for the sake of our common cause; that whether I should or should not go into the Convention was purely a matter of expediency; that I must know that there was a very strong and bitter prejudice against my race in the North as well as in the South; and that the cry of social and political equality would not fail to be raised against the Republican party if I should attend this Loyal National Convention. He insisted that it was a time for the sacrifice of my own personal feeling, for the good of the Republican cause; that there were several districts in the State of Indiana so evenly balanced that a very slight circumstance would be likely to turn the scale against us, and defeat our Congressional candidates, and thus leave Congress without a two-thirds vote to control the headstrong and treacherous man then in the presidential chair. It was urged that this was a terrible responsibility for me or any other man to take.

I listened very attentively to this address, uttering no word during its delivery; but when it was finished, I said to the speaker and the committee, with all the emphasis I could throw into my voice and manner: "Gentlemen, with all respect, you might as well ask me to put a loaded pistol to my head and blow my brains out, as to ask me to keep out of this Convention, to which I have been duly elected. Then, gentlemen, what would you gain by this exclusion? Would not the charge of cowardice, certain to be brought against you, prove more damaging than that of amalgamation? Would you not be branded all over the land as dastardly hypocrites, professing principles which you have no wish or intention of carrying out? As a mere matter of policy or expediency, you will be wise to let me in. Everybody knows that I have been duly elected as a delegate by the city of Rochester. The fact has been broadly announced and commented upon all over the country. If I am not admitted, the public will ask, 'Where is Douglass? Why is he not seen in the convention?' And you would find that enquiry more difficult to answer than any charge brought against you for favouring political or social equality; but, ignoring the question of policy altogether, and looking at it as one of right and wrong, I am bound to go into that Convention; not to do so, would contradict the principle and practice of my life." With this answer, the committee retired from the car in which I was seated, and did not again approach me on the subject; but I saw plainly enough then, as well as on the morning when the Loyalist procession was to march through the streets of Philadelphia, that while I was not to be formally excluded, I was to be ignored by the Convention.

I was the ugly and deformed child of the family, and to be kept out of sight as much as possible while there was company in the house. Especially was it the purpose to offer me no inducement to be present in the ranks of the procession of its members and friends, which was to start from Independence Hall on the first morning of its meeting.

In good season, however, I was present at this grand starting point. My reception there confirmed my impression as to the policy intended to be pursued towards me. Few of the many I knew were prepared to give me a cordial recognition, and among these few I may mention Gen. Benj. F. Butler, who, whatever others may say of him, has always shown a courage equal to his convictions. Almost everybody else on the ground whom I met seemed to be ashamed or afraid of me. On the previous night I had been warned that I should not be allowed to walk through the city in the procession; fears had been expressed that my presence in it would so shock the prejudices of the people in Philadelphia, as to cause the procession to be mobbed.

The members of the Convention were to walk two abreast, and as I was the only coloured member of the Convention, the question was, as to who of my brother members would consent to walk with me? The answer was not long in coming. There was one man present who was broad enough to take in the whole situation, and brave enough to meet the duty of the hour; one who was neither afraid nor ashamed to own me as a man and a brother; one man of the purest Caucasian type, a poet and a scholar, brilliant as a writer, eloquent as a speaker, and holding a high and influential position—the editor of a weekly journal having the largest circulation of any weekly paper in the city or State of New York—and that man was Mr. Theodore Tilton. He came to me in my isolation, seized me by the hand in a most brotherly way, and proposed to walk with me in the procession.

I have been in many awkward and disagreeable positions in my life, when the presence of a friend would have been highly valued, but I think I never appreciated an act of courage and generous sentiment more highly than I did in this brave young man, when we marched through the streets of Philadelphia on this memorable day.

Well! what came of all these dark forebodings of timid men? How was my presence regarded by the populace, and what effect did it produce? I will tell you. The fears of our loyal Governors, who wished me excluded, to propitiate the favour of the crowd, met with a signal reproof, their apprehensions were shown to be groundless, and they were compelled, as many of them confessed to me afterwards, to own themselves entirely mistaken. The people were more enlightened, and had made more progress than their leaders had supposed. An act for which those leaders expected to be pelted with stones, only brought to them unmeasured applause. Along the whole line of march my presence was cheered repeatedly and enthusiastically. I was myself utterly surprised by the heartiness and unanimity of the popular approval. We were marching through a city remarkable for the depth and bitterness of its hatred of the abolition movement; a city whose populace had mobbed anti-slavery meetings, burned temperance halls and churches owned by coloured people, and burned down Pennsylvania Hall because it had opened its doors to people of different colours upon terms of equality. But now the children of those who had committed these outrages and follies were applauding the very principles which their fathers had condemned. After the demonstrations of this first day, I found myself a welcome member of the Convention, and cordial greeting took the place of cold aversion. The victory was short, signal, and complete.

During the passage of the procession, as we were marching through Chesnut Street, an incident occurred which excited some interest in the crowd, and was noticed by the Press at the time, and may perhaps be properly related here as a part of the story of my eventful life. It was my meeting Mrs. Amanda Sears, the daughter of my old mistress, Miss Lucretia Auld, the same Lucretia to whom I was indebted for so many acts of kindness when under the rough treatment of Aunt Katy, on the "old plantation home" of Col. Edward Lloyd. Mrs. Sears now resided in Baltimore, and as I saw her at the corner of Ninth and Chesnut Streets, I hastily ran to her, and expressed my surprise and joy at meeting her, "But what brought you to

Philadelphia at this time?" I asked. She replied, with animated voice and countenance, "I heard you were to be here, and I came to see you walk in this procession." The dear lady, with her two children, had been following us for hours. Here was the daughter of the owner of a slave, following with enthusiasm that slave now a free man, and listening with joy to the plaudits he received as he marched along through the crowded streets of the great city. And here I may relate another circumstance which should have found place earlier in this story, which will further explain the feeling subsisting between Mrs. Sears and myself.

Seven years prior to our meeting, as just described, I delivered a lecture in National Hall, Philadelphia, and at its close a gentleman approached me and said, "Mr. Douglass, do you know that your once mistress has been listening to you to-night?" I replied that I did not, nor was I inclined to believe it. The fact was, that I had four or five times before had a similar statement made to me by different individuals in different States, and this made me sceptical in this instance. The next morning, however, I received a note from a Mr. Wm. Needles, very elegantly written, which stated that she who was Amanda Auld, daughter of Thomas and Lucretia Auld, and granddaughter to my old master, Capt. Aaron Anthony, was now married to Mr. John L. Sears, a coal merchant in West Philadelphia. The street and number of Mr. Sear's office was given, so that I might, by seeing him, assure myself of the facts in the case, and perhaps learn something of the relatives whom I left in slavery. This note, with the intimation given me the night before, convinced me there was something in it, and I resolved to know the truth. I had now been out of slavery twenty years, and no word had come to me from my sisters, or my brother Perry, or my grandmother. My separation had been as complete as if I had been an inhabitant of another planet. A law of Maryland at that time visited with heavy fine and imprisonment any coloured person who should come into the State; so I could not go to them any more than they could come to me.

Eager to know if my kinsfolk still lived, and what was their condition, I made my way to the office of Mr. Sears, found him in, and handed him the note I had received from Mr. Needles, and asked him to be so kind as to read it and tell me if the facts were as there stated. After reading the note, he said it was true, but he must decline any conversation with me, since not to do so would be a sacrifice to the feelings of his father-in-law. I deeply regretted his decision, and spoke of my long separation from my relations, appealing to him to give me some information concerning them. I saw that my words were not without their effect. Presently he said, "You publish a newspaper, I believe?" "I do," I said, "but if that is your objection to speaking to me, no word shall go into its columns of our conversation." To make a long story short, we had then quite a long conversation, during which Mr. Sears said that in my "Narrative" I had done his father-in-law injustice, for he was really a kind-hearted man, and a good master. I replied that there must be two sides to the relation of master and slave, and what was deemed kind and just to the one was the opposite to the other. Mr. Sears was not disposed to be unreasonable, and the longer we talked the nearer we came together. I finally asked permission to see Mrs. Sears, the little girl of seven or eight years when I left the eastern shore of Maryland. This request was a little too much for him at first, and he put me off by saying she was a mere child when I last saw her, and she was now the mother of a large family of children, and I would not know her. He could tell me everything about my people as well as she. I pressed my suit, however, insisting that I could select Miss Amanda out of a thousand other ladies, my recollection of her was so perfect, and begged him to test my memory at this point. After much parley of this nature, he at length consented to my wishes, giving me the number of his house and name of the street, with permission to call at 3 o'clock p.m. on the next day. I left him, delighted, and prompt to the hour was ready for my visit. I dressed myself in my best, and hired the finest carriage I could get to take me, partly because of the distance, and partly to make the contrast between the slave and the free man as striking as possible. Mr.

Sears had been equally thoughtful. He had invited to his house a number of friends to witness the meeting between Mrs. Sears and myself.

I was somewhat disconcerted when I was ushered into the large parlour occupied by about thirty ladies and gentlemen, to all of whom I was a perfect stranger. I saw the design to test my memory by making it difficult for me to guess which of the company was "Miss Amanda." In her girlhood, she was small and slender, and hence a thin and delicately formed lady was seated in a rocking chair, near the centre of the room, with a little girl by her side. The device was good, but it did not succeed. Glancing around the room, I saw in an instant the lady who was a child twenty-five years before, and the wife and mother now. Satisfied of this, I said, "Mr. Sears, if you will allow me, I will select Miss Amanda from this company." I started towards her, and she, seeing that I recognized her, bounded to me with joy in every feature, and expressed her great happiness at seeing me. All thought of slavery, colour, or what might seem to belong to the dignity of her position vanished, and the meeting was as the meeting of friends long separated, yet still present in each other's memory and affection.

Amanda made haste to tell me that she agreed with me about slavery, and that she had freed all her slaves as they had become of age. She brought her children to me, and I took them in my arms, with sensations which I could not, if I would, stop here to describe. One explanation of the feeling of this lady towards me was, that her mother, who died when she was yet a tender child, had been briefly described by me in a little "Narrative of my Life," published many years before our meeting, and when I could have had no motive but the highest for what I said of her. She had read my story, and learned something of the amiable qualities of her mother through me. She also recollected that as I had had trials as a slave, she had had her trials under the care of a stepmother, and that when she was harshly spoken to by her father's second wife, she could always read in my dark face the sympathy of one who had often received kind words from the lips of her beloved mother. Mrs. Sears died three years ago in Baltimore, but she did not depart without calling me to her bed-side, that I might tell her as much as I could about her mother, whom she was firm in the faith that she should meet in another, and a better world. She especially wished me to describe to her the personal appearance of her mother, and desired to know if any of her own children then present resembled her. I told her that the young lady standing in the corner of the room was the image of her mother in form and features. She looked at her daughter and said, "Her name is Lucretia—after my mother." After telling me that her life had been a happy one, and thanking me for coming to see her on her death-bed, she said she was ready to die. We parted to meet no more in life. The interview touched me deeply, and was, I could not help thinking, a strange one—another proof that "Truth is often stranger than Fiction."

If any reader of this part of my life shall see in it the evidence of a want of manly resentment for wrongs inflicted upon myself and race by slavery, and by the ancestors of this lady, so it must be. No man can be stronger than nature, one touch of which, we are told, makes all the world akin. I esteem myself a good, persistent hater of injustice and oppression, but my resentment ceases when they cease, and I have no heart to visit upon children the sins of their fathers.

It will be noticed, when I first met Mr. Sears in Philadelphia, he declined to talk with me, on the ground that I had been unjust to Capt. Auld, his father-in-law. Soon after that meeting, Capt. Auld had occasion to go to Philadelphia, and, as usual, went straight to the house of his son-in-law, and had hardly finished the ordinary salutations, when he said: "Sears, I see by the papers that Frederick has recently been in Philadelphia. Did you go to hear him?" "Yes, sir," was the reply. After asking something more about my lecture, he said, "Well, Sears, did Frederick come to see you?" "Yes, sir," said Sears. "Well, how did you receive him?" Mr.

Sears then told him all about my visit, and had the satisfaction of hearing the old man say that he had done right in giving me welcome to the house. This last fact I have from the Rev. J. D. Long, who, with his wife, was one of the party invited to meet me at the house of Mr. Sears, on the occasion of my visit to Mrs. Sears.

But I must now return from this digression, and further relate my experience in the Loyalist National Convention, and how from that time there was an impetus given to the enfranchisement of the freedmen, which culminated in the fifteenth amendment to the Constitution of the United States. From the first, the members of the Convention were divided in their views of the proper measures of reconstruction, and this division was in some sense sectional. The men from the far South, strangely enough, were quite radical, while those from the border States were mostly conservative, and, unhappily, these last had control of the Convention from the first. A Kentucky gentleman was made President, and its other officers were for the most part Kentuckians, and all opposed to coloured suffrage in sentiment. There was a "whole heap"—to use a Kentucky phrase—of halfness" in that State during the war for the Union, and there was much more there after the war. The Maryland delegates, with the exception of the Hon. John L. Thomas, were in sympathy with Kentucky. Those from Virginia, except the Hon. John Miner Botts, were unwilling to entertain the question. The result was, that the Convention was broken square in two. The Kentucky President declared it adjourned, and left the chair against the earnest protests of the friends of manhood suffrage.

But the friends of this measure were not to be out-generalled and suppressed in this way, and instantly reorganizing, elected John M. Botts of Virginia, President, discussed and passed resolutions in favour of enfranchising the freedmen, and thus placed the question before the country in such a manner that it could not be ignored. The delegates from the Southern States were quite in earnest, and bore themselves grandly in support of the measure; but the chief speakers and advocates of suffrage on that occasion were Mr. Theodore Tilton and Miss Anna E. Dickinson. Of course, on such a question, I could not be expected to be silent. I was called forward, and responded with all the energy of my soul, for I looked upon suffrage to the negro, as the only measure which could prevent him from being thrust back into slavery.

From this time onward the question of suffrage had no rest. The rapidity with which it gained strength was more than surprising to me.

In addition to the justice of the measure, it was soon commended by events as a political necessity. As in the case of the abolition of slavery, the white people of the rebellious States have themselves to thank for its adoption. Had they accepted, with moderate grace, the decision of the court to which they appealed, and the liberal conditions of peace offered to them, and united heartily with the National Government in its efforts to reconstruct their shattered institutions, instead of sullenly refusing as they did, their counsel and their votes to that end, they might easily have defeated the argument based upon necessity for the measure. As it was, the question was speedily taken out of the hands of coloured delegations and mere individual efforts, and became a part of the policy of the Republican party; and President U. S. Grant, with his characteristic nerve and clear perception of justice, promptly recommended the great amendment to the Constitution, by which coloured men are to-day invested with complete citizenship—the right to vote, and to be voted for, in the American Republic.

CHAPTER XIV: LIVING AND LEARNING.

Inducements to a political career—Objections—A newspaper enterprise—The "New National Era"—Its abandonment—The Freedmen's Savings and Trust Company—Sad experience—Vindication.

THE adoption of the fourteenth and fifteenth amendments, and their incorporation into the Constitution of the United States, opened a very tempting field to my ambition, and one to which I should have probably yielded, had I been a younger man. I was earnestly urged by many of my respected fellow-citizens, both coloured and white, and from all sections of the country, to take up my abode in some one of the many districts of the South, where there was a large coloured vote, and get myself elected, as they were sure I easily could do, to a seat in Congress—possibly in the Senate. That I did not yield to this temptation was not entirely due to my age; for the idea did not square well with my better judgment and sense of propriety. The thought of going to live among a people in order to gain their votes and acquire official honours, was repugnant to my self-respect, and I had not lived long enough in the political atmosphere of Washington to have this sentiment sufficiently blunted to make me indifferent to its suggestions. I do not deny that the arguments of my friends had some weight in them, and from their stand-point it was all right; but I was better known to myself than to them. I had small faith in my aptitude as a politician, and could not hope to cope with rival aspirants. My life and labours in the North had in a measure unfitted me for such work, and I could not readily have adapted myself to the peculiar oratory found to be most effective with the newly enfranchised class. In the New England and Northern atmosphere I had acquired a style of speaking which in the South would have been considered tame and spiritless; and, consequently, he who "could tear a passion to tatters and split the ear of groundlings," had far better chance of success with the masses there, than one so little boisterous as myself.

Upon the whole, I have never regretted that I did not enter the arena of Congressional honours to which I was invited.

Outside of mere personal considerations, I saw, or thought I saw, that in the nature of the case the sceptre of power had passed from the old slave and rebellious States, to the free and loyal States, and that hereafter, at least for some time to come, the loyal North, with its advanced civilization, must dictate the policy and control the destiny of the Republic. I had an audience ready made in the free States: one which the labours of thirty years had prepared for me, and before this audience the freedmen of the South needed an advocate as much as they needed a member of Congress. I think in this I was right; for thus far our coloured members of Congress have not largely made themselves felt in the legislation of the country; and I have little reason to think I could have done any better than they.

I was not, however, to remain long in my retired home in Rochester, where I had planted my trees and was reposing under their shadows. An effort was being made about this time to establish a large weekly newspaper in the city of Washington, which should be devoted to the defence and enlightenment of the newly emancipated and enfranchised people; and I was urged by such men as George T. Downing, J. H. Hawes, J. Sella Martin, and others, to become its editor-in-chief. My sixteen years' experience as editor and publisher of my own paper, and the knowledge of the toil and anxiety which such a relation to a public journal must impose, caused me much reluctance and hesitation; nevertheless, I yielded to the wishes of my friends and counsellors, went to Washington, threw myself into the work, hoping to be able to lift up a standard at the National Capital, for my people, which should cheer and strengthen them in the work of their own improvement and elevation.

I was not long connected with this enterprise before I discovered my mistake. The co-operation so liberally promised, and the support which had been assured, were not very largely realized. By a series of circumstances, a little bewildering as I now look back upon them, I found myself alone, under the mental and pecuniary burden involved in the prosecution of the enterprise. I had been misled by loud talk of a grand incorporated publishing company, in which I should have shares if I wished, and in any case a fixed salary for my services; and after all these fair-seeming conditions, I had not been connected with the paper one year before its affairs had been so managed by the agent appointed by this invisible company or corporate body, as to compel me to bear the burden alone, and to become the sole owner of the printing establishment. Having become publicly associated with the enterprise, I was unwilling to have it prove a failure, and had allowed it to become in debt to me, both for money loaned, and for services, and at last it seemed wise that I should purchase the whole concern, which I did, and turned it over to my sons Lewis and Frederic, who were practical printers, and who, after a few years, were compelled to discontinue its publication. This paper was the New National Era, to the columns of which the coloured people are indebted for some of the best things ever uttered in behalf of their cause; for, aside from its editorials and selections, many of the ablest coloured men of the country made it the medium through which to convey their thoughts to the public. A misadventure though it was, which cost me from nine to ten thousand dollars, over it I have no tears to shed. The journal was valuable while it lasted, and the experiment was full of instruction to me, which has to some extent been heeded, for I have kept well out of newspaper undertakings since.

Some one has said that "experience is the best teacher." Unfortunately the wisdom acquired in one experience seems not to serve for another and new one; at any rate, my first lesson at the National Capital, bought rather dearly as it was, did not preclude the necessity of a second whetstone to sharpen my wits in this my new home and new surroundings. It is not altogether without a feeling of humiliation that I must narrate my connection with the "Freedmen's Savings and Trust Company."

This was an institution designed to furnish a place of security and profit for the hard earnings of the coloured people, especially of the South. Though its title was "The Freedmen's Savings and Trust Company," it was known generally as the "Freedmen's Bank." According to its managers it was to be this and something more. There was something missionary in its composition, and it dealt largely in exhortations as well as promises. The men connected with its management were generally church members, and reputed eminent for their piety. Some of its agents had been preachers of the "Word." Their aim was now to instil into the minds of the untutored Africans lessons of sobriety, wisdom, and economy, and to show them how to rise in the world. Circulars-tracts, and other papers were scattered like snowflakes in winter by this benevolent institution among the sable millions, and they were told to "look" to the Freedmen's Bank and "live." Branches were established in all the Southern States, and as a result, money flowed into its valuts to the amount of millions. With the usual effect of sudden wealth, the managers felt like making a little display of their prosperity. They accordingly erected one of the most costly and splendid buildings of the time-on one of the most desirable and expensive sites in the National Capital, finished on the inside with black walnut, and furnished with marble counters and all the modern improvements. The magnificent dimensions of the building bore testimony to its flourishing condition. In passing it in the street I often peeped into its spacious windows, and looked down the row of its gentlemanly and elegantly-dressed coloured clerks, with their pens behind their ears and button-hole bouquets in their coat-fronts, and felt my very eyes enriched. It was a sight I had never expected to see. I was amazed with the facility with which they counted the money; they threw off the thousands with the dexterity, if not the accuracy, of old and experienced clerks. The whole thing was beautiful. I had read of this Bank when I lived in Rochester, and had indeed been solicited to become one of its trustees, and had reluctantly consented to do so; but when I came to Washington and saw its magnificent brown stone front, its towering height, and its perfect appointments, and the fine display it made in the transaction of its business, I felt like the Queen of Sheba when she saw the riches of Solomon, "the half had not been told me."

After settling myself down in Washington in the office of the New Era, I could, and did occasionally, attend the meetings of the Board of Trustees, and had the pleasure of listening to the rapid reports of the condition of the institution, which were generally of a most encouraging character. My confidence in the integrity and wisdom of the management was such that at one time I had entrusted to its vaults about twelve thousand dollars. It seemed fitting to me to cast in my lot with my brother freedmen, and help to build up an institution which represented their thrift and economy to such striking advantage; for the more millions accumulated there, I thought, the more consideration and respect would be shown to the coloured people of the whole country.

About four months before this splendid institution was compelled to close its doors in the starved and deluded faces of its depositors, and while I was assured by its President and by its Actuary of its sound condition, I was solicited by some of its trustees to allow them to use my name in the board as a candidate for its Presidency. So I awoke one morning to find myself seated in a comfortable arm-chair, with gold spectacles on my nose, and to hear myself addressed as President of the Freedmen's Bank. I could not help reflecting on the contrast between Frederick the slave boy, running about at Col. Lloyd's with only a tow linen shirt to cover him, and Frederick—President of a Bank counting its assets by millions. I had heard of golden dreams, but such dreams had no comparison with this reality. And yet this seeming reality was scarcely more substantial than a dream. My term of service on this golden height covered only the brief space of three months, and these three months were divided into two parts, during the first part of which I was quietly employed in an effort to find out the real condition of the Bank and its numerous branches. This was no easy task. On paper, and from the representations of its management, its assets amounted to three millions of dollars, and its liabilities were about equal to its assets. With such a showing I was encouraged in the belief that by curtailing expenses, doing away with non-paying branches, which policy the trustees had now adopted, we could be carried safely through the financial distress then upon the country. So confident was I of this, that in order to meet what was said to be a temporary emergency, I was induced to loan the Bank ten thousand dollars of my own money, to be held by it until it could realize on a part of its abundant securities. This money, though it was repaid, was not done so promptly as under the supposed circumstances I thought it should be, and these circumstances increased my fears lest the chasm was not so easily bridged as the Actuary of the institution had assured me it could be. The more I observed and learned, the more my confidence diminished. I found that those trustees who wished to issue cards and publish addresses professing the utmost confidence in the Bank, had themselves not one dollar deposited there. Some of them, while strongly assuring me of its soundness had withdrawn their money and opened accounts elsewhere. Gradually I discovered that the Bank had sustained heavy losses at the South through dishonest agents, that there was a discrepancy on the books of forty thousand dollars, for which no account could be given, that instead of our assets being equal to our liabilities we could not in all likelihoods of the case pay seventy-two cents on the dollar. There was an air of mystery, too, about the spacious and elegant apartments of the Bank building which greatly troubled me, and which I have only been able to explain to myself on the supposition that the employées, from the Actuary and the Inspector down to the messengers, were, perhaps, naturally, anxious to hold their places, and consequently have the business continued. I am not a violent advocate of the doctrine of the total depravity of human nature, I am inclined, on the whole, to believe it a tolerably good nature, yet instances do occur which oblige me to concede that men can and do act from mere personal and selfish motives. In this case, at any rate, it seemed not unreasonable to conclude that the finely dressed young gentlemen, adorned with pens and bouquets, the most fashionable and genteel of all our coloured youth, stationed behind those marble counters, should desire to retain their places as long as there was money in the vaults to pay them their salaries.

Standing on the platform of this large and complicated establishment, with its thirty-four branches, extending from New Orleans to Philadelphia, its machinery in full operation, its correspondence carried on in cipher, its Actuary dashing in and out of the Bank with an air of pressing business, if not of bewilderment, I found the path of inquiry I was pursuing an exceedingly difficult one. I knew there had been very lately several runs on the Bank, and that there had been a heavy draft made upon its reserve fund, but I did not know, what I should have been told before being allowed to enter upon the duties of my office, that this reserve, which the bank by its charter was required to keep, had been entirely exhausted, and that hence there was nothing left to meet any future emergency. Not to make too long a story, I was, in six weeks after my election as President of this Bank, convinced that it was no longer a safe custodian of the hard earnings of my confiding people. This conclusion once reached, I could not hesitate as to my duty in the premises, and this was, to save as much as possible of the assets held by the Bank for the benefit of the depositors; and to prevent their being further squandered in keeping up appearances, and in paying the salaries of myself and other officers in the bank. Fortunately, Congress, from which we held our charter, was then in session, and its committees on finance were in daily session. I felt it my duty to make known as speedily as possible to the Hon. John Sherman, chairman of the Senate committee on finance, and to Senator Scott of Pennsylvania, also of the same committee, that I regarded the institution as insolvent and irrecoverable, and that I could no longer ask my people to deposit their money in it. This representation to the finance committee subjected me to very bitter opposition on the part of the officers of the Bank. Its Actuary, Mr. Stickney, immediately summoned some of the trustees, a dozen or so of them, to go before the finance committee and make a counter statement to that made by me; and this they did. Some of them who had assisted me by giving me facts showing the insolvency of the bank, now made haste to contradict that conclusion, and to assure the committee that it was abundantly able to weather the financial storm, and pay dollar for dollar to its depositors if allowed to go on.

I was not exactly thunderstruck, but I was much amazed by this contradiction. I, however, adhered to my statement that the bank ought to stop. The Finance Committee substantially agreed with me, and in a few weeks so legislated as to bring this imposing banking business to a close by appointing three commissioners to take charge of its affairs.

This is a fair and unvarnished narration of my connection with the Freedmen's Savings and Trust Company, otherwise known as the Freedmen's Savings Bank, a connection which has brought upon my head an amount of abuse and detraction greater than any encountered in any other part of my life.

Before leaving the subject, I ought in justice to myself, to state that when I found that the affairs of the Bank were to be closed up, I did not, as I might easily have done, and as others did, make myself a preferred creditor and take my money out of the Bank, but on the contrary, I determined to take my chances with other depositors, and left my money, to the amount of two thousand dollars, to be divided with the assets among the creditors of the bank. And now, after seven years have been allowed for the value of the securities to appreciate, and the loss of interests on the deposits for that length of time, the depositors may deem themselves fortunate if they receive sixty cents on the dollar of what they placed in the care of this fine savings institution.

It is also due to myself to state, especially since I have seen myself accused of bringing the Freedmen's Bank into ruin, and squandering in senseless loans on bad security the hardearned moneys of my race, that all the loans ever made by the Bank were made prior to my connection with it as its President. Not a dollar, not a dime of its millions were loaned by me, or with my approval. The fact is, and all investigation shows it, that I was married to a corpse.

The fine building was there, with its marble counters and black walnut finishings, the affable and agile clerks, and the discreet and comely coloured cashier; but the Life, which was the money, was gone, and I found that I had been placed there with the hope that by "some drugs, some charms, some conjuration, or some mighty magic," I would bring it back.

When I became connected with the Bank I had a tolerably fair name for honest dealing, I had expended in the publication of my paper in Rochester, thousands of dollars annually, and had often to depend upon my credit to bridge over immediate wants, but no man, there or elsewhere, can say I ever wronged him out of a cent; and I could, to-day, with the confidence of the converted tax collector, offer "to restore fourfold to any from whom I have unjustly taken aught." I say this, not for the benefit of those who know me, but for the thousands of my own race who hear of me mostly through the malicious and envious assaults of unscrupulous aspirants, who vainly fancy that they lift themselves into consideration by wanton attacks upon the characters of men who receive a larger share of respect and esteem than themselves.

CHAPTER XV: "WEIGHED IN THE BALANCE."

THE most of my story is now before the reader. Whatever of good or ill the future may have in store for me, the past at least is secure. As I review the last decade up to the present writing, I am impressed with a sense of completeness; a sort of rounding up of the arch to the point where the key stone may be inserted, the scaffolding removed, and the work, with all its perfections or faults, left to speak for itself. This decade, from 1871 to 1881, has been crowded, if time is capable of being thus described, with incidents and events which may well enough be accounted remarkable. To me they certainly appear strange, if not wonderful. My early life not only gave no visible promise, but no hint of such experience. On the contrary, that life seemed to render it, in part at least, impossible. In addition to what is narrated in the foregoing chapter, I have to speak of my mission to Santo Domingo, my appointment as a member of the council for the government of the District of Columbia; my election as elector at large for the State of New York; my invitation to speak at the monument of the unknown loyal dead, at Arlington, on Decoration Day; my address on the unveiling of the Lincoln monument, at Lincoln Park, Washington; my appointment to bring the electoral vote from New York to the National Capital; my invitation to speak near the statue of Abraham Lincoln, Madison Square, New York; my accompanying the body of Vice-President Wilson from Washington to Boston; my conversations with Senator Sumner and President Grant; my welcome to the receptions of Secretary Hamilton Fish; my appointment by President R. B. Hayes to the office of Marshal of the District of Columbia; my visit to Thomas Auld, the man who claimed me as his slave, and from whom I was purchased by my English friends; and my visit to Lloyd's plantation, the home of my childhood, after an absence of fifty-six years; my appointment by President James A. Garfield to the office of Recorder of Deeds of the District of Columbia, are some of the matters which belong to this decade, and may come into the chapter I am now about to write.

Those who knew of my more than friendly relations with the Hon. Charles Sumner, and of his determined opposition to the annexation of Santo Domingo to the United States, were surprised to find me earnestly taking sides with General Grant upon that question. Some of my white friends, and a few of those of my own colour—who, unfortunately, allow themselves to look at public questions more through the medium of feeling than of reason, and who follow the line of what is grateful to their friends rather than what is consistent with their own convictions—thought my course was an ungrateful return for the emment services of the Massachusetts senator. I am free to say that, had I been guided only by the promptings of my heart, I should, in this controversy, have followed the lead of Charles Sumner. He was not only the most clear-sighted, brave, and uncompromising friend of my race who had ever stood upon the floor of the Senate, but was to me a loved, honoured, and precious personal friend; a man possessing the exalted and matured intellect of a statesman, with the pure and artless heart of a child. Upon any issue, as between him and others, when the right seemed in anywise doubtful, I should have followed his counsel and advice. But the annexation of Santo Domingo, to my understanding, did not seem to be any such question. The reasons in its favour were many and obvious; and those against it, as I thought, were easily answered. To Mr. Sumner, annexation was a measure to extinguish a coloured nation, and to do so by dishonourable means and for selfish motives. To me it meant the alliance of a weak and defenceless people, having few or none of the attributes of a nation, torn and rent by internal feuds, unable to maintain order at home, or command respect abroad, to a government which would give it peace, stability, prosperity, and civilization, and make it helpful to both countries. To favour annexation at the time when Santo Domingo asked for a place in our Union, was a very different thing from what it was when Cuba and Central America were sought by filibustering expeditions. When the slave power bore rule, and a spirit of injustice and oppression animated and controlled every part of our Government, I was for limiting our dominion to the smallest possible margin; but since liberty and equality have become the law of our land, I am for extending our dominion whenever and wherever such extension can peaceably and honourably, and with the approval and desire of all the parties concerned, be accomplished. Santo Domingo wanted to come under our Government upon the terms thus described; and for more reasons than I can stop here to give, I then believed, and do now believe, it would have been wise to have received her into our sisterhood of States.

The idea that annexation meant degradation to a coloured nation was altogether fanciful; there was no more dishonour to Santo Domingo in making her a State of the American Union, than in making Kansas, Nebraska, or any other territory such a State. It was giving to a part the strength of the whole, and lifting what must be despised for its isolation into an organization and relationship which would compel consideration and respect.

Though I differed from Mr. Sumner in respect to this measure, and although I told him I thought he was unjust to President Grant, it never disturbed our friendship. After his great speech against annexation, which occupied six hours in its delivery, and in which he arraigned the President in a most bitter and fierce manner, being at the White House one day, I was asked by President Grant what I "now thought of my friend Mr. Sumner"? I replied that I believed Mr. Sumner sincerely thought, that in opposing annexation, he was defending the cause of the coloured race as he always had done, but that I thought he was mistaken. I saw my reply was not very satisfactory, and said "What do you, Mr. President, think of Senator Sumner?" He answered, with some feeling, "I think he is mad."

The difference in opinion on this question between these two great men was the cause of bitter personal estrangement, and one which I intensely regretted. The truth is, that neither was entirely just to the other, because neither saw the other in his true character; and having once fallen asunder, the occasion never came when they could be brought together.

Variance between great men finds no healing influence in the atmosphere of Washington. Interested parties are ever ready to fan the flame of animosity and magnify the grounds of hostility in order to gain the favour of one or the other. This is perhaps true in some degree in every community; but it is especially so of the National Capital, and this for the reason that there is ever a large class of people here dependent upon the influence and favour of powerful public men for their daily bread.

My selection to visit Santo Domingo with the commission sent thither, was another point indicating the difference between the old time and the new. It placed me on the deck of an American man-of-war, manned by one hundred marines and five hundred men-of-wars-men, under the national flag, which I could now call mine, in common with other American citizens, and gave me a place not in the forecastle, among the hands, nor in the caboose with the cooks, but in the captain's saloon, and in the society of gentlemen, scientists, and statesmen. It would be a pleasing task to narrate the varied experiences and the distinguished persons encountered in this Santo Domingo tour, but the material is too boundless for the limits of these pages. I can only say, it was highly interesting and instructive. The conversations at the captain's table, at which I had the honour of a seat, were usually led by Messrs. Wade, Howe, and White—the three commissioners; and by Mr. Hurlburt of the New York World; the last-named gentleman impressed me as one remarkable for knowledge and refinement, in which he was no whit behind Messrs. Howe and White. As for the Hon. Benj. F. Wade, he was there, as everywhere, abundant in knowledge and experience, fully able to take care of himself in the discussion of any subject in which he chose to take a part. In a circle so brilliant, it is no affectation of modesty to say I was for the most part a listener and a learner. The commander of our good ship on this voyage, Capt. Temple, now promoted to the position of Commodore, was a very imposing man, and deported himself with much dignity towards us all. For his treatment of me I am especially grateful. A son of the United States navy as he was—a department of our service considerably distinguished for its aristocratic tendencies—I expected to find something a little forbidding in his manner; but I am bound to say that in this I was agreeably disappointed. Both the commander and the officers under him bore themselves in a friendly manner towards me during all the voyage, and this is saying a great thing for them, for the spectacle presented by a coloured man seated at the captain's table was not only unusual, but had never before occurred in the history of the United States navy. If during this voyage there was anything to complain of, it was not in the men in authority, or in the conduct of the thirty gentlemen who went out as the honoured guests of the expedition, but in the coloured waiters. My presence and position seemed to trouble them from its incomprehensibility; and they did not know exactly how to deport themselves towards me. Possibly they may have detected in me something of the same sort in respect to themselves; at any rate we seemed awkwardly related to each other during several weeks of the voyage. In their eyes I was Fred. Douglass suddenly, and possibly undeservedly, lifted above them. The fact that I was coloured and they were coloured had so long made us equal, that the contradiction now presented was too much for them. After all, I have no blame for Sam and Garrett. They were trained in the school of servility to believe that white men alone were entitled to be waited upon by coloured men; and the lesson taught by my presence on the "Tennessee" was not to be learned upon the instant, without thought and experience. I refer to the matter simply as an incident quite commonly met with in the lives of coloured men who, by their own exertions or otherwise, have happened to occupy positions of respectability and honour. While the rank and file of our race quote with much vehemence the doctrine of human equality, they are often among the first to deny and denounce it in practice. Of course this is true only of the more ignorant. Intelligence is a great leveller here as elsewhere. It sees plainly the real worth of men and things, and is not easily imposed upon by the dressed-up emptiness of human pride.

With a coloured man as conductor on a sleeping car, the last to have his bed made up at night, and the last to have his boots blacked in the morning, and the last to be served in any way, is the coloured passenger. This conduct is the homage which the black man pays to the white man's prejudice, whose wishes, like a well-trained servant, he is taught to anticipate and obey. Time, education, and circumstances are rapidly destroying these mere colour distinctions, and men will be valued in this country as well as in others, for what they are, and for what they can do.

My appointment at the hands of President Grant to a seat in the council—by way of eminence sometimes called the Upper House of the territorial legislature of the District of Columbia—at the time it was made, must be taken as a signal evidence of his high sense of justice, fairness, and impartiality. The coloured people of the district constituted then, as now, about one-third of the whole population. They were given by Gen. Grant, three members of this legislative council—a representation more proportionate than any that has existed since the Government has passed into the hands of commissioners, for they have all been white men.

It has sometimes been asked why I am called "Honourable." My appointment to this council must explain this, as it explains the impartiality of Gen. Grant, though I fear it will hardly sustain this prodigious handle to my name, as well as it does the former part of this proposition. The members of this district council were required to be appointed by the President, with the advice and consent of the United States Senate. This is the ground, and only ground that I know of, upon which anybody has claimed this title for me. I do not pretend that the foundation is a very good one, but as I have generally allowed people to call me what they pleased, and as there is nothing necessarily dishonourable in this, I have never taken the pains to dispute its application and propriety; and yet I confess that I am never so spoken of without feeling a trifle uncomfortable—about as much so as when I am called, as I sometimes am, the Rev. Frederick Douglass. My stay in this legislative body was of short duration. My vocation abroad left me little time to study the many matters of local legislation; hence my resignation, and the appointment of my son Lewis to fill out my term.

I have thus far told my story without copious quotations from my letters, speeches, or other writings, and shall not depart from this rule in what remains to be told, except to insert here my speech, delivered at Arlington, near the monument to the "Unknown Loyal Dead," on Decoration Day, 1871. It was delivered under impressive circumstances, in presence of President Grant, his Cabinet, and a great multitude of distinguished people, and expresses, as I think, the true view which should be taken of the great conflict between slavery and freedom to which it refers.

"Friends and Fellow Citizens. Tarry here for a moment. My words shall be few and simple. The solemn rites of this hour and place call for no lengthened speech. There is in the very air of this resting ground of the unknown dead a silent, subtle, and an all-pervading eloquence, far more touching, impressive, and thrilling, than living lips have ever uttered. Into the measureless depths of every loyal soul it is now whispering lessons of all that is precious, priceless, holiest, and most enduring in human existence.

"Dark and sad will be the hour to this nation when it forgets to pay grateful homage to its greatest benefactors. The offering we bring to-day is due alike to the patriot soldiers dead and their noble comrades who still live; for whether living or dead, whether in time or eternity, the loyal soldiers who imperilled all for country and freedom are one and inseparable.

"Those unknown heroes whose whitened bones have been piously gathered here, and whose green graves we now strew with sweet and beautiful flowers, choice emblems alike of pure hearts and brave spirits, reached in their glorious career that last highest point of nobleness beyond which human power cannot go. They died for their country.

"No loftier tribute can be paid to the most illustrious of all the benefactors of mankind than we pay to these unrecognised soldiers, when we write above their graves this shining epitaph.

"When the dark and vengeful spirit of slavery, always ambitious, preferring to rule in hell to serving in heaven, fired the Southern heart and stirred all the malign elements of discord;

when our great Republic, the hope of freedom and self-government throughout the world, had reached the point of supreme peril; when the Union of these States was torn and rent asunder at the centre, and the armies of a gigantic rebellion came forth with broad blades and bloody hands to destroy the very foundation of American society, the unknown braves who flung themselves into the yawning chasm, where cannon roared and bullets whistled, fought and fell. They died for their country.

"We are sometimes asked, in the name of patriotism, to forget the merits of this fearful struggle, and to remember with equal admiration those who struck at the nation's life and those who struck to save it,—those who fought for slavery, and those who fought for liberty and justice.

"I am no minister of malice. I would not strike the fallen. I would not repel the repentant, but may my "right hand forget her cunning, and my tongue cleave to the roof of my mouth," if I forget the difference between the parties to that terrible, protracted, and bloody conflict.

"If we ought to forget a war which has filled our land with widows and orphans, which has made stumps of men in the very flower of their youth; sent them on the journey of life armless, legless, maimed and mutilated; which has piled up a debt heavier than a mountain of gold— swept uncounted thousands of men into bloody graves, and planted agony by a million hearthstones; I say if this war is to be forgotten, I ask in the name of all things sacred what shall men remember?

"The essence and significance of our devotions here to-day are not to be found in the fact that the men whose remains fill these graves were brave in battle. If we met simply to show our sense of bravery, we should find enough to kindle admiration on both sides. In the raging storm of fire and blood, in the fierce torrent of shot and shell, of sword and bayonet, whether on foot or on horse, unflinching courage marked the rebel not less than the loyal soldier.

"But we are not here to applaud manly courage, save as it has been displayed in a noble cause. We must never forget that victory to the rebellion meant death to the Republic. We must never forget that the loyal soldiers who rest beneath this sod flung themselves between the nation and the nation's destroyers. If to-day we have a country not boiling in an agony of blood like France, if now we have a united country, no longer cursed by the hell-black system of human bondage; if the American name is no longer a by-word and a hissing to the mocking earth; if the star-spangled banner floats only over free American citizens in every quarter of the land, and our country has before it a long and glorious career of justice, liberty, and civilization, we are indebted to the unselfish devotion of the noble army who rest in these honoured graves all around us."

In the month of April, 1872, I had the honour to attend and preside over a National Convention of coloured citizens, held in New Orleans. It was a critical period in the history of the Republican party, as well as in that of the country. Emment men who had hitherto been looked upon as the pillars of Republicanism had become dissatisfied with President Grant's administration, and determined to defeat his nomination for a second term. The leaders in this unfortunate revolt were Messrs. Trumbull, Schurz, Greeley, and Sumner. Mr. Schurz had already succeeded in destroying the Republican party in the State of Missouri, and it seemed to be his ambition to be the founder of a new party, and to him, more than to any other man, belongs the credit of what was once known as the Liberal Republican party which made Horace Greeley its standard bearer in the campaign of that year.

At the time of the Convention in New Orleans the elements of this new combination were just coming together. The division in the Republican ranks seemed to be growing deeper and broader every day. The coloured people of the country were much affected by the threatened disruption, and their leaders were much divided as to the side upon which they should give their voice and their votes. The names of Greeley and Sumner, on account of their long and earnest advocacy of justice and liberty to the blacks, had powerful attractions for the newly enfranchised class; and there was in this Convention at New Orleans, naturally enough, a strong disposition to fraternize with the new party and follow the lead of their old friends. Against this policy I exerted whatever influence I possessed, and, I think, succeeded in holding back that Convention from what I felt sure then would have been a fatal political blunder, and time has proved the correctness of that position. My speech on taking the chair on that occasion was telegraphed from New Orleans in full to the New York Herald, and the key-note of it was that there was no path out of the Republican party that did not lead directly into the Democratic party—away from our friends and directly to our enemies. Happily this Convention pretty largely agreed with me, and its members have not since regretted that agreement.

From this Convention onward, until the nomination and election of Grant and Wilson, I was actively engaged on the stump, a part of the time in Virginia with the Hon. Henry Wilson, in North Carolina with John M. Longston and John H. Smyth, and in the State of Maine with Senator Hamlin, Gen. B. F. Butler, Gen. Woodford, and the Hon. James G. Blaine.

Since 1872 I have been regularly what my old friend Parker Pillsbury would call a "field hand" in every important political campaign, and at each National Convention have sided with what has been called the stalwart element of the Republican party. It was in the Grant Presidential campaign that New York took an advanced step in the renunciation of a timid policy. The Republicans of that State not having the fear of popular prejudice before their eyes placed my name as an Elector at large at the head of their Presidental ticket. Considering the deep-rooted sentiment of the masses against negroes, the noise and tumult likely to be raised, especially among our adopted citizens of Irish descent, this was a bold and manly proceeding, and one for which the Republicans of the State of New York deserve the gratitude of every coloured citizen of the Republic, for it was a blow at popular prejudice, in a quarter where it was capable of making the strongest resistance. The result proved not only the justice and generosity of the measure, but its wisdom. The Republicans carried the State by a majority of fifty thousand over the heads of the Liberal Republican and the Democratic parties combined.

Equally significant of the turn now taken in the political sentiment of the country, was the action of the Republican Electoral College at its meeting in Albany, when it committed to my custody the sealed-up electoral vote of the great State of New York, and commissioned me to bring that vote to the National Capital. Only a few years before, any coloured man was forbidden by law to carry a United States mail bag from one post-office to another. He was not allowed to touch the sacred leather, though locked in "triple steel;" but now, not a mail bag, but a document which was to decide the Presidential questions with all its momentous interests, was committed to the hands of one of this despised class; and around him, in the execution of his trust, was thrown all the safeguards provided by the Constitution and the laws of the land. Though I worked hard and long, to secure the nomination and the election of Gen. Grant in 1872, I neither received nor sought office under him. He was my choice upon grounds altogether free from selfish or personal considerations. I supported him because he had done, and would do, all he could to save, not only the country from ruin, but the emancipated class from oppression and ultimate destruction; and because Mr. Greeley, with the Democratic party behind him, would not have the power, even if he had the disposition, to afford us the needed protection which our peculiar condition required. I could easily have secured the appointment as Minister to Hayti, but preferred to urge the claims of my friend, Ebenezer Bassett, a gentleman and a scholar, and a man well fitted by his good sense and amiable qualities to fill the position with credit to himself and his country. It is with a certain degree of pride that I am able to say that my opinion of the wisdom of sending Mr. Bassett to Hayti has been fully justified by the creditable manner in which, for eight years, he discharged the difficult duties of that position; for I have the assurance of the Hon. Hamilton Fish, Secretary of State of the United States, that Mr. Bassett was a good Minister. In so many words, the ex-Secretary told me, that he "wished that one-half of his Ministers abroad performed their duties as well as Mr. Bassett." To those who know the Hon. Hamilton Fish, this compliment will not be deemed slight, for few men are less given to exaggeration and are more scrupulously exact in the observance of law, and in the use of language, than is that gentleman. While speaking in this strain of complacency in reference to Mr. Bassett, I take pleasure also in bearing my testimony, based upon knowledge obtained at the State Department, that Mr. John Mercer Langston, the present Minister to Hayti, has acquitted himself with equal wisdom and ability to that of Mr. Bassett in the same position. Having known both these gentlemen in their youth, when the one was at Yale, and the other at Oberlin College, and witnessed their efforts to qualify themselves for positions of usefulness, it has afforded me no limited satisfaction to see them rise in the world. Such men increase the faith of all, in the possibilities of their race, and make it easier for those who are to come after them.

The unveiling of the Lincoln Monument in Lincoln Park, Washington, April 14th, 1876, and the part taken by me in the ceremonies of that grand occasion, take rank among the most interesting incidents of my life, since it brought me into mental communication with a greater number of the influential and distinguished men of the country than any I had before known. There were present the President of the United States and his Cabinet, Judges of the Supreme Court, the Senate and House of Representatives, and many thousands of citizens to listen to my address upon the illustrious man in whose memory the coloured people of the United States had, as a mark of their gratitude, erected that impressive monument. Occasions like this have done wonders in the removal of popular prejudice, and in lifting into consideration the coloured race; and I reckon it one of the high privileges of my life, that I was permitted to have a share in this and several other like celebrations.

The following is the substance of the oration delivered by me on the occasion of the unveiling of the freedmen's monument, in memory of abraham lincoln, in lincoln park, washington, d. c., april 14, 1876.

"Friends and fellow citizens.

"I WARMLY congratulate you upon the highly interesting object which has caused you to assemble in such numbers and spirit as you have to-day. This occasion is in some respects remarkable. Wise and thoughtful men of our race, who shall come after us, and study the lesson of our history in the United States; who shall survey the long and dreary spaces over which we have travelled; who shall count the links in the great chain of events by which we have reached our present position, will make a note of this occasion; they will think of it and speak of it with a sense of manly pride and complacency.

"I congratulate you, also, upon the very favourable circumstances in which we meet to-day. They are high, inspiring, and uncommon. They lend grace, glory, and significance to the object for which we have met. Nowhere else in this great country, with its uncounted towns and cities, unlimited wealth, and immeasurable territory extending from sea to sea, could conditions be found more favourable to the success of this occasion than here.

"We stand to-day at the national centre to perform something like a national act—an act which is to go into history; and we are here where every pulsation of the national heart can be heard, felt, and reciprocated. A thousand wires, fed with thought and winged with lightning, put us in instantaneous communication with the loyal and true men all over this country.

"Few facts could better illustrate the vast and wonderful change which has taken place in our condition as a people, than the fact of our assembling here for the purpose we have to-day. Harmless, beautiful, proper, and praiseworthy as this demonstration is, I cannot forget that no such demonstration would have been tolerated here twenty years ago. The spirit of slavery and barbarism, which still lingers to blight and destroy in some dark and distant parts of our country, would have made our assembling here the signal and excuse for opening upon us all the flood-gates of wrath and violence. That we are here in peace to-day is a compliment and a credit to American civilization, and a prophecy of still greater national enlightenment and progress in the future. I refer to the past not in malice, for this is no day for malice; but simply to place more distinctly in front the gratifying and glorious change which has come both to our white fellow-citizens and ourselves, and to congratulate all upon the contrast between now and then; the new dispensation of freedom with its thousand blessings to both races, and the old dispensation of slavery with its ten thousand evils to both races—white and black. In view, then, of the past, the present, and the future, with the long and dark history of our bondage behind us, and with liberty, progress, and enlightenment before us, I again congratulate you upon this auspicious day and hour.

"Friends and fellow citizens, the story of our presence here is soon and easily told. We are here in the District of Columbia, here in the city of Washington, the most luminous point of American territory; a city recently transformed and made beautiful in its body and in its spirit; we are here in the place where the ablest and best men of the country are sent to devise the policy, enact the laws, and shape the destiny of the Republic; we are here, with the stately pillars and majestic dome of the Capitol of the nation looking down upon us; we are here, with the broad earth freshly adorned with the foliage and flowers of spring for our church, and all races, colours, and conditions of men for our congregation—in a word, we are here to express, as best we may, by appropriate forms and ceremonies, our grateful sense of the vast, high, and pre-eminent services rendered to ourselves, to our race, to our country, and to the whole world by Abraham Lincoln.

"The sentiment that brings us here to-day is one of the noblest that can stir and thrill the human heart. It has crowned and made glorious the high places of all civilized nations with the grandest and most enduring works of art, designed to illustrate the characters and perpetuate the memories of great public men. It is the sentiment which from year to year adorns with fragrant and beautiful flowers the graves of our loyal, brave, and patriotic soldiers who fell in defence of the Union and liberty. It is the sentiment of gratitude and appreciation, which often, in the presence of many who hear me, has filled yonder heights of Arlington with the eloquence of eulogy and the sublime enthusiasm of poetry and song; a sentiment which can never die while the Republic lives.

"For the first time in the history of our people, and in the history of the whole American people, we join in this high worship, and march conspicuously in the line of this time-honoured custom. First things are always interesting, and this is one of our first things. It is the first time that, in this form and manner, we have sought to do honour to an American great man, however deserving and illustrious. I commend the fact to notice; let it be told in every part of the Republic; let men of all parties and opinions hear it; let those who despise us, not less than those who respect us, know that now and here, in the spirit of liberty, loyalty, and gratitude, let it be known everywhere, and by everybody who takes an interest in human progress and in the amelioration of the condition of mankind, that, in the presence and with the approval of the members of the American House of Representatives, reflecting the general sentiment of the country; that in the presence of that august body, the American Senate, representing the highest intelligence and the calmest judgment in the country; in presence of the Supreme Court and Chief-Justice of the United States, to whose decisions we all patriotically bow; in the presence and under the steady eye of the honoured and trusted President of the United States, with the members of his wise and patriotic Cabinet, we, the coloured people, newly emancipated and rejoicing in our blood-bought freedom, near the close of the first century in the life of this Republic, have now and here unveiled, set apart, and dedicated a monument of enduring granite and bronze, in every line, feature, and figure of which the men of this generation may read, and those of after-coming generations may read, something of the exalted character and great works of Abraham Lincoln, the first martyr President of the United States.

"Fellow citizens, in what we have said and done to-day, and in what we may say and do hereafter, we disclaim everything like arrogance and assumption. We claim for ourselves no superior devotion to the character, history, and memory of the illustrious man whose monument we have here dedicated to-day. We fully comprehend the relation of Abraham Lincoln both to ourselves and to the white people of the United States. Truth is proper and beautiful at all times and in all places, and it is never more proper and beautiful in any case than when speaking of a great public man whose example is likely to be commended for honour and imitation long after his departure to the solemn shades,—the silent continents of eternity. It must be admitted, truth compels me to admit, even here in the presence of the monument we have erected to his memory, Abraham Lincoln was not, in the fullest sense of the word, either our man or our model. In his interests, in his associations, in his habits of thought, and in his prejudices, he was a white man.

"He was pre-eminently the white man's President, entirely devoted to the welfare of white men. He was ready and willing at any time during the first years of his administration to deny, postpone, and sacrifice the rights of humanity in the coloured people to promote the welfare of the white people of this country. In all his education and feeling he was an American of the Americans. He came into the Presidential chair upon one principle alone, namely, opposition to the extension of slavery. His arguments in furtherance of this policy had their motive and mainspring in his patriotic devotion to the interests of his own race. To protect, defend, and perpetuate slavery in the States where it existed, Abraham Lincoln was not less ready than any other President to draw the sword of the nation. He was ready to execute all the supposed constitutional guarantees of the United States Constitution in favour of the slave system anywhere inside the slave States. He was willing to pursue, recapture, and send back the fugitive slave to his master, and to suppress a slave rising for liberty, though his guilty master were already in arms against the Government. The race to which we belong were not the special objects of his consideration. Knowing this, I concede to you, my white fellow citizens, a pre-eminence in this worship at once full and supreme. First, midst, and last, you and yours were the objects of his deepest affection and his most earnest solicitude. You are the children of Abraham Lincoln. We are at best only his step-children; children by adoption, children by force of circumstances and necessity. To you it especially belongs to sound his praises, to preserve and perpetuate his memory, to multiply his statues, to hang his pictures high upon your walls, and commend his example, for to you he was a great and glorious friend and benefactor. Instead of supplanting you at this altar, we would exhort you to build high his monuments; let them be of the most costly material, of the most cunning workmanship; let their forms be symmetrical, beautiful, and perfect; let their bases be upon solid rocks, and their summits lean against the unchanging, blue, overhanging sky, and let them endure for ever! But while in the abundance of your wealth, and in the fulness of your just and patriotic devotion, you do all this, we entreat you to despise not the humble offering we this day unveil to view; for while Abraham Lincoln saved for you a country, he delivered us from a bondage, one hour of which, according to Jefferson, was worse than ages of the oppression your fathers rose in rebellion to oppose.

"Fellow citizens, ours is no new-born zeal and devotion—merely a thing of this moment. The name of Abraham Lincoln was near and dear to our hearts in the darkest and most perilous hours of the Republic. We were no more ashamed of him when shrouded in clouds of darkness, of doubt, and defeat, than when we saw him crowned with victory, honour, and glory. Our faith in him was often taxed and strained to the uttermost, but it never failed. When he tarried long in the mountain; when he strangely told us that we were the cause of the war; when he still more strangely told us to leave the land in which we were born; when he refused to employ our arms in defence of the Union; when, after accepting our services as coloured soldiers, he refused to retaliate our murder and torture as coloured prisoners; when he told us he would save the Union if he could with slavery; when he revoked the Proclamation of Emancipation of General Fremont; when he refused to remove the popular commander of the army of the Potomac, in the days of its inaction and defeat, who was more zealous in his efforts to protect slavery than to suppress rebellion; when we saw all this, and more, we were at times grieved, stunned, and greatly bewildered; but our hearts believed while they ached and bled. Nor was this, even at that time, a blind and unreasoning superstition. Despite the mist and haze that surrounded him; despite the tumult, the hurry, and confusion of the hour, we were able to take a comprehensive view of Abraham Lincoln, and to make reasonable allowance for the circumstances of his position. We saw him, measured him, and estimated him; not by stray utterances to injudicious and tedious delegations, who often tried his patience; not by isolated facts torn from their connection; not by any partial and imperfect glimpses, caught at inopportune moments; but by a broad survey, in the light of the stern logic of great events, and in view of that "divinity which shapes our ends, rough hew them how we will," we came to the conclusion that the hour and the man of our redemption had somehow met in the person of Abraham Lincoln. It mattered little to us what language he might employ on special occasions; it mattered little to us, when we fully knew him, whether he was swift or slow in his movements; it was enough for us that Abraham Lincoln was at the head of a great movement, and was in living and earnest sympathy with that movement, which, in the nature of things, must go on until slavery should be utterly and for ever abolished in the United States.

When, therefore, it shall be asked what we have to do with the memory of Abraham Lincoln, or what Abraham Lincoln had to do with us, the answer is ready, full, and complete. Though he loved Cæsar less than Rome, though the Union was more to him than our freedom or our future, under his wise and beneficent rule, we saw ourselves gradually lifted from the depths of slavery to the heights of liberty and manhood; under his wise and beneficent rule, and by measures approved and vigorously pressed by him, we saw that the handwriting of ages, in the form of prejudice and proscription, was rapidly fading away from the face of our whole country; under his rule, and in due time, about as soon after all as the country could tolerate the strange spectacle, we saw our brave sons and brothers laying off the rags of bondage, and being clothed all over in the blue uniform of the soldiers of the United States; under his rule we saw two hundred thousand of our dark and dusky people responding to the call of Abraham Lincoln, and with muskets on their shoulders, and eagles on their buttons, timing their high footsteps to liberty and union under the national flag; under his rule we saw the independence of the black republic of Hayti, the special object of slaveholding aversion and horror, fully recognized, and her minister, a coloured gentleman, duly received here in the City of Washington; under his rule we saw the internal slave-trade, which so long disgraced the nation, abolished, and slavery abolished in the District of Columbia; under his rule we saw, for the first time, the law enforced against the foreign slave-trade, and the first slave-trader hanged like any other pirate or murderer; under his rule, assisted by the greatest captain of our age, and his inspiration, we saw the Confederate States, based upon the idea that our race must be slaves, and slaves for ever, battered to pieces and scattered to the four winds; under his rule, and in the fulness of time, we saw Abraham Lincoln, after giving the slaveholder three months' grace in which to save their hateful slave system, penning the immortal paper, which, though special in its language, was general in its principles and effect, making slavery for ever impossible in the United States. Though we waited long, we saw all this and more.

"Can any coloured man, or any white man, friendly to the freedom of all men, ever forget the night which followed the first day of January, 1863, when the world was to see if Abraham Lincoln would prove to be as good as his word. I shall never forget that memorable night, when in a distant city I waited and watched at a public meeting, with three thousand others not less anxious than myself, for the word of deliverance which we have heard read to-day. Nor shall I ever forget the outburst of joy and thanksgiving that rent the air when the lightning brought to us the emancipation proclamation. In that happy hour we forgot all delay, and forgot all tardiness, forgot that the President had bribed the rebels to lay down their arms by a promise to withhold the bolt which would smite the slave-system with destruction; and we were thenceforward willing to allow the President all the latitude of time, phraseology, and every honourable device that statesmanship might require for the achievement of a great and beneficent measure of liberty and progress.

"Fellow citizens, there is little necessity on this occasion to speak at length and critically of this great and good man, and of his high mission in the world. That ground has been fully occupied and completely covered both here and elsewhere. The whole field of fact and fancy has been gleaned and garnered. Any man can say things that are true of Abraham Lincoln, but no man can say anything that is new of Abraham Lincoln. His personal traits and public acts are better known to the American people than are those of any other man of his age. He was a mystery to no man who saw him and heard him. Though high in position, the humblest could approach him and feel at home in his presence. Though deep, he was transparent; though strong, he was gentle; though decided and pronounced in his convictions, he was tolerant towards those who differed from him, and patient under reproaches. Even those who only knew him through his public utterances obtained a tolerably clear idea of his character and his personality. The image of the man went out with his words, and those who read them, knew him.

"I have said that President Lincoln was a white man, and shared the prejudices common to his countrymen towards the coloured race. Looking back to his times and to the condition of his country, we are compelled to admit that this unfriendly feeling on his part may be safely set down as one element of his wonderful success in organizing the loyal American people for the tremendous conflict before them, and bringing them safely through that conflict. His great mission was to accomplish two things: first, to save his country from dismemberment and ruin; and second, to free his country from the great crime of slavery. To do one or the other, or both, he must have the earnest sympathy and the powerful co-operation of his loyal fellow-countrymen. Without this primary and essential condition to success, his efforts must have been vain and utterly fruitless. Had he put the abolition of slavery before the salvation of the Union, he would have inevitably driven from him a powerful class of the American people and rendered resistance to rebellion impossible. Viewed from the genuine abolition ground, Mr. Lincoln seemed tardy, cold, dull, and indifferent; but measuring him by the sentiment of his country, a sentiment he was bound as a statesman to consult, he was swift, zealous, radical, and determined.

"Though Mr. Lincoln shared the prejudices of his white fellow-countrymen against the negro, it is hardly necessary to say that in his heart of hearts he loathed and hated slavery.* The man who could say, "Fondly do we hope, fervently do we pray, that this mighty scourge of war shall soon pass away, yet if God wills it to continue till all the wealth piled by two hundred years of bondage shall have been wasted, and each drop of blood drawn by the lash shall have been paid for by one drawn by the sword, the judgments of the Lord are true and righteous altogether," gives all needed proof of his feelings on the subject of slavery. He was willing, while the South was loyal, that it should have its pound of flesh, because he thought it was so nominated in the bond; but farther than this no earthly power could make him go.

"Fellow citizens, whatever else in the world may be partial, unjust, and uncertain, Time, time, is impartial, just, and certain in its action. In the realm of mind, as well as in the realm of matter, it is a great worker, and often works wonders. The honest and comprehensive statesman, clearly discerning the needs of his country, and earnestly endeavouring to do his whole duty, though covered and blistered with reproaches, may safely leave his course to the silent judgment of time. Few great public men have ever been the victims of fiercer denunciation than Abraham Lincoln was during his administration. He was often wounded in the house of his friends. Reproaches came thick and fast upon him from within and from without, and from opposite quarters. He was assailed by abolitionists; he was assailed by slaveholders; he was assailed by the men who were for peace at any price; he was assailed by those who were for a more vigorous prosecution of the war; he was assailed for not making the war an abolition war; and he was most bitterly assailed for making the war an abolition war.

"But now behold the change: the judgment of the present hour is, that taking him for all in all, measuring the tremendous magnitude of the work before him, considering the necessary means to ends, and surveying the end from the beginning, infinite wisdom has seldom sent any man into the world better fitted for his mission than Abraham Lincoln. His birth, his training, and his natural endowments, both mental and physical, were strongly in his favour. Born and reared among the lowly, a stranger to wealth and luxury, compelled to grapple single-handed with the flintiest hardships of life, from tender youth to sturdy manhood, he grew strong in the manly and heroic qualities demanded by the great mission to which he was called by the votes of his countrymen. The hard condition of his early life, which would have depressed and broken down weaker men, only gave greater life, vigour, and buoyancy to the heroic spirit of Abraham Lincoln. He was ready for any kind and quality of work. What other young men dreaded in the shape of toil, he took hold of with the utmost cheerfulness.

- 'A spade, a rake, a hoe,

- A pick-axe, or a bill,

- A hook to reap, a scythe to mow,

- A flail, or what you will.'

"All day long he could split heavy rails in the woods, and half the night long he could study his English Grammar by the uncertain flare and glare of the light made by a pine-knot. He was at home on the land with his axe, with his maul, with his gluts, and his wedges; and he was equally at home on water, with his oars, with his poles, with his planks, and with his boat-hooks. And whether in his flat-boat on the Mississippi river, or at the fireside of his frontier cabin, he was a man of work. A son of toil himself, he was linked in brotherly sympathy with the sons of toil in every loyal part of the Republic. This very fact gave him tremendous power with the American people, and materially contributed, not only to selecting him for the Presidency, but in sustaining his administration of the government.

"Upon his inauguration as President of the United States, an office, even when assumed under the most favourable conditions, fitted to tax and strain the largest abilities, Abraham Lincoln was met by a tremendous crisis. He was called upon not merely to administer the government, but to decide, in the face of terrible odds, the fate of the Republic.

"A formidable rebellion rose in his path before him; the Union was practically dissolved; his country was torn and rent asunder at the centre. Hostile armies were already organized against the Republic, armed with the munitions of war which the Republic had provided for its own defence. The tremendous question for him to decide was whether his country should survive the crisis and flourish, or be dismembered and perish. His predecessor in office had already decided the question in favour of national dismemberment, by denying to it the right of self-defence and self-preservation—a right which belongs to the meanest insect.

"Happily for the country, happily for you and for me, the judgment of James Buchanan, the patrician, was not the judgment of Abraham Lincoln, the plebeian. He brought his strong common sense, sharpened in the school of adversity, to bear upon the question. He did not hesitate, he did not doubt, he did not falter; but at once resolved at whatever peril, at whatever cost, the Union of the States should be preserved. A patriot himself, his faith was strong and unwavering in the patriotism of his countrymen. Timid men said before Mr. Lincoln's inauguration, that we had seen the last President of the United States. A voice in influential quarters said, "Let the Union slide." Some said that a Union maintained by the sword was worthless. Others said a rebellion of 8,000,000 cannot be suppressed; but in the midst of all this tumult and timidity, and against all this, Abraham Lincoln was clear in his duty, and had an oath in heaven. He calmly and bravely heard the voice of doubt and fear all around him; but he had an oath in heaven, and there was not power enough on earth to make this honest boatman, backwoodsman, and broad-handed splitter of rails to evade or violate that sacred oath. He had not been schooled in the ethics of slavery; his plain life had favoured his love of truth. He had not been taught that treason and perjury were the proof of honour and honesty. His moral training was against his saying one thing when he meant another. The trust which Abraham Lincoln had in himself and in the people was surprising and grand, but it was also enlightened and well-founded. He knew the American people better than they knew themselves, and his truth was based upon this knowledge.

"Fellow citizens, the fourteenth day of April, 1865, of which this is the eleventh anniversary, is now and will ever remain a memorable day in the annals of this Republic. It was on the evening of this day, while a fierce and sanguinary rebellion was in the last stages of its desolating power; while its armies were broken and scattered before the invincible armies of Grant and Sherman; while a great nation, torn and rent by war, was already beginning to raise to the skies loud anthems of joy at the dawn of peace, it was startled, amazed, and overwhelmed by the crowning crime of slavery—the assassination of Abraham Lincoln. It was a new crime, a pure act of malice. No purpose of the rebellion was to be served by it. It was the simple gratification of a hell-black spirit of revenge. But it has done good after all. It has filled the country with a deeper abhorrence of slavery and a deeper love for the great liberator.

"Had Abraham Lincoln died from any of the numerous ills to which flesh is heir; had he reached that good old age of which his vigorous constitution and his temperate habits gave promise; had he been permitted to see the end of his great work; had the solemn curtain of death come down but gradually—we should still have been smitten with a heavy grief, and treasured his name lovingly. But dying as he did die, by the red hand of violence, killed, assassinated, taken off without warning, not because of personal hate—for no man who knew Abraham Lincoln could hate him—but because of his fidelity to union and liberty, he is doubly dear to us, and his memory will be precious for ever.

"Fellow citizens, I end as I began, with congratulations. We have done a good work for our race to-day. In doing honour to the memory of our friend and liberator, we have been doing highest honours to ourselves and those who come after us; we have been fastening ourselves to a name and fame imperishable and immortal; we have also been defending ourselves from a blighting scandal. When now it shall be said that the coloured man is soulless, that he has no appreciation of benefits or benefactors; when the foul reproach of ingratitude is hurled at us, and it is attempted to scourge us beyond the range of human brotherhood, we may calmly point to the monument we have this day erected to the memory of Abraham Lincoln."

The progress of a nation is sometimes indicated by small things. When Henry Wilson, an honoured Senator and Vice-President of the United States, died in the capital of the nation, it was a significant and telling indication of national advance, that three coloured citizens, Mr. Robert Purvis, Mr. James Wormley, and myself, were selected with the Senate committee, to accompany his honoured remains from Washington to the grand old commonwealth he loved so well, and whom in turn she had so greatly loved and honoured. It was meet and right that we should be represented in the long procession that met those remains in every State between here and Massachusetts, for Henry Wilson was among the foremost friends of the coloured race in this country, and this was the first time in its history that a coloured man was made a pall-bearer at the funeral, as I was in this instance, of a Vice-President of the United States.

An appointment to any important and lucrative office under the United States Government, usually brings its recipient a large measure of praise and congratulation on the one hand, and much abuse and disparagement on the other; and he may think himself singularly fortunate if the censure does not exceed the praise. I need not dwell upon the causes of this extravagance, but I may say there is no office of any value in the country which is not desired and sought by many persons equally meritorious and equally deserving. But as only one person can be appointed to any one office, only one can be pleased, while many are offended, unhappily, resentment follows disappointment, and this resentment often finds expression is disparagement and abuse of the successful man. As in most else I have said, I borrow this reflection from my own experience.

My appointment as United States Marshal of the District of Columbia, was in keeping with the rest of my life, as a freeman. It was an innovation upon long established usage, and opposed to the general current of sentiment in the community. It came upon the people of the District as a gross surprise, and almost a punishment; and provoked something like a scream—I will not say a yell—of popular displeasure. As soon as I was named by President Hayes for the place, efforts were made by members of the bar to defeat my confirmation before the Senate. All sorts of reasons against my appointment, but the true one, were given, and that was withheld more from a sense of shame, than from a sense of justice. The apprehension doubtless was, that if appointed Marshal I should surround myself with coloured deputies, coloured bailiffs, coloured messengers, and pack the jury box with coloured jurors; in a word, Africanize the courts. But the most dreadful thing threatened, was a coloured man at the Executive Mansion in white kid gloves, swallow-tailed coat, patent leather boots, and alabaster cravat, performing the ceremony—a very empty one—of introducing the aristocratic citizens of the republic to the President of the United States. This was something entirely too much to be borne; and men asked themselves in view of it, to what is the world coming, and where will these things stop? Dreadful! Dreadful!

It is creditable to the manliness of the American Senate, that it was moved by none of these things, and that it lost no time in the matter of my confirmation. I learn, and believe my information correct, that foremost among those who supported my confirmation against the ojections made to it, was the Hon. Roscoe Conkling of New York. His speech in executive session is said by the senators who heard it, to have been one of the most masterly and eloquent ever delivered on the floor of the Senate; and this too I readily believe, for Mr. Conkling possesses the ardour and fire of Henry Clay, the subtlety of Calhoun, and the massive grandeur of Daniel Webster.

The effort to prevent my confirmation having failed, nothing could be done but to wait for some overt act to justify my removal; and for this my unfriends had not long to wait. In the course of one or two months I was invited by a number of citizens of Baltimore to deliver a lecture in that city, in Douglass Hall—a building named in honour of myself, and devoted to educational purposes. With this invitation I complied, giving the same lecture which I had two years before delivered in the city of Washington, and which was at the time published in full in the newspapers, and very highly commended by them. The subject of the lecture was, "Our National Capital," and in it I said many complimentary things of the city, which were as true as they were complimentary. I spoke of what it had been in the past, what it was at that time, and what I thought it destined to become in the future; giving it all credit for its good points, and calling attention to some of its ridiculous features. For this I got myself pretty roughly handled. The newspapers worked themselves up to a frenzy of passion, and committees were appointed to procure names to a petition to President Hayes demanding my removal. The tide of popular feeling was so violent, that I deemed it necessary to depart from my usual custom when assailed, so far as to write the following explanatory letter, from which the reader will be able to measure the extent and quality of my offence:—

"To the Editor of the Washington Evening Star:

"Sir:—You were mistaken in representing me as being off on a lecturing tour, and, by implication, neglecting my duties as United States Marshal of the District of Columbia. My absence from Washington during two days was due to an invitation by the managers to be present on the occasion of the inauguration of the International Exhibition in Philadelphia.

"In complying with this invitation, I found myself in company with other members of the Government who went thither in obedience to the call of patriotism and civilization. No one interest of the Marshal's office suffered by my temporary absence, as I had seen to it that those upon whom the duties of the office devolved were honest, capable, industrious, painstaking, and faithful. My Deputy Marshal is a man every way qualified for his position, and the citizens of Washington may rest assured that no unfaithful man will be retained in any position under me. Of course I can have nothing to say as to my own fitness for the position I hold. You have a right to say what you please on that point, yet I think it would be only fair and generous to wait for some dereliction of duty on my part before I shall be adjudged as incompetent to fill the place.

"You will allow me to say, also, that the attacks upon me on account of the remarks alleged to have been made by me in Baltimore, strike me as both malicious and silly. Washington is a great city, not a village, nor a hamlet, but the capital of a great nation, and the manners and habits of its various classes are proper subjects for presentation and criticism, and I very much mistake if this great city can be thrown into a tempest of passion by any humorous reflections I may take the liberty to utter. The city is too great to be small, and I think it will laugh at the ridiculous attempt to rouse it to a point of furious hostility to me for anything said in my Baltimore lecture.

"Had the reporters of that lecture been as careful to note what I said in praise of Washington as what I said, if you please, in disparagement of it, it would have been impossible to awaken any feeling against me in this community for what I said. It is the easiest thing in the world, as all editors know, to pervert the meaning and give a one-sided impression of a whole speech, by simply giving isolated passages from the speech itself, without any qualifying connections. It would hardly be imagined from anything that has appeared here that I had said one word in that lecture in honour of Washington, and yet the lecture itself, as a whole, was decidedly in the interest of the national capital. I am not such a fool as to decry a city in which I have invested my money and made my permanent residence.

"After speaking of the power of the sentiment of patriotism I held this language: 'In the spirit of this noble sentiment I would have the American people view the national capital. It is our national centre. It belongs to us; and whether it is mean or majestic, whether arrayed in glory or covered with shame, we cannot but share its character and its destiny. In the remotest section of the Republic, in the most distant parts of the globe, amid the splendours of Europe or the wilds of Africa, we are still held and firmly bound to this common centre. Under the shadow of Bunker's Hill monument, in the peerless eloquence of his diction, I once heard the great Daniel Webster give welcome to all American citizens, assuring them that wherever else they might be strangers, they were all at home there. The same boundless welcome is given to all American citizens by Washington. Elsewhere we may belong to individual States, but here we belong to the whole United States. Elsewhere we may belong to a section, but here we belong to a whole country, and the whole country belongs to us. It is national territory, and the one place where no American is an intruder or a carpet-bagger. The new comer is not less at home than the old resident. Under its lofty domes and stately pillars, as under the broad blue sky, all races and colours of men stand upon a footing of common equality.

" 'The wealth and magnificence which elsewhere might oppress the humble citizen has an opposite effect here. They are felt to be a part of himself and serve to ennoble him in his own eyes. He is an owner of the marble grandeur which he beholds about him,—as much so as any of the forty millions of this great nation. Once in his life every American who can, should visit Washington; not as the Mahometan goes to Mecca; not as the Catholic to Rome; not as the Hebrew to Jerusalem, nor as the Chinaman to the Flowery kingdom, but in the spirit of enlightened patriotism, knowing the value of free institutions and how to perpetuate and maintain them.

" 'Washington should be contemplated not merely as an assemblage of fine buildings; not merely as the chosen resort of the wealth and fashion of the country, not merely as the honoured place where the statesmen of the nation assemble to shape the policy and frame the laws; not merely as the point at which we are most visibly touched by the outside world, and where the diplomatic skill and talent of the old continent meet and match themselves against those of the new, but as the national flag itself—a glorious symbol of civil and religious liberty, leading the world in the race of social science, civilization, and renown.'

"My lecture in Baltimore required more than an hour and a half for its delivery, and every intelligent reader will see the difficulty of doing justice to such a speech when it is abbreviated and compressed into a half or three-quarters of a column. Such abbreviation or condensation has been resorted to in this instance. A few stray sentences, culled out from their connections, would be deprived of much of their harshness if presented in the form and connection in which they were uttered; but I am taking up too much space, and will close with the last paragraph of the lecture as delivered in Baltimore. "No city in the broad world has a higher or more beneficent mission. Among all the great capitals of the world it is pre-eminently the capital of free institutions. Its fall would be a blow to freedom and progress throughout the world. Let it stand then where it does now stand—where the father of his country planted it, and where it has stood for more than half a century; no longer sandwiched between two slave States; no longer a contradiction to human progress, no longer the hot-bed of slavery and the slave trade; no longer the home of the duellist, the gambler, the assassin; no longer the frantic partisan of one section of the country against the other, no longer anchored to a dark and semi-barbarous past, but a redeemed city, beautiful to the eye and attractive to the heart, a bond of perpetual union, an angel of peace on earth and good will to men, a common ground upon which Americans of all races and colours, all sections, North and South, may meet and shake hands, not over a chasm of blood, but over a free, united, and progressive republic."

I have already alluded to the fact that much of the opposition to my appointment to the office of United States Marshal of the District of Columbia was due to the possibility of my being called to attend President Hayes at the Executive Mansion upon state occasions, and having the honour to introduce the guests on such occasions. I now wish to refer to reproaches liberally showered upon me for holding the office of Marshal while denied this distinguished honour, and to show that the complaint against me at this point is not a well-founded complaint.

1st. Because the office of United States Marshal is distinct, and separate, and complete in itself, and must be accepted or refused upon its own merits. If, when offered to any person, its duties are such as he can properly fulfil, he may very properly accept it; or, if otherwise, he may as properly refuse it.

2nd. Because the duties of the office are clearly and strictly defined in the law by which it was created; and because nowhere among these duties is there any mention or intimation that the Marshal may or shall attend upon the President of the United States at the Executive Mansion on state occasions.

3rd. Because the choice as to who shall have the honour and privilege of such attendance upon the President, belongs exclusively and reasonably to the President himself, and that therefore no one, however distinguished, or in whatever office, has any just cause to complain of the exercise by the President of this right of choice, or because he is not himself chosen.

In view of these propositions, which I hold to be indisputable, I should have presented to the country a most foolish and ridiculous figure had I, as absurdly counselled by some of my coloured friends, resigned the office of Marshal of the District of Columbia, because President Rutherford B. Hayes, for reasons that must have been satisfactory to his judgment, preferred some person other than myself to attend upon him at the Executive Mansion and perform the ceremony of introduction on state occasions. But it was said that this statement did not cover the whole ground; that it was customary for the United States Marshal of the District of Columbia to perform this social office; and that the usage had come to have almost the force of law. I met this at the time, and I meet it now, by denying the binding force of this custom. No former President has any right or power to make his example the rule for his successor. The custom of inviting the Marshal to do this duty was made by a President, and could be as properly unmade by a President. Besides, the usage is altogether a modern one, and had its origin in peculiar circumstances, and was justified by those circumstances. It was introduced in time of war by President Lincoln, when he made his old law partner and intimate acquaintance Marshal of the District, and was continued by Gen. Grant when he appointed a relative of his, Gen. Sharp, to the same office. But again it was said that President Hayes only departed from this custom because the Marshal in my case was a coloured man. The answer I made to this, and now make to it, is that it is a gratuitous assumption, and entirely begs the question. It may or may not be true that my complexion was the cause of this departure, but no man has any right to assume that position in advance of a plain declaration to that effect by President Hayes himself. Never have I heard from him any such declaration or intimation. In so far as my intercourse with him is concerned, I can say that I at no time discovered in him a feeling of aversion to me on account of my complexion, or on any other account, and, unless I am greatly deceived, I was ever a welcome visitor at the Executive Mansion on state occasions and all others, while Rutherford B. Hayes was President of the United States. I have further to say that I have many times during his administration had the honour to introduce distinguished strangers to him, both of native and foreign birth, and never had reason to feel myself slighted by himself or his amiable wife; and I think he would be a very unreasonable man who could desire for himself, or for any other, a larger measure of respect and consideration than this at the hands of a man and woman occupying the exalted positions of Mr. and Mrs. Hayes.

I should not do entire justice to the Honourable ex-President if I did not bear additional testimony to his noble and generous spirit. When all Washington was in an uproar, and a wild clamour rent the air for my removal from the office of Marshal on account of the lecture delivered by me in Baltimore, when petitions were flowing in upon him demanding my degradation, he nobly rebuked the mad spirit of persecution by openly declaring his purpose to retain me in my place.

One other word. During the tumult raised against me in consequence of this lecture on the "National Capital," Mr. Columbus Alexander, one of the old and wealthy citizens of Washington, who was on my bond for twenty thousand dollars, was repeatedly besought to withdraw his name, and thus leave me disqualified; but like the President, both he and my other bondsman, Mr. George Hill, junr., were steadfast and immovable. I was not surprised that Mr. Hill stood bravely by me, for he was a Republican; but I was surprised and gratified that Mr. Alexander, a Democrat, and, I believe, once a slaveholder, had not only the courage, but the magnanimity to give me fair play in this fight. What I have said of these gentlemen, can be extended to very few others in this community, during that period of excitement, among either the white or coloured citizens, for, with the exception of Dr. Charles B. Purvis, no coloured man in the city uttered one public word in defence or extenuation of me or of my Baltimore speech.

This violent hostility kindled against me was singularly evanescent. It came like a whirlwind, and like a whirlwind departed. I soon saw nothing of it, either in the courts among the lawyers, or in the streets among the people; for it was discovered that there was really in my speech at Baltimore nothing which made me "worthy of stripes or of bonds."

I can say from my experience in the office of United States Marshal of the District of Columbia, it was in every way agreeable. When it was an open question whether I should take the office or not, it was apprehended and predicted if I should accept it in face of the opposition of the lawyers and judges of the courts, I should be subjected to numberless suits for damages, and so vexed and worried that the office would be rendered valueless to me; that it would not only eat up my salary, but possibly endanger what little I might have laid up for a rainy day. I have now to report that this apprehension was in no sense realized. What might have happened had the members of the District bar been half as malicious and spiteful as they had been industriously represented as being, or if I had not secured as my assistant a man so capable, industrious, vigilant, and careful as Mr. L. P. Williams, of course I cannot know. But I am bound to praise the bridge that carries me safely over it. I think it will ever stand as a witness to my fitness for the position of Marshal, that I had the wisdom to select for my assistant a gentlemen so well instructed and competent. I also take pleasure in bearing testimony to the generosity of Mr. Phillips, the Assistant-Marshal, who preceded Mr. Williams in that office, in giving the new assistant valuable information as to the various duties he would be called upon to perform. I have further to say of my experience in the Marshal's office, that while I have reason to know that the eminent Chief Justice of the District of Columbia and some of his associates were not well pleased with my appointment, I was always treated by them, as well as by the chief clerk of the courts, the Hon. J. R. Meigs, and the subordinates of the latter—with a single exception—with the respect and consideration due to my office. Among the eminent lawyers of the District I believe I had many friends, and there were those of them to whom I could always go with confidence in an emergency for sound advice and direction, and this fact, after all the hostility felt in consequence of my appointment, and revived by my speech at Baltimore, is another proof of the vincibility of all feeling arising out of popular prejudices.

In all my forty years of thought and labour to promote the freedom and welfare of my race, I never found myself more widely and painfully at variance with leading coloured men of the country than when I opposed the effort to set in motion a wholesale exodus of coloured people of the South to the Northern States; and yet I never took a position in which I felt myself better fortified by reason and necessity. It was said of me, that I had deserted to the old master class, and that I was a traitor to my race; that I had run away from slavery myself, and yet I was opposing others in doing the same. When my opponents condescended to argue, they took the ground that the coloured people of the South needed to be brought into contact with the freedom and civilization of the North; that no emancipated and persecuted people ever had or ever could rise in the presence of the people by whom they had been enslaved, and that the true remedy for the ills which the freedmen were suffering, was to initiate the Israelitish departure from our modern Egypt to a land abounding, if not in "milk and honey," certainly in pork and hominy.

Influenced, no doubt, by the dazzling prospects held out to them by the advocates of the Exodus movement, thousands of poor, hungry, naked, and destitute coloured people were induced to quit the South amid the frosts and snows of a dreadful winter in search of a better country. I regret to say there was something sinister in this so-called exodus, for it transpired that some of the agents most active in promoting it had an understanding with certain railroad companies, by which they were to receive one dollar per head upon all such passengers. Thousands of these poor people, travelling only so far as they had money to bear their expenses, were dropped on the levees of St. Louis, in the extremest destitution; and their tales of woe were such as to move a heart much less sensitive to human suffering than mine. But while I felt for these poor deluded people, and did what I could to put a stop to their ill-advised and ill-arranged stampede, I also did what I could to assist such of them as were within my reach, who were on their way to this land of promise. Hundreds of these people came to Washington, and at one time there were from two to three hundred lodged here, unable to get further for the want of money. I lost no time in appealing to my friends for the means of assisting them. Conspicuous among these friends was Mrs. Elizabeth Thompson of New York city—the lady who, several years ago, made the nation a present of Carpenter's great historical picture of the "Signing of the Emancipation Proclamation," and who has expended large sums of her money in investigating the causes of yellow-fever, and in endeavours to discover means for preventing its ravages in New Orleans and elsewhere. I found Mrs. Thompson consistently alive to the claims of humanity in this, as in other instances, for she sent me, without delay, a draft for two hundred and fifty dollars, and in doing so expressed the wish that I would promptly inform her of any other opportunity of doing good. How little justice was done me by those who accused me of indifference to the welfare of the coloured people of the South on account of my opposition to the so-called exodus will be seen by the following extracts from a paper on that subject laid before the Social Science Congress at Saratoga, when that question was before the country:

"Important as manual labour is everywhere, it is nowhere more important and absolutely indispensable to the existence of society than in the more southern of the United States. Machinery may continue to do, as it has done, much of the work of the North, but the work of the South requires bone, sinew, and muscle of the strongest and most enduring kind for its performance. Labour in that section must know no pause. Her soil is pregnant and prolific with life and energy. All the forces of nature within her borders are wonderfully vigorous, persistent, and active. Aided by an almost perpetual summer abundantly supplied with heat and moisture, her soil readily and rapidly covers itself with noxious weeds, dense forests, and impenetrable jungles. Only a few years of non-tillage would be needed to give the sunny and fruitful South to the bats and owls of a desolate wilderness. From this condition, shocking for a Southern man to contemplate, it is now seen that nothing less powerful than the naked iron arm of the negro, can save her. For him, as a Southern labourer, there is no competitor or substitute. The thought of filling his place by any other variety of the human family, will be found delusive and utterly impracticable. Neither Chinaman, German, Norwegian, nor Swede, can drive him from the sugar and cotton fields of Louisiana and Mississippi. They would certainly perish in the black bottoms of these states if they could be induced, which they cannot, to try the experiment.

"Nature itself, in those States, comes to the rescue of the negro, fights his battles, and enables him to exact conditions from those who would unfairly treat and oppress him. Besides being dependent upon the roughest and flintiest kind of labour, the climate of the South makes such labour uninviting and harshly repulsive to the white man. He dreads it, shrinks from it, and refuses it. He shuns the burning sun of the fields and seeks the shade of the verandas. On the contrary, the negro walks, labours, and sleeps in the sunlight unharmed. The standing apology for slavery was based upon a knowledge of this fact. It was said that the world must have cotton and sugar, and that only the negro could supply this want, and that he could be induced to do it only under the "beneficent whip" of some bloodthirsty Legree The last part of this argument has been happily disproved by the large crops of these productions since Emancipation; but the first part of it stands firm, unassailed and unassailable.

"Even if climate and other natural causes did not protect the negro from all competition of the labour-market of the South, inevitable social causes would probably effect the same result. The slave system of that section has left behind it, as in the nature of the case it must, manners, customs, and conditions to which free white labouring men will be in no haste to submit themselves and their families. They do not emigrate from the free North, where labour is respected, to a lately enslaved South, where labour has been whipped, chained and degraded for centuries. Naturally enough such emigration follows the lines of latitude in which they who compose it were born. Not from South to North, but from East to West "the Star of Empire takes its way."

"Hence it is seen that the dependence of the planters, land-owners, and old master class of the South upon the negro, however galling and humiliating to Southern pride and power, is nearly complete and perfect. There is only one mode of escape for them, and that mode they will certainly not adopt. It is to take off their own coats, cease to whittle sticks and talk politics at crossroads, and go themselves to work in their broad and sunny fields of cotton and sugar. An invitation to do this is about as harsh and distasteful to all their inclinations as would be an invitation to step down into their graves. With the negro, all this is different. Neither natural, artificial, nor traditional causes stand in the way of the freedman to labour in the South. Neither the heat nor the fever-demon which lurks in her tangled and oozy swamps affright him, and he stands to-day the admitted author of whatever prosperity, beauty, and civilization are now possessed by the South, and the admitted arbiter of her destiny.

"This, then, is the high vantage ground of the negro; he has labour; the South wants it, and must have it or perish. Since he is free he can now give it or withhold it, use it where he is, or take it elsewhere as he pleases. His labour made him a slave, and his labour can, if he will, make him free, comfortable, and independent. It is more to him than fire, swords, ballot-boxes, or bayonets. It touches the heart of the South through its pocket. This power served him well years ago, when in the bitterest extremity of destitution. But for it, he would have perished when he dropped out of slavery. It saved him then, and it will save him again. Emancipation came to him, surrounded by extremely unfriendly circumstances. It was not the choice or consent of the people among whom he lived, but against their will, and a death struggle on their part to prevent it. His chains were broken in the tempest and whirlwind of civil war. Without food, without shelter, without land, without money, and without friends, he with his children, his sick, his aged and helpless ones, were turned loose and naked to the open sky. The announcement of his freedom was instantly followed by an order from his master to quit his old quarters, and to seek bread thereafter from the hands of those who had given him his freedom. A desperate extremity was thus forced upon him at the outset of his freedom, and the world watched with humane auxiety, to see what would become of him. His peril was imminent. Starvation and death stared him in the face and marked him for their victim.

"It will not soon be forgotten that at the close of a five hours' speech by the late Senator Sumner, in which he advocated with unequalled learning and eloquence the enfranchisement of the freedmen, the best argument with which he was met in the Senate, was that legislation at that point would be utterly superfluous; that the negro was rapidly dying out, and must inevitably and speedily disappear and become extinct.

"Inhuman and shocking as was this consignment of millions of human beings to extinction, the extremity of the negro, at that date, did not contradict, but favoured the prophecy. The policy of the old master class dictated by passion, pride, and revenge, was then to make the freedom of the negro, a greater calamity to him, if possible, than had been his slavery. But happily, both for the old master class, and for the recently emancipated, there came then, as there will come now, the sober second thought. The old master class then found it had made a great mistake. It had driven away the means of its own support. It had destroyed the hands, and left the mouths. It had starved the negro, and starved itself. Not even to gratify its own anger and resentment could it afford to allow its fields to go uncultivated, and its tables unsupplied with food. Hence the freedman, less from humanity than cupidity, less from choice than necessity, was speedily called back to labour and life.

"But now, after fourteen years of service, and fourteen years of separation from the visible presence of slavery, during which he has shown both disposition and ability to supply the labour market of the South, and that he could do so far better as a freedman than he ever did as a slave; that more cotton and sugar could be raised by the same hands, under the inspiration of liberty and hope, than can be raised under the influence of bondage and the whip, he is again, alas! in the deepest trouble; again without a home, out under the open sky, with his wife and little ones. He lines the sunny banks of the Mississipi, fluttering in rags and wretchedness, mournfully imploring hard-hearted steamboat captains to take him on board; while the friends of the emigration movement are diligently soliciting funds all over the North to help him away from his old home to the new Canaan of Kansas."

I am sorry to be obliged to omit the statement which here follows, of the reasons given for the Exodus movement, and my explanation of them, but from want of space I can present only such portions of the paper as express most vividly and in fewest words, my position in regard to the question. I go on to say.

"Bad as is the condition of the negro to-day at the South, there was a time when it was flagrantly and incomparably worse. A few years ago he had nothing—he had not even himself. He belonged to somebody else, who could dispose of his person and his labour as he pleased. Now he has himself, his labour, and his right to dispose of one and the other as shall best suit his own happiness. He has more. He has a standing in the supreme law of the land—in the Constitution of the United States—not to be changed or affected by any conjunction of circumstances likely to occur in the immediate or remote future. The Fourteenth Amendment makes him a citizen and the Fifteenth makes him a voter. With power behind him, at work for him, and which cannot be taken from him, the negro of the South may wisely bide his time. The situation of the moment is exceptional and transient. The permanent powers of the Government are all on his side. What though for the moment the hand of violence strike down the negro's rights in the South, those rights will revive, survive, and flourish again. They are not the only people who have been, in a moment of popular passion, maltreated and driven from the polls. The Irish and Dutch have frequently been so treated. Boston, Baltimore, and New York have been the scenes of lawless violence; but those scenes have now disappeared. . . . . Without abating one jot of our horror and indignation at the outrages committed in some parts of the Southern States against the negro, we cannot but regard the present agitation of an African exodus from the South as ill-timed and in some respects hurtful. We stand to-day at the beginning of a grand and beneficent reaction. There is a growing recognition of the duty and obligation of the American people to guard, protect, and defend the personal and political rights of all the people of all the States; to uphold the principles upon which rebellion was suppressed, slavery abolished, and the country saved from dismemberment and ruin.

"We see and feel to-day, as we have not seen and felt before, that the time for conciliation and trusting to the honour of the late rebels and slaveholders has passed. The President of the United States, himself, while still liberal, just, and generous toward the South, has yet sounded a halt in that direction and has bravely, firmly, and ably asserted the constitutional authority to maintain the public peace in every State in the Union, and upon every day in the year, and has maintained this ground against all the powers of House and Senate.

"We stand at the gateway of a marked and decided change in the statesmanship of our rulers. Every day brings fresh and increasing evidence that we are, and of right ought to be, a nation; that Confederate notions of the nature and powers of our Government ought to have perished in the rebellion which they supported; that they are anachronisms and superstitions and no longer fit to be above ground. . . . .

"At a time like this, so full of hope and courage, it is unfortunate that a cry of despair should be raised in behalf of the coloured people of the South; unfortunate that men are going over the country begging in the name of the poor coloured man of the South, and telling the people that the Government has no power to enforce the Constitution and laws in that section, and that there is no hope for the poor negro but to plant him in the new soil of Kansas or Nebraska.

"These men do the coloured people of the South a real damage. They give their enemies an advantage in the argument for their manhood and freedom. They assume their inability to take care of themselves. The country will be told of the hundreds who go to Kansas, but not of the thousands who stay in Mississippi and Louisiana.

"It will be told of the destitute who require material aid, but not of the multitude who are bravely sustaining themselves where they are.

"In Georgia the negroes are paying taxes upon six millions of dollars; in Louisiana upon forty or fifty millions; and upon unascertained sums elsewhere in the Southern States.

"Why should a people who have made such progress in the course of a few years be humiliated and scandalized by exodus agents, begging money to remove them from their homes; especially at a time when every indication favours the position that the wrongs and hardships which they suffer are soon to be redressed?

"Besides the objection thus stated, it is manifest that the public and noisy advocacy of a general stampede of the coloured people from the South to the North is necessarily an abandonment of the great and paramount principle of protection to person and property in every State in the Union. It is an evasion of a solemn obligation and duty. The business of this nation is to protect its citizens where they are, not to transport them where they will not need protection. The best that can be said of this exodus in this respect is, that it is an attempt to climb up some other way, it is an expedient, a half-way measure, and tends to weaken in the public mind a sense of absolute right, power, and duty of the Government, inasmuch as it concedes, by implication at least, that on the soil of the South the law of the land cannot command obedience, the ballot-box cannot be kept pure, peaceable elections cannot be held, the Constitution cannot be enforced, and the lives and liberties of loyal and peaceable citizens cannot be protected. It is a surrender, a premature disheartening surrender, since it would secure freedom and free institutions by migration rather than by protection; by flight rather than by right; by going into a strange land rather than by staying in one's own. It leaves the whole question of equal rights on the soil of the South open and still to be settled, with the moral influence of exodus against us; since it is a confession of the utter impracticability of equal rights and equal protection in any State where those rights may be struck down by violence.

"It does not appear that the friends of freedom should spend either time or talent or furtherance of this exodus, as a desirable measure, either for the North or the South. If the people of this country cannot be protected in every State of the Union, the Government of the United States is shorn of its rightful dignity and power, the late rebellion has triumphed, the sovereignty of the nation is an empty name, and the power and authority in individual States greater than the power and authority of the United States. . . . . .

"The coloured people of the South, just beginning to accumulate a little property, and to lay the foundation of family, should not be in haste to sell that little and be off to the banks of the Mississippi. The habit of roaming from place to place in pursuit of better conditions of existence is never a good one. A man should never leave his home for a new one till he has earnestly endeavoured to make his immediate surroundings accord with his wishes. The time and energy expended in wandering from place to place, if employed in making him a comfortable home where he is, will, in nine cases out of ten, prove the best investment. No people ever did much for themselves or for the world without the sense and inspiration of native land, of a fixed home, of familiar neighbourhood and common associations. The fact of being to the manner born has an elevating power upon the mind and heart of a man. It is a more cheerful thing to be able to say I was born here and know all the people, than to say I am a stranger here and know none of the people.

"It cannot be doubted that in so far as this exodus tends to promote restlessness in the coloured people of the South, to unsettle their feeling of home, and to sacrifice positive advantages where they are, for fancied ones in Kansas or elsewhere, it is an evil. Some have sold their little homes, their chickens, mules, and pigs at a sacrifice, to follow the exodus. Let it be understood that you are going, and you advertise the fact that your mule has lost half its value, for your staying with him makes half his value. Let the coloured people of Georgia offer their six millions' worth of property for sale, with the purpose to leave Georgia, and they will not realize half its value. Land is not worth much where there are no people to occupy it, and a mule is not worth much where there is no one to drive him.

"It may be safely asserted that whether advocated and commended to favour on the ground that it will increase the political power of the Republican party, and thus help to make a solid North against a solid South, or upon the ground that it will increase the power and influence of the coloured people as a political element, and enable them the better to protect their rights, and insure their moral and social elevation, the exodus will prove a disappointment, a mistake, and a failure; because, as to strengthening the Republican party, the emigrants will go only to those States where the Republican party is strong and solid enough already with their votes, and in respect to the other part of the argument, it will fail because it takes coloured voters from a section of the country where they are sufficiently numerous to elect some of their number to places of honour and profit, and places them in a country where their proportion to other classes will be so small as not to be recognized as a political element or entitled to be represented by one of themselves. And further, because go where they will, they must for a time inevitably carry with them poverty, ignorance, and other repulsive incidents, inherited from their former condition as slaves—a circumstance which is about as likely to make votes for Democrats as for Republicans, and to raise up bitter prejudice against them as to raise up friends for them. . . . .

"Plainly enough, the exodus is less harmful as a measure than are the arguments by which it is supported. The one is the result of a feeling of outrage and despair; but the other comes of cool, selfish calculation. One is the result of honest despair, and appeals powerfully to the sympathies of men, the other is an appeal to our selfishness, which shrinks from doing right because the way is difficult.

"Not only is the South the best locality for the negro, on the ground of his political powers and possibilities, but it is best for him as a field of labour. He is there, as he is nowhere else, an absolute necessity. He has a monopoly of the labour market. His labour is the only labour which can successfully offer itself for sale in that market. This fact, with a little wisdom and firmness, will enable him to sell his labour there on terms more favourable to himself than he can elsewhere. As there are no competitors or substitutes he can demand living prices with the certainty that the demand will be complied with. Exodus would deprive him of this advantage. . . .

"The negro, as already intimated, is pre-eminently a Southern man. He is so both in constitution and habits, in body as well as mind. He will not only take with him to the North, Southern modes of labour, but Southern modes of life. The careless and improvident habits of the South cannot be set aside in a generation. If they are adhered to in the North, in the fierce winds and snows of Kansas and Nebraska, the emigration must be large to keep up their numbers. . . .

"As an assertion of power by a people hitherto held in bitter contempt, as an emphatic and stinging protest against high-handed, greedy, and shameless injustice to the weak and defenceless, as a means of opening the blind eyes of oppressors to their folly and peril, the exodus has done valuable service. Whether it has accomplished all of which it is capable in this direction, for the present, is a question which may well be considered. With a moderate degree of intelligent leadership among the labouring class of the South, properly handling the justice of their cause, and wisely using the exodus example, they can easily exact better terms for their labour than ever before. Exodus is medicine, not food; it is for disease, not health, it is not to be taken from choice, but necessity. In anything like a normal condition of things, the South is the best place for the negro. Nowhere else is there for him a promise of a happier future. Let him stay there if he can, and save both the South and himself to civilization. While, however, it may be the highest wisdom in the circumstances for the freedmen to stay where they are, no encouragement should be given to any measures of coercion to keep them there. The American people are bound, if they are, or can be bound to anything, to keep the north gate of the South open to black and white and to all the people. "The time to assert a right," Webster says, is when it is called in question. If it is attempted by force or fraud to compel the coloured people to stay there, they should by all means go—go quickly, and die if need be in the attempt."

CHAPTER XVI: "TIME MAKES ALL THINGS EVEN."

Return to the "old master"—A last interview—Capt. Auld's admission "had I been in your place, I should have done as you did"—Speech at Easton—The old gaol there—Invited to a sail in the revenue cutter Guthrie—Hon. J. L. Thomas—Visit to the old plantation—Home of Col. Lloyd—Kind reception and attentions—Familiar scenes—Old memories—Burial-ground—Hospitality—Gracious reception from Mrs. Buchanan—A little girl's floral gift—A promise of a "good time coming"—Speech at Harper's Ferry, Decoration day, 1881—Storer College—Hon. A. J. Hunter.

THE leading incidents to which it is my purpose to call attention and make prominent in the present chapter, will, I think, address the imagination of the reader with peculiar and poetic force, and might well enough be dramatized for the stage They certainly afford another striking illustration of the trite saying, that "truth is stranger than fiction."

The first of these events occurred four years ago, when, after a period of more than forty years, I visited and had an interview with Captain Thomas Auld, at St. Michaels, Talbot County, Maryland. It will be remembered by those who have followed the thread of my story, that St. Michaels was at one time the place of my home, and the scene of some of my saddest experiences of slave life; and that I left there, or, rather, was compelled to leave there, because it was believed that I had written passes for several slaves to enable them to escape from slavery, and that prominent slaveholders in that neighbourhood had, for this alleged offence, threatened to shoot me on sight, and to prevent the execution of this threat, my master had sent me to Baltimore.

My return, therefore, to this place, in peace, among the same people, was strange enough of itself, but that I should, when there, be formally invited by Capt. Thomas Auld, then over eighty years old, to come to the side of his dying bed, evidently with a view to a friendly talk over our past relations, was a fact still more strange, and one which, until its occurrence, I could never have thought possible. To me, Capt. Auld had sustained the relation of master—a relation which I had held in extremest abhorrence, and which for forty years, I had denounced in all bitterness of spirit and fierceness of speech. He had struck down my personality, had subjected me to his will, made property of my body and soul, reduced me to a chattel, hired me out to a noted slave-breaker to be worked like a beast and flogged into submission; he had taken my hard earnings, sent me to prison, offered me for sale, broken up my Sunday-school, forbidden me to teach my fellow slaves to read on pain of nine and thirty lashes on my bare back; he had sold my body to his brother Hugh, had pocketed the price of my flesh and blood without any apparent disturbance of his conscience. I, on my part, had travelled through the length and breath of this country and of England, holding up this conduct of his, in common with that of other slaveholders, to the reprobation of all men who would listen to my words. I had made his name and his deeds familiar to the world by my writings in four different languages, yet here we were after four decades once more face to face—he on his bed, aged and tremulous, drawing near the sunset of life, and I, his former slave, United States Marshalof the District of Columbia, holding his hand and in friendly conversation with him, in a sort of final settlement of past differences, preparatory to his stepping into his grave, where all distinctions are at an end, and where the great and small, the slave and his master, are reduced to the same level. Had I been asked in the days of slavery to visit this man, I should have regarded the invitation as one to put fetters on my ankles and handcuffs on my wrists. It would have been an invitation to the auction-block and the slave whip. I had no business with this man under the old régime but to keep out of his way. But now that slavery was destroyed, and the slave and the master stood upon equal ground, I was not only willing to meet him, but was very glad to do so. The conditions were favourable for remembrance of all his good deeds, and generous extenuation of all his evil ones. He was to me no longer a slaveholder either in fact or in spirit, and I regarded him as I did myself, a victim of the circumstances of birth, education, law, and custom.

Our courses had been determined for us, not by us, We had both been flung, by powers that did not ask our consent, upon a mighty current of life, which we could neither resist nor control. By this current he was a master, and I a slave; but now our lives were verging towards a point where differences disappear, where even the constancy of hate breaks down, where the clouds of pride, passion, and selfishness vanish before the brightness of infinite light. At such a time, and in such a place, when a man is about closing his eyes on this world and ready to step into the eternal unknown, no word of reproach or bitterness should reach him or fall from his lips; and on this occasion there was to this rule no transgression on either side.

As this visit to Capt. Auld had been made the subject of mirth by heartless triflers, and regretted as a weakening of my life-long testimony against slavery, by serious-minded men, and as the report of it, published in the papers immediately after it occurred, was in some respects defective and coloured, it may be proper to state exactly what was said and done at this interview.

It should in the first place be understood that I did not go to St. Michaels upon Capt. Auld's invitation, but upon that of my coloured friend, Charles Caldwell; but when once there, Capt. Auld sent Mr. Green, a man in constant attendance upon him during his sickness, to tell me he would be very glad to see me, and wished me to accompany Green to his house, with which request I complied. On reaching the house I was met by Mr. Wm. H. Bruff, a son-in-law of Capt. Auld, and Mrs. Louisa Bruff, his daughter, and was conducted by them immediately to the bed-room of Capt. Auld. We addressed each other simultaneously, he calling me "Marshal Douglass," and I, as I had always called him, "Captain Auld." Hearing myself called by him "Marshal Douglass," I instantly broke up the formal nature of the meeting by saying, "not Marshal but Frederick to you as formerly." We shook hands cordially, and in the act of of doing so, he, having been long stricken with palsy, shed tears as men thus afflicted will do when excited by any deep emotion. The sight of him, the changes which time had wrought in him, his tremulous hands constantly in motion, and all the circumstances of his condition affected me deeply, and for a time choked my voice and made me speechless. We both, however, got the better of our feelings, and conversed freely about the past.

Though broken by age and palsy, the mind of Capt. Auld was remarkably clear and strong. After he had become composed I asked him what he thought of my conduct in running away and going to the North. He hesitated a moment as if to properly formulate his reply, and said: "Frederick, I always knew you were too smart to be a slave, and had I been in your place I should have done as you did." I said, "Capt. Auld, I am glad to hear you say this. I did not run away from you, but from slavery; it was not that I loved Cæsar less, but Rome more." I told him I had made a mistake in my narrative, a copy of which I had sent him, in attributing to him ungrateful and cruel treatment of my grandmother; that I had done so on the supposition that in the division of the property of my old master, Mr. Aaron Anthony, my grandmother had fallen to him, and that he had left her in her old age, when she could be no longer of service to him, to pick up her living in solitude with none to help her, or in other words had turned her out to die like an old horse. "Ah!" he said, "that was a mistake, I never owned your grandmother; she in the division of the slaves was awarded to my brother-in-law, Andrew Anthony; but," he added quickly, "I brought her down here and took care of her as long as she lived." The fact is, that after writing my narrative describing the condition of my grandmother, Captain Auld's attention being thus called to it, he rescued her from her destitution. I told him that this mistake of mine was corrected as soon as I discovered it, and that I had at no time any wish to do him injustice; that I regarded both of us as victims of a system. "Oh, I never liked slavery," he said, "and I meant to emancipate all of my slaves when they reached the age of twenty-five years." I told him I had always been curious to know how old I was, that it had been a serious trouble to me not to know when was my birthday. He said he could not tell me that, but he thought I was born in February, 1818. This date made me one year younger than I had supposed myself from what was told me by Mistress Lucretia, Captain Auld's former wife, when I left Lloyd's for Baltimore in the Spring of 1825; she having then said that I was eight, going on nine. I know that it was in the year 1825 that I went to Baltimore, because it was in that year that Mr. James Beacham built a large frigate at the foot of Alliceana Street, for one of the South American Governments. Judging from this, and from certain events which transpired at Colonel Lloyd's, such as a boy, without any knowledge of books, under eight years old, would hardly take cognizance of, I am led to believe that Mrs. Lucretia was nearer right as to my age than her husband.

Before I left his bedside, Captain Auld spoke with a cheerful confidence of the great change that awaited him, and felt himself about to depart in peace. Seeing his extreme weakness I did not protract my visit. The whole interview did not last more than twenty minutes, and we parted to meet no more. His death was soon after announced in the papers, and the fact that he had once owned me as a slave was cited as rendering that event noteworthy.

It may not, perhaps, be quite artistic to speak in this connection of another incident of something of the same nature as that which I have just narrated, and yet it quite naturally finds place here; and that is, my visit to the town of Easton, county seat of Talbot County, two years later, to deliver an address in the Court House, for the benefit of some association in that place. This visit was made interesting to me, by the fact that forty-five years before, I had, in company with Henry and John Harris, been dragged to Easton behind horses, with my hands tied, put in gaol, and offered for sale, for the offence of intending to run away from slavery.

It may easily be seen that this visit, after this lapse of time, brought with it feelings and reflections such as only unusual circumstances can awaken. There stood the old gaol, with its whitewashed walls and iron gratings, as when in my youth I heard its heavy locks and bolts clank behind me.

Strange too, Mr. Joseph Graham, who was then Sheriff of the County, and who locked me in this gloomy place, was still living, though verging towards eighty, and was one of the gentlemen who now gave me a warm and friendly welcome, and was among my hearers when I delivered my address at the Court House. There too in the same old place stood Solomon Law's Tavern, where once the slave traders were wont to congregate, and where I now took up my abode and was treated with a hospitality and consideration undreamed of as possible by me in the olden time.

When one has advanced far in the journey of life, when he has seen and travelled over much of this great world, and has had many and strange experiences of shadow and sunshine, when long distances of time and space have come between him and his point of departure, it is natural that his thoughts should return to the place of his beginning, and that he should be seized with a strong desire to revisit the scenes of his early recollection, and live over in memory the incidents of his childhood. At least, such for several years had been my thoughts and feelings in respect to Colonel Lloyd's plantation on Wye River, Talbot County, Maryland; for I had never been there since I left it, when eight years old, in 1825.

While slavery continued, of course this very natural desire could not be safely gratified; for my presence among slaves was dangerous to the public peace, and could not more be tolerated than could a wolf among sheep, or fire in a magazine. But now that the results of the war had changed all this, I had for several years determined to return to my old home upon the first opportunity. Speaking of this desire of mine last winter, to the Hon. John L. Thomas, the efficient collector at the port of Baltimore, and a leading Republican of the State of Maryland, he urged me very much to go, and added that he often took a trip to the eastern shore in his revenue cutter "Guthrie"—otherwise known in time of war as the "Ewing"—and would be much pleased to have me accompany him on one of these trips. I expressed some doubt as to how such a visit would be received by the present Col. Edward Lloyd, now proprietor of the old place, and grandson of Governor Ed. Lloyd whom I remembered. Mr. Thomas promptly assured me that from his own knowledge I need have no trouble on that score. Mr. Lloyd was a liberal minded gentleman, and he had no doubt would take a visit from me very kindly. I was very glad to accept the offer. The opportunity for the trip, however, did not occur till the 12th of June, and on that day, in company with Messrs. Thomas, Thompson, and Chamberlain, on board the cutter, we started for the contemplated visit. In four hours after leaving Baltimore, we were anchored in the river off the Lloyd estate, and from the deck of our vessel I saw once more the stately chimneys of the grand old mansion which I had last seen from the deck of the "Sallie Lloyd" when a boy. I left there as a slave, and returned as a freeman. I left there unknown to the outside world, and returned well known; I left there on a freight boat and returned on a revenue cutter; I left on a vessel belonging to Col. Edward Lloyd, and returned on one belonging to the United States.

As soon as we had come to anchor, Mr. Thomas despatched a note to Col. Edward Lloyd, announcing my presence on board his Cutter, and inviting him to meet me, informing him it was my desire, if agreeable to him, to revisit my old home. In response to this note, Mr. Howard Lloyd, a son of Col. Lloyd, a young gentleman of very pleasant address, came on board the cutter, and was introduced to the several gentlemen and myself.

He told us that his father was gone to Easton on business, expressed his regret at his absence, hoped he would return before we should leave, and in the meantime received us cordially and invited us ashore, escorted us over the grounds, and gave us as hearty a welcome as we could have wished. I hope I shall be pardoned for speaking of this incident with much complacency. It was one which could happen to but few men, and only once in the life time of any. The span of human life is too short for the repetition of events which occur at the distance of fifty years. That I was deeply moved, and greatly affected by it, can be easily imagined. Here I was, being welcomed and escorted by the great grandson of Colonel Edward Lloyd—a gentlemen I had known well fifty-six years before, and whose form and features were as vividly depicted on my memory as if I had seen him but yesterday. He was a gentleman of the olden time, elegant in his apparel, dignified in his deportment, a man of few words and of weighty presence; and I can easily conceive that no Governor of the State of Maryland ever commanded a larger measure of respect than did this great-grandfather of the young gentleman now before me. In company with Mr. Howard was his little brother Decosa, a bright boy of eight or nine years, disclosing his aristocratic descent in the lineaments of his face, and in all his modest and graceful movements. As I looked at him I could not help the reflections naturally arising from having seen so many generations of the same family on the same estate. I had seen the elder Lloyd, and was now walking around with the youngest member of that name. In respect to the place itself, I was most agreeably surprised to find that time had dealt so gently with it, and that in all its appointments it was so little changed from what it was when I left it, and from what I have elsewhere described it. Very little was missing except the squads of little black children which were once seen in all directions, and the great number of slaves on its fields. Col. Lloyd's estate comprised twenty-seven thousand acres, and the home-farm seven thousand. In my boyhood sixty men were employed in cultivating the home-farm alone. Now, by the aid of machinery, the work is accomplished by ten men. I found the buildings, which gave it the appearance of a village, nearly all standing, and I was astonished to find that I had carried their appearance and location so accurately in my mind during so many years. There was the long quarter, the quarter on the hill, the dwelling-house of my old master, Aaron Anthony; the overseer's house, once occupied by William Sevier, Austin Gore, James Hopkins, and other overseers. In connection with my old master's house was the kitchen where Aunt Katy presided, and where my head had received many a thump from her unfriendly hand. I looked into this kitchen with peculiar interest, and remembered that it was there I last saw my mother. I went round to the window at which Miss Lucretia used to sit with her sewing, and at which I used to sing when hungry, a signal which she well understood, and to which she readily responded with bread. The little closet in which I slept in a bag had been taken into the room; the dirt floor, too, had disappeared under plank. But upon the whole, the house is very much as it was in the olden time. Not far from it was the stable formerly in charge of old Barney. The storehouse at the end of it, of which my master carried the keys, had been removed. The large carriage house, too, which in my boy's days contained two or three fine coaches, several phaetons, gigs, and a large sleigh—for the latter there was seldom any use—was gone. This carriage house was of much interest to me, because Col. Lloyd sometimes allowed his servants the use of it for festal occasions, and in it there was at such times music and dancing. With these two exceptions, the houses of the estate remained. There was the shoemaker's shop, where Uncle Abe made and mended shoes; and there the blacksmith's shop, where Uncle Tony hammered iron, and the weekly closing of which first taught me to distinguish Sundays from other days. The old barn, too, was there—time-worn, to be sure, but still in good condition—a place of wonderful interest to me in my childhood, for there I often repaired to listen to the chatter and watch the flight of swallows among its lofty beams, and under its ample roof. Time had wrought some changes in the trees and foliage. The Lombardy poplars, in the branches of which the red-winged blackbirds used to congregate and sing, and whose music awakened in my young heart sensations and aspirations deep and undefinable, were gone; but the oaks and elms where young Daniel—the uncle of the present Edward Lloyd—used to divide with me his cakes and biscuits, were there as umbrageous and beautiful as ever. I expressed a wish to Mr. Howard to be shown into the family burial ground, and thither we made our way. It is a remarkable spot—the resting place for all the deceased Lloyds for two hundred years, for the family have been in possession of the estate since the settlement of the Maryland colony.

The tombs there reminded one of what may be seen in the grounds of moss-covered churches in England. The very names of those who sleep within the oldest of them are crumbled away and become undecipherable. Everything about it is impressive, and suggestive of the transient character of human life and glory. No one could stand under its weeping willows, amidst its creeping ivy and myrtle, and look through its sombre shadows, without a feeling of unusual solemnity. The first interment I ever witnessed was in this place. It was the great-great-grandmother, brought from Annapolis in a mahogany coffin, and quietly, without ceremony, deposited in this ground.

While here, Mr. Howard gathered for me a bouquet of flowers and evergreens from the different graves around us, and which I carefully brought to my home for preservation.

Notable among the tombs were those of Admiral Buchanan, who commanded the "Merrimac" in the action at Hampton Roads with the "Monitor," March 8, 1862, and that of General Winter of the Confederate army, both sons-in-law of the elder Lloyd. There was also pointed out to me the grave of a Massachusetts man, a Mr. Page, a teacher in the family, whom I had often seen and wondered what he could be thinking about as he silently paced up and down the garden walks, always alone, for he associated neither with Captain Anthony, Mr. McDermot, nor the overseers. He seemed to be one by himself. I believe he belonged to some place near Greenfield, Massachusetts, and members of his family will perhaps learn for the first time, from these lines, the place of his burial; for I have had intimation that they knew little about him after he once left home.

We then visited the garden, still kept in fine condition, but not as in the days of the elder Lloyd, for then it was tended constantly by Mr. McDermot, a scientific gardener, and four experienced hands, and formed, perhaps, the most beautiful feature of the place. From this we were invited to what was called by the slaves the Great House—the mansion of the Lloyd's, and were helped to chairs upon its stately veranda, where we could have a full view of its garden, with its broad walks, hedged with box and adorned with fruit trees and flowers of almost every variety. A more tranquil and tranquilizing scene I have seldom met in this or any other country.

We were soon invited from this delightful outlook into the large dining room, with its old-fashioned furniture, its mahogany sideboard, its cut-glass-chandeliers, decanters, tumblers, and wine glasses, and cordially invited to refresh ourselves with wine of most exeellent quality.

To say that our reception was every way gratifying is but a feeble expression of the feeling of each and all of us.

Leaving the Great House, my presence became known to the coloured people, some of whom were children of those I had known when a boy. They all seemed delighted to see me, and were pleased when I called over the names of many of the old servants, and pointed out the cabin where Dr. Copper, an old slave, used to teach us with a hickory stick in hand, to say the "Lords Prayer." After spending a little time with these, we bade good-bye to Mr. Howard Lloyd, with many thanks for his kind attentions, and steamed away to St. Michael's, a place of which I have already spoken.

The next part of this memorable trip took us to the home of Mrs. Buchanan, the widow of Admiral Buchanan, one of the two only living daughters of old Governor Lloyd, and here my reception was as kindly as that received at the Great House, where I had often seen her when a slender young lady of eighteen. She is now about seventy-four years old, but marvellously well preserved. She invited me to a seat by her side, introduced me to her grand-children; conversed with me as freely and with as little embarrassment as if I had been an old acquaintance and occupied an equal station with the most aristocratic of the Caucasian race. I saw in her much of the quiet dignity as well as the features of her father. I spent an hour or so in conversation with Mrs. Buchanan, and when I left, a beautiful little grand-daughter of hers, with a pleasant smile on her face, handed me a bouquet of many-coloured flowers. I never accepted such a gift with a sweeter sentiment of gratitude than from the hand of this lovely child. It told me many things, and among them that a new dispensation of justice, kindness, and human brotherhood was dawning not only in the North, but in the South; that the war, and the slavery that caused the war, were things of the past, and that the rising generation are turning their eyes from the sunset of decayed institutions to the grand possibilities of a glorious future.

The next, and last noteworthy incident in my experience, and one which further and strikingly illustrates the idea with which this chapter sets out, is my visit to Harper's Ferry, on the 30th of May, this year, and my address on John Brown, delivered in that place before Storer College, an Institution established for the education of the children of those whom John Brown endeavoured to liberate. It is only a little more than twenty years ago when the subject of my discourse—as will be seen elsewhere in this volume—made a raid upon Harper's Ferry; when its people, and we may say the whole nation, were filled with astonishment, horror, and indignation at the mention of his name; when the Government of the United States co-operated with the State of Virginia in efforts to arrest and bring to capital punishment all persons in any way connected with John Brown and his enterprise; when United States Marshals visited Rochester and elsewhere in search of me, with a view to my apprehension and execution, for my supposed complicity with Brown; when many prominent citizens of the North were compelled to leave the country to avoid arrest, and men were mobbed, even in Boston, for daring to speak a word in vindication or extenuation of what was considered Brown's stupendous crime; and yet here I was, after two decades, upon the very soil he had stained with blood, among the very people he had startled and outraged, and who, a few years ago, would have hanged me upon the first tree, in open daylight, allowed to deliver an address, not merely defending John Brown, but extolling him as a hero and martyr to the cause of liberty, and doing it with scarcely a murmur of disapprobation. I confess that as I looked out upon the scene before me and the towering heights around me, and remembered the bloody drama there enacted; saw the log house in the distance where John Brown collected his men, saw the little engine house where the brave old Puritan fortified himself against a dozen companies of Virginia Militia, and the place where he was finally captured by United States troops under Col. Robert E. Lee, I was a little shocked at my own boldness in attempting to deliver an address in such presence, and of the character advertised in advance of my coming. But there was no cause of apprehension. The people of Harper's Ferry have made wondrous progress in their ideas of freedom of thought and speech. The abolition of slavery has not merely emancipated the negro, but liberated the whites; taken the lock from their tongues, and the fetters from their press. On the platform from which I spoke, sat the Hon. Andrew J. Hunter, the prosecuting attorney for the State of Virginia, who conducted the cause of the State against John Brown, that consigned him to the gallows. This man, now well-stricken in years, greeted me cordially, and in conversation with me after the address, bore testimony to the manliness and courage of John Brown, and though he still disapproved of the raid made by him upon Harper's Ferry, he commended me for my address, and gave me a pressing invitation to visit Charlestown, where he lives, and offered to give me some facts which might prove interesting to me, as to the sayings and conduct of Captain Brown while in prison and on trial, up to the time of his execution. I regret that my engagements and duties were such that I could not then and there accept his invitation, for I could not doubt the sincerity with which it was given, or fail to see the value of compliance. Mr. Hunter not only congratulated me upon my speech, but at parting, gave me a friendly grip, and added that if Robert E. Lee were alive and present, he knew he would give me his hand also.

This man's presence added much to the interest of the occasion by his frequent interruptions, approving and condemning my sentiments as they were uttered. I only regret that he did not undertake a formal reply to my speech, but this, though invited, he declined to do. It would have given me an opportunity of fortifying certain positions in my address which were perhaps insufficiently defended. Upon the whole, taking the visit to Capt. Auld, to Easton with its old gaol, to the home of my old master at Col. Lloyd's, and this visit to Harper's Ferry, with all their associations, they fulfil the expectation created at the beginning of this chapter.

CHAPTER XVII: INCIDENTS AND EVENTS.

Hon. Gerrit Smith and Mr. E. C. Delevan—Experiences at hotels and on steamboats and other modes of travel—Hon. Edward Marshall—Grace Greenwood—Hon. Moses Norris—Robert J. Ingersoll—Reflections and conclusions—Compensations.

IN escaping from the South, the reader will have observed that I did not escape from its widespread influence in the North. That influence met me almost everywhere outside of pronounced anti-slavery circles, and sometimes even within them. It was in the air, and men breathed it and were permeated by it, often when they were quite unconscience of its presence.

I might recount many occasions when I have encountered this feeling, some painful and melancholy, some ridiculous and amusing. It has been a part of my mission to expose the absurdity of this spirit of caste and in some measure help to emancipate men from its control.

Invited to accompany the Hon. Gerrit Smith to dine with Mr. E. C. Delevan, at Albany many years ago, I expressed to Mr. Smith, my awkwardness and embarrassment in the society I was likely to meet there. "Ah!" said that good man, "you must go, Douglass, it is your mission to break down the walls of separation between the two races." I went with Mr. Smith, and was soon made at ease by Mr. Delevan and the ladies and gentlemen there. They were among the most refined and brilliant people I had ever met. I felt somewhat surprised that I could be so much at ease in such company, but I found it then, as I have since, that the higher the gradation in intelligence and refinement, the farther removed are all artificial distinctions, and restraints of mere caste or colour.

In one of my anti-slavery campaigns in New York, five and thirty years ago, I had an appointment at Victor, a town in Ontario County. I was compelled to stop at the hotel. It was the custom at that time, to seat the guests at a long table running the length of the dining room. When I entered I was shown a little table in a corner. I knew what it meant, but took my dinner all the same. When I went to the desk to pay my bill, I said, "Now, landlord, be good enough to tell me just why you gave me my dinner at the little table in the corner by myself?" He was equal to the occasion, and quickly replied: "Because you see, I wished to give you something better than the others." The cool reply staggered me, and I gathered up my change, muttering only that I did not want to be treated better than other people, and bade him good morning.

On an anti-slavery tour through the West, in company with H. Ford Douglas, a young coloured man of fine intellect and much promise, and my old friend John Jones, both now deceased, we stopped at a hotel in Janesville, and were seated by ourselves to take our meals, where all the bar-room loafers of the town could stare at us. Thus seated I took occasion to say, loud enough for the crowd to hear me, that I had just been out to the stable and had made a great discovery. Asked by Mr. Jones what my discovery was, I said that I saw there, black horses and white horses eating together from the same trough in peace, from which I inferred that the horses of Janesville were more civilized than its people. The crowd saw the hit, and broke out into a good-natured laugh. We were afterwards entertained at the same table with other guests.

Many years ago, on my way from Cleveland to Buffalo, on one of the Lake steamers, the gong sounded for supper. There was a rough element on board, such as at that time might be found anywhere between Buffalo and Chicago. It was not to be trifled with especially when hungry. At the first sound of the gong there was a furious rush for the table. From prudence, more than from lack of appetite, I waited for the second table, as did several others. At this second table I took a seat far apart from the few gentlemen scattered along its side, but directly opposite a well dressed, finely-featured man, of the fairest complexion, high forehead, golden hair and light beard. His whole appearance told me he was somebody. I had been seated but a minute or two, when the steward came to me, and roughly ordered me away. I paid no attention to him, but proceeded to take my supper, determined not to leave, unless compelled to do so by superior force, and being young and strong I was not entirely unwilling to risk the consequences of such a contest. A few moments passed, when on each side of my chair, there appeared a stalwart of my own race. I glanced at the gentleman opposite. His brow was knit, his colour changed from white to scarlet, and his eyes were full of fire. I saw the lightning flash, but I could not tell where it would strike. Before my sable brethren could execute their captain's orders, and just as they were about to lay violent hands upon me, a voice from that man of golden hair and fiery eyes resounded like a clap of summer thunder. "Let the gentleman alone! I am not ashamed to take my tea with Mr. Douglass." His was a voice to be obeyed, and my right to my seat and my supper was no more disputed.

I bowed my acknowledgments to the gentleman, and thanked him for his chivalrous interference; and as modestly as I could, asked him his name. "I am Edward Marshall, of Kentucky, now of California," he said. "Sir, I am very glad to know you, I have just been reading your speech in Congress," I said. Supper over, we passed several hours in conversation with each other, during which he told me of his political career in California, of his election to Congress, and that he was a Democrat, but had no prejudice against colour. He was then just coming from Kentucky, where he had been in part to see his black mammy, for, said he, "I was nursed at the breasts of a coloured mother."

I asked him if he knew my old friend John A. Collins in California. "Oh, yes," he replied, "he is a smart fellow; he ran against me for Congress. I charged him with being an Abolitionist, but he denied it, so I sent off and got the evidence of his having been general agent of the Massachusetts Anti-Slavery Society, and that settled him."

During the passage, Mr. Marshall invited me into the bar-room to take a drink. I excused myself from drinking, but went down with him. There were a number of thirsty-looking individuals standing around, to whom Mr. Marshall said, "Come, boys, take a drink." When the drinking was over, he threw down upon the counter a twenty-dollar gold piece, at which the bar-keeper made large eyes, and said he could not change it. "Well, keep it," said the gallant Marshall, "it will all be gone before morning." After this, we naturally fell apart, and he was monopolized by other company; but I shall never fail to bear willing testimony to the generous and manly qualities of this brother of the gifted and eloquent Thomas Marshall of Kentucky.

In 1842 I was sent by the Massachusetts Anti-Slavery Society to hold a Sunday meeting in Pittsfield, N.H., and was given the name of Mr. Hilles, a subscriber to the Liberator. It was supposed that any man who had the courage to take and read the Liberator, edited by Wm. Lloyd Garrison, or the Herald of Freedom, edited by Nathaniel P. Rodgers, would gladly receive and give food and shelter to any coloured brother labouring in the cause of the slave. As a general rule this was very true.

There were no railroads in New Hampshire in those days, so I reached Pittsfield by stage, glad to be permitted to ride upon the top, for no coloured person could be allowed inside. This was many years before the days of Civil Rights Bills, black Congressmen, coloured United States Marshals, and such like.

Arriving at Pittsfield, I was asked by the driver where I would stop. I gave him the name of my subscriber to the Liberator. "That is two miles beyond," he said. So after landing his other passengers, he took me on to the house of Mr. Hilles.

I confess I did not seem a very desirable visitor. The day had been warm and the road dusty. I was covered with dust, and then I was not of the colour fashionable in that neighbourhood, for coloured people were scarce in that part of the old Granite State. I saw in an instant, that though the weather was warm, I was to have a cool reception; but cool or warm, there was no alternative left me but to stay and take what I could get.

Mr. Hilles scarcely spoke to me, and from the moment he saw me jump down from the top of the stage, carpet-bag in hand, his face wore a troubled look. His good wife took the matter more philosophically, and evidently thought my presence there for a day or two could do the family no especial harm; but her manner was restrained, silent, and formal, wholly unlike that of anti-slavery ladies I had met in Massachusetts and Rhode Island.

When tea time came, I found that Mr. Hilles had lost his appetite, and could not come to the table. I suspected his trouble was colourphobia, and though I regretted his malady, I knew his case was not necessarily dangerous; and I was not without some confidence in my skill and ability in healing diseases of that type. I was, however, so affected by his condition that I could not eat much of the pie and cake before me, and felt so little in harmony with things about me that I was, for me, remarkably reticent during the evening, both before and after the family worship, for Mr. Hilles was a pious man.

Sunday morning came, and in due season the hour for meeting. I had arranged a good supply of work for the day. I was to speak four times at ten o'clock a.m., at one p.m., at five, and again at half-past seven in the evening.

When meeting time came, Mr. Hilles brought his fine phaeton to the door, assisted his wife in, and, although there were two vacant seats in his carriage, there was no room in it for me. On driving off from his door, he merely said, addressing me, "You can find your way to the town hall, I suppose?" "I suppose I can," I replied, and started along behind his carriage on the dusty road toward the village. I found the hall, and was very glad to see in my small audience the face of good Mrs. Hilles. Her husband was not there but had gone to his church. There was no one to introduce me, and I proceeded with my discourse without introduction. I held my audience till twelve o'clock—noon—and then took the usual recess of Sunday meetings in country towns, to allow the people to take their lunch. No one invited me to lunch, so I remained in the town hall till the audience assembled again, when I spoke till nearly three o'clock, when the people again dispersed and left me as before. By this time I began to be hungry, and seeing a small hotel near, I went into it, and offered to buy a meal; but I was told "they did not entertain niggers there." I went back to the old town hall hungry and chilled, for an infant "New England north-easter" was beginning to chill the air, and a drizzling rain to fall. I saw that my movements were being observed, from the comfortable homes around, with apparently something of the feeling that children might experience in seeing a bear prowling about town. There was a grave yard near the town hall, and attracted thither, I felt some relief in contemplating the resting place of the dead, where there was an end to all distinctions between rich and poor, white and coloured, high and low.

While thus meditating on the vanities of the world and my own loneliness and destitution, and recalling the sublime pathos of the saying of Jesus, "The foxes have holes, and the birds of the air have nests, but the Son of Man hath not where to lay His head," I was approached rather hesitatingly by a gentleman, who inquired my name. "My name is Douglass," I replied. "You do not seem to have any place to stay at while in town?" I told him I had not. "Well," said he, "I am no Abolitionist, but if you will go with me I will take care of you." I thanked him, and turned with him towards his fine residence. On the way I asked him his name. "Moses Norris," he said. "What! the Hon. Moses Norris?" I asked. "Yes," he answered. I did not for a moment know what to do, for I had read that this same man had literally dragged the Reverend George Storrs from the pulpit for preaching Abolitionism. I, however, walked along with him and was invited into his house, when I heard the children running and screaming "Mother, mother, there is a nigger in the house, there's a nigger in the house"; and it was with some difficulty that Mr. Norris succeeded in quieting the tumult. I saw that Mrs. Norris, too, was much disturbed by my presence, and I thought for a moment of beating a retreat, but the kind assurance of Mr. Norris decided me to stay. When quiet was restored, I ventured the experiment of asking Mrs. Norris to do me a kindness. I said, "Mrs. Norris, I have taken cold, and am hoarse from speaking, and I have found that nothing relieves me so readily as a little loaf sugar and cold water." The lady's manner changed, and with her own hands she brought me the water and sugar. I thanked her with genuine earnestness, and from that moment I could see that her prejudices were more than half gone, and that I was more than half welcome at the fireside of this Democratic Senator. I spoke again in the evening, and at the close of the meeting there was quite a contest between Mrs. Norris and Mrs. Hilles, as to which I should go home with. I considered Mrs. Hilles' kindness to me, though her manner had been formal; I knew the cause, and I thought, especially as my carpet-bag was there, I would go with her. So giving Mr. and Mrs. Norris many thanks, I bade them good-bye, and went home with Mr. and Mrs. Hilles, where I found the atmosphere wonderously and most agreeably changed. Next day, Mr. Hilles took me in the same carriage in which I did not ride on Sunday, to my next appointment, and on the way told me he felt more honoured by having me in it, than he would be if he had the President of the United States. This compliment would have been a little more flattering to my self-esteem, had not John Tyler then occupied the Presidential chair.

In those unhappy days of the Republic, when all presumptions were in favour of slavery, and a coloured man as a slave met less resistance in the use of public conveyances than a coloured man as a freeman, I happened to be in Philadelphia, and was afforded an opportunity to witness this preference. I took a seat in a street car by the side of my friend Mrs. Amy Post, of Rochester, New York, who, like myself, had come to Philadelphia to attend an anti-slavery meeting. I had no sooner seated myself when the conductor hastened to remove me from the car. My friend remonstrated, and the amazed conductor said, "Lady, does he belong to you?" "He does," said Mrs. Post, and there the matter ended. I was allowed to ride in peace, not because I was a man, and had paid my fare, but because I belonged to somebody. My colour was no longer offensive when it was supposed that I was not a person, but a piece of property.

Another time, in the same city, I took a seat, unobserved, far up in the street car, among the white passengers. All at once I heard the conductor, in an angry tone, order another coloured man, who was modestly standing on the platform of the rear end of the car, to get off, and actually stopped the car to push him off, when I, from within, with all the emphasis I could throw into my voice, in imitation of my chivalrous friend Marshall of Kentucky, sung out, "Go on! let the gentleman alone; no one here objects to his riding!" Unhappily the fellow saw where the voice came from, and turned his wrathful attention to me, and said, "You shall get out also!" I told him I would do no such thing, and if he attempted to remove me by force he would do it at his peril. Whether the young man was afraid to tackle me, or did not wish to disturb the passengers, I do not know. At any rate he did not attempt to execute his threat, and I rode on in peace till I reached Chestnut Street, when I got off and went about my business.

On my way down the Hudson river, from Albany to New York, at one time, on the steamer "Alida," in company with some English ladies who had seen me in their own country, received and treated me as a gentleman, I ventured, like any other passenger, to go, at the call of the dinner bell, into the cabin and take a seat at the table; but I was forcibly taken from it and compelled to leave the cabin. My friends, who wished to enjoy a day's trip on the beautiful Hudson, left the table with me, and went to New York hungry, and not a little indignant and disgusted at such barbarism. There were influential persons on board the "Alida," on this occasion, a word from whom might have spared me this indignity; but there was no Edward Marshall among them to defend the weak and rebuke the strong.

When Miss Sarah Jane Clark, one of America's brilliant literary ladies, known to the world under the nom de plume of Grace Greenwood, was young, and as brave as she was beautiful, I encountered a similar experience to that on the Alida on one of the Ohio river steamers; and that lady, being on board, arose from her seat at the table, expressed her disapprobation, and moved majestically away with her sister to the upper deck. Her conduct seemed to amaze the lookers on, but it filled me with grateful admiration.

When on my way to attend the great Free Soil Convention at Pittsburg, in 1852, which nominated John P. Hale for President, and George W. Julian for Vice-President, the train stopped for dinner at Alliance, Ohio, and I attempted to enter the hotel with the other delegates, but was rudely repulsed, when many of them, learning of it, rose from the table, and denouncing the outrage, refused to finish their dinners.

In anticipation of our return, at the close of the Convention, Mr. Sam. Beck, the proprietor of the hotel, prepared dinner for three hundred guests, but when the train arrived, not one of the large company went into his place, and his dinner was left to spoil.

A dozen years ago, or more, on one of the frostiest and coldest nights I ever experienced, I delivered a lecture in the town of Elmwood, Illinois, twenty miles distant from Peoria. It was one of those bleak and flinty nights, when prairie winds pierce like needles, and a step on the snow sounds like a file on the steel teeth of a saw. My next appointment after Elmwood was on Monday night, and in order to reach it in time it was necessary to go to Peoria the night previous, so as to take an early morning train, and I could only accomplish this by leaving Elmwood after my lecture at midnight, for there was no Sunday train. So a little before the hour at which my train was expected at Elmwood, I started for the station with my friend Mr. Brown, the gentleman who had kindly entertained me during my stay. On the way I said to him, "I am going to Peoria with something like a real dread of the place. I expect to be compelled to walk the streets of that city all night to keep from freezing." I told him "that the last time I was there I could obtain no shelter at any hotel, and that I feared I should meet a similar exclusion to-night." Mr. Brown was visibly affected by the statement, and for some time was silent. At last, as if suddenly discovering a way out of a painful situation, he said, "I know a man in Peoria, should the hotels be closed against you there, who would gladly open his doors to you—a man who will receive you at any hour of the night, and in any weather, and that man is Robert J. Ingersoll." "Why," said I, "it would not do to disturb a family at such a time as I shall arrive there, on a night so cold as this." "No matter about the hour," he said; "neither he nor his family would be happy if they thought you were shelterless on such a night. I know Mr. Ingersoll, and that he will be glad to welcome you at midnight or at cock-crow." I became much interested by this description of Mr. Ingersoll. Fortunately I had no occasion for disturbing him or his family. I found quarters at the best hotel in the city for the night. In the morning I resolved to know more of this now famous and noted "infidel." I gave him an early call, for I was not so abundant in cash as to refuse hospitality in a strange city when on a mission of "good will to men." The experiment worked admirably. Mr. Ingersoll was at home, and if I have ever met a man with real living human sunshine in his face, and honest, manly kindness in his voice, I met one who possessed these qualities that morning. I received a welcome from Mr. Ingersoll and his family which would have been a cordial to the bruised heart of any proscribed and storm-beaten stranger, and one which I can never forget nor fail to appreciate. Perhaps there were Christian ministers and Christian families in Peoria at that time, by whom I might have been received in the same gracious manner. In charity I am bound to say there probably were such ministers and such families, but I am equally bound to say that in my former visits to that place I had failed to find them. Incidents of this character have greatly tended to liberalize my views as to the value of creeds in estimating the character of men. They have brought me to the conclusion that genuine goodness is the same, whether found inside or outside the Church, and that to be an "infidel" no more proves a man to be selfish, mean, and wicked, than to be evangelical proves him to be honest, just, and humane.

It may possibly be inferred from what I have said of the prevalence of prejudice, and the practice of proscription, that I have had a very miserable sort of life, or that I must be remarkably insensible to public aversion. Neither inference is true. I have neither been miserable because of the ill-feeling of those about me, nor indifferent to popular approval; and I think, upon the whole, I have passed a tolerably cheerful and even joyful life. I have never felt myself isolated since I entered the field to plead the cause of the slave, and demand equal rights for all. In every town and city where it has been my lot to speak, there have been raised up for me friends of both colours to cheer and strengthen me in my work. I have always felt, too, that I had on my side all the invisible forces of the moral government of the universe. Happily for me I have had the wit to distinguish between what is merely artificial and transient and what is fundamental and permanent, and resting on the latter, I could cheerfully encounter the former. "How do you feel," said a friend to me, "when you are hooted and jeered in the street on account of your colour?" "I feel as if an ass had kicked but had hit nobody," was my answer.

I have been greatly helped to bear up under unfriendly conditions, too, by a constitutional tendency to see the funny sides of things, which has enabled me to laugh at follies that others would soberly resent. Besides, there were compensations as well as drawbacks in my relations to the white race. A passenger on the deck of a Hudson River steamer, covered with a shawl, well-worn and dingy, I was addressed by a remarkably-religiously-missionary-looking man in black coat and white cravat, who took me for one of the noble red men of the far West, with "From away back?" I was silent, and he added, "Indian, Indian?" "No, no," I said; "I am a negro." The dear man seemed to have no missionary work with me, and retreated with evident marks of disgust.

On another occasion, travelling by a night train on the New York Central railroad, when the cars were crowded and seats were scarce, and I was occupying a whole seat, the only luxury my colour afforded me in travelling, I had lain down with my head partly covered, thinking myself secure in my possession, when a well dressed man approached and wished to share the seat with me. Slightly rising, I said, "Don't sit down here, my friend, I am a nigger." "I don't care who the devil you are," he said, "I mean to sit with you." "Well, if it must be so," I said, "I can stand it if you can," and we at once fell into a very pleasant conversation, and passed the hours on the road very happily together. These two incidents illustrate my career in respect of popular prejudice. If I have had kicks, I have also had kindness. If cast down, I have been exalted; and the latter experience has, after all, far exceeded the former.

During a quarter of a century I resided in the city of Rochester, N.Y. When I removed from there, my friends caused a marble bust of me to be carved, and since honoured it with a place in Sibley Hall, Rochester University. Less in a spirit of vanity than that of gratitude, I copy here the remarks of the Rochester Democrat and Chronicle on the occasion, and on my letter of thanks for the honour done me by my friends and fellow-citizens of that beautiful city:

Rochester, June 28, 1879

FREDERICK DOUGLASS.

"It will be remembered that a bust of Frederick Douglass was recently placed in Sibley Hall of the University of Rochester. The ceremonies were quite informal, too informal, we think, as commemorating a deserved tribute from the people of Rochester to one who will always rank as among her most distinguished citizens. Mr. Douglass himself was not notified officially of the event, and therefore could, in no public manner, take notice of it. He was, however, informed privately of it by the gentleman whose address is given below, and responded to it most happily, as will be seen by the following letter which we are permitted to publish." Then follows the letter which I omit, and add the further comments of the Chronicle. "It were alone worth all the efforts of the gentlemen who united in the fitting recognition of the public services and the private worth of Frederick Douglass, to have inspired a letter thus tender in its sentiment, and so suggestive of the various phases of a career than which the republic has witnessed none more strange or more noble. Frederick Douglass can hardly be said to have risen to greatness on account of the opportunities which the republic offers to self-made men, and concerning which we are apt to talk with an abundance of self-gratulation. It sought to fetter his mind equally with his body. For him it built no school-house, and for him it erected no church. So far as he was concerned freedom was a mockery, and law was the instrument of tyranny. In spite of law and gospel, despite of statutes which thralled him and opportunities which jeered at him, he made himself, by trampling on the law and breaking through the thick darkness that encompassed him. There is no sadder commentary upon American slavery than the life of Frederick Douglass. He put it under his feet and stood erect in the majesty of his intellect; but how many intellects as brilliant and as powerful as his it stamped upon and crushed, no mortal can tell until the secrets of its terrible despotism are fully revealed. Thanks to the conquering might of American freemen, such sad beginnings of such illustrious lives as that of Frederick Douglas are no longer possible; and that they are no longer possible, is largely due to him who, when his lips were unlocked, became a deliverer of his people. Not alone did his voice proclaim emancipation. Eloquent as was that voice, his life in its pathos and in its grandeur, was more eloquent still, and where shall be found, in the annals of humanity, a sweeter rendering of poetic justice than that he, who has passed through such vicissitudes of degradation and exaltation, has been permitted to behold the redemption of his race?

"Rochester is proud to remember that Frederick Douglass was, for many years, one of her citizens. He who pointed out the house where Douglass lived, hardly exaggerated when he called it the residence of the greatest of our citizens; for Douglass must rank as among the greatest men, not only of this city, but of the nation as well—great in gifts, greater in utilizing them; great in his inspiration, greater in his efforts for humanity; great in the persuasion of his speech, greater in the purpose that informed it.

"Rochester could do nothing more graceful than to perpetuate in marble the features of this citizen in her hall of learning; and it is pleasant for her to know that he so well appreciates the esteem in which he is held here. It was a thoughtful thing for Rochester to do, and the response is as heartfelt as the tribute is appropriate."

CHAPTER XVIII: "HONOUR TO WHOM HONOUR."

Grateful recognition—H. Beecher Stowe—Other Friends—Woman suffrage—Failure of Male Governments.

GRATITUDE to benefactors is a well recognised virtue, and to express it in some form or other, however imperfectly, is a duty to ourselves as well as to those who have helped us. Never reluctant or tardy, I trust, in the discharge of this duty, I have seldom been satisfied with the manner of its performance. When I have made my best effort in this line, my words have done small justice to my feelings. And now, in mentioning my obligations to my special friends, and acknowledging the help I received from them in the days of my need, I can hope to do no better than give a faint hint of my sense of the value of their friendship and assistance. I have sometimes been credited with having been the architect of my own fortune, and have pretty generally received the title of a "self-made man;" and while I cannot altogether disclaim this title, when I look back over the facts of my life, and consider the helpful influences exerted upon me, by friends more fortunately born and educated than myself, I am compelled to give them at least an equal measure of credit, with myself, for the success which has attended my labours in life. The little energy, industry and perseverance which have been mine, would hardly have availed me, in the absence of thoughtful friends, and highly favouring circumstances. Without these, the last forty years of my life might have been spent on the wharves of New Bedford, rolling oil casks, loading ships for whaling voyages, sawing wood, putting in coal, picking up a job here and there, wherever I could find one, holding my own with difficulty against gauntsided poverty, in the race for life and bread. I never see one of my old companions of the lower strata, begrimed by toil, hard handed, and dust covered, receiving for wages scarcely enough to keep the "wolf" at a respectful distance from his door and hearthstone, without a fellow feeling and the thought that I have been separated from him only by circumstances other than those of my own making. Much to be thankful for, but little room for boasting here. It was mine to take the "Tide at its flood." It was my good fortune to get out of slavery at the right time, and to be speedily brought into contact with that circle of highly cultivated men and women, banded together for the overthrow of slavery, of which Wm. Lloyd Garrison was the acknowledged leader. To these friends, earnest, courageous, inflexible, ready to own me as a man and brother, against all the scorn, contempt, and derision of a slavery-polluted atmosphere, I owe my success in life. The story is simple, and the truth plain. They thought that I possessed qualities that might be made useful to my race, and through them I was brought to the notice of the world, and gained a hold upon the attention of the American people, which I hope remains unbroken to this day.

Observing woman's agency, devotion, and efficiency in pleading the cause of the slave, gratitude for this high service early moved me to give favourable attention to the subject of what is called "Woman's Rights," and caused me to be denominated a woman's-rights-man. I am glad to say I have never been ashamed to be thus designated. Recognising not sex, nor physical strength, but moral intelligence and the ability to discern right from wrong, good from evil, and the power to choose between them, as the true basis of Republican Government, to which all are alike subject, and bound alike to obey, I was not long in reaching the conclusion that there was no foundation in reason or justice for woman's exclusion from the right of choice in the selection of the persons who should frame the laws, and thus shape the destiny of all the people, irrespective of sex.

In a conversation with Mrs. Elizabeth Cady Stanton, when she was yet a young lady, and an earnest abolitionist, she was at the pains to set before me, in a very strong light, the wrong and injustice of this exclusion. I could not meet her arguments except with the shallow plea of "custom," "natural division of duties," "indelicacy of woman's taking part in politics," the common talk of "woman's sphere," and the like, all of which that able woman, who was then no less logical than now, brushed away by those arguments which she has so often and effectively used since, and which no man has yet successfully refuted. If intelligence is the only true and rational basis of government, it follows that that is the best government which draws its life and power from the largest sources of wisdom, energy, and goodness at its command. The force of this reasoning would be easily comprehended and readily assented to in any case involving the employment of physical strength. We should all see the folly and madness of attempting to accomplish with a part what could only be done with the united strength of the whole. Though this folly may be less apparent, it is just as real, when one-half of the moral and intellectual power of the world is excluded from any voice or vote in civil government. In this denial of the right to participate in government, not merely the degradation of woman and the perpetuation of a great injustice happens, but the maiming and repudiation of one-half of the moral and intellectual power for the government of the world. Thus far all human governments have been failures, for none have secured, except in a partial degree, the ends for which governments are instituted.

War, slavery, injustice, and oppression, and the idea that might makes right, have been uppermost in all such governments; and the weak, for whose protection governments are ostensibly created, have had practically no rights which the strong have felt bound to respect. The slayers of thousands have been exalted into heroes, and the worship of mere physical force has been considered glorious. Nations have been, and still are, but armed camps, expending their wealth, and strength, and ingenuity, in forging weapons of destruction against each other; and while it may not be contended that the introduction of the feminine element in government would entirely cure this tendency to exalt might over right, many reasons can be given to show that woman's influence would greatly tend to check and modify this barbarous and destructive tendency. At any rate, seeing that the male governments of the world have failed, it can do no harm to try the experiment of a government by man and woman united. But it is not my purpose to argue the question here, but simply to state, in a brief way, the ground of my espousal of the cause of woman's suffrage. I believed that the exclusion of my race from participation in government was not only a wrong, but a great mistake, because it took from that race motives for high thought and endeavour, and degraded them in the eyes of the world around them. Man derives a sense of his consequence in the world not merely subjectively, but objectively. If from the cradle through life the outside world brands a class as unfit for this or that work, the character of that class will come to resemble and conform to the character described. To find valuable qualities in our fellows, such qualities must be presumed and expected. I would give woman a vote, give her a motive to qualify herself to vote, precisely as I insisted upon giving the coloured man the right to vote, in order that he should have the same motives for making himself a useful citizen as those in force in the case of other citizens. In a word, I have never yet been able to find one consideration, one argument, or suggestion in favour of man's right to participate in civil government which did not equally apply to the right of woman.

CHAPTER XIX

Interment of the late James A. Garfield—Brief references to the solemn event—Account of an interview at the Executive Mansion—His recognition of the rights of coloured citizens.

ON the day of the interment of the late James A. Garfield, at Lake View Cemetery, Cleveland, Ohio, a day of gloom long to be remembered as the closing scene in one of the most tragic and startling dramas ever witnessed in this, or in any other country, the coloured people of the District of Columbia assembled in the Fifteenth Street Presbyterian church, and expressed by appropriate addresses and resolutions, their respect for the character and memory of the illustrious deceased. On that occasion I was called upon to preside, and by way of introducing the subsequent proceedings,—leaving to others the grateful office of delivering eulogies—made the following brief reference to the solemn and touching event:—

"Friends and fellow citizens:

To-day our common mother Earth has closed over the mortal remains of James A. Garfield, at Cleveland, Ohio. The light of no day in our national history has brought to the American people a more intense bereavement, a deeper sorrow, or a more profound sense of humiliation.

It seems only as yesterday, that in my quality as United States Marshal of the District of Columbia, it was made my duty and privilege to walk at the head of the column in advance of this our President-elect, from the crowded Senate Chamber of the National Capitol, through the long corridors, and the grand rotunda, beneath the majestic dome, to the platform on the portico, where amid a sea of transcendent pomp and glory, he who is now dead, was hailed with tumultuous applause from uncounted thousands of his fellow citizens, and was inaugurated Chief Magistrate of the United States. The scene was one never to be forgotten by those who beheld it. It was a great day for the nation, glad and proud to do honour to their chosen ruler. It was a glad day for James A. Garfield. It was a glad day for me, that I—one of the proscribed race, was permitted to bear so prominent a part in its august ceremonies. Mr. Garfield was then in the midst of his years, in the fulness and vigour of his manhood, covered with honours beyond the reach of princes, entering upon a career more abundant in promise than ever invited president or potentate before.

Alas, what a contrast, as he lay in state under the same broad dome, viewed by sorrowful thousands day after day! What is the life of man? What are all his plans, purposes, and hopes? What are the shouts of the multitude, the pride and pomp of this world? How vain and unsubstantial, in the light of this sad and shocking experience, do they all appear! Who can tell what a day or an hour will bring forth? Such reflections inevitably present themselves, as most natural and fitting on an occasion like this.

Fellow citizens, we are here to take suitable notice of the sad and appalling event of the hour. We are here, not merely as American citizens, but as coloured American citizens. Although our hearts have gone along with those of the nation at large, with every expression, with every token and demonstration of honour to the dead, sympathy with the living, and abhorrence for the horrible deed which has at last done its fatal work; though we have watched with beating hearts, the long and heroic struggle for life, and endured all the agony of suspense and fear; we have felt that something more, something more specific and distinctive, was due from us. Our relation to the American people makes us in some sense a peculiar class, and unless we speak separately, our voice is not heard. We therefore propose to put on record to-night our sense of the worth of President Garfield, and of the calamity involved in his death. Called to preside on this occasion, my part in the speaking shall be brief. I cannot claim to have been on intimate terms with the late President. There are other gentlemen here, who are better qualified to speak of his character than myself. I must say, however, that soon after he came to Washington I had a conversation with him of much interest to the coloured people, since it indicated his just and generous intentions towards them, and goes far to present him in the light of a wise and patriotic statesman, and a friend of our race.

I called at the Executive Mansion, and was received very kindly by Mr. Garfield, who, in the course of the conversation said, that he felt the time had come when a step should be taken in advance, in recognition of the claims of coloured citizens, and expressed his intention of sending some coloured representatives abroad to other than coloured nations. He enquired of me how I thought such representations would be received? I assured him that I thought they would be well received; that in my own experience abroad, I had observed that the higher we go in the gradations of human society, the farther we get from prejudice of race or colour. I was greatly pleased with the assurance of his liberal policy towards us. I remarked to him, that no part of the American people would be treated with respect, if systematically ignored by the Government, and denied all participation in its honours and emoluments. To this he assented, and went so far as to propose my going in a representative capacity to an important post abroad—a compliment which I gratefully acknowledged, but respectfully declined. To say the truth, I wished to remain at home, and retain the office of United States Marshal of the District of Columbia.

It is a great thing for the Honourable John Mercer Langston to represent this Republic at Port au Prince, and for Henry Highland Garnet to represent us in Liberia, but it would be indeed a step in advance, to have some coloured men sent to represent us in white nationalities, and we have reason for profound regret that Mr. Garfield could not live to carry out his just and wise intentions towards us. I might say more of this conversation, but I will not detain you except to say, that America has had many great men, but no man among them all, has had better things said of him, than he who has been reverently committed to the dust in Cleveland to-day."

Mr. Douglass then called upon Professor Greener, who read a series of resolutions eloquently expressive of their sense of the great loss that had been sustained, and their sympathy with the family of the late President. Professor Greener then spoke briefly and was followed by Professor John M. Langston and Rev. W. W. Hicks. All the speakers expressed their confidence in President Arthur and in his ability to give the country a wise and beneficial administration.

CONCLUSION

As far as this volume can reach that point, I have now brought my readers to the end of my story. What may remain of life to me, through what experiences I may pass, what heights I may attain, into what depths I may fall, what good or ill may come to me, or proceed from me in this breathing world, where all is change, uncertainty, and largely at the mercy of powers over which the individual man has no absolute control, if thought worthy and useful, will probably be told by others when I have passed from the busy stage of life. I am not looking for any great changes in my fortunes or achievements in the future. The most of the space of life is behind me, and the sun of my day is nearing the horizon. Notwithstanding all that is contained in this book, my day has been a pleasant one. My joys have far exceeded my sorrows, and my friends have brought me far more than my enemies have taken from me. I have written out my experience here, not to exhibit my wounds and bruises, to awaken and attract sympathy to myself personally, but as a part of the history of a profoundly interesting period in American life and progress. I have meant it to be a small individual contribution to the sum of knowledge of this special period, to be handed down to after-coming generations which-may want to know what things were allowed and what prohibited; what moral, social, and political relations subsisted between the different varieties of the American people down to the last quarter of the nineteenth century; and by what means they were modified and changed. The time is at hand when the last American slave, and the last American slaveholder will disappear behind the curtain which separates the living from the dead, and when neither master nor slave will be left to tell the story of their respective relations, and what has happened in those relations to either. My part has been to tell the story of the slave. The story of the master never wanted for narrators. They have had all the talent and genius that wealth and influence could command, to tell their story. They have had their full day in court. Literature, theology, philosophy law, and learning, have come willingly to their service, and if condemned they have not been condemned unheard.

It will be seen in these pages that I have lived several lives in one. First, the life of slavery; secondly, the life of a fugitive from slavery; thirdly, the life of comparative freedom; fourthly, the life of conflict and battle; and fifthly, the life of victory, if not complete, at least assured. To those who have suffered in slavery, I can say, I too have suffered. To those who have taken some risks and encountered hardships in the flight from bondage, I can say, I too have endured and risked. To those who have battled for liberty, brotherhood, and citizenship, I can say, I too have battled; and to those who have lived to enjoy the fruits of victory, I can say, I too live and rejoice. If I have pushed my example too prominently for the good taste of my Caucasian readers, I beg them to remember that I have written in part for the encouragement of a class whose inspirations need the stimulus of success.

I have aimed to assure them that knowledge can be obtained under difficulties; that poverty may give place to competency; that obscurity is not an absolute bar to distinction, and that a way is open to welfare and happiness for all who will resolutely and wisely pursue that way; that neither slavery, stripes, imprisonment, nor proscription, need extinguish self-respect, crush manly ambition, nor paralyze effort; that no power outside of himself can prevent a man from sustaining an honourable character and a useful relation to his day and generation; that neither institutions nor friends can make a race to stand, unless it has strength in its own legs; that there is no power in the world which can be relied upon to help the weak against the strong—the simple against the wise; that races like individuals must stand or fall by their own merits; that all the prayers of Christendom cannot stop the force of a single bullet, divest arsenic of poison, or suspend any law of nature. In my communication with the coloured people I have endeavoured to deliver them from the power of superstition, bigotry, and priestcraft. In theology I have found them strutting about in the old clothes of the masters, just as the masters strut about in the old clothes of the past. The falling power remains among them long after it has ceased to be the religious fashion of our refined and elegant white churches. I have taught that the "fault is not in our stars but in ourselves that we are underlings," that "who would be free, themselves must strike the blow." I have urged upon them self-reliance, self-respect, industry, perseverance, and economy—to make the best of both worlds—but to make the best of this world first, because it comes first, and that he who does not improve himself by the motives and opportunities afforded by this world, gives the best evidence that he would not improve in any other world. Schooled as I have been among the abolitionists of New England, I recognise that the universe is governed by laws which are unchangeable and eternal, that what men sow they will reap, and that there is no way to dodge or circumvent the consequences of any act or deed. My views at this point receive but limited endorsement among my people. They for the most part think they have means of procuring special favour and help from the Almighty, and as their "faith is the substance of things hoped for and the evidence of things not seen," they find much in this expression which is true to faith but utterly false to fact. But I meant here only to say a word in conclusion. Forty years of my life have been given to the cause of my people, and if I had forty years more they should all be sacredly given to that great cause. If I have done something for that cause, I am after all more a debtor to it than it is debtor to me.

APPENDIX A.

WEST INDIA EMANCIPATION.

Extract from a speech delivered by Frederick Douglass in Elmira, N. Y., August 1, 1880, at a great meeting of coloured people, met to celebrate West India emancipation, and where he was received with marked respect and approval by the president of the day and the immense crowd there assembled. It is placed in this book partly as a grateful tribute to the noble transatlantic men and women through whose unwearied exertions the system of negro slavery was finally abolished in all the British Isles.

Mr. President;—I thank you very sincerely for this cordial greeting. I hear in your speech something like a welcome home after a long absence. More years of my life and labours have been spent in this than in any other State of the Union. Anywhere within a hundred miles of the goodly city of Rochester, I feel myself at home and among friends. Within that circumference, there resides a people which have no superior in points of enlightenment, liberality, and civilization. Allow me to thank you also, for your generous words of sympathy and approval. In respect to this important support of a public man, I have been unusually fortunate. My forty years of work in the cause of the oppressed and enslaved, have been well noted, well appreciated, and well rewarded. All classes and colours of men, at home and abroad, have in this way assisted in holding up my hands. Looking back through these long years of toil and conflict, during which I have had blows to take as well as blows to give, and have sometimes received wounds and bruises, both in body and in mind; my only regret is that I have been enabled to do so little to lift up and strengthen our long enslaved and still oppressed people. My apology for these remarks personal to myself, is in the fact that I am now standing mainly in the presence of a new generation. Most of the men with whom I lived and laboured in the early years of the abolition movement, have passed beyond the borders of this life. Scarcely any of the coloured men who advocated our cause, and who started when I did, are now numbered among the living, and I begin to feel somewhat lonely. But while I have the sympathy and approval of men and women like these before me, I shall give with joy my latest breath in support of your claim to justice, liberty, and equality among men. The day we celebrate is preeminently the coloured man's day. The great event by which it is distinguished, and by which it will for ever be distinguished from all other days of the year, has justly claimed thoughtful attention among statesmen and social reformers throughout the world. While to them it is a luminous point in human history, and worthy of thought in the coloured man, it addresses not merely the intelligence, but the feeling. The emancipation of our brethren in the West Indies comes home to us, stirs our hearts, and fills our souls with those grateful sentiments which link mankind in a common brotherhood.

In the history of the American conflict with slavery, the day we celebrate has played an important part. Emancipation in the West Indies was the first bright star in a stormy sky; the first smile after a long providential frown; the first ray of hope; the first tangible fact demonstrating the possibility of a peaceful transition from slavery to freedom of the negro race. Whoever else may forget or slight the claims of this day, it can never be other to us than memorable and glorious. The story of it shall be brief and soon told. Six-and-forty years ago, on the day we now celebrate, there went forth over the blue waters of the Carribean sea a great message from the British throne, hailed with startling shouts of joy, and thrilling songs of praise. That message liberated, set free, and brought within the pale of civilization eight hundred thousand people, who, till then, had been esteemed as beasts of burden. How vast, sudden, and startling was this transformation! In one moment, a mere tick of a watch, the twinkle of an eye, the glance of the morning sun, saw a bondage which had resisted the humanity of ages, defied earth and heaven, instantly ended; saw the slave-whip burnt to ashes; saw the slave's chains melted; saw his fetters broken, and the irresponsible power of the slave-master over his victim for ever destroyed.

I have been told by eye-witnesses of the scene, that, in the first moment of it, the emancipated hesitated to accept it for what it was. They did not know whether to receive it as a reality, a dream, or a vision of the fancy.

No wonder they were thus amazed, and doubtful, after their terrible years of darkness and sorrow, which seemed to have no end. Like much other good news, it was thought too good to be true. But the silence and hesitation they observed was only momentary. When fully assured the good tidings which had come across the sea to them were not only good, but true; that they were indeed no longer slaves, but free; that the lash of the slave-driver was no longer in the air, but buried in the earth; that their limbs were no longer chained, but subject to their own will, the manifestations of their joy and gratitude knew no bounds, and sought expression in the loudest and wildest possible forms. They ran about, they danced, they sang, they gazed into the blue sky, bounded into the air, kneeled, prayed, shouted, rolled upon the ground, embraced each other. They laughed and wept for joy. Those who witnessed the scene say they never saw anything like it before.

We are sometimes asked why we American citizens annually celebrate West India emancipation when we might celebrate American emancipation. Why go abroad, say they, when we might as well stay at home?

The answer is easily given. Human liberty excludes all idea of home and abroad. It is universal and spurns localization.

- "When the deed is done for freedom,

- Through the broad earth's aching breast

- Runs a thrill of joy prophetic,

- Trembling on from East to West."

It is bounded by no geographical lines, and knows no national limitations. Like the glorious sun of the heavens, its light shines for all. But besides this general consideration, this boundless power and glory of liberty, West India Emancipation has claims upon us as an event in this nineteenth century in which we live, for rich as this century is in moral and material achievements, in progress and civilization, it can claim nothing for itself greater and grander than this act of West India Emancipation.

Whether we consider the matter or the manner of it, the tree or its fruit, it is noteworthy, memorable, and sublime. Especially is the manner of its accomplishment worthy of consideration. Its best lesson to the world, its most encouraging word to all who toil and trust in the cause of justice and liberty, to all who oppose oppression and slavery, is a word of sublime faith and courage—faith in the truth and courage in the expression.

Great and valuable concessions have in different ages been made to the liberties of mankind. They have, however, come not at the command of reason and persuasion, but by the sharp and terrible edge of the sword. To this rule West India Emancipation is a splendid exception. It came not by the sword, but by the word; not by the brute force of numbers, but by the still small voice of truth; not by barricades, bayonets, and bloody revolution, but by peaceful agitation; not by divine interference, but by the exercise of simple human reason and feeling. I repeat that, in this peculiarity, we have what is most valuable to the human race generally.

It is a revelation of a power inherent in human society. It shows what can be done against wrong in the world, without the aid of armies on the earth or of angels in the sky. It shows that men have in their own hands the peaceful means of putting all their moral and political enemies under their feet, and of making this world a healthy and happy dwelling-place, if they will faithfully and courageously use them.

The world needed just such a revelation of the power of conscience and of human brotherhood, one that overleaped the accident of colour and of race, and set at naught the whisperings of prejudice. The friends of freedom in England saw in the negro a man, a moral and responsible being. Having settled this in their own minds, they, in the name of humanity, denounced the crime of his enslavement. It was the faithful, persistent, and enduring enthusiasm of Thomas Clarkson, William Wilberforce, Granville Sharp, William Knibb, Henry Brougham, Thomas Fowell Buxton, Daniel O'Connell, George Thompson, and their noble co-workers, that finally thawed the British heart into sympathy for the slave, and moved the strong arm of that Government in mercy to put an end to his bondage.

Let no American, especially no coloured American, withhold a generous recognition of this stupendous achievement. What though it was not American, but British; what though it was not Republican, but Monarchical; what though it was not from the American Congress, but from the British Parliament; what though it was not from the chair of a President, but from the throne of a Queen, it was none the less a triumph of right over wrong, of good over evil, and a victory for the whole human race.

Besides: We may properly celebrate this day because of its special relation to our American Emancipation. In doing this we do not sacrifice the general to the special, the universal to the local. The cause of human liberty is one the whole world over. The downfall of slavery under British power meant the downfall of slavery, ultimately, under American power, and the downfall of negro slavery everywhere. But the effect of this great and philanthropic measure, naturally enough, was greater here than elsewhere. Outside the British Empire no other nation was in a position to feel it so much as we. The stimulus it gave to the American anti-slavery movement was immediate, pronounced, and powerful. British example became a tremendous lever in the hands of American abolitionists. It did much to shame and discourage the spirit of caste and the advocacy of slavery in church and state, It could not well have been otherwise. No man liveth unto himself.

What is true in this respect of individual men, is equally true of nations. Both impart good or ill to their age and generation. But putting aside this consideration, so worthy of thought, we have special reasons for claiming the 1st of August as the birthday of negro emancipation, not only in the West Indies, but in the United States. Spite of our national Independence, a common language, a common literature, a common history, a common civilization makes us and keeps us still a part of the British nation, if not a part of the British Empire. England can take no step forward in the pathway of a higher civilization without drawing us in the same direction, She is still the mother country, and the mother, too, of our abolition movement. Though her emancipation came in peace, and ours in war; though hers cost treasure, and ours blood; though hers was the result of a sacred preference, and ours resulted in part from necessity, the motive and mainspring of the respective measures were the same in both.

The abolitionists of this country have been charged with bringing on the war between the North and South, and in one sense this is true. Had there been no anti-slavery agitation at the North, there would have been no anti-slavery anywhere to resist the demands of the slave-power at the South, and where there is no resistance there can be no war. Slavery would then have been nationalized, and the whole country would then have been subjected to its power. Resistance to slavery and the extension of slavery invited and provoked secession and war to perpetuate and extend the slave system. Thus, in the same sense, England is responsible for our civil war. The abolition of slavery in the West Indies gave life and vigour to the abolition movement in America. Clarkson of England gave us Garrison of America; Granville Sharpe of England gave us our Wendell Phillips; and Wilberforce of England gave us our peerless Charles Sumner.

These grand men and their brave co-workers here, took up the moral thunder-bolts which had struck down slavery in the West Indies, and hurled them with increased zeal and power against the gigantic system of slavery here, till, goaded to madness, the traffickers in the souls and bodies of men flew to arms, rent asunder the Union at the centre, and filled the land with hostile armies and the ten thousand horrors of war. Out of this tempest, out of this whirlwind and earthquake of war, came the abolition of slavery, came the employment of coloured troops, came coloured citizens, came coloured jurymen, came coloured congressmen, came coloured schools in the South, and came the great amendments of our national constitution.

We celebrate this day, too, for the very good reason that we have no other to celebrate. English emancipation has one advantage over American emancipation. Hers has a definite anniversary. Ours has none. Like our slaves, the freedom of the negro has no birthday. No man can tell the day of the month, or the month of the year, upon which slavery was abolished in the United States. We cannot even tell when it began to be abolished. Like the movement of the sea, no man can tell where one wave begins and another ends. The chains of slavery with us were loosened by degrees. First, we had the struggle in Kansas with border ruffians; next, we had John Brown at Harper's Ferry; next, the firing upon Fort Sumter; a little while after, we had Fremont's order, freeing the slaves of the rebels in Missouri. Then we had General Butler declaring and treating the slaves of rebels as contraband of war; next we had the proposition to arm coloured men and make them soldiers for the Union. In 1862 we had the conditional promise of a Proclamation of Emancipation from President Lincoln; and, finally, on the 1st of January, 1863, we had the proclamation itself—and still the end was not yet. Slavery was bleeding and dying, but it was not dead, and no man can tell just when its foul spirit departed from our land, if indeed it has yet departed, and hence we do not know what day we may properly celebrate as coupled with this great American event.

When England behaved so badly during our late civil war, I, for one, felt like giving up these 1st of August celebrations. But I remembered that during that war, there were two Englands, as there were two Americas, and that one was true to liberty while the other was true to slavery. It was not the England which gave us West India emancipation that took sides with the slaveholders' rebellion. It was not the England of John Bright and William Edward Foster, that permitted Alabama to escape from British ports, and prey upon our commerce, or that otherwise favoured slaveholding in the South, but it was the England which had done what it could to prevent West India emancipation.

It was the Tory party in England that fought the abolition party at home, and it was the same party that favoured our slaveholding rebellion.

Under a different name, we had the same, or a similar party, here; a party which despised the negro and consigned him to perpetual slavery; a party which was willing to allow the American Union to be shivered into fragments, rather than that one hair of the head of slavery should be injured.

But, fellow citizens, I should but very imperfectly fulfil the duty of this hour if I confined myself to a merely historical or philosophical discussion of West India emancipation. The story of the 1st of August has been told a thousand times over, and may be told a thousand times more. The cause of freedom and humanity has a history and destiny nearer home.

How stands the case with the recently emancipated millions of coloured people in our own country? What is their condition to-day? What is their relation to the people who formerly held them as slaves? These are important questions, and they are such as trouble the minds of thoughtful men of all colours, at home and abroad. By law, by the constitution of the United States, slavery has no existence in our country. The legal form has been abolished. By the law of the constitution, the negro is a man and a citizen, and has all the rights and liberties guaranteed to any other variety of the human family, residing in the United States.

He has a country, a flag, and a government, and may legally claim full and complete protection under the laws. It was the ruling wish, intention, and purpose of the loyal people, after rebellion was suppressed, to have an end to the entire cause of that calamity by for ever putting away the system of slavery and all its incidents. In pursuance of this idea, the negro was made free, made a citizen, made eligible to hold office, to be a juryman, a legislator, and a magistrate. To this end, several amendments to the constitution were proposed, recommended, and adopted. They are now a part of the supreme law of the land, binding alike upon every State and Territory of the United States, North and South. Briefly, this is our legal and theoretical condition. This is our condition on paper and parchment. If only from the national statute book we were left to learn the true condition of the coloured race, the result would be altogether creditable to the American people. It would give them a clear title to a place among the most enlightened and liberal nations of the world. We could say of our country, as Curran once said of England, "The spirit of British law makes liberty commensurate with, and inseparable from, the British soil." Now I say that this eloquent tribute to England, if only we looked into our constitution, might apply to us. In that instrument we have laid down the law, now and for ever, and there shall be no slavery or involuntary servitude in this Republic, except for crime.

We have gone still further. We have laid the heavy hand of the constitution upon the matchless meanness of caste, as well as the hell-black crime of slavery, We have declared before all the world that there shall be no denial of rights on account of race, colour, or previous condition of servitude. The advantage gained in this respect is immense.

It is a great thing to have the supreme law of the land on the side of justice and liberty. It is the line up to which the nation is destined to march—the law to which the nation's life must ultimately conform. It is a great principle, up to which we may educate the people, and to this extent its value exceeds all speech.

But to-day, in most of the Southern States, the fourteenth and fifteenth amendments are virtually nullified.

The rights which they were intended to guarantee are denied and held in contempt. The citizenship granted in the fourteenth amendment is practically a mockery, and the right to vote, provided for in the fifteenth amendment, is literally stamped out in face of government. The old master class is to-day triumphant, and the newly-enfranchised class in a condition but little above that in which they were found before the rebellion.

Do you ask me how, after all that has been done, this state of things has been made possible? I will tell you. Our reconstruction measures were radically defective. They left the former slave completely in the power of the old master, the loyal citizen in the hands of the disloyal rebel against the Government. Wise, grand, and comprehensive in scope and design, as were the reconstruction measures, high and honourable as were the intentions of the statesmen by whom they were framed and adopted, time and experience, which try all things, have demonstrated that they did not successfully meet the case.

In the hurry and confusion of the hour, and the eager desire to have the Union restored, there was more care for sublime super-structure of the Republic than for the solid foundation upon which it could alone be upheld. They gave freedmen the machinery of liberty, but denied them the steam to put it in motion. They gave them the uniform of soldiers, but no arms; they called them citizens, and left them subjects; they called them free, and almost left them slaves. They did not deprive the old master class of the power of life and death which was the soul of the relation of master and slave. They could not, of course, sell them, but they retained the power to starve them to death, and wherever this power is held, there is the power of slavery. He who can say to his fellow-man, "You shall serve me or starve," is a master, and his subject is a slave. This was seen and felt by Thaddeus Stevens, Charles Sumner, and leading stalwart Republicans, and had their counsels prevailed the terrible evils from which we now suffer would have been averted. The negro to-day would not be on his knees, as he is, abjectly supplicating the old master class to give him leave to toil. Nor would he now be leaving the South, as from a doomed city, and seeking a home in the uncongenial North, but tilling his native soil in comparative independence. Though no longer a slave, he is in a thraldom grievous and intolerable, compelled to work for whatever his employer is pleased to pay him, swindled out of his hard earnings by money orders redeemed in stores, compelled to pay the price of an acre of ground for its use during a single year, to pay four times more than a fair price for a pound of bacon, and be kept upon the narrowest margin between life and starvation. Much complaint has been made that the freedmen have shown so little ability to take care of themselves since their emancipation. Men have marvelled that they have made so little progress. I question the justice of this complaint. It is neither reasonable, nor in any sense just. To me, the wonder is, not that the freedmen have made so little progress, but, rather, that they have made so much; not that they have been standing still, but that they have been able to stand at all.

We have only to reflect for a moment upon the situation in which these people found themselves when liberated: consider their ignorance, their poverty, their destitution, and their absolute dependence upon the very class by whom they had been held in bondage for centuries, a class whose every sentiment was averse to their freedom, and we shall be prepared to marvel that they have under the circumstances done so well.

History does not furnish an example of emancipation under conditions less friendly to the emancipated class, than this American example. Liberty came to the freedmen of the United States, not in mercy but in wrath; not by moral choice, but by military necessity; not by the generous action of the people among whom they were to live, and whose good will was essential to the success of the measure, but by strangers, foreigners, invaders, trespassers, aliens, and enemies. The very manner of their emancipation invited to the heads of the freedmen the bitterest hostility of race and class. They were hated because they had been slaves, hated because they were now free, and hated because of those who had freed them. Nothing was to have been expected other than what has happened; and he is a poor student of the human heart who does not see that the old master class would naturally employ every power and means in their reach to make the great measure of emancipation unsuccessful and utterly odious. It was born in the tempest and whirlwind of war, and has lived in a storm of violence and blood. When the Hebrews were emancipated, they were told to take spoil from the Egyptians. When the serfs of Russia were emancipated, they were given three acres of ground upon which they could live and make a living. But not so when our slaves were emancipated. They were sent away emptyhanded, without money, without friends, and without a foot of land to stand upon. Old and young, sick and well, were turned loose to the naked sky, naked to their enemies. The old slave quarter that had before sheltered them, and the fields that had yielded them corn, were now denied them. The old master class in its wrath said, "Clear out! The Yankees have freed you, now let them feed and shelter you!"

Inhuman as was this treatment, it was the natural result of the bitter resentment felt by the old master class, and in view of it the wonder is, not that the coloured people of the South have done so little in the way of acquiring a comfortable living, but that they live at all.

Taking all the circumstances into consideration, the coloured people have no reason to despair. We still live, and while there is life there is hope. The fact that we have endured wrongs and hardships, which would have destroyed any other race, and have increased in numbers and public consideration, ought to strengthen our faith in ourselves and our future. Let us then, wherever we are, whether at the North or at the South, resolutely struggle on, in the belief that there is a better day coming, and that we by patience, industry, uprightness, and economy may hasten that better day. I will not listen, myself, and I would not have you listen, to the nonsense, that no people can succeed in life among a people by whom they have been despised and oppressed.

The statement is erroneous, and contradicted by the whole history of human progress. A few centuries ago, all Europe was cursed with serfdom, or slavery. Traces of this bondage still remain but are not easily discernible.

The Jews, only a century ago, were despised, hated, and oppressed, but they have defied, met, and vanquished the hard conditions imposed upon them, and are now opulent and powerful, and compel respect in all countries.

Take courage from the example of all religious denominations that have sprung up since Martin Luther. Each in its turn has been oppressed and persecuted.

Methodists, Baptists, and Quakers, have all been compelled to feel the lash and sting of popular disfavour—yet all in turn have conquered the prejudice and hate of their surroundings.

Greatness does not come to any people on flowery beds of ease. We must fight to win the prize. No people to whom liberty is given can hold it as firmly and wear it as grandly as those who wrench their liberty from the iron hand of the tyrant. The hardships and dangers involved in the struggle give strength and toughness to the character, and enable it to stand firm in storm as well as in sunshine.

One thought more before I leave this subject, and it is a thought I wish you all to lay to heart. Practise it yourselves and teach it to your children. It is this, neither we, nor any other people, will ever be respected till we respect ourselves, and we will never respect ourselves till we have the means to live respectfully. An exceptionally poor and dependent people will be despised by the opulent, and despise themselves.

You cannot make an empty sack stand on end. A race which cannot save its earnings, which spends all it makes and goes in debt when it is ill, can never rise in the scale of civilization, no matter under what laws it may chance to be. Put us in Kansas or in Africa, and until we learn to save more than we spend, we are sure to sink and perish. It is not in the nature of things that we should be equally rich in this world's goods. Some will be more successful than others, and poverty, in many cases, is the result of misfortune rather than of crime; but no race can afford to have all its members the victims of this misfortune, without being considered a worthless race. Pardon me, therefore, for urging upon you, my people, the importance of saving your earnings; of denying yourselves in the present, that you may have something in the future, of consuming less for yourselves that your children may have a start in life when you are gone.

With money and property comes the means of knowledge and power. A poverty-stricken class will be an ignorant and despised class, and no amount of sentiment can make it otherwise. This part of our destiny is in our own hands. Every dollar you lay up, represents one day's independence, one day of rest and security in the future. If the time shall ever come when we shall possess, in the coloured people of the United States, a class of men noted for enterprise, industry, economy, and success, we shall no longer have any trouble in the matter of civil and political rights. The battle against popular prejudice will have been fought and won, and in common with all other races and colours, we shall have an equal chance in the race of life.

APPENDIX B.

FREDERICK DOUGLASS was born a slave, he won his liberty, he is of negro extraction, and consequently was despised and outraged; he has by his own energy and force of character commanded the respect of the American Nation; he was ignorant, he has, against law and by stealth and entirely unaided, educated himself; he was poor, he has by honest toil and industry become rich and independent, so to speak; he, a chattel slave of a hated and cruelly-wronged race, in the teeth of American prejudice and in face of nearly every kind of hindrance and drawback, has come to be one of the foremost orators of the age, with a reputation established on both sides of the Atlantic; a writer of power and elegance of expression; a thinker whose views are potent in controlling and shaping public opinion; a high officer in the National Government; a cultivated gentleman whose virtues as a husband, father, and citizen are the highest honour a man can have.

Frederick Douglass stands upon a pedestal; he has reached this lofty height through years of toil and strife, but it has been the strife of moral ideas; strife in the battle for human rights. No bitter memories come from this strife; no feelings of remorse can rise to cast their gloomy shadows over his soul; Douglass has now reached and passed the meridian of life, his co-labourers in the strife have now nearly all passed away. Garrison has gone, Gerrit Smith has gone, Giddings and Sumner have gone,—nearly all the early abolitionists are gone to their reward. The culmination of his life-work has been reached; the object dear to his heart—the Emancipation of the Slaves—has been accomplished, through the blessings of God; he stands facing the goal, already reached by his co-labourers, with a halo of peace about him, and nothing but serenity and gratitude must fill his breast. To those, who in the past—in ante-bellum days—in any degree shared with Douglass his hopes and feelings on the slavery question, this serenity of mind, this gratitude, can be understood and felt. All Americans, no matter what may have been their views on slavery, now that freedom has come and slavery is ended, must have a restful feeling and be glad that the source of bitterness and trouble is removed. The man who is sorry because of the abolition of slavery, has outlived his day and generation; he should have insisted upon being buried with the "lost cause" at Appomattox.

We rejoice that Douglass has attained unto this exalted position,—this pedestal. It has been honourably reached; it is a just recognition of talent and effort; it is another proof that success attends high and noble aim. With this example, the black boy as well as the white boy, can take hope and courage in the race of life.

For more than forty years he has been before the world as a writer and speaker.

The first twenty-three years of his life were twenty-three years of slavery, obscurity, and degradation, yet doubtless, in time to come these years will be regarded by the student of history as the most interesting portion of his life; to those who in the future would know the inside history of American slavery, this part of his life will be specially instructive. Plantation life at Tuckahoe as related by him is not fiction, it is fact; it is not the historian's dissertation on slavery, it is slavery itself, the slave's life, acts, and thoughts, and the life, acts, and thoughts of those around him.

Col. Lloyd's plantation, where Douglass belonged, was very much like other plantations of the South. Here was the great house and the cabins, the old Aunties and patriarchal Uncles, little picaninnies and picaninnies not so little, of every shade of complexion, from ebony black to whiteness of the master race; mules, overseers, and broken down fences. Here was the negro Doctor learned in the science of roots and herbs; also the black conjurer with his divination. Here was slave-breeding, and slave-selling, whipping, torturing, and whipping to death. All this came under the observation of Douglass and is a part of the education he received while under the yoke of bondage. He was there in the midst of this confusion, ignorance and brutality. Little did the overseer on this plantation think that he had in his gang a man of superior order and undaunted spirit, whose mind, far above the minds of the grovelling creatures about him, was at that very time plotting schemes for his liberty; nor did the thought ever enter the mind of Col. Lloyd, the rich slaveholder, that he had upon his estate one who was destined to assail the system of slavery with more power and effect than any other person.

F. Douglass' fame will rest mainly, no doubt, upon his oratory. His powers in this direction are very great, and in some respects unparalleled by our living speakers. His oratory is his own, and apparently formed after the model of no single person. It is not after the Edmund Burke style, which has been so closely followed by Everett, Sumner, and others, and which has resulted in giving us splendid and highly embellished essays rather than natural and not over-wrought speeches. If his oratory must be classified, it should be placed somewhere between the Fox and Henry Clay schools. Like Clay, Douglass' greatest effect is upon his immediate hearers, those who see him and feel his presence, and like Clay, a good part of his oratorical fame will be tradition. The most striking feature of Douglass' oratory is his fire, not the quick and flashy kind, but the steady and intense kind. Years ago on the anti-slavery platform, in some sudden and unbidden outburst of passion and indignation he has been known to awe-inspire his listeners as though Ætna was there.

If oratory consists of the power to move men by spoken words, Douglass is a complete orator. He can make men laugh or cry, at his will. He has power of statement, logic, withering denunciation, pathos, humour, and inimitable wit. Daniel Webster with his immense intellectuality had no humour, not a particle. It does not appear that he could even see the point of a joke. Douglass is brim full of humour, at times of the driest kind. It is of a quiet kind. You can see it coming a long way off in a peculiar twitch of his mouth; it increases and broadens gradually until it becomes irresistible and all-pervading with his audience.

F. Douglass' rank as a writer is high, and justly so. His writings, if anything, are more meritorious than the speaking. For many years, he was the editor of newspapers, doing all of the editorial work. He has contributed largely to magazines. He is a forcible and thoughtful writer. His style is pure and graceful, and he has great felicity of expression. His written productions in finish compare favourably with the written productions of our most cultivated writers. His style comes partly, no doubt, from his long and constant practice, but the true source is his clear mind, which is well stored by a close acquaintance with the best authors. His range of reading has been wide and extensive. He has been a hard student. In every sense of the word he is a self-made man. By dint of hard study he has educated himself, and to-day it may be said he has a well-trained intellect. He has surmounted the disadvantage of not having an university education, by application and well-directed effort. He seems to have realized the fact that to one who is anxious to become educated and is really in earnest, it is not positively necessary to go to college, and that information may be had outside of college walks; books may be obtained and read elsewhere, they are not chained to desks in college libraries as they were in early times at Oxford; Professors' lectures may be bought already printed; learned doctors may be listened to in the Lyceum; and the printing press has made it easy and cheap to get information on every subject and topic that is discussed and taught in the University. Douglass never made the great mistake (a common one) of considering that his education was finished. He has continued to study, he studies now, and is a growing man, and at this present moment he is a stronger man intellectually than ever before.

Soon after Douglass' escape from Maryland to the Northern States he commenced his public career. It was at New Bedford as a local Methodist preacher and by taking part in small public meetings held by coloured people, where anti-slavery and other matters were discussed. There he laid the foundation of the splendid career, which is now about drawing to a close. In these meetings Douglass gave evidence that he possessed uncommon powers, and it was plainly to be seen that he needed only a field and opportunity to display them. That field and opportunity soon came, as it always does to possessors of genius. He became a member and agent of the American Anti-Slavery society. Then commenced his great crusade against slavery in behalf of his oppressed brethren at the South.

He waged violent and unceasing war against slavery. He went through every town and hamlet in the Free States, raising his voice against the iniquitous system,

Just escaped from the prison-house himself, to tear down the walls of the same and to let the oppressed go free, was the mission which engaged the powers of his soul and body. North, East, and West, all through the land went this escaped slave delivering his warning message against the doomed cities of the South. The ocean did not stop nor hinder him. Across the Atlantic he went, through England, Ireland, and Scotland. Wherever people could be found to listen to his story, he pleaded the cause of his enslaved and down-trodden brethren with vehemence and great power. From 1840 to 1861, the time of the commencement of the civil war, which extirpated slavery in his country, Douglass was continuously speaking on the platform, writing for his newspaper and for magazines, or working in conventions for the abolition of slavery.

The life and work of Douglass has been a complete vindication of the coloured people in this respect; it has refuted and overthrown the position taken by some writers that coloured people were deficient in mental qualifications, and were incapable of attaining high intellectual position. We may reasonably expect to hear no more of this now, the argument is exploded. Douglass has settled the fact the right way, and it is something to settle a fact.

That Douglass is a brave man there can be little doubt. He has physical as well as moral courage. His encounter with the overseer of the Eastern Shore plantation attests his pluck. There the odds were against him, everything was against him—there the unwritten rule was, that the negro who dared to strike a white man must be killed, but Douglass fought the overseer and whipped him. His plotting with other slaves to escape, writing and giving them passes, and the unequal and desperate fight maintained by him in the Baltimore ship yard, where law and public sentiment were against him, also show that he has courage. But since the day of his slavery, while living here at the North, many instances have happened which show very plainly that he is a man of courage and determination; if he had not been, he would have long since succumbed to the brutality and violence of the low and mean-spirited people found in the Free States.

Up to a very recent date it has been deemed quite safe even here in the North to insult and impose on inoffensive coloured people, to elbow a coloured man from the sidewalk, to jeer at him and apply vile epithets to him, in some localities this has been the rule and not the exception, and to put him out of public conveyances and public places by force, was of common occurrence. It made little difference that the coloured man was decent, civil, and respectably clad, and had paid his fare, if the proprietor of the place or his patrons took the notion that the presence of the coloured man was an affront to their dignity, or inconsistent with their notions of self-respect, out he must go. Nor must he stand upon the order of his going, but go at once. It was against this feeling that Douglass had to contend. He met it often; he was a prominent coloured man travelling from place to place. A good part of the time he was in strange cities stopping at strange taverns—that is, when he was allowed to stop. Frequently has he been refused accommodation in hotels. And as to riding in public conveyances, mean-spirited conductors at one time made it a rule to put all coloured people, nolens nolens, in the smoking car. Many times was Douglass subjected to this indignity.

The writer of this remembers well, because he was present and saw the transaction,—the John Brown meeting in Tremont Temple in 1860, when a violent mob composed of the rough element from the slums of the city, led and encouraged by bankers' brokers came into the hall to break up the meeting. Douglass was presiding; the mob was armed; the police were powerless; the mayor could not or would not do anything. On came the mob, surging through the aisles, over benches and upon the platform; the women in the audience became alarmed and fled. The hirelings were prepared to do anything, they had the power and could with impunity. Douglass sat upon the platform with a few chosen spirits, cool and undaunted; the mob had got about and around him; he did not heed their howling, nor was he moved by their threats. It was not until their leader, a rich banker, with his followers, had mounted the platform and wrenched the chair from under him that he was dispossessed, by main force and personal violence (Douglass resisting all the time) they removed him from the platform. Free speech was violated; Boston was disgraced; but the Chairman of that meeting was not intimidated.

GEORGE L. RUFFIN.

Boston.

APPENDIX C.

The Rev. DAVID THOMAS, D.D., ON FREDERICK DOUGLASS and His Work.

A BOOK not only reveals but often contains its author. It is a kind of incarnation of himself, a body in which he lives and works, long after the brain that thought it and the pen that wrote it have mouldered into dust. In it may be seen, not merely his passing opinions and floating feelings, but his thinking intellect and throbbing heart. A book may be less but never greater than its author. A small man, however learned, can never produce a great book. A truly great book is the spontaneous outflow of a great soul, it has not the polish of art, but the bloom of nature. A book is not to be judged by the number of its pages, the consecutiveness of its reasoning, or the rhythms of its periods, but by the amount of creative life that impregnates its sentences, and breathes in its pages.

This Volume is small in bulk, but overflowing with vitality. The Author (with whom I became acquainted soon after my advent to London, and who addressed a crowded audience in the Church at Stockwell of which I was minister) gave me an impression which continues fresh to this hour, not only of his unique history, but of his extraordinary ability and genius. In memory I see him now as he appeared on the platform some thirty-six years ago. He was then a runaway slave. In stature tall, and somewhat attenuated, with a head indicative of large brain force, his dark countenance radiating with humour and genius, his large eyes, now flashing with the fire of indignation against tyranny, and now beaming with tender sympathy for his oppressed race.

As an orator I have never heard his superior from that day to this. His voice was clear and strong, capable of every modulation, and of conveying all classes of sentiment, from the most terrific to the most gentle. His attitudes were natural, and therefore electrically commanding. He dramatised those awful memories of wrong that were at that time burning in his soul. Ten such men in our House of Commons would make quasi-patriots and hireling statesmen quail, give the genuine lovers of right courage, and effect a moral revolution. Ten such men in our

London pulpits would send charlatanic pulpiteers to their "own place;" all the little Isms would take their wing at the thunders of their voice, whilst candid enquirers would get firmly rooted in sound ethical convictions.

Having read every line of this book, and being assured that it is re-published in this country with the Author's consent, I have heartily acceded to the request of the enterprising Publisher to write this brief note. To me, the book itself supplies the interest of "Uncle Tom's Cabin," and recalls tragic adventures equal to the boldest creations of romance. It will, I trow, run as widely and live as long as "Robinson Crusoe" and kindred works, but exert at the same time a more potent and beneficent influence.

The book is an autobiography, in which a great man tells out the heartrending wrongs which he has endured, and the agonising and tremendous struggles which he put forth for freedom and justice. The Author's life was so mixed up with the most tragical period in American history, that this autobiography reveals, in aspects new and grand, the labours of the anti-slavery reformers, such as the illustrious Lloyd Garrison, and his noble colleagues; the characters of Presidents Lincoln and Garfield; and the origin, the progress, and the issues of the great Civil War between the North and the South.

It also reveals the possibilities of a human soul to change external circumstances. Here is a man, born and bred in slavery, subject for twenty-one long years to the most terrible oppression and ruthless cruelty, bleeding under the lash of the slaveholder, incarcerated in dungeous, subject to daily insults even from the conventional sainthood of the Churches, as well as from white men everywhere, and what does he do? He breaks through all, like Samson through the "withs" that bound him, until he becomes one of the first men in the State, an associate of leading Senators, a most distinguished citizen, the "Marshal of Columbia," wearing the title of "Honourable." Man need never, ought not ever, to be the creature of circumstances. He degrades his manhood when he yields to externalities. Heaven has endowed him with the power to use the most unpropitious external conditions, as the skilful mariner uses hostile waves and winds, to carry him on to his destination. In truth, to a great soul, as in the case of Frederick Douglass, the most unfavourable circumstances may be turned into triumphant chariots, to bear our manhood on to its ideal power and grandeur.

Mr. Lobb, in publishing this volume, does a work of true patriotism and philanthropy. I trust that it will find its way not only to every railway stall and every circulating library, but into every British home. All who, through this work, come in contact with Frederick Douglass, will be impressed with the dignity of human nature, and feel refreshed and encouraged. They will find a man here an existence, alas! somewhat rare.

Amongst millions of bipeds there are not many real men. Jeremiah was commissioned by the Almighty to "run to and fro through the streets of Jerusalem, and to search the broad places" in order to find a "man." The city had at that time, not been desolated by war, nor had its inhabitants, so far as is known, been thinned by any catastrophe; its streets resounded with the tread of a crowded population, its broad market-places were thronged with those who bought and sold in "order to get gain," but amidst this dense concourse of human animals—feeding, thinking, bartering, all acting with more or less energy, and some flaunting as local magnates,—to find a man was a difficult work. A man amongst a teeming population of human animals was a rare object. The grand mission of Christianity, as I understand it, is to convert the fleshly into the spiritual, the selfish into the generous, and thus all human animals into men. This book contains a man—not a man's portrait, but a man's self—breathing and thinking, weeping and rejoicing, praying and lecturing, hurling fulminations at the wrong, and smiling benedictions on the right. Truly Frederick Douglass is a grand man.

- "Nature might stand up

- And say to all the world, this was a man."

- Shakespeare.

DAVID THOMAS.

Erewyn,Upper Tulse Hill,

Feb. 24th, 1882.

Bemrose and Sons, Printers, 23, Old Bailey, London; and Derby.

[*]The following is a copy of these curious papers, both of my transfer from Thomas to Hugh Auld, and from Hugh to myself:—

"Know all men, by these presents. That I, Thomas Auld of Talbot county and state of Maryland, for, and in consideration of the sum of one hundred dollars, current money, to be paid by Hugh Auld, of the city of Baltimore, in the said state, at and before the sealing and delivery of these presents, the receipt whereof, I the said Thomas Auld, do hereby acknowledge; having granted, bargained, and sold, and by these presents do grant, bargain and sell unto the said Hugh Auld, his executors, administrators, and assigns, one negro man, by the name of Frederick Baily—or Douglass as he calls himself—he is now about twenty-eight years of age—to have and to hold the said negro man for life. And I the said Thomas Auld, for myself, my heirs, executors, and administrators, all and singular, the said Frederick BailyaliasDouglass unto the said Hugh Auld, his executors and administrators, and against all and every other person or persons whatsoever, shall and will warrant and forever defend by these presents. In witness whereof, I set my hand and seal, this thirteenth day of November, eighteen hundred and forty six (1846).

Thomas Auld. "Signed, sealed, and delivered, in the presence of Wrighton Jones, John. C. Lear."

The authenticity of this bill of sale is attested by N. Harrington, a justice of the peace of the State of Maryland, and for the county of Talbot, dated same day as above.

"To all whom it may concern: Be it known that I, Hugh Auld, of the city of Baltimore, in Baltimore county in the State of Maryland, for divers good causes and considerations, me thereunto moving, have released from slavery, liberated, manumitted, and set free, and by these presents do hereby release from slavery, liberate, manumit, and set free, my negro man, named Frederick Baily, otherwise called Douglass, being of the age of twenty-eight years, or thereabouts, and able to work and gain a sufficient livelihood and maintenance; and him the said negro man, named Frederick Douglass, I do declare to be henceforth free, manumitted, and discharged from all manner of servitude to me, my executors and administrators forever.

"In witness whereof, I the said Hugh Auld, have hereunto set my hand and seal the fifth of December, in the year one thousand eight hundred and forty six.

Hugh Auld. "Sealed and delivered in presence of T. Hanson Belt, James N. S. T. Wright."

[*]I have reason to know that this supposition did Mrs. Lincoln great injustice.

[*]"I am naturally anti-slavery. If slavery is not wrong, nothing is wrong. I cannot remember when I did not so think and feel."—Letter of Mr. Lincoln to Mr. Hodges, of Kentucky, April 4, 1864.

Made in the USA
Middletown, DE
13 September 2024

60880372R00305